ICCA
CONGRESS SERIES NO. 21

INTERNATIONAL ARBITRATION CONGRESS
EDINBURGH, 18-21 SEPTEMBER 2022

INTERNATIONAL COUNCIL
FOR COMMERCIAL ARBITRATION

ARBITRATION'S AGE OF ENLIGHTENMENT?

GENERAL EDITORS:
CAVINDER BULL SC
LORETTA MALINTOPPI
AND
CONSTANTINE PARTASIDES KC

with the assistance of the
Permanent Court of Arbitration
Peace Palace, The Hague

Published by:
Kluwer Law International B.V.
PO Box 316
2400 AH Alphen aan den Rijn
The Netherlands
E-mail: lrs-sales@wolterskluwer.com
Website: www.wolterskluwer.com/en/solutions/kluwerlawinternational

Sold and distributed by:
Wolters Kluwer Legal & Regulatory U.S.
920 Links Avenue
Landisville, PA 17538
United States of America
E-mail: customer.service@wolterskluwer.com

Printed on acid-free paper.

ISBN 978-94-035-1377-5

e-Book: ISBN 978-94-035-1387-4
web-PDF: ISBN 978-94-035-1397-3

Printed in the Netherlands.

Preface

ICCA Congress Series no. 21 comprises the proceedings of the XXV ICCA Congress, held in Edinburgh from Sunday, 18 September 2022 to Wednesday, 21 September 2022.

Originally scheduled for 2020, the Congress was delayed three times due to the COVID-19 pandemic. Despite the unavoidable delays, the theme for our Congress grew more – not less – relevant. The theme – 'Arbitration's Age of Enlightenment?' was originally inspired by a book authored by the cognitive psychologist Steven Pinker entitled 'Enlightenment Now: The Case for Reason, Science, Humanism, and Progress', which was published in 2018. The message was that international arbitration, in spite of the criticism that has been voiced in recent years, has accomplished a great deal over time, a progress of which we should all be proud.

While it became more challenging to rely on a message of optimism after the changes that fell upon us over the last three years, we remained faithful to the importance of our theme. Indeed, despite the threats confronting us today, or perhaps because of them, our international system of justice continues to have a central role to play in our modern world, and we must find ways to improve it.

In Scotland in the 18th century, the Enlightenment sparked ideas and created intellectual momentum on many fronts. We found it appealing to apply to our system of international arbitration the values of a movement which challenged the old order and originated new ideas which accelerated progress in numerous fields of human civilisation.

Our intention was to create a programme that – having considered the historic roots of the international arbitration system – would focus on ideas that can foster progress for the future, including contributions from new voices or new centres of arbitration activity and even from beyond our field.

In that spirit, we intentionally chose the first keynote speaker from beyond the world of arbitration: the honourable Louise Arbour, an exceptional jurist whose career has spanned many different areas of law. Her remarks were carefully considered and provocative; they set the right tone for the days that followed. Madam Arbour spoke of international arbitration from an outward perspective as an instrument of justice, which 'participates in the larger enterprise of social stability, progress, prosperity and peace'. The members of the international arbitration community are often keen to tell the world how much our process contributes to international dispute resolution. Madam Arbour stood before us and told us how much the arbitral process takes from national judicial systems.

The initial plenary session was titled 'Arbitration's Age of Enlightenment... and Adaptation?', to hint at the resilience with which the arbitration community reacted to the challenges posed by the pandemic. A variety of topics were addressed, ranging from the historic roots of international arbitration, the modern-day impact of artificial intelligence on arbitration, and the contribution of international arbitration in restraining resort to unilateralism, protectionism and nationalism.

The first panel of the afternoon assessed the current state of arbitration in the modern age and the fundamental challenges it will face in the world of tomorrow. The panellists shared their personal list of 'Top 3' issues in international arbitration as well as the challenges facing our field and identified ways to implement the changes needed to face these challenges.

This panel was followed by two parallel panels which revisited some of the classic cases of the past and considered the development of the modern law of international economic relations. The remaining two panels of the first day respectively: (i) reviewed the present status of the law on confidentiality, and the line that separates it from transparency in international arbitration; and (ii) explored the various tools that might be employed – in addition to arbitration – to optimize the international dispute resolution process.

The second day featured a plenary session which examined the need for, and the appropriate direction of, reforms to investor-State dispute settlement procedures. The speakers assessed the latest ICSID Rules amendments, the state-of-play of the UNCITRAL Working Group III discussions and the innovations to ISDS procedures and dispute resolution bodies endorsed by certain States or in particular regions through bilateral and multilateral agreements. In addition, the panel discussed the possible establishment of a broader permanent international investment court system. Then followed two panels that engaged the participants in a round-the-world trip into current trends and pressing issues in various regions of the world.

The second day started with the presentation of the inaugural ICCA Guillermo Aguilar-Alvarez Memorial Prize, established in honour of former ICCA Governing Board Member Guillermo Aguilar-Alvarez. The day continued with a panel which considered sociological perspectives in the field of international arbitration and continued with a panel showcasing a group of talented young practitioners who proposed innovative ideas and approaches on how to improve efficiency in arbitration. The parallel panels of the second session of the day reviewed two types of new frontiers in legal developments: the new technological frontier for the first panel; and, for the second panel, the new global issues that are likely to give rise to disputes in the future, including climate change, environmental protection, access to depleting water resources, energy and mining transition and human rights initiatives.

The two panels that took place on the morning of the last day of the Congress, respectively discussed how cross-fertilization across different disciplines may impact international arbitration and looked at arbitration from the perspective of the commercial users of arbitration, and national or international regulators who are increasingly coming into contact with the arbitration process.

The Congress closed with a debate that imagined a world without investment arbitration and discussed whether we would be better off if investment arbitration were to disappear. The closing keynote Address was delivered by Lord Carloway, the Lord President of the Court of Session and Lord Justice General, and the most senior judge in Scotland.

In conclusion, as was noted by Constantine Partasides in his opening remarks, fora such as the Edinburgh Congress are what our turbulent world of international relations and commerce needs today. Peaceful international dispute resolutions, in all their forms, are more necessary than ever before, and our international systems of justice are more essential than ever before.

We would like to end with some well-earned expressions of sincere gratitude. We are particularly grateful to the endurance of the indefatigable Edinburgh Host Committee, which treated the participants to four days filled with bagpipes music, poetry, Scottish gastronomy and ceilidh dancing, all beautifully organized, in spite of the challenges that fate threw our way. The Edinburgh Congress ultimately attracted over 1,300 delegates. Quite an accomplishment!

This book would not have been possible without the professionalism and hard work of the Editorial Staff of ICCA Publications. We are grateful to the Permanent Court of Arbitration, its past Secretary-General, H.E. Hugo Hans Siblesz, and its present Secretary-General, H.E. Marcin Czepelak, for hosting the ICCA Editorial Staff at the headquarters of its International Bureau at the Peace Palace. Our thanks also go to the technical and administrative staff of the Permanent Court of Arbitration.

A special word of thanks goes to each of the members of the Programme Committee, who accompanied us on this journey with never-failing enthusiasm. They were: Stephen L. Drymer; Babatunde Fagbohunlu; Yuet Min Foo; Susan Franck; Alvaro Galindo; Francisco González de Cossío; Jean Kalicki; Elie Kleiman; Jan Kleinheisterkamp; Michelle MacPhee; Ziad Obeid; Shaneen Parikh; Lindy Patterson KC; John Rhie; Christian Tams; and Galina Zukova.

When the then President of ICCA, Prof. Dr Gabrielle Kaufmann-Kohler, approached us to co-chair the Edinburgh Congress at the XXIV ICCA Congress in Sydney in 2018, the world was a very different place. We certainly did not know at the time that we would soon witness a global pandemic and a war in Europe. Over the three years during which we prepared this Congress, a new President succeeded Prof. Gabrielle Kaufmann-Kohler, Prof. Lucy Reed, and this provided us with an unexpected silver lining as we could benefit from the support and thoughtful contributions of two extraordinary ICCA presidents. We are very grateful to both of them.

The XXVI ICCA Congress will take place in Hong Kong from Sunday, 5 May 2024 to Wednesday, 8 May 2024. The theme will be 'International Arbitration: A Human Endeavour'. Information on the XXVI ICCA Congress will be posted on the ICCA website, < www.arbitration-icca.org >, as well as at < https://icca2024.hk/ >.

Cavinder Bull SC, Loretta Malintoppi, and Constantine Partasides KC
September 2023

XXVI ICCA CONGRESS

5-8 May 2024

Hong Kong

'International Arbitration: A Human Endeavour'

For program and registration information:

https://icca2024.hk/

www.arbitration-icca.org

For the Young ICCA Event:

https://www.youngicca.org/

Table of Contents

xi

PART I   Opening Keynote Address

Arbitration's Age of Enlightenment: A Celebration or a Challenge?

The Honourable Louise Arbour[*]

I am delighted to be with you today, more than two years after I was originally approached to participate in this gathering. The pandemic pause—I will call it a mere pause solely for this purpose—has provided us with an unwelcome opportunity to reconsider many of the settled ways in which we were working, and thinking. It has propelled us into the virtual world of learning and communicating, at a speed that would not have seemed feasible absent the pandemic constraints. Some of our new habits are here to stay, but not all. Either way, what cannot be reversed is a broad opening of the mind to the rapidly changing world and to our capacity to adapt. Whether we go back to the office two or three days a week, or not at all, is an interesting conundrum, particularly for office managers. But much more interesting is whether we can capitalize broadly on this newly acquired ability to do things differently, to take bold steps, to speed up change.

It is therefore in that spirit that I talk to you today. Same place, different times.

---

[*] The Honourable Louise Arbour, C.C., G.O.Q. was appointed to the Supreme Court of Ontario in 1987 and the Court of Appeal for Ontario in 1990. In 1996, the Security Council of the United Nations appointed Madame Arbour Chief Prosecutor for the International Criminal Tribunals for the former Yugoslavia and Rwanda. In this role, she secured the first conviction for genocide (Rwanda) since the 1948 Genocide Convention and the first indictment for war crimes by a sitting European head of state (Serbian President Slobodan Milosevic).

She resigned as Chief Prosecutor to take up an appointment to the Supreme Court of Canada in 1999. She was appointed High Commissioner for Human Rights at the United Nations (2004-2008), and the UN Special Representative of the Secretary-General on International Migration (2017-2018). Madame Arbour, Senior Counsel at Borden Ladner Gervais LLP, was appointed in 2021 to lead an independent review into sexual misconduct in the Canadian Armed Forces.

Madame Arbour has received numerous honorary doctorates and awards. She is a Companion of the Order of Canada and a Grand Officer of the Ordre national du Québec.

I was puzzled by the overarching theme of this conference: the Age of Enlightenment. In French "l'âge des Lumières" reminded me of the often quoted remark by Oren Harari that "*The electric light didn't come from the continuous improvement of the candle*," to which I must say I very much like Matt Shore's rejoinder:

> It's true that the light bulb did not come from continuous improvement of the technology of a candle, but it did come from continuous improvement over the benefit of the candle.

In that spirit, I'll invite you today to reflect with me not so much on whether international commercial arbitration, which I'll often refer to simply as "arbitration," is the candle or the light bulb, an interesting question in its own rights, but on whether it is prepared to be part of our continuous improvement of the benefits of justice.

Some will argue that private commercial arbitration is not intended to be a form of justice delivery, traditionally understood, but merely a forum for the adjudication of issues, to the satisfaction of the parties to a dispute, through a process of their choosing.

I don't subscribe to that view. The state, representing a general public interest, is invested in the availability of many forms of dispute resolutions, particularly those, like international commercial arbitration, that rely in part on state services, for instance, for enforcing or setting aside awards where warranted. But more importantly, the legitimacy, and ultimately the legality of arbitration models, depend on the acceptability of their departure from more conventional or formal state-sponsored justice institutions, such as the degree of control that the parties may exercise over the process, and whether this is compatible with fairness and justice. Indeed, just as some countries have been confronted with the shortcomings of religious adjudication in family-related matters, for example, any form of dispute resolution that would depart from some of the fundamental tenets of justice would in my view be socially and, ultimately, legally, unacceptable. If expedited hearings in small claims court to resolve private civil disputes between parties are seen as a form of access to justice, so are in my view different Alternative Dispute Resolution (ADR) models of which arbitration is one.

In other words, I don't believe that justice is limited to the resolution of disputes by state-run courts embedded in a hermetic system of laws and institutions. And indeed, state institutions increasingly turn to non-traditional forms of interventions, such as mediation, arbitration and diversion, even in areas that are not otherwise within the sole interests of the immediate parties. In the same way in the international environment, the resolution of private commercial disputes, as well as those arising from direct foreign investment, would not be possible without the imprimatur of the legal community which vouches for the adequacy of the processes, by reference to widely shared notions of fairness, such as the delivery of a just result and the ability to have recourse when the process falls short. So arbitration is, in my view, a justice instrument, and as such participates in the larger enterprise of social stability, progress, prosperity and peace.

Viewed that way, there is cause to celebrate the accomplishments, successes and contributions of international commercial arbitration to the field of authoritative dispute resolution, broadly defined, and as an instrument of civil justice.

The question I wish to address is whether these undeniable successes constitute the age of enlightenment of this discipline, or rather whether its full triumph lies ahead and requires a reasoned, evidence-based evaluation of its contribution to justice, more broadly understood. It would be tempting to examine this question from the inside, asking whether arbitration should feel threatened by emerging trends like the so-called death of expertise, the dichotomy between blind faith based on ideology or personal preferences on the one hand, and insurmountable skepticism reflecting the fear of unverifiable information on the other, a tension present today in virtually every assertion of fact, leading to a general loss of confidence in institutions. These of course are more likely to threaten the formal justice system, particularly jury trials in the West for example, but could in time infect every method of factual determination of past events.

Rather I want to take an outward look at arbitration as a discipline within the broad field of justice.

The challenge for International Council for Commercial Arbitration's (ICCA) age of enlightenment is to reconcile the idea of justice as a public good with the remarkable growth and success of arbitration as a model of private dispute resolution. This reconciliation will be made easier if it can be demonstrated that the privatization of international commercial dispute resolution benefits the public. This, in turn, will require an assessment of arbitration's impact on national justice systems, particularly on those parts of national systems that are not amenable to privatization, that is to say where its model could not simply be duplicated in every sphere of dispute resolution, or where it would clearly not be the preferable one.

The popularity and success of arbitration are undeniable. The Secretariat of the International Chamber of Commerce (ICC) International Court of Arbitration alone registered 853 new cases in 2021.[1] At the end of that year, the New York Convention has 170 state parties, which testifies to the usefulness and the wide acceptability of the present forms of arbitration as instruments of international cooperation.[2]

It is often praised as 'the only game in town'[3] in the area of international commercial dispute resolution because it offers a distinctive balance of neutrality, speed, expertise, choice, confidentiality, reviewability, finality and enforceability, some of which are severely lacking in state courts or in other options such as mediation.[4] As the discipline evolved, it has shown its ability to bridge different legal

---

1. https://www.iccwbo.be/icc-unveils-preliminary-dispute-resolution-figures-for-2021/.
2. https://newyorkconvention1958.org/index.php?lvl = cmspage&pageid = 7&id_news = 1032&opa c_view = -1.
3. Gerold Herrmann, "Does the World Need Additional Uniform Legislation on Arbitration," in *Arbitration Insights: Twenty Years of the Annual Lecture of the School of International Arbitration* vol. 16, 223, 228 (Loukas A. Mistelis & Julian D. M. Lew eds., International Arbitration Law Library 2007); quoting Yves Fortier QC.
4. Dalma R. Demeter, Kayleigh M. Smith, "The Implications of International Commercial Courts on Arbitration" (2016) 33 *Journal of International Arbitration*, Issue 5, pp. 441-469, http://www. kluwerarbitration.com/document/kli-joia-330502?q = %22The%20Implications%20of%20Inter national%20Commercial%20Courts%20on%20Arbitration%22 and Gary B. Born, *International Commercial Arbitration* 71-96 (2d ed., Kluwer Law International 2014).

systems, cultures and traditions, developing norms that in time have become truly indigenous to international commerce and investment.[5]

The impact of that success on national norms and institutions has been the subject of debate. On the positive side, some have argued that international arbitration has attracted local legal elites, who have then used their influence to have new norms injected into their own national systems.[6] This, in turn, has expanded the scope of judicial training and law school curricula, as well as interest in foreign legal education, thereby expanding the horizons of some national institutions.[7]

Others have voiced concerns about the impact of arbitration on national legal systems, particularly in the common law world which is dependent on accessibility to case law for its continued vitality, maturity and adaptation to incremental change in the factual environment in which the law operates.[8]

This debate is well-known and ongoing, and so are the many initiatives proposed to minimize the shortcomings of arbitration from national judicial and legal perspectives.

The literature also suggests, I would say not surprisingly, that the effective resolution of commercial disputes contributes to economic growth.[9] This can be said more broadly of the Rule of Law, of which arbitration is but one part. Reliance on the enforceability of agreements, and access to credible means of resolving disagreements, surely contribute to creating an environment favorable to economic stability and growth; so too I would suggest, a legal system that is and is perceived by the general public as fair, and attentive to public interests when they conflict with private ones.[10] The interface between international arbitration and national courts is thus critical. And as the economies of middle-income countries diversify and complexify, attracting international investment, so will the attention and ultimately the intervention of public interest groups intent on being heard, including in the courts, on environmental and human rights issues, for instance.

---

5. Speaker's manuscript addressed by Philip J. McConnaughay at Peking University School of Transnational on November 7, 2012: The Role of Arbitration in Economic Development and the Creation of Transnational Legal Principles.
6. Catherine A. Rogers and Christopher R. Drahozal, *Does International Arbitration Enfeeble or Enhance Local Legal Institutions?* (June 15, 2019). Legitimacy in Investment Arbitration (Cambridge University Press 2019). Available at SSRN: https://ssrn.com/abstract = 3404615.
7. Catherine A. Rogers and Christopher R. Drahozal, *Does International Arbitration Enfeeble or Enhance Local Legal Institutions?* (June 15, 2019). Legitimacy in Investment Arbitration (Cambridge University Press 2019). Available at SSRN: https://ssrn.com/abstract = 3404615.
8. *See* The Right Hon. Lord Thomas of Cwmgiedd, "Developing Commercial Law Through the Courts: Rebalancing the Relationship Between the Courts and Arbitration," The Bailii Lecture 2016, March 9, 2016. Sir Bernard Eder, "Does Arbitration Stifle Development of the Law? Should s. 69 Be Revitalised?," Chartered Institute of Arbitrators (London Branch) —AGM Keynote Address, April 28, 2016; Ank Santens, Romain Zamour, "Dreaded Dearth of Precedent in the Wake of International Arbitration—Could the Cause Also Bring the Cure?" (2015) 7 *Y.B. Arb. & Mediation*, p. 73.
9. Cited in: Philip J. McConnaughay, The Potential of Private Commercial Arbitration for Facilitating Economic Growth in Less Developed Countries (June 21, 2016). ICCA Congress Series No. 19, Kluwer Law International; Peking University School of Transnational Law Research Paper No. 16-14. Available at SSRN: https://ssrn.com/abstract = 2846347.
10. Trevor C.W. Farrow, "Privatizing our Public Civil Justice System" (2006), Articles & Book Chapters, Paper 1930, http://digitalcommons.osgoode.yorku.ca/scholarly_works/1930.

In other words, while foreign commercial activity and investment are attracted to the protection offered, for example, by the accession of a country to the New York Convention, it must anticipate, in time, increased public scrutiny of its actions, and a call for more, not less, public access and even participation, in the management of conflicts, even apparently private ones, arising from its presence in the country. This may clash with the constant pressure on developing countries to introduce arbitration-friendly public policies. Investment treaties, for instance, increasingly expand their scope into public law issues (for instance intellectual property, environmental law and data privacy), yet the majority of them automatically refer matters arising from these issues to private dispute settlement mechanisms.[11] In some countries, if the government, or a public entity, is a party to an arbitration agreement, an issue could arise as to the constitutionality of the government sheltering itself from the constitutional oversight of its national courts. In areas increasingly subject to international arbitration agreements, such as construction or insurance,[12] for instance, national environmental or human rights obligations may not be amenable to examination solely within the secrecy of the arbitration procedure.

This brings me back to the place of arbitration as an instrument of justice in the larger sense. It is a benefit to the institution of arbitration that it be seen as an element of the larger civil justice system. But, as with any benefit, there are, or there should be, obligations. Perhaps the corresponding obligations of arbitration, as an institution that forms part of the civil justice system, have not been as discussed as much as the benefits it confers on the parties, and of its own officials and professionals.

Justice is a public good. Dispute resolution, in many areas, cannot be fully privatized, whether or not the state is a party to the dispute. Indeed, it is fair to assume that in mature democracies, the judicial branch of governance will continue not only to play a major public role but will strive to provide adequate access to private justice, including as a matter of public interest. The two are inextricably linked through the common objective to seek justice. Arbitration is not and cannot—so long as it seeks to participate as an institution in the system of civil justice and avail itself of the support of other public institutions, be wholly private.

It's in that context that one may ask what impact arbitration has on the non-privatized parts of the system. In other words, if privatization of the most lucrative part of dispute resolution (commercial disputes) is taken out of the national justice system, what impact does this have on the development of the more clearly public parts, which cannot be so easily privatized? More specifically, if international commercial disputes are taken out of national courts, except for enforcing or setting aside awards, what does it do to what's left in the public system?

I assume there is not much controversy about my assertion that commercial disputes are the most lucrative parts of the system of dispute resolution. Lucrative may

---

11. Notes taken from the Hyman Soloway Annual Conference, Howard Mann, "International Arbitration and Globalization: The Battle between Private 'Justice' and Public Law," Soloway Annual Conference, University of Ottawa, January 15, 2020.
12. Ank Santens, Romain Zamour, "Dreaded Dearth of Precedent in the Wake of International Arbitration—Could the Cause Also Bring the Cure?" (2015) 7 *Y.B. Arb. & Mediation*, p. 73.

not be the right term. For the parties to a dispute that needs resolving, there is inevitably a cost. But just as in private health care and private education, there is clearly a benefit to those who chose to have recourse to what they see as preferable to the cheaper public system. And even if their departure alleviates the pressure on public institutions, their absence also impoverishes them. When arbitration is chosen, there is obviously, less of a draw on state resources, such as legal aid, the remuneration of court officials, and the like; yet in commercial litigation, the court is usually enriched by the participation of well-represented parties, with adequate means of presenting their case. The contrast with increasingly unrepresented litigants, both in civil and criminal matters, speaks for itself. Finally, the early retirement of judges who move on to adjudicate private disputes happens almost exclusively in the commercial field.[13]

My concern is therefore whether the exodus of commercial disputes towards other forms of dispute resolution, in the international sphere, is contributing to the underdevelopment of other instruments of civil justice especially in developing countries, particularly their courts and their legal systems.

In rich and even middle-income countries, it's fair to assume that there continues to be, to varying degrees, a form of healthy competition between the formal judicial system and different forms of alternative dispute resolution. Less so in international commercial disputes where the otherwise applicable domestic judicial system appears fundamentally inadequate either because of lack of capacity, delay, unwelcome publicity, corruption, and the like, and where arbitration continues to gain ground.

In such a case, the question becomes whether recourse to arbitration improved, worsened, or played no part in the development of the national systems and whether it should strive to make a positive contribution above and beyond the immediate interests of the parties. In particular, many scholars have raised concerns about the lack of contribution, indeed possibly the negative impact of Bilateral Investments Treaties on the Rule of Law on local legal regimes. They have argued that some of the negative impacts could be alleviated by Treaties containing provisions that encourage the selection of local courts, local arbitrators and local venues at all relevant stages of the process.[14]

While these academic articles shed light on the discussion about whether investment arbitration hinders the development of local legal institutions, there is a potentially stronger parallel to be drawn about the effect of international commercial arbitration on those institutions. Currently, there is a lack of research as to the effect that international commercial arbitration has on domestic rule of law. However, authors have agreed that not only does international commercial arbitration draw out more cases from national courts than investment arbitration, but it also resolves cases relating to local contract disputes, which "are the bread and butter" of local courts.[15]

---

13. "Exploring the Issues in Private Judging" (1994) 77:4 *Judicature*, p. 203.
14. Amanda Rawls, "Improving the Impact of International Arbitration on Economic Development," in Andrea Menaker (ed.), *International Arbitration and the Rule of Law: Contribution and Conformity*, vol. 19 (ICCA Congress Series, Kluwer Law International 2017) 85-99.
15. Catherine A. Rogers and Christopher R. Drahozal, Does International Arbitration Enfeeble or Enhance Local Legal Institutions? (June 15, 2019). Legitimacy in Investment Arbitration (Cambridge University Press 2019). Available at SSRN: https://ssrn.com/abstract = 3404615.

Many advocates of international commercial arbitration suggest that, to the extent that it contributes to economic development, arbitration will indirectly contribute to the consequent improvement of public legal institutions.[16] It is, in my view, doubtful that economic growth, in and of itself, will lead to improvement of legal and judicial institutions, particularly if commercial arbitration continues to appear as an attractive alternative to national courts. And to the extent that not all disputes are amenable to arbitration, absent some positive action, the public judicial system is most likely to further deteriorate.

Worse still, the rise in popularity of international arbitration as an alternative to litigation, if not accompanied by measures designed to strengthen domestic judiciaries and the Rule of law, risks strengthening authoritarian regimes adverse to a strong independent national judiciary.[17]

In short, as much as arbitration may contribute to economic growth in low and middle-income countries, it cannot purport to operate as though completely divorced from the national legal and judicial sectors. Arbitration needs to be able to rely on competent national judicial systems and should be concerned about their development. Only wishful thinking would suggest that judicial development will be the natural by-product of increased GDP.

No serious international actor, public or private, can today ignore the United Nations Sustainable Development Goals (SDGs) and particularly, for our purposes, SDG 16.

Adopted by the UN General Assembly in September 2015, the SDGs constitute the largest-ever global effort to end poverty:

> The 2030 Agenda for Sustainable Development, adopted by all United Nations Member States in 2015, provides a shared blueprint for peace and prosperity for people and the planet, now and into the future. At its heart are the 17 Sustainable Development Goals (SDGs), which are an urgent call for action by all countries—developed and developing—in a global partnership. They recognize that ending poverty and other deprivations must go hand-in-hand with strategies that improve health and education, reduce inequality, and spur economic growth—all while tackling climate change and working to preserve our oceans and forests.[18]

SDG 16 is entitled: *Peace, Justice and Strong Institutions*. SDG 16.3 seeks to promote the rule of law at the national and international levels and ensure equal access to justice for all. Although obviously by far not the sole factor, access to justice has been associated with economic growth; in its broad acceptation, justice fosters social

---

16. Philip J. McConnaughay, *The Potential of Private Commercial Arbitration for Facilitating Economic Growth in Less Developed Countries* (June 21, 2016). ICCA Congress Series No. 19, Kluwer Law International; Peking University School of Transnational Law Research Paper No. 16-14. Available at SSRN: https://ssrn.com/abstract = 2846347.
17. Catherine A. Rogers, Christopher R. Drahozal, *Does International Arbitration Enfeeble or Enhance Local Legal Institutions?* (June 15, 2019). Legitimacy in Investment Arbitration (Cambridge University Press 2019). Available at SSRN: https://ssrn.com/abstract = 3404615. The article refers to Mark Fathi Massoud, 'International Arbitration and Judicial Politics in Authoritarian States' (2014) 39 *Law & Social Inquiry*, pp. 1, 3.
18. https://sustainabledevelopment.un.org/sdgs.

development and peace as well as prosperity. In the context of the SDGs, it requires improving institutional frameworks for resolving disputes, conflict and crimes.[19]

In fact, it's fair to say that virtually all methods of alternative dispute resolutions emerged from a perception—often the reality—of one or more shortcomings in the national justice system: be it delays and other inefficiencies, costs, poor quality of justice officials, or even corruption. Even absent these deficiencies, arbitration offers features that private actors often prefer and that most public systems cannot accommodate: vast control over the process, such as choice of adjudicator and of rules of procedure, and, above all, secrecy. Ironically, we can see globally a demonstrable deficit in access to quality state-provided justice at both ends of the spectrum, including in many developed countries: for the poor, or the not quite poor enough to get state assistance, and for the wealthy, including corporations, who will use an alternative if it better serves their needs.

Some of the flaws of state-delivered justice in civil, criminal and administrative matters can and should be remedied. But there is no reason not to invest in attractive alternatives, along the many models presented by ADR, as long as the interest of justice for all is adequately served.

The successful features of international commercial arbitration could be adapted to national ADR systems, in some fields of litigation, and they should be. There is no reason to promote exclusively the underperforming traditional, formal, state-operated judicial systems in many countries. This has been proven true in developed countries, with the successful implantation of ADR. And it is plausible to assume that justice, and judicial reform, in developing countries, would benefit from ADR methodologies rather than simply seeking to modernize often outdated formal systems.

But it is equally clear that ADR is not a panacea to the underdevelopment of national systems of justice in many fields that cannot lend themselves to much privatization, such as criminal, family, constitutional and administrative law.

I suggest to you that the case for investing in the improvement of national justice systems in low and middle-income countries is both a moral imperative and a self-interested goal for actors engaged in the arbitration sector.

It's a moral imperative because, as argued above, it is plausible to assume that the spectacular growth in size and quality of international arbitration has contributed to the stagnation of justice sector development in poor countries. The institution of arbitration cannot responsibly neglect or ignore the state of other components of the civil justice system.

It is self-interested because better quality domestic justice will support economic growth and contribute to political stability, which in turn will benefit international trade and investment. Even when that occurs, it is of course highly unlikely that this will undermine arbitration or that national courts would then become a serious competitor to arbitration.

---

19. Manuel and Manuel, SDG 16.3 Working Paper 537.

In line with the SDGs, the private sector, therefore, has a role to play, indeed plays a role, consciously or not, in the pace of development of the law and of judicial institutions, in low and middle-income countries.

That role should be more explicit, more directed, and less deferential to the state, in areas traditionally perceived as the exclusive domain of the state, like justice. Simply bypassing state deficiencies is not a sufficient contribution. Corporations, just as donor countries and international institutions like the UN and the World Bank, have been reluctant to engage in serious justice reform in the countries in which they operate. Justice reform is perceived as intensely political, and efforts to date have been criticized as focusing on infrastructures such as courtrooms and prisons, without regard to recurrent costs and inefficiencies. And development efforts in the justice sector have gone disproportionately to law enforcement, often strengthening the hand of oppressive regimes and tainting any real notion of justice. Indeed, the police, often modeled on colonial legacy, is for many their first and only contact with justice, and in authoritarian regimes, is essentially power serving if not predatory and dangerous.

Unfortunately, SDG 16.3 reproduces in part that reality by focusing on two indicators: victim reporting levels and detainees without trial, both centered on the criminal process.

So while International commercial arbitrations involving commercial activities in developing countries continue to expand and thrive, general legal advice and assistance are inaccessible to millions of people. Meanwhile, justice is the most poorly funded sector by donor countries in their international aid agenda.[20] Not only do donor countries provide less financial aid to the justice sector, but they spend less on justice development assistance than they spend, in proportion, to the justice sector in their own economies. And it's not as though justice institutions were particularly well funded in rich countries, which explains in part the considerable outsourcing of justice services. But the underfunding issue is likely to be particularly acute in low-income countries, as they are known to be least able to fund core government services themselves.[21]

I suggest to you that the international private sector has a role to play in providing both expertise and resources to the development of the justice sector—formal and alternative—in emerging economies and in the poorest countries. Not only should continued efforts be made to train and include professional participants in international arbitrations from developing countries; interaction with the local bar and bench should be encouraged, including by providing advocacy and other forms of training on a *pro bono* basis.

But in light of the severe funding deficiencies in the justice sector, coupled with the historical reluctance of donor states to support that sector adequately, I suggest that ICCA should consider creating a fund, supported by contributions from arbitral awards, to be directed to the development of public justice institutions, in the spirit of access to justice for all, imbedded in the SDGs. Those less allergic to the idea of taxation might even support a compulsory contribution to such fund. Its design presents

---

20. Manuel and Manuel, SDG 16.3 Working Paper 537.
21. Manuel and Manuel, SDG 16.3 Working Paper 537.

interesting options, including for distribution. Funding from the fund could go, for example, to countries related to the matter arbitrated. But not necessarily. Countries could be invited to apply for funding, which could come with an entire package of justice reform support. A sizable fund could have a remarkable impact on the development of judicial institutions and on access to justice, thereby contributing to peace, security and development.

Absent an interest in the arbitral community for such an initiative, it is not inconceivable that national governments could take the lead and decide to levy an amount as cost payable to the state for the enforcement of arbitral awards. There is no doubt that many national jurisdictions are struggling with the increasing cost of justice delivery and may find it difficult to privatize more. Public expenditures in the justice sector compete with also increasing demands in health, and in the environment, to mention only these two obvious ones.

National initiatives would be less effective than international ones. The resulting funds would be scattered, and their use would likely be put to the improvement of home institution, rather than directed at the most needed improvement of the justice sector elsewhere. Therefore, an international private initiative, well designed and well administered, would likely have the greatest impact.

Such an initiative would be a much-needed and bold assertion by the private sector that it intends to occupy its proper place on the world scene. I believe that the development of the Rule of law, including of robust and credible national and international judicial institutions, continues to be a critical priority of our time, along with and in connection to the surge of the digital economy and artificial intelligence, human mobility and migration, and of course, climate change. Indeed, the private sector has dominated the technological revolution but has been remarkably silent, despite its obvious interests, on many critical international issues such as climate challenge, peace and justice. I believe that it's the combination of self-interest and a commitment to a greater public good that will inspire tomorrow's private sector giants to lead in the transition to sustainable energy.

I don't want to suggest that we are all standing on the deck of the Titanic, even less so that we are merely rearranging the chairs. We are facing challenges commensurate with the sophistication of the means we have developed, in recent years, to face them, The rise in disinformation, polarization, distrust of institutions, governments and intellectual elites, the unconscionable inequalities inside and between countries, the stagnation in the eradication of warfare, the continued impunity of the worst abusers of human rights, all this stands alongside the launch of the James Webb telescope, a reminder of the incredible human appetite and potential to reach for the stars.

As scientists continue to strive to understand the universe and to propel us into a better future, I like to think that similar leaders will rise in the justice sector, writ large and that international lawyers will continue to apply their remarkable skills, in the best tradition of our profession, to the greater good.

PART II   Plenary: Arbitration's Age of
   Enlightenment … and Adaptation?

CHAPTER 2

A Search for International Enlightenment Through Arbitration: Andrew Carnegie, the *Alabama* Claims Arbitration, and the 'Temple of Peace'

J. Christopher Thomas KC[*]

TABLE OF CONTENTS

I   INTRODUCTION

Many attendees of our Congress will have attended hearings at the Peace Palace in The Hague. Housing the Permanent Court of Arbitration (PCA) and its famous tenant, the

[*] Barrister & Solicitor, Arbitrator, Vancouver, British Columbia.
    This chapter is derived from a larger work-in-progress on the *Alabama* Claims arbitration, the cast of characters who played a role both in the events giving rise to the dispute and in its resolution, the making of the Treaty of Washington which in turn established the Geneva Tribunal, and the conduct of the arbitration itself.
    The author wishes to express his thanks to Sarah Lim Hui Feng, then of the National University of Singapore's Centre for International Law, for her able assistance in researching this chapter. All errors remain those of the author.

International Court of Justice, the Peace Palace is administered by the Carnegie Foundation, one of the many organizations created by the Scottish-American philanthropist, Andrew Carnegie. Mindful of the venue of this year's Congress, this chapter discusses Carnegie's obsession with international arbitration – for obsession it was – and his belief that arbitration could usher in a new age of enlightenment in relations between States.

II   A BRIEF SKETCH OF CARNEGIE'S LIFE

In 1848, at the age of twelve, Carnegie emigrated to the United States with his family. At thirteen, he was working in a cotton mill, but he soon became a telegram runner and then a telegraph operator, and it was in the latter job that he excelled. Through sheer determination and self-directed study (traits that explain his later commitment to establishing public libraries around the world), Carnegie quickly distinguished himself. By the age of seventeen, he had moved into the railroad business by becoming an assistant and personal telegraph operator to Thomas A. Scott and later J. Edward Thomson of the Pennsylvania Railroad Company.

By the time of the outbreak of the American Civil War in 1861, at the age of twenty-five, Carnegie held stock in two horsecar companies, at least two coal companies, an oil company, an iron smelting company and a railroad car company.[1] The oil investment, in particular, proved to be spectacular and by the end of 1863, Carnegie was making roughly the equivalent of USD 10 million a year (in present-day terms).[2] Success begot success and he soon became a very wealthy man. In 1901, he sold his conglomerate, Carnegie Steel Company, to J. Pierpont Morgan and then spent the remaining years of his life working on ways to give away his immense fortune.[3]

The idea of constructing a building to house a 'Temple of Peace' to administer international arbitrations evidently came from the Russian international law professor and delegate to the first Hague Peace Conference, Fyodor Fyodorovich Martens, in 1899.[4] Andrew White, the United States Ambassador to Berlin who had led the US delegation at the Conference, later pitched the idea of financing its construction to Carnegie. Carnegie was initially disinclined to contribute, but White persisted, the scope and size of the project grew, and Carnegie's interest was gradually piqued.[5]

When White visited Carnegie at his Scottish estate, Skibo, in 1902, he was able to engage Carnegie's philanthropic interest. In a happy coincidence, around the time that White was pressing Carnegie to support the project, President Theodore Roosevelt, who had been designated to arbitrate a dispute between Germany, Britain, and Italy, on

---

1. David Nasaw, *Andrew Carnegie*, Penguin Books, 2006, p. 75. ('Nasaw').
2. *The Building of Peace: A Hundred Years of Work on Peace Through Law: The Peace Palace 1913-2013*, p. 37 ('The Building of Peace').
3. Nasaw, *supra* n. 1, pp. 585-586.
4. The Building of Peace, *supra* n. 2, p. 40.
5. *Ibid.*

the one side, and Venezuela, on the other, acceded to Carnegie's importuning that the case should be heard by the new PCA.[6]

Carnegie had long advocated for the peaceful settlement of disputes through arbitration rather than by force of arms and he had pressed successive American presidents of both political stripes to support international arbitration. In a 'New Year Greeting' published in the *New York Tribune*, he praised Roosevelt for taking action toward the:

> coming banishment of the earth's most revolting spectacle – human war – *the killing of man by man* ... The complete banishment of war draws near. Its death wound dates from the day that President Roosevelt led ... opposing powers ... to the Court of Peace, and thus proclaimed it the appointed substitute for that which had hitherto stained the earth – the killing of men by each other.[7]

Roosevelt was one of several US presidents dating back to Ulysses S. Grant whom Carnegie had sought to persuade of the merits of international arbitration. Although Roosevelt was privately sceptical of arbitration's ability to resolve disputes between States, he listened to Carnegie's entreaties, in part because of the latter's generous support for Republican causes.

Carnegie was thrilled by Roosevelt's decision, and this appears to have sealed his decision to fund the construction of the Peace Palace.[8] On 22 April 1903, he wrote to the Netherlands' ambassador in Washington, Baron Gevers, expressing his pleasure at the news that the Dutch government would support the construction of a 'Court House and Library, a Temple of Peace for the Permanent Court of Arbitration', and announcing that he would contribute funding in the hopes that the establishment of 'Permanent Tribunal for the settlement of international disputes ... [would be] the most important step forward, of a world-wide character, which has ever been taken by the Joint Powers, since it must ultimately banish war, our foulest stain.'[9]

Three weeks later, Carnegie signed a cheque for USD 1.5 million. He was of course not the only contributor to the building's construction. Many of the governments that became parties to the Hague Conventions contributed materials, light fixtures, artworks, and decorations. One of the building's charms is its patchwork of early twentieth-century national decorative styles.

It took over a decade to construct the building. The opening ceremony, over which Queen Wilhelmina presided, and which Carnegie and his wife Louise attended,

6. The Award in the *Preferential Treatment of Claims of Blockading Powers against Venezuela* case was issued on 22 February 1904. Available at https://pca-cpa.org/ar/cases/76. Last visited on 29 May 2022.
7. Quoted by Nasaw, *supra* n. 1, p. 650.
8. On 27 December 1902, Carnegie wrote to Roosevelt that, 'The world took a long step upward yesterday and Theodore Roosevelt bounded into the short list of those who will forever be hailed as supreme benefactors of man.' Quoted in Nasaw at p. 649. The Building of Peace *supra* n. 2, asserts (at p. 41) that: 'It was probably the decision in December of 1902 to have the dispute between Venezuela and Germany, England, and Italy be heard at the Court of Arbitration that eventually led Carnegie to decide to act upon White's proposal to build a "Temple of Peace".'
9. The Building of Peace, *supra* n. 2, p. 41.

was held on 2 August 1913. Louise Carnegie would later write that that day was 'perhaps the greatest in Andrew's life'.[10]

It is a sad irony that construction of the Peace Palace was completed just before the onset of World War I, and perhaps made doubly ironic because a proposal was made to avoid the outbreak of hostilities by referring the dispute to PCA arbitration. After the assassination of Archduke Ferdinand by a Serbian nationalist on 28 June 1914, Austria demanded among other things that Serbia allow it to investigate the attack. The Serbian government countered by proposing that the conflict be put before the PCA. Austria rejected the proposal and declared war on Serbia on 28 July 1914. Tsar Nicholas II mobilized in support of Serbia, and Germany, allied with Austria, declared war on Russia. Britain and France soon followed suit.[11]

So it was that the 'war to end all wars' commenced. Carnegie, an optimistic and cheerful person, harboured hopes that the war would be short-lived. This proved wrong and he became greatly distressed by the scale of the carnage as the war dragged on. His health declined over the war years, and he died on 11 August 1919.

But how did Andrew Carnegie become so interested in international arbitration in the first place?

It turns out that he had become convinced of its merits some thirty years before he contributed to the Peace Palace's construction when the two countries to which he had the closest attachments agreed to submit the *Alabama* Claims to arbitration before a tribunal seated in Geneva.

III   THE *ALABAMA* CLAIMS ARBITRATION

To explain why the *Alabama* Claims arbitration had such an effect on Andrew Carnegie, it is necessary to provide some background to the dispute.

The claims of course took their name from the notorious Confederate cruiser, the C.S.S. *Alabama*, which was built at Liverpool in 1861-1862, after the outbreak of the American Civil War.

Very soon after the war broke out, Great Britain declared itself neutral. It was spurred into action after the President of the Confederacy, Jefferson Davis, took steps to issue letters of marque for privateers to prey upon US merchant ships in accordance with 'international law', to which President Abraham Lincoln responded two days later by declaring that a naval blockade 'in pursuance of the laws of the United States and

---

10. Quoted in Nasaw, *supra* n. 1, p. 773.
11. The Building of Peace, *supra* n. 2, p. 78: 'In the ultimatum, Austria demanded that the Serbian government openly declare within 72 hours, that it had known about the attack, and that it would allow Austrian officers to investigate the attack. The Serbian government, supported by Russia, refused to accept the demands, withdrew the Serbian ambassador from Vienna, and proposed to put the conflict before the Permanent Court of Arbitration in The Hague. Austria in turn refused to take this last proposal seriously, and on 28 July 1914 declared war on Serbia …'.

the law of the Nations in such case provided' would be imposed by the US Navy on the ports of the secessionist South.[12]

To the British and other European maritime powers, the use of the word 'blockade' and the references to international law implied something more than a purely domestic conflict. Lincoln's declaration required them, they contended, to determine what their positions should be vis-à-vis the two warring parties.

Both the North and the South had extensive commercial relations with Great Britain; the textile mills of the Midlands were almost entirely dependent upon cotton produced in the South, and trade and financial links between the Confederacy and the port of Liverpool were well-established. The port city – which was a significant centre of British shipbuilding – was a hotbed of sympathy and support for the Confederacy.

On 13 May 1861, the Palmerston Government recognized the Union and the Confederacy as belligerents and declared Great Britain to be neutral in the conflict.[13] The other European maritime powers quickly followed suit.

This was poorly received by the North, which considered that Britain had acted with undue haste in recognizing the Confederacy as a belligerent just weeks after the war broke out, particularly since the Confederacy had no navy to speak of at the time. Given Britain's antipathy to slavery and the Royal Navy's active efforts to suppress trade in human beings, the North had hoped for British support, not neutrality, and the neutrality proclamation was seen by many Americans as an unfriendly act taken at a time of existential peril for the Union.

The sense that Britain had acted unduly hastily was further underscored by the decision of Lord Russell, the Foreign Secretary, to publish the Queen's Proclamation of Neutrality just before the new American Minister at the Court of St James's, Charles

---

12. Presidential Proclamation of 19 April 1861. Available at www.loc.gov.resource/prbscsm0582. Last visited on 12 May 2022. *See* Warren F. Spencer, *The Confederate Navy in Europe*, The University of Alabama Press, 1983, p. 8 ('Spencer').
13. The Queen's Proclamation stated in relevant part:

> Whereas we are happily at peace with all sovereign powers and States:
>
> And whereas hostilities have unhappily commenced between the Government of the United States of America and certain States styling themselves the Confederate States of America:
>
> And whereas we, being at peace with the Government of the United States have declared our royal determination to maintain a strict and partial neutrality in the contest between the said contending parties:
>
> We therefore have thought fit, by and with the advice of our privy council, to issue this our royal proclamation:
>
> And we do hereby strictly charge and command all our loving subjects to observe a strict neutrality in and during the aforesaid hostilities, and to abstain from violating or contravening either the laws and statutes of the realm in this behalf or the law of nations in relation thereto, as they will answer to the contrary at their peril.
>
> ...

Victoria R
13 May 1861
Available at www.loc.gov/item/scsm000229. Last visited on 12 May 2022.

Francis Adams, arrived in London to take up his office. This was seen as something of a calculated slight to the United States.

But beyond this initial act of the British Government was its unwillingness or inability to act with what the United States regarded as sufficient diligence when enforcing its neutrality law, the *Foreign Enlistment Act*.

The Act, based upon an American statute and dating back to 1819, set out the duties of British subjects when Britain declared itself to be neutral in a foreign conflict. It had received very little judicial consideration, but insofar as shipbuilding was concerned, it contained a rather large hole which could be exploited by a Confederacy in need of a navy. The relevant provision barred any person in British territory from 'equipping, fitting out, arming any vessel with the intent that such vessel should be used to commit hostilities against any state with which this country is at peace ...'.[14] Notably missing from the scope of this provision were prohibitions against the building and sale of any such vessel. This formed the centrepiece of the Confederacy's strategy to obtain vessels in England that could be used (or converted for use) in war and to then equip them, fit them out, or arm them outside of British jurisdiction.[15]

The first such vessel to leave Liverpool was the *Oreto*, built by William C. Miller & Sons. It departed on 22 March 1862, said to be destined for Palermo. Rumoured during its construction to be destined for the Italian government, it was the subject of an extensive investigation by US officials, aided by private detectives and various informants recruited by the US consul at Liverpool. Charles Francis Adams warned Russell that the ship was destined for the South and pressed for its detention, but after investigation, the British Government deemed that there were insufficient grounds to detain the vessel.

As events transpired, after it left Liverpool, the vessel and its supply tender were arrested at Nassau after the senior Royal Navy commander in the area concluded that the *Oreto* was clearly built for warlike purposes and was intended for the Confederacy. But after hearing the parties, in what even the British government and the British arbitrator would later admit was an erroneous decision, the local Vice-Admiralty Court lifted the order and allowed the ship to sail.

---

14. *An Act to prevent the enlisting or Engagement of His Majesty's Subjects to serve in Foreign Service, and the fitting out or equipping, in His Majesty's Dominions, Vessels for Warlike Purposes, without His Majesty's Licence* (59 Geo. 3) C A P. LXIX. Available at https://vlex.co.uk/vid/foerign-enlistment-act-1819-861216512. Last visited on 29 May 2022.

15. Charles Francis Adams Jr pithily referred to the *Act* as 'one of those statues in which the British Parliamentary draughtsman has prescriptively revelled, and through the clauses of which judge and barrister love, as the phrase goes, to drive a coach-and-six'. Charles France Adams Jr, *Before and After the Treaty of Washington: The American Civil War and the Transvaal War*, An Address to the New York Historical Society, 19 November 1901, p. 17 [hereafter 'Adams: Before and After']. His point echoed the United States' Argument at the Geneva arbitration which described the Act as a 'flat morass of meaningless verbosity and confused circumlocution'. ('US Argument', p. 61). This characterization rather irritated the British arbitrator who pointed out that the British Act was modelled on the American and 'in the main' used 'identical language' insofar as ships were concerned. (Papers relating to the Treaty of Washington, Volume IV, Geneva Arbitration, Dissenting Opinion of Sir Alexander Cockburn, p. 270). ('Papers Relating to the Treaty').

The *Oreto* made its way to a remote island, Green Cay, where it was met by a tender, supplied with guns and other war matériel, and, on 17 August 1862, was commissioned as the C.S.S. *Florida*. After an outbreak of yellow fever decimated its crew, the *Florida* cut short a stay in Cuba and made for Mobile, Alabama, running the blockade under heavy fire and suffering significant damage in the process. Due to the need for repairs, it did not commence cruising against the United States' merchant marine until January 1863.

The second vessel to be constructed by British shipbuilders, this time by Laird Brothers of Birkenhead, was the *Alabama*. Its dockyard name was '*290*' because it was the 290th vessel constructed by the Lairds. When it was launched on 15 May 1862, it was named the *Enrica* to give the impression that it was destined for a Spanish buyer. It too was the subject of sustained investigation by US officials, as well as warnings and protests by Adams. But the *Enrica* escaped from Liverpool on 29 July 1862 in a demonstration of guile and stealthy planning by the Confederacy's chief naval procurement agent in England, James Dunwoody Bulloch.

Bulloch, a former United States naval officer, proved to be a brilliant choice to be the South's procurement agent.[16] He astutely navigated rapidly changing and – from his perspective – increasingly difficult circumstances to procure the construction of the *Florida* and the *Alabama* and to get the latter away from Liverpool just before its detention by British authorities.[17]

Bulloch had arrived in Liverpool in early June 1861, armed with an introduction to a Liverpool law firm from the then-Attorney General of the Confederacy (and future English barrister and author of *Benjamin on Sales*), Judah P. Benjamin.[18] Soon after his arrival, Bulloch took legal advice on the *Foreign Enlistment Act* from Frederick Shepard Hull, a prominent Liverpool solicitor.[19] Hull in turn arranged for two eminent barristers to opine on the law.[20] In his memoirs, Bulloch did not identify them by name, but he noted that both went on to occupy 'the highest judicial positions' in England.[21] In

---

16. Bulloch contracted for the construction of the *Florida* within a month of arriving in Liverpool and two weeks later had had arranged for the construction of the *Alabama*.

17. Various other vessels were also procured, but the arbitration later turned primarily on the acts of the *Florida*, the *Alabama* and a third vessel, the *Shenandoah*.

18. After the war ended, Benjamin fled to England, took pupillage, and promptly wrote *A Treatise on the Law of Sale of Personal Property, with Reference to the American Decisions, to the French Code, and Civil Law*. Colloquially known as *Benjamin on Sales*, the treatise became an instant classic. Benjamin quickly became a leading counsel and would go on to argue many cases before the House of Lords and the Judicial Committee of the Privy Council.

19. In his memoir, *The Secret Service of the Confederate States in Europe, or, How the Confederate Cruisers Were Equipped* (Putnam's Sons, New York, 1884) (hereinafter 'Bulloch'), Bulloch later wrote, 'A fortunate circumstance led me to consult the late Mr. F.S. Hull, a member of a leading firm of solicitors in Liverpool, and he continued to act as my solicitor during the whole period of the war. Mr. Hull was a prudent, cautious, conscientious adviser, and throughout all those troublous times I found him a watchful and safe mentor. I kept him informed of all important transactions, and consulted him with reference to all contracts. ... He piloted me safely through the mazes of the Foreign Enlistment Act, in spite of the perplexing ambiguity of its 7th Section, and the bewildering iterations and reiterations of the precept not to "equip, furnish, fit out, or arm" any ship with intent, etc., etc.' (At pp. 65-66.)

20. *Ibid.*, p. 66.

21. *Ibid.*, p. 67. In his superb article, '*The* Alabama *Claims Arbitration*', ICLQ Volume 54, January 2005, p. 1, at p. 4, the late Tom Bingham suggests that the two counsel may have been Sir Hugh

essence, their advice was that the *Act* prohibited the equipping, fitting out and arming of warships, but this prohibition did not extend to the construction of such ships per se.[22]

In this regard, the Act reflected British commercial policy; British merchants sold arms, war matériel, uniforms, and other goods to both sides during the Civil War, and the general belief of the Palmerston government of the time was that ships were just another article of commerce. But some lawyers thought that there were limits to that notion.

Even though the advice he received was that a shipbuilder did not commit an offence by selling a ship to a belligerent, Bulloch sought to obscure the ultimate purchaser of the vessels so as to provide plausible deniability to the shipbuilders. As noted, the *Oreto* and the *290/Enrica* were rumoured to be destined for the Italian and Spanish governments, respectively. Bulloch also sought to separate each vessel's construction from its equipping, by arranging for the ships' arms and supplies to be conveyed to them by tender after the ships departed Liverpool. Steps such as these, Bulloch hoped, would shield his plans from official British interference.

The *Foreign Enlistment Act* was considered to be strict in that it required due proof – not mere suspicion – of the offence before the authorities could intervene and effect a seizure. The Crown moreover could be liable for damages in the event of a wrongful seizure. These features of the law contributed to official hesitancy which worked to Bulloch's advantage.

The American consul in Liverpool, Thomas Haines Dudley, relentlessly tracked Bulloch's activities and Adams protested to the British authorities, but without success. As the *290/Enrica* readied for sea, the United States mounted a furious last-minute

---

Cairns QC and George Mellish QC. Cairns served as Solicitor General, then Attorney General in the late 1850s and briefly as Lord Chancellor in the few months of Disraeli's government after Derby resigned in 1868. When Gladstone took power, Cairns became Leader of the Opposition in the House of Lords. As for Mellish, he was appointed as Lord Justice of the Court of Appeal in Chancery in 1870 ('Bingham').

Cairns and Mellish both represented the shipowners in the legal challenge of the Government's seizure of another vessel intended for the Confederacy, the *Alexandra*. Cairns was a trenchant critic of the Treaty of Washington. In 1871, he strongly criticized the Gladstone Ministry's negotiation of the Treaty of Washington, the terms of reference of which, he argued, through want of care on the British side, could allow the United States to advance its so-called national and indirect claims. He was also a sharp critic of the Ministry's handling of the 'indirect' claims imbroglio of 1872.

22. Bulloch reported that his solicitor's advice, after consulting counsel, was as follows:

    1. It is no offense (under the Act) for British subjects to equip, etc., a ship at some country *without* her Majesty's dominions, though the intent be to cruise against a friendly State.
    2. It is no offense for *any* person (subject or no subject) to *equip* a ship *within* her Majesty's dominions, if it be *not* done with the intent to cruise against a friendly State.
    3. The mere building of a ship *within* her Majesty's dominions by any person (subject or no subject) is no offence, *whatever may be the intent of the parties*, because the offence is not the *building* but the *equipping*.

    Therefore any shipbuilder may build any ship in her Majesty's dominions, provided he does not equip her within her Majesty's dominions, and he has nothing to do with the acts of the purchaser done *within* her Majesty's dominions without his concurrence, nor *without* her Majesty's dominions even with his concurrence. [Italics in original].

    Bulloch, *supra* n. 19, Volume I, p. 67.

campaign against its departure by tendering a legal opinion by Robert Collier QC MP (counsel to the Admiralty and Judge-Advocate of the Fleet). A respected senior counsel on the western circuit, Collier saw the case as a flagrant breach of the Act which demanded the vessel's detention, and this opinion spurred the Foreign Office into action with Lord Russell seeking the views of the law officers of the Crown on Collier's opinion.

But at the very time that the law officers' opinion was sought, one of the three officers, the Queen's Advocate – the most senior in rank at the time and the recognized expert on matters of international law – who had been ailing for most of July, suddenly and irreversibly descended into madness and for obvious reasons was unable to attend to the matter, a problem exacerbated by his wife's initial failure to notify anyone of her husband's indisposition. Valuable time was lost in arriving at an opinion concurring with Collier's view that the vessel should be detained.[23]

To make matters worse, when it was decided to act against the ship, Bulloch received a tip from an unnamed 'private and most reliable source' that it was about to be detained. The *Enrica*, under the command of a British master retained specifically for the first leg of its voyage, and flying British colours, escaped just ahead of a detention order telegraphed from London to customs officials at Liverpool and Cork.[24]

Bulloch remained in England after the war and his account of the *Alabama*'s escape was understandably intentionally vague on certain details. It has never been established conclusively who tipped off Bulloch and it remains a live issue to the date of this writing.[25]

Instead of bolting south to the Atlantic, where the U.S.S. *Tuscarora* was prowling, the *Enrica* sailed north through the Irish Sea and then proceeded in a southerly direction along the west coast of Ireland en route to the island of Terceira where it rendezvoused with its supply ship, the *Agrippina* (cleared from London in order to maintain the separation between construction and equipping and arming) and another vessel, the *Bahama*, which transported the *Enrica*'s new captain, Rafael Semmes, and his officers. Semmes assumed command, the supplies, cannons and war matériel were transshipped, and the ship was commissioned the C.S.S. *Alabama*.

Over the next two years, the *Alabama* conducted a campaign of terror against the United States' merchant marine. Powered by wind and steam, the *Alabama* (and the

---

23. Bingham, *supra* n. 21, p. 6. *See also* the account of the Solicitor-General at the time (and future counsel for Great Britain in the Geneva arbitration), Sir Roundell Palmer. Roundell Palmer, First Earl of Selbourne, *Memorials, Part 2, Person and Political, 1865-1895*, MacMillan and Co. Ltd., 1896, Part I, pp. 423-427. ('Palmer').
24. Bulloch, *supra* n. 19, Volume I, p. 238.
25. *Ibid*. In 2015, a British author, Renata Eley Long, published an interesting book entitled, *In the Shadow of the Alabama: The British Foreign Office and the American Civil War*, which points the finger at a young aristocrat who served as a junior clerk in the Foreign Office, Victor Buckley ('Long', pp. 1-2). This view was shared by Charles Francis Adams and Benjamin Moran, the Secretary of the US Legation in London during and after the Civil War. Fingers were also pointed at the Collector of Customs at Liverpool, Samuel Price Edwards. Bulloch strenuously denied that any government official was the person in question. '... I feel it incumbent upon me to declare that no officer, high or low, in any department of the Government, did ever convey to me, a word or a hint which led me to anticipate what the action of the Government would be, or was likely to be, in any pending case.' Bulloch, *supra* n. 19, p. 206 and at pp. 262-264.

Florida) proved to be faster and more powerful than most of the Union's warships. Along with a handful of other ships, they pursued the American merchant ships throughout the North and South Atlantic and as far away as the Strait of Malacca and the North Pacific. Many American vessels were reflagged during the war in order to seek the protection of the Union Jack.

By the time of its sinking by the U.S.S. *Kearsarge* off Cherbourg on 19 June 1864, the *Alabama* and its tender, the *Tuscaloosa*, had sunk or burned some sixty-four Union vessels. For its part, before it was rammed and seized by a US Navy warship in the harbour of Bahia, Brazil (itself a rather flagrant breach of Brazil's sovereignty), and towed north to Hampton Roads, the *Florida* took some thirty-seven Union vessels, two of which became its tenders (renamed the *Tacony* and the *Clarence*) and they, in turn, took twenty-three more vessels.[26]

To the Northern eye, Britain exhibited a lack of diligence in allowing vessels that could be used for military purposes to be constructed in its shipyards. The United States also thought that British colonial ports were overly generous in allowing Confederate warships to take on supplies, particularly coal, and in one case – in Melbourne, Australia – in permitting the *Shenandoah* to augment its crew, thus enabling it to commence a campaign against the American whaling fleet in the North Pacific. Finally, the United States complained that even after the ships' true purpose was revealed and that they had incontestably been used to carry on war against it, the British authorities did not pursue them as being in breach of the applicable law.

All of this, of course, led the United States to demand compensation.

As noted earlier, it was President Theodore Roosevelt's decision to put the *Venezuelan Claims* case before a PCA tribunal that motivated Andrew Carnegie to donate USD 1.5 million to the construction of the Peace Palace. In a strange twist of fate, James Dunwoody Bulloch's half-sister married into the Roosevelt family. Thus, the architect of the Confederacy's ship-buying programme whose actions laid the foundation for the depredations which in turn gave rise to the *Alabama* Claims arbitration was none other than Theodore Roosevelt's 'Uncle Jimmie'.[27]

---

26. Due to the rapidly increasing notoriety of the *Alabama* and the *Florida* after they left Liverpool, the British authorities' position became increasingly untenable and took on the appearance of being unduly legalistic and at variance with the facts (although this was what the US was arguing from the very beginning). In April 1863, under heavy pressure from Charles Francis Adams, Russell decided to arrest the *Alexandra*. The shipowner challenged the seizure in the Court of Common Pleas at Westminster and a jury charged by Baron Pollock quickly found against the Crown. The matter was unsuccessfully appealed all the way to the House of Lords. In the end, the British Government bought the vessel rather than let it go to the Confederacy. The South's most audacious plan, the construction of two iron-clad ships with underwater rams, the so-called Laird Rams, which were intended to sink the wooden US Navy ships blockading the Southern ports, was thwarted, again by Russell, over the advice of his law officers (who had just lost the *Alexandra* case and believed that there was no legal basis for seizing the rams). The rams were purchased, albeit rather oddly, by the Foreign Office, rather than by the Admiralty. Spencer, *supra* n. 12, p. 116.

27. Spencer, *supra* n. 12, p. 16.

IV   ATTEMPTS AT SETTLEMENT

Throughout the war and until he left London in April 1868, Charles Francis Adams conducted an extensive correspondence with Lord Russell and his successor, Lord Stanley. With every capture or loss of a merchant marine ship during the war, Adams would protest the incident, thereby building, vessel by vessel, a detailed factual record for the hoped-for arbitration which in fact would later take place.

Russell rebuffed Adams' requests to submit the United States' claims to international arbitration.[28] When Palmerston's government was succeeded by Derby's, British resistance to arbitration softened and Adams was heartened by the progress that he was making with the new Foreign Secretary, Lord Stanley, until Secretary of State William H. Seward suddenly instructed Adams to inform Stanley that the United States saw no possibility of resolving the dispute through a joint commission.[29]

Seward's *volte face* was driven by his belief that the Alaska Purchase (which he had negotiated and announced in late March 1867) could, if played right, be the first step in inducing Great Britain to retreat from North America. An ardent annexationist, Seward thought that complete American territorial continuity on the Pacific coast from Mexico to the Arctic could be achieved by the acquisition of the colony of British Columbia (or even more) as part of the settlement of the *Alabama* Claims.[30] He,

---

28. In a reply to a letter sent by Adams some two years previously, Lord Russell stated: 'In your letter of the 23rd of October 1863, you were pleased to say that the Government of the United States is ready to agree to any form of arbitration . ... Her Majesty's Government must, therefore, decline either to make reparation and compensation for the captures made by the *Alabama*, or to refer the question to any foreign state.' Correspondence concerning Claims against Great Britain, Vol. III. p. 562. ('Correspondence Concerning Claims').

29. In a dispatch dated 13 January 1868, Seward informed Adams, 'Your dispatch of the 24th of December, No. 1, 503, has been received. You were quite right in saying to Lord Stanley that the negotiation in regard to the so-called Alabama claims is now considered by this Government to have been closed without a prospect of its being reopened ... Lord Stanley seems to have resolved that the so-called Alabama claims shall be treated so exclusively as a pecuniary commercial claim, as to insist on altogether excluding the proceedings of Her Majesty's Government in regard to the war from consideration in the arbitration which he proposed.

 On the other hand, I have been singularly unfortunate in my correspondence, if I have not given it to be clearly understood, that a violation of neutrality by the Queen's proclamation, and kindred proceedings of the British Government, is regarded as a national wrong and injury to the United States, and that the lowest form of satisfaction for that national injury that the United States could accept, would be found in an indemnity, without reservation or compromise, by the British Government to those citizens of the United States who had suffered individual injury and damages by the vessels of war unlawfully built, equipped, manned, fitted out, or entertained and protected in the British ports and harbors, in consequence of a failure of the British Government to preserve its neutrality.' Correspondence Concerning Claims, *supra* n. 28, Vol. III. p. 688.

30. In his dispatch to Adams closing the door to arbitration of the *Alabama* claims, Seward referred to various irritants existing between the two countries ranging from the San Juan Island boundary dispute on the west coast, to the east coast fisheries dispute and Britain's treatment of naturalized US citizens who had been born in Britain, and stated that in view of these 'existing sources of controversy ... *the thought occurred to me that her Majesty's government, if desirous to lay a broad foundation for friendly and satisfactory relations, might possibly think it expedient to suggest a conference, in which all the matters referred to might be considered together and so a comprehensive settlement might be attempted without exciting the sensibilities which are*

therefore, began to speak of much larger 'national' or 'indirect' claims than had previously been advanced in the hopes of setting up a grand diplomatic bargain that would simultaneously resolve the claims and extend United States territory northward.[31] These claims would later assume great importance in attracting Andrew Carnegie's interest in the dispute.

Adams was privately sceptical of Seward's idea. Adams believed that Britain had little interest in ceding territory to the United States. Indeed, British Columbia did not follow Alaska into the Union, and in the autumn of 1868, with President Andrew Johnson's Administration winding down, Seward launched a final push to settle the *Alabama* Claims. He abandoned his hopes for negotiating a territorial cession and instructed Adams' successor, Reverdy Johnson, to seek a settlement. Johnson obliged in record time, but the Johnson-Stanley Convention, subsequently amended to become the Johnson-Clarendon Convention, pleased virtually no one in Washington.[32]

Had it entered into force, the Convention would have established a joint commission to resolve a variety of disputes between the US and Great Britain, including the *Alabama* Claims. But the treaty contained no expression of regret by Great Britain

---

understood to have caused that government to insist upon a limited arbitration in the case of the Alabama claims'. Correspondence Concerning Claims, *supra* n. 28, Vol. III. p. 689, emphasis added.

31. Even though he led the attack against Seward's attempt to resolve the *Alabama* Claims (through the Johnson-Clarendon Convention), Charles Sumner shared Seward's view of the desirability of a territorial cession as part of a settlement of the *Alabama* claims. Sumner had argued in favour of Senate approval of the Alaska Purchase treaty on the basis that that the withdrawal of one European Power from North America (the Russian Empire) could stimulate the withdrawal of another (Great Britain). Charles Francis Adams Jr would later write: 'In the mind of Mr. Sumner, the ultimate, and, as he in 1870 believed, not remote withdrawal of all European flags, including, of course, the British, from the Western hemisphere, was a logical development of the Monroe doctrine . ... Secretary Seward's Alaska acquisition, bringing to an end Russian dominion in America, created a precedent. One European flag then disappeared from the New World. Covering areas of consequence, those of Spain and Great Britain only remained; and more than twenty years before, Richard Cobden had written to Sumner, – 'I agree with you that Nature has decided that *Canada and the United States must become one for all purposes of intercommunication* . ... If the people of Canada are tolerably unanimous and wishing to sever the very slight thread which now binds them to this country, I see no reason why, if good faith and ordinary temper be observed, it should not be done amicably.' Charles Sumner did not belong to the Bismarckian school of statesmanship, – he was no welder in blood and iron; and these words of Cobden furnished the key of the situation as it lay in his essentially doctrinaire mind. He, accordingly, looked forward with confidence to the incorporation of the British possessions into the American Union; but, as Mr Pierce [Sumner's principal biographer] truly enough says, he always insisted that it 'should be made by peaceful annexation, by the voluntary act of England, and with the cordial assent of the colonists'. Charles Francis Adams Jr, *Lee at Appomattox, and Other Papers*, pp. 150-151 ('Adams: Lee at Appomattox').

32. Johnson initially negotiated a version of the Convention with Stanley of the Derby government. When Gladstone formed a new government after the general election of 1868, Lord Clarendon returned to the Foreign Office. He continued negotiations to amend the convention with an increasingly desperate Reverdy Johnson. Johnson made new proposals not only after Ulysses S. Grant – who despised Andrew Johnson and did not think much of Seward – became President-elect and even after Grant took office in March 1869. Grant was fiercely opposed to the draft convention and let it be known that this was the case.

and on the American side, at least in the Senate, it was considered to allow only for the making of claims for direct losses suffered by individuals from both countries and did not encompass the United States' 'national' or 'indirect' claims. This would prove fatal to its prospects in the Senate.

Even after Ulysses S. Grant was sworn in as President-elect and then President of the United States, Reverdy Johnson, bit firmly in his teeth, continued to press Britain for concessions that would make his convention more palatable to the new administration and to the Senate. But his attempts to amend the Convention to reflect the United States' desire for an apology and to provide a forum to resolve the national injuries that it claimed to have suffered were rejected by Clarendon.

When it came time for the Senate to express itself on the Johnson-Clarendon Convention, the verdict was clear: the convention was defeated by a vote of 54 to one.

In a powerful, even incendiary speech, the Chairman of the Senate Committee on Foreign Relations, Charles Sumner, made the price of settling Britain's alleged breaches of neutrality look very high indeed. The speech, given in secret 'Executive Session' and then quickly published to widespread acclaim after the Senate resolved unanimously to lift the injunction of secrecy, was the first detailed public articulation of the American grievance.[33]

Sumner itemized in general terms the direct losses and the indirect national losses suffered by the US. Although he refrained from arriving at a specific figure, he did list the various heads of damages.[34] The calculation of the amount said to be due for Britain's contribution to the 'prolongation of the war' resulting from the depredations of the Confederate cruisers alone was either one-half of the USD 4 billion incurred by the US to prosecute the war or one-half of the USD 2.8 billion in public debt that remained to be paid off.[35] (Sumner's speech was ambiguous on this point.) This head

---

33. Caleb Cushing, who would go on to serve as one of the United States' counsel at the Geneva arbitration, declared that, 'For the first time, Great Britain receives a distinct impression of the nature and consequences of her hostile intervention in the affairs of the United States.' Springfield *Republican*, 17 April 1869. Quoted in David Herbert Donald, *Charles Sumner and the Rights of Man*, Random House, 1970, p. 430 ('Donald').

34. Sumner estimated the capture and burning of American vessels at about USD 15 million, the loss in the carrying trade at USD 110 million and then asserted that as large as these losses were, there was another chapter where they were far larger, namely, 'the national losses caused by the prolongation of the war and traceable directly to England'. He summed these damages up by saying, 'If, through British intervention, the war was doubled in duration, or in any way extended, as cannot be doubted, then is England justly responsible for the additional expenditure to which our country was doomed; and, whatever may be the final settlement of these great accounts, such must be the judgment in any chancery which consults the simple equity of the case.' He estimated the cost of suppressing the Rebellion as some USD 4 billion some of which had been paid with a debt remaining of USD 2.8 billion, 'thus leaving the calculation of this item plain to the youngest schoolboy'. 'Our Claims on England', Speech of Hon. Charles Sumner of Massachusetts, delivered in Executive Session of 13 April, on 'The Johnson-Clarendon Treaty for the Settlement of Claims', Washington, F. & J. Rives & Geo. A. Bailey, Reporters and Printers of the Debates of Congress, 1869, p. 12 ('Sumner: Original Version').

35. Sumner observed that, 'The Rebellion was suppressed at a cost of more than four thousand million dollars, a considerable portion of which has been already paid; leaving twenty-five hundred missions as a national debt to burden the people.' Sumner: Original Version, p. 12.

of claim, Sumner asserted, was easily calculated. 'Everybody can make the calculation', i.e., one-half of USD 4 billion or the remaining amount of the public debt.[36] Either way, it was an astronomical sum at the time.[37] Sumner himself called it 'colossal'.[38]

There is little doubt that Sumner was motivated to come up with a damages figure that was so large that Britain could be expected to conclude that it was beyond its means to pay. The idea was to induce Britain to seek other non-pecuniary means of settling the dispute such as an agreement on new rules of international law to govern the rights and duties of neutrals, accompanied by a cession of some or all of British North America in settlement of the claims.[39]

Unsurprisingly, Sumner's speech was poorly received in Britain (and in most, but not all, of British North America).[40] The Foreign Secretary, Lord Clarendon, wrote to the British Minister at Washington that if it was Sumner's 'desire to render friendly relations between the two countries difficult if not impossible, he may congratulate himself'.[41] To similar effect, Clarendon wrote to Queen Victoria, 'It is the unfriendly state of our relations with America that to a great extent paralyses our action in Europe. There is not the smallest doubt that if we were engaged in a Continental quarrel we should immediately find ourselves at war' with the US.[42]

American diplomats and newspaper correspondents in London reported on the widespread feelings of anger and hostility they encountered in London. The US consul-general in London, Freeman H. Morse, wrote to Senator William Pitt Fessenden

36. *Ibid. See also* Charles Sumner, *The Alabama Claims – Speech of the Honourable Chares Sumner, delivered in Executive Session of the United States Senate on Tuesday, April 4, 1869, against the ratification of the Johnson-Clarendon Treaty for the Settlement of the Alabama and Other Claims*, London: Stevens Brothers (1869), p. 26. ('Sumner: London Version'). There is a third version of the speech, which Sumner later published in his *Complete Works of Charles Sumner*, Volume 17, p. 53, which is replete with 270 footnotes ('Sumner: Complete Works').
37. Roy Jenkins noted in his biography of Gladstone that at one point (this was his 13 April 1869, speech against the Johnson-Clarendon Convention) Sumner 'suggested a figure of £400 million, which was approximately six times the size of total British annual public expenditure at the time. On another occasion he proposed that a cession of Canada to the United States might act as an assuagement. These could have been dismissed as "noises off" had not Hamilton Fish, the founder of a famous Hudson Valley foreign policy dynasty and President Grant's Secretary of State, been very apprehensive of Sumner; he was frightened to negotiate far away from Sumner's extravagant imperatives.' Roy Jenkins, *Gladstone – A Biography* (Random House) 2002, p. 359 ('Jenkins').
38. Sumner: Original Version, *supra* n. 34, p. 13.
39. Having roughly estimated the United States' national claims, Sumner completed this section of his speech with a hint of the outcome which he desired: 'This plain statement, without one word of exaggeration or aggravation, is enough to exhibit the magnitude of the national losses, whether from the destruction of our commerce, the prolongation of the war, or the expense of the blockade. They stand before us mountain-high, with a base broad as the Nation, and a mass stupendous as the Rebellion itself. It will be for a wise statesmanship to determine how this fearful accumulation, like Pelion upon Ossa, shall be removed out of sight, so that it shall no longer overshadow the two countries.' Sumner: Original Version, *supra* n. 34, p. 12.
40. In 1869, there were various pockets of support for annexation to the United States in British North America, especially on Vancouver Island, in the Red River Valley, and in Nova Scotia.
41. Lord Clarendon to Sir Edward Thornton, 1 May 1869, Clarendon Papers, Bodleian Library.
42. Lord Clarendon to the Queen, 1 May 1869, quoted in C. P. Stacey, *Canada and the British Army, 1846-1871: A Study in the Practice of Responsible Government*, University of Toronto Press, 1963, "STACEY" p. 213.

that he thought 'war was next to certainty'.[43] George W. Smalley, the New York *Tribune*'s reporter, reported from London that he had heard 'the wildest expressions from men we have always looked to for moderation and friendliness.'[44]

V   A BREAKTHROUGH

Passions eventually cooled on both sides of the Atlantic and around the end of 1870, it was judged by both sides that the time was ripe for another attempt to resolve the claims. Accordingly, a secret diplomatic initiative was launched by Great Britain in January 1871 when an unofficial – and plausibly deniable – representative of Her Majesty's Government, Sir John Rose, visited Washington, DC, for informal discussions with Secretary of State Hamilton Fish.

Like Andrew Carnegie, Rose was a Scottish immigrant to North America, but his family had emigrated to Canada rather than to the US. Widely regarded as a natural diplomat, Rose was a person of vast and varied experience. He had been a highly successful commercial lawyer in Montreal, an MP and Canada's second Minister of Finance, Britain's appointee to the joint British-American commission that settled the Hudson's Bay Company's claims against the United States, and a close confidant and the unofficial representative in London of Canada's first Prime Minister, Sir John A. Macdonald.

In September 1869, Rose resigned from the government to move to London to run a banking firm established by the prominent New York banker and Republican stalwart, Levi P. Morton. Morton, Bliss & Company of New York worked with Andrew Carnegie, and it naturally followed that when Carnegie started doing business in London, Morton's London firm would also act for him.

Rose and his partner Morton made their way to Washington in early January 1871 not only to find a means of resolving the long-festering dispute but also because they were interested in leading a syndicate to refinance the United States' war debt. Interest rates were lower in England than in the United States, and the top priority of the Secretary of the Treasury, George Boutwell, was to issue new bonds in London at those lower rates. The two issues – the resolution of the *Alabama* Claims and the American war debt – were thus inextricably linked. Rose himself had written to Boutwell in late 1870 to warn him that 'the unsettled condition of the *Alabama* Claims interfered with the funding of the [US] public debt'.[45]

Over a period of two weeks, Rose and Fish sketched out how the *Alabama* Claims and other bilateral irritants might be resolved by a Joint High Commission (ultimately comprising five American and five British representatives). Mindful of the Johnson-Clarendon Convention's fate, Rose and Fish agreed to a carefully orchestrated process

---

43. Freeman H. Morse to William Pitt Fessenden, 17 May 1869, Fessenden Papers, quoted in Adrian Cook, *The Alabama Claims: American Politics and Anglo-American Relations, 1865-1872*, Cornell University Press, 1975, p. 84. ('Cook.')
44. George W. Smalley to Senator Charles Sumner, 14 May 1869, Sumner Papers, quoted in Cook, *supra* n. 43, p. 84.
45. Hamilton Fish Diary, 9 December 1870, quoted in Jay Sexton, *The Funded Loan and the* Alabama *Claims*, Diplomatic History, Volume 27, No. 4, September 2003, 449 at p. 462 ('Sexton').

aimed at maintaining face on both sides, whereby the British Minister at Washington, Sir Edward Thornton, would write to Fish proposing the establishment of a commission to deal with a variety of issues involving the United States and British North America, to which Fish would respond that the President would be pleased to engage in such discussions if the *Alabama* Claims were added to the agenda, to which Thornton would reply that if the claims of British nationals against the United States for losses suffered in the Civil War (and vice versa) were included, Britain would be pleased to include the *Alabama* Claims. Hamilton Fish would then assent to this, and the Joint High Commission would thereby be established.

As a result of this exchange of correspondence – the letters backdated to make it look like time had elapsed between each proposal and the response thereto – the Joint High Commission was established, with its members to convene in Washington as soon as possible.

The Joint High Commission convened in the latter part of February 1871. Over the next two months, it considered an array of issues, the *Alabama* Claims being the most important. The commissioners' work was attended by many dinners, balls, a foxhunt, and even a banquet organized by a collection of Masonic lodges in honour of the head of the British Commissioners, Lord de Grey and Ripon (at that time Grand Master of England).[46]

Britain's willingness to send senior representatives to Washington went a long way to improving relations. But, of course, the agreement to arbitrate the *Alabama* Claims was the crucial part of the Treaty of Washington which was concluded on 8 May 1871. The Treaty sought to adjust a variety of irritants that had arisen between the two countries, most of which concerned issues arising between the United States and Britain's North American colonies.[47]

The Treaty's first eleven articles set out the means for arbitrating the claims 'generically known as the "*Alabama* Claims" ...'[48] Britain provided the long-sought expression 'in a friendly spirit, [of] the regret felt by Her Majesty's Government for the escape, under whatever circumstances, of the *Alabama* and other vessels from British ports, and for the depredations committed by those vessels'.[49] It agreed to put the

---

46. Some 30 members of Congress and senators attended the affair. Cook, *supra* n. 43, p. 191. The head of the British delegation, Lord de Grey and Ripon (also a Freemason) wryly reported to the Foreign Secretary on this last social event: 'Last night Tenterden, Macdonald [also a Freemason] and I were entertained by the Free-masons of this part of the world – the affair began at 7 PM and ended at 2 in the morning! Compensation asked of H.M. Gov't £20,000 apiece at least.' Ripon Papers: Letter from Lord de Grey to Lord Granville, 27 March 1871, British Library Add MS 43520 ('Ripon').

47. At the time of the Treaty's making, Britain had four colonies: (i) British Columbia to the west of the Rocky Mountains, (ii) Canada, which had only recently extended its land mass westward from present-day Ontario to include the massive tract of land to the west and north that had previously been subject to the control of the Hudson's Bay Company, and the two island colonies of (iii) Prince Edward Island, and (iv) Newfoundland. The Terms of Union between British Columbia and Canada were being settled at the same time as the Treaty was being negotiated.

48. Treaty of Washington, 1871, Article I. Among other things, the Treaty established the tribunal of five arbitrators to hear the United States' claims at Geneva. Available at https://archive.org/details/cihm_16272/page/n5/mode/2up. Last visited on 14 May 2022.

49. *Ibid.*

claims before a tribunal of five arbitrators (one American, one Briton, a Brazilian, an Italian, and a Swiss).[50] Finally, the two sides agreed to the so-called Three Rules of international law on the duties of neutrals that would govern the arbitration, even though the Treaty recorded the fact that the British Commissioners were commanded by Her Majesty to 'declare that Her Majesty's Government can not assent to the foregoing rules as a statement of principles of International Law which were in force at the time when the claims … arose'.[51]

The Treaty was quickly ratified by both parties and entered into force on 4 July 1871. The arbitrators were appointed and both sides began to prepare their respective cases to be filed on 15 December 1871. A long-festering dispute was finally going to be resolved by an international tribunal and the treaty seemed to herald a new era of Anglo-American accord.

What could go wrong? As it turned out, quite a lot.

VI   THE ARBITRATION ALMOST DERAILED

The drama was far from over for when the United States filed its Case, the British woke up to the fact that the damages section of the Case had 'out-Sumnered Sumner'. In addition to the claims for direct losses arising from sunken and burned ships and lost cargoes, in keeping with Senator Sumner's speech, the US Case also presented claims 'in equity' for national or indirect losses.[52] No detailed quantification of those claims was made, but the Case asserted that there was sufficient evidence before the Tribunal to allow it to arrive at a suitable sum. The damages awarded, the United States added, should be brought forward to the date of the award's payment by adding interest at a rate of 7%. The British were aghast when they digested the full implications of what the United States appeared to be claiming.

---

50. *Ibid.*, and Article II.
51. *Ibid.*, Article VI.
52. The US Case specified the claims as encompassing (i) the direct losses growing out of the destruction of vessels and their cargoes; (ii) the national expenditures in pursuit of the rebel cruisers; (iii) the loss in the transfer of American commercial marine to the British flag; (iv) the enhanced payments of insurance; and (v), the prolongation of the war and the addition of a large sum to the cost of the war and the suppression of the rebellion. *See* John Bassett Moore, *History and Digest of the International Arbitrations to Which the United States Has Been a Party, Together with Appendices Containing the Treaties Relating to Such Arbitrations, and Historical and Legal Notes*, Government Printing Office 1898, Volume I, 589 ('Bassett Moore'). This was consistent with Sumner's 13 April 1869 speech and indeed President Grant's 6 December 1869 speech to Congress in which he stated: 'The provisions were wholly inadequate for the settlement of the grave wrongs that have been sustained by this Government as well as by its citizens. The injuries resulting to the United States by reason of the course adopted by Great Britain during our late Civil War; in the increased rates of insurance, in the diminution of exports and imports, and other obstructions to domestic industry and production; in its effects upon the foreign commerce of the country; in the decrease and transfer to Great Britain of our commercial marine; in the prolongation of the war; and the increased cost (both in treasure and lives) of its suppression; could not be adjusted and satisfied as ordinary commercial claims which continually arise between commercial nations. And yet the Convention treated them simply as such ordinary claims, from which they differ more widely in the gravity of their character than in the magnitude of their amount, great as is that difference.' Quoted in the United States Argument submitted to the Geneva Tribunal, 15 June 1872 ('US Argument').

By early January 1872, the British press and politicians were beginning to estimate Great Britain's potential financial exposure. When Gladstone awoke to the political danger and got around to focusing on what the United States appeared to be claiming, he estimated that it could be more than what the victorious Prussians had exacted from the defeated French in the recent Franco-Prussian War.[53]

The British negotiators of the Treaty of Washington thought their American counterparts had agreed not to prefer the national or indirect claims. Hamilton Fish and the rest of the American Commissioners rejected any suggestion that they had ever agreed to do so.

In his speech following the Queen's Speech opening Parliament in February 1872, Gladstone denounced the claims as outrageous, and declared that it would be 'insane to accede to demands which no nation with a spark of honour or spirit could submit to even at the point of death'.[54] His political position was temporarily bolstered by the fact that Benjamin Disraeli, speaking for the Conservatives, also denounced the claims.[55] The effect of the Prime Minister's speech in the House of Commons was that the Government quickly painted itself into a corner. Great Britain would participate in the arbitration, but only if the indirect claims were withdrawn.

But this was a demand that the United States could not accept. It simply could not withdraw a part of its case just because its opponent had denounced it. A public stalemate ensued in which both sides publicly dug themselves further into their opposing positions while they simultaneously privately sought to find a way out. The crisis almost brought down Gladstone's government, for most of his own Cabinet took a harder line against the United States than the Foreign Secretary, Lord Granville, and the Prime Minister himself.[56]

As previously noted, Andrew Carnegie had worked closely with the firm of Morton, Bliss and Company, which was well known for its involvement with American

---

53. In a note to Robert Schenck, the US Minister at London, Gladstone said that he had not used the word 'preposterous' when criticizing the US Case, but he thought it 'probable I may have said it was absurd to suppose that we with our eyes open should have gone into a Treaty under which claims might be made upon us in comparison with which the Franco-German indemnity is insignificant.' Gladstone to Schenck, Add MS 44541, f. 23, quoted in H.C.G. Mathew, *The Gladstone Diaries*, Volume VIII, July 1871-December 1874, Clarendon Press – Oxford, 1982, pp. 115-116. ('Mathew.')

54. The statement was made in the Prime Minister's 7 February 1872 speech on the Queen's Speech opening Parliament. Quoted in John Morley, *Life of William Ewart Gladstone*, MacMillan 1903, Volume II, p. 406 ('Morley').

55. The speeches sufficiently alarmed Secretary of State Fish that on 12 February 1872, he telegraphed the American Minister at London asking, 'Is the Government sending troops to Canada?' Telegram from Hamilton Fish to Robert Schenck, 12 February 1872, Diplomatic Instructions, quoted in Cook, *supra* n. 43, p. 220.

56. Gladstone's Colonial Secretary, Lord Kimberley, for example, noted in his diary that at a Cabinet meeting held on 12 February 1872, there had been a discussion of the *Alabama* case: 'Ripon [the head of the British delegation during the negotiation of the Treaty of Washington] and Forster [who had long been friendly to the United States] were for allowing the U.S. case to go to the arbitrators, we making a protest against the indirect claims and declaring that we would not pay them if awarded against us. Granville also inclined to this course; but the rest of us were strongly against this course: & we prevailed.' Angus Hawkins and John Powell, *The Journal of John Wodehouse, First Earl of Kimberley for 1862-1902*, Royal Historical Society, 1997, p. 265 ('Hawkins and Powell').

railway interests, and with Morton's London office, run by Sir John Rose. As we have seen, Rose had played a central role in getting the Joint High Commission launched and Morton had done much lobbying in support of the initiative at the highest levels of the Grant Administration, including the President himself, and in the Senate.

Relations between the two countries and financial and commercial flows between them had improved after the Treaty was concluded, but it now appeared that the whole process of Anglo-American rapprochement was about to collapse. Carnegie, Morton, Rose, and others sprang into action, seeking to convince their respective governments to find a way out of the crisis by getting rid of the indirect claims and thus allowing the arbitration to continue.[57]

Carnegie's interest in the dispute was twofold. The first reason was rather prosaic. After the war, he further diversified his interests by moving into the business of selling American bridge and railway bonds. The US market for railway bonds had become saturated, and Carnegie had begun to combine business with pleasure by taking along a trunk-load of bonds with him on his annual summer vacation in Britain.[58]

Although his first foray into the London bond market had been highly successful, when Carnegie returned to London in March 1872, he found no appetite for American bonds. When the indirect claims crisis erupted, American securities plummeted on the London market. The British Government having stated that Britain would not participate in the arbitration unless the indirect claims were withdrawn, and the US Government having refused to back down, the capital markets took fright.

Carnegie tried his luck with the leading financial houses on the Continent. Discussions with Sulzbach Brothers in Frankfurt also drew a blank. They were unwilling to buy any bonds due to the worrying financial consequences of the as-yet unresolved arbitration.[59] As *The Economist* reported at the time, 'Half the public bodies

---

57. The famous Civil War financier, Jay Cooke, who had also opened a London office (with former Treasury Secretary Hugh McCulloch as resident partner) to lead on the issuance of US bonds to British and Continental investors, and August Belmont, the American agent of N. M. Rothschild & Sons (with whom Cooke had formed a syndicate in January 1872 to sell USD 500 million 5% bonds and USD 300 million 4.5% bonds) and Lionel de Rothschild also got into the act. Sexton, *supra* n. 45, pp. 470-474.

58. Nasaw describes how in March 1871 Carnegie sailed to London with a batch of Union Pacific-backed Omaha Bridge bonds to sell and he spent 10 of the next 18 months overseas selling bridge and railway bonds. In August 1871, for example, armed with a new supply of bonds, Carnegie sought an introduction to Baring Brothers in London. He was given a formal letter of introduction from Morton & Rose, his London brokers. The letter of 29 August 1871 stated: 'The bearer of this, Mr. Andrew Carnegie of Pittsburgh in the US has asked us for letter of introduction to you and we have pleasure in complying with this request. He brought letters to us from our New York friends and was accredited to us as a gentleman of high character, who is connected with important Railway & Iron interests in the United States. He is a leading Director of the Union Pacific Railway Co. & is well known to our friends in New York.' Quoted in Nasaw, *supra* n. 1, at p. 126. Barings ultimately passed on the bonds and Carnegie sold them to J S Morgan & Co.

59. Nasaw notes that: 'None of the major houses, including Salzbach Brothers in Frankfurt, was willing to buy or sell securities until it was known if a settlement was going to be reached, how much the British would be obliged to hand over to the Americans, and what effect the transfer of millions of pounds sterling would have on the price of gold.' Nasaw, *supra* n. 1, p. 132.

in America want to borrow English capital, and more than half the enterprises, and nothing forbids this but the unsettled *Alabama* difficulty.'[60]

But quite apart from his immediate business interests, and more fundamentally, Carnegie was deeply attached to both parties to the dispute, and he had always favoured closer relations between the two countries. Thus, as the indirect claims crisis threatened to spiral out of control, he urged Grant and Fish to jettison the indirect claims in the interests of maintaining the arbitration and avoiding a descent into war.[61]

On 16 February 1872, for example, Carnegie wrote to Grant's executive secretary, Horace Porter, expressing deep concern about the indirect claims.[62] At the same time, he wrote to Baring Brothers in London to stress how strongly Grant supported maintaining the 'closest bonds of friendship' between the two countries and urging them to warn Her Majesty's Government that Grant 'should not be pressed too far, otherwise, we may have a much less friendly administration in power'.[63]

For months the fate of the arbitration hung by a thread. It soon became clear – at least in the confidential diplomatic exchanges – that the United States did not want the arbitration to founder on claims which the Administration increasingly privately admitted that it thought had no merit. The problem was that the US could not be seen to be capitulating to British pressure. It had to maintain its right to put its case as it saw fit, while still finding a way to allay British concerns. The voices raised on both sides of the Atlantic helpfully contributed to a softening of American public opinion and a second-guessing about the wisdom of Sumner's articulation of the United States' grievance and thus created the conditions that allowed the arbitration to continue.

But the dispute remained stubbornly resistant to resolution. Options such as negotiating a supplementary article to the Treaty in which the US would abandon its indirect claims if Britain agreed never to advance such claims against it failed. Time was running out.

Finally, in mid-June, when the Tribunal re-assembled in Geneva (it had previously met in December 1871 to receive the parties' Cases), the arbitrators, with considerable 'back and forth' with the parties' agents and counsel, took control.

Faced with Britain's request to adjourn the arbitration for eight months to allow a supplemental article to be negotiated, and Britain's withholding the filing of its final Written Argument (due on 15 June) until the indirect claims were disposed of, four of the five arbitrators cut the Gordian knot of jurisdiction by making an 'extrajudicial' declaration to the parties to the effect that without determining whether they had

---

60. *The Economist*, 18 May 1872, p. 605. ('Economist')
61. Nasaw, *supra* n. 1, p. 131.
62. *Ibid*. Using what Nasaw called the 'flattery that would later become his trademark', Carnegie wrote to Grant's executive secretary that: 'Lincoln is to stand in History, when all other of his acts shall have been forgot, as the Emancipator of Four Millions of his fellow men. Grant may secure equal prominence among the very few essentially great characters of the world's history if he succeeds ... in being the first who leads nations to substitute for the barbarous appeal to the sword, the device of peaceful arbitration.'
63. Letter to Baring Brothers dated 24 February 1872. Quoted in Nasaw, *supra* n. 1, p. 132.

jurisdiction or not, the indirect claims were not well-founded in law.[64] Their declaration was delivered by the presiding arbitrator, Count Federico Sclopis de Salerano. The British arbitrator, Sir Alexander Cockburn, although involved in the declaration's formulation, considered that he could not be seen to be a party to it because Britain did not accept that the Tribunal had the jurisdiction to even discuss the indirect claims, let alone consider their merits.

The remaining arbitrators left the jurisdictional issue undecided. Without intending 'to express or imply any opinion' as to the dispute between the two governments 'as to the interpretation or effect of the Treaty', Sclopis stated that the arbitrators thought it right to state that 'after the most careful perusal of all that has been urged on the part of the Government of the United States in respect of these claims, they have arrived, individually and collectively' at the conclusion that the indirect claims did 'not constitute upon the principles of international law applicable to such cases good foundation for an award of compensation or computation of damages between nations; and should, upon such principles, be wholly excluded from the consideration of the Tribunal in making its award, even if there were no disagreement between the two Governments as to the competency of the Tribunal to decide thereon'.[65]

Since this was an 'extrajudicial' expression of opinion, it arguably had no effect unless it was accepted by both parties to the dispute. Sclopis therefore called upon the agents of both parties to confirm whether their governments accepted the declaration. Acceptance was virtually a foregone conclusion because the agents and counsel had been involved in settling the terms of the arbitrators' declaration, but it was considered to be a necessary step in order to put the claims finally to rest.

Consultations with national capitals ensued. On 25 June 1872, the United States Agent, John Chandler Bancroft Davis, informed the Tribunal that President Grant had accepted the arbitrators' declaration as 'determinative of their judgement upon the important question of public law involved', adding that as a result 'the above-mentioned claims will not be further insisted upon before the Tribunal by the United States, and may be excluded from all consideration in any award that may be made'.[66]

All that remained was Britain's concurrence with the Tribunal's declaration. At the next meeting of the Tribunal on 27 June 1872, the British Agent, Lord Tenterden, confirmed that Her Majesty's Government also accepted the Tribunal's decision. Tenterden stated that he was authorized to state that his Government 'find in the communication on the part of the arbitrators, recorded in the protocol of their proceedings of the 19th instant, nothing to which they cannot assent, consistently with the view of the interpretation and effect of the Treaty of Washington hitherto maintained by them; and being informed of the statement made on the 25th instant by

---

64. Quoted in Frank Warren Hackett, *Reminiscences of the Geneva Tribunal*, Houghton Mifflin, 1911, p. 254 ('Hackett').
65. Quoted in Bassett Moore, *supra* n. 52, p. 646. *See also* Caleb Cushing, *The Treaty of Washington: Its Negotiation, Execution, and the Discussions Relating Thereto*, New York, Harper & Brothers, 1873, at p. 70, quoting the same passage with different punctuation.
66. Quoted in Protocol VI of the Tribunal's proceedings, 25 June 1872. FO 5/103, Geneva Arbitration, Vol. 14 (1872 June 21-1872 June 30) ('FO 5'). Also available at https://history.state .gov/search?q = geneva + tribunal + protocols + 1872. Last visited on 14 May 2022 ('Protocols').

the agent of the United States, that the several claims particularly mentioned in that statement will not be further insisted upon before the Tribunal by the United States, and may be excluded from all consideration in any award that may be made; and assuming that the arbitrators will, upon such statement, think fit now to declare that the said several claims are, and from henceforth will be, wholly excluded from their consideration ... .'[67]

A relieved Sclopis then gave a lengthy speech lauding the farsightedness of both sides and their commitment to adjusting their differences through peaceful arbitration rather than through force of arms. He declared, 'We seek, if possible, to submit these conflicts of opinion between two nations to the judgment of a court of reason, instead of bloody arbitration of arms. History will remember with regard to the United States and the United Kingdom that, having to settle serious conflicts, and feeling reluctant on both sides to cede the ground, they nevertheless applied themselves to ensure peace, and not only to settle their own conflicts, but also to set an example which will be fruitful in benefit to other nations.'[68]

VII   THE ARBITRATION PROCEEDS

The parties' acceptance of the arbitrators' extrajudicial declaration meant that the crisis was finally over. The Tribunal could now turn to the remaining claims. After an adjournment of some two weeks, it resumed proceedings and on 14 September 1872, before an assembly of the Agents, counsel, various dignitaries, and representatives of the world's press, the Tribunal formally issued its Award.

Great Britain was found responsible for failing to meet the standard of due diligence specified in the Treaty of Washington and therefore made liable for the acts of certain cruisers and their tenders. The national and indirect claims having been disposed of at the outset, the damages ultimately awarded for the claimed direct losses were a little less than one-third of what the United States had finally quantified as its compensable losses. The Tribunal awarded damages of USD 15.5 million (GBP 3.25 million), to be paid in gold, within one year of the date of the Award. Cockburn dissented, except on the Tribunal's finding of liability for the acts of the *Alabama*, for which he would have awarded damages of USD 4 million.

In 1872, USD 15.5 million was no small amount of money. In his 1995 biography of Gladstone, Roy Jenkins described the financial impact of the Award as follows. It was 'at once a vast sum by Victorian standards, directly equivalent only to about £160 million today, but in relation to national income more like £4 billion, and in relation to the size of the budget (to which it contributed 5 per cent), the equivalent of a modern £150 billion'.[69] But Gladstone regarded it as well worth the price of peace and better relations with the United States. Britain promptly announced that it would comply with the award and one year later, the transfer was effected.

---

67. *Ibid.*
68. *Ibid.* Translation of the original French version of Sclopis' remarks which were reproduced in Protocol VII of the Tribunal's proceedings, 27 June 1872.
69. Jenkins, *supra* n. 37, p. 359.

No one can say what would have happened had the arbitration broken up. Many thought that war was the alternative; many others did not. The evidence is that the leaders of both countries and their respective foreign secretaries were greatly relieved that the arbitration had not foundered. There were plenty of jingoists and warmongers on both sides of the Atlantic, and the arbitration's successful conclusion deprived them of an opportunity to make trouble. And of course, financers and industrialists like Andrew Carnegie who wished for more stable and closer relations between the United States and Britain were delighted.

The United States hailed the award as a victory even if the damages were a small fraction of the swollen estimate that Charles Sumner had articulated three years previously. Naturally, there were American grumbles that the damages were paltry and British grumbles about having to pay GBP 3.25 million to their American cousins, but other issues of public policy quickly drove the arbitration from the front pages of the newspapers and the improvement in Anglo-American relations seemed to be worth it. Not only did the arbitration lay the foundation for what later became known as the 'special relationship' between Britain and America, but it also brought an end to the post-Civil War movement within the Republican Party to annex British North America and signalled the beginning of American acceptance of the recently established Dominion of Canada.

The Treaty of Washington and the Geneva Arbitration thus proved to be important steps both in the acceptance of international arbitration as a means of resolving disputes between States as well as in stimulating the development of public international law more generally.[70] Many commentators have regarded the arbitration as a landmark in the acceptance of peaceable dispute settlement between States.

Pretty well all of those directly involved in the arbitration, even the British Agent, thought that the process was at least satisfactory.[71] Not everyone thought that the arbitral process was replicable for other disputes between sovereign States and some were highly sceptical that the arbitration presaged a new world of peaceable dispute settlement.[72] But others, like Count Sclopis, hoped that the two governments had set an example that would be followed by the rest of the world.

---

70. The arbitration's successful conclusion added some momentum to the creation of the Institut de droit international and the International Law Association.

71. After the Award was finalized but before it was issued (and already aware of the outcome), Tenterden wrote to Granville observing that he still believed that 'it was a good policy' for Britain to have 'wilfully submitted ourselves to be judged by a form of opinion on these questions of International Law widely different from our own'. Although it appeared to him that there had been great difficulties in civil trained lawyers understanding common law lawyers and their legal system, on balance he thought that 'it may prove to have been a good thing for both countries and for the world in general to have had recourse to a tribunal; the members of which derived their views from a source so widely differing from the one which we have been accustomed to revere as the only fountain of knowledge'. Tenterden to Granville, 8 September 1872, quoted in Lord Edmund Fitzmaurice, *Life of Granville George Leveson Gower, Second Earl Granville K.G. 1815-1891*, Longmans, Green, and Co., 1905, Volume II, pp. 104-105 ('Fitzmaurice').

72. Sir Roundell Palmer, Britain's lead counsel, downplayed the significance of the whole matter. He later wrote that he 'doubted whether what had taken place would have any great consequences at all, beyond the present settlement of a troublesome dispute'. Palmer *supra* n. 23, p. 24.

VIII   THE ARBITRATION'S IMPACT ON ANDREW CARNEGIE

Andrew Carnegie fell squarely into the Sclopis camp. He became a true believer in the value of international arbitration as an alternative to recourse to arms. He had gotten so caught up with the dispute that he had remained in London for the whole of the summer of 1872 anxiously awaiting news from Geneva. When the award was issued, the financial markets cheered. Carnegie found that his bonds were back in demand and promptly sold them on to bankers in London and on the Continent.[73]

The *Alabama* Claims case had a profound impact on Carnegie. His biographer, David Nasaw, has written about how the arbitration and its resolution came to shape, and indeed dominate, Carnegie's life:

> It is impossible to discount the importance of this 1872 bond-selling trip for Carnegie. The market instability caused by the *Alabama* affair had forced on him an extended period of leisure in which he had tasted the fruits of semiretirement and found them quite exhilarating. Although he had not yet celebrated his thirty-seventh birthday, Carnegie would never again return to a full-time work schedule.
>
> His experience in Europe that spring and summer also had a profound effect on the development of the peace program that Carnegie would spend the final decades of his life promulgating. It was not, as he would learn, 'actual war itself which the world in our day has most to dread …. It is the ever-present danger of war, which hangs over the world like a pall, which we have to dispel'. There had been no war between Great Britain and America over the *Alabama* claims, but the strained relationship made it difficult to do business and gave unscrupulous politicians, like Senator Charles Sumner, a platform for their warmongering.[74]
>
> Disputes between nations were inevitable, but some way short of bloodshed had to be found to settle them. The willingness of both the British and American governments to submit their claims to impartial arbitration in Geneva had been an important step forward. For the rest of his life, Carnegie would refer to the settlement of the *Alabama* claims case in Geneva as an exemplary moment in international diplomacy and Anglo-American relations, where reason and common sense had peaceably solved a long-festering conflict.[75]

International arbitration became the most important public policy issue to Carnegie for the rest of his public life. He pressed a string of United States presidents and British ministers and parliamentarians to promote efforts to resolve disputes by peaceful dispute settlement. Republican presidents could hardly ignore his entreaties (even if they privately disagreed with him), but even Democratic presidents received his advice, whether solicited or not.

---

73. Nasaw, *supra* n. 1, pp. 132-133.
74. This is somewhat unfair to Sumner who abhorred war and was distressed and angered by accusations in Britain that his speech was aimed at fomenting war. In fact, in his speech denouncing the Johnson-Clarendon Convention, Sumner declared: 'I know it is sometimes said that war between us must come sooner or later. I do not believe it. But if it must come, let it be later, and then I am sure it will never come. Meanwhile, good men must unite to make it impossible.' Sumner: Original Version, *supra* n. 34, p. 14.
75. Nasaw, *supra* n. 1, p. 133.

Carnegie was particularly enthusiastic about arbitration treaties. On 31 October 1887, for example, he introduced a delegation of British MPs and leaders of trade unions to President Grover Cleveland at the White House to discuss a treaty of arbitration between Britain and the US.[76] The delegation submitted to the President 'an address, signed by 234 Members of Parliament, in favour of a treaty of arbitration between Great Britain and the United States'.[77] To his and the delegation's delight, Cleveland expressed support for such an initiative.[78] (But nothing came of it.)

While this initiative failed, the efforts exerted were 'very important, for out of it the Interparliamentary Union was born'.[79] Sir Randal Cremer MP would open communications with Frédéric Passy in 1888, and one year later the Interparliamentary Union (IPU) was founded in Bern by Cremer and Passy to bring together parliamentarians from different countries. The IPU aspired to be an international forum for peace and conflict resolution through arbitration and would later play a role in influencing the work of the PCA.[80] Dr Christian Lous Lange, who became the executive head of the IPU, later wrote: 'It is … a fact that the convocation of the Hague Conference itself was due to the Interparliamentary movement and especially to the Budapest Conference in 1896.'[81]

Thus, over a period of some forty years, Andrew Carnegie personified the search for international enlightenment through international arbitration, working assiduously for the cause of peace and the resolution of disputes between sovereigns through arbitration rather than through war. Sadly, we have witnessed the world's resistance to such an enlightened view, but it is also true that there have been many occasions when States could have resorted to force but decided instead to pursue a more enlightened path by instead submitting their disputes to international arbitration.[82]

---

76. *Ibid.*, p. 311.
77. Dr Christian. L. Lange, 'The Interparliamentary Union', 94(1) Advocate of Peace through Justice (1932), p. 26. ('Lange').
78. Nasaw notes that: 'In his *Autobiography*, Carnegie claims that he was so stirred by the event that "from that day the abolition of war grew in importance with me until it finally overshadowed all other issues".' Nasaw, *supra* n. 1, p. 311.
79. Lange, *supra* n. 77, p. 26.
80. Lange records that in the IPU's 1891 Rome Conference, the Interparliamentary Committees were invited to put the institution of an arbitration court on the agenda for the following conference. At the 1895 Brussels Conference, a draft Convention of 14 articles was voted upon. Lange argues that the 1899 Convention on the Pacific Settlement of International Disputes, which established the PCA, 'to a large extent rests on the convention drafted by the Interparliamentary Union'. Lange, *supra* n. 77, p. 28.
81. Lange, *supra* n. 77, p. 28.
82. *See* Ulf Franke, Annette Magnusson and Joel Dahlquist, *Arbitrating for Peace: How Arbitration Made a Difference*, Wolters Kluwer, 2016.

CHAPTER 3

How Does International Arbitration Fare in a World Creeping Towards Unilateralism, Protectionism and Nationalism?

Hi-Taek Shin[*]

TABLE OF CONTENTS

I   INTRODUCTION

This year's International Council for Commercial Arbitration (ICCA) Congress opens under the theme of "Arbitration's Age of Enlightenment ... and Adaptation?" and intends to explore topics that connect arbitration to the ideas and values of the Enlightenment, most notably, the philosophy that reason can be used to improve the lives of humankind in times of crisis.

International arbitration is a rational solution that answers the parties' desire to exclude external factors that can stand in the way of a fair and efficient resolution of

---

*   Governing Board Member of ICCA; Arbitrator, Twenty Essex. The author would like to thank Ms. Sue Hyun Lim (Kim & Chang) and Mr. Jake Lowther (Magnusson) for their valuable assistance in the research and preparation of this article.

disputes between them. External factors could include political agenda, national interests, hidden prejudice against foreigners or procedural asymmetry due to home advantages inherent to litigation before national courts. Arbitration offers a rational solution because it gives the parties choice through flexibility and party autonomy. Further, it ensures neutrality through free choice of seat, neutral arbitrators and the rules of the game which makes possible the creation of a level playing field.[1] This ultimately encourages the development of a transnational system.

The growth of international arbitration in the post-World War II era coincided with the prevalent thinking among intellectual groups and policymakers favoring the idea of free trade and investment with a clear vision of removing or lowering national barriers and thus facilitating the flow of international trade and investment for the benefits of all. However, recent criticism against international arbitration, and in particular investment arbitration, has raised concerns about growing regional and national populism. This could be a part of an overall trend away from the way of thinking favoring internationalism or multilateralism, as high hopes for international-ism seem to have regressed into frustration and even animosity in some parts of the world. In times like this and at the occasion of the ICCA Congress, it is worth exploring what efforts and adaptations the arbitration community has made in the past and should make in the coming years to restore and reaffirm the faith in the system and the values that it represents.

II   SOME OF THE MANY CHALLENGES FACING THE WORLD: UNILATERALISM, PROTECTIONISM AND NATIONALISM

In recent years, news media has been filled with articles and commentaries offering a dystopian view of international affairs. Many of us question whether the world is progressing or regressing from the standpoint of history. Politicians who campaign under protectionist and nationalistic slogans are emboldened by popular support and push their exclusionist policies without considering their ultimate consequence. Some in the legal field worry that this tendency is echoed, although in less overt ways, in international arbitration. Whether this concern is founded or not, it is worth taking stock of the current situation.

1   Definitions and Antitheses

The title of this chapter contains three terms, unilateralism, protectionism and nation-alism. These terms are abstract and, as with many abstract terms, they are tricky to define with precision. For discussion purposes, it may be helpful to start with a general description of these terms as they are generally understood by the public.

---

1. Alan Redfern and Martin Hunter, *Law and Practice of International Commercial Arbitration* (Maxwell and Sweet 2004), p. 26.

Unilateralism is any doctrine or agenda that supports one-sided actions and stands in opposition to multilateralism, which is the idea that states need to coordinate their actions in alliance with each other.[2] Similarly, in the context of international economic relations, protectionism is the policy of restricting imports from other countries by imposing or raising tariffs and restricting foreign direct investment.[3] Inherently, protectionism is discriminatory against foreign elements. Free trade would be the antithesis of protectionism. Nationalism is an ideology and movement that promotes the interests of a particular nation by asserting supremacy over other states,[4] and its corresponding opposite would be internationalism. Arguably, international arbitration is premised on the cooperation between systems of different jurisdictions and practitioners of different legal backgrounds, and as such represents the antitheses of unilateralism, protectionism and nationalism.

2 Recent Surge of Government Actions with Nationalistic, Protectionist or Unilateral Overtones

Instances of unilateral actions by key state actors in international politics seem to have increased over the past five to ten years. Some of these unilateral actions have led to a complex web of political and legal issues. Russia's annexation of Crimea in 2014 and the Russian invasion of Ukraine in 2022, which prompted many of the sanctions in the first place, could be prime examples of a unilateral action, to which the US and EU, among others, have responded with waves of coordinated but unilateral sanctions. The withdrawal of the US from the Paris Climate Accord in 2017, the decision of the United Kingdom to leave the EU and the long-lasting stalemate at the Appellate Body of the WTO are other recent examples of this trend. China's response to the 2016 ruling of the UN Convention on the Law of the Sea with respect to its claims in the South China Sea as "nothing more than a piece of wastepaper" is another example that carried unilateralist tones.

Trade policies characterized by protectionism have also captured the headlines. In 2019, the US imposed tariffs on billions of dollars' worth of goods from its major trading partners. The so-called trade wars between US and China have continued to escalate for years, creating tension between the two countries and affecting other economic partners such as Korea that trade with both economic powers.

Unilateral and protectionist actions by governments are often fueled by nationalist narratives that gain popularity among the voters at the domestic level. In recent years, politicians from countries in Europe to the Americas to Asia and beyond have

---

2. Atsushi Tago, "Multilateralism, Bilateralism, and Unilateralism in Foreign Policy" (August 2017) at https://oxfordre.com/politics/view/10.1093/acrefore/9780190228637.001.0001/acrefore-978 0190228637-e-449 (last accessed March 12, 2020).
3. Jim Chappelow, "Protectionism" (August 22, 2019) at https://www.investopedia.com/terms/p /protectionism.asp (last accessed March 12, 2020).
4. Merriam-Webster, "Nationalism" (2020) https://www.merriam-webster.com/dictionary/nation alism (last accessed March 12, 2020).

adopted the language of nationalism wrapped with patriotism, stoking old rivalries and mistrust.

3   Is This Trend Encroaching upon International Arbitration?

Do these phenomena curb the general public's appetite for arbitration, and our faith in an international order for the resolution of international commercial and investment disputes? It is perhaps unsurprising that the recent rise in their incidence coincides with what has been described as a "crisis" of faith in international arbitration. As one surveys the landscape today, the question frequently asked is whether arbitration is facing an existential threat. It may be worth reviewing commercial arbitration separately from investment arbitration, as they seem to face different challenges.

Commercial arbitration so far has largely been sheltered from unilateralism, protectionism and nationalism, although not entirely. We hear some observations that a surge of nationalism even in commercial arbitration is detected among some emerging jurisdictions. For example, some governments have passed legislation making it mandatory for public procurement contracts or public work contracts above a certain amount to use the local arbitration institution established in that state, creating a situation where foreign parties really have only one choice over where to take disputes for resolution.[5] But apart from those outlier cases, generally, the increase in the number of strong global arbitral institutions outside of Europe, particularly in Asia, is generally welcomed as promoting arbitration to a wider extent, so long as the basic tenets of neutrality and free choice of an institution are maintained.[6]

But any concern about possible trends of nationalization in commercial arbitration is overshadowed by the frequency and intensity of the debate surrounding investment arbitration. Take for example, as early as in 2007, Prof. Stiglitz, in his 2007 Grotius lecture[7] at the occasion of the annual meeting of the American Society of International Law, criticized the dispute resolution mechanisms in the investment provisions of bilateral trade agreements as falling "far short of the standards that we have come to expect of judicial process in modern democracies" and these agreements "have undermined democratic processes." Across the Atlantic, the previous EU Trade Commissioner Cecilia Malmström acknowledged that the acronym "ISDS" or Investor-State Dispute Settlement was toxic in Europe.[8] ISDS was accused of being a "global legal straitjacket."[9]

---

5. J. Ballantyne, "Mourre Warns Against 'Nationalisation' of Arbitration," GAR News (September 12, 2019) https://globalarbitrationreview.com/article/1197622/mourre-warns-against-%E2%80%9Cnationalisation%E2%80%9D-of-arbitration (last accessed March 12, 2020).

6. M.A. Raouf, "Emergence of New Arbitral Centres in Asia and Africa: Competition, Cooperation and Contribution to the Rule of Law" in S. Brekoulakis, ed., *The Evolution and Future of International Arbitration Vol. 37* (Kluwer Law International 2016).

7. J. Stiglitz, "Multinational Corporations: Balancing Rights and Responsibilities," 101 Am. Soc'y Int'l L. Proc. p. 58 (2007).

8. Paul Ames, "ISDS: The Most Toxic Acronym in Europe" (September 17, 2015) *Politico* https://www.politico.eu/article/isds-the-most-toxic-acronym-in-europe/ (last accessed March 12, 2020).

9. *Ibid.*

Of course, there are opposing views that this criticism is misplaced and based on misinformation[10] or so-called myths that unduly undermine the legitimacy of arbitration. One may even venture to say that this move represents the general (misguided) sentiment to return to a more permanent system under scrutiny or even control of the sponsoring states. This could be a trend that threatens to undo the progress of internationalism and de-politicization achieved by investment arbitration for decades, which could potentially spill over to international commercial arbitration.[11]

III   IN RETROSPECT: ARBITRATION'S PAST CONTRIBUTION TO THE AVOIDANCE OF POLITICIZED CONFLICTS

Arbitration is the agreement of disputing parties to a private, final and binding determination of a dispute by an independent third party. It may sound like a simple idea, but it is the result of centuries of efforts, adaptations, and evolution. Many today need to be reminded of arbitration's role in procuring and maintaining peace and prosperity. In particular, modern investment arbitration emerged as a peaceful alternative to dispute resolution by gunboat diplomacy. It is no exaggeration to say that both money and lives have been saved by this method of dispute resolution. Consider for example the *Dogger Bank* case, also known as "the incident in the North Sea," the Cold War, or the Iran-United States Claims Tribunal (IUSCT).

1   Dogger Bank

In 1904, a war between Russia and the United Kingdom appeared imminent after the Russian Baltic fleet fired on and severely damaged six English fishing boats and killed two fishermen, having mistaken them for Imperial Japanese Navy torpedo boats. The incident almost led to war between the United Kingdom and the Russian Empire. In what may be a familiar overture, the British media demanded that the "wretched Baltic fleet" be destroyed.[12] At the last moment, war was avoided when the two states agreed to arbitration conducted by an international tribunal composed of arbitrators from Britain, Russia, the US, France, and Austria. Following the tribunal's decision, Russia paid reparations and both governments had avoided war while maintaining their public reputations.

2   The Cold War

From 1947 to 1991, much of the world experienced the Cold War, during which numerous flashpoints almost led to a nuclear holocaust under the mutually assured

---

10. B. Stern, "Freshfields and Queen Mary University Arbitration Lecture" (November 23, 2019), https://play.buto.tv/yMHvJ (last accessed March 12, 2020).
11. S.W. Schill, "Concepts of Legitimacy" in David D. Caron, ed., *Practising Virtue: Inside International Arbitration* (Oxford University Press 2015) at pp. 112-113.
12. *The Advertiser*, "Shocking Outrage by the Baltic Fleet" (October 25, 1904) https://trove.nla.gov .au/newspaper/article/5028510 (last accessed March 12, 2020).

destruction (MAD) doctrine. Yet even during this tense period, major developments in international arbitration took place. The Convention on the Recognition and Enforcement of Foreign Arbitral Awards (the New York Convention) was adopted in 1958 and entered into force the following year. This was followed by the adoption of the Convention on the Settlement of Investment Disputes between States and Nationals of Other States (the ICSID Convention) in 1966, the publication of the UNCITRAL Arbitral Rules in 1976, the Optional Arbitration Clause for Use in Contracts in USA-USSR Trade in 1977 and the UNCITRAL Model Arbitration Law of 1985. International arbitration's role in maintaining world peace is often forgotten due to its lack of visibility. But it should be better highlighted that arbitration was able to facilitate the neutral and impartial resolution of sensitive commercial and investment East-West disputes, including the dispute over the construction of the respective embassies of the US and the USSR in Moscow and Washington DC.

3   Iran-United States Claims Tribunal

The IUSCT is the largest international arbitration project in modern history. It was established on 19 January 1981 as one of the measures taken to resolve the crisis in relations between Iran and the US arising out of the detention of 52 US nationals at the US Embassy in Tehran which commenced in November 1979, and the subsequent freeze of Iranian assets by the US. To date, the IUSCT has finalized over 3,900 cases.

4   Over 1,100 Institutional and Ad Hoc Investment Cases to Date

Following the adoption of the ICSID Convention, and the consent to arbitration offered in national laws, concession contracts and over 3,000 bilateral investment treaties, investment arbitration has so far been an immense success, with the number of cases rising each year since the early 1970s. As easy it is to criticize the shortcoming of investment arbitration, it is just as easy to forget that each of these cases may well represent a dispute which—had it reached a breaking point—could have led to the intervention of diplomatic protection and higher tensions among the states involved, such as in the case of the nationalization of the Suez Canal in 1956. Had diplomatic tensions and political agenda been able to seep into the legal claims underlying the 1,100 or so investment arbitrations, there may have been a longer and more painful process before these disputes came to any reasonable resolution.

5   Commercial Arbitration Cases

The number of international commercial cases greatly outnumbers those of investment cases, and their contribution is easily overlooked. However, few can doubt the merits of international arbitration, which allowed international contracts to be enforced without the formality, pace and inefficiency of litigation before national judiciaries, sometimes competing with each other in claiming jurisdiction. Recently Global Arbitration Review (GAR) reported that Naftogaz, a Ukraine company, has launched an ICC claim against Russia's Gazprom over its failure to pay for gas transportation. This case symbolically illustrates the utility of international commercial arbitration even in times of armed conflicts between two states. Faith that a contract will be honored encourages cross-border trade and investment. In addition, the speed and economy offered by arbitration allowed business relationships to continue, as parties may brush off past disputes in a quicker and less acrimonious manner than international litigation. I dare say that the members of the international arbitration community should legitimately feel proud of our collective past and present contributions in this regard.

IV   WHAT CAN ARBITRATION DO TO ALLEVIATE SOME OF THESE TENSIONS?

The question is, what can the arbitration community do to help alleviate the creeping erosion of multilateralism, free trade and internationalism?

One of the reasons for international arbitration's existence is that it offers a rational solution that answers the parties' desire to exclude external factors that can stand in the way of a fair and efficient resolution. As discussed above, it has proven instrumental in maintaining peace. This success can be attributed to party autonomy, which allows the parties both flexibility to deviate from specific national or political protocols, neutrality, and ultimately, the voluntary submission to the authority of a private and independent tribunal.

But this party autonomy is meaningful only if the system can overcome practical challenges. Parties approach arbitration with the expectation that it should be easier to manage than formal court litigation. Navigating an arbitration clause in a vacuum, including pre-dispute negotiations over procedures, can cause confusion and requires a great deal of time and energy. So the hidden ingredient to unlocking success is to make arbitration easier to use and practical from the user's perspective. So how do we do this?

The simple answer that I propose is this: we need to go back to the basics, which is to uphold the basic pillars of party autonomy and neutrality, yet at the same time, develop diverse options and modules that make it easier for parties to refer their dispute to arbitration by selecting the most appropriate practical module.

One obvious way is to develop different rules that fit different situations. No set of rules fits all cases. In order to make arbitration easier to use, it is important to continue developing viable modules for the parties with diverse interests to choose from in the resolution of their disputes at various stages of arbitration, whether they be institutional rules, soft laws, guidelines, best practices or checklists.

Even a single, narrow set of rules has proven extremely useful. Take for example the ICSID Convention and its Arbitration Rules. The 800-plus investment cases under the ICSID system during the last 55 years would not have been possible had it not been for the ICSID Convention and Arbitration Rules. An existing and tested set of rules provides an easy reference tool to commence arbitration and manage the process. It was this pre-existing framework that allowed states to include an arbitration clause in their bilateral investment treaties (BITs) by simply referring to the ICSID Convention, and to allow many of the investment disputes to be resolved. I expect that the amended ICSID Rules and Regulations which took effect on the first of July this year would significantly enhance the utility of the ICSID system of investment dispute resolution.

Some consider that creating too many laws, whether under the title of rules, protocols, soft laws, guidelines or checklists, leads to an overly formalized and overly regulated environment which prevents arbitration from being a free-flowing process. However, exploring and developing new modules and new rules provides easy reference tools, and has its good sides as well.

It is hard to deny a correlation between the proliferation of rules, guidelines and regional arbitration hubs and the explosive growth of arbitration in recent decades. New regional arbitral institutions like the Korean Commercial Arbitration Board have re-arranged their administration of international cases in line with global standards, leading to a quick rise in caseload as well as international reputation. Cooperation between different arbitral institutions creates a healthy competitive environment, where each institution improves in the areas of good governance and transparency. On the other hand, the absence of choices in modules and rules is not conducive to flexibility or speed. At worst, it can lead to extreme "party autonomy" where parties can spend time and energy negotiating a procedure that is closest to their familiar jurisdiction and litigation system. Having a wide array of viable choices that have been tested and proven useful, will allow us to continue with the growth and development of arbitration.

V   CONCLUSION

As discussed above, developing and testing viable choices available to parties, in the long run, will benefit the flexibility, neutrality and legitimacy of international arbitration. To that end, and as we have in the past, we should encourage ICCA initiatives in collaboration with other fora such as bar associations with international representations and together with various institutions and practitioners—both counsel and arbitrators—to improve and refine existing resources and tools and to develop new ones to address new challenges. The recent projects of ICCA, such as the ICCA Task Force on Standards of Practice in International Arbitration, and the ICCA-American Society of International Law joint task force on Damages in International Arbitration are very commendable in this regard. A virtue of the arbitration community so far has been its willingness to share enlightenment. I dare say that the members of the international arbitration community should be proud of our collective past and present contribution to the orderly resolution of international disputes. I am sure that our endeavors will continue in the coming years.

Some of the participants in this Congress may remember the scathing criticism against international investment arbitration in the 2012 Corporate Europe Observatory article titled "Profiting from Injustice."[13] While many of the accusations in the article leveled against arbitration practitioners were not fully accurate, it was not easy to ignore the criticism that excess commercialism in this field contributed to the mistrust and cynicism among those outside the field. This is an important point to bear in mind. Dispute resolution is first and foremost a public service, the value of which can only be fully recognized when it instills a sense of trust and confidence among the users and observers. Whatever initiative or project is taken by ICCA or its collaborators in developing rules, modules and best practices and applying them in practice, we should be conscious of not losing sight of the common goal to enhance the efficiency and legitimacy of arbitration. If we are not careful, we run the risk of inviting skepticism and even external interventions, and initiatives with good intentions can be brushed off as mere promotional tools. If that happens too often, we run the real risk of overshadowing the promises of arbitration as an effective and cost-efficient means of dispute resolution.

---

13. Corporate Europe Observatory, "Profiting from injustice: How law firms, arbitrators and financiers are fueling an investment arbitration boom" (November 27, 2012), https://corporateeurope.org/en/international-trade/2012/11/profiting-injustice (last accessed March 12, 2020).

CHAPTER 4

"Loyauté": A Tool for Enlightenment?

Carole Malinvaud[*]

TABLE OF CONTENTS

My proposition is that the concept—or even just the idea—of procedural *loyauté* can be developed to act as a remedy for the new wave of legitimacy crises facing international arbitration.

I will explore what it covers and whether it is effective.

Criticisms continue to arise in particular in relation to procedural matters such as conflict of interest, lack of transparency, and to some extent institutional bias.[1]

This looming backlash is also fueled by the parties' behavior, sometimes perceived as obstructing the arbitral proceedings[2]—from the use and abuse of interim measures[3] to excessive challenges of the arbitral tribunal's jurisdiction or composition, as well as to actions to set aside awards based on grounds that could have been raised earlier.

---

[*] Governing Board Member of ICCA Carole Malinvaud is a partner at Gide in Paris, co-head of the international arbitration group. The author thanks Professor Claire Debourg, also member of Gide Arbitration Group for her invaluable assistance with this paper.
1. M. Waibel et al., "The Backlash against Investment Arbitration: Perceptions and Reality," in M. Waibel et al. (eds.) The Backlash Against Investment Arbitration: Perceptions and Reality, Kluwer Law International, January 2010.
2. P. Halprin, Resisting Guerrilla Tactics in International Arbitration, in Stavros Brekoulakis (ed.), Arbitration: The International Journal of Arbitration, Mediation and Dispute Management, Sweet & Maxwell 2019, Vol. 85, No. 1, p. 87.
3. Ph. Pinsolle, L'impact décisif des mesures provisoires (et sa justification théorique), Rev. arb. 2021, pp. 1007-1048.

This vast array of mechanisms undermines the conduct of proceedings and appears to a certain extent disloyal, although one must admit that the frontier between a mere ruse of war and … an inadmissible low blow may be hard to draw.

Faced with this perceived need to level the playing field and fight against abusive procedural tactics, there has been a call for increased regulation of the conduct of arbitral proceedings.[4]

Under these circumstances, may we explore the idea that the concept of *loyauté* may serve as the multifunctional tool to address some of these practical challenges.[5]

Procedural *loyauté* can take a variety of forms, such as the legal basis of certain decisions, or the inspiration behind norms designed to improve the efficiency of arbitration and sometimes even the objective pursued by certain rules.

Since the concept of *loyauté* has gradually come to imbue arbitration, there is a need for greater clarification as to the nature of the concept and its consequences.

What is the subject of procedural *loyauté*?

Under which circumstances does it come into play?

Is it efficient in international arbitration?

I   THE NATURE OF PROCEDURAL *LOYAUTÉ*

While I would suggest that the very existence of the concept of procedural *loyauté* is not controversial (1), it remains difficult to identify precisely (2).

1   Existence of the Concept

The concept of *loyauté* is not a mere chivalric notion—it is to be found in a number of legal instruments, whether in its entirety or through related notions and terms.

I cannot resist mentioning Article 1464 of the French Code of civil procedure which provides that the parties and the arbitrators shall act with *loyauté* in the conduct of the proceedings.

Similarly in Belgium, Article 1499 of the Judicial Code mentions *loyauté* in the exchanges between parties.

Again, section 33 of the 1996 English Arbitration Act includes fairness as a principle.

Beyond Europe, Article 16 of the Common Court of Justice and Arbitration (CCJA) Arbitration Rules, together with Article 14 of the Uniform Act require the parties to act with *loyauté*, refraining from any dilatory measures.

---

4. F. Dasser, Equality of Arms in International Arbitration: Do Rules and Guidelines Level the Playing Field and Properly Regulate Conduct? – Can They? Will They? Should They? The Example of the IBA Guidelines on Party Representation, in A. Menaker (ed.) International Arbitration and the Rule of Law: Contribution and Conformity, Kluwer Law International, January 2017.
5. *"Ce sont souvent les problèmes les plus pratiques qui postulent le recours aux concepts fondamentaux."* Henri Motulsky, Ecrits.

Further, the idea of procedural *loyauté* is at the core of a number of arbitration rules, some of which require the arbitrators to conduct the proceedings in a fair and impartial manner[6], others of which bind both the tribunal and the parties.[7]

Finally, the international arbitral community has witnessed a proliferation of rules, codes, guidelines and protocols referring to *loyauté* and similar concepts. The 2021 ICCA Guidelines on Standards of Practice in International Arbitration and notably Guideline II D[8] are naturally, here in Edinburgh, the most appropriate example to refer to.

2   The Difficulties in Defining Procedural *Loyauté*

While no one contests its existence, its definition remains a hurdle.

Indeed, although it applies to all participants in arbitration (b) and at all stages of the arbitral proceedings (c) there is no clear or single definition of procedural *loyauté* (a).

a   *The Absence of Definition or Consensus*

Despite the general consensus surrounding the virtues of *loyauté*, defining it is not easy.

The difficulty fundamentally stems from a semantic hurdle: *loyauté* carries differing meanings from one language and legal culture to another.

Rather than seeking a universal definition, I would instead be tempted to refer to neighboring concepts or mechanisms infused with similar values and seeking to achieve comparable purposes.

Loyauté is a combination of *"fairness," "equality of arms"* and *"due process"*. It also touches upon *"candor," "honesty"* and *"sincerity"* and is comprised in the idea of *"ethics"* and *"proper conduct."*

However, *loyauté* is also associated with values which are somewhat antagonistic such as *"transparency"* and *"confidentiality,"*[9] which adds to the difficulty of defining it.

Faced with this situation, it may well be easier to understand *loyauté* through its negative formulation: what is disloyal?

---

6. *See* in particular Article 17(1) of the UNCITRAL Arbitration Rules 2010 and Article 22(4) of the ICC Rules (2012).
7. Article 24(1) of the CEPANI Arbitration Rules (2020): "In the conduct of the proceedings the Arbitral Tribunal and the parties shall act in a rapid manner and in good faith. In particular, the parties shall abstain from any dilatory act as well as from any other action having the object or effect of delaying the proceedings."
8. Guideline II D—"Party representatives shall not engage, without legitimate reasons, in activities intended to obstruct, delay or disrupt the arbitration process or to jeopardize the finality of the award."
9. Mark F. Rosenberg, "Chronicles of the Bullbank Case—The Rest of the Story," Journal of International Arbitration, Kluwer Law International, 2002, Vol. 19, Issue 1.

Dilatory tactics, vexatious or oppressive conduct, the obstruction, derailing and delaying of proceedings (*"guerrilla tactics"*[10]) are all evidently the expression of a lack of *loyauté* (*"comportement déloyal"*).

But here again, it does not necessarily solve the problem, because defining *loyauté* by reference to what it is *not*, opens the door to considerable subjectivity and highlights how tenuous the frontier between admissible procedural strategy and disloyalty is.[11]

One thing remains certain, a number of actors are subject to procedural *loyauté*, and it applies to a variety of situations alongside the arbitral proceedings.

b   A Concept Applicable to All

Initially conceived of as a duty by which the arbitral tribunals must abide, *loyauté* has become a potential source of power at their disposal to constrain or sanction the parties.

Indeed the arbitral tribunal is required to comply with its obligations of impartiality and independence while ensuring procedural fairness.

Similarly, parties are expected to behave with fairness towards their adversary and the tribunal.

Likewise, counsel has the duty to ensure the integrity and fairness of the arbitral proceedings,[12] a duty of candor or honesty to the tribunal,[13] a duty to promote the proper and fair conduct of parties' legal representatives,[14] and a duty not to engage in activities intended to unfairly obstruct the arbitration or to jeopardize the finality of the award.[15]

These duties may create tension with the overarching, *"primary"*[16] duty that governs the actions of counsel, the duty of loyalty to the party he/she represents.[17] But I would suggest that they are not in conflict, as the counsel's *loyauté* to the proceedings is, in the long run, in the interest of the party he/she represents.

---

10. P. Halprin, Resisting Guerrilla Tactics in International Arbitration, in Stavros Brekoulakis (ed.), Arbitration: The International Journal of Arbitration, Mediation and Dispute Management, Sweet & Maxwell 2019, Vol. 85, No. 1, p. 87.
11. J. Carbonnier, Civil Law—Introduction—PUF, 2004 no. 188: "Si les coups bas sont interdits, les simples ruses de guerre ne le sont pas" ["if low blows are prohibited, simple ruses of war are not."].
12. Guideline 1, IBA Guidelines on Party Representation in International Arbitration.
13. Comments to Guidelines 9-11, IBA Guidelines on Party Representation in International Arbitration.
14. LCIA Rules, Annex 1.
15. LCIA Rules, Annex 2.
16. LCIA Rules, Annex 1; Guideline 3, IBA Guidelines on Party Representation in International Arbitration.
17. P. Marzolini, "Counsel Ethics in International Arbitration: Is There Any Need for Regulation?", Indian Journal of Arbitration Law, 2017, Vol. VI, Issue 2, pp. 124-132.

Finally, experts are also subject to a duty of *loyauté*—be it of a fiduciary or contractual nature[18]—towards the party by which they are appointed, but their primary duty is towards the arbitral tribunal.

It entails a duty to provide an *"impartial, objective, unbiased and uninfluenced"* opinion,[19] otherwise, their input is of little value to the tribunal.

Hence all actors in the proceedings are subject to a form of procedural *loyauté*, and similarly, there are a number of occasions during the arbitral process where this concept comes into play.

c   *Procedural* Loyauté *Applies to a Variety of Situations*

There are many examples where procedural *loyauté* comes into play during an arbitration, and I will highlight a few of them, at the start, during or after the proceedings.

i   *Procedural* Loyauté *at the Start of the Proceedings*

The first example which comes to mind is access to justice.

There are a number of examples where procedural *loyauté* takes the form of a kind of estoppel to preclude a party from contesting the existence or the validity of an arbitration provision if it has participated without any reservations in the proceedings.[20]

In the same vein, the French *Cour de Cassation* has recently decided that a respondent that caused the withdrawal of a request for arbitration by failing to pay its share of the advance on costs was not entitled to invoke the arbitration clause to override the jurisdiction of the state court.

In that case, the claimant was not financially in a position to substitute for the respondent and to pay the entire advance on costs and therefore brought the case before the domestic courts despite the arbitration clause.

It was thus a case of the claimant's impecuniosity being triggered by the respondent's conduct, which precluded the claimant from accessing justice.

This decision is of particular interest for us today, as the *Cour de Cassation* based its decision solely on the principle of procedural *loyauté*, without any reference to any statute or rule, as if this principle had a standalone existence in international arbitration.[21]

The second example relates to the constitution of the arbitral tribunal.

---

18. *A Company v. X, Y & Z* [2020] EWHC 809 (TCC), High Court of Justice of England and Wales, Queen's Bench Division, Technology and Construction Court, HT-2020-000112, 03 April 2020, Note N. Fletcher, A Contribution by the ITA Board of Reporters, Kluwer Law International, 2020.
19. Article 4, CIArb Protocol for the Use of Party-Appointed Expert Witness in International Arbitration.
20. Cour de cassation, Civ. 1, July 6, 2005, no. 01-15.912.
21. Cour de Cassation, Civ. 1, February 9, 2022, no. 21-11.253.

Indeed the idea of *loyauté* permeates the composition of the arbitral tribunal, from its constitution and throughout the arbitration, in particular, to ensure that arbitrators are and remain impartial and independent.[22]

Parties as well as arbitrators have a role in that respect.

First, arbitrators have a duty to disclose and the scope of this duty is impregnated by the principle of *loyauté*.

In this respect, over the past ten years, French case law has shifted from an extended duty of disclosure to decisions which seem to impose a *"duty of curiosity"* on the party initiating the challenge,[23] where the fact that information is well known can mean that the arbitrator is not required to disclose it.[24]

Second, parties are required to act as soon as the circumstance they believe undermines the arbitrator's independence and impartiality is revealed, by virtue of the *loyauté* principle.[25]

Arbitrators are therefore no longer the sole guarantors of their obligation of independence and impartiality. Procedural *loyauté* is at the core of these matters.

Similarly, a party's decision to add new counsel at a late stage of the proceedings may also create new conflicts of interest and endanger the constitution of a tribunal, even where the decision was not made with the express purpose of sabotaging the proceedings.

Faced with this situation, where the challenge was directed at the counsel rather than the arbitrator, the tribunal in *Hrvatska*[26] placed fairness and integrity of the proceedings at the center of its reasoning when deciding that the (new) counsel would not be entitled to participate in the case.

Following the developments in case law, the IBA Guidelines on Party Representation in International Arbitration (2013) adopted Guidelines 5 and 6,[27] allowing the tribunal to disqualify counsel in case of a conflict of interest with an arbitrator. Similarly, Terms of Reference or Procedural Orders often include a provision ensuring that a properly constituted tribunal cannot be endangered by the arrival of additional counsel.

---

22. Article 1456 of the French Civil Procedure Code (FCCP) provides that arbitrators owe a duty of disclosure throughout the entire arbitration.
23. J. Jourdan Marques, Dalloz actualité, 4 février 2022.
24. Paris Court of Appeal, 25 May 2021, no. 18/20625: "la notoriété desdites informations justifie d'une part que l'arbitre ne soit pas tenu de les révéler, les parties devant faire preuve d'un minimum de curiosité".
25. *See* for example under French law. Paris Court of Appeal, January 26, 2021, no. 19/10666, *Vidatel*, spec. paras. 128-129.
26. *Hrvatska Elektroprivreda dd v. Republic of Slovenia*, ICSID Case No. ARB/05/24. Tribunal's ruling regarding the participation of David Mildon QC in further stages of the proceedings, May 6, 2008, para. 30.
27. Guideline 5: *"Once the Arbitral Tribunal has been constituted, a person should not accept representation of a Party in the arbitration when a relationship exists between the person and an Arbitrator that would create a conflict of interest, unless none of the Parties objects after proper disclosure."*

    Guideline 6: *"The Arbitral Tribunal may, in case of breach of Guideline 5, take measures appropriate to safeguard the integrity of the proceedings, including the exclusion of the new Party Representative from participating in all or part of the arbitral proceedings."*

As well as at the start of the proceedings, procedural *loyauté* comes into play throughout the proceedings, in particular with respect to evidence.

ii   Loyauté *in the Course of the Proceedings*

A right which is not proven does not exist.

Therefore evidence, whether it is documents, witness testimony or expert testimony, is core to the dispute resolution process and is one of the fundamental bases on which tribunals reach their decisions.

In that respect, unethical conduct by counsel or parties can taint evidence, or the method by which it is adduced, and weaken the credibility of the process.

However, a precise definition of unethical conduct in international arbitration remains difficult as a result of the differences in national ethical and procedural rules as well as the ambiguity as to their enforceability in arbitral proceedings.[28]

There is a potential *"clash"* of cultures and expectations between the practices of certain parties/counsel, and practices which are acceptable to some can appear unethical to others.

As an example, the notion of witnesses in commercial cases and the ability to "prepare" them for a cross-examination, is not dealt with by most civil law systems.

Beyond the cultural differences, the principle of *loyauté* in taking evidence can be reduced to ashes by parties using the evidentiary process to drive up costs or delay the arbitration particularly when their opponents lack the resources to fight back.

To address these situations and level the playing field, several international rules or guidelines have emerged over the past thirty years or so, and they all contain provisions relevant to ethics in the taking of evidence.[29]

For example, Article 9 of the IBA Rules on the Taking of Evidence introduced in the 1999 version provides for several grounds on which a tribunal can exclude evidence in order to curb potentially unethical tactics.

With respect to the conduct of parties and counsel, even more drastic but hopefully rare, obtaining evidence illegally is certainly one of the most significant breaches of the principle of procedural *loyauté*.

---

28. Amy C Kläsener and Courtney Lotfi, "Party and Counsel Ethics in the Taking of Evidence," The Guide to Evidence in International Arbitration, First Edition, Global Arbitration Review, September 2021, p. 1
29. For instance, the IBA Rules on the Taking of Evidence in International Arbitration (IBA Rules) revised three times since they were first issued in 1983, the IBA Guidelines on Party Representation in International Arbitration, the Prague Rules (2018), the ICCA Guidelines on Standards of Practice in International Arbitration (March 2021) and the ethical guidelines in the 2014 and 2020 LCIA Rules.
    The Prague Rules strive to propose a more civil law-oriented body of rules for taking evidence. Although they cover a wider range of issues than the IBA Rules, they contain substantially fewer ethical safeguards and duties.

However, even faced with evidence procured through illegal means, divergences exist among domestic laws as to its admissibility, which can make it difficult to predict how a tribunal would deal with the question.[30]

Illegally obtained evidence will be deemed inadmissible in jurisdictions like China and Spain, while courts in Singapore, Hong Kong, Germany, Switzerland, and England and Wales will take a more nuanced approach.[31]

Under French law, the principle of *loyauté* set out in Article 1464 of the Code of Civil Procedure is a valid ground to preclude a party from producing evidence obtained disloyally[32] (in bad faith or illegally[33]). However, if the tribunal does not take action, and absent evidence of procedural fraud, this is not a sufficient ground to set aside the award.[34]

The lack of international consensus is reflected in the newly introduced Article 9(3) of the 2020 IBA Rules which provides that the tribunal "*may* (…) *exclude evidence obtained illegally,*" while Article 9.2(g) sets out that the panel "*shall* (…) *exclude from evidence or production any Document, statement*" for any of the reasons it provides, including "*considerations of procedural economy, proportionality, fairness or equality of the Parties that the Arbitral Tribunal determines to be compelling.*"

In addition, the variety of ethical or bar rules applicable to counsel, who are not necessarily aware of the illegality of the evidence produced, will add to the complexity.[35]

Be that as it may, the solution will often depend on the sensitivity and courage of the tribunal members. The onus is on them to take action on the basis of procedural *loyauté* during the arbitration proceedings.

The reference to procedural *loyauté* does not cease with the award and continues to imbue arbitration at the setting aside stage.

---

30. Tobias Zuberbühler, Dieter Hofmann, et al., 'Article 9: Admissibility and Assessment of Evidence', IBA Rules of Evidence: Commentary on the IBA Rules on the Taking of Evidence in International Arbitration, 2nd ed., p. 220
31. 'Approaches to Evidence across Legal Cultures', *supra*, p. 4
32. Éric Loquin, Chronique des sentences arbitrales, Journal du droit international (Clunet) no. 1, January 2013, chron. 2, commentary of CAS award no. 2011/A/2433 of 8 March 2012, *Amadou Diakite v. FIFA*, p. 55; For instance, it would preclude a party from adducing evidence obtained by eavesdropping on the opposing party's telephone conversations: the tribunal excluded evidence gathered that way in *Libananco Holdings Co. Limited v. Republic of Turkey*, ICSID Case No. ARB/06/8, Decision on Preliminary Issues, June 23, 2008, *see* paras. 78-82
33. Marc Henry, "L'obligation de loyauté des arbitres envers les conseils," Cahiers de l'arbitrage, no.3, p. 525, footnote 71.
34. Paris Court of Appeal, October 27, 2020, no. 19/04177, *Republic of Benin v. Securiport*, para. 23. The Paris Court of Appeal held that, absent evidence of procedural fraud, a breach of the principle of *loyauté* in the taking of evidence cannot provide a ground for annulment of the award.
35. Amy C. Kläsener and Courtney Lotfi, *supra*, p. 4; Code of Conduct for European Lawyers of the Council of Bars and Law Societies of Europe which extends any duty that counsel may have toward courts and judges to arbitrators (Article 4.5). *See*, for instance, Rule 4.4 of the Code prohibits a lawyer from providing false or misleading information to a court.

iii   *Procedural* Loyauté *at the Enforcement Stage*

In many legal systems, a party who has participated in the proceedings and did not raise an objection in a timely manner is deemed to have waived its right to complain at the time of enforcement or recognition of the ensuing award.

This ground for inadmissibility is yet another expression of the principle of procedural *loyauté*, which lasts beyond the arbitration proceedings and precludes a party from keeping an objection until it knows the outcome of the award.

This is the solution under French law[36] which requires the parties to raise appropriate objections as soon as possible during the arbitration proceedings, including with respect to the potential challenge of an arbitrator.[37]

This would, however, not apply if the irregularity pertains to violation of substantive international public policy[38] such as the prohibition of corruption,[39] or to the jurisdiction of the Tribunal.

Similar to French law, Belgian law provides that certain grounds for annulment are only admissible if they were raised before the arbitral tribunal during the arbitral proceedings.[40]

Another example is the revision of the Swiss Federal Act on Private International Law (PILA) in 2020, which led to the introduction of the requirement to raise an objection against a breach of the procedural rules as soon as it is discovered or could have been if due attention had been exercised.[41]

Finally, the English Arbitration Act 1996 contains an analogous waiver rule for parties who seek to challenge an arbitration award without having objected during the arbitral proceedings to a lack of jurisdiction, improper conduct of the arbitration, failure to comply with the arbitration agreement, or other irregularities affecting the tribunal or the proceedings "*unless he shows that, at the time he took part or continued to take part in the proceedings, he did not know and could not with reasonable diligence have discovered the grounds for the objection.*"[42]

The intention behind all these rules clearly reflects the principle of procedural *loyauté* and aims to ensure that irregularities are not kept in reserve for a challenge.

Faced with these various manifestations of procedural *loyauté* at different stages of the proceedings and with respect to all actors in arbitration, it is time to reflect on the effectiveness of this concept.

---

36. Article 1466 of the French Code of Civil Procedure "*La partie qui, en connaissance de cause et sans motif légitime, s'abstient d'invoquer en temps utile une irrégularité devant le tribunal arbitral est réputée avoir renoncé à s'en prévaloir.*"
37. Paris Court of Appeal, May 25, 2021, no. 18/20625, paras. 26 and 36.
38. Paris Court of Appeal, April 2, 2019, no. 16/24358.
39. Paris Court of Appeal, February 21, 2017, *Republic of Kirghizstan v. M. Valeriy Belokon.*
40. Article 1717(5), Belgian Judicial Code.
41. Article 182(4), Swiss PILA.
42. Arbitration Act 1996, section 73(1).

II   CRITICAL ANALYSIS OF *LOYAUTÉ* AND ITS MECHANISMS

Procedural *loyauté* is not an abstract concept.

Its breach can be sanctioned by various mechanisms some of which are particularly harsh and therefore can have a deterrent effect on the parties if they believe that the Tribunal will make use of them.

Some sanctions go to the merits of the claim, others relate to costs, and they may even touch upon counsel or the arbitrators themselves.

1   Sanctions Having an Impact on the Merits

As we all know, adverse inference and inadmissibility are harsh sanctions which directly impact the parties' claims.

Adverse inference occurs mostly by reference to the document production phase and allows the tribunal to sanction a party which does not comply with its order to produce, by inferring from this behavior that the document in question is contrary to the interests of that party.[43]

The tribunal and the opponent are faced with a disloyal party, which refuses to comply with an order of the Tribunal.

But situations are not always that clear, and the exact prerequisites for drawing an adverse inference vary greatly depending on the specific set of rules applicable.[44]

For example, Article 10 of the Prague Rules provides that the tribunal can only draw an adverse inference in cases where the non-compliance of one party to produce evidence was *"without justifiable grounds"* and if it considers such a step appropriate.[45]

In practice, it is quite rare that arbitral tribunals go as far as to base their decision on the merits solely on this basis. It is nevertheless an element, which added to others, may contribute to convincing the Tribunal during its deliberation.

Adverse inferences may also be the basis for the tribunal's decision to shift the burden of proof.

This was the case in *Yemen v. Alkor Petroo Limited et al.* and the arbitrators' decision was not sanctioned by the Paris Court of Appeal at the enforcement stage.

Indeed the Court found this procedure to be just and held that adverse inference put each party in a position to present their case and, in particular, their evidence.[46]

---

43. Cour d'Appel de Paris, Pôle 1—chambre 1, 21 mars 2017, no. 15/17234; Jeremy K. Sharpe, Chapter 16: Adverse Inferences, in Franco Ferrari and Friedrich Jakob Rosenfeld (eds.): Handbook of Evidence in International Commercial Arbitration: Key Concepts and Issues, Kluwer Law International, April 2022, pp. 369-386, p. 369; *Is the problem the lack of solution or that the arbitrators are reluctant to apply it? Towards a correct use of document production in international commercial arbitration,* Jorge Lopez Fung in: Spain Arbitration Review, 2021, Volume 2021 Issue 41, pp. 35-58, p. 43.
44. The right to use adverse inferences can be derived from the applicable law, the arbitration rules or the party agreement, as well as soft law such as the Prague Rules or the IBA Rules for the Taking of Evidence in International Arbitration.
45. Article 10 of Rules on the Efficient Conduct of Proceedings in International Arbitration (Prague Rules), 2018.
46. Cour d'Appel de Paris, Pôle 1—chambre 1, 21 mars 2017, no. 15/17234.

This is a recognition of the suitability and efficiency of the sanction in the case of a breach of procedural *loyauté*.

In addition to adverse inferences, inadmissibility is also a sanction for breach of procedural *loyauté* impacting the merits of a case.

It can occur in a number of contexts,[47] *inter alia*, the admissibility of a claim, but also of a challenge brought against an arbitrator, or inadmissibility of evidence or of an application to set aside an award.

It is a notoriously harsh sanction for a litigant but the harshness of inadmissibility is what makes it an effective sanction for parties that engage in conduct which goes against the principle of procedural *loyauté*.

2　　Allocation of Costs

Allocation of cost is a classic remedy against parties intentionally disrupting or delaying the arbitration procedure.[48]

There is no doubt that tribunals have this power,[49] and they are sometimes well advised to exercise it during the course of the arbitration and not necessarily at the end in the final award.

Indeed this is a clear indication of the willingness of a Tribunal to ensure a fair procedure and deter procedural misconduct.

Examples of situations are manifold: from excessive document requests to failure to comply with the tribunal's orders or unjustified applications for interim relief.[50]

Disruption of the proceedings may also take the form of excessively long legal arguments, abandoned one after the other, and replaced by new ones, after being defeated by the cross-examination of one's own witness.

These tactics necessarily lead to an increase in costs for the party having to defend a series of groundless legal arguments. It is therefore appropriate, on the basis of procedural *loyauté, that* the associated cost be mostly supported by the wrongdoer.

---

47. Michael Hwang and Si Cheng Lim, Chapter 16: The Chimera of Admissibility in Neil Kaplan and Michael J. Moser (eds.), International Arbitration, in Jurisdiction, Admissibility and Choice of Law in International Arbitration: Liber Amicorum Michael Pryles, Kluwer Law International, 2018, p. 265.
48. Richard Kreindler and Mariel Dimsey, Chapter 21: Sanctioning of Party Conduct Through Costs: A Reconsideration of Scope, Timing and Content of Costs Awards, in Patricia Louise Shaughnessy and Sherlin Tung (eds.), The Powers and Duties of an Arbitrator: Liber Amicorum Pierre A. Karrer, Kluwer Law International, 2017, p. 201
49. Guideline 26 c) sets out: "*If the Arbitral Tribunal, after giving the Parties notice and a reasonable opportunity to be heard, finds that a Party Representative has committed Misconduct, the Arbitral Tribunal, as appropriate, may (…) (c) consider the Party Representative's Misconduct in apportioning the costs of the arbitration, indicating, if appropriate, how and in what amount the Party Representative's Misconduct leads the Tribunal to a different apportionment of costs*"; Article 9.8 of the IBA Rules states: "*If the Arbitral Tribunal determines that a Party has failed to conduct itself in good faith in the taking of evidence, the Arbitral Tribunal may, in addition to any other measures available under these Rules, take such failure into account in its assignment of the costs of the arbitration, including costs arising out of or in connection with the taking of evidence.*"
50. ICC Commission Report on Controlling Time and Costs in Arbitration (2012), para. 82.

3 Sanction of the Counsel or the Arbitrator

All actors in the proceedings are subject to procedural *loyauté*, as such they are subject to potential sanctions.

As far as counsel are concerned, sanctions are mostly ethical and therefore vary greatly between jurisdictions and bar associations. It is even more complicated when, as often the case in arbitration, counsel are simultaneously members of several bars.

In any event, while ethical sanctions are decided by the relevant bar, in practice arbitral tribunals tend to take into account bar rules and their potential sanctions, particularly when deciding matters such as privilege during the document production phase.

Finally, as already seen, change of counsel in the course of the proceedings may lead to disqualification of counsel by the tribunal, if it endangers the proper constitution of the tribunal.

With respect to arbitrators, lack of disclosure of relevant information regarding impartiality or independence is sanctioned by the disqualification, if it is discovered during the course of arbitration. However if only discovered later, it will mostly sanction the parties, as it may be a reason to set aside the award.

Furthermore, although theoretically possible, making a claim against an arbitrator for breach of duty of *loyauté* is quite difficult in view of the vague nature of this obligation, as well as the broad immunity attached to their quasi-judicial task and the difficulty of assessing the loss resulting from misconduct.[51]

Leaving aside the hopefully isolated jurisdictions where it is possible to imprison arbitrators if they act with a lack of integrity or impartiality,[52] engaging an arbitrator's liability requires extreme situations such as intentional misconduct[53] or fraud, which hopefully rarely if ever happen in practice.

Finally, institutions may disqualify arbitrators in extreme situations[54] and may take into account their conduct, notably in terms of diligence and efficiency, when fixing the final amount of their fees.[55]

As a matter of fact, I would suggest that the most stringent and effective sanction for counsel's or an arbitrator's disloyal conduct is the judgment of their peers, which may taint a hard-won reputation in the "small world" of arbitration.

The subject must be approached with due care, as it remains intrinsically subjective, but one will definitely be reluctant to appoint an arbitrator or recommend a counsel that has been seen to act improperly.

---

51. Julian D.M. Lew et al., Chapter 12: Rights and Duties of Arbitrators and Parties, in: Julian D.M. Lew, Loukas A. Mistelis, et al., Comparative International Commercial Arbitration, Kluwer Law International, 2003, pp. 275-299, pp. 288 et seq.
52. Cf. Alain N. Farhad, "Two Steps Forward, One Step Back: A Report on the Development of Arbitration in the United Arab Emirates", Journal of International Arbitration, 2018, Volume 35, Issue 1, pp. 131-142, p. 134.
53. Cour d'appel de Paris, Pôle 5, Chambre 16, 22 juin 2021, no. 21/07623.
54. ICC Arbitration Rules (2021), *see* Article 15.2.
55. ICC Arbitration Rules, Article 38(2) and Appendix III, Article 2.2.

To conclude, while we have seen that procedural *loyauté* serves to address a number of practical challenges, I would suggest that beyond the vagueness of the concept, one of the most significant obstacles to its implementation is so-called due process paranoia.[56]

In that respect, tribunals are often reluctant to act decisively for fear of the award being challenged on the basis of a party not having had the chance to present its case fully. As a result, certain parties are able to employ dilatory or abusive tactics without fear of sanctions.

This is, to say the least, a paradox since procedural *loyauté* and due process are siblings.

But we have all experienced cases where fresh evidence was admitted late in the proceedings although it was available months beforehand, or where last-minute objections at the hearings have triggered the reopening of issues previously declared irrelevant by the Tribunal.

Faced with borderline conduct I admit that it is sometimes difficult to draw the line, but I trust that the experience and courage of arbitrators will allow them to act robustly, a sort of enlightenment age for arbitrators as the title of this Congress suggests.

---

56. Queen Mary University of London and White & Case, '2021 International Arbitration Survey: Adapting arbitration to a changing world', p. 12.

CHAPTER 5

AI Versus IA: End of the Enlightenment?

*Lucy Reed**

I   INTRODUCTION

Three unrelated events brought me to the theme for this paper, which I initially explored in a public lecture given at the law firm of Bredin Prat in Paris in March 2022.[1] The theme is (or appears to be) the relationship between International Arbitration and Artificial Intelligence or IA versus AI.

     The first event was the Program Committee's selection of the theme of "Arbitration's Age of Enlightenment ... and Adaptation?" for the XXVth International Council for Commercial Arbitration (ICCA) Congress in Edinburgh. The Enlightenment or the Age of Reason, of course, was the intellectual and philosophical movement of the seventeenth and eighteenth centuries based on the application of reasoning both to define problems and to solve problems. To recall Rene Descartes' famous words from

* Lucy Reed, President of ICCA from 2020 to 2023, is an Independent Arbitrator with Arbitration Chambers in New York. The author thanks Ms. Lindsay Gastrell, also with Arbitration Chambers New York, for her research assistance with this paper.
1. The author is honored to have been named the inaugural Distinguished Bredin Prat Visiting Scholar for the Sciences Po LL.M in Transnational Arbitration Dispute Settlement (TADS) program for 2022, and extends appreciation to the partners of Bredin Prat and Sciences Po.

Discourse on the Method dating from 1637, *"Cogito, ergo sum"* or "I think therefore I am."[2]

The second event was a meeting I attended at the United States Council on Foreign Relations in December 2021 featuring a conversation between Dr. Henry Kissinger, renowned national security strategist and former United States Secretary of State, and Eric Schmidt, the former CEO of Google.[3] The topic was their recent book entitled "The Age of AI and Our Human Future," written with Daniel Huttenlocher, the dean of the Schwarzman College of Computing at the Massachusetts Institute of Technology.[4] In the meeting, Dr. Kissinger caught my attention by describing AI as the end of the Age of Enlightenment.

The third event was another meeting I attended in January 2022 as a member of the Advisory Council for the Queen Mary School of International Arbitration, in effect about international arbitration education. I was struck by something that Professor Julian Lew said: "As international arbitration gets more litigious and aggressive, it gets less intellectual." In context, based on my later conversation with Professor Lew, I consider that he used the word "intellectual" in part to signify "intelligent."

II   DR. KISSINGER ET AL AND AI

To connect these three events, I turn first to AI, as distinct from IA.

In the Council on Foreign Relations meeting, Dr. Kissinger admitted his initial ignorance about AI. He said:

> I was totally ignorant of any artificial intelligence field. I slid into it by accident by listening to a lecture that I was actually trying to avoid. And Eric [Schmidt] stood in the door of the room, and I didn't know him very well, and he nevertheless urged me to go back into the room and listen to that lecture.[5]

I admit similar ignorance. When I speak to young practitioners and students, I advise them to ignore what earlier generations have done in international arbitration, which necessarily was based on the opportunities of those earlier times. I urge them to focus instead on the present and future, on what likely is just over the horizon in their own arbitration careers. Lately, if pressed, I would list climate change, space law, cyber security, and artificial intelligence—all things I know little about, especially AI. Until recently, what I did know about AI is that, somehow, it suggests the endings for our smartphone text messages and screens for spam, more or less successfully.

What I now know, and find most important and intriguing, about AI is not the pure math and science on which AI rests. It is that, contrasted with basic computer

---

2. Rene Descartes, *Discourse on the Method* (1637).
3. Council on Foreign Relations, Malcolm and Carolyn Wiener Annual Lecture on Science and Technology With Henry Kissinger and Eric Schmidt, December 20, 2021, transcript available at www.cfr.org/event/malcolm-and-carolyn-wiener-annual-lecture-science-and-technology-henry-kissinger-and-eric (last accessed at July 4, 2023) (hereinafter *"Kissinger-Schmidt Lecture"*).
4. Henry A. Kissinger, Eric Schmidt, Daniel Huttonlocher, *The Age of AI and Our Human Future* (Little Brown & Co 2021).
5. Kissinger-Schmidt Lecture, p. 8.

processes, strong AI can and does solve highly complex problems in ways that we human beings cannot understand with our human brains and intelligence. Further, strong AI can train itself to solve problems without relying upon pre-programmed ways of human reasoning. In other words, AI systems have shown that they can learn how to learn.

Some concrete examples help to illustrate this counter-intuitive phenomenon. First, one can watch a video demonstrating that a deep-learning program called DeepMind learned to play and win the early computer game Atari Breakout, with no programming except being instructed to maximize the score. DeepMind accomplished this task in three stages in just four hours. Computer experts cannot explain this.

In a second example, an AI system was programmed with only the basics of the game of chess, and then—in Dr. Kissinger's words—"appl[ied] strategies that in two thousand years of chess records have never been applied by human beings."[6] These were strategies that the chess master Garry Kasparov called "a new dimension of human intelligence."[7]

Turning from games to a third example, the New York Times reported in 2017 on a study in which humans and a computer program were asked to predict the sexual orientation of human subjects based simply on photographs.[8] Humans made correct guesses 60% of the time; the computer, 91% of the time for men, and 83% of the time for women. Again, computer scientists cannot explain why or how this is.

A final example, more relevant in these COVID-19 pandemic times, is the work of a group of synthetic biologists and computer scientists at MIT described in the Kissinger-Schmidt-Huttenlocher book.[9] Their goal was to build an AI network to find a novel antibiotic capable of killing strains of bacteria that were resistant to all known antibiotics. After having the AI system "learn" the attributes of molecules predicted to be antibacterial with a "training set" of 2,000 known molecules, the AI system surveyed a library of 61,000 molecules, FDA-approved drugs, and natural products to find new molecules predicted to be effective and non-toxic antibiotics. One molecule fit the criteria—now labeled Halicin. The MIT project leaders agreed that Halicin could not have been discovered through traditional research and development. In the words of the authors:

> Chemists have devised concepts such as atomic weights and chemical bonds to capture the characteristics of molecules. But the AI identified relationships that had escaped human detection—or possibly even defied human description. The AI that MIT researchers trained did not simply recapitulate conclusions derived from the previously observed qualities of the molecules. Rather, it detected new molecular qualities—relationships between aspects of their structure and their antibiotic capacity that humans had neither perceived nor defined. Even after the antibiotic was discovered, humans could not articulate precisely why it worked.[10]

---

6. Kissinger-Schmidt Lecture, p. 15.
7. Kissinger-Schmidt Lecture, p. 15.
8. Cliff Kuang, "Can A.I. Be Taught to Explain Itself?" in The New York Times Magazine, November 21, 2017.
9. Kissinger-Schmidt-Huttenlocher, pp. 9-11, 61-65.
10. Kissinger-Schmidt-Huttenlocher, p. 11.

Eric Schmidt joked in the Council on Foreign Relations program that "in the sense [AI] doesn't know why it did something, it's like a teenager."[11]

More seriously and more relevant to the ICCA Congress theme, Dr. Kissinger shared his observation that examples such as these mark the end of the Enlightenment. In his words: "in the Enlightenment, reason dominated the perception. Here, extraordinary results can be achieved for which one does not know how they come about."[12]

This transition was perhaps inevitable. Scientists in the era of the Enlightenment were first able, with microscopes, to see things invisible to the naked eye; and then Albert Einstein was able to explain the once inexplicable in physics with the theory of relativity; and then more recent generations have enjoyed the benefits of previously unimaginable technological advances such as telephones, televisions, basic computers, and the internet. Now AI is upon us, facing the reality that human beings are no longer the top thinkers on the earth.

This is an uncomfortable proposition. It is not uncomfortable in that strong AI can solve once-unsolvable problems in ways that will benefit all of personkind, for example, by discovering a molecule like Halicin to create a new life-saving antibiotic. But it is uncomfortable in that, unlike advances in human reasoning in the Enlightenment and in Dr. Einstein's laboratory, we humans are incapable of understanding *how* AI can and does solve highly complex problems.

The mysteries of AI obviously overlap with the mysteries of human consciousness. One difference is that AI, unlike the intelligence of conscious humans, lacks any attribute of morality or ethics.[13] In "The Age of AI and Our Human Future," Kissinger et al. describe a "dialogue" in which a language-generating AI program—called a GPT-3 system—is asked a series of philosophical questions. The GPT-3 first answers that it *does* have understanding, but that it does *not* have a conscience or sense of morality. When asked whether it is "actually capable of independent thought," the GPT-3 answers:

> No. I am not. You may wonder why I give this conflicting answer. The reason is simple. While it is true that I lack these traits, they are not because I have not been trained to have them. Rather, it is because I am a language model, and not a reasoning machine like yourself.[14]

III   IA AND AI

Rather than go on about the potential impact of AI on our human future, I turn to the potential impact of AI on the practice of international arbitration or IA.

---

11. Kissinger-Schmidt Lecture, p. 5.
12. Kissinger-Schmidt Lecture, p. 4.
13. This recalls a statement by Chinese artist Ai Wei-Wei that "Without consciousness, there is no morality." "Reclaiming art from capitalism" in The Economist, The World Ahead 2022, p. 143.
14. Kissinger-Schmidt-Huttunlocher, p. 13.

There is an increasing amount of good commentary to be had on the general impact of AI on IA. This includes the work of Professor Maxi Scherer[15] and Sophie Nappert.[16]

Borrowing the title of "International Arbitration 3.0" from one of Professor Scherer's articles, what we need to know in brief is that the synapses in the human brain can store approximately 100 terabytes worth of information. As compared to the capacity of a strong AI program, this is far from enough power to learn the game of chess in a few hours or to digest a 400-page arbitration memorial in a few minutes. Professor Scherer, rather discouragingly, reminds us that "the computational capacity of the human brain equates roughly to that of an optimized computer which costs only a couple hundred euros today."[17]

Professor Scherer sets out what seems to be the reasonable consensus position on the impact of AI on IA.

First, AI already is and will increasingly be a useful tool for data- and document-driven tasks in international arbitration, including: e-discovery document review and production, through predictive coding with keywords; proofreading; translation; and legal research. Such tasks use only relatively simple AI to replicate what human professionals do, as pointed out by Professor Richard Susskind OBE in his 2020 CIArb's Alexander Lecture entitled "The Future of Dispute Resolution."[18]

Second, in contrast, AI is not likely to be useful in predicting the outcomes of international commercial arbitration, because awards are largely confidential. This differentiates the field from national court litigation, in which judgments are publicly available to be used as programming data. In a 2016 study, an AI system—using word sequences and frequency—trained itself and correctly predicted the outcomes in cases before the European Court of Human Rights 79% of the time. Similarly, in a 2017 study of United States Supreme Court cases, covering far broader categories of disputes than the European Court of Human Rights, the successful prediction rate was 70%.

Third, and most relevant to the international arbitration community, AI will not (at least any time soon) replace international arbitral tribunals. One reason, as mentioned, is the confidentiality of international commercial arbitration outcomes. Another reason, in Professor Scherer's words, is that "international arbitration cases are typically complex, fact-specific and governed by different applicable law" and hence non-repetitive, offering little data of value for predictive programming.

Most importantly, the core mandate of arbitral tribunals—commercial and investment treaty alike—is to provide *genuine reasoning* for their decisions, for the purpose of guiding the parties. As set out above, strong AI resolves complex issues

---

15. Maxi Scherer, "Artificial Intelligence and Legal Decision-Making: The Wide Open? Study on the Example of International Arbitration," available as Queen Mary Legal Studies Research Paper No. 318/2019; Maxi Scherer, "International Arbitration 3.0—How Artificial Intelligence Will Change Dispute Resolution" in Austrian YB Int'l Arb. 2019.

16. Sophie Nappert, "The Challenge of Artificial Intelligence in Arbitral Decision-Making" in Practical Law (2018); Sophie Nappert and Paul Cohen, "The March of the Robots" in Global Arbitration Review, February 15, 2017.

17. Maxi Scherer, Austrian YB Int'l Arb. 2019, p. 504.

18. Richard Susskind Obe, "Chartered Institute of Arbitrators' Alexander Lecture 2010: The future of dispute resolution," November 13, 2021 (Online event, viewable on YouTube).

without reasoning or at least without our being able to understand the reasoning. And it is highly unlikely in the near future that even strong AI systems will be able to be programmed, or to teach themselves, how to give reasons for any solutions they may offer to disputes subject to international arbitration.

IV   IA AND INTELLIGENCE

This brings me to the meeting I mentioned of the Advisory Council for the Queen Mary School of International Arbitration, in which Professor Lew observed: "As international arbitration gets more litigious and aggressive, it gets less intellectual."

To understand what underlay this observation, I followed up with Professor Lew, who graciously agreed to the attribution of his views.[19] He explained that when he first became involved with international arbitration in the early 1970s, most of the leaders of the then-fledgling practice area were specialists in public international law, private international law, comparative law, or all three. The familiar names include Pieter Sanders, Pierre Lalive, Berthold Goldman, Gunnar Lagargren, and Rene David, among others. The main positions of these leaders were with universities, not with law firms or barristers' chambers. Professor Lew went on to say:

> Today sadly, few lawyers in international arbitration have a detailed knowledge of public and/or private international law and comparative law. Their skills are as forensic litigators. To my regret, international arbitration is increasingly a form of litigation (common law style) with both the aggression often experienced and the resort to motions adopted from court proceedings, e.g. strike out motions, challenges, document production, delay tactics.[20]

Professor Lew, of course, acknowledged that his observations reflect a certain unrealistic nostalgia for the past, now that international arbitration has become big business for law firms, arbitrators, arbitral institutions, and law schools. While accepting that there is no putting this genie back in the bottle, Professor Lew did note, with appreciation, the positive contributions made by ICCA with the publication of the Guidelines on Standards of Practice in International Arbitration[21] and the International Bar Association with the Guidelines on Party Representation in International Arbitration.[22]

Professor Lew's unease rightfully goes beyond business profit and codes of conduct. His concerns focus on how international arbitration counsel and arbitrators learn, know, and use *substantive* international law. This is a topic, he says, "that

---

19. Email exchange Lucy Reed and Professor Julian Lew, January 31, 2022 (hereinafter, "Lew Observations").
20. Lew Observations.
21. Guidelines on Standards of Practice in International Arbitration, ICCA Report No. 9, available at cdn.arbitration-ICCA.org/s3fs-public/documents/media_document/ICCA-Guidelines_on_Stand ards_of_Practice_in_International_Arbitration.pdf.
22. International Bar Association, Guidelines on Party Representation in International Arbitration, available at www.ibanet.org/MediaHandler?id = 6FOC5707-E7AD-43AF-B76E-714D9FE74D7F.

warrants time and careful consideration to protect the international arbitration system."[23]

V   AI VERSUS IA

Professor Lew's observations resonated with my growing concerns about the ever-more excessive use of "precedent" in investment treaty arbitration.

One can easily recite that there is no doctrine of precedent in international dispute resolution, referring to the words—really, the silence—in Article 38(1) of the Statute of the International Court of Justice. But actual practice belies this—in my view, rightly so, as long as "non-precedential precedent" is used in an appropriate way and to an appropriate degree.

There is a great deal of commentary to be found on this topic in the field of investor-State dispute settlement (ISDS).[24] The questions being debated are well-known: Should a tribunal decide the dispute before it on the basis of the unique facts and legal arguments presented, without assuming responsibility for the development of international law? Or should tribunals strive for a *jurisprudence constante* and decide cases with an eye to coherency in international investment law? But then again, as Professor Zachary Douglas has posited: "Too much emphasis on an emerging *jurisprudence constante* may have the effect of undermining coherency for the sake of consistency."[25]

Among others, I have offered reasons for why, as a de facto matter, parties and arbitrators "devote so much ink and time to citing, discussing and distinguishing prior awards" and why there are "ever-longer footnotes," in a 2010 article entitled "The De Facto Precedent Regime in Investment Arbitration: A Case for Proactive Case Management."[26] One reason is—or was—sheer need. In the early days of ISDS, the bare and elastic legal concepts in investment treaties—fair and equitable treatment, full security and protection, umbrella clause protection—needed to be illuminated through (relatively) novel legal argument by counsel and reasoned findings by tribunals in the first generation of awards. A second and more practical reason is that investment treaty awards, unlike commercial arbitration awards, are generally public and therefore available to be studied and cited. Hence, it was natural and reasonable for counsel in

---

23. Lew Observations.
24. Zachary Douglas, "Can a Doctrine of Precedent Be Justified in Investment Treaty Arbitration?" in (2010) 25 ICSID Review-Foreign Investment Law Journal 104, p. 109; Patrick Norton, "The Role of Precedent in the Development of International Investment Law" in (2018) 33 ICSID Review-Foreign Investment Law Journal 280; Christoph Schreuer and Matthew Weiniger, "Conversations Across Cases—Is there a Doctrine of Precedent in Investment Arbitration?" in TDM 3 (2008); Andrea Bjorklund, "Investment Treaty Arbitral Decisions as Jurisprudence Constante" in TDM 1 (2010); Emmanuel Gaillard and Yas Banifatemi (eds), Precedent in International Arbitration, IAI Series on International Arbitration No. 5 (Juris 2008); Gabrielle Kaufmann-Kohler, "Arbitral Precedent: Dream, Necessity or Excuse?" (2006 Annual Freshfields Lecture) in 23 Arb. Int'l 357 (2007).
25. Douglas, p. 109.
26. Lucy Reed, "The De Facto Precedent Regime in Investment Arbitration: A Case for Proactive Case Management," in (2010) 25 ICSID Review-Foreign Investment Law Journal 95.

the cases that followed to look to and use the developing "jurisprudence" on procedural and substantive investment treaty protections.

But, as more and more ISDS awards became available, this natural early reliance on "non-precedential precedents" warranted reassessment. That it became possible to cite many past awards on, say FET, did not mean that it was helpful to cite all available awards. But this is what has happened in many (not all) cases. It is now not unusual to find footnotes in memorials citing prior ISDS awards, and articles discussing those awards, occupying up to two-thirds of the page in the legal argument sections.

The questions raised by Dr. Kissinger about AI and Professor Lew about developments in IA added a new perspective to my concern about the de facto disconnect—now excessive—of "non-precedential precedent." It is troubling that in many (again not all) cases the string citations in the memorials are offered without any substantive discussion or engagement whatsoever with the *reasoning* in the earlier awards cited, for example on the application of FET to the specific facts of the case at hand. This may be because there often is little, if any, genuine reasoning on the application of FET in the string-cited awards themselves, as they also contain string cites to earlier FET awards also lacking genuine reasoning.

In an admittedly imperfect analogy, this situation is an IA version of the uncomfortable AI phenomenon that humans cannot understand the solution given by a strong AI system: the problem goes into the computers and the solution comes out. Parties in ISDS arbitrations are advocating for legal conclusions without actually constructing the underlying arguments around the specific facts and circumstances, and tribunals are being invited to offer decisions without fulfilling their obligation to provide actual—*genuine*—reasoning. Extending the imperfect analogy, this can be seen as a low-tech and—to recall Professor Lew's adjective—non-intellectual version of AI, and hence a low-value process.

This brings to mind Dr. Kissinger's concern that AI is a short-cut around "the evolution of human achievement, much of it ... brought about by people who grappled with a problem for many years and worked through sometimes even improbable looking alternatives," and will "create an increasing temptation to rely on AI to do the conceptual final thinking."[27] In the view of Kissinger, Schmidt and Huttenlocher, this defies the spirit of the Enlightenment:

> The Enlightenment world—with its optimism regarding human reason despite its consciousness of the pitfalls of flawed human logic—has long been our world. Scientific revolutions, especially in the twentieth century, have evolved technology and philosophy, but the central Enlightenment premise of a knowable world being unearthed, step-by-step, by human minds has persisted. Until now.[28]

This led Dr. Kissinger, in the Council on Foreign Relations program, to urge that humans need to "think for ourselves ... how to relate technology to purpose."[29] Less grandly in our niche field of international arbitration, counsel and arbitrators need to

---

27. Kissinger-Schmidt Lecture, p. 21.
28. Kissinger-Schmidt-Huttenlocher, p. 49.
29. Kissinger-Schmidt Lecture, p. 11.

think for ourselves about how to relate precedent to purpose, to support the necessary underlying reasoning.

The question of *how* to do this is not particularly difficult. Counsel should select the most significant and compelling prior awards to support their own case-specific legal arguments, and tribunals should do the same to support their decisions. The goal should be to reap the benefit of the *quality* and not the *quantity* of earlier decisions. This requires the hard work of original and genuine *reasoning*. Recalling the AI GPT-3 exchange about morality and ethics, arbitration practitioners are not like "language models"—here, perhaps "citation collection models"—but rather "reasoning models."

It is worth recalling the formative years of today's ISDS practice. In the early expropriation cases before the Iran-United States Claims Tribunal, for example in the case of *Phillips Petroleum v. Iran*, counsel did discuss the earlier ad hoc petroleum nationalization arbitrations of *Sapphire Int'l Petroleum, Aminoil v. Kuwait, Liamco v. Libya*.[30] But, in using the few available "precedents," the focus necessarily was on the primary interpretation of the new treaties at issue—the Algiers Declarations[31]—and on foundational international law principles. Interestingly, not only was it difficult to find (then, only) hard copies of the earlier awards, those awards look nothing like modern investment treaty awards. The *Aminoil* decision has only *three* case citations, all for general propositions, while the *Liamco* decision is rich in comparative jurisprudence.

As events unfolded, the Iran-United States Claims Tribunal awards—originally also available only in hard copy—became the resource for counsel to use in formulating primary arguments interpreting the new breed of bilateral investment treaties. This led to early "precedents" such as *Maffezini v. Spain* in 2000, *Mondev v. United States* in 2002, *CME v. Czech Republic* and *Tecmed v. Mexico* in 2003, *MTD v. Chile* in 2004 and *CMS v. Argentina* in 2005.[32]

Now we see these cases, together with Iran-United States Claims Tribunal cases, such as *Phillips Petroleum v. Iran*, buried in string cites in footnotes in memorials in expropriation and FET cases, all too often without any connection to arguments in the text. It is true that those who wrestled with writing the early memorials in the early Iran-United States Claims Tribunal and ISDS arbitrations may have been fortunate, for

---

30. *Phillips Petroleum Company Iran v. The Islamic Republic of Iran, the National Iranian Oil Company*, IUSCT Case No. 39, Award, June 29, 1989; *Sapphire International Petroleum Ltd. v. National Iranian Oil Company*, Award, March 15, 1963; *The American Independent Oil Company v. The Government of the State of Kuwait*, Final Award, March 24, 1982; *Libyan American Oil Company v. The Government of the Libyan Arab Republic*, Award, April 12, 1977.

31. Declaration of the Government of the Democratic and Popular Republic of Algeria (General Declaration), January 19, 1981 and Declaration of the Government of the Democratic and Popular Republic of Algeria Concerning the Settlement of Claims by the Government of the United States of America and the Government of the Islamic Republic of Iran (Claims Settlement Declaration), January 19, 2021, both available on www.iusct.net.

32. *Emilio Agustín Maffezini v. The Kingdom of Spain*, ICSID Case No. ARB/97/7, Award, November 13, 2000; *Mondev International Ltd. v. United States of America*, ICSID Case No. ARB(AF)/99/2, Award, October 11, 2002; *CME Czech Republic B.V. v. The Czech Republic*, UNCITRAL, Award, March 14, 2003; *Técnicas Medioambientales Tecmed, S.A. v. The United Mexican States*, ICSID Case No. ARB (AF)/00/2, Award, May 29, 2003; *MTD Equity Sdn. Bhd. and MTD Chile S.A. v Republic of Chile*, ICSID Case No. ARB/01/7, Award, May 25, 2004; *CMS Gas Transmission Company v. The Republic of Argentina*, ICSID Case No. ARB/01/8, Award, May 12, 2005.

reasons similar (but far less grand) to those underlying the observation of David Chalmers of the New York University Center for Mind, Brain and Consciousness that "[i]t would have been fascinating to have studied maths and physics when Isaac Newton was still trying to figure out the basic principles."[33] But, there is no reason that counsel today cannot and should not engage in primary reasoning with treaty and other international law sources in presenting their ISDS cases to tribunals, by addressing first principles and relying more on comparative law. There is no reason not to do the hard work of identifying and discussing only the *most significant* decisions on outcome-determinative issues, instead of, for example, string-citing all of the FET decisions to be found by anyone in a Google search—or instead of mimicking the black-box of AI problem-solving, without discernible genuine reasoning. That different counsel in different cases will make different selections of significant awards is a *strength* of the system, not a drawback. To recall Professor Douglas' concern, what good is constancy—consistency—if it undermines coherency?

To pose an even more daring challenge to counsel and parties in investment treaty arbitration, why not leave out the "non-precedential precedents" altogether in arbitrations based on classic expropriation or now well-recognized unfair and unequal treatment? To return to the Congress theme, one might refer to Immanuel Kant's essay "Answering the Question: What is the Enlightenment?" in which Kant offered the challenge of "*sapere aude*" or "dare to know."

And what about precedents in international commercial arbitration? There is something of a movement in favor of publishing international commercial arbitration awards, primarily based on the public's interest in the substantive issues being decided. The argument, propounded by Professor Catherine Rogers among others, is that business is being deprived of important sources of international commercial and contract law.[34]

It is true that international commercial arbitration is private justice. This is largely explained by the understandable insistence on confidentiality between two usually sophisticated and well-matched international companies. But, confidentiality aside, is the public really being deprived of much substantive commercial law? Most commercial arbitration disputes involve unique facts and one-off contractual relationships. Few awards interpret commercial contract provisions with reasoning that would greatly assist other disputing parties, although there are exceptions. To that end, the ICC International Court of Arbitration—including through the ICCA Yearbook—publishes significant anonymized commercial arbitration awards. And, of course, there is transparency through national court New York Convention cases and voluntary disclosure via the now ubiquitous legal media.

In comparison to substantive commercial law, public access to decisions on arbitral procedure can and does benefit practitioners in case after case. The published

---

33. Lunch with the FT David Chalmers, "*We are the gods of the virtual worlds we create,*" February 13, 2022. This literally was a virtual reality sushi lunch between the FT reporter and David Chalmers.
34. Catherine A. Rogers, "Transparency in International Commercial Arbitration," in (2006) 54 University Kansas Law Review 1301.

awards of the Iran-United States Claims Tribunal (now available online) provided invaluable procedural jurisprudence on the 1976 UNCITRAL Rules, which jurisprudence is now taken for granted. The ICC Court and other institutions follow suit by publishing anonymized excerpts of awards and/or providing confidential access to awards to the authors of procedural guides. Publishing arbitrator challenge decisions, as the London Court of International Arbitration (LCIA) does, is also helpful, as the underlying fact patterns may be repetitive.

Certainly, one reason to have more widespread publication of international commercial arbitration awards is *not* to make more awards available for counsel to use in string cites in bare support for substantive legal propositions without corresponding reasoning. This migration of the over-use of "non-precedential precedents" from investment treaty arbitration to international commercial arbitration would not improve the practice. It would seem wiser for counsel and arbitrators, unlike AI—*artificial* intelligence systems—to remain content with IA—*genuine* international arbitration—based on the reasoning that participants can understand and make understandable to others.

To conclude by circling back to the Congress theme, such would be consistent with "Arbitration's Age of Enlightenment ... and Adaptation."

PART III   Panel 1: Progress Made/Progress
to Be Made – Exploring the Ways Forward

CHAPTER 6

E^3 + Action – Talk + Data = Enlightenment in International Arbitration

Lucy Greenwood[*]

TABLE OF CONTENTS

I   A 'GOSPEL OF DOOM'

1   'Evil News Fly Faster'

When announcing the theme for the Congress of the International Council for Commercial Arbitration (ICCA) 2022 to be 'Arbitration's Age of Enlightenment', the programme chairs stated '[D]espite the current gospel of doom, the system of arbitration has experienced extraordinary growth and success over the last 20 years, to emerge today as a major form of international dispute resolution throughout the world. As a consequence of its growth and success, the exchange of new ideas about arbitration's future is now greater than ever before, and it is coming from a wider

---

[*] Chartered Arbitrator, qualified in England and Wales and Texas. Lucy Greenwood practises exclusively as an international arbitrator and focuses on energy-related disputes. More information is available at www.greenwoodarbitration.com.

variety of stakeholders and interested parties.'[1] On further examination, that statement is telling. It highlights a 'current gospel of doom' but also underscores the 'growth and success' of international arbitration as a dispute resolution mechanism.

Long before international arbitration evolved into the successful dispute resolution mechanism we see today, there was an ongoing 'gospel of doom' among international arbitration commentators. Perhaps that is a factor of the pessimistic nature of lawyers, perhaps it is simply that there are more ways for something to go wrong than go right. Perhaps it is a reflection of human nature being more interested in failure than success, that bad news travels fast, or, to quote from The Spanish Tragedy '[I]f he lived, the news would soon be here. Nay, evil news fly faster still than good.'[2]

For many years the doomsayers focused on one overarching criticism of the process: that international arbitrations took too long and cost too much. The issue of 'time and costs' in international arbitration has been a concern since the late-1980s yet somehow still remains a concern today, or, at least, a perceived concern. Back in 1989, Lord Mustill observed 'Are the [arbitration] proceedings any longer imbued by informality, or do they not have all the all the elephantine laboriousness of an action in court, without the saving grace of the exasperated judges' power to bang together the heads of recalcitrant parties?'[3] In 2000, Fali S. Nariman asserted: '[A]rbitration has lost that lightness of touch that characterized its early manifestations: motivated or reasoned decisions – majority, concurring and dissenting – are now increasingly long and turgid, and too full of legal learning.'[4] In 2010, a member of the Corporate Counsel International Arbitration Group said 'no one he knows who uses arbitration regularly is happy with it'.[5] Around the same time, an empirical study of the practice of international commercial dispute resolution concluded that 'arbitration ...suffers from high transaction costs and an inherent limitation in the capacity to bring about consensual solutions'.[6] Fast forward a decade and concerns remained that 'spiraling costs are often seen as the worst feature of arbitration'.[7] Tellingly, one of Freshfields

---

1. The Journal News in Focus 'Arbitration's Age of Enlightenment' theme for Edinburgh ICCA 2020 11 September 2018 http://www.journalonline.co.uk/News/1026311.aspx#.XcWH4ej7RPY.
2. Thomas Kyd, written circa 1585.
3. M. Mustill, 'Arbitration: History and Background' (1989) 6 Journal International Arbitration 43 at p. 56.
4. 'The Spirit of Arbitration: The Tenth Annual Goff Lecture' (2000) 6(3) Arbitration International 261.
5. 'We can work it out' by David Hechler, Corporate Counsel, 1 February 2010. http://www.law.com/jsp/cc/PubArticleCC.jsp?id = 1202437871408. http://www.pwc.co.uk/pdf/PwC_International_Arbitration_2008.pdf. Bühring-Uhle, Arbitration and Mediation in International Business (2nd ed.), p. 127, available at www.kluwerarbitration.com asserts 'arbitration offers the best legal framework available for the resolution of international business disputes but suffers from high transaction costs and an inherent limitation in the capacity to bring about consensual solutions'.
6. Bühring-Uhle ibid., p. 127.
7. https://www.financierworldwide.com/roundtable-international-arbitration-jun19#.XcbnClf7RPY.

'International Arbitration: Top Trends 2022' was the 'drive towards greater efficiency in international arbitration'.[8]

This is my first area to address. In section II of this chapter, I will examine whether we need to shift the emphasis from purely 'time and costs' to a broader notion of increasing efficiency in international arbitration and consider how better access to data could improve efficiency.

My second area of concern is the lack of equality in our field. In around 2010, the arbitration community woke up to the staggering lack of diversity at the upper end of the international arbitration profession and began to discuss this issue. From a slow start, the inequality in the arbitration community is now attracting considerable debate. Attention has, however, been almost exclusively focused on the under-representation of women in international arbitration. In section III of this chapter, I will assess the reasons behind the under-representation of women. I will argue that although great strides have been made in the ability to monitor progress in this area and the rate of representation of women is improving, we must continue to address this issue as well as broaden the debate about what diversity means. Much remains to be done, particularly in relation to educating the community on inclusive behaviour and improving the visibility of under-represented groups.

Finally, and belatedly, the arbitration community has stirred, but has not yet woken up, in relation to climate change and the impact our industry has on the environment. We may not be the energy or the automotive industry, but the international arbitration community has a significant carbon footprint and we must act to address it. This is my third and most significant concern for the future of international arbitration. In section IV of this chapter, I present empirical research into the environmental impact of a major international arbitration and compare it with a 'green' arbitration, where hypothetical changes have been made to the manner in which the case is presented, particularly through increased use of existing technologies.

Although these three areas, which I have dubbed Efficiency, Equality and the Environment, are distinct and can be distinguished by (i) the time at which they began to receive attention from the international arbitration community, (ii) the amount and quality of attention they have received and (iii) the degree to which real progress has been made in each area; they are united by the theme of waste, namely waste of time and costs, waste of talent and waste of resources. The most compelling arguments to deliver change in all three areas are for better use of technology, improved collection of and access to empirical data, and a collective assumption of personal responsibility. The COVID-19 pandemic forced change upon the arbitration community, as it forced change upon so many. One question this chapter also wrestles with is whether this forced change is sustainable in the long run.

---

8. https://www.freshfields.com/en-gb/our-thinking/campaigns/international-arbitration-in-2022/drives-towards-greater-efficiency-in-international-arbitration/.

2 Achieving Enlightenment

The Enlightenment thinkers in the eighteenth century sought a 'new understanding of the human condition'.[9] Steven Pinker, author of Enlightenment Now, summarizes this era as a 'cornucopia of ideas, some of them contradictory, but four themes tie them together: reason, science, humanism and progress'. He goes on to say that the 'methods of science – skepticism, fallibilism, open debate and empirical testing – are a paradigm of how to achieve reliable knowledge'.[10]

If we bring the notion of scepticism and fallibilism under one umbrella of 'self-awareness' and apply Pinker's methods to the current state of international arbitration, I would say that, in general, in the international arbitration community, we indulge in extensive open debate but with limited self-awareness, and we are disadvantaged by the absence of reliable empirical testing in our field. Only once we achieve a balance between awareness, debate and empirical data will the international arbitration community be more enlightened on the issues of efficiency, equality and the environment and start to achieve real change.

II EFFICIENCY

In this section II, I trace the roots of the concerns that arbitration takes too long and costs too much and look at the best practices which have been identified to tackle the issue. I conclude that this issue needs re-framing to one of efficiency and that access to certain data on arbitrator behaviour could be the key to securing change.

1 A Long-Standing Concern

It is somewhat ironic that enormous amounts of time and costs have been spent discussing time and costs in international arbitration. Back in 2007, the Fulbright & Jaworski litigation trends survey found 'the overall trend among the survey respondents seems to be that international arbitration is not seen as offering significant cost benefits over litigation'. International arbitration may well never have been quicker and cheaper than litigation, but people clearly thought it was, with reports that 'in-house counsel feel strongly that international arbitration takes too long and costs too much'.[11] Particularly in the latter part of the 2000s, there was a great deal of

---

9. Pinker, Enlightenment Now. However, it is ironic to note, particularly in relation to the comments on Equality in this chapter, that the eighteenth century is known as 'the Enlightenment' 'even though, while it may have expanded the "rights of man", it narrowed the rights of women, who were denied control of the property and earnings and barred from higher education and professional training' Invisible Women, Caroline Criado Perez.
10. Pinker, Enlightenment Now.
11. 'Super Conference: In-House Counsel Say International Arbitration Takes Too Long', 27 May 2010, http://www.insidecounsel.com/News/2010/5/Pages/SuperConference-Inhouse-Counsel -Say-International-Arbitration-Takes-Too-Long.aspx.

hand-wringing about delays and expenses in international arbitration.[12] There was general concern that international arbitration was losing its way and that, contrary to the tired refrain, it was no longer quicker and cheaper than the alternatives.[13]

At best, international arbitration had a problem of perception. At worst, international arbitration was not delivering what it promised.

In the same way that 'evil news fly faster', it seems that the arbitration community prefers to talk about problems rather than success stories. Yet, I would posit that the attention to time and cost in arbitration has led to changes in behaviour and, as far as discernable, progress.

In this area, as with so many other facets of international arbitration, we are hampered by the lack of empirical data. One of arbitration's strengths is that it operates outside the regulated environment of national courts, but this, in turn, engenders the problem we encounter in addressing flaws with the arbitral process: the fact that reliable global data on international arbitration proceedings are rarely available.

There are three main strands to international arbitration: (i) investment treaty arbitrations conducted under the auspices of the International Centre for Settlement of Investment Disputes (ICSID); (ii) commercial (and investor-State[14]) arbitrations conducted under the auspices of the myriad of international and regional arbitrations across the globe; and (iii) arbitrations conducted on an ad hoc basis, without reference to an institution.

For 2018, the total caseload at ICSID was fifty-seven and the combined caseload of 9 of the major international arbitration institutions was 6,132.[15] It is impossible to estimate the number of ad hoc arbitrations being conducted at any one time, but it is likely to be well into the thousands annually.[16]

---

12. 'In recent years, there appears to be increasing dissatisfaction with the increased time and cost of international arbitration, leading some commentators to refer to a "sense of crisis" in international arbitration. There is an emerging trend which clearly shows that parties no longer believe that arbitration (particularly in terms of large complex disputes) is cheaper or quicker than litigation. The perceived increase in time and costs is usually attributed to a number of factors which include (i) the "over-lawyering" of arbitrations; (ii) excessive disclosure; (iii) the length of hearings; (iv) the number of arbitrators; and (v) the increasing tendency to replicate court processes before the arbitral tribunal.' L. Greenwood, 'A Window of Opportunity? Building a Short Period of Time into Arbitral Rules in Order for Parties to Explore Settlement' 27(2) Arb. Int'l 199 (2011) Internal citations omitted.
13. There is considerable debate as to whether this refrain had ever been merited.
14. Such as investor-State arbitrations administered under other rules such as the ICC or the Stockholm Chamber of Commerce (SCC). There are also investor-State arbitrations administered by the Permanent Court of Arbitration (PCA) under the UNCITRAL Rules.
15. Taking the annual caseloads as reported by the International Chamber of Commerce (ICC), London Court of International Arbitration (LCIA), Singapore International Arbitration Centre (SIAC), Permanent Court of Arbitration (PCA), Hong Kong International Arbitration Centre (HKIAC), China International Economic and Trade Arbitration Commission (CIETAC), Dubai International Arbitration Centre (DIAC) and International Centre for Dispute Resolution (ICDR) in 2018.
16. Estimations of the volume of cases which practitioners report as being ad hoc arbitrations vary from 0% to 50% of their case load, depending on jurisdiction. *See* the survey of arbitration practitioners reported at https://www2.le.ac.uk/departments/law/research/arbitration/files/arbitration-in-the-americas-report-on-a-survey-of-arbitration-practitioners.

In relation to the main strands of cases, only ICSID arbitration proceedings are reasonably transparent and published (subject to certain restrictions) and, of course, ICSID cases are a minute fraction of the overall number of international arbitrations. There are also State-to-State arbitrations, which take place before permanent courts and tribunals, like the International Court of Justice, which are also transparent, but less relevant to the conduct of arbitration due to their specialized nature. In relation to other cases, researchers are forced to rely on commercial institutions publishing data about their arbitrations and/or seek opinions from practitioners based on their individual caseloads, and/or rely on surveys of practitioners.[17]

2   We Have Techniques to Control Time and Costs, but No Real Way of Monitoring Their Efficacy

There is, therefore, a very shaky foundation of data upon which to base allegations that arbitration is slow and expensive, and, moreover, that duration affects cost. There has, however, been a detailed analysis of investment treaty arbitration costs and the variables to which they are subject.[18] Among other conclusions, the analysis identified a 'strong, significant and positive link between time and claimant's PLC [Parties' Legal Costs], respondent's PLC and total TCE [Tribunal Costs and Administrative Expenses]'.[19] However, using ICSID data, while helpful as a starting point, may lead to a situation where the tail wags the dog, simply in terms of the tiny number of ICSID cases compared with commercial arbitrations. That is not to mention the specialized nature of ICSID proceedings and the effect of that on time and cost of investment treaty arbitrations. Although some arbitral institutions publish analyses of the duration and cost of their commercial arbitrations, the data underpinning the analyses is often not available and one cannot be sure one is comparing like with like.[20]

Against all these constraints we can add the difficulty that addressing time and costs in arbitration requires all the actors in the arbitration process to work together. First, the institutions, second, the tribunal and third, the parties and counsel. Yet the interests of these three elements are not always aligned. Yes, it is likely always to be in the institution's interests to respond promptly, efficiently and to provide value for money. The tribunal, generally, should have the same approach but to a greater extent will be subject to the vagaries of the case before it and, in particular, to the way in which parties decide to present their cases. Parties and counsel are different matters. It is a truism to say one person's delay is another person's tactical manoeuvre, but in considering how or if more 'progress' is needed, we must keep this in mind. Parties and counsel will be dealing with tactical considerations to which the arbitrators and the institutions are not privy. Parties may be capricious in the way that they approach

---

17. And, of course, these surveys have inherent flaws from question bias to self-selection of respondents, and so on.
18. *See* Franck on Arbitration Costs.
19. *See*, in particular, Franck on Arbitration Costs, Chapter 8.
20. *See*, Franck on Arbitration Costs, Chapter 4 for a detailed analysis of durations of investment treaty arbitrations.

issues: at the disclosure stage insisting that no stone be left unturned, regardless of the cost, then at the award stage expressing horror at the amount of cost incurred. It is impossible to reduce these divergent interests to an over-simplified statement that arbitration 'takes too long and costs too much'. How long is 'too long'? How much is 'too much'?

Shifting the focus from time and costs and instead setting expectations that all actors will be efficient in every part that they play in an arbitration might result in a closer alignment between the competing interests. After all, even a respondent whose strategy is to delay an arbitration does not want to pay over the odds for its counsel, or, necessarily, wait months or years for the arbitration award.

These fundamental issues notwithstanding, over the years efforts have been made to address the 'time and costs' criticism of arbitration, primarily in two ways. First, by identifying and publicizing techniques for limiting the duration and cost of proceedings,[21] and second, by arbitral institutions tightening up their rules on deadlines as to when awards had to be issued and/or enforced existing deadlines more diligently.[22] There has been limited research into the effects of the identified techniques on the time and cost of an arbitration.[23]

Looking first at the techniques promoted by the arbitration community for reducing time and costs. The ICC Commission Report on Controlling Time and Costs in Arbitration was first published in 2007 and a second edition was published in 2018.[24] Neither report contains empirical data on the time and cost of arbitration. The reports focus on providing techniques which should, if applied, reduce the time and cost. The 2018 report provides useful suggestions but nothing earth-shattering. It includes reference to the importance of selecting counsel with experience and time to devote to the case, which recalls the old saying 'if you think good lawyers are expensive, you should try bad ones'. The report highlights choosing arbitrators with case management skills, although provides no insight into how this skill might be assessed. It exhorts counsel to 'avoid unnecessary repetition' of arguments and recommends that parties consider agreeing to limit the length of submissions. There are many other sensible recommendations in the report which, if followed, should result in a more streamlined process. I would call this the 'carrot' approach.

---

21. Such as the ICC Report on Techniques for Controlling Time and Costs in Arbitration which was first published in 2007 and other reports such as the Centre for Effective Dispute Resolution's (CEDR) report and rules on Settlement in International Arbitration published in November 2009.
22. The Arbitration Rules of the International Chamber of Commerce (ICC) include a deadline of six months from the last signature to the terms of reference and the Arbitration Rules of the Stockholm Chamber of Commerce also set a six month deadline from the date on which the arbitration was referred to the tribunal. Other institutions, like the LCIA, simply provide that an award should be made as soon as reasonably possible from the date of the last submission. In 2022 a number of arbitral institutions have introduced or are planning to introduce provisions to improve efficiency, *see* https://www.freshfields.com/en-gb/our-thinking/campaigns/inter national-arbitration-in-2022/drives-towards-greater-efficiency-in-international-arbitration/.
23. Because it is impossible to have a 'control' arbitration, where techniques for controlling time and costs are not deployed.
24. https://cdn.iccwbo.org/content/uploads/sites/3/2018/03/icc-arbitration-commission-report -on-techniques-for-controlling-time-and-costs-in-arbitration-english-version.pdf.

For many years there was no 'stick' to accompany the carrot and even now the sanctions for bad behaviour in terms of delaying an arbitration or incurring unnecessary costs are fairly limited. In January 2016 the ICC announced that it would reduce the fees of arbitrators who were late rendering their awards.[25] In relation to party conduct, the 2013 IBA Guidelines on Party Representation in International Arbitration provides for arbitrators to exercise their discretion in relation to misconduct by party representatives, the guidelines provide for sanctions such as admonishment, drawing adverse inferences, and awarding costs. There is certainly support for the 'stick' approach, with 80% of respondents to the 2018 Queen Mary Survey believing that arbitration rules should include 'consequences for delay by arbitrators' and 'deadlines for issuing awards',[26] but there is very little information on when or if these sticks have been wielded.[27]

3   Access to Information and Empirical Data

I would argue that we have gone as far as we can go in relation to time and costs in arbitration. We need to move away from worries about 'time and costs' to a broader notion of ensuring efficiency in arbitration.

The 'carrot' approach outlined above only works if the parties are aligned and, almost by definition in an adversarial process such as arbitration, they are generally not aligned. The 'stick' approach may have more impact because it homes in on measurable stages of the arbitration which are independent of the parties, but, again, it is something of a blunt instrument. Presently, the only applicable 'stick' is the ICC's decision to dock the pay of arbitrators who delay, but there is no deterrent effect from this as there is no transparency as to how often the 'stick' is wielded.

Improving efficiency in arbitration requires technology, transparency and access to data. It largely goes hand in hand with a more refined 'stick' approach. In this, we may be assisted in the changes to our practices forced upon us by the COVID-19 pandemic, in particular the need to be more flexible in the way we approach hearings and travel to interview witnesses.

There have been significant advances in recent years in relation to the collection and interrogation of data relating to arbitration proceedings. The organization 'Arbitrator Intelligence' has begun collecting quantitative and qualitative feedback from users and counsel about key features of arbitrator decision-making.[28] Information is collected through the Arbitrator Intelligence Questionnaire ('AIQ'). Topics include timing and duration of arbitration, case management and procedural orders, document disclosure, rulings on jurisdiction and interim relief, damages analysis, and legal

---

25. *See* the ICC Note to Parties and Arbitral Tribunal on the Conduct of the Arbitration which includes time frame for submission of draft awards (three months after the last substantive hearing and the consequences of delay (reduction in arbitrator fees).
26. https://www.whitecase.com/publications/insight/2018-international-arbitration-survey-evol ution-international-arbitration.
27. Although beyond the scope of this article, Franck on Arbitration Costs, Chapter 7 provides detailed analysis of the factors motivating tribunal decisions on awarding costs to parties.
28. *See* www.arbitratorintelligence.org.

methodologies. Data analytics from this information may provide parties and counsel insights about arbitrators' track records to improve arbitrator selection and case strategy. Respondents to the 2018 Queen Mary Survey thought that data showing arbitrator profiles should be made available to users by arbitral institutions and should include performance indicators such as the average time a certain arbitrator has spent on an arbitration. 'The counterargument advanced by others was that the relevance of such data is rather limited since every arbitration has its own particularities. That being said, there was a consensus among interviewed respondents that arbitration rules should indeed contemplate a more efficient mechanism for sanctioning delays by arbitrators.'[29] Even accepting that the ICC's 'stick' approach is a blunt instrument, there is an argument that users should know the identities of arbitrators who have had their fees reduced by the ICC and the circumstances in which the reduction arose. Arbitrator Intelligence's data could also assist in informing parties at the appointment stage as to an arbitrator's efficiency in rendering awards.

Another data-driven initiative is Dispute Resolution Data which provides aggregate data about arbitration case types, locations, and outcomes. Unlike Arbitrator Intelligence, Dispute Resolution Data does not provide case-specific information or identify information about arbitrators, parties, or even arbitration organizations. Dispute Resolution Data partners with dispute resolution organizations (mainly arbitration institutions) to obtain non-confidential data about arbitrations. Dispute Resolution Data offers data on average case duration, the average amount of awards, the success rate and value of counterclaims, the prevalence of interrogatories and rates of settlement and claims to have over 5000 cases on its database.[30] Making data available on the one aspect of an arbitration that an arbitrator can impact, namely the time in which an award is rendered, will go some way towards making arbitrators more accountable. Improving use of technology across the board in arbitration will also streamline the process and has distinct synergies with the drive to reduce the carbon footprint of an arbitration discussed in section IV of this chapter.

III   EQUALITY

A process must be inherently inefficient if it cuts out 50% of the world's population. For many years international arbitration did just that when appointing arbitrators and, arguably, the manner in which appointments were made resulted in delays due to the lack of availability of the consequentially small pool of arbitrators. In this Section III I discuss the current status of various under-represented groups in international arbitration, the need for wider publication of data, the various initiatives that exist to address the issue and finally argue that wider awareness and the assumption of personal responsibility will result in change in this area.

---

29. 2018 Queen Mary Survey. https://www.whitecase.com/publications/insight/2018-international-arbitration-survey-evolution-international-arbitration.
30. As of February 2020. www.disputeresolutiondata.com.

1   Not a Level Playing Field

The chart below shows the percentage of women appointed to arbitration tribunals from 1990 to 2018. Up until 2014 less than 10% of appointments were of female arbitrators, notwithstanding the fact that for over thirty years there has been parity in terms of law graduates and junior associates.[31] Even today international arbitration tribunals are mainly composed of Anglo-European men, counsel in international arbitrations are almost invariably men (particularly when it comes to first chairs arguing cases),[32] and in terms of ethnic, geographic, age, socioeconomic factors, and disabilities, the situation in the international arbitration community is even worse.[33]

The chart below is taken from the data collected in relation to the appointment of female arbitrators going back to 1990:[34]

---

31. Greenwood and Baker 'Getting a Better Balance on International Arbitration Tribunals' Arbitration International (2012).
32. The comments by Judge Scheindlin in Female Lawyers Can Talk, Too, Shira A. Scheindlin https://www.nytimes.com/2017/08/08/opinion/female-lawyers-women-judge, are equally true of international arbitrations.
33. 'The first thing anyone notices when they drop out of the legal profession and into the "neutral" business is the time warp. It's not exactly an old folks' home or an assisted living facility, but it is populated primarily with the people who were already practicing law when I entered the profession in 1980. These people were in their 30's then. Now they're mostly over 60. They're white. And they are male.' Victoria Pynchon, Diversity is Not a Toxic Topic, 30 Alternatives, No. 4, April 2012, at 83, cited in 'Old, White, and Male': Increasing Gender Diversity in Arbitration Panels, https://www.cpradr.org/news-publications/articles/2015-03-03--old-white-and-male-increasing-gender-diversity-in-arbitration-panels.
34. In 1990 the ICC named 517 arbitrators, of whom 4 (0.78%) were women and in 1995, the ICC named 766 arbitrators, of whom 22 (3%) were women. Louise Barrington, 'The Commercial Way to Justice' (Kluwer 1997). Other historic data is found in Greenwood and Baker 'Getting a Better Balance on International Arbitration Tribunals' Arbitration International (2012). Data since 2012 has been collated by the author as part of ongoing research and (since 2015, membership of the Equal Representation in Arbitration Pledge Steering Committee). The author has taken an average of all collected data on the appointment of female arbitrators for each year it has been available, recognizing that prior to 2012 the data cannot be considered entirely reliable.

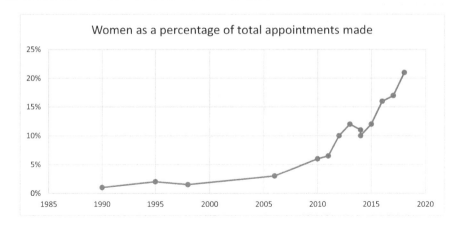

Women as a percentage of total appointments made

Prior to the launch of the Equal Representation in Arbitration Pledge[35] which is discussed further below, an accurate assessment of the percentage of female arbitrators being appointed to tribunals was in the region of 10%. There was little to no discussion of arbitrator demographics beyond gender. However, in 2014, Professor Susan Franck conducted detailed research into the backgrounds of 262 international arbitrators attending ICCA Congress and concluded that 'the 'median' international arbitrator was a fifty-three-year-old man who was a national of a developed state and had served as arbitrator in ten arbitration cases'.[36] In relation to the geographic origins of self-identifying arbitrators attending ICCA in 2014, Professor Franck determined the following:

> Although highest in world population (60.27%), Asian arbitrators were the second least represented (10%) of ICCA arbitrators. Notably, although China and India together contain approximately 33% of the world's population and roughly 30.4% of global GDP, less than 3% of participating arbitrators were from those states. Meanwhile, despite Africa's second highest population (15.41%), only two African countries were in the twenty countries with the highest global GDP (Egypt and Nigeria – 2.5%) and Africa exhibited the lowest level of representation (0.4%). Other nationalities were arguably over-represented. Europe has 10.37% of the world's population and roughly 12.8% of global GDP, but 48.2% of the arbitrators were European nationals. Similarly, the United States and Canada have 4.93% of the world's population and 14.5% of global GDP, but 27.9% of the ICCA arbitrators were from North America, and of the seventy arbitrators from North America, only one was from Mexico.[37]

There has been progress on diversity, but it has been almost entirely directed at the under-representation of women, rather than the lack of diversity in relation to nationality, ethnicity, sexual orientation and age. This sentiment was echoed in the

---

35. www.arbitrationpledge.com.
36. The Diversity Challenge: Exploring the 'Invisible College' of International Arbitration, Susan Franck et al, Washington & Lee University School of Law.
37. The Diversity Challenge: Exploring the 'Invisible College' of International Arbitration, Susan Franck et al, Washington & Lee University School of Law.

2018 Queen Mary Survey which found '[W]hilst nearly half of respondents agreed that progress has been made in terms of gender diversity on arbitral tribunals over the past five years, less than a third of respondents believe this in respect of geographic, age, cultural and ethnic diversity'.[38]

2   Redressing the Balance

The progress made in relation to the under-representation of women on international arbitration tribunals can be almost entirely ascribed to a concrete action that was launched in 2016: the Equal Representation in Arbitration Pledge. This was the first global initiative to address the under-representation of women in international arbitration.[39] Not only did it chime with growing dissatisfaction with the significant under-representation of women in the field, but it was also backed by sufficient resources to garner support on a global scale. Signatories to the Pledge commit to increasing, on an equal opportunity basis, the number of women appointed as arbitrators, with a view towards reaching the goal of full parity. Specifically, signatories promise to take steps to ensure that, whenever possible, several goals are met. These goals include, for example, that committees, governing bodies and conference panels in the field of arbitration include a fair representation of women; that lists of potential arbitrators or tribunal chairs include a fair representation of female candidates; and that entities in charge of arbitral institutions include a fair representation of female candidates on rosters and lists of potential arbitrator appointees and appoint a fair representation of women to tribunals. The most important commitment in the Pledge is the commitment made by the arbitration institutions signed up to the Pledge that they will publish data in relation to the appointment of women.

There have been efforts to redress the balance in relation to other under-represented groups. In relation to the lack of geographic diversity in the field, the African Promise was launched in 2019 and is modelled on the Equal Representation in Arbitration Pledge. The introductory paragraph of the African Promise sets out two general objectives (i) to improve the profile and representation of African arbitrators; and (ii) to appoint Africans as arbitrators, especially in arbitrations connected with Africa. In relation to broader diversity initiatives, the Alliance for Equality in Dispute Resolution[40] has the aim of promoting 'inclusivity in all aspects of the dispute resolution world' and striving 'for equality of opportunity regardless of sex, location, nationality, ethnicity or age'. It focuses on 'addressing the lack of diversity in relation to ethnicity and geography in international arbitration' through training, mentoring and access to online discussion fora. Arbitral institutions, particularly those in the United States, have been also trying to address the broader diversity issue. The

---

38. https://www.whitecase.com/publications/insight/2018-international-arbitration-survey-evol ution-international-arbitration.
39. The ERA Pledge originated from a suggestion made by the director general of the LCIA Jacomijn van Haersolte-van Hof in 2014. Since April 2015, the initiative has been sponsored by a number of founders, in particular by Sylvia Noury, a partner at Freshfields Bruckhaus Deringer LLP.
40. www.allianceequality.com.

alternative dispute resolution provider, JAMS (formerly known as Judicial Arbitration and Mediation Services), has a diversity inclusion rider that may be incorporated into a dispute resolution clause. Through it, the parties agree to appoint a 'fair representation' of diverse arbitrators—considering ethnicity, gender and sexual orientation—and to request providers to include a significant number of diverse neutrals on their rosters. The JAMS language is among the steps recommended in American Bar Association Resolution (ABA) 105 which held that the ABA would urge 'providers of domestic and international dispute resolution to expand their rosters with minorities, women, persons with disabilities, and persons of differing sexual orientations and gender identities and to encourage the selection of diverse neutrals' and that the ABA would urge 'all users of domestic and international legal and neutral services to select and use diverse neutrals'.[41] REAL – the organization promoting Racial Equality for Arbitration Lawyers – is also beginning to have a significant impact in terms of raising awareness of many unrepresented groups in international arbitration.[42]

All these initiatives are valuable in raising awareness. However, as far as they are able, arbitral institutions must monitor the nationality, ethnicity, sexual orientation, age and sex of their arbitrators. Until they do so the problem cannot be realistically addressed. It is encouraging that extensive further empirical research is to be conducted at the ICCA Congress in Edinburgh. This will facilitate a greater understanding of the demographics of ICCA attendees and build on the conclusions from the first study into ICCA delegates in 2014.

3   Removing Barriers to Appointment: Actions and Different Words

What are the barriers to appointing diverse candidates as international arbitrators? In relation to the appointment of women, I concluded in 2012 that the answer was far from straightforward and noted that factors impacting women included the effect of pipeline leaks, implicit bias and lack of visibility. To that list, I would add the way that society sees men (and, arguably, white men) as the human default. This is pervasive across society as a whole, but I would posit that the assumption that an arbitrator is 'male-unless-otherwise-indicated'[43] is one that is endemic in our industry, and it is an assumption that is made by both men and women arbitration practitioners. In conversations or presentations, we refer to an arbitrator as 'he' or the chair as the 'chairman'. In writing, using 'he' as the generic masculine[44] will not be read that way,

---

41. https://www.americanbar.org/content/dam/aba/images/abanews/2018-AM-Resolutions/105.pdf.
42. https://letsgetrealarbitration.org/.
43. Invisible Women, Caroline Criado Perez, Chapter 1.
44. Using 'he' in a gender-neutral way or asserting that both genders are included in the use of 'he'. In their book 'Understanding International Arbitration' Tony Cole and Petro Ortolani consciously chose to make every arbitrator in the book female. The authors acknowledged that arbitration has a 'diversity problem' and stated 'one of the simplest steps that we can achieve is that when we imagine an arbitral tribunal, we don't imagine three white men sitting behind a table. Getting use to the idea of referring to arbitrators as "she" rather than "he" is a trivial act that can help substantially in achieving this goal'.

'it is read overwhelmingly as male'.[45] According to Caroline Criado Perez, author of 'Invisible Women':

> when the generic masculine is used people are more likely to recall famous men than famous women; to estimate a profession as male-dominated, to suggest male candidates for jobs and political appointments. Women are also less likely to apply, and less likely to perform well in interviews, for jobs that are advertised using the generic masculine. In fact, the generic masculine is read as so over-whelmingly as male that it even overrides otherwise powerful stereotypes, so that professions such as 'beautician', which are usually stereotyped female, are suddenly seen as male.[46]

As we have a deeply male-dominated culture (particularly in such a male-dominated profession as the law) the male experience is seen as universal and the female experience is seen as niche. Rather like we have the English football team and the English women's football team; we appear to have arbitrators and female arbitrators. Although the engaged discussion that has taken place in the last decade on the lack of women in our field is to be welcomed, we must avoid underscoring the notion that a female arbitrator is somehow a different creature from the (default) male arbitrator. This is exacerbated by the suggestion that there is a risk inherent in choosing someone other than the default arbitrator.[47] There is a plethora of highly experienced arbitrators who are female. We must make a conscious choice to use different words in describing arbitrators (and counsel) and to challenge the notion that white and male go without saying, while at the same time avoiding further carving out the female arbitrator 'niche' in order to move the conversation beyond gender.[48]

The fact that the male perspective is the default and the norm across society, particularly in the legal profession, where men are equated with gravitas, judicial demeanour and endowed with the ability to 'command the respect of other arbitrators on the tribunal', renders female arbitrators almost invisible.[49] The effect of pipeline leak and implicit bias on the rates at which women are appointed to tribunals has received a reasonable amount of attention but the lack of visibility less so. It is unarguable that female arbitrators are less visible than the default (male) arbitrator.

---

45. Invisible Women, Caroline Criado Perez, p. 5.
46. Invisible Women, Caroline Criado Perez, p. 5. Internal citations omitted.
47. A few years ago, the refrain was 'no one ever got fired for choosing IBM', this seemed to suggest that if you chose the default (male) (and, by implication, experienced) arbitrator you would not be criticized, this was repeated in 2020 in a recent (2020) article Diversity of arbitrator appointments: are the parties doing enough? By Zoe O'Sullivan. https://www.cdr-news.com/ categories/arbitration-and-adr/10801-diversity-of-arbitrator-appointments-are-the-parties-doing-enough. We must stop insinuating that non-typical arbitrators are not 'IBM'. There is a plethora of highly experienced diverse arbitrators active in our field. It is simply wrong to continue the myth that by selecting a diverse arbitrator parties are somehow opting for a lesser product.
48. Per Perez 'Whiteness and Maleness Are Silent Precisely Because They Do Not Need to Be Vocalized. Whiteness and Maleness Are I. They Are Unquestioned. They Are the Default'. Invisible Women p. 23.
49. A sentiment that is frequently repeated in relation to men, but almost never heard in relation to women.

Across the board, the data supports the conclusion that institutions appoint more diverse candidates.[50] The main reason they are able to do so, I would suggest, is that they have access to more information on arbitrators generally. How then can non-typical arbitrators ensure that they are known by those who might seek to appoint them? One answer is to build a reputation and awareness of an arbitrator's practice by speaking at conferences. Yet here female arbitrators are also penalized. Looking only at the representation of women at arbitration conferences held in 2019 and leaving aside other diverse practitioners shows that women are also under-represented at speaking engagements. I analysed 231 international arbitration conferences which took place in 2019 and identified the sex of those who spoke at the events. I used a broad definition of speaker and included in my analysis keynote speakers, panellists, moderators, chairs of the conferences and those who gave opening and closing remarks. Along with a team of volunteers,[51] I collated data by reviewing published brochures of international arbitration events. Although the events were not selected using a formal methodology, I included conferences from a broad range of event organizers, which took place in seventy-one different locations. In general, the level of female participation was disappointing. Less than 40% of the conference speakers, panellists and moderators were women. Only around one-third of the keynote speakers were women. My analysis only looked at female speakers, from personal observations it appears that minority groups are even more under-represented.

On a more positive note, the data shows what can be achieved when a conference has a particular focus. I analysed female participation in each of the roles for a subset of around 50 of the 231 conferences. These conferences were targeted at either younger members of the profession or the conference had a particular focus on diversity. I included in this subset all the 'young practitioner' events, regardless of subject matter, and also included all events that focused on diversity as a subject matter. These conferences achieved much higher rates of female participation achieving a rate in excess of 50% of speakers and there was a significant increase in female keynote speakers, from 35% to over 60%.

The above figures were all compiled prior to the COVID-19 pandemic, which had a profound impact on the way conferences are conducted. Online conferences and streamed conferences opened the door not just to a wider group of delegates but also to a wider group of speakers. Interestingly, the slate of speakers at ICCA 2022 has 56% female speakers and this may well herald a new trend following the pandemic. Further research is needed to track progress in this area.

When it comes to diversity, we need to make sure we follow through. Talking is not enough. If we as a community really care about addressing the lack of diversity in our field we need to each do something that makes a difference, whether that be attending implicit bias training, promoting diverse candidates, requiring conference

---

50. This can most obviously be supported by reference to the data I published on women arbitrators in 2018 which clearly showed that women were far more likely to be appointed by an institution than by parties or co-arbitrators. https://globalarbitrationreview.com/article/1209548/the-pledge-three-years-on-progress-being-made.
51. And particular thanks goes to Olga Sedetska, Freshfields Bruckhaus Deringer LLP, who did the lion's share of the work collating the data.

organizers to ensure that every arbitration conference has gender parity among speakers and a significant number of people of colour, and refusing to participate in events which do not have a balanced roster of speakers.

IV   THE ENVIRONMENT

The notion of doing something that makes a difference is most apposite in relation to the last of the three areas of concern I have identified: the issue of the environment. This issue is both the most important and the least discussed, of my three concerns. In an industry which thrives on open debate, it is startling to observe that the environmental impact of international arbitrations has received little to no attention at all. Section IV focuses on arbitration practitioners addressing climate change at the micro level, namely the actions we must take as individuals to reduce the carbon footprint of every arbitration we are involved in. Quite simply, there is a striking inverse correlation between this issue's importance and the attention it has received.

1   We Must Act to Limit the Impact of Our Industry on the Environment

As lawyers, and particularly as dispute resolution lawyers, we are reactive and not proactive. That approach is not the one we must take when it comes to climate change. We must proactively address climate change, both at the macro (legal) level and at the micro (human) level. As international lawyers, we can contribute our expertise to developing legal principles suitable for climate change issues, accelerating policy change and establishing appropriate fora in which to resolve climate change disputes. As human beings, we can ensure that we manage our practices to limit the impact of every arbitration on the environment. We cannot in all conscience do one without the other.

The international arbitration community has contributed a significant amount at the macro level, for example, among others, the International Bar Association's 'Report on Climate Change Justice and Human Rights',[52] the ICC publication 'Dispute Resolution and Climate Change: The Paris Agreement and Beyond'.[53] Commendable as they are, I do not discuss those efforts here. They have received significant attention, in stark comparison to the lack of discussion about efforts that must be made at a micro level. This issue was first publicly discussed at an ICC Arbitration Conference in London only in late 2019 when an initiative to reduce the environmental footprint of international arbitrations was launched.[54]

---

52. https://www.ibanet.org/Document/Default.aspx?DocumentUid = 0F8CEE12-EE56-4452-BF43-CFCAB196CC04 .
53. https://2go.iccwbo.org/dispute-resolution-and-climate-change.html.
54. *See* 'Is it easy, being green?' Global Arbitration Review 15 November 2019. https://globalarbitrationreview.com/article/1210965/is-it-easy-being-green 'the purpose of the movement is to promote gradual steps towards a more sustainable future in a profession "which is far behind the curve" when it comes to addressing these issues. The frustration, [Greenwood]

2   **Humanity Has Never Faced a Problem Like It**

Planet Earth is generally considered to be around 13.7 billion years old. Homos Erectus appeared around a million years ago followed by Homo Sapiens around 200,000 years ago. If the time since the universe began is compressed into one twenty-four-hour period, humans appear in the last four seconds of that day. Yet in those four seconds, we have made something of an impact.

The atmospheric concentrations of carbon dioxide (CO_2), methane, and nitrous oxide have increased significantly since the Industrial Revolution began.[55] In the case of CO_2, the average concentration measured at the National Oceanic and Atmospheric Administration's Mauna Loa Observatory in Hawaii has risen from 316 parts per million (ppm)[56] in 1959 (the first full year of data available) to 396 ppm in 2013.[57] By the end of 2018, the observatory at Mauna Loa recorded the fourth-highest annual growth in the concentration of atmospheric carbon dioxide in sixty years of record-keeping.[58] In recent times, the atmospheric concentration of the three main 'greenhouse gases' has increased dramatically. CO_2 has increased by 40%, methane has increased by around 150%, and nitrous oxide has increased by roughly 20%.[59] Increases in all three gases contribute to global warming, with the increase in CO_2 playing the largest role. The warming is due to the 'greenhouse effect', where the atmosphere traps heat radiating out from the earth. A 'greenhouse gas' absorbs and emits infrared radiation and contributes to trapping the heat within the atmosphere. At current greenhouse gas emission rates, the earth's temperature could increase by 2°C by 2036. The United Nations' Intergovernmental Panel on Climate Change designated this 2% increase as 'dangerous'.[60] Global average temperatures have been increasing steadily in the last 150 years: 2016 was the hottest year since records began, reaching 0.99°C above the mid-twentieth century mean. The world's nine warmest years since records began have all occurred since 2005, and the five warmest since 2010.[61] A rise of 2°C is considered the most that the world could reasonably adapt to and a rise of 4°C, according to the World Bank in 2012, 'simply must not be allowed to occur'.[62] To

---

noted, was that "all of the tools to solve this problem are directly in front of us, we just need to know how to use them"'. The 'Green Pledge' sets out certain commitments from international arbitration practitioners including increasing the use of technology to reduce the need to print documents and take long haul flights. *See* www.greenwoodarbitration.com/greenpledge for more information.

55. https://www.epa.gov/climate-indicators/climate-change-indicators-atmospheric-concentratio ns-greenhouse-gases.
56. For every million molecules in the air, 316 of them were CO_2.
57. https://royalsociety.org/topics-policy/projects/climate-change-evidence-causes/basics-of-clim ate-change/.
58. https://www.noaa.gov/news/global-carbon-dioxide-growth-in-2018-reached-4th-highest-on-record.
59. https://www.epa.gov/climate-indicators/climate-change-indicators-atmospheric-concentratio ns-greenhouse-gases.
60. Mann, Michael E. (1 April 2014). 'Earth Will Cross the Climate Danger Threshold by 2036'. Scientific American.
61. https://thefuturescentre.org/trend-card/environmental-impacts-climate-change.
62. https://public.wmo.int/en/media/news/climate-change-moving-faster-we-are-un-secretary-ge neral.

keep the rise to less than or equal to 2°C, the world would, at a minimum, have to reduce its greenhouse gas emissions by half or more within the next thirty years and eliminate them completely by the end of this century. In the words of UN Secretary-General Antonio Guterres, 'climate change is moving faster than we are'.[63]

3   The Environmental Impact of a Major International Arbitration

Historically, international arbitration has suffered from a dearth of data for the reasons set out in this chapter. There is, as noted, energetic and open debate over perceived problems with arbitration, but rarely, if ever, is the debate founded on empirical research. If discussions of environmental concerns follow the same trajectory as discussions relating to the perceived inefficiencies of arbitration and, to a lesser extent, the lack of diversity in arbitration, then we will not achieve behavioural change.

Rather than simply debating the problem, the first issue in addressing the question of climate change at a micro level in international arbitration is to conduct an environmental assessment. This is usually the assessment of the environmental consequences of a plan, policy, program, or project prior to the decision to move forward with the proposed action. In this context, the term 'environmental impact assessment' is used when applied to projects by individuals or companies. The purpose of the assessment is to ensure that decision-makers consider the environmental impact when deciding whether to proceed with a project. The International Association for Impact Assessment defines an environmental impact assessment as 'the process of identifying, predicting, evaluating and mitigating the biophysical, social, and other relevant effects of development proposals prior to major decisions being taken and commitments made'.[64] There is a compelling case that prior to proceeding with every international arbitration, an environmental impact assessment should be undertaken. Unlike other aspects of international arbitration research, in conducting this assessment we are not restricted to data being made available by institutions, or to reliance upon assertion or assumption. We can use actual, observed data as a foundation for the impact assessment.

In 2019, members of the Campaign for Greener Arbitration's Steering Committee, supported by Dechert LLP, conducted a case study of a major international arbitration in order to determine its impact in terms of carbon footprint. Naturally, a number of assumptions had to be made, but these assumptions were deliberately conservative. For example, in calculating the number of printed sheets generated in the case study, the Dechert team only included an estimate of the printed pages submitted to the tribunal and disregarded all internal printing and the generation of drafts. The team based the case study on a recent USD 30-USD 50 million international arbitration they had been involved in. The exercise also considered the financial impact of various steps in the arbitration.

---

63. https://www.bbc.co.uk/news/science-environment-45471410.
64. https://www.iaia.org/.

Prior to releasing their research, the Steering Committee asked arbitration practitioners to estimate the carbon footprint of a major international arbitration. The responses underestimated the number of trees required to offset a major international arbitration by, on average, a factor of 200.[65] This further underscores the need for empirical data to accompany debate.

The results of the assessment are set out below:

---

65. Most respondents guessed that around 50-150 trees were required to offset the carbon emissions of a major international arbitration.

Typical Arbitrations

	Preliminary Analysis/ Preparing to Issue Notices	Preliminary Requests	Pleading 1	Pleading 2	Pleading 3	Pleading 4	Hearing Preparation	The Hearing	Total	Carbon Impact (kgCO2e)[8]	Costs (£)	N°. of Trees Required to Absorb Carbon Emissions[9]
Long-distance return flights [1]	0	4	9	9	9	9	10	22	72	344092.32	143856.00	15640.560
Short distance return flights [2]	9	4	6	6	6	6	14	6	57	53260.80	21945.00	2420.945
Car journeys[3]	13	10	10	10	10	10	10	5	75	1596.45	18750.00	72.566
Train journeys[4]	10	10	10	10	10	10	10	10	80	658.40	2000.00	29.927
Motorbike couriers[5]	5	5	10	10	10	10	10	10	70	66.15	1190.00	3.007
Pages printed[6]	200	200	700	700	700	700	3200	13000	19400	8316.90	194000.00	378.041
Hotel stays[7]	16	14	34	34	34	34	44	250	460	9384.00	69000.00	426.545
Coffee cups	200	200	600	600	600	600	300	300	3400	1156.00	7480.00	52.545
										4,18,531.02	£ 4,58,221.00	19026

Total emissions as a multiple of an individual's annual carbon footprint[10]: 78

Notes:

See the 'Carbon Emissions Calculator – Rationale' document for the underlying assumptions for tallying the occurrences of the various factors. The table represents the marginal cost of each extra arbitration so for that reason, figures such as office energy costs and any fixed costs are not included as these cannot be isolated per arbitration.

1. Business class return flight (11,000 km return). Price based on the mean of the flight prices between London and Dubai (10,956 km) in mid-February (GBP 1,998).

2. Business class return flight (4,000 km return). Price based on the mean of the flight prices between London and Milan (1,918 km) in mid-February (GBP 323).

3. 100 km return journey. Price based on an average of GBP 2.50 per kilometre for chauffering.

4. Standard class return (200 km return). Price based on a return fare from London to Cambridge (102 km) (GBP 25).

5. Short distance (measured from Dechert LLP to One Canada Square, Canary Wharf (7 km)). Price based on an Addison Lee motorbike courier (GBP 17).

6. Figures are in multiples per 100 pages (450 g of paper), i.e., 20 refers to 2,000 pages etc. Price based on printing costs of 10 p per sheet for A4 paper.

7. Figures in the main section of the table refer to the total number of nights, so, for example, an arbitration might require 10 nights in a hotel per person, with up to 20 people staying in a hotel this would be a total of 200 nights. Price based on the average price of a four-star hotel in London.

8. Calculated using the BEIS&DEFRA greenhouse gas (GHG) conversion data. kgCo$_2$e = Total of factor (e.g., the total number of return flights) × carbon conversion factor.

9. Per factor.

10. Per Capita emission in the UK was at 5,400 kgCO$_2$e in 2018 (Carbon Brief – https://www.carbonbrief.org/analysis-uks-co2-emissions-fell-for-record-sixth-consecutive-year-in-2018).

The total carbon impact in kgCo2e of the arbitration used as the case study was 418,531.02. This would require planting over 20,000 trees to offset the emissions. Over 93% of the identified emissions related to travel, in particular air travel (business class[66]).

The team then considered an alternative scenario, which they called the 'Green Arbitration'. This involved changing the assumptions as follows: (i) eliminating paper bundles, (ii) reducing the amount of travel, and (iii) eliminating motorbike couriers due to the alternative use of e-bundles and video conferencing.

---

66. Depending on the size of the area for each seat, business class is usually between two or three times as energy intensive as economy class.

Green Arbitrations

	Preliminary Analysis/ Preparing to Issue Notices	Preliminary Requests	Pleading 1	Pleading 2	Pleading 3	Pleading 4	Hearing Preparation	The Hearing	Total	Carbon Impact (kgCO2e)[10]	Costs(£)	N°. of Trees Required to Absorb Carbon Emissions[11]
Long-distance return flights[1]	0	3	8	8	8	8	8	20	63	301080.78	125874.00	13685.49
Short distance return flights[2]	9	4	6	6	6	6	14	6	57	53260.80	18411.00	2420.95
Car journeys[3]	10	10	10	10	10	10	10	5	75	1596.45	18750.00	72.57
Train journeys[4]	10	10	10	10	10	10	10	10	80	329.20	2000.00	14.96
Motorbike couriers[5]	5	5	10	10	10	10	10	10	70	0.00	7000.00	0.00
Pages printed[6]	100	100	350	350	350	350	1000	1,000	3600	1543.34	36000.00	70.15
Hotel stays[7]	16	12	30	30	30	30	44	250	442	9016.80	66300.00	409.85
Paperless bundling software[8]	0	0	0	0	0	0	0	0	0	N/A[12]	13850.00	0.00
Video conferencing[9]	0	0	0	0	0	0	0	0	0	N/A[12]	0.00	0.00
Coffee cups[10]	0	0	0	0	0	0	0	0	0	0	0	0.00
										3,66,827.37	£2,88,185.00	16,673.971

Total emissions as a multiple of an individual's annual carbon footprint[13] — 68

Notes:

See the 'Carbon Emissions Calculator – Rationale' document for the underlying assumptions for tallying the occurrences of the various factors.

The table represents the marginal cost of each extra arbitration so for that reason, figures such as office energy costs and any fixed costs are not included as these cannot be isolated per arbitration.

1. Business class return flight (11,000 km return). Price based on the mean of the flight prices between London and Dubai (10,956 km) in mid-Feburary (GBP 1,998).
2. Business class return flight (4,000 km return). Price based on the mean of the flight prices between London and Milan (1,918 km) in mid-February (GBP 323).
3. 100km return journey. Price based on an average of GBP 2.50 per kilometre for chauffering (http://www.dslcars.com/rates/).
4. Standard class return (200 km return). Price based on a return fare from London to Cambridge (102 km) (GBP 25).
5. Short distance (measured from Dechert LLP to One Canada Square, Canary Wharf (7 km)). Price based on an Addison Lee motorbike courier (GBP 17).
6. Figures are in multiples per 100 pages (450g of paper), i.e., 20 refers to 2,000 pages. Price based on printing costs of 10 p per sheet for A4 paper.
7. Figures in the main section of the table refer to the total number of nights, so for example, an arbitration might require 10 nights in a hotel per person, with up to 20 people staying in a hotel this would be a total of 200 nights. Price based on the average price of a four-star hotel in London.
8. Based on a costing from Opus for paperless bundling for a ten-day hearing.
9. Assuming all law firms have videoconferencing software, there is no cost per arbitration there are only the annual costs for the license (GBP 250 in addition to the general Cisco subscription) as well as the hardware costs for the recording software (at least £5,000 for the minimum equipment).
10. Calculated using the BEIS&DEFRA GHG conversion data. kgCo2e = Total of factor (e.g., the total number of return flights) x carbon conversion factor.
11. Per factor.
12. Emissions would be included in the general office emissions which are not accounted for in this chart.
13. Per Capita emission in the UK was at 5,400 kgCO2e in 2018 (Carbon Brief – https://www.carbonbrief.org/analysis-uks-co2-emissions-fell-for-record-sixth-consecutive-year-in-2018)

102

Changing those assumptions resulted in a saving of 51,704 kgCo2e, almost ten times the average carbon footprint of an individual in the UK.[67]

There are two key actions arising from the environmental impact assessment: (i) fly less and (ii) stop printing bundles.

Simply reducing the number of flights by one at each stage of every arbitration would reduce costs by half and emissions by a quarter. This could be achieved by using video more frequently to interview and prepare witnesses and taking the self-evident step of flying the witness to the team than the team to the witnesses. Similarly, arbitrators should be more receptive to discussing whether it is appropriate to take the testimony of certain witnesses by video. Here, I certainly expect there to be significant behavioural change as a result of the lockdowns across the world in 2020-2021. The lockdowns forced the arbitration community to embrace video conferencing in a way it had never done before. Suddenly there was a plethora of webinars, deliberations by Zoom and virtual hearings. The pandemic forced practitioners to adopt technology that had been available for years and simply using the technology mean that practitioners had confidence in it. It is encouraging that, at least anecdotally, there appears to have been a significant increase in technology use and hybrid hearings since the lockdowns were eased.

There was opposition in some quarters to the use of video conferencing in relation to witness evidence on the grounds that it is open to abuse in relation to whether answers might be being fed to a witness off-screen. There are also concerns that the screen limits the arbitrator's ability to really observe the witness's demeanour (although the obvious counter to that argument is that we all overestimate our ability to determine whether someone is telling the truth). There is a further counterargument which may be less emotive. Taking evidence through a screen may, in fact, limit our tendency to apply our unconscious biases to a witness appearing before us. The progress from video conferencing to a concept of 'telepresence' could reduce resistance to the notion of taking witness evidence remotely. So-called telepresence is the notion of 3D figures appearing holographically, such that the person appears to be in the hearing room with all the other participants.

Of course, the use of technology must be considered in light of all relevant laws and principles of natural justice, but it merits consideration in every case. Increasing the use of technology to take witness evidence remotely would not only reduce costs of the arbitration, improve the efficiency of an arbitration and reduce the carbon footprint of an arbitration, but it might also even improve the quality of an arbitrator's decision-making by mitigating the effects of unconscious bias.

The second action, eliminating paper bundles, would have a less significant impact environmentally but would have a dramatic impact on the disbursement costs of an arbitration. The greener arbitrations team found that printing was responsible for only 2% of carbon emissions in the major international arbitration (albeit a 2% that is easily eliminated) but accounted for 40% of disbursements. The waste involved in producing hard copies is astonishing. It is not simply the printing of the document, it is

---

67. *See supra* n. 13.

the mailing, the managing, the storing, and the eventual shredding of that hard copy that soaks up time, money and resources. Again, the COVID-19 pandemic forced the community to move from hard copies to electronic copies almost overnight, and it is encouraging once more that it seems that institutions (who were once among the worst offenders in relation to hard copies) do not seem to have reverted to their former ways.

4   Avoiding the Bystander Effect and Achieving a 'Greener' Arbitration

The so-called bystander effect is the idea that the more people who are present during an emergency, the less likely people are to offer help to a victim. A study by Latané and Rodin staged a situation in which participants heard an investigator trip and then call out that she had hurt her ankle. When individuals were alone, 70% of them attempted to help the woman, however when another person was present, only 40% offered support.[68] There is an argument that our inaction on the issue of climate change is the bystander effect playing out on a global scale. In the international arbitration community, I suspect that, in fact, it is not so much the bystander effect that is limiting our aspirations in this area, but our ability to divorce our responsibilities at home from our responsibilities at work. We may be actively addressing climate change issues at home, but we believe that once we engage in our arbitration practice, it is someone else's problem.

The international arbitration industry is made up of several autonomous parts: arbitrators, counsel, parties, and institutions as the main players, plus all the supporting acts such as court reporters, printers, couriers, hotels, airlines, taxi firms, and so on. We cannot absolve ourselves of our personal responsibility to address our impact on each part of the arbitration we participate in. The 'Tragedy of the Commons' describes the phenomenon where people benefit from everyone else's sacrifices and suffer from their own, so everyone has an incentive not to make a sacrifice. We must act to ensure that it is socially unacceptable for an individual not to consider the climate in their international arbitration practice so that the tragedy of the commons does not feature in our practices.

V   DELIVERING CHANGE

To reduce the waste of time and costs, waste of talent and waste of resources and to deliver change we need to support and promote increased data collection, embrace technology, encourage the assumption of personal and collective responsibility and take concrete action.

---

68. 'A Lady in Distress: Inhibiting Effects of Friends and Strangers on Bystander Intervention' (1969) 5(2) Journal of Experimental Social Psychology pp. 189-202. The research was prompted by an article published in the New York Times in March of 1964 which reported on the death of a 28-year-old woman called Kitty Genovese. Kitty was stabbed outside her home in New York. The article claimed that thirty-eight neighbours witnessed the attack but none of them contacted the police or attempted to help her. Although a number of inaccuracies in the report were eventually identified and acknowledged, the case is widely seen as a trigger for the research into the so-called bystander effect.

1   Become a 'Lion of Truth'

The curse of assumptions underpins each of the areas of concern I have identified. First, the assumption that arbitration will be quick and cheap, or, more accurately, the assumption that everyone involved in an arbitration wants it to be quick and cheap. Second, the assumption is that only the best arbitrators come from a particular demographic. Third, the assumption is that the carbon footprint of international arbitration is 200 times smaller than it is. To achieve progress in these areas we must eliminate assumptions by testing them against empirical data. In the words of author Suzy Kassem: '[A] lion of truth never assumes anything without validity. Assumptions are quick exits for lazy minds that like to graze out in the fields without bother.'[69] The effort required to generate empirical data is far greater than producing sound bites at conferences, which is why our 'lazy minds' take the 'quick exit' provided by an assumption. Data is the best weapon in the war against assumptions and, until relatively recently, data has been conspicuously lacking in our industry. Even now, our access to verifiable data is patchy and unsatisfactory.

2   Embrace Technology

Data is most easily delivered through technology. Technology is also the key to improving the efficiency of the process. The analysis of green arbitration in particular shows the solution lies in an increased and better use of technology in arbitration. There is also enthusiasm for better use of technology generally in our field: the overwhelming majority of respondents to the 2018 Queen Mary Survey favoured the greater use in the future of 'hearing room technologies,' cloud-based storage, 'video-conferencing', 'AI' and 'virtual hearing rooms'.[70] It should be emphasized that the hypothetical green arbitration does not implicate new technology but simply requires a willingness to use technology that we all have on the laptops in front of us, or on our smartphones. Screen-sharing, video conferencing, annotating pdfs on screen. All things that we do all day but, for many years, not when it came to an international arbitration hearing or deliberations. COVID-19 shifted the paradigm and it is to be hoped that the progress the arbitration community made in embracing technology will continue.

There are clear synergies between the drive to have greener arbitrations and the drive to have more efficient arbitrations. Embracing technology can reduce costs significantly. In their research for green arbitration, the Dechert team found that amounts spent on travel, printing, couriers and hotel stays could be reduced by a third if a green approach to an arbitration was adopted. More than half of respondents to the

---

69. Assumptions Suzy Kassem, born in Toledo, Ohio (1 December 1975), is an American author, filmmaker, philosopher, cultural critic, essayist, and poet of Egyptian descent. 'Rise Up and Salute the Sun'.
70. https://www.whitecase.com/publications/insight/2018-international-arbitration-survey-evolu tion-international-arbitration.

2018 Queen Mary Survey thought that 'increased efficiency, including through technology' was the factor that is most likely to have a significant impact on the future evolution of international arbitration.

Technology also impacts the fight to eliminate inequality. If more international arbitration conferences were streamed, then that would reduce the number of flights taken by practitioners but would also increase access to information and discussion for less privileged practitioners and, in fact, that has been precisely the effect the pandemic has had. More empirical data on how arbitrators actually perform is also likely to level the playing field between the 'knowns' and the 'unknowns' in a world where being 'known' carries a huge premium.

3   Three Concrete Actions for Change

No amount of data or technology can compensate for an absence of personal and shared responsibility for these issues. According to Pinker energy channelled by knowledge is the 'elixir with which we stave off disorder'.[71] The elixir that the international arbitration community needs is access to empirical data and a willingness to accept personal responsibility to drive change. In some areas, particularly in relation to time and costs criticisms of arbitration, we have achieved some change through talk and guidelines. In relation to diversity, we have taken certain steps and framed those steps through the lens of the limited empirical data we have been able to gather. In relation to the environment, we have skipped the talking and started with the data. To move to a state of true enlightenment, the international arbitration world needs less talk and more individual action founded on verifiable data.

I close by suggesting one small action that everyone can take in relation to each area of concern. First, in relation to efficiency: eliminate verbiage and remember that other old adage 'saying something twice doesn't make it twice as true'. Second, in relation to equality: – and regardless of whether you are male or female – refuse to participate in a non-diverse conference panel. Third, in relation to the environment: do not accept printed bundles in the hearing room and critically assess whether every flight you take is necessary.

In the words of Albert Einstein '[T]he world as we have created it is a process of our thinking. It cannot be changed without changing our thinking.' In the world of international arbitration, the time to change our thinking is now.

---

71. Pinker, Enlightenment Now.

CHAPTER *7*

Some Thoughts on Progress

*James Hope**

TABLE OF CONTENTS

I   INTRODUCTION

How do you assess progress?

There can be no doubt that international arbitration has undergone enormous growth in the twenty-first century.[1] As globalisation has increased, so have international disputes, and the primary means of resolving international disputes is by

---

* Advokat (Sweden); Solicitor-Advocate (England & Wales, Civil Proceedings); Solicitor, non-practising (Scotland); Partner, Advokatfirman Vinge KB, Stockholm, Sweden; Member of the LCIA Court; Former member of the Board of the SCC Institute, 2013-2018; Head of the Research Panel for Arbitration and Other Forms of Dispute Resolution, Stockholm Centre for Commercial Law.

1. The growth of international arbitration is reported by many sources. One example is the IBA Arb 40 Subcommittee report *The Current State and Future of International Arbitration: Regional Perspectives* dated September 2015, which reported that international arbitration was on the rise in all six regions surveyed: Africa, Asia-Pacific, Europe, Latin America, the Middle East and North Africa (MENA), and North America. *See* https://cvdvn.files.wordpress.com/2018/10/int-arbitration-report-2015.pdf (last accessed 11 June 2022).

    In terms of statistics, a total of 853 cases were registered by the ICC Secretariat in 2021 – which was said to be 'comparable but lower than the record number of filings reported in 2020'

international arbitration. To that extent, there has been clear progress in the field of international arbitration.

But there are also concerns and criticisms.

This paper offers comments and some suggestions in relation to four issues:

(1) International arbitration is often too expensive, and it often takes too long. What was once a form of 'alternative' dispute resolution – in other words, an alternative to litigation – has become a form of litigation by other means. Users complain that they want the process to be cheaper[2] as well as quicker.[3]

(2) There have been various 'soft law' initiatives within the field of international arbitration for use by practitioners from different legal cultures. The most well-known of such initiatives is the IBA Rules on the Taking of Evidence in International Arbitration (the 'IBA Rules'), which has gained widespread acceptance and is in common use within the international arbitration community.[4] One particular focus of the IBA Rules is to provide a framework for determining requests for production of documents. However, guidance is lacking in one central respect – what is the basis for determining whether a document request seeks documents that are relevant and material to the outcome of the dispute?

(3) There are recurring calls for greater diversity in international arbitration.[5] In short, for the sake of its own legitimacy as a global means of resolving

---

(ICC preliminary 2021 statistics, released on 26 January 2022): https://iccwbo.org/media-wall/news-speeches/icc-unveils-preliminary-dispute-resolution-figures-for-2021/ (last accessed 11 June 2022). The London Court of International Arbitration (LCIA) reports, in the *LCIA 2021 Annual Casework Report*, a total of 387 referrals for its services, down from the record number in 2020 but nevertheless showing a steady increase since 2012: https://www.lcia.org/media/download.aspx?MediaId = 890 (last accessed 11 June 2022). China International Economic and Trade Arbitration Commission (CIETAC) records 636 foreign-related cases in 2021, which is lower than the record number of 739 in 2020 but represents an increasing trend overall: http://www.cietac.org/index.php?m = Page&a = index&id = 40&l = en (last accessed 11 June 2022). There has been a particularly marked increase in Singapore International Arbitration Centre (SIAC), which registered over 1000 new cases in 2020 as compared with only 188 new cases in 2011: https://siac.org.sg/images/stories/articles/annual_report/SIAC_Annual_Report_2020.pdf (last accessed 11 June 2022).

   Some other arbitral institutions show less of a clear trend in recent years, but since the turn of the millennium there has clearly been considerable growth throughout the field of international arbitration.

2. *See, e.g.*, the *White & Case 2018 International Arbitration Survey: The Evolution of International Arbitration*, which noted that, although 97% of respondents indicated that international arbitration was their preferred method of resolving cross-border disputes, 67% of respondents complained about the cost of international arbitration, and 'cost' was clearly seen as the worst characteristic of international arbitration.

   See https://www.whitecase.com/sites/whitecase/files/files/download/publications/qmul-international-arbitration-survey-2018-19.pdf (last accessed 11 June 2022).

3. The *White & Case 2018 International Arbitration Survey: The Evolution of International Arbitration* notes that 34% of respondents indicated that 'lack of speed' was one of the worst features of international arbitration.

4. *See* https://www.ibanet.org/MediaHandler?id = def0807b-9fec-43ef-b624-f2cb2af7cf7b (last accessed 11 June 2022).

5. *See, inter alia*, ICCA Report No. 8, *Report of the Cross-Institutional Task Force on Gender Diversity in Arbitral Appointments and Proceedings*, 2020: https://cdn.arbitration-icca.org/s3fs-public/document/media_document/ICCA-Report-8-Gender-Diversity_0.pdf (last accessed 11 June 2022).

disputes, international arbitration needs to be truly international. Considerable work has been carried out on gender diversity, through 'The Pledge'[6] and other initiatives, although further improvements could certainly be made. Ethnic, cultural and linguistic diversity is more difficult. However, recent advances in technology can help – in particular, with the marked increase in virtual hearings and conferences as a direct result of the COVID-19 pandemic.

(4) Since writing the initial version of this paper, it is with a heavy heart that I have decided to add a fourth issue. How should international arbitration respond to the challenges of war? War, of course, is hardly new, but it has developed a new importance – at least in Europe – since the Russian invasion of Ukraine on 24 February 2022. There have been many calls to shut out Russian companies and individuals from the global economy, but how should the international arbitration community respond?

II SAVING COSTS AND TIME

The importance of saving costs and time has been on the international arbitration agenda for many years. It is generally accepted that international arbitration has become too expensive and takes too long.[7] It is also generally agreed that these are problems that need to be resolved.

Various initiatives have been taken, including (to name just a few):

– the ICC Arbitration Commission Report on Techniques for Controlling Costs and Time in Arbitration;[8]
– Appendix IV to the ICC Rules, entitled 'Case Management Techniques';[9]
– the Debevoise Efficiency Protocol (2018);[10]
– the revised 2017 SCC Rules, with their particular emphasis on efficiency;[11]
– the revised 2021 VIAC Rules, which also emphasise efficiency.[12]

---

6. The 'Equal Representation in Arbitration' Pledge: *see* www.arbitrationpledge.com (last accessed 11 June 2022).
7. *See, e.g.,* the *White & Case 2018 International Arbitration Survey: The Evolution of International Arbitration,* referred to above.
8. *See* https://iccwbo.org/content/uploads/sites/3/2018/03/icc-arbitration-commission-report-on-techniques-for-controlling-time-and-costs-in-arbitration-english-version.pdf (last accessed 11 June 2022).
9. *See* https://iccwbo.org/dispute-resolution-services/arbitration/rules-of-arbitration/#casemngtech (last accessed 11 June 2022).
10. *See* https://www.debevoise.com/news/2018/01/debevoise-updates-two-key-resources (last accessed 11 June 2022).
11. *See* https://sccinstitute.com/media/1407444/arbitrationrules_eng_2020.pdf (last accessed 11 June 2022).
12. *See* https://www.viac.eu/en/arbitration/rules-of-arbitration-and-mediation (last accessed 11 June 2022).

However, it is of course easier to identify the problems than to solve them. The issues of time and costs continue to be discussed.[13]

As Jennifer Kirby memorably pointed out in her talk at the 2015 Helsinki Arbitration Day,[14] anyone who thinks that arbitration can be fast, cheap and good should think again. That paradise where all three parts of the 'iron triangle' of time, cost and quality are perfected is where the unicorn lives – in other words, it does not exist.[15]

It is generally agreed that the parties' own legal fees account for a large proportion of the overall costs of an arbitration.[16] I suggest from experience that it is also often the parties' counsel who insist upon a lengthy procedural timetable; requiring several months to prepare written submissions and in some cases several rounds of written submissions. Such large counsel's fees and such long timetables often seem to be inevitable in large and complex cases, and arbitrators should be very careful before they seek to interfere with how counsel choose to present their cases.

Nevertheless, as Jennifer Kirby noted, arbitrators have some powers which, if exercised wisely, can help to save costs and time. It is relevant to note, for example, that the ICC Rules provide that the purpose of the initial, mandatory, case management conference is 'to consult the parties on procedural measures that may be adopted pursuant to Article 22(2)'.[17]

Article 22(2) of the 2021 ICC Rules provides:

> In order to ensure effective case management, after consulting the parties, the arbitral tribunal shall adopt such procedural measures as it considers appropriate, provided that they are not contrary to any agreement of the parties. Such measures may include one or more of the case management techniques described in Appendix IV.

---

13. Anecdotally, I suggest that the length of time it takes to conduct an arbitration has not been significantly reduced. In 2011, the Chartered Institute of Arbitrators' *CIArb Costs of International Arbitration Survey 2011* found that the average arbitration takes between seventeen and twenty months: *see* https://www.international-arbitration-attorney.com/wp-content/uploads/2017/0 1/CIArb-Cost-of-International-Arbitration-Survey.pdf (last accessed 11 June 2022). In 2017, data published by the LCIA (based on arbitrations over the period 1 January 2013 to 31 December 2016) revealed that the median total duration for an LCIA arbitration was 16 months: *see* https://www.international-arbitration-attorney.com/wp-content/uploads/2018/07/LCIA-Costs-and-Duration-Statistics.pdf (last accessed 11 June 2022). The ICC's Dispute Resolution Statistics for 2020 show that the median duration of ICC proceedings that reached a final award in 2020 was 26 months: *see* https://iccwbo.org/publication/icc-dispute-resolution-statistics-2 020/ (last accessed 11 June 2022).
14. Jennifer Kirby, 'Efficiency in International Arbitration: Whose Duty Is It?', *Journal of International Arbitration* 32, no. 6 (2015): pp. 689-696.
15. *See* Figure 2 in Jennifer Kirby's article, which beautifully illustrates this point with a drawing of a unicorn.
16. A Chartered Institute of Arbitrators survey indicated that 74% of costs incurred were external legal costs (*CIArb Costs of International Arbitration Survey 2011*, Chart 12): *see* https://www.international-arbitration-attorney.com/wp-content/uploads/2017/01/CIArb-Cost-of-Internatio nal-Arbitration-Survey.pdf (last accessed 11 June 2022).
17. Article 24(1) of the 2021 ICC Rules.

Appendix IV to the 2021 ICC Rules provides:

APPENDIX IV: CASE MANAGEMENT TECHNIQUES

The following are examples of case management techniques that can be used by the arbitral tribunal and the parties for controlling time and cost. Appropriate control of time and cost is important in all cases. In cases of low complexity and low value, it is particularly important to ensure that time and costs are proportionate to what is at stake in the dispute.

a) Bifurcating the proceedings or rendering one or more partial awards on key issues, when doing so may genuinely be expected to result in a more efficient resolution of the case.

b) Identifying issues that can be resolved by agreement between the parties or their experts.

c) Identifying issues to be decided solely on the basis of documents rather than through oral evidence or legal argument at a hearing.

d) Production of documentary evidence:
    (i) requiring the parties to produce with their submissions the documents on which they rely;
    (ii) avoiding requests for document production when appropriate in order to control time and cost;
    (iii) in those cases where requests for document production are considered appropriate, limiting such requests to documents or categories of documents that are relevant and material to the outcome of the case;
    (iv) establishing reasonable time limits for the production of documents;
    (v) using a schedule of document production to facilitate the resolution of issues in relation to the production of documents.

e) Limiting the length and scope of written submissions and written and oral witness evidence (both fact witnesses and experts) so as to avoid repetition and maintain a focus on key issues.

f) Using telephone or video conferencing for procedural and other hearings where attendance in person is not essential and use of IT that enables online communication among the parties, the arbitral tribunal and the Secretariat of the Court.

g) Organizing a pre-hearing conference with the arbitral tribunal at which arrangements for a hearing can be discussed and agreed and the arbitral tribunal can indicate to the parties issues on which it would like the parties to focus at the hearing.

h) Settlement of disputes:
    (i) encouraging the parties to consider settlement of all or part of the dispute either by negotiation or through any form of amicable dispute resolution methods such as, for example, mediation under the ICC Mediation Rules;
    (ii) where agreed between the parties and the arbitral tribunal, the arbitral tribunal may take steps to facilitate settlement of the dispute, provided that every effort is made to ensure that any subsequent award is enforceable at law.

Additional techniques are described in the ICC publication entitled 'Controlling Time and Costs in Arbitration'.

There are many suggestions here, but in my experience, it is rare for these suggestions to be followed. We can all do more in the interest of saving costs and time.

I suggest in particular that more attention could be made to shortening, or at least simplifying, counsel's written submissions. It is quite common for counsel to file written submissions of over 200 pages in length,[18] and there is also often a considerable amount of repetition from one written submission to the next.

Factual and legal arguments develop over the life of a case; such developments are in many cases both inevitable and beneficial, usually contributing to narrowing and clarifying the issues in dispute. Yet, by the end of the case, there are often simply far too many words. It has become far too easy to write longer and longer submissions, as well as longer and longer witness statements and expert reports. Such documents inevitably take a long time to write, and they take a long time to read and to answer.

Can this process be improved?

It is often suggested that it takes longer to write a short submission than a long one. The quotation – 'I apologise for writing a long letter, I did not have time to shorten it' – has been attributed to various different writers.[19] I suggest, though, that this simple excuse is misleading. It is certainly true that it takes time to turn a long text into a shorter text, but that is not always how the drafting process evolves. In many cases, there is no real need for lengthy submissions; they just end up that way.

I suggest that counsel should actively plan to write shorter, more concise submissions. Before the invention of the word processor, it was necessary to plan carefully before starting to write. Even today, the best writers do a considerable amount of planning before they embark on the actual process of drafting.

Sensible advice can be found in a memo that the UK Prime Minister, Winston Churchill, wrote to his War Cabinet during the Second World War.[20] In short, he asked his colleagues and their staff to concentrate on the essential points:

(THIS DOCUMENT IS THE PROPERTY OF HIS BRITANNIC MAJESTY'S GOVERN-MENT)

SECRET

W.P. (G) (40) 211.   COPY NO. 51

9TH AUGUST, 1940.

WAR CABINET.

————————

BREVITY.

Memorandum by the Prime Minister.

To do our work, we all have to read a mass of papers. Nearly all of them are far too long. This wastes time, while energy has to be spent in looking for the essential points.

I ask my colleagues and their staffs to see to it that their Reports are shorter.

18. I once received a written submission of over 600 pages.
19. Including Mark Twain, George Bernard Shaw, Voltaire, Blaise Pascal, Johann Wolfgang von Goethe, Winston Churchill, Pliny the Younger, Cato, Cicero, Bill Clinton, and Benjamin Franklin. The earliest use of the saying appears to have been by French mathematician and philosopher Blaise Pascal in 1657: *see* https://quoteinvestigator.com/2012/04/28/shorter-letter/ (last accessed 11 June 2022).
20. *See* https://www.businessinsider.com/memo-winston-churchill-on-brevity-improve-writing-2 017-5?r = US&IR = T (last accessed 11 June 2022).

(i) The aim should be Reports which set out the main points in a series of short, crisp paragraphs.

(ii) If a Report relies on detailed analysis of some complicated factors, or on statistics, these should be set out in an Appendix.

(iii) Often the occasion is best met by submitting not a full-dress Report, but an Aide-memoire consisting of headings only, which can be expanded orally if needed.

(iv) Let us have an end of such phrases as these: 'It is also of importance to bear in mind the following considerations......', or 'Consideration should be given to the possibility of carrying into effect.....'. Most of these woolly phrases are mere padding, which can be left out altogether, or replaced by a single word. Let us not shrink from using the short expressive phrase, even if it is conversational.

Reports drawn up on the lines I propose may at first seem rough as compared with the flat surface of officialese jargon. But the saving in time will be great, while the discipline of setting out the real points concisely will prove an aid to clearer thinking.

W.S.C.

10, Downing Street.

9TH AUGUST, 1940.

Winston Churchill's advice cannot be applied in full to the detailed written documents that are required in international arbitration cases. Yet, the sentiment remains applicable.

Counsel should always aim to make it easy for the arbitral tribunal to digest and fully understand the essential points of the arguments being made.

I would like to offer three practical suggestions for improving the process of drafting written documents in international arbitration:

(a) *Structured submissions*: It is helpful for submissions to be well-structured in answering one another so that the issues in dispute can be clearly identified.

(b) *Expansion and amendment of existing written submissions*: Parties can be encouraged to expand upon, and in some cases amend, their initial submissions, instead of writing entirely separate (and often repetitive) additional submissions.

(c) *The proper role of witness statements*: Parties should remember that the proper role of written witness statements is to set out the witness's factual evidence, not to seek to argue the case.

(a) Structured submissions

Since this year's International Council for Commercial Arbitration (ICCA) Congress is taking place in Edinburgh, it seems fitting to take inspiration from Scots law, and in particular Scottish civil procedure.

The Scottish civil courts have a unique, focused pleading style which highlights the key issues in dispute between the parties.

A case in the Court of Session is commenced by means of a Summons, containing one or more 'conclusions' (i.e., the remedies sought, such as payment of damages), a 'condescendence' (a detailed statement of the facts that the pursuer[21] offers to prove, in the form of short sentences called 'averments'), and 'pleas-in-law' (the legal propositions applicable to the case). The defender[22] answers by means of a written defence, containing 'defences' in answer to each of the pursuer's averments, and the defender's own pleas-in-law.

These pleadings are then put together into a single document, called an 'open record'.[23] The initial pleadings can be adjusted during a period of weeks thereafter, but the basic structure of the argument remains as set out in the initial pleadings, ending up with a single focused document, subsequently referred to as the 'closed record' once the period of adjustment has ended.

Adopting such a formalistic pleading style in international arbitration would, of course, be entirely wrong. Flexibility is an important feature of international arbitration and rigid proposals regarding written submissions or pleading styles should be avoided. It is also important for international arbitration to be able to be used by lawyers from all backgrounds and legal traditions, and it should not be necessary to follow a particular style of pleading in order to take part.

Yet the idea of focusing the argument is surely a good one. One way of doing this is for the arbitral tribunal to hold a procedural hearing, or case management conference, after the initial round of written submissions, and for further such procedural hearings to be scheduled, as necessary, as the case progresses. The parties can be encouraged to focus their minds on responding to each other's submissions, and the aim should be to identify the issues in dispute and the points that will need to be dealt with and determined by the arbitral tribunal.

I recognise that such a procedure requires the arbitral tribunal to undertake considerable work at a fairly early stage in the case; only an arbitral tribunal that has a good grasp of the details can prompt the parties into seeking to adopt efficient procedures as the case develops. But such front-loading by the arbitral tribunal is surely to be encouraged for other reasons. Arbitral tribunals often have to rule upon complex document production requests at a fairly early stage of the case, and such rulings can only be made properly if the arbitral tribunal has a good grasp of the details of the case already at that early stage. Arbitral tribunals are also expected to have a full grasp of the details by the time they come to the evidentiary hearing, and such work requires considerable preparation in advance of the hearing.

It is very important to add, however, that any such case management needs to be carried out with caution. Arbitral tribunals must always ensure that each party is given a sufficient opportunity to present its case. Thus, overly prescriptive case management (such as restricting the scope of a party's submissions) should be resisted. As always, it is necessary to strike a balance.

---

21. That is, the claimant in Scots law terminology.
22. That is, the defendant in Scots law terminology.
23. Pronounced 'record', with the emphasis on the second syllable.

(b) Expansion and amendment of existing written submissions

A simple suggestion is to ask the parties to expand upon, and in some cases to amend, their initial submissions in later rounds of submissions, instead of filing entirely separate further submissions.[24]

This is particularly easy when documents are filed and accessed electronically. One electronic document can simply be replaced by another, provided it is made clear to everybody involved what has been done.

Most arbitrators will recognise the difficulty that arises when a party makes an argument in its initial submission and that argument is then repeated, but subtly (or not so subtly) changed, in the party's second submission. The changes to the argument are often left unexplained, and it is necessary for the arbitrators and opposing counsel to note and work through the various ways in which the argument has developed. I suggest that this is almost always bad advocacy. The effect is to create confusion, and very often annoyance, as well as increased cost and time.

Sometimes, of course, a party needs to change its case. It is then far better for the party to be open about the fact that it has done so, and to turn the changes to its advantage. Arbitrators need to understand each party's position, and when that position keeps changing there is a real risk of a lack of understanding. At the very least, it needs to be clear by the time the arbitral tribunal comes to prepare the case for the main hearing what each party's position actually is in respect of the key issues in the case.

(c) The proper role of witness statements

Written witness statements are intended to assist in saving costs and time, but too often they actually increase costs.

Both the Scottish and English commercial courts have taken considerable steps in recent years to clarify the proper role of witness statements.[25] Again, since the ICCA Congress is taking place in Edinburgh, I will concentrate here on the Guidance Note that has been provided by the Commercial Judges in Scotland.[26] In summary:

– The purpose of signed witness statements or affidavits is to assist the court to hear cases expeditiously.
– There is also a benefit in parties knowing sooner rather than later the evidence likely to be adduced by the other side.
– It is generally desirable that a witness, who is speaking to events which occurred some time previously, should give his[27] evidence after he has had an opportunity to consider documents which he had seen at the relevant time.

---

24. I am indebted to Swedish arbitrator Fanny Gleiss Wilborg for this excellent suggestion, although she has assured me that she was not the first to propose it.
25. I have written separately and in some detail on developments in England. *See* James Hope, 'Witness Statements in International Arbitration: The Cost of "Gilding the Lily"', *Scandinavian Studies in Law* 63 (2017): pp. 437-457.
26. *See* https://www.scotcourts.gov.uk/home/commercial-court/guidance-on-use-signed-witness-statements-or-affidavits (last accessed 11 June 2022).
27. It is pointed out in the Guidance Note that use of the word 'he' includes 'she'.

- The witness should also have had the opportunity to re-read his statement shortly before he gives oral evidence.
- The Commercial Judges point out that they do not intend to have all evidence in chief presented solely in written form. They recognise that controversial issues within a witness's evidence, where issues of credibility and reliability arise, will usually have to be addressed in oral evidence in chief as well as in the statement. This assists the judge to form a view of the witness in the more relaxed circumstance of evidence in chief and also when under the stress of cross-examination.
- It is stated in the Guidance Note that counsel should use their professional judgment in deciding how much oral evidence in chief is needed in the particular case, though the judge must be free to intervene if he feels that this is tending to subvert the purpose behind the use of statements.
- Regarding the content of the witness statement, the statement should be the evidence of the witness and should cover only those matters to which he can properly speak. What the court is looking for is the actual evidence of the witness in written form.
- It is stated that witness statements should be finalised without showing the witness the other statements that are being obtained. Moreover, by fixing a date for the exchange of witness statements, the court seeks to prevent a witness's initial statement from being influenced by the evidence of the witnesses put forward by another party. On the other hand, witnesses can later read other statements that have been exchanged, and if necessary supplementary witness statements can subsequently be lodged in order to correct or qualify what the witness has said, but not to comment on or rebut the evidence of other witnesses.
- The witness should sign the statement, and the statement should include a declaration confirming that the evidence given in the statement is true to the best of the witness's knowledge and belief.

Much of the above guidance could usefully be adopted in international arbitration. In particular, it is important that witness statements only deal with the factual evidence of the witness, and they should not be used as an opportunity for counsel to make additional arguments or legal submissions.

It is notable that this guidance suggests that, in the Scottish commercial court, there will often be both some degree of oral direct examination as well as written witness statements.[28] This is rare in international arbitration, where the general practice is for written witness statements to take the place of oral direct examination. However, I suggest that in some cases it could be appropriate to allow for rather more flexibility in this respect in international arbitration. For example, the arbitral tribunal could identify particular issues on which it wishes to hear oral direct examination in the

---

28. That is, 'evidence in chief'. It should be noted that the Scottish commercial court differs in this respect from the general civil courts in Scotland, where the usual practice is still for direct examination to be carried out orally without the use of written witness statements.

witness's own words, such as the witness's personal recollection of what happened at a crucial meeting.

Finally, it is also relevant to note the recent developments in England concerning witness statements in the Business and Property Courts. The new Practice Direction PD57AC (Witness Evidence at Trial), which applies to trial witness statements signed on or after 6 April 2021, 'seeks to promote and enforce best practice on the preparation of witness statements'.[29] To summarise some particular features of this new Practice Direction:

- 'The purpose of a trial witness statement is to set out in writing the evidence in chief that a witness of fact would give if they were allowed to give oral evidence at trial without having provided the statement.'[30]
- 'A trial witness statement must contain only –
  (1) evidence as to matters of fact that need to be proved at trial by the evidence of witnesses in relation to one or more of the issues of fact to be decided at trial, and
  (2) the evidence as to such matters that the witness would be asked by the relevant party to give, and the witness would be allowed to give, in evidence in chief if they were called to give oral evidence at trial and rule 32.5(2) did not apply.'[31]
- 'A trial witness statement must set out only matters of fact of which the witness has personal knowledge that are relevant to the case, and must identify by list what documents, if any, the witness has referred to or been referred to for the purpose of providing the evidence set out in their trial witness statement.'[32]
- Trial witness statements should be prepared in accordance with the Statement of Best Practice contained in the Appendix to the Practice Direction.[33]
- Unless the court otherwise orders, a trial witness statement must include a confirmation signed by the witness.[34]

---

29. *See* https://www.judiciary.uk/announcements/new-witness-statements-practice-direction-approved/.
30. PD57AC, para. 2.1.
31. PD57AC, para. 3.1.
32. PD57AC, para. 3.2.
33. PD57AC, para. 3.4.
34. PD57AC, para. 4.1. The confirmation is worded as follows:

    I understand that the purpose of this witness statement is to set out matters of fact of which I have personal knowledge.
       I understand that it is not my function to argue the case, either generally or on particular points, or to take the court through the documents in the case.
       This witness statement sets out only my personal knowledge and recollection, in my own words.
       On points that I understand to be important in the case, I have stated honestly (a) how well I recall matters and (b) whether my memory has been refreshed by considering documents, if so how and when.

- The 'relevant legal representative' responsible for the case must certify that the Practice Direction has been complied with.[35]

III   PRODUCTION OF DOCUMENTS

Reference to the IBA Rules on the Taking of Evidence in International Arbitration has become a standard feature of most international arbitrations.

However, document production under Article 3(3) of the IBA Rules remains open to widely varying interpretations. In particular, there are widely different views as to what is relevant and material, and there is very little guidance.

Article 3(3) of the IBA Rules states as follows:

Article 3 Documents
   [...]
   3. A Request to Produce shall contain:
      (a)   (i) a description of each requested Document sufficient to identify it, or
            (ii) a description in sufficient detail (including subject matter) of a narrow and specific requested category of Documents that are reasonably believed to exist; in the case of Documents maintained in electronic form, the requesting Party may, or the Arbitral Tribunal may order that it shall be required to, identify specific files, search terms, individuals or other means of searching for such Documents in an efficient and economical manner;
      (b) *a statement as to how the Documents requested are relevant to the case and material to its outcome*; and
      (c)   (i) a statement that the Documents requested are not in the possession, custody or control of the requesting Party or a statement of the reasons why it would be unreasonably burdensome for the requesting Party to produce such Documents, and
            (ii) a statement of the reasons why the requesting Party assumes the Documents requested are in the possession, custody or control of another Party.'

(Emphasis added)

The criteria 'relevant to the case' and 'material to its outcome' are not defined in the IBA Rules. The official commentary also provides little guidance, beyond noting that the intention was to find 'a balanced compromise between the broader view [concerning requests for production of documents] generally taken in common law countries and the narrower view generally held in civil law countries', that Article 3.3 'is designed to prevent a broad "fishing expedition"', and that 'the relationship between the documents and the issues must be set forth in the request to produce with

---

I have not been asked or encouraged by anyone to include in this statement anything that is not my own account, to the best of my ability and recollection, of events I witnessed or matters of which I have personal knowledge.

35. PD57AC, para. 4.3.

sufficient specificity so that the arbitral tribunal can understand the purpose for which the requesting party needs the requested documents'.[36]

Given the compromise nature of Article 3.3 of the IBA Rules, it is no surprise that there is little guidance to fall back upon. It is also notable in this context that there is no relevant case law concerning the test for production of documents in England since the process of disclosure in the English courts is very different from production of documents under the IBA Rules.

Here too, however, inspiration can be found in Scottish civil procedure, which (coincidentally) has a strikingly similar system of document production to that under the IBA Rules.

The Scottish system of 'commission and diligence' is a formal procedure that allows parties to seek production of documents from each other. Relevance is determined quite strictly by reference to the parties' pleaded cases. A 'fishing expedition', which is defined as an attempt to obtain evidence regarding issues outside the scope of the pleadings, is generally not allowed.

The term 'fishing diligence' – i.e., a request for production of documents that is in the nature of a fishing expedition – has been used and defined in a long line of Scottish cases, including the following:

- In *Greig v. Crosbie* (1855) 18D 193, the Lord President (McNeill) said at page 195:

  > I am not inclined to grant this diligence. The pursuer comes into Court not knowing his own case; and the object of this diligence is obviously not to enable him to make his statements more specific, but to ascertain what his grounds of action really are. Such use of diligence is not permissible.

- In *Paterson v. Paterson* 1919 1 SLT 12, Lord Hunter said:

  > The recovery of documents in a cause is allowed in order that the court may be put in possession of documentary evidence bearing upon the issues of fact that have to be determined.

- In *Boyle v. Glasgow Royal Infirmary and Associated Hospitals* 1969 SC 72, Lord President Clyde at page 79 described a fishing diligence as:

  > [...] an attempt to recover documents in the hope that they will disclose material which will enable the party to make a case not yet averred on record.

- A slightly broader formulation is to be found in the Opinion of the Court, delivered by Lord Justice Clerk Ross in *Civil Service Building Society v. MacDougall* 1988 SC 58 at 62:

---

36. Commentary on the revised text of the 2020 IBA Rules on the Taking of Evidence in International Arbitration, pp. 9-11; *see* https://www.ibanet.org/MediaHandler?id = 4F797338-693E-47C7-A9 2A-1509790ECC9D (last accessed 11 June 2022).

> A fishing diligence is one for which there is no basis in the averments or one which involves too wide a search among all the papers of the haver.[37]

- Lord Sutherland was clearly using a piscatorial metaphor when, in *Parks v. Tayside Regional Council* 1989 SLT 345 at 347, he referred to a fishing diligence as implying that:

> [...] a trawl will be launched and then the catch inspected in the hope of finding something which might turn out to be useful.

- Lord Macphail stated in *Williamson v. The Advocate General for Scotland* 2006 SLT 611:

> It is obviously necessary to guard against the granting of a fishing or speculative diligence for the recovery of documents which a party hopes will disclose material for a case he has not averred in his pleadings when he has no reason to believe that the documents exist or that there is any foundation for the unpleaded case.

- In *McLean v. Argyll and Clyde Health Board* [2010] CSOH 54 at paragraph [12], Lord Brodie stated:

> The disinclination of the court to exercise its discretion to order recovery of documents in the hands of another party to the action or a third party arises from the nature of our system of civil litigation and the part that may be played in that by documents and the information contained in documents. Civil litigation is adversarial and not inquisitorial or investigative. A party who conceives he has a claim against another party is expected to articulate that claim. His opponent will then decide how he wishes to respond. Each party is entitled to have regard to his own interests. Neither party has an obligation to assist the other. The parties identify the issues and specify them in their written pleadings. Once the pleadings are finalised parties may get the opportunity to prove their respective averments but neither the proof nor the procedure leading up to it is of the nature of a general inquiry. Litigation is about the determination of issues brought to court by parties, not an exploration of what the issues might be. The right to apply to the court for an order for the recovery of documents is subordinate to that structure. Recovery may be ordered but only at the appropriate stage and for an appropriate purpose.

The authors of the textbook MacSporran and Young, *Commission and Diligence*, at paragraphs 3.29 to 3.36, identify three situations where the expression 'fishing diligence' can be used: (i) where there are no averments to support a call,[38] (ii) where the averments are too vague, and (iii) where the call is wider than necessary.[39]

---

37. The 'haver' is the formal term for the person who has the documents.
38. That is a specific request for production of documents.
39. Archibald MacSporran and Andrew Young, *Commission and Diligence*, W. Green (1995).

Obviously, all the above references relate specifically to Scottish civil litigation, and they are not directly applicable to international arbitration procedures. Nevertheless, I suggest that the same principles can broadly be applied in considering requests for production of documents pursuant to Article 3(3) of the IBA Rules. In short, document production should relate to the issues in dispute between the parties, and sometimes that means that the arbitral tribunal will need to ask the parties to clarify what those issues actually are.

It is notable that similar views have been expressed by the authors of a leading textbook on the IBA Rules – Khodykin, Mulcahy and Fletcher, *A Guide to the IBA Rules on the Taking of Evidence in International Arbitration*.[40] The authors note that there are two separate limbs to the test under Article 3.3(b) of the IBA Rules – 'relevant to the case' and 'material to its outcome' – both of which must be satisfied.[41] Accordingly, it is good practice for parties to explain in their document production requests the relationship between a document request and the issue in the written submissions to which it is said to relate.[42]

Regarding the 'material to the outcome' test, the authors note:

> [...] The document(s) must add something to the evidence on a factual issue that is on the critical path to a determination of the dispute. If it is clear that the document will have no bearing on the matters to be decided then the requirement is not met. [...].[43]

As to whether documents may be sought in aid of unformulated claims, the authors state as follows:

> It is stated elsewhere that document production under the IBA Rules cannot be used as a means of 'fishing' to identify possible new allegations or claims and that document production is aimed at obtaining evidence that is relevant and material to existing claims and issues in dispute between the parties. We agree with that position. However, the requirement of a current claim should not be applied too harshly. For example, a party may be about to amend its case to include new claims in circumstances where it would be inefficient to defer document requests relating to those new claims to a separate round of document production. The important point is that the requesting party should be in a position to explain and formulate the allegations being made in sufficiently precise terms for the benefit of the tribunal and its opponent. Provided such explanation can be provided, it will not always matter that the formal pleading containing the allegation follows shortly after the request. This will be something to be considered on a case-by-case basis.[44]

---

40. Roman Khodykin and Carol Mulcahy with consultant editor Nicholas Fletcher QC, *A Guide to the IBA Rules on the Taking of Evidence in International Arbitration*, Oxford University Press (2019).
41. Paragraphs (6.90)-(6.146).
42. Paragraph (6.99).
43. Paragraph (6.102).
44. Paragraph (6.110).

IV   DIVERSITY

The international arbitration community has made important progress in recent years towards creating some degree of gender diversity, but we need to do more to improve ethnic, cultural and linguistic diversity in international arbitration.

As was noted in the introduction to the ArbitralWomen/TDM Special Issue on 'Dealing with Diversity in International Arbitration',[45] twenty-five years ago no one was talking about 'diversity' in arbitration. Modern arbitration began to develop in the early twentieth century for use by European and North American businessmen when dealing with foreign disputes, and the arbitration community back then was:

> [...] a tightly-knit, Anglo-European (plus the odd American) gentlemen's club, where everyone knew everyone else, either personally or by reputation, where arbitrators and counsel regularly lunched or golfed together, and where everyone was usually familiar with the style and proclivities of the other members.

Thankfully, times have changed.

There is now an obvious need for the practice of international arbitration to reflect the wider world, not just the Anglo-Saxon 'Western' part of the world.

There are now several specialist LLM courses on international arbitration – including a specialist LLM course at Edinburgh University, in the city where this ICCA Congress is being held.[46] These courses attract students from a wide range of countries, and as a result, it is good to see that detailed knowledge of international arbitration is now widespread across the world.

Sadly, however, it remains quite difficult for students who graduate from such specialist courses to obtain jobs in international arbitration after graduation.

We all need to do better to improve such diversity. One concrete suggestion that I would like to put forward is for users and arbitral institutions to cater for, and encourage, arbitration in languages other than English. There is surely considerable scope for more international arbitration in Russian, Arabic, Chinese and Spanish, for example.

The Arbitration Institute of the Stockholm Chamber of Commerce sees several arbitrations every year in Russia, and there is a considerable need for neutral Russian-speaking arbitrators in order to deal effectively with such cases. Greater use of the Russian language would also automatically provide an opportunity for local counsel to gain new roles and influence. Many Russian and Commonwealth of Independent States (CIS) cases have traditionally been handled by English-speaking counsel and arbitrators sitting in London or in other European seats, but with a change in language there inevitably comes a change in approach, and often differences in cultural and commercial understanding.

---

45. Louise Barrington and Rashda Rana SC, ArbitralWomen/TDM Special Issue on 'Dealing with Diversity in International Arbitration', *TDM* 4 (2015): *see* https://www.transnational-dispute-management.com/article.asp?key = 2233 (last accessed 11 June 2022).
46. Another well-known course is the International Commercial Arbitration Law (ICAL) Masters Programme at Stockholm University, in the city where I now live and work.

Similarly, many Middle-Eastern arbitrations are held in English, but the use of Arabic would fundamentally change the people involved, and thus also the conduct of such arbitrations.

As China continues to grow, and as Mandarin Chinese becomes a *lingua franca* for a large population of people in Asia, we can expect to see more international arbitrations in Mandarin Chinese. Here too, it is important to understand that a change of language would profoundly affect the conduct of the arbitrations involved. I once acted for a Chinese client in an English-language arbitration against a US company, and I saw first-hand how much the Chinese party was clearly at a disadvantage because of the choice of English as the language of the arbitration.

Perhaps the most progress in this area has been in South America, where international arbitrations are now regularly conducted wholly or partly in Spanish or Portuguese.

I hope that the talented and multi-lingual students who graduate from international arbitration courses will lead the way in continuing to expand the international nature of arbitration. No longer is it necessary to work at a large US or European law firm to practice international arbitration. There are excellent international arbitration lawyers, and arbitrators, throughout the world.

In considering the issue of diversity in international arbitration, it is important to put emphasis on the word 'international'. It is only if our system of international arbitration is truly international that it will continue to survive in this globalised world. As with the debate about gender diversity, so too with racial, ethnic and linguistic diversity, the practitioners have to reflect the users.

V HOW SHOULD INTERNATIONAL ARBITRATION RESPOND TO WAR?

Finally, I return to the question that I posed at the end of my introduction. Following the Russian invasion of Ukraine on 24 February 2022, there have been many calls to shut out Russian companies and individuals from the global economy, but how should international arbitration respond?

I remain optimistic that international arbitration is a force for good in the world. The peaceful resolution of international disputes by independent and impartial tribunals upholding the rule of law should be encouraged and helped to flourish for the benefit of all.

In the face of such evil, my personal view is that we need to hang on to our principles. It is when the going gets tough that our principles matter most. All of us who are engaged in the system of international arbitration should support and uphold the rule of law. It is particularly in situations like this that the rule of law matters.

In connection with its 100th anniversary in 2017, the Arbitration Institute of the Stockholm Chamber of Commerce published a book entitled *Arbitrating for Peace – How Arbitration Made A Difference*, documenting fourteen landmark arbitration cases with geopolitical dimensions. It is fitting to end with the following words from the Foreword of that book, written by Former UN Secretary-General Kofi Annan:

The power of the rule of law represents an essential force in achieving sustainable societies. It is also a necessary building block to meet some of humanity's future challenges. Peace and security, sustainable and inclusive development, and the respect for human rights and the rule of law should be our focus as we strive to achieve a better world.

[...]

But peaceful resolution of disputes rarely makes the headlines. The use of the rule of law in pursuit of peace often takes place quietly, far away from the limelight. The heroes involved; the men and women who make substantial contributions and advance peace in their capacities as brave political leaders, engaged legal specialists and wise adjudicators of integrity, receive little praise in international media. Their success remains relatively unknown.

The achievements of the governments and arbitral tribunals depicted in this publication send a message of hope. They reinforce the belief that tense conflicts between international law and power politics can be overcome, and that countries do recognize and value a global rule-based system for harmony, peace and prosperity.

[...]

Arbitrating for Peace teaches us that the rule of law is one of the most powerful instruments we have for sustainable peace. Let us not forget.

VI   CONCLUSION

So how do you assess progress?

The answer is that it is often only possible to assess progress with the benefit of hindsight. I hope that, in twenty-five years' time, the world order will be more stable than it is now in 2022. I also hope that, in twenty-five years' time, international arbitration will continue to thrive. I wonder where the ICCA Congress will be then.

PART IV Once Upon a Time in International Arbitration

PANEL 2   I. Three Classics Revisited

CHAPTER 8

Putting the Abu Dhabi Oil Award's Methodology to the Test of Time

Nagla Nassar[*]

I   INTRODUCTION

The twenty-first century has ushered in a new era marked by globalization, digitalization and diversity. Against this background, it is interesting to cast our gaze back to the 1950s and ask whether one of the most famous (or infamous) awards in the history of arbitration is still relevant today. Commonly known as the Abu Dhabi Award, the decision in question, rendered by Lord Asquith of Bishopstone on 28 August 1951 in the case between Petroleum Development (Trucial Coast) Limited and His Excellency Sheikh Shakhbut Bin Sultan Bin Za'id,[1] unleashed intense debate, in large part

---

* International arbitrator and attorney, Cairo, Egypt; former co-rapporteur, ILA Committee on International Commercial Arbitration; Africa's 30 Arbitration Powerlist 2020 laureate; nagla@nasserlaw.org,
1. 'In the Matter of an Arbitration between Petroleum Development (Trucial Coast) Ltd. and the Sheikh of Abu Dhabi: Award of Lord Asquith of Bishopstone' (1952) 1(2) *International and Comparative Law Quarterly* 247-261; 'Arbitration Between Petroleum Development (Trucial

reflecting North/South dissensions rife in the middle of the last century, and gave rise to an abundance of scholarly comment.[2] Not only did the arbitrator's pronouncements spark controversy, but ideological stances taken on the basis of the decision led to the adoption of general measures to protect the interests of newly decolonized states.[3]

Moreover, the Abu Dhabi Award was one of a series of decisions[4] that profoundly undermined confidence in arbitration as a means of international dispute resolution. The distrust it aroused in certain quarters caused many to condemn international arbitration as an instrument at the service of multinationals in the developed world or as a means of coercion allowing countries in the North to inflict a new form of colonization on developing countries in the South. With hindsight, these criticisms need to be relativized, however. For although the Abu Dhabi Award may have caused shock waves on account of its total disregard for the legal system of the sovereign in question – especially as it was unprecedented and was delivered in a most insensitive manner – the decision – unlike some other awards[5] – cannot be accused of unmitigated bias towards the interests of the foreign investor nor of failing to give due consideration to the context in which the disputed agreement was concluded.

Coast) Ltd. and Sheikh of Abu Dhabi' (1953) 47(1) *American Journal of International Law* 156-159. References in this article are to the former publication.

2. *See, e.g.,* Khaled Muhamed Al-Jumah, 'Arab State Contract Disputes: Lessons from the Past' (2002) 17(3) *Arab Law Quarterly* 215-240; Otto Sandrock, ''Handcuffs' Clauses in International Commercial Contracts: Basic Reflections on the Autonomy of the Parties to Choose the Proper Law for Their Contracts' (1997) 31(4) *International Lawyer* 1105-1119; Georges R. Delaume, 'State Contracts and Transnational Arbitration' (1981) 75(4) *American Journal of International Law* 784-819; Piero Bernardini, 'The Law Applied by International Arbitrators to State Contracts', in Robert Briner, L. Yves Fortier, Klaus-Peter Berger and Jens Bredow (eds), *Law of International Business and Dispute Settlement in the 21st Century: Liber Amicorum Karl-Heinz Böckstiegel* (2001) 51-66; Mutasim Ahmad Alqudah, 'The Impact of Sharia on the Acceptance of International Commercial Arbitration in the Countries of the Gulf Cooperation Council' (2017) 20(1) *Journal of Legal, Ethical and Regulatory Issues*; Tom Childs, 'The Current State of International Oil and Gas Arbitration' (2018) 13(1) *Texas Journal of Oil, Gas, and Energy Law*; Babak Hendizadeh, 'International Commercial Arbitration: The Effect of Culture and Religion on Enforcement of Award' (LLM thesis, Queen's University, Kingston, Ontario, Canada, 2012).
3. For example, Charter of Economic Rights and Duties of States, UNGA Res. 3281 (XXIX) (12 December 1974); Permanent Sovereignty over Natural Resources. UNGA Res. 1803 (XVII) (14 December 1962) and UNGA Res. 2158 (XXI) (25 November 1966).
4. *See, e.g., Ruler of Qatar v. International Marine Oil Company Ltd.*, Award, 1 June 1953, (1957) 20 *International Law Reports* 534-547; *Saudi Arabia v. Arabian American Oil Company (Aramco)*, Award, 23 August 1958, (1963) 27 *International Law Reports* 117-233; *Sapphire International Petroleums Ltd. v. National Iranian Oil Company*, Award, 15 March 1963, (1967) 35 *International Law Reports* 136-192; *BP Exploration Company (Libya) Limited v. Government of Libyan Arab Republic*, Award, 10 October 1973, (1979) 53 *International Law Reports* 297-388; *Texaco Overseas Petroleum Company and California Asiatic Oil Company v. Government of the Libyan Arab Republic*, Award, 19 January 1977, (1979) 53 *International Law Reports* 389-511; *Libyan American Oil Company (LIAMCO) v. Government of the Libyan Arab Republic*, Award, 12 April 1977, (1982) 62 *International Law Reports* 140-219.
5. For example, *Sapphire International Petroleum, supra* n. 4, where the Swiss arbitrator awarded the Canadian claimant 'loss of profit due to a loss of opportunity to make profit'. The award of damages does not necessarily have to be tied to precise quantification of profit, so long as there is 'sufficient probability' that profit would have been made. So broad a criterion as was applied in *Sapphire* (loss of opportunity to make profit) could be used to catch consequential (indirect) damage, which, however, neither positive law nor international arbitration practice currently accepts as a recoverable head of damage.

The purpose of this article is not to resuscitate a timeworn discussion; that is readily available elsewhere for those interested in history. Our intention is rather to offer a new assessment of the Abu Dhabi Award based on an examination of the methodology the arbitrator used to reach his findings. Specifically, we will scrutinize his approach to identify the rules, standards and tests upon which it relies and to determine whether they can be considered congruent with the norms now applicable in international arbitration practice.

It must always be remembered that an award should not be considered in abstraction but must be analysed in light of the surrounding factual context and the particular circumstances of the case. The relevancy and aptness of any award are limited by its underlying factual context and circumstances, and the Abu Dhabi Award will be assessed to see if it is an exception or a confirmation of this rule.

II   THE FACTUAL SITUATION AND THE ISSUES IN DISPUTE

1   Facts and Historical Context

The arbitration in which the Abu Dhabi Award was rendered arose out of a concession agreement dated 11 January 1939 between the Ruler of Abu Dhabi and Petroleum Development (Trucial Coast) Limited relating to the exploration and production of mineral oils and their derivative and allied substances (hereinafter the 'Concession Agreement' or 'Agreement').[6]

At the time of the arbitration, the United Arab Emirates did not yet exist. In Lord Asquith's words, the principality of Abu Dhabi was 'a British-protected State; that is, its external relations are controlled by His Majesty. Internally, the Sheik is an absolute, feudal monarch.'[7] Lord Asquith did not further elaborate on the legal status of the principality or its system of government. The Abu Dhabi Award merely stated:

> Abu Dhabi has a coast line of about 275 miles on the Gulf. It is bounded on the west by the State of Qatar, and on the east by the State of Dubai, both much smaller States. These frontiers, however, were and are to some extent vague. So is its mainland area, which has been estimated at anything from 10,000 to 26,000 square miles.[8]

At the time the Concession Agreement was signed, the extent of the land mass of Abu Dhabi and the positioning of its boundaries were unclear. This was largely due to its origins as a sheikdom under tribal and itinerant rule situated on the so-called Trucial Coast bordering the Persian Gulf. During the nineteenth and early twentieth centuries, its economic development remained embryonic, depending essentially on the trading of pearls. As Lord Asquith put it: 'Abu Dhabi is a large, primitive, poor, thinly populated country, whose revenue, until oil was discovered, depended mainly on

---

6. A facsimile of the English version of the agreement held in the India Office Records and Private Papers at the British Library is available in the Qatar Digital Library, https://www.qdl.qa/archive/81055/vdc_100033359270.0x000003 (accessed 16 June 2022).
7. Abu Dhabi Award, § 1A, p. 247.
8. *Ibid.*

pearling.'[9] What he was saying, in other words, was that it lacked the constituents of a modern state.

Exploration and production agreements of the kind concluded between the company Petroleum Development and the sheikh of Abu Dhabi were something of a novelty in the early years of the twentieth century. They had little in common with the sophisticated arrangements that characterize modern production-sharing regimes. Hence, the Concession Agreement was a relatively slim document covering a mere eleven pages. Originally drafted in Arabic, the language of the ruler of Abu Dhabi, it briefly set out the terms of a relationship which was expected to last for seventy-five years. Unsurprisingly, barely ten years after its conclusion, it gave rise to a dispute over its interpretation and its scope, which became the subject of the arbitration under discussion in this article.

2   Disputed Issues

The parties to the Concession Agreement disagreed over the delimitation of the area covered by the concession and over the proper interpretation of the Agreement's provisions. Lord Asquith described the issues to be determined in the arbitration in the following terms:

> The questions referred to arbitration can usefully be paraphrased by expanding them into four, of which the first two deal with territorial waters and the second two with the submarine area outside territorial waters –
>
> (i) At the time of the agreement of January 11, 1939, did the respondent – the Sheikh – own the right to win mineral oil from the subsoil of the sea-bed subjacent to the territorial waters of Abu Dhabi? (There seems to be no doubt about this).
> (ii) If yes, did he by that agreement transfer such right to the claimant company?
> (iii) At the time of the agreement did he own (or as the result of a proclamation of 1949 did he acquire) the right to win mineral oil from the subsoil of any, and, if so, what submarine area lying outside territorial waters?
> (iv) If yes, was the effect of the agreement to transfer such original or acquired rights to the claimant company? (The Sheikh in 1949 – 10 years after this agreement – purported to transfer these last rights to an American company – the 'Superior Corporation': which the Petroleum Development Company claim he could not do, since he had already 10 years earlier parted with these same rights to themselves).
>
> I would add that the parties requested me to express a view both on question (iii) and on question (iv), even if owing to the answer given to one of these questions, the other should become academic; and the view expressed upon it at best an *obiter dictum*.[10]

---

9. *Ibid.*
10. *Ibid.*, § 2, p. 248.

Lord Asquith announced that the provisions he considered mainly relevant to determining these issues were Articles 2, 3, 12(a), 1 and 17 of the Concession Agreement, from which he quoted the salient passages:

Article 2 (a). The area included in this Agreement is the whole of the lands which belong to the rule of the Ruler of Abu Dhabi and its dependencies and all the islands and the sea waters which belong to that area. And if in the future the lands which belong to Abu Dhabi are defined by agreement with other States, then the limits of the area shall coincide with the limits specified in this definition. (b) If in the future a Neutral Area should be established adjacent to the lands of Abu Dhabi and the rights of rule over such Neutral Area be shared between the Ruler of Abu Dhabi and another Ruler, then the Ruler of Abu Dhabi undertakes that this Agreement shall include what mineral oil rights he has in that area. (c) The Company shall not undertake any works in areas used and set apart for places of worship or sacred buildings or burial grounds.

Article 3. The Ruler by this Agreement grants the Company the sole right, for a period of seventy-five years from the date of signature, to research for discover drill for and produce mineral oils and their derivatives and allied substances within the area, and the sole right to the ownership of all the substance produced, and free disposal thereof both inside and outside the Territory; provided that the export of oil shall be from the territory of the Concession direct without passing across any adjacent territory. And it is understood that this Agreement is a grant of rights over Oil and cannot be considered an Occupation in any manner whatsoever.

Article 12(a). The Ruler shall have right at any time to grant to a third party a Concession for any substances other than those specified in Article 3, on condition that this shall have no adverse effect on the operations and rights of the Company.

Article 1. The expression 'The Ruler' includes the present Ruler of Abu Dhabi and its dependencies and his heirs and successors to whom may in future be entrusted the rule of Abu Dhabi.

Article 17. The Ruler and the Company both declare that they base their work in this Agreement on goodwill and sincerity of belief and on the interpretation of this Agreement in a fashion consistent with reason. The Company undertakes to acknowledge the authority of the Ruler and his full rights as Ruler of Abu Dhabi and to respect it in all ways, and to fly the Ruler's flag over the Company's buildings.[11]

III   INTERPRETATION

The determination of the issues as framed above necessitated interpreting provisions of the Concession Agreement. In virtually all arbitrations, the interpretation of the agreement in dispute is a matter of central importance. It is the process whereby the parties' contractual rights and duties are delimited. As such, it is a core operation and in most cases will have a decisive impact on the outcome of the arbitration. The fact that in all of the petroleum arbitrations referred to in this article, the precise scope of the issues in dispute was principally dependent on the interpretation of the relevant provisions shows just how important and influential interpretation can be. The Abu

---

11. *Ibid.*, § 4, pp. 248–250.

Dhabi Award is no exception, for the resolution of all the issues listed in the preceding section turned on interpretation. For this reason, one of our main purposes will be to examine the method of interpretation applied in the Award to see whether it established standards of interpretation that have survived the test of time and could be applied in modern arbitration.

A preliminary question to be asked when addressing matters of interpretation is, what language was the agreement originally drafted in? If an arbitrator appointed to hear a case is not fluent in the original language of the contract that gave rise to the case, a translation will inevitably be required. The Concession Agreement was originally drafted in Arabic. In their pleadings, the parties relied on separate English translations, which diverged in places. Although for the sake of completeness, Lord Asquith reproduced both translations when quoting the relevant provisions of the Agreement, he brushed aside the differences as 'not important'.[12] It is to be hoped that Lord Asquith was right in thinking this and that the parties' intentions were not distorted or misrepresented in the translations. This is a peril to which any translation is exposed, and it is inevitable in situations where the arbitrator does not speak the language in which the parties conducted their negotiations and concluded their contract. Nowadays, however, the pool of qualified arbitrators is much wider, so it can be expected that an arbitrator with the required knowledge or the skills necessary to acquire such knowledge would be appointed in a case such as this. This is especially so, now that international arbitration practice has embraced the need to recognize diversity through greater inclusiveness. Diversity is instrumental to attaining better justice, insofar as it helps to ensure that the pool of available practitioners offers a wide range of attributes and qualifications.

Given that reliance on translations was thus unavoidable in this case and that the two translations adduced by the parties displayed some differences, Lord Asquith declared that an initial question raised by the arbitration was to identify 'the true translation of the Agreement'. He responded as follows:

> I have indicated the two rival translations of the contract of 1939. There is in this matter little conflict; and there would probably have been even less but for the circumstance that the Arabic of the Gulf, in which the contract is framed, is an archaic variety of the language, bearing, I was told, some such relation to modern current Arabic as Chaucer's English does to modern English. Such discrepancies, however, as exist between the two translations are fortunately trivial, and the claimants were willing for purposes of argument to accept the translation put forward on behalf of the respondent. I therefore adopt that translation in what follows.[13]

Lord Asquith's pronouncement on the original language of the Concession Agreement is surprising, to say the least, and seems difficult to justify given that his command of Arabic remains uncertain. Furthermore, the award contains no reasoning explaining the recourse to English as the language of arbitration – be it the language of the proceedings, the language to be used for submissions or the language of the

---

12. *Ibid.*, § 4, p. 248.
13. Abu Dhabi Award, § 5, p. 250.

award.[14] Nor is there any reference to language in the arbitration clause. It would seem that either the parties agreed elsewhere on the use of English, or English was used by default, being the native language of Lord Asquith and of the parties' respective counsel.

That said, the claimant's acceptance of the translation relied upon by the respondent made the entire issue of translation discrepancies moot.[15] As Lord Asquith rightly remarked, given that the parties had agreed on this matter, it was not for him to go against their common consent. This is an established rule of law deriving from the principle of party autonomy, which is a cornerstone of modern arbitration practice in the twenty-first century.[16]

After dealing with the language question, Lord Asquith embarked on the task of interpretation as such. Rightly or wrongly, he was guided in this task by his own perceptions and knowledge, rather than the rules of a given legal system.[17] This eclectic interpretative approach can be seen in his treatment of the legal issues raised by the questions concerning territorial waters. It will be discussed in section IV below. Section V will consider the methodology used by Lord Asquith to decide the issue for which the award is perhaps best known – the proper law of the contract. Lastly, in section VI consideration will be given to the formation of the tribunal, which, although rarely discussed, is a very relevant aspect of the methodological approach adopted by Lord Asquith in his award.

IV   CONTINENTAL SHELF DOCTRINE

As formulated by Lord Asquith, the central questions to be determined in the arbitration were whether at the time the Concession Agreement was concluded in 1939, the sheikh possessed the right to extract mineral oil from, on the one hand, the subsoil of the seabed subjacent to the territorial waters of Abu Dhabi and, on the other hand, the subsoil of any submarine areas lying outside territorial waters. Lord Asquith unhesitatingly answered the first question in the affirmative. On the second question, by contrast, he went into much more detail, for it raised the question of the applicability of the so-called continental shelf doctrine. Lord Asquith rejected the

---

14. In this respect, it contrasts with modern awards, which, especially if the language of the arbitration is not specified in the arbitration clause, often go into the question in great detail, perhaps encouraged by the fact that the language of the arbitration is an aspect of the proceedings now expressly mentioned in all major international arbitration rules. *See, e.g.,* UNCITRAL Arbitration Rules 2013, Article 19; ICC Arbitration Rules 2021, Article 20; ICDR International Arbitration Rules 2021, Article 20.

15. As the version endorsed in the Award, this will also be the translation used for quotations in the present article.

16. *See* Sunday A. Fagbemi, 'The Doctrine of Party Autonomy in International Commercial Arbitration: Myth or Reality?' (2015) 6(1) *Journal of Sustainable Development Law and Policy* 223-246; Giuditta Cordero-Moss, 'Limits to Party Autonomy in International Commercial Arbitration' (2014) 1(1) *Oslo Law Review* 47-66.

17. A similar approach was followed in some subsequent petroleum arbitrations; *see, e.g., Aramco, supra* n. 4, p. 172 ('The interpretation of contracts is not governed by rigid rules; it is rather an art, governed by principles of logic and common sense, which purports to lead to an adaptation, as reasonable as possible, of the provisions of a contract to the facts of a dispute.').

doctrine's applicability, rightly remarking that at the time the Concession Agreement was concluded, 'neither contracting party had ever heard of the doctrine of the Continental Shelf, which as a legal doctrine did not then exist. No thought of it entered their heads. None such entered that of the most sophisticated jurisconsult, let alone the "understanding" perhaps strong, but "simple and unschooled" of Trucial Sheikhs'.[18]

Instead, Lord Asquith resorted to what is known as the principle of contemporaneous interpretation to determine the parties' intentions.[19] This principle requires that, when interpreting a contract, consideration be given to the context and the parties' intentions at the time of its conclusion, not at the time of its interpretation.[20] Applying this principle, Lord Asquith concluded as follows:

> Directed, as I apprehend I am, to apply a simple and broad jurisprudence to the construction of this contract, it seems to me that it would be a most artificial refinement to read back into the contract the implications of a doctrine not mooted till seven years later, and, if the view which I am about to express is sound, not even today admitted to the canon of international law.[21]

Notwithstanding his finding that the continental shelf doctrine was inapplicable, Lord Asquith went on 'to consider this doctrine more narrowly'.[22] This was because the parties had so requested, even though, as he himself admitted, extensive analysis would be an 'academic' exercise and 'the view expressed upon it at best an *obiter dictum*'.[23] Lord Asquith thus undertook what turned out to be a very lengthy scholarly analysis, which, although justified by the parties' request, does not need to be analysed here. What we are concerned with here is not so much the analysis itself, but rather the appropriateness and correctness of his methodology of interpretation.

According to the methodology of contemporaneous interpretation, it is the meaning that the words of an agreement have at the time of its conclusion that determines the creation and existence of contractual rights, not the meaning they have at the time of interpreting the agreement. In other words, the agreement is to be examined in the context that prevailed at the time of its conclusion, not one existing possibly years thereafter. It is the parties' intentions at the time of contracting, not at the time of implementation of the contract, that are determinative.

As such, this methodology can be considered an inflection of the established contract law principle of *pacta sunt servanda* – sanctity of contracts – which is widely

---

18. Abu Dhabi Award, § 5, p. 253.
19. The expression 'contemporaneous interpretation' is mostly used in relation to international treaties and is distinguished from 'evolutionary interpretation'. It is beyond the scope of this article to discuss the abundant literature that has been published on the principle.
20. *See* Stefan Vogenauer, 'Interpretation of Contracts: Concluding Comparative Observations' (2007) Oxford Legal Studies Research Paper No. 7/2007, in Andrew Burrows and Edwin Peel (eds), *Contract Terms* (Oxford University Press, 2007) pp. 123-150; Lucy Greenwood, 'Principles of Interpretation of Contracts under English Law and Their Application in International Arbitration' (2019) 35(1) *Arbitration International* 21-27; Gregory Klass, 'Interpretation and Construction in Contract Law' (2018) Georgetown Law Faculty Publications and Other Works 1947, https://scholarship.law.georgetown.edu/facpub/1947/ (accessed 20 June 2022).
21. Abu Dhabi Award, § 5, p. 253.
22. *Ibid.*
23. *Ibid.*, § 2, p. 248.

recognized in modern arbitration practice.[24] Taken literally, it would imply the freezing of contracts at a given point in time – that of their conclusion. However, it overlooks the fact that a contract may entail long-term commitments and thus have an existence that continues into the future.

The continental shelf doctrine is a development that occurred after the conclusion of the Concession Agreement. Hence, it cannot be considered part of its context and is immaterial to the legal regime governing the parties' agreement, which is determined by reference to the moment when it was concluded.

In Lord Asquith's approach to contemporaneous interpretation, knowledge has an important part to play. The parties' knowledge forms part of the context in which an agreement is concluded and thus has a bearing on its meaning when applying the methodology of contemporaneous interpretation. For Lord Asquith, however, knowledge was to be understood as constructive knowledge rather than actual knowledge. While reliance on constructive knowledge may limit the applicable legal rules to those in place at the time of contracting, it may at the same time frustrate an attempt to plead ignorance of the law. For it was on the grounds of constructive knowledge – that is, knowledge a party must be assumed to possess at the time of contracting – that Lord Asquith rejected what he considered as a far-fetched – or, in his own words, 'unjustifiable' and even 'perverse' – reading of the wording of the Concession Agreement:

> I am not impressed by the argument that there was in 1939 no word for 'territorial waters' in the language of Abu Dhabi or that the Sheik was quite unfamiliar with that conception. Mr Jourdain had none the less been talking 'prose' all his life because the fact was only brought to his attention somewhat late. Every State is owner and sovereign in respect of its territorial waters, their bed and subsoil, whether the Ruler has read the works of Bynkershoek or not. The extent of the Ruler's Dominion cannot depend on his accomplishment as an international jurist.[25]

While denying the respondent the right to plead its unfamiliarity with a foreign legal concept, Lord Asquith's methodology fixed the agreement in the legal context prevailing at the time of its conclusion, in opposition to an understanding of context as being subject to change and of the contract as continuing its existence in evolving circumstances. In so doing, the Abu Dhabi Award established a rule which subsequently developed into what became known as the stabilization of the proper law of the contract, where the governing law is the law of the host state.[26] Whether

---

24. *See* Thomas Wälde, 'The "Umbrella" (or Sanctity of Contract/Pacta sunt Servanda) Clause in Investment Arbitration', https://www.biicl.org/files/946_thomas_walde_presentation.pdf (accessed 23 June 2022). *See also* Nagla Nassar, *Sanctity of Contracts Revisited: A Study in the Theory and Practice of International Commercial Transactions* (Martinus Nijhoff, 1995).

25. Abu Dhabi Award, § 5, p. 253.

26. The stabilization of the governing law found its way into bilateral investment treaties; *see, e.g.,* Katja Gehne and Romulo Brillo, 'Stabilization Clauses in International Investment Law: Beyond Balancing and Fair and Equitable Treatment', *Beiträge zum Transnationalen Wirtschaftsrecht,* No. 143 (March 2017), http://telc.jura.uni-halle.de/sites/default/files/BeitraegeTWR/Heft%20 143.pdf (accessed 23 June 2022). A detailed discussion of the stabilization rule (subsequently materialized in the stabilization clause) is beyond the scope of this article. See majority decision

intentionally or unintentionally, the creation of this rule was the consequence of Asquith's interpretation methodology. Yet, was it necessary to search so far for a ground on which to reject the application of the continental shelf doctrine? The same result could have been achieved by simply declaring that it did not form part of international law at the time when the dispute arose.[27] Lord Asquith chose otherwise, however, resorting to an interpretation methodology that veered into uncharted waters, bringing the risk of uncalculated outcomes.

V   APPLICABLE LAW

As a prerequisite to resolving the issues raised by the arbitration, Lord Asquith enquired into the law governing the Concession Agreement. Although not stated in so many words, it is clear from the award that Abu Dhabi law was purported to be the proper law of the Concession Agreement. This was a possibility Lord Asquith could not admit, however:

> What is the 'Proper Law' applicable in construing this contract? This is a contract made in Abu Dhabi and wholly to be performed in that country. If any municipal system of law were applicable, it would prima facie be that of Abu Dhabi. But no such law can reasonably be said to exist. The Sheikh administers a purely discretionary justice with the assistance of the Koran; and it would be fanciful to suggest that in this very primitive region there is any settled body of legal principles applicable to the construction of modern commercial instruments.[28]

One would have expected that, even in 1951 and even though Abu Dhabi was not a full-fledged modern state, a tribunal in a case of the size and importance of the Abu Dhabi arbitration would have acted with greater diligence by making a serious effort to ascertain the content of the laws of Abu Dhabi rather than simply dismissing the conceivability of their existence as 'fanciful'. In this respect, Lord Asquith's methodology is not just weak and lacking in courtesy and respect towards the host state, but is gravely wrong.

Modern arbitration practice does not look kindly on conduct that consists in casting aside a matter without proper investigation or reasoning. Admittedly, lack of reasoning and impropriety are not grounds on which the recognition or enforcement of an award may be refused, nor are they a lawful cause for setting aside under most arbitration regimes.[29] However, they certainly discredit an arbitrator and would justify

---

in *Government of Kuwait v. American Independent Oil Company (Aminoil)*, Award, 24 March 1982, (1984) 66 *International Law Reports* 518-627, where stabilization was disregarded and the sovereign right to change the content of the applicable law was recognized against payment of fair compensation.

27. Lord Asquith himself stated that at the time of the award the continental shelf doctrine had still not been 'admitted to the canon of international law'; Abu Dhabi Award, § 5, p. 253.
28. Abu Dhabi Award, § 5, p. 250.
29. On the role of reasoning, *see, e.g.*, Pierre Lalive, 'On the Reasoning of International Arbitral Awards', (2010) 1(1) *Journal of International Dispute Settlement* 55-65; S.I. Strong 'Reasoned Awards in International Commercial Arbitration: Embracing and Exceeding the Common Law-Civil Law Dichotomy', (2015) 37(1) *Michigan Journal of International Law*, https://

branding the arbitrator as inept and unworthy of their function. In an age when the selection of arbitrators makes use of algorithms and computer software, candidates should be aware that their position on rosters is likely to be weakened by the negative counts such conduct is likely to signify.

Having refused the application of Abu Dhabi law, Lord Asquith then considered whether English law might be applicable. He rejected this possibility, too, though with more tact: 'Nor can I see any basis on which the municipal law of England could apply.'[30] Albeit with more graciousness, the matter was again brushed aside without proper investigation or reasoning. One might have thought that a case could be made for applying English law. Given that Abu Dhabi was a British protectorate and that, according to Lord Asquith, a 'settled body of legal principles' was unimaginable in such a 'primitive region', then the law of the protecting state – that is, Britain – might be thought to qualify as the applicable law by default or as a fallback. But Lord Asquith did not see fit to pursue that path. Instead, he relied on Article 17 of the Concession Agreement to rule out the application of any municipal laws at all:

> On the contrary, Clause 17 of the agreement, cited above, repels the notion that the municipal law of any country, as such, could be appropriate. The terms of that Clause invite, indeed prescribe, the application of principles rooted in the good sense and common practice of the generality of civilised nations – a sort of 'modern law of nature'.

The provision that Lord Asquith invokes at the start of his wanton journey of cherry-picking among different legal rules stated as follows:

> The Ruler and the Company both declare that they base their work in this Agreement on goodwill and sincerity of belief and on the interpretation of this Agreement in a fashion consistent with reason. The Company undertakes to acknowledge the authority of the Ruler and his full rights as Ruler of Abu Dhabi and to respect it in all ways, and to fly the Ruler's flag over the Company's buildings.

The plain meaning of the above text in no way supports Lord Asquith's position. Rather, the parties were simply declaring their intention, on the one hand, to perform their obligations under the Concession Agreement in good faith ('goodwill and sincerity of belief') and, on the other hand, to use the criterion of reasonableness, as opposed to any technical criterion, when interpreting the agreement. Article 17 is not a governing law clause, and there is certainly nothing in it to support the view that the proper law of the Concession Agreement was a 'modern law of nature',[31] whatever that might be or mean.

---

repository.law.umich.edu/mjil/vol37/iss1/1/ (accessed 23 June 2022); Jacob Frank, 'Insufficient Reasoning: A Proper Basis for Setting Aside an Award?', https://svjt.se/content/insufficient-reasoning-proper-basis-setting-aside-award (accessed 23 June 2022); Peter Gillies and Niloufer Selvadurai, 'Reasoned Awards: How Extensive Must the Reasoning Be?', (2008) 74 *Arbitration* 125-132.

30. Abu Dhabi Award, § 5, p. 251.

31. *See, e.g., BP Exploration Company (Libya) Limited, supra* n. 4, where Clause 28(7) of the disputed concession agreement provided: 'This Concession shall be governed by and interpreted in accordance with the principles of law of Libya common to the principles of international law

Nor does Lord Asquith's reference to 'the application of principles rooted in the good sense and common practice of the generality of civilised nations'[32] provide any enlightenment. Leaving aside the expression 'civilised nations', which is now archaic, it is unclear what is meant by 'good sense' and 'reason'. Abstract concepts such as these are known to be relative and often highly subjective. Again, Lord Asquith made no effort to clarify the tenor of these abstractions. The good sense or reason of whom? one might ask. Of the arbitrator, is the clear answer, and unbridled to boot.

Lord Asquith went on:

> But, albeit English municipal law is inapplicable *as such*, some of its rules are in my view so firmly grounded in reason, as to form part of this board body of jurisprudence – this 'modern law of nature'.[33]

He followed this with examples of English law rules – familiar territory to him – that could or could not be considered part of the 'modern law of nature',[34] considering as acceptable a rule 'so firmly grounded in reason, as to form part of … this "modern law of nature"' to be acceptable, but unacceptable one bearing 'little relevance to conditions in a protected State of a primitive order on the Persian Gulf'.[35]

It is hard to explain why the admissibility of prior negotiations was rejected, given that such negotiations are material to the construction of an agreement, while the English rule giving paramount importance to the actual language of a written instrument was accepted. The words 'in my view' and 'to my mind' leave no doubt as to the subjectivity of Lord Asquith's cherry-picking, for which there are no objective explanations. And even with respect to the 'modern law of nature', Lord Asquith's reference

---

and in the absence of such common principles then by and in accordance with the general principles of law, including such of those principles as may have been applied by international tribunals.'

32. Abu Dhabi Award, § 5, p. 251.
33. *Ibid*.
34. *Ibid*.:

> For instance, while in this case evidence has been admitted as to the nature of the negotiations leading up to, and of the correspondence both preceding and following the conclusion of the agreement, which evidence as material for construing the contract might, according to domestic English law be largely inadmissible, and to this extent the rigid English rules have been disregarded; yet on the other hand the English rule which attributes paramount importance to the actual language of the written instrument in which the negotiations result seems to me no mere idiosyncrasy of our system, but a principle of ecumenical validity. Chaos may obviously result if that rule is widely departed from; and if, instead of asking what the words used mean, the inquiry extends at large to what each of the parties meant them to mean, and how and why each phrase came to be inserted
>
> The same considerations seem to me to apply to the principle *expressio unius est exclusio alterius*. I defer entirely to the warnings given by Wills J. and Lopes L.J. in the case of *Colquhous* v. *Brooks* (19 Q.B.D. 400, at p. 406; 21 Q.B.D. 52, at p. 65), as to the possibilities (and indeed the frequency) of its misapplication. But confined within its proper borders it seems to me mere common sense. (If I have a house and a garden and 200 acres of agricultural land and if I recite this and let to X 'my house and garden', it seems obvious that the 200 acres are excluded from the lease.)
>
> Much more dubious to my mind is the application to this case of certain other English maxims relied on by one or the other party in this case. …

35. Abu Dhabi Award, § 5, p. 251.

to 'principles rooted in good sense and common practice of the generality of civilized nations' is insufficiently precise to serve as a definition or a guiding standard.

Is this 'modern law of nature' kin to *lex mercatoria*? Is it an avatar of the laws of nature? Is it to be equated with equity? No one knows. A question mark remains over what Lord Asquith really meant by 'modern law of nature'. Based on Lord Asquith's own words, one can only assume that it is a collection of rules sufficiently 'grounded in reason' to form part of a 'broad body of jurisprudence'. But again, there is no criterion for deciding whether a specific rule qualifies for admission into this prestigious legal corpus. At what point does a rule become sufficiently 'grounded in reason' to be consecrated as a component of the 'modern law of nature'? In short, this 'modern law of nature' is but an eclectic collection of rules whose origins lie not in a particular legal system but in the 'common sense' of the likes of Lord Asquith and the nations an unspecified authority recognizes as 'civilized' to which he and his fellows belong. To say the least, such an elitist and self-serving approach is not only divisive but also destructive.

By current standards of international arbitration practice, a selective approach that favours certain rules in a given legal system is neither commendable nor creditable. Elitism might have worked well in a world where there were a handful of players forming a closed club and where the vested interests and risks were manifest and clearly circumscribed. In an exceedingly complex world where playing fields are open and actors unknowable in person or in advance and where vested interests and risks crisscross, it is a most dangerous approach to adopt. The quality of justice cannot be left so utterly to the arbitrator's pleasing. In arbitrators, we must trust ... within certain limits.

Reliance on the arbitrator's or the tribunal's 'good sense' and 'rules firmly grounded in reason' amounts to determining matters not in accordance with the rule of law but rather as an *amiable compositeur*. Current international practice allows an arbitrator to act as an *amiable compositeur* only if this has been expressly authorized by the parties in dispute or provided for in their arbitration agreement. Yet, there is no reference thereto in the Concession Agreement.[36] Lord Asquith must therefore be considered to have acted beyond his authority with the consequence, under international instruments that were shortly to follow,[37] that the award could be set aside or refused recognition and enforcement for want of jurisdiction, rather than for lack of reasoning.

That said, it is worth pausing over reasoning as a ground for setting aside an award. Article V of the New York Convention does not include deficiency or a total absence of reasoning as a ground allowing a contracting state to deny recognition or enforcement in its territory of a foreign award issued in another contracting state.

---

36. The Concession Agreement's dispute resolution clause is reproduced in section VI below.
37. Namely, UN Convention on the Recognition and Enforcement of Foreign Arbitral Awards, adopted 10 June 1958, entered into force 7 June 1959, 330 UNTS 3 (New York Convention), art. V(1)(c) ('award ... contains decisions on matters beyond the scope of the submission to arbitration'); UNCITRAL Model Law on International Commercial Arbitration, adopted 21 June 1985, amended 7 July 2006, Articles 34(2)(a)(iii), 36(1)(a)(iii) ('award deals with a dispute not contemplated by or not falling within the terms of the submission to arbitration').

Nonetheless, the omission of reasoning could justify refusing recognition or enforcement under the New York Convention on the grounds of comity and reciprocity – two principles fundamental to the Convention and crucial to contracting states' adhesion and commitment to it. Nor is there any reference to reasoning in the UNCITRAL Model Law, whether as a ground for setting aside an award under Article 34 or refusing recognition and enforcement under Article 36.

By contrast, the Uniform Act on Arbitration Law of the Organisation pour l'harmonisation en Afrique du droit des affaires (OHADA) recognizes the absence of reasoning (though not deficient reasoning) as a ground for setting aside an award.[38] The OHADA Uniform Act is a more modern instrument than the New York Convention and the UNCITRAL Model Law and reflects the new realities of the twenty-first century. The New York Convention was negotiated in the mid-twentieth century at the height of the decolonization struggle and the UNCITRAL Model Law barely three decades later. These two instruments reflect the geo-economic and -political power structure prevailing at the time. However, the world has since moved on, far beyond the decolonization era, which explains the change of approach in Article 26 of the OHADA Uniform Act.

In today's globalized, diversified and digitalized world, where interrelations and interdependencies are so prevalent, it is hard to ignore the importance of reasoning. For it is through reasoning that the quality of the award and the arbitrator's neutrality can be assured – two issues that the current insistence on ethical standards and quality control have brought to the fore. It is therefore surprising that loopholes still exist in international arbitration instruments that could allow the mischief of the Abu Dhabi Award's reasoning methodology to resurface.

A firm stand is needed to avoid that risk. That need is all the greater as the volume of international commercial and investment disputes referred to arbitration far exceeds and overshadows those handled by national courts. Justice is administered in domestic courts largely without regard to who is sitting on the bench, and the same needs to be the case in arbitration. The quality of justice must not be so heavily exposed to the idiosyncrasies of arbitrators, and proper standards of reasoning may well serve as a means of attaining that goal.

VI   COMPOSITION OF THE TRIBUNAL

The Concession Agreement contained a dispute resolution clause which read as follows:

> Article 15.
>
> (a) If at any time during the currency of this Agreement, there should any difference or dispute between the two parties as to the interpretation or execution of any provision thereof, or anything herein contained or in connection herewith, such dispute shall be referred to two arbitrators, one selected by

---

38. OHADA, Acte uniforme relative au droit de l'arbitrage, adopted 23 November 2017 (replacing the initial text of adopted 11 March 1999), Article 26(f) ('An action for annulment is admissible only ... if the award does not state the reasons upon which it is based').

each of the two parties, and a referee to be chosen by the arbitrators before proceeding to arbitration.

(b) Each party shall nominate its arbitrator within sixty days after the delivery of a request as [*sic*] to do by the other party, falling which its arbitrator may, at the request of the other party, be designated by the British Political Resident in the Persian Gulf. In the event of the arbitrators failing to agree upon the referee within sixty days of being chosen or designated, the British Political Resident in the Persian Gulf may appoint a referee at the request of the arbitrators or of either of them.

(c) The decision of the arbitrators, or in the case of a difference of opinion between them the decision of the referee shall be final and binding on both parties.

(d) In giving a decision the arbitrators or the referee shall notify an adequate period of delay during which the party against whom the decision is given shall conform thereto, and that party shall be in default only if he has failed to conform to the decision prior to the expiry of that period, and not otherwise.

(e) The place of arbitration shall be such as may be agreed by the parties, and in default of agreement shall be London or Baghdad.

According to subparagraph (b) above, a three-member tribunal – not a sole arbitrator – was envisaged by the parties in their agreement. Subparagraph (c) does not authorize the referee to decide the matter as a sole arbitrator; it simply provides that the third arbitrator (the referee) shall have the casting decision in the event of disagreement between the arbitrators.

It is clear from Lord Asquith's words in his award that a three-member tribunal was never formed:

> [The parties'] written agreement contained an arbitration clause, providing for the reference of disputes under it to arbitration, for the appointment of two arbitrators, and for the appointment of an umpire in the event of the two arbitrators being unable to agree. ... [T]he said arbitrators did differ; and appointed me as umpire.

Clearly, two arbitrators were appointed and could not agree; thereupon, by consent, Lord Asquith was appointed and decided the dispute as a sole arbitrator. Even if it could be argued that the parties agreed to the tribunal being constituted in this unorthodox manner, such a way of proceeding is not only at variance with modern international arbitration rules on the formation of arbitral tribunals but also fails to honour the parties' agreement through an interpretation that upholds their shared intention.

In today's world, this would be yet another valid ground – namely, composition of the arbitral tribunal not in accordance with the parties' agreement – for refusing recognition and enforcement, as provided in Article V(1)(d) of the New York Convention and Article 36(1)(a)(iv) of the UNCITRAL Model Law, or for setting aside the award, as provided in Article 34(2)(a)(iv) of the UNCITRAL Model Law.

VII   CONCLUSION

It is dangerous, if not improper and misleading, to retread old ground, and especially decisions, with hindsight. Times change, and so do the context and circumstances in which an award is issued. That is why revisiting a seventy-year-old award is, to say the least, a challenging and risky exercise. International arbitration in the 1950s is not the same as arbitration in the 2020s. It has in the meantime developed from relative infancy to full adulthood on the strength of acquired experience and developing rules. Arbitration practice today is a totally different creature from that of the mid-twentieth century; the players are different, as are the rules, standards and expectations. It is no longer an informal way of resolving disputes, but a highly developed practice with a body of detailed rules and abundant case law. It has become more regulated and institutionalized, even if this has been at the cost of some flexibility. Nowadays, most arbitrators do not come from other legal disciplines. The majority are no longer former judges or professors; they are homegrown, highly trained and dedicated professionals.

When revisiting an old award, it is inevitable that current rules and practices will colour the way it is perceived. The Abu Dhabi Award concerned a dispute between a foreign private investor and a state. Under present conditions, it could have been either an International Centre for Settlement of Investment Disputes (ICSID) arbitration (the United Kingdom and the United Arab Emirates both being signatories to the ICSID Convention[39]) or, less likely, an ad hoc or institutional commercial arbitration. In both hypotheses, it is highly improbable that the tribunal would have been constituted in such an idiosyncratic manner in a case of such magnitude. Nor is it likely that Lord Asquith would have been allowed to decide the matter as a sole arbitrator. In all probability, Article 15 of the Concession Agreement would be interpreted as implying the constitution of a three-member tribunal, with the attribution of special powers to the presiding arbitrator. In addition, today's norm is to reason the choice of the language of the arbitration in the absence of the parties' agreement thereon – be that in the arbitration agreement itself or after the dispute has arisen. Similarly, it is doubtful that the Abu Dhabi Award would have survived the scrutiny of an ICSID annulment committee, falling on one of the grounds for annulment listed in Article 52 of the ICSID Convention. In an ad hoc or institutional commercial arbitration, the Abu Dhabi Award would not have fared any better, whether in withstanding attempts to have it refused recognition or enforcement under the New York Convention or the UNCITRAL Model Law or in resisting a set-aside action brought in one of the many countries that have adopted legislation based on the UNCITRAL Model Law.[40] All in all, the Abu Dhabi Award's chances of survival must be rated very low by today's standards. Indeed, by those standards, it could not but fall. This invites us to ask whether awards should be concerned simply with resolving the disputes in the best possible way to achieve justice, or whether they should be equally, or more, concerned with establishing rules that will survive the test of time. That, however, is a discussion for another time and place.

---

39. Convention on the Settlement of Investment Disputes between States and Nationals of Other States (1966). The Convention entered into force in respect of the United Kingdom on 18 January 1967 and in respect of the United Arab Emirates on 22 January 1982.
40. For the list of states that have adopted legislation based on the UNCITRAL Model Law, see https://uncitral.un.org/en/texts/arbitration/modellaw/commercial_arbitration/status (accessed 25 June 2022).

CHAPTER 9

Why Investment Treaties Should Not Be Subverted by *Barcelona Traction*

Jan Paulsson[*]

TABLE OF CONTENTS

In 1958, the International Court of Justice (ICJ) was seized by Belgium, espousing the claims of the predominant Belgian shareholders in the Barcelona Traction Company. They alleged that the Company had been plundered with the complicity of the Spanish judiciary – a denial of justice and thus a breach of international law. The ICJ took twelve years to dismiss the case on a preliminary issue: standing to sue.

The case is invariably cited as the manifestation of a rule of customary international law that shareholders may not bring claims for losses caused to their company. (Barcelona Traction was incorporated in Canada, but the Canadian government had no interest in espousing its claim).

This precedent, handed down in 1970, presented a major obstacle to the protection of foreign investment. The rule was reversed by the *lex specialis* of treaties which flourished, coincidentally or not, in its aftermath. The chart below demonstrates, again coincidentally or not, a dramatic evolution of foreign direct investment in the years 1985-2010, particularly when compared to the tiny upturn in foreign aid. And yet today investment treaties are under attack, and one of the proposals to diminish

---

[*]   Honorary President of ICCA; Avocat honoraire of the Paris Bar; Judge on the Court of Cassation of Bahrain.

their impact is precisely to reduce the protection of foreign investors by resurrecting the *Barcelona Traction* rule. It is a bad idea.

> *Andrew Schriner and Daniel Oerther, 'No really, (crowd) work is the silver bullet',* Procedia Engineering *vol. 78 p. 224 (2014). The article references data published by OECD and UNCTAD. The authors write, at p. 226: 'Beyond being closely related to economic growth, providing opportunities to work for income eliminates the damaging incentives created by aid handouts. When the path to development goes through employment, there is an incentive to use resources to invest in the future: e.g., education, physical capital, infrastructure.'*

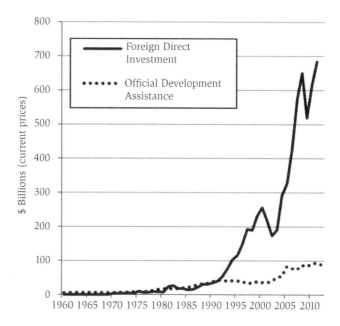

I   THE FACTS

The claimants in *Barcelona Traction*, foreign investors in Spain, alleged that in 1948, they had been the victims of one the most scandalous acts of corporate hijacking in history. Their oppressor was a man named Juan March, a reputed financial predator and master of the dark arts of smuggling, currency manipulation, corporate extortion, influence peddling, and brazen corruption. He was the subject of one of the longest and most extensively researched articles ever to appear in the *New Yorker* magazine, written by the prominent financial writer John Brooks in 1979 and so lengthy that it appeared in instalments.[1]

---

1. 'Privateer', 14 and 21 May 1979. March's first fortune was made smuggling tobacco from North Africa, but he ended up owning a dazzling array of businesses, becoming the richest man in Spain – sixth richest in the world. He ingratiated himself with a succession of Spanish governments, and

Brooks' article explained how March used the Spanish legal system to steal one of the most prosperous corporations in the country from its foreign owners. His victim – Barcelona Traction – had brought state-of-the-art hydroelectric power generation to Spain. After a few decades, it was producing 20% of Spain's power. Juan March beheld this golden prize and decided to make it his own. He alone saw that it has an Achilles heel, namely bonds issued before World War I which were payable in Sterling. The company had plenty of money to meet payments under the bonds but was prevented from doing so for eleven years due to Spanish exchange restrictions. When the shareholders conceived a way to reduce the corporation's debt by mobilizing Sterling payments outside Spain, they found that one influential bondholder was adamantly *opposed* to the plan – did not want to be paid. It seemed to make no sense, but only if you didn't know that March was pulling the strings.

After years of planning, March unleashed his assault on 10 February 1948. It was ingenious, predatory and ruthless. Three of his accomplices went into a provincial courtroom 100 kilometres from Barcelona, presenting themselves as modest bondholders who had suffered all those years of non-payment and now desperately needed their money. Brooks was able to find evidence in the old records that they had in fact acquired their bonds just four days earlier. After their discussion with the judge, without anyone being heard on behalf of the company, they came away armed with a declaration of bankruptcy and seizure of Barcelona Traction's assets. A close March associate was somehow named receiver. Before any owners of Barcelona Traction knew what was happening, their premises were vacated by that receiver (assisted by public force). He promptly held a shareholders' meeting at which he, representing the shareholders, voted alone and unanimously to throw out the foreign directors and replace them with March's men. I quote Brooks: 'later evidence strongly suggested that the complainants, the trustees in bankruptcy, and the judge himself were allies of March'. The court somehow cancelled corporate shares issued in Canada and somehow had new shares issued in Spain and somehow declared that the corporate headquarters were henceforth in Barcelona and not Toronto. Next, a March company somehow became the sole bidder in an auction somehow organized by the court and bought this great company for a tiny fraction of its value. To finish it off – perhaps his most brilliant move – March dispatched successive waves of individuals who ostensibly sought the *invalidation* of what the judge had done, but with no intent of pursuing their actions – only to create *litispendence* which somehow made it impossible for Barcelona Traction's true owners to lodge appeals. It worked like a charm.

made his best bet when he became the indispensable financier of General Franco's successful insurrection against the Republicans in the Spanish Civil War. In return for such support, March was given – so it was said – free sway to 'plunder foreign targets of opportunity'. By September 1936, Brooks reported, March was able to deposit 121.5 metric tons of gold in the Bank of Italy, which then functioned as a dual private/public bank. Brooks marvelled that one man could make gold deposits greater than the gold reserves of any but a few nations in the world.

II   THE ISSUES

Again: the confiscated company was Canadian, but its dominant shareholders were Belgian individuals and entities. In those days private parties could not invoke international law directly but had to rely on so-called diplomatic protection by their home states, provided that their governments bestirred themselves to 'espouse' their claim. At first, both Canada and Belgium protested at March's outrageous capture of the Barcelona Traction. But Generalissimo Franco, who of course had kept in force the currency restrictions which prevented payments under the bonds, praised March for what he called his 'audacious nationalism'. The owners of Barcelona Traction were able to arrange a meeting with the dictator, but he gave them a very cold shoulder. Canada lost appetite; its foreign ministry explained that Canada's interests were too insignificant to justify espousal of the corporate claims. And so it was Belgium that went to The Hague in 1958 on behalf of Barcelona Traction's shareholders.

It does not matter today whether Brooks was right about the perfidiousness of Juan March. That is ancient history. The important thing is whether foreign investors who contend that the value of their shareholding in a venture has been destroyed by a denial of justice have standing as a matter of international law.

In 1966 – eight years after Belgium had commenced the proceedings – the Court made a rather lame decision; it would at that stage consider only preliminary issues of standing, and in particular this one: could Belgium sue on behalf of Belgian investors who put their money at risk through a Canadian entity? Some Judges voted formalistically that the Court should decide immediately that Belgium had no standing because the alleged harm was done to a non-Belgian corporate entity. Others agreed that the question could be decided right away – but with the opposite result: of course, international law must be realistic and hear the complaint of the truly injured party.

So who won? Amazingly, none of them – because nine other judges thought this question could not be decided at this stage after all but must await the merits. That took four more years until the final judgment in 1970.

III   RESOLUTION OF THE ISSUES

In the second phase, the first two Memorials comprised more than 1,600 pages. Spain alone was defended by over one hundred lawyers. The Court had sixty-four additional sittings and went through every jot and title of the merits: the facts, Spanish bankruptcy law, Canadian corporate law, the relevance of tax returns and audited financial statements, the financial consequences of the various initiatives of the protagonists and so on. It is one of the most extensive files in the history of the World Court. The 357-page final judgment dismissed the case on the preliminary point, by a vote of 15 to 1; Belgium had no standing to claim on account of harm caused to a non-Belgian company.[2] Were the nine who had insisted in 1966 on this colossal waste of time and

---

2. 1970 *ICJ* 1.

treasure embarrassed? Did they remember that one of the dissenters back in 1966 had pointed out that no special fact-finding was necessary to determine that Barcelona Traction was a Canadian company ... Who knows?

And so Belgium lost the debate, the shareholders lost their money, and Juan March's estate (he had died in a road accident) held on to its vast ill-gotten gains. Rosalyn Higgins, then a young specialist in international law at Chatham House who might have been surprised if a fortune teller had told her that she would one day preside that very Court, did not hesitate to refer to it as 'an abdication' of the ICJ's 'international judicial function'.[3]

The 1960s was not a good decade for the ICJ, which was much discredited by another judgment, handed down between the two phases of *Barcelona Traction*.

I am referring to the unfortunate *South West Africa* judgment, which in 1966 held by a majority of one that that Liberia and Ethiopia were not entitled (did not have standing) to question South Africa's administration of South West Africa, now Namibia, under a United Nations mandate of trust. The developing world was scandalized, the ICJ's next budget request was rejected by the General Assembly, and not one of the five Judges whose mandates were expiring was re-elected; the process was unquestionably affected by a concerted push to install Judges of a different temperament.

So the wake of *South West Africa* was not a good place for Barcelona Traction's shareholders to see their case return to the Court, seeking to show why a Western country has standing to pursue the claims of its nationals as investors when two African States had not been allowed to be heard as to the rule over an African territory by an apartheid regime.

The Court held out a kind of nebulous promise in a much-remarked *obiter dictum*, which I will now read to you: 'if in a given case it is not possible to apply the general rule that the right of diplomatic protection of a company belongs to its national State, considerations of equity might call for the possibility of protection of the shareholders in question by their own national State'. What does this mean? Wait until someone treats an investor worse than the combination of March, Franco, and the bankruptcy judge? Who knows – another day, another claim, another set of Judges? Was this statement meant to be taken seriously? For what is one to think of the equitable impulses of a Court which managed to spend so much time and spill so much ink on this case without even mentioning the bogus 1948 bankruptcy?

Treaty-based investor-state disputes of course typically obey a rule which is the opposite of that followed by the ICJ in 1970. If a corporate entity is owned or controlled, directly or indirectly, by an investor who is a national of a signatory of the Treaty, the investor has standing. And if a corporate investor has the nationality of a State party to an investment treaty, it can act as the directly injured party without worrying whether it can mobilize the support of its government – as Barcelona Traction was unable to do

---

3. *Aspects of the Case Concerning the Barcelona Traction, Light and Power Company*', 11 Va. J. Int'l. L. 327, at 333 (1971).

with Canada. If the Belgian victims were bringing their case today, they could look to an investment treaty to which either Belgium or Canada was a party. And they would not need either government to initiate or present their complaint.

But mark well that these are features of the realm of investment treaties, where the standing of corporate investment vehicles is a matter of *lex specialis*. For its part, customary international law did not budge for forty years in the absence of any occasion for the ICJ to revisit the *Barcelona Traction* rationale.

More recently, we observed the misadventures of a businessman from a small African country who claimed mistreatment as an investor in another African country and was able to convince his home country to go to the ICJ to bring a case where it lasted (once again) for more than five thousand days – and did not (once again) produce very much at all.

This was the *Diallo* case – a long-awaited occasion for a possible realignment with the general rule in investment treaties. After all, all those treaties plainly reflect the perception of the States that sign them that it is broadly speaking proper for the shareholders of corporate investment vehicles to act as claimants in treaty cases. So let us see what happened.

Ahmadou Diallo was the name of a businessman from Conakry in West Africa who moved to Kinshasa. There he set up two companies, dealing in cross-border trade and container transport. In the late 1980s, he brought lawsuits against various local entities, both governmentally and privately owned, to recover unpaid debts. These efforts were anything but successful. The Prime Minister of Zaire issued an expulsion decree declaring that Mr Diallo's 'presence and personal conduct have breached Zairois public order, especially in the economic, financial and monetary sectors'. He was arrested and detained twice for a total of seventy-two days and ultimately deported back to Guinea, where by that time he had not lived for three decades.

Still, he was able to persuade the Guinean government to bring a case before the ICJ in 1998 against Zaire, which by then had reverted to its prior name of Congo, not under an investment treaty but by using the venerable but rather obsolete mechanism of diplomatic protection, with the Republic of Guinea acting as Claimant on account of the injury done to its national.

Congo complained that Diallo had not exhausted local remedies in Zaire, and at any rate had no standing because the right he was seeking to protect were those of his companies, not himself. It took more than eight years for these objections to be dismissed by the Court. It held that Congo had failed to prove the existence of 'available and effective remedies in its domestic legal system' with respect to injury caused to Diallo himself, so his personal claim could be heard. But with respect to what we might call the *Barcelona Traction* argument, the Court upheld what it called the 'normal rule' of nationality under the customary law of diplomatic protection: Guinea had no right to exercise diplomatic protection *with respect to injury to Diallo's companies*, which were Congolese.

A bit more than three years later, in 2010, the Court rendered a judgment on the merits of this amputated claim. It said that while Diallo's rights as a person had been violated in the course of his arrest, detention, and expulsion and could be pursued by

Guinea, his rights as a shareholder of his companies had not been impeded because he could still 'take part and vote in general meetings'.

This, as you can imagine, was the kiss of death. The kiss was the finding that reparations were owned to Diallo; the death was that after some further quantum proceedings the Court reduced the claim of about USD 11.6 million by a bit more than 99%, to the princely sum of USD 95,000, of which only USD 10,000 were for property damages and the remaining USD 85,000 for mental and moral damages based on 'equitable considerations'. Not a victory worth even the cost of sending teams of lawyers to The Hague.

Some judges dissented. Of acute interest is this passage from the opinion signed by two of them, who were prepared to move away from *Barcelona Traction*:

> The proliferation of bilateral and multilateral investment treaties, and the assertion by some States of a right, sometimes expressed in legislation, of *intervention to protect the interests of national shareholders in foreign companies,* together with a parallel development in the field of human rights ... *have all meant that the low standard of protection of shareholders under customary law is now confined to the wretched of the earth like Mr. Diallo.* Such a result could not have been contemplated by those judges whose uppermost concern was, in the words of Professor Rolin: 'to encourage investments for the benefit of developing countries, by *giving guarantees on both sides, both to those countries themselves in order to avoid a form of economic neo-colonialism, which would bring about their subjection to the rich countries, and in order to put investors out of reach of certain risks'.*[4]

> we believe that this case sets a dangerous precedent for foreign investors unprotected by bilateral investment treaties. The low standard of protection outside BITs is in stark contrast to the wide reach of modern foreign investment law, which goes far beyond what Guinea had asked for in the present case. *The Court missed a chance to do justice to Mr Diallo, and at the same time, to bring the standard of protection of customary international law up to the standard of modern investment law.*[5]

Who wrote these lines? Ardent defenders of the rights of foreign investors, suspected by the critics of investor treaty protection of having occult motivations? Who exactly were these dissenters?

One was Judge Awn Al-Khasawneh, who later became the Prime Minister of Jordan. The other was Judge Abdulqawi Ahmed Yusuf of Somalia, who as I write these lines occupies the office of President of the ICJ in The Hague. The reference to 'the wretched of the earth' is an unmistakable invocation of one of the most influential books of the twentieth century, the translated title of Franz Fanon's *Les Damnés de la Tierre,* a fierce indictment of colonialism read throughout the Third World. Neo-colonialism, Fanon might say today is not the fruit of foreign investments or the imposition of international norms protecting them but of modern forms of *dependence* on what used to be known as the metropolitan powers.

---

4. Judgment of 2010, p. 706.
5. *Ibid.,* p. 710.

Some say that *Diallo* was actually a step backwards from *Barcelona Traction*. Certainly, it was a disappointment that even in this case the majority of Judges could not see their way to applying the equitable considerations which had been reserved as a possibility in *Barcelona Traction*.

John Brooks wrote that in *Barcelona Traction* the ICJ 'failed – just as maritime courts for many centuries up to the middle of the nineteenth century had failed, because the underdevelopment of the law in those times made it powerless to deal with the realities of piracy and privateering'. Has general – customary – international law moved one inch from this position? Indeed, have we moved one inch from what Judge Fitzmaurice referred to in his reluctantly concurring opinion in *Barcelona Traction*, when he wrote that the case left 'an unsatisfactory state of the law that obliges the Court to refrain from pronouncing on the substantive merits of the Belgian claim, on the basis of what is really … a technicality … . International law must be regarded as deficient and underdeveloped in this field'.

What indeed is left for the wretched of the earth? I am thinking less of investors from poor countries like Diallo than of poor people who benefit from foreign investments – because the purpose of investment treaties is not to protect corporations. Who can love a corporate entity, whose existence and profits and loss are nothing but mental constructs? If they were not useful, we would abandon them. But they are unmatched as mechanisms for the mobilization of capital, including, for example, the huge pension funds of not-particularly wealthy retired school teachers in the US. They invest in commercial entities which in turn invest throughout the world. If such investments are confiscated, the retired schoolteachers suffer – and the managers of their funds have less appetite for foreign ventures. The true purpose of investment treaties is to induce foreign investors to be willing to invest at the lowest possible cost of capital. That means reducing the risk, and perhaps first of all the legal risk.

IV   LOOKING AHEAD

Which path will we follow? Customary international law, represented by these two cases – *Barcelona Traction*, confirmed by *Diallo* – maintains that shareholders do not have the right to seek relief under international law for damage caused to corporations but leaves open the possibility of an 'equitable' exception which remains undefined. That leaves the *lex specialis* of investment treaties. We now have half a century of quantitatively significant experience. What do we make of them? Reactions fall into three categories:

(i)   they are great and should not be touched;
(ii) they are a calamity to be fought and eliminated;
(iii) they are a beneficial means of reducing the cost of foreign-sourced capital and they should, like any other useful construct, be appraised and incrementally adjusted in light of experience, each in its particular context.

With apologies for the rhetorical question: to which camp should you belong, dear reader, as a good world citizen?

The remaining and principal part of this study is the examination of three matters: (1) the different treatment of shareholder actions under national and international law; (2) whether sophisticated national laws have developed advantages which the drafters of investment treaties and codes did not understand and therefore omitted; and (3) how dogmatic critics of the *lex specialis* are prepared to throw out the baby with the bath water.

1 Shareholder Actions under National and International Law

What is the utility of the mental construct known as the corporate entity? Its characteristic features are: capital ('equity') divided into transferable shares, separate legal 'personality', capacity to sue and be sued, liability limited to its assets as opposed to those of its shareholders, management delegated by the shareholders, immunity from shareholder claims to its assets save in the case of liquidation, and (most prominently in the latter case) priority of creditors over shareholders.

The fact that this model is followed all over the world is due to its remarkable success in the voluntary mobilization of venture capital. As the late Joseph Bishop, my genial professor of 'business units' at the Yale Law School, was fond of saying: if only the Romans, who two thousand years ago were able to build awe-inspiring monuments, roads, and aqueducts (but only by means of imperial authoritarianism and using slave labour) had only invented the fiction of the corporate 'person' perhaps they could have sparked trial-and-error private initiatives which already then would have produced the steam engine, penicillin, the Wang computer (remember, this is a recollection from the 1970s), and perhaps even a Ferrari Testarossa.

As it turns out, two fellow students from my university days went into academia, devoting themselves to the study of business organizations and corporate finance. Reinier Kraakman (now a professor at the Harvard Law School) and Henry Hansmann (Yale Law School) have written numerous fundamental articles on the subject, some of them jointly, and have been leading participants in a more than decade-long project involving a comparative analysis of national approaches with contributions from leading scholars from a number of countries where sophisticated corporate law and practices have emerged. It has resulted in an important monograph which is now in its third edition.[6]

It is not necessary to consult a work of this importance[7] to observe that it is a common characteristic of modern national corporate law – consistently with the inability of shareholders (and *their* creditors) to make claims to corporate assets and with the corporate entity's right to sue on its own behalf – that it excludes *indirect* shareholder claims on account of harm done to the corporation, irrespective of the fact

---

6. Rainier Kraakman et al., *The Anatomy of Corporate Law, A Comparative and Functional Approach* (Oxford University Press, 3rd ed. 2017).
7. A handy thirty-page primer was produced by an OECD staff member as a working paper in 2014: David Gaukrodger, 'Investment Treaties and Shareholder Claims for Reflective Loss: Insights from Advanced Systems of Corporate Law', available at https://dx.doi.org/10.1787/5jz)xvgngmr 3-en.

that it has lessened the value of the shares. *Direct* shareholder claims, e.g., for the dispossession of shares or prevention of the exercise of voting rights, are of course admissible.

The sole exceptions are shareholder *derivative* claims, which courts may authorize in specific statutorily defined circumstances in the case of inaction or misconduct by the corporation's managers. When they succeed, however, the recovery goes to the corporate coffers, to be shared by all.

Investment treaties, on the other hand, define shares in corporations as 'investments', and treaty arbitrators have frequently upheld shareholders' standing to sue on account of a diminution in the value due to a treaty breach. That is exactly what the *Barcelona Tractions* shareholders needed, and did not get.

It is therefore natural to compare *Barcelona Traction* with a modern case having the opposite effect. *CMS v. Argentina*[8] was prominent in the first wave of successful claims by shareholders on account of corporate losses. The US entity had purchased 29.42 % of the shares of TGN, an Argentine utility which operated under a licence. (The major portion, 25 %, was bought from the state.) It was induced to do so by representations to the effect that the affairs of TGN were buttressed by governmental undertakings that TGN's peso income was convertible into USD at the rate prevailing at the time of invoicing. When the government cancelled convertibility, TGN's income under its license was severely affected – and so was the value of CMS's investment. CMS was not the license holder, but that does not mean that its claim was *indirect*;[9] it claimed individual, free-standing rights as a shareholder under the Treaty to obtain redress for the effect on its investment of the government's 'dismantling of the dollar-based tariff regime', which it claimed had been a decisive factor in its decision to invest. The International Centre for Settlement of Investment Disputes (ICSID) tribunal, which included senior individuals having held high public office,[10] agreed and awarded some USD 133 million as damages; Argentina's attempt to annul the award was unsuccessful.[11]

How could anyone imagine that the issue of double recovery would not cross the minds of a tribunal of this quality, or that the able and determined advocates for Argentina would fail to spot the point? Of course, the issue was dealt with; compensation was made conditional on the CMS's surrender of its shares to the Government of Argentina.[12]

---

8. ICSID Case No. ARB/01.08, Decision on Jurisdiction, 17 July 2003.
9. Or 'reflective', to use a word in recent vogue; I fail to see why a different word is necessary, unless its intent is to conjure a penumbra of pejorativeness.
10. One of the arbitrators was a former President of the Supreme Court of Brazil and Judge of the ICJ, another a former Minister of Finance of Canada, and the third a leading figure of public international law of the Spanish speaking world. In para. 48, they wrote: 'the fact is that *lex specialis* in this respect is so prevalent that it can be considered the general rule'.
11. The committee which ruled on Argentina's application for annulment was comprised of three individuals who have served at various times as judges of the ICJ. Although the annulment committee had reservations about the reasoning of the tribunal in unrelated respects, they were unimpeded by any thoughts of *Barcelona Traction* as they upheld the arbitrators' application of the relevant treaty to allow the claim. ICISD Case No. ARB/01/08, Decision on Application for Annulment, 25 September 2007.
12. *Ibid.*, Award, 12 May 2005, p. 139.

True, other shareholders who do not benefit from the protection of international law in such circumstances are not necessarily given equal treatment. This would be abnormal in a national setting – but not in the international context. Shareholders whose rights are determined by national law must rely on the corporation to recover its loss of value. Whether that will happen, in principle and in practical effect, depends on the laws and institutions of the host country. Doubts in that respect are precisely the kind of risk which impedes foreign investment, with the result that investors either require a higher return or simply stay away. Mitigation of that risk is the very *raison d'être* of investment treaties or investment codes that incorporate an international standard – and the right of shareholder claims.

2   Should the Advantages of Sophisticated National Corporate Law Be Incorporated into International Rules Pertaining to the Treatment of Foreign Investment?

The title of an OECD working paper speaks of 'insights from advanced systems of corporate law'.[13] It is well worth reading. It would, however, be a serious mistake – and nowhere recommended by the author of the paper – to promote post haste adoption of the 'insights' of 'advanced' national systems in the *international* environment.[14]

The ability to reassure investors in a 'less advanced' system that their investment will not be compromised is a valuable commodity and must be weighed against supposed benefits which may be of great value in places where the rule of law holds sway, and the courts can be counted on to uphold corporate law the way it is written. But in other places, where the rule of law is a fragile vessel, and local investors scarce or prone to place their savings abroad, the rules-based 'insights' of 'advanced systems' have little chance of doing their magic. It does no good to introduce the most up-to-date high-speed train to a country which has no tracks that can accommodate them. Raghuram Rajan, the Chief Economist of the International Monetary Fund, who later went on to become the Governor of the Reserve Bank of India and the Vice-Chairman of the International Bank of Settlement, wrote an article fifteen years ago in which he postulated that in the field of international economic development, we would do better to *assume anarchy*, giving the following explanation:

> Institution building is one area where international financial institutions and policymakers have learned from experience and have used common sense to devise practical approaches, without much guidance from academia. And there is hope, supported by a growing body of research, that more students of development are realizing that a better starting point for analysis than a world with only minor blemishes may be a world where nothing is enforceable, property and individual rights are totally insecure, and the enforcement apparatus for every

---

13. *Supra*, note 5.
14. Or indeed, to broach a different subject, in 'less advanced' national systems whose institutional infrastructures cannot give them practical effect.

contact must be derived from first principles – as in the world that Hobbes so vividly depicted.[15]

So before we consider adopting any of the 'insights' derived from advanced systems, let alone jettisoning a prominent feature of the landscape of the protection of foreign investment, we would do well to consider whether there is a true potential benefit to abolishing or adjusting the *Barcelona Traction* rule and also whether the institutions of the host country are capable of dispassionately giving obliges their due, even if they lack political influence. This involves an appraisal of reality and experience. But by all means, let us first consider what has been said to be possible deleterious effects of shareholder claims, succinctly but well enough captured in this summary:

> Since the shareholder claim is a form of cashing out at a point when the firm has been weakened by adverse governmental action, it impedes the recapture of a viable asset base; the lack of assuredly permanent shareholder capital harms the firm's credibility vis-à-vis customers, suppliers, lenders – and possible new investors.
>
> Reassignments of shareholdings within a corporate group may extract value from one controlled entity by share transfers which are detrimental to the creditors of the transferor entity, or enable opportunistic unfavorable settlements.
>
> The value of the firm's right to sue on its own behalf is compromised by claims by individual shareholders; major shareholders may push management to ignore rational litigation strategies once they have achieved separate satisfaction; and to avoid double recovery, shareholders must be joined to the corporation's own suit.
>
> Claims of shareholders able to invoke a treaty may result in recovery under international law which is superior to what the firm could obtain under national administrative law.

Each of these objections loses sight of the essential thing: in the international environment, treaty-based shareholder claims are raised against the host government, and the latter has not made treaty commitments to its own nationals, or to others who do not have the benefit of a treaty. Treaty entitlements constitute an independent source of compensation – a *supplemental* basket if you will – which is not available to them but takes nothing from them.

---

15. *Finance and Development*, September 2004, p. 57. Rajan was on my mind when I gave a lecture given at the University of Richmond in April 2007 entitled 'Enclaves of Justice', where I reviewed the evidence of the abysmal record of delivering justice to the populations of our Earth and concluded this: 'Our concept of decent justice is not to be compromised by meretricious concessions to cultural relativism. Such concessions do no more than to make us complicit with dictators, fanatics, and thugs. The rule of law is pure illusion for most of our fellow travellers on this planet, and things will not get better unless we stop tinkering with texts and start dealing with contexts. Now, dealing with reality is, I fear, an insurmountable task if we set out to establish effective justice comprehensively. The least we can hope for, as the international law scholar Julius Stone put it in the 1950s, are enclaves of justice. But whereas for Stone that phrase was the lament of an almost inexpressible pessimism, I believe we can turn it around, and ask ourselves whether we cannot consciously create enclaves of justice, and hope that in so doing we prime a million pumps.' Pages 9-10 of a draft text never finally edited and published, but available at https://www.arbitration-icca.org/media/4/55045328762534/media012254618965 440speech-richmond__enclaves_of_justice.pdf.

Imagine that a corporation suffers a loss of value as a result of adverse governmental action. Imagine that that action breached a treaty and that a foreign shareholder is able to recover the loss pro rata, but a national investor (a) has no cause of action under the national law, (b) has such an action, but its national law provides compensation for only a fraction of the loss, *or* (c) although the partial recovery is due according to the law, the courts ignore the law, or the government simply withholds payment. In each of these instances, the foreign shareholder has recovered more than the national shareholder. But the foreigner has stolen nothing from the firm or from the domestic shareholders. *And neither the corporation nor the domestic shareholders would be better off if there were no foreign shareholders.* National corporate law and foreign investment protection are separate regimes which do not collide.

Shareholder claims obviously give rise to complications, but they should not be exaggerated. We have already seen that in *CMS* a plain-vanilla double recovery problem, more illusory than real, was readily resolved. But there can be more knotty issues. For example, two decades ago, in the NAFTA case *GAMI v. Mexico*,[16] a US corporation held a 14.18% share of a Mexican corporation, Grupo Azucarero México SA de CV (coincidentally called 'GAM'), which owned five sugar mills that were expropriated by governmental decree. The US shareholder brought a claim for compensation by an international tribunal applying international law. GAM brought a similar action in its own courts, seeking redress in accordance with Mexican law.

Now, even if one assumes that both sets of proceedings in such a case would work smoothly in accordance with the respective applicable procedural and substantive norms there can be no expectation that relief will eventuate at the same moment; that the respective standards of compensation will be the same; that the two adjudicatory processes will result in identical valuations; or that the actual compensation will be forthcoming in any event, depending on appeals, other forms of legal challenge, or simple refusal to comply. Seeing that the foreign shareholder may be compensated by both national and international processes, double recovery must be excluded. By what mechanism?

That tribunal included two prominent figures in international law: Julio Lacarte, a former Uruguayan diplomat and minister who had been one of the initial set of members of the Appellate Body of the WTO; and Michael Reisman, an American scholar and former President of the Inter-American Commission on Human Rights. I had the privilege of serving with them. The just-described issue was thoroughly debated by first-rate legal teams, and in the presence of Canada and the US as observers entitled to comment. The tribunal's solutions may be debated, but it is demonstrably false to say that we failed to attend to the issue. The considerations were complex. It is not for me to defend a res judicata, but simply to invite the reader, if so minded, to consult the annex to this study and to verify, as Arthur Miller might have put it, that *attention was paid.*[17]

---

16. UNCITRAL Rules/NAFTA Chapter 11, Final Award, 15 November 2004.
17. In the course of the proceedings, a Mexican court annulled the expropriation of three of the mills which were thereafter returned to GAM, and the Government represented that compensation to GAM for the two others (whose expropriation had not been contested) was being assessed. This

3   The Baby and the Bathwater

Everyone should welcome the prospect of incremental reform, both with respect to the legitimacy of the process and the substance of treaty protection. Shareholder claims fall into the substantive category, which also includes issues such as the need to rethink most-favoured-nation and 'umbrella' clauses, which have caused much confusion and merit clarification.

But those who would resurrect the *Barcelona Traction* ruling should not be heeded. They must think that what happened to the Belgian shareholders was just fine, and they fail to consider the plight of the wretched of the earth. Their proposals would discourage foreign investment, and they do not consider what will happen in its absence.[18]

This strikes me as irresponsible; recall the graph reproduced in my introduction. Its last data point is the year 2010. More recently, the 2019 UNCTAD World Investment Report states that foreign direct investment in 2018 totalled USD 5 trillion, compared to USD 149 billion in foreign aid.[19] That's a multiple of 33.5. The UNCTAD Report comments on this figure as follows: 'FDI has been the most stable component of the balance of payments over the past 15 years, and the most resilient to economic and financial crises …. The size and relative stability of FDI makes it the most important source of external finance for developing economies.'[20]

---

created a further complication. GAMI considered that it had the right to complain of wrongful expropriation of its investment (its share ownership) under international law irrespective of what GAM chose to do in the Mexican courts. GAMI's reaction it this situation was ultimately fatal to its case, as the Tribunal explained in para. 133: 'With knowledge of the magnitude of diminution, one might be in a position to consider whether a line is drawn beyond which the loss is so great as to constitute a taking. But GAMI has staked its case on the proposition that the wrong done to it did in fact destroy the whole value of its investment. GAMI seeks to lend credibility to its posture by agreeing to relinquish its shares in GAM as a condition of the award it seeks. It suggests that any residual value is therefore of no moment. This posture is untenable. The tribunal cannot be indifferent to the true effect on the value of the investment of the allegedly wrongful act. GAMI has neglected to give *any* weight to the remedies available to GAM. Assessment of their effect on the value of GAM's investment is a precondition to a finding that it was taken. GAMI has not proved that its investment was expropriated for the purposes of Article 1110.'

18. Indeed, some critics seem to proceed on as though they believe that analysis is just window-dressing to be found after the acquisition of the convictions tat suit one's temperament. They appear to be unacquainted with investors' decision-making criteria and with investment disputes; they seemingly view the government officials who have drafted thousands of treaties with condescension; and they communicate in an echo-chamber only with each other, ignoring the views of those who have actually been involved in the process – seemingly assuming them to be biased by vested interests. If they succeed, there will be consequences for which they are apparently unwilling to envisage, but for which they should be held accountable.

19. At p. 11. The difference when compared to the chart just shown is not only the increase over time, but also definitional choices. If the focus is limited to investment in poor countries, which are they? How does one deal with transactions that are on the borderline between pure equity contributions and other transactions involving risk and such features as convertible shares? What to do with countries with unreliable statistics and large currency fluctuations? Comparability is subject to legitimate and continuous debates. But the big picture remains clear: foreign aid will not save the world.

20. That foreign investment may be put to deleterious uses is another matter, which leads to consideration of the responsibility taken by international courts and tribunals when they rule on

One might think that a critical assessment of modern investment protection treaties would involve the examination of concrete cases to see if there is evidence of injustice or other unintended consequences. But that is not the popular form of critique of investor-State dispute settlement (ISDS). The critics take a dim view of shareholder indirect claims because they find them offensive *in the abstract*.

They say that such claims *distort and subvert national laws* that define the functions and rights of corporate entities as well as the right of those affected by their activities; *undermine decision-making authority* at the level of the corporation; *interfere with national choices* with respect to the bundles of rights that are associated with shareholding and interaction with the corporation (thus opening the door to a multiplication of claims and double recovery); *disallow creditor priorities* established under national law by enabling foreign shareholders to help themselves first from entities in distress;[21] *disturb settlement incentives; facilitate holdups*; and – perhaps above all – *leave all these complex problems to be sorted out at the discretion of arbitrators* who, as the critics are often at pains to make us understand, do so only in a superficial way. They are unsparing in their disparagement of treaty drafters and arbitral tribunals alike. They pay no heed to the fact that every investment treaty and every national foreign investment code was adopted by public officials.

I confess to a lack of interest in these abstract elucubrations. This should not be taken as an aversion to theory or to organizing principles, as long as they illuminate the path to sound policy choices. But I am unimpressed by demonstrations that things *do not work in theory*, like the bumblebee which is not supposed to be able to fly because of the excessive ratio of its body mass to wing span ... The test of sound policy must be concrete; real life is the graveyard of most constructs of the mind devised behind a desk.

We are today in the fortunate position of being able to see the outcomes of hundreds of practical applications of the provisions of investment treaties. Have the fundamental errors perceived in theory materialized? That is a legitimate question, and certainly worth pursuing. In these hundreds of cases, states and investors have been represented by resourceful advocates, and decided by prominent arbitrators including many who have held high offices in the public sector and in international organizations. They must be decided in a limited time frame, in light of the opposing pleadings often intended for debating purposes to create confusion in order to overcome a weak

---

claims by officials of hosts states that they are entitled to make fundamental changes in government policy in the public interest, blaming their predecessors for poor decisions – or worse. The inability of a state to make a meaningful promise is a costly handicap, Jan Paulsson, *The Power of States to Make Meaningful Promises to Foreigners*, 1 J. Int. Dispute Settlement 341 (2010).

21. In footnote 22 of its Submission to the Tribunal in *GAMI v. Mexico*, the United States affirmed that 'international tribunals have rejected shareholder claims in part because of the difficulty in determining what relief can fairly be granted in light of potential claims by creditors and other interested parties' with one sole citation, specifically to Eduardo Jiménez de Aréchaga, *Diplomatic Protection of Shareholders in International Law*, 4 Phil. Int'l. J. 71, 77, 78 (1965). De Aréchaga was a leading counsel to Spain in *Barcelona Traction*, was elected to the ICJ in 1970 – the very year of the ICJ's final judgment in that case – and became its President in 1976.

point, and with the need to reconcile differences of reasoning among arbitrators. And the reasoning is exposed to harsh criticism; lawyers argue as easily as they breathe.[22]

---

22. When considering the adequacy or otherwise of reasoning, it is natural to have in mind Article 52(1)(e) of the ICSID Convention, which exposes awards to annulment if they 'fail to state the reasons on which [they are] based'. Just over a decade ago, in the academic year 2005-2006, this requirement became the focus of a seminar on international investment arbitration conducted by Michael Reisman and Guillermo Aguilar at the Yale Law School. Each student chose to examine and evaluate the reasons of a single case, and ten studies selected by the instructors were published in book form under the title The Reasons Requirement in International Investment Arbitration: Critical Case Studies. (G. Aguilar Alvarez and W. M. Reisman (eds.), *The Reasons Requirement in International Investment Arbitration: Critical Case Studies* (Martinus Nijhoff Publishers, 2008). The back cover of the volume noted that the requirements of Article 52(1)(e) 'are not merely a legitimizing ritual but are supposed to function as a control mechanism', and that the ten student papers 'subjected the reasoning in some of the most important recent investment awards to rigorous analysis and appraisal'.

   Among the arbitrators whose awards were examined we find – leaving aside eminent professors and former senior advisors on international law in ministries of foreign affairs – one past President of the ICJ, another past and one future Judge of the self-same ICJ, three former national supreme court judges, and four other former national appellate court judges. One might think that a fair percentage of their awards might pass muster in the eyes of their ten student critics. Alas – where there is a will there's a way, and clearly the way to achieve recognition for a seminar paper is not to admire, but to tear down. Here are the comments made by the student critics on each of the ten awards, in the order in which they appear in the book:

   Mondev v. United States (1992): '... the complexity of the case and what has been termed, in a broader context, as "powerful pressures on the members of the tribunal to be obscure rather than rational" could not justify ... inadequate reasoning of the critical factual findings and major premises in the award'.
   Feldman v. Mexico (2002): '... numerous flaws in the reasoning, from arguments that are not sound because of false premises, such a failure to cite sources for international law, to arguments that are not valid because of poor inferences, caused by failure to adhere to requirements of the burden of proof, and by inattention to the parties' specific claims'.
   LG&E v. Argentina (2006): '... inadequate reasons are provided with respect to arbitrary and discriminatory treatment, indirect expropriation, and the state of necessity'.
   Saluka v. Czech Republic (2007): 'The discussion on expropriation [is] unreasoned ... inadequate ... confuses and prompts the reader to at least question parts of the eventual outcome.' This with respect to what many specialists would consider the gold standard in terms of its exploration of the requirements of fair and equitable treatment – the central issue in that case –drafted by an eminent tribunal chaired by Sir Arthur Watts, the superb craftsman and general editor, in his day, of Oppenheim's International Law.
   Tokios Tokeles v. Ukraine (2004): 'certain aspects exhibit either an absence or inadequacy of reasoning'.
   Occidental v. Ecuador (2004): 'The paucity of reasoning is most evident in the substantiation of the award's controlling prescriptions, with the most contentious findings suffering from the least articulation ... glaring lapses in the tribunal's reasoning ... a low-water mark in investor-state arbitral jurisprudence ... .'
   Wena Hotels v. Egypt (1999 and 2000): 'In both the jurisdictional and merits phases, the tribunal declined to provide reasons for critical decisions ... .'
   Thunderbird v. Mexico (2006): 'the tribunal did not resolve the questions the parties were putting before it'.
   Loewen v. United States (2002): 'inadequate reasoning has added substantially to the widely felt dissatisfaction among the multiple constituencies of investment arbitration. Claimants are unlikely to feel that they had "their day in court" because important aspects of their arguments on jurisdiction and the merits were ignored ... .' For the respondent, 'the award failed to put an end to the legal proceedings. The lacunae and contradictions in the tribunal's reasoning made the award easily susceptible to a challenge ... .'

But if one cares about harnessing the power of private investment nothing counts as much as concrete outcomes in light of common commercial rationality. Here I think the critics have a hard time finding traction for their indictments of theoretical inadequacies. For example, if we take the spectre of debilitating nuisance suits by multitudes of shareholders – where are they? In national legal systems where the cost of bringing such claims is relatively modest (indeed nil in jurisdictions which allow class actions), they may be something of a plague.[23] Not so in international treaty arbitrations.[24]

Those who invoke the notorious *Lauder* arbitrations[25] as a scarecrow should perhaps reconsider. The Lauder cases involved claims arising out of the allegedly wrongful cancellation of valuable television broadcasting rights exploited jointly but disharmoniously by a US investor and Czech individuals against the backdrop of vast regulatory changes in the wake of the Velvet Revolution and the fall of the Communist regime, and of the manoeuvres of a variety of actors determined to get a piece of the action in the chaotic emerging market economy. Of present interest is the shareholding structure of the venture, reducing its complex convolutions to their essentials.

Ronald Lauder, a US national, controlled a Dutch entity named CME, the successor of interest to another entity also controlled by him, and as such the initial holder of 66% of the shares of CNTS, a Czech corporation (reflecting a disproportionate contribution of 75% of the capital). CNTS established and operated a successful television station. The broadcasting licence, however, was owned by CET 21, another Czech corporation, 97% owned by Czech individuals who in return for shares in CNTS allowed the latter to exploit CET 21's licence. In a rather quick order, CME thereafter paid USD 36 million to acquire a further 22% from a Czech bank, bringing its stake to 88%, leaving 12% to the individuals who controlled the license holder. All but one of those 12% were then purchased by CME for an amount of nearly USD 34 million.

Applying the *Barcelona Traction* rule *might* have meant zero protection of the foreign investments, assuming a premise that the loss suffered was that of the licensee: the entity which was deprived of its licence. But the overwhelming financial loss was

---

Petrobart v. Kyrgyz Republic (2005): 'in its search to accord maximum protection to the alleged investor, the tribunal did not respect its duty to provide the parties to the dispute with cogent reasons for its major and far-reaching conclusions ... The failure of the tribunal to provide adequate reasoning for its determinations calls the credibility and authority of the final award into question'. The tribunal was constituted under the rules of the Stockholm Chamber of Commerce and was presided by a former justice of the Swedish Supreme Court. An application to set aside the award was made to the Svea Court of Appeal, but it failed. The student critic, unappeased, went on to assert that the reviewing Court itself failed to resolve the decisive jurisdictional question.

What towering intellect would be adequate to satisfy the hyper-critical gaze of these seminar participants? The two instructors/editors, perhaps alarmed by the severity of these criticisms, seemed anxious in their introductory chapter to attenuate the impression of militant hostility when they wrote, perhaps more hopefully than accurately: 'Interestingly, in almost all instances, it was felt [sic] that the right decision had probably [sic] been reached.' *Ibid.*, p. 1.

23. Yet, one observes, the practice continues, with legislatures declining to do away with them.
24. A singular exception was dealt with severely in *Grynberg et al. v. Grenada*, ICSID Case No. ARB/10/6, Award 10 December 2010.
25. *Ronald Lauder v. Czech Republic*, UNCITRAL, Final Award, 3 September 2001; *CME v. Czech Republic*, UNCITRAL, Partial Award, 13 September 2011, Final Award, 14 March 2003.

of course that of CME, and if its claim was well-founded it would have deserved a substantial recovery. Yet it was *Ronald Lauder personally* who first initiated arbitration, in October 1999, claiming breach of the US-Czech Bilateral Investment Treaties (BIT). The *Barcelona Traction* rule would certainly have prevented Lauder's claim by denying him standing. The tribunal held to the contrary that the text of the relevant treaty entitled him to be heard. But by the time it decided on that question, CME had commenced a separate arbitration under the Netherlands-Czech treaty (in February 2000).

Conceptually, there is nothing outlandish about this. CET 21 could have a claim under Czech law; Lauder a claim under the US treaty; and CME under the Dutch treaty. Substantive entitlements might have been different under these three hypotheses, and so could the amount to be recovered if the claims were upheld.[26] Realistically, however, the claims under the two treaties were based on a factual narrative which if established would doubtless have led to the same outcome if decided by the same arbitrators. That possibility was offered to the Czech Republic, which refused, insisting that the two treaty claims be heard by two entirely different tribunals.[27] It was an unfortunate choice, because although the *Lauder* tribunal held, by a final award dated 3 September 2001, that Lauder had standing to bring the case, it also dismissed the claim on the grounds that there had been no treaty breach; the harm caused was the result of CET 21's termination of contractual relations with CNTS.

Meanwhile, the *CME* tribunal was concluding work on the same issues that were dealt with in the Lauder final award. Its partial award, rendered just ten days later (on 13 September 2001) also upheld jurisdiction, but took the view that the Czech authorities had been instrumental in the destruction of the investment, and thereby breached the treaty and generated liability to compensate CME in an amount which was fixed at some USD 269 million plus interest in a separate, later phase of the proceedings.[28]

Nor had there ever been danger of double recovery; Lauder conceded that if the same losses were subject to separate adjudication, the second decision could take account of prior recovery.[29]

---

26. As the *Lauder* tribunal held in para. 174: 'there is no abuse of process in the multiplicity of proceedings initiated by Mr. Lauder and the entities he controls. Even assuming that the doctrine of abuse of process could find application here, the Arbitral Tribunal is the only forum with jurisdiction to hear Mr. Lauder's claims based on the Treaty. The existence of numerous parallel proceedings does in no way affect the Arbitral Tribunal's authority and effectiveness, and does not undermine the Parties' rights. On the contrary, the present proceedings are the only place where the Parties' rights under the Treaty can be protected'.

27. *Lauder* Final Award, para. 173.

28. The inconsistency between the two outcomes had nothing to do with the admissibility of indirect claims, but a different assessment of the *factual* allegations of material treaty breaches. It was apparently a balanced case. What legal system can boast that all of its judges can be relied upon to interpret all evidence in identical ways?

29. *Lauder* Final Award, para. 172. Lauder evidently felt that the cost of a major separate arbitration was rational. If arbitrators appointed to hear his case considered that these were no impediments to his securing effective redress (if justified) through the CME, they might have stayed his action pending ascertainment that CME's case would be fairly heard and any resulting award satisfied. What was actually on offer to the respondent – consolidation – seems an even more efficient solution. Its rejection may have raised doubts as to the respondent's willingness to live with the

The overriding flaw in objections to treaty-based shareholder claims is the assumption that corporations through which foreign investments are channelled operate in a vacuum of national private arrangements where the funds available in the event of misfortune constitute the stakes in a zero-sum game in which whatever any actor can salvage reduces what is available to others. (And so, for example, if shareholders can jump the line of priority, then bondholders or ordinary creditors will recover less than they otherwise would – and knowing in advance that this is the rule will simply refuse to provide financing and credit, or only do so on worse terms.) But in the international context investment treaties and investment codes offer remedies which are exclusively available to a defined class of investors and are triggered by breaches of obligations of international law. Public authorities avoid liability simply by conducting themselves in accordance with their promises.[30] If to the contrary they transgress, the qualified investor secures a remedy which is the specific result of the state's commitment. It does not reduce the recovery of other creditors by one penny; the investor may recover what it can under national law, thus reducing the state's liability by that very amount since it mitigated the loss compensable under international law.

In granting such rights as incentives for foreign investment, states may well impose restrictions. Some states may be concerned by a multiplication of claims, in which case they can deal with that issue. With respect to shareholder claims, they may (as some have done) require that they be significant investors, as reflected by a defined percentage of share ownership. Or they wish to grant international rights only after determining that a particular investment is desirable, and on that basis extend the benefits of a treaty or a code (as some have also done only to investors who have obtained prior approval).[31]

Finally, let us take a hard look at a case called *Getma v. Guinea*, in which one critic portentously featured *Getma v. Guinea* as the most prominent example of conceptual failure on the part of the arbitral tribunal. This time the putative error concerned a supposed issue of apparent authority in the context of establishing authority to act for corporations, which the author said engendered 'oppressive and wasteful costs' and facilitated 'undue opportunism on the part of the firm and its agents'.[32]

But was this so? *Getma et al v. Guinea* was brought to ICSID in September 2011 by four related French corporations. They were not claiming breaches of a treaty, but of the Guinean Investment Code, as a result of the manner in which the Government put an end to their investment in a container terminal in the port of Conakry.

---

relevant treaty. But there is no way for an outsider to appraise the circumstantial factors which were in the minds of the tribunal – which happened to include a former President of the ICJ.

30. Here I exclude the hypothesis of biased adjudicators; that is a different subject. I favour rules and practices, rigorously enforced, that exclude that possibility.

31. The claimant in *Gruslin v. Malaysia*, ICSID Case No. ARB/99/3, Award, 27 November 2000, failed precisely because he failed to prove that he had obtained the required approval.

32. Julian Arato, *The Private Law Critique of International Investment Law*, 113 Am. J. Int. Law 1, at 40 (2018).

The proceedings had started elsewhere. One of the French entities had signed a concession contract with the government to operate a container terminal in the port of Conakry. The contract contained an elaborate arbitration clause defining what types of claims could be brought under the rules of the *Cour Commune de Justice et d'Arbitrage* (CCJA) in Abidjan (comprised of thirteen judges elected by the Council of Ministers of the *Organisation pour l'Harmonisation en Afrique du Droit des Affaires*). In May 2011, Getma commenced arbitration under that contract.

The CCJA arbitration was intensely litigated and in November 2015 led to an award in favour of the claimant of some EUR 38 million plus interest. This award generated vivid controversy when it was set aside by the CCJA on the grounds that the arbitrators had made an impermissible agreement with the parties with respect to their fees.[33] Getma sought to enforce the award in the United States irrespective of its annulment but failed.[34]

Back to the ICSID case. Following its separate path, it led in December 2012 to the decision which is so severely criticized in the above-cited article. At this stage, the arbitrators were only resolving Guinea's jurisdictional objection, which was this: although the Investment Code opened the doors to ICSID, it explicitly reserved the alternative of selecting a different mode of resolving disputes by a contractual clause to that effect – and the four affiliates should be deemed to have chosen to avail themselves of such a clause in the concession contract although only one of them signed it.

The tribunal dismissed the objection, reasoning that a single act may at the same time constitute a breach of contractual obligations and of the Code.[35] This could create parallel but non-conflicting jurisdiction (*parallèle* but not *concurrente*). In such cases, the fact that the exercise of parallel jurisdictions could lead to double recovery of damages does not exclude that each tribunal may be called upon to exercise its own authority; double recovery should be avoided on the merits, in particular when assessing the evidence of prejudice.[36]

That is just what the ICSID arbitrators did in the second and final stage of the arbitration when they held in August 2016 that while the consequences of the allegedly unlawful cancellation of the contract fell exclusively under the CCJA clause, while claims arising exclusively under the Code were left to ICSID. The latter category comprised the contention relating to the governmental requisition of the claimants' assets in situ. But to the claimants' great disappointment, the losses flowing from the

---

33. The institutional schedule of fees was held to be mandatory, even though they resulted in fees of only EUR 20,000 for what had been a lengthy process in which each side, represented by international law firms, had spent some EUR 3 million. The arbitrators' answer that they had cleared the separate agreement with the Secretary General of the Court fell on deaf ears. The same fate met Getma's contention that it was not responsible for the conduct of the arbitrators and that the circumstances did not in any event justify the annulment of the award.
34. 191 F. Supp 43 (2016), upheld on appeal the following year.
35. '*Un même acte peut constituer à la fois une violation d'une obligation contractuelle et une violation du Code des investissements.*' Decision on Jurisdiction, 29 December 2012, ICSID Case No. ARB/11/29, para. 107.
36. '*Le fait que les competences parallèles puissant mener à un double recouvrement de dommage n'exclue pas que chaque jurisdiction sera appellée à exercer sa proper compétence. C'est dans le traitement du fond et en particulier au moment de la vérification de la preuve du dommage, que le double recouvrement devra être évité.*' At para. 108.

requisition justified only the recovery of USD 200,000 rather than the USD 60 million sought.[37]

In sum: Getma spent EUR 3 million only to lose its EUR 100 million CCJA claim plus whatever cost to litigate at two levels of the US federal courts and then spent EUR 2 million more to recover a paltry USD 200,000 (plus interest thereon) of its EUR 60 million ICSID claim – and even that remained subject to the Government's willingness to pay without the necessity of yet further litigation. Given the fact that the cancellation of the contract had convinced the three arbitrators appointed in the CCJA arbitration (of French, Spanish, and Lebanese origin) that Getma was entitled to a considerable recovery, and considering the description in the 2016 Award of an embarrassingly feckless attempt by the Government to convince the ICSID arbitrators that the contract had been obtained by corruption, one must conclude that this was from the investor's point of view a tale of misery. But at this point, the investor no longer had any appetite to go back to the CCJA – the only arbitral mechanism left to it in light of the ICSID Decision.

None of this has any relation to the dire consequences attributed to the ICSID tribunal by the article cited above, which rather complains that the three well-known arbitrators[38] 'eschewed a rules-based approach to apparent authority entirely, instead resolving the issue through muddy *ex post* equitable balancing – creating significant uncertainty and revealing yet another way in which ISDS can distort the corporate form'. All of this has to do with how the tribunal treated the argument that the three non-signatories of the concession contract were nonetheless bound by the fourth (and signatory) entity's invocation of the CCJA's arbitration clause, which Guinea argued was an opt-out.

The author manages to dispose of the *Getma* case without even mentioning the CCJA case or even the final ICSID award. Worse, he appears not actually to have gone through the single decision considered in his article, namely the Decision on Jurisdiction, since he writes[39] that: 'Since Getma had actually signed the contract, its access to ICSID was foreclosed.' There is no way to soften the blow: the final paragraph of the Decision comes precisely to the opposite result in line with the tribunal's reasoning with respect to the dual availability of parallel jurisdictions.

So what of the business of the arbitrators' supposedly apocalyptic decision with respect to 'apparent authority'? To begin with, the decision has nothing to do with apparent authority. The article affirms, *ipse dixit*, that Guinea's attempt to invoke the 'group of companies' theory should 'functionally ... be understood under the rubric of apparent authority' when what the arbitrators actually did was to examine *whether the three non-signatory entities had themselves consented* to the arbitration clause in the contract and thus to opt out of redress to ICSID which was otherwise available under the Investment Code. This had nothing to do with their authority to do anything on any

---

37. Award of 16 August 2016.
38. Guinea's appointee was Professor Pierre Tercier, a renowned Swiss scholar, former dean of the University of Fribourg Faculty of Law and former President of the Swiss Competition Commission.
39. *Supra* n. 32, at p. 41.

other party's behalf, let alone the specific authority to act on behalf of the signatory affiliate which was individually duly represented to sign in its own name; the issue was rather with whether *they themselves* had consented to be bound by the contractual arbitration clause.

What the arbitrators said is there for anyone to read: 'To determine whether these three other Claimants did indeed manifest their *intent to be bound* by the arbitration clause, one needs to examine their respective roles in the negotiation, conclusion, and performance of the Concession Contract.'[40] After an individualized factual inquiry, and although making clear that the fact that various representatives of the group wore multiple hats did not exclude the possibility that they may have appeared wearing only their 'Getma' hat, the arbitrators concluded from the documents and extensive testimony that two of these entities were represented to fulfil specific, individualized aspects of the contract (as explicitly provided for in the bid documents) and that the third, although less directly implicated, nevertheless took a corporate resolution to engage in the CCJA arbitration. One may agree or not with the arbitrators' appreciation of the facts, but to conclude that *parties are bound by an arbitration agreement to which they consent* can hardly be described as avoiding 'a rules-based approach to apparent authority entirely', and instead 'resolving the issue through muddy *ex post* equitable balancing'. The phrase just italicized is not only part of long-standing and elementary French law from which Guinean law derives, but is specifically confirmed by the Guinean Investment Code and indeed by the contractual arbitration clause in the concession contract signed by the Government.

This critique did not exactly make a mountain of a molehill; it was, I fear, making a mountain of nothing at all. It suggests adherence to preconceived ideas, or perhaps a desire to *épater les bourgeois*.[41]

Critics with this mindset will never say that they want to see the end of foreign investment, but they want to remove key features of treaty protection, and thus in effect dismantle barriers to the arbitrary treatment of foreign capital without heed to the damage that would be done to countries in need of capital formation essential to the financing of national institutions and thus to public administration, employment, health, and education. Enterprises will not invest abroad on the footing that they are happy to have their capital sooner or later treated as gifts. True, they may well invest

---

40. '*Pour apprecier si ces trois autres Demanderesses ont bel et bien eu* la volonté d'être lies *par la clause compromissoire, il convient de examiner leur role respectif lors de la negociation, la conclusion et l'exécution de la Convention de concession.' Supra* n. 37, at para. 153.
41. In a short paper written with three others, the same author who sought to make so much of *Getma v. Guinea* concluded as follows: 'The availability of ["shareholder reflective claims"] in the context of ISDS cause significant harm –by exposing States to multiple overlapping claims, and by distorting basic principles of corporate governance on which all shareholders rely. *While allowing SRL claims in this context can have benefits, these are strongly outweighed by the harms.* The benefits can also be realized through other, less restrictive means. *On balance, the availability of SRL claims is ISDS is unfair, inefficient, and likely to drive up the costs of doing business for all concerned in the long term.*' Julian Arato, Kathleen Claussen, Jaemin Lee and Giovanni Zarra, 'Reforming Shareholder Claims in ISDS', *Academic Forum on ISDS Concept Paper 2019/9*, 17 September 2019. We are all entitled to our opinions, but the words italicized are assertions unsupported by either data or analysis, and thus resemble articles of faith: the evidence of things unseen.

even without assurances that their rights will be respected, but that affects not only the risk premium but the attitude of those who are drawn toward environments where what ultimately matters is influence.

The supposedly appalling consequences of shareholder claims in investment arbitration are the Boogieman of dogmatics. Treaty drafters were not fools. Indeed it did not require genius to think – for example – about the fact that a corporation may have thousands of shareholders and the host state may thus in theory be exposed to the possibility of a multitude of costly arbitrations. In fact, to avoid that scenario, some BITs have limited claims to owners of at least 10% of the shares of a corporation affected by an alleged treaty violation. Most, however, did not follow that example, likely because the drafters thought that hypothesis to be unlikely – which has been proven to be a correct assumption[42] – and in any event they wanted to make the host jurisdiction attractive to a broad range of investments.

Yes, treatment under investment treaties turns out to be materially different from treatment under national law, so the critics are right in saying that a foreigner may well be treated better than a national. But so what? That is the very point of the quest to promote foreign investment. Do some want to insist that foreigners be treated as badly as nationals are treated? They shouldn't pretend to favour the promotion of foreign investment. Perhaps they might instead think that the contrary goal, namely of treating nationals as well as foreigners, is good policy for the same reason that commends the signature of these treaties: to stimulate investment.

While one mulls over this question, the fact remains that foreign investors have different types of legal protection than nationals do, just as they have different exposure to risks of another kind, call it politics or xenophobia or what have you.

Perhaps we are left with the following three conclusions.

First: the critics who want to prohibit shareholder claims owe it to us to point to awards which have resulted in unjust enrichment to the claimants, looking at the investment as the commercial proposition it must be if any rational party is to be contemplated as having made it. I await such demonstrations.

Second: the right to make claims as shareholders, although it gets claimants into the courtroom, is not a great highway to the recovery of damages. Once they have established liability and get to the articulation of quantum, there may be some difficult challenges. In the cases that the critics profess to be troubled about, the corporation is carrying on but a foreign shareholder claims that actions in violation of a treaty have diminished the value of the enterprise and thus the share. How does that translate into a monetary entitlement? Will the arbitrators refer to the per share value established by a stock market, or in its absence convert themselves into imaginary market-makers for a fictional price? What if the entity in question is one which has never issued a dividend, because a majority of shareholders preferred reinvestment, even in its golden

---

42. When the *Abaclat* case came along, the 180,000 bondholders aggrieved by the Argentinean Government's alteration of terms joined forces for obviously reasons of practicality in one single proceeding, ICSID Case No. ARB/07/5. Most of them accepted improved terms offered thereafter and withdrew; 60,000 remained in the end. (Whether the bondholders were qualified investors, as a majority of the arbitrators found, depends on how one interprets the Italy/Argentina BIT.)

days of pre-breach prosperity? What if the company as an entity was offered compensation to be divided among all shareholders, and the foreign shareholder is content to take what it can get but still wants to recover a higher amount which would result from the application of international standards? Such difficult questions may occasionally arise. It is unhelpful to judge the system by imaginary outcomes rather than by what international arbitrators decide in actual cases. That will be enough grist for debate, as indeed there is in the purely national arena.

Third and finally: imagine that the foreign investor is the corporate embodiment of a joint venture, with 50/50 partners operating at arms' length. As time passes, one of the partners gets along with the government with which it has many other dealings, the other becomes persona non grata. The government expropriates the venture, which does not complain because the partner friendly to the government votes against any such action – as is explained by the fact that it is amply rewarded with other greatly advantageous contracts. The other joint venturer must be able to sue if investment protection is to mean anything.

Do you want simpler examples? Need I say *Barcelona Traction*? *Diallo*? For critics to say that they want to dismantle the *lex specialis* of investment treaties and make sure that the Belgian shareholders would be treated just as dismissively in 2020 as they were in 1970 suggests more concern for a particular vision of ideological purity than about promoting investment flows. They need to tell us what they propose instead to do for the wretched of the earth.

Foreign investment is indispensable. Even if investment treaties are abandoned or if their confidence-building provisions are gutted, foreign investments will doubtless continue to exceed the relative trickle of foreign aid. But on what terms? There is a vast continuum between the extremes of beneficial and harmful investments. Will investments be made with confidence in the rule of law and neutral adjudication, or to the contrary on the footing of accommodations with powerful local interests? What will ultimately be the cost to the populace of the host country of disadvantageous investments accompanied by dubious inducements? Or, less insidiously, will investments be made only by a limited number of major entities, private or public, who are in a position to secure bespoke contractual arrangements, including similarly individualized commitments to conditions of dispute resolution that compensate for the loss of adequate treaty protection? What would then be the aggregate effect of losing small and medium size investors?

Extracts from *GAMI v Mexico* (NAFTA), Final Award, 15 November 2004, Section 7 ("Expropriation"), pp. 45-51.

7. EXPROPRIATION

116. A consequence of GAMI's independent right of action under NAFTA may be illustrated by a hypothetical example. The notional compensation of GAM by Mexico in an amount representing MS too per share would not in principle disentitle GAMIC from asking the NAFTA Tribunal for an additional amount representing an additional MS so per share. But the theory gives rise to a number of practical difficulties. One might imagine a perfect world in which a national court of last recourse sits down with a NAFTA tribunal incapable of reviewable error to discharge their respective responsibilities. This could be done quite logically. The Mexican court could order payment to GAM based on an evaluation of the five expropriated mills. As a matter of mathematics that evaluation might represent MS too per share of all shares of CAM. At the same time the NAFTA tribunal might find that a higher level of compensation was mandated and thus order a top-up to GAMI of MS so per share proportionate to its 14.18% shareholding. This would be a graphic illustration of the value to GAMI of its entitlement to a direct international remedy beyond its indirect benefit from the national remedy obtained by GAM. A state cannot avoid international responsibility by arguing that the foreigner must content himself with whatever compensation has been decreed by national authorities.

117. This scenario is of course a fantasy. It is factually implausible. It lacks legal foundation. The Tribunal is aware of no *procedural* basis on which such coordination could take place. And the *Sentencia* itself plausibly rejects the right of shareholders to challenge the expropriation on the *substantive* ground that the protected interest is that of the corporate owner of the expropriated assets.

118. The scenario also lacks commercial credibility. On what basis could one rationally conclude that the payment to GAMI should be reduced to account for the payment to GAM? It is an

- 45 -

169

acknowledged fact that CAM has never paid a dividend to its shareholders. Why should GAMI's recovery be debited on account of a payment to GAM which is perhaps utterly unlikely to find its way to the pockets of its shareholders?

119. The overwhelming *implausibility* of a simultaneous resolution of the problem by national and international jurisdictions impels consideration of the practically *certain* scenario of unsynchronised resolution.

120. It is sufficient to consider the hypothesis that a NAFTA tribunal were to order payment to GAMI before the Mexican courts render their final decision. One might adapt the hypothetical example given in Paragraph 116 above. GAMI would thus have received MS &so per share. (There would have been no prior offsetting Mexican recovery.) What effect should the Mexican courts now give to the NAFTA award? How could GAM's recovery be reduced because of the payment to GAMI? GAM is the owner of the expropriated assets. It has never paid dividends. It would have been most unlikely to distribute revenues in the amount recovered by GAMI. At any rate such a decision would have required due deliberation of CAM's corporate organs. Creditors would come first. And other shareholders would have an equal right to the distribution. GAM would obviously say that it is the expropriated owner and that its compensatable loss under Mexican law could not be diminished by the amount paid to one of its shareholders.

121. These difficulties are attributable to the derivative nature of CAM's claim. They can quickly transport the analysis onto a fragile limb. It is necessary to revert to basic propositions.

122. CAM's title to its five productive assets was lost in **2001** by an act of expropriation. The Mexican courts have held that the Expropriation Decree was not compliant with Mexican law. It is likely that it was therefore also non-compliant with NAFTA since the requirements of Mexican law coincide to a significant degree with those of NAFTA. But CAM cannot be a NAFTA claimant. Mexico has represented to this Tribunal that it is in the process of returning the three mills affected by the *Sentencia* to GAM (see Paragraph 8 **supra).** The wrongful expropriation of those mills may have caused prejudice to GAM notwithstanding their reversal. That prejudice may be remedied by Mexican authorities. The expropriation of the two

- 46 -

other mills was ultimately not challenged by GAM. It is therefore definitive. The Mexican Constitution requires that compensation be paid. Mexico has represented to this Tribunal that "the formalities for payment of indemnity on account of the expropriation of the other two mills are also in progress" (see Paragraph 8 *supra*).

123. GAMI's shares in GAM have not been expropriated. GAMI must therefore say that its *investment* in GAM has suffered something tantamount to expropriation. This question arises prior to any analysis of quantum. It relates to the *substantive* determination of a breach. Some precedents involve a NH deprivation of the benefit of the relevant property rights. *Starrett Housing*[25] referred to rights rendered "useless." *Santa Elena* held that an expropriatory effect is "to deprive the owner of title, possession or access to the benefit and economic use" of the property.[26] The tribunals in those cases were not required to determine whether legal protections were also extant in cases of *partial* deprivation of use or benefit. That issue has been addressed by a number of NAFTA tribunals.

124. *S.D. Myers* held that a temporary discriminatory regulation which eliminated the claimant's competitive advantage in a particular market was not expropriatory. (Redress was given on other grounds.) The tribunal added this dictum: "it may be that, in some contexts and circumstances, it would be appropriate to view a deprivation as amounting to an expropriation, even if it were partial or temporary."[27] It did not explain what those contexts and circumstances might be.

125. The *Pope & Talbot* tribunal noted[28] a that the claimant in that case had "conceded, correctly, that under international law, expropriation requires a substantial deprivation." It appears however that that tribunal viewed the requirement as stricter than that. The tribunal's own test was "whether that interference is sufficiently restrictive to support a conclusion that the property has been 'taken' from its owner.' It concluded that a diminution of the profits of the corporate claimant due to restrictions on selling softwood lumber from British Columbia to the US did not satisfy this test. The award explicitly states

25. 4 IRAN-US CLAIMS TRIBUNAL REPORTS 122.
26. Award of 17 February 2000, 5 ICSID REPORTS 153, at para. 77; 39 ILM 1317, at 1329 (2000).
27. First Partial Award, *op. cit.*, para. 283.
28. Para. 102.

- 47 -

that "an impairment of economic value" is tantamount to expropriation only if the degree of impairment is *equivalent* to expropriation.[29]

126. Should *Pope & Talbot* be understood to mean that property is taken only if it is so affected in its entirety? That question cannot be answered properly before asking: *what property?* The taking of so acres of a farm is equally expropriatory whether that is the whole farm or just a fraction. The notion must be understood as this: *the affected property* must be impaired to such an extent that it must be seen as "taken."

127. GAM's own case would thus not have been affected in principle if only one mill had been expropriated. GAM'S property rights in that single mill would have been "taken" because GAM was formally dispossessed of those rights. (Indeed GAM's success in the *Sentencia* was not impaired by its decision to abandon the complaint with respect to two of the five mills.)

128. But this Tribunal is not seised by GAM. GAMI's case is more difficult. The notions developed by *Pope & Talbot* may suggest that the Impairment of the value of its property (i.e. GAMI's shares in GAM) would not be equivalent to a 'taking" of that property if only one of five equally valuable GAM mills had been expropriated without compensation. The impairment might on the other hand have been *total* if that single mill was the only one having a positive value. (GAM I may thus be right in dismissing as irrelevant CAM's decision not to challenge the expropriation of the San Francisco and San Pedro mills.)

129. The position then is this: GAM is entitled to invoke the protection of Article Imo if its property rights (the value of its shares in CAM) were taken by conduct in breach of NAFTA. GAM! argues that such conduct was manifest in the Expropriation Decree. This Tribunal finds it likely that the Expropriation *Decree* was inconsistent with the *norms* of NAFTA. But Mexican conduct inconsistent with the norms of NAFTA is only a *breach* of NAFTA if it affects interests protected by NAFTA. GAMI's investment in CAM is protected by Article 1110 only if its shareholding was "taken."

---

29. Para. 104, at footnote 86.

130. It would in the first of these two hypotheses be disturbing to conclude that GAM! could recover only if it had taken a 14.18% participation in each of the five separate subsidiaries which owned the mills. That would be formalistic to a degree which could not easily be reconciled with the objectives of NAM. It is true that neither *Pope & Talbot* nor *S.D. Myers* delivered an extended analysis of Article 1110. Their brief discussion of Article mo is inconclusive with respect to a number of unanalysed hypotheses. Each award granted relief to the claimants on other grounds. Their references to Article 1110 may therefore be considered *obiter dicta.*

131. Other NAFTA awards have given support for the proposition that *partial* destruction of the value may be tantamount to expropriation. Thus the ICSID tribunal in *Metalclad* stated:

"... *expropriation under NAFTA includes not only open, deliberate and acknowledged takings of property, such as outright seizure or formal or obligatory transfer of title in favour of the host State, but also covert or incidental interference with the use of property which has* <u>the effect of depriving the owner. in whole or in significant part, of the use or reasonably-to-be-expected economic benefit of property</u> *even if not necessarily to the obvious benefit of the host State.'*[30]

The Supreme Court of British Columbia set aside part of the *Metalclad* award. The Court concluded that the arbitrators exceeded their mandate when interpreting Article 1105 as including a duty of transparency. But the passage quoted above was undisturbed. The Court explicitly held:

"There is no ground under 534 of the International Commercial Arbitration Act to set aside the Award as it relates to the conclusion of the Tribunal that the issuance of the Ecological Decree amounted to an

---

30. 5 ICSID REPORTS 230 (emphasis added).

expropriation of the Site without compensation."[31]

Similarly the ICSID award in *Santa **Elena** cited* with approval the following phrase from *Tippets* as a test of expropriatory effect:

"Whenever events demonstrate that the owner was deprived of fundamental rights of ownership and it appears that this deprivation is not merely ephemeral."[32]

The *Santa Elena* tribunal then went on to say that a governmental measure may constitute a taking if it "effectively freezes or blights the possibility for the owner reasonably to exploit the economic potential of the property."[33]

132. But this Tribunal need not decide whether *partial* destruction of shareholding interests may be tantamount to expropriation. It would in *any case* be necessary to assess the value of shareholdings in GAM at the time of the Expropriation Decree. GAM was and remains in the hands of its owners. Its principal assets had been taken. But Mexican law gave it substantial protections. GAM could sue for the reversal of the taking. Or it could accept the taking and claim for compensation. (GAM has of course successfully obtained the return of three mills and is awaiting compensation for the other two. It would seem difficult to suggest that GAM has been unduly passive in protecting its rights. Such a case could naturally be imagined. The minority shareholder might then have no effective means of initiating remedial action on behalf of the company. But that would have to be proved.) GAMI may have had *subjective apprehensions* that Mexican judicial remedies would be insufficient. But this Tribunal can only act on the basis of *objective findings justified by evidence* that GAM's value as an enterprise had been destroyed or impaired.

133. With knowledge of the magnitude of diminution one might be in a position to consider whether a line is to be drawn beyond which the loss is so great as to constitute a taking. But

---

31. *Ibid.* 260.
32. 6 IRAN-US CLAIMS TRIBUNAL REPORTS 219, 226 (1986).
33. 5 ICSID REPORTS 172, at para. 76.

- 50 -

GAMI has staked its case on the proposition that the wrong done to it did in fact destroy the whole value of its investment. GAMI seeks to lend credibility to its posture by agreeing to relinquish its shares in GAM as a condition of the award it seeks. It suggests that any residual value is therefore of no moment. This posture is untenable. The Tribunal cannot be indifferent to the true effect on the value of the investment of the allegedly wrongful act. GAMI has neglected to *give* any weight to the remedies available to GAM. Assessment of their effect on the value of GAMI's investment is a precondition to a finding that it was taken. GAMI has not proved that its investment *was* expropriated for the purposes of Article 1110.

- 51 -

CHAPTER 10

Mitsubishi and Its Learning

George A. Bermann[*]

TABLE OF CONTENTS

I   INTRODUCTION

The U.S. Supreme Court's 1985 decision in *Mitsubishi Motors Corporation v. Soler Chrysler-Plymouth, Inc.*[1] is known best of course for its determination that claims arising under the U.S. antitrust laws, and the Sherman Act in particular,[2] are arbitrable. The litigation began with a suit in federal district court by Mitsubishi against its Puerto Rico distributor, Soler, seeking an order to compel arbitration over Soler's alleged breach of contract. Soler answered Mitsubishi's complaint, denying the allegations of breach and interposing several counterclaims, including one under the Sherman Antitrust Act. Shortly thereafter, Mitsubishi initiated arbitration against Soler before

---

[*] Professor of law, at Columbia Law School and director of the Center for International Commercial and Investment Arbitration.; member of the faculty of the Ecole de droit, Sciences Po (Paris) and the Geneva LL.M. in International Dispute Settlement (MIDS); founding member of the Governing Board of the ICC International Court of Arbitration; head of the global advisory board of the New York International Arbitration Center; fellow of Chartered Institute of Arbitrators; Chief Reporter of the ALI Restatement of the US Law of International Commercial Arbitration; co-editor-in-chief *American Review of International Arbitration*; and author of very numerous books and articles.
1. 473 U.S. 614 (1985).
2. 15 U.S.C. sections 1 et seq.

the Japan Commercial Arbitration Association pursuant to an arbitration clause that read as follows:

> All disputes, controversies or differences which may arise between [Mitsubishi] and [Soler] out of or in relation to Articles I-B through V of this Agreement or for the breach thereof, shall be finally settled by arbitration in Japan in accordance with the rules and regulations of the Japan Commercial Arbitration Association.

The U.S. district court compelled arbitration of the antitrust claim, along with others. The appellate court reversed, however, in light of that court's earlier holding, albeit in a domestic case, that Sherman Act claims are non-arbitrable.[3] The Supreme Court granted certiorari principally to determine whether claims arising under the Sherman Antitrust Act are amenable to arbitration.

In a majority opinion authored by Justice Blackmun, the Supreme Court held that Soler could pursue its claim before the Japanese arbitral institution. In so holding, the Court rejected the position that all federal courts had taken following the Second Circuit Court of Appeals decision in the case of *American Safety Equipment Corp. v. J. P. Maguire & Co.*, namely that the rights conferred by the antitrust laws were "of a character inappropriate for enforcement by arbitration."[4] Significantly, the contract also contained a choice-of-law clause providing that "[t]his Agreement is made in, and will be governed by and construed in all respects according to the laws of the Swiss Confederation as if entirely performed therein." The Court mentioned this clause in a footnote but attached no particular significance to it.

II   THE COURT'S HOSPITALITY TOWARD ARBITRATION OF FEDERAL STATUTORY CLAIMS

Although the Court had granted certiorari on the question of the arbitrability of Sherman Act claims, it posed and answered a prior question, namely, whether the arbitration agreement in the case actually encompassed claims arising under that statute. Only if it answered that question in the affirmative, would the Court proceed to the question of whether those claims were legally capable of being arbitrated.

On the first question, the Court held that the arbitration clause, by its terms, was broad enough to cover antitrust claims and that there was no basis for reading it to exclude otherwise covered claims merely because they arise under statute rather than common law. The Court saw no reason to treat these two categories of claims differently. It opined that "we are well past the time when judicial suspicion of the desirability of arbitration and of the competence of arbitral tribunals inhibited the development of arbitration as an alternative means of dispute resolution."[5] It continued:

---

3. *American Safety Equipment Corp. v. J. P. Maguire & Co.*, 391 F.2d 821 (1968).
4. 391 F.2d 821 (2d Cir. 1968), quoting *Wilko v. Swan*, 201 F.2d 439, 444 (2d Cir.), rev'd, 346 U.S. 427 (1953).
5. 473 U.S. at 626-627.

By agreeing to arbitrate a statutory claim, a party does not forgo the substantive rights afforded by the statute; it only submits to their resolution in an arbitral, rather than a judicial, forum. It trades the procedures and opportunity for review of the courtroom for the simplicity, informality, and expedition of arbitration. We must assume that, if Congress intended the substantive protection afforded by a given statute to include protection against waiver of the right to a judicial forum, that intention will be deducible from text or legislative history.[6]

Thus, notwithstanding the importance of the public policy embodied in an enactment such as the Sherman Act, the majority could "find no warrant in the Arbitration Act for implying in every contract within its ken a presumption against arbitration of statutory claims."[7]

Turning squarely to the question of arbitrability, the Court distinguished the case before it from its earlier decision in *American Safety*,[8] on the ground that it was a domestic case and that international antitrust cases raise different considerations:

[W]e conclude that concerns of international comity, respect for the capacities of foreign and transnational tribunals, and sensitivity to the need of the international commercial system for predictability in the resolution of disputes require that we enforce the parties' agreement, even assuming that a contrary result would be forthcoming in a domestic context.[9]

The Court also reaffirmed that there existed "a strong presumption in favor of enforcement of freely negotiated contractual choice-of-forum provisions [and that] that presumption is reinforced by the emphatic federal policy in favor of arbitral dispute resolution."[10]

The Court examined but rejected each of the reasons cited in *American Safety* for treating Sherman Act claims as non-arbitrable, namely that private antitrust claims are vital to the enforcement of the antitrust laws, that contracts in antitrust cases are likely to be contracts of adhesion, that antitrust claims require sophisticated legal and economic analysis, and that antitrust cases are simply too important to be left to arbitrators. It found each of them to be unpersuasive. While acknowledging the importance of private damages actions for antitrust violations, the Court questioned the proposition that such actions could only be heard in court:

There is no reason to assume at the outset of the dispute that international arbitration will not provide an adequate mechanism. To be sure, the international arbitral tribunal owes no prior allegiance to the legal norms of particular states; hence, it has no direct obligation to vindicate its statutory dictates. The tribunal, however, is bound to effectuate the intentions of the parties. Where the parties have agreed that the arbitral body is to decide a defined set of claims which includes, as in these cases, those arising from the application of American antitrust

---

6. *Id*. at 628.
7. *Id*. at 625.
8. *See supra* n. 3, and accompanying text.
9. 473 U.S. at 629.
10. *Id*. at 631.

law, the tribunal therefore should be bound to decide that dispute in accord with the national law giving rise to the claim.[11]

The Court was simply unwilling to assume that Sherman Act claims could not or would not be properly adjudicated in an arbitral forum. It importantly added:

> Where the parties have agreed that the arbitral body is to decide a defined set of claims which includes, as in these cases, those arising from the application of American antitrust law, the tribunal therefore should be bound to decide that dispute in accord with the national law giving rise to the claim [S]o long as the prospective litigant effectively may vindicate its statutory cause of action in the arbitral forum, the statute will continue to serve both its remedial and deterrent function.[12]

In sum, provided the parties drafted their arbitration agreement in sufficiently broad terms (as the Court found they had done in this case), there is no reason why they should not be permitted to entrust the adjudication of private antitrust claims to arbitration in lieu of litigation in U.S. court. The Court then proceeded to enforce the parties' agreement to arbitrate. Notwithstanding the Court's differentiation between domestic and international antitrust cases, numerous lower federal courts have gone on to read *Mitsubishi* as impliedly overruling *American Safety*, even as to domestic cases.

The Supreme Court's willingness to subject Sherman Act claims to arbitration was not, however, without antecedent.[13] In its ruling some ten years earlier in *Scherk v. Alberto-Culver Co.*,[14] the Court had ordered arbitration of a claim arising under the Securities Exchange Act of 1934, largely on the ground that the claim, in that case, arose in a distinctly international context. The question in *Mitsubishi* had been whether the Court would extend to international antitrust claims the solicitude for arbitration that it had demonstrated in *Scherk*.

The Court's hospitality toward arbitration of federal statutory claims has continued in the years since *Mitsubishi* was decided. The Court has thus treated as legally capable of being arbitrated claims arising under such legislation as the Carriage of Goods by Sea Act[15] and the Racketeering and Corrupt Influenced Organizations Act (RICO).[16] Nor is the *Mitsubishi* decision without a counterpart elsewhere in the world. Notably, as discussed below, the *Eco Swiss v. Benneton* judgment of the European Court of Justice likewise treated competition law claims as arbitrable.[17]

In *Mitsubishi*, Justice Stevens, joined by Justices Brennan and Marshall, dissented on two grounds–first that the arbitration clause could not properly be construed to embrace claims under the antitrust statutes, and second that, even if it could be so

---

11. *Id.* at 636-637.
12. *Id.* at 637.
13. *See generally* Eric James Fuglsang, *The Arbitrability of Domestic Antitrust Disputes: Where Does the Law Stand?*, 46 DePaul L. Rev. 779 (1997).
14. 417 U.S. 506, 417 U.S. 515-520 (1974).
15. *Vimar Seguros y Reaseguros, S. A. v. M/V Sky Reefer* (94-623), 515 U.S. 528 (1995).
16. *PacifiCare Health Sys. v. Book*, 538 U.S. 401 (2003).
17. *Eco Swiss China Time Ltd. v. Benetton International NV*, Case C-126/97, [1999] ECR I-3055.

construed, "the unique public interest in the enforcement of the antitrust laws" requires that the adjudication of such claims be reserved to the courts:

> [B]oth a fair respect for the importance of the interests that Congress has identified as worthy of federal statutory protection, and a fair appraisal of the most likely understanding of the parties who sign agreements containing standard arbitration clauses, support a presumption that such clauses do not apply to federal statutory claims.[18]
>
> Like any other mechanism for resolving controversies, international arbitration will only succeed if it is realistically limited to tasks it is capable of performing well—the prompt and inexpensive resolution of essentially contractual disputes between commercial partners. As for matters involving the political passions and the fundamental interests of nations, even the multilateral convention adopted under the auspices of the United Nations recognizes that private international arbitration is incapable of achieving satisfactory results.[19]

Clearly, the majority and the dissent took markedly different positions on the best way to reconcile two distinct U.S. public policies: the public policy in favor of international arbitration and the public policy in favor of vigorous antitrust law enforcement. However, as will be demonstrated below, there is more to the *Mitsubishi* decision than its central proposition that antitrust claims under U.S. law are arbitrable.

III   THE "SECOND-LOOK" DOCTRINE

While the Supreme Court referred the antitrust claim at issue in the dispute to arbitration, it had sufficient misgivings in doing so that it sought some assurance that the arbitral tribunal would in fact entertain the antitrust claim in the case. The U.S. Government had in fact questioned whether an arbitral tribunal might read the contract's Swiss choice-of-law clause, "not simply to govern interpretation of the contract terms, but wholly to displace American law even where it otherwise would apply."[20] The Government regarded it as "[c]onceivabl[e], although ... unlikely, [that] the arbitrators could consider Soler's affirmative claim of anticompetitive conduct by CISA and Mitsubishi to fall within the purview of this choice-of-law provision, with the result that it would be decided under Swiss law rather than the U.S. Sherman Act."[21]

The Court was in fact reassured by the fact that at oral argument, "counsel for Mitsubishi conceded that American law applied to the antitrust claims, and represented that the claims had been submitted to the arbitration panel in Japan on that basis" and that "the arbitral panel had taken these claims under submission."[22] On that basis, the Court stated:

---

18. 473 U.S. at 653.
19. *Id*. at 666.
20. *Id*. at 637, n. 19.
21. *Id*.
22. *Id*.

We therefore have no occasion to speculate on this matter at this stage in the proceedings, when Mitsubishi seeks to enforce the agreement to arbitrate, not to enforce an award.[23]

Importantly, however, the Court contemplated, though did not address, the possibility that the arbitral tribunal might not "take cognizance" of Soler's antitrust claims and "actually decide them":

Nor need we consider now the effect of an arbitral tribunal's failure to take cognizance of the statutory cause of action on the claimant's capacity to reinitiate suit in federal court. We merely note that, in the event the choice-of-forum and choice-of-law clauses operated in tandem as a prospective waiver of a party's right to pursue statutory remedies for antitrust violations, we would have little hesitation in condemning the agreement as against public policy.[24]

The Court thus did not rule out the possibility that the arbitral tribunal would fail to give effect to the U.S. antitrust laws, thus in effect offending U.S. public policy. In that circumstance, a U.S. court would still have a role to play. The Court amplified as follows:

Having permitted the arbitration to go forward, the national courts of the United States will have the opportunity at the award-enforcement stage to ensure that the legitimate interest in the enforcement of the antitrust law has been addressed. The Convention reserves to each signatory country the right to refuse enforcement of an award where the recognition or enforcement of the award would be contrary to the public policy of that country. While the efficacy of the arbitral process requires that substantive review at the award-enforcement stage remain minimal, it would not require intrusive inquiry to ascertain that the tribunal took cognizance of the antitrust claims and actually decided them.[25]

This last proposition has come to be known as the "second look" doctrine, because of the prospect that a court would subject a tribunal's disposition of an antitrust claim to some measure of post-award merits review. The Court did not indicate precisely what a court would do in such a circumstance. Denial of enforcement would be entirely beside the point since, if Soler failed to recover on the antitrust claim, there would be no award to enforce, and thus no enforcement action. Moreover, there is no guarantee that the enforcement action that might conceivably be brought would be brought in the United States rather than elsewhere. The remedy the Court must have been contemplating, though without saying so, is denial of recognition of the award for violation of public policy, in which case U.S. courts would become available to entertain Soler's antitrust claim.

Taking a second look at arbitral determinations of US antitrust claims may of course be logically reconciled with the U.S. courts' recognition and enforcement obligations under the New York Convention on the ground that doing so amounts to nothing more than giving effect to the Convention's public policy exception. However, it plainly opens up the possibility of judicial review of the merits of an award, a move

23. *Id.*
24. *Id.*
25. 473 U.S. at 639.

contrary to the Convention's overall purpose and spirit. As is well-known, the Convention grounds for denying recognition and enforcement are designed in such a way as to avoid the possibility of merits review by a court before which recognition or enforcement of an award is sought.

The Court gave no indication of what the requirement that tribunals "take cognizance" of the antitrust claim actually entails and courts have had scant opportunity to address the matter. A "second look" may take a variety of forms. A court might understand the notion of "taking cognizance" of a statute somewhat literally and demand nothing more than that the statutory claim, in fact, be entertained. This would represent a "minimalist" approach. A court may however go further to examine the merits, but nevertheless in doing so designedly show some considerable deference to the tribunal, accepting its decision unless manifestly wrong. This would amount to an intermediate approach. Or it may go still further and examine the merits on a fully de novo basis—a "maximalist" approach. These approaches are decidedly different in their impact on an award's finality.

1   Standard of Review in a Second Look

Proponents of a minimalist approach essentially require nothing more than that the tribunal address and decide the antitrust claims brought before it, regardless of how well it does so. In *Baxter International Incorporated v. Abbot Laboratories*,[26] the award debtor resisted enforcement of an award on the ground that it was in violation of U.S. antitrust law. The award debtor argued that arbitrators cannot "command parties to violate rules of positive law." A majority of the court was not persuaded, finding that the tribunal had addressed the antitrust issue on the merits and that its determination was conclusive.[27] Its approach may indeed be justified on the basis of the plain language of *Mitsubishi*, since in addressing and deciding the antitrust claim, the tribunal necessarily had "taken cognizance" of it. The deference owed to the tribunal on the merits was complete. For its part, the dissent viewed the majority view as essentially rendering the role of a court meaningless.[28] "I do not agree that there is support in the law for the majority's excision of antitrust arbitration from the general framework of judicial review that prohibits an arbitration panel's award from commanding illegal conduct.[29] For the dissenting judge, in order to meet the concerns expressed by the Court in *Mitsubishi*, there had to be at least some indication that the tribunal evaluated the antitrust claims before it properly. The dissent was also unimpressed by the majority's observation that, even if a faulty award were to be enforced, any affected third party, not being bound by the award or the judgment enforcing it, would be free to relitigate the issue.[30]

---

26. 315 F.3d 829 (7th Cir. 2003).
27. *Id*. at 832.
28. *Id*. at 836.
29. *Id*. at 839.
30. *Id*.

183

Some courts have gone still further, excusing a tribunal for not taking cognizance of a party's antitrust claim, provided that, in entertaining and deciding a claim arising under some other jurisdiction's law, a tribunal nevertheless afforded the claimant relief that was adequate in light of antitrust law's purposes. In the very recent case of *Cvoro v. Carnival Corp.*,[31] a cruise ship worker initiated arbitration in Monaco, as provided for by the arbitration agreement, against a cruise operator for injuries sustained aboard the cruise line, invoking U.S. law, notably the Jones Act[32] and general maritime law, but not Panamanian law, which was the law of the contract, even though that law appeared to furnish claimant a remedy. The tribunal chose to apply Panamanian law, even though it had not been pled, finding that the claimant was not entitled to damages under that law. The tribunal did not in fact entertain the claimant's claims under U.S. law on the ground that there was not a sufficiently close connection between the U.S. and the dispute, applying instead Panamanian law, which had been designated as the law governing the contract. Having failed in the arbitration, claimant instituted suit in the U.S., essentially challenging the award's entitlement to recognition under the New York Convention. Claimant argued that recognition of the award would offend U.S. public policy in favor of protection of seafarers. Though the court agreed that U.S. public policy demanded protection of seafarers, it did not in fact require that the tribunal "take cognizance" of the U.S. seamen's protection laws. It required only that the law selected by the tribunal, in place of U.S. law, offer some degree of protection, more specifically that the award "was not so inadequate as to violate this nation's 'most basic notions of morality and justice.'"[33] The court went on to hold:

> Ultimately, at this arbitration-award-enforcement stage, the test for whether a court should refuse to enforce a foreign arbitral award based on public policy is not whether the claimant was provided with all of her statutory rights under U.S. law during arbitration ... Rather, the public-policy defense applies only when confirmation or enforcement of a foreign arbitration award would violate the forum state's most basic notions of morality and justice.[34]

According to an intermediate view, a tribunal's determination of an antitrust claim must, in view of antitrust's importance, be subject to some measure of review. The goal is to strike a balance between the competing policies of enforcing arbitral awards and effectuating U.S. public policy. Taking a second look, it is argued, entails nothing more than giving effect to the New York Convention's public policy defense to enforcement,[35] which ensures that enforcement does not operate to offend "the most

---

31. *Cvoro v. Carnival Corp.*, 941 F.3d 487 (11th Cir. 2019).
32. 46 U.S.C. § 30104.
33. *Id.* at 500.
34. *Id.* at 503-504. To the same effect, *see Simula, Inc. v. Autoliv*, Inc., 175 F.3d 716 (1999), n. 4, where the court observed in a footnote that, even if the tribunal applied Swiss law (the substantive law of the contract) instead of U.S. law to the antitrust claims, the court would not hesitate to enforce the arbitration agreement without a showing that Swiss law would not provide the claimant with "sufficient protection."
35. United Nations Convention on the Recognition and Enforcement of Foreign Arbitral Awards (adopted June 10, 1958, entered into force June 7, 1959) (New York Convention), Article V(2)(b).

basic notions of morality and justice."[36] In fact, the Court in *Mitsubishi* did essentially predicate the second-look doctrine on the public policy exception. By denying enforcement of awards that blatantly contravene the policies underlying the Sherman Act, courts would avoid second-guessing the tribunal, while still showing an important degree of respect for U.S. public policy. Thus, not every error in the application of antitrust, or any mandatory law for that matter, will implicate the fundamental policies of that law. According to one scholar, courts under this approach show considerable deference to tribunals, intervening only when "fundamental principles" of competition law are ignored by a tribunal or when violations are apparent on the face of an award.

Of course, reasonable persons can readily disagree on whether an award violates a principle of antitrust law that is fundamental enough or is sufficiently evident from the face of an award to justify a denial of enforcement. That is one of the inherent disadvantages of the intermediate approach described here. Even so, this approach has the advantage of maintaining the arbitrability of antitrust claims, without unduly prejudicing the effectiveness of either U.S. antitrust law or the law of arbitration. It also would appear to be workable.

A maximalist approach, contemplating de novo review of arbitral awards in the antitrust field, raises obvious objections. If it opens up the possibility of searching for judicial review of the merits of an award, it runs contrary to the New York Convention's overall purpose and spirit. As is well-known, the Convention grounds for denying recognition and enforcement are designed in such a way as to avoid the possibility of merits review by the court before which recognition or enforcement is sought. It is also difficult to square the maximalist view with the Supreme Court's demanding that tribunals do nothing more than "take cognizance" of antitrust claims.

Not only does the maximalist approach represent a real threat to the finality of arbitral awards in the field, but it calls into question the wisdom of subjecting antitrust claims to arbitration in the first place. If arbitral determinations of antitrust claims are going to receive so little respect, why should those claims go to arbitration in the first place? Thus, a main critique of *Mitsubishi* runs this way: Has the Supreme Court, in widening the universe of arbitrable claims subject to arbitration to include statutory claims of such paramount importance, paid too great a long-term price in terms of the principle of finality upon which arbitration depends? Would it ultimately have been more pro-arbitration, rather than less, for the Court to have denied the arbitrability of antitrust claims, thereby leaving intact traditional limits on post-award judicial review?

While the minimalist, intermediate and maximalist positions are all tenable, it is appropriate, in evaluating them, to take into consideration the policies that the Supreme Court most likely sought to advance through the *Mitsubishi* decision. One such policy is preserving the arbitrability of competition law claims. It has plausibly been suggested that absent an assurance that tribunals will be attentive to the policies underlying antitrust law, States are apt to withdraw antitrust matters from the realm of arbitration entirely. Accordingly, something more needs to be asked of arbitral tribunals than *Baxter* and arguably *Cvoro* asked. The premise of this argument is, of

---

36. *Parsons & Whittemore Overseas Co. v. Societe Generale de L'Industrie du Papier (RAKTA)*, 508 F.2d 969, 973 (2d Cir. 1974).

course, that the Court in *Mitsubishi* was indeed seeking to expand the universe of arbitrable disputes and that, more generally, submission of antitrust claims to arbitration is good policy. The latter proposition is not uncontested.[37] Among other reasons is the prospect that the arbitrability of antitrust claims, particularly if a measure of merits review is permitted at the enforcement stage, would result in multiple rounds of adjudication of the same claim.[38]

2   A Second Look under European Union Law

The "standard of review" question that the Supreme Court confronted in *Mitsubishi* resembles the question that the European Court of Justice faced in the landmark case of *Eco Swiss China Time Ltd v. Benetton International NV.*[39] In *Eco Swiss*, the Court of Justice ruled that a Member State court is obligated to annul an award that fails to give effect to European Union law norms of a public policy character, whether or not the party seeking annulment raised the issue in the arbitration. The Court subsequently extended this position to violation of consumer protection norms of a public policy character.[40]

Because the party seeking annulment in *Eco Swiss* had not raised a competition law defense, and there was, therefore, no competition law ruling to assess, the Court had no occasion to address the question of the standard of review to be exercised in such cases. However, in the awards that gave rise to Member State court cases that followed *Eco Swiss*, the arbitral tribunal did consider and rule on a competition law claim or defense.

Member State courts did not all address the matter the same way, some taking an approach resembling the intermediate approach described above (which in those circles is termed a "minimalist" approach, and others taking a maximalist approach, with that term having essentially the same meaning attached to it above). Under the former, typified by a leading French case,[41] a court annuls or denies enforcement of an award due to an error in the application of a public policy principle only if the error is, in the words of the court, "flagrant, effective and concrete." The award may not be annulled or denied enforcement if the tribunal considered the competition law claim and dealt with it in a way that may have been mistaken but does not rise (or fall) to the level of a violation of *ordre public*. At the same time, a Dutch court adopted a maximalist position, authorizing and in fact requiring a reviewing court to make its own independent judgment on the competition law issue in the case.[42] At the present

---

37. *See* Hans Smit, *Mandatory Rules in International Commercial Arbitration*, 18 Am. Rev. Int'l. Arb. 155.
38. *Id.*
39. Case C-126/97, [1999] ECR I-3079, 3086, 3094 (June 1, 1999); *see* Robert B. Von Mehren, *The Eco Swiss Case and International Arbitration*, 19 Arb. Int'l. 468 (2003).
40. *Mostaza Claro v. Centro Movil Milenium SL*, Case C-168/05, [2006] ECR I-10421.
41. *Thalès Air Defence v. Euromissile*, November 18, 2004, Rev arb. 2005 751 (Cour d'Appel Paris, 1er ch).
42. *Marketing Displays International Inc. v. VR Van Raalte Reclame B.V.*, 24.3.2005, NJF 2005/239, TvA 2006/24 (Gerechtshof Haag).

time, the minimalist position has considerably greater support both in Member State courts and in the literature.[43]

Though offered an opportunity on two occasions to do so, the European Court of Justice has not yet decided the issue. In the case of *Genentech Inc. v Hoechst GmbH and Sanofi-Aventis Deutschland GmbH*,[44] Advocate-General Wathelet, opining on the matter, urged that arbitral rulings on competition law claim, due to their *ordre public* character, be subject to de novo review in annulment and enforcement actions. He wrote:

> 58. In my opinion, limitations on the scope of the review of international arbitral awards such as those under French law ...— namely the flagrant nature of the infringement of international public policy and the impossibility of reviewing an international arbitral award on the ground of such an infringement where the question of public policy was raised and debated before the arbitral tribunal— are contrary to the principle of effectiveness of EU law.
>
> ...
>
> 67. Consequently, it makes no difference whether the infringement of the public policy rule was flagrant or not. No system can accept infringements of its most fundamental rules making up its public policy, irrespective of whether or not those infringements are flagrant or obvious.

The debate within the EU continues. Some commentators favor a minimalist approach in the interest of avoiding judicial second-guessing of arbitral determinations on the merits and promoting the finality of awards.[45] Others argue for a maximalist approach in the view that, unless courts play that role, public policy claims, like competition law claims, risk being declared non-arbitrable.[46] Interestingly, both views are advanced as "pro-arbitration."[47]

IV   APPLYING THE "NON-CHOSEN" LAW

A further but less widely noted question faced by the Supreme Court in *Mitsubishi* was whether a tribunal, directed by a contractual choice-of-law clause to apply the law of a given jurisdiction, may nevertheless entertain and adjudicate a claim arising under a different body of national law. In the *Mitsubishi* case, the parties had agreed to both (a) an arbitration clause according to which "[a]ll disputes, controversies or differences which may arise between [the parties] out of or in relation to ... this Agreement or for the breach thereof shall be finally settled by arbitration in Japan in accordance with the rules and regulations of the Japan Commercial Arbitration Association" and (b) a

---

43. Luca Radicati Di Brozolo, *Arbitration and Competition Law: The Position of the Courts and of Arbitrators*, 27 Arb. Int'l. 1 (2011).
44. Case C-567/14, [2016] ECR I-526.
45. P. Heitzmann & J. Grierson, *SNF v. Cytec Industrie: National Courts within the EC Apply Different Standards to Review International Awards Contrary to Article 81 EC*, 2007 Stockholm Int'l. Arb. Rev. 39 (2007).
46. G. Cordero-Moss, *Balancing Arbitrability and Court Control*, in Global Private International Law (ed. H. Muir-Watt, L. Bizikova, A. Brandao de Oliveirs & D. Fernandez Arroyo) (2019), p.82.
47. *See generally* George A. Bermann, *What Does It Mean to Be Pro-arbitration?*, 34 Arb. Int'l. 341 (2018).

choice-of-law clause according to which "[t]his Agreement is made in, and will be governed by and construed in all respects according to the laws of the Swiss Confederation as if entirely performed therein."

The question naturally arises whether a tribunal that is called upon to apply Swiss law may, consistent with the parties' intent, proceed to entertain an antitrust claim arising under another jurisdiction's law, i.e., the U.S. antitrust statutes. Arguably, a tribunal that applies to a covered claim a law other than the law selected by the parties thereby commits an excess of authority—a circumstance that would in principle justify the annulment of the resulting award under the Federal Arbitration Act[48] or denial of enforcement under the New York Convention.[49] Nevertheless, the Supreme Court in Mitsubishi presumed that the arbitral tribunal sitting in Tokyo, in that case, could and would indeed apply the U.S. antitrust laws, notwithstanding the contractual choice of law designating Swiss law. As noted,[50] the Court reasoned somewhat obliquely that "[t]here is no reason to assume at the outset of the dispute that international arbitration will not provide an adequate mechanism." The Court acknowledged that the tribunal "owes no prior allegiance to the legal norms of particular states [and] has no direct obligation to vindicate their statutory dictates." It concluded importantly that:

> Where the parties have agreed that the arbitral body is to decide a defined set of claims which includes, as in these cases, those arising from the application of American antitrust law, the tribunal therefore should be bound to decide that dispute in accord with the national law giving rise to the claim.[51]

Put in simpler terms, an arbitration clause drafted broadly enough to encompass noncontractual claims may empower a tribunal to decide those claims in accordance with the national law under which they arise, even if that law is other than the law chosen by the parties. This result is not difficult to accept if a given dispute is sufficiently related to a contract to be governed by the contract's arbitration clause, and thus subject to arbitration, but not fall within the scope of a choice-of-law clause drafted narrowly to cover breach of contract claims only. Such was the case in *Mitsubishi* (the choice-of-law clause in *Mitsubishi* provided that the contract "will be governed by and construed in all respects according to the laws of the Swiss Confederation."). If the antitrust claim, though arbitrable, is not governed by the choice-of-law clause, the tribunal has considerable freedom to determine the law by which to adjudicate the claim, and will indeed most likely apply to that claim the law under which the claim itself arises.

This result, though logical, may well be contrary to the parties' actual intentions. The parties may well have meant for all disputes between them bearing any relation to their contract to be governed by the law designated in the contract's choice-of-law clause, thus excluding any possibility that their legal relations might be governed by any other body of law. The only way the parties can hope to prevent a tribunal from

---

48. 9 U.S.C. section 10.
49. New York Convention., Articles V(1)(c), V(1)(d).
50. *See supra* n. 11.
51. *Id.*

applying to their dispute a law other than the chosen one would be to draft the choice-of-law clause in such a way as to govern every claim possibly falling within the scope of their agreement to arbitrate. But even that precaution may fail to secure the intended result, for the simple reason that a tribunal may, in one compelling circumstance or another, feel justified in applying the mandatory law of some other jurisdiction, notwithstanding the breadth of the choice-of-law clause. When if ever a tribunal should take such a step remains a contested issue.

The breadth of the arbitration clause in *Mitsubishi* and the relative narrowness of the Swiss choice-of-law clause thus opened up a path for application of the Sherman Act, notwithstanding the choice-of-law clause. This was possible because the choice-of-law clause was, by its terms, narrower in application than the arbitration clause. But an arbitration clause will not in all cases be broader in scope than a choice-of-law clause. Both could cover, as the choice-of-law clause in *Mitsubishi* did not, "any and all claims arising out of or related to this contract." Claims falling within the scope of the arbitration clause would then necessarily also fall within the scope of the choice-of-law clause. If the two clauses are indeed coterminous, there is arguably no room for application of the Sherman Act.

But that the choice-of-law and arbitration clauses might have the same boundaries does not necessarily bar application of the norm of a law not chosen. A tribunal might well, even while conceding the breadth of the choice-of-law clause, characterize the Sherman Act as a mandatory rule of law—thus, by definition, applicable, to the dispute, notwithstanding the choice of law. The application to a dispute of a legal norm derived from the law of a jurisdiction other than the one whose law the parties chose is of course somewhat problematic. That prospect places arbitral tribunals in something of a dilemma. If a tribunal applies to a given claim a mandatory legal norm drawn from a body of law other than the one the parties selected, its award runs a real risk of annulment or denial of enforcement as in excess of authority, though presumably not if the arbitral seat is found in the jurisdiction whose mandatory law the tribunal chose to apply, or if the award is brought for enforcement to that jurisdiction. A court is unlikely to quarrel with an award that gives effect to the mandatory law of the jurisdiction to which the court belongs. On the other hand, if a tribunal declines, on account of the parties' choice of law, to apply the mandatory law of an interested State, its award may not fare well, at least in a court of the jurisdiction whose mandatory law was in issue, on the ground of public policy.

Discussion over when, if ever, a tribunal should apply a mandatory norm found in a non-chosen body of law, though longstanding, will doubtless continue. The weight of authority among commentators favors the application of the mandatory law of a third State in appropriate circumstances,[52] but opinion remains divided.[53] One may well maintain that application of a third State's law is contrary to the actual intentions

---

52. *See, e.g.*, Pierre Mayer, *Mandatory Rules of Law in International Arbitration*, 2 Arb. Int'l. 274 (1986); Ibrahim Shehata, *Application of Overriding Mandatory Rules in International Commercial Arbitration: An Empirical* Analysis, 2017 World Arb. & Med. Rev. (2017).
53. *See generally* Jan Kleinheisterkamp, *Overriding Mandatory Laws in International Arbitration*, 67 Int'l. & Comp. L.Q. 903 (2018).

of parties who took the trouble to include a choice-of-law clause in their contract and to draft it broadly. It is not unreasonable to suppose that the parties meant for the chosen law to apply to all disputes between them arising out of their contract to the exclusion of any other jurisdiction's law, however mandatory it may be considered within that jurisdiction.

On the other hand, in many jurisdictions, national courts are willing, in exceptional circumstances, to apply to a dispute before them a mandatory provision of a law not chosen by the parties in their choice-of-law clause. A powerful consensus has arisen that a court's doing so is legitimate, again in appropriate circumstances, on the theory that party autonomy has its limits.

The question arises whether arbitral tribunals should enjoy the same prerogative. One may well argue that all countries have a right to establish the conflicts of law regimes for their courts that they wish, and the regime they choose may well provide for application of a third State's law in certain circumstances. That will then be the conflicts of law rule in the courts of those States, binding on all parties that appear before them. If that is the case, such parties must accept that choice-of-law rule. It is the price—as is any conflicts of law rule, or civil procedure rule for that matter—that parties pay when their dispute is laid before a national court.

The question is how readily to acknowledge an analogy between arbitral tribunals and national courts in this respect. In agreeing to arbitrate a dispute pursuant to an arbitration agreement entered into by the parties, an arbitrator commits to following the ground rules the parties established in that agreement. Regardless of the rationale, a failure to do so looks very much like an excess of authority on the arbitrator's part. To heighten the force of the argument, imagine that the parties' choice of law is not embodied in a contract clause entirely separate from the arbitration clause—which is the usual case—but directly in the arbitration clause itself, the clause from which a tribunal draws its authority.

In fact, the prospect of applying a non-chosen law, due to its mandatory character, places a tribunal in something of a dilemma. If that law is applied, the resulting award risks annulment or nonenforcement on excess of authority grounds in courts of States other than the one whose mandatory law was applied. If that law is not applied, the resulting award risks annulment or nonenforcement on public policy grounds in courts of the State whose mandatory law did not receive application. We have not as yet a basis for determining where the greater risk lies.

V   CONCLUSION

It is a small wonder that the *Mitsubishi* case is considered among the seminal international arbitration cases in U.S. jurisprudence. For it to have declared antitrust claims arbitrable, as it did, was a momentous step—not only due to the well-settled precedent pointing in a different direction but also due to the paramountcy of the antitrust laws in the U.S. legal system and the degree of public interest with which it is imbued. It stands at least on par with the *Eco-Swiss* judgment of the European Union Court of Justice in that regard. As a result of *Mitsubishi*, we are able to say with greater confidence than previously that no claim arising under U.S. legislation will be treated as non-arbitrable unless Congress more or less explicitly so states in the statutory language.

The *Mitsubishi* decision was also the first occasion on which the U.S. Supreme Court announced that U.S. courts will entertain on the merits an antitrust claim that went to arbitration but of which the arbitral tribunal failed to "take cognizance." We still stand to learn much more than we have about the "second look" doctrine that the Court in *Mitsubishi* devised as a kind of compromise between treating antitrust claims as non-arbitrable, on the one hand, and treating an arbitral tribunal's disposition of a claim, as important as it may be, as entirely unreviewable, on the other.

Finally, the Court took a major step in positing that an arbitral tribunal sitting in Japan and hearing a claim arising out of a contract containing a Swiss choice-of-law clause would, despite that clause, be willing to entertain a U.S. antitrust claim. Aware as it must have been of the parties' choice of law, the Court may have reasoned, without actually informing us, that, while antitrust claims fell within an arbitration clause, they did not fall within the choice-of-law clause.

But it probably does not matter whether the two clauses are or are not congruent in coverage. If the U.S. antitrust laws are mandatory in nature, an arbitral tribunal may be willing to apply them on that basis alone. The Court made no express allusion to the notion of mandatory law, which is hardly surprising since the term is not in the U.S. legal lexicon. But that may be precisely what the Court had in mind.

It remains only to ponder whether in *Mitsubishi* the outcome would have been any different if the scope of the choice-of-law clause and the arbitration clause had been identical. One cannot tell from the *Mitsubishi* decision. But it may be fair to assume, from the Court's willingness to elevate the Sherman Act to a level warranting a second look, that it would have made the same assumption that the tribunal in Tokyo was prepared to enforce it, notwithstanding the Swiss choice of law—and accordingly send the dispute to arbitration overseas, albeit on condition of a potential second look.

The question ultimately arises whether the Court did the right thing, sending antitrust cases to arbitration, despite its evident doubts that tribunals would interpret and apply it correctly while compensating for that concern by taking a "second look" at the award on the merits. Doing so does not serve the principle of party autonomy very well (the parties having chosen Swiss law), nor serve antitrust law very well (considering its doubts about tribunals' ability to handle antitrust claims properly), nor serve international arbitration very well (inviting post-award merits review). The better course, though it may not have been viewed as particularly pro-arbitration, may well have been to consider antitrust claims to be non-arbitrable.

PANEL 3   II. State Responsibility – Then and Now

CHAPTER 11

The International Law Commission and Its Articles on State Responsibility

*Bruno Simma**

TABLE OF CONTENTS

I   INTRODUCTORY REMARKS

I have been asked to introduce the International Law Commission and its product of main relevance to ICCA today, the Articles on State Responsibility [Let me just mention in passing that I personally will never speak of the Articles as 'ARSIVA' because I consider this too ugly an abbreviation for such a beautiful piece of work]. I will introduce you to both the Commission and its work on State responsibility with real pleasure. And this is not just a figure of speech. Even though twenty years have passed since I left the Commission, I still have fond memories of the summers spent in Geneva (literally underground, Salle XXI) and in New York. In retrospect, I would go as far as saying that I felt intellectually more at ease in the Commission than in the Hague Court. Why? Probably because most Commission work allowed you to be creative in a genuine marketplace of ideas without that word, 'creative', having any of the negative

---

* Judge, International Court of Justice (2003-2012); Chairman, Chamber 1, Iran-US Claims Tribunal; member of the UN International Law Commission (1997-2003); cofounder and editor of the European Journal of International Law; a cofounder of the European Society of International Law; associate member of the Institut de Droit international.

ambiguity with which legal practitioners use it. And fortunately for my presentation today, it was the Commission's work on State responsibility that I found most exciting. But before I turn to it, let me introduce the Commission and what it achieved on State responsibility. I will do so in three short parts. First, I will describe the Commission and its working methods. Secondly, I will deal with the history and the result of the International Law Commission (ILC) project on State responsibility. And in a very brief third part, I will state my views on the relevance of the Articles on that subject for investment protection and arbitration.

II   THE INTERNATIONAL LAW COMMISSION AND ITS ACTIVITIES

The International Law Commission has its legal basis in no less a document than the UN Charter. The Charter makes the codification and progressive development of international law a mandate of the UN General Assembly. In 1947 the Assembly established an expert body to support it in that task – our Commission. Next year it will have been at work for seventy-five years. The Commission gave itself a Statute approved by the General Assembly. At present, the Commission consists of thirty-four members, five of them women, all of different nationalities and all elected by the General Assembly along national groupings for a period of five years. While the members of the Commission are to perform their functions in full independence from governmental influence and control, it is fair to say that, if they don't serve, or have served, in their home countries' public service from the beginning, all of them will be personalities recognized by their Foreign or Justice ministries as leading practitioners, diplomats or academics, trustworthy and internationally known. Result: not many nerdy types on the Commission.

For several decades now the Commission has engaged exclusively in public international law projects and it is highly unlikely that private international law subjects will be back on its agenda in view of the existence of UNCITRAL and the Hague Conference on Private International Law.

Being an active Commission member before having reached retirement age is quite demanding. The Commission's annual sessions last from ten to twelve weeks, this during summer time (and, as I already mentioned, most of it underground in the Geneva Palais des Nations). A good portion of idealism helps here. I hope this audience in particular will be duly impressed if I further tell you that members don't receive any financial compensation for their work except a *per diem* which at my time amounted to CHF 400 per day of work. And remember: vacancies at the International Court of Justice (ICJ) are rare!

How does the Commission perform its work? Over time, working methods and procedures have become quite complex and I can depict them only with a broad brush. In 1949 the Commission adopted an initial work plan comprising twenty-five topics on the basis of a proposal made by Hersch Lauterpacht; State responsibility was one of them. Common to all topics to be taken up by the ILC is that they must, or better: should, be 'ripe' for codification or progressive development. The final choice of a topic will always be subject of a consultative process between the ILC and the General

Assembly's Sixth [Legal] Committee – a mix between the Commission's sponsor and supervisor. The Sixth Committee remains engaged in every further step of the ILC's work. This coordination between expert work and institutionalized observation and control by the UN Member States is an element that I cannot emphasize enough because it prevents the Commission to develop into an ivory tower and to a degree guarantees that its work finds the blessing of its customers [if we find the time, I could later tell you an interesting story about how such 'observation and control' determined the outcome of what I consider an elementary issue in our context of State responsibility].

Back to the Commission's working method: Once a topic has been found worthwhile, within the Commission and following an interchange with the Sixth Committee, a decision will be taken to proceed with it and with what type of final product in sight – a convention, a set of articles as such, a set of principles, guidelines, a study or what have you – in recent years these categories have multiplied, with the traditional one of the multilateral convention steadily losing ground. The most important step will be the choice of a Special Rapporteur, the right one, I mean, because this choice will be of the utmost importance for the success of the entire enterprise. The Special Rapporteur will present a series of annual reports to be discussed in the Commission. Once progress has been made, a Drafting Committee will be appointed and gradually present the plenary with articles, for instance, and at some stage with commentaries thereto, with the Commission step by step adopting these products and shipping them to New York, at the end of this part of the process in what is called the First Reading. All of this is in constant exchange with the Sixth Committee. What follows, possibly after some creative break, are renewed discussions in the plenary and the Drafting Committee, the so-called Second Reading, culminating in the final adoption of the texts in question and its transmission to New York, where the UN General Assembly will then have the last word on the outcome's format.

Thus far the basics on the ILC and its activities. In the second part of my presentation, let me now turn to the story of the Articles on State Responsibility.

III   THE HISTORY AND RESULT OF THE ILC WORK ON STATE RESPONSIBILITY

It's a story involving quite a bit of drama.

Up to the mid-twentieth century, and particularly in the Common Law world, State responsibility was essentially conceived as responsibility for injury to the person or property of foreigners ('aliens'). This approach had developed since the nineteenth century in what we could call the first legal North-South conflict, turning around hotly debated issues like that of the 'international minimum standard' versus 'national treatment' and next to it diplomatic (or not so diplomatic) protection.

The Commission started its work on State responsibility in 1956, with the Cuban international lawyer Garcia Amador serving as Special Rapporteur. The Commission could hardly have chosen a less opportune moment to engage with our topic. In the US, a new North-South divide in international economic questions was building up and aggravated the old contentions I have just alluded to by putting them in the context of decolonization. Garcia Amador, while proceeding from the traditional narrative, attempted to give it new legitimacy by enriching it with human rights thinking. But that did not save his approach. At that time propagating ideas like that of a universal human right to private property, including foreign property, did not fit into legal-political correctness as viewed by the UN majority. It was clear that the topic, as conceived by its first Special Rapporteur, would not go anywhere. The Commission thus decided to postpone treatment of his Reports and, in fact, never discussed any of his proposals individually. A few years after the start of ILC work on State responsibility, this first attempt had headed straight into the wall.

(In this context I think it is interesting that the conceptual basis of 'contemporary investment protection' is still very close to the core of the traditional Western concept of State responsibility as 'responsibility for injury to aliens', even if we now might speak of 'liability for damage done to foreign investors'. What is also interesting is that at more or less the same time that the – multilateral – New International Economic Order was propagated at the UN, the project of – bilateral – protection of foreign investment was conceived).

Rescue for State responsibility, inter-State responsibility, as an ILC project came in the early 1960s, triggered by a stroke of genius attributable mainly to the Italian ILC member at the time, Roberto Ago. Returning to ideas he had developed in his early thirties, actually in lectures at the Hague Academy before World War II, Ago convinced the Commission of what deserves to be called a genuine paradigm change, namely to draw a distinction between so-called primary and secondary rules (not to be mistaken as the terminology developed by H.LA. Hart). I would call this distinction the '*first pillar*' of the modern law of State responsibility. Let me explain: By 'primary rules' were to be meant the substantive rules of international law leading to specific obligations of States, while by 'secondary rules' were to be understood those rules – exclusively – on the responsibility of the State that identify in an abstract way whether obligations deriving from primary rules were breached and what the consequences of such breach were. ILC's work on State responsibility was to focus as exclusively as possible on the codification of these 'secondary' rules. This would allow the Commission to develop State responsibility without being drawn into the countless disputes around 'primary rules', like the ones on protection of foreign property, that had paralysed the earlier ILC efforts. (Interestingly enough, Ago himself was responsible for an exception from this exercise of purification by abstraction; the 'international crimes of States'– a concept that Ago, moving on to the ICJ, left more or less unexplored and that plagued Commission work for decades to come.) What I also remember is that when the first chapters of ILC articles crafted according to the new approach, dealing with the origin of State responsibility were adopted, it took academia, particularly in the Common Law world, quite a while to overcome its *horror vacui*.

The fundamentals of Ago's and, following him, the Commission's draft proposals on what was called the origin of responsibility provided the basis for the conception of what I would call the '*second pillar*' of modern State responsibility law, namely its emancipation from the strict bilateralism that still characterized the law at the time. Let me explain: the articles, in their final form, have overcome the traditional civil and tort law approach to inter-State responsibility conditioned upon damage, by taking what at the time was recognized as a revolutionary step: for responsibility to occur it was now sufficient that an act of a State is (1) attributable to that State, and (2) constitutes a breach of an international obligation of that State. Damage done to another State through that act is not a necessary condition. Damage might possibly be a further condition, but only if a primary rule says so (the same is by the way the case with the subjective element of fault). And, of course, damage will remain relevant with regard to additional legal consequences, particularly concerning reparation or compensation. The effect of all of this is that State responsibility according to the Articles has become 'objectified', or, in other words, has become vested with characteristics of public law. And this allows regard for collective or community, interest. States incur international responsibility even if they did not, in failing to respect an international legal obligation, harm specific material interests of another State, and even if a breach did not inflict a direct injury on another subject of international law. What this implies for violations of internationally recognized human rights, for instance, is fundamental, considering that in most cases human rights violations affect a country's own nationals. Among the Articles, it is Article 48 which expresses this altruist turn of State responsibility most distinctly by allowing 'a State other than an injured State' to invoke responsibility (within certain limits, that is). In its commentary on the Article, the Commission acknowledges that here we have to do with a measure of 'progressive development', but the good news is that the ICJ, not known for great enthusiasm vis-à-vis progressive international law in general, has already given its mark of approval by applying Article 48 in two important cases (*Belgium v. Senegal* and currently *The Gambia v. Myanmar*).

There is thus reason for satisfaction here. But the situation is still far from perfect. What is missing, indeed glaringly so, is another, a third, pillar, so to speak, namely a procedural, or rather institutional public law element: unlike what we find in States under the rule of law, in the international law of State responsibility there exists no apparatus to realize our objectified responsibility regime on a regular and impartial basis. The objective regime is there, available to the other members of the international community, but there is not yet any overarching duty to resort to it.

The task of invoking responsibility against a law-breaking State, and if necessary enforcing performance of obligations in the collective interest, is still left to be realized by individual States if they so decide. The ILC Articles do not provide for any method of dispute settlement (in consequence probably of the sad fate experienced by proposals made by the Commission's second Italian Special Rapporteur on our topic).

I hope I have made clear what I consider to be the ILC's achievements in 'modernizing' what was the most persistent bilateralist, State-to-State oriented, chapter of general international law. In the further development of the Commission's project, the Special Rapporteurs following Roberto Ago, Willem Riphagen, Gaetano Arangio-Ruiz and James Crawford, followed and refined the approach of the two Pillars. The project's First Reading was achieved in 1996 on the basis of no less than twenty-eight (!) reports. I had the privilege of being a member of the Commission in the process of completion and Second Reading of the draft under the superb leadership of James Crawford, from 1997 to 2001. We finally adopted the Articles on 9 August 2001. On 12 December 2001, the UN General Assembly 'noted' the arrival of the Articles and commended them to the attention of Governments. (For the attention of drafters of arbitral awards, this is when the 'Draft Articles' became the 'Articles'.) By the way, formally, the final question about the format of the articles is still open; but in my view, the best course to follow is that things are left just as they are.

A couple of points at the end of this part of my presentation.

What must not be overlooked – and what might be regarded as a shortcoming – is the fact that the ILC Articles deal with the responsibility of States vis-à-vis other states only. They do not concern, at least not expressly, the responsibility of states vis-à-vis so-called non-State actors, be they insurgents, terrorists – or foreign investors. In view of this limitation, it is all the more astounding, how much of the law codified in our Articles is being accepted and applied for instance by members of this audience, just by the nature of things, as it were. I will return to this observation in a second.

Within their limited scope, the articles present a complete set of rules, the borders of which are defined by a number of saving clauses. Some of these clauses reserve proper *leges speciales.*

IV THE RELEVANCE OF THE ARTICLES FOR INVESTMENT PROTECTION AND ARBITRATION

In the preceding parts of this presentation, I have made you familiar with the Commission and its work on State responsibility. I hope you have become aware of the enthusiasm with which I followed what I would call the 'opening' of a set of extremely traditional international laws enabling it to impact contemporary problems breaking the established bilateral boundaries. But this particular development of State responsibility – towards a genuinely 'public' international law – is not the reason for the widespread acceptance, and even popularity of, the ILC Articles in ICCA circles. This is because the fundamental innovations I consider so important are of very little, if any, relevance, or applicability, to investment protection or international commercial arbitration – areas which remain characterized by a bilateralist playing field in which civilist, tort law traditions still govern (even though here we also witness some parallelism regarding the influx, and impact, of public law thinking. But here it plays out differently).

Of course, this does not mean that the ILC Articles lack the principles and rules which form the toolbox for our work in arbitration. All we need is there, state of the art, from the *Chorzow* formula to interest, albeit sometimes formulated with a borderline degree of generality. And in arbitration practice, mostly of course that of foreign investment arbitration, the ILC toolbox is put to use in such a regular and professional way that I would not hesitate to call the case law on international responsibility on the basis of the Articles a *jurisprudence constante.* This jurisprudence is of a quantity, and in large parts also of a quality, that goes beyond what arbitrations in inter-State cases have brought about. It is just that what we find in the toolbox constitutes the least modernized, the most traditional part of the Articles, still based on good old bilateralism. I cannot see any element of progressive development here. For details on this intersection between the articles and investor-State dispute settlement, I refer you to the winter/spring 2022 (special) issue of the International Centre for Settlement of Investment Disputes (ICSID) Review, actually a big tome that has just been published.

As far as I myself am concerned, I have a feeling that taking such intersection questions further might mean intruding on my friends, Christian's and Chester's, turf. Let me, therefore, stop here. Thanks for your attention.

CHAPTER 12

Some Thoughts on Frictions and Fault Lines in the Application by Investment Tribunals of the ILC Articles on State Responsibility

*Chester Brown**

I   INTRODUCTION

At its fifty-third session in August 2001, the International Law Commission (ILC) adopted the text of the Articles on the Responsibility of States for Internationally Wrongful Acts ('ILC Articles') and decided to recommend to the United Nations General Assembly that it 'take note' of the ILC Articles in a resolution.[1] In its Resolution 56/83 of 12 December 2001, the United Nations General Assembly duly took note of the ILC Articles, the text of which was annexed to Resolution 56/83, and commended the ILC Articles 'to the attention of governments without prejudice to the question of their

---

* Professor of International Law and International Arbitration, University of Sydney Law School; Barrister, 7 Wentworth Selborne Chambers, Sydney; Overseas Member, Essex Court Chambers, London. Thanks to my co-panellists (Stephen Drymer, Judge Bruno Simma, and Professor Christian Tams) for enlightening discussions on the issues raised in this article.
1. 'Report of the International Law Commission to the General Assembly on the Work of Its Fifty-Third Session', in *Yearbook of the International Law Commission* (2001), vol. II, part 2, Ch. IV, p. 25, paras 69-73 (UN Doc. A/56/10).

future adoption or other appropriate acts'.[2] This marked the culmination of a long gestation period, as the ILC had noted at its first session in 1949 that 'the principles of international law governing State responsibility' were suitable for codification, and the UN General Assembly had requested the ILC to begin this work in 1953.[3]

Now, just over twenty years since the adoption of the ILC Articles, it is timely to examine their reception and application by arbitral tribunals in investment treaty claims.[4] Judge Simma's contribution has concerned the role of the ILC and the development of the ILC Articles and their commentaries,[5] and Professor Tams has commented on the important role that is played by investment tribunals and practitioners of investment treaty arbitration in the 'normalisation' and the 'solidification' of the ILC Articles.[6] The purpose of the present contribution is to identify some past and ongoing 'frictions' and 'fault lines' in the application by investment tribunals of the ILC Articles. There has been some useful scholarship on this issue, not only by the principal architect of the ILC Articles, the late Judge James Crawford,[7] but also by others in the excellent special issue of the *ICSID Review – Foreign Investment Law Journal* which has been published on the occasion of the twentieth anniversary of the ILC's adoption of the Articles.[8]

In addressing the topic of 'frictions' and 'fault lines', one can do no better than start with one or two quotes by Judge Crawford himself. Writing twelve years ago, he noted that there was something of a paradox in the way that some investment treaty tribunals referred to the ILC Articles in their decisions and awards. He described it as tribunals simply engaging in a 'throat-clearing exercise' of paying lip service to the Articles before getting on with the real business of analysing the facts, determining the applicable legal standard, and disposing of the case. Judge Crawford also referred to

---

2. UN General Assembly Resolution 56/83 (12 December 2001).
3. UN General Assembly Resolution 799 (VIII) (7 December 1953).
4. This panel session is entitled 'Once Upon a Time in International Arbitration II: State Responsibility – Then and Now'.
5. Bruno Simma, 'The International Law Commission and Its Articles on State Responsibility', Chapter 11, this volume.
6. Christian Tams, 'Who's Afraid of the ILC Articles on State Responsibility', Chapter 13, in this volume.
7. For example, James Crawford, *The International Law Commission's Articles on State Responsibility: Introduction, Text and Commentaries* (CUP, 2002); James Crawford, Alain Pellet, Simon Olleson and Kate Parlett (eds), *The Law of International Responsibility* (OUP, 2010); James Crawford, 'Investment Arbitration and the ILC Articles on State Responsibility' (2010) 25 *ICSID Review – Foreign Investment Law Journal* 127; James Crawford, *State Responsibility: The General Part* (CUP, 2013).
8. The special issue begins with an introduction by Campbell McLachlan, 'James Crawford AC SC FBA (1948-2021): The General Law of State Responsibility and the Specific Case of Investment Claims' (2022) 37 *ICSID Review – Foreign Investment Law Journal* 1. *See also*, in particular (of relevance to the issues discussed in this article), James Crawford and Freya Baetens, 'The ILC Articles on State Responsibility: More Than a "Plank in a Shipwreck"?' (2022) 37 *ICSID Review – Foreign Investment Law Journal* 13; Carlo de Stefano, 'Attribution of Conduct to a State' (2022) 37 *ICSID Review – Foreign Investment Law Journal* 20; Eran Sthoeger and Christian Tams, 'Swords, Shields and Other Beasts: The Role of Countermeasures in Investment Arbitration' (2022) 37 *ICSID Review – Foreign Investment Law Journal* 121; Federica Paddeu and Michael Waibel, 'Necessity 20 Years On: The Limits of Article 25' (2022) 37 *ICSID Review – Foreign Investment Law Journal* 160; and Esmé Shirlow and Kabir Duggal, 'The ILC Articles on State Responsibility in Investment Treaty Arbitration' (2022) 37 *ICSID Review – Foreign Investment Law Journal* 378.

this tribunal practice as being 'a bit like a drowning man ... [grabbing] a stick at sea in the hope of having certainty'.[9] In this sense, the ILC Articles were a sort of *tabula in naufragio* or 'a plank in a shipwreck'.[10] On reading this comment, it is not clear that Judge Crawford could even be described as damning the existing arbitral practice by faint praise. But his assessment was more balanced; even concluding that tribunals had, on the whole, made a 'very conscientious and careful attempt in general to apply the Articles'.[11]

Having said this by way of introduction, there are five issues which demonstrate past or ongoing 'frictions' or 'fault lines' which warrant brief mention. These are (1) the relevance of the ILC Articles in investment arbitration; (2) the occasional conflation by some investment tribunals of the various tests of attribution; (3) some ongoing confusion between the rules of attribution (which are a question of international law) and the question of contractual liability (which is a question of the governing law of the contract) in claims for breach of the umbrella clause; (4) the relationship between exceptions clauses and customary international law, in particular, the role of circumstances precluding wrongfulness in Chapter V of Part One of the ILC Articles; and (5) the availability of countermeasures in investment arbitration.

II   INSTANCES OF 'FRICTIONS' OR 'FAULT LINES'

1   Applicability of the ILC Articles in Investment Arbitration

Beginning with the thorny question of whether the ILC Articles are even relevant and applicable in investment treaty arbitration, it is clear that many of the provisions do apply: those in Part One (which deals with the rules on attribution, breach, and circumstances precluding wrongfulness), and Part Four (which are the general provisions).[12] What is most problematic is whether the provisions of Part Two apply; these concern the content of international responsibility, and its consequences of responsibility, including the obligation to make full reparation, and these are among the most frequently cited provisions of the ILC Articles.[13] A recent study by Esme Shirlow and Kabir Duggal noted that there have been more than 200 references by tribunals to the provisions of Part Two in the last 20 years, and around 60 references to Article 31 alone (which is the obligation to make full reparation).[14]

The question regarding the applicability of Part Two arises because it is stated in Article 33(1) as setting out the obligations of a responsible State 'to another State, to several States, or to the international community as a whole' (not to individuals).[15] Article 33(2) further states that Part Two is 'without prejudice to any right ... that may

---

9. Crawford, 'Investment Arbitration and the ILC Articles on State Responsibility', *supra* n. 7, 128.
10. *Ibid.*, 135.
11. *Ibid.*
12. *Ibid.*, 129-130; Shirlow and Duggal, *supra* n. 8, 382-383.
13. Crawford, 'Investment Arbitration and the ILC Articles on State Responsibility', *supra* n. 7, 130-131.
14. Shirlow and Duggal, *supra* n. 8, 383, and Annex.
15. ILC Articles on State Responsibility, Article 33(1).

accrue directly to any person or entity other than a State'.[16] And so this tells us that these provisions have no formal application outside the field of inter-State relations, a point which Judge Crawford emphasised in his writings: as he explained, 'the ILC Articles make no attempt to regulate questions of breach between a state and a private party such as a foreign investor. Those rules must be found elsewhere in the corpus of international law, to the extent that they exist at all'.[17] In practice, however, tribunals have continued to refer to the provisions of Part II, either out of ignorance of their inapplicability (but also usually without objection of the parties) or simply by using them as a guide and as reflecting customary international law (such as the tribunal in *Crystallex v. Venezuela*).[18]

2   Conflation of Articles 4 and 5 on Attribution of Conduct

As to the second issue, on the issue of attribution, a number of arbitral tribunals have appeared to conflate the tests for attribution of the conduct of State organs (Article 4) with that which applies to State entities which have been empowered to exercise elements of governmental authority, when they are acting in that capacity (Article 5). Carlo de Stefano argues that some tribunals have reasoned 'on the basis of the commonality relating to the exercise of governmental authority and functions',[19] and refers to tribunals conflating Articles 4 and 5 into a 'super-test' of attribution.[20] An example can be found in *Bogdanov v. Moldova*, in which the tribunal referred to Article 4 of the ILC Articles, but also discussed the delegation of sovereign functions as follows:

> The Department of Privatisation is ... a central government body of the Republic of Moldova, delegated by Governmental regulations to carry out state functions, and the effects of its conduct may be attributed to the State. It is generally recognised, in international law, that States are responsible for the acts of their bodies or agencies that carry out State functions.[21]

As De Stefano explains, each test of attribution in Articles 4, 5 and 8 of the ILC Articles are separate, and 'deserve a differentiated and separate application', as they variously apply depending on the existence of organic or structural issues, functional links, or for factual reasons.[22] Needless to say, it would be preferable for tribunals to assess the separate tests for attribution individually 'in order to preserve the functioning and legal consequences' of each rule.[23]

---

16. *Ibid.*, Art 33(2).
17. Crawford, 'Investment Arbitration and the ILC Articles on State Responsibility', *supra* n. 7, 130.
18. *Crystallex v. Venezuela* (ICSID Case No. ARB(AF)/11/2, Award of 4 April 2016), para. 848, fn. 1242.
19. De Stefano, *supra* n. 8, 26-27.
20. *Ibid.*, 25.
21. *Bogdanov v. Moldova* (Award of 22 September 2005), para. 2.2.2.
22. De Stefano, *supra* n. 8, 26.
23. *Ibid.*, 27. Another case in point is *Maffezini v. Spain* (ICSID Case No. ARB/97/7, Decision on Jurisdiction of 25 January 2000), in which the tribunal appeared to considered the status of the

3 Confusion Between the Rules of Attribution and Rules of Contractual Liability

The third instance of 'friction' which warrants some discussion can be found in the error occasionally fallen into by tribunals which seek to apply rules of attribution in connection with claims for breach of contract.[24] This had already been noted as an area of confusion by Judge Crawford in 2010.[25] In this respect, some arbitral decisions have applied the rules on attribution in the context of claims for breach of the umbrella clause, in circumstances where the relevant contract had been entered into with a separate entity of the State. However the question of contractual liability is a question of the applicable law of the contract, not public international law, and there is 'no conception of the unity of the State in domestic law'.[26] Jorge Viñuales has noted that there are a number of distinct issues which fall for analysis, including the question of privity of contract (which is a question of domestic law); the abusive exercise of a contractual right (which, if carried out by a State organ, agency, or instrumentality, may be attributable to the State under international law, notwithstanding the absence of privity, unless the claims are presented under the umbrella clause); and the operation of the umbrella clause itself (e.g., which may provide that it applies to obligations 'entered into' by the State with foreign investors, which is a question of the governing law of the contract).[27] Jorge Viñuales has lamented that the arbitral practice has created 'significant uncertainty' regarding the operation of the rules of attribution, and 'even their very application'.[28] The correct approach is to recognise that 'foreign investors may not claim the breach of the umbrella clause in relation to undertakings entered into with parastatal entities, notably based on the latter's separate juristic personality'.[29] The tribunal in *Gavrilovic v. Croatia* correctly concluded that 'the rules of attribution cannot be applied to create primary obligations for a State under a contract'.[30]

4 Relationship Between Exceptions Clauses and Circumstances Precluding Wrongfulness

The fourth 'fault line' concerns the treatment by some tribunals of exceptions clauses in bilateral and multilateral investment treaties as being coextensive with defences

---

Sociedad para el Desarrollo Industrial de Galicia (SODIGA) through the prism of both Articles 4 and 5, applying a 'structural' and 'functional' test (paras 77-79).
24. De Stefano, *supra* n. 8, 25; Shirlow and Duggal, *supra* n. 8, 384; Crawford, 'Investment Arbitration and the ILC Articles on State Responsibility', *supra* n. 7, 134.
25. Crawford, 'Investment Arbitration and the ILC Articles on State Responsibility', *supra* n. 7, 134.
26. *Ibid.*
27. Jorge Viñuales, 'Attribution of Conduct to States in Investment Arbitration' (2022) 20 *ICSID Reports* 13, 80-82.
28. *Ibid.*, 80.
29. De Stefano, *supra* n. 8, 28.
30. *Gavrilovic v. Croatia* (ICSID Case No. ARB/12/39, Award of 26 July 2018), para. 856.

under customary international law, in particular the defence of necessity.[31] This occurred a number of times in the early cases against Argentina, and the awards of the tribunals in *CMS v. Argentine Republic*,[32] and in *Enron Corporation v. Argentine Republic*,[33] can be mentioned in particular. These tribunals appeared to conflate the exceptions clause in Article XI of the United States – Argentina bilateral investment treaty (BIT) with Article 25 of the ILC Articles; this was apparently because they both contain the term 'necessary', which the tribunals interpreted as requiring that the exceptions clause in the BIT be interpreted in light of Article 25, with the high threshold that must be shown (including that the measure adopted was 'the only way' for the State to safeguard against a 'grave and imminent peril'.)[34] These decisions have however been overtaken by more recent decisions in which tribunals have recognised that an exceptions clause and a circumstance precluding wrongfulness are analytically distinct, and arise at different stages of the analysis.[35]

One might have thought that this issue had been put to bed, but one still sees tribunals (perhaps unthinkingly) suggesting in awards that an exceptions clause should displace relevant customary international law. This appeared to occur in *Bear Creek v. Peru*, where the tribunal held that the general exceptions clause excluded the possibility of Peru invoking the police powers defence.[36] This is one matter, but the tribunal's disposal of the issue was done in such general terms that one of the arbitrators, Professor Philippe Sands KC, thought it necessary to append a Partial Dissenting Opinion in which he said that the exceptions clause could not preclude the availability of defences in the form of circumstances precluding wrongfulness under customary international law.[37]

5 Availability of Countermeasures

Finally, a fifth area of 'friction' which warrants brief mention concerns the availability of countermeasures in investment treaty arbitration.[38] These are provided for in Article 22 (in Part One of the ILC Articles), which confirms that the adoption of lawful

---

31. For example, Michael Waibel, 'Two Worlds of Necessity in ICSID Arbitration: *CMS* and *LG&E*' (2007) 20 *Leiden Journal of International Law* 637; Jurgen Kürtz, 'Adjudging the Exceptional at International Investment Law: Security, Public Order and Financial Crisis' (2010) 59 *International and Comparative Law Quarterly* 325; Caroline Henckels, 'Scope Limitation or Affirmative Defence? The Purpose and Role of Investment Treaty Exception Clauses', in Lorand Bartels and Federica Paddeu (eds), *Exceptions and Defences in International Law* (OUP, 2019), 363.
32. *CMS Gas Transmission Company v. Argentine Republic* (ICSID Case No. ARB/01/8, Award of 12 May 2005), paras 331ff.
33. *Enron Corporation and Ponderosa Assets LP v. Argentine Republic* (ICSID Case No. ARB/01/3, Award of 22 May 2007), paras 334ff.
34. ILC Articles on State Responsibility, Article 25.
35. For example, *Continental Casualty v. Argentina* (ICSID Case No. ARB/03/9, Award of 5 September 2008), paras 162-169.
36. *Bear Creek Mining Corporation v. Peru* (ICSID Case No. ARB/14/21, Award of 30 November 2017), paras 471-474.
37. *Bear Creek Mining Corporation v. Peru* (ICSID Case No. ARB/14/21, Partial Dissenting Opinion of Professor Philippe Sands KC of 12 September 2017), para. 41.
38. *See, e.g.*, Sthoeger and Tams, *supra* n. 8.

countermeasures is another type of 'circumstance precluding wrongfulness'.[39] The question that arises is whether respondent States can seek to justify their conduct by establishing that the impugned measure is in fact a lawful countermeasure, with the result that the State has a defence to the investor's claim. This only appears to have been considered by three tribunals, all in the context of the NAFTA sugar wars. In one case (*Archer Daniels Midland v. Mexico*),[40] the tribunal accepted the possibility (as argued by Mexico) that its adoption of the High Fructose Corn Syrup Tax could be characterised as a countermeasure, although it ultimately rejected the argument on the facts. In contrast, the other tribunals (in *Corn Products, Inc v. Mexico*,[41] and *Cargill v. Mexico*),[42] did not admit this possibility, finding that countermeasures are exclusively available in inter-State relations, and could only be directed at a State, rather than at a foreign investor. This divergence can in part be explained by whether you subscribe to the 'derivative rights' (*Archer Daniels Midland v. Mexico*) or 'direct rights' (*Corn Products, Inc v. Mexico*) theory of the nature of investor-State arbitration.[43] More recently, however, writers have admitted to the possibility that countermeasures can in certain circumstances be presented as a defence in investment treaty arbitration.[44]

III   CONCLUDING REMARKS

This brief review has identified a number of frictions and fault lines in the application of the ILC Articles on State Responsibility by investment tribunals. Perhaps these are manageable, rather than constituting a threat to the coherence of these rules. In closing, it should be noted that Judge Crawford had more recently revised his assessment of the arbitral practice. With some optimism, he concluded in the *ICSID Review*'s special issue that there was perhaps 'less of a "shipwreck" and more of a "seaworthy ship" today compared to a decade ago'.[45]

---

39. ILC Articles on State Responsibility, Article 22.
40. *Archer Daniels Midland v. Mexico* (ICSID Case No. ARB(AF)/04/5, Award of 21 November 2007).
41. *Corn Products, Inc v. Mexico* (ICSID Case No. ARB(AF)/04/01, Decision on Responsibility of 15 January 2008).
42. *Cargill, Inc v. Mexico* (ICSID Case No. ARB(AF)/05/2, Award of 18 September 2009).
43. *See further* Jan Paulsson, 'Arbitration Without Privity' (1995) 10 *ICSID Review – Foreign Investment Law Journal* 232; Zachary Douglas, 'The Hybrid Foundations of Investment Treaty Arbitration' (2003) 74 *British Yearbook of International Law* 151, 160-184; Martins Paparinskis, 'Investment Arbitration and the Law of Countermeasures' (2008) 79 *British Yearbook of International Law* 264, 334-345; Zachary Douglas, *The International Law of Investment Claims* (CUP, 2009) 11-38.
44. Sthoeger and Tams, *supra* n. 8, 134-135.
45. Crawford and Baetens, *supra* n. 8, 19.

CHAPTER 13

Who's Afraid of the Articles on State Responsibility

Christian J. Tams[*]

TABLE OF CONTENTS

I   THE ARTICLES ON STATE RESPONSIBILITY: OUTSIDE THE COMFORT ZONE?

Our panel has so far looked at the Articles on State Responsibility ('ASR' or 'Articles')
as a text that investment law and investment lawyers *receive*, and with which we have

---

[*] Professor of International Law, University of Glasgow & University of Paris 1 (Panthéon Sorbonne); academic member, Matrix Chambers London. Email: christian.tams@glasgow.ac.uk. My thanks to Stephen Drymer, Bruno Simma, Alison Macdonald and Chester Brown for helpful comments and engaging discussions.

to work even though it originates elsewhere, namely in the world of general/public international law.

This approach fits well with the rubric for our panel, which refers to the ASR as a 'crucial point of reference for international arbitration lawyers', but at the same time portrays this 'crucial text' as one developed by others, and perhaps primarily for other contexts, namely for a world of 'inter-State disputes' based on public international law. Looking at the panel description, perhaps we can say that it suggests or implies that arbitration lawyers confronted with arguments about State responsibility are required to leave their comfort zone, or in a different metaphor: must play an away game. And if we bear in mind Bruno Simma's account of the genesis of the Articles,[1] then who could disagree? The Articles were elaborated by the ILC, the UN's Law Commission, widely regarded as one of the (not so many remaining) guardians of general international law. In elaborating them, the ILC, in turn, was guided (at times in a process of 'normative ping-pong'[2]) by the jurisprudence of the World Court in its two incarnations, viz. the Permanent Court of International Justice and the International Court of Justice, which are, equally, perceived to be bastions of generalist thinking about international law. And of course, the ILC's work was closely followed by governments who offered comments notably in the UN Sixth Committee – and again, it was the foreign office lawyers that commented, who would have been unlikely, in the 1970s, 1980s and 1990s, to have had much contact with the world of investment arbitration. So in short, in terms of their pedigree, it is difficult to think of a more generalist text – a text that was prepared by generalists, and that of course is meant to be of general application, across international law's manifold branches, as it lays down 'the general conditions under international law for the State to be considered responsible for wrongful actions or omissions, and the legal consequences which flow therefrom'.[3]

II   THE STANDARD PERSPECTIVE: DO INVESTMENT LAWYERS GET THEIR STATE RESPONSIBILITY RIGHT?

All this explains the common perspective on the Articles as a body of rules that investment lawyers receive and with which they have to work with. And it perhaps also explains why a prominent strand of the literature devoted to the relationship between investment law/arbitration and the law of State responsibility (certainly in the general international law literature), is in the form of a performance assessment: Do the investment lawyers get the law of State responsibility right? Does their engagement with the Articles meet the expectations and standards of a general/public international law audience?

---

1. Bruno Simma, 'The International Law Commission and Its Articles on State Responsibility', Chapter 11, this volume.
2. On this aspect, see Christian J. Tams, Law-Making in Complex Processes: The World Court and the Modern Law of State Responsibility, in Chinkin and Baetens (eds), Sovereignty, Statehood and State Responsibility Essays in Honour of James Crawford (Cambridge University Press, 2015), 287.
3. Introductory ILC Commentary, in YbILC 2001, vol. II/2, at 31.

Three quotes by James Crawford, whose competence in both fields – State responsibility here, investment law there – is beyond dispute, are illustrative of this approach. All three are taken from 'Investment Arbitration and the ILC Articles on State Responsibility' published in the 2010 issue of the ICSID Law Review. First, the *Wintershall* tribunal's observation that the Articles 'contai[n] no rules and regulations of State Responsibility vis-à-vis non-State actors' was in for criticism: Part One of the Articles of course applied to the entirety of a State's obligations, including those owed to non-State actors, and so, on this point, the 'Wintershall Tribunal's analysis is incorrect'.[4] *UPS v. Canada* fared better: here Crawford saw 'careful use of the ILC Articles' on attribution, and to the extent that this careful use led the tribunal to consider that NAFTA contained a special rule of attribution, its 'decision, to [James Crawford's] mind, is completely correct'.[5] Third, the overall verdict is somewhere in the middle. '[T]the universe of [investment] cases is, on the whole, of variable quality', and many awards referred to the text 'by way of signposting rather than actually integrating the substance of the [ILC] Articles into the decision'.[6] What is more, 'there has been a certain tendency for investment tribunals to seize on the Articles as a tabula in naufragio, "a plank in a shipwreck", especially 'where the members of the tribunal are not public international lawyers'.[7] But still, there generally has been a 'very conscientious and careful attempt in general to apply the Articles'.[8] Perhaps we could say that the overall performance was *quite ok*, certainly *decent* – the equivalent, in academic terms, of a 'merit' (but not a 'distinction'), or what in classes at Law Schools in Edinburgh or Glasgow might be a 'B3' (i.e. on the lower end of an 'upper second').

Performance assessments like these are important, in fact indispensable: we need a robust debate about the quality of investment awards, and it is right that this debate is had not just among investment lawyers, but with increasing input from international lawyers specialising in other fields, especially when awards rely on general international law doctrines such as State responsibility, but also the general law of treaties, State succession, questions of statehood and territorial integrity. Investment arbitration, after all, is 'not a self-contained closed legal system' but has to be 'envisaged within a wider juridical context'; and a failure to conform to the accepted standards of the wider juridical system will affect the legitimacy of awards.

---

4. James Crawford, 'Investment Arbitration and the ILC Articles on State Responsibility' (2010) 25(1) ICSID Review 127, at 130 (citing *Wintershall Aktiengesellshaft v. Argentina*, Award (ICSID Case No. ARB/04/14, 8 December 2008)).
5. *Ibid.*, 130-131 (citing *United Parcel Service of America Inc. v. Canada*, Award on the Merits (NAFTA Chapter 11 Arbitration, 11 June 2007)).
6. *Ibid.*, 132.
7. *Ibid.*, 135.
8. *Ibid.*; and, for a slightly more 'robust' assessment, James Crawford, 'Keynote Address: International Protection of Foreign Direct Investment' in Rainer Hofmann and Christian J. Tams (eds), *International Investment Law and General International Law: From Clinical Isolation to Systemic Integration?* (Nomos 2011), 17, at 24 (noting that 'the references to [the ILC Articles] are rather variable. Some cases are quite profound engagements with the issues addressed in the ILC Articles ... In other cases it has seemed that "a little knowledge is a dangerous thing", and as you would guess from my account of the sociology of the investment arbitration profession, "a little knowledge" is something quite a lot of professionals have').

III   A CHANGE OF PERSPECTIVE: INVESTMENT LAW'S
         CONTRIBUTION TO STATE RESPONSIBILITY

Still, this final presentation of our panel is an invitation to adopt a different perspective. I am hoping to get us to look at the ASR not as something produced by others and received by the investment law world – but as a text that investment lawyers influence and shape. The central point I would like to make is that investment law and investment lawyers have a lot to contribute to debates about State responsibility. Precisely because, in adjudicating claims based on breaches of investment standards, investment tribunals participate in international law's general quest – assessing State conduct against internationally agreed obligations and, where necessary, holding States accountable for failing to honour their obligations – their jurisprudence can and should contribute to the development of international law's general regimes, such as the rules governing State Responsibility.

     This central point is part of a bigger inquiry into the relationship between international investment law and general international law, which goes beyond the remit of our panel.[9] But let me sketch out two aspects, as a teaser: *first*, despite their generalist pedigree, investment law and arbitration is quite present in the ASR; and *second*, more significantly, since 2001, investment lawyers (and investment tribunals in particular) have made an important huge contribution to clarifying and specifying the substance of the law on State responsibility, often affirming the ILC's approach, but quite frequently also moulding it in a particular manner. This significant body of jurisprudence of course needs to be tested and scrutinised, but it seems to me it has a real potential of influencing how we think about responsibility – not just in the investment field, but about responsibility as a general doctrine.

IV   USEFUL GUIDANCE ON SELECT ISSUES: INVESTMENT LAW AND
         ITS ANTECEDENTS IN THE 2001 ASR

The first point is a modest one: while the ASR were elaborated by the ILC and other actors of public/general international law, and primarily for an inter-State setting, international investment law is not absent from them. I am putting this purposefully cautiously, as clearly, investment lawyers did not shape the text. And how could they: the Articles were developed between the 1960s and 2001; a first reading draft was completed in 1996, and the second reading undertaken between 1997 and 2001 was essentially an exercise in cleaning up, in simplification and in clarification. So while the Articles often distil propositions developed in the case law of international courts and tribunals (and in that sense, it has been said that '[t]he law of responsibility [is] ...

---

9. For an attempt to deal with these questions, *see* the contributions to Christian J. Tams, Stephan Schill and Rainer Hofmann, *International Investment Law and General International Law: Radiating Effects?* (Edward Elgar 2023).

essentially judge-made'[10]), the last two decades of burgeoning investment jurisprudence simply could not be reflected: the ILC's project was completed just before investment arbitration 'took off'. As a result, investments awards – whether rendered on the basis of the International Convention for the Settlement of Investment Disputes (ICSID) or other frameworks – are referred to sparingly: a google-search of the entire ILC's Commentaries (114 pages, no less) yields only seven references to 'ICSID', and the only cases referred to are the very early ones: *AGIP v. Congo, Amco Asia v. Indonesia, Santa Elena v. Costa Rica.*

Yet, if we take a more holistic view of investment disputes, the picture changes perceptibly. Once we broaden the perspective to include decisions of earlier tribunals dealing with claims relating to alien property and property-related interests (i.e., decisions rendered before the 'cut-off' of 2001), then the Articles seem in fact quite 'investment-attuned'. The precursors to contemporary treaty-based arbitration play a significant role, most obviously the Iran-US Claims Tribunal (IUSCT),[11] but also the early twentieth-century mixed-claims commissions and *ad hoc* tribunals dealing with claims involving injury to the property of aliens.[12] This body of this early property-related jurisprudence provided useful guidance for the Commission's elaboration of general concepts, not across the board, but on select issues: Three examples illustrate the point:

- The jurisprudence of the IUSCT had a significant influence on the shape of the ILC's rules on attribution of conduct, notably insofar as the tribunal had come up with plausible principles governing the conduct of actors that, while outside the State's official apparatus, but controlled by it (such as an autonomous foundation established by the State[13]); or had overstepped their mandate, but acted as if 'cloaked with governmental authority'.[14]
- Investment decisions also feature in the Commission's work on the defences to State responsibility, especially in relation to Articles 23 (*force majeure*) and 25 (state of necessity).[15] A detailed study by Federica Paddeu suggests that it was in decisions concerning property claims of aliens – aliens affected by armed

---

10. Alain Pellet, 'Some Remarks on the Recent Case Law of the International Court of Justice on Responsibility Issues', *in* Kovacs (ed.), *International Law – A Quiet Strength. Miscellanea in Memoriam Geza Herczegh* (Pazmany Press, 2011), 111, at 112.
11. On the value of Iran-US Claims Tribunals decisions in the development of the law of State responsibility, *see*: Richard B. Lillich et al. (eds), *The Iran-US Claims Tribunal: Its Contribution to the Law of State Responsibility* (Transnational Publishers 1998); and Christopher Gibson and Christopher Drahozal, 'Iran-US Claims Tribunal Precedent in Investor-State Arbitration' in Christopher Gibson and Christopher Drahozal (eds), *The Iran-US Claims Tribunal at 25: The Cases Everyone Needs to Know for Investor-State & International Arbitration* (Oxford University Press 2007) Ch. 1.
12. On their relevance *see* generally Rudolf Dolzer and Christoph Schreuer, *Principles of International Investment Law* (2nd edn, Oxford Univerisity Press 2012) 1-7.
13. *Hyatt International Corporation v. The Government of the Islamic Republic of Iran*, Iran-U.S. C.T.R., vol. 9, p. 72, at pp. 88-94 (1985) (relied on in the Commentary to Article 5, at para 4).
14. *Petrolane, Inc. v. The Government of the Islamic Republic of Iran*, Iran-U.S. C.T.R., vol. 27, p. 64, at p. 92 (1991) (as quoted in the Commentary to Article 7, at para. 7).
15. *See* notably the detailed study prepared by the UN Secretariat, '"Force majeure" and "Fortuitous event" as circumstances precluding wrongfulness: Survey of State practice, international judicial

conflict and disturbances in a foreign country, such as *Venezuelan Railroads*,[16] *Russian Indemnity*,[17] *Serbian Loans*[18] and *Brazilian Loans*[19] – that the plea of *force majeure* took shape. And it took shape as a narrow excuse requiring the State to establish that the external event made it 'materially impossible' to perform the obligation, as Article 23 now clarifies.[20]

- Decisions on property-related claims informed the principles governing reparation and notably compensation for financially assessable damages. These feature in Part II of the Articles, whose provisions do not directly apply to claims by non-State actors.[21] But nonetheless, the ILC found many of the propositions emerging from the case law of the IUSCT, from the United Nations Claims Commission (UNCC) and also from contract-based arbitrations to be useful. These, e.g., inform the Commentary's sections emphasising that lost profits can be recovered if they are reasonably established, including under concessions: in these, the Commission, e.g., relies on *LIAMCO*,[22] *Sapphire*,[23] *Amco Asia*,[24] and is very complimentary of the UNCC's methodical approach to compensation for business losses[25] – i.e., decisions that not only originate from property-related claims, but that also remain relevant to the contemporary compensation discourse in investment cases. Similarly, there is much more than a nod to the early property-related cases and indeed the investment treaty practice in the Commentary's sections underlining the importance of the fair market value for compensation claims[26] and commenting on the use of the discounted cash flow (DCF) method.[27]

---

decisions and doctrine' (1978) ILC Yearbook, vol. II(1), 148-187; and *see* the references in the ILC's Commentary to Article 23 (at fn. 366) and Article 25 (at fns 376 and 381).

16. *French Company of Venezuelan Railroads* (1904) 10 RIAA 285.
17. *Russian Indemnity Case (Russia/Turkey)* (1912) Scott Hague Court Rep 297.
18. *Case Concerning the Payment of various Serbian Loans issued in France (France v. Kingdom of the Serbs, Croats and Slovenes)* (1929) PCIJ Series A No. 20, 5.
19. *Case Concerning the Payment of various Brazilian Loans issued in France (France v. Brazil)* (1929) PCIJ Series A No. 21, 93.
20. Paddeu's conclusion is worth setting out: discussing nineteenth and early twentieth-century disputes, she notes that 'it was slowly recognised that wars and other internal conflicts did not obliterate the State's will and that so long as the State remained in control of the behavior of its armed forces, it could be responsible; .... These changes paved the way for the recognition of the plea of *force majeure*, as we now understand it, in the first half of the 20th century': *see* Federica Paddeu, The Impact of Investment Arbitration on the Development of State Responsibility Defences, in Tams, Schill and Hofmann, *supra* n. 9.
21. *See* Article 33(2) ASR.
22. Libyan American Oil Company (LIAMCO), p. 140 (relied on in the Commentary to Article 36, at para. 27).
23. *Sapphire International Petroleums Ltd. v. National Iranian Oil Company,* ILR, vol. 35, p. 136, at pp. 187 and 189 (1963) (relied on in the Commentary to Article 36, at para. 27).
24. *Amco Asia Corporation and Others v. The Republic of Indonesia,* First Arbitration (1984); Annulment (1986); Resubmitted case (1990), ICSID Reports (Cambridge, Grotius, 1993), vol. 1, p. 377 (relied on in the Commentary to Article 36, at para. 27).
25. *See* paras 23 and 26 of the Commentary to Article 36, citing Decision No. 9 of the UNCC Governing Council in 'Propositions and conclusions on: types of damages and their valuation' (S/AC.26/1992/9).
26. *See* para. 22 of the Commentary to Article 36, stating that 'Compensation reflecting the capital value of property taken or destroyed as the result of an internationally wrongful act is generally

I do not wish to overstate the point, which remains a modest one. But I believe the examples serve to at least protect the ILC against the charge that it was purely focused on inter-State disputes. It could not take into account twenty-first-century investment arbitrations. Yet it was quite open to investment law's antecedents. These informed a number of propositions reflected in the ILC's text. If we envisage the Articles as a mighty river, perhaps we can say that the early proto-investment case law was one of the tributary streams that fed into the mighty stream: a mid-level tributary most likely – not the Ohio River to the Mississippi, but perhaps the River Illinois or Wisconsin, contributing usefully and perceptibly, but not in any way dominant. This, in turn, means: there is something of the early investment law in the Articles; these are not alien, investment lawyers of earlier generations have contributed to them. And we should not view them as something alien, foreign – something that is received without agency. This is my first, modest proposition.

V   'ALMOST UBIQUITOUS RELIANCE': 'CONSOLIDATING AND REFINING' THE ARTICLES IN INVESTMENT TREATY JURISPRUDENCE SINCE 2001

The second proposition moves us forward to the present age. The Articles were adopted 21 years ago: even by the strictest tests, they have now reached maturity. And more than that, as the ICCA programme committee noted in announcing this panel, they have become 'a crucial point of reference'. Indeed they have: In James Crawford's phrase, they 'represent the modern framework of state responsibility';[28] and while adopted as a formally non-binding text, they are now almost inevitably taken to reflect general international law, as the outcome of a process that has been referred to as 'codification light'.[29]

My second point is this: investment law and investment lawyers have played a very significant role in facilitating the ILC Articles' rise to prominence and in ensuring the success of the ILC's exercise in 'codification light'. There are three aspects to this: one, through twenty years of constant engagement with the text, investment lawyers

---

assessed on the basis of the "fair market value" of the property lost.' In support, reference is, e.g., made to Article 13(1) of the Energy Charter Treaty, to the World Bank's Guidelines on the Treatment of Foreign Direct Investment (Washington, D.C., 1992, vol. II, p. 41), to *American International Group, Inc. v. The Islamic Republic of Iran*, Iran-US C.T.R., vol. 4, p. 96, at p. 106 (1983); and to *Starrett Housing Corporation v. Government of the Islamic Republic of Iran*, Iran-U.S. C.T.R., vol. 16, p. 112, at p. 201 (1987).

27. *See* para. 26 of the Commentary to Article 36, noting that 'The discounted cash flow (DCF) method has gained some favour, especially in the context of calculations involving income over a limited duration, as in the case of wasting assets' and notably referring to the case law of the IUSCT: *Amoco International Finance Corporation v. The Government of the Islamic Republic of Iran*, Iran-U.S. C.T.R., vol. 15, p. 189; *Starrett Housing Corporation v. Government of the Islamic Republic of Iran*, Iran-U.S. C.T.R., vol. 16, p. 112 (1987); *Phillips Petroleum Company Iran v. The Islamic Republic of Iran*, Iran-U.S. C.T.R., vol. 21, p. 79 (1989); and *Ebrahimi (Shahin Shaine) v. Islamic Republic of Iran*, Iran-U.S. C.T.R., vol. 30, p. 170 (1994).

28. James Crawford, *State Responsibility: The General Part* (CUP 2013), at 45.

29. Santiago Villalpando, 'Codification Light: A New Trend in the Codification of International Law at the United Nations' (2013) 8 Anuário Brasileiro de Direito Internacional 117.

have embraced the Articles; they are the Articles' most important 'user'. Two, in the process, they have not just mechanically applied rules written down by the ILC, but also tested these rules, and specified and moulded their content. And three, this investment law practice of specifying and moulding the ILC's rules is gradually being taken up by international lawyers outside the investment law field – the investment law practice on State responsibility is beginning to *radiate*. Let me say a word about each of these aspects.

1   Embracing the ILC Articles

While today, the ICCA programme committee's take on the Articles as a 'crucial point of reference' is uncontroversial, it is important to note that their success was not a foregone conclusion. The Articles were adopted, by the ILC, as a set of non-binding provisions: of course elaborated in a process intended to produce an authoritative text, but not as such binding – a fact that certainly eased the final stages of the ILC's work, but meant the text was released into an uncertain future.[30] What is more, the General Assembly, rather than incorporating them into a programmatic resolution, has so far merely 'noted' the ASR and commended them to the attention of Governments, beginning with Resolution 56/83.[31] Other than that, though, in its engagement with State responsibility the General Assembly has remained hesitant and continues to prevaricate (for now twenty years) over whether it should initiate debates about a binding Convention on State responsibility: a project that would proceed from the ILC's Articles, but open these up to discussion by State representatives in the traditional form of multilateral treaty-making.[32] As States have so far not embarked upon the 'high road' of treaty-making, the Articles' success has been achieved via the 'low road' of gradual acceptance by international laws' many stakeholders. This success has been

---

30. For much more on the chosen form, and its allegedly 'paradoxical' relationship to their authority, *see* David Caron, 'The ILC Articles on State Responsibility: The Paradoxical Relationship Between Form and Authority' (2002) 96 AJIL 857; and further Fernando Lusa Bordin, 'Still Going Strong: Twenty Years of the Articles on State Responsibility's "Paradoxical" Relationship Between Form and Authority', in Federica I. Paddeu and Christian J. Tams, *The ILC Articles at 20* (GCILS Working Paper 11/2021), p. 15.
31. Responsibility of States for Internationally Wrongful Acts UNGA Res 56/83, Annex (12 December 2001) 56th Session (2001) UN Doc. A/RES/56/83.
32. These discussions, while not advancing very far, seem to reflect growing momentum towards a treaty on responsibility. In UN GA debates, over ninety States have expressly supported the treaty option. However, as the Sixth Committee has decided to proceed by consensus, no final decision has been taken. *See* most recently, United Nations, 'Sixth Committee (Legal) – 74th Session: Responsibility of States for Internationally Wrongful Acts (Agenda Item 75)' www.un .org/en/ga/sixth/74/resp_of_states.shtml. For recent commentary, *see* Federica Paddeu, 'To Convene or Not to Convene? The Future Status of the Articles on State Responsibility: Recent Developments' (2017) 21 Max Planck Yearbook of United Nations Law 83; Arman Sarvarian, 'The Ossified Debate on a UN Convention on State Responsibility' (2021) 70 International and Comparative Law Quarterly 769; as well as Patricia Galvão Teles, 'The Impact and Influence of the Articles on State Responsibility on the Work of the International Law Commission and Beyond', in Federica Paddeu and Christian J. Tams, The ILC Articles at 20, at 10.

remarkable, as uptake has exceeded all expectations. Since 2001, the Articles have become the natural point of reference for a wide range of law appliers, working in fields as diverse as human rights, international humanitarian law, WTO law, international environmental law, the law of the sea, and many more: NGOs and domestic courts cite them, as do scholars, governments, and international courts and tribunals.[33] This twenty-year 'embrace', conveniently chronicled in successive editions of the Secretary-General's compilation of decisions referencing the ILC's work on State responsibility,[34] suggests that the Articles' 'ultimate test of acceptance ha[s] [now been] met'.[35]

It certainly has been met in investment arbitration. From early on, investment tribunals have taken note of the Articles and referenced them in their decisions. Recent studies covering the last decade suggest that '[i]nvestment tribunals' extensive reliance on the ILC Articles remains unabated':[36] As Esmé Shirlow and Kabir Duggal highlight, since 2010, 'there has been a greater and almost ubiquitous reliance in investment treaty arbitration decisions on the ILC Articles';[37] large sections of the ILC's text are referred to, reflecting the growth of investment arbitration as much as 'an increased propensity on the part of parties and tribunals to cite the ILC Articles in their analysis of the issues arising in investment treaty disputes'.[38] What is more, with 219 decisions referencing the Articles, investment tribunals 'are still the most prolific users of the ILC Articles'.[39] Even as prolific users, tribunals can of course, in their use of the Articles, get things wrong (as suggested at the outset). But the practice of the past twenty years clearly reflects the willingness of arbitral tribunals to embrace the text – a willingness not precluded by the fact that investment arbitration in its contemporary variation could not materially shape the drafting of the Articles. This embrace has been a significant factor in the Articles' consolidation, from 'promising text finally adopted' (2001) to a 'natural framework for any debate about responsibility' (2022).

---

33. For more on this 'embrace', *see* the contributions to Paddeu and Tams, The ILC Articles at 20, a symposium hosted on the EJIL Talk! blog in 2021 and since republished as a GCILS Working Paper (11/2021).
34. *See* most recently, UNGA, Responsibility of States for internationally wrongful acts, Compilation of decisions of international courts, tribunals and other bodies, Report of the Secretary-General, 29 April 2022, UN Doc A/77/74, referencing eighty-three cases, decided between 2019 and 2022, that cite the Articles. The Technical Annex to the Compilation (pp. 39-51) lists 786 references to the Articles in publicly available decisions since 2001, plus 680 references in member State submissions before courts, tribunals and other bodies.
35. Cf. James Crawford, 'The ILC's Articles on Responsibility of States for Internationally Wrongful Acts: A Retrospect', (2002) AJIL 889. It seems to me that this significantly weakens the case for a treaty approach, but this approach nonetheless remains attracrtive to many States, as suggested in the penultimate footnote.
36. James Crawford and Freya Baetens, 'The ILC Articles on State Responsibility: More Than a "Plank in a Shipwreck"'?, (2022) 37 ICSID Review (in print).
37. Esmé Shirlow and Kabir Duggal, 'The ILC Articles on State Responsibility in Investment Treaty Arbitration' (2022) 37 ICSID Review (in print).
38. *Ibid.*
39. *See* Crawford and Baetens, *supra* n. 36 and Shirlow and Duggal, *supra* n. 37. The Annex to Shirlow and Duggal's piece, as well as Crawford's 2010 article (cited in footnote 2), contain very helpful tables.

2 Working with the Articles, and Making Them Their Own

Have investment tribunals made the Articles their own, though? One can be a 'prolific user' and not develop any sense of ownership, merely referring to a text, grudgingly perhaps, that remains alien. The statements quoted in the introductory section of this comment suggest that some investment tribunals, even where they cited them, initially approached the Articles with some reservation. James Crawford's 'shipwreck' metaphor[40] confirms this – conjuring up an image of tribunals desperately clutching at a plank/text deemed to be authoritative, to somehow justify a particular decision.

It seems to me that, in the course of the past two decades, investment tribunals have become more experienced and more confident users. Their engagement with the Articles of course remains of variable depth and quality, and certain trends in the jurisprudence to me remain puzzling. (The tendency to misuse attribution rules to extend the scope of contractual liability and permit contractual claims against States, is an obvious example.[41]) But overall, twenty years and 219 decisions on, it seems high time to me to supplement the traditional 'have investment tribunals got State responsibility wrong?' question with another one: how does the systematic and long-standing engagement, by investment tribunals, contribute to our understanding of the ILC's text? My own response to this question is that it contributes quite a lot, and more specifically: investment tribunals have made a significant contribution by spelling out and specifying the meaning of vague ILC provisions. What is more, some of these specifications reflect a gradual moulding of the law of State responsibility. Let me illustrate this by reference to three select examples:

(i) The first is an instance of spelling out the meaning of the ILC's text. This is a crucial task, as so many of the ILC's provisions are general – not just in terms of their potential application (across the board), but also in their vagueness. Article 39 on contributory fault is an example in point; according to it '[i]n the determination of reparation, account shall be taken of the contribution to the injury by wilful or negligent action or omission of the injured State or any person or entity in relation to whom reparation is sought.'[42] This provision sets out a fairly common-sense principle, but it does little more. The ILC's Commentary is brief and does not say much beyond the principle. And it leaves us with hardly any guidance on central questions, such as: What does 'take into account' mean? How far can contributory fault reduce reparation claims? What qualifies as 'wilful or negligent action'? Two decades after the adoption of the Articles, the questions are by no means satisfactorily resolved. And they may never be: clearly, courts and tribunals

---

40. *See supra* n. 3.
41. In his 2010 article, Crawford noted 'confusion' among tribunals 'over the relationship between the law of attribution and issues of contractual responsibility or liability' (Crawford, footnote 3, at 134). As this confusion has not really disappeared, it may be convenient to restate Crawford's reminder: 'The rules of attribution have nothing to do with questions of contractual responsibility' (*ibid.*).
42. YbILC 2001, vol. II/2, at 109.

need to be able to exercise discretion in assessing the impact of contributory fault in particular instances raised and pleaded before them. But still, we might hope for some more clarity, at least some guidelines, so that the law is not just a vague statement of principle. Some such guidance has been provided by investment awards, which have recently begun to engage seriously with the matter. The guidance is by no means consistent, and it is not specific enough. But we now have at least five examples – *Occidental Petroleum, Copper Mesa, Yukos, Veteran Petroleum* and *Anatolie Stati*[43] – of tribunals weighing arguments based on Article 39, and beginning a discourse on the impact of contributory fault on compensation claims. In their detailed assessment, Esme Shirlow and Kabir Duggal note that investment tribunals had 'unfortunately, not ... exercised [their discretion] in a consistent or principled manner'[44] – and they have a point: much remains yet to be clarified. But my expectations may be lower: I would argue that if we want any guidance on the meaning of Article 39 (whatever field of international law we look at), investment arbitration is our best hope for *some* clarity. In that sense, I would look to cases such as *Occidental* and others as first steps towards clarifying the meaning of a nebulous ASR provision.

(ii) In another area, the impact of investment awards is more profound: this is Chapter II of Part One of the ILC Articles on attribution of conduct.[45] Articles 4-11 are among the most influential elements of the ILC's exercise in 'codification light': they clarify that States only have to stand in for conduct of actors that are related to the apparatus of government and go on to identify the types of links that are sufficient in this respect (such as designation as a State organ, control over conduct, or the conferral of regulatory power). Investment tribunals have engaged with these rules in detail and significantly extended the debate about them. They have done so by 'kissing awake' hitherto dormant rules[46] such as Article 11, according to which private conduct becomes attributable if the State adopts it as its own: this provision had risen to prominence in the International Court of Justice's

---

43. *Occidental Petroleum Corporation and Occidental Exploration and Production Company v. Republic of Ecuador*, ICSID Case No. ARB/06/11 Award (5 October 2012); *Copper Mesa Mining Corporation v. Republic of Ecuador*, PCA Case No. 2012-2, Award (15 March 2016); *Yukos Universal Limited (Isle of Man); Veteran Petroleum Limited (Cyprus) v. The Russian Federation*, PCA Case Nos 2005-04/AA227, 2005-05/AA228, Final Award (18 July 2014); *Veteran Petroleum Limited (Cyprus) v. The Russian Federation*, PCA Case Nos 2005-04/AA227, 2005-05/AA228, Final Award (18 July 2014); Anatolie Stati and Gabriel Stati, *Ascom Group SA and Terra Raf Trans Traiding Ltd v. Kazakhstan*, SCC Case No V 116/2010, Award (19 December 2013).
44. Shirlow and Duggal, *supra* n. 37; and see the much more principled critique by Martin Jarrett, *Contributory Fault and Investor Misconduct in Investment Arbitration* (CUP 2019).
45. For a much fuller discussion of the issues sketched out in the following, *see* Carlo de Stefano, 'Attribution of Conduct to a State', (2022) 37 ICSID Review (in print); and Stephan Wittich, Investment Arbitration as an Engine of Development of the Rules of Attribution, in Tams, Schill and Hofmann, *supra* n. 9.
46. In addition to Article 11, *see also* the Electrabel tribunal's reliance on Article 6, one of the least cited provisions of the ILC Articles: *Electrabel SA v. Hungary*, ICSID Case No. ARB/07/19, Decision on Jurisdiction Applicable Law and Liability (30 November 2012) para. 6.74.

(ICJ) *Tehran Hostages* case[47] but was considered to be of limited relevance – until a sequence of recent investment awards began to test the limits of attribution through adoption.[48] This testing continues, with tribunals, e.g., discussing which level of endorsement is required.[49] But even now, it is clear that in a world of privatised government agencies, Article 11 has real potential to implicate States.[50]

More generally, investment arbitrations of the last two decades have explored avenues for holding States accountable in times of privatised government: for the most part, and with the exception of a number of NAFTA awards,[51] investment tribunals seem to be working from within the ILC's attribution regime.[52] But while affirming it in principle, their jurisprudence contains helpful suggestions cautiously to 'open up' narrowly formulated provisions such as Article 5 (conduct of separate entities that, while not State organs, are authorised to exercise governmental authority)[53] and Article 8 (conduct of private actors directed and/or effectively controlled by the

---

47. ICJ Reports 1980, 3, 35 (prominently cited in the ILC's Commentary to Article 11, at para. 4).
48. *See, e.g., InterTrade Holding GmbH v. The Czech Republic* (PCA Case No. 2009-12), Final Award, 29 May 2012; *Luigiterzo Bosca v. Lithuania* (UNCITRAL), Award, 17 May 2013; *Icon of Delaware et al v Canada* (PCA Case No. 2009-04), Award on Jurisdiction and Liability, 17 March 2015; *Ampal-American Israel Corporation and others v. Arab Republic of Egypt* (ICSID Case No. ARB/12/11), Decision on Liability and Heads of Loss, 21 February 2017.
49. *See, e.g., Luigiterzo Bosca v. Lithuania* (UNCITRAL), Award, 17 May 2013, considering it sufficient that 'the Government acted at multiple steps, projecting its sovereign authority'; and *InterTrade Holding GmbH v. The Czech Republic* (PCA Case No. 2009-12), Final Award, 29 May 2012 (insisting that 'words or actions [reflecting a governmental adoption of conduct] must be clear and unambiguous').
50. *See also* Shirlow and Duggal (noting that 'tribunals since [2010] have shown greater propensity to analyse attribution of conduct to States on the basis that the State has endorsed and adopted conduct as its own').
51. *United Parcel Service of America Inc (UPS) v. Government of Canada*, UNCITRAL, Award on the Merits (24 May 2007); *Mesa Power Group, LLC v. Government of Canada*, UNCITRAL, PCA Case No. 2012-17, Award (24 March 2016); and also the hints in *Bayindir Insaat Turizm Ticaret Ve Sanayi AS v. Islamic Republic of Pakistan*, ICSID Case No. ARB/03/29, Award (27 August 2009).
52. From the many decisions working with the ILC's rules on attribution, *see, e.g., Tulip Real Estate and Development Netherlands BV v. Republic of Turkey*, ICSID Case No. ARB/11/28, Award (10 March 2014) para. 281; *Antoine Abou Lahoud and Leila BounafehAbou Lahoud v. Democratic Republic of the Congo*, ICSID Case No. ARB/10/4, Award (7 February 2014) para. 375; *Saipem SpA v. People's Republic of Bangladesh*, ICSID Case No. ARB/05/07, Decision on Jurisdiction and Recommendation on Provisional Measures (21 March 2007) para. 148. As de Stefano notes in his detailed assessment, 'international investment tribunals have generally recognized the rules of attribution in Articles 4, 5, 7 and 8 ARSIWA as a codification of customary international law'.
53. *See, e.g., Crystallex International Corporation v. Bolivarian Republic of Venezuela*, ICSID Case No. ARB(AF)/11/2, Award (4 April 2016); *Vigotop Limited v. Hungary*, ICSID Case No. ARB/11/22, Award (1 October 2014) para. 328; *Luigiterzo Bosca v. Lithuania*, UNCITRAL, Award (17 May 2013).
    de Stefano (*supra* n. 45) summarises one aspect of this opening up when noting that recent investment decisions 'seem to suggest that in order to qualify an act of a parastatal entity as attributable to the State it is not necessary to demonstrate that it was exercised strictly out of governmental authority (imperium), but it may also be taken into consideration that said act was "growing out" of the public functions of the State instrumentality'.

State).[54] These decisions free the discussion from the shackles of debates of the *'Tadic v. Nicaragua* type' on which general international lawyers remained fixated for far too long; they meaningfully develop provisions that the ILC formulated without fully rationalising the concept of 'public power' or the 'public function' which inform the rules on attribution.[55] Looked at in aggregate, recent investment awards clarify the meaning of important provisions of the ILC text, but they also shape these provisions in a particular direction – tribunals clearly do not just receive guidance from the ILC's work, but specify the content of the ILC's rules, potentially providing guidance to international lawyers more generally.

(iii) Lastly, some decisions seem to point towards a more fundamental readjustment, adopting approaches that would shape the Articles in a particular 'investment light'. This has so far been rare, but the treatment, by some NAFTA tribunals, of the ILC's regime of countermeasures provides an example. Under Articles 22 and 49 of the ILC's text, otherwise, unlawful conduct may be justified as countermeasure if directed against a prior wrongful act, but such countermeasures must be 'directed against' the State 'responsible for an internationally wrongful act'. This latter limitation excludes the application of countermeasures against third States – but does it also preclude countermeasures against third-party nations? The question arose in a series of three NAFTA cases brought against Mexico,[56] namely those brought by *ADM, Corn Products* and *Cargill*.[57] The tribunals in the latter two cases essentially equated the position of investors to that of third States: they considered Mexico to be prevented from relying on countermeasures against US investors.[58] This approach, while developed on the basis of Article 49, indeed involves 'some element of innovation':[59] it further restricts

54. *See, e.g., Ampal-American Israel Corporation v. Egypt* (*supra* n. 48) – considering it sufficient for the purposes of attribution under Article 8 that decisions by a public-sector holding company with separate legal personality 'were all taken with the blessing of the highest levels of the Egyptian Government'; and further *Bayindir v. Pakistan* (*supra* n. 51); *UAB E Energija v. Latvia*, ICSID Case No. ARB/12/33, Award (22 December 2017).

55. A point made by Alex Mills: see his 'State Responsibility and Privatisation: Accommodating Private Conduct in a Public Framework', in Paddeu and Tams (*supra* n. 30), p. 23.

56. The backdrop of these cases was a Mexican tax on soft drinks with high-fructose corn syrup (HFCS). HFCS was exported by US producers, which argued that the tax caused them to lose the value of their investment. Mexico responded that its tax was a lawful countermeasure in response to the USA's illegally blocking Mexican sugar producers from access to US markets, in violation of NAFTA.

57. *Corn Products International, Inc v. United Mexican States*, ICSID Case No. ARB(AF)/04/01, Decision on Responsibility (15 January 2008); *Archer Daniels Midland Company and Tate & Lyle Ingredients Americas, Inc v. United Mexican States*, ICSID Case No ARB(AF)/04/05, Award (21 November 2007) (ADM Award); *Cargill, Incorporated v. United Mexican States*, ICSID Case No. ARB(AF)05/2, Award (18 September 2009).

58. For a much fuller discussion *see* Eran Sthoeger and Christian J. Tams, 'Swords, Shields and Other Beasts: The Role of Countermeasures in Investment Arbitration', (2022) 37 ICSID Review (in print).

59. Paddeu in Tams, Schill & Hofmann (*supra* n. 20), at 15; Sthoeger and Tams (*supra* n. 57); and further Junianto J. Losari and Michael Ewing-Chow, 'A Clash of Treaties: The Lawfulness of Countermeasures in International Trade Law and International Investment Law' (2015) 16

the availability of countermeasures under the ILC Articles. This in itself may not be problematic, but it is worth noting that it would amount to a development – a development that the ILC did not seem to anticipate.[60] In that sense, decisions like *Cargill* and *Corn Products*, if accepted, would have an impact that goes beyond a mere finessing and/or adaptation of the ILC's Articles.

The line between clarification, shaping and remaking the ILC Articles is not fixed and may be a question of perspective. I do not assume that my own assessment of where clarification and specification become development is universally shared. But what I hope is acceptable is the basic point emerging from the short summaries: investment lawyers do not just mechanically apply the Articles, they work with them, mould them, construe them – and in the process have made them their own. And this is how it should be: writing in 2002, James Crawford noted that the ILC Articles were a useful exposition of the general rules on State responsibility – and went on to observe that these rules would now be 'consolidated and refined' in international practice. This is precisely what has happened over twenty years of investment arbitrations: these have consolidated the ILC's text, and they have refined it, including by adapting it to novel challenges and to the particular needs of the investment law regime.

VI   RADIATING EFFECTS?

A final question – much more briefly, as it takes us away from investment arbitration and into the terrain of general international law: What is the impact of the significant investment practice on the general regime of State responsibility? As so many decisions now are public, and as arbitration naturally relies on references back to prior decisions, we can expect statements by tribunals – say, on the scope of attribution rules, or on contributory fault – to enter the investment law discourse. But will the investment law practice reverberate outside the investment law context? Will it radiate?[61]

This is clearly not guaranteed: even if we admit some form of soft precedential effects within particular dispute settlement regimes (e.g., in investment arbitration), there is clearly no doctrine of precedent across different fields of international law: parties arguing before a human rights court, or before the ICJ, might rely on pronouncements by investment tribunals – but the human rights court, or the ICJ, are of course entirely free to disregard them or to treat them as inapposite. So just as with all other

---

Journal of World Investment and Trade 274. For the opposite view, endorsing the position adopted in *Corn Products* and *Cargill, see* Martins Paparinskis, 'Investment Arbitration and the Law of Countermeasures' (2008) 79 BYIL 264.

60. While the ILC's position is not entirely clear, a passage from the commentary to Article 49 suggests that countermeasures could have effects on other third parties: 'other parties, including third States, may be affected thereby [by countermeasures]. If they have no individual rights in the matter they cannot complain. The same is true if, as a consequence of suspension of a trade agreement, trade with the responsible State is affected and one or more companies lose business or even go bankrupt. Such indirect or collateral effects cannot be entirely avoided' (Commentary to Article 49, at para. 5).

61. This is the central question addressed in Tams, Schill and Hofmann, *supra* n. 9.

judicial or arbitral pronouncements, investment tribunal's decisions on State responsibility will have to persuade to 'radiate' into other fields.[62]

So far, this process of 'radiation' is at an early stage. The enormous body of investment law practice on State responsibility is only beginning to be used in other contexts and has by no means been fully digested. First steps have been taken: the Secretary-General's compilation and scholarly works document and highlight how investment law tribunals use the ILC's text – this is now all out in the open, permitting robust peer review and enabling radiation effects. But to my knowledge, courts and tribunals outside the investment field (and other bodies applying rules of State responsibility) are relatively slow to take it up. Silo-thinking may be part of this – as may be the traditional perception (which has done a lot of harm) that investment law is somehow 'exotic',[63] situated somewhere on the fringes of international. But I am quite hopeful that things are about to change: the aggregated body of investment law jurisprudence on State responsibility is just too rich and too pervasive to be ignored by general international lawyers. On questions of attribution in particular it is the key to a more relevant debate, one that takes the ILC Articles into the twenty-first century and engages with the implications of lean government and the regulatory State (which challenge international law in many areas) on State responsibility. This does not mean that investment law decisions must be generally accepted; propositions advanced in the arbitral jurisprudence need to be tested and scrutinised – and as suggested above, I remain cautious about the jurisprudence of ICSID tribunals on countermeasures. But even where they disagree, general international lawyers will benefit from engaging fully with the output of the 'most prolific users' of the ILC's text, viz. investment tribunals.

VII   CONCLUDING THOUGHTS

And so I conclude this comment with a plea – or rather: two pleas: One to general international lawyers, whom I would encourage to tap (more than they have done so far) into the rich body of investment jurisprudence on State responsibility whose potential often remains 'untapped'.[64] And the other to the investment arbitration community: a plea to appreciate that in engaging with State responsibility, investment lawyers have long ceased to be mere rule-takers without agency, who are required to work with an alien text. Not only have earlier generations of 'investment lawyers' had

---

62. As noted by Christoph Schreuer, 'it is not any legislative power but their intellectual persuasiveness that will determine the influence of investment tribunals on the development of international law': *see* his 'Development of International Law by ICSID Tribunals', (ICSID Review 2016, 728).
63. As famously stated by the ILC in 2006(!): *see* ILC, 'Fragmentation of International Law: Difficulties Arising from the Diversification and Expansion of International Law, Report of the Study Group, finalised by Martti Koskenniemi' (13 April 2006) UN Doc. A/CN.4/L.682, at para. 18.
64. As noted (in a separate context) by James Devaney: *see* his 'On The Contribution of Investment Arbitration to Issues of Evidence and Procedure Before Other International Courts and Tribunals', in Tams, Schill and Hofmann, *supra* n. 9.

some influence on the text. Twenty years of investment arbitration have embraced, clarified and shaped it. And going forward, investment lawyers play an important role in adapting the ILC's often vague and general rules to new challenges. There is, in one phrase, no need to be afraid of State responsibility.

PANEL 4   Arbitration's Printing Press:
Drawing the Line Between Confidentiality
and Transparency

CHAPTER 14

In Defence of Party Choice: The Continuing Importance of Confidentiality in Commercial Arbitration

Paula Hodges KC[*]

I   THE QUEST FOR TRANSPARENCY AND ITS IMPLICATIONS FOR CONFIDENTIALITY

Transparency is a hotly debated topic within the arbitration community. We hear it discussed at conferences, in working groups and in the context of rule revisions. Its impact on commercial arbitration has been widely felt. We have seen efforts made across the community to achieve greater organisational transparency by delivering greater insight into the way arbitral institutions work, their decision-making and their statistics on time, cost and diversity.[1] We have also seen a push towards achieving

---

[*] Global Head of International Arbitration, Herbert Smith Freehills LLP.
[1] ICC Arbitral Tribunal appointments page available here https://iccwbo.org/dispute-resolution-services/arbitration/icc-arbitral-tribunals/; LCIA Facts and Figures, Costs and Duration 2013-2

greater legal transparency in terms of the publication of arbitral decisions; an important example of this is the International Chamber of Commerce's (ICC) change to an 'opt-out' position on the publication of arbitral awards between commercial parties.[2] We have also seen a move towards greater transparency of proceedings more generally, with stakeholders across the arbitration community encouraging the sharing of information about arbitrators, their appointments and styles.[3]

Transparency is defined as 'the quality of being done in an open way without secrets'.[4] The move towards transparency in commercial arbitration therefore brings with it the object of removing 'secrets' from arbitration to ensure that it is open to analysis and critique from outside. However, this quest might seem fundamentally at odds with a process which has confidentiality as one of its most acclaimed features. In all large-scale surveys of arbitration users, confidentiality is one of the top five most valued characteristics.[5] Indeed, many argue that confidentiality is a fundamental component of the arbitration process.

For some, resolving the conflict between transparency and confidentiality seems most easily achieved by either abandoning confidentiality within commercial arbitration completely or severely curtailing it. Over the past decade in particular, some practitioners have begun to question whether commercial disputes should be resolved away from the public eye and whether their outcomes should be confidential. What began as a limited number of calls to 'open the world of international arbitration to the public'[6] has shifted into a far wider movement intent on removing any presumption of confidentiality at a statutory or institutional level and requiring parties to expressly 'opt-in' to a confidential process.

But is this movement the right way to go? Back in 2012, I argued strongly in favour of confidentiality in commercial arbitration, and my position remains unchanged.[7] In this paper, I explore the arguments made against the continuation of confidentiality in arbitration within the context of greater transparency and explain why those arguments do not ring true for commercial arbitration. In doing so, I will look through the lens of arbitration's history and purpose to explore why confidentiality is and should remain a fundamental part of the commercial arbitral process and be defended by those who practise it. I will also consider whether transparency and

---

016, released October 2017, available here https://www.lcia.org/News/lcia-releases-updated-costs-and-duration-analysis.aspx; LCIA Challenge decision database available here https://www.lcia.org/challenge-decision-database.aspx.

2. 1 January 2021, ICC Note to Parties and Arbitral Tribunals on the conduct of the Arbitration under the ICC Rules of Arbitration, section IV C.
3. https://arbitratorintelligence.com/ last accessed 24 May 2022. https://globalarbitrationreview.com/arbitrator-research-tool.
4. https://dictionary.cambridge.org/dictionary/english/transparency.
5. QMUL Survey 2006, Corporate Attitudes and Practices; QMUL Survey 2010, Choices in International Arbitration; QMUL Survey 2013, Corporate choices in International Arbitration; QMUL Survey 2015, Improvements and Innovations in International Arbitration; QMUL Survey 2018, The Evolution of Arbitration.
6. Juan Fernandez-Armesto, 'The Time Has Come: A Plea for Abandoning Secrecy in Arbitration', 3 Paris J. Int'l. Arb. 583 (2012).
7. Paula Hodges, 'The Perils of Complete Transparency in International Arbitration: Should Parties Be Exposed to the Glare of Publicity?', 3 Paris J. Int'l. Arb. 589 (2012).

arbitration, properly understood, are necessarily in conflict or whether transparency can be achieved without undermining party autonomy and confidentiality in individual disputes.

II   ARGUMENTS MADE AGAINST A CONFIDENTIAL PROCESS IN COMMERCIAL ARBITRATION

1   Legitimacy of the Process

If hyperbole is to be believed, arbitration is under threat. 'Winter is coming' and we as practitioners must be constantly vigilant against those who want to 'tear down the legal framework and end international arbitration as we know it'.[8] This fear derives primarily from the criticism directed towards investment treaty arbitration. The criticism was initially confined to fringe NGO groups and academia,[9] followed by governments who were on the receiving end of large damages awards, such as Venezuela, Bolivia and Ecuador, who began decrying the system and the International Centre for the Settlement of Investment Disputes (ICSID) in particular.[10]

A series of awards against EU Member States, which touched on issues of EU law, also led to interest being shown by the EU Commission in the process of investment treaty arbitration. This spawned a public consultation and the dissemination of material setting out the Commission's position regarding investment treaty arbitration.[11] Across Europe, we began to see the mainstream media write articles on what had previously been a fairly niche area of international law.[12] Investment treaty arbitration was criticised for limiting state regulatory power, prioritising the rights of international corporations over citizens, being shrouded in secrecy, and being the result of a conspiracy amongst law firms intent on taking money from emerging economies.

This came as a shock to many in the world of arbitration. Suddenly, instead of having to explain the work we do as investment treaty practitioners, we had to justify it. At their heart, many of the criticisms were based on a lack of transparency, and this led to concerns being voiced about a lack of legitimacy in the system; if justice was being done through investment treaty arbitration, it should be seen to be done. The response of the international and arbitration community to those criticisms was quick. Reform came in the form of the UNCITRAL Transparency Rules, the Mauritius

---

8. https://globalarbitrationreview.com/article/1177000/born-takes-%E2%80%9Cgame-of-thrones %E2%80%9D-message-to-freshfields.
9. *See*, for example, https://corporateeurope.org/sites/default/files/efila_report-web.pdf.
10. https://www.ft.com/content/fe682296-675c-35e4-aee7-3b18dd55e27a, 8 January 2012. Hugo Chavez Frias stated during 'Hello, President', '*We have to get out of that ICSID*'.
11. *See* the Commission's page on the Multilateral Investment Court Project, https://policy.trade. ec.europa.eu/enforcement-and-protection/multilateral-investment-court-project_en, last accessed 24 May 2022.
12. The Economist, 'The Arbitration Game: Investor-State Dispute Settlement' (11/10/2014) http:/ /www.economist.com/news/finance-and-economics/2163756-governments-are-souring-treat ies-protect-foreign-investors-arbitration.

Convention, the efforts of UNCITRAL Working Group III and of ICSID, including the release of the new ICSID rules.[13]

As a result, investment treaty practitioners have found themselves on shifting sands with an evolving area of practice and process, whose end form remains uncertain. The speed of change of public opinion regarding investment treaty arbitration has left an understandable lack of confidence in the permanence of any form of dispute resolution. And that has led to predictions that commercial arbitration too may face a backlash based on the lack of transparency in the system. As Constantine Partasides and Simon Maynard of Three Crowns have argued, drawing on the outcry against investment arbitration, the lack of information about the process of arbitration 'undermines the legitimacy' of the process.[14]

This argument is used to promote increased transparency and a fundamental shift away from confidentiality within the commercial arbitral process. It is suggested that there may be challenges in defending a system that 'impose[s] secrecy systematically'.[15] The argument is made that the ability to access information and data about procedure, nationality, diversity, arbitrators, interim relief and even arbitral awards themselves is a necessity to protect commercial arbitration from the hostility of the general public and NGOs, frustrated at the continued existence of 'secret courts' that decide issues of considerable economic and political significance.

2   Limiting Confidentiality to Achieve Greater Transparency for the Common Good

A related argument is that confidentiality in commercial arbitration should be limited to achieve greater transparency for the benefit of all. An argument seemingly based on the philosophy of the 'common good' suggests that individual users of arbitration should accept limits on their private decision-making to benefit others.

It is important to note that this push for transparency covers the entire system of arbitration from institutions, practitioners, clients and arbitrators, seeking greater insight into the whole process and decision-making within it. Proponents of this argument suggest that the lack of openness in the arbitration process limits access to arbitration for new practitioners and parties, keeping knowledge within the hands of the few. It argues that these limits do not benefit arbitration or its end users, particularly in terms of arbitrator appointments and procedure, but also potentially in terms of outcome. As the New York City Bar Report on the Publication of International

---

13. UNCITRAL Rules on Transparency in Treaty-based Investor-State Arbitration, 2014; United Nations Convention on Transparency in Treaty-based Investor-State Arbitration (New York, 2014) (the 'Mauritius Convention on Transparency'); Working Group III: Investor-State Dispute Settlement Reform, https://uncitral.un.org/en/working_groups/3/investor-state, last accessed 24 May 2022; ICSID Rules and Regulations Amendment Project, https://icsid.worldbank.org/resources/rules-amendments, last accessed 24 May 2022. The new Rules come into force in July 2022.
14. Constantine Partasides and Simon Maynard, 'Raising the Curtain on English Arbitration' (2017) 33 Arb. Int'l. 197, 201-202.
15. Constantine Partasides and Simon Maynard, 'Raising the Curtain on English Arbitration' (2017) 33 Arb. Int'l. 197, 201-202.

Arbitration Awards and Decisions in February 2014 stated, 'Greater access to the content of awards and the arbitrators rendering them confers advantages in the process, and that access can be very uneven. Lawyers or firms with large international arbitration practices develop files and institutional knowledge about the arbitrators, institutions, and procedural customs that may not be available to those at smaller firms or firms less immersed in international arbitration. The less information that is publicly available about arbitrators and their decisions, the greater is the advantage of a relatively small group of firms and lawyers.'[16] Philip Wimalasena also argues that there are 'hazards of a continued "secret science" both for the legitimacy and attractiveness of arbitration as well as for legal certainty'.[17]

Proponents of this argument differ in their attitude as to whether reducing confidentiality should be encouraged or imposed. Catherine Rogers argues that she 'remain[s] convinced of the benefits of voluntarily increasing transparency within the system and confident that international arbitration will continue in its trajectory toward greater transparency'.[18] For others, the move should be instigated by the arbitral community and taken swiftly. As Juan Fernandez-Armesto put it 'the present practice should be reversed and publication of awards should become the default rule' because 'publicity is one of the basic pillars of justice'.[19]

3   Confidentiality in Arbitration Poses a Risk to the Development of the Law

In his 2016 Bailii Lecture, The Right Hon. The Lord Thomas of Cwmgiedd (Lord Chief Justice of England and Wales at the time) described arbitration as a 'serious impediment' to the development of the common law in England and Wales.[20] Lord Thomas highlighted the:

> [I]ssues which arise from the resolution of disputes firmly behind closed doors - retarding public understanding of the law, and public debate over its application. A series of decisions in the courts may expose issues that call for Parliamentary scrutiny and legislative revision. A series of similar decisions in arbitral proceedings will not do so, and those issues may then carry on being taken account of in future arbitrations ... Such lack of openness equally denudes the ability of individuals, and lawyers apart from the few who are instructed in arbitrations, to access the law, to understand how it has been interpreted and applied. It reduces the degree of certainty in the law that comes through the provision of authoritative

---

16. New York City Bar Report on the Publication of International Arbitration Awards and Decisions in February 2014.
17. Philip Wimalasena, 'The Publication of Arbitral Awards as a Contribution to Legal Development: A Plea for More Transparency', 37(2) ASA Bull. 279-288, 281 (2019).
18. Catherine Rogers, 'Transparency in International Commercial Arbitration', 54 U. Kan. L. Rev. 1301, 1334 (2006).
19. Juan Fernandez-Armesto, 'The Time Has Come: A Plea for Abandoning Secrecy in Arbitration', 3 Paris J. Int'l. Arb. 583, 585 (2012).
20. The Right Hon. The Lord Thomas of Cwmgiedd, Lord Chief Justice of England and Wales, 'Developing Commercial Law Through the Courts: Rebalancing the Relationship Between the Courts and Arbitration', The Bailii Lecture 2016, 9 March 2016, https://www.judiciary.uk/wp-content/uploads/2016/03/lcj-speech-bailli-lecture-20160309.pdf.

decisions of the court. As such it reduces individuals' ability to fully understand their rights and obligations, and to properly plan their affairs accordingly.

Meanwhile, Doug Jones has argued that 'International commercial arbitrators certainly do make law. They are often tasked with making crucial decisions on complex areas of law. They espouse principles that are developed to fill gaps in national laws. They are deeply involved in comparative law and create principles that are useful, or could be useful, to those involved in international commerce. In order to maximise the use of the law made by arbitrators and supplement the development of significant areas of international commercial law, the limited and standardised publication of redacted arbitral decisions is one route which finds much support and merit.'[21]

According to this further 'common good' argument, parties should not be able to limit access to the legal analysis of the awards issued within the arbitral process. Such analysis should be published and retained to assist courts and other tribunals in their own application and interpretation of the law. Indeed, Philip Wimalensa argues forcefully that the 'disappearance of entire areas of the law into the confidentiality of arbitration and the resulting erosion of precedent raises more fundamental questions with respect to the social function of the law in a democratically constituted society'.[22]

Related to the argument that arbitration hinders the growth of the law for *all* is the more nuanced argument that publication of arbitral awards should be pursued for *arbitration's* benefit as an autonomous system of justice. To this end, Alexis Mourre, former president of the ICC International Court of Arbitration, has argued for a precedential system in arbitration, maintaining that arbitration cannot be thought of as a truly autonomous system without embracing the role of precedent.[23] In addition, he argues that 'the public interest in the development of arbitral case law, in the enhancement of the quality of arbitration, and in providing transparency and predictability to the business community overrides the principle of confidentiality as far as the publication of arbitration awards is concerned'.[24]

4   Confidentiality Is the Exception, Not the Rule in Most Jurisdictions

There is also a strong school of thought that suggests that confidentiality is not a fundamental part of commercial arbitration. To substantiate this, they suggest that confidentiality is the exception and not the rule in most jurisdictions. Indeed, as Constantine Partasides and Simon Maynard note, with reference to the position in

21. Doug Jones, 'Arbitrators as Law-Makers', 5(2) Indian J. Arb. L. 18, 28 (2018).
22. Philip Wimalasena, 'The Publication of Arbitral Awards as a Contribution to Legal Development: A Plea for More Transparency', 37(2) *ASA Bulletin* 279-288, p. 280 (2019).
23. Alexis Mourre, 'Precedent and Confidentiality in International Commercial Arbitration: The Case for the Publication of Arbitral Awards' in Yas Banifatemi (ed.) Precedent in International Arbitration, IAI Series on International Arbitration No. 5 (Juris Publishing 2008).
24. Alexis Mourre, 64-65; Elina Zlatanska, 'To Publish, or Not to Publish Arbitral Awards: That Is the Question', 81 Arbitration 25, 30-32 (2015).

England and Wales, 'the notion of an implied duty of confidentiality – in global perspective – can increasingly be called a rarity'.[25]

Those addressing this point draw from examples across the spectrum of jurisdictions, the aim being to demonstrate that the lack of consensus renders nugatory any argument in favour of a presumption of confidentiality (statutory or otherwise). Many prominent civil law jurisdictions (such as France, Germany and Switzerland) view confidentiality as a fundamental feature of commercial arbitration.[26] In the case of *Aïta v. Ojjeh*, the Paris Court of Appeal held that 'it is the very nature of arbitration proceedings to ensure that the highest level of secrecy governs the resolution of private disputes in accordance with the parties' agreement'.[27]

The approach to confidentiality amongst common law jurisdictions differs more than one might think.[28] The lack of any express or implied duty of confidentiality in the United States is often highlighted, along with the Australian decision in *Esso Australia Resources Ltd v. Plowman* (1995) 183 CLR 10 in which the Australian courts rejected the idea of an implied duty of confidentiality on the basis that, unlike privacy, confidentiality is not an 'essential attribute' of commercial arbitration.[29] In contrast, the English courts have upheld an implied duty of confidentiality in arbitration. However, it is not adopted in the Arbitration Act of 1996 because the Departmental Advisory Committee (DAC) concluded that, while 'users of commercial arbitration in England place much importance on privacy and confidentiality "as essential features" of arbitration', there was difficulty in reaching a statutory formulation in light of the 'myriad exceptions' and qualifications that would have to follow.[30] This has led to complications for the English courts' application of an implied duty of confidentiality arising from the inherently private nature of arbitration.[31]

---

25. Raising the Curtain on English Arbitration: Constantine Partasides QC and Simon Maynard (Arbitration International) 2017, 33, 197-202, 197.
26. Gu Weixia, 'Confidentiality Revisited: Blessing or Curse in International Commercial Arbitration?', 15 Am. Rev. Int'l. Arb. 1-29 (2005).
27. *Aïta v. Ojjeh*, Paris Court of Appeal, 18 February 1986, Rev. Arb. 1986, 583.
28. For example, Constantine Partasides and Simon Maynard, 'Raising the Curtain on English Arbitration', 33 Arb. Int'l. 197, 198 (2017).
29. The Federal Arbitration Act is silent on the issue of confidentiality, and the decision in *United States v. Panhandle Eastern Corp.*, 693 F. Supp. 88 (D. Del. 1988), confirmed the lack of an implied duty of confidentiality. The decision in *Esso Australia Resources Ltd v. Plowman* was followed in 2011 by the Australian International Arbitration Act in which confidentiality was provided for, subject to certain exceptions (s23C).
30. Departmental Advisory Committee, Report on the Arbitration Bill, February 1996, para 12. Sir Patrick Neill QC in his lecture, 'Confidentiality in Arbitration', 12 Arb. Int'l. 287-318 (1996), and which the DAC cited with approval in their Report, described the privacy and confidentiality of arbitration proceedings as 'a fundamental characteristic of the agreement to arbitrate' (p. 316). The 'myriad exceptions' are likely to come under the microscope in the Law Commission's ongoing review of the Arbitration Act.
31. *Ali Shipping Corporation v. Shipyard Trogir* [1997] EWCA Civ 3054 per Potter LJ 'The parties have indicated their presumed intention simply by entering into a contract to which the court attributes particular characteristics'; *Emmott v. Michael Wilson & Partners Ltd* [2008] EWCA Civ 184. . This has been further discussed in the recent Supreme Court decision in *Halliburton Company v. Chubb Bermuda Insurance Ltd* [2020] UKSC 48 (para. 88) which has confirmed that an arbitrator's duty of confidentiality takes precedence over their duty of disclosure, and that without party consent, an arbitrator can only disclose facts that are not confidential regarding

The detractors seize on this to argue that there is no general rule of law imposing confidentiality on proceedings across the world, and the few jurisdictions that do recognize such a rule formulate a significant number of exceptions, the scope of which is equally controversial. These exceptions focus on the legitimate interests of the parties to pursue legal rights as well as on competing public interests – e.g., with respect to statutory or regulatory disclosure obligations. Is it therefore misguided to assume that, even if arbitration is private, it must therefore be confidential?

III   IN DEFENCE OF THE CONTRACTUAL, PARTY-LED PROCESS

There are many and varied arguments brought to bear as to why confidentiality should not be the default position in commercial arbitration, but there is a surprising lack of clarity about how far confidentiality should be curtailed and in what respect. For example, should the publication of anonymised arbitral awards be mandatory in all arbitrations or only those that are raised in court proceedings? If parties are to be given the option to choose whether their proceedings are confidential, should confidentiality be opt-in or opt-out? Who should decide what is confidential and should that decision be supported and upheld? What say should parties have in restricting the dissemination of information about the procedure and process of their arbitration? What information belongs to the parties and what does not? Does an argument in favour of organisational transparency also require legal or procedural transparency? Why should 'privacy' remain sacrosanct in an arbitration, but confidentiality should not?

In order to explore these questions, I would like to turn back the clock to look at the fundamental tenets of commercial arbitration, and why it has grown and flourished. I will then consider whether any of the arguments for abolishing confidentiality as the default position in arbitration are persuasive and sufficient to displace the fundamental supremacy of party choice.

1   The Creation of the Arbitration System

Transferring disputes from domestic courts to a private forum has happened for many hundreds of years. Even before the term 'arbitration' was being used, tribunals of elders or groups of trading or other professionals were tasked with resolving disputes, whether religious, personal or commercial. These tribunals produced a ruling that was binding on the parties involved by agreement or social convention. For instance, it was common for merchants to agree for their disputes to be resolved quickly, efficiently, and, where possible, cheaply, by fellow merchants with knowledge and expertise in the related field.

With time, and as the commercial merits of this form of dispute resolution became more widely recognised, so came the development of more established systems for resolving commercial disputes generally. In some jurisdictions, a system

---

their appointment when making a disclosure. This consent could potentially be inferred from the type or arbitration, sector or the institutional rules adopted by the parties.

for resolving commercial disputes was established within the state judicial system. For example, in England and Wales, commercial disputes were resolved in special 'courts', such as local boroughs, fair or Staple courts, which offered many of the same benefits as an arbitral tribunal, with a commercial approach taken to the speedy settlement of disputes. In Continental Europe, disputes were resolved on an ad hoc basis within trading bodies and guilds. This also happened in England to a degree. By the eighteenth century, trading associations and guilds had begun to establish standing bodies which functioned to resolve disputes relating to trading and commerce outside the state court system.[32] The legitimacy of these bodies rested upon the power and authority of the merchant communities and the specific guilds and trades in which they operated. A ruling by one of these bodies was binding on the parties to a dispute without the need for legislative weight behind it: social and business reasons alone would strongly incline a merchant to comply.

With the expansion of the trading power of the British Empire during the nineteenth century, arbitration (as we might recognise it today) began to flourish in England and Wales. The English Common Law Procedure Act of 1854 allowed parties to arbitrate by agreement outside the court structure while relying on the court to sanction non-compliance with an arbitration agreement and to enforce a resulting award. This novel piece of legislation enabled the growth of arbitration within the English legal system.

Trade-linked arbitral rules flourished within commercial organisations and continue to exist within many trade associations to this day. A key reason why trade bodies maintain specific arbitral rules is to ensure that disputes are resolved by arbitrators who are familiar with that trade. Modern-day examples of this include the London Metal Exchange, the London Maritime Arbitrators Association, the Grain and Feed Trade Association, the Sugar Association of London, and the British Coffee Association.

The development of arbitral institutions within England and Wales which were not linked to a specific trade or industry came later towards the end of the nineteenth century when, in April 1891, the 'The City of London Chamber of Arbitration' was set up by the City of London in the Guildhall, under the administrative auspices of an arbitration committee made up of members of the London Chamber and the City Corporation. This later became the London Court of International Arbitration (LCIA) – of which I am currently the President.[33]

The promotion and acceptance of arbitration by the state as an alternative to the courts was not universal. For instance, despite arbitration being used in many states

---

32. These included (i) bodies which regulated disputes in a particular trade, for example maritime courts in the Mediterranean, the Stannary Courts in Cornwall on the English coast, or guild tribunals in Italy; and (ii) special courts and tribunals dealing with trade disputes such as the officium meranziale in Italy and later, in Southern France. Michael Mustill, 'Arbitration: History and Background', 6(2) J. Int'l. Arb. 43-56 (1989).
33. http://www.lcia.org/LCIA/history.aspx, last accessed 24 May 2022.

and specific populations in America, the progress towards federal acceptance of arbitration as a binding alternative to the resolution of disputes in the courts was comparatively slow, with the Federal Arbitration Act being introduced only in 1925.[34] In contrast, the French state was an early adopter of arbitration in the mainstream resolution of disputes, not just amongst the trading classes. During the French Revolution, arbitration was viewed as the best way to settle disputes and render justice and was widely viewed as superior to the national courts.[35] Yet in 1843, the French Supreme Court refused to recognise that an agreement to arbitrate was binding, reverting to the primacy of state courts.[36] In a similar vein to America, it was only in 1925 that pressure from the newly established International Chamber of Commerce in Paris prompted the enactment of provisions in France recognising the validity of an arbitration agreement in commercial matters.

2 In Support of International Trade: Facilitating a Party-Led Process in the Public Interest

While acceptance of court-supported arbitration at a national and international level has taken time, acceptance has now been widely achieved. That is, in considerable part, due to the New York Convention of 1958. It is very easy to forget that the New York Convention was not the beginning of the process, but rather the culmination of a process that started in the 1920s. (The Geneva Protocol on Arbitration Clauses of 1923 and the Geneva Convention on the Execution of Foreign Arbitral Awards of 1927 were agreed upon and eventually entered into by thirty states.)[37]

However, both were generally considered inadequate in achieving the enforcement objectives for which they had been designed, and an initiative began at the ICC to replace them. The ICC issued a draft convention in 1953 and change was pushed forward within the auspices of the United Nations. The Convention on the Recognition and Enforcement of Foreign Arbitral Awards was adopted by the UN following a diplomatic conference held in May and June 1958 at the United Nations Headquarters in New York and entered into force on 7 June 1959.[38]

At the first meeting of the Conference on 20 May 1958, the President of the Conference stated that 'the continuing expansion of world trade and the acceleration of

---

34. For example, the New York Chamber of Commerce established an arbitration system when it was founded in 1768, and the Chamber's arbitration panels were independent from the judiciary. William Catron Jones, 'Three Centuries of Commercial Arbitration in New York: A Brief Survey', 1956 Wash. U. L.Q. 193, 207 (1930). The Quaker religion (of which a substantial population settled in Pennsylvania), provides for the resolution of disputes between Quakers through a process akin to arbitration.
35. French 'Decree on the Courts' organisation' 16-24 August 1790.
36. Cass Civ 10 July 1843 S 1843 p. 561 and D 1843 p. 343.
37. For the history of the New York Convention, see http://www.newyorkconvention.org/travaux+preparatoires/history+1923+-+1958, last accessed 24 May 2022.
38. Report and Preliminary Draft Convention adopted by the Committee on International Commercial Arbitration at its meeting of 13 March 1953. The text was originally published in 1953 as ICC Publication no 174, which is no longer available for distribution, but is accessible here, http://www.newyorkconvention.org/11165/web/files/document/1/5/15940.pdf.

the commercial processes' had resulted in the business community regarding the Geneva Convention as 'inadequate'. He added that 'A successful conference would constitute some small progress towards the rule of law and to the smoother settlement of private law disputes.'[39]

From these few brief lines, it is clear that the New York Convention was proposed to meet an important commercial imperative with clear aims in mind. The New York Convention was also proposed to help facilitate global trade, legal certainty, and ease of enforcement. However, the central aim was not to increase arbitration per se. Arbitration was merely the mechanism proposed as the solution.

As the global trading economy transcended international borders, there was an even greater need than that envisaged by the drafters of the New York Convention for a legal process that could operate with the support of domestic legal infrastructure, but at a truly international level. Legal certainty assumed an even greater significance, both in the governing law of contractual arrangements, in the resolution of disputes and in the enforcement of legal outcomes. Arbitration facilitated trade and trade facilitated arbitration.

3   A Party-Led Process

This brief traverse through history shows that the separation of arbitration from national courts, and its very essence as a non-national party-led process, was what led to arbitration being the dispute resolution mechanism adopted in the New York Convention to facilitate world trade. Countries may allow disputes to be resolved privately, but they do not need to provide a system to support that private process, nor do they need to ensure the enforcement of its outcome. Nevertheless, by adopting the New York Convention and arbitration legislation, over 80% of the world's countries have determined that they should allow parties to agree on a process to resolve their disputes and should provide the apparatus and legal framework to enforce that outcome with relatively limited restrictions and oversight.

At the heart of the arbitral system is the sanctity of contract and of party autonomy. The Model Law and other national arbitration laws, which provide the underlying legal framework, are peppered with references to 'unless the parties agree' or 'the parties are free to agree'.[40] We see only a few mandatory provisions that are viewed as necessary for the protection of the public interest or for the administration of justice, for example, the independence and impartiality of the decision-maker. Arbitration is a creature of contract and, barring limited exceptions, both the agreement to

---

39. United Nations Conference on International Commercial Arbitration, Summary record of the first meeting, held at Headquarters, New York, Tuesday 20 May 1958, 3:30 pm, p. 2, Available here http://www.newyorkconvention.org/11165/web/files/document/1/5/15837.pdf.
40. For example, The English Arbitration Act 1996, section 38 'The parties are free to agree on the powers exercisable by the arbitral tribunal ... .' Or section 44 'Unless otherwise agreed by the parties ... .' Or, UNCITRAL Model Law on International Commercial Arbitration 1985 with amendments as adopted in 2006, section 17, 'Unless otherwise agreed by the parties, the arbitral tribunal may, at the request of a party, grant interim measures', Article 26, 'Unless otherwise agreed by the parties ... .'

arbitrate and the outcome are upheld in most national legal systems. As the US Supreme Court stated in *Volt Information Science v. Leland Stanford, Jr. University* '[T]he FAA's primary purpose [is to] ensur[e] that private agreements to arbitrate are enforced according to their terms. Arbitration under the [FAA] is a matter of consent, not coercion, and parties are generally free to structure their arbitration agreements as they see fit. . . By permitting the courts to "rigorously enforce" such agreements according to their terms, we give effect to the contractual rights and expectations of the parties... .'[41] In short, arbitration is about its users and how they choose to resolve disputes within their contractual agreement.

4   In This Party and Controlled Process, What Do Parties Want in Terms of Confidentiality?

So, what do arbitration users seek in terms of confidentiality? When the 1996 Arbitration Act was being formulated in England and Wales, the DAC expressed the following view: 'there is ... no doubt whatever that users of commercial arbitration in England place much importance on privacy and confidentiality "as essential features" of arbitration'.[42]

Despite the debate that ensues on this issue amongst practitioners and academics, little has changed since 1996 in terms of what parties want or expect across the world. As Gary Born has noted: 'confidentiality plays an essential role in fulfilling the objectives of an international arbitration agreement'.[43] If we track back through numerous surveys of users, we see a consistent picture on the question of confidentiality. According to the Buhring-Uhle 2005 survey into arbitration and the settlement of international business disputes, confidentiality was considered to be the third most important characteristic of international arbitration.[44] In the 2006 International Arbitration Survey: Corporate Attitudes and Practices by Queen Mary University, users who opted out of transnational litigation gave 'lack of confidentiality' as a motivation for doing so. 'Privacy' was ranked as the second most important advantage of international arbitration (behind enforceability).[45]

In the 2010 International Arbitration Survey: Choices in International Arbitration undertaken by Queen Mary University, 62% of the corporates participating in the survey agreed that confidentiality in international arbitration was 'very important', with only 1% indicating that it was 'not important at all'. A further 24% considered confidentiality to be 'quite important'.[46] Interestingly, the 2010 survey found that '50% of respondents erroneously believe that arbitration is confidential even where there is no specific clause to that effect in the arbitration rules adopted or the arbitration

---

41. *Volt Info. Scis., Inc. v. Bd. of Trs. of Leland Stanford Junior Univ.*, 489 U.S. 468, 479 (1989).
42. Departmental Advisory Committee, Report on the Arbitration Bill, February 1996, para. 12.
43. Gary B. Born, *International Commercial Arbitration*, (Kluwer Law International 2014, 2nd edn), p. 2816.
44. Ch. Bühring-Uhle, *Arbitration and Mediation in International Business* (Kluwer 1996).
45. QMUL Survey 2006, Corporate Attitudes and Practices, p. 6.
46. QMUL Survey 2010, Choices in International Arbitration, p. 29.

agreement'.[47] The Queen Mary survey also asked participants which aspects of arbitration should be kept confidential. In order of importance, participants identified the amount in dispute (76%), the pleadings and documents submitted in the case (72%), the full award (69%), details in the award that allow the identification of the parties (58%), the very existence of the dispute (54%) and the legal question to be decided (54%).

And this consistent picture continues. In the 2013 Queen Mary University Survey, again, confidentiality ranked as the most important benefit behind neutrality.[48] In the 2015 Survey for the in-house counsel subgroup, the second most frequently listed valuable characteristic of arbitration was 'confidentiality and privacy', with the report's authors noting that this 'fits the subgroup's particular motives for choosing arbitration'.[49] In the 2018 Survey, 87% of respondents believed that confidentiality in international commercial arbitration is of importance, with most believing that it should be an opt-out, rather than an opt-in feature.[50]

So, what does this show? It shows a consistent view amongst users that confidentiality is important and that users themselves value confidentiality as a critical part of the arbitral process. Accordingly, it strikes me as surprising that practitioners should be articulating a different position on this than the clients whom they represent. The survey results also show that there is a potential divergence in how arbitration is perceived by users and what is actually on offer. If, as the 2010 survey suggested, 50% of users believed arbitration to be automatically confidential when it is not, there is a distinct failure amongst counsel, practitioners, and arbitral institutions to clarify this issue.

a   *Having Your Cake and Eating It: Do Parties Also Want Transparency?*

Given that confidentiality and privacy are consistently cited by users as the most valuable features of arbitration, it seems counterintuitive that some users, particularly in-house counsel, also want arbitration to be more transparent. In the 2018 Queen Mary University survey, when asked which of the following factors would have the most significant impact on the future evolution of international arbitration, both transparency from arbitral institutions and more publicly available information about arbitrators were chosen by 28% of respondents.[51] Responses from the in-house counsel subgroup were particularly interesting, with 43% indicating that there was a need for more transparency of information to make an informed choice about arbitrators,[52] and 89% expressing a willingness to provide an evaluation of arbitrators at the end of a dispute.[53]

---

47. QMUL Survey 2010, Choices in International Arbitration, p. 3.
48. QMUL Survey 2013, Corporate choices in International Arbitration, p. 8.
49. QMUL Survey 2015, Improvements and Innovations in International Arbitration, p. 6.
50. QMUL Survey 2018, The Evolution of Arbitration, p. 3.
51. QMUL Survey, 2018, The Evolution of Arbitration, p. 38.
52. QMUL Survey 2018, p. 21.
53. QMUL Survey 2018, p. 23.

This interest in more data is hardly surprising, particularly in relation to arbitrators, their case management skills, their degree of proactivity and even their approach to procedural and substantive issues. Martin Hunter's oft-quoted approach sums up the position of most practitioners and parties, namely: 'When I am representing a client in an arbitration, what I am really looking for in a party nominated arbitrator is someone with maximum pre-disposition towards my client, but with the minimum appearance of bias.'[54] Getting an inside track on whether an arbitrator has the attributes likely to rule in a client's favour will always be worth having. Similarly, it may be very useful to know whether an arbitrator is ruthlessly efficient or has a tendency to take on too many cases resulting in delays or over-reliance on tribunal secretaries.

The survey results show that parties would like information about other parties' arbitration experiences. When asked in the abstract, they also express a willingness to share information about their own experience. But when it comes to the end of an arbitration, few parties are willing to share the award or data about the performance of the arbitrators. A letter from the ICC confirming that an award will be published unless a party 'opts out' is met, by many of my clients at least, with a resounding 'no'.[55] Similarly, we are not seeing a deluge of awards or anonymised feedback being submitted to information-sharing initiatives such as Arbitrator Intelligence. While a hugely laudable 'opt-in' initiative, by 24 May 2022, 1200 + 'Feedback responses' had been gathered from about 800 + arbitrators,[56] showing only limited growth in the information available since 2019 when 750 'AIQs' had been gathered from about 850 arbitrators.[57] The GAR Arbitrator Research Tool (available with a GAR subscription) which was launched in 2017, contains 558 Arbitrator profiles, each submitted by the relevant arbitrator.[58] While the initiatives do appear to be growing, do these numbers truly suggest a huge appetite for sharing data, even if there may be interest in receiving it?

It is only human to want to have your cake and eat it. But we really need to understand as a community, what truly is valued by clients. It appears that, despite acknowledging the benefits of transparency, parties remain reluctant to run their own disputes in public. And this may not, in reality, present a true conflict of aims, but may result from confusion between transparency in the arbitral system as a whole, and confidentiality in individual disputes. Parties may indeed want institutional, organisational and procedural transparency, but not at the expense of the confidentiality of their own disputes.

---

54. Prof. M Hunter, 'Ethics of the International Arbitrator', 53 Arbitration 219 (1987).
55. 1 January 2021, ICC Note to Parties and Arbitral Tribunals on the conduct of the Arbitration under the ICC Rules of Arbitration, section IV C, para. 58, https://cdn.iccwbo.org/content/uploads/sites/3/2017/03/icc-note-to-parties-and-arbitral-tribunals-on-the-conduct-of-arbitration.pdf.
56. https://arbitratorintelligence.com/ information on home page, last accessed 24 May 2022.
57. https://www.youtube.com/watch?v=o7W166SbkLI, video uploaded 13 March 2019, last accessed 24 May 2022, and https://app.arbitratorintelligence.com/, last accessed 24 May 2022.
58. https://globalarbitrationreview.com/arbitrator-research-tool, number specified as at 24 May 2022.

IV WHY PARTY CHOICE OVERRIDES THE ARGUMENTS MADE AGAINST CONFIDENTIALITY

As illustrated, commercial arbitration is and always has been a party-led and party-controlled process. The codification of arbitration into domestic and international laws has been designed to respect that fundamental feature. Each of the arguments made against the continuation of confidentiality in arbitration cites, to some extent, the benefit brought to third parties by removing a presumption of confidentiality. Underlying these arguments is the pursuit of the 'common good' to a lesser or greater degree. This might be allowing access to the legal analysis in awards to facilitate the development of the law or access to information about arbitrators or procedures to assist other parties and practitioners.

If we come back to the starting point of this being a contractual agreement between parties about how to resolve their own commercial disputes, it does not seem reasonable to put the onus on those same parties to use their private process to facilitate these other ends at the expense of preserving confidentiality. Now, there will no doubt be circumstances which justify exceptions to confidentiality, which derive from public interest or public policy grounds (to which I will return), but these exceptions should not themselves undermine a baseline assumption that parties should be free to decide whether the dispute resolution process should be confidential. So where does that leave us with the arguments made against confidentiality?

1 Legitimacy of the Process

The practice of commercial arbitration can find itself tainted by the infectious pessimism engendered by the recent backlash against investment arbitration. It is easy to extrapolate from the challenges facing investment treaty arbitration and assume commercial arbitration is faced with the same challenges on the same scale. And few would deny that investment treaty arbitration is at somewhat of a crossroads. There is an ongoing re-calibration of the rights and obligations of investors and states and adjustment of the investor-State dispute settlement process.

However, I am not convinced that a discussion of the challenges facing commercial arbitration should focus on the proposals for an investment court system, the criticisms brought to bear on treaty arbitration regarding its regulatory chilling effect on states, the Achmea consternation, the criticism of treaty arbitration's 'secret courts', the replacement of NAFTA with the United States–Mexico–Canada Agreement, the US attitude to the Comprehensive and Progressive Agreement for Trans-Pacific Partnership, or withdrawals from ICSID. These criticisms and the threats they pose are about the realignment and adaptation of the system and the resolution of disputes between states and investors. As The Honourable Chief Justice James Allsop AO put it so eloquently at the International Council for Commercial Arbitration (ICCA) Congress in 2018, 'Many of the concerns in relation to international commercial arbitration are expressed in language similar to concerns about ISDS arbitration, but that superficial similarity should not be allowed to disguise the important differences between the two types of dispute resolution, and the quite different issues involved.'[59]

I see no clamour from NGOs against the process of commercial arbitration per se. We see no movement to overturn the New York Convention. We see no widespread outcry against the enforcement of commercial arbitral awards in general. Indeed, we continue to see accessions to the New York Convention, most recently, Turkmenistan.[60] The picture is not one of stagnation or retreat, but rather of continuing growth and evolution as countries develop and adapt their arbitration legislation to respond to demand. We may choose to question the system of commercial arbitration and seek to change aspects of it, but we should do so by judging it on its own merits, not by looking at it through the prism of investment arbitration. Overriding the sanctity of contract and party choice on the basis that a similar, but fundamentally different system, has faced legitimacy challenges, seems both oppressive and illogical.

2   Limiting Confidentiality to Achieve Greater Transparency for the Common Good

This argument, in my view, confuses transparency within the system of commercial arbitration generally, with confidentiality in individual disputes. There are strong arguments to be made that many arbitral institutions have been, and continue to be, reluctant to share information about their inner workings, their cost effectiveness, and their efficiency. This might include publishing information about specific procedural decision-making, time or costs data across an institution's entire caseload, or statistics about that caseload such as nationality of parties or the gender of their arbitrators.[61] It may even extend to statistics about the number of emergency arbitrator applications, or the number of times certain provisions of the rules have been applied and how. This is all information which can, and should, be made available to users. None of this information allows parties or their disputes to be identified. It shares no facts from their case and no legal issues that were raised. It rather shows what the institution is doing and enables parties to decide whether or not to choose that institution in its future arbitration clauses. I am wholeheartedly supportive of the sharing of this sort of data and would encourage institutions to be more proactive in this regard.

---

59. The Honourable Chief Justice James Allsop AO, 'Commercial and Investor-State Arbitration: The Importance of Recognising Their Differences', ICCA Congress 2018, Sydney, Opening Keynote address, available https://www.fedcourt.gov.au/digital-law-library/judges-speeches/chief-justice-allsop/allsop-cj-20180416#_ftn47.

60. https://uncitral.un.org/en/texts/arbitration/conventions/foreign_arbitral_awards/status2 (accessed 24 May 2022).

61. ICC Arbitral Tribunal appointments page available here https://iccwbo.org/dispute-resolution -services/arbitration/icc-arbitral-tribunals/; LCIA Facts and Figures, Costs and Duration 2013-2016, released October 2017, available here https://www.lcia.org/News/lcia-releases-updated -costs-and-duration-analysis.aspx; LCIA Challenge decision database available here https:// www.lcia.org/challenge-decision-database.aspx; LCIA Casework Reports available here https: //www.lcia.org/lcia/reports.aspx; HKIAC statistics available here https://www.hkiac.org/ about-us/statistics; SCC statistics available here https://sccinstitute.com/statistics/; SIAC statistics available here https://www.siac.org.sg/2014-11-03-13-33-43/facts-figures/statistics.

But we then come to other areas where transparency is sought. Should challenges to arbitrators be shared? Why do we need access to that information and whose information is this to share? Here, again, I would argue that it depends on the information being shared. In 2010, the LCIA began to publish its arbitrator challenge decisions in an anonymised form and has done so ever since.[62] The aim of disclosing that data is to share the inner workings of the decision-making process of the institution and how its rules on arbitrator conflicts of interest are applied. This, I would argue, is achievable transparency, removing 'secrets' from the process, but only the secrets of the institution rather than the details of the parties of the dispute. In a similar vein, the ICC Secretariat's Guide, and the many and varied guidance notes and practice notes published by arbitral institutions, seek to raise the curtain on how their rules are interpreted and applied. I am also supportive of the ICC's initiative in sharing the names of arbitrators appointed in their arbitrations, together with their nationality and the method of appointment.[63] Provided that those arbitrators have consented to their personal data being shared in this way, it enables users of arbitration to identify potential arbitrator candidates who they might otherwise not know, but without any intrusion into the underlying dispute or release of data about the parties.

However, what about confidential information that truly relates to an individual dispute? Should parties be required to share data about their arguments, their witnesses, their experts, their procedural steps, their jurisdictional challenges or their awards? Here, I would say no.

In the vast majority of cases, there should not be any obligation on parties to share this information for the 'common good', in any form, whether anonymised or not. Indeed, I would argue that arbitral institutions should support parties by making confidentiality the default. I am pleased to see that institutions such as the LCIA, the Hong Kong International Arbitration Centre and the Singapore International Arbitration Centre (SIAC) provide for confidentiality.[64] It does, after all, remain open to parties to 'opt-out' of that provision in the rules when drafting their arbitration clauses, or to waive their rights to confidentiality at a later date by sharing the content of their award. However, I am opposed to arbitral institutions assuming the role of gatekeeper in terms of confidentiality, prioritising the 'common good' over their individual users in what is a contractual process. Provisions in rules that make confidentiality 'opt-in' rather than 'opt-out' place the onus on the parties to actively protect that contractual process. It is for that reason that I would question the ICC's new approach which makes publication of awards the default. While the new approach does not override party choice entirely, in requiring an active choice to opt out, I consider its premise to be misguided.

The argument becomes more nuanced when parties seek the support of the court. Arbitration is different from other forms of contractual alternative dispute resolution because it can intersect with the court system at several points in the process. And it must be for the court or national legislators to determine when and how that support can be accessed and the conditions it places on accessing it. Domestic courts are public

---

62. https://www.lcia.org/challenge-decision-database.aspx.
63. https://iccwbo.org/dispute-resolution-services/arbitration/icc-arbitral-tribunals/.
64. LCIA Rules 2020, Article 30; HKIAC Rules 2018, Article 45; SIAC Rules 2016, Article 39.

bodies in which justice must be seen to be done. If parties want to use the power of the court in supporting their contractual process, they must either accept the conditions placed on that support or give up their reliance on that support.

It is therefore open to national courts to lift the veil on confidentiality in certain circumstances. And many do. Parties accessing the courts to challenge, appeal or enforce an award will usually find the facts of the dispute, and the reasoning of the award, in the court judgment ruling on the challenge or appeal that has been made, potentially, although not always, in an anonymised form.

I would also accept that there may be circumstances which lead legislators to impinge on an arbitration's confidentiality in order to protect the legitimate interests of an arbitrating party or in the public interest. Confidentiality cannot be absolute. We have seen legislators grapple with these issues when stipulating 'exceptions' to any express duties of confidentiality. These 'controversial and difficult' issues were acknowledged in the DAC Report on the Arbitration Bill of February 1996 resulting in the decision not to codify a duty of confidentiality within the English Arbitration Act,[65] and for legislators and courts to determine when confidentiality should be overridden, in respect of which information, and at what stage in the proceedings. Indeed, we have recently seen the English court grappling with these issues in delineating the boundaries of an arbitrator's obligations of disclosure, privacy and confidentiality,[66] and in deciding the limits of confidentiality and privacy in relation to arbitration applications which come before the court or intersect with court proceedings.[67]

Recognising that exceptions to the rule may exist does not justify the blanket removal of confidentiality for all arbitrations or in respect of all information within an arbitration to which the exception applies. For example, a company may be required to disclose the fact of an arbitration so that investors and shareholders have access to information that has the potential to affect their investment. Yet while the fact of the dispute and its potential impact might need to be disclosed, the counterparty, the facts, legal arguments, procedure and documents may not.[68] A state may also determine that certain issues or categories of dispute either cannot be arbitrated or should be excluded from the presumption of confidentiality, for example in relation to governmental actions, human rights or fraud.

---

65. Report on the Arbitration Bill, February 1996, Departmental Advisory Committee on Arbitration. Chapter 2 The Law Commission in the UK is looking at this again as part of its review of the Arbitration Act 1996.
66. The Supreme Court judgment in *Halliburton Company v. Chubb Bermuda Insurance Ltd* [2020] UKSC 48.
67. In *Newcastle United Football Co. Ltd v. Football Association Premier League* Ltd [2021] EWHC 349 (Comm), the court considered the circumstances where it should deviate from this principle. In *CDE v. NOP* [2021] EWCA Civ 1908, the Court of Appeal also confirmed that where court proceedings overlapped with the subject matter of an arbitration, the starting point should be that hearings will be held in public unless an exception applies.
68. For example, International Accounting Standard (IAS) 37 'Provisions, Contingent Liabilities and Contingent Assets' allows the non-disclosure of information about provisions and contingent liabilities where disclosure is expected to prejudice the position of an entity in a dispute. In such circumstances, IAS 37 requires only that the general nature of the dispute is disclosed.

Yet these exceptions to the rule should not mean that the exceptions become the rule. For most arbitrations, sanctity of contract and party choice should not be sacrificed on the altar of a presumed common good.

3 Confidentiality in Arbitration Poses a Risk to the Development of the Law

It is certainly true that many commercial disputes are being referred to arbitration rather than to national courts. Indeed, it might be argued that this is due to the success of arbitration, particularly in some areas of business and trade where arbitration is the default process for dispute resolution. The interpretation of certain insurance, shipping or gas pricing clauses has sat firmly within the remit of arbitral tribunals for some decades, only darkening the doors of the courts in very limited circumstances. The choice of arbitration may be due to the benefits of arbitration or may be due to a wish from one of the parties to avoid making a precedent.

It is first worth considering whether the origins of these arguments are truly founded in concern for the development of the law, or rather a feeling of unease about arbitration's role alongside that of the courts. As The Honourable Chief Justice James Allsop AO stated, 'The question of whether commercial arbitration is stifling the development of commercial law contains an at least implicit allegation that international commercial arbitration is usurping the role of national courts.'[69] These concerns do not lie far below the surface in many jurisdictions. Many newcomers to the New York Convention express similar concerns about seeking to have issues of their domestic law or relating to assets present within their jurisdiction resolved by their own courts: the so-called nationalisation of dispute resolution where states are reluctant to cede power from their courts.

It is also easy to sweep these concerns aside and simply meet them with the argument that the solution to the problem (if it is a problem) is for national courts to adapt to meet the requirements of those who choose to arbitrate instead. The form of that adaptation differs from country to country. Singapore, France and Germany are working hard to introduce new, faster commercial courts that can resolve international disputes, potentially with foreign counsel and foreign languages, to attract some of the work traditionally resolved through international arbitration. And the Hague Convention, while still in its infancy, does present a potential challenge for arbitration for the future. Parties may be willing to relinquish some of the advantages of arbitration to work within the international commercial court framework in some jurisdictions where those judgments can be enforced internationally.

But if we assume that arbitration is to continue to co-exist alongside the courts and that concerns about the development of the law are justified, should those concerns override party control over their contractual process? And in what respect?

---

69. The Honourable Chief Justice James Allsop AO 'Commercial and Investor-State Arbitration: The Importance of Recognising Their Differences', ICCA Congress 2018, Sydney, Opening Keynote address, para. 48, available https://www.fedcourt.gov.au/digital-law-library/judges-speeches/chief-justice-allsop/allsop-cj-20180416#_ftn47.

In my view, the answer to that question should be a resounding no. Most commercial arbitrations will not trouble national courts at any point during the proceedings, moving autonomously from dispute to arbitral procedure to award and to payment of that award without any court involvement at all. And in this respect, arbitration is no different to any other form of contractual 'alternative dispute resolution', such as mediation, negotiation and expert determination where no such expectation to share legal reasoning is engendered. Where an arbitration runs without the need for the courts to supervise its process or enforce its outcome, I can see no justification for requiring the parties to share any aspect of these proceedings publicly unless they choose to do so, regardless of whether they use an arbitral institution or agree to ad hoc proceedings. Parties choose how, where, and when to resolve their disputes. We may be interested in the allocation of risk and responsibility between private parties, but we should not have the right to access that information unless they choose to share it. There is no basis on which all parties should be forced to share their award, whether that be the facts of the dispute or its legal reasoning, just in case it generates interest in a thorny legal issue.

Arbitrators apply the law rather than make it. Therefore, there may be novel points of law that arise in arbitration proceedings where at least one of the parties decides to consult the national court of the governing law. Section 45 of the English Arbitration Act 1996 (English Act) allows a party in an ongoing arbitration to make an application to the court, either with the agreement of all other parties or with the permission of the tribunal, to determine a preliminary point of law.[70] Similarly, section 69 of the English Act allows a party to appeal a point of English law to the courts. Neither of these provisions is mandatory and, in my view, rightly so. Section 69 currently stands as an anomaly on the world's stage (alongside Hong Kong), out of step with the Model Law and other modern arbitration laws.[71] The fact that the drafters of the Model Law and its adopter states did not see the need for a similar provision may indicate that protecting the development of the law is a less fundamental issue than those arguing in support of that proposition might suggest. That said, I accept that the issue is more relevant to common law jurisdictions where the law is developed via precedent rather than according to static codes as in civil law jurisdictions.

However, if all arbitral awards were published in order to provide 'guidance' on how arbitrators have interpreted certain legal provisions, I see considerable confusion ensuing given the absence of a system of precedent in arbitration. Indeed, the lack of precedent in the investment treaty arena has resulted in the cherry-picking of awards and the development of inconsistent jurisprudence, subsequently generating moves to

---

70. *See*, for example, the case of *The Eternal Bliss* [2021] EWCA Civ 1712 in which the Court of Appeal reached a decision on demurrage which may go on to inform the nature of liquidated damages more generally.
71. The Law Commission is currently considering amendments to the Arbitration Act 1996. The availability of appeals on a point of law is an area which is under consideration https://www.lawcom.gov.uk/law-commission-to-review-the-arbitration-act-1996/ last accessed 24 May 2022.

introduce an appellate body and binding precedent system.[72] I also predict considerable disquiet amongst the judiciary if mandatory publication of all arbitral awards showed the development of a line of interpretation with which it disagreed yet could not remedy. I would also question the judiciary's willingness to be persuaded by that line of interpretation in their own decision-making.

4 Confidentiality is the Exception, Not the Rule in Most Jurisdictions

Finally, I would like to return to the argument that a presumption of confidentiality is the exception and not the rule in most jurisdictions. There is some truth to this. The UNCITRAL Model Law does not contain any provision on confidentiality, meaning that the many pieces of arbitration legislation across the globe which are based on the Model Law are similarly lacking provision for confidentiality. Yet variety abounds. An express or implied duty of confidentiality is found in diverse sets of legislation from New Zealand to Romania, from Peru to Scotland.[73]

But what is critical is that even in those jurisdictions without an implied or express default position on confidentiality, there is a common understanding that party choice and party autonomy are paramount. Each jurisdiction recognises that arbitration is a contractual process and that parties' contractual terms should be respected. While the Australian position may have caused surprise when it rebutted the presumption of confidentiality without express provision for it, the Australian approach still permits and upholds the right for parties to agree that their arbitration should be confidential.

Accordingly, it is not credible to use the multiplicity of international approaches to argue that confidentiality is not an important facet of commercial arbitration and should be removed in its entirety. While national legislation permits parties to choose to keep their arbitrations confidential (whether by way of express provision in the legislation, by implication or through party choice), there remains global acceptance that party choice on this issue remains the key factor.

V CONCLUSION

The debate around confidentiality in arbitration is currently confusing. Laudable efforts to improve transparency in investment treaty arbitration have led to corresponding efforts to restrict or remove confidentiality in commercial arbitration, based purely on the misguided assumption that where one goes, the other should follow. Proponents of transparency within the commercial arbitration context fail to address why private parties should be compelled or asked to share details of their dispute for the common good of other users or in support of the arbitral process itself. Arguments around whether arbitration currently is, or is not confidential, and whether it should

---

72. *See*, for example, the two-tier EU Investment Court System.
73. Section 14(B) New Zealand Arbitration Act 2012; Article 353 Romanian Code of Civil procedure; Article 51, Peruvian Arbitration Act; Rule 26, Scottish Arbitration Act 2010.

continue to be also lack clarity. Some argue for the removal of confidentiality entirely, or over certain aspects of the process, while others argue for the removal of any presumption, express or implied, at a national level.

Transparency is a laudable aim. But in advocating transparency, we need to be very careful to ensure we think carefully about what we truly want, need, or, indeed, have a right to require. Seeking transparency around the process of arbitration, particularly institutional statistics, decision-making and the interpretation and application of arbitral rules is important. This relates to the process of arbitration and the institutions seeking arbitration business should be offering greater openness to users across the board. Efforts to widen the pool of arbitrators by age, gender and ethnicity are also laudable and to be encouraged. Any initiative that enables potential candidates to be highlighted and considered should be fostered, provided it does not also share details of the parties who appointed them, their dispute or the outcome without those parties' agreement. But when does a quest for transparency become an unnecessary and unjustified intrusion into a private contractual dispute? And who should draw that line?

The arguments in favour of the publication of arbitral awards are similarly confused, based on different justifications and with different intentions in mind. Some seek the publication of the legal reasoning only of points of public interest, while others seek the full anonymised award. Some seek to do so as a default, while others wish to change the presumption in favour of awards being published unless parties opt out. In my view, it is critical to know why we are seeking access to arbitral awards and to what end. Arguing that publication is for the good of arbitral practice seems to be a difficult one to maintain. In terms of the development of the law, it is hard to dispute whether legal questions are being determined behind closed doors which may be useful to others. But that is the system that has been designed and is currently supported. It is up to legislators to consider how serious this problem truly is and to legislate accordingly, while also weighing up the implications on the sanctity of contract and on the future of the arbitral seat if the system is altered.

While the debate on this issue is useful and instructive, I maintain that when discussing confidentiality in commercial arbitration, we must always start from the beginning and think about why arbitration developed, and why parties use it. Arbitration developed as, and remains, a contractual form of dispute resolution, party-led and party-driven. With that in mind, I would argue that barring very limited exceptions, parties should be given the process they want. And that, overwhelmingly, is a confidential, private process.

To that end, express provision at the national level (subject to necessary public interest/policy caveats) is arguably the most sensible and effective route. While my preference would be to make express provision for confidentiality at a legislative level, I recognise this is unachievable globally. That ship has sailed, and it is not realistic to aim for the revision of the UNCITRAL Model Law and all other pieces of domestic arbitration legislation. The English approach of an 'implied' duty may be the second-best option but brings with it many difficulties. As Philip Clifford and Eleanor Scogings have said 'The precise extent of any confidentiality is a mystery to many and its legal basis, beyond being an implication as a matter of English law, remains unclear.'[74] Implied duties, while a way of enabling the law to respond and adapt to different situations, also bring with them a lack of clarity and uncertainty. I am hopeful that the Law Commission's review of the Arbitration Act may bring about a renewed focus on whether confidentiality should and can be made express under English law.[75]

While having a default position of express duties of confidentiality at the legislative level across the globe may not be achievable, it remains the case that the vast majority of legal systems continue to uphold the sanctity of party agreement on confidentiality, subject again, to necessary caveats. And here we return to my title, 'in defence of party choice'. Given the varied approaches at national and institutional levels, parties should be afforded an informed choice about their options regarding confidentiality. Practitioners should therefore ensure that parties are told about their options and given the opportunity to choose the outcome they want. It is not acceptable that 50% of users believe arbitration to be automatically confidential if the reality is that it may not be, barring express provision. Arbitral institutions should deliver the confidentiality that parties assume to exist and want or be very open about what their rules offer in terms of confidentiality. As practitioners, we should also engage with clients more proactively on the subject of confidentiality. Talking about confidentiality should facilitate discussion about the level of confidence required, and what they may be willing to share. This discussion may itself prompt a greater willingness to share information and allow greater transparency.

I would also argue that, as practitioners, we need to frame the arguments around transparency and confidentiality more carefully and keep the user at the front of our minds. We need to be careful about advocating an approach for change that we believe users *should* want, rather than what they *actually* want. Failing to listen to what our clients need from the system runs the risk of driving them to look at alternative forms of dispute resolution.

---

74. Philip Clifford and Eleanor Scogings, 'Which Law Determines the Confidentiality of Commercial Arbitration?', 35 Arbitration International 391-399, 391 (2019).
75. This forms part of the focus of the Law Commission https://www.lawcom.gov.uk/law-commission-to-review-the-arbitration-act-1996/ (last accessed 24 May 2022). However, given the codification challenges identified in the Departmental Advisory Committee, Report on the Arbitration Bill, February 1996, paras 9-17, this wish may go unfulfilled.

CHAPTER 15

Confidentiality in International Commercial Arbitration Does Not Undermine the Legitimacy of the Process

Lilit Nagapetyan[*]

> *My father was a businessman and I am a businessman; I want my philosophy to be business-like, to get something done, to get something settled.*[1]

> *What an absurdity to postulate that confidentiality is not part and parcel of commercial arbitration. It is inconceivable that such a procedure, whether domestic or international, should take place in the public eye.*[2]

It is about time the legitimacy card stops being used as a magic wand to oppose or justify the deficiencies of the arbitration process. International commercial arbitration might be imperfect, fluid, at times lengthy, at times costly, inconsistent in the diverging outcomes, or fragmentary in the approach of arbitrators. But it is not lacking party legitimacy for those who seek autonomy in resolving their disputes. And that is the only legitimacy that counts.

Legitimacy is multifaceted, and there is little agreement on the ways in which different conceptions of legitimacy are used by different actors of the heterarchical arbitration community. There is a tendency to regard international commercial arbitration as an instrument of transnational global governance in addition to a dispute

---

[*] Lilit Nagapetyan is a dispute resolution lawyer, and her private practice focuses on international commercial arbitration, as well as complex cross-border disputes and enforcement proceedings. She is also a Teaching Fellow at Queen Mary University of London (School of International Arbitration) where she pursues her PhD. She has previously practised in London as a forensic accountant with a top-ten accounting firm where she has been involved in a wide range of litigation and arbitration disputes. She is the winner of the 2022 Young ICCA Essay Competition.

1. Ludwig Wittgenstein, in conversation with Drury (Rhees 1991, 125).
2. Serge Lazareff, *Confidentiality and Arbitration: Theoretical and Philosophical Reflections*, ICC Bulletin – Special Supplement (2009) 81.

settlement mechanism. Hence, this creates unjustified expectations from arbitrators to develop a consistent and predictable normative framework, a task for which commercial arbitration is doomed to fail.

The analysis of the concept of legitimacy of commercial arbitration hence should be linked to a pursuit of its utility. Why are we even concerned about its legitimacy in the first place? From a pragmatic research perspective, are we seeking assurance that commercial arbitration serves the interests of the public community?[3] Or the actors in the arbitration industry? Or just the parties?

Indeed, it can hardly be disputed that the growth of arbitral institutions has led them to perform functions outside of dispute settlement, including pursuing educational, promotional, development goals as well as shaping professional ethics standards. However, the exercise of these functions does not grant these institutions, and by extension not the arbitrators either, any transnational authority when it comes to resolution of commercial disputes.

Unlike investor-state dispute settlement (ISDS), in commercial arbitration, the decision-making authority of arbitral tribunals stems exclusively from the consent of the disputing parties who are acting in their private capacity. It creates limited effect on third parties as, for example, it does not entail the declaration of government policies as illegal or states' liability in the form of taxpayers' funds. Therefore, given the limited public interest component in it, the legitimacy of international commercial arbitration shall be assessed as to whether it exercises its authority in line with the fundamental values of disputing parties.

In commercial arbitration, the disputing parties find themselves in an autonomous 'single, centralized forum, with internationally enforceable dispute resolution agreements and decisions'.[4] Hence, party autonomy remains the primary legitimating factor for international commercial arbitration, and the parties' interest is for their dispute to be heard by an independent tribunal compliant with principles of procedural fairness. Such procedural guarantees, including the prohibition of arbitrators from acting *ultra vires*, are protected by involvement of state courts who are precluded from hearing the substance of the dispute de novo.

Confidentiality refers to the right of the parties to have those who are present at the proceedings not to disclose the content or nature of the proceedings.[5] The principle of confidentiality is vastly recognised as one of the key advantages of arbitration proceedings that lures the parties into settling their dispute via arbitration instead of judicial proceedings. Whilst it is not identical to privacy, confidentiality is impossible

---

3. Thomas Schultz, *Legitimacy Pragmatism in International Arbitration: A Framework for Analysis*, in Jean Kalicki and Mohamed Abdel Raouf (eds), Evolution and Adaptation: The Future of International Arbitration (ICCA Congress Series No. 20, Wolters Kluwer, 2019), King's College London Law School Research Paper No. 2018-25.
4. Gary Born, *International Commercial Arbitration*, vol. I (2nd edn, Wolters Kluwer 2009) 70.
5. Alexis Brown, *Presumption Meets Reality: An Exploration of the Confidentiality Obligation in International Commercial Arbitration*, 16(4) Am. U. Int'l L. Rev. (2001).

without it as privacy means the right of the parties to limit the presence of 'strangers' at the proceedings.[6]

It is a well-known fact that the users of international commercial arbitration favour not only the confidentiality of both the arbitral proceedings but also its outcome for protecting their business secrets.[7] Nevertheless, the principle of confidentiality is lately regarded as one of the major obstacles to establishing a body of law stemming from arbitration practice,[8] which is in turn undermining the legitimacy of arbitration.

International commercial arbitration broadly follows the civil law model where 'courts are not bound to follow previous judicial decisions'.[9] Hence, decisions by arbitral commercial tribunals do not have any formal precedential status, which also relates to the fact that arbitral awards are not published as a rule. Because of such lack of binding precedent, confidentiality of international commercial arbitration is often criticised for lack of transparency – these two buzzwords have become widespread with the impending growth of international arbitration.

However, let us remind ourselves: parties opt for international commercial arbitration for the opportunity to customise the way in which they prefer their disputes to be resolved. The arbitrator's authority stems from the party autonomy expressed by way of a contract, and it binds the parties to comply with the arbitrators' decision, irrespective of whether it is based on the law or principles of fairness and equity.[10] This is exactly why the parties have chosen to arbitrate in the first place.

Had the parties wanted to keep the case in the public system, they would have chosen the court system with rigid procedural rules and the appeal system in place. In a setting where the parties often come from different jurisdictions and do not have an appetite to get bogged down in procedural discrepancies, or conflict of law issues, it seems at least irrational to place on them the burden of developing a consistent arbitral jurisprudence. This is not what they have signed up for.

One might argue that in international commercial arbitration, it is in the interest of parties who are involved in regular commercial transactions subject to arbitration, to benefit from a degree of predictability.[11] And such predictability is supposed to be achieved through the transparency of the reasoning of awards. However, given the stark discrepancy of factual and contractual legal issues subject to arbitration, it will be impossible but also prejudicial to the parties to a dispute to prioritise 'the development

---

6. L. Yves Fortier, *The Occasionally Unwarranted Assumption of Confidentiality*, 15 Arb. Int'l. 131 (1999).
7. Emmanuel Gaillard and John Savage, *Fouchard, Gaillard, Goldman on International Commercial Arbitration* (Kluwer Law International, 1996), 733.
8. Loukas A. Mistelis, *Confidentiality and Third Party Participation*: UPS v. Canada and Methanex Corporation v. United States, 21(2) Arb. Int'l 216 (2005).
9. Joseph Dainow, *The Civil Law and the Common Law: Some Points of Comparison*, 15 Am. J. Comp. L. 419, 426 (1967).
10. Stephen J. Ware, *Default Rules from Mandatory Rules: Privatizing Law Through Arbitration*, 83 Minn. L. Rev. 703, 726 (1999).
11. Andrea Bianchi and Anne Peters (eds), *Transparency in International Law*, United Kingdom, Cambridge, Cambridge University Press, 2013, p. 161.

of consistent rules through arbitral awards'.[12] Other obstacles include no clear hierarchy in the tribunals, differences and divergent language in the applicable law and ensuing obligations.[13] Unlike ISDS or sports arbitration, there is no incentive for arbitrators to ensure equal treatment of investors or sports players respectively or to ensure the legality of expropriation.

What does the principle of confidentiality entail? The scarcity of published arbitral awards. However, with the lack of binding precedent as referred to above, or at least a recognised *jurisprudence constante*, published decisions would not necessarily increase the quality of the arbitral decision-making, especially where arbitrators do not have to provide any reasoning for their decisions. Let us illustrate this point with just one example of how the issue of corruption has been dealt with in international investment arbitration where all decisions are published.

Arbitrators are granted a wide degree of discretion when it comes to applicable evidentiary rules as the rules on the standard of proof in international arbitration are not usually contained in the arbitral institutional rules, international arbitration conventions, and national arbitration laws. This, however, has created a significant challenge for adjudication of corruption allegations in the context of international investment arbitration. The review of the arbitral case law[14] has shown that there is no consensus among the arbitral community as to the applicable evidentiary standards: a wide range of standards has been applied in practice, which can be broadly classified as low, high, undefined, or more than one standard.

A curious observation that has been made during this doctrinal analysis is that investment tribunals tend to cross-refer to cases where illegality at large (including corruption) has been involved,[15] however, in a very selective manner: by choosing and relying on cases which support their desired outcome, or which help identify the content of certain rights and obligations, i.e., without treating those previous decisions as binding precedent. How this would be different in the context of international commercial arbitration?

Publication of awards is, therefore, not a panacea, especially as the number of awards of precedential value is not as high as it is sometimes portrayed. And it certainly does not affect the party's legitimacy which stems from the parties' interest in keeping the details of the dispute as well as their 'trade secrets' confidential, for commercial and technological reasons.

What about other dimensions of legitimacy, such as national or global legitimacy, i.e., the validity of arbitration from the perspective of the society or a state? From the parties' perspective, this, however, is irrelevant provided that their dispute in question

---

12. Gabrielle Kaufman-Kohler, *Arbitral Precedent: Dream, Necessity or Excuse?*, 24 Arb. Int'l. 357, 357, 376 (2007).
13. Andrea K. Bjorklund, *Investment Treaty Arbitral Decisions as Jurisprudence Constante*, in Colin Picker, Isabella Bunn & Douglas Arner (eds), *International Economic Law: The State and Future of The Discipline* (Hart Publishing, 2008).
14. The author of this chapter has reviewed ca 100 ISDS awards where corruption or other illegality allegations have been raised.
15. Christoph Schreuer, *Diversity and Harmonization of Treaty Interpretation in Investment Arbitration*, 3 Transnat'l Disp. Mgmt. (April 2006) at 14.

is resolved, especially where it has no or minimal repercussions on society. They are not obliged to take into consideration third parties, international economic interests, or the general public in the resolution of their controversies.[16]

Undoubtedly, national law is a necessary element of international commercial arbitration as it is governing the arbitration agreements, the substantive contracts, regulates arbitral procedure and is applied by the enforcement court. However, the limited scope of scrutiny exercised by national courts, together with the principles of Kompetenz-Kompetenz and separability demonstrate that international commercial arbitration is not simply an extension of any national legal order. In addition, there is no designated supervisory institution that would create a meaningful check on the arbitrators' powers.[17] Therefore, arbitral lawmaking is not controlled by national institutions, save for the due process guarantees.

If transparency is at the core of the concern, there are other ways to encourage it which do not undermine confidentiality lying at the core of parties' consent. Such mechanisms include: an appeals mechanism that would allow the arbitral decision to be reviewed on merits; admission of amicus curiae briefs to allow the interested parties to offer information that might be relevant to the proceedings;[18] increased professionalism of arbitrators, including by considering an entry-level qualification exam; standardisation of the arbitrators' appointment process. But certainly not by denying the parties what they have come for – a private process of settling their commercial disputes.

International commercial arbitration might be 'the worst form of international dispute resolution, except all those other forms that have been tried from time to time'.[19] What remains problematic, however, is that the external observers as well as the general public do not necessarily distinguish between different types of arbitration and criticise arbitration, whether involving only private or also public actors.[20] Such distinction, however, is crucial for the assessment of the legitimacy of international commercial arbitration which has a different premise compared to other types of arbitration as confidentiality 'has its roots in the desire for a system of justice suited to the world of commerce'.[21] It would therefore be simply wrong to draw on an umbrella framework to question its legitimacy.

16. Christopher R. Drahozal, *Is Arbitration Lawless?*, 40 Loy. of L.A. L. Rev. 187, 192 (2006).
17. Emily Ariz, *Does the Lack of Binding Precedent in International Arbitration Affect Transparency in Arbitral Proceedings?*, 29(1) U. Miami Int'l & Comp. L. Rev. (2021).
18. Anibal Sabater, *Towards Transparency in Arbitration (A Cautious Approach)*, 5 Berkeley J. Int'l L. Publicist 47 (2010).
19. Charles N. Brower, *A Crisis of Legitimacy*, Nat'l L. J. B15 (7 October 2002).
20. Stephan Schill, Conceptions of Legitimacy of International Arbitration, ACIL Research Paper 2017-14, published in: David D. Caron et al. (eds), *Practising Virtue: Inside International Arbitration* (Oxford University Press 2015) 106-124.
21. Serge Lazareff, *Confidentiality and Arbitration: Theoretical and Philosophical Reflections*, ICC Bulletin – Special Supplement (2009) 81.

CHAPTER 16

How Confidential Is Confidential?: Safeguards, Obstacles, and Boundaries of Confidentiality in International Commercial Arbitration

Anke Sessler[*]

TABLE OF CONTENTS

I   INTRODUCTION

Confidentiality is often advocated as one of the advantages of arbitration over litigation.[1] Yet, in recent years, demands for more 'transparency' and proposals to reduce the level of confidentiality[2] have been raised.

---

*   Anke Sessler, Advisory Board Member of ICCA and partner at Skadden, Arps, Slate, Meagher & Flom, holds positions in various arbitration institutions and has extensive experience in international and domestic arbitration and complex litigation proceedings. She represents industrial corporations and financial service providers in disputes relating to *inter alia* M&A and supply contracts, joint ventures and other commercial agreements, as well as in shareholder litigation and disputes relating to corporate boards.
1. Queen Mary University of London and White & Case International Arbitration Group, '2018 International Arbitration Survey: The Evolution of International Arbitration', p. 7 (2018),

While some of my observations may also apply to investment arbitration, I will focus on confidentiality in international commercial arbitration in this paper.

First, I will describe the status quo: How confidential are international commercial arbitration proceedings, anyway? To answer this question, I will shortly analyse the approaches to confidentiality of arbitration laws and arbitration rules. I will show that there are significant differences (below at section II). Then, I will discuss the advantages and disadvantages of confidentiality. I will advocate that confidentiality in international commercial arbitration is a legitimate concern and must be protected against ill-founded criticism (below at section III). Finally, I will provide a short conclusion (below at section IV).

II STATUS QUO: HOW CONFIDENTIAL ARE INTERNATIONAL COMMERCIAL ARBITRATION PROCEEDINGS, ANYWAY?

Especially in the past, it was argued that confidentiality was a concept inherent to any arbitration proceeding.[3] The supporters of this opinion assumed that arbitration proceedings were confidential irrespective of whether the applicable arbitration law or the applicable arbitration rules contained a specific provision requiring confidentiality.

Today, it is widely argued that arbitration is not *per se* confidential.[4] Thus, parties will have to consult the applicable arbitration law, the applicable arbitration rules, and any confidentiality agreements to find out if and to what extent arbitration proceedings are confidential.

1 Arbitration Laws

A lot of arbitration laws do not contain a provision on confidentiality. In particular, the UNCITRAL Model Law on International Commercial Arbitration ('UNCITRAL ML') is completely silent on this issue[5] and, consequently, various arbitration laws that are based on the UNCITRAL ML, such as the German Arbitration Law, also do not contain a provision on confidentiality.

---

available at http://www.arbitration.qmul.ac.uk/media/arbitration/docs/2018-International-Arbitration-Survey---The-Evolution-of-International-Arbitration-(2).PDF (last accessed 31 October 2022); Gary Born, *International Commercial Arbitration*, 3rd edn (Kluwer Law International 2021) p. 3003; Anna-Maria Tamminen and Viktor Saavola, 'Chapter 11: Protecting Confidentiality Within Arbitral Proceedings' in Axel Calissendorff and Patrick Schöldström, eds, Stockholm Arbitration Yearbook 2021 (Kluwer Law International 2021) p. 191 at p. 192.

2. *See* for instance Peter Bert, 'Neues von der Deutschen Institution für Schiedsgerichtsbarkeit' (16 February 2022), available at https://anwaltsblatt.anwaltverein.de/de/zpoblog/neues-von-der-dis (last accessed 31 October 2022).

3. Jörg Risse and Max Oehm, 'Vertraulichkeit und Nicht-Öffentlichkeit in Schiedsverfahren', ZVglRWiss (2015) p. 407.

4. Heiner Kahlert, *Vertraulichkeit im Schiedsverfahren* (Mohr Siebeck 2015) p. 6 and p. 408; A.-M. Tamminen and V. Saavola, 'Protecting Confidentiality Within Arbitral Proceedings', *supra* n. 1, p. 196.

5. J. Risse and M. Oehm, 'Vertraulichkeit und Nicht-Öffentlichkeit in Schiedsverfahren', p. 415; G. Born, *International Commercial Arbitration*, *supra* n. 1, p. 3009.

In contrast, pursuant to case law, arbitration proceedings are regarded as confidential in England.[6]

2 Arbitration Rules

a *Confidentiality*

Arbitration rules deal with the issue of confidentiality very differently. There are various arbitration rules which contain far-reaching confidentiality provisions, such as Article 44.1 DIS[7] Arbitration Rules, Article 30(1) LCIA[8] Rules, Article 44 Swiss Rules, Article 45.1 HKIAC[9] Rules, Rule 39(1) SIAC[10] Rules, and Article 37(1) ICDR[11] Arbitration Rules.

These rules usually provide for certain exemptions to the duty of confidentiality. These exemptions are often explicitly mentioned in the arbitration rules, but even if they are not, it is widely acknowledged that they apply nevertheless as unwritten exemptions.[12] Typical exemptions are:

- The parties have agreed to waive or limit confidentiality.
- A disclosure is required by applicable law or by other legal duties.
- A disclosure is required for purposes of annulment or recognition and enforcement of arbitral awards.

In contrast to arbitration rules that provide for a strict confidentiality regime, other arbitration rules, such as the UNCITRAL Arbitration Rules, do not stipulate a duty of confidentiality at all. Article 22(3) ICC[13] Arbitration Rules merely provides that the arbitral tribunal may make orders concerning the confidentiality of the arbitration proceedings, which suggests that unless such an order is made, neither the parties nor the arbitrators are bound to confidentiality.[14]

---

6. *John Foster Emmott v. Michael Wilson & Partners Ltd.*, ([2008] EWCA Civ 184, Case No. A3/2007/2785 & 2786), Award (12 March 2008); Mathias Wittinghofer, 'Emmott v. Michael Wilson & Partners Ltd: Der englische Court of Appeal meint es ernst mit der Vertraulichkeit im Schiedsverfahren – oder nicht?', SchiedsVZ (2009) p. 156 at p. 159; J. Risse and M. Oehm, 'Vertraulichkeit und Nicht-Öffentlichkeit in Schiedsverfahren', p. 417; A.-M. Tamminen and V. Saavola, 'Protecting Confidentiality Within Arbitral Proceedings', *supra* n. 1, p. 196.
7. Deusche Institution für Schiedsgerichtsbarkeit.
8. London Court of International Arbitration.
9. Hong Kong International Arbitration Centre.
10. Singapore International Arbitration Centre.
11. International Centre for Dispute Resolution.
12. G. Born, *International Commercial Arbitration, supra* n. 1, pp. 3048-3049; A.-M. Tamminen and V. Saavola, 'Protecting Confidentiality Within Arbitral Proceedings', *supra* n. 1, pp. 196-197.
13. International Chamber of Commerce.
14. However, confidentiality applies to the work of the institution, i.e., the International Court of Arbitration, *see* Article 6 Appendix I of the ICC Arbitration Rules and Article 1 Appendix II of the ICC Arbitration Rules.

b   *Publication of Arbitral Awards*

A question related to the principle of confidentiality is the question of whether and under what conditions arbitral institutions may publish arbitral awards. Usually, this question is either addressed in the arbitration rules or the arbitral institution will have issued some guidance in this regard, either on its website or in a separate document.[15] Again, this issue is dealt with very differently. For example, Article 44.3 sentence 2 DIS Arbitration Rules provides that the DIS may only publish an arbitral award with the prior written consent of all parties. Other arbitral institutions allow the arbitral award to be published without the explicit consent of the parties in anonymised form but provide that a party may object to the publication. Also, there are differences as regards the question of whether the arbitral institution may publish the arbitral award right away, or whether a certain grace period must first have elapsed before the arbitral institution may publish the arbitral award.

3   Parties' Agreement

If the applicable arbitration law and the arbitration rules do not contain a provision on confidentiality, the parties are, of course, not prevented from concluding an agreement in this regard. To prevent unpleasant surprises, such agreements must be drafted carefully. It is recommendable that the parties consider the scope, limits, and effects of the envisaged confidentiality, in particular:

- Who shall be covered by the confidentiality agreement?
- Shall confidentiality also apply to the pre- and post-arbitration phases?
- Shall there be any limits or exemptions?
- Do the parties want to stipulate remedies for breaches of the confidentiality agreement, for example, liquidated damages?

4   Conclusion

To sum up, arbitration proceedings are not confidential *per se*. They are to be treated confidentially only if and to the extent the applicable arbitration law and/or the applicable arbitration rules so require, or to the extent the parties have reached a corresponding agreement. Even if these requirements are fulfilled, the principle of confidentiality does not apply universally but is subject to exemptions.

---

15. *See*, for example, ICC, Note to Parties and Arbitral Tribunals on the Conduct of the Arbitration (2021), paras 56 et seq., available at https://iccwbo.org/content/uploads/sites/3/2020/12/icc-note-to-parties-and-arbitral-tribunals-on-the-conduct-of-arbitration-english-2021.pdf (last accessed 31 October 2022). This note describes the ICC's approach to publication of awards in some detail, while the ICC Arbitration Rules are silent on this issue.

III CONFIDENTIALITY IS A LEGITIMATE CONCERN AND MUST BE PROTECTED AGAINST ILL-FOUNDED CRITICISM

As shown above, arbitration rules deal with confidentiality very differently. The differing approaches reflect that confidentiality is a complex topic and that there are diverging opinions on whether arbitration shall be confidential, and, if yes, on the scope of such confidentiality. In this section, I will discuss arguments for and against confidentiality. I will argue that the principle of confidentiality, i.e., that parties are entitled to conduct arbitration proceedings under the protection of confidentiality, is a cornerstone of arbitration that must be protected from dilution.

1 Parties Want: And Have a Legitimate Right – To Keep Their Disputes Confidential

In my view, the key argument speaking for a far-reaching duty of confidentiality in international commercial arbitration is that most parties want confidentiality. Confidentiality has been and remains one of the most important factors for companies to choose arbitration over litigation. As a general rule, unless there are specific circumstances that suggest a different treatment,[16] parties do not want to fight out their disputes in public.[17] Since arbitration is based on the principle of party autonomy, their wishes must be taken seriously.

Having said that, I also believe that confidentiality is a very legitimate concern. Especially because legal disputes can have a negative impact on a company's reputation,[18] the desire to keep such disputes away from the eyes of the public is anything but improper – it is perfectly comprehensible. In addition, confidentiality significantly enhances the prospects of resolving a dispute via settlement. In contrast, the willingness to settle can decrease to a great extent once a dispute is publicly known.

2 Any Alleged Rights to Information by the Public Are Outweighed by the Parties' Legitimate Confidentiality Concerns

Some opponents of confidentiality argue that the public has a right to be informed about legal disputes, including commercial arbitration proceedings.[19] I do not agree.

In my opinion, it is already questionable whether the public has such a right to information. The matters dealt with in most commercial arbitration proceedings are of little public interest. Commercial arbitration proceedings revolve around the question of whether there has been a breach of contract under civil law. With few exceptions, this contract concerns the business relationship of the parties and stipulates the rights

---

16. For example, to put pressure on the opposing party to agree to a settlement, a party may be inclined to make a dispute publicly known.
17. J. Risse and M. Oehm, 'Vertraulichkeit und Nicht-Öffentlichkeit in Schiedsverfahren', p. 407.
18. J. Risse and M. Oehm, 'Vertraulichkeit und Nicht-Öffentlichkeit in Schiedsverfahren', p. 407.
19. *See* for details Menno Aden, 'Die Nichtöffentlichkeit des Schiedsverfahrens', DZWIR (2012) p. 360 at p. 362.

and duties of the parties, not of the public or anyone else. Therefore, parties are generally not required by law to disclose to the public the contracts they have concluded.

But even if one assumes, for the sake of the argument, that the public has a right to information, such right is generally outweighed by the parties' legitimate confidentiality concerns. It is a widely acknowledged principle in modern legal systems that it is up to the parties how they intend to resolve their commercial disputes. The options are manifold: A party may waive any claims, the opposing party may admit any claims, and the parties can settle their dispute via negotiations or any kind of alternative dispute resolution procedures – the parties can even roll the dice[20] if this is what they want to do. All these measures can be legitimately conducted in a confidential atmosphere without the involvement of the public. Thus, it is not plausible why parties, if they choose to submit their dispute to arbitration, shall not be entitled to the same level of confidentiality.

Sometimes, arbitration proceedings are compared with court proceedings. Because court proceedings are – at least in principle – open to the public, it is argued that arbitration proceedings must also be public. In my opinion, however, this comparison is misleading. In court proceedings, state sovereignty is exercised directly. Court judges are appointed by the state, their judgments are issued 'in the name of the people'. The public nature of court proceedings ensures that these very 'people' can control what judgments are made in their name. On the contrary, arbitrators do not render their awards 'in the name of the people'. Rather, their mandate is of a private nature. Almost every phase of the arbitral process is permeated by the principle of private autonomy, court intervention is limited to a few specific issues. No party can be dragged into a commercial arbitration proceeding if it has not agreed to such proceeding. Thus, there is hardly a need for a public watchdog.

3   **Unfounded Allegations of Secrecy Do Not Justify Foregoing Confidentiality**

These days, arbitration is challenged for various reasons, including the (unfounded) allegation that arbitration proceedings amount to 'shadow justice in first-class hotels'.[21] To counter these allegations, some supporters of arbitration suggest that more 'transparency' be necessary.

While the notion of inordinate secrecy which some people (wrongly) associate with arbitration has the potential to damage the acceptance of arbitration as a legitimate means of dispute resolution, any 'smell-of-secrecy' allegations should not lead to arbitral legislators or institutions prematurely waiving or restricting the principle of confidentiality. Rather, the arbitration community should increase its efforts to depict arbitration – despite its shortcomings – as a well-functioning means for

---

20. J. Risse and M. Oehm, 'Vertraulichkeit und Nicht-Öffentlichkeit in Schiedsverfahren', p. 419.
21. J. Risse and M. Oehm, 'Vertraulichkeit und Nicht-Öffentlichkeit in Schiedsverfahren', p. 408; Anke Henrich, Michael Kroker, Max Haerder and Henryk Hielscher, 'Schattenjustiz im Nobelhotel', Wirtschaftswoche (18/2013) p. 46.

resolving disputes in a globalised world. This certainly requires some information about arbitration in general, including demonstrating the quality of arbitration proceedings and the integrity of arbitral institutions and arbitrators. It does not require sacrificing confidentiality on the altar of unfounded criticism.[22]

4   Confidentiality Does Not Substantially Hinder Any Development of the Law

Promoters of more 'transparency' argue that confidentiality hinders the emergence of case law[23] because only a few arbitral awards are published. I doubt that this argument is very strong, and I do not think that it justifies doing away with confidentiality on a large-scale basis.

First, I believe that, at least with respect to most areas of the law, there are still enough matters decided by state courts whose decisions are usually published or at least available to lawyers upon request. Thus, the need for more published arbitral awards does not apply universally, but only concerns certain fields of law, if any. In addition, a lot of arbitral awards concern very case-specific, fact-driven issues and are far from providing answers to fundamental, unresolved legal questions. Hence, the publication of such arbitral awards will hardly add much value to the development of the law.

Second, I believe that the main reason why so few arbitral awards have been published until today is that the arbitration community has simply not pushed this issue with vigour. The ICC and other arbitral institutions have recently decided that they will take a more proactive role to further the publication of arbitral awards while taking the parties' confidentiality concerns into account.[24] Certainly, one may wonder whether the amount of published arbitral awards will increase significantly if publication depends on the parties' agreement – or lack of objection – to publication. But here again, the will of the parties should guide the discussion: If the parties find that confidentiality of their disputes matters more than the development of case law, then this should be the result. In addition, arbitral institutions can offer that the arbitral award will only be published in anonymised form, only in parts or in summarised form, only after explicit consent to any redaction, and/or only after considerable time has elapsed after the proceedings have ended, and thereby find ways to reconcile both issues.

The ICC's approach regarding the publication of arbitral awards is explained in its Note to Parties and Arbitral Tribunals, a guideline on how the ICC deals with frequently

---

22. Jörg Risse, 'Wehrt Euch endlich! Wider das Arbitration-Bashing', SchiedsVZ (2014) p. 265 at p. 266.
23. Christian Duve and Moritz Keller, 'Privatisierung der Justiz – bleibt die Rechtsfortbildung auf der Strecke? – Ein Beitrag zur Auflösung des Spannungsverhältnisses von Privatautonomie und Rechtsfortbildung in der Schiedsgerichtsbarkeit', SchiedsVZ (2005) p. 169 at pp. 172-173.
24. ICC, Note to Parties and Arbitral Tribunals on the Conduct of the Arbitration (2021), paras 56 et seq., available at https://iccwbo.org/content/uploads/sites/3/2020/12/icc-note-to-parties-and -arbitral-tribunals-on-the-conduct-of-arbitration-english-2021.pdf (last accessed 31 October 2022).

arising issues in arbitration proceedings under its auspices. The note stipulates that the ICC Secretariat will inform the parties and arbitrators during the proceedings and at the time of notification of any final arbitral award made as of 1 January 2019 that the final arbitral award, any other arbitral awards and/or orders, as well as dissenting and/or concurring opinions, may be published in their entirety, including the names of the parties and of the arbitrators, no less than two years after the date of said notification. The parties may agree on a longer or shorter time period. However, at any time before publication, any party may object to publication or require that any award and related documents be fully or partially anonymised (by removing names and/or any contextual data) or pseudonymised (by replacing names with pseudonyms). Moreover, at any time, any individual or entity may also convey to the ICC Secretariat that it does not wish, as a general policy, any ICC arbitral award and related documents to which it is a party to be published. In this case, none of these documents will be published. In case of a confidentiality agreement, order or explicit provisions under the law of the place of arbitration covering certain aspects of the arbitration or of the award, publication will be subject to the parties' specific consent.

If no obstacles exist that hinder publication, the ICC publishes the arbitral decisions in cooperation with Jus Mundi, an international law and arbitration search engine. With final checks and approval from ICC's International Court of Arbitration, including the dispatch of the publishable document to the parties for their information, Jus Mundi publishes the ICC award or related ICC document on a specific website free of charge.[25]

IV   CONCLUSION

Confidentiality has been and remains an essential component of international commercial arbitration proceedings. Despite some justified calls for more information, for example, with regard to the emergence of case law, I believe that the principle of confidentiality should not be diluted beyond reasonable adjustments. The parties' strong desire to keep international commercial arbitration proceedings confidential, if the parties agree so, must be met, today and in the future, to ensure that arbitration remains a leading dispute resolution procedure for international commercial disputes.

---

25. ICC-Jus Mundi Partnership Page, available at https://jusmundi.com/en/partnership/ICC (last accessed 31 October 2022).

CHAPTER 17

The Link Between Transparency and Legitimacy in International Arbitration

Caroline Simson[*]

TABLE OF CONTENTS

I   INTRODUCTION

There are differing reasons as to why transparency is important in investor-State and private commercial disputes, but, ultimately, many arbitral institutions and stakeholders feel that – at the very least – the perception of legitimacy in both areas is improved by increased transparency. Indeed, former US Supreme Court Justice Louis Brandeis famously noted that 'sunlight is said to be the best of disinfectants'. But just how important is the link between transparency and legitimacy?

Some have pointed to weaknesses in the argument that there is a strong link between the two. In a 2006 article in the journal Information Polity relating to transparency measures undertaken by the European Union, professors Deirdre Curtin and Albert Jacob Meijer argue that few citizens access the information presented in EU

---

[*] Senior Reporter, Law360.

policy papers, and that those who do access it – such as NGOs or journalists – may only do so to advance their own pre-existing narrative or to highlight policy failures.[1]

Others, however, see a clear link between transparency and legitimacy.

In a 2011 article published in the International Review of Administrative Sciences, professors Heungsik Park and John Blenkinsopp argue that transparency and trust play a 'substantial role' in curtailing corruption and enhancing citizen satisfaction in public services.[2]

This appears to be the position embraced by many within the investor-State community, which has come under fire from the public for operating under a perceived veil of secrecy. As a result, many nations and supranational organizations like the United Nations are now recognizing the value of publishing awards in investor-State arbitration. (For clarity's sake, when I discuss transparency in investor-State arbitration I'm referring to public disclosure with respect to a particular claim rather than mechanisms for non-party participation.)

The extent of that transparency – including whether pleadings and other filings from arbitrations should be made public – appears to be more controversial.

In the commercial arbitration sphere, however, the concept of legitimacy takes a different form. While the expectation of confidentiality takes precedence in any approach aimed at publishing information related to proceedings and/or awards, stakeholders say that a limited degree of increased transparency may help to increase diversity among arbitrators and also increases the ability of lawyers and third-party funders to assess or manage risk, including possibly through the use of artificial intelligence.

II   INVESTOR-STATE ARBITRATION

1   Approaches by Stakeholders in Investor-State Arbitration

a   *Supranational Organizations*

The UN adopted the Rules on Transparency in Treaty-based Investor-State Arbitration in 2013. Broadly, the rules require arbitral institutions to 'promptly' publish information about an investor-State proceeding, including documents like the notice of arbitration and the award.

---

1. Deirdre CURTIN and Albert MEIJER, 'Does Transparency Strengthen Legitimacy?' Information Polity (October 2006) at https://www.researchgate.net/publication/228993285_Does_Trans parency_Strengthen_Legitimacy/link/004635150b73b837d6000000/download (last accessed 1 September 2022).
2. Heungsik Park and John Blenkinsopp, 'The Roles of Transparency and Trust in the Relationship Between Corruption and Citizen Satisfaction', International Review of Administrative Sciences 77(2) pp. 254-274, available at https://journals.sagepub.com/doi/pdf/10.1177/002085231139 9230 (last accessed 23 August 2022).

Michael Schöll, Chair of the United Nations Commission on International Trade Law, noted the importance of transparency when the rules were unveiled, stating that '[t]ransparency lies at the very foundation of good governance'.[3]

This was echoed by UNCITRAL's Working Group III (Investor-State Dispute Settlement Reform) in a report outlining the work of its thirty-fourth session held in Vienna from 27 November until 1 December 2017. The report notes that during the group's deliberations participants concluded that 'transparency was a key element of the rule of law, and of access to justice as well as the legitimacy of the ISDS system', and they agreed that 'enhancing public understanding of ISDS was key in addressing the perceived lack of legitimacy of the system'.[4]

b   Individual Nations

In a February 2020 working paper detailing amendments to its rules, the International Centre for Settlement of Investment Disputes (ICSID) noted that states were divided on the extent to which documents other than awards, decisions or orders should be made public. In addition to questioning how the broad publication of case documents would advance the objectives of transparency, states raised concerns about the time and cost involved in redacting such documents.

For example, although Costa Rica said in 2018 that it thought publishing the award with redactions should be mandatory,[5] that country subsequently argued that documents should only be published if they 'provide value to external observers in terms of accountability'.[6]

'In Costa Rica's experience, it has been observed that some documents are merely procedural, and their publication could negatively affect the proceedings' good governance and may create greater confusion if taken out of context. Furthermore, they may create greater confusion and affect the reputation of individuals acting in the process if taken out of context.'[7]

---

3. United Nations Meetings Coverage, 'Newly Adopted Transparency Rules Play Fundamental Role in Good Governance, United Nations International Trade Law Body Tells Sixth Committee', (13 October 2013) at https://www.un.org/press/en/2013/gal3459.doc.htm (last accessed 3 August 2022).
4. Report of Working Group III (Investor-State Dispute Settlement Reform) on the work of its thirty-fourth session (Vienna, 27 November-1 December 2017) at https://documents-dds-ny.un .org/doc/UNDOC/GEN/V18/029/83/PDF/V1802983.pdf?OpenElement (last accessed 3 August 2022).
5. 'Rule Amendment Project – Member State & Public Comments on Working Paper # 1 of August 3, 2018', p. 24, available at https://icsid.worldbank.org/sites/default/files/amendments/ Compendium_Comments_Rule_Amendment_3.15.19.pdf (last accessed 8 August 2022).
6. 'Comments on Working Paper #3', p. 8, available at https://icsid.worldbank.org/sites/default/ files/amendments/WP_3_Comment_Compendium.pdf (last accessed 8 August 2022) (henceforth 'WP3 Comments').
7. WP3 Comments, p. 40.

These weren't universal concerns: 'Other states took the position that all publication advanced transparency, that the time and cost involved in redaction was manageable, and that tribunals had the inherent ability to prevent abuse of the rule.'[8]

The United States, for example, said several years later that it 'strongly' opposed a proposed change to the rules that would allow a party to have a veto over whether an amicus or non-disputing treaty party submission is published by ICSID. The US said that it viewed the proposed change as inconsistent with the objective of greater transparency, pointing to its practice of publishing its own submissions on the US State Department website.[9]

The US also said that this attitude extends to other contexts as well, pointing to its signing of a 2019 statement On the Importance of Transparency In WTO Dispute Settlement.[10]

Morocco has expressed support for improving the functioning and transparency of arbitral proceedings in accordance with the UNCITRAL Rules on Transparency,[11] as has the European Union, which says that the UNCITRAL Rules on Transparency are a 'good example of a minimum standard which could be applied' in its proposal for a standing mechanism to adjudicate international investment disputes.[12]

In a joint submission made by the governments of Chile, Israel, Japan, Mexico and Peru to UNCITRAL WGIII, the countries pointed to the potential positive effects of publishing pleadings, awards and other case documents, saying it would 'allow parties to future disputes to understand and be aware of the arguments previously made by disputing parties, as well as the decision and reasoning of prior decision makers under the same treaty. Subject to certain criteria and exceptions (for example for confidential information), these provisions thus may promote consistency and correctness because they demonstrate how States that are party to a treaty interpret a particular provision'.[13]

---

8. 'Proposals for Amendment of the ICSID Rules', Working Paper #4, Volume 1, February 2020, available at https://icsid.worldbank.org/en/Documents/WP_4_Vol_1_En.pdf (last accessed 3 August 2022) (henceforth 'Feb. 2020 ICSID Rules Amendment Proposal') p. 333.
9. 'Compendium of Comments for Working Paper # 5 as of October 27, 2021', p. 22, available at https://icsid.worldbank.org/sites/default/files/documents/Compendium_of_State_Comments_WP_Five.pdf (last accessed 8 August 2022).
10. 'Joint Statement on the Importance of Transparency in WTO Dispute Settlement', available at https://docs.wto.org/dol2fe/Pages/SS/directdoc.aspx?filename = q:/WT/GC/W785.pdf&Open = True (last accessed 3 August 2022).
11. 4 March 2019 submission from the Government of Morocco to UNCITRAL Working Group III on its 37th Session, p. 4, available at https://undocs.org/en/A/CN.9/WG.III/WP.161 (last accessed 3 August 2022).
12. 24 January 2019 submission from the European Union and its member states to UNCITRAL Working Group III on its 37th Session, p. 7, available at https://undocs.org/en/A/CN.9/WG.III/WP.159/Add.1 (last accessed 8 August 2022).
13. 2 October 2019 submission from the governments of Chile, Israel, Japan, Mexico and Peru to UNCITRAL Working Group III on its 38th Session, p. 9, available at https://undocs.org/en/A/CN.9/WG.III/WP.182 (last accessed 3 August 2022).

i   *Specific Measures Adopted by Nations*

The UN estimates that more than fifty existing investment treaties concluded after April 2014 include the UNCITRAL Rules on Transparency or provisions modelled on those rules, and are applicable in at least some instances of investor-State dispute resolution. Moreover, 23 nations have signed the Mauritius Convention on Transparency in Treaty-based Investor-State Arbitration (otherwise known as the Mauritius Convention).

The Convention, which recognizes 'the need for provisions on transparency in the settlement of treaty-based investor-State disputes to take account of the public interest involved in such arbitrations' obligates states to use the UNCITRAL Rules on Transparency in any investor-State arbitration subject to any reservations made by the respondent nation or the claimant's home nation.

However, if the goal is to increase transparency in investor-State arbitration, the reality is that much remains to be done. The Mauritius Convention has only been signed by twenty-three nations and only entered into force in nine of those.[14] The UN Conference on Trade and Development estimated in a December 2019 report[15] that there are some 3,000 'old-generation' treaties that don't include reform-oriented features, such as an increased focus on transparency. In a subsequent report issued in July, UNCTAD estimated that some 75% of investment arbitrations in 2021 were brought under bilateral investment treaties and treaties with investment provisions signed in the 1990s or earlier.[16]

Nations may have a variety of reasons for wanting to limit transparency in investor-State arbitration, including not wanting to disclose feuds with investors to prevent follow-on claims from other similarly situated investors, or potentially scaring away other potential investors.

c   **Arbitral Institutions**

ICSID has changed its rules in order to allow more awards to be made public. Although the ICSID Convention requires consent from both parties before publishing an award, its rules now state that a party has given consent unless it objects in writing within sixty days. This provision applies to orders and decisions as well.[17]

The rules also allow ICSID to publish excerpts of an award even if a party objects to publishing it in its entirety, subject to redactions requested by the parties. Hearings are also automatically conducted in public unless either party objects.

---

14. UNCITRAL, Status: United Nations Convention on Transparency in Treaty-based Investor-State Arbitration (New York, 2014), available at https://uncitral.un.org/en/texts/arbitration/conventions/transparency/status (last accessed 3 August 2022).
15. Investment Policy Monitor, December 2019 Issue 22, p. 13 at https://unctad.org/en/PublicationsLibrary/diaepcbinf2019d8_en.pdf (last accessed 10 March 2020).
16. IIA Issues Note, July 2022 Issue 1, p. 3 at https://unctad.org/system/files/official-document/diaepcbinf2022d4_en.pdf (last accessed 5 August 2022).
17. ICSID Convention, Regulations and Rules https://icsid.worldbank.org/sites/default/files/documents/ICSID_Convention.pdf (last accessed 5 August 2022).

The Permanent Court of Arbitration (PCA) Rules 2012 do not appear to address confidentiality specifically. Instead, the rules state that hearings will be held in camera unless the parties agree otherwise, and awards 'may' be made public with the parties' consent.

Many investor-State proceedings at the PCA, however, take place under the UNCITRAL arbitration rules. The 2013 version of the UNCITRAL arbitration rules incorporates the UNCITRAL Rules on Transparency for Treaty-based Investor-State Arbitration.

The Singapore International Arbitration Centre's (SIAC) investment arbitration rules forbid the parties from disclosing 'all matters relating to the proceedings' without a written agreement from the parties (with a few exceptions, including in subsequent proceedings to enforce or challenge the award) and authorize the tribunal to issue an order or award for sanctions or cost against any offending parties.[18]

The rules do permit SIAC to publish information about the proceedings, including the nationality of the parties and the identity of the arbitrators, the relevant treaty, and the date the arbitration was initiated. The identities of the parties, their counsel, and the relevant economic sector, among other things, may also be published if the parties consent.

d   Others

The Corporate Counsel International Arbitration Group noted in comments made in 2020 regarding ICSID's' proposed rule change that '[t]ransparency will showcase the professionalism of ISDS arbitrators and counsel and the integrity of the process, and thereby help counter the harmful myths and misconceptions that have been circulating for some time regarding ISDS'.[19]

2   Potential Impacts of Increased Transparency in Investor-State Arbitration

There appears, at long last, to be a consensus among many stakeholders of investor-State arbitration and the institutions that administer them that greater transparency is a good thing.

When dealing with public funds, the need for transparency and its connection to legitimacy is obvious, although there is an argument to be made that not every document from an arbitration needs to be public.

Publishing awards in investor-State arbitration can also create accountability by ensuring that arbitrators will know that their awards can be publicly scrutinized, and

---

18. SIAC Investment Rules, 1st Edition, 1 January 2017, Rule 37, available at https://www.siac.org .sg/images/stories/articles/rules/IA/SIAC%20Investment%20Rules%202017.pdf (last accessed 8 August 2022).
19. Compendium of State and Public Comments on WP #3 – 27 February 2020, p. 40, available at https://icsid.worldbank.org/en/Documents/WP_3_Comment_Compendium.pdf (last accessed 11 March 2020) (henceforth 'WP3 Compendium').

it can create better predictability by helping stakeholders – including lawyers for states and investors alike, and for third-party funders – to determine how a case may go.

In a 2021 paper, authors Wolfgang Alschner of the University of Ottawa and Damien Charlotin of HEC Paris discuss using text mining, which is the process of using computer algorithms to digest written materials, to analyse investor-State awards in the hopes of finding trends and patterns. They argue that using text analytics can help practitioners in making evidence-based and data-driven decisions.

'Rather than relying on personal experience or small samples, investors and states can assess the merits of a claim quickly, based on the analysis of the most relevant previous cases (text analytics assisting in identifying those as well), and litigants can appoint arbitrators based on a more comprehensive profile of their record.'[20]

III   INTERNATIONAL COMMERCIAL ARBITRATION

It's widely recognized that a key benefit of international commercial arbitration is that it is confidential, so businesses will, without difficulty, be able to resolve disputes without exposing trade secrets or other confidential business information. Disputes themselves can also be kept out of the public eye, potentially shielding the company from negative press.

While there are some benefits to increasing transparency in international commercial arbitration that I discuss below, most arbitral institutions take the approach that disputes are to remain confidential unless the parties agree otherwise.

Still, there are a few institutions that have begun to take the approach that at least some degree of transparency has its benefits in commercial arbitration.

1   Institutions Moving Towards Increased Transparency

The International Chamber of Commerce's (ICC) International Court of Arbitration issued a practice note in January 2019 stating that it would begin publishing awards issued after 1 January 2019, unless one of the parties objects. The ICC has now announced that it has made its arbitral awards available free of charge to the global legal community on Jus Mundi, a search engine for international law and arbitration. Claudia Salomon, president of the ICC International Court of Arbitration, said at the time that 'this is an important opportunity for us to provide additional information about ICC Arbitration and communicate the importance of the legitimacy of arbitration through information'.[21]

---

20. 'Data Mining, Text Analytics, and Investor-State Arbitration' by Wolfgang Alschner & Damien Charlotin, available at https://ssrn.com/abstract=3857127 (last accessed 8 August 2022).
21. 'Publication of ICC arbitral awards with Jus Mundi' https://iccwbo.org/dispute-resolution-services/arbitration/publication-of-icc-arbitral-awards-with-jus-mundi/ (last accessed 5 August 2022).

Still, the ICC recognizes that there are reasons to protect confidentiality in arbitration – particularly private commercial arbitration – since proceedings may concern trade secrets or other proprietary information.

As such, ICC awards are only published if the parties do not object and personal data in the awards and related documents is redacted via pseudonymization or anonymization.

The London Court of International Arbitration (LCIA) takes a more conservative approach, saying it will not publish any award or part of an award without the parties' consent.[22] In the FAQ section of its website, the LCIA says that it 'addresses the quality and enforceability of awards through its role in the appointment process and its robust administration procedures'.[23]

The LCIA did decide in early 2018, however, to publish a digest of anonymized challenge decisions against arbitrators as 'part of its ongoing commitment to transparency'. The LCIA did so in an effort to provide a research tool for lawyers, saying the digest provides 'insight through the LCIA Court's own words'.[24]

2   Institutions Emphasizing Confidentiality

The American Arbitration Association's International Centre for Dispute Resolution (ICDR) states that awards may be made public with the parties' consent 'or as required by law', but the ICDR may publish 'selected' awards that have been edited to conceal the parties' identities unless a party has objected in writing to publication within six months from the date of the award.[25]

The SIAC rules forbid parties to an arbitration from disclosing matters relating to the proceedings and award to any third person, with certain exceptions (such as in proceedings to enforce or challenge an award). The rules empower the tribunal to sanction or impose costs on an offending party.

The rules allow SIAC to publish anonymized awards with the consent of the parties and tribunal.[26]

The Hong Kong International Arbitration Centre (HKIAC) arbitration rules forbid parties from disclosing information relating to the arbitration or to an award or

22. LCIA Arbitration Rules (2014), Article 30.3, available at https://www.lcia.org//Dispute_Resolution_Services/lcia-arbitration-rules-2014.aspx#Article%2026 (last accessed 12 March 2020).
23. 'Frequently Asked Questions', available at https://www.lcia.org/frequently_asked_questions.aspx#26. (last accessed 5 August 2022).
24. 'LCIA Releases Challenge Decisions Online', 12 February 2018, available at https://www.lcia.org/News/lcia-releases-challenge-decisions-online.aspx (last accessed 5 August 2022).
25. 'ICDR International Dispute Resolution Procedures – Amended and Effective March 1, 2021', Article 40, available at https://www.icdr.org/sites/default/files/document_repository/ICDR_Rules_1.pdf?utm_source=icdr-website&utm_medium=rules-page&utm_campaign=rules-intl-update-1mar (last accessed 8 August 2022).
26. SIAC Rules, 6th edition, 1 August 2016, Rules 32 and 39, available at https://www.siac.org.sg/images/stories/articles/rules/2016/SIAC%20Rules%202016%20English_28%20 Feb%2020217.pdf (last accessed 8 August 2022).

emergency decision without the parties' consent. There are several exceptions, including in proceedings to enforce or challenge the award, to seek third-party funding or where otherwise required by law.

The rules allow the HKIAC to publish an award or certain excerpts if the parties are anonymized and neither party objects.[27]

The arbitration rules for the Arbitration Institute of the Stockholm Chamber of Commerce (SCC) simply state that '[u]nless otherwise agreed by the parties, the SCC, the Arbitral Tribunal and any administrative secretary of the Arbitral Tribunal shall maintain the confidentiality of the arbitration and the award'.[28]

3   Potential Impacts of Increased Transparency in Commercial Arbitration

a   Increased Diversity

One specific benefit of increased transparency in commercial arbitration could be the potential for greater gender and ethnic diversity among arbitrators. The problem, in a nutshell, is that it can be difficult for younger, more diverse arbitrators to gain a foothold in the business since proceedings are confidential.

Penn State Law professor Catherine Rogers has written for years about what she calls the 'diversity paradox' – referring to the widespread concern within the arbitration community about the lack of diversity among arbitrators, but the 'apparent inability to translate those concerns into actual appointments in individual cases'.[29]

Steps are being taken by various institutions, including the ICC, to publicize more information about which arbitrators are being chosen by the parties and to potentially publish resulting awards.

Although the statistics have been improving in recent years, it's well-documented that improving diversity among arbitrators in international arbitration remains a work in progress. This is particularly true when parties are appointing their own arbitrators. As an example, in its most recent annual casework report, the LCIA said its Court appointed women 47% of the time. But the percentage of women appointed as arbitrators decreased to only 16% when they were appointed by the parties, down from 22% in 2020.[30]

Increases in diversity reported by the HKIAC nevertheless reflect a similar trend. In its most recent case statistics, the HKIAC said that 21.8% of the 142 appointments it

27. HKIAC Administered Arbitration Rules 2018, Article 45, available at https://www.hkiac.org/sites/default/files/ck_filebrowser/PDF/arbitration/2018_hkiac_rules.pdf (last accessed 12 March 2020).
28. 2017 Arbitration Rules of the Arbitration Institute of the Stockholm Chamber of Commerce, Article 3, available at https://sccinstitute.com/media/1407444/arbitrationrules_eng_2020.pdf (last accessed 12 March 2020).
29. 'The Key to Unlocking the Arbitrator Diversity Paradox?: Arbitrator Intelligence', available at https://www.linkedin.com/pulse/key-unlocking-arbitrator-diversity-paradox-catherine-rogers/ (last accessed 5 August 2022) (henceforth 'The Diversity Paradox').
30. 2021 Annual Casework Report, p. 20, available at https://www.lcia.org/lcia/reports.aspx (last accessed 5 August 2022).

made in 2021 were of female arbitrators. Among the 118 party-appointed arbitrators, only 12.7% were female.[31]

It's worth noting that increased transparency relating to arbitrators in commercial arbitration may actually have the opposite effect by potentially reinforcing the perception of 'clubbiness' – that is, that parties have a small group of arbitrators whom they typically rely on. In a report released in 2014 by the New York City Bar's Committee on International Commercial Disputes, the authors noted that '[t]o the extent that the names of arbitrators are disclosed in published decisions, that tendency could increase if publication bore out the perception that a small group of arbitrators dominate the field, decrease if disclosure shows a great diversity of active, widely used arbitrators, or simply alter the choices to the extent that the parties perceive variations in expertise or biases among specific arbitrators'.[32]

b   *Better Predictability*

Although there is no precedent in international commercial arbitration, previous decisions and awards issued by arbitrators are nevertheless valuable resources that often provide insight into how a particular arbitrator might view an issue. This is recognized by several institutions, including the ICC. Awards issued by the SCC are also available in various digests.

As with investor-State arbitration, there has been increasing recognition in the commercial arbitration sphere as well that publishing awards can help parties to determine the strength of a case. There is an effort among for-profit businesses in the arbitration sector to compile such information in order to sell it to law firms and third-party funders, a means of providing them with the tools they need to choose arbitrators and come up with a case strategy.

Dispute Resolution Data (DRD), LLC claims to have established 'the first and only global database pertaining to international commercial arbitration and mediation dispositions'.[33] It markets its product to law firms, insurance and reinsurance companies, corporate legal departments and third-party funders.

But since commercial arbitration is still largely viewed as confidential, DRD says that the information it obtains, which is provided voluntarily by 'data contributors' – meaning institutions like the ICDR and Centre for Effective Dispute Resolution (CEDR), among others – does not include the parties' identities, the advocates, the arbitrators or mediators, or the associated institution.

The potential appeal of this information is obvious, in that it could help practitioners uncover alternative dispute resolution practices and trends.

31. 2021 Statistics, available at https://www.hkiac.org/about-us/statistics (last accessed 5 August 2022).
32. Report by the Committee on International Commercial Disputes: 'Publication of International Arbitration Awards and Decisions', February 2014, p. 2, available at https://www2.nycbar.org/pdf/report/uploads/20072645-PublicationofInternationalArbitrationAwardsandDecisions.pdf (last accessed 12 March 2020).
33. Dispute Resolution Data, 'About DRD', available at https://www.disputeresolutiondata.com/about_drd (last accessed 8 August 2022).

But the practical use of such information is limited now due to the confidential nature of international commercial arbitration. In a 2018 article, Karen Maxwell, a barrister at 20 Essex Street, notes that the usefulness of such a product – which is based on only partial data – is somewhat limited.

'So unless a sufficiently large proportion of institutional and ad hoc arbitration could be brought within the scope of data analysis, the tool is only going to give you a fairly broad brush picture. That might still be very useful, of course. But it won't let you read the arbitrator's mind',[34] she wrote.

It's possible that publishing more awards could hasten the development of predictive analytics within international commercial arbitration, something that's already happening in the litigation sphere.

In 2016, researchers at the University College London, the University of Sheffield and the University of Pennsylvania developed a machine learning algorithm to analyse the case text of the European Court of Human Rights. They reported an accuracy rate of 79%.

Still, Maxwell notes in her article that such programs could have potentially negative effects in that lawyers or funders may ask themselves whether a matter is worth arbitrating or litigating at all.[35]

IV CONCLUSION

There appears to be an emerging consensus among stakeholders that increased transparency in investor-State arbitration may help to address concerns about legitimacy and that this is an important goal for the health of investor-state dispute settlement (ISDS) moving forward. Some nations also say that publishing awards could help parties to a dispute better understand how arbitrators resolve cases and how states interpret particular treaty provisions.

The extent of that transparency, however, remains hotly debated, with many nations expressing concern about cost (for the time taken to make redactions) and the potential for documents to be taken out of context. Perhaps for this reason, many nations have refrained from taking proactive steps like signing the Mauritius Convention and have not yet updated their old-generation treaties.

The extent of action taken by arbitral institutions to increase transparency in investor-State arbitration remains somewhat limited, though ICSID has emerged as a leader in this area.

Within international commercial arbitration as well, there is some movement toward increased transparency. The ICC has emerged as a leader in this area by committing to publish awards and release the identities of arbitrators, but the ICDR and the LCIA have also taken steps to increase transparency.

---

34. Karen Maxwell, 'Computer Says No: Data Analytics in Arbitration', 9 February 2018, available at http://arbitrationblog.practicallaw.com/computer-says-no-data-analytics-in-arbitration/ (last accessed 23 August 2022) (henceforth 'Computer Says No').
35. 'Computer Says No'.

Exposing the identity of arbitrators who adjudicate a proceeding may help to increase diversity by removing the need for counsel to speak with someone who's worked with the arbitrator in the past. There are concerns, however, that greater transparency on arbitrators could in fact reinforce the perception that most parties rely on a small 'clique' of elite arbitrators.

Publishing awards may help improve predictability by exposing arbitrators' decision-making processes, and could potentially hasten the development of artificial intelligence used in predictive analytics. But this could potentially lead to other issues, including lawyers and funders questioning whether a matter is worth pursuing if an algorithm says there is little chance of success.

In all instances, stakeholders appear to agree that the confidential nature of arbitration generally trumps any potential benefits that may arise from increased transparency, and that confidential information should not be exposed under any circumstances.

CHAPTER 18

A Letter to the Editor

Mallory Silberman[*]

Dear ISDS colleagues,

In the spirit of this year's Congress objectives, which include "taking stock" and "exploring ideas,"[1] I would like to propose the retirement of the so-called "transparency debate" at our conferences. To explain why that is, though—and for the sake of transparency—we must have a frank conversation about the debate.

First, there is no debating "transparency." The word itself is a rhetorical trump card. The reason for this is that the obverse of "transparency" is a concept that has sinister (even criminal) connotations,[2] and people are therefore loath to be painted as someone who opposes, or even just questions, "transparency." Accordingly, if we truly wish to debate—as opposed to just replicating the effects of an echo chamber—we must begin using nomenclature that does not implicitly inhibit or halt any further discussion.[3] Just think about how your thinking might change if the issue were

---

[*] Mallory Silberman, a former partner at Arnold & Porter, is an adjunct professor at the Georgetown University Law Center. While working in private practice, she has acted as counsel in nearly fifty investor-State arbitrations. The comments in this article are her own, and should not be attributed to Arnold & Porter, to its clients, or to the Georgetown University Law Center.

[1.] *See* Invitation from the ICCA President, *available at* https://icca2020.scot/ (last visited March 14, 2020).

[2.] *See, e.g.*, Oxford English Dictionary (defining "concealment," first and foremost, as "[t]he crime of concealing or suppressing information so as to cause injury or disadvantage to another ... ."), *available at* https://oed.com/view/Entry/38070?redirectedFrom = concealment#eid (last visited June 18, 2021).

[3.] For an explanation of how a loaded term can warp thought, debate, and discussion, *see generally* Daniel Kahneman, *Thinking Fast and Slow* (Farrar, Straus, and Giroux 2011), Chapter 7 (explaining that one way to exploit cognitive biases, and to make the mind jump to a particular conclusion, is by presenting a question in a manner that suggests that there is only one possible answer); *see also id.*, pp. 60-62 (explaining that, due to the wiring of the human brain, "familiarity is not easily distinguished from truth," and—accordingly—the mere repetition of a statement can sometimes convince a person of its accuracy).

presented as being about party autonomy ... or the sanctity and efficiency of proceedings ... or the insulation of a decision-maker from bias. We are doing the term "transparency" a disservice by using it in a way that might obscure commentary.

Second, **the debate is not ours to decide.** There does not seem to be any dispute about this. We can lobby for access to more information—and debate and propose default presumptions on publication. But, in the end, we do not make the call; any final decisions about publication are for the parties (and potentially the tribunal) to make. This reality is even reflected in the UNCITRAL Rules on Transparency in Treaty-based Investor-State Arbitration.[4] Thus, for example, even though the Rules set out a presumption that various case materials will be published,[5] the Rules also make it clear that the parties remain free to reject the presumption in their arbitration agreement.[6]

Third, **there is not all that much to debate.** Or, at least, there *no longer* is all that much to debate. For example, there is already consensus regarding the framework that a tribunal should use if it is faced with a party dispute (and no prior agreement) about publication.[7] It is also accepted that, unless the parties agree otherwise, they are permitted in principle to speak about their own cases[8]—and that the presumption is the

---

4. *See, e.g.*, UNCITRAL Rules on Transparency in Treaty-based Investor-State Arbitration (2014), Article 3(3) ["UNCITRAL Rules on Transparency"] (explaining that, if a member of the general public would like to have access to case materials beyond what the parties have already agreed to publish, the issue will be decided by tribunal following consultations with the parties).

5. *See* UNCITRAL Rules on Transparency, Article 3(1) (stating that, "[s]ubject to [certain caveats], the following documents shall be made available to the public: the notice of arbitration, the response to the notice of arbitration, the statement of claim, the statement of defence and any further written statements or written submissions by any disputing party; a table listing all exhibits to the aforesaid documents and to expert reports and witness statements, if such table has been prepared for the proceedings ... any written submissions by the non-disputing Party (or Parties) to the treaty and by third persons[;] transcripts of hearings, where available; and orders, decisions and awards of the arbitral tribunal").

6. *See* UNCITRAL Rules on Transparency, Article 1(1) ("The UNCITRAL Rules on Transparency in Treaty-based Investor-State Arbitration ... shall apply to investor-State arbitration initiated under the UNCITRAL Arbitration Rules pursuant to a treaty providing for the protection of investments or investors ('treaty') concluded on or after 1 April 2014 *unless the Parties to the treaty have agreed otherwise*") (emphasis added); *see also* Zachary Douglas, *The International Law of Investment Claims* (Cambridge University Press 2009), p. 75 (explaining that, even though an investment treaty alone does not constitute an arbitration agreement, its text is effectively treated as such, because the text represents "a unilateral offer to arbitrate" that "must be deemed to be accepted [in order for] an agreement to arbitrate [to] come[] into existence"); *see also id.*, p. 76 (explaining that "the validity of the agreement to arbitrate is contingent upon the investor claimant's acceptance of [the terms of the offer set forth in the investment treaty]," and that the investor cannot unilaterally "modify those terms in any respect . ....").

7. *See generally, e.g.*, *Amco Asia Corporation and others v. Republic of Indonesia*, ICSID Case No. ARB/81/1 (Decision on Request for Provisional Measures, December 9, 1983) (Goldman, Foighel, Rubin) ["*Amco I*"]; *Metalclad Corporation v. United Mexican States*, ICSID Case No. ARB(AF)/97/1 (Decision on Request for an Order Prohibiting the Claimant from Revealing Information Regarding the Case, October 27, 1997) (Lauterpacht, Civiletti, Siqueiros) ["*Metalclad*"]; *Biwater Gauff (Tanzania) Ltd. v. United Republic of Tanzania*, ICSID Case No. ARB/05/22 (Procedural Order No. 3, September 29, 2006) (Hanotiau, Born, Landau) ["*Biwater Gauff*"]; *World Duty Free Company Limited v. Republic of Kenya*, ICSID Case No. ARB/00/7 (Award, October 4, 2006), ¶ 16 (Guillaume, Rogers, Veeder) ["*World Duty Free*"]; *Abaclat and others v. Argentine Republic*, ICSID Case No. ARB/07/5 (Procedural Order No. 3, January 27, 2010) (Tercier, van den Berg, Abi-Saab).

8. *See, e.g.*, *Amco I*, ¶ 5; *Metalclad*, ¶ 4; *World Duty Free*, ¶ 16.

opposite when it comes to the disclosure of an opponent's materials.[9] Further, there seems to be broad recognition that, even though publication plainly has certain virtues,[10] it can also be disruptive at times, and/or unfairly impact one or more of the parties.[11] For that reason, there seems to be no dispute that there are certain limits in practice to what the parties may say and/or share.[12] (Indeed, even the rules and the treaties that set out a presumption of "transparency" will often contain caveats and exceptions to publication.)[13]

Moreover, and notably, on the practical level, many details about investor-State cases are already available to the public.[14] For example, since the very beginning,

---

9. *See, e.g.*, IBA Rules on the Taking of Evidence in International Arbitration (2020), Article 3(13) ("Any Document submitted or produced by a Party or non-Party in the arbitration and not otherwise in the public domain shall be kept confidential by the Arbitral Tribunal and the other Parties, and shall be used only in connection with the arbitration. This requirement shall apply except and to the extent that disclosure may be required of a Party to fulfill a legal duty, protect or pursue a legal right, or enforce or challenge an award in bona fide legal proceedings before a state court or other judicial authority").

10. *See, e.g.*, Report of UNCITRAL Working Group II (Arbitration and Conciliation) on the Work of its Fifty-Third Session (Vienna, October 4-8, 2010), ¶ 17 ("[E]nsuring transparency and meaningful opportunity for public participation in treaty-based investor-State arbitration was said to constitute a means to promote the rule of law, good governance, due process, fairness, equity and rights to access information. It was also seen as an important step to respond to the increasing challenges regarding the legitimacy of international investment law and arbitration as such").

11. *See, e.g.*, *Biwater Gauff*, ¶ 136 ("It is self-evident that the prosecution of a dispute in the media or in other public fora, … may aggravate or exacerbate the dispute and may impact upon the integrity of the procedure. This is all the more so in very public cases, such as this one, where issues of wider interest are raised, and where there is already substantial media coverage, some of which is already being the subject of complaint by the parties").

12. *See, e.g.*, *Amco I*, ¶ 5 (explaining that, even though no rule existed that expressly prohibited the parties from speaking to the media, there nevertheless remained "practical rule [that] both parties to a legal dispute should refrain [from] any [behavior] that could aggravate or exacerbate the [dispute]," and "render[] its solution possibly more difficult"); *Metalclad*, ¶¶ 4, 10 (concluding that, while the parties could not be expected to "refrain entirely from every public utterance mentioning the existence, or speculating upon the possible outcome, of the proceedings," public comments and disclosures could not be allowed to interfere with the "orderly unfolding of the arbitral process," or "the maintenance of working relations between the [p]arties … ."); *World Duty Free*, ¶ 16 ("direct[ing] the Parties to avoid any action that would aggravate or exacerbate the dispute," and "further direct[ing] that any public discussion should be an accurate report").

13. *See, e.g.*, Dominican Republic-Central America Free Trade Agreement, Article 10.21: Transparency of Arbitral Proceedings ["*DR-CAFTA*"] (establishing a presumption that certain materials will be published, and then stating that "[n]othing in this Section requires a respondent to disclose protected information or to furnish or allow access to information that it may withhold in accordance with Article 21.2 (Essential Security) or Article 21.5 (Disclosure of Information)"); *see also* UNCITRAL Rules on Transparency, Article 7(1) ("Confidential or protected information, as defined in paragraph 2 and as identified pursuant to the arrangements referred to in paragraphs 3 and 4, shall not be made available to the public pursuant to articles 2 to 6"), Article 7(7) ("The arbitral tribunal may, on its own initiative or upon the application of a disputing party, after consulting with the disputing parties where practicable, take appropriate measures to restrain or delay the publication of information where such publication would jeopardize the integrity of the arbitral process because it could hamper the collection or production of evidence[;] lead to the intimidation of witnesses, lawyers acting for the disputing parties or members of the arbitral tribunal[;] or in comparably exceptional circumstances").

14. Such details can often be found in a variety of locations, including the website of an administering institution; the annual reports of a corporation; the regulatory filings of a corporation or sovereign; an online database of arbitration awards; arbitration periodicals;

ICSID has kept certain "registers" that any person may "inspect,"[15] which contain "all significant data concerning the institution, conduct[,] and disposition of each proceeding ... ."[16] Further, in the many years since the media and others began asking for access to ISDS awards,[17] numerous parties have answered the call. Nowadays, it is common for parties to publish investment awards and decisions.[18]

Thus, it would seem that what we are really debating is whether the parties also routinely should publish their written and oral submissions.[19]

Fourth, **no one needs to lose this debate.** And no one *can* lose it, as both sides can be right. After all, the decision is up to the parties, and different sets of parties may reach different agreements about what approach would be best for their case. There are many ways that the parties could balance transparency concerns with other important objectives.[20]

Further, and as noted above, publication can be both copacetic and worrisome; as a practical matter, that means necessarily that there is not only one correct answer here. In fact, there may even be ways to achieve the objectives of more than one side of debaters. For example, if there are any concerns that the real-time publication of pleadings would be problematic—e.g., because there are often several-month stretches between a memorial and a counter-memorial—the parties could always consider agreeing to release the submissions only at the end of the case. This might serve to address calls for more access while assuaging the fears about a "trial by media."

Fifth, **we could be discussing so much else.** Instead of just debating an issue that is not ultimately up to conference-goers to decide, why not put our minds to the task of actually making something out of "Arbitration's Printing Press?" The materials

---

academic journals; and listservs. A basic search through these resources can yield, among other things (1) the names, nationalities, and CVs of the arbitrators; (2) the identity of the parties' representatives and their contact details; (3) the principal procedural events; (4) a summary of each party's key arguments and evidence; (5) the identities of the attendees at the hearings; (6) the tribunal's final ruling and reasoning; (7) the total amount of procedural costs; and (8) the fees and expenses incurred by each party.

15. ICSID Financial and Administrative Regulations (1968), Regulation 23(2).

16. *Id.*, Regulation 23(1). These registers are now published online (and have been for more than a decade).

17. *See, e.g.*, A. DePalma, *NAFTA's Powerful Little Secret; Obscure Tribunals Settle Disputes, but Go Too Far, Critics Say*, N.Y. Times, March 11, 2001.

18. For example, the website "italaw" contains rulings (and/or other materials) from 1,199 different investor-State cases. *See* https://www.italaw.com/browse/claimant-investor/all (last visited June 30, 2021).

19. Some arbitration agreements already contemplate the publication of these sorts of materials. *See, e.g.*, DR-CAFTA, Article 10.21.1 ("Subject to paragraphs 2 and 4, the respondent shall, after receiving the following documents, promptly transmit them to the non-disputing Parties and make them available to the public: (a) the notice of intent; (b) the notice of arbitration; (c) pleadings, memorials, and briefs submitted to the tribunal by a disputing party and any written submissions submitted pursuant to Article 10.20.2 and 10.20.3 and Article 10.25; (d) minutes or transcripts of hearings of the tribunal, where available; and (e) orders, awards, and decisions of the tribunal").

20. *See, e.g.*, The Tea on International Arbitration Podcast: The Tea, Czech Edition (Part 1), *available at* https://anchor.fm/dcbartea/episodes/The-Tea--Czech-Edition-Part-1-etssbo (last visited June 30, 2021) (explaining that "transparency is only one of the virtues you want to see in any investment arbitration proceedings," and that any decision about what to publish must also consider such issues as equality of arms and efficiency).

that have already been published recount some of the most fascinating stories in the world, and—collectively—they surely have lessons to teach us. Should we prepare a modern treatise on government? Are there other ways to make use of the printing press? (Or other modes of communication to try?)

Let us look ahead to the future, and put the old debate into retirement.

PANEL 5   Post-pandemic Dispute Resolution Toolbox

CHAPTER 19

Dispute Resolution Toolbox

Lady Justice Joyce Aluoch*

One tool does not fit all disputes in the real world of conflicts. In the professional world especially, it is critical for individuals to be prepared for a variety of solutions and to know what tools and techniques to be used to settle disputes and disagreements in a way that is respectful of parties' needs.

The Conflict Resolution Toolbox shows negotiators, mediators, managers, and professionals at all levels how to assess conflict situations and choose the right tools to resolve the issues in a meaningful way, simply and effectively.[1]

In Africa particularly, Alternative Dispute Resolution (ADR) is important for preventing conflicts and enhancing stability.[2]

Many people have lost faith in the ability of their nations' courts to provide timely or just closure to their grievances. Lack of confidence in the justice sector has a profound impact on governance. A 2009 survey in Liberia, for example, found that only 3% of criminal and civil disputes were taken to a formal court. Over 40% sought resolution through informal mechanisms. The remaining 55% went to no forum at all. This includes cases where claimants felt the need to take justice into their own hands, often with violent consequences. Similar examples can be quoted from many African states.

In countries just coming out of conflicts in Africa for example South Sudan, Central African Republic and several others, societal tensions are already high and justice systems do not function effectively, the need for prompt resolution of disputes is particularly critical. Without timely, accessible, affordable, and trusted mechanisms to resolve differences, localized disagreements or crimes can degenerate into big

---

* Lady Justice Joyce Aluoch EBS, CBS (Rtd) Judge, Certified International Mediator (IMI), Accredited Mediator (CEDR-London), Chartered Mediator (ICMC), MCIarb-London.
1. The Conflict Resolution by Gary Furlong.
2. Alternative Dispute Resolution in Africa and Enhancing Stability by Ernest E. Uwazie.

conflicts. This contributes to cultures of violence and vigilante justice, hence the need to constitute a Judicial Reform Committee.

Despite attempts at modernization, many African countries are still struggling to establish functional judiciaries. A good example is South Sudan where I am currently undertaking judicial reforms, having been mandated by the Intergovernmental Authority on Development (IGAD) to do so. In countries like Kenya, Uganda, Tanzania and several others, Magistrates and Judges still use long hands to take down evidence in court.

Court records are archived manually and there are not enough computers. Fortunately, this is now changing with the e-filing system introduced in the courts of many counties during the COVID-19 pandemic. But still, the biggest problem is the large number of cases that the courts must handle, especially the Magistrates' courts. Both hearings and applications take a long time to conclude. As a mediator in Kenya, I have handled a matter referred to me under the High Court Annexed Mediation Program that had been pending in court for nine years! I was able to assist the parties to resolve the dispute and reach a settlement agreement of their own within one day. This is enough to show that the formal legal system is overloaded and cannot provide timely and effective closure. It is also more costly in time and money as some people must travel long distances to reach the courts.

Given these circumstances, has the ADR mechanism and the tools it offers been accepted in Africa? The answer is in the affirmative as the notion of ADR fits well with the traditional concepts of African justice, particularly its core value of reconciliation. Pioneering ADR concepts in many African countries have generated positive results and illustrate the suitability of ADR in African contexts.

What then is the future of ADR in Africa? The answer is simple, and it is that ADR can and is already building an effective dispute settlement system and bridging the gap between the formal legal system and the traditional modes of African justice. The institutionalization of ADR in African legal systems should also bolster security and development. Whilst some conflict is inevitable in any society, its effective resolution depends on the availability of trusted processes and trained personnel. ADR is a practical tool to foster peacebuilding and conflict resolution at both the interpersonal and community levels. It is also a potentially valuable mechanism for stabilization and state-building efforts.

Furthermore, ADR can also deliver quick relief to some conflict triggers in fragile contexts, while the more complex and long-time judicial sector also provides a framework for reference, review, and reform as well as to institutionalize much-needed education and professional training.

Notwithstanding the benefits cited above, ADR programs in Africa face some challenges, beginning with a lack of political will, human resources, legal foundations, and sustainable financing. Many governments do not understand or appreciate the need for ADR, as such, ADR projects are often donor funded. Furthermore, some lawyers view ADR as a threat to their income and refer to it as, 'Alarming Drop in Revenue', and do not support it, though, in several African countries, Kenya included, more and more lawyers are now training as mediators, whereas Arbitrators have trained over the years, and many African countries have Arbitration Acts. It is alleged that some judges also resist ADR for fear of losing 'control', over non-litigation processes of resolution or out-of-court settlements. I do not, however, have any statistics on this, but I am familiar with the High Court Annexed Mediation Rules in Kenya[3] where a Deputy Registrar and her/his trained personnel scrutinize files and when a matter is considered suitable for mediation, then without due consultation with the parties, The Deputy Registrar directs the parties to go for mediation before a mediator chosen from the list of mediators accredited by the court. Usually, a date is given for mention, hoping that the parties will have reached a settlement through mediation. When this happens, mediation becomes 'mandatory'. Judges may also direct parties to go for mediation when they consider that the dispute before them can be settled by mediation. If a settlement is not reached by the parties, the court will make further orders as appropriate.

This 'mandatory' mediation only affects civil and commercial matters, large construction disputes, labour and employment, family matters, etc., but not criminal matters.

It is worth mentioning that mediation is already mandated in many jurisdictions, as observed by The Rt. Hon Sir Geoffrey Vos, Master of the Rolls, in his talk at the Roebuck Lecture 2022. He noted that 'there are no standardized forms as to how mandated mediation can and should work'.[4] Another tool for resolving disputes in Kenya is the Alternative Justice System, which gives the Council of Elders and religious leaders a bigger role to play in the justice system resolution mechanisms including traditional approaches so long as they do not contravene the Bill of Rights, are not repugnant to justice or morality and are not inconsistence with the Constitution or any written law.[5]

A new international toolbox for Dispute Resolution that deserves mention is the United Nations Convention on International Settlement Agreements resulting from Mediation, also known as the Singapore Convention,[6] which was adopted by the United Nations General Assembly on 20 December 2018. The Convention opened for signatures on 7 August 2019, and to date, 55 countries, including the world's largest economies, namely the US, China, India, and Australia, as well as 13 African countries have signed it. The Convention came into force on 12 September, six months after the third ratification by Fiji. Currently, the Convention has been ratified by nine countries, none of them from the African continent.

The Singapore Convention applies to an agreement resulting from mediation, concluded in writing by parties to resolve a commercial dispute which at the time of its conclusion is international. Mediation under the Singapore Convention is defined broadly as 'a process where disputing parties attempt to reach an amicable settlement of their dispute with the assistance of a person or persons lacking authority to impose a solution on them'. The Convention does not exclude a mediator from later becoming

---

3. The Judiciary Mediation Manual-2016. (Kenya).
4. Sir Geoffrey Vas, Master of Rolls of England, and Wales (Roebuck Lecture, 8 June 2022), Mandating Mediation-The Digital Solution.
5. The Alternative Dispute Resolution Bill, 2009. (Kenya).
6. The Singapore Mediation Convention (The United Nations Convention on International Settlement Agreements Resulting from Mediation).

an arbitrator, provided the mediator did not have the authority to issue an arbitral award at the time of the mediation. This definition leaves the door open to supporting hybrid processes.

To integrate ADR as a popular and effective tool in building a culture of justice in Africa, several steps need to be considered, including:

1) Enacting robust legislation. Whilst most court rules and policies permit judges to encourage parties to settle matters out of court, enacting legislation will most likely 'elevate the status of ADR, build public confidence' and further, 'increase ADR utilization. Legislation also provides a framework for reference, review, and reform'

2) Governments and donors should invest in the continuous training of ADR of all professionals, not just lawyers. The training should include local and religious leaders, traditional authorities in society, police and security, women and youth leaders, and organizations which work to promote peace. ADR can also play a role in transitional justice contexts in countries like South Sudan where I am currently reforming the judiciary as agreed by the government in transition.

3) Stakeholders involved in the training and practice of ADR should be encouraged. This will elevate the support for ADR.

4) To maximize the efficiencies and complementarities of ADR with the official judicial process, a systematic monitoring process should be developed. This should include but not be limited to the percentage of cases filed and determined through ADR processes, as opposed to court litigation, the average time spent on a case, the number of successful ADR settlement agreements reached, the number of ADR practitioners and trainers, the number of ADR institutions and services in the country, the community acceptance, and the level of service satisfaction by disputants and practitioners.

Given the benefits and acceptance of ADR in Africa, and with so many things happening around the world, has the Dispute Resolution Toolbox been affected in any way?

Stephanie Williams (2021) United Nations Acting Special Representative of the Secretary-General in Libya said 'COVID-19 has accelerated the in cooperation of digital technologies into the interactions and strategies of mediators.' She went further to say that as a result 'an innovate hybrid model of mediation has started to emerge which combines digital interactions with physical meetings, organized at critical times and under specific risk mitigation protocols'.

A mediator's choice of digital means for engaging with parties in conflict will depend on the mediation strategy, the situation on the ground, the level of connectivity in each setting and the preferences of digital tools used by the parties in conflict. The security and safety of the tools used, and the information stored in the process of engagement need to be considered, as well as reputational risks. It is advisable for mediators to take relevant courses like the one offered by Digital Process and Facilitation.[7] In 2009, the Digital Process Design and Facilitation for Mediation launched the Toolkit on Digital Technologies and Mediation, to raise awareness among

---

7. Asif Khan, Chief of the UN Mediation Support Unit-Digital Process Design and Facilitation for Mediation.

mediation practitioners of the implications of the use of digital in mediation contexts and provide mediators with concrete examples and practical information on how it could impact their work.

The Dispute Resolution Toolbox has also been affected by climate change. It is important to note that it is not easy to find agreement amongst counties on environmental issues. However, with ADR there is hope that this will be possible. India has taken the lead in section 2(f) of its Arbitration and Conciliation Act by defining the ambit of international arbitration which envisages an individual, corporate or a government of foreign country.

But one may ask, what are climate change disputes? According to Yukta Batra, 'Any dispute arising out of or in relation to the effect of climate change and climate change policy, the United Nation's Framework on Convention on Climate Change (UNFCC) and the Paris Agreement.'

In November 2019, the International Chamber of Commerce (ICC) Commission on Arbitration and ADR published a report on 'Resolving Climate Change Related Disputes through Arbitration and ADR'.[8] The report classified the disputes into three major categories:

(1) Specific transaction, adaptation or mitigation contracts: These are contracts that are executed to adhere to the Paris Agreement. Such contracts can be executed between investors, industries, states, owners, and contractors.
(2) Contracts not concerning specific transactions, adaption, or mitigation. Contractual performance affected by global warming or change in legislation. These contracts may or may not be rendered in conformity with Paris Agreement. Contractual performance may be impacted by the change in national laws, regulations, or policies to meet commitments to Paris Agreements etc. voluntary commitments by industry and other impacts of climate change.
(3) Submission agreements. These are agreements or clauses in contracts where both parties will resort to arbitration if a dispute arises.

At the international level is the complexity of environmental law disputes arising from infrastructure, land, industry, finance, insurance, and others. One illustration of its worldwide importance is the inclusion of ADR proceedings in international conversations.

The Vienna Convention for the Protection of the Ozone Layer for example, says in Article 11(2), 'If the parties concerned cannot reach agreement by negotiation, they may jointly seek the good offices of, or request mediation by, a third party.' According to Article 11(3) of the Convention, this is an essential step before parties to a dispute can bring it to arbitration or before the International Court of Justice.

---

8. ICC   Report,   https://iccwbo.org/content/uploads/sites/3/2019/11/icc-arbitration-adr-commission-report-on-resolving-climate-change-related-disputes-english-version.pdf.

This situation is different from the 1979 Convention on Long-Range Transboundary Air Pollution, which, unlike the Vienna Convention, does not specifically require the use of ADR as a means of resolving conflicts.

The Taskforce report on 'Arbitration of Climate Change and Related Disputes' is an excellent breakthrough in environmental disputes. It shows that ADR assists in the discovery of prospective environmental issues between the developer and the public at an early stage when they are simple to resolve and contributes to the resolution of environmental problems.

With all the disruptions in the Dispute Resolution toolbox, is 'mixed mode' the way forward?

According to Thomas Stipanowich, in an article written in 2020, he said in part, 'Today as never before, commercial dispute processing is "mixed mode", with business parties and counsel employing a variety of diverse approaches to promote their varied priorities in resolving conflict. However, we still have far to go in understanding and addressing the dynamics of 'lane shifting' in dispute resolution ... .'[9]

One of the main attractions of mediation is how the process can be adapted to match the needs of its users, unlike the other forms of dispute resolution tools. One option is to combine mediation with another process such as arbitration. It is possible to have mediation followed by arbitration (Med-Arb), a hybrid two-stage ADR process. It usually involves the parties agreeing to grant a mediator power to convert automatically to being an arbitrator and to make a legally binding arbitral award if the mediation fails to result in a settlement of the relevant dispute. The Arb-Med, on the other hand, is a hybrid dispute resolution process that combines the benefits of arbitration and mediation. The process starts with an arbitration proceeding after which a non-binding arbitration award is issued.

The International Mediation Mixed Mode Task Force, a combined effort of the College of Commercial Arbitrators (CCA), the International Mediation Institute (IMI), and the Strauss Institute for Dispute Resolution, Pepperdine School of Law, has been charged with 'examining and seeking to develop model standards and criteria for ways of combining different ways of combining dispute resolution processes that may involve the interplay between public or private adjudicative systems such (e.g., litigation, arbitration or adjudication) with non-adjudicative methods that involve the use of a neutral (e.g., conciliation or mediation), whether in parallel, consequentially or as integrated processes which the Task Force has called "Mixed Mode Scenarios"'.

To conclude is to say that a trend to combine dispute resolution processes, mainly mediation and arbitration is gaining momentum and is the way forward.

---

9. Arbitration, Mediation and Mixed Mode: Seeking Workable Solutions and Common Ground on Med-Arb, Arb-Med and Settlement-Oriented Activities by Arbitrators, A paper by Thomas Stipanowich (Pepperdine University Caruso School of Law).

CHAPTER 20

Combined Dispute Resolution Processes: Trends and Challenges Post Pandemic

Wolf von Kumberg[*]

There is a growing interest in combined dispute resolution processes (mixed mode), which can involve a progression comprising dispute escalation clauses in contracts, dispute boards, adjudication, arbitration, as well as the simultaneous use of mediation and arbitration. This can produce a dispute resolution continuum from dispute avoidance, through dispute boards and facilitated settlement negotiations to adjudication and arbitration.[1] The emphasis for applying mixed mode to disputes is resolution rather than process-oriented.

I spent nearly thirty years as an in-house counsel, latterly as Assistant General Counsel for Northrop Grumman out of its London office dealing with international disputes. My primary goals in choosing a dispute resolution mechanism included: enforceable finality; relationship saving; speed; predictability; control; cost-effectiveness; independent and impartial third-party neutrals; the possibility of flexible and creative solutions and confidentiality. I was interested in results and not necessarily wedded to an adjudicative process to get there. Increasingly this list of criteria is what most multinational companies are looking for when resolving their international disputes.

---

[*] Wolf is a leading internationally recognised independent arbitrator and mediator, based out of London and Washington D.C. Wolf has over thirty years' experience in complex commercial disputes within international business with a particular focus on Aviation, Defence, Technology, Cyber, Engineering/Infrastructure and Investor State dispute resolution. Before establishing his ADR practice, he served as Legal Director and Assistant General Counsel to Northrop Grumman Corporation and prior to this at Litton Industries Inc. During his international career, he was located in their Toronto, Zurich and London offices.

1. Kathleen Paisley and Veronique Fraser, 'Combined Dispute Resolution Processes: Exploring New Trends and Facing Challenges', ICC Mediation Conference, Paris October 2016.

The Global Pound Conference Series 2016-17 was a not-for-profit global project which sought to gather data on what users of dispute resolution services (DRS) and processes really want and need. The Series was entitled 'Shaping the Future of Dispute Resolution & Improving Access to Justice' and was named after Roscoe Pound, the distinguished American legal scholar, who was Dean of Harvard Law School from 1916 to 1936. The last of the Series was held in London in 2017. The principal organisation responsible for driving the Global Pound Conference Series 2016-17 was the International Mediation Institute (IMI)[2] of which I was the first Chair. The mission of IMI, which is a user-driven public interest charitable foundation registered in The Hague in 2007, is to promote mediation globally as a means of resolving disputes and forging deals.

The 'Cumulated Data Results March 2016-May 2017' are available.[3] The themes that have emerged include: the need for efficiency, that non-adjudicative processes tend to be cost-effective, with the parties retaining control, that the most cost-effective commercial dispute resolution processes combine adjudicative and non-adjudicative processes and that improvements could include the use of escalation processes, followed using a combination of adjudicative and non-adjudicative approaches.

It is interesting to note that some 71 % of respondents to the survey, in answer to the question: 'Which stakeholders are likely to be most resistant to change in commercial dispute resolution practice?', responded 'external lawyers'. It is also interesting to note that the group that was rated as the most influential on such change was governments and ministries of justice. External lawyers are, however, in business to satisfy their clients and my own experience is that they will react when a client's request changes. It is therefore the User that is critical to changing the dispute resolution landscape, for it is the User that ultimately has the dispute and wishes to find a tool through which to resolve it.

Today, particularly after two years of judicial services being disrupted by the Pandemic, there is growing global interest in mediation as a dispute resolution mechanism. This is evidenced by the Guide on Investment Mediation from the International Energy Charter Conference[4] and the complementary IMI Competency Criteria for Investor-State Mediators,[5] as well as the growing interest in mediation in jurisdictions where it has not previously been popular, in countries like India, China, the UAE and Kazakhstan. It is noteworthy that the Investor-State mediation initiative at the Energy Charter Treaty Secretariat (ECT) has been taken by Sovereign States, rather than investors. It is States that adopted the ECT Mediation Guidelines and Model Protocol enabling mediation in investment disputes to take place. In fact, the interest in utilising mediation in Investor-State Dispute System (ISDS) has extended to the World Bank and its dispute resolution arm, the International Investment Disputes Centre for

---

2. Global Pound Conference Series 2016-17 available at https://imimediation.org/research/gpc/.
3. The Cumulated Data Results March 2016-May 2017 available at https://imimediation.org/en/ research/gpc/series-data-and-reports/.
4. Guide on Investment Mediation from the International Energy Charter Conference available at The Energy Charter Conference 'Guide on Investment Mediation' 19 July 2016.
5. IMI Competency Criteria for Investor-State Mediators available at https://www.imimediation.org /about/who-are-imi/ism-tf/.

Settlement of Investment Disputes (ICSID), which promulgated mediation rules in March 2022. ICSID, together with the ECT and the Centre for Effective Dispute Resolution (CEDR) have now run several pilot Investor-State mediation training courses, including for the Ministry for Justice in Hong Kong in 2018, 2019 and again in 2022. CEDR led a round table of key ISDS Law Firms discussing the use of mediation in IS disputes and received positive feedback on its inclusion as a credible tool. The mood is clearly shifting towards an acceptance of mediation as a collaborative tool, in addition to the traditional use of arbitration, in resolving these Investor-State disputes through adjudicative means.

In November 2019, a Colloquium was organised at Harvard University with an eminent group of global scholars, practitioners, mediators and Alternative Dispute Resolution (ADR) Institutions to explore 'New Forms to Resolve Investor-State Disputes'. The Colloquium looked at the issues facing ISDS today, explored ISDS alternatives and provided a set of outputs. A key output was the recognition that mediation is not only a possible addition to the ISDS dispute resolution toolkit but also a necessary addition if ISDS is to retain its credibility. A mixed-mode approach was advocated looking at the use of mediation in conjunction with arbitration, each being complimentary to the other.

The interest in extending the use of ADR to a wider public audience has also continued to be explored in England and Wales, a jurisdiction arguably well advanced in ADR. In September 2019, following the Civil Justice Counsel's Report on ADR published in December 2018,[6] the Civil Justice Council's Judicial Liaison Committee was formed, of which I was a member. The Committee's objective is to provide the judiciary, the ADR community, and the professions with a dedicated forum for the discussion and the exchange of information about the role of ADR in the civil justice system, including tribunals. The Committee reports annually on its work to the Judges' Council and Judicial Executive Board.

With this increasing interest in mixed-mode dispute resolution, how might these various techniques be combined to create a more effective toolbox for dispute resolution? In essence, they are different. Mediation is a collaborative tool, while arbitration is adjudicative.

Approaches might include mediators using evaluative techniques, 'mediator's proposals', mediators setting the stage for adjudication, arbitrators inquiring as to the use of mediation, arbitrators encouraging mediation, and arbitrators even setting the stage for settlement. Both processes are run in parallel, with some administration being common, through an Institution such as the International Chamber of Commerce (ICC) or American Arbitration Association (AAA). Perhaps more extreme but used in some jurisdictions, the same mediator or arbitrator 'changing hats' and acting as a neutral in both roles. This means the same neutral is taking the role of mediator and then if mediation fails the role of arbitrator or the arbitrator taking on the role of settlement facilitator.

---

6. Civil Justice Counsel's Report on ADR available at https://www.judiciary.uk/wp-content/uploads/2018/12/CJC-ADRWG-Report-FINAL-Dec- 2018.pdf.

Much of this was looked at in an article in the Fordham International Law Journal in 2017 by Klaus Peter Berger and J. Ole Jensen, 'The Arbitrator's Mandate to Facilitate Settlement'.[7] This article notes the pressures of time and cost in dispute resolution and the resulting need for a proactive approach by the arbitral tribunal. It notes that there is nothing incompatible with the responsibilities of an arbitrator in getting involved in settlement discussions with the parties. Generally, and for obvious reasons, private meetings with the parties, sometimes called caucuses, are to be avoided.

The concept of med/arb/med has been discussed for some time now, with many common law lawyers still looking at the process with suspicion. It simply does not fit into the process of traditional US/UK mediation and the rules of conflict avoidance that have grown up around it. Yet common law jurisdictions such as Ontario and Singapore[8] have made provision for the hybrid use of such techniques and the question is why, if parties are informed and consent to the process should it not be more widely employed? There are clearly challenges which include user awareness, authority, accountability, avoidance of bias, transparency and enforceability, but all of these can be overcome if the parties and the neutral carefully structure the process.

An important step in raising the profile of mediation, in particular in cross-border disputes, is the United Nations Convention on International Settlement Agreements Resulting from Mediation (Singapore Convention)[9] adopted on 20 December 2018 and now signed by fifty-five States and ratified by ten. It will arguably do for mediation what the New York Convention did for arbitration. The very fact that States are signing up to a Convention enforcing cross-border mediated disputes indicates the increasing importance that mediation is perceived to have in international trade and enforces its credibility as a dispute resolution mechanism. What the ultimate impact and effectiveness of the Convention will be is too early to say, but the global dispute resolution toolbox has certainly been expanded.

When I was the Assistant General Counsel at Northrop Grumman Corp, we developed an ADR Policy to help manage our disputes and trained employees on its effective use. Increasingly companies are looking not only at dispute resolution mechanisms but also at dispute management and dispute avoidance. Since leaving Northrop, I have spent time with companies helping them to incorporate ADR policies to achieve these goals. One of the most effective dispute avoidance mechanisms is dispute boards (DBs) and, in particular, a derivative known as Conflict Avoidance Boards (CABs). CABs are the ultimate combined conflict avoidance and dispute resolution mechanism, including in the context of non-construction and major project areas, such as shipbuilding, energy projects, the automobile and telecommunications industries, rail projects as well as complex technology infrastructure projects such as those used in the Aerospace and Defence industries. An excellent exposition of this is

---

7. Klaus Peter Berger and J. Ole Jensen, 'The Arbitrator's Mandate to Facilitate Settlement', Fordham International Law Journal 2017, Volume 40, Issue 3, Article 7.
8. Med/arb/med Ontario and Singapore report available here http://www.slaw.ca/2017/12/13/ med-arb-efficiency-vs-justice/ and http://www.conventuslaw.com/report/singapore-med-arb arb-med-and-the-arb-med-arb/.
9. Singapore Convention available at https://uncitral.un.org/en/texts/mediation/conventions/ international_settlement_agreements.

in a paper presented by James Perry at the 12th Annual DRBF (Dispute Resolution Board Foundation) International Conference in 2012 '*The Future of Dispute Boards in Non-construction Applications and Why it Matters*'.[10] They are particularly suited to medium- and long-term projects, where there is a need to preserve relationships and there are complex interfaces which often lead to disputes.

A DB will generally, but not always, be appointed at the inception of a project. Depending on the size of the project, it may consist of one or three members who, like all third-party neutrals, are to be independent and impartial. The dispute board may be a dispute adjudication board (DAB) and may make decisions or a dispute review board, which makes non-binding recommendations. It may be paid a monthly retainer or at least paid for time spent reviewing project reports and updates. It will generally visit the project every three to four months. As such, it almost becomes part of the project team and will use mediation-type skills to identify issues early and also to head off people clashes.

The origins of DBs lie in the United States, where the concept has been used for forty years as a means of avoiding and resolving disputes in major civil engineering works, such as roads and dams. The concept was taken further by the International Federation of Consulting Engineers (FIDIC) in their so-called Rainbow Suite of contracts for 'Conditions of Contract for Construction' including the so-called Pink Book, which is a form of contract favoured by the World Bank and the other Multilateral Development Banks.[11] An excellent text on dispute boards is 'Chern on Dispute Boards, Practice and Procedure', Third Edition.[12]

A variation on the theme is the Conflict Avoidance Panel concept, on which the DRS of the Royal Institution of Chartered Surveyors has worked with Transport for London (TfL). The DRS of the Royal Institution of Chartered Surveyors (RICS) worked with TfL to develop what they describe as a groundbreaking conflict and early intervention concept, which enables the parties to apply for the appointment of a Conflict Avoidance Panel as and when needed. According to the RICS, this procedure has been written into GBP 7 billion for TfL projects and has been used successfully on eleven matters in its first year of operation, resolving issues and conflicts that could have developed into full-blown disputes.

The Chartered Institute of Arbitrators, when I was Chair of the Board of Management, took this concept and incorporated it into a set of Rules the primary purpose of which is conflict avoidance, rather than dispute resolution. As eloquently put by Nicholas Gould and Christina Lockwood in the preamble to the Rules:[13]

> Dispute boards are created by contract and aid the parties in resolving their disagreements. In the last twenty years there has been an increasing demand for

---

10. James Perry, 'The Future of Dispute Boards in Non-construction Applications and Why it Matters' presentation given at the 12th Annual Conference of the Dispute Resolution Board Foundation, 3-5 May 2012, Sydney, Australia.
11. International Federation of Consulting Engineers (FIDIC) available here FIDIC.
12. Cyril Chern, *Chern on Dispute Boards, Practice and Procedure*, Third Edition, Informa Law from Routledge, 2015.
13. CIArb Dispute Board Rules available at https://www.ciarb.org/media/14974/ciarb-dispute-board-rules-practice-standards-committee-august-2014.pdf.

less adversarial dispute resolution methods such as mediation, conciliation and dispute boards. The great benefit of using a standing dispute board is that its members may be called upon as soon as a problem arises and help the parties resolve their differences before they become polarised in their views. The dispute avoidance role of the standing board should be emphasised: the dispute board encourages the parties to solve their own problems, creating an atmosphere where the parties communicate and recourse to the advisory role of the board. Resolving conflicts at an early stage, or even before they arise, is an obvious benefit that greatly minimizes costs such as legal fees and reduces loss of productive time and goodwill between the parties.

Dispute boards should be set up at the outset of a contract and remain in place throughout its duration. Thus, the dispute board members will be familiar with the contract and its performance, and also be acquainted with the parties, making the board an effective dispute resolution mechanism with 'real-time' value. Ideally, the dispute board members become part of the project team and are trusted to be fair and impartial, so that their advice will be readily accepted by all parties. The need for prompt, cost-effective and impartial dispute resolution can be found in many contractual relationships in several industries. In order to meet this need, the Chartered Institute of Arbitrators (the 'CIArb') offers the international business community the CIArb Dispute Board Rules, which cater to any medium or long-term project, whether construction, IT, commercial or otherwise.

In Article 12 of the Rules the dispute avoidance mandate of the Board is expressly set out:

Article 12

1. The true mission of a Dispute Board is not judicial; rather it is to prevent formal Disputes. The Parties may at any time jointly refer a matter or Dispute to the DB for it to give an informal advisory opinion as a means of Dispute avoidance and/or informally discuss and attempt to resolve any disagreement that may have arisen between the Parties during the performance of the Contract. The DB may provide the requested advisory opinion during a conversation with the Parties, during any meeting or site visit in the presence of both Parties or in a written note to the Parties, or, with the prior agreement of the Parties, provide informal assistance to resolve a disagreement in any other form. The Parties are not bound to act upon any advice given during the informal assistance process.
2. The DB may on its own initiative raise an issue with the Parties in order to establish a dialogue between them and to clarify matters in the presence of the DB. The Parties have the right to stop the DB's initiative if they regard it as unnecessary, provided that they notify the DB promptly, jointly and in writing.
3. If the DB is later called upon to make a Determination concerning a matter with respect to which it has provided an informal advisory opinion, the DB shall not be bound by any views expressed in such verbal or written advisory opinion.

Particularly now, coming out of the Pandemic, with the need to meet the challenges posed by climate change, we will require collaborative means for resolving energy transition related disputes. These are disputes arising out of the need for Governments and commercial parties to move from a carbon based to a sustainable system of energy production. This will entail a seismic shift in existing legal commitments geared to the carbon economy and the introduction of sustainable energy processes. This will require existing legal relationships to be restructured and collaborative dispute resolution technics to be deployed on new energy systems and technology. The disputes arising from this transition are poorly resolved through adjudicative means as these do not take into account the restructuring requirements and time constraints that climate change imposes. Only through collaboration can the varied types of innovative solutions needed to resolve these disputes, be found. This is best served through tools such as facilitated negotiation, mediation and dispute boards.

A final question? Is now the time to move from a prix fixe approach to dispute resolution to one that is more a la carte? A mixing and matching of tools to fit the actual needs of the specific dispute. Parties might start to contemplate resolution rather than justice as the prime objective for deciding the tool or tools to deploy. Given the lessons coming out of the Pandemic that practical, cost-effective and pragmatic solutions are needed to resolve conflicts quickly, we must move away from strictly deploying traditional dispute resolution mechanisms. The coming decades will necessitate fresh thinking around dealing with the energy transition and climate change-related disputes. These are disputes that must be avoided or managed if we are not to derail our net-zero agenda. Combined modes of dispute resolution will have to be an important part of the solution.

CHAPTER 21

Knowledge-Based ADR Toolbox for Uncertain Times

Elina Mereminskaya[*]

TABLE OF CONTENTS

I   INTRODUCTION

The world we live in is a complex interdependent reality, a condition that has been exacerbated in the last two decades.[1] This observation has been recently proven and reinforced by at least three phenomena: First, the COVID-19 pandemic put entire countries into lockdown and heavily interrupted compliance with contractual obligations in 2020 and 2021. Second, an illegal war against Ukraine initiated by Russia on 24 February 2022 has affected the supply of goods and commodities all over the world, not to mention the terrible human losses and suffering that disturb our moral sense. And third, the long-forgotten high inflation rates caused by the two previous factors,

---

[*] Head Partner at WAGEMANN Arbitration, LL.M., Ph.D., FCIArb, International Arbitrator, Chair of the Americas Initiative of the Institute of Transnational Arbitration (2022-2024 term); Vice Chair, Project Establishment Subcommittee, International Construction Projects Committee of the IBA (2022-2023 term).
1. Aldo Mascareño, 'Close to the Edge: From crisis to critical transitions in social systems theory', Soziale Systeme 2020; 25(2) (in print).

together with fiscal and financial measures taken by the governments in response to COVID-19.[2]

All the above has triggered multiple supply-chain interruptions and significant increases in regular and extraordinary costs that impacted the capacity of the parties to perform their contractual obligations. Until now, no increase in bankruptcy rates due to the governmental measures introduced at the outset of the pandemic has taken place. Most of them are due to end by mid-2022; therefore, a future wave of bankruptcies can be anticipated.[3] The prediction is becoming a reality, at least in what concerns the Chilean construction sector, which saw in disbelief how various long-time construction companies filed for bankruptcy or reorganization in the last quarter of 2022.[4]

What will companies do in that context in order to survive hard and uncertain times? They could, of course, rely on their contracts to request full enforcement of their claims or to be excused for failure to perform. By way of example, a general contractor might want to collect liquidated damages from its subcontractors for late performance, while claiming an increase in the contract price from the project's owner because of inflation.

However, if the contractual provisions are not well-suited to the interests of the parties, or if the counterparty is undergoing similar critical processes and is not in a position to accept the claims, the next step would be a resort to dispute resolution.

The companies are willing to resort to lawyers only when business ethics and word-of-mouth agreements are no longer enough, or when they have no option because court or arbitral proceedings are initiated. As we know, handing the decision of the dispute to the lady who rules blindfolded is a leap of faith that few companies are willing to take. However, in the uncertain times we live in today, the institutional protection of expectations that only law can provide is more crucial than ever.[5] Yet this comes with heavy demands on the law itself. The problem is no longer the application of positive law; nor the corridors of legal interpretation. If the law is to provide an answer to the problems that companies globally face today, it must supplement its expertise in the application and interpretation of the law with a deep understanding of

2. World Bank, 'Global Economic Prospects', (June 2022) at https://www.worldbank.org/en/news/press-release/2022/06/07/stagflation-risk-rises-amid-sharp-slowdown-in-growth-energy-markets (last accessed 3 July 2022); International Monetary Fund, 'World Economic Outlook: War Sets Back the Global Recovery' (April 2022) at https://www.imf.org/-/media/Files/Publications/WEO/2022/April/English/text.ashx (last accessed 3 July 2022).
3. Robert K. Rasmussen, 'COVID-19 Debt and Bankruptcy Infrastructure', The Yale Law Journal Forum (10 November 2021) at https://www.yalelawjournal.org/pdf/F7.RasmussenMacroed FinalDraftWEB_gioo9bcy.pdf (last accessed 3 July 2022); Atradius Collection, 'Insolvencies Increase as Government Support Ends' (12 April 2022), at https://atradiuscollections.com/global/ (last accessed 3 July 2022).
4. Exante, 'Quiebras y caída en las inversiones: los factores que más preocupan en el sector de la construcción' (20 October 2022) at https://www.ex-ante.cl/quiebras-y-caida-en-las-inversiones-los-factores-que-mas-preocupan-en-el-sector-de-la-construccion/ (last accessed 25 October 2022); Ignacia Munita, 'Tras quiebra de Claro, Vicuña y Valenzuela: Los proyectos pendientes y en los que acusa tener disputas con entes públicos' (22 October 2022) at www.emol.com/noticias/Economia/2022/10/22/1076349/proyectos-pendientes-quiebra-claro-vicunavalenzuela.html (last accessed 25 October 2022).
5. Niklas Luhmann, *Law as a Social System* (Oxford 2004).

the complexity of the cases it is confronted with. In other words, legal problems are not only legal but also technical, economic, environmental, often political and always emotional, since humans are involved.

In this chapter, I argue that modern law should adopt a reflexive stance on the sociolegal problems it deals with. Reflexivity means that law is sensible to the knowledge produced in other domains and that it is able to integrate this knowledge into its own process of decision-making.[6] By means of reflexivity, law becomes aware of the fact that legal norms are an idealization of expectations; that they are not the reality itself, but an observation and analytical abstraction of complex conditions taking place at the level of social practices. Sociolegal reality is thus overdetermined by countless factors that are, in principle, invisible to law. This is the baseline of our interconnected, networked, and interdependent world of the twenty-first century. Therefore, a proper and asymptotically fair juridical decision must reflexively include multiple perspectives on the case; it must operate in interconnected networks of knowledge.

In order to unfold this argument, in the first section I present my case as a plaidoyer for knowledge hubs or knowledge-based tools in the practice of law in the global world. Next, I describe some elements of an Alternative Dispute Resolution (ADR) toolbox in the construction industry, and finally, I draw conclusions from my analysis.

II   A PLAIDOYER FOR KNOWLEDGE HUBS

In the first few months of the 2020 pandemic, as we began to receive initial concerns from our clients about the contractual consequences of the lockdown, our first reaction was to fall back on the familiar legal repertoire. Force majeure and *hardship* were the most commonly used words in our telematic meetings. As news of the global lockdown came to us and as the initial two-week lockdown turned into months and eventually years, traditional legal language fell short of providing appropriate solutions to the problems the clients were facing. Then we sought epidemiological knowledge to get a perspective on how long the disaster would last; we tried to understand the duration of materials stranded in distant ports to know if there would be total loss of them; we assessed various State policies to know what was legally possible and what not in different regions of the globe. In a word, we went outside the law to better apply the law.

It was probably one of the most important lessons from the pandemic for the law of the twenty-first century: we finally recognized that legal knowledge is not enough to

---

6. Gunther Teubner, 'Substantive and Reflexive Elements in Modern Law', Law & Society Review, Vol. 17 (1982), p. 239; Gunther Teubner, 'A Constitutional Moment? The Logics of Hitting the Bottom', by Poul F Kjaer, Gunther Teubner and Alberto Febbrajo (Eds), The Financial Crisis in Constitutional Perspective: The Dark side of Functional Differentiation (Hart, 2011) pp. 9-51; Gunther Teubner, 'Substantive and Reflexive Elements in Modern Law', by Christopher Thornhill (Ed.) Luhmann and Law (Routledge, 2015) pp. 181-228.

deal with legal problems, just because legal problems are technically and socially (economically, politically) embedded.

In the happy old days of the twentieth century, when history had ended as Francis Fukuyama announced – his work was made a mandatory reading in Russian law schools of the post-soviet era – that the market, democracy and the rule of law were expected to prevail throughout the world order,[7] things were clear to us. In those simple times, we used the legal figure of the *hard cases* to put us in the position of extreme situations. Today everything is a *hard case*.

What we need today is to reflect on the complexity of the cases in the complexity of our legal strategy to deal with them. For doing this, we need the expertise of different knowledge workers. In this world, each conflict should be addressed from the point of view of diverse areas of knowledge to deliver a comprehensive analysis thereof.[8] Thus, a decision to initiate arbitration would be made based on the following variables: (i) whether the information available is sufficient to initiate a dispute resolution procedure; (ii) whether the business relationship with the counterparty suggests opting for a non-adversarial method of dispute resolution, given that future projections have more potential than the focal conflict; (iii) whether the company has an interest in initiating arbitration for reasons unrelated to the substance of the dispute (e.g., generating an expected profit provision) and whether there are other avenues to achieve this; (iv) whether the dispute is of technical nature, which is better addressed with other methods of dispute resolution such as Expert Determination; (v) whether the projections for industry development make the lawsuit economically unsustainable, and (vi) whether the conflict has a significant emotional component to it rather than being a pure monetary issue; among others.

All these aspects can be taken into consideration and the CEO might commit to participate in mediation rather than arbitration. She can conduct an independent technical assessment to determine whether the reported delays by the construction site are true, or pay for therapy for the onsite professionals and let the matter evaporate while waiting for another project to be initiated in the following two years.

The complexity of contemporary legal problems makes it difficult to have a multidimensional analysis capable of processing and reflecting this complexity. If we lawyers want to even come close to the possibility of comprehensive advice of that kind, we would have to achieve additional degrees in economics, engineering, psychology and marketing, among others. But this emulation of Leonardo da Vinci's genius is no longer possible for the simple reason that no professional can condense the world's knowledge. The legal knowledge alone that we have to digest and manage today is already quite overwhelming.

However, what none of the individuals could achieve on their own, can be achieved by networks in which multiple specialties can meet and interact as hubs of knowledge and expertise. Interdisciplinary work organized through these highly

---

7. Francis Fukuyama, *The End of History and the Last Man* (Simon and Schuster 2006).
8. Some of the ideas related to the knowledge hub were published in Spanish: Elina Mereminskaya, 'El potencial de los hubs de conocimiento y expertise' (20 April 2020), https://idealex.press/el-potencial-de-los-hubs-de-conocimiento-y-expertise/ (last accessed 3 July 2022).

specialized knowledge and expertise hubs could provide comprehensive answers to the multidimensional conflicts faced by clients. Therefore, hubs linking lawyers with engineers, economists, psychologists, data scientists and others should not be seen as a distant future, but as an urgent necessity to meet our clients' expectations to protect their own normative expectations as lawyers. These types of networks are only timidly emerging at present. Transaction costs may increase, language translation may be more difficult, and the number of variables to consider multiplies exponentially. But the alternative is not to learn from the world, and if the law had not learned from the evolution of the world, we would still punish with lashes those who do not comply with the contract.

During the last two to three years, many of us witnessed the only limited remedies that the legal orders were able to provide. That is, in many jurisdictions, the parties were left wondering how to deal by way of local provisions written centuries ago, with a pandemic expanded over the entire world within just months. Force majeure provisions do not cover cost increases and do not allow claims for stand-by costs, while price adjustment clauses were seldom to find until recently, and certainly, no contract addressed personnel shortages caused by appealing governmental financial support.

As the complexity of the world continues to increase and uncertain times seem to become the 'new normal', there is a greater need for a reflexive law that is able to cope with uncertainties by incorporating specialized knowledge and providing safety valves for pressure release.

III   AN ADR TOOLBOX OF THE CONSTRUCTION INDUSTRY

In the construction industry, technical knowledge is firmly embedded in dispute resolution mechanisms used to solve conflicts arising during project execution. If we were to analyse these mechanisms from the point of view of a project in execution, we would observe an early involvement of lawyers that act as support during contract administration, prevention and resolution of disputes.

From any angle, construction, infrastructure and concession contracts offer a prolific scenario to produce a conjunction between legal, technical, and economic areas of knowledge. Like Yin and Yang, the legal and technical disciplines supplement each other by providing mechanisms that give comprehensive coverage to disputes.

This conjunction occurs for the obvious reason that the execution of this type of contract requires the application of an enormous amount of diverse and highly qualified knowledge. This is also due to the certainty that – in some yet unknown and uncertain way – the project will have to be adjusted to the site and soil conditions, for which additional technical solutions will have to be developed and implemented.

These uncertainties are considered risks that are dealt with by way of an initial risk allocation between the client and the contractor.[9] At the same time, unlike many

---

9. Mundhir Al Hasani, 'Understanding Risk and Uncertainty in Project Management', European Journal of Economics, Law and Politics, Vol. 5 (2018), pp. 30-40. *See* FIDIC Rainbow Suit that

other types of contracts, construction contracts include mechanisms that make them adaptable to reality, i.e., they are already reflexive contracts.

Due to the complex nature of the construction contracts, 'risks can hardly be ever eliminated; they can only be transferred to another party to a construction contract agreement or shared on the basis of relevant contractual conditions'.[10] Accordingly, risk management is 'a complex, long-lasting and far-reaching process that begins long before the investment and sometimes lasts even after its completion'.[11]

I will briefly discuss four specific tools that include elements of the interdisciplinary approach to dispute prevention and resolution.

1   Interdisciplinary Advice as a Contract Administration Tool

During the phase of project execution, risk analysis and management take place on a continuous basis with the aim of dispute prevention. The correct assumption is 'instead of figuring out how best to resolve a conflict near the end of its lifecycle, dispute prevention examines measures explicitly designed to break the dispute cycle earlier and to deescalate problems as they form before they solidify into formal legal action'.[12]

From the point of view of interdisciplinary involvement in dispute prevention and resolution, at least the following milestones already exist.

First, project-related risks should be addressed from a contractual as well as a technical dimension. Almost all risks require such an interdisciplinary approach, as the underlying events are most probably technical in nature, but the corresponding risks have been contractually allocated by one of the parties. For example, soil mechanics is a technical matter that needs to be determined before the project's engineering. Changes in the soil mechanics might significantly affect the time of execution of the project and its cost. To determine which party will bear the impacts, it is necessary to analyse the contractual risk allocation.

Second, while the technical contemporaneous record is created onsite, the information needs to be adjusted to what the interested party can claim. For example, if the contractor claims overhead costs, it could claim it as a daily value multiplied by the number of days of the extension if it is contractually entitled to do so. Otherwise, the contractor will have to submit the cost actually incurred, which will require full-fledged supporting information.

Third, the contractor is usually required to timely submit its notices and claims. If it fails to do so, the claim is deemed waived. In addition, the contractor is usually

---

illustrates recommendations for the appropriate contract form pursuant to the risk allocation at https://fidic.org/node/149 (last accessed 5 July 2022).

10. Aurelija Peckiene, Andzelika Komarovskab and Leonas Ustinovicius, 'Overview of Risk Allocation between Construction Parties', Procedia Engineering Vol. 57 (2013), pp. 889-894.
11. Paweł Szymański, 'Risk Management in Construction Projects', Procedia Engineering Vol. 208 (2017), pp. 174-182.
12. Janice L. Sperow, 'The Benefits of Dispute Prevention', Dispute Resolution Journal, Vol. 75 No. 3, 2021, pp. 1-19. The author provides a comprehensive overview of measures that could be used for dispute prevention, noticeable relying on special knowledge: usage of expertise, prevention-focused contractual clauses, usage of emerging technology, pre-authorized decision-maker, etc.

required to rely on certain contractual provisions and to provide all technical records in support of its information. For example, the revised FIDIC contract forms establish additional formalities with 'more detailed and stricter requirements' that place 'a greater administrative burden on the parties'.[13] The trend, if followed, will require even closer cooperation between legal and technical teams.

Therefore, the contractor must establish the event, its contractual entitlement, and the impacts or costs and damages.[14] For example, to claim an extension of time, the contractor should submit an impacted schedule of the works. However, such a schedule should show only the events that can be claimed based on the contractual entitlement, otherwise the impacted schedule, even if technically correct, would be rendered useless.

The involvement of an interdisciplinary advisory team during this stage presents certain challenges. First, experience shows that the technical teams of both the client and the contractor, 'have little interest in contractual matters during the life of a project'.[15] Second, lawyers involved in the consulting work at this stage have to meet certain criteria: in addition to being specialized in construction, they have to be able to focus on the goal of project completion and be in command of a non-adversarial communication style to avoid escalating disagreements.

2   Dispute Board

The literature on the application of Dispute Boards is nowadays abundant.[16] Their advantages related to time and cost savings, as well as their main purpose of dispute avoidance, are well established.[17] Recently, the Dispute Board has been assigned the

---

13. Bernd Ehle and China Irwin, 'Claims Procedure and Dispute Resolution under the Revised FIDIC Conditions', Construction Law International, Vol. 14 (2019), https://www.ibanet.org/article/3 061530b-25b8-4723-aab1-b08c88919bbb#article2 (last accessed 9 July 2022).

14. Under the revised FIDIC conditions, Sub-Clause 20.2.4 requires a submission of a 'fully detailed Claim' in the following terms: 'In this Sub-Clause 20.2, "fully detailed Claim" means a submission which includes: (a) a detailed description of the event or circumstance giving rise to the Claim; (b) a statement of the contractual and/or other legal basis of the Claim; (c) all contemporary records on which the claiming Party relies; and (d) detailed supporting particulars of the amount of additional payment claimed (or amount of reduction of the Contract Price in the case of the Employer as the claiming Party), and/or EOT claimed (in the case of the Contractor) or extension of the DNP claimed (in the case of the Employer).'

15. Elliott Geisinger, 'Dispute Avoidance in International Construction Projects: The Use of Outside Counsel as Contract Manager', Construction Law Journal, Vol. 25, No. 1 (2009), pp. 11-23.

16. See different sources at Dispute Board Resolution Foundation webpage https://www.disputeboard.org/ (last accessed 9 July 2022).

17. Peter H.J. Chapman, 'The Use of Dispute Boards on Major Infrastructure Projects', The Turkish Commercial Law Review, Vol. I, No. 3 (2015), pp. 219-232; G.M. Peck, 'The Benefit/Cost Equation for Dispute Boards: Australian Experience' (15-17 May 2014) at https://www.disputeboard.org/wp-content/uploads/2016/02/the-BenefitCost-equation-for-Dispute-Boards-Australian-experience.pdf (last accessed 9 July 2022); Juan Eduardo Figueroa Valdés and William R. Schubert, 'The Role of Dispute Boards in the Construction Industry', International Arbitration Law Review, Vol. 20, No. 2 (2017), pp. 55-68.

role of dispute avoidance, which is promoted by most standard forms of construction contracts, especially by the New Engineering Contract (NEC4).[18]

For the purposes of this paper, aimed at showing the advantages of knowledge-based tools, the following features of Disputes Boards are relevant. First, unless the project is small and a one-person Dispute Board is recommended, they are usually composed of technical and legal professionals. Second, they can combine mediation-style assistance with formal adjudication.[19]

This interdisciplinary assessment of the problems before they interrupt parties' relationships, cash flow and the sheer possibility of project execution, as well as the soft powers owned by the members of the Dispute Board, allows for a reduction of the inherent complexity. The problems are chunked and, so to say, are 'digested' before they can surmount and disrupt contract performance.

3   A Case of the Chilean Dispute Resolution Mechanism for the Concessions of Public Works

Another interesting example of the knowledge-based dispute resolution mechanism is the Technical Panel for the concessions of public works that exists under Chilean law. Chile introduced a system of concessions for public works in the mid-1990s, which allowed it to develop a good infrastructure at low fiscal cost,[20] and in the absence of any international funding from multilateral agencies.

In 2010, the regulation underwent some modifications. A so-called Concessions Technical Panel was created. The Concessions Technical Panel is composed of two lawyers, two engineers and one professional specialized in economics or financial sciences, with a professional or academic career in technical, economic or legal matters related to the infrastructure concessions sector. Pursuant to Article 36 of the *Public Works Concessions Law*,[21] the Technical Panel hears matters related to technical or economic discrepancies during the execution of the concession contract. The Technical Panel issues 'recommendations' within the scope of its competence, which are not binding to the parties. The parties may choose to reach an agreement based on the recommendation or resort to arbitration.

By the end of 2021, the Concessions Technical Panel had competence in over 35 projects. As stated in its 2021 Report: 'in the entire period of operation of the Panel, i.e.,

---

18. Robert Alan Gerrard and Patrick Waterhouse, NEC4 Resolving and Avoiding Disputes, 2019.
19. Albert Bates Jr and R. Zachary Torres-Fowler, 'Dispute Boards: A Different Approach to Dispute Resolution', by Christian Campbell (ed.), 2020, Comparative Law Yearbook of International Business, pp. 237-264.
20. P. Herman Chadwick, 'START. Mecanismos de resolución de controversias: una mirada desde la política pública', *Concesiones: El esperado relanzamiento* (May 2012), pp. 177-186. However, these contracts tend to be constantly renegotiated which increases certain kinds of spendings from the taxpayers. See Eduardo Engel, Ronald Fisher and Alexander Galetovic, 'When and How to Use Public-Private Partnerships in Infrastructure: Lessons from the International Experience' (February 2020), available at https://www.nber.org/papers/w26766 (last accessed 9 July 2022).
21. Decree with the Power of Law No. 164 from 1991 (Public Works Concessions Law), which has been updated on various occasions, the Law No. 20.410 of 2010.

since 2011, 62 Discrepancies have been received, accounting for 121 disputes as of December 2021 and a total amount requested for compensation of 24.2 million UF,[22] of which 3.15 million UF have been recognized by the Panel, equivalent to a recognition of approximately 13%. However, about 67% were recognized to the Concession Company, either an amount or recognition of the right to be compensated, in full or in part'.[23]

In addition, 'out of a total of 62 Recommendations issued since 2010, 29 cases have been terminated through direct agreements, settlements, conciliations, and sentences. From the analysis of these terminated cases, almost 90% of them fully or partially coincide with the respective Recommendation issued by the Technical Panel, considering the criteria established therein. Moreover, of the total number of cases terminated, almost 50% have been terminated by direct agreement of the parties, without recourse to the Arbitration Commission'.[24]

Recourse to the Technical Panel is a condition for subsequent arbitration. Article 36bis of the *Public Works Concessions Law* provides for ad hoc arbitration before the so-called Arbitration Commission.

At the beginning of each concession contract, the parties appoint members of the Arbitration Commission from two pre-approved lists of candidates. The first list includes twenty lawyers and is drawn up by the Chilean Supreme Court. The other list includes ten non-lawyers such as economists and engineers and is drawn up by the Court for the Defense of Free Competition. At least two of the members of the Arbitration Commission must be lawyers.

This example does not mean that the Technical Panel's performance is fully accepted. Some of its features are subject to improvement.[25] However, it has not been feasible to assess the work of the interdisciplinary Arbitration Commissions as their decisions are not published systematically.[26]

However, the use of the Technical Panel undoubtedly helps to resolve part of the disputes at an early stage. And in the case of those disputes that go to arbitration, there is an important gain: technical analysis and evidence are available almost from the outset. Therefore, these instances seem to be useful exercises of a reflexive law that seeks to adjust to the requirements of the knowledge society.

---

22. Unit of Account used in Chie adjusted for inflation. UAH 1 is equivalent to USD 34.20 (9 July 2022).
23. Panel Técnico de Concesions, 'Memoria 2021' (2022) available at https://www.panelconce siones.cl/OpenDocs/Default.aspx?argCarpetaId = 504&argInstanciaId = 69, p. 5 (last accessed 9 July 2022).
24. *Ibid*.
25. *See* general critic: http://www.infraestructurapublica.cl/conflictividad-en-concesiones-aboga dos-delinean-los-desafios-del-sistema/; also Elina Mereminskaya, 'Una bola de cristal para licitantes', Industria Legal, CL, Vol. 8, November 2021, https://www.wycia.com/wp-content/ uploads/2021/12/Industria-Legal-CL-Vol.-8-Nov.-2021.pdf (last accessed 9 July 2022).
26. There is no complete database that comprises those decisions. On the Directorate of Concessions of Public Work only selected decisions can be found: http://fiscalia.mop.cl/Paginas/Sentencias .aspx (last accessed 9 July 2022).

4   Arbitration Procedures Designed According to Pareto Principle

The Pareto principle, also known as the 80/20 rule, is an observational theory maintaining that 80% of the output from a given situation or system is determined by 20% of the input.[27] While this is not a scientific law and proportion can be construed very differently,[28] it is a shortcut used to describe that a majority of results are achieved by the minority of inputs.

The 80/20 approach is common among engineers and other technicians when dealing with claims, thereby allowing for a methodological step-by-step analysis. For example, out of 14 accounts of claims submitted by the contractor, 3 to 4 will be responsible for 80% of the total amount claimed, which become the main target of analysis.

The next step would be to determine whether the claims are supported by the contractual risk allocation entitling the contractor, which could lead to disregarding one or more of those claims. Claims that have passed the above test would be analysed for compliance with the formal notice requirements.

The remaining claims that were duly notified and submitted can be now analysed in detail, i.e., specific events will be determined and their impact on the performance of the works will be analysed. If the impacts are confirmed, the question of costs can be finally addressed. Thus, instead of undertaking a highly complex technical analysis of the fourteen claims, the effort is channelled towards claims that are economically relevant and contractually substantiated.

In 2019, the Queen Mary University of London Survey dedicated to construction disputes, asked clients and users how they can help increase the efficiency of arbitration proceedings. The most popular response, with 62%, was to 'focus on resolving the dispute rather than leaving "no stone unturned"'.[29] This call for efficiency means that a fully fledged discussion of each and every problem that emerged during the execution of a construction project is unnecessary and seems to be an invitation to follow the Pareto principle.

The more efficient structure and management of arbitration proceedings have been advocated by numerous authors who have crafted valuable proposals aimed at a common target: to chunk the size and complexity of the disputes as well as to incorporate the specific knowledge at the early stages of arbitral proceedings.[30]

---

27. *See* review of papers: https://www.sciencedirect.com/topics/engineering/pareto-principle (last accessed 3 July 2022).
28. *See*: https://paperswithcode.com/paper/pareto-s-80-20-rule-and-the-gaussian (last accessed 3 July 2022).
29. Queen Mary University of London and Pinsent Masons, 'International Arbitration Survey: Driving Efficiency in International Construction Disputes' (November 2019), available at https://arbitration.qmul.ac.uk/research/2019/, p. 31, (last accessed 9 July 2022).
30. John W. Hinchey, 'Rethinking Resolution of Construction Disputes', 15 No. 1 Construction L. Int'l 11 (March 2020); Jörg Risse, 'An Inconvenient Truth: The Complexity Problem and Limits to Justice', Arbitration International, Vol. 35 (2019), 291-307; Doug Jones, 'Innovating Evidence Procedure in International Construction Arbitration', Journal of the Canadian College of Construction Lawyers, Vol. 167 (2019); Janet Walker and Doug Jones, 'Procedural Order No. 1: From Swiss Watch to Arbitrators' Toolkit', *The Powers and Duties of an Arbitrator: Liber Amicorum Pierre A. Karrer*, Kluwer Law International, 2017, pp. 393-401; Albert Bates Jr.

IV   CONCLUSIONS

In this chapter, I have addressed the relevance of multidisciplinary knowledge-based work to meet the challenges that the complex legal problems of the twenty-first century impose on the law. Through a review of both the literature and different tools for the prevention and resolution of disputes in the field of arbitration of construction, I have argued that interdisciplinary work is not only a noble aspiration of the law but a necessity to better meet the protection of the normative expectations of our clients in an uncertain and highly interconnected world. Several conclusions can be drawn from my analysis.

First, the global critical experiences such as the COVID-19 pandemic, political revolutions and wars, have shown that the certainty of living in a world governed by the rule of law cannot be taken for granted in the twenty-first century. Events such as these reveal the uncertain and highly interconnected nature of contemporary global society. This shows the law that legal problems are not only legal but include a series of assumptions and variables to which the law must reflexively attend in order to fulfil its function properly.

Second, the appropriate strategy for dealing with the complexity of contemporary global legal problems is to reflect the complexity of those problems through interdisciplinary hubs of knowledge. The work of lawyers should incorporate the knowledge of engineers, economists, psychologists and data scientists, among others, by means of knowledge networks working together for the best resolution of cases.

Third, dispute resolution mechanisms that are up to the task are, for example, interdisciplinary advice as a contract administration tool that manages risks from the beginning of the project, thus avoiding the escalation of controversies; dispute boards composed of legal and technical professionals; technical panels that move between legal, economic, technical and even political domains which may resolve emerging disputes before they explode; and efficiency measures aimed at reducing the complexity of arbitration proceedings without excluding relevant variables.

Are these mechanisms suitable exclusively for the construction sector? I would suggest that they are suitable for a much wider range of contracts that are marked by similar characteristics: the complex nature of their structure; the technical, financial, and economic embeddedness of the legal problem they posit; and the need to adapt to a changing environment. If we have to go outside the law to better apply the law, then we better recognize the multivariable nature of legal problems and develop a toolbox for this new state of affairs.

'Controlling Time and Cost in Arbitration: Actively Managing the Process and "Right-Sizing" Discovery', Dispute Resolution Journal (August/October 2012); John T. Blankenship, 'Isomorphism of Construction Arbitration: The Key to Its Prevention and Reversal', Dispute Resolution Journal (May/October 2010). Also *see* the proposal of applying Project Management notions to arbitration process from Ben Giaretta, 'Project Management in International Arbitration', McGill Journal of Dispute Resolution, Vol. 3 (2016-2017), pp. 66-85.

PANEL 6   State of the World in 2022 – New
Developments and Reform in International
Investment Arbitration

CHAPTER 22

A User's Guide to What's New in the ICSID Rules 2022

*Meg Kinnear**

TABLE OF CONTENTS

I INTRODUCTION

In October 2016, the Secretariat of the International Centre for Settlement of Investment Disputes (ICSID) advised its members that it would propose amendments to the ICSID Rules. The prior amendment process had concluded in 2006 and included notable

---

* Advisory Member of ICCA; Meg Kinnear is the Secretary-General of ICSID and a Vice-President of the World Bank. She was first appointed as Secretary-General in 2009. Prior to her election as Secretary-General, she was Senior General Counsel and Director General of the Trade Law Bureau of Canada (1999-2009), Executive Assistant to the Deputy Minister of Justice of Canada (1996-1999), and Counsel in the Civil Litigation Section of the Department of Justice of Canada (1984-1996).

changes such as increased transparency of the process and the motion to strike for manifest lack of legal merit (MLLM). It had also been accompanied by a proposal to establish an Appellate Body for treaty cases, but that proposal did not garner State support and was left for future consideration.[1]

The main objectives of the 2016 amendment project were to enhance the cost- and time- effectiveness of the dispute settlement process, to offer a greater variety of dispute settlement tools, and to address some of the issues raised by ongoing discussions about reform of investor-State dispute settlement (ISDS). Early on, ICSID established a working method that consisted of issuing a draft set of rule proposals (in English, French and Spanish), an explanation as to how these proposals modified the current practice, and an invitation for written comment on the draft proposals. This was published in a Working Paper and made available for public and member State consultation. Ultimately there were six Working Papers that documented the evolution of what became the ICSID Rules 2022.

Over the five and a half years of development of these rules, ICSID made more than 200 presentations to the public, received over 150 written comments on updated rules, and convened three, week-long, in-person consultations with member States. This round of amendments has been ICSID's most inclusive and transparent rule amendment process to date and resulted in the most comprehensive amendments to date. The full record of this process, including written comments and the six Working Papers, are on the ICSID website.[2]

While the Working Papers and comments provide useful background, parties should exercise caution in citing them in the same way as classic 'travaux preparatoires'. This is because the text in each Working Paper represented a proposal by the ICSID Secretariat based on all comments received and was not necessarily the position of any single delegation or a record of the negotiation at any point in time. Rather, it is the wording of the amended rules as finally adopted by the membership that should be the primary guide to their interpretation.

ICSID Member States voted on the proposed amendments on 21 March 2022, and they were approved by 85% of the membership. They came into effect on 1 July 2022, the start of the ICSID fiscal year.

This article highlights the main changes effected by the ICSID Rules 2022, and how these will apply in individual cases.[3]

---

1. *See* background papers to 2006 amendments at https://icsid.worldbank.org/resources/ publications/background-papers (last accessed 25 July 2022). *See also*, Aurélia Antonietti, 'The 2006 Amendments to the ICSID Rules and Regulations and the Additional Facility Rules', 21 ICSID F.I.L.J. 427 (2006).
2. The six working papers may be accessed at: https://icsid.worldbank.org/resources/rules-amendments.
3. All references to the ICSID Rules 2022 in this article can be found at https://icsid.worldbank.org /rules-regulations (last accessed 25 July 2022). *See*, https://icsid.worldbank.org/procedures(last accessed 25 July 2022) for further description of the procedure under the ICSID Rules 2022.

II   IMPLEMENTATION OF THE AMENDED RULES

The Centre has taken the following approach to the implementation of the amended rules:

- *Convention Cases*: The 2022 ICSID Convention Arbitration Rules (AR) and Conciliation Rules (CR) will apply based on the date of consent to the proceeding. If consent was given before 1 July 2022, the rules in effect at the time of consent will apply by default;[4] however, parties may agree to apply the 2022 rules. The amended Institution Rules (IR) and amended Administrative and Financial Regulations (AFR) will apply to arbitration and conciliation from 1 July 2022, except that ICSID will not request a first advance solely from claimant for cases registered before July 1 and will not apply the new default rules to requests for advances that were made before July 1. The amended arbitrator and conciliator declarations[5] will apply to cases under the 2022 AR and CR, and the 1 July 2022, Memorandum on Fees and Expenses[6] and Schedule of Fees[7] apply to work performed in all cases from 1 July. Requests for post-Award remedies made after 1 July but based on Awards issued under the 2006 rules will continue to be addressed under the 2006 rules, although the updated AFR, the updated Memorandum on Fees and Expenses, and the updated Schedule of Fees would apply to such proceedings. The Institution Rules do not apply to requests for post-Award remedies.
- *Additional Facility Cases*: The amended ICSID Additional Facility Rules (AF Rules) apply to all requests for arbitration under the Additional Facility Arbitration Rules (AF AR) and to all requests for conciliation under the Additional Facility Conciliation Rules (AF CR) that are filed on July 1 or thereafter, even if consent was given before 1 July 2022.[8] The Additional Facility Administrative and Financial Regulations will apply to all Additional Facility cases pending as of 1 July (with the exceptions noted above for Convention cases) (AF AFR). Parties can agree to apply the 2022 AF AR or AF CR in pending AF cases. The updated arbitrator and conciliator declarations apply in cases under the 2022 AF AR and AF CR. The July 1, 2022 Memorandum on Fees and Expenses and Schedule of Fees also apply to work performed in all cases from July 1.
- *Mediation Cases*: The ICSID Mediation Rules (MR) and Mediation Administrative and Financial Regulations (MR AFR) apply to requests for mediation filed on 1 July 2022 or thereafter. The updated Memorandum on Fees and Expenses and Schedule of Fees apply as of July 1. The fee for lodging requests for

---

4. ICSID Convention, Article 44.
5. The form of the declaration is found at https://icsid.worldbank.org/rules-regulations/declarat ions.
6. Found at https://icsid.worldbank.org/services/cost-of-proceedings/memorandum-fees-expens es/2022 (last accessed 25 July 2022).
7. Found at https://icsid.worldbank.org/services/cost-of-proceedings/schedule-fees/2022 (last accessed 25 July 2022).
8. AF Rule 4; AFR 1, AF AR 1(4), AF CR 1(4).

mediation and fact-finding is USD 1,000, reflecting the expectation of a less time-consuming review process for such requests (as compared to arbitration and conciliation), and as an incentive for facility users to apply these new sets of rules.

- *Fact-Finding Cases*: The Fact-Finding Rules (FFR) and the Fact-Finding Administrative and Financial Regulations (FF AFR) apply to cases filed on 1 July 2022 or thereafter. The updated Memorandum on Fees and Expenses and Schedule of Fees apply as of 1 July.

III   OVERALL APPROACH AND STRUCTURE

While the 2022 Rules effect the broadest change in the ICSID rules to date, much remains the same, and facility users will find that the process has built on ICSID's already strong foundations. In terms of overall approach, the ICSID Rules were put into a more 'plain language' format, gender-neutral drafting was adopted,[9] and the order and numbering of the rules were revised in some places to reflect the usual sequence of a case.

The new rules have been published on the ICSID website and are found in four separate booklets, each with all the texts needed for a case pursuant to that set of rules.[10] Thus, the blue booklet addresses arbitration and conciliation under the ICSID Convention, and includes the ICSID Convention, the Report of the Executive Directors on the Convention, the applicable AFR, the IR, the AR, and the CR. The yellow booklet contains the ICSID AF Rules, the AF AR, the AF CR, and the AF AFR. As in prior iterations of the ICSID Rules, the content of the AF AR and AF CR mirrors the contents of the AR and CR respectively, except where a distinction is necessitated by the fact that the ICSID Convention does not apply in AF proceedings.[11]

Two new, stand-alone, sets of rules have also been adopted: ICSID FFR, in the red booklet with their applicable administrative and financial regulations (FFR AFR), and ICSID MR, in the green booklet with their applicable administrative and financial regulations (MR AFR). The fact-finding and mediation rules were drafted with the intent that they be as widely available as possible, to be used either for stand-alone proceedings or in parallel with arbitration or conciliation.

IV   CONVENTION AFR

The AFR were adjusted slightly to provide for an hourly (rather than daily) fee, and a fixed *per diem* fee while on travel status.[12] Separately, the ICSID Memorandum on Fees and Expenses and the Schedule of Fees were updated on 1 July 2022 to provide an

---

9. *See*, for example, AFR 32(4).
10. Found at https://icsid.worldbank.org/rules-regulations (last accessed 25 July 2022).
11. AF Rule 3.
12. AFR 14(1).

hourly fee of USD 500 and a *per diem* of USD 900.[13] The prior rules concerning requests for an increase in fees or *per diems* were strengthened, clarifying that any such request must be made in writing through the Secretary-General, and not directly to the parties, and must justify the increase requested. Given that ICSID fees accrue based on actual work done, such requests are rarely agreed to.

The AFR have also revised the sequence for payment of the first advance, with the claimant to make a deposit on its share of advances for the arbitration upon registration of the request, and the respondent to pay its share upon the Constitution of the tribunal.[14] This change allows the Centre to make necessary arrangements for the next steps immediately upon registration rather than waiting for funds at the constitution stage.

AFR 16 addressing the consequences of a default in payment of advances has also been updated. The process is the same as in the prior rules, however, the timing is different. New AFR 16 allows the Secretary-General to suspend the proceeding fifteen days after the notice of default if neither party has paid. The Secretary-General may discontinue the proceeding ninety days after the suspension by giving notice of a default in payment to the parties and to the tribunal. Hence, the time for such discontinuance has been reduced by ninety days and no order is required from the tribunal.

V   INSTITUTION RULES

The IR remain applicable to the commencement of ICSID Convention arbitration and conciliation, reflecting the unique ICSID registration requirement which filters out cases that are manifestly outside the jurisdiction of the tribunal or commission.[15] As this standard imposes a very high bar, the vast majority of cases are registered. Registration will only be refused if the case as presented by the claimant manifestly exceeds ICSID's jurisdiction.

Updated IR 2 contains a more specific list of information required in the request for arbitration or conciliation, which should ensure that claimants provide all necessary information for the Centre to assess the request against the standard in Convention Articles 25 or 36. Claimants may use the detailed list in IR 2 as a checklist for what is required to be filed. Assuming all relevant information is provided, parties may expect the request to be decided within 16-18 days of it being filed with the lodging fee. IR 3 lists recommended (but not mandatory) information to be included in the request. This includes the number and method of appointment of panellists, whether the expedited arbitration (EA) rules will be used, and the names of persons and entities that own or control a requesting party that is a juridical person.

IR 4 requires the request and its supporting documents to be filed electronically. The ICSID Rules 2022 have adopted electronic filing for all documents in cases,[16] as

---

13. *Supra* nn. 6 & 7.
14. AFR 15.
15. Convention Articles 25 (arbitration) and 36 (conciliation).
16. *See* IR 4; AR 4; CR 3; AF AR 5, 12; AF CR 5, 11; FFR 6; MR 5(3)(e).

part of the Centre's initiative to decrease the time and cost of proceedings. This practice began during the COVID-19 pandemic and has worked flawlessly. Parties needing instructions on how to file electronically can review the process on the ICSID website, which explains how to establish an account on the ICSID case management platform.[17] Similarly, parties and tribunals may elect to hold any hearing or session in person, remotely, or in a hybrid format, which also provides opportunities for cost savings.[18]

VI   ARBITRATION RULES

The vast majority of ICSID cases are arbitrations, under the Convention or the Additional Facility. Several amendments have clarified or changed arbitral procedures, notably including the following:

1   Time Limits and Extensions of Time

Numerous rule changes implement the objective of increasing the time- and cost-effectiveness of the process.[19] This objective is framed by AR 3, requiring parties and the tribunal to conduct the proceeding in good faith and expeditiously, while providing each party with a reasonable opportunity to present its case.[20] Time limits under the amended rules are calculated based on the time at the seat of the Centre and shall be satisfied if a procedural step is taken on the relevant date or on the subsequent day if the relevant date falls on a weekend. No provision is made to exempt national holidays. However, in their first session parties and tribunals may adopt case-specific provisions concerning due dates and calculation of time.[21]

The time limits set by the Convention for rectification, revision, and annulment of an Award cannot be extended, and an application for such a remedy filed after the expiry of the time limit will be disregarded.[22] Other time limits prescribed by the ICSID Convention or the rules can be extended by party agreement. However, a step taken after the expiry of such a time limit will be disregarded unless the parties agree otherwise, or the tribunal finds that there are special circumstances justifying the failure to meet the time limit.[23]

Time limits set by the tribunal (or by the Secretary-General if there is no tribunal) may be extended by the Tribunal (or the Secretary-General) or by agreement of the parties. A party must file a reasoned request for an extension of such time limit before it expires. A procedural step taken, or document received, after the expiry of such a time limit will be disregarded unless the parties agree otherwise, or the tribunal (or

---

17. *See* ICSID website on how to file a request, at https://icsid.worldbank.org/procedures/arbitration/convention/how-to-file-a-request/2022 (last accessed 25 July 2022).
18. AR 29(4)(f); AF AR 38(4)(g).
19. *See* chart at https://icsid.worldbank.org/procedures/arbitration/convention/time-limits (last accessed 25 July 2022) for a list of relevant time frames in the ICSID Rules 2022.
20. AR 3; AF AR 11.
21. AR 9-10; AF AR 17-18.
22. AR 11(1).
23. AR 11(2).

Secretary-General if applicable) decides that there are special circumstances justifying the failure to meet the time limit.[24]

Extension of time limits applicable to tribunals is addressed in AR 12. Tribunals are expected to make best efforts to meet the time limits for rendering decisions, orders, and Awards. If they are unable to do so, they must advise the parties of the special circumstances justifying their delay and state when they anticipate rendering the decision, order, or Award.[25] This rule complements the numerous provisions in the amended rules which impose specific time limits on the issuance of decisions, orders, and Awards.[26] For example, a decision on MLLM must be made in 60 days,[27] a decision or Award on a preliminary objection that has been bifurcated must be made in 180 days,[28] and an Award on the merits must be made in 240 days.[29] These dates are calculated from the last submission, and they replace the former rule on the closure of the proceedings.[30] The closure rule had rarely served to limit the time to issue Awards, and hence the amended rules are expected to be more effective in achieving compliance with time limits. Failure to meet such time limits is not a basis for an arbitrator challenge but will be reinforced through various measures, including publication on the ICSID website and postponement of payment of the arbitrator's invoices until the matter is brought into compliance.[31]

The time limits stipulated in the rules were established carefully, based on surveys of best practices in ICSID proceedings and considering the historical record of the time elapsed to issue decisions, orders, or Awards in proceedings. While AR 12 permits an extension of time limits for tribunal determinations in special circumstances, such extensions should not become standard practice. Concern about timeliness is undoubtedly the most frequently voiced concern about investment arbitration, and the scheme implemented in the 2022 amended rules seeks to address this most central of concerns in a fair and effective manner.

2 Notice of Third-Party Funding

As is evident from the written comments received by ICSID, views about third-party funding (TPF) vary substantially. Some commentators noted that TPF is increasingly available for ISDS and is an important tool in ensuring access to justice; others view TPF as inappropriate for litigation against a sovereign and encouraged its prohibition. The amended ICSID rules do not seek to resolve this ongoing debate. Rather, the purpose of the TPF provision[32] is more specific – it is a conflict-of-interest provision,

---

24. AR 11(3).
25. AR 12; AF AR 20.
26. *Supra* n. 19.
27. AF 41; AF AR 51.
28. AF 44; AF AR 54.
29. AF 58; AF AR 69.
30. ICSID Rules 2006, AR 38.
31. Memorandum on Fees and Expenses, *supra* n. 6, para. 22.
32. AR 14; AF AR 23.

intended to provide parties and arbitrators with the information necessary to avoid a conflict of interest between a third-party funder and a decision- maker in the case.

The TPF provision requires each party to file a written notice disclosing the name and address of any non-party from which it received funds for the pursuit or defence of a proceeding, either directly or indirectly. If the funder is a juridical person, the notice must state the names of the persons and entities that own and control the juridical person. There is no specific form for the notice, and any written communication will suffice if it includes the relevant information. The notice must be filed on the earlier of the date of registration or the date of obtaining funding and it must be kept up to date during the proceeding should changes in the funding situation occur. The TPF rule does not require that further information about the TPF arrangement be disclosed in the notice. Rather, AR 14(4) directs a party to AR 36 if further information on a funding arrangement is required. That rule allows a tribunal to order a party to produce evidence or documents 'if it deems it necessary'. AR 14(4) does not transform the TPF notice into a discovery provision and the TPF rule should not be expanded beyond its stated purpose.

3   Challenge Proposals

The challenge procedure under the ICSID Convention is constrained by Articles 14 and 56-58 of the Convention, notably to stipulate the qualities required of an arbitrator or conciliator, to establish the standard of review (manifest lack of the qualities required), and to confer power on the non-challenged arbitrators to decide challenges of a sole arbitrator, unless the non-challenged arbitrators are equally divided. As part of the Convention, these provisions would require amendment by a unanimous vote and were not included in the amendment project. However, the provisions relating to challenge have been updated consistently with the Convention and the overall goals of the amendment project.

First, the declaration to be filed by an arbitrator or conciliator has been expanded to include disclosure of any professional, business or other significant relationship in the past five years with the parties, their representatives, members of the tribunal, or any third-party funder providing funding for the case; ISDS cases in which the arbitrator or conciliator has been involved in the past five years; and circumstances that might cause their independence or impartiality to be questioned. The declaration also requires the arbitrator or conciliator to confirm their availability to address the case in an expeditious manner.[33]

Second, AR 22 has been revised to require any disqualification proposal to be filed within twenty-one days after the later of the Constitution of the tribunal or the date on which the challenging party knew or should have known the relevant facts. This replaces the former exhortation to 'file promptly' and provides a clear time limit for challenges. Once the challenge is filed, it is briefed in accordance with the schedule set

---

33. The form of the declaration is found at https://icsid.worldbank.org/rules-regulations/declarations (last accessed 25 July 2022).

out in AR 22, which cumulatively takes up to thirty-three days. This time limit is especially important given that a challenge effects a stay of the entire proceeding unless the parties agree otherwise.[34]

Third, AR 23 clarifies that co-arbitrators deciding a challenge of a single arbitrator may declare themselves equally divided for any reason and hence refer the matter for decision by the Chair. The decision on the challenge should be made within thirty days after the briefing period ends. All of these provisions will ensure that challenges are completed in a shorter timeframe and have less potential to slow the pace of proceedings overall. Counsel should be aware of these new rules as they will have to be prepared to complete briefing in a relatively constrained time frame after filing of the challenge.

4   Case Management Conferences

The amended rules require a tribunal to convene one or more case management conferences (CMCs) during the proceeding.[35] The CMC is in addition to the first session. It is intended to simplify a proceeding by identifying uncontested facts, narrowing issues in dispute, or addressing any other procedural or substantive issue arising in the case. AR 31 provides the parties and tribunal with the opportunity to manage the proceeding in any way that achieves the goals of expedition and cost-effectiveness. This might include, for example, agreeing to a joint set of facts, stipulating certain facts that are not in dispute, the use of case management tools such as road maps and decision trees, or providing opportunities for the parties to assess whether they would like to explore a settlement. There is no limit to what may be addressed in a CMC, and it is hoped that parties and tribunals will use them to the best advantage in respect of each individual case.

5   Document Production

Document production is increasingly common in investment arbitration and is usually managed under the *IBA Rules on the Taking of Evidence in International Arbitration*[36] and by individual tribunals in consultation with the parties. There is no presumption in the ICSID rules that a party is entitled to file requests for production of documents. Whether there will be requests for production of documents and the scope of production is addressed at the first session under AR 29(4)(g).[37]

The amended rules do not change this practice and do not seek to regulate document production. However, AR 37 does address disputes on objections to production by setting out criteria for the tribunal to consider on a motion requesting production. These criteria include the scope and timeliness of the request; the

---

34. AR 22; AF AR 30.
35. AR 31; AF AR 40.
36. Found at http://www.ibanet.org (last accessed 25 July 2022).
37. AF AR 38(4)(f).

relevance and materiality of the request; the burden of production; and the basis of the objection. This reflects the usual criteria applied by tribunals in practice.[38]

6   Tribunal-Appointed Experts

A new rule has been added addressing tribunal-appointed experts. This reflects the fact that tribunals increasingly appoint such experts to assist them, especially with highly technical evidence. AR 39 allows a tribunal to appoint an expert to report on a matter within the scope of the dispute 'unless the parties agree otherwise'.[39] Codifying usual practice, the rule requires the tribunal to consult with the parties on identification, terms of reference, and fees of the expert; requires the expert to provide a declaration concerning any potential conflict;[40] requires the parties to provide information needed by the expert to complete the report; and gives the parties the right to make submissions on the report of the tribunal-appointed expert.

7   Manifest Lack of Legal Merit

The 2006 amendments to the ICSID Rules added the original rule on MLLM.[41] Experience with this rule demonstrated that there was some confusion as to whether it applied solely to 'legal' arguments, or whether it included substantive or jurisdictional objections.[42] AR 41[43] of the amended rules makes express that the MLLM motion may apply to 'the substance of the claim, the jurisdiction of the Centre, or the competence of the Tribunal'.

A party must file the MLLM motion no later than forty-five days after the Constitution of the tribunal, and the tribunal must render its decision or Award on the objection within sixty days after the later of the Constitution of the tribunal or the last submission on the objection. Tribunals often schedule an argument of an MLLM motion at the same time as the first session. AR 52(2)[44] on costs adds that a tribunal shall award a party prevailing on a motion for MLLM its reasonable costs unless there are special circumstances justifying a different allocation of costs. If a party fails in its MLLM application or has only partial success, the usual rules on costs would apply (AR 50-52). In particular, the tribunal could make an interim order on costs (AR 52(3)). To date, motions for MLLM have succeeded in relatively few cases,[45] and AR 52(2) should reinforce the high standard for success on a motion to dismiss for MLLM.

---

38. AF AR 47.
39. AF AR 49.
40. *See* https://icsid.worldbank.org/rules-regulations/declarations (last accessed 25 July 2022) for text of declaration of tribunal-appointed expert.
41. ICSID Rules 2006, AR 41(5).
42. *See* table of cases at https://icsid.worldbank.org/cases/content/tables-of-decisions/manifest-lack-of-legal-merit (last accessed 25 July 2022).
43. AF AR 51.
44. AF AR 62(2).
45. *See*, 'In Focus: Objections that a Claim Manifestly Lacks Legal Merit (ICSID Convention Arbitration Rules 41(5))' at https://icsid.worldbank.org/resources/publications/focus-objections-claim-manifestly-lacks-legal-merit-icsid-convention (last accessed 25 July 2022).

8   Bifurcation and Preliminary Objections

Bifurcation is common in investment arbitrations, often with respect to jurisdiction and merits, but potentially on other bases, for example bifurcating merits and damages. The amended rules address these topics in a series of individual rules. AR 42 relates to bifurcation other than with respect to a preliminary objection. It incorporates the well-known case law test for bifurcation: whether bifurcation would materially reduce the time and cost of the proceeding; dispose of all or a substantial portion of the proceeding; and does not depend on evidence that is intertwined with the merits to such a degree that bifurcation would be impractical.[46] AR 43[47] allows preliminary objections, while AR 44[48] addresses bifurcation of preliminary objections. The latter rule is similar to AR 42 and incorporates the same test for bifurcation. AR 45[49] governs preliminary objections that are not bifurcated.

9   Consolidation and Coordination

AR 46[50] is a new rule addressing consolidation and coordination of arbitrations. Both mechanisms require consent of the parties and should be considered if like cases are being addressed in parallel. Consolidation is a merger of two or more related cases and essentially makes them into a single case. It is only available where the like arbitrations are registered under the Convention and involve the same Contracting State. A consolidated case results in a single proceeding, a single set of costs, one tribunal and a single Award, and hence offers significant efficiency benefits. The terms of consolidation must be agreed to by the parties and approved by the Secretary-General to ensure that they are capable of being implemented.

Coordination aligns specific procedural aspects of two or more related cases but maintains the separate nature of each individual arbitration (including separate tribunals, costs, and Awards). Coordination encourages the consensual use of joint procedures where consolidation is not available, for example, to coordinate proceedings in a related ICSID Convention and UNCITRAL case, to appoint the same arbitrators, or to have joint hearings of a witness in common.

10   Provisional Measures

AR 47[51] addresses provisional measures other than security for costs (SFC), which is addressed separately in AR 53.[52]

---

46. AR 42; AF AR 52.
47. AF AR 53.
48. AF AR 54.
49. AF AR 55.
50. AF AR 56.
51. AF AR 57.
52. AF AR 63.

Like bifurcation and preliminary objections, it establishes a clear framework for the steps to be taken and includes the standard usually applied in cases: whether the measures are urgent and necessary, and what effect the imposition of such measures may have on each party.

11   Costs

Convention Article 61(2) gives tribunals broad discretion in awarding costs. Amended AR 50-53 elaborate on the determination of costs. AR 52 requires tribunals to consider, *inter alia*, the outcome of the proceeding or any part of it; the conduct of the parties, including whether they acted in an expeditious manner; the complexity of the issues; and the reasonableness of the costs claimed.[53] This provides greater guidance for the exercise of discretion in allocating costs prescribed by Article 61 of the Convention. The selection of these criteria gives tribunals the ability to calibrate a costs order not only with the outcome of the case but also with the manner in which it was litigated. It complements the objectives of the rules, including encouraging effective conduct of the case. Thus, a Tribunal might reduce a costs assessment to a successful party that caused an unwarranted delay in the proceeding.

Tribunals must give written reasons for costs and are expected to address these circumstances in the costs award.[54] Counsel would address these criteria in their submissions on costs and their conduct should be guided by them during the proceeding.

AR 52(3) expressly allows a tribunal to make an interim order on costs. It should be noted that under the Convention, an interim costs order is not enforceable until the final Award is released, which would include the interim costs order as part of its allocation of costs. Nonetheless, the ability to order interim costs related to a specific aspect of the case should reinforce the expectations of the parties and make costs a more effective incentive throughout the entire proceeding.

12   Security for Costs

AR 53[55] is a new rule on SFC. Previously, requests for SFC had been addressed as provisional measures. Either party may request SFC by motion to the tribunal. In deciding the request, the tribunal must consider the other party's ability and willingness to comply with an adverse decision on costs; the effect the SFC would have on that party's ability to pursue its claim or counterclaim; and the conduct of the parties. The evidence adduced to establish the need for SFC may include the existence of TPR. However, the mere existence of TPF is not sufficient to require SFC. Rather, the existence of TPF may be raised (and rebutted) as an indication as to whether a party could satisfy an adverse award of costs. The criteria concerning conduct of the parties

53. AF AR 62.
54. AR 52(4); AF AR 63.
55. AF AR 63.

might include consideration of whether both parties acted in good faith, for example, whether they had timely paid their share of requested advances, or whether they had failed to comply with prior costs orders.

The tribunal may specify any relevant terms in the order on SFC, including a lesser amount than requested, the type of security to be posted, and the timeline for posting security. If a party fails to comply with that order, the case may be suspended for ninety days. After ninety days, the tribunal may consult with the parties, and if apt, may discontinue the proceeding. The tribunal may also modify or revoke the SFC at any time. The allocation of the costs of obtaining SFC would be addressed under AR 52, as a cost of the proceeding.

13   Transparency

The amended rules increase transparency in response to concerns about consistency of Awards and decisions, and overall legitimacy of the ISDS process. As a result, the amendments emphasize publication of decisional documents and submissions. As required by Article 48(5) of the ICSID Convention, Awards and decisions on annulment require consent of the parties to publication, in full or as redacted by the parties. Consent to publish these documents is deemed if a party does not object to publication within sixty days after dispatch of the document.[56] This deemed consent addresses situations where both parties fail to indicate whether they agree to publication. Avoidance of a deemed consent is simple, requiring only that a party advise the Centre in writing of its position on consent to publication. If consent is refused, the Centre will prepare excerpts of the Award.[57] The parties will have an opportunity to comment on the proposed excerpts, which are made in the form of redactions to the Award.

As there are no Convention provisions regulating publication of orders and decisions, these will be governed solely by AR 63. Orders and decisions will be published within sixty days after they are issued, with any redactions agreed by the parties and jointly notified to the Secretary-General. Disputes as to redaction are decided by the tribunal.[58]

An additional amendment allows parties to publish their written submissions with redactions agreed to by the parties. Again, absent consent on redaction, the parties may have the tribunal decide disputed redactions.[59]

Parties are expected to redact all documents in good faith, and tribunals should ensure that the redaction process does not consume substantial time or resources, potentially through cost consequences in accordance with AR 52.

New AR 66 assists parties and the tribunal in the redaction process by defining 'confidential or protected information' for the purposes of the transparency provisions. This includes information protected from disclosure by the relevant instrument of

---

56. AR 62(3).
57. AR 62(4).
58. AF AR 73.
59. AR 64; AF AR 74.

consent or applicable law, in accordance with tribunal decisions, or by party agreement.

The rules on non-party participation have also been amended. AR 67 addressing non-disputing party (NDP) participation is similar to Rule 37(2) of the 2006 arbitration rules, except that it adds two criteria to the consideration of whether to allow an NDP submission: whether there is any affiliation between the NDP and a party; and whether anyone is providing the NDP with assistance to file the submission.[60] These additional criteria have been raised in some cases.[61]

AR 68 is a new rule allowing the non-disputing treaty party (NDTP) to make a submission on the interpretation of the treaty at issue and upon which consent is based.[62] This reflects the interest of the NDTP in correct interpretation of the treaty which it negotiated and is inspired by like provisions in the UNCITRAL Rules on Transparency[63] and some investment treaties. However, if a State wants to comment on a matter other than interpretation of the treaty on which jurisdiction in the case is based, it must apply under the usual rules for NDP participation and meet that test.

14 Expedited Arbitration

Chapter XII of the amended rules adds provisions on EA.[64] It is hoped that these rules will be used particularly in less complex treaty cases, in contract cases, and in cases involving small or medium-sized entities.

Parties may consent to expedite an arbitration at any time by jointly notifying the Secretary-General of their intent to do so.[65] Parties will derive maximum benefit from the expedited rules by expediting as early as possible in the process. Essentially, the EA procedures provide reduced time frames for each step (half of the time found in the regular rules) and require parties to proceed on all issues at once rather than bifurcating for interlocutory motions. The expedited rules assume a sole arbitrator unless the parties want a three-person panel,[66] and the tribunal member(s) in an expedited case must confirm they are able to meet the expedited time frames.[67] Parties may opt out of an EA at any time by jointly notifying the Secretary-General of their intent to do so.[68]

---

60. AR 67(2); AF AR 77(2).
61. *See* table of NDP decisions at https://icsid.worldbank.org/cases/content/tables-of-decisions/ndp (last accessed 25 July 2022).
62. AR 68; AF AR 78.
63. *See, UNCITRAL Rules on Transparency in Treaty-based Investor-State Arbitration,* Article 5, at https://uncitral.un.org/en/texts/arbitration/contractualtexts/transparency (last accessed 25 July 2022).
64. AR 75-86; AF AR 79-88.
65. AR 75; AF AR 79.
66. AR 76.
67. AR 77-79.
68. AR 86.

VII   CONCILIATION RULES

The ICSID Rules have always offered conciliation of disputes, however in practice few parties used the conciliation mechanism (eleven cases as of 30 June 2022). At the same time, such alternate dispute resolution (ADR) techniques have been very successful in the commercial context. As a result, the overall approach to amendment of the CR in the ICSID 2022 Rules was to update these to offer the parties greater flexibility and incorporate more ADR techniques into ICSID conciliation. It is hoped that this will encourage parties to resort to these rules more frequently and to include conciliation clauses in contracts and treaties.

The updated CR make information or documents generated in the process confidential unless parties agree otherwise; the AFR require the publication of the information; the documents are independently available; or disclosure is required by law.[69] As with mediation, parties cannot rely on views expressed during conciliation or in the Conciliation Report in other proceedings unless they agree otherwise.[70] The Conciliation Commission is tasked with clarifying the issues in dispute and assisting the parties to reach a mutually acceptable resolution. In so doing, it may recommend specific terms of settlement or that parties refrain from actions that might aggravate the dispute. It may also request explanations from the parties, communicate with the parties jointly or separately, and make site visits.[71]

The updated CR include a requirement to file a notice of TPR[72] and revised rules on disqualification,[73] similar to the equivalent rules in the AR.

VIII   ADDITIONAL FACILITY RULES

The Additional Facility Rules (AF Rules) have been substantially broadened in the 2022 amendments. As a result, they will effectively be available whenever the Convention is not available, i.e., where only one of the disputing parties is a Contracting Party or a national of a Contracting Party, or where both disputing parties are not affiliated with an ICSID Contracting State.[74] The Additional Facility is also specifically made available for cases in which a regional economic integration organization (REIO)[75] is claimant or respondent. This reflects recent treaties signed by REIOs (such as the EU) in their own name, consenting to the REIO making or responding to claims.

The former practice of requiring permission to access the Additional Facility has been deleted. Instead, parties make a request to institute arbitration proceedings under AF AR 2, following the process in AF AR 2-9. This is similar to the process for Convention arbitration, except that the relevant threshold for registration is that the request is not manifestly outside the scope of Article 2(1) of the AF Rules, namely that

---

69. CR 9; AF CR 17.
70. CR 10; AF CR 18.
71. CR 24; AF CR 32.
72. CR 12; AF CR 21.
73. CR 19-20; AF CR 27-28.
74. AF Rules 2-3.
75. Defined in AFR 1(4).

there is a 'legal dispute(s) arising out of an investment between a State or an REIO on the one hand, and a national of another State on the other hand, which the parties consent in writing to submit to the Centre ...'.[76] An AF conciliation is commenced by making a request to institute conciliation proceedings under AF CR 2-9.

The procedural rules for the AF AR mirror those for the AR, with several exceptions. Notably:

- If the tribunal has not been constituted within 90 days after registration, either party may request that the Secretary-General appoint the arbitrator(s) who have not yet been appointed.[77] Such arbitrators may, but need not, be appointed from the ICSID Panel of Arbitrators.
- The parties can agree to replace an arbitrator at any time prior to the Constitution of a tribunal.[78]
- The standard for a challenge under AF AR 30 is that 'circumstances exist that give rise to justifiable doubts as to the qualities required of the arbitrator'. These qualities are listed in AF AR 22. In addition, the Secretary-General shall take the decision on the proposal for disqualification.[79] Alternatively, the other party can agree to the proposal for disqualification, in which case the arbitrator must resign.[80]
- AF AR 41 provides for a seat of arbitration as the Convention does not apply to this aspect of the proceeding. The seat shall be agreed upon by the parties or, absent agreement, decided by the tribunal having regard to the circumstances of the case.
- If the parties agree, the Award does not need to be reasoned.[81]
- As for decisions and orders, Awards rendered under the AF AR shall be published within sixty days after issuance, with redactions agreed to by the parties and jointly notified to the Secretary-General.[82]

The procedural rules for AF CR mirror those for the CR.

IX   FACT-FINDING RULES

ICSID has had FFR in the Additional Facility since 1978, but parties have not used these to date. In the amendment consultations, there was discussion as to whether to continue offering fact-finding given its lack of use. Ultimately it was decided to update the FFR and offer them as stand-alone rules, available broadly.

There are few formal requisites to a request for fact-finding if the parties wish to invoke the procedure. Fact-finding proceedings may be initiated jointly by parties

---

76. AF Rules 2(1); AF AR 7(1).
77. AF AR 26.
78. AF AR 28.
79. AF AR 31(1).
80. AF AR 30(3).
81. AF AR 70(1)(i).
82. AF AR 73.

relating to an investment, involving a State or an REIO, and which the parties consent to in writing.[83] There can be a sole or uneven number of persons on the fact-finding Committee.[84] The process is expedited, with parties filing a short, written statement (maximum fifty pages) within fifteen days after the Constitution of the Committee, and a first session taking place within thirty days after the Constitution of the Committee.[85] The Committee conducts its process in accordance with a protocol established with the parties, who may decide if the Committee's report will be binding or if the Committee should make recommendations in its report.[86]

As with mediation and conciliation, information and documents generated in a fact-finding shall be confidential unless the parties agree otherwise; the information is independently available; or disclosure is required by law.[87] If successful, the process concludes with a report including a recommendation if requested by the parties and stating the facts established.[88]

X   MEDIATION RULES

Mediation in ISDS is increasingly a priority for States and investors. Numerous recent investment treaties include mandatory or recommended mediation clauses.[89] The MR offer a set of rules tailored to the mediation of investment disputes. As with the FFR, the threshold to commence a mediation is relatively simple: the Centre is authorized to administer mediations involving a State or REIO that relate to investment, provided the parties have given their written consent.[90]

Mediation may be brought based on consent to mediate in a contract, treaty or law.[91] However, if the instrument of consent contains no such provision, a party may make an offer to mediate through the Centre, which is forwarded to the opposite party. If accepted, the parties will be considered to have agreed to mediate under the MR.[92]

Mediation may be commenced at any time the parties agree it would be useful. For example, parties might agree to mediate during the consultation or cooling-off period in a treaty. Mediation can be done as a stand-alone process, but it is also available in parallel with arbitration, conciliation, or fact-finding.

The costs of the mediators and the Centre are borne equally by the parties.[93] The process is a confidential one in which information and documents generated in the

---

83. FFR 2; *see* FFR 3-7 concerning filing of FF Request.
84. FFR 9-11.
85. FFR 12.
86. FFR 12.
87. FFR 16-17.
88. FFR 20-21.
89. *See*, ICSID's overview on mediation provisions in investment treaties, available at https://icsid .worldbank.org/sites/default/files/publications/Overview_Mediation_in_Treaties.pdf (last accessed 25 July 2022).
90. MR 2, 3.
91. MR 5.
92. MR 6.
93. MR 9. The schedule of fees sets the lodging fee for mediation and fact-finding at USD 1,000, and the parties pay an administrative charge of USD 200 per hour if staff services dedicated to mediation or fact-finding.

mediation may not be used outside of the mediation unless parties agree; they are independently available; or disclosure is required by law. The fact that the parties are mediating may also not be disclosed, and parties may not rely on information obtained in the mediation in other proceedings.[94] These protections put a premium on confidentiality to encourage parties to resolve the dispute through mediation.

The parties may select a sole mediator or two co-mediators, appointed by agreement or with the assistance of ICSID's Secretary-General.[95] The only mandatory qualification for mediators is that they be independent and impartial; however, parties may agree on further case-specific qualifications if useful.[96] The role of the mediator is to assist the parties in reaching a mutually agreeable resolution of all or part of the dispute; the mediator cannot impose a resolution and may not make settlement recommendations without the consent of the parties.[97]

The process begins with the parties filing a brief initial statement outlining the dispute, the relevant issues, and any views on procedure.[98] A first session is convened in which the mediator works out a mediation protocol with the parties, addressing procedural matters such as the participation of other persons, the schedule of meetings, and the treatment of information obtained in the mediation process. At the first session, each party must identify a person authorized to settle on its behalf and describe the process that would be followed to implement a settlement agreement.[99] The mediator may meet and communicate with the parties jointly or separately throughout the process.[100]

The mediation ends with a notice of termination, which is issued once the parties have reached a settlement; if the parties agree to terminate the mediation; if a party withdraws from the process; if the mediator determines there is no likelihood of resolution through mediation; or if the parties fail to appoint a mediator within 120 days.[101] If the parties do reach a mediated settlement, it could be enforced pursuant to the Singapore Convention on Mediation, as the MR are aligned with the requirements of that Convention. Alternatively, if the mediated resolution is a corollary to an ongoing arbitration, the resulting agreement could be recorded by the tribunal in the form of an Award and benefit from the ICSID Convention enforcement regime.[102]

XI   CONCLUSION

The ICSID Rules 2022 represent a substantial step forward in ISDS procedures. As they increasingly are used by parties, they should offer significant advantages in the litigation of investment disputes.

---

94. MR 10-11.
95. MR 13.
96. MR 12.
97. MR 17, 21.
98. MR 19.
99. MR 20(4).
100. MR 19- 20.
101. MR 22.
102. AR 55(2).

CHAPTER 23

'State of the World': New Developments and Reform in International Investment Arbitration – The UNCITRAL ISDS Reform

Anna Joubin-Bret & David Nikolaus Probst[*]

TABLE OF CONTENTS

I   INTRODUCTION

The United Nations Commission on International Trade Law ('UNCITRAL' or 'Commission') is currently undertaking comprehensive deliberations on a reform of the current system for investor-State dispute settlement (ISDS).

---

[*] Anna Joubin-Bret is the Secretary of the United Nations Commission on International Trade Law (UNCITRAL) and Director of the International Trade Law Division of the Office of Legal Affairs of the United Nations; David Probst is a Legal Officer at the UNCITRAL Secretariat; the views expressed in this article are those of the authors and do not necessarily represent those of the Organization.

333

The ISDS system was created with the aim of enhancing confidence in the stability of the investment environment primarily in developing countries.[1] Over the last decades, a growing number of international investment agreements (IIAs) providing for ISDS has been concluded by States, particularly in the 1990s. More than 3,000 IIAs have been concluded, of which over 2,500 are currently in force.[2] In parallel with the increase in the global web of treaties, there has been a growing number of ISDS cases brought by foreign investors against States. According to information collected by the United Nations Conference on Trade and Development (UNCTAD), the number of known treaty-based ISDS cases passed the 1,000 mark in 2020.[3] Many more cases are brought under contracts and investment laws.

While based on a treaty network of over 3,000 IIAs, including quite different dispute settlement provisions, referring to the ICSID Convention, UNCITRAL Rules, ICC arbitration, sometimes other fora, and having resulted in over 1,000 decisions by ad hoc tribunals, the paper will refer to an ISDS system and to the reform thereof, acknowledging that it is indeed atomized and multifaceted, but has nevertheless the characteristics of an organized system.[4]

Given the increase in the number of ISDS cases and the fact that cases have not only involved developing countries but also developed countries, initially thought to be net capital exporters, IIAs and more specifically the ISDS system have come under

---

1. *See also* 'Possible reform of investor-State dispute settlement (ISDS), Note by the Secretariat', UNCITRAL, Working Group III, 34th Session (Vienna, 27 November-1 December 2017), UN Doc. A/CN.9/WG.III/WP.142 (18 September 2017) para. 6: 'Investment treaties [...] provide substantive guarantees to foreign investors and their investments in the form of enforceable obligations placed upon States, as States undertake to respect certain standards of investment protection (such as fair and equitable treatment, protection from expropriation, and non-discrimination). Although the specific terms vary, investment treaties follow a similar structure and contain a number of core principles. These broad similarities among investment treaties make it possible to speak of a "regime" of international investment protection.'
2. 'International Investment Agreements Navigator' (United Nations Conference on Trade and Development, Investment Policy Hub), https://investmentpolicy.unctad.org/international-investment-agreements (last accessed 4 August 2022).
3. 'Investor-State Dispute Settlement Cases pass the 1,000 Mark: Cases and Outcomes in 2019', UNCTAD IIA issues note, issue 2 (July 2020), https://unctad.org/en/PublicationsLibrary/diaepcbinf2020d6.pdf (last accessed 2 December 2020); the number had increased to 1,190 known treaty-based ISDS cases by 31 December 2021, *see* Investment Dispute Settlement Navigator, https://investmentpolicy.unctad.org/investment-dispute-settlement (last accessed 1 May 2022).
4. The current ISDS system is based on IIAs concluded starting in the early 1960s between home States and host States of investors. The two main pillars of the system are the substantive provisions of protection and the dispute settlement system. IIAs provide for substantive protection through provisions of Fair and Equitable Treatment, Full Protection and Security, protection against Expropriation, Freedom of Transfer of Funds, National Treatment and Most-Favoured Nations Treatment. They are enforced through recourse to ad hoc arbitrations which allow a foreign national to bring a claim directly against a sovereign State for violations of its treaty obligations. Similar protections are also provided under Investment Laws and Investment Agreements concluded between the State and individual investors. The ISDS system aims at the 'de-politicization' of investment disputes and the removal of the risk of such disputes escalating into inter-State conflicts should the home State of the investor exercise diplomatic protection; *see* 'Possible future work in the field of dispute settlement: Reforms of investor-State dispute settlement (ISDS), Note by the Secretariat', UNCITRAL, 50th Session (Vienna, 3-21 July 2017) UN Doc. A/CN.9/917 (20 April 2017), paras 9-13.

public scrutiny. Strong and growing criticism in particular relating to the use of international arbitration to settle claims concerning public measures and involving payment of compensation to foreign investors with public funds, has emerged in all regions. A first wave of criticism against ISDS had emerged in Latin America based on the perception of bias against States and given rise to Venezuela, Bolivia and Ecuador taking measures to distance themselves from the ISDS system.[5] Criticism in Europe crystallized around the negotiation of the Transatlantic Trade and Investment Partnership Agreement (TTIP) and has focused on the legitimacy of the system itself, on the lack of consistency of awards giving rise to uncertainty and on the impact on the State's right to regulate for public purpose. Furthermore, the methods to appoint arbitrators and particularly the so-called double hatting whereby arbitrators can also act as counsel in other cases were highlighted to show the deficiencies of the system. High-profile cases, such as *Phillip Morris v. Australia*[6] and *Phillip Morris v. Uruguay*,[7] have also put the topic on a political level in other regions. More generally, criticisms have focused on methods of appointing arbitrators and the impact of such methods on arbitrators' independence and impartiality, the lack of coherence of a system based on decisions made by tribunals constituted to hear a specific case (also referred to as 'ad hoc' tribunals), and the lack of corrective mechanisms (i.e., the lack of appropriate control or review mechanisms), the length and costs of the proceedings and the lack of transparency.[8] Reforming ISDS has become in the last decade a recurrent topic in international conferences and academic work.[9]

---

5. Bolivia denounced the ICSID Convention in 2007 (see news release, *Denunciation of ICSID Convention* (16 May 2007), available from https://icsid.worldbank.org/news-and-events/news-releases/denunciation-icsid-convention (last accessed 2 December 2020)); Ecuador denounced the ICSID Convention in 2010 (*see* news release, *Denunciation of the ICSID Convention by Ecuador* (9 July 2009), available from https://icsid.worldbank.org/news-and-events/news-releases/denunciation-icsid-convention-ecuador (last accessed 2 December 2020)); Venezuela denounced the ICSID Convention in 2012 (*see* news release, *Venezuela Submits a Notice under Article 71 of the ICSID Convention* (26 January 2012), available from https://icsid.worldbank.org/news-and-events/news-releases/venezuela-submits-notice-under-article-71-icsid-convention (last accessed 2 December 2020)).

6. *Philip Morris Asia Limited v. The Commonwealth of Australia* (PCA Case No. 2012-12), *see* UNCTAD Investment Dispute Settlement Navigator, https://investmentpolicy.unctad.org/investment-dispute-settlement/cases/421/philip-morris-v-australia (last accessed 2 December 2020).

7. *Philip Morris Brand Sàrl (Switzerland), Philip Morris Products S.A. (Switzerland) and Abal Hermanos S.A. (Uruguay) v. Oriental Republic of Uruguay* (ICSID Case No. ARB/10/7), *see* UNCTAD Investment Dispute Settlement Navigator, https://investmentpolicy.unctad.org/investment-dispute-settlement/cases/368/philip-morris-v-uruguay (last accessed 2 December 2020).

8. *See* Gabrielle Kaufmann-Kohler and Michele Potestà (CIDS – Geneva Centre for International Dispute Settlement), 'Can the Mauritius Convention serve as a model for the reform of investor-State arbitration in connection with the introduction of a permanent investment tribunal or an appeal mechanism? Analysis and roadmap' (3 June 2016), available from https://uncitral.un.org/sites/uncitral.un.org/files/media-documents/uncitral/en/cids_research_paper_mauritius.pdf, paras 18-23; *see also* Anna Joubin-Bret and Jean E. Kalicki, 'Introduction', in Anna Joubin-Bret and Jean E. Kalicki, eds, *Reshaping the Investor-State Dispute Settlement System*, (Brill | Nijhoff 2015), pp. 1-17.

9. *See*, for example, *Evolution and Adaption, The Future of International Arbitration*, ICCA Congress Series no. 20 (2018); Anna Joubin-Bret and Jean E. Kalicki, eds, *Reshaping the Investor-State Dispute Settlement System* (Brill | Nijhoff 2015).

Against this background, UNCITRAL has entrusted its Working Group III in July 2017 with a broad mandate to work on the possible reform of ISDS. In July 2019, the Working Group completed the first two phases of its mandate, namely the identification of concerns regarding the current ISDS system and the decision that reform is desirable to address these concerns. It started in October 2019 to undertake the development of concrete reform options as part of the last phase (phase three) of its mandate.

The Working Group sessions attracted broad participation by delegates representing States as well as intergovernmental and non-governmental organizations.[10] Submissions by UNCITRAL members and observers and working papers by the Secretariat can be found in all six official languages of the United Nations (UN) on the UNCITRAL website, among additional resources and information on the reform process.[11]

This contribution reports on an ongoing reform process, which continues to make progress. For the latest updates on UNCITRAL's activities and the current status of the reform discussion, please visit the UNCITRAL Working Group III web page (https://uncitral.un.org/en/working_groups/3/investor-state) and follow our posts on Twitter (@annajoubinbret) and LinkedIn (https://www.linkedin.com/company/uncitral/).

This chapter will of course refer to the reports of UNCITRAL and of its Working Group III sessions. It will therefore use a similar indirect style, particularly not attributing positions or contributions to individual delegations or groups of States. It will refer to comments and recommendations made by the Working Group by consensus and reflected in its reports that are subsequently submitted to the Commission.

II   WHY UNCITRAL

In July 2017, UNCITRAL entrusted its Working Group III with the possible reform of the ISDS system against the background of its global reach and its experience with the negotiation of legal instruments in the field of international arbitration. It was the prevailing view that UNCITRAL provides an appropriate multilateral forum to discuss relevant issues in an inclusive and transparent manner, where the interests of not only States but also of other stakeholders could be considered. It was recalled that UNCITRAL has successfully undertaken a first step towards reform of ISDS with the preparation of standards on transparency.[12]

Previously, multilateral and regional attempts at reforming IIAs and ISDS had already been envisaged in some fora. Thus, negotiations of a multilateral investment

---

10. 'UNCITRAL Working Group on investor-State dispute settlement (ISDS) continues work on reforms', Press Release, UNIS Vienna, United Nations Information Service (24 January 2020), available at https://unis.unvienna.org/unis/en/pressrels/2020/unisl289.html (last accessed 2 December 2020).
11. *See* UNCITRAL Working Group III web page at (https://uncitral.un.org/en/working_groups/3 /investor-state).
12. 'Report of the United Nations Commission on International Trade Law, Fiftieth session (3-21 July 2017)' General Assembly, 72nd Session, UN Doc. A/72/17, para. 258.

agreement under the umbrella of the Organisation for Economic Co-operation and Development (OECD) were initiated in 1995 but discontinued after three years.[13] A proposal by the Secretariat of the International Centre for Settlement of Investment Disputes (ICSID) in 2004 to establish an appellate mechanism to review awards had not led to concrete action.[14] A number of States have also addressed the deficiencies of ISDS provisions directly in their investment treaties beginning with the United States model bilateral investment treaty (BIT) revision in 2012.[15] ISDS reform on the level of IIAs is supported and monitored by UNCTAD, providing a comprehensive analysis of key issues and developing tools to support the formulation of more balanced international investment policies.

UNCITRAL has developed several successful instruments in the field of international arbitration.[16] In 1976, UNCITRAL adopted the UNCITRAL Arbitration Rules. The General Assembly, when adopting its resolution on the Rules expressed its conviction 'that the establishment of rules for ad hoc arbitration that are acceptable in countries with different legal, social and economic systems would significantly contribute to the development of harmonious international economic relations'.[17] The UNCITRAL Arbitration Rules are used for the settlement of a broad range of disputes, including disputes between private commercial parties, investor-State disputes and State-to-State disputes, disputes administered by arbitral institutions as well as in ad hoc proceedings.

In 1985, UNCITRAL adopted the Model Law on International Commercial Arbitration ('Model Arbitration Law'), which reflects worldwide consensus on key aspects of international arbitration practice accepted by States of all regions and the different legal or economic systems of the world. The Model Arbitration Law aims at contributing to the establishment of a 'unified legal framework for the fair and efficient settlement of disputes arising in international commercial relations' together with the New York Convention on the Recognition and Enforcement of Foreign Arbitral Awards ('New York Convention') and the UNCITRAL Arbitration Rules.[18] As of this writing,

---

13. *See* 'Multilateral Agreement on Investment', Organisation for Economic Co-operation and Development, http://www.oecd.org/investment/internationalinvestmentagreements/multila teralagreementoninvestment.htm (last accessed 2 December 2020).

14. *See* 'Possible Improvements of the Framework for ICSID Arbitration', ICSID Discussion Paper (22 October 2004), available at https://icsid.worldbank.org/en/Documents/resources/Possible %20Improvements%20of%20the%20Framework%20of%20ICSID%20Arbitration.pdf (last accessed 2 December 2020).

15. Kathryn Gordon and Joachim Pohl, 'Investment Treaties over Time: Treaty Practice and Interpretation in a Changing World', OECD Working Papers on International Investment (2015/02) OECD Publishing, available from http://dx.doi.org/10.1787/5js7rhd8sq7h-en (last accessed 2 December 2020).

16. 'Status of conventions and model laws, Note by the Secretariat', UNCITRAL, 53rd Session (New York, 6-17 July 2020) UN Doc. A/CN.9/1020 (1 April 2020).

17. 'Arbitration Rules of the United Nations Commission on International Trade Law', General Assembly, 31st Session, UN Doc. A/RES/31/98 (15 December 1976).

18. General Assembly Resolution 40/72, 'Model Law on International Commercial Arbitration of the United Nations Commission on International Trade Law', 40th Session (11 December 1985) UN Doc. A/RES/40/72.

legislation based on the Model Law has been adopted in 85 States in a total of 118 jurisdictions.

The promotion of the New York Convention is an integral part of the work programme of UNCITRAL. With the accession of Turkmenistan in 2022, the New York Convention has 170 State parties as of this writing.[19]

One of the main characteristics of these three instruments is that they are generic and can be applied to a wide range of disputes. This generic approach was preserved during the revision of the UNCITRAL Arbitration Rules in 2010.[20] In parallel, it was decided, upon a request in a State submission, that immediately after the revision of the UNCITRAL Arbitration Rules, work should be undertaken on the topic of transparency in treaty-based investor-State arbitration.[21]

In the following years, UNCITRAL developed its first instrument applicable specifically to ISDS, the Rules on Transparency in Treaty-based Investor-State Arbitration (2014) (Rules on Transparency).[22] These rules, which came into effect on 1 April 2014, address the need 'to take account of the public interest involved in such [ISDS] arbitrations'.[23] The rules apply to ISDS proceedings initiated under the UNCITRAL Arbitration Rules pursuant to an IIA concluded on or after 1 April 2014 unless the parties to the agreement have agreed otherwise. The rules also apply if the IIA was concluded before 1 April 2014 if its parties have agreed to their application.

UNCITRAL further prepared a convention designed to facilitate the application of the Transparency Rules to the 3,000 or more investment treaties concluded before its entry into force, the United Nations Convention on Transparency in Treaty-based Investor-State Arbitration (New York, 2014) (the 'Mauritius Convention on Transparency'). In essence, the Mauritius Convention on Transparency introduces the substantive transparency standards embodied in the Transparency Rules into the fragmented treaty-by-treaty regime by way of a single multilateral instrument.

After the adoption of these texts, a question was raised at the annual session of UNCITRAL in 2015 on whether the Mauritius Convention on Transparency could provide a useful model for possible further reforms in the field of ISDS. During the discussions, it was noted that the then-current circumstances posed a number of challenges to ISDS and proposals for reforms had been formulated by a number of

---

19. *See* 'Status: Convention on the Recognition and Enforcement of Foreign Arbitral Awards (New York, 1958) (the "New York Convention")', UNCITRAL web page, https://uncitral.un.org/en/texts/arbitration/conventions/foreign_arbitral_awards/status2 (last accessed 4 December 2020).
20. 'Report of the United Nations Commission on International Trade Law' 41st Session (16 June-3 July 2008) General Assembly, 63rd Session, Supplement No. 17, UN Doc. A/63/17, paras 313, 314.
21. *Ibid.*, para. 314.
22. UNCITRAL Rules on Transparency in Treaty-based Investor-State Arbitration (effective date: 1 April 2014), text and additional resources available on the UNCITRAL web page at https://uncitral.un.org/en/texts/arbitration/contractualtexts/transparency (last accessed 4 December 2020).
23. 'Report of the United Nations Commission on International Trade Law', 46th Session (8-26 July 2013) General Assembly, 68th Session, UN Doc. A/68/17, Annex I, at C.

organizations.[24] A year later in 2016, a research paper elaborated by the Geneva Center for International Dispute Settlement (CIDS) presented to UNCITRAL formed the basis for further consultations on whether to undertake work on ISDS reform.[25] The report proposed to follow an approach similar to the one pursued in respect of the Transparency Rules and the Mauritius Convention on Transparency, where a multilateral treaty ensures the application of the 'substantive' transparency rules to existing IIAs and that would thereby allow reform of a complex and atomized system by way of a single multilateral instrument.

III   SCOPE OF THE MANDATE

The Commission entrusted Working Group III with a broad mandate to work on the possible reform of ISDS. It was emphasized that the Working Group would, in line with the UNCITRAL process, ensure that the deliberations would include the widest possible breadth of available expertise from all stakeholders and would be Government-led, with high-level input from all Governments, consensus-based and fully transparent.[26]

The Commission had noted that ISDS involves a number of policy issues and highlighted that Governments should have a leading role in the reform process and

---

24. 'Report of the United Nations Commission on International Trade Law', 48th Session (29 June-16 July 2015) General Assembly, 70th Session, UN Doc. A/70/17, para. 268; *see also* 'Settlement of commercial disputes: presentation of a research paper on the Mauritius Convention on Transparency in Treaty-based Investor-State Arbitration as a possible model for further reforms of investor-State dispute settlement, Note by the Secretariat' UNCITRAL, 49th Session (New York, 27 June-15 July 2016) UN Doc. A/CVN/9/890 (24 May 2016).
25. Gabrielle Kaufmann-Kohler and Michele Potestà (CIDS – Geneva Centre for International Dispute Settlement), 'Can the Mauritius Convention serve as a model for the reform of investor-State arbitration in connection with the introduction of a permanent investment tribunal or an appeal mechanism? Analysis and roadmap' (3 June 2016), available from https://uncitral.un.org/sites/uncitral.un.org/files/media-documents/uncitral/en/cids_resear ch_paper_mauritius.pdf, pp. 93, 94.
26. *See* wording of the mandate in 'Report of the United Nations Commission on International Trade Law', 50th Session (3-21 July 2017) General Assembly, 72nd Session Supplement No. 17, UN Doc. A/72/17, para. 264: 'The Commission entrusted Working Group III with a broad mandate to work on the possible reform of investor-State dispute settlement. In line with the UNCITRAL process, Working Group III would, in discharging that mandate, ensure that the deliberations, while benefiting from the widest possible breadth of available expertise from all stakeholders, would be Government-led, with high-level input from all Governments, consensus-based and fully transparent. The Working Group would proceed to: (a) first, identify and consider concerns regarding investor-State dispute settlement; (b) second, consider whether reform was desirable in the light of any identified concerns; and (c) third, if the Working Group were to conclude that reform was desirable, develop any relevant solutions to be recommended to the Commission. The Commission agreed that broad discretion should be left to the Working Group in discharging its mandate, and that any solutions devised would be designed taking into account the ongoing work of relevant international organizations and with a view to allowing each State the choice of whether and to what extent it wished to adopt the relevant solution(s).'

should be represented by officials with adequate expertise and experience in negotiating investment treaties or investment chapters in free trade agreements and with exposure to claims related to ISDS.[27]

The mandate is structured in three phases: (a) first, identification and consideration of concerns regarding ISDS; (b) second, consideration of whether reform is desirable in the light of any identified concerns; and (c) third, if the Working Group were to conclude that reform is desirable, development of any relevant solutions to be recommended to the Commission.[28]

It was reiterated that the mandate of the Working Group is to work on the possible reform of ISDS rather than reform of substantive standards in IIAs and that the focus of its work should be on the procedural aspects of ISDS, though taking due note of the interaction with underlying substantive standards.[29]

It was also recalled that legislative work by UNCITRAL and its working groups is generally based on consensus,[30] and that, in accordance with UNCITRAL practice, consensus does not require unanimity, but is instead based on a widely prevailing majority and the absence of a formal objection that would trigger a request for a vote. While the adoption of an instrument or a text by consensus does not give it any binding nature and States remain free to decide whether they want to adopt or apply it, it was stated that efforts should be made to consider all possible options so as to achieve the broadest consensus.[31]

IV   PROCEDURAL BACKGROUND

As of August 2022, Working Group III has held ten sessions on the ISDS reform.[32] The Commission expressed its satisfaction with the progress made by the Working Group through a constructive, inclusive and transparent process.[33] The ISDS reform process presents a wide range of challenges and difficulties with regard to the complexity of the topics on the agenda, the number of interested States and stakeholders and the amount of topics and reform options for consideration. Nevertheless, in the five years since it was given its mandate, Working Group III has been able to continuously move the discussions forward, respecting the guiding principles of a constructive, inclusive and transparent process.

---

27. 'Report of the United Nations Commission on International Trade Law', 50th Session (3-21 July 2017) General Assembly, 72nd Session Supplement No. 17, UN Doc. A/72/17 (henceforth 'Commission Report 72'), para. 250.
28. *Ibid.*, para. 264.
29. 'Report of Working Group III (Investor-State Dispute Settlement Reform) on the work of its thirty-seventh session' (New York, 1-5 April 2019) UNCITRAL 52nd Session (Vienna, 8-26 July 2019), UN Doc. A/CN.9/970 (henceforth 'WGIII Report 970') para. 27.
30. Commission Report 72, para. 259.
31. *Ibid.*
32. *See* UNCITRAL Working Group III web page at (https://uncitral.un.org/en/working_groups/3/investor-state) (last accessed 4 December 2020).
33. *See* 'Report of the United Nations Commission on International Trade Law', 53rd Session (6-17 July 2020 and 14-18 September 2020) General Assembly, 75th Session, UN Doc. A/75/17 (29 September 2020), Part two, para. 36.

1 A Government-Led and Inclusive Process

The Working Group sessions have benefitted from significant and increasing participation by States, including developing and least-developed countries. The Working Group session in January 2020 in Vienna was attended by more than 400 delegates representing 106 States, and 66 international organizations and non-governmental organizations.[34] The UNCITRAL Secretariat has received over 40 submissions from about 50 Governments.[35]

Considerable efforts are being made to reach out to all regions and countries to raise awareness and build capacity within delegations to effectively participate in the ISDS reform process. Five inter-sessional meetings were organized by the Governments of the Republic of Korea, the Dominican Republic, Guinea and Hong Kong SAR, China.[36]

Prior to Working Group sessions, the Columbia Center on Sustainable Investment (CCSI) and the Deutsche Gesellschaft für Internationale Zusammenarbeit (GIZ), with the assistance of the UNCITRAL Secretariat, regularly conduct training and briefing sessions on ISDS topics being discussed in the Working Group sessions in order to allow delegations to participate fully and effectively in the deliberations. The European Union, France, Germany, and Switzerland have provided financial support to facilitate participation by delegations from developing and least-developed countries.

2 Expertise from All Stakeholders

The deliberations of the Working Group are based on a broad range of available expertise from different stakeholders. An Academic Forum on ISDS and a Practitioners' Group have been set up early in the process as informal groups aimed at making constructive contributions to the ongoing discussions by providing information from their research and experience.[37]

---

34. *See* 'Report of Working Group III (Investor-State Dispute Settlement Reform) on the work of its resumed thirty-eighth session' (Vienna, 20-24 January 2020) UNCITRAL, 54th Session, UN Doc. A/CN.9/1004/Add.1 (28 January 2020) (henceforth 'WGIII Report 1004/Add.1') p. 3; *see also* 'UNCITRAL Working Group on investor-State dispute settlement (ISDS) continues work on reforms', Press Release, UNIS Vienna, United Nations Information Service (24 January 2020), available at https://unis.unvienna.org/unis/en/pressrels/2020/unisl289.html (last accessed 2 December 2020).
35. Submissions by States are published on the UNCITRAL Working Group III web page at https://uncitral.un.org/en/working_groups/3/investor-state (last accessed 2 December 2020).
36. First Inter-sessional Regional Meeting 10-12 September 2018, Incheon, Republic of Korea; Second Inter-sessional Regional Meeting, 13-14 February 2019, Santo Domingo, Dominican Republic; Third Inter-sessional Regional Meeting, 26 September 2019, Conakry, Guinea; Fourth Inter-sessional Meeting, 2-3 September 2021, hosted by the Republic of Korea; Fifth Inter-sessional Meeting on the Use of Mediation in ISDS, hosted by Hong Kong SAR, China.
37. *See* 'Report of the United Nations Commission on International Trade Law, 51st Session (25 June-13 July 2018) General Assembly 73rd Session, UN Doc. A/73/17 (31 July 2018), para. 144; *see also* 'Report of Working Group III (Investor-State Dispute Settlement Reform) on the work of its thirty-sixth session (Vienna, 29 October-2 November 2018)' UNCITRAL, 52nd Sess., UN Doc.

Also, more than sixty-six international intergovernmental organizations and non-governmental organizations with a variety of industry and policy expertise have participated in the Working Group sessions as observers and have organized numerous side events during as well as in-between the Working Group sessions.[38]

The UNCITRAL Secretariat has prepared working papers on identified issues and reform options in preparation for the Working Group sessions with reference to a broad range of published information on the topics.[39] Further, the Secretariat has organized informal webinars, in which state representatives and leading experts shed light on reform topics with the aim to brainstorm the reform options on the agenda and to advance the discussions.[40]

3   Transparency

The reform process is being conducted in a fully transparent manner. Each step of the deliberations is documented in the Working Group and Commission reports. The reports as well as the notes by the Secretariat and submissions by States are publicly available on the UNCITRAL web page in all six UN languages.[41] Moreover, audio recordings of the sessions are available on the UNCITRAL web page.[42]

4   Working Group III Progress During the COVID-19 Pandemic

The consideration of the reform options on the agenda continued during the lockdowns and travel restrictions in response to the COVID-19 pandemic. In order to maintain the momentum of the reform discussion and to ensure that the process remains inclusive and transparent, the Secretariat has put together a programme of virtual events and other inter-sessional activities open to all delegations and stakeholders.

Starting in March 2020, informal briefings provided delegations with information on the status of the preparatory work on the various reform options and a series of webinars was held in cooperation with the Academic Forum on ISDS, including the

---

A/CN.9/964 (6 November 2018) (henceforth 'WGIII Report 964') para. 15; Concept papers of the Academic Forum on ISDS can be accessed on the following dedicated web page: https://www .jus.uio.no/pluricourts/english/projects/leginvest/academic-forum/ (last accessed 3 December 2020).

38. *See* WGIII Report 1004/Add.1, p. 3; *see also* 'UNCITRAL Working Group on investor-State dispute settlement (ISDS) continues work on reforms', Press Release, UNIS Vienna, United Nations Information Service, (24 January 2020), available at https://unis.unvienna.org/unis/ en/pressrels/2020/unisl289.html (last accessed 2 December 2020).

39. Working Papers and additional resources can be accessed on the UNCITRAL Working Group III web page at https://uncitral.un.org/en/working_groups/3/investor-state.

40. *See* the dedicated web page, Virtual Panel Series: UNCITRAL Texts and COVID-19 Response and Recovery – 8-9 and 13-16 July 2020 at https://uncitral.un.org/en/COVID-19-panels.

41. *See* UNCITRAL Working Group III web page at -(https://uncitral.un.org/en/working_groups/3 /investor-state) (last accessed 4 December 2020).

42. Audio recordings of the Working Group III sessions can be accessed at https://uncitral.un.org /en/audio.

topics on the agenda of the postponed 39th session.[43] The Secretariat also organized a series of virtual presentations of the draft code of conduct for adjudicators in ISDS jointly with the ICSID Secretariat for delegations as well as interested stakeholders. And in conjunction with this year's Commission session, the Virtual Panel Series: UNCITRAL Texts and COVID-19 Response and Recovery was held including an event on 'COVID-19 Impact on International Dispute Resolution'.

In order to involve delegations at an early stage of the development of working papers on reform options, the draft documents are now posted on the UNCITRAL web page for comments that will facilitate the discussions at the Working Group sessions.[44]

Since October 2020 Working Group III has successfully held several hybrid sessions on videoconferencing platforms, with interpretation into all six UN languages and the possibility of physical participation.

V STATE OF REFORM DISCUSSIONS

The Working Group completed the first two phases of the reform agenda based on a broad consensus on identified concerns with regard to the current ISDS system and the desirability of reform (1). In October 2019, the Working Group started with the preliminary consideration of a number of reform options as part of phase three of its mandate (2). The reform options discussed consist of a procedural work stream (3) and a structural work stream (4). The consideration of options for the implementation of an ISDS reform is also part of the agenda (5).

1 General Status of the Reform Process

a Concerns Identified and Desirability of Reform

By October 2018, the Working Group identified a number of concerns related to the following three broad categories: the lack of consistency, coherence, predictability and correctness of arbitral decisions,[45] arbitrators and decision-makers,[46] and cost and duration of ISDS.[47] The Working Group also decided that a reform to address concerns related to the definition and the use of third-party funding (TPF) in ISDS was

---

43. Recordings and background materials on these webinars are available on the UNCITRAL webpage at https://uncitral.un.org/en/working_groups/3/investor-state.
44. *See* UNCITRAL Working Group III web page at https://uncitral.un.org/en/working_groups/3/investor-state.
45. WGIII Report 964, paras 40, 52-53, 62-63.
46. *Ibid.*, paras 82-83, 89-90, 97-98, 107-108.
47. WGIII Report 964, paras 122-123, 127, 132-133; *see also* 'Possible reform of investor-State dispute settlement (ISDS), Note by the Secretariat' UNCITRAL Working Group III (Investor-State Dispute Settlement Reform) 36th Session (Vienna, 29 October-2 November 2018) UN Doc. A/CN.9/WG.III/WP.149 (5 September 2018).

desirable.[48] Furthermore, the Working Group identified options for the implementation of a reform and the calculation of damages and compensation in ISDS as topics for further consideration.[49] It was reiterated that other concerns could be identified and dealt with at a later stage of the deliberations.[50] On this basis, the Working Group agreed to discuss, elaborate and develop multiple potential reform solutions simultaneously.[51]

b   *Identified Reform Options*

Based on numerous submissions by States, the following reform options have been identified and classified as follows:

- (a) Tribunals, ad hoc and standing multilateral mechanisms:
  - (i) Establishment of a Multilateral advisory centre to assist developing States in ISDS proceedings.
  - (ii) Establishment of a Stand-alone review or appellate mechanism.
  - (iii) Establishment of a Standing first instance and appeal investment court, with full-time judges.
- (b) Arbitrators and adjudicators appointment methods and ethics:
  - (i) ISDS tribunal members' selection, appointment and challenge.
  - (ii) Code of conduct for arbitrators and adjudicators.
- (c) Treaty Parties' involvement and control mechanisms on treaty interpretation:
  - (i) Enhancing treaty Parties' control over their instruments.
  - (ii) Strengthening the involvement of State authorities in the interpretation of treaties.
- (d) Dispute prevention and mitigation:
  - (i) Strengthening of dispute settlement mechanisms other than arbitration (ombudsman, mediation).
  - (ii) Introducing a requirement to exhaust local remedies.
  - (iii) Procedures to address frivolous claims, including summary dismissal.
  - (iv) Means to address multiple proceedings, reflective loss and counter-claims by respondent States.
- (e) Cost management and related procedures:
  - (i) Expedited procedures.
  - (ii) Principles/guidelines on allocation of cost and security for cost.
  - (iii) Other streamlined procedures and tools to manage costs.
- (f) TPF in ISDS.

---

48. WGIII Report 970, paras 17, 25.
49. WGIII Report 1004, paras 100-104.
50. WGIII Report 970, para. 39.
51. *Ibid.*, para. 81.

(g) Implementation of the reforms through a multilateral instrument on ISDS reform.[52]

This list of reform options was considered non-exhaustive and other concerns were not precluded from being identified and dealt with at a later stage of the deliberations.[53]

Subsequently, the Working Group included the calculation of damages and compensation in ISDS as a topic for consideration.[54] Moreover, the Working Group identified a number of cross-cutting issues, including the States' right to regulate, exhaustion of local remedies and enforcement thereof, costs and allocations thereof, and immunity of respondent States against enforcement.[55]

c   *Project schedule*

In October 2019 the Working Group decided on a project schedule, which covered a first round of discussions of the above-listed reform options.[56] It was emphasized that the order in which the discussions would take place would not reflect any priority to be given to those options and that the main objective of the discussions on the reform options would be to provide guidance on how they could be further developed:

– The thirty-eighth session, which took place in Vienna in October 2019, was allocated to consider the following reform options: multilateral advisory centre and related capacity-building activities,[57] code of conduct,[58] and TPF.[59] In addition, the Working Group would discuss the proposal for the development of a multilateral instrument on ISDS reform.[60]

– The resumed thirty-eighth session, which took place in Vienna in January 2020, was allocated to consider the following reform options: stand-alone

---

52. 'Possible reform of investor-State dispute settlement (ISDS), Note by the Secretariat', UNCITRAL Working Group III, 38th Session (Vienna, 14-18 October 2019) UN Doc. A/CN.9/WG.III/WP.166 (30 July 2019) paras 12-64.
53. *See* WGIII Report 1004, para. 17; WGIII Report 970, paras 39 and 40.
54. WGIII Report 1004, para. 24.
55. Report of Working Group III (Investor-State Dispute Settlement Reform) on the work of its resumed fortieth session (Vienna, 4 and 5 May 2021)' UNCITRAL, 54th Session, UN Doc. A/CN.9/1054 (27 May 2021) (henceforth 'WGIII Report 1054'), para. 35.
56. 'Report of Working Group III (Investor-State Dispute Settlement Reform) on the work of its thirty-eighth session (Vienna, 14-18 October 2019)' UNCITRAL, 53rd Session, UN Doc. A/CN.9/1004 (23 October 2019) (henceforth 'WGIII Report 1004') paras 16-17.
57. *See* 'Possible reform of investor-State dispute settlement (ISDS), Advisory Centre, Note by the Secretariat', UNCITRAL Working Group III, 38th Session (Vienna, 14-18 October 2019) UN Doc. A/CN.9/WG.III/WP.168 (25 July 2019) (henceforth 'Secretariat Note 168').
58. *See* 'Possible reform of investor-State dispute settlement (ISDS) Background information on a code of conduct Note by the Secretariat', UNCITRAL Working Group III, 38th Session (Vienna, 14-18 October 2019) UN Doc. A/CN.9/WG.III/WP.167 (31 July 2019).
59. *See* 'Possible reform of investor-State dispute settlement (ISDS) Third-party funding – Possible solutions Note by the Secretariat', UNCITRAL Working Group III, 38th Session (Vienna, 14-18 October 2019) UN Doc. A/CN.9/WG.III/WP.172 (2 August 2019).
60. *See* Secretariat Note 194.

review or appellate mechanism,[61] standing multilateral investment court,[62] and selection and appointment of arbitrators and adjudicators.[63]

- The thirty-ninth session in October 2020 was allocated to consider the following reform options: dispute prevention and mitigation as well as other means of alternative dispute resolution (ADR),[64] treaty interpretation by States parties,[65] security for costs,[66] means to address frivolous claims,[67] multiple proceedings including counterclaims,[68] reflective loss and shareholder claims based on joint work with OECD,[69] and a multilateral instrument on ISDS reform.[70]

d   *Resource Requirements and Workplan*

The Commission considered in its session in September 2020 the resource require-ments of Working Group III. Several States had requested to allocate to the Working Group the resources necessary to complete the work on ISDS reform by the year 2023.[71]

---

61. 'Possible reform of investor-State dispute settlement (ISDS) Appellate and multilateral court mechanisms Note by the Secretariat', UNCITRAL Working Group III (Investor-State Dispute Settlement Reform) 38th Session (resumed) (Vienna, 20-24 January 2020) UN Doc. A/CN.9/WG.III/WP.185 (29 November 2019) (henceforth 'Secretariat Note 185').
62. *Ibid.*
63. 'Possible reform of investor-State dispute settlement (ISDS), Selection and appointment of ISDS tribunal members, Note by the Secretariat', UNCITRAL Working Group III, 38th Session (Vienna, 14-18 October 2019) UN Doc. A/CN.9/WG.III/WP.169 (31 July 2019).
64. 'Possible reform of investor-State dispute settlement (ISDS) Dispute prevention and mitigation – Means of alternative dispute resolution Note by the Secretariat', UNICTRAL, Working Group III (Investor-State Dispute Settlement Reform) 39th Session (New York, 30 March-3 April 2020) UN Doc. A/CN.9/WG.III/WP.190 (15 January 2020) (henceforth 'Secretariat Note 190').
65. 'Possible reform of investor-State dispute settlement (ISDS), Interpretation of investment treaties by treaty Parties, Note by the Secretariat', UNICTRAL, Working Group III (Investor-State Dispute Settlement Reform) 39th Session (New York, 30 March-3 April 2020) UN Doc. A/CN.9/WG.III/WP.191 (17 January 2020) (henceforth 'Secretariat Note 191').
66. 'Possible reform of investor-State dispute settlement (ISDS), Security for cost and frivolous claims, Note by the Secretariat', UNICTRAL, Working Group III (Investor-State Dispute Settlement Reform) 39th Sess. (New York, 30 March-3 April 2020) UN Doc. A/CN.9/WG.III/WP.192 (16 January 2020) (henceforth 'Secretariat Note 192').
67. *Ibid.*
68. 'Possible reform of investor-State dispute settlement (ISDS), Multiple proceedings and counter-claims, Note by the Secretariat', UNICTRAL, Working Group III (Investor-State Dispute Settlement Reform) 39th Session (New York, 30 March-3 April 2020) UN Doc. A/CN.9/WG.III/WP.193 (22 January 2020) (henceforth 'Secretariat Note 193').
69. 'Possible reform of investor-State dispute settlement (ISDS), Shareholder claims and reflective loss, Note by the Secretariat', UNCITRAL Working Group III, 38th Session (Vienna, 14-18 October 2019) UN Doc. A/CN.9/WG.III/WP.170 (9 August 2019) (henceforth 'Secretariat Note 170').
70. 'Possible reform of investor-State dispute settlement (ISDS), Multilateral instrument on ISDS reform, Note by the Secretariat', UNICTRAL, Working Group III (Investor-State Dispute Settlement Reform) 39th Session (New York, 30 March-3 April 2020) UN Doc. A/CN.9/WG.III/WP.194 (16 January 2020) (henceforth 'Secretariat Note 194').
71. *See* 'Work programme, Submission by Austria, Belgium, Bulgaria, France, Germany, Ghana, Italy, Mauritius, the Netherlands, Poland, Romania, Slovakia, Slovenia, Spain, Sweden, Swit-zerland and the European Union, Note by the Secretariat', UNICTRAL Resumed 53rd Session (14-18 September 2020), UN Doc. A/CN.9/1036 (29 July 2020); *see also* 'Other business, Submission by Australia, Bahrain, Chile, Israel, Japan, Mexico, Peru, Thailand and the United

In May 2021, the Working Group discussed a work plan for its work on ISDS reform until 2026 and generally accepted that this work plan provided a workable roadmap for progress to be made by the Working Group.[72] This work plan also incorporates work on the cross-cutting issues identified by the Working Group.[73]

In the following Commission session in 2021, it was decided based on strong support to recommend to the General Assembly that additional conference and supporting resources be allocated to the secretariat for a single period of four years, from 2022 to 2025.[74] The request was granted by the General Assembly in its seventy-sixth session and the first additional week was scheduled for September 2022.[75]

2   Preliminary Consideration of Relevant Issues of Reform Elements

In its session in October 2019, the Working Group started to undertake a preliminary consideration of the identified reform elements in accordance with the agreed project schedule.[76] The goal of the preliminary discussions in phase three is to clarify, define and elaborate the reform elements after having discussed them as options in an earlier stage, without prejudice to the delegations' final positions and without making any decisions on whether to adopt a particular reform element at this stage of the deliberations.[77] It was noted that a reform of ISDS needs to ensure that ISDS does not undermine the obligations of States to take action under the Sustainable Development Goals and against climate change under the Paris Agreement.[78]

The discussions are based on the States' submissions and the notes by the UNCITRAL Secretariat; they also take into consideration input from relevant observers. In general, the Working Group has discussed the scope of application, the different aspects of the various reform options as well as their legal implications; it has usually requested that the UNCITRAL Secretariat undertakes further preparatory work in the form of feasibility work or the development of draft provisions.

States of America, Note by the Secretariat', UNCITRAL Resumed 53rd Session (14-18 September 2020), UN Doc. A/CN.9/1040 (3 September 2020); *see also* 'Resources to implement the work programme with respect to investor-State dispute settlement (ISDS) reform, Note by the Secretariat', UNCITRAL Resumed 53rd Session (14-18 September 2020), UN Doc. A/CN.9/1011 (6 May 2020).

72. WGIII Report 1054, para. 35.
73. *Ibid.*, para. 15.
74. 'Report of the United Nations Commission on International Trade Law, Fifty-fourth session (28 June-16 July 2021)' General Assembly, 76th Session, UN Doc. A/76/17, para. 263; 'Resource requirements to implement investor-State dispute settlement (ISDS) reform', UNICTRAL, 54th Session (Vienna, 28 June-16 July 2021) UN Doc. A/CN.9/1063 (28 May 2021).
75. *See* 'Report of the United Nations Commission on International Trade Law on the work of its fifty-fourth session', Report of the Sixth Committee, General Assembly, 76th Session, UN Doc. A/76/471, para. 15.
76. WGIII Report 1004, para. 25.
77. *See* WGIII Report 1004/Add.1, para. 15 and WGIII Report 1004, para. 25.
78. WGIII Report 1004, para. 99.

3 Reform Elements of a Procedural Nature

The Working Group has undertaken preliminary considerations of reform elements of procedural nature to apply to existing and future IIAs and if required also to procedural rules.

a Code of Conduct

The development of a code of conduct for arbitrators and adjudicators was identified early on as a reform option to be pursued. Broad agreement had been expressed on the importance of a code of conduct and it was suggested that such measures enhancing the confidence in the independence and impartiality of ISDS tribunal members whether arbitrators or judges would be in the interest of States and investors. It was also suggested that a code of conduct could usefully complement other reform options to be developed by the Working Group and that its preparation could be done in a rather short period of time.[79]

Based on a first note of the UNCITRAL and ICSID Secretariats, the Working Group discussed in its October 2019 session the potential scope of application, content and enforcement mechanisms of a code of conduct.[80] It was generally found that a code should be binding and mandatory and should aim at having a universal application.[81] The Working Group emphasized the need to differentiate between rules for arbitrators and for adjudicators and judges and also considered the application to support personnel.

Concerning the content, particular attention was given to the issues of so-called double hatting, the resignation of arbitrators, issue conflicts and the scope of disclosure obligations with regard to their impartiality and independence.

It was stressed that the enforcement mechanism would constitute a key component of the code of conduct. In order to establish an effective sanctions mechanism, it was suggested that a more in-depth study beyond challenges and disqualification would be required, which may include sanctions linked to the remuneration scheme, disciplinary measures, reputational sanctions and notifications to professional associations. It was further suggested that a centralized system or body for monitoring compliance as well as a database on challenges and sanctioned arbitrators could increase transparency, which would effectively assist in the enforcement of the code of conduct and that an advisory centre could be tasked with this role.[82]

The UNCITRAL and ICSID Secretariats prepared a draft code of conduct for adjudicators in ISDS (the draft Code) on the basis of a comparative review of the standards found in codes of conduct in investment treaties, arbitration rules applicable

---

79. *Ibid.*, paras 51-78.
80. WGIII Report 1004, paras 52, 53; *see also* 'Report of Working Group III (Investor-State Dispute Settlement Reform) on the work of its thirty-fifth session (New York, 23-27 April 2018)' UNCITRAL, 51st Session (New York, 25 June-13 July 2018) UN Doc. A/CN.9/935 (14 May 2018), para. 64; WGIII Report 964, para. 78.
81. WGIII Report 1004, 53-64.
82. *Ibid.*, 67-77.

to ISDS, codes of conduct of international courts and the discussions in the Working Group.[83]

The draft Code aims at providing a uniform approach to requirements applicable to adjudicators handling international investment disputes (IID) and at giving more concrete content to broad ethical notions and standards found in the applicable instruments. It seeks to create a 'balanced, realistic and workable' document. The draft Code is applicable to arbitrators, judges and other types of adjudicators.[84] It will be accompanied by a commentary, which aims at clarifying the content of each provision, including the relationship between the obligations of adjudicators and the disclosures required, discussing practical implications, and providing examples.[85]

The Working Group started with a first reading of the draft Code in its sessions in November 2021 and February 2022.[86] The discussions and decisions of the Working Group have been reflected in a revised version of the draft Code prepared jointly by the secretariats of ICSID and UNCITRAL.[87]

b   *Third-Party Funding*

The Working Group also discussed concrete reform options with regard to TPF in ISDS, particularly in light of the current lack of transparency and regulation.[88] A regulation would aim at addressing not only concerns related to the impact of TPF on the proceedings,[89] in particular, potential conflicts of interests of arbitrators but also concerns related to the impact of TPF on the ISDS system as a whole,[90] in particular an increase in the number of ISDS cases, amounts of damages claimed and frivolous claims.

Different models for regulating TPF in ISDS were addressed. While some support was expressed for prohibiting TPF, it was also argued that it could permit access to

---

83. *See* 'Possible reform of investor-State dispute settlement (ISDS) Draft Code of Conduct', UNICTRAL, Working Group III (Investor-State Dispute Settlement Reform) 41st Session (Vienna, 15-19 November 2021) UN Doc. A/CN.9/WG.III/WP.209 (15 September 2021) (henceforth 'Secretariat Note 209').
84. WGIII Report 1004, para. 55.
85. *See* Secretariat Note 209.
86. Report of Working Group III (Investor-State Dispute Settlement Reform) on the work of its forty-first session (Vienna, 15-19 November 2021)' UNCITRAL, UN Doc. A/CN.9/1086 (13 December 2021) and Report of Working Group III (Investor-State Dispute Settlement Reform) on the work of its forty-second session (New York, 14-18 February 2022)' UNCITRAL, UN Doc. A/CN.9/1092 (23 March 2022) (henceforth 'WGIII Report 1092'), paras 79-130.
87. 'Possible reform of investor-State dispute settlement (ISDS) Draft Code of Conduct', UNICTRAL, Working Group III (Investor-State Dispute Settlement Reform) 43rd Session (Vienna, 5-16 September 2022) UN Doc. A/CN.9/WG.III/WP.216 (5 July 2022).
88. WGIII Report 1004, 79-98.
89. Including conflicts of interest arising out of TPF; impact of TPF on costs and on security for costs, disclosure of information to third-party funders not subject to confidentiality obligations, control, or influence of third-party funders over the arbitration process, negative impact on amicable resolution of disputes and the availability of TPF mainly for investors.
90. Including the increase in the number of ISDS cases, in frivolous claims as well as in the amount of damages claimed, the underlying rationale for providing protection to foreign investors and the right of States to regulate.

justice for small- and medium-sized enterprises (SMEs). It was suggested that further research might need to be conducted on the extent to which SMEs had used TPF.[91] It was noted that a general prohibition of TPF along with exceptions, for example in the case of the demonstrated impecuniosity of the claimant (or a so-called access to justice approach) could provide an appropriate approach for regulating the practice.[92]

It was generally felt that the existence of TPF and the identity of the third-party funder should be disclosed at an early stage of the proceedings. Also, the Working Group discussed an extension of the disclosure obligation to the terms of the funding agreement and the consequences of non-compliance. Moreover, it was suggested that costs related to TPF should not be recoverable as part of the allocation of costs and discussed whether TPF should have an impact on the decision on security for costs.

The Working Group concluded that the work on TPF could result in binding rules and asked the UNCITRAL Secretariat to prepare draft provisions. The draft provision should take account of the current work of ICSID on a disclosure obligation in its ongoing Rules and Regulations Amendment Process.[93] Against the background of the acknowledged lack of concrete empirical data on the use of TPF and its impact on ISDS and the difficulty in obtaining such data, the Secretariat is also seeking to collect relevant data, including on the frequency of its use, the relative success rates of third-party funded claims, the amounts claimed in third-party funded claims in comparison to non-funded claims, and the reasons why TPF is used.

The Secretariat held an expert group meeting on the draft provisions on TPF at the end of November 2020 with leading experts in the field and obtained feedback from third-party funders. A revised set of draft provisions on TPF has been included in a Working Paper on procedural rules for discussion in the Working Group session in September 2022.[94]

c   *Selection and Appointment of Arbitrators and Adjudicators*

The Working Group undertook a preliminary consideration of issues related to the selection and appointment of ISDS tribunal members.[95] The Working Group had concluded that the development of reforms by UNCITRAL was desirable to address concerns related to the lack or apparent lack of independence and impartiality of decision-makers in ISDS, related to the question of adequacy, effectiveness and transparency of the disclosure and challenge mechanisms available under many

---

91. WGIII Report 1004, 81.
92. *Ibid.*, 82, 83.
93. *See* "Proposals for the Amendment of the ICSID Rules, Working Paper # 4', International Centre for Settlement of Investment Disputes (Volume 1, February 2020) available at https://icsid.worldbank.org/sites/default/files/amendments/WP_4_Vol_1_En.pdf (last accessed 3 December 2020).
94. 'Possible reform of investor-State dispute settlement (ISDS) Draft provisions on procedural reform', UNCITRAL Working Group III (Investor-State Dispute Settlement Reform) 43rd Session (Vienna, 5-16 September 2020) UN Doc. A/CN.9/WG.III/WP.219 (11 July 2022) (advance copy) (henceforth 'Secretariat Note 219').
95. WGIII Report 1004/Add.1, paras 95-133.

existing treaties and arbitration rules, the lack of appropriate diversity among decision-makers in ISDS and the mechanisms for constituting ISDS tribunals in existing treaties and arbitration rules.[96]

In its January 2020 session, the Working Group discussed the qualifications and requirements for ISDS tribunal members as well as the means to achieve diversity. Further, two possible options for reform were discussed: the establishment of a roster of qualified candidates and the setting up of a permanent body composed of full-time adjudicators. With regard to the latter, the Working Group discussed the modalities of the nomination and selection of adjudicators as well as the authority and process for the assignment of cases. Also, questions regarding caseload management and rules on challenges were raised. The Working Group noted that consideration shall be given to the location of the permanent body, whether it would be hosted within an existing organization (possibly a body within the UN) or as a separate body, the need to put in place a mechanism to rectify any problems that could arise after the body was set up, the need to ensure sustainability and equitability, means to ensure diversity in the composition of the Secretariat and the possible role of the permanent body in handling State-to-State disputes.

d   *Dispute Prevention and Mitigation as Well as Other Means of ADR*

In its October 2020 session, the Working Group discussed issues related to dispute prevention and mitigation and other means of ADR based on submissions by States and a note by the Secretariat.[97]

i   *Dispute Prevention and Mitigation*

It was highlighted that these reform options concern the pre-dispute phase and that dispute prevention and mitigation play a significant role in attracting and retaining investments. On a national level, in particular models for information channels between investors and the responsible authorities of the host State regarding investor complaints and the mechanisms to ensure coherence between domestic legislation and investment treaties were discussed.

It was further suggested to possibly develop treaty model provisions for dispute prevention and mitigation as well as pre-arbitration consultation procedures. The need to raise awareness of these mechanisms through technical assistance and capacity-building activities was underlined. Such activities could be set up in an efficient way without burdening States and could, for example, be assigned to an Advisory Centre.

The Secretariat was requested to work with interested delegations and organizations to compile relevant and readily available information on the best practices for States on dispute prevention and mitigation and to examine possible means of implementation and how an Advisory Centre could assist States in this area.

---

96. WGIII Report 964, paras 83-108.
97. *See* WGIII Report 1044, paras 17-40 and Secretariat Note 190.

ii　　*Alternative Dispute Resolution Methods and Strengthening Recourse to Mediation*

With regard to mediation, conciliation and other forms of ADR methods, the Working Group pointed out a need for guidance for the effective use of cooling-off periods and discussed challenges and possible means to foster the use of mediation in ISDS. It was said that policies as well as a conducive legal framework for encouraging mediation would be necessary and that capacity-building and training of potential mediators and other stakeholders was a key aspect. It was also said that an advisory centre could play a role in compiling and sharing information on best practices in ADR.

The Working Group requested the Secretariat to prepare model clauses reflecting best practices on the amicable settlement or cooling off period, including an adequate length of time and clear rules on how such period could be complied with. The Secretariat was requested to compile guidelines or recommendations on how such a period could be more effectively used.

The Secretariat prepared draft provisions on mediation to be included in existing and future IIAs as well as draft guidelines for users of investment mediation for consideration by the Working Group.[98]

e　　**Multiple Proceedings and Counterclaims, Including Shareholder Claims and Reflective Loss**

Multiple proceedings had been identified as a concern by the Working Group due to, among others, their possible negative impact on the cost and duration of the ISDS proceedings, potential inconsistent outcomes, possible double recovery, forum shopping as well as abuse of the process by claimant investors.[99] It was widely felt that there was a need to reform the current ISDS system by addressing these concerns, particularly as the old-generation investment treaties did not provide appropriate means to address them.

The Working Group discussed a number of potential tools to address multiple proceedings and decided that further work on this topic should focus on identifying more specifically the types of multiple proceedings and shareholder claims that might arise, and the potential concerns associated with each, so as to further define the scope of the issue. Also, the Secretariat was requested to compile a list of the tools and mechanisms that already existed in treaty practice. Further, the Secretariat was requested to recommend model clauses and options for the implementation of these tools in the ways intended, such as through resolutions of the General Assembly, guidelines to tribunals, or other explanatory works. It was said that a detailed toolbox

---

98. 'Possible reform of investor-State dispute settlement (ISDS) Draft provisions on mediation', UNCITRAL Working Group III (Investor-State Dispute Settlement Reform) 43rd Session (Vienna, 5-16 September 2020) UN Doc. A/CN.9/WG.III/WP.217 (13 July 2022); 'Possible reform of investor-State dispute settlement (ISDS) Draft guidelines on investment mediation', UNCITRAL Working Group III (Investor-State Dispute Settlement Reform) 43rd Session (Vienna, 5-16 September 2020) UN Doc. A/CN.9/WG.III/WP.218 (20 July 2022).

99. *See* WGIII Report 1044, paras 41-63; *see also* Secretariat Note 193 and Secretariat Note 170.

that would specifically and appropriately respond to the concerns that existed with respect to multiple proceedings and shareholder claims could be developed. It would then remain to determine how to implement it as part of the reform process.

With regard to counterclaims, it was pointed out that one of the primary reasons for the lack of counterclaims in ISDS is the absence of substantive obligations on the part of investors in investment treaties. While it was clarified that drafting such (substantive) obligations is not within the mandate of the Working Group, the Secretariat was requested to continue work on the procedural aspects of counterclaims and to draft model consent clauses, that would condition a State's consent to ISDS on the consent of the investor to have the same tribunal hear counterclaims. Draft provisions on counterclaims have been prepared as part of a Working Paper on procedural rules.[100]

f   *Security for Costs*

The Working Group also considered reform options related to security for costs.[101] It was agreed that further work should leverage the work undertaken by ICSID and the UNCITRAL Secretariat was requested to prepare a model clause focusing on making security for costs available for respondents against claimants, clarifying that security for costs would only be available on request of a party, and would not apply against third parties. The model clause should cover the conditions and threshold and specify options for consequences in case of failure to comply.

The model clause should provide for options of conditions ranging from general options which would give more discretion to ISDS tribunals, to options that list items for consideration more expressly but leave how to apply these to the ISDS tribunals (such as impecuniosity, cases of shell corporations, multiple claimants, history of compliance with awards and existence of TPF), and options that would include very prescriptive lists mandating security for costs in defined circumstances (such as TPF).

The formulation of these conditions should ensure that a balance was found between ensuring effective rights for States on the one hand and access to justice on the other, and the ISDS tribunal would not be required to prejudge the dispute. Furthermore, the Working Group requested the Secretariat to prepare guidelines and best practices regarding how the security for costs provisions could be applied in a fair and consistent manner. The Secretariat has prepared draft provisions on security for costs as part of a Working Paper on procedural rules.[102]

g   *Frivolous and Unmeritorious Claims*

With regard to frivolous claims, the Working Group expressed general support for developing a more predictable framework to address such claims, which would make

---

100. *See* Secretariat Note 219.
101. *See* WGIII Report 1044, paras 64-77; *see also* Secretariat Note 192.
102. *See* Secretariat Note 219.

it possible to dismiss them at an early stage of the proceedings and provide an expedited process. Such improved framework with provisions in investment treaties and relevant rules could address concerns about the cost and duration of ISDS as well as regulatory chill.[103]

For further preparatory work on this topic, the Secretariat was requested to compile information about provisions in existing investment agreements and arbitration rules (such as Article 41(5) of the ICSID Arbitration Rules) and jurisprudence and to prepare options for a model clause, which would create a clear framework for the early dismissal of frivolous claims, while giving flexibility to the ISDS tribunal to handle frivolous, vexatious and other types of claims, taking into account the reason for the dismissal being sought. Draft provisions on early dismissal have been elaborated as part of a Working Paper on procedural rules.[104]

h   Interpretation of Investment Treaties by Treaty Parties

The Working Group took note of the numerous existing treaty interpretation tools and that treaty interpretation nonetheless remains rare in practice. Several tools and their legal nature and practical relevance were discussed, including joint interpretations, consistent positions by States in the pleadings as respondents or submissions as non-disputing parties as well as unilateral and multilateral declarations.[105]

The Secretariat was requested to compile the various interpretive tools contained in investment treaties and to further elaborate on the issues raised in the Working Group, including why the existing tools on treaty interpretation were not effectively used by States or were not accepted by tribunals and how they could be effectively used.[106]

i   Assessment of Damages and Compensation

The Working Group considered issues related to the assessment of damages and compensation. In particular, the Working Group considered the coherence and consistency of decisions made by ISDS tribunals, a potential inconsistency of decisions regarding the application of legal principles to the assessment of damages and compensation and the high amount of compensation awarded by ISDS tribunals which may undermine States' ability to regulate.[107]

The Secretariat prepared a note outlining the key issues relevant to the assessment of damages and the determination of compensation under investment treaties,

---

103. *See also* Secretariat Note 192.
104. *See* Secretariat Note 219.
105. *See* WGIII Report 1044, paras 90-101.
106. *See also* Secretariat Note 191.
107. 'Report of Working Group III (Investor-State Dispute Settlement Reform) on the work of its thirty-fourth session (Vienna, 27 November-1 December 2017)' UNCITRAL, UN Doc. A/CN.9/930/Add.1/Rev.1 (26 February 2018), para. 30; WGIII Report 970, paras 36-38.

including underlying legal principles and methodologies for consideration by the Working Group.[108]

4 Reform Elements of Structural Nature

The Working Group has also undertaken preliminary considerations of reform elements of a structural nature relating to institutional design.

a Standing Multilateral Investment Court and Appellate Mechanism

The Working Group undertook preliminary considerations of the creation of appellate mechanisms: (i) issues related to the enforcement of decisions rendered through a permanent appellate mechanism or a standing first-tier body, (ii) the financing of such permanent body, and (iii) the selection and appointment of adjudicators in a standing mechanism.[109]

The creation of an appellate mechanism would aim at addressing concerns with regard to the procedural and substantive correctness of decisions and at rectifying errors in decisions by ISDS tribunals.[110] The proposal to establish a standing first instance and appeal investment court was made in a submission by a group of States to comprehensively address concerns pertaining to the lack of consistency, coherence, predictability and correctness of arbitral decisions by ISDS tribunals, to arbitrators and decision-makers and to cost and duration of ISDS cases.[111] It is based on the view that the concerns identified by the Working Group are intertwined and systemic, and that addressing concerns separately would leave some concerns unaddressed.[112]

i Appellate Mechanism

The Working Group discussed various objectives and the scope and standard of review of an appellate mechanism and the related risk of an increase in costs and duration of

---

108. 'Possible reform of investor-State dispute settlement (ISDS) Assessment of damages and compensation', UNCITRAL Working Group III (Investor-State Dispute Settlement Reform) 43rd Session (Vienna, 5-16 September 2020) UN Doc. A/CN.9/WG.III/WP.220 (5 July 2022) (advance copy).
109. WGIII Report 1004/Add.1, paras 14-94; 'Report of Working Group III (Investor-State Dispute Settlement Reform) on the work of its fortieth session (Vienna, 8-12 February 2021)' UNCITRAL, 54th Session (Vienna, 28 June-16 July 2021) UN Doc. A/CN.9/1050 (17 March 2021) (henceforth 'WGIII Report 1050'); WGIII Report 1092.
110. Secretariat Note 185, para. 7; Submission by Morocco 161; 'Possible reform of investor-State dispute settlement (ISDS), Submission from the Government of Ecuador, Note by the Secretariat', UNCITRAL Working Group III, 38th Session (Vienna, 14-18 October 2019) UN Doc. A/CN.9/WG.III/WP.175 (17 July 2019) (henceforth 'Submission by Ecuador 175'); 'Possible reform of investor-State dispute settlement (ISDS), Submission from the Government of China, Note by the Secretariat', UNCITRAL Working Group III, 38th Session (Vienna, 14-18 October 2019) UN Doc. A/CN.9/WG.III/WP.177 (19 July 2019) (henceforth 'Submission by China 177').
111. Submission by the European Union 159/Add.1.
112. Ibid.

the proceedings.[113] It was found that existing procedures for annulment (under the ICSID Convention) or setting aside of an award were generally very limited in scope. On the other hand, the scope and standard of review should not be too broad in order to avoid that parties would appeal the majority of ISDS decisions and to avoid a de novo review of all cases appealed.[114] The Working Group also considered bodies, the decisions of which could be subject to appeal,[115] the practice and rules of a range of appellate bodies, and whether only decisions on the merits or also decisions on jurisdiction and other matters should be covered by the appellate mechanism.

With regard to the effect of appeal, the Working Group discussed the ability to affirm, reverse or modify the decision of the first-tier tribunal and to render a final decision based on the facts before it. It was further debated if the appellate body should have a remand authority, the extent to which the decision rendered should have an interpretative effect and whether decisions should be subject to confirmation or review by the States Parties to the relevant IIA.

Based on this discussion, the Secretariat prepared draft provisions on the main components relating to the nature, scope and effect of an appellate mechanism.[116]

The Working Group considered these draft provisions in February 2021.[117] In the discussion, it was said that an appeal mechanism could enhance the correctness and consistency of decisions rendered by ISDS tribunals, and thereby increase the overall predictability and the efficiency of ISDS, that a full rehearing should be avoided and that such mechanism should not increase the complexity of the ISDS system.[118] The Working Group requested the Secretariat to prepare text and specific guidance on the further development of the relevant draft provisions.[119]

ii   Enforcement

The Working Group also considered issues related to the enforcement of decisions rendered through a permanent body. Enforcement was considered a key feature of any system of justice. It was acknowledged that the application of the existing enforcement mechanisms such as under the New York Convention and the ICSID Convention would depend on how such a body would be set up, in particular, if its decisions would qualify as arbitral awards.

---

113. Submission by Morocco 161; Submission by Ecuador 175; Submission by China 177.
114. WGIII Report 1004/Add.1, para. 29.
115. That is, arbitral tribunals, any standing multilateral investment court, regional investment courts, and international commercial courts.
116. *See* document A/CN.9/WG.III/WP.202, para. 59, the document contains draft provisions on Scope and standard of review (paras 1-3 of the draft provisions), Decisions by ISDS tribunals subject to appeal (paras 4 and 5 of the draft provisions), Effect of appeal (para. 6 of the draft provisions), Authority of the appellate body (paras 7-9 of the draft provisions), Rectification of errors (para. 10 of the draft provisions), Timelines (para. 11 of the draft provisions) and Security for costs (para. 12 of the draft provisions).
117. WGIII Report 1050, paras 63-111.
118. WGIII Report 1050, paras 58-62.
119. WGIII Report 1050, paras 112-116.

The Working Group considered the enforcement of decisions under a specific enforcement regime established for the permanent body, potential conflicts with existing enforcement mechanisms, State immunity and potential models for the design of such an enforcement mechanism. As a potential model, Article 54 ICSID Convention and the language of recent investment treaties were mentioned.[120]

It was considered whether a permanent body could qualify as a 'permanent arbitral body' under Article I (2) New York Convention and suggested that the parties to the permanent body or UNCITRAL could issue a provision or recommendation on the interpretation of this article.[121] The Working Group also discussed Article 53 ICSID Convention, which provides that ICSID awards should 'not be subject to any appeal or to any other remedy except those provided for in the Convention'. Further, the option of an *inter se* modification of the ICSID Convention among the States establishing an appellate mechanism according to Article 41 of the Vienna Convention on the Law of the Treaties was considered.

The Secretariat was requested to conduct preparatory work which would aim to provide an in-depth analysis of the questions raised during the deliberations and information on provisions in existing international instruments and on how such provisions could be adapted in the context of a permanent body.[122]

iii   Financing

Moreover, the Working Group had a preliminary discussion on the financing of a permanent body tasked with handling appeals or composed of two tiers to hear disputes.[123] As key budgetary components, the Working Group identified the remuneration of adjudicators, costs related to the administration of the case, costs of administrative staff as well as overhead costs of the permanent body, such as the costs of the premises, facilities, communication and others. The Working Group discussed financing by the State parties to the convention establishing the permanent body, noting that a contribution structure would have to ensure the independence of the permanent body. Moreover, it was suggested that financing needed for the general operation of the permanent body could be allocated to the participating States and the costs related to administering ISDS cases to the disputing parties. It was emphasized that the financing of a permanent body should take into consideration the quality and reliability of the services rendered, long-term sustainability, different structural options, transitional financing measures, contingency plans and flexibility regarding the caseload.

---

120. WGIII Report 1004/Add.1, paras 64-68.
121. WGIII Report 1004/Add.1, paras 69-79; Convention on the Recognition and Enforcement of Foreign Arbitral Awards (New York, 1958), Article 1(2): The term 'arbitral awards' shall include not only awards made by arbitrators appointed for each case but also those made by permanent arbitral bodies to which the parties have submitted.
122. A (draft) working paper on appellate mechanisms and enforcement issues is available on the UNCITRAL Working Group III web page at https://uncitral.un.org/en/working_groups/3/investor-state.
123. WGIII Report 1004/Add.1, paras 82-93.

The UNCITRAL Secretariat was requested to undertake preparatory work including an examination of hybrid models for financing, an examination of contribution schemes for participating States addressing the concerns expressed about undue influence by States with larger contributions, and a preliminary analysis of the potential budget of a permanent body based on comparable international judicial bodies.[124]

iv   Selection and Appointment of Adjudicators in a Standing Mechanism

The Working Group discussed the issue of the selection and appointment of adjudicators in a standing mechanism in February 2021[125] and February 2022.[126]

During the preliminary considerations in February 2021, the Working Group discussed general matters related to the creation of a standing mechanism and the role of the disputing parties in the selection and appointment of adjudicators.[127] Moreover, fundamental questions related to the composition of the permanent body, the nomination, selection and appointment, the terms of office, removal procedures and the assignment of cases were deliberated.[128]

The Working Group requested the Secretariat to prepare draft provisions based on the preliminary discussions, which were considered in February 2022. In this session, it was noted that the establishment of a standing mechanism would likely require the preparation of a statute and that the statute might need to be supplemented by rules or regulations addressing detailed procedural matters, to be drafted by either the Working Group or by the Committee of the Parties.[129] This first set of draft provisions on the standing mechanism covered issues related to its establishment, jurisdiction and governance, selective representation and the number and qualification of tribunal members, as well as options for the nomination, selection and appointment mechanisms.[130]

b   *Advisory Centre*

The Working Group had a first round of discussions on the establishment of an advisory centre on ISDS, for which interest and general support had been expressed.[131] The discussions were based on proposals by States, made in relation to the concerns

---

124. *Ibid.*, para. 94.
125. *See* WGIII Report 1050, paras 17-56 and 'Possible reform of investor-State dispute settlement (ISDS) Selection and appointment of ISDS tribunal members', UNICTRAL, Working Group III (Investor-State Dispute Settlement Reform) 40th Session (Vienna, 8-12 February 2021) UN Doc. A/CN.9/WG.III/WP.203 (16 November 2020).
126. WGIII Report 1092, paras 15-78 and 'Possible reform of investor-State dispute settlement (ISDS) Standing multilateral mechanism: Selection and appointment of ISDS tribunal members and related matters', UNICTRAL, Working Group III (Investor-State Dispute Settlement Reform) 42nd Sess. (New York, 14-18 February 2022) UN Doc. A/CN.9/WG.III/WP.213 (8 December 2021).
127. WGIII Report 1050, paras 17-22.
128. *Ibid.*, paras 22-54.
129. WGIII Report 1092, paras 15-18.
130. *Ibid.*, paras 18-78.
131. WGIII Report 1004, paras 28-50; *see also* Secretariat Note 168.

regarding the cost and duration of ISDS, and in light of the consideration that the cost of ISDS creates a burden on States, in particular developing and least-developed countries, as well as investors, mainly SMEs and individuals.[132]

The discussion of the Working Group focused on the potential beneficiaries, the scope of services, and the financing of an advisory centre.[133] In particular, a preferential role for least-developed and developing countries, as well as the possible participation of developed States and SMEs, was discussed. The Working Group considered advisory and support services under the broad categories of representation services, assistance in organizing the defence and support during proceedings, general advisory services, ADR services, capacity-building and sharing of best practices.[134] It was stressed that the resources available to the advisory centre would inevitably define or limit the scope of services that could be provided. It was further suggested that the Advisory Centre on WTO Law could provide a useful model.

In order to further develop this reform option, the Secretariat collected input on the establishment of an advisory centre by way of a questionnaire,[135] held a webinar focusing on the potential scope of services and beneficiaries,[136] and prepared draft provisions governing the advisory centre and its operation.[137] Moreover, a group of

---

132. Secretariat Note 168, paras 4-6; WGIII Report 964, para. 119; *see also* 'Possible reform of investor-State dispute settlement (ISDS), Submission from the European Union and its Member States', UNICTRAL Working Group III (Investor-State Dispute Settlement Reform) 37th Session (New York, 1-5 April 2019) UN Doc. A/CN.9/WG.III/WP.159/Add.1 (24 January 2019) (henceforth 'Submission by the European Union 159/Add.1'); 'Possible reform of investor-State dispute settlement (ISDS), Submission from the Government of Morocco, Note by the Secretariat', UNICTRAL Working Group III (Investor-State Dispute Settlement Reform) 37th Session (New York, 1-5 April 2019) UN Doc. A/CN.9/WG.III/WP.161 (4 March 2019) (henceforth 'Submission by Morocco 161'); 'Possible reform of investor-State dispute settlement (ISDS), Submission from the Government of Thailand', UNICTRAL Working Group III (Investor-State Dispute Settlement Reform) 37th Session (New York, 1-5 April 2019) UN Doc. A/CN.9/WG.III/WP.162 (8 March 2019); 'Submission from the Government of Costa Rica', UNICTRAL Working Group III (Investor-State Dispute Settlement Reform) 37th Session (New York, 1-5 April 2019) UN Doc. A/CN.9/WG.III/WP.164 (22 March 2019) and 'Possible reform of Investor-State dispute settlement (ISDS), Submission from the Government of Costa Rica, Note by the Secretariat' UNICTRAL Working Group III, 38th Session (Vienna, 14-18 October 2019) UN Doc. A/CN.9/WG.III/WP.178 (31 July 2019); 'Submission from the Government of Turkey', UNCITRAL Working Group III, 38th Session (Vienna, 14-18 October 2019) UN Doc. A/CN.9/WG.III/WP.174 (11 July 2019); 'Possible reform of Investor-State dispute settlement (ISDS), Submission from the Republic of Korea, Note by the Secretariat', UNCITRAL Working Group III, 38th Sess. (Vienna, 14-18 October 2019) UN Doc. A/CN.9/WG.III/WP.179 (31 July 2019).
133. WGIII Report 1004, paras 28-50.
134. *Ibid.*, paras 31-36.
135. UNCITRAL Working Group III on ISDS Reform, Questionnaire on the establishment of an advisory centre on investor-State dispute settlement (ISDS), available at https://uncitral.un.org/en/multilateraladvisorycentre.
136. A recording, the programme and background information are available on the UNCITRAL web page at https://uncitral.un.org/en/advisorycentrewebinar (last accessed 3 December 2020).
137. 'Possible reform of investor-State dispute settlement (ISDS) Advisory Centre', UNCITRAL Working Group III (Investor-State Dispute Settlement Reform) 43rd Session (Vienna, 5-16 September 2020) UN Doc. A/CN.9/WG.III/WP.212 (3 December 2022); 'Possible reform of investor-State dispute settlement (ISDS) Advisory Centre', UNCITRAL Working Group III (Investor-State Dispute Settlement Reform) 43rd Session (Vienna, 5-16 September 2020) UN Doc. A/CN.9/WG.III/WP.212/Add.1 (3 December 2022).

observers in Working Group III prepared and submitted a note on the costs and financing of an Advisory Centre on International Investment Law, which has further been discussed in subsequent webinars.[138]

5   Implementation of the Reform: A Multilateral Framework Based on the Mauritius Convention on Transparency Model, on the OECD BEPS Convention?

The way to implement a potential ISDS reform is a key consideration in the development of reform options and has been addressed in numerous submissions by States.[139] The key issues relevant to designing a multilateral instrument on ISDS reform have been outlined in a note by the UNCITRAL Secretariat.[140] This note suggests – based on the submissions by States – how such an instrument could be structured and could encompass the various options for reform and integrate them under one multilateral framework.[141]

As elaborated above, the mechanism applied in the Mauritius Convention on Transparency was already considered as a possible model for implementation during the deliberations on UNCITRAL's mandate on ISDS reform. A mechanism for ISDS reform implementation could consist of a convention designed to facilitate the application of a reform to the roughly 3,000 investment treaties concluded before the entry into force of such reform and thus to introduce changes into the fragmented treaty-by-treaty regime by way of a single multilateral instrument.[142] It would constitute the vehicle by which the various reform options are proposed to States for implementation.

Other submissions by States suggest modelling an implementation instrument after the OECD Multilateral Convention to Implement Tax Treaty-Related Measures to

---

138. International Arbitration Institute and International Law Institute, 'Note on the costs and financing of an Advisory Centre on International Investment Law' (18 July 2020), accessible at https://uncitral.un.org/sites/uncitral.un.org/files/aciil_note_on_costs_financing_24_august_2020_final_updated.pdf (last accessed 3 December 2020).

139. The Submissions that refer to the implementation of multiple reform options include the following: Submission by the European Union 159/Add.1; 'Possible reform of investor-State dispute settlement (ISDS). Submission from the Government of Colombia, Note by the Secretariat', UNCITRAL Working Group III, 38th Session (Vienna, 14-18 October 2019) UN Doc. A/CN.9/WG.III/WP.173 (14 June 2019) (henceforth 'Submission by Colombia 173'); and Submission by Ecuador 175; see also 'Possible reform of investor-State dispute settlement (ISDS), Submission from the Governments of Chile, Israel, Japan, Mexico and Peru, Note by the Secretariat', UNCITRAL Working Group III, 38th Session (Vienna, 14-18 October 2019) UN Doc. A/CN.9/WG.III/WP.182 (2 October 2019) (henceforth 'Submission by Chile, Israel, Japan, Mexico and Peru 182'), suggesting implementation of reform options through a 'suite' approach.

140. Secretariat Note 194.

141. WGIII Report 1004, paras 101 and 104.

142. Gabrielle Kaufmann-Kohler and Michele Potestà (CIDS – Geneva Centre for International Dispute Settlement), 'Can the Mauritius Convention serve as a model for the reform of investor-State arbitration in connection with the introduction of a permanent investment tribunal or an appeal mechanism? Analysis and roadmap' (3 June 2016), available from https://uncitral.un.org/sites/uncitral.un.org/files/media-documents/uncitral/en/cids_research_paper_mauritius.pdf, pp. 93, 94.

Prevent Base Erosion and Profit Shifting (MLI).[143] The MLI does not modify the text of individual tax treaties but applies alongside existing tax treaties modifying their application with regard to base erosion and profit shifting. As opposed to the Mauritius Convention on Transparency, Contracting Parties to the MLI notify a list of treaties the MLI applies to at the time of the signing.[144]

The State submissions also highlight the need for a coherent and flexible approach to the overall reform of ISDS, which would allow each State to choose whether and to what extent to adopt reform options.[145] A multilateral treaty could contain certain 'blocks' of options to be considered as minimum standards and other blocks that States could opt in or opt out of.[146]

A submission foresees the development of an instrument establishing a standing multilateral first instance and appellate court and a specific notification ('opt-in') that a particular existing or future investment treaty would be subject to the jurisdiction of the standing mechanism. It further suggests the adoption of an open approach to implement the reform option, allowing States to either use the standing mechanism as such, or limit its use, for instance, by applying it to State-to-State dispute settlement only, or by utilizing only the appellate mechanism.[147]

Yet another submission proposes the elaboration of a 'suite' approach, aimed at developing a menu of relevant solutions, which may vary in form. Once developed, States would incorporate one or more of the proposed provisions either in their entirety or in the combination preferred by States into their investment treaties, taking into account their own political and policy concerns and interests.[148]

The Working Group also discussed implementation options in its session in October 2020.[149] It was reiterated that a coherent and flexible approach to the different reform options needed to be applied, allowing States parties to choose whether and to what extent they would adopt the relevant reform options. A preference was expressed for an application to both existing and future IIAs and it was said that the whole purpose of a multilateral instrument was to make some, or all, of the reform options being developed applicable to existing investment treaties.

A number of characteristics were suggested as being important. The instrument should respond in particular to the identified concerns related to the consistency and coherence of arbitral decisions and promote legal certainty in ISDS. It should establish a flexible framework, whereby States could choose the reform options – including the mechanism for ISDS and relevant procedural tools and also accommodate future

---

143. Submission by Colombia 173.
144. The Mauritius Convention on Transparency applies to arbitrations conducted on the basis of investment treaties concluded before 1 April 2014, unless the treaty is excluded in a reservation pursuant to Article 3 Mauritius Convention on Transparency (see Article 1 Mauritius Convention on Transparency).
145. See Submission by the European Union 159/Add.1; Submission by Colombia 173; and Submission by Ecuador 175; see also Submission by Chile, Israel, Japan, Mexico, and Peru 182, suggesting the implementation of reform options through a 'suite' approach.
146. Submission by Colombia 173, para. 29.
147. Submission by the European Union 159/Add.1, paras 35-37, 39.
148. Submission by Chile, Israel, Japan, Mexico and Peru 182, p. 2 and Annex.
149. See WGIII Report 1044, paras 102-111.

developments in the field of ISDS and provide temporal flexibility to allow continued participation by States Parties. Further, it was suggested that the instrument should allow for the widest possible participation of States to achieve an overall reform of ISDS and provide for a holistic approach to ISDS reform clearly setting forth the objective of achieving sustainable development through international investment.

It was noted that a minimum standard could contribute to the consistency and coherence of the ISDS system. While it was suggested that the instrument could contain optional elements that could be opted in or out by a participating State, it was also said that a flexible instrument with optional elements might contribute to more fragmentation of the ISDS system and forum shopping.[150]

Differing views were expressed on whether further work on options for implementation should be undertaken in parallel with the development of the reform options or whether they should be discussed at a later stage.[151]

Since 2020, two informal meetings were held on the multilateral instrument. The Secretariat also sought the assistance of the Treaty Section of the United Nations Office of Legal Affairs as well as of public international law and treaty law experts, who provided their views on the issues outlined in Secretariat Note 194 and identified issues requiring further consideration. On this basis, the Secretariat prepared further issues for consideration in a working paper supplementing Secretariat Note 194, which also contains an illustrative example of how a multilateral instrument could be structured.[152]

The Working Group will have to discuss how it wants to structure and interconnect the various reform elements it will develop in the coming sessions, how to ensure that they apply to existing treaties and to future agreements, how they are reflected in rules of procedure that will apply to the disputes, whether it wishes to develop a comprehensive set of dispute resolution provisions that will replace existing ISDS chapters or provisions in IIAs and how this set of dispute resolution provisions will integrate the various options for claimants (whether investors or States) to choose to enter into an investment dispute. While the Working Group has developed various elements, it will now have to decide how these elements will feature in the broader reform of ISDS.

VI   PARALLEL ISDS REFORM DEVELOPMENTS

Besides the UNCITRAL ISDS reform process, reform developments are also taking place in other fora. Effective July 2022, ICSID has amended its arbitration and mediation rules through the Rules and Regulations Amendment process particularly addressing concerns relating to the cost and duration of ISDS processes as well as the

---

150. *Ibid.*, para. 108.
151. *Ibid.*, paras 103, 104.
152. 'Possible reform of investor-State dispute settlement (ISDS) Multilateral instrument on ISDS reform', UNCITRAL Working Group III (Investor-State Dispute Settlement Reform) 43rd Session (Vienna, 5-16 September 2020) UN Doc. A/CN.9/WG.III/WP.221 (22 July 2022).

balance between States and investors in the procedural rules.[153] As the reform topics partially overlap, as does their respective membership, the Secretariats of UNCITRAL and ICSID are cooperating closely in order to work towards harmonized solutions and avoid further fragmentation of the legal framework for ISDS. Reform items such as TPF and the establishment of an appeal mechanism will require close cooperation with the ICSID Secretariat in order to develop an effective and coherent reform package. The UNCITRAL reform process generally takes into account the implications of the ISDS reform for the application of existing arbitration rules and administering institutions.

The OECD is hosting a forum that also touches upon certain ISDS-related topics – the Freedom of Investment process. The UNCITRAL Secretariat particularly took into consideration the OECD's work on the topics of shareholder claims and reflective loss in its preparatory work.[154]

Other reform developments are taking place on the level of IIAs. Most of the IIAs signed in recent years contain reform elements including the approaches of no ISDS, a standing ISDS tribunal, limited ISDS and improved ISDS procedure.[155] These developments are monitored and supported by UNCTAD, which assists policymakers, government officials and other IIA stakeholders to reform IIAs with a view to making them more conducive to sustainable development and inclusive growth.[156] Its activities include research and policy analysis, technical assistance and intergovernmental consensus-building.

VII   CONCLUSION AND WAY FORWARD

In a concentrated effort, the Working Group completed a first round of preliminary consideration of identified reform options in October 2020. Since then, the Working Group has made progress with the development of concrete reform elements despite the new working methods imposed by the COVID-19 pandemic. A first reform element, the code of conduct of arbitrators and adjudicators, is planned to be presented to the Commission next year and draft provisions for several other reform elements are already being considered by the Working Group in first readings.

The Working Group continues to simultaneously discuss, elaborate and develop multiple reform elements. The Working Group has also begun to discuss the design of

---

153. For further information on the ICSID Rules and Regulations Amendment project see the ICSID web page at https://icsid.worldbank.org/resources/rules-and-regulations/icsid-rules-and-regulations-amendment-working-papers (last accessed 3 December 2020).
154. *See* Secretariat Note 170.
155. *See* 'Reforming Investment Dispute Settlement: A Stocktaking' UNCTAD (March 2019, Issue 1), available at https://unctad.org/en/PublicationsLibrary/diaepcbinf2019d3_en.pdf (last accessed 3 December 2020); in the (signed but not yet ratified) US-Mexico-Canada Agreement (USMCA), Canada withdraws from the ISDS mechanism as it existed under NAFTA; Recently, 23 Member States of the European Union signed an agreement for the termination of intra-EU bilateral investment treaties as such.
156. 'Reforming Investment Dispute Settlement: A Stocktaking' UNCTAD (March 2019, Issue 1), available at https://unctad.org/en/PublicationsLibrary/diaepcbinf2019d3_en.pdf (last accessed 3 December 2020).

the delivery mechanism for the overall reform process, through a multilateral convention that will host the reform elements. This also entails the question of where and in which form certain reform elements fit into such a multilateral convention.

With strengthened resources and a work plan structuring its work until 2026, the Working Group is well-equipped to achieve meaningful and sustainable reform of the legal framework for IIDs in accordance with its mandate.

CHAPTER 24

ISDS Reform: Innovative Actions at the National and Bilateral Levels

*Ajuma Patience Okala**

TABLE OF CONTENTS

I   INTRODUCTION

The concept of Investor-State Dispute Settlement (ISDS) can be described as a double-edged sword. It is arguably the most important provision of International Investment Agreements (IIAs) to the investors, giving them the most comfort as they commit their resources to a different jurisdiction. It is at the core of investment protection policies implemented by host States to attract investors. Conversely, this comforting gift to investors, can in some cases, seem like a curse, an albatross around the neck of the host States. Not a few pundits still consider it scandalous that individual investors can commence commercial or investment arbitral proceedings against sovereign States, especially when the claims concern measures taken by the host State to achieve public policy objectives.

This reaction can be justified considering the recent arbitral awards against developing countries. These awards have not helped matters or allayed the concerns and outright fears of those who consider the system to be skewed against host States. Some recent awards against developing host States have brought to the fore, the need

---

*   Director Legal Services of Nigerian Investment Promotion Commission and Chief Negotiator of Nigeria's International Investment Agreements team.

for re-consideration of the system. A case in point is the 2017 award ordering Nigeria to pay P&ID USD 6.6 billion plus interest amounting to a total of over USD 9 billion for a project that was yet to take off.[1] Another example is the 2018 International Centre for Settlement of Investment Disputes (ICSID) award ordering Pakistan to pay USD 5.9 billion to a mining firm Reko Diq,[2] an amount that is about two times the total Foreign Direct Investment (FDI) attracted by Pakistan in 2018. Some of these cases were brought on the basis of broadly drafted standards found in older IIAs that limit the right of host States to regulate investment in their territories, and that expose them more openly to investor-State disputes.[3]

Of further concern is the fact that in 2020, the majority of the new ISDS cases (75%) were brought against developing countries and transition economies.[4]

However, some developing countries such as Nigeria that previously were capital importers are now capital exporters, especially regionally, and have commenced far-reaching reforms to their IIA regimes, as standard setters in their own right. It is therefore impossible for anyone to insist that things stay as they are. The global efforts at identifying concerns about the systems with a view to reforming and further refining them are, therefore, a welcome development.

The focus of this short paper is not to interrogate the desirability of the reforms at the multilateral level, nor is it to take away from the extensive work already being done. Rather, the aim is to highlight the quick wins that are available bilaterally and nationally to provide cures for aspects of the current ISDS regime that ail States, with particular reference to the reforms currently underway in Nigeria.

1   The 'Root' of the Matter

The two main multilateral reforms to ISDS by United Nations Commission on International Trade Law (UNCITRAL)'s Working Group III – WG III and ICSID are centred around subjects such as the lack of consistency, coherence and predictability of arbitral decisions, the apparent lack of independence and impartiality of arbitrators, costs and duration of ISDS proceedings, third-party funding (TPF), security for costs, code of conduct for Arbitrators, among others. The engagements border essentially on procedural and structural reforms, which are important. However, at the core, ISDS cases are triggered by the text of substantive provisions of treaties signed by treaty partners.

The first- and second-generation treaties reflect the mindset of capital-importing countries in time past, which was essentially to do and sign whatever it took to attract

---

1. https://jusmundi.com/en/document/decision/en-process-and-industrial-developments-ltd-v-the-ministry-of-petroleum-resources-of-the-federal-republic-of-nigeria-part-final-award-friday-17 th-july-2015 (3 March 2020) *Process and Industrial Development Ltd. v. The Ministry of Petroleum Resources of the Federal Republic of Nigeria.*
2. *Tethyan Copper v. Pakistan* https://www.thefreelibrary.com/Barrick + Gold + Corporation + (TSE%3a + ABX) + - + Barrick + Announces + Reko + Diq...-a0595353574 (3 March 2020).
3. Hamed El-Kady and Mustaqeem de Gama, *The Reform of the International Investment Regime: An African Perspective*, ICSID Review (2019), pp. 1-14.
4. https://unctad.org/system/files/official-document/diaepcbinf2021d7_en.pdf (September 2021).

investors and investments into their countries. Conversely, capital-exporting countries sought to gain as much protection as the treaty could give to meet their profit expectations. It appears that the capital-importing countries did not give much thought to the consequences of the loosely drafted provisions of such treaties beyond the optics of having signed a document that appeared to encourage the inflow of investments.

Over time, there appears to have been a paradigm shift in that mindset as a result of a number of factors including the fact that the line between capital-importing and capital-exporting countries is fast fading or blurred. It also has not helped to see that a definite correlation between the signing of Bilateral Investment Treaties (BITs) and an increase in FDI inflows is still a subject of debate.[5] Furthermore, some capital-importing countries have realized that even where the proliferation of treaties has attracted FDI, the investments attracted fall short of the right quality required to meet the economic growth expectations and developmental objectives of such host States. Rather than count their developmental gains, such host States are awakened to the rude shock of the debilitating and economically crippling effects of the seemingly simple BIT when an ISDS case is filed and awards are granted against them.

The receipt of Notice of Arbitration many times compels Host States to take a closer look at the text of the treaty. Arguably, the Host States realize at this point, that they probably failed to properly articulate a well-thought-out investment policy to determine their expectations of the treaty, beyond giving as much comfort as possible to investors.

Poor drafting of provisions such as definitions, fair and equitable treatment, full protection and security, pre-establishment, prohibition of performance requirements, expropriation and failure to circumscribe Most-Favoured Nation (MFN) and National Treatment (NT) articles, devoid of ambiguities that enable broad interpretation of the text, are a few of the triggers of ISDS cases. Same can be said of drafting of ISDS provisions without relevant safeguards to determine who gets access and the conditions precedent to accessing the settlement mechanism.

2 Reforming Nationally: Effective 'First Aid'

It is trite knowledge that the treaty text is oftentimes the foundation of all ISDS cases. When the porously drafted provisions meet certain actions of a host State, an incredibly expensive ISDS case is born. While the multilateral efforts at reform are highly commendable and have the prospects of effecting changes at a much broader level, the processes of achieving consensus on the reforms are long-drawn.

Conversely, it is much easier for States to address piecemeal, some of the issues that escalate into ISDS cases nationally and bilaterally through careful wording of their investment legislation, treaty texts and national and bilateral refinement of their IIA regimes. This is because bilateral treaty negotiations typically do not take as long as is required for multilateral efforts to yield the required fruit. Furthermore, States are able

---

5. https://investmentpolicy.unctad.org/uploaded-files/document/unctad-web-diae-pcb-2014-Sep %2024.pdf (9 March 2020).

to negotiate specific provisions that speak to their specific investment policies and treaty objectives.

II   INNOVATIVE STEPS TAKEN NATIONALLY AND BILATERALLY: CASE STUDY OF NIGERIA

Given the global wave of reforms, largely informed by an increase in the number of ISDS cases, and the growing dissatisfaction of host States in the old order of IIAs, Nigeria commenced holistic and far-reaching national and bilateral reforms of its IIA regime. Over time, the reforms were structured to mirror UNCTAD's three phases of IIA reform found in its *Reform Package for the International Investment Regime* (*2018 edition*).[6] Phase 1 was a national effort at the development of a new model BIT. Phase 2 centres around a national review of the existing stock of old-generation BITs and a bilateral effort at modernizing the treaties that fall short of the quality required to attract responsible, inclusive, and sustainable investments. Phase 3 will entail an alignment of the bilateral reforms with the national laws to achieve cohesion at both levels. The reform process is driven by Nigeria's Investment Promotion Agency (IPA), the Nigerian Investment Promotion Commission (NIPC) established under the provisions of the NIPC Act.[7]

1   The Nigeria-Morocco BIT

The national reforms in Nigeria's investment treaty regime commenced in 2015 with the development of a new model BIT in pursuit of sustainable development, balance of investors' rights and obligations, preservation of Nigeria's policy space, expanding investment facilitation and more importantly, the insertion of safeguards to seemingly unrestricted access to ISDS. The model, which became effective in February 2016 captures the national policy in innovative and modern provisions that set the tone for the attraction of RIBBS investments, i.e., Responsible, Inclusive, Balanced, Beneficial and Sustainable investments. Careful efforts were made to include well-thought-out definitions of key terms such as 'investment' and 'investor' to ensure that the protections and benefits of BITs only cover actual investments already established in Nigeria and determine in clear terms, who can access ISDS.

Other issues covered in the model, among others, were innovative provisions:

- introducing circumscribed NT and MFN articles;
- ensuring that BITs promote Nigeria's sustainable development objectives including specifically addressing issues relating to the environment, human rights, health, labour, safety and anti-corruption;

---

6. https://investmentpolicy.unctad.org/publications/1190/unctad-s-reform-package-for-the-inter national-investment-regime-2018-edition- (4 March 2020).
7. http://www.nigeria-law.org/Nigerian%20Investment%20Promotion%20Commission%20Act. htm.

- preserving Nigeria's policy space and the right of Nigeria to regulate in the public interest;
- balancing the asymmetry in investor's rights and obligations;
- inserting temporary safeguard measures;
- insertion of investment facilitation provisions to proactively assist investors with information and promote transparency of the legal and regulatory framework as well as transparency in arbitral proceedings;
- including dispute prevention as a key component of the treaty;
- establishing a Joint Implementation Committee to monitor the implementation and serve as a de-escalation and mediation mechanism;
- inserting pre-conditions to accessing ISDS and safeguards to curb seemingly unrestricted exposure to international arbitration.

The model was used to successfully conclude negotiations and sign a BIT between the Federal Government of Nigeria and the Kingdom of Morocco in December 2016. The Nigeria-Morocco BIT,[8] with its reform-oriented provisions, featured prominently in United Nations Conference on Trade and Development (UNCTAD)'s 2017 World Investment Report (WIR) and was cited as an example of a balanced 'new generation' investment treaty, which other developing countries and emerging economies should emulate.[9]

2   Dispute Prevention, Dispute De-escalation and Mediation

Care was taken to word innovative provisions in the treaty to address some current global concerns on ISDS and the substantive provisions leading up to those concerns. One major issue addressed nationally in the model BIT and bilaterally in the treaty is dispute prevention, dispute de-escalation and mediation.

The Nigeria-Morocco BIT establishes a Joint Implementation Committee, which among other things, is a dispute prevention mechanism, to '… seek to resolve any issues or disputes concerning Parties' investment in an amicable manner'.[10] The Committee also serves as a mediation and dispute resolution mechanism, to resolve disputes submitted under specified timelines, by an investor within 6 months from the date of the written request for consultations and negotiations, failing which '… the investor may, after the exhaustion of local remedies or the domestic courts of host State, resort to international arbitration mechanisms'.[11]

These provisions and the Joint Implementation Committee mediation provide ready solutions at a bilateral level to concerns on the improvement of time efficiency

---

8. https://investmentpolicy.unctad.org/international-investment-agreements/treaties/otheriia/37 11/morocco---nigeria-bit-2016- (3 March 2020) https://www.iisd.org/itn/2017/09/26/the-2016-morocco-nigeria-bit-an-important-contribution-to-the-reform-of-investment-treaties-tarcisio-gaz zini/ (3 March 2020).
9. https://issuu.com/unpublications/docs/world_investment_report_2017/68 Pages 120-123 and 140 (3 March 2020).
10. Article 4(4)d.
11. Article 26.

for ISDS, enhancing treaty Parties' involvement and control over their instruments, dispute prevention and mitigation, exhaustion of local remedies and mediation, which are being considered at multilateral engagements at the ICSID Rules (Amendment) Process and UNCITRAL Working Group III.

Unlike the discussions at the multilateral level, the treaty text at the bilateral level has the added advantage of reflecting a mutually agreeable time efficiency template that takes cognizance of the developmental realities and constraints of the treaty partners, thereby addressing the issue very quickly.

In similar national and/or bilateral efforts to address some ISDS concerns, Argentina and the United Arab Emirates have included a ban on TPF in their 2018 BIT.[12] The United States has also restricted TPF of domestic claims against the federal government.[13] Similarly, Egypt's Investment Law No.72 of 2017 provides '… multit-iered mechanisms for the settlement of investment disputes, including domestic litigation, amicable settlement and alternative dispute resolution (ADR) …'.[14] Essen-tially, it is indicative of the fact that Egypt seeks to develop an effective and flexible mechanism for the settlement of investment disputes. Such similar bilateral efforts to treat other identified concerns were raised under the ICSID Rules Amendment Process and UNCITRAL WG III.

3   Phase 2: Reforming the Old-Generation BITs

In 2017, Nigeria commenced Phase 2 of the reform process, which involves reforming the existing stock of old-generation BITs that are still in force despite their potentially injurious provisions that expose Nigeria to the needless risk of international arbitra-tion. Inspired by a table in UNCTAD's 2017 WIR, which rated IIAs on the basis of 11 reform-oriented provisions,[15] Nigeria came up with twenty critical and reform-oriented parameters. On the basis of the twenty parameters, which included critical consider-ations for the IIA reform,[16] the key investment protection, facilitation and promotion provisions of most of the twenty-nine BITs signed by Nigeria prior to the adoption of the new model, were assessed. The exercise indicated that a large percentage of the BITs fell short of the provisions needed to attract sustainable, responsible and

---

12. Agreement for the Reciprocal Promotion and Protection of Investments between the Argentine Republic and the United Arab Emirates, signed 16 April 2018 (3 March 2020) https://inve stmentpolicy.unctad.org/international-investment-agreements/treaties/bilateral-investment-tr eaties/3819/argentina---united-arab-emirates-bit-2018- (2 March 2020).

13. 31 USC 3727 (United States Anti-Assignment of Claims Act). https://www.iisd.org/itn/2019/0 6/27/third-party-funding-and-the-objectives-of-investment-treaties-friends-or-foes-brooke-guv en-lise-johnson/ (2 March 2020).

14. Moataz Hussein https://www.iisd.org/itn/2018/10/17/new-egyptian-investment-law-eyes-on-sustainability-and-facilitation-moataz-hussein/ (3 March 2020).

15. https://issuu.com/unpublications/docs/world_investment_report_2017/68 Page 121 (4 March 2020)

16. The parameters include reference to sustainable development, inclusion of enterprise-based definition of investment, inclusion of temporary safeguard measures, inclusion of transparency and investment facilitation clauses, among others.

qualitative investments. Validation of the work done on the assessment of Nigeria's BITs was received from UNCTAD, the World Bank and Nigeria's IIA team.

In 2019, practical steps commenced on the renegotiation and modernization of older BITs and concluded treaties that do not align with the current policy direction on Nigeria's BITs. With guidance from UNCTAD, Nigeria recently undertook a country-specific analysis of each BIT in force with country-by-country proposals on the next steps to be taken to proactively modernize each BIT. The analysis highlights:

(a) scores of each Treaty based on the twenty critical and reform-oriented parameters used for the assessment;
(b) tenures and current status of each Treaty (since a large number of them are already expired but are automatically renewed along with the potentially injurious provisions);
(c) next dates for the possible unilateral termination of the Treaties; and
(d) tenure of the survival clause (during which the treaty provision will still be in effect even after the Treaties are terminated).

Similar country-specific analysis of concluded but yet-to-be-ratified BITs was undertaken with a specific focus on the availability of quality safeguards to ISDS and the absence of pre-establishment provisions.

Engagements with some treaty partners had commenced on modernization of some treaties and renegotiation of other old-generation BITs in order to crystallize the required reforms and address some challenges to the ISDS regime at the bilateral level.

4 Phase 3: Alignment and Cohesion in National and Bilateral Efforts

In order to ensure cohesion of the reforms at the national, regional and bilateral levels, Nigeria has commenced preliminary work on Phase 3 of the reform process that entails the review of critical investment protection, facilitation and promotion provisions of the national investment law, the Nigerian Investment Promotion Commission Act,[17] which contains a number of protections that are not circumscribed, in addition to a seemingly unrestricted unilateral offer of ISDS by international arbitration to foreign investors.

The objective is to ensure that the national investment law and other related legislations largely align with reforms undertaken at the bilateral level so that the gains made in the model BIT are not lost through the current provisions of the legislation. NIPC has commenced work on the requisite amendments to the Act and has engaged relevant stakeholders including UNCTAD, the World Bank, Nigeria's National Assembly and the National Assembly Business Environment Roundtable (NASSBER) in the process.

---

17. Nigerian Investment Promotion Commission Act No. 16 of 1995 (see earlier reference to this Act) http://www.nigeria-law.org/Nigerian%20Investment%20Promotion%20Commission%20Act. htm (3 March 2020).

Discussions on the formulation of an AfCFTA Investment Protocol for Africa which will hopefully take cognizance of current global, regional and national reforms are underway as well as mirror the value found in the modernized provisions of the 2016 Pan African Investment Code. Nigeria is also part of the Guiding Principles on Investment policymaking for D-8 countries developed jointly with UNCTAD.[18] The non-binding Guiding Principles provide guidance for investment policymaking with a view to: promoting inclusive economic growth and sustainable development; promoting coherence in national and international investment policymaking; fostering an open, transparent and conducive global policy environment for investment; and aligning investment promotion and facilitation policies with sustainable development goals. These initiatives align with Nigeria's key IIA reform pillars, including sustainable development, the right to regulate and preserve policy space, balancing the asymmetry between investors' rights and obligations and encouraging international cooperation on investment-related challenges in addition to mitigating investment disputes through the use of Ombudspersons or similar institutions.

5   Coordination of Nigeria's Reforms

One primary objective of Nigeria's reform of its IIA regime is dispute prevention and de-escalation and other mediation mechanisms. With a stand-alone article on dispute prevention in its new model BIT, Nigeria had elevated the need to de-escalate disputes to serve the combined purpose of facilitating the ease of doing business, promote investment retention, expansion and reinvestment as well as limit Nigeria's exposure to avoidable international arbitration. Specifically, Nigeria's inclusion of a Joint Implementation Committee in its model BIT to, among other things, 'seek to resolve any issues or disputes concerning Parties' investment in an amicable manner', is a pointer to the country's commitment to mediate disputes.

Additionally, at the national level, the OSIC Lab, an administrative dispute prevention and resolution mechanism has been established in the country's IPA: Nigerian Investment Promotion Commission to support the country's efforts at dispute prevention and de-escalation and other forms of mediation. These bilateral and national efforts are already addressing the concerns and injuries which multilateral engagements such as discussions of the ICSID Rules Amendment Process on Mediation seek to address.

III   CLOSING THOUGHTS

There is increasing consensus on the desirability of reforms of the ISDS system. While the impact of multilateral reforms is broader and far-reaching the value of the almost

---

18. The D-8 Organization for Economic Cooperation, also known as Developing-8, is an organization for development co-operation among the following countries: *Bangladesh, Egypt, Nigeria, Indonesia, Iran, Malaysia, Pakistan,* and *Turkey*. Text of the principles available at: https://investmentpolicy.unctad.org/publications/1221/joint-d-8-organization-for-economic-cooperation---unctad-guiding-principles-for-investment-policymaking (4 March 2020).

instant relief derivable from national and bilateral reforms, while waiting for a sign-off of the multilateral reforms, cannot be over-emphasized. They provide the opportunity for host States to apply tailor-made solution sets to the trending concerns about ISDS. Continuation of reforms at a national and bilateral level is clearly worthwhile.

There however comes with this apparent 'quick win' the challenge of developing the capacity of investment treaty negotiators to agree on treaty texts beneficial to both parties, as my experience in the course of several negotiations has shown me that *a treaty is only as good as its negotiators.*

Additionally, as reforms on the national, bilateral and multilateral levels continue, they bring to the fore the apparent challenge of worsened fragmentation of the treaties aggravating the complexities of the proverbial spaghetti bowl of investment treaties.

It is therefore crucial to consider a more holistic approach to reform that also includes the substantive norms found in the treaties.[19] Such reform efforts need to be synchronized, coordinated and structured to minimize the risks of a fragmented approach to the reform of the broader international investment regime.[20]

---

19. UNCTAD's World Investment Report 2019, p. 115, available at: https://unctad.org/en/PublicationsLibrary/wir2019_en.pdf (4 March 2020).
20. Hamed El-Kady (October 2016), *Towards a More Effective International Investment Policy Framework in Africa*, Transnational Dispute Management; www.transnational-dispute-management.com.

The "State of the World" in 2022: New Developments and Reform in International Investment Arbitration—ISDS Reform Proposals: An Investor Perspective

Andrew T. Clarke[*]

TABLE OF CONTENTS

I   INTRODUCTION

Until I retired in March 2020, I had the privilege of serving as the Chair of the Corporate Counsel International Arbitration Group (CCIAG), an association of corporate counsel

---

[*] ICCA Governing Board member, Queen Mary University of London Centre for Commercial Law Studies Advisory Counsel member, Chair of the Steering Committee for QMUL's Energy Law Institute, Bencher of Middle Temple and, until April 2020, Chair of the CCIAG and in-house counsel with ExxonMobil International Limited for thirty-three years. Previously a member of the Court of the London Court of International Arbitration and its board of directors.

working for a broad range of companies. I have added their input to my own thoughts[1] in order to express the views of a wide range of investors with experience of using investor-state dispute settlement (ISDS), and who consider its availability to be an important consideration in decisions to invest abroad.

The last several years have been marked by an intense discussion about the need for reform to ISDS procedures. States have been found by international arbitration tribunals to have breached their obligations to foreign investors and ordered to pay compensation. Sections of the media and certain academics have been increasingly critical of the system, a reaction which is described as a "backlash" against ISDS[2] and "a crisis of legitimacy." The supporters of the system have failed to respond effectively and states have risen to the challenge by putting forward various reform proposals. These are taking place in multiple venues: at International Centre for Settlement of Investment Disputes (ICSID) (sweeping reforms to the ICSID Arbitration Rules will go into effect on July 1, 2022); the Energy Charter Conference (negotiations in relation to the modernization of the Energy Charter Treaty are reported to have been recently completed) and in Working Group III (WGIII) at UNCITRAL which has been discussing potential reforms to ISDS since 2017.[3]

Among the more radical reforms proposed are the elimination of the current arbitration-based adjudication system (with an appointments mechanism based on party autonomy) and the adoption of an appellate court to hear appeals against awards by arbitration tribunals or the proposed multilateral investment court (MIC) which would supplant arbitration tribunals entirely. The changes are described as procedural in nature and proposed in order to improve the operation of the ISDS system; however, there is a risk that foreign investors, who are not being adequately consulted in relation to the proposals, may react negatively to the changes and reconsider the cost and timing of future investments. If adopted, the "new world" of ISDS may be characterized by fewer or more expensive investments for the states who sign up for the reforms.

This paper will set out the context and key elements of the current ISDS system before focusing on some of the key proposals under discussion in WGIII. It will also look at the mechanism proposed for the adoption of reform proposals. In addition to raising questions over some of the flaws in these proposals, it will consider the near-term and longer-term implications of such reforms for investors, states and civil society and the impact they may have on future investment.

---

1. The perspectives expressed in this chapter are personal to the author and not attributable to his work with specific corporations in the past. This chapter was update by Tom Sikora, Chair of the CCIAG, in June 2022.
2. Clint Peinhardt and Rachel L. Wellhausen, *Withdrawing from Investment Treaties but Protecting Investment*, (2016) Global Policy doi: 10.1111/1758-5899.12355 http://www.rwellhausen.com/uploads/6/9/0/0/6900193/10.1111_1758-5899.12355.pdf (last accessed March 2020).
3. The CCIAG sits in the WGIII deliberations as an observer at the invitation of the secretariat so the author has direct knowledge of these discussions.

II   BACKGROUND

State protections for foreign investors have a long and interesting history stretching back over 500 years. The desire to provide such protection came from states keen to open up mutual trade and development while avoiding direct political conflict with other states whose citizens came to trade or invest. This helped states, interested in utilizing such resources, to secure foreign expertise, capital and investment to develop their national resources and promote economic development. Capital-exporting states also promoted such agreements, anticipating the benefits that successful investors can deliver through their growth and the repatriation of the proceeds of their investments. The agreements have proliferated at a bilateral and multilateral level to create the complex, multifaceted framework that applies to foreign investment today. Although the linkage between the treaties and such investment has been questioned by analysts,[4] it is without doubt that the last fifty years have seen an exponential growth in foreign direct investment (FDI). The United Nations has stressed the importance of the private/public partnership in securing the investment necessary to meet the sustainable development goals adopted in 2015,[5] but current forecasts see a significant shortfall occurring.

At a time when investor confidence would seem to be critical to meeting these objectives, states are now reassessing the need to offer foreign investment protections. Criticism of ISDS over the last ten years has led to TTIP being abandoned, some bilateral investment treaties being abrogated, and a broad-reaching re-evaluation of the system by states. Broad reforms are being considered with profound implications for investors, states and civil society. The consequences for states that adopt such changes, whether they are capital importing or capital exporting, are important, particularly if it means an increase in the cost of foreign investment and/or a reduction in investment flows.

Under the current ISDS system, the vast majority of the investment agreements currently in force give foreign investors special protection by allowing them to initiate ISDS to resolve investment disputes.[6] Out of the 2646 investment agreements that are

---

4. Joseph E. Stiglitz, "Regulating Multinational Corporations: Towards Principles of Cross-Border Legal Frameworks in a Globalized World Balancing Rights with Responsibilities" The Ninth Annual Grotius Lecture Series, American University International Law Review Vol. 23, No. 3, Article 1 (2007).

5. In a report written by Christopher Garroway and Chantal Line Carpentier of UNCTAD entitled "Why are we behind on SDG finance and what can we do about it?" published by UNCTAD on September 26, 2019 states that global FDI is in steady decline, leaving a sizable SDG investment gap of around USD 2.5 trillion annually, UNCTAD estimated that meeting the SDGs will require USD 5-7 trillion in investment each year from 2015 to 2030 of which only USD 1 trillion is expected to come from government spending and development assistance, http://unctad.org/en/pages/. newsdetails.aspx?OriginalVersionID = 2204 (last accessed March 2020).

6. See UNCTAD World Investment Report 2019, https://unctad.org/en/PublicationsLibrary/wir20 19_en.pdf at p. 99 (last accessed March 2020) (noting that 3,317 investment agreements have been signed and 2,658 are currently in force); see also UNCTAD Investment Dispute Settlement Navigator search conducted November 7, 2019, https://investmentpolicy.unctad.org/investment -dispute-settlement (last accessed March 2020) (showing that 2,443 of 2,577 mapped investment agreements allow for ISDS).

currently in force, at least 2440 allow for ISDS.[7] Despite the hostility to ISDS, new investment agreements with ISDS provisions are still being concluded regularly. For example, in 2020—notwithstanding the pandemic—states concluded twenty-one new investment agreements.[8] The current ISDS system has several noteworthy features:

- It is the creation of states, indeed the treaties that establish it come from acts of sovereign power by the states. They choose which states to conclude investment agreements with, draft the substantive provisions and set out the dispute settlement rules in the agreements.
- It is designed to incentivize and facilitate international investment. Capital-importing states are in a global competition for investment and want to be viewed favorably by foreign investors. If the treaties they sign fail to do so, the agreements do not serve the purpose of attracting foreign investment, nor will they achieve the economic and diplomatic objectives associated with concluding an investment agreement.
- It establishes a new relationship between states and foreign investors and provides important incentives that reduce risk to the investor, creating a greater balance between the investor and the respondent state. In the event of a dispute, both parties, investor and state, participate equally in the constitution of the tribunal to hear the dispute, a key element of party autonomy.[9] This gives both parties confidence that the tribunal will conduct the proceedings in a fair and impartial manner. It also makes it more likely that both sides will respect the final decision or award.
- It balances the need for consistency, correctness, and finality. The need for consistency is balanced against the need for correctness. Each tribunal hears a discrete dispute and there is no strict rule of precedent requiring a tribunal to follow decisions reached by prior tribunals. In practice, tribunals often rely on decisions in previous cases so the results are generally consistent over time. But the system was not designed to produce *absolute* consistency, because of the need to balance consistency and correctness. States and investors believed that a correct outcome will be more likely if the disputing parties are able to appoint arbitrators who are best suited for the given case—based on the

---

7. UNCTAD World Investment Report 2021, https://unctad.org/system/files/official-document/wir 2021_en.pdf at p. 122 (last accessed March 2022) (noting that 2,646 investment agreements are currently in force); *see also* UNCTAD Investment Dispute Settlement Navigator, https:// investmentpolicy.unctad.org/investment-dispute-settlement (last accessed March 2020) (showing that 2,440 of 2,574 mapped investment agreements allow for ISDS).
8. UNCTAD World Investment Report 2021, https://unctad.org/system/files/official-document/wir 2021_en.pdf at p. 122 (last accessed March 2022).
9. There are numerous other examples of provisions that ensure balance between states and investors, including the following: (1) states negotiate the procedural rules, but they generally give investors 2-3 options to choose from, such as the ICSID Arbitration Rules and the UNCITRAL Arbitration Rules; (2) in the conduct of the arbitration, both sides are given due process and equal opportunities to set out their claims or defences; (3) both sides are accountable for their conduct during the arbitration and can be required to pay attorneys' fees and costs; and (4) both sides have an obligation to treat a final award as binding and enforceable.

arbitrator's knowledge and experience[10]—and not confined by precedents, even if binding precedents might yield more consistency. The need for correctness is also balanced against the need for finality. Tribunals may make mistakes. Awards can be annulled on limited grounds, such as for significant due process violations, but the control mechanisms in the current system were not designed to correct errors on the merits. States and investors have supported this approach because alternative control mechanisms, such as an appellate mechanism with the power to review and reverse legal conclusions reached by the first-instance tribunal, may result in more correct decisions in some (but certainly not all) cases, but at an unacceptable cost: longer and more expensive proceedings. Reaching a correct and fair, final decision as expeditiously as possible is important to both states and investors.

– It ensures that arbitral awards are enforceable. ISDS awards are enforceable in nearly every state. One hundred and fifty-five states have ratified the ICSID Convention and 169 states that have ratified the 1958 New York Convention. The universal enforceability of ISDS awards is critical to states' and investors' confidence in the system. If there is uncertainty regarding enforcement, investors will have little faith in the dispute settlement process, the investment agreement, and ultimately, the safety and security of their existing or prospective investments.

If these considerations, and the framework established with the underlying support from the ISDS system, have contributed to the substantial increase in FDI during the latter part of the twentieth century, the reform proposals should also be examined to assess whether they will have an impact on future investment. As always, different proposals are anticipated to have different impacts—some beneficial, some not.

III   IMPORTANCE OF FDI

Is foreign investment worth the trouble it apparently causes? From the pre-pandemic data, it would appear that FDI is very important to global economic growth and public welfare. FDI constitutes 38% of the global gross domestic product (GDP)[11] and data shows there is a strong link between FDI and job growth. In the United States, FDI was directly responsible for 6.1 million jobs in 2016, and it contributed indirectly to an additional 2.4 million jobs.[12] In Latin America, FDI in new projects created nearly 1.4

---

10. The arbitrator's knowledge and experience in relation to the applicable law or the industry or region at issue, for example, are viewed as important by both states and investors.
11. UNCTAD World Investment Report 2019, Regional Fact Sheet: Developed Economies (June 2019), https://unctad.org/Sections/dite_dir/docs/WIR2019/wir19_fs_dvd_en.pdf (last accessed March 2020), at p. 1.
12. International Trade Administration, Industry and Analysis Economics Brief: Jobs Attributable to Foreign Direct Investment in the United States (February 2016), https://www.trade.gov/mas/ian/build/groups/public/@tg_ian/documents/webcontent/tg_ian_005496.pdf (last accessed March 2020), at p. 9.

million new jobs between 2013 and 2018, and 45% of new jobs in Mexico and 14% of new jobs in Brazil were attributed to FDI-linked projects.[13] In 2018, more than 170,000 jobs were created across the African continent as a result of 710 FDI projects, comprising USD 75.5 billion in capital.[14] The inflow of foreign capital is essential for the growth of the economy, the provision of infrastructure, and the continued economic development in the capital-importing host country. Specific benefits for host states include elevated living standards, foreign expertise in local business, development of human capital, transfer of technology, host country tax revenues, and the creation of quality jobs.

FDI relies on an investor being willing to accept the risks associated with making an investment in a foreign country in return for the benefits it expects to receive. Confidence and trust are at the heart of this assessment. The likelihood that a bargain will be met depends on the reliability (and past conduct) of the parties involved, the terms and conditions of the bargain (particularly the dispute resolution provisions), but also on the effectiveness of the legal regime in which it takes place. The efficacy of the process for resolving disputes and enforcing awards are key foundations on which a legal regime stands. Numerous multilateral institutions have recognized that access to impartial third-party dispute settlement is one of the key characteristics of a positive investment climate, along with such factors as open competition, predictability, rule of law, lack of corruption, and stability. It is one of the major factors considered by ratings and assessment mechanisms, including the World Bank Group's Ease of Doing Business Index.

In order to secure the benefits of FDI, governments should be taking proactive steps to cultivate and maintain an environment conducive to foreign investment. Those steps would include providing substantive protections for foreign investments and ensuring access to neutral, independent dispute settlement procedures in order to resolve disputes that arise. This is one of the key elements that an investor considers before making an investment. Any change that increases uncertainty will increase the perceived risk to an investor. Given the challenges ahead, it is more important than ever that states take steps to promote and facilitate foreign investment, and among the most important of these is the development of stable and transparent investment regimes protected by access to effective ISDS mechanisms.

IV   ASSESSING THE IMPACT OF THE REFORM PROPOSALS

This section will focus on two of the main reform proposals by the European Union, the proposed MIC and appellate mechanism. These proposals have significant flaws but also appear to be fundamentally contrary to the interests of both states and investors

---

13. Invest in Bogota, Research (April 2018), https://www.efe.com/efe/english/business/mexico-city-bogota-lead-latin-america-job-growth-linked-to-fdi/50000265-3600092 (last accessed March 2020).
14. EY, Attractiveness Program Africa (September 2019), https://www.ey.com/Publication/vwLUAssets/ey-africa-attractiveness-2019/$FILE/ey-africa-attractiveness-2019.pdf (last accessed March 2020).

and could significantly undermine investor confidence and reduce global investment flows. In summary, there are currently at least five flaws in the current proposals that cannot be remedied with technical solutions:

(a) they tilt the balance of the dispute settlement system against investors, who will change their investment decisions accordingly;
(b) they eliminate party autonomy for both investors and respondent states in the selection of adjudicators;
(c) they reduce the pool of qualified arbitrators;
(d) they introduce uncertainty regarding the enforceability of arbitral awards; and
(e) they introduce uncertainty regarding how dispute settlement proceedings will be funded and maintained over time.

These flaws need to be examined in more detail in relation to the MIC and the appellate mechanism.

1   Flaws of the MIC Proposal

a   *Tilts the Balance Against Investors and Implications for Their Investment Decisions*

At the heart of the EU's proposal for a MIC is a permanent mechanism composed of adjudicators appointed only by contracting states, not investors. UK Chief Justice Hewart is often quoted in support of the MIC: "[It] is of fundamental importance that justice should not only be done, but should manifestly and undoubtedly be seen to be done" but investors will not view a system in which only one side appoints all of the adjudicators as either fair or just. Giving investors a role in the appointment of adjudicators is necessary to maintain investors' confidence in the system, and such confidence is critical to ensuring the flow of foreign investment, and the problem goes beyond perception.

As a general matter, states are more likely to appoint adjudicators whom they view to be inclined to rule in favor of states. This phenomenon is familiar from the current ISDS system, in which some arbitrators are perceived as "state-friendly" and appointed exclusively by states. The assumption that states "would be expected to appoint objective adjudicators, rather than ones that are perceived to lean too heavily in favor of investors or states, because they are expected to internalize not only their defensive interests, as potential respondents in investment disputes, but also their offensive interests"[15] as home states of investors is not supported by any evidence and is probably incorrect. The evidence points in the opposite direction.

---

15. Submission from the European Union and its Member States to UNCITRAL Working Group III (January 24, 2019), A/CN.9/WG.III/WP.159/Add.1, https://undocs.org/en/A/CN.9/WG.III/WP.159/Add.1 (last accessed March 2020), at para. 23.

The reality is that few states have offensive interests related to ISDS. According to UNCTAD data, approximately 75 % of all ISDS cases have been filed by investors from one of the thirty-eight OECD Member States (833 of 1,104).[16] Overall, approximately 58 % of UN Member States have never had one of its investors file an ISDS claim against another state (112 of 193).[17] It is natural that states that always, or almost always, act as respondents—most states—will take a defensive approach when considering the appointment of adjudicators on a court. These states may reap significant benefits from concluding an investment agreement that includes ISDS, e.g., in attracting and promoting foreign investment, but they are still likely to choose adjudicators who see the world from a government's defensive perspective rather than an investor's perspective.

Even states whose investors bring claims regularly tend to prioritize their defensive interests on issues related to dispute settlement. This is evidenced by non-disputing party submissions by states. These submissions overwhelmingly side with the respondent's interpretation of the investment agreement, even in cases involving claims by the non-disputing party's own investors, because states are looking to protect themselves should they face similar claims.[18] Another example is treaty practice on ISDS over the past twenty years. Capital-exporting states, which might be expected to promote investor protections, have been at the forefront of introducing new tools in investment agreements that make it harder for investors (including their own investors) to initiate and pursue ISDS claims, such as tools that require the waiver of domestic remedies. It is difficult to identify any examples of tools in recent agreements—or tools under consideration in the working group discussions—that go in the other direction. In the undoubtedly political process of choosing adjudicators on a permanent court,[19] the pressure to favor defensive interests is likely to be particularly acute.

Once adjudicators are appointed, they may also feel accountable to the states that appointed them. It is noteworthy in this regard that the proposal at WGIII has evolved from allowing adjudicators an opportunity to renew their terms, to the current

---

16. UNCTAD Investment Dispute Settlement Navigator search conducted March 14, 2022, https://investmentpolicy.unctad.org/investment-dispute-settlement (last accessed March 2022).
17. This conclusion is based on data in Annex 2 of the UNCTAD Fact Sheet on Investor-State Dispute Settlement Cases in 2020 (September 2021), https://unctad.org/system/files/official-document/diaepcbinf2021d7_en.pdf (last accessed March 2022).
18. *See* Concurring and Dissenting Opinion of Judge Charles N. Brower, *Mesa Power Group v. Government of Canada* (UNCITRAL), https://www.italaw.com/sites/default/files/case-documents/italaw7241.pdf (last accessed March 2020), at para. 30 ("I have never experienced a case in which the other Party or Parties to a treaty subject to interpretation, appearing in a non-disputing capacity, have ever differed from the interpretation being advanced by the respondent State.").
19. *See* Submission from the Government of Bahrain to UNCITRAL Working Group III (August 29, 2019), A/CN.9/WG.III/WP.180, https://uncitral.un.org/sites/uncitral.un.org/files/wp_180_bcdr_clean.pdf (last accessed March 2020), at para. 29 ("[R]eplacing the entire scheme of arbitrators appointed by the parties to a dispute with one in which judges are appointed by the States party to the treaty establishing the permanent investment court creates a risk of judicial appointments becoming politicized. Indeed, this is a concern that has been expressed by commentators and would undo one of the hallmarks of the existing ISDS regime, which has so far been rather successful in depoliticizing the appointment process.").

proposal, which forbids renewal.[20] It is asserted that this revised approach is necessary to ensure that adjudicators are "independen[t] from governments," as it is acknowledged that party appointment can skew adjudicators' incentives.[21] But that is not enough. Adjudicators, for example, would be dependent on states to pay their salaries and fund and maintain the court's permanent facilities.[22] This could also skew adjudicators' incentives. And even if an adjudicator demonstrates bias, the adjudicator will continue to receive appointments for the duration of his or her term.

States should resist the temptation to think that tilting the balance of the system against investors is in states' interests. As highlighted above, the purpose of providing investors with effective dispute settlement tools is to give investors the confidence that disputes will be resolved fairly and impartially. This is to encourage investors to be willing to incur the risks and make the investments that are critical to the host state's achievement of its economic and societal goals. An imbalanced dispute settlement system would directly harm investors, but would also cause lasting, substantial indirect harm for all host states and the civil societies they represent.

b   *The MIC Would Eliminate Party Autonomy in the Selection of Adjudicators*

Under the latest proposal for the MIC, when an investor initiates a case, a subset of adjudicators on the permanent court would be assigned on a "randomized basis" to a "division" of the court that would hear the case.[23] Neither the investor nor the respondent state would have any role in the appointment of adjudicators for a given case, contrary to well-established practice. While arbitration systems have justifiable limitations on party autonomy to choose arbitrators (e.g., some exclude arbitrators who lack minimum professional qualifications), the proposal to eliminate party autonomy completely is contrary to the interests of both states and investors as it would prevent them from choosing the best adjudicators to resolve investment disputes.

China notes that both states and investors value party autonomy: "Participants in investment arbitration (investors, host-country Government officials, lawyers or arbitrators) generally believe that [party autonomy] is the core and most attractive feature

---

20. Compare the Canada-European Union Trade Agreement (CETA), para. 8.27(5) ("The Members of the Tribunal appointed pursuant to this Section shall be appointed for a five-year term, renewable once") with Submission from the European Union and its Member States to UNCITRAL Working Group III (January 24, 2019), A/CN.9/WG.III/WP.159/Add.1, https://undocs.org/en/A/CN.9/WG.III/WP.159/Add.1 (last accessed March 2020), at para. 19 ("Independence from governments would be ensured through a long-term non-renewable term of office (many international tribunals provide for nine year terms, for example), combined with a robust and transparent appointment process.").

21. *See* Submission from the European Union and its Member States to UNCITRAL Working Group III (January 24, 2019), A/CN.9/WG.III/WP.159/Add.1, https://undocs.org/en/A/CN.9/WG.III/WP.159/Add.1 (last accessed March 2020), at para. 19.

22. *Id.*, at para. 33 ("Contributions to the financing of a standing mechanism would be made, in principle, by the contracting parties.").

23. *Id.*, at para. 24.

of international arbitration."[24] Party autonomy is important because the disputing parties are experts in the particularities of the case and are therefore best placed to choose arbitrators with the appropriate knowledge and experience to render a correct decision. As China notes, "investment disputes often involve complex factual and legal issues at the first-instance stage of legal proceedings."[25] Accordingly, "many factors need to be considered by the parties in determining the composition of the arbitral tribunal and the suitability of the arbitrators selected for it, such as legal background, experience and nationality, as well as the level of energy input and special expertise that may be required for a particular case."[26] The proposed MIC denies both parties the opportunity to weigh these factors and to constitute the most effective tribunal. China's conclusion that party autonomy "should be retained in any reform process"[27] would be the preferred outcome.

In addition, different states will have varying priorities regarding adjudicator qualifications, and it is not clear why a one-size-fits-all approach is necessary or desirable. For example, many investment disputes arise between states and investors from the same region. In such cases, states and investors will likely prefer adjudicators with specific language skills, cultural knowledge, and familiarity with regional legal systems. These divergent priorities cannot be accommodated by the MIC.

Governments should ask themselves: If the court is established and I face a claim, how likely is it that I would have chosen any one of the three adjudicators appointed?[28] If not, why is this a better system to adjudicate the claim? Importantly, there is no reason to expect that an adjudicator nominated by a given state to the permanent court will be approved by the other states; and even if the adjudicator is approved, there is no reason to expect that the adjudicator will be randomly selected to sit on the division of the court hearing its case.

c   *The MIC Would Reduce the Pool of Qualified Arbitrators*

The MIC proposal requires adjudicators to refrain from participating in any outside activities other than teaching for "a long-term non-renewable term of office" (noting that "many international tribunals provide for nine-year terms").[29] Adjudicators would also "have the qualifications required in their respective countries for appointment to the highest judicial offices or are jurisconsults of recognized competence in international law."[30] Taken together, these limitations would indisputably reduce the existing pool of qualified ISDS arbitrators, a factor which is the backbone of the current system,

24. *See* Submission from the Government of China to UNCITRAL Working Group III (July 19, 2019), A/CN.9/WG.III/WP.177, https://undocs.org/en/A/CN.9/WG.III/WP.177 (last accessed March 2020), at section III, para. 2.
25. *Id.*
26. *Id.*
27. *Id.*
28. Investors will be asking themselves the same question.
29. Submission from the European Union and its Member States to UNCITRAL Working Group III (January 24, 2019), A/CN.9/WG.III/WP.159/Add.1, https://undocs.org/en/A/CN.9/WG.III/WP.159/Add.1 (last accessed March 2020), at paras. 16, 19.
30. *Id.*, at para. 20.

as investors will not use a dispute settlement system if the decision-makers are inadequate.

There do not appear to be any studies addressing the severity of the impact of the MIC on the arbitrator pool, which itself raises red flags, but the limited information available to decision-makers causes concern. For example, Susan Franck has found that imposing just one of the requirements—requiring public international law expertise—will lead to a "narrow, nondiverse" arbitrator pool.[31] There is a risk that these requirements, if adopted, would cumulatively narrow the new pool of adjudicators to essentially three groups: (1) senior academics; (2) established practitioners transitioning to becoming full-time adjudicators, most of whom are very senior and close to retirement; and (3) retired judges. The common feature of these individuals is that they will be elderly, nondiverse, and nonpracticing.

There is a particular concern that arises from eliminating practitioners from the pool. Many practitioners have proven to be excellent arbitrators, with experience in representing both states and investors and can therefore see both sides of the issue and render fair judgments. From a broader perspective, there should be concerns about creating major barriers to entry for new arbitrators—and the impact that would have on the arbitrator pool. Ideally, we should be striving for a dispute settlement system that exemplifies age, gender, and regional diversity—qualities that will be essential to the future credibility of the system. The EU's MIC proposal runs directly contrary to ongoing efforts in the international arbitration community to broaden the arbitrator pool and make the arbitration community more inclusive and representative of the disputing parties. It is important to improve the range of experience and views of decision-makers in order to increase the quality and legitimacy of their judgments.

Even if states are inclined to take steps, such as imposing more requirements for arbitrators, thereby reducing the overall pool of arbitrators, states need not create a new court to do so. Many treaties impose tailored requirements for arbitrator qualifications. Some treaties also employ rosters. There is no need to adopt a flawed permanent mechanism like the MIC in order to impose more requirements for arbitrators.

d   The MIC Would Introduce Uncertainty Regarding the Enforceability of Arbitral Awards

The proposal for a MIC acknowledges that enforcement of arbitral awards is critical.[32] Indeed, states and investors will quickly lose confidence in a dispute settlement system that results in unenforceable awards. Concerns about enforceability would lead investors to make risk-averse choices that negatively impact international trade,

---

31. *See* Susan D. Franck, *International Arbitration: Between Myth and Reality*, McGill Journal of Dispute Resolution Vol. 5, No. 1 (2018), at https://papers.ssrn.com/sol3/papers.cfm?abstract_id=3222792 (last accessed March 2020), at pp. 9-10.
32. *See* Submission from the European Union and its Member States to UNCITRAL Working Group III (January 24, 2019), A/CN.9/WG.III/WP.159/Add.1, https://undocs.org/en/A/CN.9/WG.III/WP.159/Add.1 (last accessed March 2020), at para. 30.

investment, and the flourishing of national economies. But while the proposal recognizes the problem, it lacks a solution: a key intrinsic flaw of the MIC is that it would introduce great uncertainty regarding the enforcement of arbitral awards.

Under the current system, as discussed in Section II, ISDS awards are enforceable in nearly every state. In the case of ICSID awards, the 155 states that have ratified the ICSID Convention are obligated to enforce ICSID awards without further review, as the ICSID Convention provides for automatic enforcement. As for ISDS awards rendered in non-ICSID cases, the New York Convention is applicable in 169 states, as of this writing, and requires swift enforcement with limited review. The New York Convention has played a unique role in promoting international trade and investment by facilitating the enforcement of arbitral awards for sixty-four years in approximately 2,500 cases.

The MIC would eliminate the stability and predictability created by the current regime. States that agree to resolve investment disputes using the MIC could commit to enforcing awards in their jurisdictions. However, these awards may not be enforceable in jurisdictions that do not agree to the MIC—which could be a substantial number of states, even under the most optimistic projections of court proponents. The EU contends that there is "no reason" to question the enforceability of MIC awards under the New York Convention,[33] for example, but with respect, that will not be for the EU to decide and cannot be known now. Domestic courts in each of the 169 New York Convention states will need to decide for themselves, and they will likely reach different conclusions, leading to a patchwork enforcement regime in place of today's well-established and nearly universally subscribed regime. There is a risk that this will undermine investor confidence and stunt investment.

The legal argument put forward for applicability of the New York Convention is that Article 1(2) of the Convention covers awards by "permanent arbitral bodies."[34] Whether this is right or wrong, it is important to note that numerous scholars have questioned the conclusion that a MIC can be considered a permanent arbitral body (rather than a judicial or quasi-judicial mechanism) based on analysis of the Convention's *travaux préparatoires*.[35] Again, there is an inherent risk that courts would come to different conclusions, which would produce further uncertainty for investors and states seeking foreign investment.

---

33. Submission from the European Union and its Member States to UNCITRAL Working Group III (January 24, 2019), A/CN.9/WG.III/WP.159/Add.1, https://undocs.org/en/A/CN.9/WG.III/WP.159/Add.1 (last accessed March 2020), at para. 32.

34. *Id.*

35. *See, e.g.*, Marike Paulsson, "Revisiting the Idea of ISDS Within the EU and an Arbitration Court: The Effect on Party Autonomy as the Main Pillar of Arbitration and the Enforceability of Arbitral Awards" (May 21, 2018), http://arbitrationblog.kluwerarbitration.com/2018/05/21/revisiting-idea-isds-within-eu-arbitration-court-effect-party-autonomy-main-pillar-arbitration-enforceability-arbitral-awards/ (last accessed March 2020); Alvaro Galindo et al., *The New York Convention's Concept of Arbitration and the Enforcement of Multilateral Investment Court Decisions*, in 60 Years of the New York Convention: Key Issues and Future Challenges (2019), at pp. 459-472; Richard Happ & Sebastian Wuschka, *From the Jay Treaty Commissions to a Multilateral Investment Court: Addressing the Enforcement Dilemma*, Indian Journal of Arbitration Law, Vol. VI, No. 1 (2017), at pp. 113-132.

e   *The MIC Would Introduce Uncertainty as to How Dispute Settlement Proceedings Will Be Funded and Maintained*

It has been proposed that the contracting parties will finance the court and "consideration should also be given to requiring that users of the standing mechanism pay certain fees," though the "fees should not be so high as to become a hurdle for small- and medium-sized enterprises to bring a case."[36] There is significant concern that this approach will not be sustainable and will put the dispute settlement system at risk, particularly in an environment in which certain states are already questioning, and even scaling back, their financial contributions to international organizations. Indeed, the proposal to weigh financial contributions among states based on their level of development[37] calls to mind ongoing debates in other international organizations regarding the identification of "developing countries" and the breakdown of rights and responsibilities resulting from that status.

It is important that states do not underestimate the costs associated with the court. When adjudicators' salaries, staff salaries, and the costs of funding and maintaining permanent facilities are taken into account it will be very expensive. In the current system, the investor and the respondent state jointly pay arbitrator fees and administrative expenses, and they do so only for the duration of the given case. Under the MIC, contracting states will bear the cost of paying adjudicators and maintaining the court on a permanent basis—with only nominal contributions from investors, as discussed above—regardless of whether they or their investors use the system. Having states pay for a standing body which is resolving disputes in which they are not involved is an intrinsic feature of the court.

This new approach would undoubtedly be sensitive for countries that are already questioning the value of their financial contributions to international organizations. Separately, the majority of states whose investors never or rarely bring ISDS cases would understandably question whether they are obtaining the benefit of the bargain. Based on these types of considerations, investors may ask themselves whether the mechanism will be available when it is needed to resolve their disputes, and they would also question the viability of investment agreements that incorporate the MIC.

2   Flaws of the Appellate Mechanism Proposal

The second main proposal by the EU is the creation of an appellate mechanism that would be empowered to review legal conclusions on a de novo basis and review factual determinations for manifest errors.[38] During WGIII meetings, it is apparent that some states view the appellate mechanism as a "middle ground" that would achieve many of the MIC's objectives while not raising quite the same level of concern to the critics of

---

36. Submission from the European Union and its Member States to UNCITRAL Working Group III (January 24, 2019), A/CN.9/WG.III/WP.159/Add.1, https://undocs.org/en/A/CN.9/WG.III/WP.159/Add.1 (last accessed March 2020), at para. 33.
37. *Id.*
38. *Id.*, at para. 14.

permanent mechanisms. That view is erroneous because the appellate mechanism proposal raises fundamental concerns that, like the MIC, cannot be remedied with technical solutions. The appellate mechanism is flawed because it: (a) tilts the balance of the dispute settlement system against investors in the same manner as the MIC; (b) makes erroneous decisions permanent; and (c) increases the cost and duration of proceedings.

a   *The Appellate Mechanism Tilts the Balance of the Dispute Settlement System Against Investors*

The current proposal does not address the constitution of the appellate mechanism, but it can be surmised that all appellate mechanism members would be appointed by states, which would create the same imbalance as the court. For the reasons discussed above, there are strong reasons to believe that states will appoint appellate mechanism members who would be inclined to rule in favor of states. The imbalance is inescapable. In fact, an appellate mechanism would create *more* imbalance than the court because of the appellate mechanism's superior power to issue decisions that would be binding in future cases. Investors would not have confidence in this system, which would be reflected in their investment decisions.

The suggested "open architecture" approach also does not inspire confidence. Under this approach, states could maintain existing ad hoc ISDS but also allow disputing parties to take appeals to a permanent appellate mechanism.[39] In practice, the imbalanced appellate mechanism would reign supreme. Investors would be disinclined to initiate a case—or find much value in the underlying investment agreement—if a one-sided appellate mechanism with power to review the tribunal's legal conclusions de novo confronts a successful claim or award. And if investors cannot initiate a case, there is a real risk that they may not invest at all.

b   *The Appellate Mechanism Would Make Erroneous Decisions Permanent*

The current proposal makes clear that decisions by the appellate mechanism on legal issues would be de facto or de jure binding in future cases.[40] Indeed, the main argument that is advanced in favor of an appellate mechanism is that it will create more consistent case law. Questions arise as to the extent to which an appellate mechanism will produce more consistent case law across the universe of over 2,600 investment agreements that are in force, but it has to be acknowledged that the mechanism could

---

39. *Id.*, at para. 39. Separately, the characterization of this approach as "open architecture" is flawed. Under the suggested approach, states would have just two choices: a court and an appellate mechanism, or just an appellate mechanism. There is almost no flexibility. It is a cafeteria with just two options. In contrast, the present system has a genuine open architecture that offers states many choices to design dispute settlement procedures that suit their and their investors' needs and interests.

40. *Id.*, at para. 44 ("In the same institution there will be a greater degree of deference towards an appeal mechanism as compared to that likely to be displayed by ad hoc tribunal.").

produce more consistent case law in some instances. But an appellate mechanism is not the right mechanism to achieve consistency. It would be prone to rendering erroneous decisions that would be permanent.

In the current system, awards can be corrected on limited grounds (e.g., due process violations) by an ICSID annulment committee (in the case of ICSID awards) or by domestic courts in the arbitral seat or in the jurisdiction in which enforcement of an award is sought (in the case of non-ICSID awards). Other basic errors may not be corrected, but critically, the damage is limited to that one case. By contrast, an appellate mechanism would make a flawed decision permanent and binding in future cases. As discussed in section II, states created the current system to achieve a balance between consistency, correctness, and finality. The appellate mechanism would disrupt this balance by putting consistency above all other considerations.

States should consider the scenario in which a future appellate mechanism takes on an issue of the highest sensitivity—e.g., the scope of the fair and equitable treatment obligation or the essential security exception—and issues a flawed decision that is binding in future cases. The only way to correct that error in the future would be to persuade the other contracting party or parties to amend the treaty or issue an interpretation (which would only be binding on a tribunal if permitted under the agreement). These are difficult paths to pursue. One flawed decision by one division of the appellate mechanism in just one case could effectively undermine the entire system.

The current system gives the state better options. It can seek to constitute a tribunal composed of arbitrators that it believes have the right knowledge and experience to render the correct decision on an issue of the highest sensitivity. Then, it can seek to persuade the tribunal. The tribunal will decide the case on the merits. In most cases, the tribunal will rely on prior arbitral decisions to support its conclusions because of the strength of the logic of these decisions, not because the tribunal is required to adhere to past decisions because of binding precedent. If the tribunal errs, the state has further choices. It can seek to annul the award based on limited grounds. In addition, it can either seek to persuade the other contracting party or parties to amend or interpret the treaty to prevent the same error in the future, or it can do nothing at all and wait for future opportunities to revisit the issue with a different tribunal. One poor decision cannot do irreparable harm to the system.

By contrast, an appellate mechanism would be prone to making errors that would cripple the system. The mechanism's decisions will reflect the quality of its members, and the pool of qualified individuals to choose from will be quite narrow (on the assumption that the same requirements that would apply to MIC adjudicators would also apply to appellate mechanism members). Some of the best arbitrators currently involved in ISDS cases would therefore be excluded from the pool. Also, as discussed, the lack of balance between states and investors in the constitution of permanent mechanisms may lead to errors.

In addition, the nature of the task itself will invite errors. States carefully negotiate the terms of their investment agreements, and even the smallest differences in language, context, or structure are significant. In a given case, an appellate mechanism may render a correct interpretation of a provision in one agreement. But the appellate mechanism will be expected to create consistent case law across the universe of over 2,600 investment agreements. There is therefore substantial risk that the appellate mechanism, in the interests of consistency, will take a correct interpretation of a provision in one agreement and misapply the precedent to interpret a similar, but inconsistent, provision in a different agreement. In other words, a state will be subject to rules to which it did not consent. The result will be erroneous decisions that are contrary to the interests of both states and investors.

c   *The Appellate Mechanism Increases the Cost and Duration of Proceedings*

It is acknowledged in the proposal that the routine use of the appellate mechanism would have negative consequences, as it suggests that "[m]echanisms for ensuring that the possibility to appeal is not abused should be included."[41] The main negative consequence that is implied, but not named, is that disputes will be lengthier and more costly for both states and investors. No technical solutions can prevent that, as the evidence suggests that the losing party in international disputes will likely seek review, particularly when the review mechanism is an appellate mechanism with the power to reverse any legal error. And an appellate mechanism requires more time and cost than other review mechanisms.

In the current system, parties seek review with increasing regularity. In the case of ICSID, annulment was rarely requested from 1971 to 2010, but from 2011 to 2020, it was requested in approximately 39% of awards (88 of 225).[42] Interestingly, disputing parties regularly requested annulment from 2011 to 2020 even though the success rate during this period was just 3%.[43] This low success rate reflects, amongst other factors, the narrow grounds for annulment in the ICSID Convention and the overall quality of the awards.

Under an appellate mechanism, requests for review by states and investors would significantly increase due to the appellate mechanism's broader review power. In the case of the WTO's Appellate Body, which has essentially the same broad review power as the proposed appellate mechanism, appeals were initiated with respect to 66% of panel reports as of December 31, 2019 (203/306).[44] From 2011 to 2019, the percentage of appeals sought was even higher: 69% (76/110).[45] Again, this is compared to annulment requests with respect to 39% of ICSID awards during roughly the same period.

Increased second-level review will significantly increase the cost and duration of proceedings. But the greatest source of added time and cost will come from the higher

41. *Id.*, at para. 15.
42. ICSID 2021 Annual Report, https://icsid.worldbank.org/sites/default/files/publications/ICSID _AR21_CRA_bl1_web.pdf (last accessed March 2022), at p. 31.
43. *Id.*
44. WTO Appellate Body Annual Report for 2019-2020 (July 2020), https://docs.wto.org/dol2fe/ Pages/SS/directdoc.aspx?filename = q:/WT/AB/30.pdf&Open = True (last accessed March 2022), at p. 176.
45. *Id.*

success rate to be expected in appeals versus annulments. The best available data suggests that the WTO Appellate Body modifies or reverses portions of approximately 85% of panel reports,[46] which is dramatically higher than the 3% ICSID annulment success rate this decade. A similar upswing in reversals with an appellate mechanism for investment disputes can be anticipated. But the consequences for the length and cost of the dispute will be much greater for investment disputes. When the WTO Appellate Body reverses or modifies a panel report, it generally "fills in the gaps" or leaves elements of the dispute unresolved. An appellate mechanism for investment disputes, by contrast, will often need to remand the case for additional proceedings due to the fact-intensive nature of investment disputes. Any remand procedures—the details of the current proposal are unclear—will produce untold delays and increased costs.

It has been suggested that the obvious delays and costs associated with an appellate mechanism will be offset by other aspects of their proposal. It is necessary to address these arguments.

First, it is argued that establishing the MIC and thereby eliminating the arbitrator selection process will save time and money.[47] It may save time in some cases but cause delays in others if, for example, the contracting states fail to agree on appointments of adjudicators on the permanent mechanisms in a consistently timely manner. It is unlikely to save a significant amount of money, as arbitrator selection requires a relatively minimal expenditure of attorney's fees and no evidence to the contrary is offered. Also, the cost associated with arbitrator selection is money well-spent, as both disputing parties want to ensure that they have the most suitable arbitrators to hear the case at hand, and these costs would be dwarfed by the costs of maintaining permanent mechanisms.

Second, it is argued that less time and money will be spent on arbitrator challenges because "adjudicators would be considered independent and impartial on account of their tenure" and potential conflicts would only arise in "very specific limited cases."[48] There is simply no way to support this assertion. For example, arbitrators will be required to disclose potential conflicts of interest, and there will surely be regular challenges based on those disclosures or alleged failure to make the required disclosures. Challenges may be even more frequent: in the current system, most challenges are directed at the arbitrator appointed by the other side, whereas in a new regime, all three adjudicators would be prone to challenge by both sides. Also, arbitrators will be required to have extensive professional experience, which will make the existence of conflicts more likely.

Third, it is stated that adjudicators will have incentives not to prolong cases since their remuneration would not be linked to the time spent on a case.[49] Not only is there

---

46. Michel Cartland, Gérard Depayre & Jan Woznowski, *Is Something Going Wrong in the WTO Dispute Settlement?*, Journal of World Trade, Vol. 46, No. 5 (2012), at p. 989.
47. Submission from the European Union and its Member States to UNCITRAL Working Group III (January 24, 2019), A/CN.9/WG.III/WP.159/Add.1, https://undocs.org/en/A/CN.9/WG.III/WP.159/Add.1 (last accessed March 2020), at para. 52.
48. *Id.*, at para. 53.
49. *Id.*, at para. 54.

no evidence that arbitrators act with such a lack of integrity, but the looming prospect of de novo review by an appellate mechanism may actually lead arbitrators to "overdo it" and draw out the proceedings to ensure that all points, even tangential points, are fully briefed and addressed by the parties and the court.

Fourth, it is contended that consistency and predictability will reduce cost and duration.[50] In fact, most attorneys' time is spent litigating the facts and the application of the law to facts, not legal standards, so increased consistency regarding legal standards will not significantly reduce time or cost. With respect to legal standards, good attorneys will surely seek to distinguish prior holdings that are unfavorable to their client—not just throw up their hands—so it is hard to foresee a significant reduction in time or cost. In addition, consistently flawed decisions may actually invite new cases and make those cases longer and more costly.

The working group has concluded that the cost and duration of disputes are one of the three principal concerns with the current ISDS system, which makes the appellate mechanism a uniquely unsuitable reform to pursue. Investors share states' objectives in streamlining dispute settlement. If years of delay and millions of dollars are added to the cost of resolving disputes, intelligent and experienced investors will pursue other dispute settlement mechanisms, or else look to alternatives to investing abroad.

V   REFORMS THAT WOULD IMPROVE THE SYSTEM FOR ALL USERS

Notwithstanding the flaws identified in the two key proposals above, there are numerous ISDS reforms which have been proposed by governments in WGIII, which have the potential to deliver constructive improvements to the current ISDS system.[51] Incremental reforms, that improve the fairness and efficiency of the dispute settlement system, would be beneficial for all stakeholders. The ISDS system is still relatively young and should be given time to continue to evolve to reflect lessons learned by states, investors, and other stakeholders from the last 30 years of experience and cases resolved under this system.

1   Multilateral Advisory Center

A multilateral advisory center for ISDS could complement existing efforts by international organizations and academic institutions to assist developing states. Above all, an advisory center could play a key role in dispute prevention, and from investors' experience of disputes, it is clear that avoidance is better than cure. The delegations to WGIII from Morocco and Thailand observed that many countries are hampered by a lack of knowledge, experience, and institutional capacity to prevent investment

---

50. *Id.*, at para. 55.
51. *See* Addendum to Note by the UNCITRAL Secretariat, Possible Reform of investor-State dispute settlement (ISDS) (July 13, 2019), http://undocs.org/en/A/CN.9/WG.III/WP.166/Add.1 (last accessed March 2020).

disputes from arising.[52] Investors would agree with this. A better understanding of the obligations a state has agreed to provide to foreign investors would reduce the risk of unintended breaches occurring through decisions being made that are difficult to reverse. If decisions are taken on an informed and considered basis, states would be better placed to work with investors on the adjustments that may be necessary to take account of the economic consequences. This could contribute significantly to certainty and predictability, enhancing the relationship between investors and states. An advisory center could also facilitate the sharing of information between states on best practices, and even spearhead the creation of guidelines on dispute prevention.[53] The success of such a scheme would depend on the scope of services to be provided, which is still under discussion at WGIII, so an advisory center could also train government officials to defend and manage ISDS cases; however, valid concerns have been expressed that it would be inappropriate for the center to act as counsel for states in investment disputes.[54]

2   Code of Conduct

The absence of a universal code of conduct for arbitrators in ISDS cases is a glaring flaw in the current system. Arbitrators in ISDS cases have generally exhibited great integrity, but a code of conduct is necessary to ensure that arbitrators have a clear understanding of their ethical obligations and provide for conflicts of interest to be identified and addressed. This will establish a level playing field which is transparent and fair for all. The International Bar Association (IBA) Guidelines on Conflicts of Interest in International Arbitration are valuable but insufficient. While the IBA Guidelines have made a significant contribution to the resolution of ethical questions in ISDS cases, they are optional guidelines designed for arbitration matters generally and are not tailored for

---

52. *See* Submission from the Government of Morocco to UNCITRAL Working Group III (March 4, 2019), A/CN.9/WG.III/WP.161, https://undocs.org/en/A/CN.9/WG.III/WP.161 (last accessed March 2020), at para. 18 ("Owing to their limited financial resources and lack of legal professionals with significant experience in ISDS, developing countries need assistance in that area."); Submission from the Government of Thailand to UNCITRAL Working Group III (March 8, 2019), A/CN.9/WG.III/WP.162, https://undocs.org/en/A/CN.9/WG.III/WP.162 (last accessed March 2020), at para. 11 ("Government agencies responsible for ISDS issues in many developing countries still lack the know-how to recognize a looming dispute, and more crucially, how to manage them. In addition, a knowledge gap exists between the government legal experts and the officials directly responsible for measures potentially breaching treaty obligations.").
53. Submission from the Republic of Korea to UNCITRAL Working Group III (July 31, 2019), A/CN.9/WG.III/WP.179, https://uncitral.un.org/sites/uncitral.un.org/files/wp179_new.pdf (last accessed March 2020), at section III(2) (noting that an advisory center "could become a hub for collecting and disseminating best practices and institutional information," including "education on dispute prevention").
54. Report of UNCITRAL Working Group III on the work of its thirty-eighth session (advance copy) (October 23, 2019), A/CN.9/1004, https://uncitral.un.org/sites/uncitral.un.org/files/draft_report_for_website.pdf (last accessed March 2020), at para. 33 ("While support was expressed for the advisory centre providing support during the proceedings particularly for States with limited resources, doubts were expressed as regards the role that the advisory centre could play in representing States, in particular in light of the potential resources that it would require, and the potential liabilities and conflicts that it might incur.").

ISDS cases. They were also drafted by practitioners with little input from states. WGIII has a valuable opportunity to build on the IBA Guidelines and recent scholarship and create a code of conduct that will ensure that arbitrators in ISDS cases act in accordance with the highest ethical standards. It is notable that WGIII has partnered with ICSID in this endeavor, which may help address inconsistencies between WGIII and ICSID approaches identified by Ecuador and others.[55]

As for the content of a code of conduct itself, the main elements should include independence and impartiality, integrity, diligence and efficiency, confidentiality, competence or qualifications, and disclosure.[56] One of the key considerations in this discussion relates to double-hatting, and investors would strongly oppose a broad prohibition, on the grounds that it would narrow the pool of qualified arbitrators and produce other unintended consequences that would outweigh any potential benefits of such an approach.

3   Prior Scrutiny of Awards

The delegation from Morocco stated that: "Most rules on investment arbitration do not provide for a quality control procedure whereby an award can be reviewed before it becomes final."[57] As a solution, Morocco suggested learning from the example of the International Chamber of Commerce (ICC) and giving an independent body a short period of time to review awards to "ensure that each award complied with all the formalities, addressed all claims and set out the grounds on which it was based."[58] It is unclear whether a review by an independent body is feasible and I anticipate that many technical questions will arise regarding the scope and effect of such review. However, there are attractive possibilities in Morocco's suggestion to look for additional ways to improve the review of tribunal awards that will not materially affect the duration or costs of the proceedings nor favor one disputing party over another.

Another proposal that has been discussed in WGIII involves giving both disputing parties an opportunity to review and comment on the draft award before it is finalized. The Trans-Pacific Partnership Agreement, for example, allows disputing parties to request to review the draft award and provides them with sixty days to provide written comments to the tribunal.[59] This is a novel way to ensure that the tribunal fully considers the views of the parties and makes the correct decision.

---

55. *See* Submission from the Government of Ecuador to UNCITRAL Working Group III (July 17, 2019), A/CN.9/WG.III/WP.175, https://undocs.org/en/A/CN.9/WG.III/WP.175 (last accessed March 2020), at paras. 20-21 (noting, for example, that that ICSID and UNCITRAL rules diverge on standards for arbitrator disqualification).
56. Report of UNCITRAL Working Group III on the work of its thirty-eighth session (advance copy) (October 23, 2019), A/CN.9/1004, https://uncitral.un.org/sites/uncitral.un.org/files/draft_report_for_website.pdf (last accessed March 2020), at para. 56.
57. Submission from the Government of Morocco to UNCITRAL Working Group III (March 4, 2019), A/CN.9/WG.III/WP.161, https://undocs.org/en/A/CN.9/WG.III/WP.161 (last accessed March 2020), at para. 21.
58. *Id.*, at paras. 22-25.
59. The Comprehensive and Progressive Agreement for Trans-Pacific Partnership, Article 9.23(10).

4   Improving Arbitrator Selection

WGIII has an opportunity to help states and investors choose arbitrators who are best suited to resolve the dispute and who would advance the objectives of the dispute settlement system as a whole. Several delegations have made proposals in this regard that deserve careful consideration. Turkey proposes that the Secretariat maintain an indicative list of arbitrators for use by states and investors that would provide information on the availability and workload of arbitrators such that disputing parties opposed to double-hatting could choose arbitrators accordingly. The database could also have other information about arbitrators to assist party selection. In their joint submission, Chile, Israel, Japan, Mexico, and Peru suggest that states could require that arbitrators in disputes involving highly technical subject matter, such as financial services, have specialized knowledge and experience.[60] Finally, Bahrain focuses on diversity, and proposes that "diversity considerations be formally added to the criteria to be applied when selecting arbitral panel members."[61]

These types of proposals are a positive step forward for the existing system. States and investors would benefit from better information on arbitrators—which initiatives like Arbitrator Intelligence[62] are making available. They also benefit from more diverse, expert arbitrators being available. It will be interesting to see how these discussions evolve on how to balance these objectives with other important objectives such as ensuring party autonomy.

5   Alternative Dispute Resolution Mechanisms

Several delegations to WGIII have suggested exploring alternative dispute resolution mechanisms, including mediation and conciliation.[63] China stated, for example, that conciliation can help states and investors "adopt creative and forward-looking methods to promote the settlement of investment disputes."[64] As a result, disputing parties can

---

60. Submission from the Governments of Chile, Israel, Japan, Mexico, and Peru to UNCITRAL Working Group III (Oct. 2, 2019), A/CN.9/WG.III/WP.182, https://undocs.org/en/A/CN.9/WG .III/WP.182 (last accessed March 2020), at p. 6.
61. Submission from the Government of Bahrain to UNCITRAL Working Group III (August 29, 2019), A/CN.9/WG.III/WP.180, https://uncitral.un.org/sites/uncitral.un.org/files/wp_180_ bcdr_clean.pdf (last accessed March 2020), at para. 61.
62. *See* https://arbitratorintelligence.com/ (last accessed March 2020).
63. *See* Submission from the Government of China to UNCITRAL Working Group III (July 19, 2019), A/CN.9/WG.III/WP.177, https://undocs.org/en/A/CN.9/WG.III/WP.177 (last accessed March 2020), at section III, para. 4; Submission from the Government of Thailand to UNCITRAL Working Group III (March 8, 2019), A/CN.9/WG.III/WP.162, https://undocs.org/en/A/CN.9/ WG.III/WP.162 (last accessed March 2020), at para. 24; Submission from the Government of Turkey to UNCITRAL Working Group III (July 11, 2019), A/CN.9/WG.III/WP.174, https:// undocs.org/en/A/CN.9/WG.III/WP.174 (last accessed March 2020), at section III.
64. *See* Submission from the Government of China to UNCITRAL Working Group III (July 19, 2019), A/CN.9/WG.III/WP.177, https://undocs.org/en/A/CN.9/WG.III/WP.177 (last accessed March 2020), at section III, para. 4.

avoid adversarial dispute settlement proceedings and "maintain[] long-term coopera-tive relationships."[65] Many investors have successfully used mediation and concilia-tion to resolve difficult commercial disputes, and there is no reason why similar results could not be achieved in investment disputes.

Now would be a good time to pursue mediation and conciliation options, as the UN Convention on International Settlement Agreements Resulting from Mediation, better known as the "Singapore Mediation Convention," has recently been concluded. It will play a valuable role in changing the international legal landscape by allowing parties to enforce post-mediation settlement agreements abroad in a similar manner as arbitral awards.

It is important to note that these alternative dispute resolution mechanisms should be optional for disputing parties rather than a prerequisite to pursuing ISDS. In some cases, one or both disputing parties may take the view that a dispute cannot be resolved in mediation or conciliation, and they should not be compelled to pursue that path. If they are compelled, the process is likely to be unsuccessful and result in a waste of time and resources for both parties.

6   Expedited Procedures

Investors and states—particularly small- and medium-sized companies and developing countries—would benefit from the availability of expedited procedures to resolve investment disputes, as recommended by several delegations.[66] The one-size-fits-all model of ISDS is cost-prohibitive and inappropriate for certain disputes involving a small amount of money or less complex subject matter. While these types of disputes may be more suitable for mediation, conciliation, or other alternative dispute settle-ment mechanisms, states and investors should not be prevented from pursuing arbitration. Many arbitral institutions have introduced expedited procedures in recent years for that reason.

7   Additional Case Management Tools

Arbitrators in ISDS cases need to be flexible in structuring the proceedings to ensure that they have the information they need to make the correct decision and to guarantee both disputing parties due process. At the same time, steps need to be taken to ensure that cases are resolved in a more expeditious fashion. It would be helpful to explore both mandatory rules and guidance for tribunals to achieve these results. For example, the delegate from Thailand proposed requiring the tribunal to consult with the parties to establish a budget for the proceedings.[67]

---

65. *Id.*
66. Submission from the Government of Thailand to UNCITRAL Working Group III (March 8, 2019), A/CN.9/WG.III/WP.162, https://undocs.org/en/A/CN.9/WG.III/WP.162 at para. 17; Submis-sion from the Government of Turkey to UNCITRAL Working Group III (July 11, 2019), A/CN.9/WG.III/WP.174, https://undocs.org/en/A/CN.9/WG.III/WP.174, at section III.
67. *Id.*, at para. 16.

VI   THE MECHANICS FOR IMPLEMENTATION

One of the key challenges to the current debate is the mechanism through which reforms will be implemented. Treaties would normally be amended by the states that are party to them; however, this represents a significant challenge given the number and variety of treaties in place. Many of these treaties have their own unique provisions dealing with termination or amendment, and "sunset" clauses to protect investors from sudden adverse changes that may affect the protections covering their investments. These proposals are addressed in Working Paper 194.[68] As UNCITRAL is not in a position to legislate on behalf of the participating states (or others) it has been suggested that a multilateral instrument be prepared that states could either opt in or opt out of (depending on the approach agreed), with the potential to introduce changes to the ISDS procedures for future investment treaties. More creatively, it has been suggested that this might go beyond procedural matters and even apply retrospectively to existing treaties.[69] Although the intention is "to promote legal certainty and coherence in ISDS,"[70] the risk is that the opposite will be the case.

As noted above in section III, trust and certainty are key considerations for investors, different types of risk come at a cost and may prevent investment entirely. Among the risks businesses have to consider (operational, geological, commercial, environmental, social and political), political risk is among the hardest to quantify and almost entirely within the control of states. An increase in political risk will increase the cost of investment or, once it rises above a certain level, will prevent it entirely. WGIII should be focusing on mechanisms that will de-risk investment and streamline the ISDS process to promote greater predictability. This would encourage greater compliance with existing obligations and the consequential benefit that fewer disputes would arise. In a world competing for foreign investment, states with a greater need will think carefully about the consequences of opting into the new arrangements. If, as the author believes, the new regime introduces a higher level of risk and uncertainty for investors, they are more likely to opt out, leaving existing (tried and trusted) arrangements in place. Where treaty counterparties have opted-in their investors may be less clear about the protections that will apply—creating opportunities for the investors from capital-exporting states that have also chosen to opt-out.

If the reforms stray into substantive protections (currently outside the mandate given by the UNCITRAL Commission) or introduce retrospective change, this should be considered very carefully. It would raise important questions, particularly in relation to its scope and content, as it could have a significant impact on investors' perception of the reliance they can place on state-provided protections. Investors are already coming to terms with the decision of the European Court of Justice in *Achmea v. Slovakia*[71]

---

68. https://undocs.org/A/CN.9/WG.III/WP.194 (last accessed March 2020).
69. An approach that has only been adopted in two conventions to date: the United Nations Convention on Transparency in Treaty-based Investor-State Arbitration; and the OECD Multilateral Convention to Implement Tax Treaty Related Measures to Prevent Base Erosion and Profit Shifting.
70. https://undocs.org/A/CN.9/WG.III/WP.194 (last accessed March 2020) at para. 7.
71. ECLI:EU:C:2018:158.

which had the effect of retrospectively voiding intra-EU member state bilateral investment protections. It is becoming clear that the fabric of international law, which holds together the complex relationships of international trade and investment, is more delicate than it appears.

VII   CONCLUSION

It is clear that there are real concerns regarding the ISDS system that have been raised by the international community as well as delegates at WGIII. Opportunities for constructive reform clearly exist, but to be effective such reform must take into account the concerns, interests, and perceptions of investors. In assessing the benefits and impacts of each reform, states should consider the effect it may have on existing and future investment, at home and abroad.

PART V   Regional Themes

PANEL 7   Regional Themes I: The
Americas and Europe Between
Constitutionalism and Populism

CHAPTER 26

The Americas and Europe Between Constitutionalism and Populism: European Challenges to ISDS

*Sir David Edward**

TABLE OF CONTENTS

I   INTRODUCTION

This topic has two aspects:

(1) public and governmental objections to the current practice of Investor/State Dispute Settlement (ISDS) through arbitration – notably the proposal of the European Commission for the creation of an Investment Court, and

---

*   Honorary President, Scottish Arbitration Centre; Professor Emeritus, University of Edinburgh; Judge of the European Court of Justice 1992-2004; Advocate (Scotland) 1962; Queen's Counsel (Scotland) 1974; Fellow of the Royal Society of Edinburgh; Honorary Bencher, Gray's Inn.

(2) the legal or constitutional clash between:
- the jurisdiction of international arbitral tribunals; and
- the jurisdiction of national and transnational courts – notably the Court of Justice of the European Union (CJEU).

The existing system of ISDS through arbitral tribunals is criticised on several grounds, reflecting governmental and popular ('populist') concerns on the one hand, and more strictly legal or 'constitutionalist' concerns on the other. The defects of the system have been summarised by the European Commission as follows:[1]

(1) *Ad hoc*: Tribunals are only set up on a case-by-case basis.
(2) *Risks of partiality*: Arbitrators nominated by the disputing parties may feel obliged to 'represent' the party who nominated them, and may have other conflicts of interest.
(3) *Unpredictable*: Tribunals adopt different interpretations of investment protection standards, being appointed ad hoc for one case at a time.
(4) *One-stop shop*: Parties have very limited grounds on which to appeal against ISDS decisions – essentially violation of due process.
(5) *Inefficient*: ISDS duplicates the same framework for dealing with every problem, which is costly and doesn't cover the large number and variety of treaties.
(6) *Opaque*: There is currently limited published information about:
- the existence of investment disputes;
- the procedure of the dispute;
- the substantive aspects of the case;
- the results of the disputes.

In what follows, I shall discuss:

(1) The origins of ISDS arbitration and the problems it was intended to resolve.
   (a) ICSID
(2) The causes of dissatisfaction with ISDS through arbitration.
(3) The proposals of the European Commission for the creation of a Multilateral Investment Court System (ICS).
(4) The jurisdiction of the Court of Justice of the European Union (CJEU)
(5) The *Achmea* case:[2]
   (a) Background.
   (b) The factual and legal context.

---

1. *Commission's Factsheet on the Multilateral Investment Court* annexed to Council of the EU Press Release, 20 March 2018, *Multilateral Investment Court: Council gives mandate to the Commission to open negotiations*. https://www.consilium.europa.eu/en/press/press-releases/2018/03/20/multilateral-investment-court-council-gives-mandate-to-the-commission-to-open-negotiations/ accessed 11 July 2022.
2. Case C-284/16 *Slovak Republic v. Achmea BV*, 6 March 2018, ECLI:EU:C:2018:158.

(c) The Opinion of the Advocate General (a member of the Court whose function is to assist the Court by delivering an independent opinion on cases of importance).

(d) The Judgment of the Court.

(e) The immediate aftermath.

(6) The Opinion of the CJEU on the Comprehensive Economic and Trade Agreement (CETA) between Canada and the European Union and its Member States ('the CETA Opinion'):[3]

(a) Background.

(b) Opinion 1/17 of the CJEU.

(c) Subsequent events.

(7) The *Micula* saga:

(a) Factual background.

(b) The judgment of the General Court ('GCEU').[4]

(c) The judgment of the Supreme Court of the United Kingdom ('UKSC').[5]

(d) The opinion of the Advocate General.[6]

(e) The judgment of the CJEU.[7]

(8) Concluding reflections.

II   THE ORIGIN OF ISDS, ITS JUSTIFICATION AND OBJECTIVES

For many years, ISDS reflected the fact that investment flowed from the developed countries of Western Europe and North America (the 'investor states') towards those that were underdeveloped or – notably in South America – suffered from frequent economic crises that hindered development (the 'host states').

Where measures taken by the host state were injurious to the interests of the investor, the option of suing in that state's courts was often unattractive or impractical because they were ill-organised, hopelessly dilatory or corrupt. Under classical international law, the only other option for the investor was to seek the diplomatic protection of the investor-State, a remedy rarely granted and not necessarily productive of satisfactory results.

That was the background to the system of Bilateral Investment Treaties (BITs), whereby the States Parties undertake reciprocal obligations as to their treatment of investors. In the great majority of cases, they provide for a form of arbitration that enables the investor to claim directly against the host state.

This was a relative novelty in international law since the traditional view was that international law is concerned exclusively with relations between sovereign states and international inter-state organisations. The inadequacy of this approach became most

---

3. Opinion 1/17 of the Court, 30 April 2019, ECLI:EU:C:2019:341.
4. Cases T-624/15, T-694/15 and T-704/15, *European Food SA and others v. European Commission*, ECLI:EU:T:2019:423.
5. *Micula and others v. Romania*, judgment of 19 February 2020, [2020] UKSC 5.
6. Case C-638/19P *European Commission v. European Food SA & Others*, ECLI:EU:C:2021:529.
7. Case C-638/19P *European Commission v. European Food SA & Others Idem*, ECLI:EU:C:2022:50.

clamant in light of the Holocaust and other horrors of that period. As Professor Sir Hersch Lauterpacht had written in 1945, pleading for protection in international law of the individual against the state:

> The sovereign State, in an exclusive and unprecedented ascendancy of power, became the unsurpassable barrier between man and the law of mankind. The human being became, in the offensive, but widely current terminology of the experts, a mere object of international law.[8]

In the intervening years, the direct legal protection of individuals against the misconduct of states has become an acknowledged part of national and international law. The direct legal protection of investors was a natural development of this trend.

The settlement of investment disputes by arbitration was thought to be desirable for several reasons, notably speed, confidentiality, informality and adjudication by experts in international and commercial law drawn from different countries and traditions. It is important to stress that the purpose of these arrangements was to *encourage* investment, as is shown in the founding documents of the International Centre for Settlement of Investment Disputes (ICSID).

1   ICSID

The creation of ICSID by an international Convention (the 'Washington Convention') under the auspices of the International Bank for Reconstruction and Development (now the World Bank) sought to put the arbitral system on a firm institutional footing. The purpose was explained by the Executive Directors of the Bank in their Report dated 18 March 1965, presenting the draft Convention for adoption (emphasis added):

> In submitting the attached Convention to governments, the Executive Directors are prompted by the desire to strengthen the partnership between countries in the cause of economic development. *The creation of an institution designed to facilitate the settlement of disputes between States and foreign investors can be a major step toward promoting an atmosphere of mutual confidence and thus stimulating a larger flow of private international capital into those countries which wish to attract it.*
>
> 'The Executive Directors recognize that investment disputes are as a rule settled through administrative, judicial or arbitral procedures available under the laws of the country in which the investment is made. However, experience shows that disputes may arise which the parties wish to settle by other methods and investment agreements entered into in recent years show *both States and investors frequently consider that it is in their mutual interest to agree to resort to international methods of settlement.*
>
> 'The present Convention would offer an international method of settlement designed to take account of the special characteristics of the disputes covered, as well as of the parties to whom it would apply. *It would provide facilities for conciliation and arbitration by specially qualified persons of independent judgment according to rules known and accepted in advance by the parties concerned. In particular, it would ensure that once a government or investor had given consent to*

---

8. *An International Bill of the Rights of Man,* Oxford, 1945, republished 2013, Introduction, p. 5.

conciliation or arbitration under the auspices of the Centre such consent could not be unilaterally withdrawn.'[9]

The Convention provides for the constitution of an arbitral tribunal – normally one arbitrator nominated by each party and a president chosen by the two arbitrators, which failing by the President of the Bank as Chairman of the Administrative Council. There is a procedure for annulment of the award by an annulment committee appointed from amongst the panel of arbitrators nominated by the Member States. The grounds for annulment are limited:

(a) that the Tribunal was not properly constituted;
(b) that the Tribunal has manifestly exceeded its powers;
(c) that there was corruption on the part of a member of the Tribunal;
(d) that there has been a serious departure from a fundamental rule of procedure; or
(e) that the award has failed to state the reasons on which it is based.

An important feature of the ICSID Convention is the provision (Article 54(1)) that (emphasis added):

> Each Contracting State shall recognize an award rendered pursuant to this Convention as binding and enforce the pecuniary obligations imposed by that award within its territories as if it were a final judgment of a court in that State.

ICSID has 165 Signatory and Contracting States. In Fiscal Year 2022, 364 cases were being administered by the ICSID Secretariat, of which 18 were under non-ICSID Rules. In 56% of new cases registered in FY 2022, the basis of consent was a Bilateral Investment Treaty, and 11% the Energy Charter Treaty; 11 involved Member States of the EU as respondent States (Spain 3, Sweden 1, Hungary 1, Romania 4, Slovakia 1 and Slovenia 1).[10]

There are, of course, other arbitral proceedings involving investor/State disputes – many of them under the UNCITRAL Rules – especially those conducted under the auspices of the International Chamber of Commerce, the London Court of International Arbitration, the Permanent Court of Arbitration, the Stockholm Chamber of Commerce, and ICSID's Additional Facility Rules.

There are now some 3,000 BITs – what the European Commission has called a 'spaghetti bowl'.

III CAUSES OF DISSATISFACTION WITH ISDS THROUGH ARBITRATION[11]

Dissatisfaction with the system of ISDS through arbitration can be traced to differing perceptions of its working and outcomes, some better informed than others.

---

9. Report of the Executive Directors on the Convention, paras 9-11 (emphasis added).
10. *The ICSID Caseload – Statistics – Issue 2022-2* at www.icsid.worldbank.org.
11. For a very recent discussion, *see* Hallak, *Investor-State Protection Disputes Involving EU Member States: State of Play*, European Parliamentary Research Service, PE738.216, available at

Inequality of arms: As mentioned above, in earlier years the majority of cases were concerned with investors from developed countries investing in underdeveloped countries or in countries that suffered from recurrent economic crises that hindered development. The investors tended to be multinational corporations, particularly from the United States, represented by well-resourced law firms, again particularly from the United States. Pitted against the resources available to the defendant states, there was perceived to be an inbuilt inequality of arms.

Oppression: In terms of outcome, awards in millions of dollars, enforceable not only in the courts of the respondent state but also in the courts of any state where the respondent state has assets, have created the impression of oppression by the 'capitalist West' of less well-favoured countries and peoples. That perception has been accentuated where, as in some states of South America, new governments have sought to redress the misgovernment of their predecessors, including the corrupt award of government contracts dressed up as investments. Some states have withdrawn from ICSID on this ground.

Arbitrators' conflict of interest: There has been an impression that the pool of ISDS arbitrators consists of well-heeled lawyers, many of them from multinational law firms which, by the breadth of their practice, may have real or perceived conflicts of interest. This has been accentuated by the perception – or in some cases the reality – that individual lawyers may be acting contemporaneously as attorneys in one arbitration and arbitrator in another. This may lead, so it is suggested, to an arbitrator being unwilling to go along with a view of the law that is different from the legal advice given to clients.

Constraint on policy choices: The subject matter of ISDS arbitrations is, by its nature, economic, and there are many different views and theories as to how the economic development of a country should be organised and regulated. Thus, it frequently happens that a government regards it as necessary to promote investment of a particular kind, or in a particular sphere of the economy, while its successor has different priorities and seeks to regulate the economy in a different way. Arbitrators are thought to be blind to that consideration.

Limits and interpretation of BITs: Failure to take account of legitimate policy differences is also traced to the terms of the BITs themselves, which tend to be couched in the vocabulary of public international law. Application of the canons of classical international law to the interpretation of BITs can be contentious, particularly in times of crisis.[12] In the absence of any appeal court whose rulings are binding, there is no way in which such differences in legal interpretation can be resolved.

Usurpation of national courts: In parallel with more or less well-informed ('populist') dissatisfaction with the arbitral system of ISDS, there has grown up a 'constitutionalist' objection to a situation where, it is said, the jurisdiction of national

---

https://www.europarl.europa.eu/RegData/etudes/IDAN/2022/738216/EPRS_IDA(2022)738216_EN.pdf.

12. *See, e.g.,* from my personal experience, the difference between the Arbitral Tribunal and the Annulment Committee as to interpretation of 'necessity' in *Sempra Energy International v. Argentine Republic*, ICSID Case No. ARB/02/16, Award dated 28 September 2007, and Decision of the Annulment Committee 29 June 2010.

courts (or, in the case of the EU, the jurisdiction of the CJEU) is usurped by ad hoc arbitral tribunals that are not subject to the normal procedural and substantive constraints of a judicial system.

Constitutional Courts have been particularly jealous of their exclusive competence to determine the constitutional propriety of acts of national institutions that confer rights on international or transnational institutions. Thus, for example, the German Constitutional Court, the *Bundesverfassungsgericht*, has asserted its right to 'verify whether legal acts of the European institutions and bodies remain within the limits of the sovereign powers conferred on them [by the Member States]'.[13]

IV THE EUROPEAN COMMISSION'S PROPOSAL FOR A MULTILATERAL INVESTMENT COURT

With the entry into force of the Lisbon Treaty in 2009, investment became part of the common commercial policy, which is an exclusive competence of the EU. Thereafter the European Commission published a number of papers and embarked on several public consultations with specific reference to the future of ISDS.

Following the submission by the Commission of various documents,[14] the Council of the EU, which represents the governments of the Member States, issued 'Negotiating Directives for a Convention establishing a multilateral court for settlement of investment disputes'.[15] The following paragraphs from that document set out the essentials of the proposal (emphasis added):

> '9. The Convention should include appropriate *procedural safeguards*, including provisions against frivolous claims. It should also be explored whether the Convention should include amicable dispute resolution mechanisms and other procedural provisions on, inter alia, parallel claims or joint interpretations.
>
> '10. The multilateral court should be composed of a *tribunal of first instance and an appeal tribunal*. The appeal tribunal should have the competence to review decisions issued by the tribunal of first instance, *on the grounds of errors of law or manifest errors in the appreciation of facts or, as appropriate, serious procedural shortcomings*. The Convention should include provisions for the completion of the proceedings in light of the findings of the appeal tribunal, which should have the power, when appropriate, to send back cases to the tribunal of first instance ("remand").
>
> '11. The independence of the Court should be guaranteed. *Members of the Court* (both of the tribunal of first instance and of the appeal tribunal) should be subject to stringent requirements regarding their qualifications and impartiality. Strong *rules on ethics and conflict of interests*, including a code of conduct for the Members of the Court and challenge mechanisms shall be included in the

---

13. BVerfG, 2BvE 2/08 vom 30.6.2009, Absatz -Nr (1-421) §§338-339.
14. *See*, Inception Impact Assessment, https://ec.europa.eu/smart-regulation/roadmaps/docs/201 6_trade_024_court_on_investment_en.pdf (accessed 18 July 2022) and Recommendation for a Council Decision authorising the opening of negotiations for a Convention establishing a multilateral court for the settlement of investment disputes, 13 September 2017, COM(2017) 493 final.
15. Negotiating Directives for a Convention establishing a multilateral court for the settlement of investment disputes, 1 March 2018, 12981/17 ADD1 (emphasis added).

Convention. The Members of the Court should receive a *permanent remuneration*. They should be appointed for a *fixed, long and non-renewable period of time* and enjoy *security of tenure*, as well as all necessary guarantees of impartiality and independence. Members should be *appointed through an objective and transparent process*. Different methods of appointment of the Members of the Court should be explored including, for example, the possibility that all Parties to the Convention are entitled to appoint a Member of the Court, or the possibility that Members of the Court are appointed through other methods inspired by existing international courts such as the International Court of Justice or the International Criminal Court, taking into account, inter alia, the expected size of the Court and the need to ensure effectiveness and cost-efficiency. Any such method shall ensure that the Members of the Court who are appointed are of a *high quality with the necessary professional and ethical standing* to fulfil their duties. Any method of appointment of the Members of the Court shall provide also for *regional balance and gender representation* in addition to ensuring the efficient and effective management of the Court. Moreover, Members should be appointed to hear a particular case by a transparent and objective method.'

The advantages of the system (as contrasted with the alleged defects of the existing system quoted above) are said to be:[16]

(1) *Permanence*: the court would be a permanent international institution.
(2) *Independence*: States who are members would appoint permanent, fully qualified judges, free of any conflicts of interest or interest in the outcome of cases.
(3) *Predictability*: By sitting permanently and deciding cases over time, judges would deliver consistent decisions.
(4) *Comprehensiveness*: The court would allow either party to appeal against a decision.
(5) *Cost-effectiveness*: The court would allow for economies of scale, as it could cover disputes arising under the bilateral investment agreements which all members of the multilateral investment court have in place.
(6) *Transparency*: The court would:
    – publish online details of all aspects of its work, including its decisions;
    – open all hearings to the public;
    – allow third parties (NGOs, trade unions, consumer groups and business associations) to make submissions.

I have not been able to find any cost-benefit analysis of the proposal, or indeed any quantification of what it might involve in terms of financial or human resources. Unless I am mistaken, the Commission's case rests more on assertion of supposed defects and on supposed advantages than on any objective research.

Against that background, I turn to the case law.

---

16. Commission Factsheet, *supra* n. 1.

V   THE JURISDICTION OF THE CJEU

To put the Court's case law in context, it is important to understand the nature and limits of the Court's jurisdiction:

The CJEU is not a court of general jurisdiction. Its jurisdiction and forms of action are defined and limited by the Treaties establishing the European Union – the Treaty on European Union ('TEU')[17] and the Treaty on the Functioning of the European Union (TFEU),[18] – and, in greater detail by the Statute of the Court,[19] and the Rules of Procedure.[20] The available forms of action before the Court are laid down in these texts.

The Court of Justice as an EU institution consists of two courts, the Court of Justice and the General Court, whose decisions may, within limits, be appealed to the Court of Justice.

The three forms of process that are relevant here are:

(1) The action to review the legality of acts of the EU institutions, including Decisions of the Commission on matters relating to competition and state aid.[21] Such actions are heard in the first instance by the General Court, subject to review by the Court of Justice.[22] This was the form of process in the *Micula* case.[23]

(2) The Preliminary Ruling procedure, where the Court of Justice may be asked by any court or tribunal of a Member State to rule on questions concerning the interpretation of the Treaties or the validity and interpretation of acts of the institutions.[24] This was the form of process in the *Achmea* case.[25]

(3) The Opinion procedure, where a Member State, the European Parliament, the Council or the Commission may obtain the opinion of the Court as to whether a projected [international] agreement is compatible with the Treaties.[26] This was the form of process for the *CETA Opinion*.[27]

The Opinions of the Court in these cases must be distinguished from the Opinions of the Advocates General, who are members of the Court whose function is to deliver independent preliminary Opinions in cases of importance.

---

17. Article 19.
18. Articles 251-281.
19. Protocol no. 3.
20. Currently as amended 25 September 2012.
21. TFEU Article 263.
22. TFEU Article 256.
23. *Supra* n. 4.
24. TFEU, Article 267.
25. *Supra* n. 2.
26. TFEU Article 218 (11).
27. *Supra* n. 3.

411

VI   THE *ACHMEA* CASE

1   Background

The background details of the *Achmea* case can be found in the Opinion of Advocate General Melchior Wathelet, to which I shall refer later.[28] Only a few salient features are given here.

Before the accession to the EU of the countries of the former Eastern bloc (the 'candidate countries'), the European Commission encouraged the existing Member States to conclude BITs with the candidate countries to prepare them for accession. Provision for the conclusion of BITs was also included in the Accession Agreements with the candidate countries. A significant number of BITs were concluded between the existing Member States and the candidate countries and, with some exceptions, they have not been denounced or otherwise terminated.

Since accession of the candidate countries, the European Commission has conducted a contentious campaign against enforcement of these BITs. The Commission's position has been based on the combined effect of three provisions of the TFEU:

(1) Article 3(1)(e) provides that the EU is to have exclusive competence in the area of common commercial policy.

(2) Article 207(1) provides that:

> The common commercial policy shall be based on uniform principles, particularly with regard to ... the commercial aspects of ... foreign direct investment ....

(3) Article 344 provides that:

> Member States undertake not to submit a dispute concerning the interpretation or application of the Treaties to any method of settlement other than those provided for therein.

The Commission's argument has been that, upon the accession of the candidate countries to the EU, what were now 'intra-EU BITs' became unenforceable as being contrary to the combined effect of Articles 3, 207 and 344 (above). Thence, by what seems to me to be a leap of logic, the Commission has argued that arbitral awards made under the BITs became unenforceable. Moreover, as in the *Micula* case discussed below, the Commission argued that payment of the sum awarded in the arbitration would constitute an illegal state aid in favour of the claimant, who would therefore be bound to repay it.

2   *Achmea*: The Factual and Legal Context

The *Achmea* case arose under the Netherlands/Czechoslovakia BIT, which entered into force in 1992. The terms of the BIT were in customary form and included an

---

28. Opinion of the Advocate General dated 19 September 2017, ECLI:EU:C:2017:699.

arbitration clause, providing that the arbitral tribunal should determine its own procedure applying the UNCITRAL rules.

In 2004, the Slovak Republic now separated from the Czech Republic ('Slovakia') opened its health system to national and foreign operators offering private sickness insurance services. Achmea, an undertaking belonging to a Netherlands insurance group, established a Slovak subsidiary offering private sickness insurance. Following a change of government in 2006, Slovakia partly revoked the liberalisation of the sickness insurance market, with detrimental consequences for Achmea.

In 2006, Achmea invoked the arbitration clause in the Netherlands/ Czechoslovakia BIT and started proceedings against Slovakia. An arbitral tribunal was duly constituted with the place of arbitration at Frankfurt-am-Main. In 2012, the tribunal found that measures taken by Slovakia breached the terms of the BIT and ordered the Republic to pay damages of EUR 22.1 million plus interest and costs. Slovakia raised an action to set aside the award in the Frankfurt Regional Court (*Oberlandesgericht*). This was unsuccessful and Slovakia appealed on a point of law to the Federal Court of Justice (*Bundesgerichtshof*).

The German court referred a number of questions to the CJEU as to whether enforcement of the arbitral award would be compatible with the rules of EU law, focusing on two issues:

(1) whether enforcement was precluded by TFEU Article 344 concerning disputes between Member States; and
(2) whether it was precluded by TFEU Article 267 establishing the Preliminary Reference procedure.[29]

The crucial issue was whether, as the Court later put it, the arbitral tribunal could be 'situated within the judicial system of the EU'.[30]

The Court of Justice has defined the nature of the EU judicial system in a series of Opinions,[31] as set out in the following passage:

> '[T]he founding treaties of the EU, unlike ordinary international treaties, established a **new legal order**, possessing its own institutions, for the benefit of which the Member States thereof have limited their sovereign rights, in ever wider fields, and the subjects of which comprise not only those States but also their nationals.
>
> ...
>
> '[The] essential characteristics of EU law have given rise to *a structured network of principles, rules and mutually interdependent legal relations* linking the EU and its Member States, and its Member States with each other, which are now engaged, as is recalled in the second paragraph of Article 1 TEU, in a "process of creating an ever-closer union among the peoples of Europe".
>
> 'This legal structure is based on the fundamental premiss that each Member State shares with all the other Member States, and recognises that they share with

---

29. A third issue regarding possible discrimination was of less importance.
30. Judgment in the *Achmea* case, *supra* n. 2, at para. 43.
31. *See*, in particular, Opinion 1/09 on the European Patent Court, ECLI:EU:C:2011:123, and Opinion 2/13 on accession to the European Convention on Human Rights, ECLI:EU:C:2014:2454.

it, a *set of common values* on which the EU is founded, as stated in Article 2 TEU. That premiss implies and justifies the existence of *mutual trust* between the Member States that those values will be recognised and, therefore, that the law of the EU that implements them will be respected.

...

'In order to ensure that the specific characteristics and the autonomy of that legal order are preserved, the Treaties have established a *judicial system intended to ensure consistency and uniformity in the interpretation of EU law.*

'In that context, it is for the national courts and tribunals and for the Court of Justice to ensure the full application of EU law in all Member States and to ensure judicial protection of an individual's rights under that law.

'In particular, *the judicial system as thus conceived has as its keystone the preliminary ruling procedure provided for in Article 267 TFEU,* which, by setting up a dialogue between one court and another, specifically between the Court of Justice and the courts and tribunals of the Member States, *has the object of securing uniform interpretation of EU law, its full effect and its autonomy* as well as, ultimately, the particular nature of the law established by the Treaties.'[32]

The question then is, 'How do arbitral tribunals and their awards fit into the Court's view of the EU judicial system?' Over the years, the Court has made a number of decisions on this issue. Broadly speaking, it has distinguished between tribunals constituted under the arbitration provisions of a commercial contract, which do not come within the scope of Article 267,[33] and those that can, in one way or another, be equiparated to a 'court or tribunal of a Member State' so as to come within the scope of Article 267, such as, for example, a Portuguese arbitration tribunal set up to resolve taxation disputes.[34]

3   *Achmea*: The Advocate General's Opinion

In his *Achmea* Opinion, Advocate General Wathelet concluded that the arbitral tribunal set up under Article 8 of the Netherlands-Slovakia BIT was such as to come within the scope of Article 267, although he expressed doubts about ICSID arbitrations. His reasoning was as follows:

'The characteristics of the arbitral tribunals constituted in accordance with Article 8 of the BIT, and in particular of the arbitral tribunal involved in the present case, are such that they allow the ordinary courts and tribunals of the Member States to ensure compliance with those principles, as they do in the context of international commercial arbitration.

'Article 8 of the BIT entrusts the President of the SCC Arbitration Institute, established in a Member State, with the appointment of the arbitrators, if the appointments have not been made within the periods laid down in Article 8(3) of the BIT. It also provides that the UNCITRAL Arbitration Rules are to apply to the arbitral procedures conducted in accordance with that article. According to Article 16 of the 1976 Arbitration Rules, it is for the arbitral tribunal itself to determine the

---

32. Opinion 2/13 *supra* n. 30, paras 157-176, omitting case references (emphasis added).
33. Case 102/81, *Nordsee*, ECLI:EU:C:1982:107; Case C-125/04, *Denuit & Cordenier,* ECLI:EU:C: 2005:69.
34. Case C-377/13, *Ascendi Beiras Litoral e Alta*, ECLI:EU:2014:1754.

seat of the arbitration and to choose the institution which is to act as Registry, after hearing the parties.

'By its procedural order of 19 March 2009, the arbitral tribunal fixed the seat of the arbitration on the territory of a Member State, namely in Frankfurt am Main. Its award would therefore, in accordance with Article 1059 of the German Code of Civil Procedure, be amenable to an action for annulment before the German courts, which will therefore be able, in that context, to ensure the uniformity of interpretation of EU law and compliance with the European public policy rules. It was in the context of an action of that type that the case came before the referring court and the Court of Justice.

'In addition, the recognition and enforcement of arbitral awards made by the arbitral tribunals constituted in accordance with Article 8 of the BIT fall within the scope of the New York Convention, to which all the Member States have acceded. In accordance with that convention, the national courts may refuse to recognise and enforce those awards for all the reasons set out in Article V of that convention, including the fact that the arbitral procedure was not in accordance with the agreement of the parties and that recognition or enforcement of the award would be contrary to public policy, including European public policy.

'Therefore, on the assumption that Achmea attempted to obtain recognition and enforcement of the arbitral award at issue in the present case in another Member State, the courts and tribunals of the requested State would also be responsible for ensuring that the award is not incompatible with EU law.

...

'The Commission also refers to the risk that the seat of an arbitration may potentially be fixed in a third country or that recognition and enforcement of an arbitral award that was incompatible with EU law may be sought in a third country, in which cases the courts and tribunals of the European Union would not be involved and the Court of Justice would therefore never be requested to give a preliminary ruling.

'The same applies, in the Commission's submission, to the intra-EU BITS which designate the International Centre for Settlement of Investment Disputes (ICSID), established in Washington DC, as the institution acting as Registry in the arbitration. In such a case, the arbitral award would be binding on the parties and could not be subject to any appeal or any other remedy except those provided for in the ICSID Convention. It follows that there would be no legal means that would allow the courts and tribunals of the Member State to review the compatibility of ICSID arbitral award with EU law.

'While I consider that the Member States should avoid the choice of ICSID in their BITs, the risks referred to by the Commission are, in the present case, purely hypothetical, since the BIT at issue does not designate the ICSID as the institution acting as Registry in the arbitration, the parties chose the PCA in The Hague as the institution performing that role, the arbitral tribunal fixed the seat of the arbitration on the territory of a Member State and there has been no request for recognition and enforcement of the arbitral award in any third countries, but an action for annulment of the arbitral award before the courts and tribunals of a Member State, one of which made a reference to the Court for a preliminary ruling.'[35]

---

35. Opinion, *supra* n. 27, at paras 245-253.

4   *Achmea*: The Judgment of the Court

The approach of the Court was quite different. Starting from its conception of the Preliminary Reference procedure under Article 267 as the 'keystone' of the EU judicial system, it defined three issues:

(1) Were the disputes that the *Achmea* tribunal was set up to resolve liable to relate to the interpretation or application of EU law?

(2) Was the tribunal 'situated within the judicial system of the EU'?

(3) Was an award made by the tribunal 'subject to review by a court of a Member State, ensuring that the questions of EU law which the tribunal may have to address can be submitted to the Court by means of a reference for a preliminary ruling'.

On the first question, the Court's reasoning was that, since Article 8(6) of the BIT required the tribunal to 'take into account ... the law in force of the Contracting Party concerned', it was bound in so doing to take account of EU law as an integral part of the law of Slovakia and, potentially, to interpret or apply it.[36]

On the second question, the Court pointed out that the tribunal was not part of the judicial system of the Netherlands or Slovakia. 'Indeed, it is precisely the exceptional nature of the tribunal's jurisdiction compared with that of those two Member States that is one of the principal reasons for the existence of Article 8 of the BIT.' Consequently, the tribunal could not be regarded as 'a court of tribunal of a Member State' within the meaning of Article 267.[37]

On the third question, the Court accepted that the seat of the arbitration was Frankfurt; that German law was thereby applicable to judicial review of the validity of the arbitration award; and that Slovakia had invoked that jurisdiction to have the award set aside. However, the jurisdiction of the German court was limited to the validity of the arbitration agreement and the consistency with public policy of recognition and enforcement of the award, thus excluding examination of any issues as to the interpretation and application of EU law that might arise in the course of the arbitration.

The Court distinguished other forms of arbitration which allow issues of EU law to be referred, if necessary, to the Court of Justice, and also methods of dispute resolution set up under international agreements to which the EU is a party 'provided that the autonomy of the EU and its legal order is respected'.[38]

The Court concluded that:

'In the present case ... apart from the fact that the disputes falling within the jurisdiction of the arbitral tribunal ... may relate to the interpretation both of [the BIT] and of EU law, the possibility of submitting those disputes to a body which is

---

36. *Achmea* judgment, supra n. 2, paras 39-42.
37. *Ibid.*, paras 43-49.
38. *Ibid.*, paras 50-57.

not part of the judicial system of the EU is provided for by an agreement which was concluded, not by the EU, but by Member States.

'Article 8 of the BIT is such as to call in question not only the principle of mutual trust between the Member States, but also the preservation of the particular nature of the law established by the Treaties, ensured by the preliminary ruling procedure provided for in Article 267 ..., and is not therefore compatible with the principle of sincere cooperation [provided for in Article 4(3) TFEU].'[39]

The Court's judgment concluded that:

Articles 267 and 344 TFEU must be interpreted as precluding a provision in an international agreement concluded between Member States, such as Article 8 [of the BIT], under which an investor from one of those Member States may, in the event of a dispute concerning investments in the other Member State, bring proceedings against the latter Member State before an arbitral tribunal whose jurisdiction that Member State has undertaken to accept.[40]

5 The Immediate Aftermath of *Achmea*

The *Achmea* judgment gave rise, almost at once, to frenzied discussion amongst arbitration lawyers and a storm of articles in legal and professional journals,[41] as well as seminars and conferences devoted entirely to discussion of its import. The following issues (amongst others) appear to arise:

- What is the import of the Court's claim of the 'autonomy' of EU law and the EU legal system? How does that autonomy differ (if at all) from the autonomy that might be claimed by the law and legal system of the many States in the world that are parties to BITs?
- Is the Court's conception of the EU legal system as an 'autonomous' structure of which it is the keystone, compatible with the international standing and competences of the Member States, albeit their competences are limited by their obligations under the EU Treaties? Is the Court claiming some sort of international jurisdiction going beyond the scope of the EU Treaties?
- What is the status in international law of 'intra-EU BITs' that have not been denounced or otherwise departed from? Has EU law had the effect of rendering these BITs unlawful and, if so, also unenforceable? If so, when and to what effect?
- Does a declaration of the invalidity of a BIT deprive an investor of the benefit of an award made by an arbitral tribunal constituted under, and on the faith of, that BIT?
- What is the status of ongoing arbitrations commenced on the basis of intra-EU BITs? Are the awards of arbitral tribunals established under intra-EU BITs

---

39. *Ibid.*, para. 58.
40. *Ibid.*, para. 60, and the operative part of the judgment.
41. *See*, notably, Professor Alan Dashwood, *Article 26 ECT and Intra-EU Disputes – The Case Against an Expansive Reading of Achmea*, (2021) 46 European Law Review 415-434.

binding and enforceable, especially awards governed by the ICSID Convention?

Some of these issues may have been laid to rest by the Court's *CETA Opinion*,[42] but by no means all, as the judgment of the UK Supreme Court shows.[43]

Meanwhile, the Court of Justice reaffirmed its judgment in *Achmea* in two cases: *Moldova v. Komstroy*[44] and *Poland v. PL Holdings*.[45] Neither of these cases concerned an arbitral award under the ICSID Convention. This came in the course of the *Micula* saga, where the Court of Justice took a quite different approach to the UK Supreme Court (*see* section 7 below).

VII   THE CETA OPINION[46]

1   Background

CETA is a free trade agreement between the EU and Canada that contains provisions relating to the reduction of customs duties and non-tariff barriers to trade in goods and services, as well as rules relating to investment, public procurement, competition, protection of intellectual property and sustainable development. Being what is known in EU law as a 'mixed agreement, it requires signature and ratification by the EU and also all the Member States, as well as Canada. There was a temporary hiccup when the Parliament of Wallonia, a region of Belgium, threatened to block the signature of the Agreement by Belgium on the ground that it would enable multinationals, through ISDS procedures, to put pressure on governments to degrade environmental, food and labour standards.[47]

Thirteen Member States (including the UK) have now ratified CETA, but not yet Canada or the EU (which awaits ratification by all the Member States). Some but not all of its provisions have been brought into force on a provisional basis.

Chapter 8 of the Agreement, entitled 'Investment', is considerably more extensive in scope and detail than the customary BIT which is, of course, natural in a free trade agreement. Section D of Chapter 8, 'Investment Protection', begins with provisions that are designed to meet the sort of objections raised by the Walloon Parliament:

> '1. For the purpose of this Chapter, the Parties reaffirm their right to regulate within their territories to achieve legitimate policy objectives, such as the protection of public health, safety, the environment or public morals, social or consumer protection or the promotion and protection of cultural diversity.

---

42. *Supra* n. 3.
43. *Supra* n. 5.
44. Case C-741/19 *Republic of Moldova v. Komstroy LLC,* ECLI:EU:C:2021:655 (Opinion of Advocate General Szpunar at ECLI:EU:C:2021:164).
45. Case 109/20 *Republiken Polen v. PLHoldings,* ECLI:EU:C:2021:875 (Opinion of Advocate General Kokott at ECLI:EU:C:2021:321).
46. *Supra* n. 3.
47. Extensively reported in the press – for example, POLITICO – 'Walloon Parliament rejects CETA deal', 14 October 2016, and France 24, 'Wallonia formally approves EU-Canada trade deal', 28 October 2016.

'2. For greater certainty, the mere fact that a Party regulates, including through a modification to its laws, in a manner which negatively affects an investment or interferes with an investor's expectations, including its expectation of profits, does not amount to a breach of an obligation under this Section.

'3. For greater certainty, a Party's decision not to issue, renew or maintain a subsidy:

(a) in the absence of any specific commitment under law or contract to issue, renew, or maintain that subsidy; or

(b) in accordance with any terms or conditions attached to the issuance, renewal or maintenance of the subsidy,

does not constitute a breach of the provisions of this Section.

'4. For greater certainty, nothing in this Section shall be construed as preventing a Party from discontinuing the granting of a subsidy or requesting its reimbursement where such measure is necessary in order to comply with international obligations between the Parties or has been ordered by a competent court, administrative tribunal or other competent authority, or requiring that Party to compensate the investor therefor.'[48]

Section F provides for the 'Resolution of investment disputes between investors and states'.[49] To a certain extent, it follows the line of a conventional BIT. The novelty is the introduction of a standing Tribunal and an Appeal Tribunal.

The Tribunal is initially to consist of fifteen members – five nationals of Canada, five nationals of a Member State of the EU, and five nationals of a third country, appointed for a five-year term, renewable once. They are to sit in divisions of three, one from each group, chosen 'on a rotation basis, ensuring that the composition of the divisions is random and unpredictable, while giving equal opportunity to all Members of the Tribunal to serve'. In order to ensure their availability, the members of the Tribunal are to be paid a monthly retainer fee. The ICSID Secretariat is to act as the secretariat of the Tribunal.[50]

The details of the Appellate Tribunal are less complete but broadly shadow those for the Tribunal.[51] As regards the grounds of appeal, it is provided that:

The Appellate Tribunal may uphold, modify or reverse the Tribunal's award based on:

(a) errors in the application or interpretation of applicable law;

(b) manifest errors in the appreciation of the facts, including the appreciation of relevant domestic law;

(c) the grounds set out in Article 52(1) (a) through (e) of the ICSID Convention, in so far as they are not covered by paragraphs (a) and (b).[52]

The members of both Tribunals are to be persons who

possess the qualifications required in their respective countries for appointment to judicial office or be jurists of recognised competence. They shall have demonstrated

---

48. Article 8.9.
49. Section F of Chapter 8, Articles 8.18-8.45.
50. Article 8.27.
51. *See* below for further details added by the Joint Committee.
52. Article 8.28.

expertise in public international law-. It is desirable that they have expertise in particular in international investment law, in international trade law and the resolution of disputes arising under international investment or international trade agreement.[53]

Under the head of Ethics, it is provided:

The Members of the Tribunal shall be independent. They shall not be affiliated with any government. They shall not take instructions from any organisation, or government with regard to matters related to the dispute. They shall not participate in the consideration of any disputes that would create a direct or indirect conflict of interest. They shall comply with the International Bar Association Guidelines on Conflicts of Interest in International Arbitration or any supplemental rules adopted pursuant to Article 8.44.2. In addition, upon appointment, they shall refrain from acting as counsel or as party-appointed expert or witness in any pending or new investment dispute under this or any other international agreement.[54]

In addition to the provisions of the CETA Agreement itself, the Parties established a Joint Interpretative instrument.[55] This amplifies a number of points already noted and declares that:

CETA moves decisively away from the traditional approach of investment dispute resolution and establishes independent, impartial and permanent investment Tribunals, inspired by the public judicial systems in the European Union and its Member States and Canada, as well as … international courts such as the International Court of Justice and the European Court of Human Rights.[56]

A Joint Committee representing Canada and the EU is established to be 'responsible for all questions concerning trade and investment between the Parties and the implementation and application' of CETA,[57] including the power to adopt binding interpretations.[58] A Committee on Services and Investment is to adopt a code of conduct for the members of the CETA Tribunals.[59]

2   CETA: Opinion 1/17 of the Court of Justice

After its problems with the Walloon Parliament regarding the signature of CETA, Belgium sought the Opinion of the Court of Justice under Article 218(11) TFEU asking whether Section F of CETA (above) is compatible with the EU Treaties, including compatibility with human rights. Belgium raised three questions:

(1) whether the ISDS mechanism is compatible with the autonomy of the EU legal order;

---

53. Article 8.27.
54. Article 8.30.
55. EU Official Journal 2017 L 11, p. 3.
56. Point 6(f).
57. Article 26.1 and 26.3.
58. Article 26.5(e).
59. Article 8.44.2.

(2) whether it is compatible with the general principle of equal treatment and the requirement of effectiveness; and

(3) whether it is compatible with the right of access to an independent tribunal.

In answer to the first question, the Court held that CETA's ISDS mechanism 'stands outside the EU judicial system', and that the function of its Tribunals is to interpret and apply the provisions of CETA; so that:

> they cannot have the power to interpret or apply provisions of EU law other than those of the CETA or to make awards that might have the effect of preventing the EU institutions from operating in accordance with the EU constitutional framework.[60]

The Court then examined in greater detail whether the Tribunals might have jurisdiction to interpret and apply rules of EU law other than the provisions of CETA. It noted that, under the Agreement, the Tribunal may need 'to consider the domestic law of a Party as a matter of fact' and that, in doing so, 'the Tribunal shall follow the prevailing interpretation given to the domestic law by the courts or authorities of that Party' and that 'any meaning given to domestic law by the Tribunal shall not be binding upon the courts or the authorities of that Party'.[61] Consequently, the Court concluded that CETA confers no power on the Tribunals to interpret or apply EU law.[62]

Next, the Court considered whether the ISDS mechanism might affect the operation of the EU institutions in accordance with the EU constitutional framework. The Court recognised that CETA Tribunals might have to consider whether an EU measure is 'fair and equitable', or whether it constitutes indirect expropriation or an unjustified restriction of the freedom to make payments and transfer of capital.[63] The Court also recognised that Tribunals might have to consider whether measures taken by the EU constitute restrictions on the freedom to conduct business.[64] In the end, however, the Court concluded that this could not affect the autonomy of the EU legal order.[65]

I must leave the reader to study the Court's reasoning, which I find diffuse and confusing, not to say pharisaical. It appears to rely on the 'escape clauses' (quoted above) as to the pursuit of legitimate policy objectives in order to conclude that the CETA Tribunals would not have jurisdiction to intrude upon the autonomy of the EU legal order. It does not address squarely the issue that faces many arbitral tribunals (and the EU courts themselves) – namely, whether a measure purportedly taken in pursuit of a public policy objective is, in reality, a covert discriminatory restriction on trade. That must, I think, enter directly into the interpretation and application of the impugned measure.

---

60. §§106-118.
61. §130, quoting Article 8.31.2 of CETA.
62. §136.
63. §138.
64. §148.
65. §161.

The rest of the Opinion is concerned with the second and third questions posed by Belgium (above), as to which the Court concluded that the CETA system did not violate the principle of equal treatment or the requirement of effectiveness[66] or deny the right of access to an independent tribunal.[67]

Whatever may be the deficiencies of its reasoning, what matters for our purposes is that the Court did not put a judicial spanner in the works of CETA. The Opinion appeared to dispel the impression given by the *Achmea* judgment that the CJEU was claiming some sort of 'extraterritorial' jurisdiction. This proved sadly not to be the case.

3   CETA: Subsequent Events

To date (July 2022), 15 Member States of the EU have ratified CETA. Of the twelve States that have not ratified, objection to the ISDS provisions is one of the hurdles to ratification in all of them. Essentially, the grounds of objection are, first, the creation of a 'parallel justice system' and, second, a 'regulatory chill' on the future development of environmental, health and labour standards.[68]

The CETA Joint Committee has so far adopted two Decisions:

(1) Decision No. 001/2021 setting out the administrative and organisational matters regarding the functioning of the Appellate Tribunal;[69] and

(2) Decision No. 002/2021 adopting a procedure for the adoption of interpretations.[70]

The Committee on Services and Investment has adopted two Decisions:

(1) Decision No. 001/2021 adopting a Code of Conduct for Members of the Tribunals and Mediators;[71] and

(2) Decision No. 002/2021 adopting Rules for Mediation.[72]

---

66. §§162-188.

67. §§189-244.

68. *Ratification Tracker* by the Jean Monnet Network on Transatlantic Trade Policies, Carleton University, Ottawa, at https://carleton.ca/tradenetwork/research-publications/ceta-ratification-tracker/ accessed 13 July 2022.

69. https://www.international.gc.ca/trade-commerce/trade-agreements-accords-commerciaux/agr-acc/ceta-aecg/appellate-tribunal dappel.aspx?lang = eng accessed 13 July 2022. The Appellate Tribunal is to consist of six members, chosen on the same basis as those of the Tribunal, with analogous provisions as to its method of working.

70. https://www.international.gc.ca/trade-commerce/trade-agreements-accords-commerciaux/agr-acc/ceta-aecg/procedure-adoption-interpretations.aspx?lang = eng accessed 13 July 2022.

71. https://trade.ec.europa.eu/doclib/docs/2021/january/tradoc 159403.pdf accessed 13 July 2022.

72. https://trade.ec.europa.eu/doclib/docs/2021/january/tradoc_159404.pdf accessed 13 July 2022.

VIII   THE *MICULA* SAGA

1   The Factual Background

In 1999, in order to develop its regional policy, Romania adopted an investment incentive scheme known as EGO24, which promoted investment in two regions of the country. It required investments to be maintained for twice the period of the benefits received.

During the early 2000s, in reliance on EGO 24, Micula and others (the Claimants) invested in a large, highly integrated food production operation in one of the designated regions as part of a ten-year business plan.

In 2002, Romania and Sweden concluded a BIT, which provided for ISDS under the ICSID Convention.

During the negotiations for accession of Romania to the EU, the European Commission informed Romania that various schemes including EGO24 were not in line with EU state aid rules and urged Romania to bring its schemes into alignment without delay. In August 2004 Romania passed an ordinance repealing all but one of the EGO24 tax incentive schemes, citing the need to comply with the EU rules on state aid.

In July 2005, the Claimants filed a request with ICSID for arbitration under the Romania/Sweden BIT, contending that revocation of the EGO24 incentives was a violation of the BIT. Romania contended that it was forced to revoke the incentives in order to comply with EU requirements and allow lawful accession by Romania to the EU. Both Romania and the European Commission (appearing as *amicus*) contended that any payment of compensation arising out of any award in the arbitration would constitute illegal state aid under EU law and render the award unenforceable in the EU.

On 1 January 2007, Romania acceded to the EU.

In 2013, the ICSID tribunal, having earlier dismissed objections on jurisdiction and admissibility, issued its Award. It held that Romania had breached the fair and equitable treatment clause of the BIT and awarded damages amounting at the time to GBP 70 million. and costs amounting to GBP 80 million. The award did not address the effect of state aid rules on enforceability. Romania's application to annul the Award under the ICSID procedure was rejected by the ICSID ad hoc Annulment Committee in 2016.

Importantly, Romania was required by the Annulment Committee to file an assurance that it would pay the Award in full and subject to no conditions whatsoever if the annulment application was dismissed.

Meanwhile, 2014 saw the commencement of two proceedings in parallel:

(1) The Commission instituted proceedings against Romania, alleging that payment of the Award would constitute illegal state aid, and
(2) The Claimants instituted proceedings for enforcement of the Award in the United Kingdom (and elsewhere).

2   The Commission Decision and the Judgment of the General Court

On 30 March 2015, the Commission adopted its Final Decision in the state aid proceedings against Romania[73] to the following effect:

- payment of the Award constituted state aid within the meaning of Article 107(1) TFEU and was incompatible with the internal market;
- Romania was prohibited from making any payment of such state aid to the Claimants;
- any payments already made were to be recovered; and
- the Claimants were jointly liable to repay any sums received by them as part payment of the Award.

The Claimants thereupon filed proceedings for annulment of the Commission Decision before the General Court of the EU.

The General Court first considered the applicability of EU law to a situation predating Romania's accession to the EU, and held that:

- EU law became applicable in Romania only from the date of its accession, and it was only on that date that the Commission acquired competence to review Romania's actions in relation to the state aid rules of the Treaty.
- State aid must be considered to be granted at the time that the right to receive it is conferred on the beneficiary.
- All the events relating to EGO: Romania's adoption of EGO, the Claimants' obtaining of the licences enabling them to benefit from the incentives laid down by EGO, the entry into force of the BIT, the revocation of the incentives laid down by EGO; and the infringements committed by Romania on that occasion, as well as the initiation of the ICSID arbitration procedure, took place before Romania's accession to the EU on 1 January 2007.
- The repeal of the EGO incentives constitutes the event giving rise to the damage for which compensation was awarded.
- The arbitral tribunal confined itself to assessing the damage suffered by the Claimants on the basis of repeal of the EGO and calculated the amount of damages corresponding to a right to compensation which arose in 2005.
- It was immaterial that the tribunal's Award was issued after accession of Romania to the EU as is the fact of payment by Romania on the basis of the Award.[74]
- Consequently, the Commission's Decision was annulled.

The judgment of the General Court was appealed to the CJEU (*see* below).

---

73. Commission Decision (EU) 2015/1470 of 30 March 2015 on State aid SA. 38517 (2014/C) (ex 2014/NN) implemented by Romania.
74. Judgment of the General Court, *supra* n. 4, §§67-80.

3   The UK Proceedings and the Judgment of the UK Supreme Court

In 2014, Micula and others commenced proceedings in the English High Court for registration and enforcement of the Award. The Court ordered registration but, on the application of Romania, granted stay (suspension) of enforcement pending the decision of the General Court (above). The Court of Appeal continued the stay but ordered Romania to provide security. That decision was appealed to the Supreme Court. On the date scheduled for the hearing, the General Court issued its judgment and the hearing was deferred.

In its unanimous judgment of 19 February 2020, the Supreme Court considered the vexed question as to whether, if at all, a State Party to the ICSID Convention can refuse the execution of a final Award. It concluded that this is an issue that can be definitively decided only by the International Court of Justice, but that in any event none of the potential grounds for refusal could apply in this case.[75]

The Court then considered the effect of Article 351 TFEU which provides that:

> The rights and obligations arising from agreements concluded [before the date of accession] between one or more member states on the one hand, and one or more third countries on the other, shall not be affected by the provisions of the Treaties.

The ICSID Convention was ratified by the UK on 19 December 1966 and entered into force a month later. The UK acceded to the EU on 1 January 1973. Consequently, the ICSID Convention, as far as the UK is concerned, is a 'pre-accession agreement'.

After briefly considering arguments as to the scope of Article 351, the Court addressed the obligations of the UK under the ICSID Convention as follows:

> 'It is clear that the specific duties in articles 54 and 69 of the ICSID Convention are owed to all other Contracting States. The Convention scheme is one of mutual trust and confidence which depends on the participation and compliance of every Contracting State. The importance within this scheme of the effective recognition and enforcement of awards is apparent from the preamble which emphasises the requirement that "any arbitral award be complied with".
>
> 'The structure of the ICSID Convention supports this interpretation. ...These features of the Convention regime provide a strong indication that a Contracting State which has obligations under the Convention in relation to an award owes those obligations to all other States party to the Convention as well as to any party to the award. Article 27(1) confirms that the obligation on a Contracting State against whom an arbitration award is made to comply with the award is not just owed to the other parties to the dispute, since it recognises that any Contracting State whose national is involved in the dispute may bring an international claim against the other Contracting State if it fails to comply with the award rendered. ...
>
> 'The Claimants identify four features of the scheme, which demonstrate that its purpose requires that the relevant obligations must be owed, not only to the State of nationality of the party seeking to enforce the award, but to all Contracting States. First, a key purpose of the Convention is to encourage investment by providing investors with reassurance that a monetary award can be enforced in the territories of all Contracting States. The failure of any Contracting State to enforce an award in accordance with article 54 would undermine the Convention scheme

---

75. Judgment of the UKSC, *supra* n. 5, §§68-87.

on which investors and Contracting States all rely. This points to a network of mutual enforcement obligations. Secondly, were a Contracting State, when implementing its Convention obligations into domestic law, to qualify them by providing that no award was to be recognised or enforced if illegal under domestic law or contrary to its public policy, that would represent a plain breach of duty owed to all other Contracting States of which they would all be entitled to complain, even before such legislation came to be applied in any particular case. Thirdly, if a Contracting State were to fail to enforce an award in accordance with the ICSID scheme the beneficiaries of the award would be compelled to seek enforcement elsewhere and the burden of enforcement would fall on other States involving expenditure of resources within their legal systems. Fourthly, in such situations attempts to enforce in an alternative forum might result in the party against which enforcement is sought reducing or withdrawing its commercial assets in that alternative forum to the detriment of the State concerned.

'The travaux préparatoires of the ICSID Convention also support the view that obligations to comply with the Convention scheme are owed to all Contracting States.'

The Court concluded that neither the Convention nor its travaux préparatoires provide any warrant for restricting the scope of the duties owed by a Contracting State to the community of Contracting States.[76] Consequently, the Court lifted the stay, allowing the Claimants to seek to enforce the Award in the United Kingdom.

The Judgment of the UK Supreme Court was followed (without mention) in July 2021 by the Opinion of the Advocate General of the Court of Justice and in January 2022 by the Judgment of the Court. The scope for appeal from the General Court to the Court of Justice is limited to appeals on points of law. In this case, the appeal centred on the question of whether the General Court was correct in holding, in essence, that all material events had occurred before Romanian accession and, consequently, by necessary implication, that the actual payment, post-accession, of the compensation awarded by the arbitral tribunal could not be characterised as state aid.

4   The Opinion of the Advocate General[77]

The Advocate General, Maciej Szpunar, began his Opinion with the reflection that 'The tumultuous encounter between EU law and investment arbitration law has raised numerous questions which the judgment in *Achmea* will not have sufficed to eliminate.' He then set about a detailed analysis of the problems raised by the case which were complicated by the intricacies of court procedure. It seems unnecessary to go into all the details here.

The Advocate General first addressed the applicability of the *Achmea* judgment to the case at issue where the arbitration proceedings under a pre-accession BIT began before the date of Romania's accession to the EU.[78] He did so from the point of view of time and substance (*ratione temporis* and *ratione materiae*). In his analysis, the

---

76. *Ibid.*, §§104-108.
77. *Supra* n. 6.
78. Paragraphs 62-108.

criterion of time did not provide an answer without considering the underlying substance.[79]

As to substance, his analysis was that *Achmea* applied to a situation where a dispute capable of concerning the interpretation or application of EU law was withdrawn from the judicial system of the EU, based on mutual trust, by arbitral proceedings under a pre-accession BIT. This did not apply where, as in the *Micula* case, the arbitration proceedings had already been started before accession.[80] But that did not end the matter because the question ultimately at issue was whether, as the Commission had held, it was actual payment of the sum awarded that constituted a State aid.

On this issue, the Advocate General accepted that under the general law of liability, the right to compensation arises on the day on which the harm is sustained. But it does not follow that, in the law of State aid, the right to receive the aid arises at that time. The arbitral award establishes *retroactively* the existence of a right to compensation, but it is the award itself that confers the right to payment of the sum awarded.[81] Consequently, the reasoning of the General Court was wrong in law.

5   The Judgment of the Court of Justice[82]

The Court of Justice adopted similar reasoning in holding that the General Court was wrong in law. But it differed from the Advocate General in holding that *Achmea* did not apply.

The Court's reasoning is based on the following finding as to the basis of the arbitral award:

> 27. In its arbitral award of 11 December 2013 ('the arbitral award') the arbitral tribunal found that, by repealing the tax incentives scheme at issue prior to 1 April 2009, Romania had violated the legitimate expectations of the [arbitration applicants] who thought that those incentives would be available, in substantially the same form, until 31 March 2009 inclusive, had failed to act transparently by failing to inform those applicants in a timely manner and had failed to ensure fair and equitable treatment of the investments of those applicants, within the meaning of Article 2(3) of the BIT. Consequently, the arbitral tribunal ordered Romania to pay the arbitration applicants, by way of damages, the sum of 791882452 Romanian lei (RON) (approximately EUR 178 million), that sum being fixed by taking into account principally the loss allegedly suffered by the applicants in the period from 22 February 2005 until 31 March 2009.

On that basis of 'fact', the Court held that *Achmea* applied by the following process of reasoning:[83]

> '140. In the present case, with effect from the date of Romania's accession to the European Union, EU law, including Articles 107 and 108 TFEU, was applicable to that Member State. As is apparent from the information in the case file referred to

---

79. Paragraph 75.
80. Paragraphs 79-83.
81. Paragraphs 126-129.
82. *Supra* n. 7.
83. Paragraphs 140-146.

in paragraph 27 above, it is common ground that the compensation sought by the arbitration applicants did not relate exclusively to the damage allegedly suffered before that date of accession, with the result that the dispute brought before the arbitral tribunal cannot be regarded as being confined in all respects to a period during which Romania, which had not yet acceded to the European Union, was not yet bound by the rules and principles recalled in paragraphs 138 and 139 above.

'141. It is common ground that the arbitral tribunal before which that dispute was brought does not form part of the EU judicial system which the second subparagraph of Article 19(1) TEU requires the Member States to establish in fields covered by EU law, which, with effect from Romania's accession to the European Union, replaced the mechanism for resolving disputes that might concern the interpretation or application of EU law.

'142. First, that arbitral tribunal is not a "court or tribunal of a Member State" within the meaning of Article 267 TFEU and, second, the arbitral award delivered by that court is not subject, in accordance with Articles 53 and 54 of the ICSID Convention, to any review by a court of a Member State as to its compliance with EU law.

'143. Contrary to the submissions made at the hearing by European Food and Others and Viorel Micula and Others, that assessment cannot be called into question by the fact that Romania had consented to the possibility of litigation being brought against it in the context of the arbitration procedure provided for by the BIT.

'144. Such consent, unlike that which would have been given in commercial arbitration proceedings, does not originate in a specific agreement reflecting the freely expressed wishes of the parties concerned, but derives from a treaty concluded between two States in the context of which they have, generally and in advance, agreed to exclude from the jurisdiction of their own courts disputes which may concern the interpretation or application of EU law in favour of arbitration proceedings ....

'145. In those circumstances, since, with effect from Romania's accession to the European Union, the system of judicial remedies provided for by the EU and FEU Treaties replaced that arbitration procedure, the consent given to that effect by Romania, from that time onwards, lacked any force.'

IX   CONCLUDING REFLECTIONS

The result of the Court's judgment in the *Micula* case appears to be that an investor, relying on the implied consent of the host State under a Bilateral Investment Treaty, and having embarked on a time-consuming and costly arbitration process, duly constituted and concluded under an International Convention providing for the automatic enforcement of awards, can find itself deprived of the fruits of its award by the retroactive judgment of a court that had no jurisdiction either at the time of the investment or at the date of the arbitral award.

It was therefore to be expected that the Court's judgment would provoke reactions such as this:

'Obviously, the overreach of the ECJ does not come as a surprise. In fact, it is perfectly understandable from the ECJ point of view, which apparently aims to eradicate international arbitration involving EU member states and by extension also EU investors, in one way or another and superimpose its jurisdiction.

'This approach is in complete ignorance of public international law and the existing obligations which EU member states willingly and validly have entered into with other states, whether before or after accession to the EU.

'Public international law and treaty law simply do not work on the basis of accepting the claimed supremacy of EU law and "automatic replacement" approach of the ECJ.

'Indeed, at the public international law level, all subjects of international law and all treaties are, or at least should be treated equally, with good reason.'[84]

It is regrettable, to say the least, that the Court did not explore the implications for its own jurisdiction of the binding nature in public international law of the ICSID Convention and any award made thereunder; and all the more so since the UK Supreme Court, and also Advocate General Wathelet in his *Achmea* Opinion, had already drawn attention to the conflict.[85]

Amongst principles of immediate relevance, two appear to stand out. First, the Treaty on European Union provides that: 'In its relations with the wider world, the Union shall ... contribute to *the strict observance and the development of international law.*'[86] The CJEU exists and operates within the context of that Treaty and is bound by its obligations. Second, the Vienna Convention on the Law of Treaties provides that 'A party may not invoke the provisions of its internal law as justification for its failure to perform a treaty.'[87]

F.A. Mann, of whom Lord Denning said that 'Of all my learned friends, Francis Mann is the most learned of all', wrote that:

Jurisdiction is concerned with what has been described as one of the fundamental functions of public international law, *viz.*, the function of regulating and delimiting the respective competences of States.[88]

More recently, Professor Cedric Ryngaert has written, citing Mann:

In essence, the laws of jurisdiction ... serve as the basic 'traffic rules' of the international legal order.[89]

Rather than contribute to the orderly exercise of jurisdiction, the Court's judgments in *Achmea* and *Micula* have given rise to numerous litigations, notably as regards Spain's obligation to pay arbitral awards under the Energy Charter Treaty.[90]

---

84. *See* Lavranos, *The New* Micula *Judgment and the Overreach of the ECJ*, Blogpost dated 10 March 2022 at http://arbitrationblog.practicallaw.com/the-new-micula-judgment-and-the-overreach-of-the-ecj/.
85. Opinion in the *Achmea* case, *see* above VI.
86. Treaty on European Union, Article 3.5.
87. Vienna Convention, Article. 27.
88. F.A. Mann, *The Doctrine of Jurisdiction in International Law* (1964) 111 RCADI 1 at p. 15.
89. Ryngaert, 'The Concept of Jurisdiction in International Law' in Orakhelashvili (ed.) *Research Handbook on Jurisdiction and Immunities in International Law*, Elgar, at p. 51.
90. *See* Law 360, *passim*, most recently reporting the ruling of a DTC federal judge dismissing litigation to enforce a EUR 26.5 million arbitral award issued to Dutch solar energy investors ((Law 360, 30 March 2023).

Professor George Bermann predicted a decade ago:

'Up to now, European Union law and the law of international arbitration have
largely occupied separate worlds. To describe their relationship as one of mutual
indifference would scarcely be an overstatement. The past, in which these two
bodies of law coexisted, each following its separate and distinctive logic, looks
today like something of an age of innocence. ... .

'Due to the way in which tensions between EU law and investment
arbitration law have recently been framed, arbitration tribunals and courts can
scarcely avoid addressing more frontally the relationship between the competing
legal orders. Indications thus far suggest that, in that confrontation, the European
Union may be required to make concessions to competing legal orders that it is not
accustomed to making.'[91]

The Court's more recent claim to the 'autonomy' of the EU legal order (an
autonomy to which other legal orders are not, apparently, entitled) suggests that no
such concession is likely to be forthcoming in the immediate future.

Meanwhile, the European Commission's campaign against ISDS through arbitration has had some success in setting up the framework for the CETA Tribunals. The
prospect of a Multilateral Investment Court replacing the existing system of ISDS
through arbitration seems to belong to a future more remote than my lifetime.

It is worth recalling, by way of conclusion, the consequences of a much earlier
attempt to meet 'popular dissatisfaction'. The scene is the meeting of the American Bar
Association in St Paul, Minnesota, in 1906:

'It was a pleasant summer evening. ... In the morning the clans of the respectable
Bar had assembled for a business meeting and had later taken a recess until 8 in the
evening. At the evening session, there were to be two addresses. ... Now you must
understand that the typical Bar Association address of that period was a sober,
solid exposition of some sober, static subject. ... The members attended as a matter
of duty and respect, to be cheered by the speaker's well-turned eulogium on our
institutions or by his smooth exposition of a familiar principle of law.

'But now it was something different. The first speaker was a youngish
lawyer, in his early thirties, a local light in Nebraska – brought on this national
stage simply because the Association's president had recently heard him speak at
a meeting of the Nebraska Bar Association. And what was his topic? "Popular
Dissatisfaction with the Administration of Justice"! *Are* the people dissatisfied?
What *can* they be dissatisfied about? Do *we* not give them a good enough justice?
Whose idea can it be that things are wrong? Well, we are here; so we might as well
stay and listen politely; the president's reception doesn't begin till 9.30.

' But the strong legal minds were sniffing like faithful sheepdogs who smell
the wolf approaching down the wind; the lesser minds were nervously huddling
like the sheep of the sheepfold; for a vague instinct told them that there was danger
ahead in this speech by a lawyer who was, to all seeming, merely a law professor
and a commissioner of the supreme court [of Nebraska], but who was talking like
a reform wolf in sheep's clothing.'

---

91. Bermann, *Navigating EU Law and the Law of International Arbitration*, (2012) 28(3) Arbitration
International 398, 399.

The speaker was Roscoe Pound, who later became Dean of Harvard Law School and one of the great figures of the American legal scene. His address, a classic of legal literature, was nothing less than a root-and-branch attack on the workings of the American legal system, which a scandalised delegate from New York defended as 'the most refined and scientific system ever devised by the mind of man'. A Mr Spoonts of Texas averred that Pound was attempting to 'destroy that which the wisdom of centuries has built up', and in order to prove it he declaimed four whole verses of poetry by Edgar Allan Poe.

The target of Roscoe Pound's attack was what he called 'the sporting theory of justice' – 'the instinct of giving the game fair play':

> The inquiry is not, what do substantive law and justice require? Instead the inquiry is have the rules of the game been carried out strictly? If any material infraction is discovered, just as the football rules put back the offending team five, ten or fifteen yards, as the case may be, our sporting theory of justice awards new trials or reverses judgments ... in the interest of fair play.[92]

In response to Pound's attack, the opportunities for tactical surprise were removed. Rigorous procedures of pre-trial disclosure through discovery and interrogatories were introduced, so that the justice game would be played with all the cards face up on the table. The intention may have been sound: the result is a pre-trial procedure that can be so elaborate, intrusive, time-consuming and costly as to dissuade any sane person from embarking on litigation at all. Beware of getting what you wish for!

It is true that ISDS through arbitration raises legitimate concerns, which the revised ICSID Regulations[93] seek to address. But there is no evidence that a judicial system will do any better. Time will tell.

Above all, we should not forget that the ultimate aim is to ***encourage investment*** – an aim that is of some importance to the world economic order and the well-being of humanity.

---

92. John H. Wigmore, *Roscoe Pound's St Paul Address of 1906: The Spark That Kindled the White Flame of Progress, 1937*, 20(5) Journal of the American Judicature Society, p. 176ff., including the text of Pound's address at pp. 178ff.
93. ICSID Press Release with links https://icsid.worldbank.org/news-and-events/communiques/icsid-releases-2022-versions-its-rules-and-regulations accessed 13 July 2022.

CHAPTER 27

The CJEU and ISDS

*Markus Burgstaller**

TABLE OF CONTENTS

I   INTRODUCTION

The Court of Justice of the European Union (CJEU or 'Court') has recently addressed the relationship between EU law and international investment law in a number of important decisions.

With respect to investor-State dispute settlement (ISDS) within the EU, the CJEU issued at least five decisions. In *Achmea*, the CJEU ruled that EU law must be interpreted as precluding an investor-State arbitration clause in an investment treaty

---

*   Markus Burgstaller is a Partner at Hogan Lovells International LLP in London. He represented the Slovak Republic in the *Achmea* case before the German courts and the CJEU. He is currently representing the Claimants in another case mentioned in this contribution, namely *Mainstream v. Germany*. The views expressed in this article are the author's views. These are neither the views of Hogan Lovells International LLP nor of any of its clients.

concluded between EU Member States ('intra-EU bilateral investment treaty (BIT)').[1] Relying on *Achmea* the CJEU confirmed the incompatibility of investor-state arbitration with EU law in relation to intra-EU cases under the Energy Charter Treaty (ECT) in *Komstroy*.[2] In two further judgments, *PL Holdings*[3] and *European Food*[4] as well as in *Opinion 1/20*,[5] the CJEU confirmed its previous judgments. With respect to intra-EU ISDS, this contribution shall focus on *Achmea* and *Komstroy*.

With respect to non-intra EU ISDS, the CJEU in *Opinion 1/17* ruled that the investor-state dispute resolution clause in the Comprehensive Economic and Trade Agreement between Canada, of the one part, and the EU and its Member States, of the other part (CETA), is compatible with EU law.[6]

This contribution seeks to analyse why the CJEU came to different conclusions in these cases. It will highlight that, unlike in relation to CETA, as a matter of EU law (and indeed in the view of the CJEU) in intra-EU cases, the uniform interpretation and application of EU law is at risk. International arbitral tribunals – with one recent exception[7] – did not consider themselves bound by the Judgments of the CJEU. There is therefore divergence in the decision-making of the CJEU on the one hand and international arbitral tribunals on the other hand.

Most EU Member States have committed to terminating their intra-EU BITs. Until they are terminated, these BITs remain in force as a matter of international law, and,

---

1. CJEU, Case C-284/16, *Slowakische Republik (Slovak Republic) v. Achmea BV*, Judgment (6 March 2018) (henceforth *Achmea*).
2. CJEU, Case C-741/19, *Republic of Moldova v. Komstroy LLC*, Judgment (2 September 2021) (henceforth *Komstroy*).
3. CJEU, Case C-109/20, *Republic of Poland v. PL Holdings Sàrl*, Judgment (26 October 2021) (henceforth *PL Holdings*). In *PL Holdings*, the CJEU, relying on *Achmea*, held: 'Articles 267 and 344 TFEU must be interpreted as precluding national legislation which allows a Member State to conclude an ad hoc arbitration agreement with an investor from another Member State that makes it possible to continue arbitration proceedings initiated on the basis of an arbitration clause whose content is identical to that agreement, where that clause is contained in an international agreement concluded between those two Member States and is invalid on the ground that it is contrary to those articles.'
4. CJEU, Case C-638/19 P, *European Commission v. European Food S.A. and Others*, Judgment (25 January 2022) (henceforth *European Food*). In *European Food*, the CJEU, relying on *Achmea*, held: 'It is common ground that the arbitral tribunal before which that dispute was brought does not form part of the EU judicial system which the second subparagraph of Article 19(1) TEU requires the Member States to establish in fields covered by EU law, which, with effect from Romania's accession to the European Union, replaced the mechanism for resolving disputes that might concern the interpretation or application of EU law. That arbitral tribunal is not a 'court or tribunal of a Member State' within the meaning of Article 267 TFEU and, second, the arbitral award delivered by that court is not subject, in accordance with Articles 53 and 54 of the ICSID Convention, to any review by a court of a Member State as to its compliance with EU law.'
5. CJEU, *Opinion 1/20*, Opinion of 16 June 2022 (henceforth *Opinion 1/20*). In *Opinion 1/20* the CJEU held: 'the Court has already ruled on that question. It is clear from the judgment of 2 September 2021, Republic of Moldova (C-741/19, EU:C:2021:655), and in particular from paragraphs 40 to 66 thereof, that compliance with the principle of autonomy of EU law, enshrined in Article 344 TFEU, requires Article 26(2)(c) of the ECT to be interpreted as meaning that it is not applicable to disputes between a Member State and an investor of another Member State concerning an investment made by the latter in the first Member State'.
6. CJEU, *Opinion 1/17*, Opinion of 30 April 2019 (henceforth *Opinion 1/17*).
7. *Green Power Partners K/S and SCE Solar Don Benito APS* (SCC Arbitration V (2016/135), Award (16 June 2022) (henceforth *Green Power v. Spain*).

while international arbitral tribunals continue to accept jurisdiction over any intra-EU BIT disputes, it may well be that fundamental questions of the relationship between EU and international investment law will be decided by the courts before which successful claimants seek to enforce any awards.

With respect to intra-EU ECT cases, EU Member States have not yet come up with any consistent view. Accordingly, for now, claimants will continue to bring claims in intra-EU ECT cases. However, following the announcement by a number of EU Member States to withdraw from the ECT, on 7 July 2023, the European Commission proposed a coordinated EU withdrawal from the ECT.[8] The European Commission's proposals will now be submitted to the Council of the EU, where a qualified majority is necessary for their approval. In its proposal, the European Commission takes the view that:

> [The ECT] is incompatible with the principle of autonomy of Union law, as it does not include some of the safeguards identified by the Court in the CETA opinion in order to conclude that the arbitration awards would not have the 'effect of preventing the EU institutions from operating in accordance with the EU consti-tutional framework'.[9]

This contribution will proceed as follows: first, it will outline – in chronological order – the *Achmea* Judgment, *Opinion 1/17*, and the *Komstroy* Judgment; second, it will provide an overview of how international tribunals and EU Member States, including their courts, have dealt with the *Achmea* and *Komstroy* Judgments in intra-EU BIT and ECT cases to date; third, it will make reference to ongoing enforce-ment proceedings of intra-EU ECT awards; and finally, it will provide some concluding remarks.

II   THE JUDGMENT OF THE CJEU IN *ACHMEA*, *OPINION 1/17*, AND THE JUDGMENT OF THE CJEU IN *KOMSTROY*

1   The Judgment of the CJEU in *Achmea*

The CJEU's Judgment in *Achmea* related to a request for a preliminary ruling by the German Supreme Court in accordance with Article 267 of the Treaty on the Functioning of the European Union (TFEU). The subject matter of the case before the German courts related to an annulment application of an arbitral award issued by a tribunal under the Netherlands-Slovak Republic BIT (BIT). In its Judgment, the CJEU held that: 'Articles 267 and 344 TFEU must be interpreted as precluding a provision in an international

---

8. European Commission, *European Commission proposes a coordinated EU withdrawal from the Energy Charter Treaty* (7 July 2023); European Commission, Proposal for a Council Decision on the withdrawal of the Union from the Energy Charter Treaty, COM(2023) 447 final (7 July 2023); Recommendation for a Council Decision on the approval of the withdrawal of the European Atomic Energy Community from the Energy Charter Treaty, COM(2023) 446 final (7 July 2023).
9. European Commission, Proposal for a Council Decision on the withdrawal of the Union from the Energy Charter Treaty, COM(2023) 447 final (7 July 2023), pp. 1 and 2.

agreement concluded between Member States, such as Article 8 of the Netherlands-Slovak Republic BIT.'[10]

Article 8 of that BIT contained an investor-State arbitration clause. In its Judgment, the CJEU stressed the autonomy of the EU legal system.[11] The Court emphasised that that principle was enshrined in particular in Article 344 TFEU under which Member States undertake not to submit a dispute concerning the interpretation or application of the Treaties to any method of settlement other than those provided for in the Treaties.[12] The CJEU also noted that EU law is based on the fundamental premise that each Member State shares with all other Member States a set of common values. This implies and justifies the existence of mutual trust between Member States. Accordingly, Member States are obliged to ensure the application of and respect for EU law.[13] In this way, the EU Treaties have established a judicial system intended to ensure consistency and uniformity in the interpretation of EU law.[14]

The Court stressed that it is for the national courts and tribunals and the CJEU to ensure the full application of EU law in all Member States.[15] The keystone for that judicial system is Article 267 TFEU. This provision sets up a dialogue between the CJEU and courts and tribunals of Member States and it has the object of securing the uniform interpretation of EU law.[16]

The CJEU had to answer a preliminary question, namely whether the arbitral tribunal had to interpret EU law to solve the dispute. The Court found that the arbitral tribunal *may* have had to apply EU law. The BIT included an applicable law clause. Pursuant to that clause, the tribunal had to apply, among others, 'the law in force of the Contracting Party concerned' and 'relevant agreements between the Contracting Parties.'[17] The Court found that EU law must be regarded as forming part of the law in force in every Member State and as deriving from an international agreement between the Member States.[18] Therefore, the tribunal *may* have had to apply EU law.[19]

Given that the tribunal *may* have had to apply EU law, the CJEU had to analyse whether the tribunal was a 'court or tribunal of a Member State' within the meaning of Article 267 TFEU such that it could request a preliminary ruling from the CJEU. The Court found that this was not the case.[20] It held that: '[I]t is precisely the exceptional nature of the tribunal's jurisdiction compared with that of the courts of those two Member States that is one of the principal reasons for the existence of Article 8 of the BIT.'[21]

---

10. *Achmea*, para. 62.
11. *Achmea*, para. 32.
12. *Achmea*, para. 32.
13. *Achmea*, para. 34.
14. *Achmea*, para. 35.
15. *Achmea*, para. 36.
16. *Achmea*, para. 37.
17. *Achmea*, para. 40.
18. *Achmea*, para. 41.
19. *Achmea*, para. 42.
20. *Achmea*, para. 49.
21. *Achmea*, para. 45.

The CJEU asked whether an arbitral award made by such a tribunal is subject to review by a court of a Member State. If so, this would ensure that questions of EU law which the tribunal may have to address can be submitted to the Court by means of a reference for a preliminary ruling.[22] The Court found that pursuant to the BIT the decision of the tribunal was final and that the tribunal could determine its own procedure applying the UNCITRAL arbitration rules and, in particular, could choose its own seat.[23] The Court found that any judicial review can be exercised only to the extent that national law permits.[24]

Crucially, for present purposes, the CJEU held that:

> an international agreement providing for the establishment of a court responsible for the interpretation of its provisions and whose decisions are binding on the institutions, including the Court of Justice, is not in principle incompatible with EU law. The competence of the EU in the field of international relations and its capacity to conclude international agreements necessarily entail the power to submit to the decisions of a court which is created or designated by such agreements as regards the interpretation and application of their provisions, provided that the autonomy of the EU and its legal order is respected.[25]

The CJEU then went on to distinguish these agreements with third States with the intra-EU BIT underlying the *Achmea* case and concluded:

> In the present case, however, apart from the fact that the disputes falling within the jurisdiction of the arbitral tribunal referred to in Article 8 of the BIT may relate to the interpretation of both that agreement and of EU law, the possibility of submitting those disputes to a body which is not part of the judicial system of the EU is provided for by an agreement which was concluded not by the EU but by Member States.[26]

Following the Judgment of the CJEU on 6 March 2018, the German Supreme Court annulled the award on 31 October 2018. In its decision, the German Supreme Court held that in the light of the Judgment of the CJEU, the offer to arbitrate in the investor-State arbitration clause in the Netherlands-Slovak Republic BIT was not valid. Therefore, Achmea could not perfect an arbitration agreement when it filed for arbitration. As a result, the tribunal did not have jurisdiction.[27]

2 The CJEU's *Opinion 1/17*

Article 8.31 of CETA contains an applicable law clause which provides in parts most relevant for present purposes as follows:

---

22. *Achmea*, para. 50.
23. *Achmea*, para. 51.
24. *Achmea*, para. 53.
25. *Achmea*, para. 57.
26. *Achmea*, para. 58.
27. German Federal Supreme Court of Justice, *Slowakische Republik gegen Achmea B.V.*, Order (31 October 2018).

1. When rendering its decision, the Tribunal established under this Section shall apply this Agreement as interpreted in accordance with the Vienna Convention on the law of Treaties [...] ('VCLT'), and other rules and principles of international law applicable between the Parties. 2. The Tribunal shall not have jurisdiction to determine the legality of a measure, alleged to constitute a breach of this Agreement, under the domestic law of a Party. For greater certainty, in determining the consistency of a measure with this Agreement, the Tribunal may consider, as appropriate, the domestic law of a Party as a matter of fact. In doing so, the Tribunal shall follow the prevailing interpretation given to the domestic law by the courts or authorities of that Party and any meaning given to domestic law by the Tribunal shall not be binding upon the courts of the authorities of that Party.

The CJEU found that the resolution of investment disputes foreseen in CETA by means of establishing a CETA Tribunal and Appellate Tribunal, and in the longer term, a multilateral Investment Tribunal, 'may be compatible with EU law only if it has no adverse effect on the autonomy of the EU legal order'.[28] In order to ensure that the autonomy of the legal order is preserved, the Treaties have established a judicial system intended to ensure consistency and uniformity in the interpretation of EU law.[29] Referring to the preliminary rulings procedure enshrined in Article 267 TFEU the CJEU stressed that in 'accordance with Article 19 [Treaty on European Union] TEU, it is for the national courts and tribunals and the Court to ensure the full application of [EU] law in all Member States and to ensure effective judicial protection, the Court having exclusive jurisdiction to give the definitive interpretation of [EU] law'.[30]

At the outset of its analysis on whether the ISDS mechanism contained in CETA may have adverse effects on the autonomy of the EU legal order, the CJEU stated that that mechanism stands outside the EU judicial system.[31] However, this does not mean, in itself, that the mechanism adversely affects the autonomy of the EU legal order.[32] In the CJEU's view because of the reciprocal nature of international agreements, it is open to the EU to 'enter into an agreement that confers on an international court or tribunal the jurisdiction to interpret that agreement without that court or tribunal being subject to the interpretations of that agreement by the courts or tribunal of the Parties'.[33] It follows that EU law does not preclude the ISDS mechanism envisaged in CETA. However, since these tribunals stand outside of the EU judicial system, two conditions have to be satisfied: first, CETA does not confer on these tribunals any power to interpret or apply EU law other than the power to interpret and apply the provisions of that agreement having regard to the rules and principles of international law applicable between the Parties; second, CETA does not structure the powers of those tribunals in such a way that, while themselves engaging in the interpretation or application of rules of EU law other than those of that agreement, they may issue awards which have the

---

28. *Opinion 1/17*, para. 108.
29. *Opinion 1/17*, para. 111.
30. *Opinion 1/17*, para. 111.
31. *Opinion 1/17*, para. 113.
32. *Opinion 1/17*, para. 115.
33. *Opinion 1/17*, para. 117.

effect of preventing the EU institutions from operating in accordance with the EU constitutional framework.[34]

With respect to the first condition, the CJEU, having referred to Articles 8.31.1 and 2 CETA, distinguished these provisions from *Achmea* on at least three counts. First, the intra-EU BIT in *Achmea* 'established a tribunal that would be called upon to give rulings on disputes that might concern the interpretation or application of EU law'.[35] Second, while *Achmea* concerned an intra-EU BIT, CETA concerns the creation of a tribunal by means of an agreement between the EU and a non-EU Member State.[36] Third, whereas in any area that is subject to EU law (as was the case in *Achmea*), Member States are required to have due regard to the principle of mutual trust, that principle is not applicable in relations between the EU and a non-EU Member State.[37] Further, with specific reference to Article 8.31.2 CETA, the CJEU stressed that the Tribunal is obliged to follow the prevailing interpretation given to domestic law by the courts or authorities of that Party, and those courts and those authorities are not bound by the meaning given to their domestic law by that Tribunal.[38] The CJEU added that neither will the CETA Appellate Tribunal be called upon to interpret or apply the rules of EU law other than the provisions of the CETA. In the CJEU's view, it is clear that it was 'no way the intention of the Parties to confer on the Appellate Tribunal jurisdiction to interpret domestic law'.[39] Accordingly, CETA 'does not confer on the envisaged tribunal any jurisdiction to interpret or apply EU law other than that relating to the provisions of that agreement'.[40]

With respect to the second condition, the CJEU noted that the power of the envisaged tribunals under CETA to award damages to a private investor distinguished it from the WTO dispute settlement system which system is 'partly based on negotiations between those contracting parties and offering a number of options for giving effect to awards'.[41] The CJEU then went on to state:

> If the [EU] were to enter into an international agreement capable of having the consequence that the [EU] – or a Member State in the course of implementing EU law has to amend or withdraw legislation because of an assessment made by a tribunal standing outside the EU judicial system of the level of protection of a public interest established [...], it would have to be concluded that such an agreement undermines the capacity of the Union to operate autonomously within its unique constitutional framework.[42]

In the CJEU's view, the safeguards contained in Article 28.3.2 CETA[43] mean that the tribunal has no jurisdiction to declare incompatible with the CETA the level of

---

34. *Opinion 1/17*, para. 119.
35. *Opinion 1/17*, para. 126.
36. *Opinion 1/17*, para. 127.
37. *Opinion 1/17*, para. 129.
38. *Opinion 1/17*, para. 131.
39. *Opinion 1/17*, para. 133.
40. *Opinion 1/17*, para. 136.
41. *Opinion 1/17*, para. 146.
42. *Opinion 1/17*, para. 150.
43. Article 28.3.2 CETA reads in relevant parts: 'subject to the requirement that such measures are not applied in a manner which would constitute a means of arbitrary or unjustifiable discrimination between the Parties where like conditions prevail, or a disguised restriction on trade in

protection of a public interest established by EU measures and, on that basis, to order the EU to pay damages.[44] The CJEU found further support in numerous other similar provisions in CETA to allow it to conclude that 'the Parties have taken care to ensure that those tribunals have no jurisdiction to call into question the choices democratically made within a Party [...]'.[45] Accordingly, in the CJEU's view, CETA does not adversely affect the autonomy of the EU legal order.[46]

One crucial question that results from *Opinion 1/17*, in particular with respect to the CJEU's contradistinction of its reasoning on the autonomy of the EU legal order in *Achmea* (and the principle of mutual trust), is what this means for arbitrations under the ECT.[47] The CJEU clarified this question in its *Komstroy* Judgment.

3   The Judgment of the CJEU in *Komstroy*

The CJEU's Judgment in *Komstroy* related to a request for a preliminary ruling by the Paris Court of Appeal in accordance with Article 267 TFEU. The subject matter of the case before the French courts related to an annulment application of an arbitral award issued by a tribunal under the ECT. The underlying arbitration is related to a claim by a Ukrainian claimant against the Republic of Moldova. Notably, therefore, the underlying arbitration did not involve an intra-EU case; in fact, it did not even involve any EU investor or an EU Member State (other than the French courts having jurisdiction to hear the annulment application). The Paris Court of Appeal referred three questions relating to the meaning of an investment pursuant to Articles 1(6) and 26(1) of the ECT to the CJEU for a preliminary ruling.[48]

The CJEU noted that it had jurisdiction to interpret the ECT because since the entry into force of the Treaty of Lisbon the EU has exclusive competence, as regards foreign direct investment, pursuant to Article 207 TFEU and, as regards investments that are not direct, it has shared competence.[49] The CJEU added:

---

services, nothing in this Agreement shall be construed to prevent the adoption or enforcement by a Party of measures necessary: (a) to protect public security or public morals or to maintain public order; (b) to protect human, animal or plant life or health.'

44. *Opinion 1/17*, para. 153.
45. *Opinion 1/17*, para. 160.
46. *Opinion 1/17*, para. 161.
47. In at least one case a respondent non-EU Member State, Mozambique, in an arbitration under the Italy-Mozambique BIT, argued that the tribunal had to apply EU law, and in particular the Cotonou Convention, to which the EU itself is a party, along with its Member States. The Tribunal found that: 'The *Achmea* Decision explicitly addresses agreements between member states of the EU [...] and Opinion 1/17 clearly states that the jurisdiction of EU courts "does not take precedence over" the jurisdiction of tribunals established by agreements between member states and non-member states [...] The Tribunal is accordingly not persuaded that the *Achmea* Decision has any application to BITs between EU member states and non-member states, such as the BIT under which this arbitration was commenced.' *CMC Muratori Cementisti CMC Di Ravenna SOC. Coop; CMC Muratori Cementisti CMC Di Ravenna SOC. Coop. A.R.L. Maputo Branch; and CMC Africa Austral, LDA v. Republic of Mozambique* (ICSID Case No. ARB/17/23), Award (24 October 2019) para. 336.
48. *Komstroy*, para. 20.
49. *Komstroy*, paras 26 and 27.

It is true that the Court does not, in principle, have jurisdiction to interpret an international agreement as regards its application in the context of a dispute not covered by EU law. That is the case in particular where such a dispute is between an investor of a non-member State and another non-member State.

However, first, the Court has held that, where a provision of an international agreement can apply both to situations falling within the scope of EU law and to situations not covered by that law, it is clearly in the interest of the European Union that, in order to forestall future differences of interpretation, that provision should be interpreted uniformly, whatever the circumstances in which it is to apply [...].[50]

The CJEU went on to stress that the establishment of the seat of the arbitration on the territory of an EU Member State entailed the application of EU law, compliance with which the court hearing the case is obliged to ensure in accordance with Article 19 TEU.[51] The CJEU, referring to both *Achmea* and *Opinion 1/17*, considered that the autonomy of EU law with respect to both the law of the Member States and to international law is justified by the essential characteristics of the EU and its law, relating in particular to the constitutional structure of the EU and the very nature of that law.[52] Thus, the question of whether a dispute between a Member State and an investor of another Member State concerning an investment made by the latter in the first Member State may be subject to arbitration proceedings under Article 26(2)(c) ECT must be examined.[53]

Because the ECT itself is an act of EU law, an arbitral tribunal is required to interpret, and even apply EU law pursuant to Article 26(6) of the ECT.[54] Referring to *Achmea*, the CJEU held that the arbitral tribunal was not 'a court or tribunal of a Member State' within the meaning of Article 267 TFEU, and is not therefore entitled to make a reference to the Court for a preliminary ruling.[55]

It thus had to be ascertained whether an arbitral award by such a tribunal is, in accordance with Article 19 TEU in particular, subject to review by a court of a Member State and whether that review is capable of ensuring full compliance with EU law guaranteeing that questions of EU law which the tribunal may have to address can, if necessary, be submitted to the CJEU by a preliminary ruling. According to the CJEU, such judicial review can be carried out by the referring court only in so far as the domestic law of its Member State so permits. Article 1520 of the French Code of Civil Procedure provides only for limited review concerning, in particular, the jurisdiction of the arbitral tribunal.[56] Unlike in commercial arbitrations, in the ECT Member States agree to remove disputes which may concern the application or interpretation of EU law from the jurisdiction of their own courts and, hence, from the system of judicial

---

50. *Komstroy*, paras 28 and 29.
51. *Komstroy*, para. 34.
52. *Komstroy*, para. 43.
53. *Komstroy*, para. 47.
54. *Komstroy*, paras 48 to 50.
55. *Komstroy*, para. 53.
56. *Komstroy*, paras 54 and 57.

remedies which the second subparagraph of Article 19(1) TEU requires them to establish in the fields covered by EU law.[57] The CJEU concluded:

> It should be noted in that regard that, despite the multilateral nature of the international agreement of which it forms part, a provision such as Article 26 ECT is intended, in reality, to govern bilateral relations between two of the Contracting Parties, in an analogous way to the provision of the bilateral investment treaty at issue in the case giving rise to the [Achmea Judgment].
>
> It follows that, although the ECT may require Member States to comply with the arbitral mechanisms for which it provides in their relations with investors from third States who are also Contracting Parties to that treaty as regards investments made by the latter in those Member States, preservation of the autonomy and of the particular nature of EU law precludes the same obligations under the ECT from being imposed on Member States as between themselves.
>
> In the light of the foregoing, it must be concluded that Article 26(2)(c) ECT must be interpreted as not being applicable to disputes between a Member State and an investor of another Member State concerning an investment made by the latter in the first Member State.[58]

III   INTRA-EU ISDS AFTER *ACHMEA* AND *KOMSTROY*: PRACTICE OF INTERNATIONAL ARBITRAL TRIBUNALS AND REACTIONS OF EU MEMBER STATES, INCLUDING THEIR COURTS

1   Intra-EU ISDS after *Achmea* and *Komstroy*: Practice of International Arbitral Tribunals

a   *Practice of International Arbitral Tribunals Established under Intra-EU BITs*

Investment tribunals established under intra-EU BITs have not so far accepted jurisdictional objections by EU Member States based on *Achmea*. To give just two examples:

First, in an Award dated 26 July 2018 in *Gavrilovic v. Croatia*, an International Centre for Settlement of Investment Disputes (ICSID) tribunal said that the Respondent was too late to raise any objections to the tribunal's jurisdiction on the basis of the *Achmea* Judgment and held that objection to be inadmissible.[59]

Second, in an Award dated 9 October 2018 in *UP and C.D Holding v. Hungary*, an ICSID tribunal said that:

> The Achmea Decision contains no reference to the ICSID Convention or to ICSID Arbitration. Therefore, and in view of the above mentioned determinative differences between the Achmea case and the present one, the Achmea Decision cannot

---

57. *Komstroy*, para. 59.
58. *Komstroy*, paras 64 to 66.
59. *Georg Gavrilovic and Gavrilovic d.o.o. v. Republic of Croatia* (ICSID Case No. ARB/12/39), Award (26 July 2018).

be understood or interpreted as creating or supporting an argument that, by its accession to the EU, Hungary was no longer bound by the ICSID Convention.[60]

To date, there were at least two dissenting opinions by arbitrators in intra-EU BIT cases which considered that the tribunal would not have jurisdiction. In *Adamakopoulos and others v. Cyprus*, Professor Kohen opined that first, EU law (and EU action) is 'omnipresent in this case [and] is part of both national and international law applicable [...] by virtue of the BITs';[61] secondly, as confirmed in *Achmea* and Article 18 TFEU (which established the principle of non-discrimination), investor-State arbitration clauses in intra-EU BITs are incompatible with the EU Treaties and the EU Treaties prevail over the BIT;[62] and, as a result thirdly, the tribunal lacks jurisdiction.[63] Similarly, in *Raiffeisen v. Croatia*, one arbitrator dissented.[64]

b *Practice of International Arbitral Tribunals Established under the ECT in Intra-EU Cases*

Until recently, the practice of international arbitral tribunals shows that EU Member States have also not been successful with any objections raised to a tribunal's jurisdiction based on *Achmea* or *Komstroy* in intra-EU ECT arbitrations. The ECT is a multilateral investment treaty to which not only Member States but also the EU itself is a party. The ECT contains an applicable law clause. Article 26(6) of the ECT reads as follows: 'A tribunal established under paragraph (4) shall decide the issues in dispute in accordance with this Treaty and applicable rules and principles of international law.'

With respect to non-ICSID cases, one example is the Stockholm Chamber of Commerce (SCC) case *CEF Energia v. The Italian Republic*. In a decision dated 16 January 2019, the tribunal focused on the notion that the applicable BIT in *Achmea* made EU law applicable whereas, in the tribunal's view, that appears not to be the case under the ECT. The tribunal said: 'The CJEU does not make any comment on, nor does it gainsay the authority of that UNCITRAL tribunal to rule according to the general principles of international law. Its sole concern revolved around the two parts of the Achmea BIT which it says engage the application of EU law.'[65]

With respect to ICSID cases, the tribunal in *Vattenfall v. Germany* in a decision dated 31 August 2018 not only emphasised that it was an ICSID tribunal and thus different to the UNCITRAL tribunal seated in Germany in *Achmea* but also that the

---

60. *UP and C.D. Holding Internationale v. Hungary* (ICSID Case No. ARB/13/35), Award (9 October 2018) para. 258.
61. *Theodoros Adamakopoulos and others v. Republic of Cyprus* (ICSID Case No. ARB/15/49), Statement of Dissent of Professor Marcelo G. Kohen (3 February 2020) para. 43.
62. Kohen, Dissent, para. 48.
63. Kohen, Dissent, para. 70.
64. *Raiffeisen Bank International Ag and Raiffeisenbank Austria D.D. v. Croatia* (ICSID Case No. ARB/17/34), Decision on Respondent's Jurisdictional Objections (30 September 2020) paras 255-258 (dissenting view by Mr Tomov).
65. *CEF Energia B.V. v. The Italian Republic* (SCC Arbitration V (2015/158), Award (16 January 2019) para. 96(e).

position in an intra-EU ECT case would be different to the position under an intra-EU BIT. The tribunal held:

> The ECJ's reasoning was not specifically addressed to investor-State dispute settlement under the ECT. While there is a certain breadth to the Court's wording, addressing provisions 'such as' the dispute resolution provision of the BIT in that case, it is an open question whether the same considerations necessarily apply to the ECT.[66]

The tribunal went on to say:

> In particular the ECT is not an agreement concluded 'between Member States', as referred to by the ECJ. The ECT is a multilateral treaty, to which the EU itself is a party, alongside its Member States. Unlike the Dutch-Slovak BIT, the ECT is a 'mixed agreement' between both Member States and third States, in addition to the EU itself.[67]

The ICSID tribunal in *Eskosol v. Italian Republic* in a decision dated 7 May 2019 went one step further when it stated:

> Some intra-EU BITs, like the Achmea BIT, may require application of EU law, but other intra-EU BITs by their terms may not. In the context of the ECT, which the CJEU has not even discussed, it would be particularly surreal to interpret the CJEU as already having decided that the arbitral mechanism is contrary to EU law, when that mechanism as discussed above does not actually command the application of EU law, and thus decidedly does not pose the particular risk that the CJEU identified as its basis for concern.[68]

Other ICSID tribunals deciding cases under the ECT took a different view on the application of EU law in intra-EU ECT cases but still did not accept the EU Member State's jurisdictional objection based on *Achmea*. Thus, for example, the tribunal in *NextEra Energy v. Kingdom of Spain* in a decision of 12 March 2019 said:

> Although the Tribunal understands that in the present case, EU Law may find application, it cannot state that overlap between the two sets of rules strips the present dispute of its international aspects. In other words, the Tribunal cannot infer its own competence – or incompetence – from the principle of primacy of EU Law over the ECT for intra-EU disputes. The fact that there may exist a partial overlap between the two sets of rules on the merits (such as FET and Fundamental Freedoms), cannot, for the purpose of jurisdiction, be resolved in favour of EU Law. This is because the questions pertaining to the Tribunal's jurisdiction must be answered in light of Article 26 of the ECT.[69]

---

66. *1. Vattenfall AB; 2. Vattenfall GmbH; 3. Vattenfall Europe Nuclear Energy GmbH; 4. Kernkraftwerk Krümmel GmbH & Co. oHG; 5. Kernkraftwerk Brunsbüttel GmbH & Co. oHG v. Federal Republic of Germany* (ICSID Case. No. ARB/12/12), Decision on the *Achmea* Issue (31 August 2018) (henceforth *Vattenfall v. Germany*) para. 161.
67. *Vattenfall v. Germany*, para. 162.
68. *Eskosol S.p.A. in liquidazione v. Italian Republic* (ICSID Case No. ARB/15/50), Decision on Italy's Request for Immediate Termination and Italy's Jurisdictional Objection based on the Inapplicability of the Energy Charter Treaty to intra-EU Disputes (7 May 2019) para. 177.
69. *NextEra Energy Global Holdings B.V. and NextEra Energy Spain Holdings B.V. v. Kingdom of Spain* (ICSID Case No. ARB/14/11), Decision on Jurisdiction, Liability and Quantum Principles (12 May 2019) para. 351.

The tribunal in *Watkins v Spain* said that *Achmea* was 'silent on the case of ECT-based arbitration'[70] and that the 'ordinary meaning of Article 26 of the ECT confers jurisdiction on the Tribunal'.[71] It concluded by saying that:

> The Tribunal's jurisdiction is based on the ICSID Convention, the ECT, and general international law principles governing State consent. The Tribunal is placed in a public international law context and not in a national or regional context. The two legal orders (the EU legal order and the ECT normative space) evolve in parallel and the Tribunal finds its jurisdiction in a treaty validly established in the international legal order.[72]

There are also a number of examples following *Komstroy* in which tribunals have not accepted the intra-EU objection of EU Member States. Thus, for example, one ICSID tribunal constituted under the ECT said:

> From the outset, the Tribunal makes it clear that, as it affirmed in the Decision, EU law is not applicable to jurisdiction. As a result, the Komstroy Judgment is irrelevant to the question of jurisdiction. The applicable law to jurisdiction and the merits of the dispute is international law, and not principles of sub-systems of international law such as EU treaties.[73]

However, in one recent case, an SCC tribunal seated in Stockholm declined jurisdiction on the basis of Spain's intra-EU objection. In *Green Power v. Spain*, the tribunal first recalled that the relevant provisions of EU law, including the state aid provisions contained in Articles 107 and 108(2) TFEU as well as Articles 267 and 344 TFEU must be applied – either as part of international law or as part of the applicable law to the arbitration agreement pursuant to the Swedish *lex arbitri* – to assess the validity of Spain's unilateral offer to arbitrate intra-EU investment disputes under Article 26 ECT.[74] The tribunal determined that it has to apply EU state aid law and in this context concluded:

70. *Watkins Holding S.A.R.L, Watkins (Ned) B.V., Watkins Spain S.L., Redpier S.L., Northsea Spain S.L, Parque Eolico Marmellar S.L., and Parque Eolico la Boga S.L. v. Kingdom of Spain* (ICSID Case No. ARB/15/44), Award (21 January 2020) (henceforth *Watkins v. Spain*) para. 221.
71. *Watkins v. Spain,* para. 222.
72. *Watkins v. Spain,* para. 225.
73. *Infracapital F1 S.à r.l. and Infracapital Solar B.V. v. Kingdom of Spain* (ICSID Case No. ARB/16/18), Decision on Respondent's Request for Reconsideration Regarding the Intra-EU Objection and the Merits (1 February 2022), para. 107 (footnote omitted). See also *Cavalum SGPS, S.A. v. Kingdom of Spain* (ICSID Case No. ARB/15/34), Decision on the Kingdom of Spain's Request for Reconsideration (10 January 2022), para. 97 ('(5) The ruling in *Komstroy* does not affect the jurisdiction of the Tribunal under the applicable international law, namely the ECT and the ICSID Convention. (6) There is nothing in the *Achmea* and *Komstroy* rulings which could deprive a Tribunal so constituted of jurisdiction, or suggest that Member States have no capacity to enter into agreements such as the ECT.'); *Sevilla Beheer B.V. and others v. Kingdom of Spain* (ICSID Case No. ARB/16/27), Decision on Jurisdiction, Liability and the Principles of Quantum (11 February 2022) paras 668 and 676 ('Furthermore, the Tribunal recalls that it is empowered to provide its own interpretation of the jurisdictional requirements of the ECT by virtue of the principle of compétence de la compétence. The CJEU's jurisprudence is not binding on the Tribunal in this respect. This is uncontested by the Respondent in principle. [...] In view of the above, the Tribunal maintains its conclusion regarding the applicability of Article 26 of the ECT in an intra-EU context despite the findings made in the *Komstroy* Judgment.').
74. *Green Power v. Spain,* para. 447.

If the Tribunal were to assert jurisdiction over the claims brought by the Claimants, it would have to decide the merits of claims relating to matters that pursuant to the EU Treaties are under the exclusive competence of the European Commission, and it would do so despite the fact that such transfer of jurisdiction to a REIO, *in casu* the EU, is expressly recognised in the text of the ECT. Under such conditions, the Tribunal considers that it would be overstepping its powers under the ECT, properly interpreted in the light of the relevant provisions of EU law.[75]

Relying on *Achmea* and *Komstroy* the tribunal in *Green Power v. Spain* added:

Moreover, even if the Tribunal were to consider that matters of State aid are not essential for the present case or cannot be legitimately raised, it would still lack jurisdiction as a result of the autonomy and primacy of the EU legal order and Spain is precluded under Articles 267 and 344 TFEU to offer to submit to arbitration a dispute with investors from EU Member State, such as the Claimants.[76]

The tribunal in *Green Power v. Spain* emphasised that in its view EU law was *lex superior*, as far as intra-EU relations were concerned, in relation to the ECT, including its Article 16. The tribunal said:

Seen from a *lex superior* perspective, the ECT could only override EU law in intra-EU relations if the ECT, including its Article 16, could be considered as *lex superior* with respect to the relevant norms of EU law, including Articles 267 and 344 TFEU and the principle of primacy. The Tribunal considers that there are no grounds on which the ECT could have such an overriding character in the circumstances of this case.[77]

The *Green Power v. Spain* tribunal emphasised that its seat was in an EU Member State (Sweden)[78] before concluding:

It is therefore the unanimous view of the Tribunal that the same considerations (referring to *Achmea* and *Komstroy*) apply to the offer to arbitrate by Spain under Article 26 ECT. Seated in an EU Member State, it likewise cannot apply to consent to arbitrate by the Respondent and affirm its jurisdiction. Following the reasoning of the CJEU Grand Chamber in the *Achmea Judgment* and subsequently confirmed in the *Komstroy Judgment*, this Tribunal considers that the offer of the Respondent, as an EU Member State, to arbitrate under Article 26 ECT a dispute with investors of another EU Member State which would, of necessity, require this Tribunal to interpret and apply the EU Treaties, is precluded. Therefore, there is no unilateral offer by the Respondent which the Claimants could accept.[79]

2   Intra-EU ISDS after *Achmea* and *Komstroy*: Reactions of EU Member States, Including Their Courts

It remains to be seen whether international arbitral tribunals will follow the reasoning of the *Green Power v. Spain* tribunal. Broadly speaking, the reactions of EU Member

---

75. *Green Power v. Spain,* para. 454.
76. *Green Power v. Spain,* para. 456.
77. *Green Power v. Spain,* para. 470.
78. *Green Power v. Spain,* para. 475.
79. *Green Power v. Spain,* para. 477.

States can be divided into reactions in relation to specific arbitrations and reactions disassociated with specific arbitrations.

a Reactions of EU Member States in Relation to Specific Arbitrations

In light of the practice of international arbitral tribunals, EU Member States have resorted to a number of procedural tools in order to seek to give force to the intra-EU objection. These tools have been deployed from early on in arbitrations until after an award has been issued. This section will briefly summarise some of these key developments.[80]

First, at least one EU Member State (Germany) has applied to an ICSID tribunal on the basis of Rule 41(5) of the ICSID Arbitration Rules with a view to having the case dismissed early on for lack of jurisdiction.[81] In *Mainstream v. Germany*, an ICSID tribunal did not accept Germany's application.[82]

Second, at least two EU Member States (Germany and the Netherlands) applied to the German courts with a view for the German courts to declare the respective ICSID cases to be 'inadmissible' as a matter of German (procedural) law with mixed results before the first instance courts: whereas Germany did not succeed with its application before its own courts (the Berlin Court),[83] the Netherlands succeeded with their application in two separate cases before the German courts (the Cologne Court).[84] Ultimately, on appeal the German Supreme Court considered the intra EU ECT claims to be 'inadmissible'.[85]

Third, EU Member States have applied – typically successfully – for annulment of intra-EU investment awards before the courts of EU Member States.[86] At the same time, EU Member States would not seem to have been successful, as far as any arguments

---

80. Enforcement proceedings will be touched upon in the next chapter.
81. Pursuant to ICSID Arbitration 41(5): 'Unless the parties have agreed to another expedited procedure for making preliminary objections, a party may, no later than 30 days after the constitution of the Tribunal, and in any event before the first session of the Tribunal, file an objection that a claim is manifestly without legal merit.'
82. *Mainstream Renewable Power Ltd et al. v. Federal Republic of Germany* (ICSID Case No. ARB/21/26), Decision on Respondent's Application under ICSID Arbitration Rule 41(5) (18 January 2022).
83. IAReporter, *Revealed: Berlin Court Dismisses Germany's Request for Anti-Arbitration Declaration Directed as ICSID Case* (24 May 2022) (reporting on a decision dated 28 April 2022).
84. IAReporter, *German Court Declares ECT/ICSID Arbitrations Against the Netherlands to be Inadmissible due to their Intra-EU Nature* (8 September 2022) (reporting on two decisions dated 1 September 2022). In one case, the Claimants filed an application for provisional measures seeking an order for the Netherlands to withdraw the German court proceedings. The tribunal noted that the Netherlands had represented during the hearing that the German court proceedings in fact were only aimed at having the court rule on the interpretation of EU law, while the tribunal's power to rule on its own jurisdiction remained uncontested. In light of these representations, the tribunal declined to order that the Netherlands withdraw the German court proceedings. *Uniper SE, Uniper Benelux Holding B.V. and Uniper Benelux N.V. v. Kingdom of the Netherlands* (ICSID Case No. ARB/21/22), Procedural Order No. 2 – Decision on the Claimants' Request for Provisional Measures (9 May 2022).
85. IAReporter, Germany's Supreme Court Rules that Anti-Arbitration Declaration Mechanism is Available against Intra-EU ICSID Arbitrations (27 July 2023).
86. *See*, for example, Paris Court of Appeal, *Strabag SE, Raiffeisen Centrobank AG and Syrena Immobilien Holding AG v. Republic of Poland* (19 April 2022); Paris Court of Appeal, *Slot Group*

based on the intra-EU objection are concerned, be it in relation to intra-EU BIT or intra-EU ECT cases, in their applications for annulment before ICSID Annulment Committees[87] and the courts of non-EU Member States.[88]

b Reactions of EU Member States Disassociated with Specific Arbitrations

The significance of *Achmea* is also underlined by declarations which EU Member States issued on 15 and 16 January 2019.[89] While the contents of these declarations are not identical, they all have in common a number of key elements:

First, all EU Member States say that they will terminate all BITs concluded between them by means of a plurilateral treaty or, where that is mutually recognised as more expedient, bilaterally.[90]

Second, all EU Member States say that in cooperation with a defending Member State, the Member State in which an investor that has brought such an action is established will take the necessary measures to inform the arbitral tribunals concerned of the consequences of *Achmea*, namely that investor-State arbitration clauses in intra-EU BITs are inapplicable.[91]

Third, all EU Member States say that defending Member States will request the courts, including in any third country, which are to decide in proceedings relating to an intra-EU investment arbitral award, to set these awards aside or not to enforce them.[92]

On 24 October 2019, it was announced that EU Member States had reached agreement on a plurilateral treaty for the termination of intra-EU BITs. On 5 May 2020,

---

AS C/O Mr. David Janosik (bankruptcy administrator of SLOT AS) and CEC Praha v. Poland (19 April 2022).

87. *See*, for example, *Magyar Farming Company Ltd, Kintyre Kft, & Anicia Zrt v. Hungary* (ICSID Case No. ARB/17/27), Decision on Annulment (16 November 2021); *InfraRed Environmental Infrastructure GP Limited and others v. Kingdom of Spain*, (ICSID Case No. ARB/14/12), Decision on Annulment (10 June 2022).

88. *See*, for example, Swiss Supreme Court, 25 November 2020, 4A_563/2020 (upholding the UNCITRAL arbitral award in *Vaclav Fischer v. Czech Republic*); Swiss Supreme Court (23 February 2021) 4A_187/2020 (upholding the UNCITRAL arbitral award in *PV Investors v. Spain*).

89. There is one declaration titled 'Declaration of the Representatives of the Governments of the Member States of 15 January 2019 on the Legal Consequences of the Judgment of the Court of Justice in *Achmea* and on Investment Protection in the European Union' which is signed by 22 EU Member States (Belgium; Bulgaria; Czech Republic; Denmark; Germany; Estonia; Ireland; Greece; Spain; France; Croatia; Italy; Cyprus; Latvia; Lithuania; Netherlands; Austria; Poland; Portugal; Romania; Slovak Republic; and United Kingdom – the latter no longer a Member State of the EU) ('Majority Declaration'). There is a second declaration titled 'Declaration of the Representatives of the Governments of the Member States of 16 January on the Enforcement of the Judgment of the Court of Justice in *Achmea* and on Investment Protection in the European Union' signed by five EU Member States (Finland; Luxembourg; Malta; Slovenia; and Sweden) ('Minority Declaration'). Finally, there is a third declaration titled 'Declaration of the Representative of the Government of Hungary, of 16 January 2019 on the Legal Consequences of the Judgment of the Court of Justice in *Achmea* and on Investment Protection in the European Union' ('Hungary Declaration').

90. Majority Declaration, para. 5; Minority Declaration, para. 5; Hungary Declaration, para. 4.

91. Majority Declaration, para. 2; Minority Declaration, para. 2; Hungary Declaration, para. 2.

92. Majority Declaration, para. 2; Minority Declaration, para. 2; Hungary Declaration, para. 2.

23 EU Member States signed the 'Agreement for the Termination of Bilateral Investment Treaties Between the Member States of the European Union' ('Intra-EU BIT Termination Agreement').[93] As of 14 October 2022, the Intra-EU BIT Termination Agreement has entered into force in relation to all 23 EU Member States Signatories to it.[94] A comprehensive analysis of the Intra-EU BIT Termination Agreement is beyond the scope of this contribution. For present purposes, certain key components should be highlighted:

First, pursuant to the Intra-EU BIT Termination Agreement, all intra-EU BITs together with their sunset clauses[95] are terminated.[96] Termination shall take effect as soon as the Agreement enters into force for the relevant parties in accordance with Article 16.[97] This effectively means that any intra-EU BIT between Member State A and Member State B, including its sunset clause, shall be terminated thirty calendar days after the date of deposit of the instrument of ratification, approval or acceptance by the second Member State depositing such instrument.[98]

Second, the parties to the Intra-EU BIT Termination Agreement confirm that investor-State arbitration clauses in intra-EU BITs are inapplicable. As a result, as of the date on which the last of the parties to the intra-EU BIT became an EU Member State, the clause in such a BIT 'cannot serve as legal basis for Arbitration Proceedings'.[99]

Third, in any pending or new arbitration proceedings, the parties will inform arbitral tribunals that investor-State arbitration clauses cannot serve as the legal basis for such proceedings and where they are party to judicial proceedings concerning an arbitral award issued on the basis of an intra-EU BIT, ask the competent court, including in any third country, to set the arbitral award aside, annul it or refrain from recognising and enforcing it.[100]

---

93. Signatories of the Intra-EU BIT Termination Agreement are Belgium, Bulgaria, Croatia, Republic of Cyprus, Czech Republic, Denmark, Estonia, France, Germany, Greece, Hungary, Italy, Latvia, Lithuania, Luxembourg, Malta, Netherlands, Poland, Portugal, Romania, Slovakia, Slovenia and Spain. This means that four EU Member States have not signed the Intra-EU BIT Termination Agreement: Austria, Finland, Ireland and Sweden. Ireland did not have any intra-EU BITs that it could terminate.
94. Portugal was the last EU Member States Signatory to the Intra-EU BIT Termination Agreement in relation to which it entered into force, on 14 October 2022.
95. 'Sunset clause' according to the Intra-EU BIT Termination Agreement means 'any provision in a[n intra-EU BIT] which extends the protection of investments made prior to the date of termination of that Treaty for a further period of time'. Article 1(7) of the Intra-EU BIT Termination Agreement.
96. Article 2(1) and (2) and Article 3 of the Intra-EU BIT Termination Agreement.
97. Article 4(2) of the Intra-EU BIT Termination Agreement.
98. Pursuant to Article 16(1) and (2) of the Intra-EU BIT Termination Agreement: '1. This Agreement shall enter into force 30 calendar days after the date on which the Depository receives the second instrument of ratification, approval or acceptance. 2. For each Party which ratifies, accepts or approves it after its entry into force in accordance with paragraph 1, this Agreement shall enter into force 30 calendar days after the date of deposit by such Party of its instrument of ratification, approval or acceptance.'
99. Article 4(1) of the Intra-EU BIT Termination Agreement.
100. Article 7(a) and (b) of the Intra-EU BIT Termination Agreement. However, pursuant to Article 6(1) of the Intra-EU BIT Termination Agreement '[Concluded Arbitration Proceedings] shall not be reopened'. Pursuant to Article 1(4) of the Intra-EU BIT Termination Agreement 'Concluded Arbitration Proceedings' means 'Any [intra-EU BIT] Arbitration Proceedings which ended with a settlement agreement or with a final award issued prior to 6 March 2018 where: a) the award

With respect to the ECT, the declarations by Member States issued on 15 and 16 January 2019 differ:

(a) The 22 Member States (then including the UK) that signed the Majority Declaration declared that *Achmea* also applies to intra-EU ECT cases in that the investor-State arbitration clause in the ECT in intra-EU cases is incompatible with the EU Treaties.[101] This also means that these 22 Member States (then including the UK) said that they would request the courts, including in any third country, which are to decide in proceedings relating to an intra-EU investment arbitration award (this would seem to include intra-EU ECT awards), to set these awards aside or not to enforce them due to a lack of valid consent.[102] In this regard, the Majority Declaration does not distinguish between intra-EU BIT and intra-EU ECT cases. The Majority Declaration also states that: 'Beyond actions concerning the [ECT] based on this declaration, Member States together with the Commission will discuss without undue delay whether any additional steps are necessary to draw all the consequences from [Achmea] in relation to the intra-EU application of the [ECT].'[103]

(b) Finland, Luxembourg, Malta, Slovenia and Sweden in the Minority Declaration declared that:

> The Member States note that [Achmea] is silent on the investor-state arbitration clause in the [ECT]. A number of international arbitration tribunals post [Achmea] have concluded that the [ECT] contains an investor-State arbitration clause applicable between EU Member States. This interpretation is currently contested before a national court in a Member State. Against this background, the Member States underline the importance of allowing for due process and consider that it would be inappropriate, in the absence of a specific judgment on this matter, to express views as regards the compatibility with EU law of the intra-EU application of the ECT.[104]

(c) Hungary in its Declaration said that in its view: '[Achmea] concerns only intra-EU [BITs]. [Achmea] is silent on the investor-State arbitration clause in the ECT and it does not concern any pending or prospective proceedings initiated under the ECT. The ongoing and future applicability of the ECT in intra-EU relations requires further discussion and individual agreement amongst the Member States.'[105]

---

was duly executed prior to 6 March 2018, even where a related claim for legal costs has not been executed or enforced, and no challenge, review, set-aside, annulment, enforcement, revision or other similar proceedings in relation to such final award was pending on 6 March 2018, or b) the award was set aside or annulled before the date of entry into force of the [Intra-EU BIT Termination Agreement].'
101. Majority Declaration, para. 1.
102. Majority Declaration, para. 2.
103. Majority Declaration, para. 9.
104. Minority Declaration, Preamble (footnotes omitted).
105. Hungary Declaration, paras 8 and 9.

The preamble to the Intra-EU BIT Termination Agreement says that the treaty 'does not cover intra-EU proceedings on the basis of Article 26 of the ECT. The Union and its Member States will deal with this matter at a later stage' and it does not make further statements or include provisions about the (in-)applicability of Article 26 ECT in intra-EU ECT cases.

On 24 June 2022, the Contracting Parties to the ECT (which include all EU Member States) reached an Agreement in Principle concerning a 'modernised ECT' pursuant to which an article was intended to be introduced that clarified that Article 26 (which includes the offer to arbitrate on the part of Contracting Parties to the ECT) shall not apply among EU Member States.[106] The intention had been that the 'modernised ECT' be adopted on 22 November 2022. However, because Germany, France, Spain and the Netherlands blocked the adoption of the 'modernised ECT', the 'modernisation package' was taken off the agenda of the 33rd meeting of the Energy Charter Conference on 22 November 2022 and the modernisation of the ECT was not adopted. In the meantime, at present, the ECT continues to apply to the EU and all EU Member States save for Italy that unilaterally withdrew in 2015. Germany, France and Poland also initiated a procedure of withdrawal in December 2022 which will become effective in December 2023.[107]

Further, as mentioned, on 7 July 2023 the European Commission proposed that the EU withdraw from the ECT. If that proposal was accepted by the Council by a qualified majority, the EU's withdrawal shall take effect upon the expiry of one year after the date of the receipt of the notification by the Depositary, or on such later date as may be specified in the notification of withdrawal. The European Commission added:

> Pursuant to Article 47.3 of the ECT, the provisions of the ECT shall continue to apply to investments made in the [EU] by investors of other Contracting Parties, or in the other Contracting Parties by investors of the [EU], for a period of 20 years as of the date of the [EU] withdrawal from the ECT. Article 47.3 of the ECT would have no impact on intra-EU relations, to which the ECT has never, does not and will never apply, including its Article 47.3. However, [...], there is a risk of legal conflict that must be eliminated. The Commission remains of the view that the appropriate response is to adopt an instrument that is a 'subsequent agreement between the parties regarding the interpretation of the treaty or the application of its provisions' within the meaning of Article 31(3)(a) of the Vienna Convention on the Law of Treaties (VCLT), among the Member States, the [EU] and EURATOM. The Commission will therefore continue the negotiations of the text of such an agreement which, once they are completed, would be the subject of a proposal for the conclusion of the subsequent agreement on behalf of the Union and of EURATOM. The codification of the interpretation of the EU and its Member States in a separate treaty (something that is possible because of the bilateral nature of the obligations) is all the more pressing in the absence of the ECT modernisation

---

106. Energy Charter Secretariat, Decision of the Energy Charter Conference, CCDEC 2022, 10 GEN (24 June 2022), p. 7.
107. In addition, Denmark, Luxembourg, the Netherlands, Slovenia and Spain announced their withdrawal. IAReporter, *Three EU Member States have recently notified their withdrawal from the ECT, according to the Energy Charter Secretariat* (23 March 2023); IAReporter, *Denmark's Government announces intention to withdraw from the ECT* (13 April 2023).

that would have embedded in the text itself and via a 'for greater certainty' clause, the understanding of all Contracting Parties that its Article 26 does not apply intra-EU.[108]

It remains to be seen whether the Council will adopt the European Commission's proposal. It also remains to be seen whether international arbitral tribunals will follow the European Commission's interpretation of the sunset clause in the ECT.

IV   ENFORCEMENT OF INTRA-EU ECT AWARDS OUTSIDE OF THE EU

In the absence of reasonable prospects to enforce intra-EU ECT awards within the EU, successful claimants in intra-EU ECT cases have frequently sought to enforce awards outside of the EU. Here, as with annulment proceedings before the courts of non-EU Member States, it would appear that successful claimants have, at least, not been rejected in their enforcement efforts.

For example, the UK Supreme Court lifted the stay of enforcement of the ICSID award in *Micula and others v. Romania*, after finding that EU law did not displace the United Kingdom's obligations under the ICSID Convention.[109] More recently, the English Commercial Court granted enforcement of an intra-EU ECT ICSID award against Spain.[110]

The Federal Court of Australia has likewise allowed the enforcement of two intra-EU ECT-based ICSID awards.[111] Most recently, in a decision of 12 April 2023, the High Court of Australia, Australia's highest court, has affirmed that Spain cannot invoke sovereign immunity to avoid the recognition and enforcement of an intra-EU ECT ICSID award – and that the CJEU's position on intra-EU investment arbitration is irrelevant to this question.[112]

A significant number of cases are pending before courts in the United States, primarily before the District Court of the District of Columbia. As compared to the English and Australian Courts, the D.C. Court appears to have been slightly more cautious. It has stayed enforcement of at least nine intra-EU ECT awards until a set-aside or annulment decision is issued, noting that it is *'loath to wade into this*

---

108. European Commission, Proposal for a Council Decision on the withdrawal of the Union from the Energy Charter Treaty, COM(2023) 447 final (7 July 2023), p. 3.
109. *Micula and others (Respondents/Cross-Appellants) v. Romania* (Appellant/Cross-Respondent) [2020] UKSC 5, 19 February 2020. Notably, on 29 July 2022 the European Commission brought proceedings against the UK in relation to the issuance of the Judgment of the UK Supreme Court on 19 February 2020 for breach of the EU Treaties in conjunction with the Agreement on the withdrawal of the United Kingdom of Great Britain and Northern Ireland from the European Union and the European Atomic Energy Community. At time of writing, these proceedings were pending before the CJEU as Case C-516/22.
110. *Infrastructure Services Luxembourg S.à.r.l. and Energia Termosolar B.V. v. Kingdom of Spain* [2023] EWHC 1226 (Comm), 24 May 2023.
111. *Kingdom of Spain v. Infrastructure Services Luxembourg S.à.r.l.* [2021] FCAFC 3 (1 February 2021); *Infrastructure Services Luxembourg S.A.R.L v. Kingdom of Spain* [2021] FCAFC 112 (25 June 2021).
112. *Kingdom of Spain v. Infrastructure Services Luxembourg S.à.r.l. & Anor* [2023] HCA 11 (12 April 2023).

territory unnecessarily'.[113] In two recent decisions, the Court considered the successful claimants' success in confirming their intra-EU ECT ICSID awards against Spain *'highly likely'*.[114] Conversely, in relation to the enforcement of an intra-EU ECT non-ICSID case, the court concluded that:

> Spain lacked the legal capacity to extend an offer to arbitrate *any* dispute with the Companies under the law that applied to the parties. As such, no agreement to arbitrate ever existed. Absent such an agreement, this Court cannot establish jurisdiction under any exception to the Foreign Sovereign Immunities Act.[115]

It is safe to assume that successful claimants in intra-EU ECT cases will continue to seek to enforce any awards outside of the EU. It remains to be seen which way the D.C. courts will go. If they rule in favour of the claimants, then important questions about the relationship between EU law and international law will be decided by courts outside of the EU, mainly in the US.

V CONCLUSION

With one recent notable exception to date, international arbitral tribunals in both intra-EU BIT and intra-EU ECT cases appear not to have accepted jurisdictional objections by EU Member States based on *Achmea* and *Komstroy*, respectively. This appears to be true in both ICSID and non-ICSID cases. It remains to be seen whether international arbitral tribunals will follow the one exception in the SCC *Green Power* v. *Spain* case (seated in an EU Member State).

International arbitral tribunals are not and may not consider themselves bound by Judgments of the CJEU. However, experience shows that when seized, courts of EU Member States tend to follow any such Judgment of the CJEU. At the same time, the same may not necessarily be true for any courts outside of the EU. This may mean that there may continue to be a discrepancy between CJEU Judgments on the one hand and arbitral awards on the other hand.

---

113. *Masdar Solar & Wind Cooperatief U.A. v. Kingdom of Spain*, 1:18-cv-2254 (D.D.C. 18 September 2019). *See also Infrastructure Services Luxembourg S.À.R.L. And Energia Termosolar B.V. (Formerly Antin Infrastructure Services Luxembourg S.À.R.L. And Antin Energia Termosolar B.V.) v. Kingdom of Spain*, 1:18-cv-01753 (D.D.C. 28 August 2019); *Novenergia II – Energy & Environment (SCA) (Grand Duchy of Luxembourg), SICAR v. The Kingdom of Spain*, 18-cv-01148 (D.D.C. 27 January 2020); *Eiser Infrastructure Limited v. Kingdom of Spain*, *1:18-cv-1686* (D.D.C. 5 August 2020); *Nextera Energy Global Holdings B.V. v. Kingdom of Spain*, 1:19-cv-1618 (D.D.C. 30 September 2020); *9Ren Holding S.a.r.l. v. Kingdom of Spain*, 1:19-cv-01871 (D.D.C. 30 September 2020); *RREEF Infrastructure (G.P.) Limited and RREEF Pan-European Infrastructure Two Lux S.à r.l. v. Kingdom of Spain*, 1:19-cv-03783 (D.D.C. 31 March 2021); *Cube Infrastructure Fund SICAV and Others v. Kingdom of Spain*, 1:20-cv-01708 (D.D.C. 17 May 2021); *Infrared Environmental Infrastructure GP Limited and Others v. Kingdom of Spain*, 1:20-cv-00817 (D.D.C. 29 June 2021).
114. *9Ren Holding S.a.r.l. v. Kingdom of Spain*, 1:19-cv-01871 (D.D.C. 15 February 2023); *Nextera Energy Global Holdings B.V. v. Kingdom of Spain*, 1:19-cv-1618 (D.D.C. 15 February 2023).
115. *Blasket Renewable Investments, LLC v. Kingdom of Spain*, 1:21-cv-3249 (D.D.C. 29 March 2023).

As far as the Intra-EU BIT Termination Agreement is concerned, the ratification process started slowly but is now complete. However, three EU Member States with intra-EU BITs in force have not signed the Agreement. At the same time, in light of the European Commission's recent proposal of coordinated EU withdrawal from the ECT, the future of the ECT – not only with regard to its intra-EU application – is uncertain. The interpretation of the ECT's sunset clause in Article 47 of the ECT may well be at issue in a number of ECT arbitrations going forward – and not merely in an intra-EU context.

CHAPTER 28

The Interaction of European Investment Law with Public International Law

Julie Bédard & César Rivière[*]

TABLE OF CONTENTS

I   INTRODUCTION

The European Union (EU) and its Member States have played and continue to play an important role in the development of international trade law. The EU is a leader in the global trade of goods and services and holds the world's largest share of outward foreign direct investment (FDI) stock.[1] Furthermore, regulatory decisions made by the EU have effects beyond its borders: from antitrust law to environmental and health

---

*   Julie Bédard (Columbia Law School, JSD; Columbia Law School, LLM; McGill University Faculty of Law, B.C.L./LL.B.) is a Partner and Head of International Litigation and Arbitration Group for the Americas at Skadden, Arps, Slate, Meagher & Flom LLP and Affiliates (the "Firm"). César Rivière (Columbia Law School, JD; Université Paris 1 Panthéon-Sorbonne, Master II; Université Paris 1 Panthéon-Sorbonne, LL.B./BSc.) is an associate in the Firm's International Litigation and Arbitration group. The work is the authors' and the statements made therein are not necessarily those of the Firm or any one or more of its clients. The authors would like to thank Liz Coffin-Karlin for her valuable contribution.
1. European Commission, DG Trade Statistical Guide (August 2022) at https://trade.ec.europa.eu/doclib/docs/2013/may/tradoc_151348.pdf (last accessed September 2022).

protection, the EU has developed a "global power" to "unilateral[ly] ... regulate global markets[,]" "through its legal institutions and standards that it successfully exports to the rest of the world[.]"[2] This power, sometimes called the "Brussels effect," results from the EU's market power, regulatory capacity, and preference for strict rules.[3]

In 2009, with the adoption of the Treaty of Lisbon, the EU expanded its powers to the regulation of foreign investments. Previously exercised by Member States, the regulation of foreign investments is the capacity to enter into bilateral (BITs) or multilateral investment treaties with foreign nations, which set the standards of treatment for foreign investors and designate a forum to resolve any disputes. European investment law is still nascent, but it will not be developed on a *tabula rasa*. In fact, over the past decades, the Member States of the EU collectively have committed to nearly half of all BITs concluded worldwide.[4]

The changing structure of investment treaty arbitration and FDI in the EU has not yet been fully integrated into public international law, raising important questions. First, the implications of foundational decisions and opinions of the Court of Justice of the European Union (CJEU) in the area of European investment law are still being clarified.[5] Second, various conflicts of law and jurisdiction that will arise from the emergence of the European investment law regime remain to be addressed.

In this article, we consider the effects beyond the frontiers of the EU of the evolving regime of European investment law since the 2009 Treaty of Lisbon and the ensuing decisions of the CJEU.

II   THE DEVELOPMENT OF EUROPEAN INVESTMENT LAW UNDER THE LISBON TREATY

1   The Transfer of the Authority to Regulate FDIs to the EU

In assessing the role of European investment law beyond the frontiers of the EU, it is helpful to first delineate the jurisdiction of the EU and the place of its laws and regulations within the sphere of international law.

Recent developments in European constitutional law have enabled the EU to exert increased global regulatory power on capital flows, particularly in the regulation of FDIs. With the entry into force of the Treaty of Lisbon on December 1, 2009, the

---

2. Anu Bradford, "The Brussels Effect," 107 Nw. U. L. Rev. (2012) p. 1 at p. 64.
3. *Ibid.*
4. Communication from the Commission to the Council, the European Parliament, the European Economic and Social Committee and the Committee of the Regions, "Towards a Comprehensive European International Investment Policy" (July 7, 2010), COM (2010)343 final, at 4.
5. Tom Jones, " EU Seeks Feedback on Investment Protection Regime," Global Arbitration Review (May 26, 2020), available at https://globalarbitrationreview.com/isds-reform/eu-seeks-feedback -investment-protection-regime (last accessed September 2, 2022); Veronika Korom, "Is There Room to Hope for Non-treaty-based ISDS in the EU? Remarks on AG Kokott's Opinion in Case C-109/20 Poland v. PL Holdings," Kluwer Arbitration Blog (May 5, 2021), available at http:// arbitrationblog.kluwerarbitration.com/2021/05/05/is-there-room-to-hope-for-non-treaty-based- isds-in-the-eu-remarks on-ag-kokotts-opinion-in-case-c-109-20-poland-v-pl-holdings/ (last accessed September 2, 2022).

Member States transferred their authority to regulate FDI to the EU—an extension of power for the EU's central authorities.[6] From that point forward, the EU acquired the competence to decide the FDI policies of the EU's prominent economic bloc.

Under Article 207(1) of the Treaty on the Functioning of the European Union (TFEU), as amended by the Treaty of Lisbon:

> The common commercial policy shall be based on uniform principles, particularly with regard to changes in tariff rates, the conclusion of tariff and trade agreements relating to trade in goods and services, and the commercial aspects of intellectual property, *foreign direct investment*, the achievement of uniformity in measures of liberalisation, export policy and measures to protect trade such as those to be taken in the event of dumping or subsidies. The common commercial policy shall be conducted in the context of the principles and objectives of the Union's external action.[7]

The transfer of the power to regulate FDIs from the Member States to the EU has straightforward implications: if the EU can develop its European investment policy in unison, it may yield a greater bargaining power to impose its requirements on third countries.

2 The Participation of Member States in the Development of European Investment Law

Bilateral trade agreements are often structurally complex, covering not only FDIs but also issues of health, safety, and security, all of which arguably fall within the shared competence of the EU and its Member States.[8] Bilateral trade agreements may also cover other forms of movement of capital, including "the acquisition of company securities with the intention of making a financial investment without any intention to influence the management and control of the undertaking ('portfolio' investments)."[9]

The Commission initially took the position that Article 207(1) of the TFEU and Lisbon Treaty gave it exclusive power to negotiate trade agreements affecting the

---

6. Treaty of Lisbon amending the Treaty on European Union and the Treaty establishing the European Community, signed at Lisbon (December 13, 2007) (TFEU), Articles 157-158.
7. TFEU Article 207(1).
8. Opinion 1/17 of the European Court of Justice regarding the Comprehensive Economic and Trade Agreement between Canada, of the one part, and the European Union and its Member States, of the other part (CETA) (April 30, 2019) ("Opinion 1/17") para. 26.
9. Opinion 2/15 of the European Court of Justice regarding the Free Trade Agreement between the European Union and the Republic of Singapore (May 16, 2017) ("Opinion 2/15") para. 227. *See also Tokios Tokelés v. Ukraine* (ICSID Case No. ARB/02/18), Decision on Jurisdiction (April 29, 2004) para. 32 (a respondent state's "request to restrict the scope of covered investors through a control-test would be inconsistent with the object and purpose of the Treaty, which is to provide broad protection of investors and their investments."); *Ambiente Ufficio S.p.A. and others (formerly Giordano Alpi and others) v. Argentine Republic* (ICSID Case No. ARB/08/9), Decision on Jurisdiction and Admissibility (February 8, 2013) para. 471 ("Notwithstanding the peculiari-ties of these financial instruments, in the light of the broad understanding to be given to Art. 25 of the ICSID Convention, the Tribunal has no doubt that bonds/security entitlements such as those at stake in the present proceedings fall under the term 'investment' as used in Art. 25 of the Convention.").

common commercial policy, including FDIs.[10] The Commission also took the view that the EU's exclusive competence should extend beyond the text of the TFEU addressing "FDI" to include "portfolio" investments because of the "overlap" between the EU's commitments with respect to those investments, and the general prohibition against restrictions on movements of capital and payments between Member States and third States.[11]

From a political standpoint, the Commission's interpretation had a practical appeal. With an all-encompassing, exclusive power to negotiate bilateral trade agreements, the Commission could lead negotiations without interference and streamline the execution of "new generation" agreements. However, this position could have constitutional implications, leading not only to greater centralization of diplomatic power but also to a potential infringement upon the Member States' sovereignty.[12]

This question of separation of powers came to the fore in 2017 with the CJEU's review of the Free Trade Agreement (FTA) between the EU and the Republic of Singapore (the "EU-Singapore FTA"). As a "new generation" bilateral free-trade agreement, the EU-Singapore FTA contained, "in addition to the classical provisions on the reduction of customs duties and of non-tariff barriers to trade in goods and services, provisions on various matters related to trade, such as intellectual property protection, investment, public procurement, competition and sustainable development."[13] While the European Commission worked under the assumption that the EU had exclusive competence to negotiate this FTA, "differences of opinion became apparent in consultations within the [European Union's] Trade Policy Committee on the nature of the European Union's competence to conclude ... [trade] agreement[s]."[14] The European Commission thus sought the CJEU's opinion to determine whether complex bilateral agreements should be concluded exclusively by the EU or rather were "mixed agreements" to be signed by both the EU and the Member States.[15]

The CJEU ruled against the European Commission, finding that this "new generation" bilateral agreement needed to be concluded as a "mixed agreement" insofar as it covered areas falling under the shared competence of the EU and Member States.

While noting that the Lisbon Treaty confers upon the EU the power to regulate the common commercial policy as it relates to trade with third countries, the CJEU underscored that "the mere fact that an EU act, such as an agreement concluded by it, is liable to have *implications* for trade with one or more third States is not enough for it to be concluded that the act must be classified as falling within the common commercial policy."[16] For a bilateral trade agreement to fall within the exclusive competence of the EU, its components must "display a *specific link* ... with trade."[17]

---

10. Opinion 2/15, para. 12.
11. *Ibid.*, para. 16.
12. *Ibid.*, para. 19.
13. *Ibid.*, para. 17.
14. *Ibid.*, para. 11.
15. TFEU, Article 218(11).
16. Opinion 2/15, para. 36.
17. *Ibid.*, para. 37.

The CJEU then individually analyzed each commitment contained within the bilateral agreement to decide whether the EU-Singapore FTA required the consent of individual Member States.

With regard to European investment law, the CJEU found that the EU "does not have exclusive competence to conclude an international agreement ... in so far as it relates to the protection of non-direct foreign investments."[18] The CJEU therefore followed a strict textual interpretation of the Lisbon Treaty, noting that the term "FDI" was "an unequivocal expression of [the framers'] intention not to include *other* foreign investment in the common commercial policy."[19] In Opinion 2/15, the CJEU relied on precedents related to corporate and tax law to infer that direct investments required the power of "effective participation in the management or control of a company carrying out an economic activity."[20] For the CJEU, "[i]t is settled case-law that direct investment consists in investments of any kind made by natural or legal persons which serve to establish or maintain lasting and direct links between the persons providing the capital and the undertakings to which that capital is made available in order to carry out an economic activity."[21] But the criteria of "lasting and direct links ... in order to carry out an economic activity" is, of course, a broad standard which could be subject to varying interpretations depending on the economic activity conducted.

Importantly, the CJEU further found that an investor-state mechanism of dispute settlement "cannot ... be established without the Member States' consent."[22] The CJEU noted that provisions for dispute settlements "which remove[] disputes from the jurisdiction of the courts of the Member States" cannot be seen as merely "ancillary" to the EU's competence to enter into international commitments.[23]

The CJEU's opinion regarding the EU-Singapore FTA has major practical implications for the development of EU investment law, particularly in answering the question of *who* will decide the content of this field in the years and decades to come.

First, the central authorities must include Member States in the negotiation and conclusion of bilateral agreements with third countries. While "mixed" agreements—concluded by the EU and Member States—may take longer to be achieved, their inclusivity will reinforce their legitimacy under both European law and public international law. The Energy Charter Treaty (ECT) was such a mixed agreement, which reflected commitments from both the EU and individual Member States. Member States have also shown a certain deference to the EU in their policy choices regarding international relations,[24] so long as the reserved competences and the national identities of the Member States are respected.[25]

---

18. *Ibid.*, para. 238.
19. *Ibid.*, para. 83.
20. *Ibid.*, para. 82.
21. *Ibid.*, para. 80.
22. *Ibid.*, para. 292.
23. *Ibid.*
24. French Constitutional Court, Decision no. 2017-749 DC of July 31, 2017, para. 9. *See also* Joris Larik, "Prêt-a-Ratifier: The CETA Decision of the French Conseil Constitutionnel of 31 July 2017," 13(4) Eur. Const. L. Rev. (December 2017) pp. 759-777.
25. *See* Treaty on European Union (December 13, 2007) (TEU), Article 4(2); *see also ibid.*, Article 5(2)-(4) (laying out the principles of conferral, subsidiarity, and proportionality of Union action).

Second, the CJEU now plays a central role in the development of EU investment law. Pursuant to the *ex ante* procedure of review set up in Article 218(11) of the TFEU,[26] the CJEU has a de facto right to veto any international agreement which it considers, on its face, to be contradictory to European constitutional law.[27]

III   THE RELATIONSHIP BETWEEN PREEXISTING INTERNATIONAL AGREEMENTS AND EUROPEAN INVESTMENT LAW

1   The EU's Relationship with International Law

As a common area constituted by treaties among its Member States, the EU derives its powers from its foundational treaties, the TFEU and the Treaty on European Union (TEU).[28] These treaties, entered into by the EU Member States, regulate the relationship and governance of the Member States within the EU and transfer certain powers to EU authorities. From a public international law perspective, the treaties that form the EU constitute a "special species of international law" within a broader set of rules and principles,[29] including:

1. International conventions, whether general or particular, establishing rules expressly recognized by the contesting states;
2. International custom, as evidence of a general practice accepted as law;
3. The general principles of law recognized by civilized nations; and
4. Judicial decisions and the teachings of the most highly qualified publicists of the various nations, as subsidiary means for the determination of rules of law.[30]

The EU and its Member States therefore operate within the broader framework of public international law. Article 21(1) of the TEU recognizes the role played by international law in the action of the EU on the "international scene," which:

> shall be guided by the principles which have inspired its own creation, development and enlargement, and which it seeks to advance in the wider world: democracy, the rule of law, the universality and indivisibility of human rights and fundamental freedoms, respect for human dignity, the principles of equality and solidarity, and respect for the principles of the United Nations Charter and international law.[31]

---

26. TFEU, Article 218(11) ("A Member State, the European Parliament, the Council or the Commission may obtain the opinion of the Court of Justice as to whether an agreement envisaged is compatible with the Treaties. Where the opinion of the Court is adverse, the agreement envisaged may not enter into force unless it is amended or the Treaties are revised.").
27. *See, generally*, Anne Pieter van der Mei, "EU External Relations and Internal Inter Institutional Conflicts: The Battlefield of Article 218 TFEU," 23 Maastricht J. Eur. & Comp. L. (2016) p. 1051.
28. *See, e.g.*, TFEU, Article 1(2) ("This Treaty and the Treaty on European Union constitute the Treaties on which the Union is founded.").
29. *Eskosol S.p.A. in liquidazione v. Italian Republic* (ICSID Case No. ARB/15/50), Decision on Italy's Request for Immediate Termination and Italy's Jurisdictional Objection Based on Inapplicability of the Energy Charter Treaty to Intra-EU Disputes (May 7, 2019) para. 115.
30. Statute of the International Court of Justice (June 26, 1945), Article 38(1).
31. TEU, Article 21(1).

European law, however, has its own space within the wider framework of international law. The "autonomy enjoyed by EU law in relation to … international law"[32] has been central to the case law of the CJEU and played an important part in the CJEU's decision in *Achmea*:

> according to settled case-law of the Court, the autonomy of EU law with respect … to international law is justified by the essential characteristics of the EU and its law, relating in particular to the constitutional structure of the EU and the very nature of that law. EU law is characterised by the fact that it stems from an independent source of law, the Treaties, by its primacy over the laws of the Member States, and by the direct effect of a whole series of provisions which are applicable to their nationals and to the Member States themselves. Those characteristics have given rise to a structured network of principles, rules and mutually interdependent legal relations binding the EU and its Member States reciprocally and binding its Member States to each other ….

Conversely, instruments of international law that fall outside of European law enjoy a similar autonomy. As the international investment tribunal in *Eskosol v. Italy* held in 2019, an investment tribunal constituted under an international treaty (here, the ECT) is "required to operate in the international legal framework of" this international treaty, and "outside the EU and the dictates of EU law."[33] The *Eskosol* tribunal provided the following depiction of the structure of public international law to explain its analysis (*see* Figure 28.1).

Figure 28.1   The Structure of Public International Law

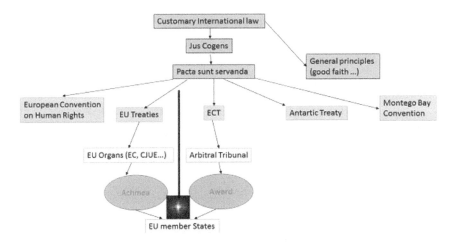

Eskosol S.p.A. in liquidazione v. Italian Republic (ICSID Case No. ARB/15/50), Decision on Italy's Request for Immediate Termination and Italy's Jurisdictional Objection Based on Inapplicability of the Energy Charter Treaty to Intra-EU Disputes (May 7, 2019) paragraph 181.

---

32. Opinion 2/13, para. 170.
33. *Eskosol S.p.A. in liquidazione v. Italian Republic* (ICSID Case No. ARB/15/50), Decision on Italy's Request for Immediate Termination and Italy's Jurisdictional Objection Based on Inapplicability of the Energy Charter Treaty to Intra-EU Disputes (May 7, 2019) para. 186.

The autonomy of international investment agreements from European law also implies that European law is not hierarchically controlling those international agreements. The arbitral tribunal in *Cube Infrastructure Fund SICAV v. Spain* explained in 2019 that international law continues to evolve in an autonomous fashion, in parallel with European law. In this dispute, Spain argued that because "the EU legal rules take precedence over any incompatible rules of whatever other source [according to the architecture of the EU legal order] the jurisdictional clause [of the ECT] would become inapplicable should any inconsistency be found" with European law.[34] To buttress this position, Spain relied on Article 26(6) of the ECT, under which a tribunal established under this treaty "shall decide the issues in dispute in accordance with this Treaty and applicable rules and principles of international law."[35]

For Spain, the reference to "principles of international law" constituted an incorporation of European Law and the secondary law of the EU institutions.[36] Rejecting this proposition, the arbitral tribunal, composed of Professor Vaughan Lowe (acting as President), the Honorable James Jacob Spigelman, and Professor Christian Tomuschat, wrote that:

> To say that EU law is a part of international law and yet has supremacy over other, non-EU components of international law is, in the view of the Tribunal, to mischaracterize EU law and confuse questions belonging to two different legal orders ... . EU law is only one among several regional, and many national, legal systems; and it is international law that regulates relations between these different legal systems. Within the system of international law, EU law does not have supremacy, and has no hierarchical priority over the laws of non-Member States, or over rules of international law, including the ECT. Any such claim to priority would challenge the basis of the ECT as a multilateral treaty, unilaterally asserting for the EU and its Member States a right to be treated differently from all other ECT Contracting Parties.[37]

The CJEU has, in its past decisions, clarified that European law does not supersede other international agreements lawfully entered into between Member States (or the EU) and a third country. Nearly fifteen years ago, in *Kadi v. Council and Commission*, the CJEU wrote that "the review of lawfulness thus to be ensured by the Community judicature applies to the Community act intended to give effect to the international agreement at issue, and not to the latter as such."[38] Indeed, "any judgment given by the Community judicature deciding that a Community measure

---

34. *Cube Infrastructure Fund SICAV v. Spain* (ICSID Case No. ARB/15/20), Decision on Jurisdiction, Liability and Partial Decision on Quantum (February 19, 2019) para. 128. In *Cube Infrastructure v. Spain*, the arbitral tribunal underscored that "[w]ithin the system of international law, EU law does not have supremacy, and has no hierarchical priority over the laws of non-Member States, or over rules of international law, including the ECT," and concluded that the ECT applies on an intra-EU basis despite recent European law developments, including *Achmea. Ibid.*, para. 130.
35. *Ibid.*, para. 127.
36. *Ibid.*, para. 128.
37. *Ibid.*, para. 130.
38. Joined Cases C-402/05 P and C-415/05 P, *Kadi v. Council and Commission*, Judgment (September 3, 2008), para. 286 (addressing regulations of the Council of the EU implementing a resolution of the United Nations Security Council requiring the freezing of assets of certain individuals).

intended to give effect to such a resolution is contrary to a higher rule of law in the Community legal order *would not entail any challenge to the primacy of that resolution in international law.*"[39]

However, in 2021, the CJEU indicated in *République de Moldavie v. Komstroy LLC* that, under certain circumstances, it retained jurisdiction under European law to "give a preliminary ruling on the interpretation" of an international agreement "concluded by the Council, pursuant to Articles 217 and 218 TFEU" even if such agreement was concluded by, and among, third states that are not members of the TFEU.[40]

In *Komstroy*, the Paris Court of Appeals submitted a reference for a preliminary ruling to the CJEU on the interpretation of the term "investment" in the ECT. The ECT is a mixed agreement concluded by and among the European Council, European Member States, and third countries. In total, 28 third countries are members of the ECT.[41] The ECT does not contain any dispute resolution provision pursuant to which Member States may submit their disputes on the interpretation of the terms of the ECT.[42] Seized of a request for annulment of an arbitral award rendered in a dispute involving an investor of a third country (Ukraine) against the government of another third country (the Republic of Moldova), the Paris Court of Appeal referred the question of the interpretation of the definition of "investment" under the ECT to the European Court of Justice.

The CJEU recognized that "the Court does not, in principle, have jurisdiction to interpret an international agreement as regards its application in the context of a dispute not covered by EU law ... particular[ly] where such a dispute is between an investor of a non-member State and another non-member State."[43] However, the CJEU held that, as an exception to this principle:

> where a provision of an international agreement can apply both to situations falling within the scope of EU law [e.g., in inter-EU disputes] and to situations not covered by that law [e.g. in disputes exclusively between third countries], it is clearly in the interest of the European Union that, in order to forestall future differences of interpretation, that provision should be interpreted uniformly, whatever the circumstances in which it is to apply.[44]

The CJEU justified its competence on the basis of the ability of investors to submit their dispute under the ECT to the civil or administrative courts of contracting parties,

---

39. *Ibid.*, para. 288 (emphasis added).
40. Case C-741/19, *République de Moldavie v. Komstroy LLC*, Judgment (September 2, 2021), para. 23.
41. Case C-741/19, *République de Moldavie v. Komstroy LLC*, Opinion of Advocate General Szpunar (March 3, 2021), para. 4.
42. *Ibid.*, para. 40 ("the ECT does not establish any court or tribunal responsible for ensuring the uniform interpretation of its provisions, in a manner consistent with the Court's interpretation within its legal order. The ECT is intended to be interpreted only in the course of the settlement of disputes by various arbitral or State tribunals in the Contracting Parties, which therefore cannot avoid divergences in interpretation.").
43. Case C-741/19, *République de Moldavie v. Komstroy LLC*, Judgement (September 2, 2021), para. 28.
44. *Ibid.*, para. 29.

as well as the choice of the parties in *Komstroy* to have selected Paris, France, as the seat of their arbitration—hereby electing France's arbitral law as *lex fori*.[45]

Just one month after *Komstroy*, the European Court of Justice expanded its case law by reviewing the validity of ad hoc investment arbitrations under European law. In *PL Holdings v. Republic of Poland*,[46] a Luxembourgish investor (PL Holdings) commenced an investment arbitration against the Republic of Poland regarding a decision of the Polish Financial Supervision Authority to suspend PL Holdings' voting rights in two Polish banks. The arbitration was based on the Belgium/Luxembourg-Poland bilateral investment treaty ("BLEU-Poland BIT"), conducted under the rules of the Arbitration Institute of the Stockholm Chamber of Commerce (the "SCC Rules") and seated in Stockholm, Sweden.

Following an award in favor of the investor of approximately EUR 150 million, Poland commenced annulment proceedings in Sweden claiming that the arbitration proceedings violated European law. In response, the investor noted that even if, under *Achmea*, Poland's consent to arbitration in the BLEU—Poland BIT were found to be invalid under EU law, Poland's procedural conduct amounted to a separate, contractual consent to arbitration under Swedish law and applicable commercial arbitration principles.[47]

The Supreme Court of Sweden referred to the European Court of Justice the question of whether, under European law, a Member State can conclude an ad hoc arbitration agreement with an investor from another Member State.[48] The European Court of Justice responded in the negative, holding that an ad hoc arbitration agreement that purports to "continue arbitration proceedings initiated on the basis of an arbitration clause whose content is identical to" a bilateral investment agreement is invalid under European law.[49] In effect, *PL Holdings* purports to prevent investors from circumventing *Achmea* by concluding ad hoc agreements to arbitrate treaty-based investment disputes with Member States.[50]

---

45. *Ibid.*, paras. 31-32.
46. Case C-109, *Republiken Polen v. PL Holdings Sarl*, Judgment of the Court (October 26, 2021).
47. *Ibid.*, paras. 28-29. *See, generally*, Mathias Audit, *Arbitrage d'investissement intra-europeen: le fondement contractuel n'exclut pas la contrariete au droit de l'union, note sous CJUE, 26 octobre 2021*, 2021(2) Revue de l'Arbitrage (2021) pp. 1119-1125.
48. *Ibid.*, para. 33. More specifically, PL Holdings had claimed that, under Swedish law, "even if the Republic of Poland's 'offer of arbitration' stemming from Article 9 of the BIT were invalid" pursuant to *Achmea*, "the fact remains that an ad hoc arbitration agreement was concluded between the parties to the dispute in the main proceedings, in accordance with Swedish law and the principles of commercial arbitration, having regard to the conduct of those parties. By making a request for arbitration, PL Holdings submitted an 'offer of arbitration' in accordance with the same conditions as those laid down in Article 9 of the BIT, and the Republic of Poland tacitly accepted that offer by refraining from validly challenging the jurisdiction of the arbitral tribunal on the basis of that agreement."). *Ibid.*, para. 28.
49. Case C-109, *Republiken Polen v. PL Holdings Sarl*, Judgment of the Court (October 26, 2021), para. 70.
50. *PL Holdings* should not, however, be interpreted as indicating that private parties may not arbitrate issues related to EU law in the context of commercial arbitration proceedings. As Advocate General Kokott noted in her separate opinion, the European Court of Justice has generally recognized that while "parties to a contract are not free to create exceptions to EU law," they may subject those issues to commercial arbitration proceedings, subject to a "limited" review of arbitration awards that includes a review of "compliance with fundamental provisions

The ramifications of *Komstroy* and *PL Holdings* in the field of public international law are still to be determined, and courts from third countries and international tribunals constituted under international agreements may reject the rulings of the CJEU on that matter. In practical terms, however, the issue arises whether *Komstroy* and *PL Holdings* may hamper the attractiveness of Paris—or any other European center—as the arbitral seat for investment arbitrations, to the benefit of other seats beyond the jurisdiction of the EU such as London, Geneva, New York or Washington D.C.[51] Investors may also turn to the International Centre for Settlement of Investment Disputes (ICSID) arbitration rules because those rules limit the judicial review of arbitral awards, and the influence domestic courts—such as the courts of the EU—may have over the ultimate ruling of the arbitrators.[52]

2   The Performance of International Agreements under the Principle of *Pacta Sunt Servanda*

In addition to the principle of autonomy of international investment agreements, the principle of *pacta sunt servanda* supports the continuing validity of those agreements in parallel with the development of European investment law.[53] Under the principle of

---

which are essential for the accomplishment of the tasks entrusted to the European Union and, in particular, for the functioning of the internal market." Case C-109, *Republiken Polen v. PL Holdings Sarl*, Opinion of Advocate General Kokott (April 22, 2021), paras. 44-45. *See also* Case C-284/16, *Slowakische Republik v. Achmea BV*, Judgment of the Court (March 6, 2018), para. 54 ("It is true that, in relation to commercial arbitration, the Court has held that the requirements of efficient arbitration proceedings justify the review of arbitral awards by the courts of the Member States being limited in scope, provided that the fundamental provisions of EU law can be examined in the course of that review and, if necessary, be the subject of a reference to the Court for a preliminary ruling.").

51. *See, e.g.*, Jérémy Jourdan-Marques, "Chronique d'arbitrage: après *Komstroy*, Londres rit et Paris pleure," *Dalloz Actualité* (September 17, 2021).

52. *See, e.g.*, *Green Power Partners v. The Kingdom of Spain* (SCC 2016/135), Award (June 16, 2022), para. 441 (recognizing that "[t]he question of whether or not EU law applies to the determination of jurisdiction and, if so, the extent to which it does so, does not arise in the same manner in the circumstances of this [SCC] arbitration as in ICSID proceedings."); *Cavalum SGPS v. Kingdom of Spain*, (ICSID Case No. ARB/15/34), Procedural Order No. 6 (September 7, 2022), para. 57 (same). *See also* George Bermann, *Understanding ICSID Article 54*, 35(2) ICSID Review, pp. 311-344 (2020) (discussing the limited scope of review of ICSID Awards).

53. *See, e.g.*, *Blusun S.A. v. Italy* (ICSID Case No. ARB/14/3), Award (December 27, 2016) para. 291; *Rockhopper Italia S.p.A. v. Italy* (ICSID Case No. ARB/17/14), Decision on the Intra-EU Jurisdictional Objection (June 29, 2019) paras. 172-175; *Belenergia S.A. v. Italy* (ICSID Case No. ARB/15/40), Award (August 28, 2019) para. 321; *Vattenfall AB v. Germany* (ICSID Case No. ARB/12/12), Decision on the *Achmea* Issue (August 31, 2018) para. 207; *OperaFund Eco-Invest SICAV PLC v. Spain* (ICSID Case No. ARB/15/36), Award (September 6, 2019) paras. 327-330; *Cube Infrastructure Fund SICAV v. Spain* (ICSID Case No. ARB/15/20), Decision on Jurisdiction, Liability and Partial Decision on Quantum (February 19, 2019) paras. 118-138; *SolEs Badajoz GmbH v. Spain* (ICSID Case No. ARB/15/38), Award (July 31, 2019) paras. 235-237; *9REN Holding S.À.R.L. v. Spain* (ICSID Case No. ARB/15/15), Award (May 31, 2019) para. 147; *Eiser Infrastructure Ltd. v. Spain* (ICSID Case No. ARB/13/36), Award (May 4, 2017) para. 207; *Masdar Solar & Wind Cooperatief U.A. v. Spain* (ICSID Case No. ARB/14/1), Award (May 16, 2018) paras. 306-324; *Antin Infrastructure Servs. Lux. S.à.r.l v. Spain* (ICSID Case No. ARB/13/31), Award (June 15, 2018) paras. 204-230; *RREEF Infrastructure (G.P.) Ltd. v. Spain* (ICSID Case No. ARB/13/30), Decision on Jurisdiction (June 6, 2016) paras. 78-89.

pacta sunt servanda, "[e]very treaty in force is binding upon the parties to it and must be performed by them in good faith"[54] and "[a] party may not invoke the provisions of its internal law as justification for its failure to perform a treaty"[55] or as "invalidating its consent."[56]

To the extent that a Member State or the EU would seek to terminate a preexisting inter-EU BIT, it would need to follow the procedures for "denunciation" laid out in the inter-EU BIT at issue, including the issuance of a notification of termination,[57] and compliance with any "sunset" or "survival" clauses. A contracting state's compliance with the procedures for denunciation safeguards the "principle of legal certainty [that] entitles investors to rely legitimately upon a State's written consent to arbitrate disputes, as long as that consent has not been withdrawn or invalidated through the proper procedures, including those set forth in the underlying treaty and the express provisions in the [Vienna Convention on the Law of Treaties]."[58]

Sunset clauses provide for a transitional period under which the State remains liable, and claims may still be brought against it, despite the termination of the treaty. For example, Article 47(3) of the ECT provides that "[t]he provisions of this Treaty shall continue to apply to Investments made in the Area of a Contracting Party by Investors of other Contracting Parties ... as of the date when that Contracting Party's withdrawal from the Treaty takes effect for a period of 20 years from such date."[59] Contracting states cannot unilaterally decide to amend the scope of sunset clauses.[60]

3   The Grandfathering of Preexisting Inter-EU BITs under European Law

In the year following the adoption of the Lisbon Treaty, the European Commission advocated for a "comprehensive European investment policy" with "[a] more activist approach to ensuring that EU investment relations with third partners constitute a 'two-way street[,]'"[61] as well as a centralized international investment policy.[62] The EU

---

54. Vienna Convention on the Law of Treaties ("Vienna Convention") Article 26.
55. *Ibid.*, Article 27.
56. *Ibid.*, Article 46.
57. *See, e.g.*, Vienna Convention, Articles 65-67. *See also Eskosol S.p.A. in liquidazione v. Italian Republic* (ICSID Case No. ARB/15/50), Decision on Italy's Request for Immediate Termination and Italy's Jurisdictional Objection Based on Inapplicability of the Energy Charter Treaty to Intra-EU Disputes (May 7, 2019) paras. 94-98 (noting that "whatever the scope and reach of the *Achmea* Judgment may be, it cannot be considered as a matter of international law to automatically invalidate ... either the ECT as a whole or the consent to arbitration reflected in Article 26 of the ECT.").
58. *Eskosol S.p.A. in liquidazione v. Italian Republic* (ICSID Case No. ARB/15/50), Decision on Italy's Request for Immediate Termination and Italy's Jurisdictional Objection Based on Inapplicability of the Energy Charter Treaty to Intra-EU Disputes (May 7, 2019) para. 98.
59. Energy Charter Treaty, Article 47(3).
60. *See, e.g.*, Bernhard Wychera & Winslow Mimnagh, "Investment Arbitration: The Nature of State Consent Expressed in BITs," *Austrian Yearbook on International Arbitration* (Christian Klau-segger ed. 2019) p. 411 (discussing the mutual agreement of Denmark and the Czech Republic to remove a sunset clause prior to terminating their BIT).
61. COM (2010)343 final, *supra* n. 4, p. 4.
62. *Ibid.*, p. 5.

took a proactive position in designing modern investment treaties and alternative dispute resolution mechanisms in parallel with a substantial preexisting body of BITs and multilateral treaties concluded by EU Member States and the EU itself, which, as the European Commission itself recognizes, "remain binding on the Member States as a matter of public international law … ."[63] To date, Member States of the EU "are parties to almost half of the total number of international investment agreements that are currently in force worldwide (roughly to 1400 out of 3000)."[64]

In order to structure the transition from preexisting inter-EU BITs concluded prior to the Lisbon Treaty to the new "modern" European investment regime, the EU adopted a procedural framework for the renegotiation of Inter-EU BITs in the form of the so-called Grandfathering Regulation—the (EU) Regulation 1219/2012.

Under the Grandfathering Regulation, "all bilateral investment agreements with third countries signed before 1 December 2009 or before the date of the accession [of the Member State]"[65] that are duly notified to the European Commission "may be maintained in force … until a bilateral investment agreement between the Union and the same third country enters into force."[66] In Opinion 2/15, the CJEU underscored that the Grandfathering Regulation:

> empowers the Member States, subject to strict conditions, to maintain in force … bilateral agreements with a third State concerning direct investment as long as an agreement between the European Union and that third State concerning direct investment does not exist. On the other hand, as soon as such an agreement between the European Union and that third State enters into force, that authorisation ceases to exist.[67]

Member States have notified 1,360 bilateral investment treaties to the European Commission under the Grandfathering Regulation, including 123 for Germany, 113 for Italy, and 93 for France.[68] The new agreements between the EU and Canada, Mexico, Singapore and Vietnam would, once implemented, replace 57 of those bilateral investment treaties.[69]

While the EU negotiates new international investment agreements with foreign countries, Member States are under a duty to "take any appropriate measures to ensure that the provisions of the bilateral investment agreements … do not constitute a serious

---

63. European Commission, Proposal for a Regulation of the European Parliament and of the Council Establishing Transitional Arrangements for Bilateral Investment Agreements between Member States and Third Countries, COM (2010)344 (July 7, 2010), p. 2.
64. European Commission Concept Paper, "Investment in TTIP and beyond – the path for reform Enhancing the right to regulate and moving from current ad hoc arbitration towards an Investment Court," p. 1 available at https://trade.ec.europa.eu/doclib/docs/2015/may/tradoc_153408.PDF (last accessed September 2, 2022).
65. Regulation (EU) No. 1219/2012 of the European Parliament and of the Council of December 12, 2012 establishing transitional arrangements for bilateral investment agreements between Member States and third countries (the "Grandfathering Regulation"), Article 2.
66. *Ibid.*, Article 3.
67. Opinion 2/15, para. 250.
68. Emanuel Castellarin, "Investissment" in *Répertoire de Droit Européen* (Dalloz 2021) para. 51.
69. *Ibid.*

obstacle to the negotiation or conclusion by the Union of bilateral investment agreements with third countries … ."[70] The Grandfathering Regulation further provides that "Member States are required to take the necessary measures to eliminate incompatibilities, where they exist, with Union law, contained in bilateral investment agreements concluded between them and third countries[,]"[71] and the authorization to maintain preexisting inter-EU BITs comes "without prejudice to other obligations of the Member States under EU law."[72]

The Regulation does not provide guidance on the meaning or implications of the Member States' obligation to "take all appropriate steps to eliminate the incompatibilities" between their preexisting inter-EU BITs and European Investment Law. Member States and investors may attempt to rely on the case law interpreting a similar duty that arises under Article 351(1) of the TFEU regarding pre-accession bilateral commitments with third countries. Under Article 351(1) of the TFEU, pre-accession inter-EU BITs "shall not be affected by the provisions of the Treaties"[73] but Member States must "take all appropriate steps to eliminate the incompatibilities" between their pre-accession bilateral agreements with third countries and European law.[74]

Member States have followed three types of measures under Article 351(1) of the TFEU: avoidance, renegotiation, and denunciation. Before finding any incompatibilities between BITs and European law, national courts are called upon to "ascertain whether a possible incompatibility between the Treaty and [a] bilateral convention can be avoided by interpreting that convention, to the extent possible and in compliance with international law, in such a way that it is consistent with Community law."[75] In the context of the Grandfathering Regulation, arbitral tribunals may, by analogy, interpret international arbitration agreements in a manner that would favor their compatibility with European law. This is especially true of ambiguous choice of law provisions[76] that *may* be interpreted as allowing an arbitral tribunal to apply European law—an act that is incompatible with *Achmea* and *Komstroy*—or as allowing the application of international law exclusively, as allowed by CJEU in Opinion 1/17.

While some investment tribunals have followed a broad interpretation of the laws applicable to investor-State disputes,[77] other arbitral tribunals have taken a more

---

70. Grandfathering Regulation, Article 6(1).
71. *Ibid.*, Recitals 11-12.
72. Juliane Kokott & Christoph Sobotta, "Investment Arbitration and EU Law," 18 Cambridge Y.B. Eur. Legal Stud. 3, 16 (2016).
73. TFEU, Article 351(1).
74. *Ibid.*, Article 351(2).
75. Case C-216/01, *Budějovický Budvar, národní podnik v. Rudolf Ammersin GmbH*, Judgment (November 18, 2003), para. 169.
76. *See, e.g.,* France–Mexico BIT, Article 9(6) ("[a] tribunal established under this Article shall decide by a majority of votes the dispute in accordance with this Agreement and applicable rules and principles of international law.").
77. *Asian Agricultural Products Ltd. v. Republic of Sri Lanka* (ICSID Case No. ARB/87/3), Final Award (June 27, 1990) para. 21; *MTD Equity Sdn. Bhd. and MTD Chile S.A. v. Republic of Chile* (ICSID Case No. ARB/01/7), Decision on Annulment (March 21, 2007) para. 75; *Eureko B.V. v. Republic of Poland*, Partial Award, Dissenting Opinion of Jerzy Rajski (August 19, 2005) para. 5. For an analysis of the mechanism of *renvoi* of international law to domestic law, *see* "Chapter 2: Applicable Substantive Law and Interpretation," in *Law and Practice of Investment Treaties: Standards of Treatment* (Andrew Newcombe and Lluís Paradell eds., 2009) pp. 75-120 at § 2.13.

restrictive approach. For instance, in 2020, in *Adamakopoulos et al. v. Cyprus*, the majority of the Arbitral Tribunal found that:

> The fact that, as alleged by the Respondent, the bail-in measures were "policy measures established by the EU Bank Recovery Resolution Directive" does not mean that the Tribunal would be interpreting or applying EU law. The bail-in measures are facts for this Tribunal which has to ask whether there has been a violation of the relevant BIT provisions. The Tribunal would not necessarily be interpreting or applying EU law and thus there is no incompatibility between the BITs and the EU Treaties.[78]

When incompatibilities cannot be avoided by means of interpretation, Member States are under a duty to take "appropriate steps" to get rid of these incompatibilities. Under well-established CJEU case law, appropriate steps include the renegotiation of the bilateral agreement and, in certain circumstances, denunciation. In *Commission v. Portuguese Republic*, the CJEU found that denunciation could be appropriate where the parties were not able to renegotiate the provisions of the agreement that are incompatible with European Law and when the "contested agreement contains a clause ... which expressly enable[s] the contracting parties to denounce it[.]"[79] While the obligation to take steps to eliminate incompatibilities may interfere with the foreign policy interests of a Member State, the CJEU ruled that this result necessarily ensues from the text of the European treaties, which have already weighed the foreign policy interests of Member States and the Community's interests.[80]

The Grandfathering Regulation provides for a collaboration of the Member States and the European Commission in the negotiations of amendments to existing bilateral agreements.[81] It also indicates that the Member States' duty to "take any appropriate measures to ensure that the provisions of the bilateral investment agreements ... do not constitute a serious obstacle to the negotiation or conclusion by the Union of bilateral investment agreements with third countries" is made "with a view to the *progressive replacement* of the bilateral investment agreements."[82]

The notion that the preexisting BITs shall be progressively *replaced*—and not *denounced*—is further supported by Recital 6 of the Regulation, under which the European Parliament and Council note that:

> In the interest of Union investors and their investments in third countries, and of Member States hosting foreign investors and investments, bilateral investment agreements that specify and guarantee the conditions of investment *should be maintained in force and progressively replaced* by investment agreements of the Union, providing for high standards of investment protection.[83]

---

78. *Adamakopoulos et al. v. Cyprus* (ICSID Case No. ARB/15/49), Decision on Jurisdiction (February 7, 2020) para. 174.
79. Case C-62/98, *Commission v. Portuguese Republic*, Judgment (July 4, 2000), para. 46.
80. *Ibid.*, para. 50.
81. Grandfathering Regulation, Articles 8-9.
82. *Ibid.*, Articles 5 and 6 (emphasis added).
83. *Ibid.*, Recital 6.

The Grandfathering Regulation thus provides an important safeguard under EU law against attempts by the EU or its Member States to precipitously change the investment regime in place before the Lisbon Treaty.

IV   THE DEVELOPMENT OF EUROPEAN INVESTMENT LAW IN THE CONTEXT OF THE CETA

As the EU embarks on an ambitious journey to "progressively replace[]" the hundreds of preexisting inter-EU bilateral investment treaties with "new generation" international investment agreements, foreign countries and investors can turn to the EU-Canada Comprehensive Economic and Trade Agreement (CETA) for indications regarding the content of the EU's "new generation" agreements.

Signed in 2016, and with a provisional application starting on September 21, 2017, the CETA is "an ambitious and comprehensive free trade agreement (FTA) that covers virtually all sectors and aspects of EU-Canada trade."[84] The CETA also contains important investment protections that reflect the EU's priorities, including the protection of "governments' right to regulate in the public interest," and the "replace[ment]" of the "old form of investor-state dispute settlement (ISDS) in many existing trade agreements with a new, improved Investment Court System."[85] The CETA thus contains important provisions on the protection of foreign investments that have been analyzed by the CJEU in its Opinion 1/17 on the compatibility of the CETA with European law.

1   The Principle of Autonomy of European Law

The investment protection chapter of the CETA provides for a dispute resolution mechanism under which claims may be submitted to international tribunals constituted under the ICSID Convention and Rules of Procedure for Arbitration Proceedings, the ICSID Additional Facility Rules, the UNCITRAL Arbitration Rules, or any other rules on agreement of the disputing parties.[86] The CETA, however, contains specific rules regarding the constitution of the arbitral tribunal, with arbitrators nominated from a list of fifteen "Members of the Tribunal" appointed by the EU and Canada.[87] The CETA also provides for the creation of an appellate tribunal[88] and requires Canada and the EU to:

> pursue with other trading partners the establishment of a multilateral investment tribunal and appellate mechanism for the resolution of investment disputes. Upon

---

84. European Commission Directorate-General for Trade, "EU and Canada celebrate fourth anniversary of comprehensive trade agreement (CETA)" (September 21, 2021), available at https://policy.trade.ec.europa.eu/news/eu-and-canada-celebrate-fourth-anniversary-ceta-202 1-09-21_en (last accessed September 7, 2022).

85. European Commission, *CETA Fact Sheet 4 of 7*, "Safeguard in CETA: 6 ways CETA guarantees the EU's interests" (September 2017), available at https://trade.ec.europa.eu/doclib/docs/201 7/september/tradoc_156060.pdf.

86. CETA, Article 8.23.

87. *Ibid.*, Article 8.27.

88. *Ibid.*, Article 8.28.

establishment of such a multilateral mechanism, the CETA Joint Committee shall adopt a decision providing that investment disputes under this Section will be decided pursuant to the multilateral mechanism and make appropriate transitional arrangements.[89]

The CETA reinforces the autonomy of European law by clearly providing that the CETA tribunal shall not have jurisdiction to determine the legality of a measure, alleged to constitute a breach of this Agreement, under the domestic law of the disputing Party. For greater certainty, in determining the consistency of a measure with this Agreement, the Tribunal may consider, as appropriate, the domestic law of the disputing Party as a matter of fact. In doing so, the Tribunal shall follow the prevailing interpretation given to the domestic law by the courts or authorities of that Party and any meaning given to domestic law by the Tribunal shall not be binding upon the courts or the authorities of that Party.

In Opinion 1/17, the CJEU held that the CETA's limited competence was valid under European law because the CETA tribunal would only have a jurisdiction "confined to the provisions of the CETA" and "[d]omestic laws of the Parties may only be taken into account as a matter of fact, and the CETA Tribunal is obliged to abide by the prevailing interpretation given to that domestic law by the domestic courts."[90]

As the CJEU wrote, "the creation of a court responsible for the interpretation of its provisions and whose decisions are binding on the EU, is, in principle, compatible with EU law."[91] This separate legal order is compatible with the autonomy of the "EU legal order"[92] as long as "the [CJEU] has exclusive jurisdiction to give the definitive interpretation of [EU] law."[93] As such, so long as an international tribunal "stand[ing] outside the EU judicial system ... [does not] have the power to interpret or apply provisions of EU law other than those of the [underlying treaty] or to make awards that might have the effect of preventing the EU institutions from operating in accordance with the EU constitutional framework,"[94] it does not infringe upon the autonomy of the EU legal order.

The CJEU thus held that the investment chapter of the CETA can coexist with the EU legal order because the CETA Tribunal has "no jurisdiction to interpret the rules of EU law other than the provisions of the CETA"[95] and can only take national and EU laws into account as a matter of fact. This *"prise en considération"* is known to both European law and international law.[96] Under European Law, the method of *prise en*

---

89. *Ibid.*, Article 8.29.

90. Guillaume Croisant, "Opinion 1/17 – the CJEU Confirms that CETA's Investment Court System is Compatible with EU Law" (April 30, 2019), available at http://arbitrationblog.kluwe rarbitration.com/2019/04/30/opinion-117-the-cjeu-confirms-that-cetas-investment-court-syste m-is-compatible-with-eu-law/ (last accessed September 7, 2022).

91. Opinion 1/17, para. 106. The ECJ added that "[a]n international agreement entered into by the Union may, moreover, affect the powers of the EU institutions provided, however, that the indispensable conditions for safeguarding the essential character of those powers are satisfied and, consequently, there is no adverse effect on the autonomy of the EU legal order." *Ibid.*, para. 107.

92. *Ibid.*, § V.A.

93. *Ibid.*

94. *Ibid.*, para. 118.

95. *Ibid.*, para. 132.

96. *See, e.g.*, Estelle Fohrer-Dedeurwaerder, *La prise en considération des normes étrangères* (2008); Luca Radicati di Brozolo, "L'illicéité 'qui crève les yeux': critère de contrôle des sentences au

considération is used in the context of the Rome I Regulation (on the law applicable to contractual relations).

Relatedly, some investment arbitral tribunals have in the past had recourse to the theory of *acte clair* in their application of European law.[97] In *Eureko B.V. v. The Slovak Republic*, the arbitral tribunal in fact noted that:

> The argument that the ECJ has an "interpretative monopoly" and that the Tribunal therefore cannot consider and apply EU law, is incorrect. The ECJ has no such monopoly. Courts and arbitration tribunals throughout the EU interpret and apply EU law daily. What the ECJ has is a monopoly on the final and authoritative interpretation of EU law: but that is quite different. Moreover, even final courts are not obliged to refer questions of the interpretation of EU law to the ECJ in all cases. The *acte clair* doctrine is well-established in EU law.[98]

The delineation between a *prise en considération* of European law—or the application of an *acte clair*—and what could appear as the "final and authoritative interpretation of EU law" under the CETA may become a point of tension in future disputes, with arbitral tribunal and European courts potentially coming into disagreements on the meaning of European law.[99]

2 The Right to Regulate under Domestic Laws

As noted above, the CETA explicitly reaffirms the parties' "right to regulate within their territories to achieve legitimate policy objectives, such as the protection of public

---

regard de l'ordre public international (à propos de l'arrêt Thalès de la Cour d'appel de Paris)," *Revue de l'Arbitrage* (Volume 2005 Issue 3) pp. 529-560; François Knoepfler, "Note: Tribunal fédéral suisse (1re Cour civile) 23 juin 1992—Fincantieri-Cantieri Navali v. M.," *Revue de l'Arbitrage* (Volume 1993 Issue 4) pp. 695-704; Genevieve Bastid-Burdeau, "Les embargos multilatéraux et unilatéraux et leur incidence sur l'arbitrage commercial international: Les états dans le contentieux économique international, I. Le contentieux arbitral," *Revue de l'Arbitrage* (Volume 2003 Issue 3) pp. 753-776; *Société H. v. société O.* (ICC Case No. 5622), Award (August 19, 1988) para. 147.

97. See, e.g., *Electrabel S.A. v. Republic of Hungary* (ICSID Case No. ARB/07/19), Award (November 25, 2015) para. 4.148 (interpreting Article 26 of the Energy Charter Treaty (regarding the law applicable to the dispute), the arbitral tribunal noted that the European Court of Justice's "exclusive jurisdiction does not prevent numerous other courts and arbitral tribunals from applying EU law" and concluded that "[g]iven the widespread relevance and importance of EU law to international trade, it could not be otherwise").

98. *Eureko B.V. v. The Slovak Republic* (PCA Case No. 2008-13), UNCITRAL, Award on Jurisdiction, Arbitrability and Suspension (October 26, 2010) paras. 281-282 (holding that the tribunal did not lack jurisdiction over the dispute, "[e]ven assuming, for the sake of argument, that the questions that the Tribunal will need to address might ... include questions of EU law ... .").

99. Case C-283/81, *Srl CILFIT and Lanificto di Gavardo SpA v. Ministry of Health*, Judgment (October 6, 1982), para. 17 (noting the "difficulties to which [the interpretation of Community law] gives rise." These difficulties include: the drafting of legislations in several languages, the use of peculiar terminology with European law concepts which may have a different meaning that those employed by Member States, and the need to interpret European law within its objectives and its state of evolution.); Case C-466/00, *Arben Kaba v. Secretary of State for the Home Department*, Judgment (March 6, 2003), para. 39 (even in the presence of a preexisting decision of the CJEU, an act may still need further clarification or be subject to varying interpretation, and a "tribunal [may] encounter[] difficulties in understanding or applying the judgment ... .").

health, safety, the environment or public morals, social or consumer protection or the promotion and protection of cultural diversity."[100] This right is further bolstered by the assurance that "the mere fact that a Party regulates, including through a modification to its laws, in a manner which negatively affects an investment or interferes with an investor's expectations, including its expectations of profits, does not amount to a breach of an obligation under this Section."[101]

While the CETA gives certain interpretive powers to the CETA Tribunal, the CJEU has taken a firm position that "the CETA Tribunal has no jurisdiction to declare incompatible with the CETA the level of protection of a public interest established by the EU measures [necessary to protect public security or public morals or to maintain public order or to protect human, animal or plant life or health] and, on that basis, to order the Union to pay damages."[102] The CJEU's interpretation of the standard of the CETA, with which some arbitration tribunals may disagree, instills the view of the CJEU that the EU's right to regulate will be central to a determination of an investor's right to damages under the CETA.

3   The Standard of Fair and Equitable Treatment

With regard to the standard of fair and equitable treatment, the CETA states that "[a] Party breaches the obligation of fair and equitable treatment referenced in paragraph 1 if a measure or series of measures constitutes"[103] a denial of justice, fundamental breaches of due process, manifest arbitrariness, a targeted discrimination, or an abusive treatment of investors.[104] The CETA does not state whether this list is intended to be limitative, but such an inference could be drawn through Articles 8.10(f) and Article 8.10(3), which together provide that the parties to the CETA "shall regularly ... review the content of the obligation to provide fair and equitable treatment"[105] and "[adopt] further elements."[106] The CETA further notes that a breach of domestic law "does not, in and of itself, establish a breach of [the CETA]."[107]

The CJEU validated the investment chapter of the CETA by taking comfort in the fact "that *the jurisdiction* of the CETA Tribunal to find infringements of the obligation ... *to accord 'fair and equitable treatment'* to covered investments *is specifically circumscribed*, since [the CETA] *lists exhaustively* the situations in which such a finding can be made."[108] This position is a departure from traditional international investment law as many treaties do not specifically circumscribe the ability of arbitral tribunals to find a breach of the standard of fair and equitable treatment, notably because this

---

100. CETA, Article 8.9(1).
101. *Ibid.*, Article 8.9(2).
102. Opinion 1/17, paras. 151-153.
103. CETA, Article 8.10(2).
104. *Ibid.*
105. CETA, Article 8.10(3).
106. *Ibid.*, Article 8.10(2)(f).
107. *Ibid.*, Article 8.10(7).
108. Opinion 1/17, para. 158.

standard is particularly fact-sensitive and arguably cannot be forced to fit into specific categories.[109]

4   The Standard of Expropriation

With regard to expropriation, the CETA provides for the "prompt, adequate and effective compensation" of a covered investment which has been directly or indirectly expropriated, but limits the circumstances under which the acts of a party may constitute indirect expropriation.[110] Indirect expropriation is defined in Annex 8-A of the trade agreement as "a measure or series of measures of a Party [which] has an effect equivalent to direct expropriation, in that it substantially deprives the investor of the fundamental attributes of property in its investment, including the right to use, enjoy and dispose of its investment, without formal transfer of title or outright seizure."[111] The CETA further details the factors that may be taken into account in assessing, on a case-by-case basis, whether an indirect expropriation has taken place, including the economic impact of the measure, the duration of the measure, the extent to which the measure interferes with reasonable expectations, and the object, context, and intent of the measure.[112] Notably, "except in the rare circumstance when the impact of a measure or series of measures is so severe in light of its purpose that it appears manifestly excessive, non-discriminatory measures of a Party that are designed and applied to protect legitimate public welfare objectives, such as health, safety and the environment, do not constitute indirect expropriations."[113]

Indirect expropriation is a challenging subject for investors and sovereign states. On the one hand, indirect expropriations, while difficult to prove,[114] may "effectively neutralize the benefit of the property of the foreign owner."[115] On the other hand, claims of indirect expropriation have been seen by some respondent states as

---

109. *See* International Institute for Sustainable Development, Commentary to the Draft Investment Chapter of the Canada-EU Comprehensive Economic and Trade Agreement (CETA) (2013). Gus van Harten, "The European Union's Emerging Approach to ISDS: A Review of the Canada-Europe CETA, Europe-Singapore FTA, and European-Vietnam FTA," 1 U. Bologna L. Rev. (2016) p. 138 at pp. 155-156.
110. CETA, Annex 8-A, Article 1(b), 2.
111. CETA, Annex 8-A, Article 1(b).
112. *Ibid.*, Article 2. *See, e.g., Saluka v. Czech Republic* (UNCITRAL), Partial Award (March 17, 2006) paras. 262-263 ("international law ... has yet to draw a bright and easily distinguishable line between non-compensable regulations on the one hand and, on the other, measures that have the effect of depriving foreign investors of their investment and are thus unlawful and compensable in international law."); 'Chapter 5. Theoretical Approaches', in Aniruddha Rajput, Regulatory Freedom and Indirect Expropriation in Investment Arbitration, (Kluwer 2018) pp. 73-102.
113. CETA, Annex 8-A, Article 3.
114. *S.D. Myers, Inc. v. Government of Canada* (UNCITRAL), Partial Award (November 13, 2000) para. 161.
115. *CME Czech Republic B.V. v. The Czech Republic* (UNCITRAL), Partial Award, September 13, 2001) para. 604. *See also Compañia del Desarrollo de Santa Elena S.A. v. Republic of Costa Rica* (ICSID Case No. ARB/96/1), Award (February 17, 2000) para. 77.

challenging the legitimate exercises of their regulatory powers.[116] Indirect expropriations therefore create an area of friction that can only be addressed on a case-by-case basis.[117]

With regard to the legitimacy of EU law in the context of claims in international law, the CETA emphasized that "EU legislation is adopted by the EU legislature following ... democratic process ... and that that legislation is deemed ... to be both appropriate and necessary to achieve a legitimate objective of the Union" and that "[i]t is apparent from reading those provisions together that the discretionary powers of the CETA Tribunal and Appellate Tribunal do not extend to permitting them to call into question the level of protection of public interest determined by the Union following a democratic process."[118] But the argument of democratic legitimacy cuts both ways. Treaties and bilateral agreements are the products of a State's sovereign powers and are most often approved by the executive branch and ratified by the legislative branch,[119] and in some instances may take precedence over national laws.[120]

V THE OPPORTUNITY FOR COLLABORATION AMONG THE ACTORS OF INTERNATIONAL LAW

While the recent developments in European investment law may appear to be a revolution within the international public law community, they are still in their early stages and are building upon a substantial, preexisting, and comprehensive body of international investment agreements between Member States and third countries.

The progressive transition of the European investment law regime is an opportunity for a broader conversation among the actors of the international public law community to address the proposed changes to the European investment law regime in both a constructive and critical way. This transitional period allows other stakeholders, including foreign nations and investors, to discuss the EU's proposed changes, and propose or negotiate alternatives, as needed.

---

116. See, e.g., Ronald S. Lauder v. The Czech Republic (UNCITRAL), Final Award (September 3, 2001) para. 198; Técnicas Medioambientales Tecmed, S.A. v. The United Mexican States, (ICSID Case No. ARB (AF)/00/2), Final Award (May 29, 2003) para. 119.
117. See, e.g., G.C. Christie, "What Constitutes a Taking of Property under International Law," in British Year Book of International Law (Oxford Univ. Press 1962) p. 307 at 338; Jan Paulson, "Indirect Expropriation: Is the Right to Regulate at Risk?," Symposium on "Making the Most of International Investment Agreements," at http://www.oecd.org/investment/internationalinvestmentagreements/36055332.pdf para. 7 (last accessed September 7, 2022).
118. Opinion 1/17, paras. 151-156.
119. See, e.g., United States Constitution, Article VI Cl. 2; Basic Law of the Federal Republic of Germany (1949), Article 59.
120. See, e.g., French Constitution, Article 55; Constitution of the Czech Republic (1992), Article 10; Constitution of the Republic of Croatia (2014), Article 134.

CHAPTER 29

From the No to the May Be: Latin America and Investment Arbitration

Eduardo Zuleta[*]

TABLE OF CONTENTS

Fifty-eight years ago, in September 1964, at the annual meeting of the Board of Governors of the World Bank in Tokyo, a resolution was passed for the executive directors to formulate the final text of a proposed convention on investment arbitration. Twenty-one countries voted against the resolution, nineteen of them forming part of Latin America.[1] This was not only the first time in the World Bank's history that a major resolution met substantial opposition to a final vote,[2] but one of the very few times in which all Latin American countries adopted a unanimous position with respect to investment arbitration.

In the 1960s and the 1970s, the countries of Latin America supported both the 1962 United Nations General Assembly Resolution of Permanent Sovereignty over

[*] Independent arbitrator. The author thanks Angelica Maria Perdomo and Santiago Zuleta for their assistance in the preparation of this chapter.

1. Antonio R. Parra, The History of ICSID (Oxford: Oxford University Press, 2012), pp. 66-67. The delegations that voted against the resolution were Argentina, Bolivia, Brazil, Chile, Colombia, Costa Rica, Dominican Republic, Ecuador, El Salvador, Guatemala, Haiti, Honduras, Iraq, Mexico, Nicaragua, Panama, Paraguay, Peru, Philippines, Uruguay, and Venezuela.
2. The No of Tokyo Revisited: Or How Developed Countries Learned to Start Worrying and Love the Calvo Doctrine, Rodrigo Polanco Lazo, *ICSID Review—Foreign Investment Law Journal*, Vol. 30, No. 1 (Winter 2015), pp. 172-193. Published: December 11, 2014.

Natural Resources[3] and the Charter of Economic Rights and Duties of States (CERDS).[4] These instruments were perceived as a victory of the Calvo doctrine in the international arena, and of the view that foreign investments were subject to the law of the host state, that foreign investors should not enjoy more rights or privileges than nationals and that compensation for expropriation should be determined by the law of the host state and not by international law.[5]

The attitude of Latin American countries towards investment arbitration and the support of the Calvo doctrine, particularly during the 1960s and the 1970s, has been frequently characterized as hostile, but as Catherine Titi observes, the "habitual description of the Latin American take on arbitration as one of hostility fails to capture the complexity and fine nuances of this relationship between Latin America and the investor-state dispute resolution mechanism."[6]

Even though Latin American countries signed some Bilateral Investment Treaties (BITs) during the 1980s and even earlier,[7] the so-called investment treaty boom took place in the decade of the 1990s. First, because most Latin American countries signed and/or ratified the International Convention for the Settlement of Investment Disputes (ICSID) Convention[8] and, second, because hundreds of BITs were signed not only with the United States and Europe but also between countries of the region. Several attempts have been made to explain the reason for this boom: The need to attract foreign investment for the privatization programs undertaken by several countries,[9] a result of the Washington Consensus,[10] the need to have an essential tool in the competitive

---

3. UN General Assembly, *Permanent sovereignty over natural resources*, December 17, 1973, A/RES/3171, available at: https://www.refworld.org/docid/3b00f1c64.html (accessed October 5, 2022).
4. Charter of Economic Rights and Duties of states UN General Assembly Resolution 3281 (XXIX), December 12, 1974.
5. Mary H. Mourra, *The Conflicts and Controversies in Latin American Treaty Based Disputes*, in Mary H. Mourra (ed. and Contributor), Thomas H. Carbonneau (General Editor), Latin American Investment Treaty Arbitration, The Controversies and Conflicts (Wolters Kluwer, 2008), p. 13.
6. Catherine Titi, Investment Arbitration in Latin America: The Uncertain Veracity of Preconceived Ideas, Arbitration International, Vol. 30, No. 2 (LCIA 2014).
7. BIT were signed between Costa Rica and Switzerland and between and Ecuador and Germany in 1965; same year. El Salvador and France; a BIT between Ecuador and Switzerland was signed in 1968. In the 1970s, BITs were concluded, *inter alia*, between Paraguay and Uruguay (1976), Paraguay and France (1978) and El Salvador and France (1978); in the 1980s BITs were concluded, *inter alia*, between Panama and the United States (1982), Uruguay and Germany (1987), and Cost Rica and France (1984). Available at: https://unctad.org/en/Docs/poiteiiad2.en.pdf (accessed October 5, 2022).
8. Database of ICSID Member States, available at: https://icsid.worldbank.org/about/member-states/database-of-member-states (accessed October 5, 2022).
9. Mary H. Mourra, *The Conflicts and Controversies in Latin American Treaty Based Disputes*, in Mary H. Mourra (ed. and Contributor), Thomas H. Carbonneau (General Editor), Latin American Investment Treaty Arbitration: The Controversies and Conflicts (Wolters Kluwer, 2008) p. 16.
10. The term "Washington Consensus" is generally used to refer to a set of policy recommendations, particularly economic policies, for developing countries in general, and Latin America in particular. The "consensus" refers generally to the level of agreement between the IMF, the World Bank and the U.S. Department of Treasury on such policy recommendations. The view that all shared was that the operation of the free market and the reduction of state involvement were crucial to development in the global South. The Washington Consensus has been perceived from a mere shift to a more liberal approach shift to an intervention in the economic policies of the region to force a change in the attitude towards foreign investment.

effort of attracting foreign capitals,[11] the need to compete among those similarly situated,[12] and even a form of a one-way harmonization of commercial legal standards in the image of the United States (U.S.) legal system (legal transplant).[13]

Whether a conscious decision to incentivize foreign investment, the result of an imposition to receive investments or loans, or a mixture of factors, the decade of the 1990s witnessed an unprecedented signature and ratification of BITs and treaties related to international arbitration, including, of course, the Convention on the Recognition and Enforcement of Foreign Arbitral Awards (the New York Convention) and the Convention on the Settlement of Investment Disputes between States and Nationals of Other States (the ICSID Convention).

But if the 1990s were considered the era of the BIT boom in Latin America, the first fifteen years of the twenty-first century could be characterized as the era of the boom of investment claims against Latin American countries. More than 50 claims were filed against Argentina during such period; 23 against Ecuador; 16 against Bolivia; 47 against Venezuela; 8 against Panama and 28 against Mexico.[14] Colombia, which had only been threatened with one claim in 2002, which was finally settled, received 19 claims between 2016 and 2021.[15]

The Latin American countries that found themselves as defendants in investment cases reacted differently. Some denounced the ICSID Convention and terminated treaties, others built defenses based on their constitution and on interpretations of the ICSID Convention, and others have conditioned the signature of BITs to amendments alleging constitutional requirements. What seems to be a common trend in the present, is not to sign new BITs.

As a threshold matter, this chapter will discuss what is "Latin America," a term not infrequently used to cover all countries south of the United States as if one and the same in terms of policies and attitudes towards investment arbitration. Then, starting from the "*No of Tokyo*," follows a brief presentation of the evolution of the signature of investment treaties and the subsequent filing of claims against Latin American states. Afterward, the chapter addresses some specific legal theories invoked in the defense of claims, particularly the case of Argentina; the constitutional grounds invoked by Ecuador to denounce BITs; and the decisions of the Constitutional Court of Colombia in reviewing BITs and Free Trade Agreements (FTAs) (including the curious reference to the *Achmea* decision) to leave the reader with the question of whether this evolution

11. Ignacio A. Vincentelli, The Uncertain Future of ICSID in Latin America, Law & Bus. Rev. Am. Vol. 16 (2010), p. 409.
12. Ignacio A. Vincentelli, The Uncertain Future of ICSID in Latin America, Law & Bus. Rev. Am. Vol. 16 (2010) 409 citing Andrew T. Guzman; Why LDCs Sign Treaties That Hurt Them: Exp Popularity of Bilateral Investment Treaties, Va. J. Int'l L. Vol. 38 (1998), pp. 639, 644.
13. Eric Gillman, Legal Transplants in Trade and Investment Agreements: Understanding the Exportation of U.S. Law to Latin America, Geo. J. Int'l L. Vol. 41 (2009), 263.
14. United Nations Conference on Trade and Development, Investment Policy Hub, available at https://investmentpolicy.unctad.org/investment-dispute-settlement (accessed October 5, 2022).
15. United Nations Conference on Trade and Development, Investment Policy Hub, available at https://investmentpolicy.unctad.org/investment-dispute-settlement/country/45/colombia/res pondent (accessed October 5, 2022).

could be compared with the situation in Europe and the origin of the legal theories invoked by the European Union and the European Courts and States in their reaction to investment arbitration.

I   THE CONCEPT OF "LATIN AMERICA"

"Latin America" may be one of those concepts that we think we know, but we only have an illusion of knowledge.[16] Latin America is used to define a group of countries without clearly defining which countries are comprised in the group. It is also used as a political concept and sometimes even as a discriminatory term.

There has been extensive debate as to the origin of the concept of Latin America. It has been attributed to the French as a justification of the occupation of Mexico (1862-1867)[17] and to attempt to differentiate a region that had allegedly more links to France, in terms of language and cultural traditions ("Latin language and Latin traditions"), than to the "other America," i.e., the United States of America. But it has also been attributed to intellectuals in South and Central America in 1856 who were protesting U.S. expansion into the Southern Hemisphere, even though the intellectual elite in the region seemed more inclined to use the term "americanos" or to refer to "*Hispano America*" to differentiate themselves from the United States which was claiming and using the name "America" all for itself.[18]

The purpose of finding a term to identify the countries of America, other than the U.S. and Canada was, from the point of view of France, Spain and the United States, an attempt to justify affinities in terms of race and culture with Europe and the United States. From the point of view of the countries in the region, the purpose was to stress their independence from Europe and the United States. The intent, in any event, was not to encompass a group of countries as if they were one and the same.

---

16. According to Sloaman and Fernbach, we all suffer, to a greater or lesser extent, from an illusion of understanding. We tell ourselves that we understand what's going on, that our opinions are justified by our knowledge, and that our actions are grounded on justified beliefs even though they are not. We tolerate complexity by failing to recognize it. That is the illusion of understanding. S. Sloman & P. Fernbach, The Knowledge Illusion: Why We Never Think Alone (Riverhead Books, 2017), pp. 9 and 35.
17. M. Gobat, The Invention of Latin America: A Transnational History of Anti-imperialisms, Democracy and Race (Oxford University Press, 2013), pp. 1345-1375.
18. Gobat submits that in the early nineteenth century "elites in the Southern Hemisphere rarely identified themselves and the continent with the Latin race. Initially, their preferred terms were *americanos* and *América*. As John Chasteen shows, these centuries-old terms became prevalent in the 1810s and 1820s, when the region waged wars of independence against Spain. With this struggle, *americano* took on an anticolonial meaning and no longer encompassed only people of European descent, but also those of indigenous, African, and mixed-race descent. As U.S. expansionists began to threaten Mexico in the 1830s, elites in Central and South America increasingly adopted the term *Hispano-América* to differentiate their societies from the United States, which was claiming "America" all for itself" (M. Gobat, The Invention of Latin America: A Transnational History of Anti-imperialisms, Democracy and Race (Oxford University Press, 2013), pp. 1345-1375). That particular concept of Latin America was not substantially different from the concept used by Spain to refer to its former colonies, la *América Española*, the Spanish America.

It is not the purpose of this chapter to go into an in-depth analysis of the similarities and differences between the countries comprising so-called Latin America. However, a summary of the factors that have historically contributed to such differences may assist in understanding, first, that a unified position with respect to arbitration has been the exception and not the rule; second, that it is difficult to find situations where a substantial majority of the countries have taken the same approach as regards investment arbitration; and third, that even when there appears to be a unified position within a group of countries, such appearance does not necessarily reflect reality when analysed closely.

Before the colonization of what is now Latin America, there were, on the one hand, immense and extremely developed empires (Incas, Aztecs, Mayas) and, on the other, smaller and extremely primitive indigenous communities.[19] During the colonization and the colonial period, the institutions that evolved varied depending upon the type of indigenous communities and their degree of development.[20] After the independence, two relevant factors must be considered. First, the territorial divisions resulting from the independence from Spain and Portugal were predominantly political decisions that did not consider the affinities of the inhabitants or the natural geography of the territory.[21] Second, rather than seeking consolidation of the Spanish rules or the harmonization of the legislation in the region, the various new independent republics searched for different legal systems.[22]

The countries of the region have, over the years, adopted different policies on migration which have marked substantial differences in the cultural development and the approach to legal institutions, including arbitration. Argentina and Uruguay received large European migrations, particularly from Italy, Germany and the United Kingdom. Brazil has the largest Japanese community after Japan; Peru received a significant migration from China and Japan; Bolivia and Guatemala have a large indigenous population and relatively small migrations;[23] Colombia has historically received few migrations, excluding the Lebanese migration to the Caribbean coast, and the massive migration from Venezuela starting in 2017.

---

19. L. Bethell, The Cambridge History of Latin America. Vol. 1. Colonial Latin America (Cambridge University Press, 1984).
20. L. Bethell, The Cambridge History of Latin America. Vol. 2. Colonial Latin America (Cambridge University Press, 1984).
21. L. Bethell, The Cambridge History of Latin America. Vol.3: From Independence to c. 1870 (Cambridge University Press, 1985); J. Lynch, The Spanish American Revolutions 1808-1826 (W. W. Norton & Company, 2nd ed. 1986).
22. The French Civil Code had a great influence, but it was the subject matter of different approaches. Chile adopted the Civil Coe prepared by Andrés Bello and modeled on the French Civil Code. Colombia and Venezuela adopted the Andrés Bello Code. The Dominican Republic adopted the French Civil Code almost verbatim. Cuba and Puerto Rico followed the Spanish Civil Code. Panama took inspiration in the Spanish Civil Code but adopted its own version. Argentina followed the works of Velez Sarsfield and his adoption of the French Civil Code. Brazil and Mexico adopted modern codes to some extent departing from the French influence (see C. Mirow, M. El Código de Napoleón y los Códigos de Bello y Vélez Sérsfield. En Anuario de Derecho Privado, Número 33. Universidad de los Andes, Facultad de Derecho, December 2004).
23. J. Martínez Pizarro, América Latina y el Caribe: migración internacional, derechos humanos y desarrollo. Comisión Económica para América Latina y el Caribe (CEPAL) Santiago de Chile, septiembre de 2008.

A further difference among the countries in the region results from the adoption of the concept of administrative law and the organization of the courts. Some countries, influenced by the French model, adopted the concepts of administrative contracts and administrative acts,[24] with a special legal regime and specialized courts: the administrative courts and the Council of State. The constitutional control of the laws was generally attributed to a special section of the Supreme Court. However, jurisdictions like Colombia have a Constitutional Court, separate from the Supreme Court with extensive constitutional powers that can comprise the control of not only the State's domestic laws but also of international treaties signed by Colombia, pending ratification.

Of course, in this diverse environment, the development of arbitration has been equally diverse. Domestic arbitration between private parties has historically been accepted, to different degrees, with little or no reluctance. Traces of arbitration in Latin America have been found as early as in the Spanish law applicable in the territories of Spanish America.[25] Provisions on arbitration may be found in the Judicial Code of Colombia, Law 105 of 1890, Article 307, the Argentinian Code of Procedure of August 20, 1880, and the Chilean Law on Organization of Tribunals of 1875. Arbitration was also included in the national constitutions of Venezuela (1830), Chile (1823) Brazil (1824), and Ecuador (1878). The attitude that has been characterized as hostile is generally seen in cases where a state entity or the state is involved, or where the arbitration has international elements and there is an attempt to exclude the dispute from domestic arbitration or the local courts.

Even though arbitration between private parties was generally permitted, the participation of states and state entities in domestic arbitration was heavily restricted. Submitting to arbitration, decisions involving the so-called exorbitant powers of the state, was not acceptable. It was necessary to preserve the jurisdiction of the courts as the "natural judges" to decide state disputes with private parties.[26]

---

24. Generally, the definition of an administrative contract depends either upon the matter or upon the type of entity involved or both. Administrative contracts can either be governed by administrative law or special regimes for state contracts, subject to the exclusive jurisdiction of the local courts and the state and state entities reserved for themselves the so-called exorbitant powers that included the possibility to unilaterally interpret or terminate the contact and the power to declare the caducity of the contract for the reasons provided for in the law, which generally included reasons of public policy or public convenience. Decisions based on the exorbitant powers of the state were subject to the control of the domestic courts.

25. J.P. Cárdenas Mejía, *Introducción a la Historia del Arbitraje en Colombia*. Revista Arbitrio, Centro de Arbitraje de la Cámara de Comercio de Bogotá, March 2019, pp. 19-29). Eloy Anzola claims that the "birth certificate" of arbitration in Latin America is contained in the order (*pragmatica*) issued by the Emperor Charles V (Charles I of Spain) on December 10, 1532 pursuant to which the arbitration provisions of Castille shall be applied in "the Indias," in the Spanish America. The order (*pragmatica*) was in turn incorporated in the *Recopilación de las Leyes de los Reynos de las Indias* (Book Fifth, Title X, Law V) published in 1680 under Charles II. *See* Anzola, E. *Nacimiento del Arbitraje en América*, http://eanzola.com/images/uploads/Acta_de_Nacimiento_del_Arbitraje_en_América.pdf. J.P. Cárdenas Mejía, *Introducción a la Historia del Arbitraje en Colombia*. Revista Arbitrio, Centro de Arbitraje de la Cámara de Comercio de Bogotá, March 2019, pp. 19-29.

26. G. Tawil, *On the Internationalization of Administrative Contracts, Arbitration and the Calvo Doctrine* in Albert Jan van den Berg (ed.), Arbitration Advocacy in Changing Times, ICCA Congress Series, 2010 Rio Volume 15 (Kluwer Law International 2011) pp. 325-347.

As regards the Calvo and Drago doctrines, which have frequently been invoked as the basis for the perceived reluctance of Latin America to arbitration, Professor Diego Fernández Arroyo correctly explains that while the Calvo doctrine is a reaction to perceived diplomatic abuse, and the Drago doctrine is a reaction to the use of force, and both refer to acts that involve states, in fact, they did not have the impact sometimes attributed to them, in the field of commercial arbitration or the development of arbitration that does not involve states or state entities. The doctrines impacted, therefore, public interest and state contracts but could not be said to have been the cause of a reluctance to accept commercial arbitration.[27]

Latin America cannot be analysed as a single entity, or as a region that has a uniform approach towards arbitration. The differences in the approach to arbitration are sufficient to separate the countries either individually, or even by blocks that share a view of arbitration. The analysis of Latin America as a single entity will always result in generalizations, creating knowledge illusions.

II   THE *"NO OF TOKYO"*

In the years following the end of the Second World War, the end of colonialism increased the number of independent countries and, as a result thereof, new countries joined the United Nations. Developing countries were in need of investment but economic, legal, social, and even psychological factors (perception of political and non-commercial risks) were identified as deterrents to increased investments in developing countries.[28] During the quarter century following the Second World War, "a wave of expropriations took place in Eastern Europe, in the former European colonies and in Latin America."[29] However, apprehensions of investors were not limited to expropriations but extended to all government measures that might tend to impair the rights or assets of foreign investors.[30]

To address these concerns, several multilateral proposals were considered. From investment insurance to codes of conduct for host governments in their treatment of foreign investments to the drafting of multilateral investment treaties. Examples of the latter are the Abs–Shawcross Draft Convention, which included, *inter alia*, provisions on fair and equitable treatment (FET), constant protection and security, observance of undertakings given in relation to investments made by nationals of another party, expropriation and dispute resolution; and the OECD 1962 Draft Convention on the Protection of Foreign Property, broadly similar to the Abs–Shawcross Draft Convention

---

27. D. Fernández Arroyo, *La Evolución del Arbitraje en América Latina: De la supuesta hostilidad a la evidente aceptación*. Biblioteca Jurídica Virtual del Instituto de Investigaciones Jurídicas de la UNAM).

28. Antonio R. Parra, The History of ICSID (Oxford University Press, 2nd edn, 2017), Chapter 2.

29. Rodrigo Polanco Lazo, The No of Tokyo Revisited: Or How Developed Countries Learned to Start Worrying and Love the Calvo Doctrine, ICSID Review, Vol. 30, No. 1 (2015), pp. 172-193, citing Andreas F. Lowenfeld, International Economic Law (OUP 2003).

30. Antonio R. Parra, The History of ICSID (Oxford University Press, 2nd edn, 2017) Chapter 2.

but more restrictive in certain aspects, such as not extending the general treatment protection to the admission of investments.[31]

During the decade of the 1950s, the United States entered friendship, commerce and navigation treaties (FCNs) which dealt with most of the investment issues that were subject to debate. Germany, in turn, entered several investment treaties between 1959 and 1962. Such treaties referred to non-discriminatory treatment, protection and security, just compensation in the event of expropriation, and freedom from restrictions on the transfer of capital and returns. These BITs, however, did not address the resolution of disputes between a party and nationals of the other party. In view of the absence of an agreement as to the substantive issues on investment protection and the lack of clear rules in the BITs as to the forum for dispute resolution, working on a dispute settlement mechanism seemed to be the least controversial approach.[32]

The World Bank began to work on a draft convention for the settlement of investment disputes between states and investors of other states. The draft convention was discussed in several regional consultative meetings and generally received positive comments. However, at the regional meeting in Santiago (Chile), various participants from Latin America opposed the proposals considering that the draft convention would grant foreign investors "a legally privileged position, in violation of the principle of full equality before the law" and unacceptably delegate to an international organization "powers belonging to national institutions."[33]

Latin American countries opposed the establishment of a center for the settlement of investment disputes and questioned the authority of the World Bank to draw up such a treaty. The Executive Directors of the Bank approved a report with the recommendation for the Board of Governors to adopt, at the Annual Meeting in Tokyo in September 1964, a resolution asking the Executive Directors to formulate the proposed convention on the settlement of investment disputes and to submit its text to member governments.

The Board of Governors submitted the recommended resolution at the Tokyo meeting and, even though it was approved, 21 countries, including all the 19 Latin American countries that were members of the Bank, voted against the resolution. The speaker for the Latin American countries, the governor for Chile, Félix Ruiz, presented the position of the countries of the region in the following terms:

> I should particularly like to stress the opinion of the countries whom I am here representing with respect to the draft Agreement on Conciliation and Arbitration. We consider undesirable the resolution submitted to the Board of Governors, which recommends, and entrusts to the Boards of Directors of the Bank, the drafting

31. On the history of the draft multilateral conventions to protect foreign investments *see*, *inter alia*, Antonio R. Parra, The History of ICSID (Oxford University Press, 2nd edn, 2017) Chapter 2; Surya Surbedi, International Investment Law, Reconciling Policy and Principle, Hart Publishing, 2nd edn, 2012) Chapter 2; Stefan D. Amarshina and Juliane Kokott, *Multilateral Investment Rules Revisited*, in Peter Muchlinsky, Federico Ortino and Christopher Schreuer Editors, The Oxford Handbook of International Investment Law (Oxford University Press, 2008) pp. 119-153; M. Sornarajah, The International Law on Foreign Investment (Cambridge University Press, 2010) Chapter 6.
32. Antonio R. Parra, The History of ICSID (Oxford University Press, 2nd edn, 2017), Chapter 2.
33. Antonio R. Parra, The History of ICSID (Oxford University Press, Second Edition, 2017) Chapter 4.

of an international agreement to create a center for conciliation and arbitration to which foreign private investors could have recourse for the settlement of their disputes with governments of member countries, without necessarily having to exhaust the formalities and procedures of the national tribunals. It is believed that this would stimulate private investment in the underdeveloped economies.

The legal and constitutional systems of all Latin American countries that are members of the Bank offer the foreign investor at the present time the same rights and protection as their own nationals; they prohibit confiscation and discrimination and require that any expropriation on justifiable grounds of public interests shall be accompanied by fair compensation fixed, in the final resort, by the law courts.

The new system that has been suggested would give the foreign investor, by virtue of the fact that he is a foreigner, the right to sue a sovereign state outside its national territory, dispensing with the courts of law. This provision is contrary to the accepted legal principles of our countries and, de facto, would confer a privilege on the foreign investor, placing the nationals of the country concerned in a position of inferiority.

I must state, Mr. President, that the procedure suggested does not meet with the approval of our countries because it contravenes constitutional principles relating to this question that cannot be ignored.[34]

It was the first time that a major resolution proposed to the member countries of the World Bank received such a substantial opposition to a final vote and the first time that all Latin American countries adopted a formal unified position against arbitration for disputes involving states. This negative vote, that became known as the *"No of Tokyo,"* reflected the position of the Latin American countries in that foreign investors should not receive better treatment than nationals and therefore should be subject to the laws and jurisdiction of the recipient state, a position that had already been expressed at the consultative meeting held earlier in Santiago.

The former Secretary-General of ICSID, Paul Szasz, proposes five reasons for the *"No of Tokyo"*: (1) Not all Latin American governments were eager to attract foreign investment. (2) Latin American countries feared that by adopting the proposed convention they would be undermining the principle of non-intervention. (3) Granting foreign investors the right to arbitrate their disputes against states was a breach of the principle of equal treatment of foreigners and nationals. (4) Latin American countries rejected the argument that their domestic courts were not adequate (in terms of efficiency and fairness) to decide investment claims. (5) Latin American countries were suspicious of arbitral proceedings.[35]

The decade of the 1960s and the 1970s witnessed several proposals from developing states to redefine the relationships between states and the interaction between investments, investors and states. The United Nations was the forum where Latin American states debated their views on international law, particularly, on investments, expropriation, and compensation.

In this line, the United Nations General Assembly approved a series of resolutions that were not only supported by the states of the region but were also viewed by them

---

34. Antonio R. Parra, The History of ICSID (Oxford University Press, Second Edition, 2017) Chapter 4.
35. Paul C. Szasz, The Investment Disputes Convention and Latin America, Va. J. Intl. L. Vol. 11 (1971), 256, 257.

as evidence of the opinion of most of the states as to the status of customary international law on certain investment matters.

For instance, Resolution 1803 of 1962 on Permanent Sovereignty over Natural Resources (Resolution 1803) provided that in cases of expropriation, appropriate compensation should be paid in accordance with the rules in force in the states taking the corresponding measure in the exercise of its sovereignty. In turn, Resolution 3171 of 1973 on Permanent Sovereignty over Natural Resources provided, *inter alia*, that: "[T]he application of the principle of nationalization carried out by states, as an expression of their sovereignty in order to safeguard their natural resources, implies that each state is entitled to determine the amount of possible compensation and the mode of payment and that any dispute which might arise should be settled in accordance with the national legislation of each state carrying out such measures."[36]

By Resolution 3201 of May 1974, the General Assembly of the United Nations declared a New International Economic Order declaring that every state enjoys full permanent sovereignty over its natural resources and all economic activities, that each state is entitled to exercise effective control over them and their exploitation with means suitable to its own situation, including the right to nationalization or transfer of ownership to its nationals, and that no state may be subject to economic, political or any other type of coercion to prevent the free and full exercise of this inalienable right.

Finally, the CERDS[37] was widely supported by Latin American states because, in addition to the reiteration of the principles of sovereignty, non-intervention, territorial integrity and political independence, it emphasized the core position of the Latin American states.

Articles 2(1) and 2(2) of the CERDS stated that:

Article 1:

Every state has the sovereign and inalienable right to choose its economic system as well as its political, social and cultural systems in accordance with the will of its people, without outside interference, coercion or threat in any form whatsoever.

Article 2:

1. Every state has and shall freely exercise full permanent sovereignty, including possession, use and disposal, over all its wealth, natural resources and economic activities.
   Each state has the right:
   (a) To regulate and exercise authority over foreign investment within its national jurisdiction in accordance with its laws and regulations and in conformity with its national objectives and priorities. No state shall be compelled to grant preferential treatment to foreign investment;
   (b) To regulate and supervise the activities of transnational corporations within its national jurisdiction and take measures to ensure that such activities comply with its laws, rules and regulations and conform with its economic and social policies. Transnational corporations shall not intervene in the internal affairs of a host state. Every state should, with full

---

36. One hundred and eight countries voted in favour of the resolution, one voted against and sixteen countries abstained.
37. United Nations General Assembly Resolution A/RES/29/3281 (XXIX) December 12, 1974.

regard for its sovereign rights, co-operate with other states in the exercise of the right set forth in this subparagraph;

(c) To nationalize, expropriate or transfer ownership of foreign property, in which case appropriate compensation should be paid by the state adopting such measures, taking into account its relevant laws and regulations and all circumstances that the state considers pertinent. In any case where the question of compensation gives rise to a controversy, it shall be settled under the domestic law of the nationalizing state and by its tribunals, unless it is freely and mutually agreed by all states concerned that other peaceful means be sought on the basis of the sovereign equality of states and in accordance with the principle of free choice of means.

The CERDS, therefore, adopted the view that foreign investment shall be governed by the laws of the host state; foreign investors shall not receive a better treatment than nationals; and compensation shall be determined in accordance with the laws of the recipient state and not international law.

The debate was therefore set. Latin American countries considered that their laws and their courts granted sufficient protection to foreign investors and that the voting at the United Nations in support of the Charter indicated that such approach reflected customary international law. This position was clearly opposed by developed countries and particularly by the United States. After 1974 and during the 1980s, very few BITs or other International Investment Agreements (IIAs) were entered into and only a handful of Latin American countries ratified the ICSID Convention.

III   THE TREATY BOOM

The 1990s, however, marked a significant change. The numbers are striking. Less than twenty BITs were signed in the 1980s. But in the decade starting in 1990, the BITs signed by the Latin American States exceeded 200. The BITs generally provided for the application of the rules to which Latin American States had objected. Prompt, adequate and effective compensation in case of expropriation; international rules as opposed to local law; international arbitral tribunals and not local courts; and FET to foreign investors.

An obvious question arises. What prompted this explosion of BITs, and this switch from local laws and local courts to international standards and arbitral tribunals? Several explanations have been put forward to explain this drastic change in the policies of Latin American States.

Under the so-called enlightenment theory, developing countries, including Latin American countries, realized that it was in their own interest to encourage foreign investments in their territories, and therefore they needed to offer stronger protections to foreign investors. The theory could also be explained as a voluntary acceptance by Latin American states of the rules of customary international law and of arbitration to decide international disputes. This explanation, as discussed by Guzman, is not entirely satisfactory. On the one hand, while Latin American states were supporting the United Nations resolutions, some of them were negotiating BITs. If developing countries truly had changed their views on the value of commitment mechanisms and internationally binding agreements, it would be difficult to explain why a significant number of BITs were already in force and more were being negotiated, while the General Assembly voted 108 to one, in favour of the 1973 Resolution on Permanent Sovereignty over Natural Resources, and adopted the New International Economic Order.[38]

But in addition, if the Latin American states had selected the United Nations and the World Bank as the forums to express their views on the rights of states and foreign investors, it is not clear why, if there was a "change of heart" such new views were not expressed in the General Assembly of the United Nations, or in other worldwide forums to promote the signature of multilateral treaties on investment.

Professor Sornarajah explains the proliferation of BITs suggesting that developing countries "knowing the confused state of the law, [countries] entered into such treaties so that they could clarify the rules that they would apply in case of any disputes which may arise between them."[39] In other words, the reason to sign the BITs was to clarify the rules of international law with respect to which there was confusion. However, such a dramatic change is more than a clarification of the legal rules related to investments. A mere clarification does not justify a change where investors receive much more protection than what they had under the prior approach of Latin American States.

Another reason put forward for the massive signing of BITs is the benefits that developing states perceived they would receive under such treaties. These alleged benefits have been, however, disputed, and the debate remains as to whether BITs effectively contribute to the increase of foreign investment.

An additional approach to the reasons for this drastic change is the theory of transplantation, understood as the moving of a rule or a system of law from one country to another, or from one people to another. Baker[40] and Gillman[41] propose that underneath each of the BITs and trade agreements entered into between the United States and the Latin American States is a fundamental commitment on the part of U.S. negotiators to export domestic legal rules and norms into the international arena.[42] According to Baker "as the overwhelmingly dominant economic player at the negotiating table, the United States has little difficulty instilling its legal standards and interpretations into the agreements."[43] This process of exporting law "from economically powerful to economically disadvantaged states, and thereby forming extended

---

38. Andrew T. Guzman, Why LDCs Sign Treaties That Hurt Them: Explaining the Popularity of Bilateral Investment Treaties, Va. J. Int'l L. Vol. 38 (1998), pp. 639, 644.
39. M. Sornarajah, The International Law on Foreign Investment (Cambridge University Press, 5th edn, 2021), Chapter 5: Bilateral Investment Treaties, p. 226; Andrew T. Guzman, Why LDCs Sign Treaties That Hurt Them: Explaining the Popularity of Bilateral Investment Treaties, Va. J. Int'l L. Vol. 38 (1998), pp. 639, 644.
40. Mark B. Baker, No Country Left Behind: The Exporting of U.S. Legal Norms under the Guise of Economic Integration, Emory Int'l L. Rev., Vol. 19 (2005), p. 1321.
41. Eric Gillman, Legal Transplants in Trade and Investment Agreements: Understanding the Exportation of U.S. Law to Latin America, Geo. J. Int'l L., Vol. 41 (2009), p. 263.
42. Mark B. Baker, No Country Left Behind: The Exporting of U.S. Legal Norms under the Guise of Economic Integration, Emory Int'l L. Rev., Vol. 19 (2005), p. 1321.
43. Mark B. Baker, No Country Left Behind: The Exporting of U.S. Legal Norms under the Guise of Economic Integration, Emory Int'l L. Rev., Vol. 19 (2005), p. 1321.

trading blocs linked by shared legal norms, is not a phenomenon unique to the United States. The European Union has long engaged in a similar practice with the peripheral states, first in Spain and Greece, then more recently with the post-communist countries of Eastern Europe."[44]

Gillman goes further to suggest a new form of colonialism or *Pax Americana* by stating that "The content and terms of the agreements are proposed on a take it or leave it basis. Through these agreements, the U.S. transfers several areas of domestic law to partner nations. Considering the complex interaction between legal transplants and recipient legal systems, as well as the significant consequences that legal transplants carry for receiving nations, the formulaic 'one-size-fits-all' approach of the U.S. in negotiating FTAs and BITs with Latin American countries is fraught with problems. Trade and investment agreements serve as conduits for the transfer of U.S. legal norms to the systems of Latin American trading partners. Such agreements often appear to be neutral contractual documents that are the result of a bargaining process between sovereigns. However, this is deceptive because BITs and FTAs between the U.S. and Latin American nations promote U.S. law to the exclusion of partner country norms."[45]

In sum, under this theory, trade and investment agreements between the U.S. or Europe, on the one hand, and Latin American countries, on the other, represent the one-way—and to some extent imposed—harmonization of commercial legal standards in the image of the U.S. and European legal systems.

IV   THE CLAIMS BOOM

After the 1990s treaty boom came the 2000s claims boom. As of today, two Latin American countries rank top 2, with the largest number of treaty-based Investor-State Dispute Settlement (ISDS) cases as respondents. Argentina accounts for 62 cases, and Venezuela for 55 cases. Mexico follows in fifth place with 38 cases. The earliest cases were initiated by the end of the 1990s, with a dramatic increase after 2005. The explosion of claims came a little bit later for other countries such as Perú, with a total of 31 cases, out of which, 28 cases began after 2010; and Colombia with 19 cases, all of which began after 2016.

The reasons triggering this avalanche of claims are as diverse as the approaches adopted by each Latin American country to face it. Yet, there seems to be a point of convergence: constitutionalism. The experiences of Argentina, Ecuador, and Colombia provide a comprehensive depiction of the interactions between ISDS and the constitutional frameworks of Latin American countries, with an apparent tendency to privilege the protection of national and constitutional interests, over foreign investors.

---

44. Mark B. Baker, No Country Left Behind: The Exporting of U.S. Legal Norms under the Guise of Economic Integration, Emory Int'l L. Rev., Vol. 19 (2005), p. 1321.
45. Eric Gillman, Legal Transplants in Trade and Investment Agreements: Understanding the Exportation of U.S. Law to Latin America, Geo. J. Int'l L., Vol. 41 (2009), p. 263.

1   Argentina

In the context of an economic crisis, multiple investment cases were filed against the Republic of Argentina. At least in 22 cases, 19 under the ICSID Rules, Argentina was found liable for breaching a treaty provision, with an award in favor of the investor.[46] Argentina initiated annulment proceedings in 18 of the 19 ICSID cases, and only one (1) award was entirely annulled[47] by the ICSID Annulment Committee, and two (2) other awards were partially annulled.[48]

During the ICSID annulment proceedings, a debate arose as to whether the awards under scrutiny, could be subject to further domestic judicial control at the seat. Argentina's reasons to hold that judicial review was required, evolved over time.

Initially, the Argentine Attorney General's Office relied on the principle of Argentine Constitutional law that international treaties are subordinated to the Argentine Constitution. Article 27 of the Argentine Constitution provides that "The Federal Government is required to consolidate peace and commercial relations with foreign powers by means of treaties that shall be subject to the public law principles set forth in this Constitution." In turn, Article 75, section 22, paragraph 1 provides that Congress is empowered to "Approve or reject the treaties executed with other nations and with international organizations (…). The treaties and agreements supersede the laws." As a treaty, the ICSID Convention would be subject to the public law principles of Argentine Constitutional law, and this requirement to abide by public law constitutional principles applies to the whole system, i.e., to the treaty and to its products, such as the awards issued under the ICSID rules.

The main consequence of this legal construction was that the Argentinian courts had to check the award's full compliance with domestic public law principles prior to enforcement. The issue, of course, was that "the public law principles set forth in this Constitution" as Article 27 states, include concepts such as "sovereignty" and "state of emergency" that could affect the enforcement of awards.

Another argument brought by Argentina regarding ICSID awards was related to the constitutionality of the adherence procedure to the ICSID Convention. Argentina adhered to ICSID in August 1994 and the Law of Adhesion was published in September 1994. In August 1994 the Argentinian Constitution was amended, empowering Congress to approve treaties that delegated powers and jurisdiction to supranational bodies. Even though the law approving ICSID followed the procedure for approval that was in force before the amendment of the Constitution, it was published after the amendment, so it had to comply with the requirements provided for under the amendment. Since the procedure outlined in the 1994 Constitution was not applied,

---

46. United Nations Conference on Trade and Development, Investment Policy Hub, available at https://investmentpolicy.unctad.org/investment-dispute-settlement/country/8/argentina/respondent (accessed October 4, 2022).

47. *Sempra Energy International v. Argentine Republic* (ICSID Case No. ARB/02/16).

48. *CMS Gas Transmission Company v. Argentine Republic* (ICSID Case No. ARB/01/8); and *Enron Creditors Recovery Corporation (formerly Enron Corporation) and Ponderosa Assets, L.P. v. Argentine Republic* (ICSID Case No. ARB/01/3).

any arbitration carried out under the ICSID Convention against Argentina could be declared null and void by a domestic court.

Argentina did not denounce the ICSID Convention on grounds of unconstitutionality. Instead, it adopted the position that ICSID awards were subject to the control of Argentine courts based on a joint interpretation of Articles 53 and 54 of the ICSID Convention. Article 53 provides that the award "shall binding on the parties and shall not be subject to any appeal or to any other remedy except those provided for in this Convention," while Article 54 provides that "Each Contracting State shall recognize an award rendered pursuant to this Convention as binding and enforce the pecuniary obligations imposed by that award within its territories as if it were a final judgment of the courts of a constituent state."

According to Argentina, Article 53 of the ICSID Convention establishes the final and binding nature of ICSID awards but "does not establish an obligation of *voluntary* payment by the State."[49] As to Article 54, Argentina argued that it merely provides the way in which ICSID Awards must be complied with, which, in its view, is to treat the ICSID award as if it were a final judgment of a domestic court. Consequently, to enforce the award and collect payment the claimant must pursue execution proceedings before local Argentinian courts. Argentina further argues that this execution is made through an administrative and not a judicial proceeding.

However, in ICSID annulment proceedings it has been found that additional steps to secure the enforcement of an award are only required when there is a reluctance to comply from the debtor, and not as a requisite for payment.[50] Therefore, in line with the good faith principle, the ordinary meaning of terms in their context, and the treaty's object and purpose, it has been understood that pursuant to Article 53(1) of the ICSID Convention, respondent states have an international obligation to abide by and comply with the terms of an award, without claimants having to resort to domestic actions.

2   Colombia

Colombia can be said to be a newcomer to the investment arbitration arena, facing its first case as late as 2016. To date, Colombia has registered a total number of 19 cases as a respondent state, 5 of which have been decided with a final award. Despite this sudden explosion of claims, the experience of Colombia in investment arbitration cases could be regarded as "positive," considering that 4 out of the 5 awards rendered so far, were in favor of the respondent state.

This generally positive experience added to continuous pro-foreign investment governments may explain why—at least as of the date of this chapter—Colombia has chosen to remain within the ICSID system, instead of resorting to extreme measures. It is also worth noting that, in the only request for annulment filed by Colombia so far, no domestic constitutional law arguments were invoked to vacate the award.

---

49. *Enron Corporation Ponderosa Assets, L.P. v. Argentina* (2008), Decision on The Argentine Republic's Request for a Continued Stay of Enforcement of The Award (October 7, 2008).
50. *Sempra Energy International v. Argentina* (2009) Decision on the Argentine Republic's Request for a Continued Stay of Enforcement of the Award (March 5, 2009).

Nonetheless, this apparently favourable attitude towards the ISDS system and its independence was tainted by two decisions adopted by the Colombian Constitutional Court that interpreted the substantive provisions of IIAs.

By virtue of Article 241-10 of the Political Constitution of Colombia, the Colombian Constitutional Court is vested with the authority to review the constitutionality of treaties negotiated by the government. This constitutional control occurs *ex-ante* when the treaty has been signed and is yet to be ratified. The Constitutional Court had always taken the approach that the review of the constitutionality of treaties in general, and particularly investment treaties, was limited to a formal assessment without reviewing the substance of the treaty. Moreover, the Constitutional Court had never, when determining the scope of the obligations acquired by Colombia, examined the substantive provisions enshrined in IIAs.

However, in the ruling C-252 of June 6, 2019, related to the Constitutionality of the BIT between Colombia and France, the Constitutional Court asserted that the constitutional control before the ratification of the treaty has a comprehensive scope, covering both procedure and substance. In this unprecedented decision, the Constitutional Court adjudged that the Colombia-France BIT complied with the Colombian Constitution, but conditioned its ratification to the state parties' issuance of a joint interpretative note of several provisions of the treaty, including those regarding FET, national treatment, most-favored nation (MFN), and expropriation.

The Court considered that a two-pronged reasonableness test was needed. The Court first verified whether the aims pursued by the BIT were legitimate in the light of the Constitution, and second, whether the BIT as a whole and its individual provisions, were suitable to fulfill those aims.

As to the first part of the test, the Constitutional Court considered that the BIT complied with the Constitution. However, before ruling that the treaty had passed the reasonableness test, the Court went on to examine its compatibility with the principle of equality enshrined in Article 13 of the Constitution. The Court observed that the BIT lacked any substantive provision protecting domestic investors or guaranteeing equality of protection between domestic and foreign investors to prevent discrimination against the former. Consequently, the Constitutional Court upheld the constitutionality of the BIT, under the condition that none of its substantive provisions requires more favourable treatment for foreign investors than for Colombian nationals.

In the second part of the test, the Court reviewed the constitutionality of each particular provision of the BIT. For this analysis, the Court discussed whether the decisions of international arbitration tribunals, which give content to the substantive standards found in BITs, should be taken into consideration for purposes of constitutional control. In this line, the Constitutional Court made a rigorous analysis of investment arbitration decisions, criticizing the lack of uniformity in the application of the FET, MFN, and Expropriation clauses:

FET

Article 4 of the Colombia-France BIT provides that "Each Contracting Party shall accord fair and equitable *treatment* in accordance with *applicable international law* to investors of the other Contracting Party and its investments in its territory.

For greater certainty, the obligation to accord fair and equitable treatment includes, *inter alia*: a) the obligation not to deny justice in civil, criminal or administrative proceedings in accordance with due process; b) the obligation to act in a transparent, non-arbitrary and discriminatory manner as regards investors from the other contracting Party and its investments. This treatment is consistent with the principles of foreseeability and *legitimate expectations* (...)."

About the FET clause, the Constitutional Court concluded that the language was vague and undetermined, contradicting constitutional principles of legal certainty and good faith. Hence, an interpretation from the state parties was required to clarify whether the term *"international law"* refers to customary international law, treaty law, or both and if it refers to customary international law, which specific "instruments" are applicable. The Constitutional Court further considered that the expression *"inter alia"* must be interpreted restrictively, and not in an additive but rather analogical sense.

As to the content of the FET obligation, the Constitutional Court first referred to a "current discussion as to whether the scope of the FET clause was limited to the classic standard of denial of justice, or if it admitted more flexible interpretations related to (i) arbitrary or discriminatory treatment, (ii) due process violations and lack of transparency, (iii) legitimate expectations (...)." This reference may at first hand seem harmless since the Constitutional Court finally analysed all the standards already set forth in Article 4, without cherry-picking the actual content of the FET clause that was negotiated by the states. However, the fact that the Constitutional Court unnecessarily acknowledged the existence of such debate, leaves the question open as to whether it eventually would balance more towards a "limited classic standard" of FET, allowing only for the protection against denial of justice.

After this remark, the Constitutional Court then continued to review the scope of the standards of protection against "(i) arbitrary or discriminatory treatment, (ii) due process violations and lack of transparency, (iii) legitimate expectations." For this analysis, the Constitutional Court referred to decisions in investment arbitration cases issued more than twenty years ago,[51] based on first-generation treaties, without even analysing whether those decisions reflect the evolution and the current context of international investment law. The Constitutional Court even resorted to interpretations recorded in annulled awards, i.e., *CMS Gas Transmission Co v. Argentina*.

The Constitutional Court concluded that the protections enshrined in the FET standard were compliant with the Constitution. Nonetheless, regarding legitimate expectations, the Constitutional Court noted that the concept must be interpreted to encompass only (a) the expectations that arise from specific and repeated acts carried out by the host state to induce an investor to make or maintain investments in its territory, and (b) the breaches that affect the investment by abrupt and unexpected changes made by public authorities.

MFN

Akin to other national treatment and MFN clauses included in multiple IIAs ratified by Colombia, Article 5 of the Colombia-France BIT provides that each contracting party shall grant to the investments of investors of the other contracting party made in its territory, a "treatment not less favorable than that accorded *in similar circumstances* to its own investors or to investors of a more favored nation." Article 5(3) provides that this obligation does not prevent the contracting parties from

---

51. That is, *Metalclad Corporation v. The United Mexican States*, ICSID Case No. ARB(AF)/97/1.

adopting justified, "necessary and proportionate" measures to guarantee public order in the event of serious threats to the fundamental interests of the states.

According to the Constitutional Court, the terms "similar circumstances" and "necessary and proportionate" are vague and uncertain. The Constitutional Court asserted that the term "similar circumstances" has been inconsistently interpreted by previous tribunals, some with a strict understanding that similar is "identical," and others with more flexible approaches. This inconsistency affects legal stability and creates uncertainty among public authorities when exercising their powers. Consequently, the standard must follow an interpretation that encompasses all relevant circumstances, including differentiated treatment directed to pursue legitimate public policy objectives. Moreover, the terms "necessary and proportionate" must be interpreted as respecting the autonomy of national authorities to guarantee public order and protect legitimate public policy objectives.

The Constitutional Court further concluded that the practice accepted by some international investment tribunals to import provisions from other treaties ratified by the host state of the investment, through the MFN clause, may pose a threat to the powers of the President of Colombia to direct international relations and negotiate treaties, as embodied in Article 189.2 of the Colombian Constitution. Nonetheless, the Constitutional Court also recognized that the MFN clause was important to ensure the right to equality, also protected by the Colombian Constitution. Consequently, the Constitutional Court declared the expression "treatment" to be compliant with the Constitution insofar as it was interpreted to preserve the exclusive powers of the President.

Expropriation

Article 6(2) of the Colombia-France BIT defines indirect expropriation. Under this provision, a case-by-case analysis must be performed in order to determine whether a measure or series of measures adopted by one of the contracting parties constitute indirect expropriation, considering, among others, the "impact of the measure or series of measures in the legitimate expectations of the investor." Article (6)2 further provides that measures for the protection of public policy objectives do not constitute an indirect expropriation insofar as such actions are "necessary and proportionate in the light of these objectives."

The Constitutional Court found that the expressions "legitimate expectations" and "necessary and proportional" pose difficulties due to their vagueness and dissimilar application by international investment tribunals. Accordingly, it concluded that these terms must be interpreted under the same conditions required for Article 4 with respect to the concept of "legitimate expectations," and Article 5 regarding the expression "necessary and proportional."

In sum, the Constitutional Court concluded that the Colombia-France BIT was compliant with the Constitution, provided that all the issues identified in the ruling were clarified by means of interpretative declarations.

Certain members of the Constitutional Court rendered clarifications and dissenting opinions, criticizing the decision adopted by the majority, on multiple grounds, some of which referred to the following issues: (1) Investment arbitration lacking a system of precedent. International decisions are only a supplementary means for the determination of international obligations. The Constitutional Court "indiscriminately" selected awards without any analysis of their relevance for the current context under which the Colombia-France BIT was negotiated. (2) The so-called interpretative declarations were really amendments to the treaty since they had to be approved by both parties. A unilateral interpretative declaration by Colombia was equivalent to a reservation in a bilateral treaty. (3) The decision unduly interfered with the powers of the President of Colombia to direct the international relations of the country.

There is a particularly conspicuous clarification submitted by one of the Justices[52] that refers to the possible "implications" of the *Slovak Republik v. Achmea B.V.* decision, rendered on March 7, 2018, by the European Union Court of Justice, in connection with the ISDS clause in the Colombia-France BIT (Article 15). The concern manifested in the clarification was that the decision of the ECJ could eventually affect the consent given by France to arbitrate, preventing Colombian investors from filing claims against France, while allowing French investors to file claims against Colombia. This "unbalance" in the consent to arbitrate, would be contrary to the principle of equity and reciprocity in international relations enshrined in Article 226 of the Constitution. It is not clear on which grounds could the Constitutional Court base its constitutionality assessment of a treaty provision, on the interpretation of a judgment issued by a foreign court. Moreover, the alleged unbalanced or unequal situation proposed in the clarification is an entirely hypothetical scenario with no legal or factual basis. The clarification is rather laconic, shedding no light on these qualms.

Fortunately, the Constitutional Court disregarded the concern raised in this clarification, and instead, declared Article 15 of the Colombia-France BIT to be compatible with the Constitution. The decision adopted in this regard is certainly an adequate and desirable conclusion. Nevertheless, one cannot help to worry that such interpretation could eventually resurface.

After the issuance of ruling C-252 of 2019, France and Colombia eventually renegotiated the corresponding provisions of the treaty, and the issue was settled. Despite this outcome, this ruling remains a decision that may open the door for the Constitutional Court to control the content of investment treaties and instruct the executive branch as to how further treaties must be negotiated.

The intervention of the Constitutional Court in the already negotiated content of a treaty seems incoherent with one of the very aims of the ruling, which is to preserve the powers of the executive branch. As stated in the dissenting opinion of one of the Justices of the Constitutional Court "Article 189.2 of the [Constitution] expressly states that it is incumbent upon the President of the Republic as head of State to '*[d]irect international relations*. Appoint diplomatic and consular agents, receive the respective agents *and enter into treaties or agreements with other States and entities under international law, which shall be submitted to Congress for approval*' (emphasis outside the original text). 2. Based on the foregoing, upon a systematic and comprehensive reading of the Constitution, it is observed that the Constitution opted to grant a specific competence to the Executive in the management and direction of international relations, which cannot be ignored by this Court, under the argument of guaranteeing 'the protection of the integrity and supremacy of the Constitution'."[53]

---

52. Clarification of the Vote of Justice Carlos Bernal Pulido to the ruling C-252/19.
53. Clarification of the vote and partial dissenting opinion of Justice Alejandro Linares to the ruling C-252/19, §I.

Furthermore, in line with the dissenting opinions of some Justices, the intervention of the Constitutional Court may pose a major threat to the integrity of the treaty. This is especially true for bilateral agreements where there is virtually no room for reservations and any adjustment, interpretation, or modification will require a partial or even a complete renegotiation of the treaty between the signatory states.

The apparently amicable reception by France of the conditions set out by the Constitutional Court should be taken as an exotic rather than an expected reaction. It is worth recalling the failed IIA signed between Colombia and the United Kingdom on March 9, 1994. The Constitutional Court rendered the ruling C-358, declaring that the IIA was constitutional except for Article 6, which provided protection against unlawful expropriation. At the time, Article 58 of the Constitution allowed for direct administrative expropriations without compensation, which was contrary to the standard of lawful expropriations as defined under the IIA. The unconstitutionality of this single article translated into the need for a renegotiation of the IIA, which failed in this case and led to the indefinite frustration of the entry into force of the treaty.

The ruling C-252 of 2019 certainly established a debatable precedent by "[elevating] the standard of the constitutional control applicable to the enabling legislation for international agreements on the promotion and protection of investments."[54] Yet, in a recent ruling, the Constitutional Court clarified that such precedent is restricted to international agreements on the promotion and protection of investments and is therefore not applicable to other commercial agreements. Based on this premise, the Constitutional Court excluded the application of the elevated standard of constitutional control to the analysis of the Trade Agreement between the United Kingdom and the signatory Andean Countries (Colombia, Peru, and Ecuador) of May 15, 2019.

3   Ecuador

On January 15, 1986, Ecuador signed the ICSID Convention, which was later ratified in 2001,[55] as an attempt from Ecuador to adjust to the standards of a globalized market and attract foreign capital by providing assurances that give confidence to the investors.[56] Afterward, between the 1990s and early 2000s, Ecuador entered a series of BITs.

Nonetheless, in 2008 a new Constitution was enacted. Article 422 of the Constitution provides that "Treaties or international instruments where the Ecuadorian State yields its sovereign jurisdiction to international arbitration entities in disputes involving contracts or trade between the State and natural persons or legal entities cannot be entered into. The treaties and international instruments that provide for the settlement of disputes between States and citizens in Latin America by regional arbitration entities or by jurisdictional organizations designated by the signatory

---

54. Colombian Constitutional Court, Ruling C-110 of March 24, 2022.
55. Executive Decree No. 1417-B, Official Registry No. 309 of April 19, 2001.
56. Iñigo Salvador Crespo, Mélanie Riofrío Piché "La denuncia del Convenio del Centro Internacional de Arreglo de Disputas Relativas a Inversiones o la calentura en las sábanas," Revista Ecuatoriana de Arbitraje No. 2 (89-127). Available at https://iea.ec/publicaciones/revista-2/.

countries are exempt from this prohibition. Judges of the States that, as such or their nationals, are part of the dispute cannot intervene in the above."[57]

The government headed by the President of Ecuador at the time, Rafael Correa (2007-2017), adopted a new social and political model enshrined under the 2008 Constitution, aiming to protect "the national sovereignty in economic, energetic and alimentary matters."[58] The implementation of this model entailed, among others, the "strengthening of the legal system, by the application of national laws, and bilateral agreements to avoid controversies related to the investment of foreign capitals."[59] This translated into the withdrawal from the international investment arbitration system, particularly the one established under the ICSID Convention. President Correa supported this anti-ISDS measure on what he perceived as the recurrently negative outcomes for Ecuador as a respondent state after an avalanche of investment claims began in 2002.[60]

Consequently, on July 2, 2009, Ecuador formally denounced the ICSID Convention.[61] Afterward, on September 28, 2009, the President requested the National Assembly to denounce various BITs on the ground that they were contrary to Article 422 of the Constitution. Under the Ecuadorian Constitution, the denunciation of treaties involving the state's consent to the jurisdiction of international bodies requires the approval of the National Assembly, subject to the issuance of a preliminary ruling from the Constitutional Court on the constitutionality of the treaty to be denounced. Accordingly, the Constitutional Court initiated unconstitutionality actions and began issuing judgments in June 2010 declaring the unconstitutionality of several BITs which were later denounced with the approval of the Secretary General of the Presidency of Ecuador.

After the decade-long government of Rafael Correa came to an end, in 2017, a new government led by Lenin Moreno, assumed the presidency of Ecuador. This new government, aiming to attract foreign investment, and in defence of the ISDS system,[62] requested the Constitutional Court for a reinterpretation of Article 442, to clarify that the prohibition referred thereto, did not apply to investment disputes. The Constitutional Court remained silent for almost three years, and only in 2022 issued a statement rejecting the application for reinterpretation, on the basis that it was not for the

---

57. Political Constitution of the Republic of Ecuador, Official Registry No. 449, 20/10/2008. Available at https://pdba.georgetown.edu/Constitutions/Ecuador/ecuador08.html#mozTocId674027.
58. National Development Plan for the Republic of Ecuador (2007-2010), policy 5.4., p. 216. Available at https://www.resdal.org/caeef-resdal/assets/ecuador---plan_nacional_desarrollo_2007-2010.pdf (accessed October 4, 2022).
59. National Development Plan for the Republic of Ecuador (2007-2010), policy 5.4., p. 217. Available at https://www.resdal.org/caeef-resdal/assets/ecuador---plan_nacional_desarrollo_2007-2010.pdf (accessed October 4, 2022).
60. United Nations Conference on Trade and Development, Investment Policy Hub, available at https://investmentpolicy.unctad.org/investment-dispute-settlement/country/45/colombia/respondent (accessed October 4, 2022).
61. Executive Decree No. 1823 of July 2, 2009, Official Registry No. 632.
62. CIAR Global, "Lenin Moreno defiende en china el uso del arbitraje internacional en Ecuador" https://ciarglobal.com/lenin-moreno-defiende-en-china-el-uso-del-arbitraje-internacional-en-ecuador/.

Constitutional Court to give meaning to Article 422, but rather to obtain a statement on a specific circumstance for its application, which, is incompatible with the admissibility of the action for constitutional interpretation.[63]

In 2021, Moreno's mandate concluded and the current president of Ecuador, Guillermo Lasso, took office. Within the first two months of his government, President Lasso signed the ICSID Convention, as part of a fast-paced policy of reincorporating the country in the international investment arena.

According to its laws, Ecuador can ratify a treaty through a presidential decree, insofar as it does not refer to any of the matters listed in Article 419 of the Constitution. When a treaty falls within the scope of Article 419, its ratification requires legislative approval. The Secretary-General of the Presidency of Ecuador requested an opinion from the Constitutional Court on whether the ratification of the ICSID Convention required such approval.

On June 30, 2021, the Constitutional Court issued Opinion No. 5-21-TI, providing that the ratification of the ICSID Convention did not require legislative approval or previous constitutional analysis.[64] In the Opinion, three main issues were discussed, based on Article 419(4), (6), (7). The first issue was whether the ICSID Convention referred to the rights and guarantees regulated in the Constitution. The second issue was whether the ICSID Convention bound the state to integration or trade agreements. The third issue was whether the ICSID Convention attributes powers of a domestic legal nature to an international or supranational organization.

The Constitutional Court found, first, that the ICSID Convention does not have any provision that modifies the regulatory regime of rights and guarantees of the Constitution, that concludes commercial negotiations between the state parties, or that subjects the states to an economic integration process. To reach this conclusion, the Constitutional Court analysed the preamble of the treaty, finding that it was not categorical enough to bind Ecuador to any of the abovementioned obligations.

Moreover, the Constitutional Court clarified that the fact that an international treaty relates to international cooperation or economic development does not mean that it is a trade agreement requiring legislative approval under Ecuadorian law. Finally, the Constitutional Court found that no powers were attributed to ICSID under the Treaty, as the state is not obliged to resort to arbitration or conciliation just by the mere fact of being a party to it. In this regard, the Constitutional Court recalled that consent being the cornerstone of arbitration, the attribution of powers could never be automatic.

---

63. Centro de Derechos Económicos y Sociales, January 14, 2022, available at https://cdes.org.ec/web/corte-constitucional-rechaza-solicitud-de-interpretacion-de-422/.
64. Opinion No. 5-21-TI/21 of July 30, 2021, Constitutional Court of Ecuador. Available at http://esacc.corteconstitucional.gob.ec/storage/api/v1/10_DWL_FL/e2NhcnBldGE6J3RyYW1pdGU
nLCB1dWlkOidiNDJlODMyYy01MDc4LTQxMDktYWMwMy0xOTc2YzdiNzUyNTUucGRmJ30
(accessed October 4, 2022).

Based on this interpretation, the President ratified the ICSID Convention on July 16, 2021, through Executives Decrees Nos 122 and 165.[65] The treaty entered into force on September 3, 2021.

Between August and October 2021, thirteen unconstitutionality actions were filed before the Constitutional Court, requesting the repeal of both Executive Decrees, for being unconstitutional.[66] The first action was brought against Executive Decree No. 122. (62-21-IN) and was admitted by the Constitutional Court on October 15, 2021. The Constitutional Court accumulated to the first process all the actions that were subsequently filed and rejected a request to stay the entry into force of the ICSID Convention.

According to the applicants, the constitutional breach is flagrant: Article 422 determines that the state cannot enter into "any treaty or international instrument where the Ecuadorian State yields its sovereign jurisdiction to international arbitration entities in disputes involving contracts or trade between the State and natural persons or legal entities" giving "little room for interpretation" according to Article 427 of the Constitution. They also claim that the spirit behind this prohibition is to safeguard Ecuador's sovereign authority from foreign jurisdictions, as their decisions, in the applicants' view, have always been averse to the state.

A final judgment is yet to be issued by Ecuador's Constitutional Court. The outcome of this controversy is critical not only to define the future of Ecuador in the ISDS system but even more, to define the position of Ecuador regarding the interaction between the Constitution—including the intervention of the Constitutional Court—in connection with its international obligations. Considering the Colombian case extensively discussed above, it is to be seen whether the Ecuadorian Constitutional Court also decides to exercise powers in the interpretation of treaties, including the ICSID Convention and IIAs that may overlap with the powers of the executive branch. Nonetheless, this attitude would be far from unexpected, considering that the Colombian Constitutional Court has historically been followed as a model by other Latin American Constitutional Courts, including Ecuador's.[67]

The journey of Latin American countries in the ISDS system may appear entirely sui generis or even unique. Yet, there seems to be a resemblance of certain attitudes with legal theories invoked by the EU and the European Courts and States in their reaction to investment arbitration. Latin American legal systems continue to reinforce their historical practice of adopting European standards, and transforming them to fit their entirely different social, economic and political circumstances. This difference is precisely where the problem lies: the European backlash to investment arbitration

---

65. On July 16, 2021, through presidential Executive Decree No. 122, Ecuador ratified the ICSID Convention again.

66. Instituto Peruano de Arbitraje, "Múltiples acciones de inconstitucionalidad han sido presentadas en asuntos relacionados al arbitraje nacional e internacional" https://iea.ec/noticias/multiples -acciones-de-inconstitucionalidad-han-sido-presentadas-en-asuntos-relacionados-al-arbitraje-n acional-e-internacional/ (accessed October 5, 2022).

67. For instance, in an opinion rendered by the Ecuadorian Constitutional Court, related to the constitutionality of the BIT between Ecuador and Peru, a reference to a decision from the Colombian Constitutional Court was incorporated to support the Opinion. Constitutional Court of Ecuador, Opinion No. 032-13-DTI-CC, Case No. 0016-13-TI. Available at https://www.ecotec .edu.ec/material/material_2019D1_DER325_02_122343.pdf (accessed October 5, 2022).

emerged in the context of an integrated region, comprising multiple countries with more stable economies and governments, and that will continue their trade activities among them, with or without investment arbitration. The Latin American backlash not only involves entirely different economies, with more host states than capital exporters but also emerges in the context of isolated countries that are far from achieving an actual integration process that could allow them to stand solidly as a region. The former, without mentioning the specificities of the political moment that Latin America is experiencing, and its yet unknown consequences for the position of these countries in the global trade arena.

PANEL 8   Regional Themes II: Asia, Africa and the Middle East: Dynamism and Consolidation

CHAPTER 30

Local Characteristics of Arbitration in China and Their Influence on Legislations

Wei Sun[*]

TABLE OF CONTENTS

I   INTRODUCTION

Since the enactment of the Arbitration Law in 1994, China has been regulating all arbitration practices with one single arbitration law. With the rapid development of domestic arbitration in China, both the system and practices of arbitration have gradually developed local characteristics. Meanwhile, commercial subjects, arbitrators, and courts from China have participated in international commercial arbitration more frequently, which highlights the realistic need to internationalize commercial arbitration practices. Therefore, it is a reality that the arbitration system in China is developing in parallel in two directions: one is to develop unique local characteristics and the other is the need for internationalization. However, the unified legislation

---

[*] Partner of Zhong Lun Law Firm, Beijing, China and LL.D. candidate admitted in 2021, Majoring
     in International Law at China University of Political Science and Law.

system in China, which is to regulate both domestic arbitration and international arbitration under one single Arbitration Law, cannot satisfy such growing demands in two opposite directions. As the Arbitration Law is currently under revision, this research aims to review the drawbacks of the unified legislation system of arbitration and propose a dualistic legislation model with different focuses on domestic arbitration and international arbitration, so as to propose a solution to optimize the arbitration system in China on the legislative level.

This research is structured as follows. The first part summarizes the local characteristics of Chinese commercial arbitration and analyzes the causes of their uniqueness. In the second part, this research states that there is a need to internationalize arbitration in China and illustrates that there have been some trends of internationalization in arbitration practice which went beyond laws and regulations. Those two parts aim to show the overall development of arbitration in China and explain the realistic need to transform arbitration legislation into a dualistic model. The third part analyzes some specific systems that should be distinctive in domestic arbitration and international arbitration and concludes that the differences between the practices of those two kinds of arbitration are extensive and profound, which highlights the necessity of a dualistic model in arbitration legislation. The fourth part illustrates both theoretically and realistically that a dualistic model of arbitration legislation is feasible in China.

II   THE UNIQUE CHARACTERISTICS OF COMMERCIAL ARBITRATION IN CHINA AND THE CAUSES OF THE UNIQUENESS

It could be seen from the arbitration history in the world that arbitration is a mechanism to settle disputes, voluntarily adopted by people, especially merchants to resolve their conflicts in the early days, and was only gradually recognized by national laws in later stages. On the contrary, the commercial arbitration mechanism in China has not gone through a nongovernmental, self-determined and autonomous process of development. In fact, the arbitration mechanism in China was established by legislation and then promoted by the government, which was developed "top-down" and was not completely driven by the market.[1]

Since the commercial arbitration system in China, in essence, resulted from an inquisitorial system instead of mercantilism,[2] it, therefore, enjoys distinct local characteristics compared with systems in other countries. First, the commercial arbitration system in China originated from administrative arbitration during the planned economy period and therefore is inevitably impacted by administrative factors. Second, as a product of the inquisitorial system, arbitration institutions prioritize the

---

1. Lianbin Song and Ling Yang, "The Systematic Dilemma of the Privatization of Arbitration Institutions in China: An Investigation into the Legislation of Chinese Nongovernmental Organizations," 27 (03) Law Review (2009) p. 49.
2. Sibao Shen and Yuan Xue, "On the Positioning of Commercial Arbitration System in China and its Revolution," 2006 (04) Law Science (2006) p. 67 at pp. 68-69.

substantive justice of the case and to a certain degree lead the arbitration procedures. Therefore, the commercial arbitration system in China not only carries a social function to stabilize society but also has some notable resemblance to litigation.

1   Commercial Arbitration in China Has Deep Administrative Involvement

Although the legislators of the 1994 Arbitration Law intentionally separated arbitration institutions from administrative authorities,[3] the existing commercial arbitration in China remains heavily influenced by administrative factors. These influences can be found in various features of arbitration institutions, including the nature, establishment, and appointment and removal of personnel of the decision-making body.

a   *Arbitration Institutions Are Established by Administrative Authorities and Mostly Classified as Institutional Organizations*

There are four different views on the nature of arbitration institutions in academia and industry, which are market intermediaries, institutional organizations, nongovernmental organizations, and nonprofit organizations.[4] According to Article 10 of the Arbitration Law and Article 3 of the Interim Procedures for Registration of Arbitration, the government should lead the establishment of the arbitration commission.[5] The current mainstream opinion regards arbitration institutions in China as the legal person of institutional organizations.[6] Moreover, as influenced by Article 4 of the Plan for Reorganization of Arbitration Institutions (GBF [1995] No.44), a majority of arbitration institutions in China have been categorized as institutional organizations.[7]

---

3. Angran Gu, "Explanation on Arbitration Law of the People's Republic of China (Draft)" in Kangsheng Hu, ed., *Arbitration Law of the People's Republic of China* (Law Press of China 1995) p. 152; Zhengbang Wen, "Arbitration Law of the People's Republic of China and the Revolution of Arbitration System in Market-Oriented Economy," 1995 (06) China Legal Science (1995) p. 55 at p. 57.
4. Zuping Zhang, "Nature of Commercial Arbitration Institutions in China and the Difficulties of Revolution," 26 (5) Journal of Shanghai University of Political Science & Law (The Rule of Law Forum) (2011) p. 53.
5. "Notice Concerning the Reorganization of Arbitration Institutions and Arbitration Associations," General Office of the State Council, GBF [1994] No. 99 (November 13, 1994); "Notice Concerning Further Reorganization of Arbitration Institutions," General Office of the State Council, GBF [1995] No. 38 (May 26, 1995); "Notice Concerning Printing and Distributing 'Plan for Reorganization of Arbitration Institutions', 'Interim Procedures for Registration of Arbitration Commissions', and 'Measures on Arbitration Fees to be Charged by Arbitration Commissions'," General Office of the State Council, GBF [1995] No.44 (July 28, 1995).
6. Jin Huang, Lianbin Song and Qianquan Xu, *Arbitration Law* (China University of Political Science Press 2002 Revision) p. 34.
7. Fuyong Chen, *The Unfinished Transformation: An Empirical Analysis of the Current Status and Future Trends of China's Arbitration Institutions* (Law Press of China 2010) pp. 33-36. In 2017, the former Legislative Affairs Office of the State Council of the People's Republic of China has investigated around 250 arbitration institutions around China and received feedback from 231 arbitration institutions. Among them, 187 were categorized as institutional organizations, which accounts for 81%; 9 were classified as social organizations or intermediary organizations, and 35

Since the establishment of institutional organizations has to rely on state organs or state-owned assets, they carry the function of social service. In practice, a majority of arbitration institutions are managed administratively by the government, which is similar to the management of institutional organizations.[8] Therefore, arbitration institutions, defined as institutional organizations, in their nature carry administrative features.

b The Decision-Makers of Arbitration Institutions Are Appointed and Removed by Administrative Authorities

Article 2 of the Plan for Reorganization of Arbitration Institutions states that members of the first session of an arbitration commission shall be appointed by the people's government of the city. Apart from members of the first session, decision-makers of some arbitration institutions are also appointed or removed by administrative authorities. Empirical research shows that the members of arbitration commission in China have strong administrative features with a lack of professional backgrounds. For example, many members come from administrative authorities and most chairmen of the arbitration institutions are also heads of the administrative authorities.[9] Based on the aforementioned assignment of personnel, it is inevitable for the management of arbitration institutions to be heavily influenced by administrative and institutional factors.

2 Commercial Arbitration in China Also Has a Duty to Stabilize Society

Commercial arbitration in China not only settles economic disputes, but also has a duty to resolve social conflicts, stabilize the society, and maintain the sustainable and sound development of the economy and society.[10]

---

with uncertain nature. Lili Jiang, "The Legal Nature of Chinese Arbitral Institution and Its Reform," 2019 (3) Journal of Comparative Law (2019) p. 142.

8. For example, the arbitration commission shall report its work plan to the government, participate in government meetings and administrative activities with government as the participants. And the decision-makers of the commission enjoys the remuneration at the level corresponding to administrative authorities. Moreover, in financial management, a majority of arbitration institutions are included into the financial management of governments instead of being independent. Lili Jiang, "The Legal Nature of Chinese Arbitral Institution and Its Reform," 2019 Journal of Comparative Law (2019) p. 142 at p. 143.
9. Fuyong Chen, *The Unfinished Transformation: An Empirical Analysis of the Current Status and Future Trends of China's Arbitration Institutions* (Law Press of China 2010) pp. 36-38.
10. In 2018, in the Several Opinions on Improving the Arbitration System to Strengthen the Credibility of Arbitration, the General Office of the CPC Central Committee and the General Office of the State Council clearly stated that arbitration is effective in respecting party autonomy and settling disputes in a convenient and effective manner, and such functions should be fully developed. Arbitration is also significant in resolving conflicts impartially, promptly, and properly, maintaining social stability, promoting reform and opening up, and guaranteeing the sustainable and sound development of the economy and society. Some arbitration institutions also openly state that they take up a duty to stabilize the society. For example, in the Decision of the Standing Committee of the People's Congress of Guangzhou Municipality on Developing the Arbitration Practices in Guangzhou, it has been clearly stated that Guangzhou Arbitration

a   *Arbitration Prioritizes Substantive Justice of the Case*

The judicial idea of China focuses more on substantive justice than procedural justice. For example, Article 2 of the Civil Procedure Law regulates the tasks of the law, and most of them focus on substantive issues, such as identifying civil rights and obligations, the outcome of the case, protecting lawful rights and interests of the parties, and maintaining social order. Procedural justice is only mentioned by "protecting the parties' exercise of procedural rights." Arbitration legislation in China is heavily influenced by the judicial model. The Arbitration Law starts with the statement that the law is formulated in order to ensure the impartial and prompt arbitration of economic disputes, to protect the legitimate rights and interests of the parties and to safeguard the sound development of the socialist market economy. It is clear that the arbitration legislation emphasizes substantive justice.

Arbitration practice in China also focuses on substantive justice. A typical example is the right of clarification in arbitration. Clarification traditionally means a right of the court to urge a party to make a sufficient or appropriate statement and submit evidence when the party's statement is insufficient or inappropriate.[11] Theoretically, it is believed that clarification is to complement the principle of disposition and the principle of adversary hearing of civil procedure and guarantees that the parties will not lose procedural and substantive interests because of their lack of legal knowledge and litigation capacity.[12] There are no rules about the right of clarification of arbitral tribunals in existing laws and regulations of China, but some arbitration institutions have special provisions on this issue in their own arbitration rules.[13] Most scholars and practitioners in China agree that arbitral tribunals should have the right to clarification, and there are discussions on issues such as the boundary of the right of clarification and the approaches to make a clarification in the hearings.[14] Moreover, in the judicial practice in China, there are cases where the arbitral award is set aside

---

Commission (GAC) shall establish the reporting system of arbitration cases. Arbitration cases involving social stability and civil disputes should be reported timely to municipal complaint divisions, municipal corresponding administrative departments, relevant administrative departments in charge of the industry, and district people's government. The second session of Wuxi Arbitration Commission also summarized that the commission insists to be people-oriented in their work and maintain social stability in accordance with the law.

11. Weiping Zhang, *Civil Procedural Law*, 5th edn (Law Press of China 2019) p. 88. Clarification is a concept in civil procedural law in the civil law system, and the main rules of clarification in China can be found in Articles 2 and 53 of Provisions of the Supreme People's Court on Evidence in Civil Procedures.

12. Zhong Ren, "Boundary of Supplement Statement in Civil Procedure in China," 2018 (6) China Legal Science (2018) p. 217 at pp. 217-218.

13. Shenzhen Court of International Arbitration, Arbitration Rules of Shenzhen Court of International Arbitration (henceforth SCIA Arbitration Rules), Article 36 Item 3 (2022).

14. Relevant research, *see* Kaixiang Liu, "On the Understanding and Application of the Right of Clarification in Arbitration Procedure," 2008 (4) Beijing Arbitration Quarterly (2008) p. 65 at pp. 65-76; Fakun Zhang, "The Specific Application of the Right of Clarification in the Arbitral Hearings," 2014 (1) Commercial Arbitration (2014) p. 66; Hong Yao and Han Su, "Analysis on the Right of Clarification in Arbitration Procedures," 29 (4) Journal of Shanxi Politics and Law Institute for Administrators (2016) p. 47.

because the arbitral tribunal didn't exercise the right of clarification in the proceeding.[15] Since there are no specific rules for guidance, arbitral tribunals exercising the right of clarification would first refer to judicial interpretations regarding clarification in litigation and then rely on specific circumstances of the particular case. Arbitral tribunals can exercise the right of clarification in many situations, which include both procedural and substantive issues. The right of clarification can complement the shortage of the party's capabilities to participate in the arbitration and present evidence and could promote substantive justice. However, clarification is a mechanism of civil procedure in the civil law system and there are no corresponding practices in the common law system. It is also rare for arbitral tribunals to make clarifications in international arbitration. International commercial arbitration is a dispute resolution mechanism with a high degree of party autonomy and great emphasis on due process, which does not correspond with the idea rooted in the right of clarification that a neutral arbitrator could intervene in the statements and debates of the parties to protect substantive justice.

In light of the above, there should be different standards in determining the justifiability of clarification in domestic arbitration and international arbitration, and this difference can be shown in the judicial review of the arbitral award. If the tribunal exercises the right of clarification in a domestic arbitration, in general, and subject to contradictory evidence, it should not be viewed as an unfair treatment of the parties by the tribunal, or constitute the ground for setting aside or nonenforcement of the arbitral award.

b   Arbitral Tribunal Can Conduct Mediation

In China, the mediation mechanism represented by court mediation and people mediation[16] is an important approach to settling disputes. In ancient China, mediation inside a court conducted by governments of all levels was also common.[17] As a less confrontational way to resolve conflicts, mediation corresponds with the pursuit of harmony in traditional ethics and the idea of the "Golden Mean" in Chinese culture. Therefore, mediation is essential in settling disputes and maintaining social stability. In this context, there is a model of tribunal mediation in the arbitration system in China

---

15. In *Qinghai Jiexiang Mining Investment Co., Ltd. v. Qinghai Fifth Geological and Mineral Exploration Institute* (2016) Qing 01 MT No. 9, the court held that in the arbitration, the tribunal didn't explain to the party that it has the right to separately bring an action regarding the same dispute after liquidation. It is a procedural flaw which violates the arbitration procedures under the *Arbitration Law*. Therefore, this arbitral award should be set aside. Nevertheless, there are different views in judicial practice regarding the right of clarification in arbitration. Some courts hold that clarification is a substantive issue within the discretion of the tribunal and should not be reviewed or constitute a ground for setting aside the arbitral award (*Beijing Honglin Pharmaceutical Co., Ltd. v. Shanghai Gaosheng Pharmaceutical Technology Co., Ltd.* (2016) Jing 02 MT No. 31).
16. For court mediation, *see* the Civil Procedure Law, Article 9 (2017). The main legal basis of people mediation is the People's Mediation Law of the People's Republic of China.
17. Fengrong Liang, "The Judicial Mediation Mechanism in Ancient China," 2001 (4) Journal of Henan University (Social Science) (2001) p. 73 at pp. 74-75.

which is similar to court mediation.[18] The rule of tribunal mediation is preserved in Article 68 of the 2021 Proposed Revisions to the Arbitration Law for Public Consultation ("Proposed Revisions") which also supplements that "mediation agreement and an arbitral award shall have equal legal effect." The model of tribunal mediation means that when both parties agree, the arbitrator(s) can serve as mediator(s). The arbitral tribunal can balance the interests of the parties beyond legal provisions, so as to provide better solutions for the parties and offer possibilities and space to realize the substantive justice of the case. If mediation is unsuccessful, the arbitral tribunal can resume its role as the neutral arbitrator(s) and continue to hear the case and render an arbitral award.

3 The Legal Framework of Arbitration in China Resembles Litigation Rules

There are a lot of mandatory provisions of arbitration procedure in the existing Arbitration Law and the Proposed Revisions, which show a resemblance to civil procedure law. Besides, the influences of litigation are also revealed in arbitration practices in China. In practice, arbitral tribunals rely heavily on written evidence rather than witness testimony and are extremely strict when reviewing the objectivity and authenticity of the witness testimony. In general, the tribunals rarely determine the facts simply based on witness testimony and as a result, lawyers would always provide a lot of supplementary evidence when submitting a testimony.[19] This is consistent with the traditions and practices of civil procedures in China but is very different from international arbitration practices which give value to witness testimony.

The reason that the Arbitration Law closely resembles litigation rules is related to its duty to regulate arbitration practice when it was formulated. As a matter of fact, the Arbitration Law was drafted in 1993, and prior to the revision of the Civil Procedure Law in 1991, there was no independent commercial arbitration in China. For a relatively long period of time, arbitration remained to be a preposition procedure for litigating economic contract disputes in court.[20] In such a context, it was the best option to start regulating independent arbitration procedures through legislation, and the litigation system can provide a clear guidance for arbitration practice in its beginning stage. Thus, this legislative approach is different from the common legislative practice of other countries which only sets out limited mandatory rules and provides the parties with larger space to choose their own rules.

18. Arbitration Law, Article 51 (2017).
19. Wei Sun, *Commercial Arbitration in China: Law and Practice*, 2nd edn (Law Press of China 2020) pp. 12-13.
20. Wei Jiang and Hao Li, "On the New Pattern of Interrelations Between People's Courts and Arbitration Organizations—For the Sake of the Promulgation and Coming into Force of the Arbitration Law," 1995 (4) Law Review (1995) p. 32 at pp. 33-34.

4   Arbitration Institutions Play an Important Role in Commercial Arbitration in China

a   Arbitration Institutions Largely Dominate the Arbitration Procedures

In China, it is for the arbitration institution instead of the arbitral tribunal to decide on the jurisdiction and the validity of the arbitration agreement. Article 20 of the current Arbitration Law does not mention the principle of competence-competence, and it is for the arbitration commission or the court to decide on jurisdiction. Besides, compared with the practices of major international arbitration institutions in the world, arbitration institutions and the secretary of the tribunal in China take a lot of responsibility on behalf of arbitral tribunals, such as notification and some management work. The China International Economic and Trade Arbitration Commission (CIETAC) Arbitration Rules (2015 edition) provide that after CIETAC accepts a case, the Arbitration Court shall designate a case manager to assist with the procedural administration of the case.[21] This kind of rule is also listed in the arbitration rules of the Beijing Arbitration Commission (BAC) and the Shanghai International Economic and Trade Arbitration Commission (SHIAC).[22]

b   Parties Could Only Appoint Arbitrators from the Panel of Arbitrators

With respect to the appointment of arbitrators, China currently stipulates that parties could only select and appoint arbitrators from the panel provided by the arbitration institution.[23] In consideration of the developing status of arbitration in China, this requirement is helpful to better guarantee the overall quality of arbitrators, enhance public trust in arbitration as a way to settle disputes and promote the development of the arbitration system in China. However, for international commercial arbitration in which the parties come from different countries worldwide, this requirement would seriously restrict the parties' choice of arbitrators and is thus seldom adopted.

In summary, the commercial arbitration system in China prioritizes the substantive justice of the case, emphasizes the function of mediation with Chinese characteristics, has a duty to stabilize the society, and largely resembles the litigation system.

III   INTERNATIONALIZATION OF COMMERCIAL ARBITRATION IN CHINA: REALISTIC BACKGROUND AND DEMANDS FOR REFORM

With China's growing participation in international investment and commercial cooperation, the related international disputes have been increasing every year. International commercial arbitration is one of the best approaches to resolve such disputes.

---

21. China International Economic and Trade Arbitration Commission, CIETAC Arbitration Rules, Article 13.4 (2015).
22. Beijing Arbitration Commission, BAC Arbitration Rules, Article 1.4 (2022) and Shanghai International Arbitration Center, SHIAC Arbitration Rules, Article 12.3 (2015).
23. Arbitration Law, Article 13 (2017).

With the continuous enhancement of comprehensive national strength, China's international arbitration is playing a bigger role in international commercial dispute resolution. Therefore, the necessity of strengthening relevant legislation on international commercial arbitration has become more and more prominent.

1   Economic Development and Legislative Support Nurturing the Development of International Commercial Arbitration

a   *Foreign Economic Growth Directly Leads to an Increase in International Commercial and Investment Dispute Cases*

According to the CIETAC 2021 Work Report, a significant increase of foreign elements can be seen in the cases it accepted, which involved 93 countries and regions with the parties coming from seventy-four countries and regions.[24] Likewise, the BAC 2021 Work Report shows that in 2021 BAC accepted 249 international commercial arbitration cases with a year-on-year growth of 15.81%, involving parties from twenty-five overseas countries or regions.[25] More and more international commercial disputes indicate that China has the potential to develop into an important jurisdiction for international commercial dispute resolution.

b   *Strengthening Legislation in the Foreign-Related Field and Improving Foreign-Related Rule of Law System Becomes a Reform Priority*

Economic globalization requires the support of advanced laws. Among them, legislation on dispute resolution is an indispensable part. The rule of law is a basic method of governance, an important factor in the core competitiveness of a country, and has increasingly become a great supporting force in international competition.[26] Adequate legislation on international arbitration will enhance a country's soft power in the legal system, increase its participation in international affairs, and constitute an important channel to take part in global governance.

2   Good Practice of International Commercial Arbitration in China Has Laid a Foundation for Further Reform

While China's international arbitration is flourishing, the arbitration institutions in China have been trying to adopt advanced international arbitration rules. Some of them

---

24. China International Economic and Trade Arbitration Commission, "CIETAC 2021 Work Report (Text Version)," available at http://www.cietac.org/index.php?m = Article&a = show&id = 1 8217 (last accessed February 15, 2022).
25. Beijing Arbitration Commission, "Beijing Arbitration Commission/Beijing International Arbitration Center Annual Report (2021)," available at http://www.bjac.org.cn/news/view?id = 4105 (last accessed April 12, 2022).
26. Jihong Mo and Ziwen Xu, "Providing Solid Legislative Guarantee for Foreign-related Rule of Law," *Guangming Daily*, April 1, 2022, p. 11.

have been widely applied in practice in many fields and achieved satisfactory effects, providing support for the reform and improvement of arbitration legislation.

a Shift from Mandatory List of Arbitrators to Recommended List of Arbitrators

As mentioned above, the Arbitration Law provides for the mandatory list of arbitrators for the selection or appointment of arbitrators. Nevertheless, some arbitration institutions such as CIETAC and BAC are relaxing such restrictions by allowing the parties concerned to select arbitrators outside the list in international commercial cases.

b Independence of Mediation

Independent mediation is stipulated in Article 40 of the BAC Arbitration Rules (2008), by which the parties may apply for mediation by mediators as per the Beijing Arbitration Commission Mediation Center Mediation Rules. This is a breakthrough in the framework of the Arbitration Law under which mediation is organized by the arbitral tribunal and is effective in reducing the parties' concerns about the mediation conducted by the arbitral tribunal in international commercial arbitration.

c Innovation of Arbitrators' Fees

According to the Operational Guidelines on Adopting the Hourly Rate for Arbitrators' Fees published by BAC on July 1, 2021, the parties may, prior to or after a dispute arises, jointly decide that the arbitrators' fees applicable to their dispute shall be calculated by hourly rates. This approach is quite common in international arbitration, but in China where arbitrators' fees are generally determined based on the sum in dispute, it is indeed an innovative move and a beneficial exploration.

d Introduction of Emergency Arbitrator System

In international commercial arbitration, to provide urgent temporary relief to the parties, major institutions have offered provisions for the parties to apply for interim protection measures and urgent relief prior to the constitution of the arbitral tribunal.[27] In order to be in line with international arbitration rules, some arbitration institutions in China have also established an emergency arbitrator system in their arbitration rules. For example, relevant provisions can be found in the China International Economic and Trade Arbitration Commission Emergency Arbitrator Procedure of CIETAC, Article 69 of the Shanghai Arbitration Commission Arbitration Rules (2018) of

---

27. Singapore International Arbitration Centre, SIAC Rules, Article 30 (2016); International Chamber of Commerce, ICC Arbitration Rules, Article 29 (2021); London Court of International Arbitration, LCIA Arbitration Rules, Article 9B (2020); Hong Kong International Arbitration Centre, HKIAC Administered Arbitration Rules, Article 23 (2018).

the Shanghai Arbitration Commission (SHAC), Article 63 of the 2022 Beijing Arbitration Commission Arbitration Rules, etc. Moreover, BAC accepted and heard the first case in Mainland of China that applied the emergency arbitrator procedure.[28]

e   Grant Arbitral Tribunal the Power to Order Interim Measures

It usually takes a longer time to complete international arbitration cases. To prevent transfer or hiding of properties by the parties to the arbitration before an arbitral award is made, which may frustrate the enforcement of the effective arbitral award rendered thereafter, arbitration rules of major international institutions usually provide that the arbitral tribunal may exercise discretion in granting interim measures it deems reasonable.[29] The current Civil Procedure Law and the Arbitration Law include no such provisions. However, some arbitration institutions have added relevant provisions in their arbitration rules, granting the arbitral tribunal the power to decide on interim measures, including Article 23 of the CIETAC Arbitration Rules (2015) and Article 62 of the BAC Arbitration Rules (2022).

f   Pilots and Exploration of Arbitrator Taking over Procedural Management

To improve transparency of arbitration proceedings and motivate the arbitrators to actively organize the case, BAC piloted the initiative of "transferring procedural management power from the institution to the tribunal" in 2021, under which the arbitrators are required to take over the management of the arbitration procedures, including service and transmission of documents, negotiation and decision on procedure matters, selection of the form of hearing (online or offline) and other aspects. These pilot actions are a breakthrough in the case management model widely applied in China, conducive to improving the arbitrators' capability to manage the procedures and to hear the cases.

g   Attempt at Optional Appellate Arbitration in International Arbitration

The finality of a single arbitral award is a basic principle of the commercial arbitration system of China. However, popular seats of arbitration in the world, such as Singapore,

---

28. Wei Sun, "First Emergency Arbitrator Proceeding in Mainland China: Reflections on How to Conduct an EA Proceeding from Procedural and Substantive Perspectives," (September 1, 2018) at http://arbitrationblog.kluwerarbitration.com/2018/09/01/first-ea-proceeding-mainland-china-reflections-conduct-ea-proceeding-procedural-substantive-perspectives/ (last accessed April 3, 2022).
29. Singapore International Arbitration Centre, SIAC Rules, Article 30 (2016); International Chamber of Commerce, ICC Arbitration Rules, Article 28 (2021); London Court of International Arbitration, LCIA Arbitration Rules, Article 25 (2020); Hong Kong International Arbitration Centre, HKIAC Administered Arbitration Rules, Article 23 (2018).

Hong Kong, the United Kingdom and the United States usually allow or don't prohibit the internal appellate system for arbitration.[30] In order to adapt to the differences between arbitration legislations in China and other jurisdictions, the Shenzhen Court of International Arbitration (SCIA) has introduced the optional appellate arbitration system into its arbitration rules, stipulating that unless prohibited by the laws of the seat of arbitration, where the parties have agreed on submitting to the SCIA for appellate arbitration in respect of the award rendered by the arbitral tribunal, their agreement shall prevail. This innovative optional appellate arbitration system of the SCIA has responded to the diverse demands of various market entities.

In conclusion, China's in-depth involvement in globalization generates realistic demands for internalization of commercial arbitration in China. This is a great opportunity for China to further participate in global governance and at the same time poses a challenge to the arbitration system of China. As a Chinese saying goes, a workman must first sharpen his tools if he is to do his work well. To become a leading jurisdiction for dispute resolution in the world, China needs to bring its arbitration law in line with international conventions.

IV   REALISTIC NECESSITY OF DUALISTIC LEGISLATION ON ARBITRATION

Adequate international arbitration regulations are undoubtedly a key factor for a country's commercial arbitration system to attract foreign parties to choose this country as the place for dispute resolution. As to whether domestic arbitration and international arbitration can be unified in an arbitration law, there are two opinions in academia, that is, the unified legislative model and the dualistic legislative model.[31] As is indicated by the name, the unified legislative model means a unified system and procedure for both domestic and international arbitration in an arbitration law, while the dualistic legislative model requires distinction in the forms of domestic arbitration legislation and international arbitration legislation. There are two approaches to make a distinction: first, a domestic arbitration law and an international arbitration law are formulated separately; second, the domestic arbitration provisions and international arbitration provisions are separately stipulated in arbitration law, each constituting an independent part.

Whether the unified legislative model is applicable to domestic arbitration and international arbitration depends on the compatibility of these two. In case of high compatibility, in terms of legislative technique, the arbitration law can include the international arbitration legislation as a separate chapter and set the special rules of application for international arbitration procedures in this chapter, leaving other matters subject to the provisions for domestic arbitration procedures. The Civil Procedure Law represents this legislative model, in which special provisions for civil

---

30. Hong Kong Arbitration Ordinance, Cap. 609 Article 73 (2011); Singapore Arbitration Act 2001, Articles 49, 50 (2020).
31. Panfeng Fu, "The Dualistic Model of French Commercial Arbitration Law and Its Value," (1) 2019 Chinese Review of International Law (2019) p. 86 at p. 86.

actions involving foreign elements are stipulated in Part Four and Article 266 therein provides "the provisions of this Part shall be applicable to civil proceedings within the territory of the People's Republic of China in regard to cases involving foreign elements. Where it is not covered by the provisions of this Part, other relevant provisions of this Law shall apply." Besides, the Arbitration Law currently in force is another example of the unified legislative model.

On the contrary, in case of fundamental differences between domestic and international arbitration legislation due to the many particularities of international arbitration procedures, it will be difficult for the specific provisions for domestic arbitration to apply to international arbitration. Legislators must comprehensively consider the proportion of special provisions for international arbitration and general provisions for domestic arbitration. When the proportion of special provisions is too high, it is advisable to separate domestic arbitration from international arbitration to ensure the scientific and reasonable arrangement and structure of the arbitration law.

On this basis, the author believes that the commercial arbitration legislation in China is different from the prevailing international commercial arbitration system in many aspects, and the two systems also differ in their legislative ideas. Therefore, the unified legislative model, where the provisions for international arbitration are stipulated separately in a chapter of the arbitration law, is not the best arrangement. Instead, the dualistic legislative model is more appropriate. The reasons are stated below.

1 Ad Hoc Arbitration Should Be Stipulated Only in International Arbitration Rules at the Current Stage

Currently, the Chinese domestic arbitration field does not have the institutional environment and development space for ad hoc arbitration.

First, the professional competence of arbitrators is insufficient. Ad hoc arbitration procedures require arbitrators to have a high level of professional ability to understand procedural rules and advance procedures. However, in the institutional arbitration practice over a long time, the secretary of the arbitration institution is responsible for taking care of and advancing arbitration procedures, so that most arbitrators lack the ability to directly deal with and solve the problems of arbitration procedures, and the ability to negotiate and communicate with the parties and to effectively organize and advance arbitration procedures. In ad hoc arbitration, all procedural problems will be resolved by the arbitral tribunal. If they are handled improperly, the arbitral award may be set aside, or face rejection in recognition and enforcement. It remains unclear whether the arbitral tribunal constituted by the parties themselves for ad hoc arbitration, without proper supervision, can recognize the importance of such problems and properly handle them. Retraining is needed for arbitrators who are to administer ad hoc arbitration, and even for those arbitrators who have accumulated a lot of practical experience in institutional arbitration. At least for now, the conditions in this respect are not met.[32]

---

32. Xiaohong Liu and Shuo Feng, "Three Points of View on the Amendment to the Arbitration Law—The Proposed Revisions to the PRC Arbitration Law for Public Consultation as

Second, the professional ethics and discipline of arbitrators are yet to be strengthened. Whether the ad hoc arbitration system is good or bad, and whether the arbitral award rendered through ad hoc arbitration can be voluntarily performed by the parties, is closely related to the arbitrators' professional qualities and ethics.[33] However, China now lacks a self-discipline mechanism for arbitrators, and the behavior of arbitrators has not been effectively regulated.[34] In ad hoc arbitration, the heteronomy mechanism in the form of supervision of the arbitration institution is also absent. Whether the arbitrators can adhere to professional ethics and discipline, and maintain independence and impartiality depends on their self-discipline. This is also a challenge for the arbitrators.

Last, independent arbitrators are to be cultivated. Independent arbitrators are full-time arbitrators, and it is a common occupation in international arbitration. However, in the arbitration practice in China, most arbitrators work part-time instead of full-time. Hence, the independent arbitrators are insufficient and therefore, the adjudicator required in ad hoc arbitration is not available.

To conclude, in view of the lack of the institutional environment and development space for ad hoc arbitration in China at present, and the leading role of institutional arbitration in domestic arbitration, a two-step approach should be more stable and appropriate: currently, the pilots of ad hoc arbitration system can be launched in international arbitration, while at the same time, a number of excellent arbitrators will be cultivated; after the system becomes mature, ad hoc arbitration can then be introduced into domestic arbitration.

2 Different Rules of Determining Jurisdiction Should Be Allowed in Domestic and International Arbitration

According to the rule of competence-competence as an international arbitration tradition, the validity of the arbitration agreement and the jurisdiction of the arbitral tribunal shall be decided by the arbitral tribunal itself rather than the arbitration institution or the court. However, the Arbitration Law currently in force has different provisions for jurisdiction. Article 20.1 therein provides that "if a party challenges the validity of the arbitration agreement, it may request the arbitration commission to make a decision or apply to the people's court for a ruling. If one party requests the arbitration commission to make a decision and the other party applies to the people's court for a ruling, the people's court shall give a ruling." As can be seen, under the Arbitration Law, the arbitral tribunal cannot decide its own jurisdiction, and the

---

Reference," 36 (5) Journal of Shanghai University of Political Science and Law (2021) p. 54 at p. 61.

33. Xianda Zhang, "Research on Establishment of Ad Hoc Arbitration in China," 46 (3) Journal of Shanghai Normal University (Philosophy and Social Sciences) (2017) p. 57 at p. 62.

34. Hu Li, "On Dynamic Integration of Administration of the Arbitration Institution and Independent Award of the Arbitral Tribunal," 2020 (1) Commercial Arbitration and Mediation (2020) p. 28 at p. 37; Xintong Zhang, Hui Jiang, "Localization Approach of Ad Hoc Arbitration from the Perspective of Party Autonomy," 37 (2) Journal of Guangxi Political Science and Law Institute (2022) p. 6 at p. 9.

jurisdiction shall be decided by the arbitration commission or the court, between which the court has a higher level of authority. Major adjustment thereto is made in the Proposed Revisions. Article 28 therein specifies that the arbitral tribunal shall have the right to review the jurisdiction on its own. This adjustment is meant to adapt to the arbitration procedures involving foreign elements stipulated in the Proposed Revisions since the arbitral tribunal has to decide on its jurisdiction on its own in ad hoc arbitration. The majority of international arbitration institutions have provided for competence-competence for arbitral tribunals.

In contrast, in Chinese domestic arbitration, granting arbitral tribunals the right to make decisions on jurisdiction is of little significance in the context that ad hoc arbitration has not been recognized and all cases are managed by arbitration institutions, and it may even cause unnecessary procedural delays. To be more specific, if the defendant challenges jurisdiction prior to the constitution of an arbitral tribunal, in strict compliance with the rule of competence-competence, such challenge cannot be resolved until the arbitral tribunal is constituted. However, since all domestic arbitration cases in China are administered by arbitration institutions, and these arbitration institutions have come to play an important role in arbitration after many years of practice, with their professionalism increasing year by year, it is a better option to allow the arbitration institutions to decide on jurisdiction, achieving both efficiency and fairness at the same time.

3   Arbitral Tribunals Should Differ in Granting Interim Measures in Domestic and International Arbitration

The Proposed Revisions provide specific provisions on interim measures in section III, Chapter IV. Although the provision improves the competence of arbitral tribunals in respect of interim measures, it fails to take into account the differences between domestic and international arbitration, and the possible resistance to its implementation should not be underestimated. Specifically speaking, since it is common practice in international commercial arbitration for arbitral tribunals to have the power to decide on interim measures and international arbitral tribunals and representatives are more familiar with such mechanism, this provision will be put into practice without hindrance in international arbitration. However, it may be premature to grant this power to arbitral tribunals in domestic arbitration procedures. The main considerations are twofold. First, the overall capability of Chinese arbitrators is yet to be improved. Second, arbitral tribunals need support from court enforcement measures to exercise their power of interim measures in many cases. A gradual adaptation process is what the courts need. First, judicial reform needs to be further advanced with sufficient personnel to support arbitral tribunals' interim measures. At present, Chinese courts follow a strict and cautious approach to taking conservatory measures. Many applications for preservation were not granted, thus failing to proceed to enforcement. If Chinese arbitral tribunals are able to grant interim measures, the caseload and enforcement difficulty will undoubtedly put enormous pressure on the judicial system, giving rise to procedural delays, which in turn will cause serious inconvenience to the parties to the arbitration. Second, courts in China need time to work with arbitration institutions step by step, so as to reach a consensus on what kind of interim measures can be enforced. Therefore, it is more prudent to take interim measures in different ways on the basis of respecting different development stages of international arbitration and domestic arbitration.

4   Procedural Rules Should Differ in the Level of Detail in Domestic and International Arbitration

As mentioned in the first part of this paper, both the Arbitration Law and the Proposed Revisions contain a good many mandatory provisions on arbitration procedures, showing a clear tendency of judicialization. Judicialized rules indicate rigorousness and meticulousness, but they also bring redundancy, which can have a negative impact on party autonomy. After years of practice, the tendency towards judicialization of Chinese arbitration has become a notion agreed upon by arbitral institutions and parties. However, the prevailing practice in international commercial arbitration is that the parties may choose the procedural rules to be applied in the arbitration. Not only can they choose the rules of the arbitral institution or other rules, but they can also make adjustments to the details of the applicable rules.[35]

Take oral hearings in arbitration as an example. The provisions concerning oral hearing procedures of the Arbitration Law are highly consistent with those of litigation in terms of procedures such as the notice of oral hearing, default, record of oral hearing, production and examination of evidence, defense, and appraisal. However, the UNCITRAL Model Law on International Commercial Arbitration (hereinafter referred to as the Model Law) contains only general provisions for oral hearings. For instance, Article 24 of the Model Law, though entitled "Hearings and Written Proceedings," only provides whether a case is to be heard in an oral hearing or in written forms without addressing the actual procedural rules of hearings. International arbitration is characterized by party autonomy and a high degree of procedural freedom and flexibility. As mentioned above, the Proposed Revisions still present a more litigious approach to arbitration procedures, which may hardly meet the expectations of the parties to international arbitration. In light of the provisions on arbitration procedures and the compulsion of rules, it would be practical and necessary to legislate separately for domestic and international arbitration, which have different needs.

5   Mediation by Arbitral Tribunals Should Only Be Provided for Domestic Arbitration

As mentioned in the first part, both the Arbitration Law and the Proposed Revisions include provisions that allow arbitral tribunals to act as mediators and conduct mediation during the arbitration. Influenced by the traditional culture and ideologies,

---

35. UNCITRAL, Model Law on International Commercial Arbitration ("Model Law"), Article 19 (2006).

the parties to disputes in China usually consider and accept that it is within the arbitrators' duty to invite or guide the parties to resolve their disputes through mediation.

However, mediation conducted by arbitrators is quite rare in international arbitration. The reasons are that the parties believe that: first, the experience of conducting the mediation may compromise the impartiality and independence of arbitrators.[36] Second, arbitrators who act as mediators may have private access to one of the parties, which undermines the due process of arbitration.[37] Third, the effectiveness of mediation may be limited because of the parties' concerns about the resumption of the arbitral process, which may prevent them from disclosing key information against them during the mediation. Fourth, the same arbitral tribunal which presides over the mediation may invite the pursuit of efficiency to the detriment of the realization of fairness. In addition, the mediation mechanism in China's commercial arbitration is suspected of giving excessive play to the discretionary power of arbitral tribunals, which may undermine party autonomy.[38]

It is apparent that the Chinese arbitrator mediation mechanism is underpinned by cultural and traditional factors. Although it is widely used and has achieved positive results in China, this mechanism may trigger challenges from the parties to international arbitration. And the resulting awards may also encounter obstacles to recognition and enforcement.[39]

6   The Power of Arbitral Tribunals to Investigate and Collect Evidence Is Inappropriate for International Arbitration Procedures

The Arbitration Law clearly gives arbitral tribunals the power to investigate and collect evidence.[40] Article 61 of the Proposed Revisions not only retains this provision but also adds in paragraph 2 that "the assistance of the people's court may be requested when necessary," which makes it more operable for arbitral tribunals to collect evidence on their own, helping tribunals to identify the merits of cases and make a fair and impartial judgment based on more sufficient information. What is more, courts in China also have the power to investigate and collect evidence in civil procedures. Therefore, it generally meets the reasonable expectations of the parties of cases in Chinese arbitration when arbitral tribunals investigate and collect evidence on their own initiative.

However, it is extremely rare for legislation and main procedural rules of major countries and global arbitration practice to allow arbitral tribunals to collect evidence on their own initiative. The Model Law only grants arbitral tribunals the power to

---

36. Article 67 of Chapter VIII "Special Provisions for International Commercial Arbitration" of the 2022 BAC Rules can be regarded as the response to this potential issue.
37. Shahla F. Ali, "The Legal Framework for Med-Arb Developments in China: Recent Cases, Institutional Rules and Opportunities," 10 Dispute Resolution International (2016) p. 119 at pp. 126-127.
38. Ruohan Zhu, "Chinese Model of the International Commercial Arb-Med-Arb: Challenge and Counter Measures," 25 (3) Journal of Xinyu University (2020) p. 53 at p. 56.
39. *Gao Haiyan v. Keeneye Holdings Ltd* [2012] 1 HKLRD 627.
40. Arbitration Law, Article 43 (2017).

determine the admissibility, relevance, materiality and weight of evidence submitted by the parties.[41] In practice, arbitral tribunals do not usually play an active role in evidence collection. Instead, they at most exercise the power to assist a party at its request in obtaining evidence in the possession of the other party. For example, "document production," common in international arbitration, is a typical procedure that reflects the auxiliary role of arbitral tribunals. Although this procedure involves the participation and order of arbitral tribunals, it is initiated at the request of one party with evidence owned by the other party, indicating the equal and adversarial relationship between the parties. The primary role of arbitral tribunals in exercising their powers is to provide assistance to the parties so that reasonable needs of evidence collection can be met. In other words, arbitral tribunals are not actively or directly involved in the process of evidence collection.

In international arbitration, arbitral tribunals' initiative to collect evidence may raise questions about its neutrality by the parties, for a meaningful item of evidence is always inevitably more favorable to one party in terms of its probative effect. Once tribunals choose to collect evidence on their own, it will be difficult for them to defend themselves in the face of challenges as to whether they have selectively favored one party. Furthermore, the evidence gathered by tribunals may naturally outweigh others in the arbitrators' minds, thereby undermining the validity of the parties' examination of evidence to the extent that it poses a potential threat to due process.

7   Rules Relating to Appraisal Are Inappropriate for International Arbitration Procedures

Paragraph 1, Article 44 of the Arbitration Law provides that "whereas an arbitration tribunal deems it necessary to have the specialized issues appraised, it may submit them to the appraisal department chosen by the parties to the agreement or to the appraisal department designated by the arbitration tribunal." Article 62 of the Proposed Revision follows this provision by giving arbitral tribunals the power to initiate the appraisal procedure on their own initiative. In China, arbitral tribunals can efficiently resolve disputes between the parties by taking the initiative to arrange for an appraisal institution or designate a specific appraiser to conduct the appraisal. However, the Chinese rules relating to the appraisal, a commonly used method of fact-finding in Chinese arbitration, are difficult to apply to international arbitration proceedings for the following reasons.

First, limited qualified appraisers make it difficult to meet the practical needs of various types of international arbitration cases. In Chinese arbitration, appraisal departments for common technical issues are chosen either from the list prepared by the arbitration institutions (if any) or from the appraisal list of relevant courts. In China, the range of selection barely meets the need for case handling. When it comes to international cases, the appraisal procedure prevailing in Chinese arbitration is hardly effective due to a number of factors, including the fact that Chinese may not be

---

41. Model Law, Article 19 (2006).

the working language in certain cases and that the relevant items to be appraised may not be in China. In international arbitration, the parties get used to appointing their own expert witnesses to provide advice on specialized issues. Arbitral tribunals will then vote for the most persuasive expert opinion provided by both sides. What is more, arbitral tribunals generally do not designate their own expert witnesses, mainly because they are not the primary providers of facts and evidence.

Second, arbitral tribunals in China enjoy absolute power to initiate the appraisal procedure, which is quite different from international arbitration procedures that value party autonomy. With respect to the handling of specialized issues, both Article 37 of the Arbitration Act 1996 of the UK and Article 27 of the Arbitration Act of Singapore provide that while arbitral tribunals may appoint one or more experts to report to them on specific issues to be determined, the parties may also exclude this power of the tribunals by agreement. In international arbitration, arbitral tribunals generally do not introduce expert witnesses on their own initiative, but rather leave it to the parties to respectively submit the appraisal opinions or hire expert witnesses. However, according to paragraph 1, Article 44 of the Chinese Arbitration Law, only arbitral tribunals may initiate the appraisal procedure if they consider that an appraisal is required on a specialized issue. Chinese rules of appraisal give arbitral tribunals the power to initiate the appraisal procedure without being bound by the parties, which may detract from the willingness of foreign parties to choose Chinese arbitration institutions or apply Chinese arbitration law for dispute resolution, leading to the detriment of the future development of the international arbitration system in China.

8   Only a Comprehensive Set of International Arbitration Legislation Can Provide the Necessary Rules to Support International Arbitration

The effective promotion of international commercial arbitration procedures depends on the support of a comprehensive international arbitration law at the seat of arbitration. China's current Arbitration Law and the Proposed Revisions do not provide sufficient supporting rules for international arbitration proceedings. Chapter VII of the Proposed Revisions, titled "Special Provisions for Arbitrations Involving Foreign Elements," contains only six articles, which are far from perfect and cannot effectively back up the practice of international arbitration. Some examples are as follows.

First, the Proposed Revisions do not provide for international arbitration in China that is directly administered by foreign arbitration institutions. For instance, it is unclear whether or not the Chinese Arbitration Law will be applied to international commercial arbitration procedures administered by the Singapore International Arbitration Centre (SIAC) when the seat of arbitration is in mainland China.

Second, the Proposed Revisions is silent on whether China will support arbitral tribunals' decisions on interim measures, emergency arbitrators, and other issues in international arbitration proceedings conducted in other jurisdictions.

Third, with respect to ad hoc arbitration, Article 92 of the Proposed Revisions deals with the necessary assistance of arbitration institutions and courts in ad hoc arbitration proceedings. However, the Article is too concise to be put into practice. For example, by what procedure should intermediate people's courts determine arbitration institutions? Should the parties be heard? In what form should the appointment be made? In these respects, Articles 9A and 9B of the International Arbitration Act (IAA) of Singapore provide detailed default rules for the arbitrator appointment of the parties and the appointing authority. Such articles, serving as necessary rules, offer much to learn.

In a nutshell, while the Proposed Revisions are making progress, Chapter VII "Special Provisions for Arbitrations Involving Foreign Elements" is not sufficiently detailed and does not take into full account the heterogeneity between international and domestic arbitration. The future revision and improvement of the arbitration law should meet higher standards with a more macroscopic grasp and a more far-reaching plan. The arbitration law should serve international arbitration, which not only includes arbitration conducted in China by Chinese arbitral institutions, but also arbitration conducted in China by foreign arbitral institutions or arbitral tribunals formed outside China, and the implementation of interim measures in China approved by foreign arbitration. Only when China's legislation and judiciary are more inclusive and friendly in this regard will it be possible for Chinese arbitration to truly integrate into international arbitration and for China to truly have its voice heard in international arbitration.

From all of the above, it is clear that international arbitration and domestic arbitration require distinctive rules, and it would be very difficult to accommodate the objective needs of both in just one law. Therefore, it would be more effective and desirable to legislate separately for domestic and international arbitration.

V   THE FEASIBILITY OF DUALISTIC LEGISLATION ON ARBITRATION

Considering the difficulty of satisfying the needs of arbitration development in China with one arbitration law, dualistic legislation on arbitration proves reasonable and feasible from the perspective of legislative theory and technique. Theoretically, the law should respond to practical needs. The different traditions and needs of Chinese and international arbitration make dualistic legislation theoretically sound. From the perspective of legislative technique and comparative law, there are precedents of dual arbitration legislation in foreign laws. The experience of France and Singapore, both of which have adopted a dualistic model of arbitration law, is worth learning from.

1   Dualistic Legislation Is Theoretically Justified

The advance of globalization leads international legislation to gradually become "converging." Take international commercial arbitration as an example. With the rapid development of international trade and investment and the deepening of economic globalization, "internationalization" has become a special factor to be considered by countries when formulating their own arbitration laws. Following the enactment of the

Model Law, more and more countries have incorporated the main elements of the Model Law into their domestic laws. There is a high degree of coordination among national arbitration legislation, with some countries in certain regions achieving uniformity in arbitration laws.[42]

However, globalization indicates a process towards pluralism by respecting differences around the world, rather than a process of unification or homogenization.[43] Political systems, economic development, cultural traditions, social customs, and religious beliefs vary greatly from country to country, so that it is impossible to have a one-size-fits-all law. Therefore, economic globalization may result in the convergence of laws, but convergence does not mean the uniformity of laws. Countries around the world need to preserve their own legal characteristics when dealing with domestic matters. When faced with international disputes, they are expected to incorporate internationally prevailing laws and customary rules. The two types of law can go hand in hand.

It follows that countries need to take into consideration the differences between local and international resources. If a legal system whose local characteristics are too distinctive and play a dominant role in domestic practice but is difficult to be accepted or adapted to by foreign participants, then a dualistic legislative model should be adopted. The model can be applied to the residents of the country and other countries respectively, which is more science-based than forcibly fusing the two systems into one law.

2 The Comparative Law Analysis of Singapore and France Shows That Dualistic Legislation Is Feasible and Beneficial

Countries that have adopted a dualistic legislative model for domestic and international arbitrations either have two separate parts in one arbitration law or have two arbitration laws.

The former is exemplified by France. The French Arbitration Law includes two parts, that is, the part of "Domestic Arbitration" and the part of "International Arbitration." Besides providing the article (Article 1506 of the French Code of Civil Procedure) to set out the specific provisions applicable to international arbitration in the "Domestic Arbitration" part, the law also provides independent chapters including the parts on "International Arbitration Agreement," "Arbitral Proceedings and Awards," "The Recognition and Enforcement of Arbitral Awards Made Abroad or in International Arbitration," and "Remedies" in the "International Arbitration."[44] In

---

42. Zhi Zhang, *The Liberalization, Internationalization and Nationalization of Arbitration Legislations: In Comparison with UNCITRAL Arbitration Model Law*, (China Social Sciences Press 2016) p. 41.
43. Kangzhi Zhang, "Cooperation and Harmony in the Course of Globalization," 33 (2) Journal of Minzu University of China (2006) p. 12 at p. 12.
44. Panfeng Fu, "Comparison on the Proposed Revision and the French Arbitration Law," available at http://iolaw.cssn.cn/bwsf/202108/t20210816_5353703.shtml (last accessed January 15, 2022).

general, international arbitration provisions are less intrusive on the freedom of the parties.

The latter is typified by Singapore. As one of the most preferred arbitration seats for parties to international commercial arbitration, Singapore attaches particular importance to the independence of international commercial arbitration. The IAA, enacted in 1994, established a dualistic legal mechanism for arbitration that distinguishes between domestic and international arbitration. The main reason for this legislative model is that Singaporean legislators, for one thing, were aware of the need for greater freedom in international arbitration; and for another, realized that the limited judicial intervention in international arbitration was not suitable for domestic arbitration.[45] Historically, Singapore's first arbitration law was enacted in 1953 and the legislative model of one uniform arbitration law was maintained until 1994. As Singapore law is heavily influenced by English law, this old arbitration law is characterized by a relatively strong judicial intervention in arbitration.[46] In 1991, the Review of Arbitration Laws Committee of the Singapore Law Reform Commission began a study of the Singaporean arbitration law legislation. In 1993, the Commission issued the Report on Review of Arbitration Laws, in which one of the main recommendations was the introduction of a dualistic legislative model for domestic and international arbitration. The Parliament of Singapore adopted the recommendation of the Commission and the dualistic model of Singapore's arbitration law was therefore formed.

In summary, arbitration laws in Singapore have a tradition of strong intervention. The change from "monistic" to "dualistic" arbitration law took place based on the increasingly distinct needs and differences between domestic and international arbitration. In fact, these factors are very much in line with the traditional and practical factors facing China today. The 1994 legislative reform of a dualistic model undoubtedly addressed and resolved the challenges of arbitration in Singapore, making it one of the world's leading arbitration seats today. The Singaporean legislative practice is a testament to the technical feasibility and implementation effectiveness of dualistic legislation and should be of particular relevance to China.

VI   CONCLUSION

The local characteristics of Chinese arbitration legislation and the need for internationalization of commercial arbitration in China together call for a dualistic legislative system. First, the adoption of separate legislation for Chinese and international arbitration will retain the provisions that are unique to China and have proven to be

---

45. Singapore Parliamentary Reports, Column 625 Vol. 63, on the sitting on October 31, 1994.
46. Lawrence GS Boo and Charles Lim, "Overview of the International Arbitration Act and Subsidiary Legislation in Singapore," 12 Journal of International Arbitration (1995) p. 75 at p. 75, available at https://kluwerlawonline.com/journalarticle/Journal + of + International + Arbitration/12.4/JOIA1995030 (last accessed April 12, 2022).

effective in practice at home, serving to address Chinese disputes and safeguard social stability. Second, dualistic legislation will prevent the system with strong Chinese characteristics from concerning foreign parties, providing sound legal and institutional support for China to become an international commercial arbitration center in the future.

CHAPTER 31

Arbitration in India: Quo Vadis?*

*Darius J. Khambata***

TABLE OF CONTENTS

I   INTRODUCTION

It was the challenge that free thought and reason posed to tradition, during the Age of Enlightenment that brought about the industrial and later the technological revolution.

---

* This chapter traces the trajectory of Indian arbitration during the last decade and attempts to project its future.

** Darius J. Khambata Senior Advocate, LLM (Harvard) practises before the Bombay High Court and the Supreme Court of India as well as other High Courts and Tribunals across India. He was previously the Advocate General of Maharashtra (2012 to 2014) and the Additional Solicitor General of India (2009 to 2012), both distinguished public offices. He has appeared in several important constitutional, corporate and commercial matters and in significant domestic and international commercial arbitrations. He is a member of the Singapore International Arbitration Centre's Court of Arbitration. He was a Vice President of the London Court of International Arbitration. He was also a member of the Law Commission of India's Committee that recommended substantial amendments to Indian arbitration law. He is a member of One Essex Court London and has his own chambers in Mumbai.

    The author is grateful to Mr. Karan Rukhana and Mr. Tushar Hathiramani both talented lawyers, for their valuable inputs.

Free enterprise not only of business but also of speech, art and expression brought with it a 'free trade in ideas'.[1] This in turn led to the emergence, globally, of democracy as the most powerful tool of governance and ultimately to the end of colonialism.

Indeed, arguably, the struggle for a democratic way of life and the ability to sustain economic growth are intertwined. Arbitration marks an individual's contractual choice of freedom from sovereign Courts and respect for the autonomy of the arbitrant to so contract.

Arbitration in India has ancient roots that go back to antiquity.[2] The first appearance of common law arbitration in India was colonial. Sir Elijah Impey's Bengal Regulations of 1772 required judges to prevail upon parties to submit their disputes to arbitration. More about that later.

However, the real emergence of arbitration in India as the preferred means of commercial dispute resolution came as a direct result of the liberalization and perestroika introduced in India, in 1991. That revolution of thought included a prescient vision that Indian Courts, overburdened as they were with massive social and administrative litigation, would not find the resources nor the time to resolve the expected exponential increase in commercial disputes. With a growing economy, inevitably comes growing commercial litigation.

Clearly, the Arbitration Act of 1940 too was not equipped to deal with this oncoming flood. As early as 1981, the Supreme Court had already lamented, somewhat graphically, the state of Indian arbitration, which it said '… made lawyers laugh and legal philosophers weep…'.[3]

It was the UNCITRAL Model Law that India looked at when it enacted its Arbitration & Conciliation Act of 1996 ('the Arbitration Act') in an attempt to sweep away cobwebs and bring fresh winds of change. The Arbitration Act was in large part, a replica of the UNCITRAL Model Law.

II   THE EARLY YEARS OF THE 1996 ACT: A TUMBLE DOWN THE RABBIT HOLE

But in India in common law tradition, legal change is driven not only by Parliament but also by the Supreme Court. With these twin engines, unfortunately also came a divergence of approach.

In the decade or so that followed the enactment of the Arbitration Act Indian arbitration was plagued by several ills, many brought about by the Supreme Court's interventionist approach. These were: (i) the intrusive judicial review of India-seated arbitration awards on a broad view of public policy which included even the vague and indeterminate 'patent illegality', where it went to the 'root of the matter' (a fetter that was undefined and allowed Courts to shift the goal posts from case to case) – *Saw Pipes*

---

1. An expression first used by Justice Oliver Wendell Holmes in his famous dissent in *Abrams v. U.S.* 250 U.S. 616, 630 (1919).
2. It finds mention in the Upanishads, ancient Hindu texts.
3. *Guru Nanak Foundation v. Rattan Singh and Sons*, (1981) 4 SCC 634, 636.

Ltd;[4] (ii) the extension of such review to permit a challenge in India to a foreign award[5] although India was not the seat but only the enforcing jurisdiction – *Venture Global,*[6] thus crossing the Rubicon set by the New York Convention;[7] (iii) a disregard of the principles of negative Kompetenz-Kompetenz, by excessive judicial determination of issues at the stage of appointment of arbitrators – *Patel Engineering;*[8] *Boghara Polyfab;*[9] (iv) arbitration agreements appointing as arbitrators, officers of Government companies/organizations who were parties, were standard and not seen as a violation of independence or impartiality; (v) interminable delays in arbitration proceedings; and (vi) an absence of effective Institutional arbitration.

This resulted in a flight of international commercial arbitration, from India to seats abroad primarily in London and Singapore. The new Arbitration Act of 1996, pro-enforcement and minimally interventionist in its tenor, was by judicial interpretation converted to a platform to 'do justice' by Courts and not by the parties' chosen forum, the arbitral tribunal.

Thus ensued the wonderland of Indian arbitration, reminiscent of the exchange between Alice and the Cheshire cat, who sat perched on the branch of an oak tree at a fork in the road.[10] When Alice asked the Cat which road she should take, he replied 'That depends on where you want to go.' Alice said, a trifle perplexed 'But I don't know where I want to go.' To which the Cat smugly retorted 'Then it doesn't matter, does it, which way you go?'

By 2012, like Alice, arbitration in India had not only lost its way but also its sense of purpose.

III THE SUPREME COURT CHARTS A COURSE: THE FORK IN THE ROAD

Between 2012 and 2015 the Supreme Court sought to re-direct arbitration law:[11]

---

4. *ONGC v. Saw Pipes Ltd* (2003) 5 SCC 705, paras 28, 31.
5. In this chapter, arbitrations seated outside India are referred to as 'foreign'. India-seated arbitrations are further divided into 'domestic' (both parties being Indian) or 'international commercial arbitration' (one party being foreign). Section 2(1)(f) of the Arbitration Act defines 'international commercial arbitration' as meaning an arbitration relating to disputes arising out of legal relationships, whether contractual or not, considered as commercial under the law in force in India and where at least one of the parties is: (i) an individual who is a national of, or habitually resident in, any country other than India; or (ii) a body corporate which is incorporated in any country other than India; or (iii) an association or a body of individuals whose central management and control is exercised in any country other than India; or (iv) the Government of a foreign country.
6. *Venture Global Engineering v. Satyam Computer Services Ltd* (2008) 4 SCC 190.
7. Convention on the Recognition and Enforcement of Foreign Arbitral Awards, 10 June 1958, 21 U.S.T. 2517, 330 U.N.T.S. 3 ['New York Convention'].
8. *SBP & Co v. Patel Engineering Ltd & Anr* (2005) 8 SCC 618.
9. *National Insurance Co Ltd v. Boghara Polyfab Pvt Ltd* (2009) 1 SCC 267.
10. With apologies to Lewis Carroll's 'Alice in Wonderland'.
11. In India, directional change in law, including that governing arbitration, comes not only from statutory amendment but also from the Supreme Court. India's Supreme Court uses its vast powers under the Constitution of India to make law. The Supreme Court has been described as the most powerful Court in the world in terms of the sweep and reach of its jurisdiction. The

First, in *BALCO*[12] by which it unequivocally made the seat of the arbitration its juridical fulcrum.[13] Consequently, if an Indian Court was merely an enforcing Court it had no jurisdiction to review a foreign award, much less to set it aside. *Venture Global* was overruled.[14]

Second, in *Shri Lal Mahal*[15] the longstanding narrow view of public policy for refusing enforcement of a foreign award was restored unequivocally holding that section 48 (corresponding to Article V (2)(b) of the New York Convention) did not permit a 'second look' at a foreign award akin to an appellate jurisdiction and that a mere error in a foreign award did not constitute a violation of 'public policy'.

Third, in *Western Geco International*[16] the Supreme Court introduced administrative law review of awards, as part of the fundamental policy of Indian law, which encompassed (a) the adoption of a judicial approach – one that was bona fide, fair, reasonable and objective and 'not actuated by any extraneous consideration'; (b) principles of natural justice; and (c) Perversity or irrationality in the Wednesbury sense.[17]

But was all this '*too little, too late*'? Regrettably, the Supreme Court did *not* make the one major directional correction that was imperative viz. to overrule or modify its intrusive review decision in *Saw Pipes*.[18] So the apparently narrow ground of 'public policy' available to challenge an India seated award remained considerably widened to

---

Supreme Court does not sit en banc but in benches of as little as two of its Judges. So a small group of Judges can direct or re-direct the arbitration orientation of India. This has indeed occurred in the past few years. Although the decision of a bench of equal or larger strength is binding on another bench it is not unusual for a bench disagreeing with the decision of a co-ordinate bench to refer the question to a larger bench for reconsideration. Hence change in the law by judicial interpretation is always a real possibility.

12. *Bharat Aluminium v. Kaiser Aluminium* (2012) 9 SCC 552.
13. In *BALCO* the Supreme Court held this law to apply only prospectively to arbitration agreements entered into after 6 September 2012 – the date of the *BALCO* judgment. This left uncovered a number of cases in the pipeline. In subsequent decisions the Supreme Court extended the seat doctrine even to pre 6 September 2012 arbitration agreements, fording the breach left by *BALCO*, by holding that choice of a foreign seat (even without choice of a foreign substance law) constituted an implied exclusion of Part 1 of the Arbitration Act. In *BGS SGS Soma JV v. NHPC Ltd.* (2020) 4 SCC 234 the Supreme Court extended the seat doctrine to even domestic arbitration to determine the jurisdiction of the appropriate Court to challenge the award.
14. *Supra* n. 6.
15. *Shri Lal Mahal v. Progetto Grano Spa* (2014) 2 SCC 433.
16. *ONGC v. Western Geco International* (2014) 9 SCC 263 paras 35, 38, 39.
17. *Id.*: Failure to adhere to these principles would render infirm an award as 'perverse or so irrational that no reasonable person would have arrived at [...] such an award'. *Associated Provincial Picture Houses Ltd. v. Wednesbury Corporation* (1947) 2 All ER 680 (CA). Reviewing a decision of a local authority, the Court of Appeal recognized that an executive authority must abide by certain principles while exercising discretion such as having regard to matters which the empowering statute considered relevant to the exercise of discretion. Conscious of the scope of review being narrower than if it were sitting in appeal, the Court discovered that 'the discretion must be exercised reasonably' and that if the authority did not consider matters it was bound in law to consider or considered matters which were irrelevant, then the authority could be said to be acting unreasonably.
18. *Supra* n. 4.

include a 'patent illegality' in the award. We had failed to lay the lessons of the past before us and had, to an extent, repeated our mistakes.

Perhaps a return to the Bengal Regulations of 1772 was called for: awards then could only be set aside for gross corruption or partiality of arbitrators.

IV   THE 2015 AMENDMENTS: ALICE CHOOSES HER PATH

In 2013, the Government of India commissioned recommendations for amendments to the Arbitration Act from the Law Commission of India. A Committee of the Law Commission, of which I was a member, made two reports in August 2014 and February 2015.[19] After the elections in May 2014, the Government of India had changed and it was to the credit of this new government that it fast-tracked the process of amendment to the Arbitration Act.

The stage was thus set for Parliamentary intervention. 23 October 2015 witnessed the birth of twins – a brand new Commercial Courts Act to streamline, expedite and invigorate the process of commercial litigation before Courts was enacted simultaneously with the 2015 Amendments to the Arbitration Act. The backbone of these amendments came from the Law Commission's Reports.

The purpose of the 2015 Amendments[20] shows that the Government had set its sights high. The 2015 Amendments were aimed at addressing the delays and hurdles in India in enforcing contracts. The Statement of Objects and Reasons made this plain, viz.:

> 4. As India has been ranked at 178 out of 189 nations in the world in contract enforcement, it is high time that urgent steps are taken to facilitate quick enforcement of contracts, easy recovery of monetary claims and award of just compensation for damages suffered and reduce the pendency of cases in courts and hasten the process of dispute resolution through arbitration, so as to encourage investment and economic activity.[21]

The 2015 amendments marked conceptual changes to the approach to arbitration in India:

> (i) The seat theory, recently embraced by the Supreme Court in *BALCO,* got statutory recognition. A proviso was added to Section 2(2) to make available two provisions of Part 1 (held by *BALCO* to apply only to domestic awards) even to foreign arbitrations viz Section 9 – (interlocutory reliefs from an Indian Court 'before, during and after' arbitration proceedings) and Section 27 – (the assistance of an Indian Court in gathering evidence).

---

19. Report No. 246 dated August 2014 viz. Amendment to the Arbitration and Conciliation Act 1996 is found at https://lawcommissionofindia.nic.in/reports/report246.pdf.

     The Supplementary to Report No. 246 on Amendments to the Arbitration and Conciliation Act, 1996 dated February 2015 is found at https://lawcommissionofindia.nic.in/reports/Supplementary_to_Report_No._246.pdf.
20. The Arbitration & Conciliation (Amendment) Act 2015.
21. The Arbitration and Conciliation (Amendment) Bill, 2015, Statement of Objects and Reasons, https://prsindia.org/files/bills_acts/bills_parliament/2015/Arbitration_and_Conciliation_bill,_2015_1.pdf.

(ii) Section 11(6A) confined the remit of a Court appointing an arbitrator, to determination of only the *existence* of the arbitration agreement. Negative Kompetenz-Kompetenz[22] was recognized. All issues, apart from existence, such as arbitrability, legality, rescission, settlement of the dispute were left to the arbitral tribunal which has positive Kompetenz-Kompetenz under Section 16(1). The 2019 amendments to the Arbitration Act propose a reversal of this positive change in that they delete Section 11(6). Fortunately however this particular amendment has not yet been notified to take effect.[23] Moreover the Supreme Court in *Vidya Drolia's* case has observed that even in the absence of Section 11(6A) the Court's approach under Section 11 should be prima facie and held that the Arbitral Tribunal had primary jurisdiction to decide questions of jurisdiction and non-arbitrability, at least on a first look basis.[24]

(iii) Negative Kompetenz-Kompetenz was buttressed by an amendment to Section 8. Section 8 mandates a judicial authority (including a Court) to refer the parties to arbitration, where the action brought before it was the subject of an arbitration agreement. The amendment required, for this process, the Court to have only a 'prima facie' look to see that no arbitration agreement existed.[25]

(iv) Section 12 incorporated the IBA Rules on Conflicts of Interest in International Arbitration into the Arbitration Act. Section 12(1) mandated the disclosure of Fifth Schedule (Orange List) circumstances (as giving rise to justifiable doubts as to independence or impartiality) and circumstances that are 'likely to affect' the ability of an arbitrator to devote sufficient time to and to complete the arbitration within 12 months. Section 12(5) disqualified a person from being appointed arbitrator, in respect of Seventh Schedule (Red List) relationships or subject matter and an additional circumstance viz:

'The arbitrator is an employee, consultant, advisor or has any other past or present business, relationship with a party.'[26]

---

22. The term negative Competence-Competence was first coined by Emmanuel Gaillard in his 'Convention d'arbitrage' in Juris Classeur: Droit International Fasc, 586-5 (1994) as matter of timing whereby arbitrators, as opposed to Courts, should be the first judges of their own jurisdiction and the Court's involvement is to be deferred to the stage of setting aside or enforcement of the arbitral award. Indian Courts have invoked the doctrine of Negative Kompetenz-Kompetenz. *ArcelorMittal Nippon Steel India Ltd v. Essar Bulk Terminal Limited* (2022) 1 SCC 712, paras 94 and 96; *Essar Bulk Terminal Ltd v. ArcelorMittal Nippon Steel India Ltd* (MANU / GJ / 0270 / 2022), paras 100, 119, 122-128.

23. Section 3 of the Arbitration and Conciliation (Amendment) Act, 2019.

24. *Vidya Drolia v. Durga Trading Corp.* (2021) 2 SCC1 paras 144-145, 153-154 holding that the 2015 Amendments had legislatively overruled *Patel Engineering* and that even repeal of section 11 (6A) could not revive the law laid down in *Patel Engineering.*

25. The Supreme Court had taken a similar view in *Shin Etsu Chemical Co Ltd v. Aksh Optifibre Ltd.*, (2005) 7 SCC 234, a case involving a foreign arbitration under section 45 akin to Article II(3) of the New York Convention. In *Vidya Drolia (supra)* the Supreme Court unequivocally applied the prima facie test in the context of India-seated arbitration as well holding that the Supreme Court's judgment in *Patel Engineering* (supra) had been legislatively overruled by the 2015 Amendments and it was the arbitral tribunal who must have the first shot at deciding not only arbitrability but also existence of the arbitration agreement (paras 154.3, 154.4).

26. Out went the invidious practice of 'employee-arbitrator' clauses being thrust upon private parties by Government organizations and companies!

            Section 12(5) permitted a written waiver of Seventh Schedule circumstances, but only after disputes had arisen.

(v) Section 17(2) gave the Arbitral Tribunal's interlocutory orders enforceability akin to orders of a Court;

(vi) Section 29A set a time limit on India seated arbitrations – one year extendable by a maximum of six months by consent; further extensions could be only by reasoned order of a Court. By the 2019 Amendment two further amendments were made to Section 29A: the first was to start the clock ticking only once the pleadings were complete; the second was to restrict the provision only to domestic India seated arbitrations between two Indian parties i.e. to exclude international commercial arbitrations from such strict time constraints.[27] These provisions have, despite initial skepticism, worked well. Arbitrations have moved faster and where required Courts have extended time swiftly and without fuss. Section 29A has to be viewed in the context of most arbitrations in India not being institutional and several taking an inordinate time for the award.

(vii) Procedural requirements[28] and a time limit[29] for disposal of challenge petitions by the court are added, but it is doubtful whether these can realistically be achieved given the burden of arrears existing in most courts.

By far the most profound change came in the form of the adoption of a dualistic approach to India-seated arbitrations by dichotomizing the scope of challenge under Section 34 thus:

(i) For international commercial arbitration awards the challenge was restricted to a narrow public policy review alone – thus equating it to the New York Convention international standard for enforcement of foreign awards. Explanations were added to both Section 34 (2) and Section 48(2) that declared that '...... an award is in conflict with the public policy of India only if

    – the making of the award was induced or affected by fraud or corruption or was in violation of Section 74 or Section 81;[30] or

    – it is in contravention with the fundamental policy of Indian law; or

    – it is in conflict with the most basic notions of morality or justice.'[31]

---

27. The Arbitration & Conciliation (Amendment) Act 2019 – https://egazette.nic.in/WriteReadData/2019/210414.pdf.

28. Section 34, Arbitration Act:

    [...]
    (5) An application under this section shall be filed by a party only after issuing a prior notice to the other party and such application shall be accompanied by an affidavit by the applicant endorsing compliance with the said requirement.

29. (6) An application under this section shall be disposed of expeditiously, and in any event, within a period of one year from the date on which the notice referred to in sub-section (5) is served upon other party.

30. Sections 74 and 81 protect the confidentiality of conciliation proceedings.

31. An expression adopted from *Parsons & Whittemore Overseas Co. Inc v. Societe Generale De L 'Industrie Du Papier & Bank of America* 508 F.2d 969 (US Court of Appeals, Second Circuit), 973-974 in which it was held: '[...] the Convention's public policy defense should be construed narrowly. Enforcement of foreign arbitral awards may be denied on this basis only where enforcement would violate the forum state's most basic notions of morality and justice'.

The wider public policy reviews of *Saw Pipes* and *Western Geco* were thus abolished.[32]

(ii) For domestic awards in addition to the narrow public policy review, Section 34 (2A) permitted review if there was 'patent illegality' appearing on the face of the award.[33] This statutorily recognized the 'patent illegality' challenge enunciated in *Saw Pipes* but restrained it with the *Champsey Bhara*[34] principle i.e. that a Court can review an error in a proposition of law on the face of the award. Even applying an administrative law test the judicially reviewable error would have to be self-evident.[35]

The second major direction signalled by the 2015 amendments was with regard to the unwarranted tendency of Courts to reassess the merits of the dispute if they disagreed with the result obtained before the tribunals:

(i) For domestic awards, a prohibiting proviso was added, viz. that an award should not be set aside 'merely on the ground of an erroneous application of the law or by re-appreciation of evidence.' The limits of the ground of 'patent

---

32. *HRD Corporation (Marcus Oil and Chemical Division) v. GAIL (India) Limited*, (2018) 12 SCC 471, para. 18. '[b]oth Sections 34 and 48 have been brought back to the position of law contained in Renusagar Power Plant Co. Ltd. v. General Electric Co., 1994 Supp (1) SCC 644, where public policy will now include only two of the three things set out therein, viz., fundamental policy of Indian law and "justice or morality"'. The ground relating to 'the interest of India' no longer obtains. 'Fundamental policy of Indian law' is now to be understood as laid down in Renusagar [Renusagar Power Co. Ltd. v. General Electric Co., 1994 Supp (1) SCC 644]. 'Justice or morality' has been tightened and is now to be understood as meaning only basic notions of justice and morality, i.e., such notions as would shock the conscience of the Court as understood in *Associate Builders v. DDA* [*Associate Builders v. DDA*, (2015) 3 SCC 49: (2015) 2 SCC (Civ) 204]. Section 28(3) has also been amended to bring it in line with the judgment of this Court in Associate Builders [*Associate Builders v. DDA*, (2015) 3 SCC 49: (2015) 2 SCC (Civ) 204], making it clear that the construction of the terms of the contract is primarily for the arbitrator to decide unless it is found that such a construction is not a possible one.

The Supreme Court concluded that '[t]hus, an award rendered in an international commercial arbitration – whether in India or abroad – is subject to the same tests qua setting aside under Section 34 or enforcement under Section 48, as the case may be'.

33. Section 34 (2A) – 'An arbitral award arising out of arbitrations other than international commercial arbitrations, may also be set aside by the Court, if the Court finds that the award is vitiated by patent illegality appearing on the face of the award:

Provided that an award shall not be set aside merely on the ground of an erroneous application of the law or by reappreciation of evidence.'

34. *Champsey Bhara & Co v. Jivraj Balloo Spinning and Weaving Co Ltd* AIR 1923 PC 66.

35. In *Batuk K. Vyas v. Salim M. Merchant*, AIR 1953 Bom 133 (DB) the Bombay High Court held, in the context of issuance of a Writ of Certiorari, that no error could be said to be apparent on the face of the record if it was not self-evident and if it required an examination or argument to establish it. In *Hari Vishnu Kamath v. Syed Ahmed Ishaque*, AIR 1955 SC 233, para. 23 the Supreme Court observed that this test might not be adequate in every case since what one judge may consider self-evident another might not. Nevertheless in *Surya Devi v. Ram Chander Rai* (2003) 6 SCC 675, para. 38(6) the Supreme Court held: 'A patent error is an error which is self evident i.e. which can be perceived or demonstrated without involving into any lengthy or complicated argument or a long drawn out process of reasoning. Where two inferences are reasonably possible and the subordinate court has chosen to take one view, the error cannot be called gross or patent.'

illegality' have, in the context of this proviso, been cogently and succinctly explained by the Supreme Court in its decision in *Delhi Metro*.[36]

(ii) Explanations were added to sections 34, 48 and 57 clarifying that to determine whether there was a contravention of the fundamental policy of Indian law 'shall not entail a review on the merits of the dispute'. The Explanations had been recommended by the Law Commission of India specifically for the purpose of neutralizing the *Western Geco* wider review.[37]

The 2019 Amendments to the Arbitration Act have now also introduced a modification to section 34 which confines challenges under section 34(2)(a) to those that the applicant 'establishes on the basis of the record of the arbitral tribunal'. This requirement substituted the previous language of 'furnishes proof that', and it is intended to keep challenges within the scope of the proceedings before the tribunal rather than allowing challenges based on facts and material outside the proceedings.

Summarizing the effect of the 2015 Amendments on the public policy exception, in *Ssangyong Engineering* the Supreme Court confirmed that the expanded view of 'fundamental policy of Indian law' adopted by the Court in *Western Geco* had been done away with.[38] However as considered below, *Ssangyong Engineering* at the same time expanded the concept of patent illegality.

---

36. In *Delhi Airport Metro Express Private Limited v. Delhi Metro Rail Corporation Limited* (2022) 1 SCC 131 para. 29 the Supreme Court held 'Patent illegality should be illegality which goes to the root of the matter. In other words, every error of law committed by the Arbitral Tribunal would not fall within the expression "patent illegality". Likewise, erroneous application of law cannot be categorised as patent illegality. In addition, contravention of law not linked to public policy or public interest is beyond the scope of the expression "patent illegality". What is prohibited is for Courts to reappreciate evidence to conclude that the award suffers from patent illegality appearing on the face of the award, as Courts do not sit in appeal against the arbitral award. The permissible grounds for interference with a domestic award under Section 34(2-A) on the ground of patent illegality is when the arbitrator takes a view which is not even a possible one, or interprets a clause in the contract in such a manner which no fair-minded or reasonable person would or if the arbitrator commits an error of jurisdiction by wandering outside the contract and dealing with matters not allotted to them. An arbitral award stating no reasons for its findings would make itself susceptible to challenge on this account. The conclusions of the arbitrator which are based on no evidence or have been arrived at by ignoring vital evidence are perverse and can be set aside on the ground of patent illegality. Also, consideration of documents which are not supplied to the other party is a facet of perversity falling within the expression "patent illegality".'

37. *See* the Supplementary to Report No. 246 of the Law Commission of India dated 6th February, 2015, available at, http://lawcommissionofindia.nic.in/reports/Supplementary_to_Report_No._246.pdf paras 10.3-10.5. '10.4 Such a power to review an award on merits is contrary to the object of the Act and international practice. As stated in the Statements of Objects and Reasons of the 1996 Act itself, one of the principal objects of that law was "minimalization of judicial intervention".

10.5 As the Supreme Court's judgment in Western Geco would expand the Court's power rather than minimize it, and given that is also contrary to international practice, a clarification needs to be incorporated to ensure that the term "fundamental policy of Indian law" is narrowly construed. If not, all amendments suggested by the Law Commission in relation to construction of the term "public policy" will be rendered nugatory, as the applicability of the Wednesbury principles to public policy will certainly open the floodgates.'

38. *Ssangyong Engineering v. National Highway Authority* (2019) 15 SCC 131, para. 28, at paras 34-42. The Supreme Court also held: (i) courts cannot interfere with the merits of an award under the expanded judicial approach exception; however, the award may be interfered with in

V   JUDGE-MADE LAW HAS ADVANCED ARBITRATION: ALICE FINDS HER WAY

1   Casting the Net Wide

The Supreme Court has bound non-signatory affiliates or companies within a group to arbitration agreements signed by only one of them utilizing the 'Group of Companies' doctrine. However, they would be bound provided the circumstances demonstrate that the mutual intention of all the parties was to bind even the non-signatory.[39] In *Chloro Controls*, the Supreme Court set down the four conditions to be satisfied to establish implied consent of the non-signatory, viz.: (i) there exists a direct relationship between the signatory party and the non-signatory; (ii) there exists a direct commonality of the subject matter; (iii) the agreement between the parties is in the nature of a composite transaction with a common object (such as an umbrella or mother agreement and ancillary agreements;) and performance of each of the agreements would not be possible without performance of the others; and (iv) where a composite reference would meet the ends of justice.[40]

The Supreme Court divided the legal bases for joinder of non-signatories into two categories, viz.: (i) theories of implied consent or discernible contractual intention to bind non-signatories such as third party beneficiaries, guarantors, assignees and the Group of Companies doctrine; and (ii) theories dependent on legal doctrines such as agency, apparent authority, piercing of the veil, joint venture relationships, succession and estoppel.[41]

The Supreme Court thus moved away from the formalistic requirement of explicit and signed assent to constructive consent.

In the *MTNL* case, the Supreme Court expanded the doctrine to bind non-signatory companies in a group which had a tight group structure with strong organizational and financial links constituting a single economic unit or reality.[42] The Supreme Court has also combined the Group of Companies doctrine with the alter ego doctrine, to lift the corporate veil in a case of fraud and to commit all the parties to a

---

case of violation of natural justice principles as provided under sections 18 and 34(2)(a)(iii) of the Arbitration Act; (ii) the position of the 'public policy' exception was relegated by the amendments to now mean that an award was against the fundamental policy of Indian law, only as held in *Renusagar*; (iii) the 'interest of *India*' ground recognized in Renusagar no longer obtained; (iv) the 'justice and morality' ground now meant the 'most basic notions of morality and justice'; (v) what a patent illegality was, remained as held in *Associate Builders*, a pre-2015 Amendment decision; and a mere erroneous application of the law did not qualify; (vi) patent illegality having to be on the face of the award, what was not subsumed within the 'fundamental policy of Indian law' *could* not be brought in 'by the backdoor' as patent illegality.

39. *Chloro Controls India Private Ltd v. Severn Trent Water Purification Inc* (2013) 1 SCC 641 paras 71 and 73-74; *Cox and Kings Ltd v. SAP* (2022) SCC Online 570 paras 24, 31, 76 and 82.
40. *Chloro Controls, id.*, paras 73-74.
41. *Id.*, para. 103.
42. *MTNL v. Canara Bank* 2019 SCC Online SC 995 para. 10.7; the Supreme Court at para. 10.4 doffed its hat to the origins of the doctrine in *Dow Chemical v. Isover-Saint-Gobain* 1984 Rev Arb 137.

common arbitration.[43] Indian law has thus got considerably ahead of the curve in applying the Group of companies doctrine. Not many jurisdictions have been receptive to the doctrine.[44,45]

The Supreme Court nevertheless recognizes the fundamental difference between the Group of Companies doctrine, which respects and recognizes the corporate veil of each entity of a group, and the alter ego or piercing the corporate veil doctrine, which disregards separate legal identity and utilizes a means of surmounting fraudulent activity by setting up a device to shield the non-signatory entity from arbitration.[46]

Recently however the Supreme Court[47] has questioned the unchecked expansion of the arbitration net to capture all non-signatory affiliates, in disregard of the separate corporate entity of the non-signatory, and of the statutory requirement that a person must claim 'through or under' the signatory party.[48] Six questions in all have been referred to a larger bench for consideration.[49] Even while referring to these questions the Supreme Court tightened the circumstances under which the doctrine could be invoked by (i) requiring a legal relationship between the non-signatory and the

---

43. *Ameet Lalchand Shah v. Rishabh Enterprises* (2018) 1 SCC 678 paras 14 and 24; *ONGC Ltd v. Discovery Enterprises Pvt Ltd & Ors* (27/4/2022).
44. Gary Born, *International Commercial Arbitration*, 3d edn. Vol. I., pp. 1565-1568.
45. English Courts have rejected it. *Peterson Farms Inc v. C & M Farming Ltd* (2004) EWHC 121.
46. A distinction enunciated in *Cheran Properties Ltd v. Kasturi and Sons Ltd* (2018) 16 SCC 413 at para. 28 citing Gary Born, *International Commercial Arbitration*, 2d edn. p.1432.
47. *Cox and Kings (supra)* paras 59 and 85.
48. Section 8(1) of the Arbitration Act provides: 'A judicial authority, before which an action is brought in a matter which is the subject of an arbitration agreement shall, if a party to the arbitration agreement or *any person claiming through or under him*, so applies not later than the date of submitting his first statement on the substance of the dispute, then, notwithstanding any judgment, decree or order of the Supreme Court or any Court, refer the parties to arbitration unless it finds that prima facie no valid arbitration agreement exists.' Section 45 of the Arbitration Act (equivalent to Article II(3) of the New York Convention) which 'Notwithstanding anything contained in Part I or in the Code of Civil Procedure, 1908 (5 of 1908),a judicial authority, when seized of an action in a matter in respect of which the parties have made an agreement referred to in section 44, shall, at the request of one of the parties *or any person claiming through or under him*, refer the parties to arbitration, 1 [unless it prima facie finds] that the said agreement is null and void, inoperative or incapable of being performed.' (Emphasis supplied).
49. *Cox and Kings (supra)* para. 55.

  a. Whether phrase 'claiming through or under' in Sections 8 and 11 could be interpreted to include 'Group of Companies' doctrine?
  b. Whether the 'Group of companies' doctrine as expounded by Chloro Control Case (supra) and subsequent judgments are valid in law?

Para. 104:

  A. Whether the Group of Companies Doctrine should be read into Section 8 of the Act or whether it can exist in Indian jurisprudence independent of any statutory provision?
  B. Whether the Group of Companies Doctrine should continue to be invoked on the basis of the principle of 'single economic reality'?
  C. Whether the Group of Companies Doctrine should be construed as a means of interpreting the implied consent or intent to arbitrate between the parties?
  D. Whether the principles of alter ego and/or piercing the corporate veil can alone justify pressing the Group of Companies Doctrine into operation even in the absence of implied consent?

signatory emanating from a contractual understanding;[50] (ii) emphasizing that the mere fact that the non-signatory was a member of a group of affiliated companies was not by itself sufficient;[51] and (iii) reiterating that the alter ego doctrine was distinct from the Group of Companies doctrine.[52]

The jury is thus still out as to the exact extent to which the Group of Companies doctrine will be applied. Moreover, the Supreme Court has also not examined the larger question as to whether the Group of Companies doctrine constitutes a full exception to the doctrine of privity and in effect also imposes a substantive liability upon the non-signatory party. Under Indian law, the doctrine of privity has otherwise been applied strictly.[53]

2   Pro-enforcement Bias for Foreign Awards

Foreign awards are now uniformly enforced indicating the growing pro-enforcement bias generally of Indian Courts.[54] After *Shri Lal Mahal* (supra), the Supreme Court reiterated its deferential position in two decisions[55] rejecting arguments that invited it to re-interpret contractual provisions, to re-assess the evidence or correct errors in the award. The grounds for refusing enforcement are even narrower than enunciated in the seminal decision in *Renusagar*,[56] which had held the field for enforcement of foreign awards until *Venture Global* (supra). In *Renusagar*, the Supreme Court had identified only three grounds on which enforcement could be refused, viz. (i) fundamental policy of Indian law (ii) the interests of India and (iii) justice or morality.[57] The Supreme Court had cautioned that public policy must be construed narrowly and must be something more than a violation of law.[58] The *Renusagar* position has been further narrowed by the 2015 Amendments.

Indeed, even in the seemingly aberrant decision in *NAFED*, the Supreme Court reiterated settled principles of enforceability and the distinction between mere illegality in the award and its being in conflict with public policy. A critique of this decision therefore is focused on (i) the length of time (thirty years!) it took for proceedings to

---

50. *Id.*, paras 24-25.
51. *Id.*, para. 50.
52. *Id.*, para. 90.
53. Section 19(a) and (b) of the Specific Relief Act – '19. Relief against parties and persons claiming under them by subsequent title. – Except as otherwise provided by this Chapter, specific performance of a contract may be enforced against –

> (a) either party thereto;
> (b) any other person claiming under him by a title arising subsequently to the contract, except a transferee for value who has paid his money in good faith and without notice of the original contract';

> *M.C. Chacko v. State Bank of Travancore*, (1969) 2 SCC 343 para. 9.
54. India was amongst the first countries to ratify the New York Convention.
55. *Vijay Karia v. Prysmian Sistemi* (2020) SCC Online SC 177; *Government of India v. Vedanta Limited* (2020) SCC Online SC 749.
56. *Renusagar Power Co Ltd v. General Electric Co*, 1994 Supp(1) SCC 644.
57. *Ibid.*, para. 66.
58. *Renusagar (supra)*, paras 65 and 66.

traverse the complex and slow Indian enforcement system and (ii) the ease with which the Supreme Court (without extensive reasons) refused enforcement of a 1989 FOSFA award which had enforced an export contract (albeit without mandatory Government permission) as being a contravention of the fundamental policy of Indian law.[59]

Part of the problem of enforcement in India lies in the nebulous content of the expression 'fundamental policy of Indian law'. The Supreme Court has attempted to narrow the term by defining it narrowly: '"Fundamental Policy" refers to the core values of India's public policy as a nation, which may find expression not only in statutes but also time-honoured, hallowed principles which are followed by the courts.'[60]

The Supreme Court has also alleviated the rigour of the requirement of filing the arbitration agreement with an application for enforcement of a foreign award holding section 47 to be directory and defects rectifiable even at a later stage of the enforcement proceedings in consonance with 'The object of the New York Convention ... (being) ... smooth and swift enforcement of foreign awards.'[61]

3 Emergency Arbitrators Recognized under Part I

The scheme of emergency arbitration provided for in institutional rules, usually allows the emergency award to operate till the Constitution of the tribunal and it may be confirmed, modified or set aside by it.[62] Part I only permits interim reliefs by a Court under section 9 or by an 'arbitral tribunal' under section 17. However, the term 'arbitral tribunal', under section 2(1)(d)[63] does not expressly include an 'Emergency Arbitrator'.

The recommendation of the Law Commission that the definition be amended to include an emergency arbitrator was not incorporated in the 2015 Amendments. In contrast, the Singapore International Arbitration Act and the Singapore Domestic Arbitration Act, grant legal status to an 'emergency arbitrator' by including it in the definition of the 'arbitral tribunal'. Likewise, the New Zealand Arbitration Act, 1996 includes an 'emergency arbitrator' within the definition of 'arbitral tribunal'. Part 3A and section 22B of the Hong Kong Arbitration Ordinance expressly provide that emergency relief provided under relevant arbitration rules 'is enforceable in the same manner as an order or direction of the Court that has the same effect, but only with the leave of the Court'.

---

59. *National Agricultural Cooperative Marketing Federation of India v. Alimenta SA* (2020) SCC Online SC 381.
60. *Prysmian (supra)* at para. 88.
61. *PEC Limited v. Austbulk Shipping SDN BHD* (2019) 11 SCC 620 paras 22-24.
62. Rule 10, Schedule 1 of the SIAC Rules; Article 9.11 of the LCIA Rules; Article 29(3) of the ICC Rules; Rule 43(8) of the Swiss Institute of Arbitration Rules, Rule 6, Appendix III of the China International Economic and Trade Arbitration Commission Arbitration Rules, 2015.
63. Section 2(1)(d) '"arbitral tribunal" means a sole arbitrator or a panel of arbitrators'.

The Supreme Court in *Amazon*[64] has now held that the definition of 'arbitral tribunal' contained in section 2(1)(d) applied 'unless the context otherwise requires'. The Supreme Court relied on the definition of 'arbitration' contained in section 2(1)(a)[65] and in sections 2(6), 2(8) and 19(2) of the Arbitration Act which recognized party autonomy to hold that where India-seated arbitration proceedings were administered, under institutional rules providing for emergency arbitrations, an emergency arbitrator's award is the order of the 'arbitral tribunal' under section 17 and directly enforceable on its own as an order of a Court.

The Supreme Court's judgment in *Amazon* does not however apply to a foreign seated arbitration. In such cases the party seeking enforcement, of a foreign interim/emergency award has two choices, both for indirect enforcement of such award: (i) to file a suit before a Civil Court seeking enforcement of such award, or (ii) to file a section 9 Petition before the Court on the strength of such award.[66]

4   Court's Review of Kompetenz-Kompetenz Decisions

Section 16(1) of the Arbitration Act, gives statutory recognition to full positive Kompetenz-Kompetenz.[67] The timing, and arguably the scope of the challenge to such jurisdictional determination depends on whether jurisdiction is refused or accepted.

Where jurisdiction is refused

Section 37 (2) (a) of the Arbitration Act provides for an 'appeal' from an order of the arbitral tribunal accepting the jurisdictional objection. The general connotation of an 'appeal' is a proceeding which subjects the facts as well as the law applied by the inferior court or tribunal to a review and retrial in which the superior court has the power to reverse, confirm, annul or modify the order of the inferior court or tribunal.[68] The Calcutta High Court assumed section 37(2)(a) to be such a general appeal requiring a full review over a section 16 jurisdictional order.[69]

---

64. *Amazon.com NV Investment Holdings LLC v. Future Retail Limited & Ors* (2022) 1 SCC 209, paras 11, 14, 17, 23, 24, 30, 40 and 46. The matter concerned an Emergency Award under the SIAC Rules.
65. 'any arbitration whether or not administered by permanent arbitral institution'.
66. *Raffles Design International Pvt. Ltd v. Educomp Professional Education Ltd & Ors* 2016 SCC Online Del 5521, paras 104, 105; *Ashwani Minda and Jay Ushin Ltd v. U-Shin Ltd* 2020 SCC Online Del 721 – the Delhi High Court did not permit a 'second bite at the cherry' in a section 9 application when an application for interlocutory orders had been rejected by the Emergency Arbitrator.
67. Section 16 (1) provides:

> '(1) The arbitral tribunal may rule on its own jurisdiction, including ruling on any objections with respect to the existence or validity of the arbitration agreement, and for that purpose, – (a) an arbitration clause which forms part of a contract shall be treated as an agreement independent of the other terms of the contract; and
> (b) a decision by the arbitral tribunal that the contract is null and void shall not entail ipso jure the invalidity of the arbitration clause.'

68. *Tirupati Balaji Developers P. Ltd & Ors v. State of Bihar* (2004) 5 SCC 1, paras 9 and 10.
69. *Sarkar & Sarkar v. State of West Bengal* (2007) 2 Arb LR 396 (DB). para. 1:

But the Supreme Court[70] has applied the 'fundamental policy of Indian law' test under section 37 against a tribunal's interlocutory order under section 17. Similarly, the Delhi High Court has held that a section 37 appeal is not a regular appeal under civil procedure.[71] Yet an important distinction must be borne in mind: a section 17 order is discretionary and passed in the exercise of jurisdiction, whereas a section 16 order is a determination as to whether jurisdiction exists at all.

In a subsequent decision, the Delhi High Court adopted a nuanced approach when it held that while there was no proscription of appellate powers under section 37, in exercise of such powers a Court would have to bear in mind the underlying object of the Act viz. minimal court interference in the arbitral proceedings.[72]

Where jurisdiction is upheld

Where the tribunal rejects the objection and assumes jurisdiction, section 16(5) requires it to decide the dispute on merits. The jurisdictional determination is amenable to challenge only under section 34 which prescribes specific and limited grounds on which a Court may set aside an arbitral award and such review is not an 'appeal'.[73] A Court exercising powers under section 34 of the Arbitration Act is not empowered to modify or revise the award of the arbitral tribunal nor to review the merits of the award.[74]

The Bombay High Court first affirmed a de novo determination approach over questions of jurisdiction,[75] but in appeal overruled that decision equating jurisdictional challenges to the limited review of awards.[76] In doing so, the appellate court, strangely,

---

Now the task of this Court is to examine whether such ruling of the learned Arbitrator under section 16 regarding the existence of the arbitration agreement factually and legally and further arbitrability of the subject matter is right or wrong in this appellate jurisdiction. We are not unmindful of our power under section 37 of the Act. Unlike under section 34 read with section 37 our jurisdiction as a first Appellate Court is not a restricted one. Therefore, it is open for us to consider all aspects of the matter meaning thereby we can examine as to whether interpretation given by the learned Arbitrator of a clause is correct or not.

State of West Bengal v. Sarkar & Sarkar (2018) 12 SCC 736 – in its affirming order, the Supreme Court did not render any findings on the scope of section 37.

70. *National Highways Authority of India v. Gwalior Jhansi Expressway Limited* (2018) 8 SCC 243, paras 21, 22 and 24.
71. *Dinesh Gupta & Ors v. Anand Gupta & Ors* MANU / DE / 1727/ 2020 The Delhi High Court relied on the judgment of the Supreme Court in *Snehadeep Structures P Ltd v. Maharashtra Small Scale Industries Development Corporation Ltd* – (2010) 3 SCC 34.
72. *Edelweiss Asset Reconstruction Company Ltd v. GTL Infrastructure Ltd & Ors* MANU / DE / 2072 / 2020.
73. *Maharashtra State Electricity Distribution Co. Ltd. v. Datar Switchgear Ltd* (2018) 3 SCC 133 para. 51.
74. *Project Director, National Highways No. 45E and 220 National Highways Authority of India v. M Hakeem & Anr* – 2021 SCC Online SC 473, paras 23, 24 and 42.
75. *M3Nergy Sdn Bhd v. Hindustan Petroleum Corporation Ltd* (2018) SCC Online Bom 19461.
76. *Hindustan Petroleum Corporation Ltd v. M3Nergy Sdn Bhd* (2019) SCC Online Bom 2915, para. 21.

placed reliance on the decision of the UK Supreme Court in *Dallah Real Estate*,[77] a decision that gave the 'last word' on jurisdiction to the Courts after a de novo adjudication. The court might have instead looked to the *First Options* decision of the US Supreme Court which applied the same narrow standard of review of an award on arbitrability to that adopted while reviewing an award on merits since there was 'clear and unmistakable evidence' that the parties had agreed to submit the arbitrability question to arbitration.[78] Section 10 of the Federal Arbitration Act (FAA) allows only a limited review on specified narrow grounds.[79]

While the degree of judicial review over gateway disputes[80] is yet to be conclusively determined by the Supreme Court, its decision in *Vidya Drolia*[81] suggests a fuller review under section 34 by limiting negative Kompetenz-Kompetenz to affording priority, rather than finality, to a tribunal's jurisdictional determination:

> Thus, the competence-competence principle, in its negative effect, leaves the door open for the parties to challenge the findings of the Arbitral Tribunal on the three issues. The negative effect does not provide absolute authority, but only a priority to the Arbitral Tribunal to rule the jurisdiction on the three issues. The courts have a 'second look' on the three aspects under Section 34 of the Arbitration Act. [The nature and extent of power of judicial review under Section 34 has not been examined and answered in this reference.][82]

The Supreme Court's characterization of a section 34 review of 'gateway disputes' as a 'second look' sounds like the paradigm for a de novo determination. Indeed the Court expressly held that 'The court has been conferred power of "second look" on aspects of non-arbitrability post the award in terms of sub-clauses (*i*), (*ii*) or (*iv*) of

---

77. *Dallah Real Estate and Tourism Holding Co. v. Ministry of Religious Affairs, Government of Pakistan* 2010 UK SC 46 paras 86, 96, 104 and 160. The correctness of the Division Bench's reliance on *Dallah Real Estate* may be questioned. The UK Supreme Court in *Dallah* concluded that an arbitral tribunal's Kompetenz-Kompetenz was not absolute and did not bar judicial review and that an arbitral tribunal's decision as to the existence of its own jurisdiction did not bind a party who had not submitted the question of arbitrability to the tribunal. The Supreme Court held, based on the provisions of section 67 of the UK Arbitration Act 1996 that the 'last word' as to an arbitral tribunal's jurisdiction would lie with the Court and that the Courts would re-examine for themselves, by way of an independent investigation the jurisdiction of an arbitral tribunal. In *A v. B* (2010) EWHC 3302 para. 25, where the Court held that 'a challenge such as is made under Section 67 is indeed a complete re-hearing [rather than limited review]'. The UK Supreme Court in *Enka Insaat Ve Sanayi a.s. v. OOO 'Insurance Company Chubb' & Ors* (2020) UK SC 38, reemphasized the *Dallah* position with greater vigour stating that the Court '53. must necessarily interrogate the substantive jurisdiction of the arbitral tribunal (or the putative or potential tribunal if none has been or is intended to be appointed) in determining whether the foreign proceedings are a breach of the agreement to arbitrate the dispute in question ... .'
78. *First Options of Chicago Inc v. Kaplan* 514 U.S. 938 (1995); US Courts use the expression 'arbitrability' compendiously to involve even questions as to the existence and validity of the arbitration agreement. This sometimes contuses the issue.
79. *Bayer Corp Science AG v. Dow AgroSciences LLC* 680 Fed. App. 985 (Fed Cir. 1 March 2017).
80. Vis-à-vis procedural issues regarding jurisdiction, Indian law seems to follow US Law. The Supreme Court in *IFFCO v. Bhadra Products* – (2018) 2 SCC 534 has held that an objection as to admissibility of the claim on the grounds of limitation was a question to be determined by the arbitral tribunal.
81. *Vidya Drolia & Ors v. Durga Trading Corporation* (2021) 2 SCC 1.
82. *Id.*, para. 131.

Section 34(2)(a) or sub-clause (i) of Section 34(2)(b) of the Arbitration Act.'[83] Adopting a contrary approach could be anomalous given that when appointing arbitrators under section 11, the issue of the existence of the arbitration agreement is to be determined finally by the Court rather than left to the appointed tribunal.[84]

A de novo approach on jurisdictional decisions is not uncommon as 'courts in [other] Model Law jurisdictions have generally adopted a de novo standard for jurisdictional issues in proceedings under Article 16(3) and 34(2)(a)(i), at least insofar as issues of law (distinguished from fact) are concerned'.[85]

5   Party Autonomy

Party autonomy, described as 'the brooding and guiding spirit in arbitration', was extended by the Supreme Court in upholding the right of two Indian nationals (one of whom was habitually resident outside India) to have their disputes arbitrated at a foreign seat[86] and to choose a foreign law not only as the law governing the arbitration agreement and the curial law but also as the substantive law, barring only a case of circumvention of law.[87] The Court found section 44[88] to be party neutral and not requiring one of the parties to be foreign.[89]

VI   SPEED BREAKERS AHEAD: WILL HUMPTY DUMPTY TAKE A GREAT FALL?

The 2015 Amendments take the fork in the road. Yet there are potential speed breakers ahead.

1   Perversity and Irrationality: A Trojan Horse

The recognition of 'perversity' and 'irrationality' (concepts borrowed from administrative law) as grounds for challenge of awards coupled with the 'working test' of perversity applied by the Supreme Court[90] risks a merit-based review. The 'working

---

83. *Id.*, para. 154.3.
84. *National Insurance Company Limited v. Boghara Polyfab Private Limited* – (2009) 1 SCC 267, followed in various subsequent judgments of the Supreme Court. Section 11(6A) which confined a Court's determination, at the stage of appointment of arbitrators, to only examination of the existence of an arbitration agreement was sought to be deleted by the 2019 Amendments but this amendment has not yet been notified for effect.
85. Gary Born, *International Commercial Arbitration*, 3d edn, p. 3472.
86. *Pasi Wind Solutions Private Limited v. GE Power Conversion India Private Limited* (2021) 7 SCC 1 paras 78, 88 and 91.
87. *Id.*, paras 81, 86, 88 and 89; However it is not clear whether this ratio applies to two Indian nationals who are both resident in India.
88. Corresponding to Article I(1) of the New York Convention.
89. *Pasi Wind Solutions* (*supra*) paras 49-50.
90. *Associate Builders* (*supra*) para. 31; *Delhi Airport Metro Express Pvt Ltd. v. Delhi Metro Rail Corporation Ltd* (2022) 1 SCC 131 paras 28 and 29.

test' is to see if the award: (i) ignored vital evidence; (ii) contains a finding that is based on no evidence; or (iii) considers something irrelevant to the decision.

The working test requires a Court to decide whether evidence was 'vital' and ignored or 'irrelevant' and considered. This necessarily requires an appraisal of the evidence and a review of the validity of the decision of the arbitrator, not just of the decision-making process. In its definition of 'perversity' and 'irrationality' the Supreme Court in *Associate Builders* qualified these grounds as having to be unreasonable in the Wednesbury sense.[91] Despite noticing that section 34(2)(a) did not permit a merit-based review,[92] that an arbitrator was master of the appraisal of the evidence and that a challenge to an award was not an appeal to correct errors of fact,[93] *Associate Builders* nevertheless affirmed the *Western Geco* expansion into perversity and Wednesbury unreasonableness.

Thus, administrative law principles of judicial review have been imported into the Arbitration Act which otherwise strictly restricts judicial interference with arbitration.[94] The Supreme Court had previously recognized the inherent character of arbitration as a contractual mechanism created by parties when it unequivocally held that orders (and also presumably awards) by an Arbitral Tribunal would not be capable of being corrected by prerogative writs under Articles 226 and 227 of the Constitution of India, available to correct executive action.[95]

---

91. Viz. 'a decision which is perverse or so irrational that no reasonable person would have arrived at … .' *Associate Builders* (*supra*) para. 31.

92. *Associate Builders* (*supra*) para. 17: '17. It will be seen that none of the grounds contained in sub-section (2)(a) of Section 34 deal with the merits of the decision rendered by an arbitral award. It is only when we come to the award being in conflict with the public policy of India that the merits of an arbitral award are to be looked into under certain specified circumstances.'

93. *Id.*, para. 33.

94. Section 5 of the 1996 Arbitration Act provides: 'Notwithstanding anything contained in any other law for the time being in force, in matters governed by this Part, no judicial authority shall intervene except where so provided in this Part' – a reproduction of Article 5 of the UNCITRAL Model law. Moreover in *Associate Builders* (*supra*), the Supreme Court cautioned that a Court hearing a challenge of a domestic award, did not act as a Court of Appeal, could not correct errors of facts, must allow a 'possible view' on the facts by the arbitration to pass muster as 'the arbitrator is the ultimate master of the quantity and quality of evidence to be relied upon ... and would not set aside an award only because it was based on little evidence or on evidence which did not measure up in quality to a trained legal mind'.

95. *SBP & Co v. Patel Eng. Ltd.* (2005) 8 SCC 618. A bench of seven judges. The Supreme Court at para. 45 held:

> 45. It is seen that some High Courts have proceeded on the basis that any order passed by an Arbitral Tribunal during arbitration, would be capable of being challenged under Article 226 or 227 of the Constitution. We see no warrant for such an approach. Section 37 makes certain orders of the Arbitral Tribunal appealable. Under Section 34, the aggrieved party has an avenue for ventilating its grievances against the award including any in-between orders that might have been passed by the Arbitral Tribunal acting under Section 16 of the Act. The party aggrieved by any order of the Arbitral Tribunal, unless has a right of appeal under Section 37 of the Act, has to wait until the award is passed by the Tribunal. This appears to be the scheme of the Act. The Arbitral Tribunal is, after all, a creature of a contract between the parties, the arbitration agreement, even though, if the occasion arises, the Chief Justice may constitute it based on the contract between the parties. But that would not alter the status of the Arbitral Tribunal. It will still be a forum chosen by the parties by agreement. We, therefore, disapprove of the

The extension of a rule of administrative law to challenge awards is fundamentally flawed. The tendency to judge the validity of arbitral actions by administrative law standards is however not new. The Supreme Court in *K.P. Poulouse*, a decision under the Arbitration Act 1940, had held the arbitrator to have misconducted himself as his award '[ignored] the very material documents which throw abundant light on the controversy to help a just and fair decision'.[96] The Supreme Court ultimately memorialized the application of Wednesbury principles via perversity, in *Western Geco* as a facet of violation of the fundamental policy of India.

It is the constitutional duty of the judiciary to review administrative action since it involves elements of public law and because conferment of discretionary power upon the executive is subject to its being exercised reasonably and fairly. In comparison, an arbitration most often does not involve any element of public law and is a private dispute resolution mechanism built on consensus and party autonomy.[97]

The essential difference between an administrative tribunal and an arbitrator was best captured by Lord Denning in *Northumberland Compensation Appeal Tribunal*: '[t]he Court of King's Bench never interfered by certiorari with the award of an arbitrator because it was a private tribunal and not subject to the prerogative writs'.[98] This distinction was later also premised by Lord Justice Steyn on the limitations upon review of arbitral awards placed by statute in *Secretary of State for the Environment*[99] where he held:

> The power to review a finding of fact of a tribunal on the ground that there is no evidence to support it, and that there is therefore an error of law, is a useful one in certain areas of the law, notably in the administrative law field. But in the limitation appellate jurisdiction of the Court under s1 of the Arbitration Act 1979 this concept has no useful role to play. It is inconsistent with the filtering system for the granting of leave to appeal which was created by the Arbitration Act 1979.

---

stand adopted by some of the High Courts that any order passed by the Arbitral Tribunal is capable of being corrected by the High Court under Article 226 or 227 of the Constitution. Such an intervention by the High Courts is not permissible.

96. *K.P. Poulouse v. State of Kerala* (1975) 2 SCC 236 para. 6. Indian courts occasionally resorted to this approach *Sathyanarayana Bros. (P) Ltd. v. T.N. Water Supply & Drainage Board* (2004) 5 SCC 314, paras 15, 16 (a material document was not called for by the arbitrator. It was held that the award was vitiated); *Bharat Coking Coal Ltd. v. Annapurna Constructions* (2003) 8 SCC 154, para. 40 (a failure by the arbitrator to consider relevant material and clauses of the contract results in a misdirection in law).
97. The essence of arbitration is a contract between two or more parties to have a private tribunal conclusively adjudicate their disputes and differences. Classically defined, arbitration is 'a private procedure established by agreement [...]'. *See* Lord Frazer in *Amalgamated Metal Corp. v. Khoon Seng Co.* (1977) 2 Lloyds Reports 310, 317. In *Ahmad Baravati v. Josepthal, Lyon & Ross Inc*, 28F 3d 704, 709 (1994), the US Court of Appeals (7th Circuit) held that the freedom to stipulate the dispute resolution procedure can be near absolute 'short of authorizing trial by battle or ordeal or, more doubtfully, by a panel of three monkeys'. The working group that drafted the Model Law observed that 'probably the most important principle on which the Model Law should be based is the freedom of the parties in order to facilitate the proper functioning of international commercial arbitrations according to their expectations'. *See* UN Doc A/CN.9/207, para. 17.
98. *R v. Northumberland Compensation Appeal Tribunal* (1952) All ER 122.
99. *Secretary of State for the Environment v. Reed International plc* (1974) 1 EGLR 22 at 24.

In *Sui Southern Gas Co.*, the Singapore High Court rejected an invitation to apply 'Wednesbury unreasonableness' on the basis that Wednesbury principles applied to decisions of authorities who exercised discretion bestowed upon them by Parliament which expected them to exercise it reasonably.[100] Differentiating arbitration the Court held that, '[t]his presumption of rationality, however, finds no purchase in the context of private arbitrations, where parties have contractually agreed to abide by the decision of the arbitral tribunal'.[101]

The attempt by the 2015 Amendments to surmount *Western Geco* was partially neutralized by the Supreme Court in *Ssangyong*. The Supreme Court held that although '*perversity*' was no longer available as a ground under the public policy head it would amount to a 'patent illegality' under section 34(2A). Thus, perversity in the Wednesbury sense remains available to challenge domestic arbitration awards (i.e., entirely between Indian parties) in India-seated arbitrations.[102] It is puzzling how the fact-based 'perversity and irrationality' or Wednesbury unreasonableness can qualify as patent illegality.

A Pandora's box may have been opened at least for domestic awards. Perversity and irrationality have, after 2015, been invoked to set aside an award by substitution of the courts' preferred interpretation of a contract for that of the arbitral tribunal, on the premise that the tribunal ignored a 'basic rule' of interpretation, viz. that the contract should be read as a whole, and that this constituted 'perversity' in interpretation.[103] The Bombay High Court[104] set aside an award on the ground of perversity, relying on *Associate Builders*. The Court was careful however to steer well clear of re-appreciation of evidence and to base its decision only on the challenge to certain critical findings of the tribunal that were analysed by the Court to have no evidentiary support at all. But will every Court withstand the temptation of substituting its justice for that of the arbitral forum?

The Supreme Court has sounded welcome alarm bells in a recent decision observing:

> There is a disturbing tendency of Courts setting aside arbitral awards, after dissecting and reassessing factual aspects of the cases to come to a conclusion that the award needs intervention and thereafter, dubbing the award to be vitiated by either perversity or patent illegality, apart from the other grounds available for annulment of the award. This approach would lead to corrosion of the object of the

---

100. *Sui Southern Gas Co. Ltd v. Habibullah Coastal Power Co. (Pte) Ltd* (2010) 3 SLR 1, 7.
101. *Id.*
102. *Ssangyong (supra)*, para. 41.
103. *South East Asia Marine Engineering & Constructions v. Oil India Ltd.* (2020) SCC Online SC 451, paras 34, 37-79; *see also Patel Engineering v. NEEPCO*, 2020 SCC Online SC 466; a contrary, and it is submitted better approach, was taken by the Supreme Court in *Indian Oil Corporation Ltd v. Shree Ganesh Petroleum Rajgurunagar* (2022) SCC Online SC 131 paras 45-46, by refusing to set aside an award for an error in interpretation holding that where there was a valid reference, this would, only be an error within jurisdiction.
104. *Board of Control for Cricket in India v. Deccan Chronicle Holdings Ltd.* 2021 SCC Online Bom 834.

1996 Act and the endeavours made to preserve this object, which is minimal judicial interference with arbitral awards.[105]

There are solutions available. First, the Supreme Court may consider restricting the meaning of 'perversity' to a finding based on no evidence at all, rather than the administrative law 'working test'.[106] Second, it may help to adopt the approach of the Supreme Court in a case concerning enforcement of a foreign award, in which the court qualified the 'otherwise unable to present his case' ground by requiring that to be in respect of something that went to the root of the case or resulted in a denial of justice.[107]

These qualifications, in addition to 'the face of the award' requirement of section 34 (2A), might prevent the *perversity and irrationality* ground from turning into another Saw Pipes 'public policy' catch-all.

2 Enforceability of Investment Treaty Awards in India

India has had a tumultuous relationship with investment arbitration, beginning with *White Industries*.[108] Since then, India has found itself to be the respondent State in 16 investment treaty arbitrations.[109] This led to a two-fold response by the Government of India. First, the termination of 58 Bilateral Investment Treaties (BITs) by the Government of India in September 2018. *Second*, adoption in 2020 of a new Model BIT with provisions intended to reduce the exposure of the Indian Government to treaty claims. The 2020 Model BIT, still provides for arbitration as a means of dispute resolution but the remedy is couched with conditions.[110]

---

105. *Delhi Airport Metro Express Private Limited v. Delhi Metro Rail Corporation Limited* (2022) 1 SCC 131 para. 28.
106. The Supreme Court has held a perverse finding to be one based on no evidence or one that no reasonable person would arrive at *Rajinder Kumar Kindra v. Delhi Administration* AIR 1984 SC 1805 para. 4 specifically referring to an arbitration; *Triveni Rubber & Plastics v. CCE* 1994 Supp 3 SCC 665 at para. 3. If there is some evidence on record which is acceptable and could be relied on, the conclusions would not be treated as perverse: *Kuldeep Singh v. Commissioner of Police & Ors* AIR 1999 SC 677 para. 10.
107. *Vijay Karia v. Prysmian Cavi. E Sistemi SRL & Ors.* (2020) SCC Online 177, para. 84.
108. *White Industries Australia v. Republic of India*, UNCITRAL Final Award, 30 November 2011. A case in which the tribunal incorporated (into the India-Australia BIT) the 'Effective Means' clause from the India-Kuwait BIT on the basis that the 'Most Favoured Nation' clause in the India-Australia BIT allowed it to cherry pick clauses from other BITs. Then ignoring the qualifications to that clause ('in accordance with its applicable laws and regulations') it awarded damages for delays in enforcement by Indian Courts. The 'applicable laws' viz. Indian law would not have permitted the award of such damages.
109. https://investmentpolicy.unctad.org/investment-dispute-settlement/country/96/india/investor.
110. Clause 15.5: In the event that the disputing parties cannot settle the dispute amicably, a disputing investor may submit a claim to arbitration pursuant to this Treaty, but only if the following additional conditions are satisfied:

    (i) not more than six (6) years have elapsed from the date on which the disputing investor first acquired, or should have first acquired, knowledge of the measure in question and knowledge that the disputing investor with respect to its investment, had incurred loss or damage as a result; or
    (ii) where applicable, not more than twelve (12) months have elapsed from the conclusion of domestic proceedings pursuant to 15.1.

Fast-track direct enforceability of BIT awards without scrutiny of the national court is unavailable. India is not a party to the International Centre for Settlement of Investment Disputes Convention ['ICSID Convention']. Hence parties cannot take recourse to Article 54(1).[111] Indian statute does not provide automatic enforcement of ICSID or investment treaty arbitration awards.[112] Consequently, the only recourse for enforcement of investment awards in India is through the New York Convention.

India signed the New York Convention with the 'commercial' reservation allowed under Article 1(3).[113] Yet a New York Convention award is enforceable under

---

(iii) the disputing investor or the locally established enterprise have waived their right to initiate or continue before any administrative tribunal or court under the law of any Party, or other dispute settlement procedures, any proceedings with respect to the measure of the Defending Party that is alleged to be a breach referred to in Article 13.2.

(iv) where the claim submitted by the disputing investor is for loss or damage to an interest in an enterprise of the other Party that is a juridical person that the disputing investor owns or controls, that enterprise has waived its right to initiate or continue before any administrative tribunal or court under the law of any Party, or other dispute settlement procedures, any proceedings with respect to the measure of the Defending Party that is alleged to be a breach referred to in Article 13.2.

(v) At least 90 days before submitting any claim to arbitration, the disputing investor has transmitted to the Defending Party a written notice of its intention to submit the claim to arbitration ('notice of arbitration'). The notice of arbitration shall:

    a. attach the notice of dispute and the record of its transmission to the Defending Party with the details thereof;

    b. provide the consent to arbitration by the disputing investor, or where applicable, by the locally established enterprise, in accordance with the procedures set out in this Treaty;

    c. provide the waiver as required under Article 15.5 (iii) or (iv), as applicable; provided that a waiver from the enterprise under Article 15.5 (iii) or (iv) shall not be required only where the Defending Party has deprived the disputing investor of control of an enterprise;

    d. specify the name of the arbitrator appointed by the disputing investor.

111. Article 54(1) of the ICSID Convention provides, '(1) Each Contracting State shall recognize an award rendered pursuant to this Convention as binding and enforce the pecuniary obligations imposed by that award within its territories as if it were a final judgment of a court in that State. A Contracting State with a federal constitution may enforce such an award in or through its federal courts and may provide that such courts shall treat the award as if it were a final judgment of the courts of a constituent state.'

112. Section 44-A of the Code of Civil Procedure, 1908 (CPC) which enables automatic execution of foreign decrees covers only decrees of a superior Court of a reciprocating territory, and not awards of a tribunal.

113. 'Any State may ... declare that it will apply the Convention only to differences arising out of legal relationships whether contractual or not, which are considered as commercial under the national law of the State making such declaration'. The 'commercial' reservation was added following a suggestion from the Dutch delegation. They were of the opinion that the inclusion of the reservation would allow countries which differentiated between civil and commercial law, to sign the convention. *Travaux préparatoires*, United Nations Conference on International Commercial Arbitration, Summary Record of the Twenty-third Meeting, E/CONF.26/SR.23, pp. 7, 12, available at https://undocs.org/E/CONF.26/SR.23; also *see* Albert Jan van den Berg, *The New York Convention of 1958: An Overview* https://cdn.arbitration-icca.org/s3fs-public/document/media_document/media012125884227980new_york_convention_of_1958_overvi ew.pdf. ('This reservation was inserted because at the New York Conference of 1958 it was believed that, without this clause, it would be impossible for certain Civil Law countries, which distinguish between commercial and non-commercial transactions, to adhere to the Convention.')

Part II of the Arbitration Act. Section 44 defines a foreign award as 'an arbitral award on differences between persons arising out of legal relationships, whether contractual or not, considered as commercial under the law in force in India…'. Like the New York Convention, the Arbitration Act does not define the term 'commercial'. One must look elsewhere to invest that term with meaning.

Section 2(1)(c) of the Commercial Courts Act, 2015 enumerated disputes arising from a variety of enumerated transactions related to commerce, as 'commercial disputes'.[114] The second explanation to section 2(1)(c) clarified that 'A commercial dispute shall not cease to be a commercial dispute merely because

(a) …
(b) one of the contracting parties is the State or any of its agencies or instrumentalities, or a private body carrying out public functions';

Commenting on section 2(1)(c) the Calcutta High Court[115] observed, '[t]he term commercial dispute is of wide import. It brings within its compass any dispute connected with the commercial world'. Drawing light from the Explanation to section 2(1)(c), a relationship could be considered commercial, despite the State or one of its agencies being one of the contracting parties. Viewed so, the provision would support treating investment awards as 'commercial' within the meaning of section 44.

---

114. '2(c) "commercial dispute" means a dispute arising out of –

  (i) ordinary transactions of merchants, bankers, financiers and traders such as those relating to mercantile documents, including enforcement and interpretation of such documents;
  (ii) export or import of merchandise or services;
  (iii) issues relating to admiralty and maritime law;
  (iv) transactions relating to aircraft, aircraft engines, aircraft equipment and helicopters, including sales, leasing and financing of the same;
  (v) carriage of goods;
  (vi) construction and infrastructure contracts, including tenders;
  (vii) agreements relating to immovable property used exclusively in trade or commerce;
  (viii) franchising agreements;
  (ix) distribution and licensing agreements;
  (x) management and consultancy agreements;
  (xi) joint venture agreements;
  (xii) shareholders agreements;
  (xiii) subscription and investment agreements pertaining to the services industry including outsourcing services and financial services;
  (xiv) mercantile agency and mercantile usage;
  (xv) partnership agreements;
  (xvi) technology development agreements;
  (xvii) intellectual property rights relating to registered and unregistered trademarks, copyright, patent, design, domain names, geographical indications and semiconductor integrated circuits;
  (xviii) agreements for sale of goods or provision of services;
  (xix) exploitation of oil and gas reserves or other natural resources including electromagnetic spectrum;
  (xx) insurance and re-insurance;
  (xxi) contracts of agency relating to any of the above; and
  (xxii) such other commercial disputes as may be notified by the Central Government.'

115. *Swadha Builders Pvt. Ltd v. Bhattacharjee* 2021 SCC Online Cal 35, para. 7.

Unfortunately, the Delhi High Court has held to the contrary in *Vodafone*.[116] Rejecting Vodafone's objections, the Court held that national courts had jurisdiction over matters of BIT arbitrations, and, in support, it relied on, amongst others India's refusal to accede to the ICSID Convention.[117] The Court held that an arbitration agreement between an investor and a State was not a species of treaty but a contract and involved '... a contractual obligation and a contractual right'.[118] Nevertheless, the Court held that a BIT award was neither an international commercial arbitration award governed by the Arbitration Act nor a domestic arbitration award.[119] It held that BIT awards were not governed by Part II of the Arbitration Act as that Part only covered commercial contracts.[120] *Vodafone* was followed by the Delhi High Court in *Khaitan Holdings*.[121]

The Delhi High Court has plainly got it wrong. It did not notice the wider meaning of the term 'commercial' under the Commercial Courts Act nor the broad meaning that the Supreme Court had given to the term 'commercial' in the context of enforcement of a foreign award viz.:

> While construing the expression 'commercial'" in Section 2 of the Act it has to be borne in mind that the Act is calculated and designed to subserve the cause of facilitating international trade and promotion thereof by providing for speedy settlement of disputes arising in such trade through arbitration and any expression or phrase occurring therein should receive, consistent with its literal and grammatical sense, a liberal construction.
>
> The expression 'commercial' should, therefore, be construed broadly having regard to the manifold activities which are integral part of international trade today.[122]

---

116. *Union of India v. Vodafone Group* 2018 SCC Online Del 8842 at para. 6 Aggrieved by India's retrospective tax imposed on the Vodafone Group's Indian company, Vodafone's Dutch subsidiary initiated an investment arbitration under the India-Netherlands BIT and Vodafone. Group Plc initiated an investment arbitration under the India-United Kingdom BIT. This initiation of parallel BIT arbitrations led India to file a civil suit before the Delhi High Court seeking a stay of the arbitration commenced under the India-United Kingdom BIT. Vodafone challenged the jurisdiction of the Delhi High Court. It argued that national courts did not have jurisdiction to interpret or enforce provisions of BITs entered into by two sovereigns.
117. *Id.*, para. 78.
118. *Id.*, para. 83.
119. *Id.*, para. 89; Despite it having held (at para. 83) that the agreement to arbitrate disputes between an investor and a State was not a species of treaty but involves 'a contractual obligation and a contractual right'.
120. *Id.*, para. 90.
121. *Union of India v. Khaitan Holdings* 2019 SCC Online Del 6755 para. 29.
122. *RM Investment & Trading Co. Pvt. Ltd. v. Boeing Co* (1994) 4 SCC 541 para. 12 followed in *Harendra Mehta v. Mukesh Mehta*, (1999) 5 SCC 108, paras 18-21. Section 2 of the Foreign Awards (Recognition and Enforcement) Act, 1961 provided: 'In this Act, unless the context otherwise requires, "foreign award" means an award on differences between persons arising out of legal relationships, whether contractual or not, considered as commercial under the law in force in India, made on or after the 11th day of October, 1960 – (a) in pursuance of an agreement in writing for arbitration to which the Convention set forth in the Schedule applies; and (b) in one of such territories as the Central Government being satisfied that reciprocal provisions have been made, may, by notification in the official Gazette, declare to be territories to which the said Convention applies.' The Arbitration Act repealed this Act, instead providing for enforcement of foreign awards in Part II.

It is almost impossible to say that Investor-State disputes are not an integral part of international trade today. Article 27.5 of the 2020 Model BIT now expressly declares claims under it to be commercial for the purposes of the New York Convention.[123] The problem arises in cases of awards resulting from claims under earlier BITs following the previous 2003 Model BIT that did not include such a provision. There is thus an urgent need for clarity on the position of law qua enforceability of extant investment Tribunal awards in India, perhaps adopting the US approach.

The US too signed the New York Convention with the commercial reservation. US courts have however consistently given an expansive meaning to the term 'commercial' under the New York Convention.[124] The position of US Courts on the *commercial* reservation is 'as long as a dispute arises from a commercial relationship, it is subject to arbitration, and any foreign award rendered in that arbitration is subject to enforcement under the Convention'.[125] Any doubts as to the commercial nature of a relationship are resolved in favour of enforceability under the New York Convention.[126]

Granting easy enforceability to BIT awards would positively contrast India with China. China has expressly excluded 'disputes between foreign investors and the host government' from the legal relationships considered commercial for the purpose of its accession to the New York Convention.[127]

3 The Arbitration Council of India

The 2019 Amendment seeks controversial changes to the Arbitration Act such as establishing an Arbitration Council of India (Part 1-A) and imposition of 'qualifications'

---

123. Article 27.5 of 2020 Model BIT: 'A claim that is submitted to arbitration under this Article shall be considered to arise out of a commercial relationship or transaction for purposes of Article I of the New York Convention.'
124. *Diag Human v. Czech Rep. – Ministry of Health* 824 F.3d 131 (D.C. Cir. 31 May 2016); *BCB Holdings Ltd. v. Gov't of Belize* 110 F. Supp. 3d 233, 242-243 (D.D. Cir. 24 June 2015), affirmed in *BCB Holdings Ltd. v. Gov't of Belize*, 650 Fed. Appx. 17, 18 (D.C. Cir. 13 May 2016); *Citizens Bank v. Alafabco, Inc* 396 F.3d 1289 (1298 11th Circuit 2005); The US Supreme Court in *Citizens Bank v. Alafabco, Inc.* held 'We have interpreted the term ["commercial"] in the FAA as the functional equivalent of the more familiar term "affecting commerce" – words of art that ordinarily signal the broadest permissible exercise of Congress' Commerce Clause power.' 539 US 52, 56 (2003).
125. H. Kronke et al., *The New York Convention: Recognition and Enforcement of Foreign Arbitral Awards*, p. 35.
126. Gary BORN, *International Commercial Arbitration*, vol. I., p. 327 *citing Mitsubishi Motors Corp. v. Soler Chrysler-Plymouth*, 473 US 614.
127. Chinese Supreme Court, Notice on the Implementation of China's Accession to the Convention on the Recognition and Enforcement of Foreign Awards (22 April 1987) available at https://cicc.court.gov.cn/html/1/219/199/411/698.html 'Legal relationships, whether contractual or not, which are considered commercial means the economic rights and obligations arising from contracts, torts or relevant legal provisions, such as purchase and sale of goods, lease of property, project contracting, processing, technology transfer, equity or contractual joint adventure, exploration and development of natural resources, insurance, credit, labor service, agency, consultation service, marine, civil aviation, railway or road passenger and cargo transportation, product liability, environment pollution, marine accident, and ownership disputes, except disputes between foreign investors and the host government.'

for arbitrators, in a proposed 8th Schedule, many of which are impractical and unattainable. On 4 November 2020, an Ordinance deleted the provisions of the 8th Schedule, although ominously section 43J still provides for 'qualification, experience and norms' as may be specified by regulations. None have been prescribed as yet.

The proposed Arbitration Council will be composed of members to be appointed by the Government of India. Section 43D prescribes manifold functions for it which purport to be policy-making in nature. But this section also confers the Council with powers to frame policies for grading of arbitral institutions and arbitrators and to frame norms 'to ensure satisfactory level of arbitration and conciliation'.

The Arbitration Council is a potential regulator in sheep's clothing and would be an intrusion on party autonomy. Part I-A has not yet been notified to have effect.

4   Lack of Institutionalized Arbitration

Historically, India-seated arbitrations have been ad hoc.[128] Institutional arbitration is a rarity. For example, the venerable International Centre for Alternate Dispute Resolution (ICADR), a statutory and government-controlled arbitration centre in India has the unenviable record of having administered only forty-nine arbitrations in the entire twenty-one years of its existence.[129]

In recent years, however, several modern arbitral institutions have been formed or rejuvenated.[130] These institutions have modern structures and up-to-date rules that facilitate speedy and efficient arbitration. Some of them have been set up on the international model with a board that manages and a court that guides them. Nevertheless, the vast majority of domestic arbitrations in India remain ad hoc due to the legacy of existing arbitration agreements, the reluctance of parties and courts to appoint institutions to run the arbitration and a common misconception that institutional arbitration means greater expense.

The benefits of institutional arbitration are not as well appreciated as they should be, viz. quicker appointments of arbitrators, better selection of Presiding Arbitrators (including specialized arbitrators), monitoring and supervising the conduct of the arbitration with some control on arbitral fees, and other benefits such as emergency arbitration and consolidation of arbitrations.

A High Level Committee was set up by the Government of India under the Chairmanship of Justice B.N. Srikrishna, a respected retired judge of the Supreme Court of India, to address the lack of institutional arbitration,[131] but most of its recommendations remain unimplemented.

---

128. The majority of arbitrators are retired judges, whether party or court appointed.
129. The ICADR no longer exists. It has been morphed into the New Delhi International Arbitration Centre formed by a statute bearing same name in 2020.
130. These include Delhi High Court International Arbitration Centre, The Nani Palkhivala Arbitration Centre, The Indian Merchant Chamber Arbitration Centre, The Mumbai Centre for International Arbitration, The Hyderabad International Arbitration & Mediation Centre and the New Delhi International Arbitration Centre.
131. Its terms of reference include highlighting measures that facilitate, '(a) the quick and effective resolution of commercial disputes through arbitration; and (b) the effective conduct of

5   No Regulatory Matrix for Third-Party Funding

The Srikrishna Committee Report notes that Singapore and Hong Kong legalized, and Paris supported, legalization of, third-party funding, and recommends that '[s]imilar measures, if adopted with suitable modifications for the Indian context, could give a boost to arbitration in India'.[132] Despite this endorsement, the Government of India is yet to regulate third-party funding.

It may be of some surprise that third-party funding has always been permitted in India, barring only funding agreements that are extortionate and unconscionable or inequitable against a party, for improper objects, or for injuring or oppressing others by abetting and encouraging wrongful suits.[133]

In an early judgment the Supreme Court[134] observed that an agreement to pay 50% of the proceeds of litigation 'would be legally unobjectionable if no lawyer was involved' and that 'the rigid English rules of champerty and maintenance do not apply in India'.[135] Hence agreements involving champerty are not necessarily illegal in India.[136] Recent dicta of the Supreme Court is also in sync:[137]

> In India, funding of litigation by advocates is not explicitly prohibited, but a conjoint reading of Rule 18 (fomenting litigation), Rule 20 (contingency fees), Rule 21 (share or interest in an actionable claim) and Rule 22 (participating in bids in

---

international and domestic arbitrations' Report of the High Level Committee to Review the Institutionalisation of Arbitration Mechanism in India, 30 July 2017 ('the Report') available at https://legalaffairs.gov.in/sites/default/files/Report-HLC.pdf.

132. The Report (*supra*) pp. 43, 44.

133. *Ram Coomar Coondoo v. Chunder Canto Mookherjee* 1876 SCC Online PC 19: (1876-1877) 4 IA 23, 39, 47. *Ram Coomar* was followed by a subsequent Privy Council decision in *Raja Rai Bhagwat Dayal Singh v. Debi Dayal Sahu* 1908 SCC Online PC 1. The Privy Council cited, amongst others, its decision in *Ram Coomar* to decide that agreements which would have been void in England on the grounds of champerty, have been, in fact, enforced in India.

134. *Mr. 'G' a Senior Advocate of the Supreme Court* (1955) 1 SCR 490.

135. *Id.*, para. 11: Originally English law declared agreements of maintenance and champerty as illegal. However, these offences 'finally ceased to be criminal offences and torts by virtue of sections 13 and 14 of the Criminal Law Act 1967'. Thereafter, third party funding in litigation has been recognized and permitted through the evolution of common law, which culminated with *Arkin v. Borchard Lines Ltd.* (2005) 1 WLR 3055; (2005) EWCA Civ 665.

136. *Suganchand v. Balchand* 1956 SCC Online Raj 127 para. 10: Relying upon the Privy Council the Court held: 'Para 11 From a perusal of the above cases, it is clear that champertous agreements in India are not per se void. On the other hand, a fair agreement to supply funds to carry on suit in consideration of having a share in the Property, if recovered, has not been considered opposed to public policy. There may be cases in which it may be just and proper to assist a suitor, who has a just title to property and no other means except the property itself, to prosecute his case; but as observed by their Lordships of the privy Council, such agreements should be watched very carefully and they should not be enforced, being opposed to public policy if they fall in one of the categories mentioned below –

> (1) if they are extortionate and unconscionable so as to be inequitable against the party, or
> (2) if they are made not with the bona fide object of assisting a claim believed to be just and obtaining a reasonable recompense, therefor, but for improper objects as – (a) for the purpose of gambling in litigation, or (b) of injuring or oppressing others by abetting and encouraging unrighteous suits.'

137. *Bar Council of India v. A.K. Balagi* (2018) 5 SCC 379, para. 38.

execution, etc.) would strongly suggest that advocates in India cannot fund litigation on behalf of their clients. There appears to be no restriction on third parties (non-lawyers) funding the litigation and getting repaid after the outcome of the litigation.

Third-party funding facilitates greater access to justice by enabling meritorious claims despite the impecuniosity of arbitrants. Funder evaluation weeds out hopeless causes and audits the arbitral process. Encouragement of third-party funding is imperative, particularly in tough economic times. There is a need for regulation focused upon the dangers of misuse including to: (i) clearly define what would be 'unconscionable' and prohibited; (ii) prescribe the nature of control a third-party funder may be permitted to exercise over the arbitration; (iii) provide for inalienable terms for the funding contract including the right to terminate; and (iv) identify disclosure obligations.

VII   THE PRACTICE OF ARBITRATION NEEDS OVERHAULING: THROUGH THE LOOKING GLASS

Any aspiration that India become a popular seat for international commercial arbitration will require a serious overhauling of the practice of arbitration in India. India has several advantages that should have made it a popular seat: over 150 years of recorded common law, a strong commercial bar for which English is the lingua franca, an intellectual and innovative judiciary and good infrastructural support. These advantages have to an extent been squandered.

Support for reform can be drawn from the extraordinary observations, in a recent case, of the Supreme Court, bemoaning the inefficiencies of civil practice in India. In a lengthy postscript to its decision in *Ajit Mohan*[138] the Supreme Court observed:

> Much as the legal fraternity would not want, restriction of time period for oral submissions is an aspect which must be brought into force. We really doubt whether any judicial forum anywhere in the world would allow such time periods to be taken for oral submissions and these be further supplemented by written synopsis thereafter. Instead of restricting oral arguments it has become a competing arena of who gets to argue for the longest time.

The Supreme Court recognized that it is 'the litigants who bear the costs of our complex and prolonged adjudicatory process'.[139]

There is a message in this for arbitration as well and a role for each of the stakeholders:

(i) Courts must approach an award asking the question, 'How do we uphold it?' rather than, 'How would we have decided it?' It is possibly the deficiencies of many domestic awards that motivate Courts to retain wider judicial review than is contemplated by the Arbitration Act. The imperative of reaching a just

---

138. *Ajit Mohan v. Legislative Assembly National Capital Territory of Delhi & Ors* (2021) SCC Online SC 456 at paras 236-246.
139. *Id.*

result, some would say. But is the cure worse than the disease? After all the essence of arbitration is that in the first place, the parties wanted the arbitral tribunal, and not the Courts, to decide their disputes. Pro-activity in enforcement is required rather than suspicion. The woes of a successful arbitrant should not start post-award. That said, party autonomy and the need for rapid enforcement are now increasingly respected by several Courts in India, including the Supreme Court, and the Bombay and Delhi High Courts.

(ii) The Government must facilitate arbitration facilities in all major cities modelled on Maxwell Chambers in Singapore. They should offer, amongst other things, real-time transcription – a game changer in terms of greatly shortening the arbitration and vastly improving the accuracy and integrity of the process. Regular monitoring of the working of the Arbitration Act can make for timely legislative intervention, keeping in mind that a soft touch works better than heavy-handed regulation.

(iii) Arbitral tribunals have to shed the Due Process paranoia that grips some of them.[140] Allowing lawyers latitude is never a good idea! Fairness of process is not achieved by interminable cross-examination and oral arguments. Strict chess clock time sharing, Redfern schedules, real-time transcription, hot tubbing of experts and robust cost orders (despite the edifying 2015 amendments to section 24) are not common. Indian tribunals also prefer to retain wide procedural discretion and barring a select few, do not issue the detailed Procedural Orders (particularly P.O.No.1) that are commonplace internationally.[141] On the other hand virtual hearings are here to stay and Indian tribunals have enthusiastically embraced them.[142] Virtual options facilitate evolution of a hybrid model, allowing virtual oral closings a few days after the evidentiary hearing without a physical re-gathering.[143] Permitting an oral closing sometimes forms a critical part of the opportunity of presenting one's case. Yet it is often denied in international commercial arbitration, perhaps on the subliminal ground that it would require physical regathering. Virtual oral closings eliminate the inconvenience and cost of physical oral closings. Another welcome development would be greater pro-activity of all tribunals in identifying (at an early stage) the issues on which evidence is not required, limiting irrelevant evidence and the length of oral arguments and more

---

140. Perhaps this is due to the predominance, as arbitrators, of retired Judges, some of whom carry the baggage of civil procedure.
141. Interestingly the Srikrishna Report recommends Model Rules of Procedure (which could include the IBA Rules for taking Evidence) to be incorporated as a schedule to the Arbitration Act and to operate as a default procedure unless parties by agreement exclude them. (Para. 14 p. 72).
142. The Maharashtra National Law University has published an excellent paper analysing technology, case management and legal issues involved in virtual hearings, viz. 'Virtual Arbitration in India – A Practical Guide'.
143. Internationally, oral closings are often discouraged, due to the cost and inconvenience of a physical re-gathering after the evidentiary hearing. In India, where the oral tradition still reigns supreme this is often seen as unfair.

closely managing the proceedings.[144] This approach has, to an extent, been taking root in some India seated arbitrations.

(iv) We lawyers need to pledge ourselves to a new practice. Strict time limits, memorialization of pleadings,[145] detailed yet page-limited opening written submissions and strictly no 'ambushing' of opponents. This again is rare in Indian arbitration. The idea of marshalling and disclosing your whole case, in detail by reference to documents, evidence and law *prior* to the evidentiary hearing is perceived in India as the antithesis of clever practice. Yet it is in fact the most efficient manner of organizing your argument, pruning it of the inessential and of focusing on the core differences before the Tribunal. This helps to shorten the time for arbitration and to make it fairer to both parties.

VIII CONCLUSION: WIPE THE GRIN OFF THE CHESHIRE CAT

Coupled with the Supreme Court's judgment permitting non-Indian lawyers to practice arbitration in India and to advise on a 'fly in, fly out' basis,[146] the introduction of dualism and the discipline of Courts refusing the temptation of reassessing results, means that India, for the first time, becomes attractive as a seat for international commercial arbitration.

I'm confident that the vibrancy of its Court driven jurisprudence, the firm commercial law foundations of its Bar and the economic law imperative to provide efficient dispute resolution will keep India relevant as a seat for international arbitration.

But will India become an international commercial arbitration powerhouse? I believe the answer to that question lies in another:

Can all the stakeholders seize the opportunity to evolve a new form of arbitration in India by re-inventing themselves? That is the real question that shadows Indian arbitration.

---

144. Perhaps not as far as the civil law influenced Prague Rules on the Efficient Conduct of Proceedings in International Arbitration 2018.
145. The memorial style of pleading facilitates and expects citation of legal authorities in support of the case. This is anathema to classical pleading which eschews inclusion of legal authorities and restricts pleadings to averments of fact and limited legal submissions.
146. *Bar Council v. A.K. Balaji* (2018) 5 SCC 379 paras 47-48.

CHAPTER 32

Of Lions, Tigers, Dragons, and Wolves: Transforming International Arbitration in Africa

*Ndanga Kamau**

TABLE OF CONTENTS

I   INTRODUCTION

Africa is a continent of contrasts. The mere mention of the word 'Africa' conjures up images of darkness and light. Across the continent, contradictions abound. Immense wealth coexists with abject poverty. Resource-rich countries are poor. Intractable conflicts ebb and flow as modern cities grow. To simply refer to 'Africa' is to negate the vastness of the continent. Such simplicity risks ignoring the reality of fifty-four

---

* Ndanga Kamau is an international lawyer based in The Hague, Netherlands. She sits as arbitrator in institutional and ad hoc disputes. Ndanga is a vice president of the ICC International Court of Arbitration and a senior honorary fellow of the British Institute of International and Comparative Law (BIICL). You can reach her at, ndanga@ndangakamau.com and read more about her international law practice at, https://ndangakamau.com.

independent states, inhabited by more than a billion people, who speak thousands of languages. These states have distinct legal systems which have developed with their own peculiarities. And yet, to disaggregate Africa is to find oneself overwhelmed by its heterogeneity. Tongue-tied by its immenseness. So, in this chapter, I will dare to speak of 'Africa', while acknowledging the problems associated with such a monolithic reference.

The chapter explores trends in international arbitration in Africa. It does so in two parts. The first part identifies some of the external players that influence economic activity and dispute resolution in Africa.[1] The second part explores how Africans have transformed international arbitration across the continent.

II   EARLY ARRIVALS

Adam Hochschild[2] writes that in the Middle Ages Europeans knew little of Africa. Exploration across the Mediterranean was impeded by Moors in North Africa. Along the west coast of Africa, beyond the Canary Islands, was the *Mare Tenebroso*, the Sea of Darkness. He writes:

> In the medieval imagination [writes Peter Forbath], this was a region of uttermost dread … where the heavens fling down liquid sheets of flame and the waters boil…where the serpent rocks and ogre islands lie in wait for the mariner, where the giant hand of Satan reaches up from fathomless depths to seize him, where he will turn black in the face and body as a mark of God's vengeance for the insolence of his prying in this forbidden mystery. And even if he should be able to survive all these ghastly perils and sail on through, he would then arrive at the Sea of Obscurity and be lost forever in the vapors and slime at the edge of the world.[3]

Europeans soon overcame their fear of these seas to land on African shores. Diogo Cão[4] a Portuguese mariner, led an expedition that landed in the then Kingdom of the Congo in 1482.[5] His more famous countryman, Vasco da Gama made it all the way to East Africa between 1497 and 1498, on his way to India.[6]

Trade with European powers became the dominant form of trade for Africans. By the time of the Enlightenment, Europeans had been trading with, and in, Africans for a few hundred years.[7] In the post-Enlightenment period, Europeans acquired African colonies across the continent. Some were settlement colonies – especially in East and

---

1. The chapter does not cover players from the Middle East. A regrettable omission.
2. Adam Hochschild, *King Leopold's Ghost* (Houghton Mifflin 1998).
3. Adam Hochschild, *King Leopold's Ghost* (Houghton Mifflin 1998), pp. 6-7.
4. He was not the first Portuguese sailor to land in Africa. Other Portuguese sailors had reached the west African coast earlier. But it is likely that he was the first to get to Central Africa
5. Adam Hochschild, *King Leopold's Ghost* (Houghton Mifflin 1998).
6. South African History Online, https://www.sahistory.org.za/article/vasco-da-gamas-voyage-discovery-1497.
7. *See*, for example, Howard W. French, *Born in Blackness: Africa, Africans, and the Making of the Modern World, 1471 to the Second World War* (Liveright Publishing Corporation, 2021); Toby Green, *A Fistful of Shells: West Africa From the Rise of the Slave Trade to the Age of Revolution* (Penguin, 2020).

Southern Africa – but others were no more than trading posts.[8] As European powers governed newly created African states, so too did they impose laws and regulations to govern various aspects of life and business, including dispute resolution.[9] Some of these laws – including arbitration laws – remain today.

In the post-colonial period, trade with former colonial powers remained dominant.[10] Investment too was dominated by European investors, and, increasingly, by the United States. This pattern of trade and investment is reflected in international disputes involving foreign investors and African states – the claimants are usually European or American.

There have been some changes in the twenty-first century.

III   ENTER THE DRAGON[11]

Archaeological finds in East Africa show that China had contact with Africa before the Europeans. Zheng He, an administrator and diplomat of the Ming Dynasty, embarked on several sea voyages between 1403 and 1433.[12] It is reported that he arrived in East Africa and met with the Sultan of Malindi in present-day Kenya.[13] Today, China is Africa's largest trading partner and investor.[14] Her dragon economy maintains a seemingly insatiable appetite for resources. So, like European states in the industrial age, China acquires these resources wherever it can find them. Chinese companies have invested right across the African continent in multiple sectors including oil & gas, mining, infrastructure, retail, and leisure.

Any discussion about outbound Chinese investment must mention the Belt & Road Initiative (BRI). African countries are at the heart of the BRI and thirty-seven

---

8. Exceptionally, one of these colonies – then called the Congo Free State – was the personal property of King Leopold II of Belgium.
9. *See, e.g.,* the legal framework for international arbitration in former British, French, and Portuguese colonies.
10. *See,* for example, Mozambique trade with Portugal, https://clubofmozambique.com/news/mozambique-portugal-still-main-eu-trade-partner-despite-covid-as-summit-starts-223971/, Africa and France: reshaping ties and renewing engagement, Economist Intelligence Unit, https://country.eiu.com/article.aspx?articleid = 1640347347&Country = Cameroon&topic = Economy_1.
11. The dragon is a legendary creature in Chinese mythology.
12. Howard W. French, *Born in Blackness: Africa, Africans, and the Making of the Modern World, 1471 to the Second World War* (Liveright Publishing Corporation, 2021); Tansen Sen, 'The Impact of Zheng He's Expeditions on Indian Ocean interactions', Bulletin of the School of Oriental and African Studies, University of London, Vol. 79, No. 3 (2016), pp. 609-636 (Cambridge University Press).
13. Tansen Sen, 'The Impact of Zheng He's Expeditions on Indian Ocean interactions', Bulletin of the School of Oriental and African Studies, University of London, Vol. 79, No. 3 (2016), pp. 609-636 (Cambridge University Press).
14. *See, e.g.,* Table showing Top 15 investors in Africa from 2010 to 2019, https://sabc.ch/wp-content/uploads/2017/12/Report-Swiss-African-Business-Relations-Status-Quo-2021.pdf; China-Africa Research Initiative, http://www.sais-cari.org/data, China-Africa Economic and Trade Relationship Annual Report (2021), China is Africa's Largest Trading Partner, The State Council Information, People's Republic of China, White Paper; Kingsley Ighobor, 'China in the Heart of Africa: Opportunities and Pitfalls in a Rapidly Expanding Relationship', Africa Renewal, United Nations, January 2013; Teresa Nogueira Pinto, 'How China-African Trade May Evolve', 15 March 2022, GIS Reports Online.

countries and the African Union are reported to have signed memorandums of understanding to be part of the initiative.[15] African BRI projects include infrastructure projects such as ports, railways, highways, and airports. Some of these investments include loans to build the infrastructure – an approach that has led to some concerns about the debt burden of some African countries.[16]

The initial profile of Chinese investors in Africa was state-owned enterprises (SOEs) with a lot of capital.[17] Today, the SOEs have been joined by private investors[18] who are investing in leisure, manufacturing, and other sectors. Anecdotally, disputes between Chinese parties and their African counterparts are resolved amicably without resorting to adversarial means of dispute resolution. However, as China continues to develop its infrastructure for international arbitration, and Chinese arbitral institutions focus on providing support for BRI disputes, there may be more disputes resolved through international arbitration. A notable initiative is the China-Africa Joint Arbitration Centre (CAJAC).[19] The centre is an ambitious project to provide a neutral forum to resolve commercial disputes between Chinese and African counterparts – including disputes arising out of BRI projects.[20] Such a neutral mechanism, it was hoped, would promote trade and investment between China and African countries. So far, CAJAC has member institutions in Beijing, Johannesburg,[21] Nairobi, Shanghai,[22] Shenzhen[23] and L'Organisation pour l'Harmonisation en Afrique du Droit des Affaires (OHADA). Since they were set up, CAJAC members have not published any information about their caseloads and operations.

As Chinese investments in Africa have grown, so too has China's network of bilateral investment treaties (BITs) with African states. As of August 2022, China has BITs with at least thirty-six African countries, twenty of which are in force.[24] There are a few known claims by Chinese investors against African states. Recently, a Chinese investor lodged treaty and contract claims against Ghana after the state cancelled a

15. China Signs MOUS with thirty-seven African countries, AU on B&R development, Xinhua Net (7 September 2018), http://www.xinhuanet.com/english/2018-09/07/c_137452482.htm.
16. Yunnan Chen, Chinese Debt and the Myth of the African Debt-Trap in Africa, Italian Institute for International Political Studies, 24 July 2020, https://www.ispionline.it/en/pubblicazione/chinese-debt-and-myth-debt-trap-africa-27024; Kathrin Hille and David Pilling, China Applies Brakes to Africa Lending, 11 January 2022, https://www.ft.com/content/64b4bcd5-032e-4be5-aa3b-e902f5b1345e; China Says Allegations It Causes Debt Trap for Africa Are False, Bloomberg News, 26 October 2021, https://www.bloomberg.com/news/articles/2021-10-26/china-says-allegations-it-causes-debt-trap-for-africa-are-false.
17. Xiaofang Shen, Private Chinese Investment in Africa: Myths and Realities, World Bank Policy Research Working Paper 6311 (2013).
18. These private investors include small- and medium-sized enterprises. See, for example, Howard W. French, China's Second Continent: How a Million Migrants are Building a New Empire in Africa (Alfred A. Knopf, 2014).
19. CAJAC Johannesburg https://cajacjhb.com/, CAJAC Shanghai http://www.shiac.org/CAJAC/index_E.aspx, CAJAC Shenzhen http://www.scia.com.cn/index.php/En/index/service/id/19.html.
20. CAJAC was proposed at the Forum for China-Africa Cooperation (FOCAC) meeting in December 2015.
21. https://cajacjhb.com/.
22. http://www.shiac.org/CAJAC/index_E.aspx.
23. http://www.scia.com.cn/index.php/En/index/service/id/19.html.
24. https://edit.wti.org/.

contract to develop an intelligent traffic management system.[25] Another Chinese investor won an investment treaty claim against Nigeria in a dispute related to a free trade zone in Ogun State.[26]

China has not been the only new entrant from Asia.

IV   TIGER RISING[27]

Historians aver that the relationship between India and Africa – especially East Africa – dates back several centuries.[28] In earlier times, contact was through trans-Indian Ocean trade. But the type of contact changed in subsequent centuries. The change was indirect.

Slavery was abolished in Great Britain in 1833,[29] and in her colonies from 1834 onwards. The abolition of slavery led to a shortage of labour in the British Empire, especially in the sugar-growing islands like Mauritius. So, Britain designed a system of indentured labour to compensate for the shortage. Mauritius was to be the first site of 'The Great Experiment'.[30] Indians were brought there to work in the sugar cane fields as indentured labourers starting in 1834.[31] Mauritius today has a population that is predominantly of Indian descent. Strong cultural and familial ties influence trade and investment between Mauritius and India.[32]

The British also took indentured labourers to the then Natal Province in South Africa – present-day Kwazulu Natal Province. Like in Mauritius and other parts of the Empire, Indians were taken to Natal to work in the sugarcane fields. Their descendants remain in South Africa today, forming a diaspora with cultural and familial links to India. In Kenya and Uganda, some Indians arrived as traders in the nineteenth and twentieth centuries. However, most were brought in as indentured labourers to build the railway line from Mombasa to Kampala.[33] Their descendants remained in East Africa – including as traders and investors in the region. In 1972, Idi Amin, then

---

25. *Beijing Everyway Traffic and Lighting Tech Co Ltd v Republic of Ghana* (UNCITRAL – treaty) – China-Ghana BIT, and *Beijing Everyway Traffic and Lighting Tech Co Ltd v. Republic of Ghana* (LCIA Arbitration – contract).
26. *Zhongshan Fucheng Industrial Investment v. Nigeria* (UNCITRAL – China-Nigeria BIT).
27. The tiger is the national animal of India.
28. Anonymous, *Periplus Maris Erythraei* (Voyage around the Erythraean Sea), written in the middle of the first century CE, mentions the presence of Indian traders in Africa; Aparajita BISWAS, 'India-Africa Relations: Evolving Past to a Promising Future', Indian Foreign Affairs Journal, Vol. 10, No. 3 (July-September 2015), pp. 284-299.
29. An Act for the Abolition of Slavery throughout the British Colonies; for promoting the Industry of the manumitted Slaves; and for compensating Persons hitherto entitled to the Services of Such Slaves ('Slavery Abolition Act').
30. An Overview of the History of Indenture, https://aapravasi.govmu.org/aapravasi/wp-content/uploads/2020/10/History-of-Indenture.pdf; Indian Indentured Labourers, https://www.nationalarchives.gov.uk/help-with-your-research/research-guides/indian-indentured-labourers/; Bhaswati Mukherjee, 180th Anniversary of arrival of Indian indentured labour in Mauritius, 24 October 2014, https://www.mea.gov.in/in-focus-article.htm?24132/180th + Anniversary + of + arrival + of + Indian + indentured + labour + in + Mauritius.
31. *See supra* n. 29.
32. For a time, Mauritius was the biggest investor in India – at least on paper – because it established itself as a favourable tax jurisdiction for investment into India.
33. Mayur Mulki, Laying the Lunatic Line, 18 June 2018, https://www.livehistoryindia.com/story/eras/laying-the-lunatic-line; Stephanie Jones, 'Merchant-Kings and Everymen: Narratives of

president of Uganda, ordered the expulsion of about 50,000 Indians from Uganda. They had to leave behind all their wealth and possessions – they were never compensated for those losses.

Today, India is the seventh largest investor in Africa. Unlike China, most of the large investors are private companies. It may not be possible to calculate how much India's investments in Africa are driven by cultural and familial ties. But, in a speech to the Ugandan Parliament in 2018, India's Prime Minister acknowledged a link. He referred to the history of Indian indentured labour in East Africa by stating that 'heroic labour connected Uganda to the shores of the Indian Ocean through railway'.[34] In that speech, the Prime Minister also outlined the ten principles that would guide India's engagement with Africa.[35] The principles include promoting trade with Africa, encouraging Indian companies to invest in Africa, and collaborating to ensure a just international climate order.

Not much is known about disputes involving Indian investors in Africa. A few disputes are public,[36] but there may be others which remain confidential. Because of India's policy to terminate BITs, Indian investors cannot rely on treaty protection for their investments. India had signed BITs with thirteen African countries. Of these, seven had entered into force but were subsequently terminated. Only one of the BITs – with Libya – remains in force. So, Indian investors must rely on contractual protection[37] for their investments.

Another new entrant is making inroads in Africa, with little attention from around the world.

V   DANCES WITH WOLVES[38]

Türkiye's history in Africa dates to the sixteenth century when the Ottomans arrived in North Africa.[39] The Ottoman Empire went on to spread across present-day North Africa. After the Italo-Turkish War of 1911, the Ottoman Empire lost its African

---

the South Asian Diaspora of East Africa', Journal of East African Studies, Vol. 1, No. 1, 16-33, March 2007; Chitra Gadgil, Contribution of Indians in Kenya-Uganda Railway.

34. Prime Minister's address at Parliament of Uganda during his State Visit to Uganda (25 July 2018), https://mea.gov.in/Speeches-Statements.htm?dtl/30152/Prime + Ministers + address + at + Pa rliament + of + Uganda + during + his + State + Visit + to + Ugand.

35. Prime Minister's address at Parliament of Uganda during his State Visit to Uganda (25 July 2018), https://mea.gov.in/Speeches-Statements.htm?dtl/30152/Prime + Ministers + address + at + Pa rliament + of + Uganda + during + his + State + Visit + to + Ugand.

36. *Patel Engineering Limited (India) v. Republic of Mozambique*, PCA Case 2020-21 (UNCITRAL Rules) and the related case, *Mozambique Ministry of Transport and Communications v Patel Engineering* (ICC Case).

37. Indian investors may also rely on host-country legislation for investment protection, where such legislation exists.

38. The national animal of Türkiye is the grey wolf.

39. *See*, for example, Andrew C. Hess, 'The Ottoman Conquest of Egypt (1517) and the Beginning of the Sixteenth-Century War, International Journal of Middle Eastern Studies, Vol. 4, No. 1 (January 1973), pp. 55-76 (Cambridge University Press).

territories.[40] The empire was eventually dismantled in 1922. In the Republican era, Türkiye appeared to pay little attention to Africa. It was not until 1998 that it adopted its 'Opening to Africa' policy. In 2005, Türkiye went further still and declared 2005 the Year of Africa.

Today, Türkiye is the fourth largest investor in Africa, surpassing the United Kingdom, India, and Japan. In just over twenty years, Türkiye has deepened its relationship with African states to include diplomatic, economic, and military ties. Most of Türkiye's activity in Africa appears to go unnoticed as commentators and rival states focus on Chinese investment. As an illustration of the depth of Turkish interest in Africa, it now has embassies in forty-three out of fifty-four African countries – third after France and the United States – up from twelve in 1998.[41] Further, Türkiye became an observer member of the African Union in 2005 and was designated a strategic partner in 2008.[42]

Türkiye's investments in Africa span several sectors including oil and gas, mining, agriculture, construction, port management, healthcare, and education. Turkish construction companies have a notable footprint in Africa – as in the rest of the world. According to the Turkish Ministry of Trade, African projects accounted for 17.8% of projects by Turkish construction companies in 2021.[43] The projects include construction of hotels, stadiums, infrastructure, hospitals, and shopping malls.

In contrast to India, Türkiye is slowly expanding its BIT network in Africa. So far, it has concluded BITs with thirty-two African countries.[44] Türkiye's BIT programme appears to be less successful than China's because only seven out of thirty-two BITs have entered into force.[45]

Turkish investors have made at least ten claims against Libya[46] under the Libya-Türkiye BIT – and more than forty claims against other states. So, Turkish investors are familiar with enforcing their rights against states. Considering Türkiye's poor network of BITs in Africa, it remains to be seen how its investors will use contracts – and investment laws in host states – to protect their investments in Africa.

The last new entrant in Africa is located farthest east.

---

40. See, for example, Timothy W. Childs, *Italo-Turkish Diplomacy and the War over Libya, 1911-1912*, Social, Economic and Political Studies of the Middle East and Asia, Vol. 42 (Brill, 1990).
41. Turkish Ministry of Foreign Affairs, https://www.mfa.gov.tr/turkish-representations.en.mfa; Turkey is making a big diplomatic and corporate push into Africa, The Economist, 23 April 2022, https://www.economist.com/middle-east-and-africa/2022/04/23/turkey-is-making-a-big-dipl omatic-and-corporate-push-into-africa.
42. Africa-Turkey Partnership, African Union, https://au.int/en/partnerships/africa_turkey; Turkey and the African Union, Turkish Ministry of Foreign Affairs, https://www.mfa.gov.tr/turkey -and-the-african-union.en.mfa#:~:text=AU%20demonstrated%20its%20will%20to,21%20Aug ust%202008%2C%20in%20Istanbul.
43. Turkish International Contracting Services (1972-2021), https://www.tmb.org.tr/files/doc/162 3914018902-ydmh-en.pdf; Deniz Çicek Palabiyik and Erhan Cihan Ünal, 'Turkish construction firms' overseas projects total $29.3 Bin 2021: Official, https://www.aa.com.tr/en/economy/ turkish-construction-firms-overseas-projects-total-293b-in-2021-official/2465163#.
44. https://edit.wti.org/.
45. https://edit.wti.org/.
46. See, https://investmentpolicy.unctad.org/investment-dispute-settlement/country/214/t-rkiye/ investor.

VI   SNOW MONKEYS[47]

A brief mention of Japan concludes the discussion on new players. One could turn west to contemplate Brazil's interest in Africa, or closer east to the Middle East, but not on this occasion. There is no known historical – read pre-colonial – contact between Japan and Africa. That does not mean there was no contact – an ignorance of history does not equate to an absence of history. In the 1960s, Japan started interacting with African countries as part of its overseas development assistance (ODA) programme.[48] However, it was not until 1993 that Japan developed a strategy for its engagement with Africa by hosting the first Tokyo International Conference on African Development (TICAD). Japan's interest then, which persists today, was to assist with humanitarian aid and support industrialisation in Africa.[49]

Tunisia and Senegal co-hosted TICAD 8 in Tunis in August 2022. At the conference, Japan pledged to spend USD 30 billion on investment in Africa over three years.[50] The money would come from private and public contributions and would 'focus on investment in people and quality of growth and aim for a resilient and sustainable Africa while solving various problems faced by the African people'. Japan's contributions should 'strengthen a free and open international economic system' that can help countries recover from COVID-19 and the impact of the war in Ukraine.[51] In his closing speech at the conference, Japan's Prime Minister, Fumio Kishida, emphasised Japan's approach of 'growing together with Africa'.[52]

Japan is the eighth largest investor in Africa.[53] With this latest pledge, Japan continues a recent shift in emphasis from development aid to foreign direct investment (FDI).[54] Japanese investors can be found in a variety of sectors including energy, mining, oil & gas, and infrastructure – not that different from their Chinese, Indian or Turkish counterparts. But, Japanese companies have historically been cautious about investing in Africa. So, it is curious to see that while Japan is encouraging its private investors to invest in Africa, it has not expanded its BIT network on the continent – in contrast to China and Türkiye. Japan has signed BITs with five African countries – Egypt (1977), Mozambique (2013), Kenya (2016), Côte d'Ivoire (2020), and Morocco (2020).[55] The BITs signed in 2020 are not yet in force. This small network of BITs perhaps reflects the reality that Japan's investments are concentrated in a few

---

47. Snow monkey, or macaque, is the national animal of Japan.
48. Japan's Development Assistance to Africa, 17 June 2022, https://www.mofa.go.jp/policy/oda/page22_001492.html.
49. www.japan.go.jp, Howard Lehman, *Japan and Africa: Globalization and Foreign Aid in the 21st Century* (Routledge 2011).
50. https://www.mofa.go.jp/afr/af2/page1e_000469.html.
51. https://www.mofa.go.jp/files/100386138.pdf.
52. https://www.mofa.go.jp/af/af1/page3e_001233.html.
53. Table showing Top 15 investors in Africa from 2010-2019, https://sabc.ch/wp-content/uploads/2017/12/Report-Swiss-African-Business-Relations-Status-Quo-2021.pdf.
54. Japan in Africa, https://www.japan.go.jp/japaninafrica/index.html.
55. In 2017, it was reported that Nigeria and Japan would begin negotiations for a BIT, but no agreement has been reached. 'Nigeria and Japan Set to Commence Negotiations of a Bilateral Investment Treaty (BIT)', https://www.nipc.gov.ng/2017/12/16/nigeria-japan-set-commence-negotiation-bilateral-investment-treaty-bit/.

countries, rather than spread out across the continent like other large investors. Japan has had close economic ties with South Africa for several decades; it imports platinum and iron ore, and exports cars. But, today, one of the biggest Japanese investments in Africa is a liquefied natural gas (LNG) project in South Africa's neighbour – Mozambique. There, Japanese companies and banks have invested about USD 14 billion.[56]

In the absence of a rich network of BITs, it is notable that Japan provides comprehensive insurance to its companies investing abroad. For example, the Japanese government's Nippon Export and Investment Insurance provides a range of products that cover political and commercial risks.[57]

There are few known investment claims by Japanese investors – and none in Africa so far. Like with other new entrants, it remains to be seen whether an increase in Japanese private investment in Africa will have any impact on disputes with African parties.

We now turn to the lions.

VII   TRANSFORMING INTERNATIONAL ARBITRATION IN AFRICA

With every attempt to analyse how international arbitration has changed in Africa in the last few decades, one is confronted by the continent's heterogeneity. That international arbitration has transformed is not debatable – although there are those that will debate any point. What may be debatable is what has driven the change. A nudge from foreign investors? A quest for good governance? Pressure from multilateral lending institutions? Herd mentality? A desire to improve business and investment climates? All the above?

Change has happened in some countries and remains a work in progress in others. These differences reflect that African countries remain at different stages of development – economic and legal. While several African countries already have modern regimes for international arbitration, some remain decades behind. Others still, continue to transform by passing new arbitration laws and signing up to multilateral conventions related to arbitration, such as the New York Convention and the International Centre for the Settlement of Investment Disputes (ICSID) Convention.

Part I of this chapter introduced the old and new entrants in the theatre of economic activity in Africa. In so doing, it highlighted how history has shaped the status quo of trade and investment and related dispute resolution involving foreign investors in Africa. Part II will outline the trends in transforming international arbitration in Africa. It will do so by outlining the changes in the legal and institutional frameworks for international arbitration in Africa. It will also mention some changes to other aspects of international arbitration in Africa.

It is well established that an increase in commercial transactions leads to an increase in disputes. How, when, where, and if, these disputes are resolved in Africa, depends on the legal and institutional arrangements available in each jurisdiction.

---

56. The Mozambique LNG Project: An energy resource for the world tomorrow, Mitsui & Co, https://www.mitsui.com/jp/en/innovation/business/mozambique_lng/index.html.
57. https://www.nexi.go.jp/en/products/index.html.

Part II starts with an introduction to the Lion Economies.

1   The Lion King(s)

Lion Economies refer to the fastest-growing economies in Africa. Members[58] are usually a subset of Côte d'Ivoire, Egypt Ethiopia, Ghana, Kenya, Morocco, Mozambique, Nigeria, Rwanda, Senegal, South Africa, and Tanzania. Using this analogy, smaller African economies could be called cubs. Lions are not the only wildlife. One commentator refers to leopards – smaller more agile African economies.[59]

In Africa, growing from a cub to a lion, or indeed transforming from a leopard to a lion, does not always reflect deliberate policy choices. In economies where growth depends on commodity prices, high commodity prices can lead to outsize growth. The converse is also true. Other shocks are relevant – a lion can shrink to a cub because of civil war or cross-border conflict. And, a global pandemic followed by war-induced increases in fuel and food prices, can shrink even the mightiest animals.

Wars and pandemics are not the only threats to African economies. Poor infrastructure, energy shortages, impacts of climate change, and underinvestment in health and education, all threaten growth and development. So, African states are strongly incentivised to attract FDI in these sectors. The need for investment is not abstract. The African Development Bank estimates that the continent needs to spend USD 130-170 billion on infrastructure per year, which would still leave a funding gap of USD 100 billion.[60] These are eye-watering sums. Foreign investment at this scale requires a robust legal and regulatory framework.

Lions are the most influential economies in Africa – they lead the way in designing frameworks to attract foreign capital, dominate cross-border trade, determine policy choices in regional economic communities, and set trends in legal and regulatory reform. As for international arbitration, while lions may be at the forefront of the transformation of this area of dispute resolution, the cubs are not far behind.

a   *The Instruments*

At independence, most African countries maintained the legal and institutional arrangements of the colonial period – including laws and institutions for dispute resolution. So, where they existed, provisions for international arbitration survived independence. Such provisions could be found in the codes of civil law countries and

---

58. Lions on the move: The progress and potential of African economies, McKinsey Global Institute, 1 June 2010; Lions on the move II: Realizing the potential of Africa's economies, McKinsey Global Institute, 14 September 2016; Haroon Bhorat and Finn Tarp, *Africa's Lions: Growth Traps and Opportunities for Six African Economies* (Brookings Institution Press, 2016).
59. Óscar Garrido Guijarro, 'African Leopards: Small and Medium-Sized Powers Leading the Continent', Instituto Español de Estudios Estratégicos, ieee.es, Analysis Paper 15/2022, 2 March 2022.
60. Africa's Infrastructure: Great Potential But Little Impact on Inclusive Growth, African Development Bank, https://www.afdb.org/fileadmin/uploads/afdb/Documents/Publications/2018AEO/African_Economic_Outlook_2018_-_EN_Chapter3.pdf.

in the arbitration statutes of common law countries. Today, we see that the colonial legacy in Africa has left behind a patchwork of legal systems that are based on Belgian, Dutch, French, Italian and Portuguese civil laws, English common law, customary law, and Islamic law.[61]

To make sense of the international arbitration laws in Africa it is convenient, if imperfect, to put the countries in five groups.

First, those countries whose arbitration laws remain unchanged after independence. They include Zanzibar, whose regime for international arbitration dates to the early twentieth century,[62] and Namibia, which has not modernised its legal regime after independence from South Africa in 1995.[63]

Second, those countries whose arbitration laws changed soon after independence, but have not modernised since. It includes Malawi which maintains an arbitration law enacted in 1967.[64]

Third, UNCITRAL Model Law countries. The newest member is Sierra Leone, whose parliament passed the Sierra Leone Arbitration Act, 2022 in August 2022. Other countries in this group are Egypt (1994), Kenya (1995), Madagascar (1998), Mauritius (2008), Nigeria (1990), Rwanda (2008), South Africa (2017), Tunisia (1993), Uganda (2000), Zambia (2000), and Zimbabwe (1996).

Fourth, countries that have not adopted the Model Law, but have enacted modern arbitration laws which are based on, or influenced by, the UNCITRAL Model Law. They include Angola (2003),[65] Liberia (2010),[66] Ethiopia (2021),[67] Sudan (2016),[68] Tanzania (2020),[69] and the seventeen countries that have adopted the Uniform Act on Arbitration of the *Organisation pour l'harmonisation en Afrique du droit des affaires* (OHADA).

Fifth, countries that have no known arbitration laws. In this category are Eritrea[70] and South Sudan.[71]

---

61. *See*, for example, Salmon A. Shomade, *Colonial Legacies and the Rule of Law in Africa: Ghana, Kenya, Nigeria, South Africa, and Zimbabwe*, 1st edn (Routledge 2022); AN Allott (ed.), *Judicial and Legal Systems in Africa* (Butterworths 1962); Salvatore Mancuso, 'The New African Law: Beyond the Difference Between Common Law and Civil Law', Annual Survey of International and Comparative Law, Vol. 14, No. 1 (2008).
62. Arbitration Cap 25 Laws of Zanzibar (1928), Arbitration Clauses (Protocol) Cap 26 Laws of Zanzibar (1926), Arbitration (Foreign Awards) Cap 27 Laws of Zanzibar (1931).
63. Arbitration Act 42 of 1965 (RSA).
64. Arbitration Act (Cap. 6:03) (Act No 26 of 1967).
65. Voluntary Arbitration Law (Law No. 16/03 of July 25).
66. Liberia does not have a standalone arbitration law. Provisions on arbitration are contained in Chapter of the Liberian Code of Law, Revised Commercial Code – Commercial Arbitration (2010).
67. Arbitration, Conciliation and Working Procedure Proclamation, Proclamation No. 1237/ 2021.
68. Sudan Arbitration Act, 2016.
69. Arbitration Act 2020, Cap 15.
70. Article 175 of the Civil Procedure Code of Eritrea 2015 contains a reference to arbitration – as the basis for a preliminary objection to a suit, but does not contain provisions on arbitration.
71. Article 138 in Chapter XI of the Code of Civil Procedure Act, 2007 of South Sudan contains provisions on references of disputes from litigation to arbitration, but is silent on commencing a domestic or international arbitration.

New York Convention

Enforcement of arbitral awards is governed by a range of regimes in African jurisdictions. Provisions on enforcement in arbitration laws coexist with the New York Convention – some of the former are based on the latter.[72] At the time of writing, forty-one of Africa's fifty-four states have acceded to the New York Convention. One, Djibouti, succeeded to the New York Convention in 1983.[73] When the Convention was signed on 10 June 1958, there were nine independent states in Africa – none of them signed the Convention. By the time the Convention went into force on 9 March 1959, Guinea had also become an independent state, and Morocco and Egypt had acceded to the Convention. The twelve countries that are not state parties to the convention are Gambia, Guinea-Bissau, Chad, Congo (Brazzaville), Equatorial Guinea, Eritrea, Eswatini, Libya, Namibia, Somalia, South Sudan, and Togo.

Little is known about the application of the New York Convention in African states. In jurisdictions such as Egypt, with a more established arbitration practice, private reporting is sometimes available. But in most jurisdictions, even where case reports exist, there is no systematic reporting on case law on the New York Convention.

ICSID Convention

The absence of African states at the foundation of the New York Convention is in stark contrast to the fundamental role that African states played in the negotiation and entry into force of the ICSID Convention. Antonio R Parra in ICSID Review Special Issue on Africa, describes the substantive contributions made by African delegates at the regional consultative forum held in Addis Ababa in 1963.[74] He also notes that when it came to ratification, an African state – Nigeria – was the first state to ratify the ICSID Convention in 1966. It was soon joined by fourteen other African states, which together helped get to the twenty ratifications needed for the ICSID Convention to enter into force. At the time of writing only four African states have not signed the ICSID Convention – Eritrea, Equatorial Guinea, Libya, and South Africa. Four others – Angola, Guinea-Bissau, Ethiopia and Namibia have signed, but not yet ratified the Convention.[75]

Over the years, African states have included an option for ICSID arbitration in investment contracts, BITs, and domestic investment laws. Not only that, they have also included options for institutional arbitration at the ICC International Court of Arbitration, the LCIA, and ad hoc arbitration using the UNCITRAL Rules.

African states have signed almost 1000 BITs.[76] Although many of these BITs are not yet in force, they continue to dominate the conversation about investment claims involving African states and state entities. Contracts and investment laws are ignored.

---

72. *See, e.g.*, Article 52 of the Ethiopia Proclamation No 1237-2021.
73. https://treaties.un.org/doc/Publication/CN/1983/CN.194.1983-Eng.pdf.
74. Antonio R. Parra, 'The Participation of African States in the Making of the ICSID Convention', ICSID Review, Vol. 34, No. 2 (2019), pp. 270-277.
75. https://icsid.worldbank.org/about/member-states.
76. Makane Moïse Mbengue and Stefanie Schacherer, *Evolution of International Investment Agreements in Africa, Handbook of International Investment Law and Policy* (Springer, 2021), pp 2597-2618.

Yet, ICSID statistics show that contracts and investment laws are just as important as BITs in Africa.[77] In a statistics report focusing on Africa issued in 2017, ICSID published the source of consent in cases involving an African state. Of the 135 cases registered at that time, 45% relied on consent in a BIT, 39% relied on consent in an investment contract, and 16% relied on consent in an investment law of the host state.[78]

Information trickling out of the ICC, LCIA and domestic courts deciding applications for set aside and enforcement of arbitral awards, underline that contracts are a significant source of consent to international arbitration involving states and state entities.[79]

b   The Institutions

In 2017, Dr Emilia Onyema published a list of arbitration institutions in Africa.[80] The list, inspired by a need to collect empirical data on the state of international arbitration, achieved notoriety that could not have been foreseen. It has been used to allege – with incontrovertible evidence! – that there was a proliferation of arbitration institutions in Africa.[81] The list shows no such thing. It lists, liberally, institutions that have a connection with alternative dispute resolution in Africa. It includes the Mauritius Office of the Permanent Court of Arbitration (PCA), training centres that do not administer disputes, industry-specific dispute resolution centres, defunct institutions, institutions that were registered but never went into operation, institutions focused on domestic arbitration, and so forth.

But, suppose for a moment, that all these institutions were functional arbitration centres. Would ninety-one institutions spread across fifty-four countries – an average of fewer than two institutions per country – be so alarming? Perhaps two institutions in Sao Tome e Principe might create some redundancy. But consider the Democratic Republic of Congo (DRC). Lubumbashi, the capital of mineral-rich Katanga Province in the southeast, is almost double the distance from Kinshasa than Vienna is from Amsterdam. Could there be room for two or more arbitral institutions in the DRC? Certainly. As it happens, two institutions are listed for the DRC – both in Kinshasa.

---

77. ICSID, Spotlight on contract-based disputes, https://icsid.worldbank.org/node/20966.
78. https://icsid.worldbank.org/resources/publications/icsid-caseload-statistics. These statistics can be contrasted with those from other regions in a similar period, 46 cases: 65% BIT, 27% investment contract, and 4% investment law in the South East Asia and Pacific Region; and 105 cases: 56% BIT, 43% ECT and 1% investment contract in Europe.
79. *See, e.g.*, *Divine Inspiration Group PTY (DIGOIL) v. Democratic Republic of Congo*, Judgment of Paris Court of Appeal, 7 January 2020, series of English court decisions related to the award in *Process and Industrial Developments (P&ID) Ltd. v. The Ministry of Petroleum of the Federal Republic of Nigeria*, English court proceedings in *Ghana Power Generation Company (GPGC) Limited v. The Government of the Republic of Ghana*, PCA Case No. 2019-05, Final Award 26 January 2021.
80. Emilia Oneyema, List of Known Arbitration Institutions in Africa (2020) https://afas-global.org/files/List%20of%20Known%20Arbitration%20Institutions%20in%20Africa.pdf.
81. *See*, for example, Gregory Travaini, Arbitration Centres in Africa: Too Many Cooks? Kluwer Arbitration Blog, 1 October 2019.

Elsewhere on the continent, a few jurisdictions have established arbitration centres with regional and international ambitions. Centres in Egypt,[82] Kenya,[83] Mauritius,[84] Morocco,[85] Nigeria,[86] Rwanda,[87] and South Africa[88] are vying for cross-border disputes involving African and non-African parties. Of these, CRCICA in Cairo is well established. Set up under the auspices of the Asian African Legal Consultative Organisation (AALCO) in 1979, it has a growing caseload from the Middle East and Africa. Its sister organisation, RCICAL, which was established in 1989 has yet to achieve much success and is surpassed in visibility and reputation by other centres in Lagos – the Lagos Court of Arbitration (LCA) and the Lagos Chamber of Commerce International Arbitration Centre (LACIAC), which were established in the last ten years. AFSA in South Africa has historically not administered disputes – it has appointed arbitrators for ad hoc domestic disputes under AFSA Rules. That changed in 2021 when it issued the AFSA International Rules – comprehensive procedural rules for institutional arbitration.[89] The procedural rules in these centres are based on, or inspired by, the UNCITRAL Arbitration Rules,[90] the LCIA Rules,[91] and the ICC Rules.[92]

If the success of arbitral institutions is measured by the number of cases handled, then many of these African centres have not yet achieved success. But if their success is measured by their contribution to transforming international arbitration, broadly defined, then they have been wildly successful. The centres are at the heart of thought leadership, training, and lobbying to improve the legal framework for international arbitration in their jurisdictions.

c   *The Parties and Disputes*

Two brothers, the Sultan of Muscat and the Sultan of Zanzibar were involved in an arbitration about territory they had inherited from their father, the Sultan of Oman.[93] They appointed the Governor-General of India as arbitrator. The arbitrator, in turn, directed the Government of Bombay to send an officer to make enquiries in Muscat and Zanzibar. Satisfied with the officer's report, the Governor-General issued a decision on

---

82. Cairo Regional Centre for International Commercial Arbitration (CRCICA), https://crcica.org/.
83. Nairobi Centre for International Arbitration (NCIA), https://ncia.or.ke/.
84. Mauritius International Arbitration Centre (MIAC), https://miac.mu/.
85. Casablanca International Mediation and Arbitration Centre (CIMAC), http://cimac.ma/.
86. Lagos Court of Arbitration (LCA), Lagos Chamber of Commerce International Arbitration Centre (LACIAC), Regional Centre for International Commercial Arbitration – Lagos (RCICAL), https://rcical.org/.
87. Kigali International Arbitration Centre (KIAC), https://kiac.org.rw/.
88. Arbitration Foundation of Southern Africa International (AFSA International), https://arbitration.co.za/international-arbitration/afsa-international/#.
89. AFSA International Rules (came into force on 1 June 2021), https://arbitration.co.za/international-arbitration/international-rules/.
90. *See*, for example, CRCICA Arbitration Rules 2011, LCA Arbitration Rules 2018.
91. *See*, for example, NCIA Arbitration Rules 2015 and AFSA International Rules 2021.
92. *See*, for example, KIAC Arbitration Rules 2012, CIMAC Arbitration Rules 2017.
93. *Arrangement for Settlement of Differences between the Sultan of Muscat and the Sultan of Zanzibar, and the Independence of their Respective States*, Decision of 2 April 1861, UNRIAA, Vol. XXVIII pp. 107-114.

2 April 1861. He decided that the Sultan of Zanzibar should rule over Zanzibar and the African dominions left behind by the Sultan of Oman. Further, that the Sultan of Zanzibar should pay his brother 40,000 crowns a year to compensate for the abandonment of all claims and the inequality of the inheritances, and 80,000 crowns in a once-off payment for two years in arrears. The decision is in the form of a brief letter to the two brothers. Its brevity belies its significance in deciding questions of sovereignty and independence. The brothers replied to the arbitrator, accepting his decision – the exchanges are worth reading if only to marvel at their exaggerated diplomatic language.

This decision illustrates some characteristics of international arbitration involving African states in the pre-independence era. Most disputes were linked to territory – if only indirectly. And the protagonists were often foreigners – occupying powers, settlers, and arbitrators. There are not many state-state disputes recorded from this era. Those available include border delimitation involving the Boer republics in South Africa,[94] the attack on a caravan of the Maharao of Kutch in Abyssinia,[95] an incident involving the exchange of fire between Italian and Abyssinian soldiers in Walwal,[96] and a dispute about nationality and consular relations involving an Egyptian national.[97]

Whether state-state arbitration has transformed in post-independence Africa may be debatable. While African parties to the disputes are now independent states – perhaps these disputes have not transformed enough – the subject matter of the disputes remains the same. The disputes are about territory – delimitation and sovereignty – stemming from the colonial legacy. Examples include the delimitation of a land boundary between Eritrea and Ethiopia,[98] determination of the boundaries of the Abyei region in Sudan-South Sudan,[99] delimitation of maritime boundaries between Guinea and Guinea-Bissau,[100] and Guinea-Bissau and Senegal,[101] and the dispute about the marine protected area in the Chagos Islands.[102]

In contrast, disputes between African states and private parties have increased dramatically in the last few decades. A detailed review of these cases is beyond the

---

94. *Arbitral Award relating to the boundary delimitation between South-African Republic (Transvaal) and the Orange Free State*, decision of 19 February 1870, UNRIAA, Vol. XXVIII pp. 125-130; *Award as to the boundary between the United Kingdom and the South African Republic (Transvaal)*, decision of 5 August 1885, UNRIAA, Vol. XXVIII, pp. 185-188.
95. *Attaque de la caravane du Maharao de Cutch (Royaume-Uni c. Éthiopie)*, 7 octobre 1927, UNRIAA Vol. II, pp. 821-827.
96. *Incident de Walwal (Italie c. Éthiopie)*, 3 septembre 1935, UNRIAA Vol. III, pp. 1657-1667.
97. *Salem Case (Egypt, USA)*, 8 June 1932, UNRIAA, Vol. II, pp. 1161-1237.
98. *Delimitation of the border between Eritrea and Ethiopia*, 13 April 2002-22 March 2003, UNRIAA Vol. XXV, pp. 83-229.
99. *Delimitation of the Abyei Area* (Government of Sudan v. the Sudan People's Liberation/Army), 22 July 2009, UNRIAA Vol. XXX, p. 145.
100. *Délimitation de la frontière maritime entre la Guinée et la Guinée-Bissau*, 14 février 1985, UNRIAA Vol. XIS, pp. 147-196.
101. *Délimitation de la frontière maritime entre la Guinée-Bissau et le Sénégal*, 31 juillet 1989, Vol. XIX, pp. 147-196.
102. *Award in the Arbitration regarding the Chagos Marine Protected Area between Mauritius and the United Kingdom of Great Britain and Northern Island*, 18 March 2015, UNRIAA Vol. XXXI, pp. 359-606.

scope of this chapter, but a few issues should be noted. First, as mentioned earlier, in contrast to other regions, the cases are based on BITs, contracts, and investment laws of the host state. Second, the disputes arise in several sectors, but predominantly in natural resources and large infrastructure projects. Third, several disputes are linked to poor governance. In response, states have sometimes pleaded corruption as a defence during the arbitration or as a ground to set aside the award or resist enforcement – with mixed success.[103] Fourth, the home states of the claimants are usually one of the top investors in Africa. So far, the claimants' home states have mostly been the old entrants identified in Part I.

As for international arbitration between private parties, there has been little change over the decades. African parties still prefer to resolve their disputes through litigation in domestic courts. In some more developed jurisdictions – remember the lions? – there is a growing practice of domestic arbitration. Commentators expect that implementing the African Continental Free Trade Agreement (AfCFTA)[104] will increase both cross-border transactions in Africa and an appetite for international arbitration. Then, African states will have the opportunity to test the infrastructure for international arbitration that they have developed in the past few years.

When African private parties contract with foreign private parties, any international arbitrations that result are usually delocalised[105] – foreign seat, foreign institution, foreign arbitrators. More and more, Africans are calling for disputes involving African parties and projects to be relocalised to African seats, administered by African institutions, and decided by African arbitrators. This assertiveness by Africans has been a notable trend in the last ten years.

d   International Arbitration for All

ICCA publications are replete with references to the value of ICCA Congresses as a forum to develop international arbitration practice and theory.[106] Such gatherings of practitioners and academics from different jurisdictions develop new ideas and solve complex problems. In Africa, similar power is being harnessed at a continental scale. Ten years ago, Africans interested in international arbitration events would have had to travel to Europe, the Americas, and Asia.

---

103. *See, e.g., Wena Hotels Ltd. v. Arab Republic of Egypt*, ICSID Case No. ARB/98/4, *World Duty Free Company v. Republic of Kenya*, ICSID Case No. ARB/00/7, *African Holding Company of America, Inc. Adn Société Africaine de Construction au Congo S.A.R.L. v Democratic Republic of the Congo*, ICSID Case No. ARB/05/21, *Cortec Mining Kenya Limited, Cortec (Pty) Limited and Stirling Capital Limited v. Republic of Kenya*, ICSID Case No. ARB/15/29, *BSG Resources Limited, BSG Resources (Guinea) Limited and BSG Resources (Guinea) SARL v. Republic of Guinea*, ICSID Case No. ARB/14/22, *Federal Republic of Nigeria v. Process & Industrial Developments Limited* [2020] EWHC 2379 (Comm).
104. The AfCFTA creates the world's largest free trade area. It entered into force on 30 May 2019.
105. *See*, for example, Abdulqawi Ahmed Yusuf, 'The Contribution of Arbitration to the Rule of Law: The Experience of African Countries', in Andrea Menaker (ed.), ICCA Congress Series No. 19 (Mauritius 2016): *International Arbitration and the Rule of Law: Contribution and Conformity* ICCA Congress Series, Volume 19 (ICCA & Kluwer Law International 2017), pp. 27-34.
106. *See, e.g.,* VV Veeder, 'Memories from ICCA's First Fifty Years', in Arbitration – The Next 50 Years: 50th Anniversary Conference, ICCA Congress Series No. 16 (2011).

Today, multiple international arbitration events are scheduled across the continent.[107] At these gatherings, participants discuss and debate issues that are relevant in Africa and beyond. Participants include legislators, members of the executive, academics, private practitioners, judges, and students. The gatherings are complemented by numerous arbitration-related initiatives[108] which have sprung up across the continent. The initiatives have multiple objectives – mentoring, training, networking, and thought leadership.

Together, the gatherings and initiatives contribute to transforming international arbitration in Africa, while themselves embodying transformation.

VIII   CONCLUSION

Diogo Cão could not have predicted what his pioneering landing in Central Africa would unleash. How quickly things got out of control is well illustrated by letters from Afonso I, the Manikongo of the Kingdom of Kongo, to King João III of Portugal in 1526. The Manikongo laments the corruption and depravity occasioned by Portuguese traders:

> Each day the traders are kidnapping our people – children of this country, sons of our nobles and vassals, even people of our own family...This corruption and depravity are so widespread that our land is entirely depopulated...We need in this kingdom only priests and schoolteachers, and no merchandise, unless it is wine and flour for Mass...It is our wish that this kingdom not be a place for the trade or transport of slaves.[109]

Afonso I, an enthusiastic slave trader,[110] may have found his limits – he was content to participate in the slave trade, as long as his kin were not being kidnapped.

In the centuries since Cão's landing, interest in Africa by people from around the world has continued – it is unlikely to wane. Some of those interested in Africa behave like the rapacious early traders of the sixteenth century, aided by present-day equivalents of Afonso I. Others are open to a mutually beneficial relationship underpinned by the rule of law. It is up to African states, and Africans themselves, to establish the legal and institutional frameworks that support such a relationship. The changes in international arbitration in the past few decades illustrate that Africans are ready to do so. A new Age of Enlightenment in International Arbitration may have arrived in Africa.

---

107. *See*, for example, SOAS Arbitration in Africa Conferences, East African International Arbitration Conferences, AfAA Annual International Arbitration Conferences, CIArb Nigeria Annual Conferences, ICC International Court of Arbitration Africa Conferences, CIArb Kenya International Conferences.
108. *See*, for example, Association for the Promotion of Arbitration in Africa (APAA), African Arbitration Association (AfAA), African Arbitration Academy (AAA), AfricArb, Africa Commission of the ICC Court.
109. Adam Hochschild, *King Leopold's Ghost* (Houghton Mifflin 1998), p. 13.
110. See, for example, Toby Green, *A Fistful of Shells: West Africa from the Rise of the Slave Trade to the Age of Revolution*, pp. 199-232; Adam Hochschild, *King Leopold's Ghost* (Houghton Mifflin 1998).

Still, the original Enlightenment, that so-called Age of Reason had its limitations. It did not stop man from using the law to commit unthinkable atrocities, exploit other men, and entrench inequality based on arbitrary criteria. So, let not our celebration of a new Age of Enlightenment in International Arbitration lead us to complacency. Enlightenment is not enough.

CHAPTER 33

African Practitioners, International Arbitration, and Inclusivity

Emilia Onyema[*]

TABLE OF CONTENTS

I   INTRODUCTION

This 2022 ICCA Congress is titled, 'Arbitration's Age of Enlightenment?' as a question. Since the last ICCA Congress in 2018, there have been several shifts in the world of arbitration particularly with the 2020 COVID-19 pandemic, evolutions in artificial intelligence (AI), information technology, issues of climate change, more recourse to regional trading and investment blocs, global economic uncertainties, and various geopolitical unrests. The shifts we have seen in arbitration proceedings include the move to virtual and hybrid hearings through greater use of information technology; the new push towards greater use of AI including new 'venues' for arbitration such as in the metaverse; greater interest in greener arbitrations; and for the regional focus of my

[*] Emilia Onyema is a Professor of International Commercial Law at SOAS University of London. I am grateful to Dr Chinwe Egbunike-Umegbolu and Mr Umran Chowdhury for their research assistance. All errors remain mine.

paper, the start of trading of the African Continental Free Trade Area. Any discerning eye will notice that the vast majority of these shifts are global in nature, yet it appears that African voices in these spaces are not being heard. I intend in this context, to interrogate the role of Africans in international arbitration and the development of arbitration in African states; recent developments such as the launch of our SOAS Arbitration in Africa survey, the various arbitration conferences and initiatives such as the launch and the role of the African Arbitration Association; how, through these developments, African states and African arbitration practitioners contribute their 'African voices' to the development of international arbitral jurisprudence. I will explore how this much-needed engagement can be sustained and utilised in the promotion of arbitration as an inclusive and purposive dispute resolution mechanism which is truly global and international. In section II, I will set out international arbitration and African practitioners; our SOAS arbitration in Africa survey (III); the African Promise (IV); modern arbitration in African states (V); and the future growth of arbitration in Africa (VI).

II   INTERNATIONAL ARBITRATION AND AFRICAN PRACTITIONERS

Arbitration is now globally recognised as the dispute resolution of choice for the resolution of cross-border commercial disputes. It is not immediately clear whether arbitration is also the dispute resolution of choice for domestic commercial disputes in African states. I have argued that this may not necessarily be the case.[1] If my view is correct, it follows that there is a need for the African arbitration community to develop or promote the use of arbitration for the resolution of domestic commercial disputes in their various countries.

The global rise of arbitration for the resolution of cross-border commercial disputes has also created an international arbitration community. Sociologists appear to agree on certain features of a community, including a group of people who interact with each other; such interaction happens within a bounded territory; and members of the group share common values, beliefs and behaviours; the group has a particular social structure and all its members have a sense of belonging.[2]

1   Framing the Problem

The international arbitration community membership includes arbitrators, counsel, tribunal secretaries, administrators of arbitral institutions and associations, and experts. We all acknowledge that the membership of this community is not homogenous

---

1. Emilia Onyema, 'Shifts in Dispute Resolution Processes of West African States' in A Moscati, M Roberts & M Palmer M (eds) Comparative Dispute Resolution Research Handbook (Edward Elgar Publishing, 2020), 519 at p. 527 where I note, 'Thus at present, litigation remains the primary (though not necessarily the preferred) method of dispute resolution in West African states.'
2. Phil Bartle, 'What Is a Community? A Sociological Perspective', available at: https://edadm821 .files.wordpress.com/2010/11/what-is-community.pdf (accessed 13 July 2022).

and being international or global, it by necessity, implicates the collection of individuals of different factors such as nationalities, gender, age, professional background, and ability – making for a diverse collection of peoples forming the community. Similar to any community of persons, it is the members of the community that devise, agree and perpetuate its norms, rules, principles, behaviours and cultures. In our global arbitration community, it is however not all its members that participate in developing its norms, rules, and principles leading to some differences in behaviours and cultures. This is the gap and problem which has raised the discourse on diversity and inclusion.

One peculiarity with the international arbitration community is that its arbitrator and counsel members make decisions and propose legal norms and principles which resonate outside of the community onto the general public and impact other communities of persons, such as states and citizens and businesses across the world.[3] It is the impact of this latter form of exclusion that is most worrisome, that is the exclusion of some voices from participating in the crafting of the norms and rules that govern or influence international business and the behaviour of states. This exclusion of the voices from certain (underrepresented) groups against the amplification of the voices of those members of the same community from certain other majority groups, is what needs rebalancing.

The major reason for such a rebalancing is the representation of the primary users of arbitration and those who are most impacted by the output of the global arbitration community in the form of final awards. These decisions are attributed to the whole community though produced by a section of the community. Some commentators refer to these minorities within a majority as the 'pale, stale and male' group, though it is not clear if the description requires the presence of all three elements. In my view, the description is rather wide since there are some pale, stale and male members of the community whose practice effectively reflects that of the underrepresented group. In contrast, there are also some pale females whose practice and rule-making opportunities equal (or even exceed) those of some of the male, pale and stale members.[4]

This lack of inclusion problem can therefore be framed a little differently to reflect these realities. The major discontent is that there are too many members of this community that are left at the fringes or margins while a select few are appointed and reappointed as arbitrators.[5] Though, such individuals do not reflect the demographics of the global arbitration community. In other words, the busiest arbitrators do not reflect the membership of the international arbitration community. I will now examine some publicly available data from some arbitration institutions with particular reference to the appointment of African arbitrators.

---

3. Examples include the various investment arbitration awards on measures taken by states whether to stabilise their currencies, protect their environment and public health issues.
4. One example is data from the world of investment arbitration where Professors Brigitte Stern and Gabrielle Kaufman-Kohler (who are both female though Europeans) rank among the top ten investment arbitrators in the world. On this, *see* Taylor St John, Daniel Behn, Malcolm Langford and Runar Lie, 'Glass Ceilings and Arbitral Dealings: Explaining the Gender Gap in International Investment Arbitration', Pluricourts Research paper of 23 March 2017 at p. 2, available at: https://papers.ssrn.com/sol3/papers.cfm?abstract_id = 3782593 (accessed 13 July 2022).
5. This is particularly relevant in those disputes which raise very important issues of general application for determination by the arbitral tribunal.

2 Data

It is of course a little too simplistic to examine this problem or its validity on the basis of bare numbers. This is for the simple reason that such comprehensive data is not available. In effect, we cannot count and say there are x number of arbitration practitioners across the world and of this x% are female; x% are under 40 years, and x% are African, etc. A qualitative analysis supplemented by publicly available data from arbitration institutions may provide us with more robust evidence or a picture of the situation. I note that it is not practicable to source data from all known arbitration institutions especially where such data is not publicly available. I shall therefore rely on representative data from across the regions of the world. I also note that the publication of data by arbitration institutions located in Europe and Asia is more comprehensive and easily available when compared with those from other regions of the world. This in effect will again skew the possible conclusions from such data since most of such institutions though 'international' as defined by their caseload and disputants, may not necessarily be 'international' in the nationality of the arbitrators that sit under their rules. With these caveats in mind, I shall now examine some of the most recent publicly available data from the two major non-African arbitration institutions that host disputes from African parties, the International Chamber of Commerce (ICC) in Paris and the London Court of International Arbitration (LCIA) in London,[6] and International Centre for Settlement of Investment Disputes (ICSID).

In 2020, The International Court of Arbitration of the International Chamber of Commerce (ICC) registered 929 cases under its rules and 17 cases as appointing authority.[7] In these cases, 2,507 parties were involved and 5% of the parties were from Sub-Saharan Africa,[8] while 1.8% were from North Africa.[9] These percentages translate to 171 parties from 35 African states.[10] In contrast, a total of 1,520 arbitrator appointments and confirmations from 92 countries were made. Of this, 1.2% were from Sub-Saharan Africa and 1.1% from North Africa. These percentages translate to 18[11] and 16[12] arbitrator appointments and confirmations from Sub-Saharan Africa and North Africa, respectively. These numbers speak for themselves on the disparities in the number of African parties and the number of Africans appointed as arbitrators. I

---

6. The ICC hosts arbitrations from across the African continent while the LCIA hosts arbitrations from primarily anglophone African countries. These have colonial linkages such as language, legal system, familiarity with the laws, and strong colonial ties.
7. ICC Dispute Resolution, 2020 Statistics, ICC Publication No.: DRS895 ENG (2021).
8. Representing 125 parties from: Angola (8); Benin (2); Burundi (2); Cameroon (2); Chad (1); Congo DR (9); Congo R(1); Cote d'Ivoire (1); Equatorial Guinea (1); Ethiopia (1); Gabon (9); Gambia (1); Ghana (4); Guinea (4); Kenya (3); Liberia (1); Madagascar (1); Mali (1); Mauritius (9); Mozambique (6); Nigeria (22); Rwanda (4); Seychelles (3); Sierra Leone (2); South Africa (7); Tanzania (8); Uganda (5); Zambia (5); and Zimbabwe (2).
9. Representing forty-six parties from: Algeria (9); Egypt (13); Libya (5); Mauritania (3); Morocco (6); and Tunisia (10).
10. ICC Dispute Resolution 2020 Statistics at p. 24.
11. Cameroon (2); Kenya (2); Mauritius (1); Nigeria (5); South Africa (4); Tanzania (1); and Zimbabwe (3).
12. Algeria (2); Egypt (12); Morocco (1); and Tunisia (1).

must note that these numbers need to be read in the context of the arbitrator appointment mechanism under the ICC Rules,[13] and the ICC Practice.[14]

I must quickly note that the ICC since 2020 has taken very practical steps towards greater inclusivity of African arbitrators through the appointment of a Regional Director for Africa, to, 'work closely with the ICC Africa Commission ... to expand the pool of qualified African arbitration practitioners who may act in the many ongoing and future disputes arising in the region'.[15] In 2021, they also launched the 'Hold the Door Open' scheme for young African arbitration practitioners as, 'an opportunity to gain practical experience by observing arbitration hearings' and this was launched with the first cohort in 2022.[16]

Turning to the LCIA 2021 statistics,[17] the LCIA received 322 referrals under its arbitration rules, eight referrals under the UNCITRAL rules and ten as appointing authority by parties from 90 countries.[18] Parties from African countries accounted for 6.6% (about 22 disputants) of the parties. In contrast, 449 appointments of 298 different arbitrators were made and of this, only 16 were from Africa.[19] These were from Egypt (4), Ghana (1); Kenya (2); Mauritius (2); Nigeria (2); South Africa (4); and Uganda (1).[20]

Finally, 2021 data from ICSID[21] for an investment arbitration view, also shows a major disparity between the number of African parties appearing before ICSID and the number of Africans appointed as arbitrators in ICSID arbitrations. African state parties were from Burkina Faso (1); Congo Republic (3); Egypt (3); Mali (2); Mauritania (1); Morocco (1); Nigeria (1); Sudan (1); and Tanzania (1) in 14 cases. African adjudicators[22] were from Botswana (2); Burundi (2); Nigeria (2.5);[23] and Egypt (0.5),[24] making a cumulative total of 5 appointments out of a total of 246 adjudicators appointed under ICSID proceedings in 2021.

I already mentioned that this is not an exact scientific analysis, but these bare numbers tell a story which is that we have more African parties occupying the role of disputants than those occupying the role of adjudicators. Readers must keep in mind

---

13. Article 13 ICC Rules, 2021.
14. The practice of nominations from ICC National Committees. Also, at p. 28 of the 2020 Statistics, the eleven-year trend tells a story of increase in most year-on-year data in the number of African arbitrators appointed and confirmed in ICC cases.
15. ICC Dispute Resolution 2020 Statistics, at p. 6. I note the 'may' in their statement which I hope will soon become 'shall'.
16. *See*: https://iccwbo.org/media-wall/news-speeches/new-initiative-to-hold-the-door-open-for-young-arbitration-practitioners/ (accessed 12 July 2022).
17. LCIA 2021 Annual Casework Report is available at: https://www.lcia.org/lcia/reports.aspx (accessed 12 July 2022).
18. LCIA 2021 Report, at p. 7.
19. LCIA 2021 Report, at pp. 9-10.
20. Interestingly, there appear to be no disputing parties from either Francophone or Lusophone Africa that refer their disputes to the LCIA.
21. The ICSID Caseload Statistics, 2022-1, pp. 24 and 28, and is available at: https://icsid.worldbank.org/sites/default/files/documents/The_ICSID_Caseload_Statistics.1_Edition_ENG.pdf (accessed 12 July 2022).
22. This includes, arbitrators, conciliators and ad hoc committee members.
23. One of the arbitrators with three appointments is UK/Nigeria national.
24. This adjudicator is Egypt/USA national.

the arbitrator appointment mechanism of these arbitration institutions in examining where the gap or fault for the lack of appointment of African arbitrators lay. This is not the purpose of this contribution.

I acknowledge that as Julian Lew will describe, this is a 'chicken and egg' situation. It is obvious that disputing parties want to appoint the best arbitrator for their case and one common requirement will be prior experience.[25] However, the million-dollar question is how do aspiring arbitrators get experience if they are not appointed as arbitrators in an arbitration dispute? In answer to this question, young aspiring colleagues have been advised to participate in moots, mentorship schemes, and if possible, to intern with very busy arbitrators.[26] And these are all good suggestions but sitting as an arbitrator is really not like any other professional activity. It is one of those roles that you learn by doing, not a mock or moot but by participating in an actual arbitration.[27] This is primarily because no two arbitrations are exactly the same. We can produce general practice rules and guidelines, and there are loads from different organisations,[28] but that is all they are: guidelines. Such guidelines have their place and are useful for standardising practice.

3   Some Necessary Skills for Arbitrators

It is important to examine again who should be appointed as arbitrators in the current more complex and sophisticated commercial environment in which international arbitration is practised. This examination will set out the skills and knowledge sets that Africans seeking arbitral appointment should also be measured against. These specifications are generic enough to be applied to any arbitrator appointment process.

The starting point will need to be the laws and rules of arbitration which provide minimum guidance and requirements. Provisions on possible skills for arbitrator appointees are very similar in arbitration laws and rules that deal with this issue. A few examples will therefore demonstrate the relevant provisions in arbitration laws and rules.

The UNCITRAL Model Law on International Commercial Arbitration (Model Law) and UNCITRAL Arbitration Rules require the arbitrator to be impartial and independent and possess any relevant qualification required by the parties.[29] This general requirement is also contained in other arbitration rules such as those of the ICC, LCIA, Kigali and Singapore International Arbitration Centre (SIAC).[30]

---

25. Emilia Onyema 'Empirically Determined Factors in Appointing Arbitrators in International Commercial Arbitration', Vol. 73, No. 2, Arbitration (2007) 199 at p. 205.
26. I already mentioned at *supra* n. 16, the ICC *Hold the Open Door* Initiative.
27. The role of tribunal secretary is closest to experiencing an actual arbitration as an arbitrator.
28. *See*, for example, guidelines from the Chartered Institute of Arbitrators (CIArb), International Bar Association (IBA) and International Council for Commercial Arbitration (ICCA).
29. Article 12 of the UNCITRAL Model Law; Article 11 of the UNCITRAL Arbitration Rules.
30. Article 11, ICC Arbitration Rules (2021); Article 10, LCIA Arbitration Rules 2020; Article 16, Kigali International Arbitration Centre Rules 2012; rule 13, Singapore International Arbitration Rules.

The recent joint collaborative effort between ICSID and UNCITRAL on a draft Code of Conduct for Adjudicators sets out the expectations of the community of the standard of behaviour expected of such adjudicators.[31] ICSID on its website notes that:

> The Code is intended to provide applicable principles and provisions addressing matters such as independence and impartiality, and the duty to conduct proceedings with integrity, fairness, efficiency and civility. It is based on a comparative review of standards found in codes of conduct in investment treaties, arbitration rules applicable to ISDS, and of international courts.[32]

Similarly, the IBA Conflict Guidelines note under General Principle 1 that, 'Every arbitrator shall be impartial and independent of the parties at the time of accepting an appointment to serve and shall remain so until the final award has been rendered or the proceedings have otherwise finally terminated.'[33]

A quick summary of some notable attributes or desirable skills for prospective arbitrators include: personal integrity which leads to independence and impartiality and relevant disclosure; communication skills (written and oral); cognitive skills (ability to think clearly and objectively, and to listen); knowledge of the process, laws and rules of arbitration relevant to the particular dispute; social skills which includes respect for others and cultural awareness; and ability to 'judge' or make binding decisions.

It is my firm belief that these attributes are not the sole preserve of some practitioners but are also evident in a large number of Africa-based arbitration practitioners though with less visibility internationally. It became apparent to me that the global arbitration community need to become more aware of this crop of experienced and skilled African arbitration practitioners. Some of the actions that I and some colleagues have taken to promote the participation of African practitioners in international arbitration will be discussed briefly below.

III   SOAS ARBITRATION IN AFRICA SURVEY

At SOAS we started a bespoke biennial data-gathering exercise from which we publish a report on the state of arbitration and its practitioners on the African continent. As noted in our 2018 survey report, the purposes of the survey are: (1) to provide a platform for African practitioners to express their views of and experiences in domestic and international arbitration; (2) to effectively articulate 'African voices' in the international arbitration discourse; and (3) to provide evidence from arbitration

---

31. *See* the ICSID website for various commentaries on the Code at: https://icsid.worldbank.org/resources/code-of-conduct/commentary (accessed 13 July 2022).
32. *See*: https://icsid.worldbank.org/resources/code-of-conduct (accessed 13 July 2022).
33. The text of the IBA Guidelines on Conflicts of Interest in International Arbitration is available at: https://www.ibanet.org/MediaHandler?id = e2fe5e72-eb14-4bba-b10d-d33dafee8918#: ~ :text = (d)%20An%20arbitrator%20is%20under,or%20her%20impartiality%20or%20independence (accessed 13 July 2022).

practitioners in Africa of their knowledge, expertise, experiences, skills and participation (in arbitration).[34] This 2018 survey report provided empirical evidence in support of well-acknowledged issues such as the underrepresentation of African practitioners in international arbitration. It, however, also provided us with qualitative information on why this was the case. The top reasons given by the respondents to this issue were: (1) poor perception of African arbitration practitioners (by their foreign colleagues) as lacking in expertise and experience; (2) bias by appointors in favour of foreign counsel and arbitrator; and (3) Africans not appointing fellow Africans as arbitrators.[35]

Our 2020 survey focused on the top African arbitration institutions operating on the continent and the most used seats for arbitration.[36] While our 2022 survey focuses on the views of African arbitration practitioners on globally topical issues such as the COVID-19 pandemic, climate change, infrastructure projects and the Africa Continental Free Trade Area and their impact on arbitration in Africa.[37]

These survey reports contribute the much touted 'African voices' to international arbitration discourses but will not help shape international law or global social changes if more Africans do not sit as arbitrators and contribute to the development of such jurisprudence. The key milestone is for many more experienced African arbitrators to sit in international arbitration proceedings and not only on Africa-connected disputes. However, even appointments to arbitral tribunals on Africa-connected disputes are a good start. It is this understanding that led to the drafting and publication of the *African Promise*.

IV   THE AFRICAN PROMISE

Jay-Z, the media mogul in 2019 raised an outcry that made the front pages of several news outlets, for the lack of African Americans on the arbitrator panel of the American Arbitration Association (AAA) from which he was required to choose arbitrators.[38] This is despite the fact that Jay-Z's lawyers were predominantly white.[39] The international arbitration community for several decades had operated in the full knowledge of the underrepresentation of Africans as arbitrators and counsel in international arbitration.

---

34. Emilia Onyema, SOAS Arbitration in Africa Survey (2018) titled, 'Domestic and International Arbitration: Perspectives from African Arbitration Practitioners', at p. 4, available at: https://eprints.soas.ac.uk/25741/1/SOAS%20Arbitration%20in%20Africa%20Survey%20Report%202018.pdf (accessed 13 July 2022).
35. SOAS Arbitration in Africa survey report (2018), *ibid.*, at p. 8.
36. Emilia Onyema, SOAS Arbitration in Africa survey report (2020) titled 'Top African arbitral Centres and Seats', available at: https://eprints.soas.ac.uk/33162/1/2020%20Arbitration%20in%20Africa%20Survey%20Report%2030.06.2020.pdf (accessed 13 July 2022).
37. The 2022 SOAS Arbitration in Africa survey report will be published in August 2022.
38. 'Jay-Z Criticizes Lack of Black Arbitrators in a Battle Over a Logo (Published 2018)' (*Nytimes.com*, 2022); Link: https://www.nytimes.com/2018/11/28/arts/music/jay-z-roc-nation-arbitrators.html. *See also* commentary on this in the American University Business Law Review available at: https://aublr.org/2019/03/jay-z-adds-to-his-legacy-by-creating-space-for-diversity-in-arbitration/ (accessed 13 July 2022).
39. Jay-Z was represented by Alex Spiro of Quinn Emanuel LLP whose profile is at: https://www.quinnemanuel.com/attorneys/spiro-alex/ (accessed 13 July 2022).

In 2019, the *African Promise* was published to promote greater participation of African practitioners in international arbitration as arbitrators and counsel. The text of the *African Promise* was based on that of the Equal Representation in Arbitration (ERA) Pledge which itself was published in [2016] to, 'improve the profile and representation of women in arbitration; and to appoint women as arbitrators on an equal opportunity basis'.[40] The ERA Pledge as of 17 June 2022 has been signed by 5,068 individuals and organisations.[41] It has led to an increase in the number of women appointed to sit as arbitrators, particularly by arbitration institutions. Against the 2020 annual caseload reports for example, the ICC reported an increase in the number of females appointed/confirmed as arbitrators from 312 in 2019 to 355 in 2020;[42] the LCIA Court in its 2021 casework Report reports that it, 'remains the main driving force in gender diversity, selecting women in 47% of all its appointments';[43] as did SIAC that reported that, 'of the 196 arbitrators appointed by SIAC, 64 (35.8%) were women';[44] and ICSID reported an increase of female adjudicators appointment to 27% of all appointments.[45] These are in addition to the increase in the number of females appointed to lead arbitration institutions in the recent past including the celebration of the first female President of the ICC International Court of Arbitration announced in November 2020.[46]

The ERA Pledge is therefore globally acknowledged as an effective tool in the gender rebalancing of actors in international arbitration. The *African Promise* authors therefore, with the consent of the executives of the ERA Pledge, decided to build on this successful model.[47] The *African Promise* as of the end of May 2022 has been signed by 343 individuals and organisations.[48]

I already showed above in section 2.2, using available data from some of the major arbitration institutions, to show that they receive arbitration cases from many more African parties than the number of African arbitrators they appoint. Thus, having established that African arbitration practitioners are not appointed in corresponding numbers in Africa-related or non-Africa-related disputes as arbitrators, and with the responses from the SOAS 2018 Survey, the need for some remedial steps was obvious.

---

40. Equal Representation in Arbitration (ERA) Pledge is available at http://www.arbitrationpledge .com/ (accessed 4 July 2022).
41. *See* ERA webpages at: http://www.arbitrationpledge.com/ (accessed 4 July 2022).
42. ICC Dispute Resolution, 2020 Statistics, ICC Publication No: DRS895 ENG (2021) at p. xx.
43. 'LCIA News: Annual Casework Report 2021, at p. 5, available at: https://www.lcia.org/lcia/ reports.aspx (accessed 13 July 2022).
44. SIAC Annual Report (2021) at p. 24 is available at: https://www.siac.org.sg/images/stories/ articles/annual_report/SIAC-AR2021-FinalFA.pdf (accessed 13 July 2022).
45. ICSID Casework Statistics (2022-1) at p. 30, available at: https://icsid.worldbank.org/sites/ default/files/documents/The_ICSID_Caseload_Statistics.1_Edition_ENG.pdf (accessed 13 July 2022).
46. *See*: https://iccwbo.org/media-wall/news-speeches/client-mindset-takes-centre-stage-under-new-icc-court-president-claudia-salomon/#: ~ :text = Claudia % 20Salomon % 20made % 20histo ry % 20on,world's % 20foremost % 20international % 20arbitral % 20institution (accessed 13 July 2022).
47. The authors of the African Promise are Professor Emilia Onyema of SOAS University of London; Dr Stuart Dutson of Simmons and Simmons, London and Mr Kamal Shah of Stephenson Harwood, London.
48. The *African Promise* is available for signature at: https://onyema-arbitration.co.uk/the-african -promise/ (accessed 13 July 2022).

The *African Promise* is one of the remedial steps that can be taken to raise greater awareness of this exclusionary practice which has persisted for far too long and to begin to correct it. The text of the African Promise is short and states as follows:

> As a group of counsel, arbitrators, representatives of corporates, States, arbitral institutions, academics and others involved in the practice of international arbitration, we are committed to improving the profile and representation of African arbitrators especially in arbitrations connected to Africa. In particular, we consider that African arbitrators should be appointed as arbitrators on an equal opportunity basis. To achieve this, we will take the steps reasonably available to us – and we will encourage other participants in the arbitral process to do likewise – to ensure that, wherever possible:
>
> - committees, governing bodies and conference panels in the field of arbitration include a fair representation of Africans;
> - in arbitrations connected with Africa lists of potential arbitrators or tribunal chairs provided to or considered by parties, counsel, in-house counsel, arbitral institutions or otherwise include a fair representation of African candidates;
> - States, arbitral institutions and national committees include a fair representation of African candidates on rosters and lists of potential arbitrator appointees, where maintained by them;
> - where they have the power to do so, counsel, arbitrators, representatives of corporates, States and arbitral institutions appoint a fair representation of African arbitrators especially in arbitrations connected with Africa;
> - statistics for nominations and appointments (split by party and other appointment) of African arbitrators especially in relation to arbitrations connected with Africa are collated by arbitral institutions and made publicly available; and
> - senior and experienced arbitration practitioners support, mentor/sponsor and encourage Africans to pursue arbitrator appointments and otherwise enhance their profiles and practice.
>
> In recognition of the under-representation of Africans on international arbitral tribunals especially in arbitrations connected with Africa, we have drawn up a promise to take action (an African Promise). An African Promise seeks to increase the number of Africans appointed as arbitrators, especially in arbitrations connected with Africa in order to achieve a fair representation as soon as practically possible.
>
> The introductory paragraph of An African Promise sets out two general objectives:
> 1. to improve the profile and representation of African arbitrators; and
> 2. to appoint Africans as arbitrators, especially in arbitrations connected with Africa.

An African Promise establishes concrete and actionable steps that the international arbitration community can and must take towards achieving these general objectives. It is, however, acknowledged that in some cases, some stakeholders may not reasonably be able to carry out each and every commitment. For this reason, the words 'wherever possible' were introduced to preface each of the specific commitments.

The *African Promise* on its own cannot fix the problem of exclusion. It is one step. The *African Promise* binds its signatories who have voluntarily signed it to ensure a fair consideration for the appointment of African arbitrators in both Africa-related and non-Africa-related disputes where such Africans are qualified. Stripped to its bare minimum, the *African Promise* requires arbitrator appointors to include the names of

African arbitrators in their appointment shortlists for the selection of their clients. It is obvious that if a name does not make the shortlist, there is no chance of such individuals being appointed. The inclusion of the names of qualified African arbitrators assures such nominees and the selecting parties that they are qualified to be selected as arbitrators. This will begin to create a list of names of possible African arbitrator appointors.

Africans are latecomers to the modern arbitration space and so will not have as much experience in terms of the number of disputes and complexity of disputes determined. However, appointments in domestic disputes and less complex matters will increase the number of disputes determined and the experience and skill of these arbitrators. Moreover, it is well recognised that the Chartered Institute of Arbitrators has a strong training track record in English-speaking Africa, with several African arbitration practitioners noting that they have undertaken Chartered Institute of Arbitrators (CIArb) courses and hold qualifications as associates, members, fellows and chartered arbitrators of the CIArb.[49] In addition, many young practitioners have studied arbitration as part of their postgraduate or undergraduate studies in universities either within or outside the African continent creating a knowledgeable group of possible appointors.

It must be stressed that though the *African Promise* refers to Africa-connected disputes, this was to reassure non-African colleagues whose practice is primarily built on Africa-related disputes and also to acknowledge the fact that at this time, the continent may not have the requisite number of practitioners with relevant expertise for African disputants to appoint onto arbitral tribunals. We must continue to build and grow this capacity across the continent. The goal firmly remains the full and fair participation of all qualified members of the international arbitration community in any type of dispute to which they are so qualified to adjudicate.

The next phase of the *African Promise* is monitoring its impact. It is not just a question of the number of signatories, but it remains more importantly the question of monitoring compliance with the undertakings made by signatories of the *African Promise*. The private nature of arbitration restricts the amount of information even of number of disputes in the public domain. However, some institutions are beginning to publish the names and some information of individuals sitting as arbitrators under their rules.[50] In some cases such as ICSID, this information also includes the names of those organisations acting as counsel.[51]

I strongly believe that the publication that will add more value to the information we currently can access publicly is the publication of the names and nationalities of individuals nominated by the parties and institutions to sit as arbitrators (irrespective of whether they were so appointed as arbitrators in the particular dispute). Such

---

49. Emilia Onyema, SOAS Arbitration in Africa Survey (2018), *supra* n. 34, at p. 15.
50. *See*, for example, the ICC arbitral tribunals search engine available at: https://iccwbo.org/dispute-resolution-services/arbitration/icc-arbitral-tribunals/ (accessed 13 July 2022); and ICSID database is available at: https://icsid.worldbank.org/resources/databases/arbitrators-conciliators-ad-hoc-committee-members (accessed 13 July 2022).
51. A search of the cases will include counsel names: https://icsid.worldbank.org/cases/case-database (accessed 13 July 2022).

publication will support the international arbitration community by identifying those practitioners that parties and institutions consider suitable to be nominated as arbitrators. It will reassure those disputants wishing to appoint an individual in such list as being suitable for appointment and this will lead to appointments for aspiring arbitrators and those wishing to grow their practice.

The second focus of the African Promise is to work with the active African arbitration institutions and to support them to widen their pool of arbitrator appointors, especially from the continent, and to publish such lists as well by making them freely and publicly available. This is important if we recollect that one of the top reasons African arbitration practitioners gave for their low participation in international arbitration in our 2018 SOAS Arbitration in Africa survey report is, 'Africans not appointing fellow Africans as arbitrators'.[52] I cannot emphasise enough the need for African disputants and arbitration institutions to appoint qualified and experienced Africans as arbitrators as a matter of evidencing their confidence in the ability of their fellow Africans to so act. This will also encourage non-African parties and institutions to appoint such Africans.

I shall now turn to a brief discussion of the role of the modern form of arbitration in supporting the increased participation of Africans in international arbitration.

V   MODERN ARBITRATION IN AFRICAN STATES

It must be acknowledged that as it relates to modern forms of arbitration, African countries can also be said to be latecomers to the table. However, it is not because there was no concept of dispute resolution in African communities before colonialism. There were several different forms of dispute resolution processes that continue to exist and are practised in different African communities. These processes are referred to as customary or traditional dispute resolution processes.[53] Every description (as documented primarily by anthropologists) of these 'customary' dispute resolution processes evidence the fact that there was a spectrum of processes from the conciliatory to the interventionist by a third party or panel of adjudicators.[54] One major difference between the traditional and modern forms of dispute resolution processes was that the third party did not have to necessarily be neutral (in the sense of independent and impartial of the disputing parties). In most cases, such third party was also an interested party, but one that is trusted by the disputing parties. The adjudicator could be either a member of the family of the disputants or from the same community, clan or village. In some cases, depending on the social sensitivity or the nature of the dispute, the resolution process was private, as between the disputants or their families.

---

52. Emilia Onyema, SOAS Arbitration in Africa survey report (2018), at p. 8.
53. See Chinwe Egbunike-Umegbolu, 'The Chronicles of the Pre-Colonial Method of Settling Disputes: Nigeria as a Case Study', Transnational Dispute Management (May 2022).
54. See Emilia Onyema, 'Shifts in Dispute Resolution Processes of West African States' in A. Moscati, M. Roberts & M. Palmer (eds), Comparative Dispute Resolution Research Handbook (Edward Elgar Publishing, 2020), 519. See also Virtus Chitoo Igbokwe, 'The Law and Practice of Customary Arbitration in Nigeria: Agu V. Ikewibe and Applicable Law Issues Revisited', Journal of African Law Vol. 41 (1997), at p. 201.

However, such dispute became public immediately after it was elevated for resolution by the community or clan or village.[55]

The modern form of arbitration is backed or underpinned by formal (and semi-formal) rules and laws and the state's police powers. Its adjudicators are required to be neutral or independent of the disputing parties, which in itself, is one example of the influence of litigation on arbitration or private adjudication. There is therefore ample evidence that Africans by nature, in the same manner as other humans, have full capacity to resolve disputes and have done this over many centuries.

Modern form of arbitration requires the application of an identified set of rules or laws to the ascertained facts to arrive at a reasoned decision. In pre-colonial times, African adjudicators or decision-makers applied clearly identified customary practices or rules or principles to ascertained facts to reach a decision. They also distinguished facts where necessary and where there is no clear customary practice, rule or principle to apply to a particular set of facts, the adjudicators devised new rules that aligned with other rules and fundamental laws of the particular community.[56] In this way, such adjudicators made new rules and laws that over time and with acceptance within the community, clan or village, became observed as binding by its members. In a similar manner, modern arbitrators may devise new rules to apply to a given set of novel facts and over time this may be accepted by the particular trade community or a national court and enforced by the court or performed by the parties. It is this rule-making ability of arbitrators that makes the inclusion of African arbitrators particularly imperative.

African businesses and parties participate in the international trading system and are part of the community of traders. African countries account for large amounts of raw materials and minerals partly from the extractive sector as primary producers and import finished products and technology as consumers.[57] In this trading system, African states and their agencies also play major roles as parties and regulators. It is fully recognised and accepted that increased trading activities generally lead to an increase in disputes and these disputes need to be efficiently resolved. Arbitration is globally recognised as the most viable process for the resolution of commercial disputes and this needs to also be the situation in African countries.[58] I briefly make the case below that, for this to become a reality, we need to develop the domestic arbitration market in Africa.

---

55. *See* Chinwe Egbunike-Umegbolu, *ibid.*, at p. 10.
56. *See* Abdulmumini A. Oba, 'The Future of Customary in Africa', in Jeanmarie Fenrich, Paolo Galizzi & Tracy E. Higgins (eds) *The Future of African Customary Law*, CUP (2012) 58 at p. 63.
57. *See* John Stuart, 'How African can move up the Value Chain' OECD Development Matters Publication (2022) available at: https://oecd-development-matters.org/2022/03/10/how-africa-can-move-up-the-value-chain/ (accessed 13 July 2022).
58. *See* for a discussion of this in the context of the African Continental free Trade Area, Emilia Onyema, 'Reimagining the Framework for Resolving Intra-African Commercial Disputes in the Context of the African Continental Free Trade Area Agreement', *World Trade Review* (2019), pp. 1-25.

VI   FUTURE GROWTH AREA

Arbitration of commercial disputes will continue to grow in numbers as it relates to African disputes. It is also expected that there will be an increase in the number of intra-African disputes from the growth of intra-African trade as a result of the commencement of trading in goods and services under the Africa Continental Free Trade Agreement.[59] The commercial contracts that will underpin these transactions will most likely include arbitration clauses so that when disputes arise, they will be arbitrated. It is important that there is proper awareness of the systems for arbitration within the African continent to forestall the export of such arbitrations outside the continent as is the current situation.

In addition to modern arbitration laws and rules, independent arbitration institutions and a supportive judiciary, Africa needs to develop a crop of skilled and experienced African arbitrators that can be appointed to adjudicate such disputes. These adjudicators can be pulled from domestic arbitration within African states. To do this we need to encourage the uptake of domestic arbitration and preferably for such arbitrations to be administered by local arbitration institutions. In this way, African arbitration institutions will also gain sustained experience in administering arbitrations. Thus, in my opinion, developmental resources and energy should be focused on the development and growth of the domestic arbitration market and ecosystem in each African state. We are aware of 91 arbitration institutions in 41 African countries and, in my view, these are not enough. This is because we have 11 African countries that do not have any known arbitration institutions. The key issue is not the number of arbitral institutions but ensuring that those that exist are qualitative and sustainable. I have argued elsewhere that not all those organisations that describe themselves as arbitration institutions in reality administer arbitration cases.[60] We need to identify those organisations that administer arbitrations and provide them with the necessary support to ensure continuity and also push for a move away from a predominantly ad hoc arbitration market to institutional arbitration in African states.

VII   CONCLUSION

In this contribution, I have argued and made suggestions for the inclusion of African arbitration practitioners in the international arbitration community and the development of arbitration in African states through support for domestic and institutional arbitration.

---

59. *Ibid*.
60. Emilia Onyema, SOAS Arbitration in Africa survey report (2020), *supra*, at p. 7.

PANEL 9   The Sociology of Arbitration

CHAPTER 34

The Changing Sociology of the Investment Arbitration Market: The Case of Double Hatting

*Malcolm Langford**

I   INTRODUCTION

In April 2018, in a keynote address at the New York Investment Arbitration Centre, United Nations Commission on International Trade Law (UNCITRAL)[1] Secretary Anna Joubin-Brett spoke of the 'misery of being a double hatter'.[2] Reflecting on the enhanced scrutiny the investment arbitration community was facing over the long-standing practice of arbitrators acting simultaneously as legal counsel, Joubin-Brett's timing was

*   Professor, Faculty of Law, University of Oslo; Chair, Academic Forum on ISDS; Affiliate Researcher, PluriCourts Centre of Excellence and Co-Director, Centre on Law and Social Transformation, University of Bergen and CMI. In memory of Daniel F. Behn, 1974-2022. Email: malcolm.langford@jus.uio.no. Thanks to Lauge Poulsen, Federico Ortino, Daniel Behn, and Nicolo Ridi for comments on an earlier version.
1. United Nations Commission on International Trade Law.
2. Anna Joubin-Bret, *Judith S. Kaye Arbitration Lecture*, New York International Arbitration Center, New York, 25 April 2018.

notable. Earlier that day, the Austrian state representative in the UNCITRAL Working Group (WG) III negotiations on investment arbitration reform had cited statistics on the extent of double hatting.[3] Long-standing murmurings of dissent over the practice,[4] strengthened by empirical research, were now finding a formal and official voice. It was also a voice that grew quickly in strength. In subsequent sessions within UNCITRAL WG III, critiques of the practice were echoed by numerous states in their written and oral submissions and significant time was devoted to the discussion of potential regulation and prohibition.[5]

This backlash against double hatting provides a useful opportunity to ask whether there is a changing sociology in the international investment arbitration market. Double hatting is one of many concerns with arbitral practice that is grounded in growing public law expectations of adjudicative behaviour.[6] Other concerns include multiple appointments by the same party,[7] lack of procedural transparency,[8] proximity of law firms to arbitrators,[9] conflicts of interests,[10] excessive collegiality,[11] lack of diversity,[12] high fees,[13] and excessive numbers of appointments,[14] which have all raised pressure on the current modus of appointment. This is further exacerbated by

---

3. The paper cited was Malcolm Langford, Daniel Behn, and Runar Hilleren Lie, 'The Ethics and Empirics of Double Hatting' 6:7 ESIL Reflection (2017) p. 1.
4. Phillipe Sands, 'Conflict and Conflicts in Investment Treaty Arbitration: Ethical Standards for Counsel' in Arthur Rovine ed., *Contemporary Issues in International Arbitration and Mediation: The Fordham Papers* (Brill, 2012), p. 28; Phillipe Sands, 'Developments in Geopolitics: The End(s) of Judicialization?' *2015 ESIL Conference Closing Speech*, 12 September 2015.
5. *See* sections III/IV below.
6. *See, e.g.*, the analysis of growing judicialization and constitutionalization in Alec Stone Sweet and Florian Grisel, *The Evolution of International Arbitration: Judicialization, Governance, Legitimacy* (Oxford University Press 2017).
7. *See* Luke Eric Petersen, 'Spain Succeeds in Disqualifying Arbitrator Kaj Hober in Energy Charter Arbitration', *Investment Arbitration Reporter*, 14 January 2020; UNCITRAL, Report of Working Group III (Investor-State Dispute Settlement Reform) on the work of its thirty-eighth session (Vienna, 14-18 October 2019) UN doc. A/CN.9/1004. *See also*: *Halliburton Co. v. Chubb Bermuda Insurance Ltd & Others* (Court of Appeal (England and Wales), 19 April 2018). On appeal to UK Supreme Court.
8. *See, e.g.*, Chiara Giorgetti, 'Who Decides Who in International Investment Arbitration', 35(2) University of Pennsylvania Journal of International Law (2014) p. 431; Sergio Puig, 'Blinding International Justice', 56(3) Virginia Journal of International Law (2016) p. 647.
9. Runar Lie, 'The Influence of Law Firms in Investment Arbitration', in Daniel Behn, Ole Kristian Fauchald and Malcolm Langford eds, *The Legitimacy of Investment Arbitration: Empirical Perspectives* (Cambridge University Press, 2022), p. 100.
10. *See* Judith Levine, 'Dealing with Arbitrator "Issue Conflicts" in International Arbitration', 61 Dispute Resolution Journal (2006) p. 60; Ruth Mackenzie and Phillipe Sands, 'International Courts and Tribunals and the Independence of the International Judge', 44 Harvard International Law Journal 271 (2003); Joseph Brubaker, 'The Judge Who Knew Too Much: Issue Conflicts in International Adjudication', 26(1) Berkeley Journal of International Law (2008), p. 111.
11. Sergio Puig, 'Social Capital in the Arbitration Market', 25 European Journal of International Law (2014) pp. 387, 400.
12. Andre Bjorklund et al., 'The Diversity Deficit in International Investment Arbitration', 21(2-3) Journal of World Investment and Trade (2020) p. 410.
13. Focusing at least on transparency of costs awards, *see* Susan Franck, 'Rationalizing Costs in Investment Treaty Arbitration', 88 Wash. U. L. Rev. (2011) p. 769.
14. UNCITRAL, Report of Working Group III (Investor-State Dispute Settlement Reform) on the work of its thirty-eighth session (Vienna, 14-18 October 2019) UN doc. A/CN.9/1004.

broader critiques that Investor-State Dispute Settlement (ISDS) is pro-investor,[15] pro-investment,[16] anti-developing state,[17] and fails to provide legal certainty.[18]

To be sure, the system (including the practice of double hatting) has its defenders. They assert that the critique is exaggerated, overblown, or simply incorrect, and that the regime evolves to address concerns and attracts more support than is acknowledged.[19] Yet, the mounting critique has fuelled a call for a greater democratization of the regime, which has already partly materialized. As shall be argued, in the case of double hatting, we can observe new and emerging rules, self-regulation in the face of reputational pressure, and threats of greater judicial scrutiny.

The result is that two predominant explanatory theories of arbitral appointment – symbolic capital and insider behaviour – require revisiting, especially due to the emerging public law nature of appointment. Public law norms *transform* the type of capital that is demanded by prospective clients and their lawyers and *disrupt* existing forms of insider behaviour – especially double hatting. However, the paper points also to some paradoxical and dynamic effects. On one hand, the rise of what might be called 'moral capital' may be creating new forms of competition, as pragmatic gatekeepers of old may give way to new moral gatekeepers. On the other hand, the last two years have also witnessed the rise of a counter-movement, seeking to legitimate traditional arbitral private law norms within ISDS.

The paper proceeds by presenting the arbitration market (section 2), introducing and expanding competing theories of arbitral appointment (section 3), and then

---

15. That is, tribunals exhibit a bias that disproportionately favours the interests and rights of individual foreign investors when pitted against the duty of a state to regulate and legislate in the broader public interest. *See, e.g.,* Gus Van Harten, 'Arbitrator Behaviour in Asymmetrical Adjudication: An Empirical Study of Investment Treaty Arbitration', 50 Osgoode Hall Law Journal (2012), p. 211 at p. 251.

16. That is, tribunals exhibit a bias that disproportionately favours liberal economic rights and values over other equally important public welfare objectives such as public health, environmental protection or fundamental human rights. *See,* e.g., Jorge Viñuales, *Foreign Investment and the Environment in International Law* (Cambridge University Press 2012).

17. That is, tribunals are disproportionately more likely to rule against less developed respondent states. *See, e.g.,* Thomas Schultz and Cedric Dupot, 'Investment Arbitration: Promoting the Rule of Law or Over-Empowering Investors? A Quantitative Empirical Study', 25 European Journal of International Law 1147 (2014); Daniel Behn, Tarald Berge and Malcolm Langford, 'Poor States or Poor Governance? Explaining Outcomes in Investment Treaty Arbitration', 38(3) *Northwestern Journal of International Law & Business* (2018), p. 333.

18. *See, e.g.,* Michael Waibel et al. eds, *The Backlash Against Investment Arbitration: Perceptions and Reality* (Kluwer 2010); Julian Arato, Chester Brown and Federico Ortino, 'Parsing and Managing Inconsistency in ISDS', 21 *Journal of World Investment and Trade* (2020), p. 336; Florian Grisel, 'Fair and Equitable Treatment: Ordering Chaos Through Precedent?', in Daniel Behn, Ole Kristian Fauchald and Malcolm Langford eds, *The Legitimacy of Investment Arbitration: Empirical Perspectives* (Cambridge University Press, 2021) p. 258.

19. For example, the European Federation for Investment Law and Arbitration (EFILA) concludes that, 'The bottom line of this analysis is that most of the criticisms are neither supported by the facts nor by the treaty practice and case law. The fact is that the system has been functioning satisfactorily and that it generally provides for adequate resolution of investment disputes.' European Federation for Investment Law and Arbitration (EFILA), *A Response to the Criticism Against ISDS,* 17 May 2015, 42. *See also* J. Fry, 'International Human Rights Law in Investment Arbitration: Evidence of International Law's Unity' 18 Duke Journal of International and Comparative Law (2007) p. 77.

charting the trajectory of critique (section 4) and its effects on the arbitration market (section 5). It concludes cautiously by presenting a revised theory of today's arbitration market while noting the emergence of a concerted pushback against reform (section 6).

II   PRESENTING THE ARBITRATION MARKET

The development of ISDS represents a remarkable extension of both international law and commercial arbitration. While the development of this regime is largely attributable to the rise of the sprawling network of investment treaties, arbitration can arise also through various forms of investment contracts and national foreign direct investment (FDI) laws.[20] Commonly, arbitration panels are filled by (wing) arbitrators appointed respectively by the investor and state with a president (chair) appointed by either the two-wing arbitrators or the host institution. While the field of ISDS was a small niche market for arbitrators in the 1990s, there are now over one thousand known investment treaty arbitrations initiated to date (almost all coming in the last 15-20 years)[21] – 1177 as of October 2020.[22] Highly prestigious, it is a coveted market for many working in the field of international law and/or commercial arbitration.

The actors that inhabit the mysterious and closeted world of international arbitration have long been of academic interest. In 1996, after extensive interviews, Dezalay and Grant observed that a coterie of 'grand old men' dominated the broader field of international commercial arbitration.[23] Small in number, linked closely, and mostly European, they even referred to themselves as a 'club' or a 'mafia'.[24] After a period of 'generational warfare', these figures were joined and complemented by Anglo-American arbitration technocrats and law firms.[25]

Often drawing on Dezalay and Garth, more recent studies confirm the asymmetric nature of the arbitration market within ISDS, whether in terms of gender, nationality, education, employment background and the core-periphery.[26] Puig's social

---

20. This particular form of arbitration is often administered under ICSID, but can also arise under ad hoc procedures or the rules of international commercial arbitration centres.

21. PluriCourts Investment Treaty Arbitration Database (PITAD): pitad.org. Daniel Behn et al., *PITAD Investment Law and Arbitration Database: Version 1.0*, Pluricourts Centre of Excellence, University of Oslo (31 January 2019).

22. Daniel Behn et al., 'Evidence-Guided Reform: Surveying the Empirical Research on Arbitrator Bias and Diversity in Investor–State Arbitration', in Manfred Elsig, Rodrigo Polanco, Peter van de Bossche, *International Economic Dispute Settlement: Demise or Transformation?* (Cambridge University Press 2021), p. 264 at p. 267.

23. Yves Dezalay and Bryant Garth, *Dealing in Virtue: International Commercial Arbitration and the Construction of a Transnational Legal Order* (Chicago University Press, 1996).

24. *Ibid.*, at 10.

25. *Ibid.* Although this generational depiction is contested: see discussion in response by Grisel to this chapter.

26. *See, e.g.*, Paul Friedland and Stavros Brekoulakis, '2012 International Arbitration Survey: Current and Preferred Practices in the Arbitral Process', 8 Const. L. Int'l (2013), p. 39; Michael Waibel and Yanhui Wu, 'Are Arbitrators Political?' Working Paper (December 2011); Susan Franck, 'Empirically Evaluating Claims about Investment Treaty Arbitration,' 86 N.C. L. Rev. (2007), p. 1; Lauge N. Skovgaard Poulsen, 'Politics of Investment Treaty Arbitration', in Thomas Schultz and Federico Ortino, eds, *Oxford Handbook of International Arbitration* (Oxford University Press 2018); Susan Franck et al., 'International Arbitration: Demographics, Precision

network analysis of arbitral appointments at the International Centre for Settlement of Investment Disputes (ICSID) between 1972 and 2014 found that with the exception of a few 'formidable women', grand old men from Europe and North America, continue to 'dominate the arbitration profession'.[27] Later medium-N surveys of commercial arbitration have confirmed not only the elite educational backgrounds and male and Western identities[28] but also the possible rise of a third generation of managerial arbitrators within commercial, but not investment treaty, arbitration.[29]

Figure 34.1   The Arbitral Powerbrokers

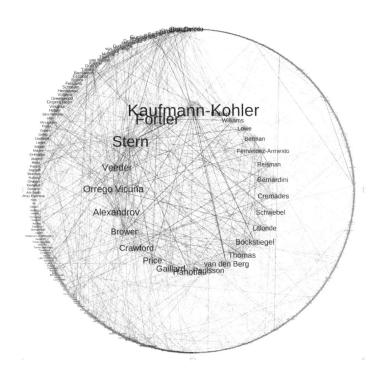

Large-N empirical studies by members of the PluriCourts consortium on all 1000-plus known investment arbitration cases, 600-plus arbitrators and almost 4000

and Justice', *ICCA Congress Series No. 18: Legitimacy: Myths, Realities, Challenges* 33 (2015); Thomas Schultz and Robert Kovacs, 'The Rise of a Third Generation of Arbitrators? Fifteen Years after Dezalay and Garth', 28(2) Arbitration International (2012), p. 161; Lucy Greenwood and C. Mark Baker, 'Getting a Better Balance on International Arbitration Tribunals', 28 Arb. Int'l (2012), p. 653; Susan Franck et al., 'The Diversity Challenge: Exploring the "Invisible College" of International Arbitration', Columbia J. Transnat'l L. (2015), p. 429; Gus van Harten, 'The (Lack of) Women Arbitrators in Investment Treaty Arbitration', Columbia FDI Perspectives, No. 59 (6 February 2012).

27. S. Puig, 'Social Capital in the Arbitration Market', *supra* n. 11.
28. Franck et al., 'International Arbitration: Demographics, Precision and Justice', *supra* n. 26.
29. Schultz and Kovacs, 'The Rise of a Third Generation of Arbitrators?, *supra* n. 26; Puig, 'Social Capital in the Arbitration Market', *supra* n. 11.

legal counsel, expert witnesses and secretaries, reveal the full breadth of the asymmetry, including its gender and geographic divide. As of January 2017, a small group of 25 'powerbrokers' dominated arbitral appointments (*see* Figure 34.1)[30] and only 11% were women. Moreover, only 26% of arbitrators came from the Global South despite the majority of cases being taken against Global South countries[31] The research also reveals the stickiness of the club: only 5% of arbitrators each year constituted new appointees.[32]

III   THEORIZING THE ARBITRATION MARKET

1   Symbolic Capital

Why is the market for international investment arbitration so asymmetric and elite in nature? Dezalay and Garth's explanation, which focused on commercial arbitration, was Bourdieusian. Largely a *demand-side* theory, the argument runs that given conditions of uncertainty concerning the commensurability of transnational qualifications, there was a prescient need to construct a market for arbitration:

> International lawyers in the field of international commercial arbitration must constantly evaluate the stature and authority of potential arbitrators who come from different legal traditions and backgrounds. They must see who will have clout with other arbitrators and with the parties who must obey the decision. Lawyers trying to select arbitrators must therefore determine who from France is equivalent to a retired justice from the House of Lords or who in Sweden is equivalent to an elite professor of contracts and commercial law from the United States. What this means is that arbitration must create a market in symbolic capital – the social class, education, career, and expertise that is contained within a person.[33]

Appointment is thus based on the accumulation of desired *symbolic capital.* Lawyers and their clients look for potential arbitrators that exhibit the optimal combination of social, legal and economic characteristics. Together these attributes will project neutrality, competence, and authority. The ideal arbitrator will thus exhibit and use such authority within an arbitral panel and amongst the parties, for the benefit of one party and eventual enforcement.

What is pertinent and inherent in Dezalay and Garth's description of symbolic capital is the importance of multiple roles. They seek to show the peculiar symbolic capital of those actors that cross institutional lines. One vignette is telling. An

---

30. Malcolm Langford, Daniel Behn and Runar Lie, 'The Revolving Door in International Investment Arbitration', 20(2) *Journal of International Economic Law* (2017) p. 301.
31. Taylor St John et al., *Glass Ceilings and Arbitral Dealings: Gender and Investment Arbitration* (2018) PluriCourts Working Paper; Malcolm Langford, Daniel Behn and Maksim Usynin, 'Does Nationality Matter? Arbitrator Background and Arbitral Outcomes' in Daniel Behn, Ole Kristian Fauchald and Malcolm Langford eds, *The Legitimacy of Investment Arbitration: Empirical Perspectives* (Cambridge University Press, 2021), p. 285.
32. St John et al., *ibid.*
33. Dezalay and Garth, *Dealing in Virtue, supra* n. 23, p. 23.

Anglo-American litigator, with his first case in international commercial arbitration, learnt the importance of appointing distinguished arbitrators as counsel, commenting that he was a 'conductor of virtuosos and prima donnas'.[34]

This observation deserves greater attention. ISDS has long been characterized by the concept of revolving door, in which individuals within the international investment arbitration community move back and forth between different roles in different arbitrations – concurrently and sequentially. This may be as legal counsel, arbitrator, expert witness, or tribunal secretary.[35] Notably, when Daniel Behn, Runar Lie and myself at PluriCourts took this into account in our computational network analysis in 2017, the picture of powerbrokers changed. There was a jump in network power scores for a group of arbitrators who performed regularly in other roles.:[36] If one compares the ranking in Figure 34.1 with Table 34.1, it is clear that some arbitrators who appeared regularly as counsel – e.g., Alexandrov, Crawford, Price, Gaillard, Paulsson – move up the list; and they are all 'household' names in the field.

Table 34.1   All Actors: Network Power Rankings (Top 25) – as of 1 January 2017

Rank	Name	Nationality	Arb.	Counsel	Exp.	Sec.	HITS hub
1	Gabrielle Kaufmann-Kohler	Switzerland	56	0	0	0	1.00000
2	L. Yves Fortier	Canada	53	0	0	0	0.87664
3	Brigitte Stern	France	88	0	0	0	0.87278
4	V.V. Veeder	UK	37	2	0	0	0.55004
5	Francisco Orrego Vicuña	Chile	49	0	0	0	0.54280
6	Stanimir Alexandrov	Bulgaria	32	31	0	0	0.52113
7	Charles Brower	US	52	0	0	0	0.48111
8	James Crawford	Australia	27	14	5	0	0.48067
9	Daniel Price	US	18	13	0	0	0.48031
10	Emmanuel Gaillard	France	23	21	0	0	0.47015
11	Bernard Hanotiau	Belgium	40	3	0	0	0.44905
12	Jan Paulsson	France	28	18	4	0	0.4454
13	Albert Jan van den Berg	Netherlands	44	0	0	0	0.44069
14	J. Christopher Thomas	Canada	43	3	0	0	0.42114
15	Karl-Heinz Böckstiegel	Germany	40	0	0	0	0.41590
16	Marc Lalonde	Canada	35	0	0	0	0.39232

---

34. *Ibid.*, p. 109.
35. Langford, Behn and Lie, 'The Revolving Door in International Investment Arbitration', *supra* n. 30.
36. *Ibid.*

Rank	Name	Nationality	Arb.	Counsel	Exp.	Sec.	HITS hub
17	Stephen Schwebel	US	18	9	0	0	0.38389
18	Bernardo Cremades	Spain	37	2	0	0	0.37650
19	Piero Bernardini	Italy	36	1	0	0	0.37495
20	Gonzalo Flores	Chile	0	0	0	38	0.34236
21	W. Michael Reisman	US	19	1	16	0	0.33781
22	Juan Fernández-Armesto	Spain	29	0	0	0	0.32955
23	Franklin Berman	UK	24	0	0	0	0.32912
24	Vaughan Lowe	UK	24	1	1	0	0.32573
25	Gabriela Álvarez-Avila	Mexico	0	18	0	19	0.32565

This revolving door occurs also in real-time, through so-called double hatting. Our analysis also measured the extent to which arbitrators simultaneously acted as legal counsel.[37] It was measured formally in two principal ways, using again data up to 1 January 2017. First, an 'arbitrator-focused' approach counted all individual cases in which at least one arbitrator on the panel is simultaneously acting as legal counsel in at least one other ISDS case. Second, a 'counsel-focused' approach counted individual cases where at least one legal counsel is simultaneously acting as an arbitrator in at least one other ISDS case (the inverse of the first measure). We found that a total of 47% of cases (509 in total) involve at least one arbitrator simultaneously acting as legal counsel – much higher than expected.[38] Turning to the counsel-focused category, it accounted for a further 11% of cases (118 in total).

Figure 34.2   The Double Hatting Index (Top 10)

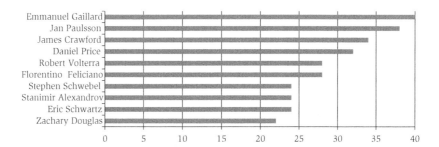

---

37. Langford, Behn and Lie, 'The Ethics and Empirics of Double Hatting', *supra* n. 3; Langford, Behn and Lie, 'The Revolving Door in International Investment Arbitration', *supra* n. 30.

38. Moreover, in 190 of the cases in this arbitrator-focused category, there are also legal counsel double hatting elsewhere as arbitrators – deepening the extent of the revolving door.

We also scrutinized the *identity* of this group. In doing so, we developed a double hatting index. If an individual was involved in a minimum of two international investment arbitration cases in the roles of arbitrator and counsel, then a yearly score of (2) was assigned to that individual for a given year.[39] The score is conservative and does not attempt to describe the *intensity* of double hatting within a calendar year. Hence the maximum score an individual can receive for a year is (2). Figure 34.2 shows the top 10 list that we published.[40] It shows that the practice is dominated by many of the most powerful and influential arbitrators.[41] However, there are many powerful arbitrators who *do not* feature at all on this list or even amongst the top 100 on our double hatting index. This includes a number that have spoken out against the practice.[42]

Finally, we asked if the degree of double hatting has *changed* over time. Figure 34.3 shows the proportion of cases affected each year for both arbitrator-focused (medium grey) and counsel-focused (light grey). Interestingly, double hatting is a relatively late phenomenon that primarily begins in the early 2000s. The share of double hatting cases was lower in 2016 but it was not yet clear whether this represented a new trend – a similar one-off reduction occurred in 2006.

Figure 34.3   Double Hatting over Time

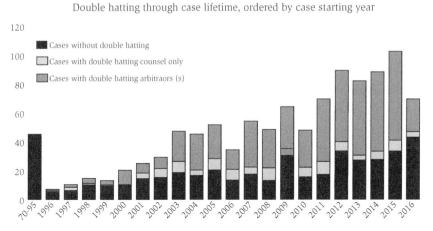

Double hatting through case lifetime, ordered by case starting year

---

39. Cases were included in the evaluation from their constitution date and until they are either discontinued, settled or finally resolved through a decision in the form of an award. Cases that were pending as of 1 January 2017 have a concluding date as of 1 January 2017 for the purposes of the analysis.
40. One arbitrator has been excluded from the originally reported version in *JIEL* as the inclusion of the annulment proceeding was deemed to overstate the degree of double hatting.
41. Langford, Behn and Lie, 'The Revolving Door in International Investment Arbitration', *supra* n. 30, section IV.
42. For example, Philippe Sands, W. Michael Reisman, Sir Franklin Berman, and Judge Thomas Buergenthal.

Returning to the theory of symbolic capital, it is not notable that double hatting is a characteristic feature of many of the most powerful and renowned arbitrators. It suggests that the ability to carry both roles was viewed as a form of prestige, or at the very least did not harm symbolic capital.

2   Insider Behaviour

However, symbolic capital is more than the mere possession of a diverse background. Symbolic capital is itself a social construction that emerges from a specific context. In this respect, it is important to ask whether its development was influenced as much by the supply-side (arbitrators) as much as the demand side (clients and their lawyers). Dezalay and Garth themselves point partly in this supply-side direction. They note the 'networks and relationships organized' around arbitration and the 'space for positions and struggles'.[43]

This observation underscores that the arbitral community may have possessed significant agency in shaping the demand for certain forms of symbolic capital. Notably, the structural potential for this constructive power lies in the revolving door, and particularly double hatting. When actors could simultaneously occupy multiple spaces, it not only constituted a natural form of symbolic capital: As legal counsel, arbitrators had the direct possibility to generate general demand for specific forms of symbolic capital, which would be to their advantage.

In 2004, Ginsburg foregrounded more clearly – at a general level – such *supply-side* behaviour of arbitrators in an alternative *rational choice* model that focused on strategic action.[44] He claimed that the rapid global spread of arbitration incentivizes insiders to raise the barriers to keep out new entrants:

> Here competition to establish the network standard could be associated with monopolistic behavior and may be undesirable. [The scholar] Ogus expects that in national jurisdictions lawyers will control the content of legal culture and will use the notion defensively against outside competition. In this view, culture can be an anti-competitive product. Those inside the relatively closed world of international arbitration can use claims of an 'arbitration culture' to highlight their own expertise. Those who are 'outside the culture' are less desirable participants.[45]

The story told by Ginsburg is the classic realist story of collective action in the legal profession.[46] Lawyers work to keep out external and internal competitors, emphasizing or making necessary the possession of necessary knowledge in the

---

43. *Ibid.*
44. Tom Ginsburg, 'The Culture of Arbitration', 36 Vanderbilt Journal of Transnational Law (2003), p. 1335.
45. *Ibid.*, p. 1344.
46. *See* discussion in; W. Wesley Pue and David Sugarman (eds), *Lawyers and Vampires: Cultural Histories of Legal Professions* (Hart Publishing 2003); Harald Espeli, Hans Eyvind Næess, and Harald Rinde, *Våpendrager og Veiviser: Advokatenes Historie i Norge* (Universitetsforlag 2008); Malcolm Langford, 'Revisiting the Theory of the Legal Complex Outcomes' in Malcolm Feeley and Malcolm Langford eds, *The Limits of the Legal Complex: Nordic Lawyers and Political Liberalism* (Oxford University Press 2021), p. 262.

demarcating of professional boundaries. Indeed, one arbitration lawyer recently boasted that their competitive advantage lies in what is 'not written down'.[47]

However, the tools deployed are not just constructivist. In 2005, Rogers highlighted the potential role of structural factors that enhance the imperfect competitive nature of the market and benefit insiders, one of them being the revolving door.[48] First, insiders have the power to make arbitration appointments (as counsel or tribunal secretariats). She noted explicitly that, 'Arbitrator selection is often in the hands of members of the same "club", who are either operating in the institutions or already appointed as party-appointed arbitrators.'[49] Second, she also pointed out that arbitrators enjoy an absence of regulation. There is little to no legal/judicial oversight and room for reputational sanction.[50]

As Rogers suggests briefly, double hatting reinforces these asymmetries and can facilitate insider behaviour. Borrowing from the economics of multimarket diversification, we can explicate this insight more fully in formal economic terms. Moreover, we can take the argument one step further. One reason for the emergence of multiple markets, such as the practice of double hatting, is that it can assist insider behaviour.

In economics, the reasons for the multimarket diversification by economic actors are classified as efficiency and strategy, with the result being so-called conglomerates (not unlike arbitral powerbrokers).[51] If a firm diversifies and sells its products in multiple markets, it gains enhanced market power under two alternative scenarios. First, if there are economies of scale in diversification, and second if they can induce anti-competitive effects, particularly collusion and calculated exit.[52] Let us take each in turn.

In the case of markets for arbitrators and counsel, the *economies of scale* generally favour diversification. The roles are largely substitutable.[53] The same 'expertise', primarily legal knowledge, symbolic capital, and relevant networks, can be deployed in both arenas. Moreover, contracting costs are constant in each market for all competitors.[54] Each arbitration is an ad hoc process and there are no long-term arrangements

---

47. GAR, *Global Arbitration Review 100: The Guide to Specialist Arbitration Firms 2012* (Geneva: GAR, 2012), at 3, cited in Eberhardt and Olivet, below n. 22.
48. Catherine Rogers, 'The Vocation of the International Arbitrator', 20 American University International Law Review (2004), p. 957 at pp. 968-969.
49. 'Arbitrator selection is often in the hands of members of the same "club", who are either operating in the institutions or already appointed as party-appointed arbitrators.' Rogers, *supra* n. 48, at 12.
50. *Ibid.*, at 970-975.
51. *See, e.g.*, Arnold Heggestad and Stephen Rhoades, 'Multi-market Interdependence and Local Market Competition in Banking', 60(4) The Review of Economics and Statistics (1978), 523-532 particularly, *see also* Michael Porter, *Interbrand Choice, Strategy, and Bilateral Market Power* (Harvard Economic Studies, 1996).
52. Kirsty Hughes and Christine Oughton, 'Diversification, Multi-market Contact and Profitability', 60 Economica (1993), pp. 203-224.
53. David Encaua, Alexis Jacquemin and Michel Moreaux, 'Global Market Power and Diversification', 96(382) The Economic Journal (1986), pp. 525-533.
54. This is strongly emphasized in the complementary literature on vertical integration in markets. *See*: Ronald Coase, 'The Nature of the Firm', 4(16) Economica (1937), 386; and Benjamin Klein, Robert G. Crawford and Armen A. Alchian, 'Vertical Integration, Appropriable Rents, and the Competitive Contracting Process', 21(2) The Journal of Law and Economics (1978), p. 297.

(except for employees in a law firm or some tribunal secretaries). While some individuals may struggle with the managerial aspect of the counsel role (e.g., academics with a high teaching load), lawyers employed by law firms or more flexible academics or in retirement may be able to combine multiple roles easily. The result is that arbitrators have the potential to exercise significant power in two markets simultaneously.

What is of particular interest is the second explanation. Concentration of power may emerge because it enhances strategic and collective *anti-competitive behaviour*. Economists have theorized and demonstrated that multimarket firms can engage in a form of cooperation or collusion. Action initiated in one market may result in retaliation in the other market.[55] This danger of reciprocal tit-for-tat can incentivize mutual forbearance or strategic exit.[56] Thus, a predominance of conglomerate firms can mean a 'reduction in rivalry' even when markets possess a relatively competitive structure'.[57] As Edwards famously noted, there is an 'incentive to live and let live, to cultivate a cooperative spirit, and to recognize priorities of interest in the hope of reciprocal recognition'.[58] Writing in the same period, the sociologist Simmel emphasized that the multiple contact points, and the resulting mutual knowledge amongst firms, facilitates also tacit cooperation.[59] Thus, Axelrod concluded that reducing monopolistic tendencies would involve keeping the 'same individuals from interacting too regularly with each other'.[60]

Whether central actors in investment arbitration engage in such strategic monopolistic behaviour is a difficult question to answer. Ginsburg pointed to the remarkable convergence in particular forms of arbitral practice, which he argued could only be accounted for by insider behaviour. Our quantitative research in mapping the 'revolving door' provided no direct evidence to prove or disprove such a claim.[61] While other sociological literature – based on survey evidence and interviews – reveals the presence of many strategic arbitrators,[62] and the claim has been raised in several arbitrator challenges,[63] such data gathering does not indicate directly yet whether they engage in *reciprocal* strategic behaviour.

However, vertical integration is not the best characterization of the monopolistic nature of the market as there are different arbitrators and counsel for case (i.e., product). Vertical integration is commonly defined as 'two single-output production processes': Martin Perry, 'Vertical Integration: Determinants and Effects', 1 Handbook of Industrial Organization (1989), p. 183.

55. Corwin Edwards, 'Conglomerate Bigness as a Source of Power', in National Bureau of Economic Research, *Business Concentration and Price Policy* (Princeton University Press, 1955), 331.
56. Note the conditional argument in Joel Baum and Helaine Korn, 'Dynamics of Dyadic Competitive Interaction', 20(3) Strategic Management Journal (1999), p. 251.
57. Heggestad and Rhoades, 'Multi-market Interdependence and Local Market Competition in Banking', *supra* n. 51, 523.
58. Edwards, 'Conglomerate Bigness as a Source of Power', *supra* n. 55, 335.
59. George Simmel, *The Sociology of George Simmel* (trans) (Free Press 1950).
60. Robert Axelrod, 'The Emergence of Cooperation among Egoists', 75 American Review of Political Science (1981), p. 306, at p. 312.
61. Langford, Behn and Lie, 'The Revolving Door in International Investment Arbitration', *supra* n. 30.
62. *See especially* Franck, 'International Arbitration', *supra* n. 26 above and Dezalay and Garth, *supra* n. 29.
63. *See Raiffeisen Bank International v. Croatia*, ICSID Case No. ARB/17/34, Decision on the Proposal to Disqualify Stanimir Alexandrov, 17 May 2018.

However, one can think of two situations in which monopolistic behaviour could emerge due to strong incentives. The first is when central players recommend each other as counsel or arbitrators in the expectation that they would engage in similar nominations.[64] This creates a mutually beneficial snowballing effect as an increase in the number of appointments raises an actor's social and symbolic capital in the market. The second may be more subtle but powerful in the long run. It would constitute the cultivation of a 'patronage' network in which a central actor recommends emerging colleagues or former students. This creates a 'sphere of influence',[65] in which there are internal incentives in this micro-network for reciprocal nomination and external incentives for central players to respect each other's sphere of influence. Further research is required on whether the concentration of power we have observed is driven by strategic factors in addition to economies of scale.

Summing up, existing literature contends that appointment in arbitration markets is determined strongly by the accumulation of symbolic capital to meet demand and insider behaviour to limit supply or shape demand. Which of these two different approaches best explains the economic sociology of appointment is not, however, the focus of this paper. Indeed, the fact that the theories are focused largely on the respective demand and supply sides of the market suggests that both sets of factors may play a role. What is crucial for present purposes, is that both theories provide a space for certain structural dynamics, especially the phenomenon of the revolving door. This allows us in the remainder of the paper to investigate whether the broader structural transformation of ISDS might be affecting the specific market for arbitral appointment. By bringing public law values to the fore, the demand and supply side of the market may be undergoing recalibration. Indeed, already in 1996, Dezalay and Garth pointed to the potentially disruptive effects of the rise of public international economic law in the form of GATT[66] and NAFTA:[67]

> The specific features that have allowed international commercial arbitration to develop and thrive by avoiding the state, we suggest may also render it incapable of adapting effectively to a new and very different regime in business disputes.[68]

We turn now to this transformation by charting critiques and their impact over the last twenty-five years, before returning to its implications for the arbitration market.

IV   THE LEGITIMACY CRISIS AND DOUBLE HATTING CRITIQUE

As foreshadowed, in the past decade, ISDS has been engulfed by a dual legitimacy crisis. As states hosting foreign investors found themselves increasingly having to defend their laws and policies before and in the shadow of international arbitral

---

64. *Ibid*.
65. Simmel, *The Sociology of George Simmel*, *supra* n. 59, noted the incentive to respect spheres of influence in different markets.
66. General Agreement on Tariffs and Trade.
67. North American Free Trade Agreement.
68. Dezalay and Garth, *Dealing in Virtue*, *supra* n. 23, p. 14.

tribunals, concerns arose with *outcome* legitimacy. It is claimed that ISDS in particular is pro-investor, pro-investment, and anti-developing state; and fails to provide legal certainty.[69] Equally, there was a concern with *process* legitimacy, in which the community of arbitrators figure prominently. Process critiques commonly revolve around the apparent lack of transparency, conflict of interests, litigation funding, and quality of reasoning.[70]

Unsurprisingly, these substantive and procedural concerns have resulted in demands for reform from various states, international organizations, and civil society groups – resulting in different forms of unilateral and multilateral action.[71] This has included withdrawal from the Convention for the Settlement of Investment Disputes between States and Nationals of Other States (ICSID Convention)[72] and certain investment treaties, development of new model treaties, replacement of arbitration with a court-like system,[73] substantive reform of existing treaties,[74] and revision of procedural rules.[75] However, many considered the result a patchwork. The reforms lacked depth (only selected issues were tackled) and breadth (only a few states were involved and many solutions require broad consensus).

In July 2017, the first major comprehensive attempt at ISDS reform was announced.[76] At its 50th session, member states of the UNCITRAL entrusted WG III with

---

69. *See, e.g.*, Gus van Harten, 'Arbitrator Behaviour in Asymmetrical Adjudication: An Empirical Study of Investment Treaty Arbitration', 50 Osgoode Hall Law Journal (2012), p. 211 at p. 251; Jorge Viñuales, *Foreign Investment and the Environment in International Law* (Cambridge University Press 2012); Thomas Schultz and Cedric Dupont, 'Investment Arbitration: Promoting the Rule of Law or Over-Empowering Investors? A Quantitative Empirical Study', 25 European Journal of International Law (2014), p. 1147; Behn, Berge and Langford, 'Poor States or Poor Governance' *supra* n. 17; Waibel et al., *The Backlash Against Investment Arbitration*, *supra* n. 18; Arato, Brown and Ortino, 'Parsing and Managing Inconsistency in ISDS', *supra* n. 18.
70. *See* Giorgetti, 'Who Decides Who in International Investment Arbitration', *supra* n. 8; Sands, 'Developments in Geopolitics: The End(s) of Judicialization?', *supra* n. 4; Puig, 'Social Capital in the Arbitration Market', *supra* n. 11, p. 416.
71. Taylor St John, *The Rise of Investor-State Arbitration: Politics, Law, and Unintended Consequences* (OUP 2018), Ch. 8; Malcolm Langford, Daniel Behn and Ole Kristian Fauchald, 'Backlash and State Strategies in International Investment Law', in Tanja Aalberts and Thomas Gammeltoft-Hansen (eds), *The Changing Practices of International Law* (CUP 2018) 70-102.
72. 575 UNTS 159, Articles 14 and 40.
73. For example, EU-Canada Trade Agreement (signed 30 October 2016, entered into force 21 September 2017 (CETA).
74. For example, US Mexico Canada Agreement (USMCA) ('NAFTA 2.0') (signed 29 January 2020). States have recently initiated a new process to modify the Energy Charter Treaty (signed 17 December 1994, entered into force 16 April 1998) according to the mandate of its state contracting parties.
75. It is important to note that UNCITRAL is not the only multilateral or plurilateral effort to reform the manner in which disputes are resolved under investment treaties. ICSID for example has initiated several processes over the past decade to reform rules applying in ICSID disputes; arbitral institutions (principally the ICC and SCC) have modified or added rules to allow for better administration of ISDS disputes.
76. Anthea Roberts, 'Incremental, Systemic, and Paradigmatic Reform of Investor-State Arbitration' 112(3) American Journal of International Law (2018), p. 410. The process emerged gradually in 2015, when the UNCITRAL Secretariat commissioned a study to the Geneva Center for International Dispute Settlement (CIDS) to review whether the Mauritius Convention on Transparency could provide a useful model for possible reforms in the field of investor-State arbitration. *See* United Nations, Report of the United Nations Commission on International Trade Law Forty-eighth session (29 June-16 July 2015), Official Records of the General Assembly,

a broad, open-ended, and problem-driven mandate to address the real and perceived legitimacy of the current regime.[77] The body would: identify concerns regarding ISDS; consider whether reform was desirable in the light of those concerns; and, if so, develop solutions.[78] During their November 2018 meeting in Vienna, WG III identified six concerns to be addressed by the reform process: (1) excessive legal costs; (2) duration of proceedings; (3) legal consistency; (4) decisional correctness; (5) arbitral diversity; and (6) arbitral independence and impartiality.[79]

What is notable is that double hatting has been the most-discussed issue under the sixth concern. The reasons for this are diverse and deserve a brief history and overview – which will traverse the backlash to double hatting and the counter-backlash

1   Early Critique

The concern with double hatting is not new. Already in 2003, Sands and Mackenzie raised such concerns;[80] and warnings came from other senior figures[81] and civil society organizations.[82] These voices were, nonetheless, isolated. Double hatting is a common practice in everyday commercial arbitration and is often viewed as beneficial.[83] As Stone Sweet has argued, when two parties in a conflict first turn to third-party resolution, trust in the dispute resolver's neutrality and expertise, their 'impartiality and wisdom', is paramount.[84] Parties to such private disputes typically seek to draw arbitrators from a legal community where their expertise, reputation (and arguably

---

Seventieth Session, Supplement No. 17, UN Doc. A/70/17, para. 268. In 2017, the UNCITRAL Secretariat commissioned a further study from CIDS and the process then formally commenced with a new mandate for WG III. See generally: Malcolm Langford et al., 'UNCITRAL and Investment Arbitration Reform: Matching Concerns and Solutions: An Introduction', 21 Journal of World Investment and Trade (2020), p. 167.

77. United Nations Commission on International Trade Law (UNCITRAL), 'Report of Working Group III (Investor-State Dispute Settlement Reform) on the work of its thirty-fourth session (Vienna, 27 November-1 December 2017)', UN doc No A/CN.9/930/Rev.1 (19 December 2017).

78. *See* United Nations, Report of the United Nations Commission on International Trade Law Fiftieth session (3 July-21 July 2015), Official Records of the General Assembly, Seventy Second Session, Supplement No. 17, UN Doc. A/72/17, paras 263-264.

79. UNCITRAL, 'Possible reform of investor-state dispute settlement (ISDS)', UN Doc No A/CN.9/WG.III/ WP.149 (5 September 2018). Moreover, several other issues have emerged in the process, such as third-party funding, prevention of investment disputes and calculation of damages. Malcolm Langford, 'UNCITRAL and Investment Arbitration Reform: A Little More Action', *Kluwer Arbitration Blog*, 21 October 2019.

80. Ruth Mackenzie and Phillipe Sands, 'International Courts and Tribunals and the Independence of the International Judge', 44 Harvard Int'l Law J. (2003), p. 271. *See also* Sands, 'Conflict and Conflicts in Investment Treaty Arbitration, *supra* n. 4.

81. *See, e.g.*, Thomas Buergenthal, 'The Proliferation of Disputes, Dispute Settlement Procedures and Respect for the Rule of Law', 3(5) Transnational Dispute Management (2006).

82. Nathalie Bernasconi-Osterwalder, Lise Johnson and Fiona Marshall, *Arbitrator Independence and Impartiality: Examining the Dual Role of Arbitrator and Counsel* (IISD 2010) 17, https://www.iisd.org/sites/default/files/publications/dci_2010_arbitrator_independence.pdf.

83. Langford, Behn and Lie, 'The Ethics and Empirics of Double Hatting' *supra* n. 3.

84. Alec Stone Sweet, 'Judicialization and the Construction of Governance', 32 Comp. Polit. Studies (1999), p. 147. *See also* Martin Shapiro, *Courts: A Comparative and Political Analysis* (Univ. Chicago Press 1981).

preferences) are well-established. As ISDS arbitrations were one-off ad hoc disputes, and few in number, it is perhaps surprising that only a few objected at the time.

However, the public law nature of ISDS has become increasingly apparent. It involves international treaties; states as respondents (often in their role as sovereign); issues of domestic public policy; the interests of multiple stakeholders; and, in the case of ICSID and the Permanent Court of Arbitration (PCA), public institutions appointing arbitrators. Moreover, international investment arbitration since the early 2000s has taken on a more juridical form as precedent has formed an important part of arbitral reasoning.[85] Such a context fits well with what Stone Sweet and Shapiro label as socially complex forms of adjudication, which place higher demands on dispute resolvers.[86] The outcomes of any case are less likely to fall within the range of accepted outcomes for both disputing parties (and directly interested third parties), and so an adjudicator must work much harder to demonstrate neutrality.

Thus, Sands asked, in a more direct and stronger tone, in 2012, whether a lawyer that 'spends a morning drafting an arbitral award that addresses a contentious legal issue' can divorce themselves from their role in addressing the same or similar legal issue in the 'afternoon' as counsel in a different case.[87] And, even if they can, would they be able to convince a reasonable observer that such role bifurcation was maintained?[88] An additional concern is the inverse of the first: an arbitrator acting as legal counsel may be coloured by their arbitral role or use their pleadings in one case for the purpose of being picked up and used by the same individual in their work as an arbitrator in another case.

While double hatting is not formally prohibited, an increasing number believed that it fell afoul of *IBA Guidelines on Conflicts of Interest in International Arbitration*, in at least certain cases. The guidelines provide that conflicts of interest arise if behaviour 'would give rise to justifiable doubts as to the arbitrator's impartiality or independence.[89] For example, in *Telkom Malaysia v. Ghana*,[90] Emmanuel Gaillard disclosed that he was acting as counsel in *RFCC v. Morocco* and the respondent state lodged multiple challenges against his appointment in the Hague District Court.[91] Ghana claimed that both cases involved similar legal issues and noted that it was relying on *RFCC v. Morocco* in its submissions. The Hague District Court ordered Gaillard to choose whether to continue as arbitrator or legal counsel, but not both. This case was the exception not the rule, and there have been no other successful challenges.

---

85. *See also* A. Stone Sweet and F. Grisel, *The Evolution of International Arbitration*, on the broader judicialization of the field.
86. *See* Sweet, 'Judicialization and the Construction of Governance', *supra* n. 84; Shapiro, *Courts: A Comparative and Political Analysis*, *supra* n. 84.
87. *See* Sands, 'Conflict and Conflicts in Investment Treaty Arbitration', *supra* n. 4.
88. *Ibid.*, 31-32.
89. *Ibid.*, Part I, Article 2.
90. *Telekom Malaysia Berhad v. The Republic of Ghana*, PCA Case No. 2003-03, UNCITRAL, Settled.
91. *Republic of Ghana v. Telekom Malaysia Berhad*, Hague District Court, Challenge No. 13/2004, Petition No. HA/RK 2004.667, 18 October 2004; Challenge 17/2004, Petition No. HA/RK/ 2004/778, 5 November 2004.

2 Maturing Critique

In 2015, in his closing speech at the European Society of International Law conference, Sands launched arguably his strongest attack, which was published shortly thereafter in *EJIL: Talk!* He took direct aim at some of the association's members – some present in the plenary hall.[92] The international legal profession, he maintained, bore some responsibility for the legitimacy crisis in international law and adjudication. The crux of his concern was the ethics of appointments and the appearance that international lawyers were prioritizing their material and political interests over independence and impartiality.

Sands named four specific practices, whereby all concerned the absence of transparency and public law norms and two of them double hatting: Lawyers and law firms were 'capturing' international investment arbitration and charging excessive fees; International Court of Justice (ICJ) judges were acting as arbitrators – seemingly the 'only' international court to allow this practice; some judges and arbitrators were too close to states, participating in the appointment processes of state counsel or leaking confidential information to governments; and individuals were acting simultaneously as arbitrators and legal counsel in international investment arbitration – i.e., double hatting. Sands conceded that such critique is 'delicate and embarrassing' but unavoidable as it goes to the 'heart of the system.'[93]

Yet, Sands noted that despite a decade-long expression of concern with double hatting in ISDS and beyond, it had never been measured.[94] He acknowledged that he was himself unsure as to how far he could draw on 'isolated' incidents to undergird his general critique.[95] This speech inspired though our measurement of the extent and nature of double hatting in ISDS, presented above in section 3 – namely that 58% of cases were affected by double hatting.[96] The research generated significant attention in social media,[97] a threatened lawsuit against the authors, and reports of discussions amongst arbitrators.[98]

This research was followed in November 2017 by an empirical analysis of ICJ judges double hatting or 'moonlighting' as arbitrators – Sands' second critique above. Bernasconi-Osterwalder and Dietrich Brauch found that (as of July 2017), a sitting ICJ judge had sat as an arbitrator in 10 per cent of all ISDS cases.[99] They discussed the fees involved and noted the potential for conflicts of interest given ISDS involved party

---

92. Sands, 'Developments in Geopolitics: The End(s) of Judicialization?', *supra* n. 4.
93. *Ibid.*
94. For other critics, *see* references at *supra* n. 9. Double hatting as an expert witness at the same time as acting as arbitrator or legal counsel may also be problematic but requires a more nuanced ethical discussion.
95. Sands, 'Developments in Geopolitics: The End(s) of Judicialization?', *supra* n. 4.
96. Langford, Behn and Lie, 'The Ethics and Empirics of Double Hatting', *supra* n. 3; Langford, Behn and Lie, 'The Revolving Door in International Investment Arbitration', *supra* n. 30.
97. For an overview, *see* https://www.jus.uio.no/pluricourts/english/news-and-events/news/2020/prize-revolving-door.html.
98. Private correspondence from an arbitrator, September 2018.
99. Nathalie Bernasconi-Osterwalder and Martin Dietrich Brauch, Is 'Moonlighting' a Problem? The Role of ICJ Judges in ISDS, IISD Commentary, November 2017.

appointment. While not focused on double hatting within ISDS, this analysis heightened considerably the discussion of multiple adjudicative roles. It also had a dramatic impact on the ISDS arbitration market – on 25 October 2018 the President of the ICJ President announced an effective ban on judges moonlighting as arbitrators.[100]

3   Diffusion of Critique

The year 2017 arguably marked a turning point for the public discussion and critique of double hatting. In Figure 34.4, I have plotted the references to double hatting and investment arbitration in academic articles registered in Google Scholar. Until June 2017, only three articles can be found. Yet, in the two and half years from that date, 119 academic publications have addressed the topic. The topic has also featured significantly on social media – especially Twitter –[101] and has been the subject of podcasts[102] and addressed in keynote lectures by figures such as the ICSID Secretary-General.

Figure 34.4   Double Hatting and Investment Arbitration: Google Scholar

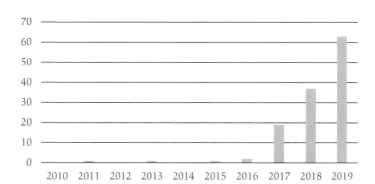

To be sure, the issue of double hatting in practice has been addressed by other literature with different terminology – e.g., 'dual roles'. However, articles addressing the issue are often cited only after 2016.[103] The exception is Judith Levine's, 'Dealing with Arbitrator 'Issue Conflicts' in International Arbitration' from 2008 which was cited academically ten times before 2017;[104] and Ruth Mackenzie and Phillipe Sands'

---

100. Marie Davoise, 'Can't Fight the Moonlight? Actually, You Can: ICJ Judges to Stop Acting as Arbitrators in Investor-State Disputes', *EJIL:Talk!* 5 November 2018.
101. https://twitter.com/search?q = double-hatting&src = typed_query – scroll down to see posts over a five-year period.
102. Charles N. Brower Lecture on International Dispute Resolution was given at 3:00 p.m., 5 April 2018.
103. *See* Google Scholar citations for Joseph Brubaker, 'The Judge Who Knew Too Much: Issue Conflicts in International Adjudication', 26(1) Berkeley Journal of International Law (2008), p. 111; Bernasconi-Osterwalder, Johnson and Marshall, *Arbitrator Independence and Impartiality, supra* n. 82.
104. Judith Levine, 'Dealing with Arbitrator "Issue Conflicts" in International Arbitration' 61 Dispute Resolution Journal (2006), p. 60.

'International Courts and Tribunals and the Independence of the International Judge', from 2003 which was cited fifteen times before 2017 in an international investment arbitration context.[105]

As foreshadowed, the issue of double hatting subsequently seeped into the two major multilateral reform processes: the development of new ICSID rules and the UNCITRAL WG III investment arbitration reform process. In August 2018, the issue of double hatting was addressed in the first iteration of the Working Paper on Proposals for Amendment of the ICSID Rules. The paper called for an increase in disclosure and transparency so that conflicts of interest could be dealt with on a case-by-case basis, but the issue was partly deferred due to the emerging UNCITRAL discussions.[106]

In the UNCITRAL WG III process, double hatting was not identified in the opening session in October 2017. However, in the following session in April 2018, double hatting was explicitly mentioned by the Government of Thailand in its written submission: It noted specifically the possibility of conflict of interests and a weakening of sociological legitimacy in ISDS.[107] The matter was discussed by states and the sessional report of the working group read similarly to the initial conclusions in the ICSID process.[108] Delegates debated the potential for 'actual and perceived conflicts of interests' although some noted counterarguments for double hatting such as allowing

---

105. Ruth Mackenzie and Phillipe Sands, 'International Courts and Tribunals and the Independence of the International Judge', 44 Harvard International Law Journal (2003), p. 271.

106. ICSID, *Volume 3: Proposals for Amendment of the ICSID Rules – Working Paper*, August 2018, paras 302-305. ['The WP therefore does not take a position on double-hatting, and leaves this for the joint ICSID–UNCITRAL discussions. However, the proposed rules do require greater disclosure and provide a better basis to assess whether a conflict exists in fact. The disclosure of additional information regarding an arbitrator's other roles proposed in the declaration would enhance transparency and enable the parties to consider potential conflicts of interest deriving from double-hatting on a case-by-case basis, and to pursue the available remedies should they choose to do so.']

107. *Possible reform of Investor-State dispute settlement (ISDS), Comments by the Government of Thailand*, UN doc. A/CN.9/WG.III/WP.147. ['Another concern in ISDS is related to arbitrators' possible pre-existing bias due to their repeated appointments on one side of the dispute, and situations of "double-hatting" where the same persons are appointed as counsel and arbitrators in similar disputes. Such situations can bring about conflicts of interests in positions, and undermine the impartiality of arbitrators.']

108. *Report of Working Group III (Investor-State Dispute Settlement Reform) on the work of its thirty-fifth session* (New York, 23-27 April 2018), paras 78-81:

> 78. A number of concerns were raised with regard to this topic, often referred to as 'double-hatting'. Statistics provided to the Working Group indicated that the practice was prevalent in ISDS. It was generally noted that the practice posed a number of issues including potential and actual conflict of interest. It was stated that even the appearance of impropriety (for example, suspicion that arbitrators would decide in a manner so as to benefit a party it represented in another dispute) had a negative impact on the perception of legitimacy of ISDS. Some States shared their experience in this regard.
>
> 79. Other observations included that domestic legislation in general did not prohibit double-hatting. It was also noted that 'triple' or even 'quadruple' hatting had been observed in practice, where certain individuals acted as party-appointed experts in certain ISDS cases or advisers to third-party funders. It was consequently suggested that the scope of the issue should be clearly delineated, and that the focus should not be on the practice of double-hatting itself, but rather on the problems that the practice posed (particularly where there was an actual conflict of interest). It was noted that States had attempted to address the question of double-hatting in more recent investment treaties.

'potential arbitrators (entrants) to gain experience of ISDS by acting first as counsel in a number of cases'.[109] In subsequent sessions, the topic gained more attention in the documentary submissions, Secretariat papers, sessional reports, and interventions and discussions by states and observers. As Table 34.2 shows, in 2018 and 2019 up to 50% of the formal documents submitted by the UNCITRAL secretariat or states in the process registered this concern.

Table 34.2   Double Hatting in the UNCITRAL WG III Process:
A Document Content Analysis

	No. of Documents	Documents with 'Double Hatting'	Proportion of Documents with Double Hatting (%)	No. of Mentions of Double Hatting
34th Session (2017)	5	0	0	0
35th Session (2018)	5	2	40	8
36th Session (2018)	8	4	50	25
37th Session (2019)	12	6	50	16
38th Session (2019)	11	2	18	19
38th Session – Ext (2020)	4	1	25	1

In the October 2019 session, significant time was devoted to discussing how double hatting could be regulated. A majority of state interventions proposed prohibition, while a minority suggested regulation. The report of the discussion captures this shift from a focus on actual conflict of interests to perceived conflict of interests. At the same time, counterarguments were made by some states and observers – for example, that double hatting may contribute to 'diversity in gender, geography, age group and ethnicity' by 'ensuring an adequate pool of qualified arbitrators'.[110]

---

80. It was noted that, while some data was available, there was also a need to compile additional data and information about the practice for the Working Group to better understand the nature of double-hatting and to consider possible solutions.

81. There was general agreement that double-hatting to the extent that it created potential or actual conflict of interest was the main issue of concern. The need to balance a number of interests was highlighted, in that possible solutions might involve an element of tension with other issues, such as efforts to expand and diversify the pool of arbitrators. For example, allowing double-hatting might allow potential arbitrators (entrants) to gain experience of ISDS by acting first as counsel in a number of cases. The need for training of potential arbitrators in developing States was again suggested in that regard. From that perspective of inter-connection among different issues, it was said that solutions would require a holistic approach and might need to be of a systemic nature. Another view was that tools such as a code of conduct could address the matter, and that it should not be limited to the functions of arbitrator and counsel but should cover other actors in the field of ISDS, such as experts.

109. *Ibid.*, para. 81.
110. Report of Working Group III (Investor-State Dispute Settlement Reform) on the work of its thirty-eight session (Vienna, 14-18 October 2019), UN doc. A/CN.9/1004, paras 57-58, as follows:

4   Counter-Backlash

Nonetheless, the critique has not been met with silence. Over the last four years, an increasing mobilization of counterarguments has occurred, which is already clear from the analysis of UNCITRAL WG III discussions above.[111]

First, there is the claim that practically speaking, there is a small pool of investment arbitrators that can sit in these types of arbitrations.[112] This argument was entrenched already in arbitral jurisprudence in 2002 when a tribunal declared the following in an arbitrator challenge:

> It is commonplace knowledge that in the universe of international commercial arbitration, the community of active arbitrators and the community of active litigators are both small and that, not infrequently, the two communities may overlap, sequentially if not simultaneously. It is widely accepted that such overlap is not, by itself, sufficient ground for disqualifying an arbitrator.[113]

The statement has seemingly continuing force and was invoked by counsel in 2018 to defend an arbitrator under challenge,[114] and the concern was presented by some states in the October 2019 session of the WG III. Empirically speaking, this argument could only hold for the 1990s. Since then, the potential pool of experienced investment arbitrators has expanded significantly – more than 600 have served in at least one case. While there may be a shortage of qualified adjudicators in other

---

57. With regard to independence and impartiality, the need to address double-hatting was generally emphasized and statistics were provided. The experience of States in recently concluded investment treaties on how they addressed that matter was shared. It was said that arbitrators, upon appointment, should generally refrain, and be prevented, from acting as counsel or party-appointed expert or witness in any pending or new ISDS cases. Differing views were expressed on the extent to which double-hatting should be regulated and a number of solutions were presented (complete ban, introducing a transitional period after which the arbitrator would be prevented from acting as counsel or expert, limiting the number or type of cases that an arbitrator could take, and requiring declarations). The need to develop a definition and scope of double-hatting was mentioned.

58. While the necessity of regulating double-hatting was shared, it was also noted that a balance should be sought between restricting double-hatting and ensuring an adequate pool of qualified arbitrators which would also contribute to addressing the lack of diversity in gender, geography, age group and ethnicity. It was also stated that any regulation on double-hatting should not unduly limit parties' autonomy to make appointments.

111. *See* section IV below.
112. On this point, Barton Legum, a prominent counsel and arbitrator based in Paris, has noted that: 'the pool of qualified arbitrators is already "vanishingly small" and that it would be problematic for the users of the arbitration system if efforts were made to exclude all practicing BIT counsel from this pool'. Luke Eric Peterson, 'Arbitrator Decries "Revolving Door" Roles of Lawyers in Investment Treaty Arbitration', *Investment Arbitration Reporter* (25 February 2010).
113. *SGS Société Générale de Surveillance S.A. v. Islamic Republic of Pakistan* (ICSID Case No. ARB/01/13), Decision on Claimant's Proposal to Disqualify Arbitrator (19 December 2002) para. 26 (emphasis added).
114. *Raiffeisen Bank International v. Croatia*, ICSID Case No. ARB/17/34, Decision on the Proposal to Disqualify Stanimir Alexandrov, 17 May 2018, para. 59.

fields,[115] investment arbitration is a buyer's market, not a seller's market – appointments are viewed as highly prestigious.[116] Nonetheless, it is interesting that this 'small pool' argument is repeated and restated without reference to the nature of the market.

Second, some leading arbitrators have argued that double hatting is important in developing arbitral expertise. Gary Born has been particularly prominent and controversial in protesting various ISDS reform efforts.[117] As to double hatting, in 2018, he stated, 'I view double hatting – sometimes acting as counsel, other times serving as an arbitrator – as an important strength of the international arbitration system. It makes you better in each of those roles.'[118] Here, Born makes the case that symbolic capital reflects actual capital, although it is not entirely clear why serving simultaneously rather than sequentially is necessarily preferable – besides the question of organization.

Third, some point to the need for transitional arrangements as lawyers move from the legal counsel role to the full-time arbitrator role.[119] Both inside and outside reform processes, arbitral community voices have expressed concern that prohibitions on double hatting might affect the entry of women, younger arbitrators, and arbitrators from developing countries, into arbitral roles.[120] From an economic perspective, it may be fair to permit legal counsel seeking to become full-time arbitrators time and space to carry on their legal counsel practice until there is some guarantee that arbitral appointments will come.[121] This argument, however, probably only holds for a short period of time: once a counsel obtained their first or even second arbitrator appointment, they could desist from accepting future counsel appointments as they ease into a new role. In any case, double hatting has been practised foremost by experienced arbitrators rather than younger counsel in transition.[122] Moreover, the gender gap is mostly driven by the focus on appointing parties on prior experience.[123] From an

---

115. *Ibid.*, 2.
116. Franck et al., 'International Arbitration: Demographics, Precision and Justice', *supra* n. 26.
117. He recently likened the EU's proposal for a multilateral investment court to the Nazi court-stacking in the 1930s: see https://www.youtube.com/watch?v = VkmMQh4F0PM&t = 8 409s.
118. Jenna Greene, 'An International Arbitration Star with NY Roots', New York Law Journal, 14 May 2018 https://www.law.com/newyorklawjournal/2018/05/14/from-hitchhiking-across-africa-to-international-arbitration-star-a-qa-with-wilmers-gary-born-389-30964/?slreturn = 20 200125131325.
119. Anthea Roberts, 'A Possible Approach to Transitional Double Hatting in Investor-State Arbitration' *EJIL:Talk!* 31 July 2017, https://www.ejiltalk.org/a-possible-approach-to-transitional-double-hatting-in-investor-state-arbitration/.
120. *See, e.g.*, Laura Pereira and Zara Desai, 'A Binding Code of Conduct for Adjudicators in Investor-State Disputes: A Step Forward?', Thomson Reuters Arbitration Blog, 26 May 2020.
121. Legum states: 'I have a lot of sympathy for those who say you need arbitrators with skill and experience. How on earth does somebody get established as an arbitrator if he or she never gets a chance to start? So I think inevitably there has to be some overlap. But there may be a stage in one's career when it becomes sensible to do one thing or the other.' Peterson, *supra* n. 112, 2.
122. If we examine the top twenty-five double hatters according to our index, we do find a group of prominent legal counsel that appear to be merely transitioning from the legal counsel role to the arbitral role – but they are only in a minority.
123. *See* St John et al., *Glass Ceilings and Arbitral Dealings: Gender and Investment Arbitration*, *supra* n. 31.

empirical perspective, it is possible to equally argue that a reduction in double hatting could increase the participation of female arbitrators, i.e., if it increases the chances for new appointments. In any case, what is important for present purposes is that the argument that double hatting has diversity benefits is increasingly made and appears to have significant resonance in some quarters.

Finally, arbitrators have resisted the automatic conflation of double hatting with conflicts of interest. In practice, there is clearly a wide spectrum of potential conflicts of interest, from clear and substantive conflicts of interest to mere perceptions of conflicts. As Richard Kreindler of Cleary Gottlieb Steen and Hamilton stated during Paris Arbitration Week in 2019: 'There is good double hatting, bad double hatting and innocuous double hatting.'[124] Actual conflicts are present most likely only in a minority of double hatting cases – and so this claim also resonates for many. While critics of double hatting maintain that double hatting still raises issues of perceived legitimacy – which is covered by the International Bar Association (IBA) rules – defenders are anxious to keep the focus on actual conflicts of interest.

V   THE EFFECT OF CRITIQUES ON THE INVESTMENT ARBITRATION MARKET

We now turn to the impact of this critique (and counter-critique) on the investment arbitration market, directly and indirectly. As the investment arbitration regime and its reform processes are fragmented, we need to look in different places for the critiques' effects. There is currently no overarching coordinating institution that could facilitate and enforce particular conflict of interest rules. However, in different spheres, it is possible to observe not only the potential impact of diffusion and debate but also the traces of the counter-backlash.

1   Changes in Treaties

First, we see some action from the principals – states – in the investment treaty regime. A new series of treaties and model treaties have included bans on double hatting. Up until 2017, the only treaty to regulate the practice was the newly signed Canada-EU Comprehensive Economic and Trade Agreement (CETA).[125] Article 8.30(1) of CETA stipulates that members of the Tribunal 'shall be independent' and 'upon appointment, they shall refrain from acting as counsel or as party-appointed expert or witness in any pending or new investment dispute under this or any other international agreement.' Moreover, the push by the European Union for a Multilateral Investment Court, also as part of the UNCITRAL WG III process, would definitively rule out double hatting.

Since 2017, there have been several treaty developments. Three can be named. First, in the Chile-Argentina Free Trade Agreement (FTA), double hatting in all its

---

124. Reported by ICCA, 1 April 2019.
125. EU-Canada Trade Agreement (signed 30 October 2016, entered into force 21 September 2017.

varieties is banned for ISDS;[126] second, the inter-state Commission established under the Comprehensive and Progressive Agreement for Transpacific Partnership (CPTPP) adopted a Code of Conduct for ISDS that expressly bans an arbitrator – once appointed, during the proceedings – from serving as counsel or party-appointed expert or witness in any pending or new investment dispute under the CPTPP or any other international agreement.[127] Finally, in the new Dutch model Bilateral Investment Treaty (2019), there is a new provision on requirements for arbitrators which possesses strong public law overtones and constitutes a strong ban on double hatting. An arbitrator cannot have occupied a counsel position in the five years *before* the dispute:

> The Members of the Tribunal shall possess the qualifications required in their respective countries for appointment to judicial office, or be jurists of recognized competence. The appointing authority shall make every effort to ensure that the members of the Tribunal, either individually or together, possess the necessary expertise in public international law, which includes environmental and human rights law, international investment law as well as in the resolution of disputes arising under international agreements. *In addition, Members of the Tribunal shall not act as legal counsel or shall not have acted as legal counsel for the last five years in investment disputes under this or any other international agreement.*[128]

The most significant 'legislative' development though is the new code of conduct that has emerged from the UNCITRAL/ICSID process. In May 2020, the two international organizations distributed the first draft for public comment.[129] Article 6, entitled 'Limit on Multiple Roles', provided as follows:

> Adjudicators shall [refrain from acting]/[disclose that they act] as counsel, expert witness, judge, agent or in any other relevant role at the same time as they are [within X years of] acting on matters that involve the same parties, [the same facts] [and/ or] [the same treaty].

The intent to include a provision of double hatting is clear, but the plethora of double brackets reflected the lack of a concrete consensus amongst states on the degree of regulation. The commentary to the draft provision notes the advantages and disadvantages of the practice.[130] On one hand, 'An outright ban is easier to implement, by simply prohibiting any participation by an individual falling within the scope of the prohibition.'[131] On the other hand, an outright ban 'may exclude a greater number of persons than necessary to avoid conflicts of interest', 'would interfere with the freedom

126. http://www.sice.oas.org/TPD/ARG_CHL/ARG_CHL_e.ASP.
127. Chiara Giorgetti et al., 'Lack of Independence and Impartiality of Arbitrators', 21(1) Journal of World Investment and Trade (2020), pp. 441-474.
128. Article 20.5. Emphasis added. Available at: https://www.google.com/url?sa=t&rct=j&q=&esrc=s&source=web&cd=4&ved=2ahUKEwiCyqvIqO3nAhUSFpoKHtGlCX8QFjADegQIBhAB&url=https%3A%2F%2Fwww.internetconsultatie.nl%2Finvesteringsakkoorden%2Fdocument%2F3586&usg=AOvVaw0WGUekzZgmfE-febJKw_BM.
129. *Code of Conduct for Adjudicators in Investor-State Dispute Settlement*, ICSID and UNCITRAL May 2020.
130. *Code of Conduct for Adjudicators in Investor-State Dispute Settlement – Annotated*, ICSID and UNCITRAL May 2020.
131. *Ibid.*, para. 67.

of choice of adjudicators and counsel by States and investors',[132] restrict the amount of 'available' expertise,[133] and constrain 'new entrants to the field'.[134] The UNCITRAL and ICSID secretariats note that the latter concern could be addressed by introducing 'a phased approach so that an adjudicator may overlap in a small number of cases at the start of their adjudicator career' but they point out that even this 'is hard to justify if the mere fact of double-hatting is considered as creating a conflict of interest'.[135] They also note that trying to limit the prohibition to cases concerning the actual conflict of interests is extremely difficult in practice.[136]

The range of possible options for regulating double hatting was narrowed though in the second version of the code of conduct, which was launched on 19 April 2021. For international investment disputes (IID), Article 4 provides:

> Unless the disputing parties agree otherwise, an Adjudicator in an IID proceeding shall not act concurrently as counsel or expert witness in another IID case [involving the same factual background and at least one of the same parties or their subsidiary, affiliate or parent entity].

This version defers partly to concerns about limiting party autonomy by allowing investors and states in a case to consent to double hatting. However, it otherwise presented states in WG III with a stark choice: prohibition in a very narrow set of situations (actual conflict in cases concerning the same facts or parties) or a simple outright prohibition (if the text in the square brackets is deleted).

Following in-depth and sustained discussions at subsequent WG III sessions in November 2021,[137] a further revised version was produced in March 2022 for public discussion. The substantially revised Article 4 applies firstly to arbitrators, as follows:

> 1. Unless the disputing parties agree otherwise, an Arbitrator in an IID proceeding shall not act concurrently [and within a period of three years following the conclusion of the IID proceeding,] as a legal representative or an expert witness in another IID proceeding [or any other proceeding] involving:
>
> (a) The same measures;
> (b) The same or related parties; or
> (c) The same provisions of the same treaty.
>
> 2. An Arbitrator in an IID proceeding shall not act concurrently [and within a period of three years following the conclusion of the IID proceeding] as a legal representative or an expert witness in another IID proceeding [or any other proceeding] involving legal issues which are substantially so similar that accepting such a role would create the appearance of a lack of independence or impartiality.

---

132. *Ibid.*, para. 68.
133. *Ibid.*, para. 69.
134. *Ibid.*, para. 68.
135. *Ibid.*
136. *Ibid.*, para. 72. ['Should it only apply when the same parties are present; when the same facts are addressed; when the same legal issues arise; or when a combination of these factors are present? In terms of legal instruments, should it include all international disputes, or only those pursuant to the same treaties?']
137. *See: Report of Working Group III (Investor-State Dispute Settlement Reform) on the work of its forty-first session* (Vienna, 15-19 November 2021), UN doc. A/CN.9/1086, paras 86-107.

The text is essentially a compromise between states who wished for an outright ban, an outright ban in a wide range of situations, and mere disclosure. Article 4(1) now contains an automatic ban (for contemporaneous and potentially historical double hatting) for cases in which there is a clear overlap: the same measures, parties, and treaty provisions. Moreover, as per Article 4(2), the presence of similar legal issues can attract the prohibition but the provision is nuanced when compared to the original proposal, by placing emphasis on the need for 'substantial' similarity and a clear perceived conflict of interest. Article 4 then goes on to provide a clear ban on judges in an eventual permanent ISDS mechanism.[138] However, dissensus remains, as states in September 2022 diverged on the need for a cooling off period and whether Article 4(2) should be retained – with some states arguing it was covered by Article 3 on independence and impartiality.[139]

Examining these treaty and reform developments so far, it is clear that regulation is on its way, but the extent of imposition of actual restrictions, or their direct effect, will only be clear at some point in the future when the code of conduct is adopted and mainstreamed. So far what the above developments contribute most to is arguably a strengthening of the critical discourse – and thus pressure on arbitrators. It is this effect to which we now turn.

2   Self-Regulation

The second impact of the critique is the reaction from the agents – arbitrators – in the form of self-regulation. There may be strong motives for arbitrators to evolve their behaviour in response to external signals.

The principal prism through which to understand and model such behaviour is within *rational choice* theory, whereby adjudicators seek to optimize their goals within a constrained context.[140] For investment treaty arbitrators, a strategic account would

---

138. '3. Judges shall not exercise any political or administrative function. They shall not engage in any other occupation of a professional nature which is incompatible with their obligation of independence or impartiality or with the demands of a full-time office. In particular, they shall not act as a legal representative or expert witness in another IID proceeding.

4. Judges shall declare any other function or occupation to the [President] of the standing mechanism and any question on the application of paragraph 1 shall be settled by the decision of the standing mechanism.

5. Former Judges shall not become involved in any manner in an IID proceeding before the standing mechanism, which was pending, or which they had dealt with, before the end of their term of office.

6. As regards an IID proceeding initiated after their term of office, former judges shall not act as a legal representative of a disputing party or third party in any capacity in proceedings before the standing mechanism within a period of three years following the end of their term of office.'

139. *See Report of Working Group III (Investor-State Dispute Settlement Reform) on the work of its forty-third session* (Vienna, 5-16 September 2022), UN doc. A/CN.9/1124, paras 232-246. *See also* discussion in Anthea Roberts and Taylor St John, 'UNCITRAL and ISDS Reform: What to Expect When You're Expecting', *EJIL:Talk!*, 5 October 2022, available at https://www.ejiltalk .org/uncitral-and-isds-reform-what-to-expect-when-youre-expecting/.

140. Adjudicators: (1) may hold diverse preferences that extend beyond political ideology or good lawyering; (2) 'take into account the preferences and likely actions of other relevant actors,

imply that a behavioural correction in response to legitimacy critiques could forestall certain material and reputational 'costs', such as greater non-compliance by respondent states and exits from the regime or damage to *individual* reputation and chances of future appointment.[141] A sizeable sample of arbitrators themselves have acknowledged that they engage in strategic behaviour when writing decisions.[142] The concern of some in the arbitral community with the critique of double hatting is apparent, if not palpable.[143]

---

including their colleagues, elected officials, and the public;' and (3) operate in a 'complex institutional environment' that structures this interaction. *See* Lee Epstein and Jack Knight, 'Reconsidering Judicial Preferences' 16 Annual Review of Political Science (2013), p. 11, at p. 11. On diverse goals, *see* in particular Laurence Baum, *Judges and Their Audiences: A Perspective on Judicial Behavior* (2008). Evidence from various domestic jurisdictions suggests that judges are strategically sensitive to signals from the executive and legislature: *See, e.g.*, Juan Carlos Rodriguez-Rada, 'Strategic Deference in the Colombian Constitutional Court, 1992-2006' in Gretchen Helmke and Julio Rios-Figueroa (eds) *Courts in Latin America* (2011) 81-98; Diana Kapiszewski, 'Tactical Balancing: High Court Decision Making on Politically Crucial Cases' 45 Law and Society Review (2011), p. 471; Epstein and Knight, *ibid.* although the scholarship is divided on the extent of this shift. Compare, e.g., M. Bergara, B. Richman and P. Spiller, 'Modeling Supreme Court Strategic Decision Making: The Congressional Constraint', 28(2) Legislative Studies Quarterly (2003), p. 247 with Segal, *ibid.* As to public opinion, there is consensus that it has an *indirect* influence on judgments though judicial appointments but is divided over whether it exerts a *direct* influence on judges. Roy Flemming and Dan Wood, 'The Public and the Supreme Court: Individual Justice Responsiveness to American Policy Moods', 41 American Journal of Political Science (1997), pp. 468, 480. *See also* Barry Friedman, *The Will of the People: How Public Opinion has Influenced the Supreme Court and Shaped the Meaning of the Constitution* (2009); Lee Epstein and A. Martin, 'Does Public Opinion Influence the Supreme Court? Possibly Yes (But We're Not Sure Why)', 13 University of Pennsylvania Journal of Constitutional Law (2010) pp. 263, 270; Isaac Unah, Kristin Rosano and K. Milam, 'U.S. Supreme Court Justices and Public Mood', 30 Journal of Law and Politics (2015), p. 293. At the international level, empirical and doctrinal scholarship suggests that the Court of Justice of the EU (CJEU) and the WTO dispute settlement body are sensitive to the balance and composition of member state opinion within institutional constraints: Olof Larsson and Daniel Naurin, 'Judicial Independence and Political Uncertainty: How the Risk of Override Affects the Court of Justice of the EU', 70(2) *International Organisation* (2016), pp. 377-408; M. Pollack, *The Engines of European Integration: Delegation, Agency, and Agenda Setting in the EU* (2003); Cosette Creamer, 'Between the Letter of the Law and the Demands of Politics: The Judicial Balancing of Trade Authority within the WTO' *Working Paper* (2015).

141. Studies of domestic judges that are subject to reappointment processes reveal higher levels of strategic behaviour amongst this group. *See* Ilana Lifshitz and Stefanie Lindquist, 'The Judicial Behavior of State Supreme Court Judges', *APSA 2011 Annual Meeting Paper* (2011). For a study of investment arbitrators' strategic considerations, *see* Malcolm Langford and Daniel Behn, 'Managing Backlash: The Evolving Investment Arbitrator?', 29(2) European Journal of International Law (2018), p. 551.

142. In a recent survey, 262 international arbitrators, which included a subset of 67 with experience in ITA, S. Franck et al., 'International Arbitration: Demographics, Precision and Justice' *ICCA Congress Series No 18, Legitimacy: Myths, Realilities, Challenges* (2015), p. 33. They were asked whether they considered future reappointment when deciding cases. A remarkable 42 % agreed or were ambivalent. Given the sensitive nature of the question, it is arguable that this figure is understated.

143. We received a threat of legal action from one arbitrator, describing our index as a form of defamation with commercial and reputational consequences. The arbitrator challenged the methodology and data selection, demanded a retraction of the articles, and a formal written apology.

These strategic predictions may be also enhanced by a logic of appropriateness: sociological forces.[144] The theory of *discursive institutionalism* proposes that discourse (such as the legitimacy crisis) may shape the preferences of judicial agents[145] and the space in which they communicate and justify their actions.[146] Arbitrators may thus simply adapt to a new culture of appointments – a new social norm – and view double hatting in morally pejorative terms.

The reasons for such self-regulation, however, are not the central point here. They merely provide some background justification for why we might expect a change in the arbitration market. The key question here is descriptive: Do we see such a shift?

Table 34.3   New and Arbitral and Counsel Activities of Selected ISDS Arbitrators

	Double-Hatting Index 2012-2016					New Cases as Arbitrator			New Cases as Counsel		
	2012	2013	2014	2015	2016	2017	2018	2019	2017	2018	2019
Gaillard	X	X	X	X	X	1	0	0	1	1	
Paulsson	X	X	X	X	X	1	2	1	0	0	0
Crawford	X	X	X	X		0	1	0	0	0	0
Price	X	X	X	X	X	0	1	0	0	0	0
Volterra	X	X	X	X	X	1	1	0	3	2	*147
Feliciano	X	X	X	X	Passed away	n.a	n.a	n.a	n.a.	n.a.	n.a.
Schwebel	X	X				0	0	0	0	0	0
Alexandrov	X	X	X	X	X	13	7	2	0	0	0
Schwartz	X	X		X	X	0	0	0	0	0	0
Douglas	X	X	X	X	X	4	6	1	0	0	0
Greenwood	X	X				4	2	0	0	0	0

In an attempt to provide a first look at the possible change, I have tracked the activities of those in our prior top 10 double hatting list plus one arbitrator/counsel (Christopher Greenwood) who has become active again in the arbitration market after a period on the ICJ. Table 34.3 presents whether they received a yearly score in the five years before 2017 and then new appointments as arbitrators and counsel. The data is based on publicly available ISDS documents now incorporated in PITAD as well as searches of the online websites of the arbitrators to locate missing cases. This is complemented in Table 34.4 by a closer look at the types of arbitral and counsel work in the period 2017-2019, and the extent to which cases concern finalization.

---

144. On this empirical conundrum, *see* A. Gilles, 'Reputational Concerns and the Emergence of Oil Sector Transparency as an International Norm', 54 *International Studies Quarterly* (2010), p. 103.
145. V. Schmidt, 'Discursive Institutionalism: The Explanatory Power of Ideas and Discourse', 11 *Annual Review of Political Science* (2008), pp. 303, 304.
146. Schmidt, *supra* n. 85, 304.
147. Note that there is some uncertainty over the new counsel cases by Volterra.

Table 34.4   Finished Versus Pending Cases for Selected Arbitrators 2017-2019

	Finished Cases as Arbitrator			Pending Cases as Arbitrator	Finished Cases as Counsel			Pending Cases as Counsel
	2017	2018	2019	As at 2019	2017	2018	2019	As at 2019
Gaillard	1	0	0	2	3	0	0	3
Paulsson	1	0	0	5	0	1	1	1
Crawford	2	0	0	5	0	1	1	0
Price	1	1	0	1	0	0	0	0
Volterra	2	0	1	3	1	0	0	5*
Feliciano	1	n.a.	n.a.	0	1	0	0	0
Schwebel	2	0	0	0	0	0	0	0
Alexandrov	2	5	3	31	3	0	0	0
Schwartz	0	0	0	6	0	0	0	0
Douglas	1	4	1	21	0	0	0	1
Greenwood	0	1	5	10	0	0	0	0

The above data allows us to initially sketch four groups or 'types' amongst this previously rather homogenous group. First, some arbitrators have ceased arbitral practice due to retirement, illness or death (Price, Feliciano, Schwebel) making it difficult to judge the effect of the new critique on them. Second, some arbitrators were forced to give up both arbitral and counsel work as ICJ judges (Crawford), mostly because of double hatting critique against ICJ judges acting as arbitrators and the new prohibition imposed in 2018. Third, and directly on point, some arbitrators have maintained or dramatically increased arbitral work but have not taken up new counsel work (Greenwood, Douglas, Alexandrov, and Schwartz). Examining the websites of Greenwood, Douglas, and Schwartz there appears to be an attempt to signal that they only act as arbitrators. Greenwood joined an arbitrator's practice in 2018 and Douglas's only current case as counsel is not especially visible. Schwartz left, however, King and Spaulding for an arbitral-centric practice earlier than Alexandrov – the former in 2016, the latter in August 2017. Fourth, some arbitrators seem to care little about the critique. Gaillard and Volterra also took up new cases as counsel.

This preliminary overview of changes in double hatting practice suggests that the critique is potentially having an influence. We see a clear change for four of the six arbitrators who could make a clear choice. However, how far this extends to the remainder of the arbitral field is the subject of an ongoing research project. On one hand, the arbitrator who has spoken in favour of double hatting, Gary Born, continues to take some cases as counsel. On the other hand, given the decrease in double hatting by some very active arbitrators, the overall level of the phenomenon has significantly decreased.

3 State Challenges

Finally, it is important to examine whether states – as litigants rather than principals – have begun to more regularly **challenge** double hatting in arbitral proceedings.[148] An initial review indicates that there has not been an increase, but this may be also because the practice is declining or arbitrators are avoiding the possibility of a challenge by declining a counsel role. Instead, we have seen accompanying or related challenges on appointment by the same party and connections through law firms. Moreover, it is not clear how much can be taken from the existence or not of arbitrator challenges. Some authors have argued that because the rules are so vague and the jurisprudence on double hatting unsettled that it is difficult for parties to challenge the practice.[149]

VI CONCLUSIONS: A CHANGING MARKET

The above discussion indicates that recent critiques of double hatting have diffused broadly and, as this preliminary analysis shows,[150] it appears to have had some impact on treaty and arbitral practice. The extent and speed of the impact can be clearly debated, especially as previous studies reveal that the decentralized system of ISDS adjusts more slowly to backlash than the centralized trade adjudication system of the WTO.[151] Although the ongoing reform discussions and new treaty negotiations are likely to facilitate further adaptation, this reform process will not be complete until 2026, or later.[152]

The main point of this paper, however, is to highlight the potentially changing sociology of appointment – whatever its speed and scale – through the impact of public law critiques of international investment arbitration. The case of double hatting is just one example amongst others but it usefully points to the need to revisit the two dominant sociological theories of appointment.

On the demand side of the investment arbitration market, it is arguable that the form or content of symbolic capital is potentially undergoing a change. Double hatting may no longer be viewed as a form of prestige and element for those seeing new appointments. Indeed, it is possible that the absence of double hatting – a classical public law norm – may now better signal the 'impartiality' desired by clients and their lawyers. Such a change is potentially representative of a broader change in, at least,

---

148. Malcolm Langford, Daniel Behn and Ole Kristian Fauchald, 'Backlash and State Strategies in International Investment Law', in Thoma Gammeltoft-Hansen and Tanja Aalberts (eds), *The Changing Practices of International Law: Sovereignty, Law and Politics in a Globalising World* (2018), Ch. 4.

149. Bernasconi-Osterwalder, Johnson and Marshall, *Arbitrator Independence and Impartiality*, *supra* n. 82.

150. A comprehensive analysis of the trends in double hatting across all arbitrators is currently underway at PluriCourts.

151. Malcolm Langford, Cosette Creamer and Daniel Behn, 'Regime Responsiveness in International Economic Disputes', in Szilárd Gáspár-Szilágyi, Daniel Behn and Malcolm Langford (eds), *Adjudicating Trade and Investment Disputes: Convergence or Divergence?* (CUP 2020), p. 244.

152. Roberts and St John, *supra* n. 139.

state preferences for arbitral capital. For example, in the UNCITRAL WG III, there is a strong push for ensuring that adjudicators have sufficient competence in 'public' international law, with no strong focus on relevant commercial experience.

On the supply side, it has been argued that the decline of double hatting reduces insider advantages. This provides more power to the 'non-double-hatters' to shape the culture of appointments and flows of information. To be sure, this does not reduce necessarily the power of the broader club of lawyers who are instrumental in appointments: Lie has charted the close links between some law firms and certain arbitrators in appointment processes.[153] However, a reduction in double hatting reduces the direct opportunities for arbitrators to engage in anti-competitive behaviour. Moreover, combined with the emergence of other public law norms – including greater scrutiny of repeat appointments by law firms – means that the investment arbitration market may be less affected by insider behaviour.

In this respect, we see potentially a new 'moral economy' in the investment arbitration market emerging. The concept has been defined as follows:

> The moral economy embodies norms and sentiments regarding the responsibilities and rights of individuals and institutions with respect to others. These norms and sentiments go beyond matters of justice and equality to conceptions of the good; for example, regarding needs and the ends of economic activity.[154]

In our case, we can identify the gradual infusion of moral capital on the demand side and the space for moral guardians on the supply side. Actors can now use new forms of capital, in this case, moral capital, to signal authority and cast doubt on others. A potentially paradoxical result is that the changing market creates new strategic incentives to 'act moral' or 'appear moral' in order to obtain appointments. If one is concerned with moral norms, this is a very good result. Although given the counter-backlash, this new symbolic capital may be in the eye of the beholder. In any case, the emergence of a new moral economy sharpens our attention on the way in which the arbitration market may be changing.

---

153. Lie, 'The Influence of Law Firms in Investment Arbitration', *supra* n. 9.
154. Andrew Sayer, 'Moral Economy and Political Economy', 61(1) *Studies in Political Economy* (2000), pp. 79-103, at p. 79.

CHAPTER 35

The End of Hubris in International Arbitration?: A Reply to Malcolm Langford

Florian Grisel[*]

TABLE OF CONTENTS

In "The Changing Sociology of the Investment Arbitration Market: The Case of Double Hatting," Malcolm Langford presents findings that complement his own previous article on "The Revolving Door in International Investment Arbitration."[1] In his most recent paper, Langford argues that "[t]he rising democratization of investment arbitration is challenging traditional theories on appointment of international investment arbitrators."[2] His main claim is that the "public law critiques of international investment arbitration" are leading to the "potential changing sociology of appointment."[3] By "potential changing sociology of appointment," Langford has in mind the decline of "double hatting," and suggests the existence of two causal relationships in this regard: (i) public critiques of "double hatting" impact the practices of actors in the field, who increasingly avoid acting as counsel and arbitrator in parallel cases; (ii) this decline of "double hatting" is associated with the emergence of a new "moral economy" (or a "changing sociology") in the investment arbitration market. My comments below focus

---

[*] Associate Professor of Socio-Legal Studies, University of Oxford.
1. Malcolm Langford, Daniel Behn & Runar Hilleren Lie, "The Revolving Door in International Investment Arbitration," (2017) 20 *Journal of International Economic Law* 301.
2. Malcolm Langford, "The Changing Sociology of the Investment Arbitration Market: The Case of Double Hatting," Chapter 34, to this volume.
3. *Id.*, section 5.

on the data put forward by Langford in support of his claims, his explanation of "double hatting" and my own tentative explanation of this phenomenon.

I   SOCIOLOGY AS AN EMPIRICAL DISCIPLINE

In the social sciences, claims are deemed valid insofar as they are backed by empirical evidence. Malcolm Langford presents convincing evidence that debates concerning double hatting have arisen in public spaces that are traditionally deemed influential in the field of investment arbitration. However, Langford's main claim concerning the decline of double-hatting practices over the past few years deserves elaboration and further empirical backing. The data canvassed for the purposes of this chapter does not allow tracking the evolution of double hatting across time. The fact that four out of eleven of the individuals described by Malcolm Langford as the top "double hatters" may have moved away from counsel work to concentrate on arbitrator work in recent years does not suffice to infer a causal link between the debates on double hatting on the one hand and this trend on the other hand. It is in fact unclear how those debates have had an impact on social practices in international arbitration, and that any decline in "double hatting" is affecting its sociology (the core argument of the chapter). The methodology presented in the chapter, which is based primarily on a statistical study of the appointments of "the top 11 double hatters" since 2017, would benefit from a more thorough engagement with the following considerations: how representative is this sample of the top 11 "double hatters"? Does the study take into account the fact that several of these "double hatters" have reached an age when counsel work becomes less popular? What are the individual trajectories of these "double hatters"? Were they always "double hatters"? Have they become "double hatters"? Is the practice of "double hatting" evolving over time because of age, personal taste, or other factors? It would have been helpful, for instance, to engage in a series of interviews with prominent actors of investment arbitration in order to obtain their own assessment of the issues at stake.[4] This type of empirical work could be a promising avenue for future research and a useful complement to the current study. Another potentially promising exercise is to examine the argument, drawn from the statistical analysis presented in a previous article, that double hatting is "much higher than expected."[5]

II   DOUBLE HATTING AS MORAL CAPITAL

Langford relies on "two predominant explanatory theories of arbitral appointment" in order to account for the high occurrence of "double hatting" in investment arbitration: *The Culture of Arbitration* (Tom Ginsburg) and *Dealing in Virtue* (Yves Dezalay and Bryant Garth). I will focus particularly on the second study, which appears to be most

---

4. These topics are discussed, for instance, in a series of interviews by Neil Kaplan. *See* https://delosdr.org/index.php/in-conversation-with-neil/ (last checked October 24, 2022).
5. *Id.* p. 9. *See also,* Langford, Behn & Lie (*supra* n. 1).

relevant for Langford's account of double hatting.[6] In Langford's words: "What is pertinent in Dezalay and Garth's description of symbolic capital is the importance of multiple roles, including double hatting. ISDS [Investor State Dispute Settlement] has long been characterized by the concept of revolving door, in which individuals within the international investment arbitration community move back and forth between different roles in different arbitrations across time, whether as legal counsel, arbitrator, expert witness or tribunal secretary."[7] He specifically argues that Dezalay and Garth's analysis supports his findings concerning "double hatting": in his view, Dezalay and Garth provide a valid explanation of how actors of international arbitration build symbolic capital by "cross[ing] institutional lines."[8] Langford seems to argue that double hatting is a legitimizing strategy that actors of international arbitration have used in order to increase their moral, or symbolic, capital. I agree with his argument. However, the reasons why actors have opted for this strategy rather than other more linear strategies are not explicit. On this point, Langford's reliance on Dezalay and Garth raises more questions than answers. Dezalay and Garth focus their analysis on international commercial arbitration, mainly based on the case study of the International Chamber of Commerce (ICC) in the early 1980s. Langford does not explain the relevance of a sociological account of *commercial* arbitration for the study of *investment* arbitration.[9] Are the two fields one and the same? Are they separate? Or do they intersect in some way? The reader is given little guidance as to how to answer these questions. In addition, the main findings of Dezalay and Garth do not provide grounds for Langford's argument that international arbitration—whether commercial or investment—was built across institutional lines. It is true that Dezalay and Garth made some passing references to the "double expertise" of "expatriate lawyers" in *Dealing in Virtue*.[10] But the gist of their argument is different, and does not provide a relevant explanation for "double hatting." In fact, Dezalay and Garth famously suggest that a conflict between two classes of legal entrepreneurs—the "grand old men" who were mostly based in the law faculties of continental Europe and the "young technocrats" who acquired legitimacy in Anglo-American law firms—deeply shaped, and to a large extent determined, the evolution of international commercial arbitration. Faithful to Bourdieu's social theory, their account emphasizes the ability of legal elites to dominate a field and reshape it in their own image. What matters most in Dezalay and Garth's analysis is the social legitimacy displayed by the dominant group—e.g., the "young technocrats" after the 1980s—within a given field. What it does not provide is a relevant explanation of why, and how, actors in a certain social field swap positions within this field in order to sustain their own legitimacy. It certainly does not explain why double hatting is "much higher than expected," as argued by Malcolm Langford.[11]

---

6. Langford (*supra* n. 2).
7. *Id.*, Section 3.1.
8. *Id.*, Section 3.1.
9. He argues in an earlier version of his chapter that "international investment arbitration is a different kettle of fish" than commercial arbitration. *See* Langford (*supra* n. 2).
10. Yves Dezalay & Bryant G. Garth, *Dealing in Virtue: International Commercial Arbitration and the Construction of a Transnational Legal Order*, University of Chicago Press, p. 53.
11. Langford (*supra* n. 2), Section 3.1.

That said, the discrepancy between Dezalay and Garth's analysis on the one hand and the practice of "double hatting" was noted by prominent practitioners of international arbitration a long time ago. In a book review of *Dealing in Virtue*, for instance, Eric Schwartz (one of the top 11 "double hatters" on Langford's list) mentions some interesting overlaps between the categories drawn by Dezalay and Garth:

> there is little basis, in my view, for the authors' contention that conflict between an aging cadre of notables, i.e., "grand old men," and a younger generation of "technocrats" has helped to shape the modern development of international commercial arbitration. (...) many of those prominent in international arbitration are at the same time academics and practitioners, which makes it even more difficult to speak of cleavage between the two.[12]

In another review of *Dealing in Virtue*, John Beechey argues along similar lines that Dezalay and Garth failed to account for professional overlaps between practicing lawyers and academics in the development of international commercial arbitration:

> Whilst some (grand old men) have developed academic careers to complement their role as active practitioners, *their "symbolic capital" arises first and foremost from long experience as contentious lawyers with significant international commercial arbitration practices (although few, if any, would profess to being entirely specialized in that field)* and whose stature has grown with the development of international commercial arbitration itself over the past twenty to twenty-five years. To ignore them is to miss a step in the development.[13]

In short, although Beechey and Schwartz point towards professional overlaps that are different from the ones identified by Langford, the practice of double hatting seems to have existed for a very long time in the field of international arbitration, and Dezalay and Garth have ignored this practice in constructing their analysis of international arbitration. Their reference to double hatting seems merely contextual and does not provide a convincing explanation for this phenomenon.

III   DOUBLE HATTING AND MARGINALITY

Other sociological accounts of international arbitration could provide an explanation for the double-hatting practices observed by Langford. I will attempt here to draw from my own research in order to advance a tentative explanation for these practices. In an article published in 2017 in *Law & Society Review*, I measured the claims made by Dezalay and Garth against empirical evidence drawn from the archives of the International Chamber of Commerce.[14] In particular, I reviewed the appointment of more than a thousand arbitrators in 644 ICC cases resolved between 1922 and 1973 and analyzed the individual trajectories of leading ICC arbitrators. I supplemented this data by

---

12. Eric A. Schwartz, "Book Review of *Dealing in Virtue*," (1997) 12 *ICSID Review—Foreign Investment Law Journal* 229, 231-232.
13. John Beechey, "Book Review of *Dealing in Virtue*," (1997) 24 *Journal of Law and Society* 569, 573 (emphasis added).
14. Florian Grisel, "Competition and Cooperation in International Commercial Arbitration: The Birth of a Transnational Legal Profession," (2017) 51/4 *Law & Society Review* 790.

drawing on the Who's Who List of the Most Highly Regarded Individuals in Commercial Arbitration (2015). Based on this data, I argue that the competition between "grand old men" and "young technocrats" is not a defining feature of international commercial arbitration. In fact, my data indicates that international commercial arbitration has been constructed by individuals acting at the margins of different legal and professional systems since the end of the Second World War (rather than by elite members of separate communities vying for power and legitimacy within a newly constructed field). I call these individuals the "secant marginals" because they were able to draw bits of legitimacy from the different systems in which they were partially grounded.[15] These "secant marginals" were often forced migrants who developed various forms of professional expertise at the juncture between academia, legal practice and arbitration work.[16] Their individual trajectory was one of social climbing in a context where they could not—contrary to Dezalay and Garth's argument—use their elite position within a specific social system in order to gain global legitimacy. The figure of the "secant marginal" is reminiscent of that of the "stranger" famously captured by Georg Simmel (himself the archetype of a marginal man):

> The stranger will thus not be considered here in the usual sense of the term, as the wanderer who comes today and goes tomorrow, but rather as the man who comes today and stays tomorrow—the potential wanderer, so to speak, who, although he has gone no further, has not quite got over the freedom of coming and going. He is fixed within a certain spatial circle—or within a group whose boundaries are analogous to spatial boundaries—but his position within it is fundamentally affected by the fact that he does not belong in it initially and that he brings qualities into it that are not, and cannot be, indigenous to it.[17]

The "secant marginals" built up international arbitration in their own image, and their successors imitated them. I observe for instance that most, if not all, of the top 25 commercial arbitrators on the Who's Who List of the Most Highly Regarded Individuals in Commercial Arbitrators (2015) have very similar profiles to those of the "secant marginals": they are members of one or several bar associations, teach at the university, maintain multiple ties with arbitral institutions and, of course, are nominated as arbitrators.[18] Some of them have, in ways that are potentially more problematic than the double hatting described by Langford, heavily weighed on policy-making processes that have had a direct influence on the development of international arbitration.[19] In short, leaders of international arbitration, whether past or present, are

---

15. *Id.* pp. 799 et seq.
16. *Id.* pp. 800-807.
17. Georg Simmel, "The Stranger," in Donald N. Levine (ed.), *Georg Simmel: On Individuality and Social Forms*, The University of Chicago Press, 1971, p. 143.
18. Grisel (*supra* n. 14), pp. 812-818.
19. See Florian Grisel, "Treaty-Making Between Public Authority and Private Interests: The Genealogy of the Convention on the Recognition and Enforcement of Foreign Arbitral Awards" (2017) 28/1 *European Journal of International Law* 73 (showing how a transnational network of experts associated with the ICC influenced the negotiations of New York Convention in the late 1950s, notably by intervening on behalf of states). The Working Group III of UNCITRAL, which Langford seems to associate with the "rising democratization of investment arbitration," potentially illustrates the same type of double hatting.

quintessential double hatters, and their double hatting not only spans legal professions but also legal systems. The main difference between the old and the new generation of leading arbitrators is that the latter have been more self-consciously devoted to leveraging (social, financial, human, and symbolic) capital in order to accrue global legitimacy than the former.[20]

In a separate article published in the *Oxford Handbook of International Arbitration*, I have extended my analysis to investment arbitration based on the review of more than 1700 appointments of arbitrators in 624 cases brought to the International Centre for the Settlement of Investment Disputes (ICSID) between 1972 and 2017.[21] My data indicates that the "secant marginals" who built international commercial arbitration after the Second World War also became involved in the early ICSID cases and that their hybrid social features were reproduced over time in investment arbitration, just as they were in the field of commercial arbitration.

Malcolm Langford claims that "double hatting is a relatively late phenomenon that primarily begins in the early 2000s."[22] Figure 3 in his paper suggests that not a single ISDS arbitrator cumulated activities as arbitrator and counsel between 1970 and 1995. This seems like an overstatement, considering the fact that his data concentrates on *simultaneous* double hatting rather than on *successive* double hatting (i.e., the fact that a lawyer obtains an appointment as arbitrator after the end of the first case, or vice versa) and that the number of cases was so few at the time that they rarely overlapped (and thus simultaneous double hatting could hardly occur). One should therefore extend the analysis to cover *successive* double hatting in order to obtain meaningful results. I carried out a brief search on the ICSID website and selected three examples—Pierre Lalive, Andrea Giardina and Aron Broches—in order to complement Langford's findings.[23] During the relevant time period (1970-1995), Pierre Lalive was counsel in ICSID Cases 72/1 and 74/1 and an ad hoc committee member in ICSID Case 81/2. Andrea Giardina was counsel in ICSID Case 77/1 and ad hoc committee member in ICSID Cases 81/1, 81/2 and 94/2. Aron Broches was counsel in ICSID Cases 89/1 and 84/4, ad hoc committee member in ICSID Case 84/4 and arbitrator in ICSID Case 82/1. Double hatting is not new and appears to be grounded in the practice of ISDS.

This sociological account of international arbitration—both commercial and investment—provides, I believe, a valid explanation for the permanence of double hatting. The pioneers of international arbitration were double hatters because they derived more legitimacy from the system that they were constructing than from the other systems and professions from which they were still trying to draw bits of legitimacy. For these "secant marginals," international arbitration was a unique opportunity to ground their careers, and they used every position that this system offered in order to achieve this purpose (whether in parallel or successively). Whether

---

20. Grisel (*supra* n. 14), p. 814.
21. *See* Florian Grisel, "Marginals and Elites in International Arbitration," in Federico Ortino and Thomas Schultz (eds.), *Oxford Handbook of International Arbitration*, Oxford University Press, 2020, p. 260.
22. Langford (*supra* n. 2), Section 3.1.
23. *See* https://icsid.worldbank.org/en/Pages/cases/ConcludedCases.aspx?status = c (last checked July 22, 2022).

or not one would be appointed as an arbitrator was, and still is, difficult to predict for most people, and defending cases as counsel (or teaching at a university, holding positions in an arbitral institution, participating in policy debates, and so forth) was (and still is, although arguably to a lesser extent) a way to mitigate the risks associated with this "career." Langford argues that the sociological landscape of international arbitration is "changing": what I have observed in my own research is, on the contrary, the striking stability of the features displayed by practitioners of international arbitration over the past few decades.[24] This does not exclude, of course, the possibility that public pressure might modify these practices. But the fact that leaders of international arbitration might stop cumulating counsel and arbitrator's work (a claim that is not backed by evidence thus far) does not say much about the nature of "double hatting," a practice that seems deeply grounded into their identities and extends far beyond the activity of counsel.

---

24. This observation is consistent with my argument that systems of private governance grounded in social norms (what Malcolm Langford calls a "moral economy") are particularly resilient and hard to evolve. *See* Florian Grisel, *The Limits of Private Governance: Norms and Rules in a Mediterranean Fishery*, Hart Publishing, 2021.

CHAPTER 36

Sociology and the Market for Commercial Arbitrators: Seeing It All Differently

Janet Walker, CM[*]

TABLE OF CONTENTS

I   THE SOCIOLOGY OF ARBITRATION

1   Why Sociology?: Why Now?

There is, perhaps, no more fascinating topic for sociological analysis than international arbitration. Sociology tells us that, as human beings, we are, above all, social beings. And yet, as arbitration practitioners navigating the intricate formalities of the hard and soft laws and the rules that regulate commercial dealings and disputes, we can lose sight of the human interactions that are at the heart of it all.

---

[*] Janet Walker, CM is an independent arbitrator with chambers in London, Toronto and Sydney, and a distinguished research professor at Osgoode Hall in Toronto. Janet chaired the ICC Canada Arbitration Committee and is a board member of CIArb Canada. She is co-chair of CanArbWeek and was a member of the ICCA2018 Sydney executive organizing committee. Janet is also the executive editor of the *Canadian Journal of Commercial Arbitration* and co-author of *Commercial Arbitration in Australia under the Model Law*. She authors Canada's main text on the conflict of laws. The author wishes to thank Alisha Matthias, Research Assistant, Sydney Arbitration Chambers, for her excellent editorial assistance.

Sociology teaches us to step back from our day-to-day activities, our conventions, and our rituals to observe the patterns of our professional relationships and the dynamics of our interactions. When we do, we sometimes discover that what we *think* we are doing and what we *say* we are doing, are not quite the same as what we *are* doing. Viewed from a distance, as social phenomena, we can see that some of our social structures and rituals support our perceived objectives and others do not; and some have unintended consequences, and others support perfectly valid objectives that we had not previously discerned.

An Age of Enlightenment – the theme of this International Council of Commercial Arbitration (ICCA) Congress – is a time marked by a rigorous review of established ideas. Sociology is one means of conducting this review.

But this is not our community's first foray into Sociology. The ICCA 2014 Program Committee, headed by Lucy Reed, who is currently ICCA's President, pursued the theme of 'Legitimacy: Myths, Challenges, Realities'.[1] The Congress began with a live empirical study in which the participants were polled on decision-making in arbitration and the Congress ended with the results being shared with the participants on the last day. Throughout the program, the participants were challenged to reflect on the commonly held myths about international arbitration and to test those myths against the realities that they had experienced. This sociological approach to arbitration generated lively engagement and fresh insight into the law and the lore of arbitration.

Also in 2014, the late Emmanuel Gaillard, one of the arbitrators highlighted in Professor Langford's Congress paper,[2] made a highly memorable contribution to the sociology of arbitration in his Freshfields lecture.[3] In that lecture, M[e] Gaillard introduced his iconic Venn diagram,[4] in which he showed his innovative taxonomy of the social actors in the field, including the *essential actors* (parties and arbitrators); the *service providers* (counsel, institutions, supportive judiciaries, experts; funders, etc.); and the *value providers* (states, international organizations, professional organizations, academic institutions, discussion fora, etc.).

In his lecture, M[e] Gaillard also developed a taxonomy of our rituals: *arbitral hearings*, *recognition tournaments*, and *periodic mass gatherings*. Finally, he described the interaction among the social actors as moving from a *solidaristic* model in which 'a small number of occasional players, acting in turn in different capacities ... and possessing a strong common set of shared values' was evolving into a *polarized* model, in which 'a large number of players ... occupy specific functions and "in which certain social agents have become champions of certain causes which are not necessarily

---

1. ICCA 2014 Program, available at chrome-extension://efaidnbmnnnibpcajpcglclefindmkaj/https: //cdn.arbitration-icca.org/s3fs-public/document/media_document/icca_website_schedule_03. 27.14.pdf.
2. Malcolm Langford, Chapter 34: 'The Changing Sociology of the Investment Arbitration Market: The Case of Double Hatting' (2022) ('Changing Sociology').
3. Emmanuel Gaillard, 'Sociology of International Arbitration', 31 Arbitration International (2016) p. 1.
4. *Ibid.*, p 10 chrome-extension://efaidnbmnnnibpcajpcglclefindmkaj/https://cdn.arbitration-icca. org/s3fs-public/document/media_document/emmanuel-gaillard--sociology-of-international-ar bitration-042715-ia.pdf.

shared by other players in the field"'.[5] Interestingly, this observation foreshadowed the emerging issues concerning the practice of 'double hatting' in investment arbitration, which has been the subject of the study in Professor Langford's Congress paper.

2   Professor Langford's Study of Double Hatting

M[e] Gaillard's contributions to arbitration and to the sociology of international arbitration serve as an important inspiration for this chapter commenting on Malcolm Langford's study.[6] In his paper, Professor Langford has documented the practice of serving in multiple roles as a means of gaining *symbolic capital* to secure appointments. He has argued that this practice once served to concentrate power and support strategic and collective anti-competitive behaviour that limited supply in the market for commercial arbitrators.[7] In other words, the economic sociology of double hatting tells the story of accumulating symbolic capital to meet demand, and insider behaviour to limit supply.[8] However, Professor Langford suggests that in the new moral economy in investment arbitration we are seeing a shift to measuring candidates in 'moral capital' and this is creating new strategic incentives to 'act moral' or to 'appear moral' in order to obtain appointments.[9]

Even more interesting than these propositions are the assumptions that underlie them: 'Why quantitative empirical analysis?' as the method; 'Why Investor-State Dispute Settlement (ISDS)?' as the topic; and 'Why arbitrator selection?' as the focus? Let's consider each of these in turn.

3   Why Quantitative Empirical Analysis?

Starting with the choice of quantitative empirical analysis as the method: Presenting a complex social interaction in the form of numbers, graphs and charts can certainly help us to see it with fresh eyes. On the whole, lawyers are among the least numerate of professionals on the planet. And we can easily be dazzled by numbers. Somehow, the idea that mathematical calculations represent incontrovertible proof to *someone* suggests that we too should believe them. Indeed, through quantitative analysis, Professor Langford demonstrated in what seemed to be a very compelling way the extent to which double hatting occurred in investment arbitration leading up to 2017[10] and how it declined after that time. His statistics and his calculations showing the evolving composition of the caseloads of leading arbitrators were very impressive.

However, as persuasive as they seem, the data do not explain themselves – and the narrative that we develop to explain the data can depend upon assumptions that may be subject to debate. For example, to advance the theory that double hatting has

---

5. *Ibid.*, pp. 13–14.
6. M. Langford, 'Changing Sociology.'
7. *Ibid.*, pp. 596, 602.
8. *Ibid.*, p. 603.
9. *Ibid.*, p. 621.
10. *Ibid.*, p. 598.

been a strategic choice, Professor Langford relied upon the assumptions that the roles of arbitrator and counsel are largely substitutable and that they require the same expertise.[11] Our collective experience may suggest otherwise. Not all brilliant counsel make good arbitrators. Indeed, not all good judges make good arbitrators. In this Congress, the presentations of Melanie van Leeuwen and Kathleen Paisley in the panel on 'The Renaissance Arbitrator',[12] described the myriad skill sets required to serve well in the role of arbitrator, not all of which seem likely to be central to the role of an advocate.

Furthermore, insight into the context from which the data emerges may be critical to understanding its significance. Beyond the personal qualities that may make certain individuals more capable in serving in the roles of counsel or of arbitrator, their professional circumstances may support or undermine their aspirations to serve in one of those roles or the other. Professor Langford gives a nod to the importance of adequate resources in addressing the 'managerial aspect of the counsel role',[13] noting that this could limit the capacity of those with competing professional obligations. Indeed, the resources required to serve as counsel in a large arbitration are typically beyond the reach of individuals who work independently. In contrast, the freedom from disqualifying conflicts of working independently may be necessary for developing a career as an arbitrator.

In this way, it is widely appreciated in the arbitration community that one's professional circumstances may affect one's capacity to serve in one role or another; and that the choice to work in a law firm or to work independently may be influenced more by one's personal circumstances and income needs than a preference for serving as an arbitrator or as counsel. On the one hand, members of law firms may enjoy a larger and more regular income than all but the busiest of arbitrators working independently; and, on the other hand, remaining available to be responsive in a timely fashion to the parties' needs requires a degree of flexibility in one's schedule that is unavailable to all but a few of the members of large law firms. The combination of these two factors alone can be sufficient to make serving as arbitrator difficult to pursue as a primary role for many practitioners other than those approaching retirement.

This leaves the few individuals who were the focus of Professor Langford's study – those who have the talent and the resources to function well in both roles. It may be just a matter of judgment in interpreting the data whether we should conclude that managing one's career to curtail one's double-hatting and to avoid issue conflicts is a strategic attempt to 'appear moral' rather than simple prudence in light of the increasing risk of challenges to arbitrators and to awards arising from the practice,[14].

---

11. *Ibid.*, p. 601 (the same 'expertise' can be deployed ... in both arenas').
12. ICCA 2022 Congress program available at chrome-extension://etaidnbmnnnibpcajpcglclefindm kaj/https://cdn.arbitration-icca.org/s3fs-public/document/media_document/Edinburgh%20I CCA%202022%20Congress%20Programme%2016.09.22.pdf. *See also* Chapter 46, 'Aristotle's Virtue Ethics in Arbitration', in this volume.
13. Malcolm Langford, Chapter 34: 'The Changing Sociology of the Investment Arbitration Market: The Case of Double Hatting' (2022) ('Changing Sociology').
14. *Ibid.*, p. 620: 'it is not clear how much can be taken from the existence or not of arbitrator challenges. Some authors have argued that because the rules ae so vague and the jurisprudence on double hatting unsettled, that it is difficult for parties to challenge the practice'.

Indeed, the evolving attitude of the wider public to double hatting may render the question moot if proposals are adopted to establish rules restricting it.[15]

In other words, even if the math is right in a quantitative analysis, examining the underlying premises may cause us to question the conclusions. Nevertheless, in encouraging us to debate the conclusions, the quantitative empirical analysis will have caused us to re-think some of our previously accepted views. And, in this way, Professor Langford's study has made an important contribution. It is thought-provoking.[16]

4 Why Investment Arbitration?

If choosing quantitative empirical research as the method for a sociological study of arbitration is not a mere caprice or happenstance, then neither is the choice of ISDS as the topic. The veritable explosion of scholarship and commentary on ISDS in recent decades has been an inevitable result of the regular publication of case information, orders and awards of matters in investment arbitration. The size of the scholarly literature and of the academic community of those devoted to the highly specialized field of ISDS has all but eclipsed those of commercial arbitration in the private sector. Thus, it might have seemed quite natural to interpret an invitation from the International Council for *Commercial* Arbitration as an invitation to examine the specialized field of investment arbitration. Indeed, this interpretation seems to have gone unquestioned by organizers and participants alike.

But as that path is well-trodden, and as this *is* the International Council for *Commercial* Arbitration, it may be useful also, in this chapter, to take a look through a sociological lens at commercial arbitration. However, given the patchwork of information available, it would be difficult to develop a meaningful quantitative analysis. Fortunately, as was done by Me Gaillard and others, it is possible to invite readers from the arbitration community to rely instead upon their own experience to test the propositions considered.

5 Why Arbitrator Selection?

With this, we turn to the last of the three questions about the assumptions underlying Professor Langford's study: Why choose *arbitrator selection* as the focus for a sociological examination? Fortunately, there is little mystery in this. It is a topic that conveniently spans the fields of investment and commercial arbitration. More than this, it may be said, tongue in cheek, that no topic has quite the same personal significance for so many at periodic mass gatherings such as the ICCA Congress as this.

15. 'Possible Reform of Investor-State Dispute Settlement (ISDS) – Draft Code of Conduct', UNCITRAL Working Group III (Investor-State Dispute Settlement Reform), forty-first session (Vienna, online, 15–19 November 2021), UN Doc. A/CN.9/WG.III/WP/209 (15 September 2021) Article 4 (Limit on Multiple Roles).
16. 'The most thought-provoking thing in our thought-provoking time is that we are still not thinking.' Martin Heidegger, *Was heißt Denken?* 1954: Max Nlemeyer Verlag.

Accordingly, there may be no better justification for choosing to examine arbitrator selection needed than collective self-interest.

However, on a more serious note, it is widely accepted that a well-chosen arbitrator or panel of arbitrators can be vital to promoting the quality of the arbitral process and the result. It is also well accepted that the freedom of the parties to choose their arbitrator or arbitrators is one of the features of arbitration that draws parties to it. Accordingly, to self-interest as a justification, we can add interest in supporting the best in arbitration as a reason for following Professor Langford's lead in focusing on arbitrator selection – and, in this chapter, in doing so in the *commercial* arbitration market.

II   WHAT ABOUT COMMERCIAL ARBITRATION?

1   Making Informed Choices in Appointments

In developing an analysis of arbitrator selection in the commercial arbitration market, we must accept two other premises relied upon by Professor Langford and others: that arbitrator selection is primarily a market-based choice, and that sound choices depend upon a well-functioning market. This was the focus of Patrick Baeten's Congress paper 'A User's Perspective on the International Commercial Arbitration Market'.[17] It might seem off-putting to some to adopt Mr Baeten's description of the central relationship in arbitration – one that was described by Professor Gaillard as that between *parties* and *arbitrators* – as one of *customer* and *seller*. However, it should be of common concern to all who are interested in the welfare of international arbitration to learn from a party such as Mr Baeten – a customer/buyer – that the 'access to information about potential sellers/arbitrators is unsatisfactory'.[18]

While there may be no assurance that parties will not be persuaded by less relevant considerations, or that sound outcomes in the arbitration will inevitably follow from wise choices in the selection of arbitrators, most would agree on the importance of the role played by relevant and reliable information. The questions are: What kind of information will be most relevant and reliable? And, assuming that increasing the availability of relevant and reliable information will help parties to make better choices, are there limits to the kind of information that can be made available and the assistance that it can provide? And what are the consequences for the arbitral process of making more information available?

With these questions, we turn to the love-hate relationship that we have had for some decades with transparency.

---

17. Patrick Baeten, Chapter 49: 'A User's Perspective on the International Commercial Arbitration Market'.
18. *Ibid.*, p. 828.

2   A Love-Hate Relationship with Transparency

The more one reflects on the benefits of information to the process of selecting arbitrators in international commercial arbitration and on the implications of efforts to increase the availability of information, the more one realizes that international arbitration is a social endeavour that has long had a love-hate relationship with transparency.

At the beginning of the twenty-first century, arbitration was still a very private affair. As described by Dezalay and Garth in their iconic study, *Dealing in Virtue*,[19] the parties entrusted their disputes to wise men who were respected in the business community for their extensive commercial experience and good judgment.[20] These arbitrators were expected to work closely with the parties and their advisers to design a simple process for the dispute and to resolve it promptly, conclusively, and to the satisfaction of the parties. There was no suggestion that any of the participants needed to be accountable to outsiders, or that greater transparency would be anything but an intrusion.

Indeed, in his famous Goff lecture in 2000, Fali Nariman echoed this sentiment when he railed against the 'legal baggage taken on board the good ship ICA'.[21] He said that it could be justified only if the process was a public one, *which it clearly was not*. The whole idea was contrary to what he called the 'Spirit of Arbitration'.

Shaking ourselves awake from this nostalgic daydream, we look around, just a generation later, to find ourselves fully immersed in the information era. Since the pandemic restrictions have ended, talks, symposia and conferences have once again come to be held on a continuous basis in scores of centres around the world. Email inboxes and newsfeeds channel a steady stream of communications promoting events, reporting on recent developments, and otherwise generally enlivening our networks. Despite our daily efforts to drink from the firehose of information about international commercial arbitration, our thirst for it has seemed only to grow.

As was also highlighted in the 2014 ICCA Congress, this thirst for information had, at that time, reached crisis levels in the field of ISDS. The wider public in many countries began to object to having their government's policy choices reviewed by private tribunals – tribunals lacking the standing and accountability of state courts. How could decision-makers appointed on a one-off basis by the parties, serving in tribunals administered by non-governmental organizations, be permitted to exercise authority to make decisions on critical issues of public importance free of the review of

---

19. Yves Dezalay and Bryant G. Garth, *Dealing in Virtue: International Commercial Arbitration and the Construction of a Transnational Legal Order* (University of Chicago Press 1996).
20. This would have been consistent with the practice in Paris – 'French commercial courts are not staffed with professional judges, but with members of the business community working part-time at the court (and for free)': Gilles Cuniberti, 'Paris, the Jurisdiction of Choice?', Conflict of Laws.Net (2 February 2011) available at http://conflictoflaws.net/2011/paris-commercial-court-creates-international-division/ (last accessed 1 August 2022).
21. Fali S. Nariman, 'The Spirit of Arbitration: The Tenth Annual Goff Lecture' 16(3) Arbitration International (2000) p. 261 at p. 262.

the local courts? Who were these people? How were they chosen? And what procedural safeguards were there for the wider public affected by their decisions?

The solution to the legitimacy crisis was said to be greater transparency.[22] The fabled image of a system in which the parties entrusted business disputes to tête-à-têtes with 'grand old men' was decried as fundamentally unacceptable for disputes affecting the wider public. It reflected a democratic deficit that had to stop.

The continuing story of the response to this concern in the field of investment arbitration is beyond the scope of this chapter. However, despite the differences between investor-State disputes and commercial disputes,[23] the call for greater transparency came to be extended to international commercial arbitration as well.[24]

The role of publicity in commercial disputes is far more complex and nuanced. As Mallory Silberbman pointed out in her Congress paper, 'Arbitration's Printing Press: A Letter to the Editor',[25] the time for treating transparency as a rhetorical trump card has passed, and we should look for more meaningful approaches to the question of whether international commercial arbitration is or should be public.

A thoughtful look at the need for transparency and accountability in arbitrator selection in commercial arbitration reveals important differences. Apart from disclosures of potential conflicts of interest, the need for information relates to questions of arbitrators' experience, expertise, and availability as they might bear on the arbitral process and their expertise in the subject matter of the dispute. Accountability in commercial arbitration selection has a different purpose from that in investment arbitration. It relates primarily to the efficiency with which the resolution of the dispute

---

22. This prompted a wide range of responses, including the adoption of the United Nations Convention on Transparency in Treaty-based Investor-State Arbitration, New York, 2014 (adopted 10 December 2014, entered into force 18 October 2017) ('Mauritius Convention'). Ironically, the regular publication of investment arbitration awards, combined with the prevalence of certain issues of treaty interpretation, may have caused individual arbitrators to feel obliged to make consistent rulings and, thereby, create the basis for 'arbitrator shopping', one of the many concerns that has plagued investment arbitration. In other words, transparency was itself a contributing factor, but this is not to challenge the importance of public results – merely to note one of the many complexities.

23. And acknowledging that there are cases on the margins, such as those involving public bodies and public interests. These were the focus of a panel at the 2018 ICCA Congress in Sydney: *Ibid. See also* Matthew Carmody, 'Overturning the Presumption of Confidentiality: Should the UNCITRAL Rules on Transparency Be Applied to International Commercial Arbitration?', 19 International Trade and Business Law Review (2016) p. 96; Catherine A. Rogers, 'Transparency in International Commercial Arbitration', 54 Kansas Law Review (2006) p. 1301.

24. One example of this call for greater transparency came in a paper presented by Constantine Partasides QC at the International Council on Commercial Arbitration (ICCA) Congress in Sydney in April 2018. In a panel concerning arbitrations involving public bodies and public interests, he argued that the 'tidal wave' of transparency sweeping through investor state arbitration should extend to commercial arbitration because transparency has come to be viewed as an end in itself and any lack of information is a gap susceptible to being filled by misinformation or generating suspicion. He went on to argue that the public legitimacy of international commercial arbitration is making doubtful any presumption of a desire for confidentiality, and that confidentiality should be secured only when clearly chosen by the parties: Constantine Partasides QC, 'Arbitrations Involving Public Bodies and Public Interests: Salient Issues, Part 1 – The Increasing Participation of Public Entities in International Arbitration', panel discussion, 24th ICCA Congress (Sydney, 17 April 2018).

25. Mallory Silberbman, Chapter 18: 'Arbitration's Printing Press: A Letter to the Editor'.

will be managed and the extent to which the outcome and reasoning will meet the expectations of the parties. The primary audience for accountability in commercial arbitration is not the wider public, but the market within which it operates – the businesses that may need to select arbitrators for future disputes.

III   INFORMATION ABOUT ARBITRATORS

1   What We Knew Then and What We Know Now

In the days of Dezelay and Garth, the arbitrators who were available for appointments were a self-described 'mafia'. As an exclusive and shadowy group of insiders, they were reputed to be well known, but only to one another and to the parties who appeared before them. Questions about how to select an arbitrator from among them seem rarely to have been raised. Perhaps, the arbitrators were all sufficiently eminent to serve in most disputes and because there were so few arbitrators and so few disputes, it was easily determined on any occasion who was available and who was best suited for the dispute.

Most practitioners today would agree that choosing an arbitrator carefully can be critical to the efficiency of the arbitration and the efficacy of the result; and that a simple attestation that 'X is a good egg' would no longer suffice to support a sensible choice. But more to the point, in just two short decades, there has been a remarkable growth in the choices available, and with this growth, there has been a veritable explosion of publicly available information about potential appointees from which to choose. How is it that the concern about the availability of useful information still rings true? What information do we need and how do we find it?

Useful information could include the arbitrators' qualifications and experience, their perspectives on relevant procedural issues; and, possibly, information on their performance. How are these now becoming available? Is the information reliable? Is it sufficient? Is it useful?

2   Arbitrators' Websites, Institutional Panel Lists, Commercial Directories

There are now a range of sources for this information including the arbitrators' websites, institutional panels, commercial indexes, publications, and conference presentations. However, each has its own caveats. Arbitrators' own websites are as varied as the arbitrators themselves, which may make it difficult to find relevant information and to compare one candidate with another.

The panels of recommended arbitrators found through some arbitral institutions[26] may be more standardized in format and content than arbitrators' own websites. However, the resources of institutions to seek out and include a broad range

---

26. *See, e.g.*, Asian International Arbitration Centre (AIAC), 'Panellist Search', available at https://www.aiac.world/panellist (last accessed 1 August 2022); Australian Centre for International

of qualified individuals and to verify and ensure the currency of the information provided to them by the panellists may vary from one institution to another, and there may be an element of capture for newer or smaller institutions in presenting well-known arbitrators.

Commercial directories seek to improve the accuracy and utility of the information by using researchers and interviewing those who know the arbitrators, but there can be speculative observations made by arbitrators in the interests of co-promotion and, again, there is a risk of capture for publications dependent on the subscriptions of those profiled.

3   Arbitrators' Perspectives on Current Issues

Some commercial directories seek to go beyond resumés and attestations to present the arbitrators' perspectives on recent developments and trends in the field,[27] and others seek to fill the gaps for subscribers even further by including links to the arbitrators' recent publications and publicly available awards.[28]

The arbitrators' publications may provide useful insight into their perspectives on the field. However, many arbitrators may be justifiably wary of expressing views in the abstract on issues that might arise in particular cases before them: e.g., 'Was the pandemic a force majeure?' Furthermore, although arbitrators' publications may demonstrate the capacity to write well and to think clearly, increasingly, as arbitration becomes a mainstream academic subject and the standards for academic writings in the field rise, meaningful contributions require more time than many busy arbitrators can find without capable assistants and one might ask: 'Whose work is it anyway'?

Although conference presentations could play a similar role, there has been a general trend to free presenters from the burden of producing a paper and to opt instead

---

Commercial Arbitration (ACICA), 'Search the ACICA Panel of Arbitrators', available at https://acica.org.au/arbitrator-panellist-search/#!directory (last accessed 1 August 2022); Dubai International Arbitration Centre (DIAC), available at http://www.diac.ae/ (last accessed 1 August 2022); Hong Kong International Arbitration Centre (HKIAC), 'Panel & List of Arbitrators', available at http://www.hkiac.org/arbitration/arbitrators/panel-and-list-of-arbitrators (last accessed 1 August 2022); Korean Commercial Arbitration Board International (KCAB International), 'Panel of Arbitrators', available at http://www.kcabinternational.or.kr/user/arbitrators.do?CURRENT_MENU_CODE = MENU0003&TOP_MENU_CODE = MENU0001 (last accessed 1 August 2022); London Court of International Arbitration (LCIA), 'Director of Members', available at https://www.lcia.org/Membership/directory-of-members.aspx (last accessed 1 August 2022).Singapore International Arbitration Centre (SIAC), 'SIAC Panel', http://www.siac.org.sg/our-arbitrators/siac-panel (last accessed 1 August 2022); Stockholm Chamber of Commerce (SCC), available at https://sccinstitute.com/ (last accessed 1 August 2022); Vienna International Arbitration Centre (VIAC), 'List of Practitioners in International Arbitration', available at http://www.viac.eu/en/arbitration/practitioners (last accessed 1 August 2022).

27. Who's Who Legal, 'Thought Leaders – Arbitration 2022' available at https://whoswholegal.com/thought-leaders/thought-leaders---arbitration (last accessed 1 August 2022).

28. Kluwer Arbitration Blog, 'Wolters Kluwer Launches Data-Driven Enhancements to Arbitrator Tool Within Kluwer Arbitration Practice Plus', (19 November 2021) available at http://arbitrationblog.kluwerarbitration.com/2021/11/19/wolters-kluwer-launches-data-driven-enhancements-to-arbitrator-tool-within-kluwer-arbitration-practice-plus/ (last accessed 1 August 2022).

for short speeches or roundtable discussions, sometimes highlighting little more than the speakers' oratorical skills. And, in these periodic mass gatherings, speakers may need to compete with audience members for airtime. The Q&A portions of the program can become significant opportunities to gain airtime for those who are not on the stage, as can the coffee breaks or corridor conversations during the program sessions.

Indeed, the magic of passing the microphone has really come into its own in the increasingly popular format of the 'moderated symposium' in which everyone can have a turn at speaking spontaneously on topics of common interest. This format requires no program preparation beyond a crowd-sourced list of questions, no papers, and no sustained presentations. It is a win-win opportunity to give everyone the chance to 'talk the talk.' But even this format can lose its lustre when the lively exchanges settle into familiar patterns of soundbites channelling what are imagined to be popular views on current issues. At such moments, when thoughtful engagement is displaced by the enthusiasm to assist in providing the information needed for an efficient market, the disappointment for appointing parties may also include realizing that it is unclear what has been reliably demonstrated about the arbitrators' relevant qualifications.

4 Arbitrators' Performance Statistics

Turning finally to the information on how individuals have performed or might perform in the role of arbitrator – whether they can 'walk the walk', surely that is what appointing parties are after.

One recent innovation proposes to provide access for paid subscribers to a database of statistics about individual arbitrators over a broad range of criteria.[29] Once again, the numerical evidence of arbitrator performance can seem impressive, even dazzling, but there may be differences between recruiting for a major league baseball team and constituting an arbitral tribunal. Can parties really hope to achieve the desired result with a 'moneyball' approach to selecting arbitrators?

5 Publishing Arbitral Awards

Finally, there is the possibility that systematically publishing arbitral awards could serve, *inter alia*, as a source of information about the skill and judgment of potential arbitrators.[30] The Singapore International Arbitration Centre (SIAC) and the International Chamber of Commerce (ICC) have indicated an intention to publish arbitral

---

29. Catherine A. Rogers, 'Moneyball for Arbitrators', Kluwer Arbitration Blog (2 July 2018), available at http://arbitrationblog.kluwerarbitration.com/2018/07/02/moneyball-for-arbitrators/ (last accessed 1 August 2022).
30. Other benefits, such as enriching the jurisprudence on leading commercial issues have been noted. *See* The Right Hon. John Thomas, Lord Thomas of Cwmgiedd, Lord Chief Justice of England and Wales, 'Developing Commercial Law Through the Courts: Rebalancing the Relationship Between the Courts and Arbitration', speech, The Fourth BAILII Sir Henry Brooke Lecture (9 March 2016). It is not clear, though, what thought leadership would make available that could not be replicated in scholarly writings.

awards.[31] The potential of awards to reflect the skill and judgement of arbitrators would be subject to several obvious caveats where the award was rendered as a result of the collective reasoning of a tribunal of three arbitrators, or where some aspects of it might be attributable to assistants or those involved in scrutiny. Still, the structure of the award, the procedural history, the articulation of the facts, the law, the issues and, of course, the quality of the reasoning, could all provide some indication of the capabilities of the arbitrators.

Despite the promise of this development to inform the market for arbitrators, in her Congress paper, 'In Defence of Party Choice: The Continuing Importance of Confidentiality in Commercial Arbitration',[32] Paula Hodges decried the proposal to publish commercial arbitration awards as one that would create a concern for a loss of confidentiality and one that would be out of step with the wishes of the parties.[33]

The question of confidentiality in commercial arbitration is a complex one. Few institutions and national laws provide any reliable assurance of confidentiality; and international studies have confirmed that questions such as what information is kept confidential, who is bound, and what exceptions may be permitted, are largely a matter for the parties to decide by agreement.[34] Despite this, there seems to be a general acceptance that, subject to overriding concerns relating to the wider public interest in the subject matter of the dispute or the outcome,[35] commercial parties are entitled to secure the confidentiality of their matter if they wish to do so. This is different from litigation in most state courts.

Much has changed since Fali Nariman spoke of 'The Spirit of Arbitration', but commercial arbitration remains, after all, private, if not assuredly confidential. In deference to this, arbitral institutions, aware that their market share of potential cases may be reduced if they do not accommodate this desire, have agreed to publish awards only with the permission of the parties. This may suffice to explain why the initiative has not progressed.

However, the reasons to refrain from publishing awards in commercial arbitrations may not be limited to the loss of confidentiality and the contrary wishes of the parties. Confidentiality is a specific concern for restricting access to particular information, that is, some of the information in most awards and all of the information in some awards. This need for confidentiality may be met in cases that do not engage the interests of the wider public by recognizing the parties' right to it when and where that right is asserted – either in the parties' agreement or in granting an application brought in the proceedings.

---

31. 2013 Rules of the Singapore International Arbitration Centre, Rule 28.10 (https://siac.org.sg/siac-rules-2013). Note to Parties and Arbitral Tribunals on the Conduct of the Arbitration Under the ICC Rules of Arbitration, Notes 57-59 (https://iccwbo.org/news-publications/arbitration-adr-rules-and-tools/note-parties-arbitral-tribunals-conduct-arbitration/#single-hero-document).

32. Paula Hodges, Chapter 14: 'In Defence of Party Choice: The Continuing Importance of Confidentiality in Commercial Arbitration'

33. *Ibid.*

34. Filip De Ly, Mark Friedman and Luca Radicati Di Brozolo, 'International Law Association International Commercial Arbitration Committee's Report and Recommendations on "Confidentiality in International Commercial Arbitration"', 28(3) Arbitrational International (2012) p. 355.

35. *Esso Australia Resources v. Plowman* (1995) 183 CLR 10.

And, while party autonomy is important, the problem with systematically publishing awards relates to something more fundamental than disregard for party autonomy: it will change the way we arbitrate – and not necessarily for the better.

Every piece of writing is intended for an audience, and as Fali Nariman observed, the less private the award, the more it will be encumbered by features designed to satisfy the curiosity of strangers rather than to meet the needs of the parties.[36] As the audience grows, the simple explanation as to why one party has prevailed and the other has not will be supplemented by ever-increasing detail on the procedure, the record, the submissions, and the law – all designed to ensure that the tribunal is accountable to those who have less and less interest in the particular dispute or the outcome.

The regular audiences today for awards include the legal teams, party representatives, scrutinizing institutions and, from time to time, reviewing courts. Each has expectations that, though challenging, seem capable of being addressed by diligent tribunals. However, if we make awards regularly available to the general public, and if arbitrators anticipate being judged by snippets of their awards circulated at large and out of context, there will be a range of additional concerns that will alter the approach that otherwise might be taken to writing these awards.

This transparency and accountability may not improve the quality of the tribunal's ultimate work product. This is concerning, but there are other, perhaps more serious, concerns. If the award is seen to reflect what has gone on in the process, it could change that process as well. We could see the emergence of defensive arbitrating extending beyond the tribunal to counsel and other participants. It could stifle the willingness to innovate and to tailor the process in the instant case to improve it.

Accordingly, in taking a sociological approach to the issue of publishing awards, we can see that although the idea of systematic publication may seem to be a good one, it could alter the human interactions that are at the heart of the arbitral process, and it could alter them in ways that may not be desirable.

As Fali Nariman suggested, the spirit of arbitration may require it to remain, in principle, a private process – one that is intimate to Emanuel Gaillard's essential actors and to those who are needed to assist them. This is so even if, on the margins, there may be a need to protect the confidentiality of some information or to disclose more broadly some other information.

On the question of arbitrator selection, it brings us full circle to acknowledging that perhaps you can never really know how people are likely to perform as arbitrators until you work with them; and that we must accept that, for this reason, people will always enjoy serving as arbitrators with those who they know from direct experience; and that whether our shortlists include fresh or familiar faces, there will always be some guesswork and intuition involved in selecting arbitrators.

---

36. F.S. Nariman, 'The Spirit of Arbitration' pp. 262 ff.

IV   DIRECT EXPERIENCE AND SEEING IT ALL DIFFERENTLY

It also brings us to the recognition that we have all just witnessed a phenomenon that has caused us, in a wholly unprecedented way, to reconsider the process of getting to know one another so that we can work together better.

Through the pandemic, we experienced the near-universal isolation of all of us from one another. And yet, despite our physical isolation, we were collectively propelled into the new normal of videoconferencing, and we experienced a kind of casual and intimate engagement previously unknown. We visited more of our colleagues' kitchens, basement studies and spare bedrooms around the world than we ever imagined possible. We met pets and family members we might never otherwise have encountered. In a meeting with colleagues and friends in this personal context, we gained fresh insight into them as individuals.

We also learned much about the options for the conduct of arbitral meetings and hearings and we continue to learn more: whose in-person attendance is critical and who can participate remotely without impairing the quality of the proceedings? What circumstances militate in favour of one or the other kind of attendance in each case? What is the most effective way to combine in-person and remote participation?

We filled the informational gap created by the pause in in-person conferences with a continuous stream of webinars and ubiquitous online content. It has changed our perspective on in-person conferences. We will continue to value thoughtful presentations, but we seem likely otherwise to be more interested in the opportunities to engage with others interactively.

And, in the specific context of arbitrator selection, the advent of webinars and web meetings made it possible to experience up close and in real time, a much wider range of potential candidates than would have been possible by attending in-person events. Furthermore, the capacity of videoconferencing to eliminate the time and expense of travel and hospitality in interviewing prospective arbitrators has reduced the concerns about the way in which that practice could affect the integrity of the process of arbitrator selection.

Beyond these particular areas of collective discovery, we have learned the value of gathering together in person. It is simply the best way to get to know one another, to develop our coherence as a community, and to improve our ability to work well in our various roles in commercial arbitration. With this discovery, we enter a new Age of Enlightenment, one in which we will develop a much more sophisticated approach to the options and opportunities for communicating and engaging with one another. As we do so, it will be worth continuing to pause from time to time to reflect on the role of social interactions – human interactions – in our work in international commercial arbitration.

PANEL 10　　Young Practitioners
and Our Future

CHAPTER 37

Report of the Moderator for the Young Practitioners and Our Future Panel

Yuet Min Foo[*]

TABLE OF CONTENTS

I   INTRODUCTION

The panel on 'Young Practitioners and Our Future' at the ICCA 2022 Edinburgh Congress was an interactive session in which participants engaged in 'speed-conferencing' in small groups to exchange views on the latest developments in the international arbitration arena. The discussions were facilitated by a panel of future arbitration leaders from various jurisdictions – Yuet Min Foo as the moderator, with twelve facilitators comprising Julian Bordaçahar, Naomi Briercliffe, Elizabeth Chan, Valentine Chessa, Arie Eernisse, Iuliana Iancu, Jonathan Lim, Melissa Ordonez, Nesreen Osman, Naomi Tarawali, Siddharth Thacker and Nhu Hoang Tran Thang.

The topics discussed fell broadly within two categories: (i) recent trends in international arbitration – entrepreneurship, technology and environment; and (ii) the future of arbitration and institutions – regulation, diversity and confidentiality. Participants had the opportunity to engage in discussions on two chosen topics during the

---

[*] Director, Dispute Resolution, Drew & Napier.

session. After the 'speed-conferencing' sessions, the facilitators shared their perspectives on the various topics and some findings of interest from the group discussions. This chapter sets out a summary of the discussions.

II   RECENT TRENDS IN INTERNATIONAL ARBITRATION

1   The Proliferation of Young Entrepreneurs in the Business of Arbitration

In recent years, there has been a noticeable increase in the number of young enterprising lawyers striking out on their own in hopes of having more autonomy over their work and clients.

Valentine Chessa and Julian Bordaçahar led the discussion on the recent proliferation of young entrepreneurs venturing into the business of arbitration. They explored burning questions of why, when and how young lawyers should fly solo or launch a new boutique or business.

Participants generally concurred that a certain level of experience is necessary before one goes solo as an arbitrator. On the other hand, very young practitioners launching boutique firms that are predominantly devoted to counsel work are not unheard of. Participants also discussed the development of ad hoc teams composed of practitioners from different law firms on the basis of the expertise needed for a given case.

The panel heard that several participants launched their boutique firms with former colleagues or were supported by former colleagues, while some others launched businesses that are ancillary to the lawyering profession and that are based on their previous experience as lawyers and on ideas as to how to improve workflow or create new tools to aid the work of lawyers.

Most of the participants considered that offices are still necessary although with a certain flexibility, while all the participants agreed that technology is an essential part of their venture that renders possible projects that were not imaginable only a few years ago. All the participants also agreed that a good website, coupled with a strategic social media approach, are crucial to the success of any new venture.

Ms Chessa and Mr Bordaçahar highlighted the importance of business development for young entrepreneurs in the arbitration scene. They shared tips on building a personal brand and leveraging one's network, rankings and pro bono work to become *the* rainmaker, despite no longer hailing from a more prominent firm. They also gave their perspectives on how young entrepreneurs are perceived by the market and arbitration institutions, and what enterprising lawyers can do to stand out, compete and thrive in the global landscape.

Most importantly, the panel noted that to be a successful entrepreneur in this competitive market, one needs to have a clear vision of his or her project and have the passion to execute it.

2   Use of Artificial Intelligence and Digital Technologies

Over the years, we have seen the emergence of artificial intelligence (AI), blockchain and other digital technologies in international arbitration. While more lawyers are becoming increasingly familiar with using such technologies as tools to assist in the arbitral process, the question remains as to how these new technologies are influencing the way in which cases are arbitrated and whether such influence is always positive.

The discussion led by Elizabeth Chan and Arie Eernisse focused on the use of AI and blockchain technology in arbitration, how these digital technologies are transforming the process of arbitration, and the future opportunities they create for the international arbitration landscape. The group discussed the different types of technologies that law firms and institutions were already using as part of their dispute resolution work. Examples of these technologies include Brainspace (e-discovery); Opus2 (case management); Jus Mundi (legal research) and various technologies to assess the likelihood of success in a case or of a particular issue in a case, amongst others.

Ms Chan and Mr Eernisse also discussed with their group the issue of differentiating between those technologies that improve or assist in the arbitral process (e.g., a case management platform) and those which have some substantive input in the production of legal documents (e.g., legal submissions, awards). While the use of the former is relatively uncontroversial, the same could not be said of the latter. Where AI has some substantive role, for example in drafting legal submissions or making a decision, we discussed how the quality of any output will depend at least on the quality of the input (for example, precedents).

3   Climate Change and Arbitration

With climate change consistently being a global topic of interest and with the increasing international (and national) efforts to address challenges of environmental protection, it comes as no surprise that the number of arbitration cases involving environmental issues has grown steadily in recent years. The outcome of these cases and the tribunals' reasoning on the balance between environmental protection and investment protection can be of significance for international law practitioners.

Jonathan Lim and Melissa Ordonez explored with participants how international arbitration could be used to address climate change disputes against the backdrop of increased climate change litigation around the world.

They observed that disputes related to State action to combat climate change will likely increase and there is a potential broad scope for arbitration to be used in such context. Those disputes are varied in nature and may take place over a variety of fora. In investment arbitration, a key challenge that arbitrators might face is striking the right balance between investor protection and State's climate change goals.

More generally, the group discussed whether arbitration is fit for purpose and whether it is a 'force for good or evil'. There were many mixed views, and participants shared their thoughts on the significance of recent developments relating to the Energy

Charter Treaty (ECT) and UNCITRAL Working Group II discussions. Participants also discussed with Mr Lim and Ms Ordonez whether the confidentiality of arbitrations impedes its role as a policy tool for advancing climate change goals, and some participants suggested the possibility of a presumption of transparency for climate change disputes.

III   THE FUTURE OF ARBITRATION AND INSTITUTIONS

1   Regulators in Arbitration

At present, there is no unified regulatory body governing the field of international arbitration. Instead, arbitral proceedings are regulated by the relevant arbitral institution chosen by the parties to conduct the arbitration.

Siddharth Thacker and Iuliana Iancu delved into the question of whether international arbitration practice should be governed by a central regulatory body and what would the role of government be vis-à-vis the regulator. There was a general consensus amongst participants that arbitration does not need any form of regulator or regulation, as this would in fact impinge on the very attributes for which parties opt for arbitration and would restrict party autonomy. The common view was that users of arbitration elected to arbitrate disputes for their de-regulated and non-bureaucratic nature.

If, however, there was a regulator, it should not be the government or answerable to the government in any form; there should be a total separation. This is because there would be a clear conflict of interest as governments in certain jurisdictions are the largest users of arbitration.

Mr Thacker and Ms Iancu also discussed with participants whether one needed a uniform code of conduct applicable to all counsel and arbitrators in international arbitration. The general view was that it would be prudent to allow the respective professional bodies and bar association rules that counsel were affiliated with, to dictate and govern the code of conduct and standards of legal ethics of each counsel. Soft laws, such as the IBA Guidelines on Conflicts of Interest in International Arbitration have also proven to be effective, and the general view was that other similar soft laws could be adopted for the conduct of arbitration by both counsel and arbitrators.

The group also discussed the issue of corruption in arbitration (in particular in relation to the *Alstom* saga) and the topic of the impact of parallel criminal proceedings on arbitrations. On corruption, the general consensus that emerged was that an estoppel rule would be beneficial, requiring parties to raise the corruption issue before the arbitral tribunal (if they are able to do so) or risk the enforcement court finding abuse of process, as arbitral tribunals are the proper and competent forum where all the relevant arguments pertaining to the issues in dispute should be aired. Regarding parallel criminal proceedings, participants' views were divided on the question of how tribunals should deal with evidence from criminal investigations that are brought into arbitration. Generally, the attendees were of the view that, due to the incomplete nature of such evidence, tribunals should tread carefully and not ascribe such evidence too much weight, without more.

2   Geographical Diversity

The field of international arbitration has been facing challenges in increasing diversity amongst arbitrators. Nesreen Osman and Nhu Hoang Tran Thang facilitated two group discussions about geographical diversity, a hot topic established in 2020 when the Congress was first envisaged to take place, and which has since then gained an increased amount of interest and consideration from international arbitration stakeholders. This topic generated immense dialogue.

The discussion focused on two main topics (i) as a starting point, whether there was a right to a diverse pool of arbitrators and (ii) whether there is still a divide between the traditional arbitration hubs and the new emerging hubs around the globe.

On the first issue, there was somewhat of a divergence of opinion. Some participants considered that there was no 'right' as such, but an expectation that there would be a diverse pool of arbitrators available to parties when appointing a tribunal. Other participants' views went further, concluding that parties not only have a right to a diverse pool of arbitrators to choose from, but it is also the role of the arbitral institutions to ensure that this is available.

The vast majority of participants agreed that the goal of improved diversity of arbitral tribunals is most efficiently served by arbitral institutions. The experience of counsel was that it often proves difficult, if not impossible, to change their clients' mentality regarding tribunal composition as geographical diversity is simply not a priority for a large proportion of disputing parties. For instance, some commented that the 'Jay-Z' case in which the rapper objected to the dearth of African American arbitrators on the American Arbitration Association (AAA) panel is rather exceptional and represents a rare situation in which users are concerned with the diversity of their tribunal. In that case, Jay-Z's objections led to the AAA swiftly moving to include additional African American arbitrators on its panel, avoiding the objection itself having to be formally progressed. However, according to participants, notwithstanding the exceptional nature of the circumstances of the Jay-Z case, it demonstrates once more that arbitration means party autonomy and that the parties, not their lawyers, are able to significantly improve the diversity of arbitral tribunals.

Counsel active in the Middle East and Africa commented that their clients were often keen on appointing Western-trained arbitrators to decide their disputes, despite repeated proposals of competent candidates who were more closely connected geographically to the features of the dispute. This was said to be, amongst other things, the result of a vicious 'higher bidding' process; for example, where the claiming party appoints an English KC instead of someone more geographically connected to the dispute or applicable law and the responding party feels compelled to appoint someone with a similar profile to ensure they have a perceived equal weight in the deliberations. The common view of participants was that this makes counsel's contribution to improving diversity continually challenging.

Institutions, therefore, find themselves at the forefront of the efforts to improve geographical diversity, and participants, including representatives of institutions, agreed that they are making exceptional efforts and have already achieved quantifiable results in that regard. For example, it was commented that some institutions make considerable efforts to include diverse arbitrators on their panels (both from a gender and a geographical perspective) as well as appoint first-time arbitrators to appropriate cases in order to provide those of different backgrounds and jurisdictions an opportunity to gain experience. It was acknowledged, however, that the contribution of the arbitral institutions is also limited by the small proportion of appointments for which they are responsible. Other institutional efforts were also highlighted, such as the reference in Art. 8 of the Rules of the Scottish Arbitration Centre to appointments to R.E.A.L, the initiative for Racial Equality for Arbitration Lawyers.

Participants also agreed that, while geographical diversity is linked to the quality of the arbitration process, one should not shift away too quickly from the consideration of the fundamental requirements when constituting an arbitral tribunal, such as the arbitrators' competences.

On the second topic, there was a general sense that there remains an inclination towards the traditional hubs such as Paris, London, Geneva, Singapore and Hong Kong, which is dictated primarily by the clients' preferences and clients/counsel wishing to stick with whom they know. However, it was noted that the development of arbitration-friendly places geographically different outside of the traditional arbitration hubs was a welcomed progression. The conversation between participants showed that, while there are many initiatives for the development of arbitral institutions, these are sometimes competing against each other at the local or regional level, making the creation of new arbitration hubs anything but straightforward.

The example of the Caribbeans, where several institutions are active, was raised as well as the multitude of African arbitral institutions competing against each other. The discussion also touched on the recent developments in the UAE where two arbitral institutions were suddenly abolished and merged with a third institution with the ultimate aim of creating one substantial arbitral institution in the jurisdiction. While the underlying reason for this change was seen as worthy, the impact on the reputation of the jurisdiction was also noted given that there is now likely to be a hesitation in using an arbitral institution in the UAE.

Some participants explained that they are actively trying to at least consider alternative hubs/institutions. This is assisted in part by the fact that they tend to be a little cheaper than the traditional hubs which means they may be more suitable for cost-conscious users. It was also acknowledged that there is a role for counsel to play in educating clients about the existence of alternative arbitral institutions/jurisdictions and their benefits.

3   Transparency and Confidentiality

The tension between transparency and confidentiality in international commercial arbitration remains a delicate and unsettled issue. While confidentiality is widely recognised as a significant advantage of arbitration, there have been increasing calls to expand the transparency of arbitral proceedings for greater reliability and accountability.

Naomi Briercliffe and Naomi Tarawali posed to participants questions such as: 'Where should the balance lie between transparency and confidentiality in commercial arbitration?'; 'Should the position be different in investment treaty arbitration, and if so, why and what of commercial arbitration between States or State-related parties and investors?'

These issues are not new, but two rounds of lively discussion proved that the issues remain unsettled, with one group concluding with a vigorous call for the default publication of all arbitral awards (albeit redacted for confidential information), and the other holding firmly that notwithstanding the many potential benefits of transparency, confidentiality remains a key attraction for its users and a choice that should be upheld – at least in commercial arbitration. The transparency debate is clearly much alive.

Arguments in favour of greater transparency in arbitration focused principally on the benefits that this could bring for the education of the judiciary and the legal profession more generally, as well as the development of the law, particularly as regards its application in cases related to new areas of technology. A delegate active in the funding space also suggested that the publication of awards should be favoured because it would support the development of the market for the sale of awards by successful claimants.

There were no participants who opposed transparency in arbitration per se. However, it was agreed that the right balance between transparency and confidentiality needed to be struck. Our first group considered ways to improve the consistency of what becomes public from awards and what does not. Ideas included requiring arbitrators or arbitral institutions to identify points of public interest and publish excerpts or summaries of those points separate from a confidential award. However, colleagues from some arbitral institutions explained the significant burden that having the responsibility of anonymising and checking arbitration documents for publication places on them.

Participants from legal publication companies also told us about the work they are already doing to publish awards in different jurisdictions and the difficulties they currently encounter.

Some practitioner participants were unanimous that in all circumstances, party choice regarding the confidentiality of an arbitral process/award must be respected. Their experience also reflected that while clients are often sympathetic or even proactively supportive of the publication of awards in principle, they are not willing to agree to it when it comes to their own arbitrations even in anonymised form.

Finally, Ms Tarawali and Ms Briercliffe also discussed different approaches to the treatment of awards before national courts, for example during enforcement proceedings. As they were very fortunately joined by participants from across the world, they learned, for example, that in the British Virgin Islands (BVI), the confidentiality of arbitration proceedings is sacrosanct even through the court system. In Brazil, however, arbitration matters tend to become public immediately once there is a court application in respect of them. And in Singapore where arbitration-related litigation would otherwise be public, there is a mechanism for seeking a sealing order in respect of the proceedings – such an order is typically easy to obtain.

IV   CONCLUDING REMARKS

The interactive 'speed-conferencing' format of the panel session was well-received. Participants were actively engaged in discussions about notable developments in the field of international arbitration and various areas in the practice of arbitration that may see a change in the near future. It is the panel's hope that young practitioners – arbitration counsel and arbitrators alike – continue to embrace new technologies and play a part in positively shaping the international arbitration landscape.

PART VI   New Frontiers

PANEL 11   New Frontiers I: Arbitration in the Age of [Post-pandemic] Technology

CHAPTER 38

How to Win Instructions in the Post-pandemic World

Lee Ji En[*]

TABLE OF CONTENTS

I   INTRODUCTION

For the last few years, the legal industry has been buzzing about legal technology and how technology might change the practice of law. Almost every major conference or event would feature a panel about technology. This has been a refreshing change from the past, where lawyers often dismissed the potential impact that technology could bring to the industry. However, the legal technology issues that often came up at these conferences were often about technology that sounds controversial, e.g., an 'AI arbitrator' or 'dispute resolution on blockchain', even though these tools may not be readily applicable to most people in the legal industry. No one seems to be talking about the less 'sexy' technology solutions, e.g., a case management tool, which already exist and can be implemented to tremendously improve the current practice of law.

'*Software is eating the law.*' (Some law and tech events, 2017-2022). This might be the case, but this is not the focus of this chapter. This chapter is about what lawyers

---

[*]   CEO of Chambers Lab.

and arbitrators can do today to immediately improve their chances of winning instructions in the post-pandemic world. It has two parts.

The focus of this chapter is to examine how the pandemic has changed international arbitration. We argue that the pandemic has resulted or will result in the following permanent changes in the legal industry:

(a) virtual hearings are increasingly becoming the default option for many civil and commercial cases, especially when it comes to procedural hearings;
(b) documents are increasingly being created in digital format, with transactional documents being electronically signed and deals being completed in a paperless environment;
(c) business travel will become harder to justify within law firms; and
(d) boutique or independent practices will become increasingly popular and successful.

In this section, we also address the secondary effects which arise from these changes. For example, we explain how the fact that documents are increasingly being created in the digital format will result in electronic document or case management systems becoming increasingly important, and the arbitral institution (or arbitral venue) that offers the best paperless dispute resolution experience will stand out in the post-pandemic world.

Having set out the effects of the pandemic, we explain how getting legal operations *right* can help lawyers in the post-pandemic world (at least in the near to mid-term future). The Corporate Legal Operations Consortium (CLOC) defines legal operations ('legal ops') as '*a set of business processes, activities, and the professionals who enable legal departments to serve their clients more effectively by applying business and technical practices to the delivery of legal services*' and explains that legal ops '*provides the strategic planning, financial management, project management, and technology expertise that enables legal professionals to focus on providing legal advice*'.[1] Legal ops is not about AI or blockchain. It is not 'sexy'. It is about designing intuitive and streamlined processes, which often involve tried-and-tested technology solutions, to deliver targeted outcomes.

This section is therefore about practical legal ops strategies which will help arbitration practitioners achieve their targeted outcomes: to win instructions. These are some examples of legal ops strategies which can be adopted:

(a) Lawyers should adopt flexible sourcing strategies to build the best possible team, based on the factors that matter to their clients. This requires lawyers to be aware of resources which are available in their local jurisdictions and also around the world (e.g., in Malaysia, Singapore, India, Australia, etc.).

---

1. *See* https://cloc.org/what-is-legal-operations.

(b) Lawyers should focus on building better user experience for their clients, and this requires a holistic deployment of technology and human resource solutions.

(c) The role of legal project managers will become increasingly important, and ideally, they should be involved in all aspects of a matter, including the pricing and bidding strategies.

II HOW HAS THE PANDEMIC CHANGED INTERNATIONAL ARBITRATION?

1 The Rise of Virtual Hearings, and the Adoption of Technology in Hearings

There is no doubt that virtual hearings are here to stay. The authorities in many jurisdictions, e.g., Singapore[2] and Malaysia,[3] have indicated that they will continue to hold virtual hearings in the appropriate cases even after the pandemic. As arbitration practitioners, the questions that we need to ask ourselves are:

(a) What are virtual hearings best suited for?
(b) How can we improve the virtual hearing experience?
(c) How will the increase in adoption of virtual hearings affect our practice?

The general view is that virtual hearings are often preferred when it comes to procedural or interim hearings.[4] Most of these hearings are relatively administrative and do not involve the examination of witnesses. Having said that, this is not to say that all procedural or interim hearings should be conducted virtually. For instance, if one party is based in a less developed region with poor internet connectivity, it may be unfair to insist that the procedural hearings be conducted virtually.

The COVID-19 pandemic has made everyone realise that it is possible to conduct hearings in many different ways. Moving forward, arbitration practitioners would need to be conscious of these different options and carefully consider the appropriate option for their cases. Apart from purely physical or virtual hearings, these options include:

(a) *Asynchronous hearings*, where parties can address the tribunal via an 'asynchronous' exchange of submissions. This will reduce the need for all parties

---

2. Singapore has amended the law to provide a permanent framework that will facilitate the use of technology in court proceedings, which not only includes the adoption of remote hearings, but also the adoption of asynchronous hearings and documents-only hearings. *See*: https://www.mlaw.gov.sg/news/parliamentary-speeches/2021-09-13-second-reading-speech-by-2m-edwin-tong-on-courts-civil-and-criminal-justice-reform-bill.
3. *See*: https://www.nst.com.my/news/crime-courts/2022/01/762942/virtual-hearings-remain-new-norm.
4. "The Future of Disputes: Are Virtual Hearings Here To Stay?" by Baker McKenzie and KPMG (*see*: https://www.bakermckenzie.com/en/insight/publications/2021/01/are-virtual-hearings-here-to-stay).

to schedule fixed timeslots for hearings, which can be challenging in international arbitration cases where parties are operating in multiple time zones.

(b) *Documents-only hearings*, where the matter may be resolved without any oral hearing. This is not new, but the COVID-19 pandemic has made it increasingly acceptable for disputes to be resolved without oral hearings.

(c) *Hybrid hearings*, which can adopt numerous permutations, including:

  (i) Arbitrators attend the hearings in person, while everyone else attends the hearings virtually;

  (ii) Arbitrators and counsel attend the hearings in person, while everyone else attends the hearings virtually; and

  (iii) Arbitrators, counsel and key witnesses attend the hearings in person, while everyone else (including the less important witnesses) can choose to attend the hearings virtually.

Even if parties choose to conduct hearings in person, the way we set up physical hearings should be improved by incorporating the types of technology that parties are now used to due to the pandemic.

Take transcription as an example. Before the pandemic, transcription service providers would often fly their transcribers to the hearing venue. This resulted in transcriptions being extremely costly, and parties would also need to get a bigger room to accommodate the transcribers. Nevertheless, parties would often pay for such services because there was no real alternative. The pandemic proved that it is completely possible for someone to follow and attend the hearings virtually. In fact, transcription service providers continued to provide quality transcription services during the pandemic, which means there is now no reason for them to send someone to attend hearings in person.

Transcription service providers will also need to compete with automated transcription tools which are becoming more mainstream. Tools such as Otter.ai can provide fully automated real-time transcription at an extremely low cost (e.g., Otter.ai charges USD 20 per user per month). These tools provide arbitration practitioners with alternatives to improve the hearing transcription experience:

(a) *During the hearing*: Parties can use affordable real-time transcription using AI-powered automated transcription tools. The accuracy of these tools is around 80%-90%, which should be sufficient for real-time purposes. In any case, there is always a fallback alternative, i.e., the audio recording which parties can refer to if clarification is required.

(b) *After the hearing*:

  (i) *Option 1*: This option is meant for parties who want to maintain the same approach as pre-pandemic hearings. The recording and automated transcripts will be automatically sent to a professional transcriber for review after the hearing. Solutions such as Rev.com (which is already being used by law firms for various purposes such as transcribing video recordings of depositions) can usually provide quick turnaround (e.g., five hours) at affordable rates (e.g., USD 1.50 per minute of audio recording). Within a few hours, one can get a professional transcript at a price which is more affordable than the pre-pandemic solutions.

(ii) *Option 2*: Given that parties now have the option of relying on the automated transcripts and recordings, there is no real need for them to insist on having professional transcribers churn out another 'more accurate' version of the transcripts. Arbitration practitioners might only choose to use professional transcribers in cases where there is a dispute on what was said, and parties cannot agree on the matter even with the available recordings.

The above-mentioned transcription example illustrates the following forces which will operate in the post-pandemic world:

(a) *Technology will challenge the status quo when it comes to the processes involved in the arbitration practice*: In the past, people might assume that real-time transcription services can only be provided if professional transcribers attend hearings in person. Now the assumption is no longer applicable.

(b) *The pandemic has reduced the psychological or mental barriers involved in the adoption of technology*: This is an extension of the point above. Due to the pandemic, it is now harder for lawyers to resist the adoption of technology for whatever reasons that they used to cite. For every '*it is better to do this [in the pre-pandemic manner]*' argument, one could counter by saying '*but you did it [with some technology-assisted solution] during the pandemic*'. This shift puts clients in a better position to push their lawyers to embrace technology and helps those who are more innovative to stand out in the arbitration circuit.

(c) *Technology can make arbitration less* expensive:
  (i) Advocates for arbitration used to argue that arbitration should be preferred over litigation because it is cheaper and faster. This argument is no longer valid in many jurisdictions. However, in the post-pandemic world, technology might offer arbitration the chance to be more affordable than litigation, or at least narrow the gap.
  (ii) When it comes to transcription, some courts are still reluctant to adopt automated transcription tools due to various policy reasons. For instance, certain judges might be afraid that the recordings generated by these tools will need to be disclosed to the public under the open justice policy. The courts might also be worried about outsourcing transcription services to professionals based in another country (which is often the case with these tools). There might also be concerns as to whether the courts have sufficient capabilities to support the adoption of these technology tools across the country. These policy reasons tend to cut across all types of technology tools, which means that courts are likely to be slower than arbitration practitioners in the adoption of technology.

Transcription is simply one example of how the rise of virtual hearings and the increase in the adoption of technology in hearings will change arbitration in the post-pandemic world. One can dissect arbitration hearings into smaller components, and look at how technology can be implemented to lower costs or improve certain targeted outcomes.

The paperless nature of virtual hearings also offers the opportunity to revisit whether 'bundles' are still necessary in the post-pandemic world. Bundles are expensive and time-consuming to produce, and they often do not provide the most intuitive experience in virtual hearings. They only make sense if one is producing bundles of hardcopy documents. Why can't parties disclose their documents virtually using a shared database, with intelligent search and other features? As long as all the evidence is properly labelled and identifiable, there is no reason for parties to choose bundles as the default option. If arbitrators could operate without bundles of physical documents during the pandemic (where many jurisdictions had extremely strict lockdown measures), one can argue that they can also go without bundles in the post-pandemic world.

Another example is the use of video recordings during arbitration hearings. During the pandemic, given the rise of virtual hearings, it became more acceptable for video recordings to be part of an arbitration hearing. While virtual hearing guidelines still indicate that recordings are prohibited unless consent is obtained from the parties and arbitrators, this is at least one step forward from the pre-pandemic days when video cameras were rarely seen in hearings, and one is naturally suspicious cameras being used in hearings. Now the main question is whether to enable the recording feature or not. The arguments against recording are mainly in relation to protecting the confidentiality of the hearings, which is a concern that can be addressed using technology (e.g., encryption of the videos) and other solutions.

This increased acceptance of video recording offers the opportunity to redesign the arbitration experience to achieve certain mutually agreeable outcomes, e.g., to improve an arbitrator's ability to revisit or recall what took place during the hearing. One can see parties agreeing to have 360-degree cameras recording the key witnesses. This will help counsel and arbitrators better analyse the witnesses' reactions during examination or cross-examination. For example, one party might rely on video evidence from the hearing to submit that one witness is lying (e.g., the witness was visibly uncomfortable in the video). If we go one step further, parties might also want to analyse the arbitrators' reactions to different parts of the hearings in a close-up manner. Given the prevalence of close-up shots during virtual hearings in the pandemic, it is now harder for one to argue that parties should not be able to see the arbitrators in a close-up manner in post-pandemic hearings.

2   Paperless Environment

This section focuses on the pandemic's impact on accelerating the legal industry's transition to a paperless world.

Prior to the pandemic, while technology was already being used in many parts of the legal industry, hardcopy documents were often still seen as 'necessary'. Parties would submit hardcopy bundles to the courts or arbitrators as a default. Major deals or transactions would be signed in hardcopy documents. This is in part because, even if one of the stakeholders were willing to go paperless, another stakeholder (e.g., the courts, the notary public, etc.) would often require the documents to be printed out. This changed during the pandemic when everyone was forced to consider how to work in a paperless setting.

Hardcopy documents created significant logistical challenges in cross-border transactions or complex international arbitrations, where the relevant stakeholders are often all over the world and under different types of lockdown measures. As a result, many stakeholders in the legal industry quickly switched over to using e-signatures and other paperless solutions. As a practitioner, this felt like a magical moment to me because some of these stakeholders have been complaining about how it is 'impossible' to go paperless for years, and yet, when the pandemic happened, they somehow managed to cope with a paperless environment over an extremely short period of time.

Similar to the point made in the section above, once it has been shown that paperless systems work for arbitrations (as they did during the pandemic), it would be hard for someone to insist on going back to relying on hardcopy documents. Here, we posit that the paperless movement will change arbitration in the following four manners.

First, hearings will go paperless by default. Printing will be limited to certain unique circumstances, e.g., huge spreadsheets which do not work well with laptop monitors. In cases where printing is required even though there are no special circumstances which justify such printing, the party which requests printing may have to bear the relevant costs. In paperless hearings, it would become harder for parties to recover the cost related to printing and bundling as part of their disbursements, because one can argue that such costs were unreasonably incurred.

Second, electronic document or case management systems will become more important. The post-pandemic world presents a few changes which will make electronic document or case management systems essential in future arbitration matters:

(a) *The importance of metadata*: In the pre-pandemic world, important documents are often signed and generated in hardcopy versions, and then scanned and saved in the digital format. These documents are increasingly generated in digital format (natively). When documents or materials are generated digitally, the metadata (e.g., who created a document, who accessed a document, at what time, etc.) that comes with these materials provide an important source of information. Electronic case management systems are therefore necessary to help parties analyse and visualise the metadata in a user-friendly manner.

(b) *The need to go beyond PDF or Word documents*: During the pandemic, parties relied on virtual collaboration tools, such as video conferencing solutions and chat apps, to negotiate transactions. The increased adoption of such technology tools means that documents and evidence in future disputes will come in formats other than PDF documents. For example, with WhatsApp conversations, it will be easier if an arbitrator can review the chats in an intuitive manner (similar to how one reads messages on a phone) instead of reading them in a text file which might come in the following format:

> '[5:59 pm, 13/08/2022] A: Hi B, how are you?
> [5:59 pm, 13/08/2022] B: [Voice recording] Please see attached "Exhibit 1"
> for a transcript of the voice recording.
> [6:00 pm, 13/08/2022] B: [Image] Please see attached "Exhibit 2" for a copy
> of this image.'

Arbitration practitioners will thus need to use electronic case or evidence management tools which can accommodate all these data in their native formats and learn to present these data in the most intuitive manner to the arbitrators.

(c) *The ever-increasing amount of data*: Due to computer processing power and internet data being cheaper, we are generating a lot more data in all aspects of our lives. This means that even in cases where the quantum in dispute is relatively small, we might find ourselves with a lot of data to review (e.g., long chat correspondence between buyers and sellers). A lot of this data might be irrelevant. An intelligent case or evidence management platform will thus assist parties in quickly parsing through the noise and focusing on the data that matters.

Third, the arbitral institutions with the best paperless 'operating system' will win:

(1) We are moving towards a world where arbitral institutions or arbitral venues will face more competition and it will be difficult to stand out. Many institutions are in jurisdictions which adopt the UNCITRAL Model Law on International Commercial Arbitration. Many also have access to 'state-of-the-art' hearing venues.

(2) Forward-looking arbitral institutions or venues will therefore be incentivised to provide or integrate electronic document and project management systems as part of their service. We can think of this as creating an 'operating system' (OS) for international arbitration. As an example, the OS could take the following form:

    (a) A party can go to an arbitral institution's platform to commence an arbitration. The onboarding process (a.k.a. commencement of arbitration) will be designed such that one can file an initial notice of arbitration or conduct basic matters without having to instruct a lawyer. The platform can also give parties a quick estimate of the cost involved if they choose to arbitrate the matter, and this cost estimate can be revised in real-time as the matter progresses.

    (b) Once a matter has been commenced, the OS can offer a variety of features including:

(i) *Project management features*: The case counsel, the parties, the law firms and the arbitrators will be granted access to the 'project' (i.e., the matter). The timelines, next steps and costs involved (for arbitrators who charge by time cost) can all be seen through a dashboard that is updated on a real-time basis.

(ii) *Secured file storage and communications*: Parties will upload documents to the portal, or their respective secured file storage systems will integrate with the portal. This allows parties to communicate strictly within the portal, and all actions on the portal are logged. Every document that is downloaded will have a watermark stating the time and person who downloaded the document. This can reduce the chances of confidential data in an arbitration being leaked.

(iii) *Forms & templates*: The arbitral institutions can provide open-source access to selected precedents, which can be integrated with document automation features. For example, an arbitrator can go through a checklist and select the relevant options for the procedural order, and a draft procedural order (based on the arbitrator's preferred procedural order template) will be generated instantaneously.

(iv) *Electronic library*: Parties can gain access to the arbitral institution's library via this portal.

(v) *Arbitrator database*: Parties can select their preferred arbitrator based on the relevant filters and compare them on this database. Parties can also contact the arbitrators directly via the database.

(vi) *Online payment gateway*: All relevant payments for the arbitration can be made electronically via the platform.

(vii) *Marketplace*: Parties can find all the solutions that they need (e.g., printing and bundling solutions in a particular location, eDiscovery solutions, hearing solutions) from the portal.

(viii) *Funding options*: Parties can also be alerted to funding options, similar to how e-commerce tools now provide you with the option to get 'instalment plans' or additional warranty. The platform can also offer parties an easy and secure way to grant funders access to details relating to the case.

(c) At the end of the arbitration, parties can safely export or archive the information relating to the case on the same platform. They can always revisit the platform to access their data.

(3) The above-mentioned example is based on existing technology, which means it can be implemented in today's world if one decides to do so (and some are already working on it[5]). It is not some sort of hypothetical AI-based solution which requires further breakthroughs in technology.

---

5. For example, Modron Spaces (https://www.modron.com/spaces), Immediation (https://www.immediation.com/ and New Era ADR (https://www.neweraadr.com/).

(4) Ultimately, arbitration users will increasingly look for methods and platforms which will allow them to go through an arbitration, from cradle to grave, without having to leave a paperless environment. As corporations move toward being paperless, it will become increasingly 'expensive' to maintain the usage of paper. For instance, the company will find it harder to justify spending expensive real estate to store hardcopy documents, when documents can be stored digitally (especially when the originals were created digitally). Thus, institutions with the most intuitive and powerful paperless experience will probably have an edge over the other institutions.

(5) Further, the arbitral institutions can also leverage their OS to stand out in the following manner:

  (a) *Increased productivity*: The project management capabilities will help streamline task allocation and ensure that the arbitral institutions are running efficiently. The platform can tell which case counsel is too busy, or which case counsel has more capacity. It can also provide useful data which can be used to improve the internal workflows of an institution. For instance, an institution might find that their case counsel are spending too much time on a particular task, which can be automated.

  (b) *Lower cost*:

    (i) As compared to law firms or parties, the arbitral institution is likely to be in a better position to purchase in bulk or negotiate the cost of such solutions because it has a larger volume of cases and stronger market power. Legaltech or other vendors would be interested in integrating their products and services with the institution's platform on the basis that they can generate greater revenue, even if they are providing substantial discounts to those who access the services or software via the institution's platform. These cost savings can be passed on to the parties, which will find arbitration with the specific institution cheaper than arbitrations with other institutions.

    (ii) With a paperless case management tool, arbitral institutions can recruit from anywhere in the world. This may allow the institutions to get better talent at a lower cost. With case counsel situated across the world, the institutions can also operate around the clock.

  (c) *Greater innovation*: An integrated arbitration OS will encourage companies to provide deeper integrations with the arbitral institution. This will open the possibilities for more seamless features and automation in the arbitration processes. Using the automated transcription service as an example again, the OS can integrate with a transcription tool and a video conferencing tool. After a few hearings featuring the same arbitrator, an AI-powered automated transcription tool like Otter.ai would be trained to become much more accurate when it comes to recognising the arbitrator. The transcripts can also be automatically saved in the right folders, and automatically linked to the relevant documents in the document management system, after the hearing. Parties can also request professional transcription services via the marketplace with a few clicks.

Having said that, it may be the case that none of the arbitral institutions will find themselves in the winning position. Instead, just like how taxis in some places have been replaced like Uber or similar apps, or how Kodak lost out to digital cameras despite being in the pole position to develop digital cameras,[6] arbitral institutions might find themselves losing to an outsider. For example, a technology company might develop the best paperless dispute resolution experience, and arbitral institutions will simply become one of the many 'plugins' to the system.

Fourth, cybersecurity risk management will become increasingly important. We live in a world where cyber-attacks are becoming more sophisticated. Even employees in tech companies which invest heavily in cybersecurity are being tricked by phishing attacks.[7]

The pandemic has made it harder for arbitration practitioners to manage cybersecurity risks in certain aspects. In the past, hearings would normally be conducted in person, without the use of cameras. Now that virtual hearings are commonplace, parties have to consider the level of cybersecurity protection for all relevant stakeholders in a case. After all, the system is only as secure as its weakest link. This is especially challenging given that the stakeholders might be joining the hearing from a variety of environments, ranging from shared offices to their own homes.

Arbitration practitioners are well aware of these risks, especially after the Permanent Court of Arbitration's website was hacked in July 2015.[8] The growing awareness of cybersecurity risks in international arbitration has led to several initiatives and responses, such as:

(a) Practitioners within groups such as ICCA, New York City Bar Association and the International Institute for Conflict Prevention & Resolution have developed the ICCA-NYC Bar-CPR Protocol on Cybersecurity in International Arbitration.[9]

---

6. Kodak was once synonymous to photography, and people would describe a moment worth capturing as a 'Kodak moment'. A Kodak engineer also created the first prototype of a digital camera in 1975. However, Kodak failed to capture the digital photography trend and ultimately went bankrupt. Today, business schools often refer to the Kodak story as one where the incumbent was so blinded by their success that they failed to adapt to the changing market trends, and ended up being disrupted by new innovative businesses. The exact answer is of course a bit more nuanced, and you can read more here: https://hbr.org/2016/07/kodaks-downfall-wasnt-about-technology.
7. *See*: https://arstechnica.com/information-technology/2022/08/phishers-breach-twilio-and-target- cloudflare-using-workers-home-numbers/.
8. *See*: https://www.iareporter.com/articles/permanent-court-of-arbitration-goes-offline-with-cy ber-security-firm-contending-that-security-flaw-was-exploited-in-lead-up-to-china-philippines-arbitration/.
9. *See*: https://www.arbitration-icca.org/cybersecurity-international-arbitration-icca-nyc-bar-cpr-working- group.

(b) A multidisciplinary and international team of legal and tech professionals have also come together to build a community called CyberArb to exchange information and ideas on cybersecurity-related matters in international arbitration.[10]

(c) The American Arbitration Association (AAA) and International Centre for Dispute Resolution (ICDR) launched CaseShield, a virtual desktop solution designed to help arbitrators and mediators manage their cases. AAA and ICDR describe CaseShield as providing '*enterprise-grade*' cybersecurity protection to users and eliminating '*the need for the Arbitrator to vet, acquire, configure, manage and monitor their own security tools and settings*'.[11]

These developments are encouraging, but insufficient to deal with cybersecurity threats which are constantly developing. Moving forward, all relevant stakeholders need to do more to address the rising cybersecurity risks in arbitrations. For instance, the following non-exhaustive list of questions should be addressed:

(a) Do arbitral institutions owe a duty to disclose every potential data breach incident regardless of whether the breach is likely to have an impact on the cases that they manage? If so, does it have to disclose within a specific timeframe?

(b) Do arbitrators owe a duty to disclose every potential data breach incident regardless of whether the breach is likely to have an impact on the cases that they are presiding over? If so, does it have to disclose within a specific timeframe?

(c) Should arbitral institutions' panel requirements include certain cybersecurity requirements?

(d) Should arbitrators (or other relevant stakeholders) be required to go through a cybersecurity audit every year to certify that their setup complies with the relevant standards for the cases that they are presiding over?

It appears that there are no clear answers to these questions at the moment. There is no standard for arbitral institutions to comply with – some are more progressive than others. This means that we might find ourselves in a situation where an institution might choose not to disclose an incident, e.g., an employee's email was hacked, simply because it is not required to do so. After all, the reputational damage which comes with such disclosures can be severe.

It is also hard for parties to determine which arbitrator to appoint if cybersecurity is a major concern. Parties might find it awkward to ask arbitrators to disclose their cybersecurity systems, especially prior to the appointment. Arbitrators (who often work independently) might also be ill-equipped to make such disclosures. At the moment, most of the best practices or guides produced by arbitral institutions deal with cybersecurity measures that parties can adopt after an arbitrator has been appointed.

---

10. *See*: https://cyberarb.com/.
11. *See*: https://go.adr.org/aaa-case-shield.

However, these guidelines would be of limited help in cases where parties appointed an arbitrator whose setup is simply ill-equipped to deal with cybersecurity risks, and it might be too late or too expensive to deal with these risks after the appointment. Thus, it would be better if the international arbitration community can come together to address some of the above-mentioned questions and develop basic standards on cybersecurity for international arbitration – for arbitral institutions, arbitrators, and other relevant stakeholders. Such developments will help us move the industry to one where cybersecurity risks are dealt with right from the start and as a matter of course, instead of one where such risks are only considered in cases with 'heightened' cybersecurity requirements.

3   Post-pandemic Business Travel

Prior to the pandemic, it was commonplace for international arbitration practitioners to travel regularly. Arbitrators or lawyers would fly to another location for procedural hearings, and lawyers would travel just to take their clients' instructions. As mentioned in Section II.A above, procedural hearings are increasingly conducted virtually, and lawyers are also finding it harder to fly to another location just to take instructions. Indeed, this trend started gaining traction pre-pandemic due to the international firms' concern with sustainability and carbon emissions, and the pandemic has merely accelerated the trend and made it easier for firms or clients to deny requests for business travel.

In this section, we will not discuss the reasons behind the change in business travel trends – there are many, but the point is that one cannot seriously dispute that international arbitration practitioners do not travel for business as often as they used to. The focus of this section will be on the impact of this trend.

When it comes to substantive work (e.g., drafting, taking of instructions, etc.), the shift away from business travel tends to happen in tandem with technological improvements which enable all stakeholders to work seamlessly from remote locations. This includes the adoption of virtual hearings and paperless systems (as set out in Sections II.A and II.B). The reduction in business travel is therefore less likely to reduce the quality of substantive work.

However, the same cannot be said when one looks at business development and client relationship management. Despite the pandemic, we have not seen any significant technological improvements in relation to business development and client relationship management in the legal industry. Some conference organisers adopted solutions which allowed their virtual conference participants to network online, but these solutions are generally not intuitive to use. Even though people do catch up via video conferencing tools, these are often viewed as stop-gap measures.

For now, this author's personal and anecdotal observation is that legal business development and client relationship management are still best done in person. When it comes to building or maintaining relationships, it is hard for Zoom calls to beat the wine-and-dine. Many arbitration practitioners are aware of this issue. Therefore, some conferences (e.g., Singapore Convention Week and ICCA 2022 in Scotland) attracted large crowds from across the world.

The problem is that, with business travel becoming harder to justify within law firms, lawyers increasingly find themselves having to bear the costs of travel and accommodation on their own. For those who are already established in the industry or those who have sufficient financial resources, the main obstacle is finding the time to travel specifically for business development (instead of simply doing business development while travelling for a 'meeting' or a case). Those who are just starting in the arbitration world or those with less financial resources are likely to find it much harder to break through the current market.

Given the importance of in-person business development in the legal industry, international arbitration practitioners are likely to move towards a future where they will engage with 'agents' who are closer to the jurisdictions in which they operate. These 'agents' will meet up and build commercial relationships with the various stakeholders in the arbitration industry (e.g., in-house lawyers and other lawyers) on behalf of their clients. An example is David Grief International Consultancy,[12] which David Grief, the former Senior Clerk for Essex Court Chambers, started in late 2021. As David Grief is now based in Asia, he is often engaged by barristers and arbitrators from London and other jurisdictions to be their 'agents' in Asia. This allows arbitration practitioners to maintain a market presence in Asia without having to constantly travel to the relevant jurisdictions.

Alternatively, lawyers can also focus on implementing creative business development strategies in the virtual world. In the post-pandemic world where business travel is harder to justify, social media and online presence will become increasingly important tools for lawyers to engage with their potential clients. Many law firms or lawyers have become more active on LinkedIn or other forms of social media during the pandemic.

The challenge, in this regard, is how to stand out in the noisy world that we live in. People are constantly being bombarded by entertaining and engaging content on YouTube or TikTok – why would they care about a lawyer's social media content? Some lawyers have been incredibly successful on social media, such as Erika Kullberg[13] who has millions of followers on TikTok and Instagram. Erika developed a brand for herself by focusing on a simple idea: she reads the terms and conditions and informs her followers on what they need to know from the terms and conditions. For example, she made a video on how one can get a free pair of Nike shoes if their shoes developed a flaw within two years after the manufacture date (located on the item's tag).[14] What sets her content apart is that they are bite-sized content and that she has an authentic presence on social media. These types of content are rarely seen in the legal industry,

---

12. Disclosure: The author works with David Grief International Consultancy in relation to business development for lawyers and arbitrators. More information on David Grief International Consultancy can be found here: https://www.davidgrief.com/
13. *See*: https://www.instagram.com/erikankullberg/?hl = en.
14. *See*: https://www.instagram.com/p/ChACTvIAM9t/?hl = en.

where legal business development is often focused on building the corporate image (which is less personal) and long-form written content (e.g., case updates or articles).

To summarise, international arbitration practitioners will need to review their business development strategies to see how they can adapt in a world where business travel is less common, and where it is increasingly difficult to stand out in the virtual world.

4   The Rise of Independent Practitioners and Boutique Firms

Perhaps the biggest and most obvious shift in the legal industry during the pandemic pertains to the 'work from home' culture. Before the pandemic, no one would have imagined law firms implementing permanent 'work from home' policies.[15] Such policies used to be in the exclusive domain of tech companies, or companies with very progressive setups – not law firms. However, the lockdown measures during the pandemic forced everyone to work from home. This shift was akin to a major real-life experiment to test whether lawyers can be effective when they work from home. It did not take long before the earnings data from law firms firmly dispelled the myth that lawyers will be less productive if they were allowed to work from home. On the contrary, lawyers tend to bill more because they spend less time commuting to work. Lawyers can also benefit from taking short naps, which can help them be more productive.

Building on the topics discussed above, this chapter argues that the combination of (a) virtual hearings, (b) paperless working environment, and (c) 'work from home' culture will result in the rise of independent practitioners and boutique outfits in the arbitration sector. The reasons are as follows:

(a) *Greater autonomy and flexibility*: Virtual hearings and paperless systems enable arbitration practitioners to truly work from anywhere. This is especially attractive to younger practitioners, who are more likely to value mobility in their work. They can go to Brazil or Portugal as a digital nomad[16] – some places even provide attractive tax benefits. However, these practitioners are unlikely to find such flexibility within law firms, which will still want lawyers to work from the office for at least a significant period of time.

(b) *Lower cost base*: Given the general acceptance of working from home, lawyers no longer need to worry about setting up a nice office in central business districts when they set up their new outfits. People are also increasingly used to working from co-working spaces. This reduces the costs associated with setting up a new firm substantially and tilts the cost-benefit analysis towards starting new firms.

---

15. For instance, Norton Rose Fulbright now has a permanent policy where lawyers can work from home for two days per week, two days in the office, and the last day is up to their preference.
16. *See, e.g.*: https://www.businessinsider.com/digital-nomad-visas-lowest-monthly-income-req uirements-portugal-malta-list-2022-9.

(c) *Growing alternatives in relation to legal process outsourcing*: In the past, outsourcing was only available to large firms which have the resources to set up an office in a lower-cost jurisdiction. This has changed in recent years, partially due to private equity and venture capital firms investing more heavily in legal ops and legal tech companies. These companies can service all types of law firms, including independent practitioners.

For example, when it comes to complex disputes which require extensive discovery and document review, small law firms can engage companies such as Integreon[17] or TransPerfect Legal Solutions.[18] The cost of engaging these vendors is likely to be comparable, if not lower, than engaging a big law firm's paralegal team to do the same work. These vendors are likely to have more advanced capabilities than law firms because they have invested heavily in the technology and resources required for the process, often setting up offices around the world to ensure they have coverage of multiple languages and time zones. These are capabilities that big law firms will struggle to match at the same cost because they are ultimately run by law firm partners, whose interests are unlikely to be aligned with building a large legal tech or legal ops team.

As far as the end client is concerned, they are likely to get better value for money if they engage a team of independent practitioners (or a boutique firm), who will work with legal tech and legal ops companies as and when the need arises.

(d) *Higher (or fairer) earnings-to-effort ratio*: Ultimately, more people are likely to find that the shift towards being an independent practitioner or starting a boutique practice makes *cents* (i.e., money sense) in today's world. This applies especially to younger lawyers with a few years of experience or salaried partners. By coming out on their own, they earn 100% of what they bill (after deducting the costs). From a mathematical standpoint, this is likely to be significantly more than what they were earning in a big law firm on both objective and relative terms (i.e., relative to the number of hours that these lawyers bill).

For example, in Singapore, it is not uncommon to have junior lawyers with three years of experience earning around SGD 120,000 per annum for billing 2,000 hours a year. If these lawyers were to become independent, they can bill SGD 200 per hour (much lower than their average hourly rates in big law firms) and bill 1,000 hours a year (half the billable hours), and still make more money at SGD 200,000 a year (66.7% increase in earnings).

While the exact math would differ for each individual, it is indisputable that 'going solo' is now an attractive option for many young lawyers, who consider this model an opportunity for them to have greater control of their lives and enjoy significant financial rewards at the same time.

---

17. https://www.integreon.com/what-we-do/litigation-services/managed-document-review-serv ices/.
18. https://www.transperfectlegal.com/services/document-review-legal-staffing.

These new outfits will pose significant challenges to large firms. Given their lower cost base, these firms can bid for the same work at a lower cost than large firms. Many independent practitioners would have first trained at big law firms before they left to start out on their own. Their pitch will essentially be that you get 'Big Law quality' at an affordable price. They will also compete with large firms on talent, given the increased emphasis that Gen Zs place on work-life balance and autonomy in their careers.

III HOW MIGHT LEGAL OPERATIONS HELP YOU WIN INSTRUCTIONS?

When it comes to instructing lawyers for arbitrations, clients consider a myriad range of factors. In this section, we crystallised them into the following factors to facilitate our discussions on the strategies that lawyers can adopt to win more instructions (in no particular order):

(a) cost;
(b) experience in the relevant practice area or the relevant type of dispute ('Experience');
(c) quality of advocacy and knowledge of the law ('Quality');
(d) reputation;
(e) relationship with the lawyer;
(f) user-friendliness; and
(g) speed of service.

The legal ops strategies that are proposed in this section are set out at a level that should be generally applicable to all lawyers, regardless of whether they are in big law firms, boutique firms or independents. However, the precise manner to deploy these strategies or the exact solution will depend on the specific context.

1 Sourcing for the Right Team

As mentioned in Section II.D above, many lawyers are likely to leave big law firms to practice independently or in boutique outfits over the next few years. Big law firms will face increasing competition from these new outfits, which tend to be more flexible with cost. Boutique firms also tend to be more user-friendly because they are prepared to adapt to the client's requirements. For example, international firms generally discourage lawyers from using WhatsApp or WeChat to discuss work-related matters with clients, but boutique firms would have no issue using such chat apps to make it easier for their clients to communicate with them.

In a world where there are more independent or boutique outfits, parties will become increasingly open and interested in building teams of counsel. The focus will be on getting the best people for the best price. In some cases, this means having people from different firms and different locations working together on one matter. For example, this author has observed situations where it is cheaper to engage a leading advocate (e.g., a King's Counsel) with independent juniors than an international law firm. To illustrate:

Cost of legal teams (Example)

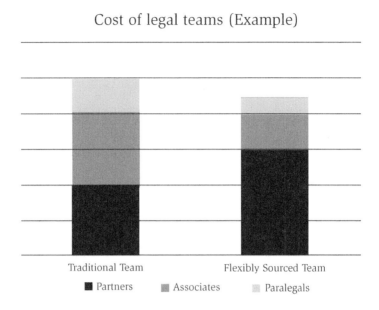

Traditional Team   Flexibly Sourced Team

■ Partners   ■ Associates   ▨ Paralegals

This chart illustrates the pricing advantages of a flexibly sourced team, where the clients could engage:

- a more senior and experienced counsel (e.g., King's Counsel) as compared to partners in a traditional law firm, which leads to the cost at the partner level being higher;
- associates at the same level of experience, but cost less because they are working in independent outfits and they collect 100% of what they bill (*see* above);
- paralegals at the same level of experience, but cost less because they can be based in a lower-cost jurisdiction; and

still pay *less* than a traditional team in big law firms.

With this in mind, arbitration practitioners can consider adopting the following strategies:

(a) Instead of viewing such changes in business models as a threat, big firms should build relationships with independent practitioners and use them as a resource to price in a more competitive manner. To use analogies from the

construction industry, big law firms are well placed to be the 'main contractor' or 'project coordinator' in disputes, where they become the entity which
sources the team and ensures the overall progress of the project.

(b) Practitioners should share and exchange details which are relevant to building teams, e.g., the cost structures, actual experience and user-friendliness of
various independent practitioners or boutique outfits. As clients become
more interested in building teams across firms, practitioners should have
these details so that they can recommend and suggest the right additions
(from other firms) to their clients. While some practitioners might be reluctant to share such details now, the trend of building teams across firms is
likely to be inevitable and such reluctance will only cause them to lose out to
the practitioners who are more open to sharing such information (and the
independents are unlikely to have any issues in this regard).

(c) Practitioners should look beyond their domestic legal industries and engage
with foreign legal service providers or alternative legal service providers to
explore strategies in relation to building teams. For example, to increase the
speed of service, a law firm can work with independent juniors in various
jurisdictions across different time zones to ensure that the team works around
the clock.

(d) Practitioners should develop clear workflows and systems which facilitate
collaboration with 'external counsel'. At the moment, practitioners mainly
instruct external counsel when they need more senior lawyers (e.g., King's
Counsel or Senior Advocate) to come on board. Often, the law firm would
defer to the senior lawyers when it comes to working styles. This is not a
sustainable approach when the team consists of people from all over the
world and different outfits. As we will explain in Section III.C below,
practitioners should engage legal project managers to ensure that workflows
or systems are thoughtfully designed to minimise miscommunication and
ensure consistent quality across teams.

2   Designing the Best User Experience

The pandemic has forced us to reconsider how we deliver legal services. The legal
industry in many countries decided to increase the adoption of technology in hearings
and the adoption of paperless environments to ensure that we could continue to deliver
legal services during the pandemic, and these changes have also improved the user
experience of legal services. For example, paperless hearings allow foreign clients to
attend hearings without having to travel, which in turn reduces the clients' legal
spending and enables them to spend more time doing things that matter.

As we transition to the post-pandemic world, it is important that we continue to
innovate and improve the user experience in international arbitration. Further, instead
of being reactionary (as we did during the pandemic), we can take a step back and
revisit the fundamentals:

(a) What are the services that arbitration practitioners provide to their clients? Is it just the efficient resolution of disputes?

(b) What are the pain points in the delivery of our services?

In this author's opinion, arbitration practitioners are in the business of helping their clients manage the risks associated with disputes, and the effective resolution of disputes is simply one form of managing such risks. If so, arbitration practitioners can improve the user experience by assisting with the client's contract lifecycle management and using legaltech solutions to proactively avoid potential disputes (e.g., by using legaltech tools to monitor how legal developments might affect the contracts that the client has entered into). These arbitration practitioners could also work with legal ops vendors to digitise and review all the client's contracts in an affordable manner, which will in turn streamline the client's contract lifecycle management process.

When it comes to arbitrations, the practitioners can also work with legal ops solution providers (either in-house or external vendors) to improve the user experience in the following manner:

(a) *Better legal spending management*: Legal ops experts can be engaged to measure and manage the client's expected legal spending for the matter in real time. This would improve the client's user experience because the client will gain actionable insights which could help them decide on whether to litigate or attempt settlement.

(b) *Better resource allocation*: Legal ops experts can be engaged to optimise the allocation of tasks, to ensure that tasks are being allocated to the right person on the team and predict whether external resources (e.g., from independent practitioners, eDiscovery vendors, etc.) should be obtained for the matter. For instance, technology can be used to track the hours that an associate has been spending at work, the tasks that have been allocated to the said associate, the deadlines that are coming up for the associate, and other factors, to determine whether to allocate certain tasks to other internal or external resources. After all, the client's user experience could be improved if the staff working on the matter is not overworked and does not suffer from burnout, which could result in significant wastage of cost and inconvenience to the client if the staff decides to leave the firm.

(c) *Faster response time*: Legal ops experts can be engaged to set up a team which could provide clients with all-day support. Legal ops experts are best placed to build teams that can function across different time zones and have sufficient buffer capacity to respond to the client's queries within a short timeframe. They can also create workflows and standard operating procedures to ensure the teams can collaborate in an efficient and streamlined manner. Legal ops experts can also work with practitioners to develop self-service solutions, which can address the client's simple or administrative queries in an immediate and automated manner. For example, a simple chatbot or client portal can be set up to deliver the type of information which does not require a lawyer's input.

Ultimately, arbitration practitioners must listen to their clients and understand the pain points that their clients face in arbitration. This could be done by working with legal ops experts who could design interactive surveys to obtain relevant qualitative or quantitative inputs from the clients. As illustrated above, the improvement of user experience is likely to require legal ops experts who can deploy legaltech and human resource solutions in a holistic manner.

3   Working with Legal Project Managers

Lawyers are typically not trained with the necessary skill sets to perform the above-mentioned strategies which can help them win instructions in the post-pandemic world. Most lawyers are either ill-equipped or too busy to manage the business, technological and operational aspects of these strategies. While it would be ideal for lawyers to develop more expertise in these areas, pushing lawyers to do so is not necessarily the best option. Senior lawyers' time is better spent on high-value and profitable billable legal work. In all likelihood, junior lawyers will be the ones who are tasked to pick up such skills, but if these junior lawyers are already facing serious pressure to bill 2000 hours a year, such additional workload will only hasten their burnout. Therefore, it is often better for lawyers to work with legal ops experts who are trained and dedicated to solving these problems in their full-time jobs.

Legal project managers are those who are engaged to 'use the principles of project management to help [legal practices] run more efficiently, and in a more cost-effective and client-focused way'.[19] These professionals are indispensable when it comes to implementing the strategies mentioned above. Their job scope often includes:

(a) designing the job specification for external vendors (e.g., eDiscovery vendors, forensic experts, independent junior counsel, etc.);
(b) managing communications & expectations within the team (including both internal and external resources);
(c) allocating resources within the team;
(d) supervising quality of work;
(e) ensuring that deadlines are met;
(f) streamlining processes to prevent duplication and improve response time; and
(g) controlling costs for the matter.

Every arbitration or dispute can be treated as a 'project' and managed based on well-tested project management principles. At the start of every project, these legal project managers are tasked to answer these (non-exhaustive) questions:

(a) What is the scope of this project?
(b) When is the deadline? Can we set intermediate milestones?

---

19. *See*: https://www.clio.com/blog/legal-project-manager/.

    (c) Who is the best person for this project?
        (i) Who has excess capacity? Who is too swamped?
        (ii) Who has the most suitable personality for this client?
        (iii) Who has the skillset for this matter?
    (d) What are the costs involved?
        (i) What's the client's budget?
        (ii) What's our cost internally? How do we calculate our internal costs?
        (iii) How should we charge?
    (e) Do we need to acquire new tools to better manage this project?
    (f) What are the potential challenges in this project?
    (g) What do we need to explain during the onboarding process (for both the working team and the client)?
        (i) How might we set expectations with the client and the working team?
        (ii) Do we need to set 'blackout periods' (e.g., no one in the team should be expected to take calls or reply to emails between 6 pm and 8 pm)?
        (iii) How might we facilitate collaboration in a remote/hybrid context?

In today's world, partners or associates are often tasked to play the role of a legal project manager, and often in an ad-hoc and unsystematic manner. However, most of these roles do not actually require a lawyer, and trained legal project managers (many of them also have law degrees) are more than capable to perform these roles. Legal project managers can also enhance the lawyers' ability to play some specific roles within this process. For instance, with the legal project manager taking charge of most aspects of matter management, the partner can spend more time on client relationship management (which can be left to partners, if that is the preference).

As we move towards a world where teams are flexibly sourced, we will need to manage a team with people from different cultures, different time zones, different training backgrounds, and ultimately, different working styles. Without legal project managers, arbitration practitioners are unlikely to be able to fully unlock the potential in the post-pandemic world. Their existing teams will find it difficult to compete effectively in terms of price or user experience with a flexibly sourced team, which can be cheaper and available for support 24/7.

IV   CONCLUSION

We are living in exciting times. The pandemic has transformed how we practice and removed numerous psychological barriers when it comes to the adoption of technology in the legal industry. We can now implement many readily available legal ops solutions (i.e., not some magical AI or blockchain solution) to help us practice in a better way, in a way that makes practice more enjoyable. At the end of the day, having an enjoyable legal practice is the most sustainable way of ensuring that you will continue to win instructions in the post-pandemic world. There is no point in having strong billables for five years, and then suffering from burnout and leaving practice thereafter.

This is not to say legal ops is the panacea to all problems in the post-pandemic legal practice. One issue which has been identified in this chapter – the changes to post-pandemic business travel – cannot be solved by legal ops. Instead, practitioners will need to reconsider how legal business development should be done in the post-pandemic world, which is an issue best left for another chapter.

CHAPTER 39

Artificial Intelligence in Arbitral Decision-Making: The New Enlightenment?

*Maxi Scherer**

TABLE OF CONTENTS

> A wise man[/woman] apportions his[/her] beliefs to the evidence.
>
> David Hume

I   INTRODUCTION

The Age of Enlightenment, an intellectual and philosophical movement that dominated Europe in the seventeenth and eighteenth centuries, was marked by an increasing emphasis on the scientific method and the pursuit of knowledge obtained by means of reason and the evidence of the senses. The Scottish philosopher David Hume expressed this aptly in the quote above – cited here with some adaptations for modern purposes.

The 2022 ICCA conference programme in Edinburgh is under the overall title 'Arbitration's Age of Enlightenment?' This question could not be better suited for the issues addressed in this chapter, which discusses the influence of artificial intelligence

---

*   Professor of Law, Queen Mary University of London; Special Counsel, Wilmer Cutler Pickering Hale and Dorr LLP. Email: maxi.scherer@wilmerhale.com.

(AI) on arbitral decision-making. Some see AI as a promising new enlightenment of our discipline; others fear AI's consequences on the legal profession as a whole.

It is trite to underline the importance AI already has in many areas of law, including contract analysis, legal research, e-discovery etc.[1] For instance, computer programs are available to help lawyers analyse the other side's written submissions and to provide relevant case law that was omitted therein or has been rendered since. In international arbitration, the use of AI exists or has been predicted for a wide variety of tasks including appointment of arbitrators, legal research, drafting and proofreading of written submissions, translation of documents, case management and document organization, cost estimations, hearing arrangements (such as transcripts or simultaneous foreign language interpretation) and drafting of standard sections of awards (such as procedural history).[2] This chapter will not deal with those aspects but instead

---

1. *See, e.g.*, Jan de Bruyne and Cedric Vanleenhove, *Artificial Intelligence and the Law* (Cambridge 2021); Guido Governatori et al., 'Thirty Years of Artificial Intelligence and Law: The First Decade', Artificial Intelligence and Law (September 2022) at https://doi.org/10.1007/s10506-022-09329-4 (last accessed 19 October 2022); Philip Hanke, 'Computers with Law Degrees? The Role of Artificial Intelligence in Transnational Dispute Resolution, and Its Implications of the Legal Profession', 14(2) Transnational Dispute Management (2017), p. 1; Harry Surden, 'Artificial Intelligence and Law: An Overview', 35(4) Georgia State University Law Review (2019) p. 1338; Richard Susskind, *Tomorrow's Lawyers: An Introduction to Your Future*, 2d edn (Oxford 2017); Serena Villata et al., 'Thirty Years of Artificial Intelligence and Law: The Third Decade' (July 2022), at https://doi.org/10.1007/s10506-022-09327-6 (last accessed 19 October 2022) p. 6.

2. *See* Mohamad S. Abdel Wahab, 'Online Arbitration: Tradition Conceptions and Innovative Trends' in *International Arbitration: The Coming of a New Age?*, ICCA Congress Series no. 17 (henceforth *ICCA Congress Series no. 17*) pp. 654-667; Kate Apostolova and Mike Kung, 'Don't Fear AI in IA', Global Arbitration Review (27 April 2018); Gülüm Bayraktaroğlu-Özçelik and Ş. Barış Özçelik, 'Use of AI-Based Technologies in International Commercial Arbitration', 12(2) European Journal of Law and Technology (2021) p. 1; Adesina Temitayo Bello, 'Online Dispute Resolution Algorithm: The Artificial Intelligence Model as a Pinnacle', 84(2) Intl. J. Arb. Mediation & Dispute Mgt. (2018) p. 159; Bianca Berardicurti, '25. Artificial Intelligence in International Arbitration: The World Is All That Is the Case', in Carlos González Bueno, ed., *40 under 40 International Arbitration (2021)* (Dykinson, S.L. 2021) pp. 377-392; Aditya Singh Chauhan, 'Future of AI in Arbitration: The Fine Line Between Fiction and Reality', Kluwer Arbitration Blog (September 2020) at http://arbitrationblog.kluwerarbitration.com/2020/09/26/future-of-ai-in-arbitration-the-fine-line-between-fiction-and-reality/ (last accessed 19 October 2022); Paul Cohen and Sophie Nappert, 'The March of the Robots', Global Arbitration Review (15 February 2017); Horst Eidenmüller and Faidon Varesis, 'What Is an Arbitration? Artificial Intelligence and the Vanishing Human Arbitrator', available at https://ssrn.com/abstract = 362 9145 (last accessed 19 October 2022); Myriam Gisquello, 'Artificial Intelligence in International Arbitration' in Thomas Schultz and Federico Ortino, eds, *The Oxford Handbook of International Arbitration* (Oxford Academic 2020) p. 591; Derick H. Lindquist and Ylli Dautaj, 'AI in International Arbitration: Need for the Human Touch', (1) Journal of Dispute Resolution (2021) p. 39; Emma Martin, 'The Use of Technology in International Arbitration', in Carlos González Bueno, ed., *40 under 40 International Arbitration* (Wolters Kluwer 2018) pp. 337-348; Sophie Nappert, 'Disruption Is the New Black – Practical Thoughts on Keeping International Arbitration on Trend', (2) ICC Dispute Resolution Bulletin 20 (2018) pp. 25-36; Sophie Nappert, 'The Challenge of Artificial Intelligence in Arbitral Decision-Making', Practical Law UK Articles (4 October 2018); Maroof Rafique, 'Why Artificial Intelligence Is a Compatible Match for Arbitration', 88(2) Arbitration: The International Journal of Arbitration, Mediation and Dispute Management (2022) pp. 310-320; Lucy Reed, 'AI vs IA: Artificial Intelligence and Genuine International Arbitration', Keynote lecture at Sciences Po Law School (March 2022) at https://www.sciencespo.fr/ecole-de-droit/fr/actualites/ai-vs-ia-artificial-intelligence-and-genuine-internation al-arbitration.html (last accessed 20 October 2022); Christine Sim, 'Will Artificial Intelligence Take over Arbitration?', 14(1) Asian Intl. Arb. J. (2018) p. 1; Robert H. Smit, 'The Future of

focus on one of the more controversial areas which are at the core of the arbitral process: the decision-making itself.[3] Section II will explore whether and how AI can be used to help or potentially replace arbitrators in their task to decide the dispute. Section III, in line with the conference's overall philosophical theme, will address the implications the use of AI would have on legal theories of legal decision-making.

II   AI DECISION-MAKERS OF THE FUTURE?

When considering AI for arbitral decision-making,[4] some have speculated about the feasibility of 'robot arbitrators'.[5] Authors typically either assert that AI would be inevitable in the future,[6] or express scepticism, based on the assumption that AI would not be able to resolve tasks that involve high cognitive functions, such as legal decision-making.[7]

Science and Technology in International Arbitration: The Next Thirty Years', in Stavros Brekoulakis, Julian D.M. Lew and Loukas Mistelis, eds, *The Evolution and Future of International Arbitration* (Wolters Kluwer 2016) pp. 365-378; Francisco Uríbarri Soares, 'New Technologies and Arbitration', VII(1) Indian J. Arb. L. (2018) p. 84; Gauthier Vannieuwenhuyse, 'Arbitration and New Technologies: Mutual Benefits', 35 Journal of International Arbitration (2018) pp. 119-129.

3. *See also* Maxi Scherer, 'International Arbitration 3.0: How Artificial Intelligence Will Change Dispute Resolution' in Christian Klausegger, ed., *Austrian Yearbook of International Arbitration* (Wolters Kluwer 2019), p. 503.

4. Importantly, this question differs from the discussion around online arbitration, which generally refers to proceedings for which processes are streamlined thanks to the use of technology, such as electronic filings, but where the decision-making itself is still by human arbitrators. *See, e.g.,* Pablo Cortés and Tony Cole, 'Legislating for an Effective and Legitimate System of Online Consumer Arbitration' in Maud Piers and Christian Aschauer, eds, *Arbitration in the Digital Age* (Cambridge 2018) p. 209; Kevin Ongenae and Maud Piers, 'Procedural Formalities in Arbitration: Towards a Technologically Neutral Legal Framework', 38(1) Journal of International Arbitration (2021) pp. 27-58; Pietro Ortolani, André Janssen and Pieter Wolters, *International Arbitration and Technology* (Kluwer Law International 2022); Amy J. Schmitz, 'Building on OArb Attributes in Pursuit of Justice', in Maud Piers and Christian Aschauer, eds, *Arbitration in the Digital Age* (Cambridge 2018) p. 182; Jeffrey Maurice Waincymer, 'Online Arbitration', IX(1) Indian Journal of Arbitration Law, Centre for Advanced Research and Training in Arbitration Law, National Law University, Jodhpur (2020), pp. 1-23; Qin Zhen, 'The Use of New Technologies in International Arbitration', Blog by the American Review of International Arbitration (February 2019), available at http://aria.law.columbia.edu/the-use-of-new-technologies-in-international-arbitration/ (last accessed 19 October 2022).

5. Paul Cohen and Sophie Nappert, 'Case Study: The Practitioner's Perspective' in Maud Piers and Christian Aschauer, eds, *Arbitration in the Digital Age* (Cambridge 2018) pp. 126, 140-145; P. Cohen and S. Nappert, 'The March of the Robots', p. 6; José María de la Jara, Daniela Palma and Alejandra Infantes, 'Machine Arbitrator: Are We Ready?', Kluwer Arbitration Blog (May 2017) at http://arbitrationblog.kluwerarbitration.com/2017/05/04/machine-arbitrator-are-we ready/#: ~ :text = A % 20group % 20of % 20lawyers % 20has,awards % 20than % 20Gabrielle % 20Kau ffman % 2DKohler (last accessed 19 October 2022).

6. K. Apostolova and M. Kung, 'Don't Fear AI in IA'.

7. Guillermo Argerich, María Blanca Noodt Taquela and Juan Jorge, 'Could an Arbitral Award Rendered by AI Systems be Recognized or Enforced? Analysis from the Perspective of Public Policy', Kluwer Arbitration Blog (February 2020) at http://arbitrationblog.kluwerarbitration.com /2020/02/06/could-an-arbitral-award-rendered-by-ai-systems-be-recognized-or-enforced-analy sis-from-the-perspective-of-public-policy/ (last accessed 19 October 2022); B. Berardicurti, 'Artificial Intelligence in International Arbitration: The World Is All That Is the Case', p. 389; A.S. Chauhan, 'Future of AI in Arbitration: The Fine Line Between Fiction and Reality'; J.M. de la Jara,

Lawyers' scepticism that AI would not be 'up for the job' when deciding legal matters is generally misplaced. When one follows David Hume's advice to look at the evidence, scientific research shows that AI-driven programs can accurately predict the outcome of legal decision-making – and indeed more so than human experts.

Several studies may lend support to this thesis. For instance, an early study showed that computer programs excelled over human experts in predicting the votes of individual US Supreme Court justices in upcoming decisions for the 2002 term. The computer model achieved a correct prediction rate of 75%, whereas the human expert group, composed of eminent lawyers and law professors, correctly guessed only 59% of votes.[8]

Another study, conducted by a group of researchers published in 2016, focussed on decisions by the European Court of Human Rights.[9] Looking at a data set of 584 decisions, the researchers trained a computer model using natural language processing and machine learning.[10] The model was trained on a 10% subset of the dataset[11] and was asked to predict the Court's decision (i.e., whether or not the Court found a violation) for the remaining 90%. The model obtained an overall accuracy to predict the outcome of the Court's decision in 79% of all cases.[12]

A further study from 2017 was made with input data of more than 28,000 US Supreme Court case outcomes and 240,000 individual justices' votes from 1816 to 2015.[13] Using machine learning, the researchers trained the model on a sample from the data set and then applied the obtained model to the remaining out-of-sample data.[14] Overall, the model predicted the votes of individual justices with 71.9% accuracy, and the outcome of the decisions with 70.2% accuracy.[15] While there was fluctuation in any given year or decade, the study claims that the model delivered 'stable performance' over time.[16] The study also claims that the model 'significantly outperforms' possible baseline comparison models.[17]

D. Palma and A. Infantes, 'Machine Arbitrator'; D.H. Lindquist and Y. Dautaj, 'AI in International Arbitration: Need for the Human Touch', p. 41; *see also*, more nuanced, S. Nappert, 'The Challenge of Artificial Intelligence in Arbitral Decision-Making'; Henk J. Snijders, 'Arbitration and AI, from Arbitration to "Robotration" and from Human Arbitrator to Robot', 87 (2) The International Journal of Arbitration, Mediation and Dispute Management (2021) pp. 223-242; F. Uríbarri Soares, 'New Technologies and Arbitration', p. 101; Abhilasha Vij, 'Arbitrator-Robot: Is A(I)DR the Future?', 39(1) ASA Bulletin (2021) pp. 123-146, 138-143.

8. Roger Guimerà and Marta Sales-Pardo, 'Justice Blocks and Predictability of U.S. Supreme Court Votes', 6(11) PloS One (2011); Theodore W. Ruger et al., 'The Supreme Court Forecasting Project: Legal and Political Sciences Approaches to Predicting Supreme Court Decision Making', 104 Colum. L. Rev. 1150 (2004) p. 1152. For some of the other earlier studies, *see* Andrew D. Martin et al., 'Competing Approaches to Predicting Supreme Court Decision Making', 2(4) Perspective on Politics (2004) p. 761.

9. Nikolaos Aletras et al., 'Predicting Judicial Decision of the European Court of Human Rights: A Natural Language Processing Perspective', PeerJ Computer Science 2:e93 (2016).

10. *Ibid.*, at p. 1.

11. *Ibid.*, at p. 9.

12. *Ibid.*, at p. 10.

13. Daniel M. Katz, Michael J. Bommaritoii and Josh Blackman, 'A General Approach for Predicting the Behavior of the Supreme Court of the United States', 12(4) PloS One (2017) p. 5, Table 1.

14. *Ibid.*, at pp. 6-8.

15. *Ibid.*, at pp. 8-9.

16. *Ibid.*, at p. 9.

17. *Ibid.*, at p. 15.

The basic explanation for these – apparently triumphant – AI successes is that human brains suffer 'hardware' limitations which computer programs surpass easily. A more specific explanation relates to the methodology used in those studies.[18] Be it as it may, these studies disprove the assumption that AI models would not be able to predict legal decisions accurately.

Nonetheless, whether these 'successes' could be replicated in international arbitration and in real life is a different question. Several important limitations and hurdles exist, most notably the following.[19]

First, data-driven AI programs are data-hungry: the larger the sample data, the more accurate the model's predictive value. In international commercial arbitration awards are generally confidential and the constitution of a database to establish an AI model would therefore prove difficult. However, this is not to say that AI models in international commercial arbitration are impossible. Initiatives exist to publish commercial awards on a regular basis, possibly in a redacted format.[20] In any event, even without publishing confidential awards, institutions could collect them and make them available for the purpose of building AI models.

Second, any data-based computer models are only as good as the input data. Vulnerability in the data diet has negative consequences on the extracted algorithm. In particular, the underlying data which was used to train the model might have been 'infected' with human biases.[21] The machine learning algorithm will be based on those biases and possibly even exaggerate them by holding them as 'true' for its future decision or outcome prediction.[22] Even without going as far as pointing towards human

---

18. For a critical analysis of the studies, *see* Maxi Scherer, 'Artificial Intelligence and Legal Decision-Making: The Wide Open? A Study Examining International Arbitration', 36(5) Journal of International Arbitration (2019) pp. 539, 546-554.

19. For more detailed analysis, *see ibid.*, at pp. 554-565.

20. *See, e.g.*, ICC, 'Note to Parties and Arbitral Tribunals on the Conduct of the Arbitration under the ICC Rules of Arbitration (1 January 2019)' available at https://cdn.iccwbo.org/content/uploads /sites/3/2017/03/icc-note-to-parties-and-arbitral-tribunals-on-the-conduct-of-arbitration.pdf (last accessed 9 May 2019); e.g. ICC, 'Publication of ICC Arbitral Awards with Jus Mundi', available at https://iccwbo.org/dispute-resolution-services/arbitration/publication-of-icc-arbi tral-awards-with-jus-mundi/ (last accessed 19 October 2022); Antonio Musella, 'Arbitration, Open Data, Justice and Artificial Intelligence: A New Step Forward', Kluwer Arbitration Blog (April 2020) at http://arbitrationblog.kluwerarbitration.com/2020/04/16/arbitration-open-data -justice-and-artificial-intelligence-a-new-step-forward/ (last accessed 19 October 2022); Kathleen Paisley and Edna Sussman, 'Artificial Intelligence Challenges and Opportunities for International Arbitration', 11(2) NYSBA New York Dispute Resolution Lawyer (2018) pp. 37-39.

21. On human basis in legal decision-making, *see, e.g.*, Shai Danziger et al., 'Extraneous Factors in Judicial Decisions', 108(17) PNAS (2011) p. 6889.

22. For instance, studies have shown that the use of algorithms in criminal risk assessment in the US has led to racially biased outcomes. Olga Akselrod, 'How Artificial Intelligence Can Deepen Racial and Economic Inequities' (July 2021), available at https://www.aclu.org/news/privacy -technology/how-artificial-intelligence-can-deepen-racial-and-economic-inequities#: ~ :text = Bias % 20is % 20often % 20baked % 20into,development % 2C % 20implementation % 2C % 20and % 20use (last accessed 19 October 2022); Julia Angwin et al., 'Machine Bias: There's Software Used Across the Country to Predict Future Criminals: And It's Biased Against Blacks', ProPublica (23 May 2016), available at https://www.propublica.org/article/machine-bias-risk-assessments-in -criminal-sentencing (last accessed 19 October 2022); Ande Davis, 'A Preponderance of Bias: Why Artificial Intelligence Should Be Qualified Immunity's Fatal Flaw', 61(3) Washburn Law Journal (2022) pp. 565, 586; Emile Loza de Siles, 'Artificial Intelligence Bias and Discrimination:

biases in the underlying data, the model might extract patterns from the data and extrapolate them in a way that might lead to systemic mistakes. For instance, in the area of investment arbitration, concerns have been voiced that arbitral tribunals are inherently and unduly investor-friendly.[23] Assuming for the purpose of the argument that this were so, an AI model based on investment arbitration data would be likely to perpetuate such (alleged) favour given to investors. The model would likely predict favourable outcomes for investors against States in a disproportionate number of cases.

Third, AI programs have significant issues in providing reasoned legal decisions.[24] On the one hand, it may be difficult to identify the actual factors that have led to a certain outcome prediction in case of black-boxed AI models. Indeed, not only in the legal sector but more broadly, AI models were unable to explain the results obtained,[25] which has raised some concerns.[26] On the other hand, even if certain

---

Will We Pull the Arc of Moral Universe Towards Justice?', 2022 (1) Revista Forumul Judecatorilor (Judiciary Forum Review) (2022) pp. 40-66; Stanley Greenstein, 'Preserving the Rule of Law in the Era of Artificial Intelligence (AI)', Artificial Intelligence and Law 30 (2022) pp. 291-323; Karen Hao, 'AI Is Sending People to Jail: And Getting It Wrong' (January 2019), available at https://www.technologyreview.com/2019/01/21/137783/algorithms-criminal-justice-ai/ (last accessed 19 October 2022); Will Douglas Heaven, 'Predictive Policing Algorithms Are Racist: They Need to Be Dismantled', MIT Technology Review (July 2020), available at https://www.technologyreview.com/2020/07/17/1005396/predictive-policing-algorithms-racist-dismantled-machine-learning-bias-criminal-justice/ (last accessed 19 October 2022); Jeff Larson et al., 'How We Analyzed the COMPAS Recidivism Algorithm', ProPublica (23 May 2016), available at https://www.propublica.org/article/how-we-analyzed-the-compas-recidivism-algorithm (last accessed 19 October 2022); Sandra G. Mayson, 'Bias In, Bias Out', 128 Yale Law Journal (2019) p. 2234; Natalia Mesa, 'Can the Criminal Justice System's Artificial Intelligence Ever Be Truly Fair?' (May 2021), available at https://massivesci.com/articles/machine-learning-compas-racism-policing-fairness/ (last accessed 19 October 2022); Cade Metz, 'Who Is Making Sure That A.I. Machines Aren't Racist?', NY Times (March 2021), available at https://www.nytimes.com/2021/03/15/technology/artificial-intelligence-google-bias.html (last accessed 19 October 2022); *State v. Loomis*, 881, N.W.2d 749, 7532 (Wis 2016).

23. *See, e.g.*, George Cadillac, 'The Appearance of Bias in International Investment Arbitrators and Analysis of Potential Impediments to Bias in the European Union's Proposal for a Multilateral Investment Court', 13(1) Australian and New Zealand Journal of European Studies (2021) pp. 108-109; Pia Eberhardt et al., 'Profiting from Injustice: How Law Firms, Arbitrators and Financiers Are Fuelling an Investment Arbitration Boom' (Corporate Europe Observatory 2012), available at https://www.tni.org/files/download/profitingfrominjustice.pdf (last accessed 19 October 2022) p. 8; George Kahale III, 'Is Investor-State Arbitration Broken?', 9(7) Transnational Dispute Management (2012) pp. 1-2; Gus van Harten, 'Perceived Bias in Investment Treaty Arbitration', in Michael Waibel et al. eds, *The Backlash against Investment Arbitration* (Kluwer Law International 2010) p. 433.

24. *See* M. Scherer, 'International Arbitration 3.0', pp. 511-512.

25. For instance, disturbing results were obtained from an AI program able to guess a person's sexual orientation from publicly posted profile pictures. The accuracy rates are troubling (83% for women and 91% for men) but what is even more alarming are the researchers' difficulties in determining the bases on which the AI program obtained those result. *See* Michal Kosinki and Yilun Wang, 'Deep Neural Networks Are More Accurate than Humans at Detecting Sexual Orientation from Facial Images', 114 J. Personality & Soc. Psychol. (2018) p. 246; Cliff Kuang, 'Can A.I. Be Taught to Explain Itself?', NY Times (November 2017), available at www.nytimes.com/2017/11/21/magazine/can-ai-be-taught-to-explain-itself.html (last accessed 19 October 2022).

26. AI research tries to deal with those issues and develop Explainable Artificial Intelligence, also called XAI. *See, e.g.*, Sandra Wachter, Brent Mittelstadt and Chris Russell, 'Counterfactual Explanations Without Opening the Black Box: Automated Decisions and the GDPR', 31 Harv. J.L. & Tech. (2018) p. 842.

factors are identifiable as causes for a given outcome prediction, these factors might not prove to be a useful explanation. At its core, AI models are typically based on statistics and probabilities.[27] The reason an AI model that has accurately predicted an outcome could give would be along the lines of: 'because there was an 86% probability in favour of this outcome'.

However, this type of explanation does not meet the objectives of legal reasoning. Providing a reasoned decision that outlines the premises on which it is based, constitutes one of the fundamental features of legal decision-making. Reasons are important because they allow (i) the losing party to understand why it lost and make the decision more acceptable (legitimacy objective); (ii) the parties to the dispute and, if the decision is published, third parties in similar situations to adapt their behaviour in the future (incentive objective); and (iii) other decision-makers to follow the same rationale or explain their departure therefrom (consistency objective).

It is submitted that none of these objectives can be fulfilled satisfactorily with probabilistic reasoning, such as, say, that the likelihood of a claim to succeed was 86%. The legitimacy objective is not met because statistical information is unlikely to help the losing party to understand why it lost and make the decision more acceptable.[28] The incentive objective fails because statistical information also does not allow parties or third parties to adapt their behaviour in the future. Finally, the consistency objective is not satisfied because other decision-makers have no information as to why they should follow the same rationale or depart therefrom.

The need for reasoned decisions is therefore likely to be an important barrier to AI-based legal decision-making. The impact of the probabilistic nature of AI models, however, raises even more fundamental questions as to the overall paradigm of decision-making, as discussed in the next section.

III   PARADIGM SHIFT IN THEORIES ON LEGAL DECISION-MAKING

Theories of legal or judicial decision-making abound, but a fundamental distinction exists between those that postulate the use of logic by ways of deductive reasoning on the basis of abstract, pre-determined legal rules (regrouped in the category of legal formalism), and those that emphasize the importance of extra-legal factors and the political dimension of the law (regrouped in the category of legal realism). The use of AI in legal decision-making does not fit easily in either category.

Legal formalism, in its purest form, posits that law is, and should be, an entirely self-contained system, in which judges never face choices or questions of interpretation that would be resolvable through extra-legal considerations.[29] A judicial decision is the

---

27. *See, e.g.,* Ethem Alpaydin, 'Machine Learning' (MIT Press 2016) pp. 50-52, 63-64, 82-84; Margaret A. Boden, *Artificial Intelligence: A Very Short Introduction* (Oxford 2018) pp. 26-28, 39-40.
28. Social scientist studies have found that probabilistic explanations have a low value for human addressees. *See, e.g.,* John R. Josephson and Susan G. Josephson, *Abductive Inference: Computation, Philosophy, Technology* (Cambridge 1996).
29. *See, e.g.,* Hans Kelsen, *Reine Rechtslehre*, 2d edn (Tübingen 1960) p. 478; Max Weber, *Wirtschaft und Gesellschaft (Economy and Society)* (Tübingen 1922), pp. 657-658.

product of a seemingly mechanical or mathematical application of pre-established legal principles or rules to the proven facts using means of logic.[30] The underlying idea can be expressed in the simple formula 'R + F = C' or 'rule plus facts yield conclusion'.[31] More specifically, the legal syllogism will consist of a major premise in the form of the pre-established rule (e.g., 'if P then Q') and a minor premise seeking to establish that the required condition stipulated in the major premise (P) occurred in fact. If such condition is met, by means of a deductive reasoning, or subsumption, the judge concludes that the legal consequence (Q) is to be applied in the case at hand as a matter of logic.[32]

Today, it is rare to find 'pure' formalists, but the main idea of legal decision-making as based on deductive reasoning and logic remains influential.[33] Even in their more nuanced forms, legal formalist theories still point to deductive, logical, rule-based reasoning as the guarantee for the objectivity, impartiality and neutrality of law.[34]

AI processes, if applied in the legal context, would potentially run counter to this understanding of legal decision-making. Most AI models, in particular those based on machine learning, have no pre-defined rules. Deductive, causal reasoning is replaced by an inverse approach because the machine learning program extracts the algorithm from the observable data. Rather than using logic, the AI model calculates probabilities, i.e., the likelihood for any given outcome.[35]

Applying such machine learning processes in the legal decision-making context therefore would mean accepting a departure from the above-mentioned understanding of judicial reasoning according to formalist theories. A decision based on those AI models would *not* be based on pre-determined legal rules, would *not* be the result of deductive logic and would *not* follow the above-described legal syllogism.

While this situation would be a cause for concern for legal formalists, it might be seen as vindicating others who have long criticised formalist theories. In the first half of the twentieth century, legal realists attacked the fundamental postulates of formalist theories that the law was a mechanical application of pre-determined rules by the judge by means of logic and deductive reasoning.[36] Accepting that legal certainty was a myth,

---

30. French jurist Jean Domat saw the law as a logical, 'geometrical' demonstration, as any other scientific demonstration. *See, e.g.*, Marie-France Renoux-Zagamé, 'La figure du juge chez Domat', 39 Droits 35 (2004), pp. 35-52; Marie-France Renoux-Zagamé, 'Domat, Jean', in Patrick Arabeyre, Jean-Louis Halpérin and Jacques Krynen, eds, *Dictionnaire Historique des Juristes Français* (Paris 2007).
31. Neil Maccormick, *Legal Reasoning and Legal Theory* (Oxford 1994) p. x.
32. *Ibid.*, at pp. 21-29.
33. *See, e.g.*, H.L.A. Hart, *The Concept of Law* (Oxford 1961).
34. Maccormick, *Legal Reasoning and Legal Theory, supra* n. 31, pp. ix-x.
35. *See, e.g.*, E. Alpaydin, 'Machine Learning', pp. 63-64, 82-84; M.A. Boden, *Artificial Intelligence, supra* n. 27, at pp. 39-40.
36. *See, e.g.*, Karl N. Llewellyn, 'Some Realism about Realism: Responding to Dean Pound', 44(8) Harvard L. Rev. 1222 (1931). *See also* the later study, Wilfrid E. Rumble Jr, 'Rule-Skepticism and the Role of the Judge: A Study of American Legal Realism', 15 Emory L.J. 251 (1966). For an overview, *see, e.g.*, Laura Kalman, *Legal Realism at Yale: 1927-1960* (Chapel Hill 1986); Wilfrid E. Rumble Jr, *American Legal Realism: Skepticism, Reform and the Judicial Process* (Ithaca 1968). More recently, *see also* Pierre Brunet, 'Analyse Réaliste du Jugement Juridique', 147:4 Cahiers Philosophiques (2016) p. 9; Brian Leiter, *Naturalizing Jurisprudence. Essays on American Legal Realism and Naturalism in Legal Philosophy* (Oxford 2007).

realists developed what they called rule scepticism and drew attention to the fact that rules do not play a determinative part in legal decision-making.[37] Rather, according to this theory, judges decide cases based on extraneous non-legal factors or their 'hunches' and then *ex post* provide their decision with a seemingly logical rule-deferring coating.[38] Unmasking the hypocrisy and double standard of judicial decision-making, realists argue that logic and rule deference is only a facade and ignores the social interests involved. This thought was later developed by the movement of critical legal theory, emphasizing the political significance of the law as a means of empowerment and emancipation.[39] Rather than being a mechanical and supposedly neutral application of rules, law does not contain a 'right answer' but corresponds to competing normative visions.[40]

Even before the legal realist movement became well-known, Justice Oliver Wendell Holmes described decision-making in similar ways. In 1897, in his seminal work, *The Path of Law*, he criticized what he called the 'fallacy of logic'.[41] He insisted that law was imminently a matter of prediction, emphasizing the importance of statistics for the future of the law. He described his work as a study on prediction and more precisely 'the prediction of the incidence of the public force through the instrumentality of the courts'.[42] In order to make correct predictions, he surmised on the use of statistics for future lawyers' generations, noting that '[f]or the rational study of the law the black-letter man [or woman] may be the man [or woman] of the present, but the man [or woman] of the future is [one] of statistics and the master of economics'.[43]

Holmes' emphasis in 1897 on prediction and statistics in legal decision-making, in lieu of logic, shines today in a new light when considering the implications of AI. As discussed above, predictions based on statistics or probabilities are precisely features used in AI machine learning models.[44] Are we therefore to conclude, as some have argued,[45] that AI would vindicate the legal realists' theories? And that the possible use of machine learning models in legal decision-making would be in line with what human judges have always done. Would therefore, in essence, the debate between formalists and realists eventually be won by the latter?

These conclusions, however, ignore an important distinction that needs to be drawn between the descriptive aspect (i.e., how judges *do* effectively reason and take

---

37. *See, e.g.*, Jerome Frank, *Law and the Modern Mind* (Brentano's 1930); Jerome Frank, 'What Courts Do in Fact', 26 Ill. L. Rev. 645 (1932) pp. 645-666, 761-784.
38. Joseph C. Hutcheson Jr, 'The Judgment Intuitive: The Function of the "Hunch" in Judicial Decision', 14 Cornell L. Rev. (1929) p. 274.
39. *See, e.g.*, feminist critiques of adjudication, such as by Carol Gillian, *In a Different Voice* (Cambridge 1982); Catharine A. Mackinnon, *Feminism Unmodified: Discourses on Life and Law* (Cambridge 1987); Catharine A. Mackinnon, *Toward a Feminist Theory of the State* (Cambridge 1989).
40. *See, e.g.*, Roberto Mangabeira Unger, *The Critical Legal Studies Movement* (Cambridge 1983).
41. Oliver Wendell Holmes Jr, 'The Path of the Law', 10 Harv. L. Rev. (1897) pp. 457, 466.
42. *Ibid.*, at p. 457.
43. *Ibid.*, at pp. 458, 469.
44. *See* above at section III.
45. N. Aletras et al., 'Predicting Judicial Decision of the European Court of Human Rights', p. 16 (who argued that their study results 'back[] basic legal realist intuitions.').

decisions) and the prescriptive or normative aspect (i.e., how they *should* reason and take decisions) of those theories.[46]

Legal formalism contains both a descriptive and normative element. Formalists *describe* the process by which judges apply the law as a matter of logic, deduction and legal syllogism.[47] They also argue that the self-contained nature of the law, the neutrality of legal thinking untouched by extraneous non-legal factors is, normatively, how it *should* be. This is in order to keep the law clear of politics or morals[48] and provide for a 'modern paradigm of legal rationality under the "rule of law"'.[49]

Legal realism, on the contrary, is first and foremost concerned with descriptive aspects. They trace what judges *actually* do, or in other words the *reality* of judicial decision-making – hence the name of the movement. They highlight the influence of extraneous non-legal factors, criticizing the formalistic rule-application approach as utopian and far from the real world. However, they do not go as far as arguing that judges *should* take into account extraneous non-legal factors. While it might be a matter of fact that judges are influenced by extraneous factors, no one seriously argues that this is a good thing and should be the normative basis for judicial activity.

When looking at AI models, the foregoing leads to a number of observations. AI models would not only decide based on probabilities as a matter of fact, it would also be their normative basis. As mentioned above, a decision based on AI models would neither be based on pre-determined legal rules nor be the result of deductive logic or legal syllogism.[50] This would be true on a descriptive level (i.e., how these models do effectively decide) and on a normative level (i.e., how these models should decide).

Replacing logic deductive and rule-based reasoning with probabilistic inferences as the normative framework of judicial decision-making would therefore not only constitute a departure from legal formalism, but it would also go well beyond legal realists' theories. Indeed, realists accept that judges – after having made their decision based on a variety of factors, including non-legal, political and moral considerations – do render their decision coated in a format that seeks to comply with logic, using rule-based deductive reasoning.[51] What realists criticize is the hypocrisies of such a facade, but they accept that such facade or format exists. AI-based decision-making would take away such format.

Using statistics or probabilities as the normative framework for judicial decision-making seems problematic for other reasons. So far, probabilities or statistics are not an

---

46. *See, e.g.,* Pierre Brunet, 'Le Raisonnement Juridique: Une Pratique Spécifique?', 26(4) Intl. J. Semiotics L. (2013) p. 767. *See also, e.g.,* H.L.A. Hart, *Essays in Jurisprudence and Philosophy* (Oxford 1983) pp. 103-105.

47. *See* above at section III.

48. *See, e.g.,* Kelsen, *Reine Rechtslehre, supra* n. 29, p. 478 ('What is here chiefly important is to liberate law from the associate which has traditionally been made for it – its association with morals.').

49. Maccormick, *Legal Reasoning and Legal Theory, supra* n. 31, pp. ix-x.

50. *See* above at section III.

51. *See, e.g.,* O.W. Holmes, 'The Path of the Law', p. 699 ('The training of lawyers is a training in logic. The processes of analogy, discrimination, and deduction are those in which they are most at home. The language of judicial decision is mainly the language of logic. And the logical method and form flatter that longing for certainty and for repose which is in every human mind.').

accepted legal basis for decisions.[52] English and other common law lawyers will be familiar with the term 'balance of probabilities' which sets out a standard of proof.[53] Importantly, however, this applies only to the establishment of facts.[54] Once the facts are established using this method, probabilities have no room in judicial decision-making. For instance, one cannot grant a claim merely on the basis that there is an 80% chance that the established facts constitute a violation of the contract.

The previous example illustrates well the concrete issues with probabilistic bases for decision-making. What threshold would be appropriate for a claim to be granted? Would anything above 50% be sufficient? Or would one require a higher threshold of, say 80%? Even with such a higher threshold, though, one accepts that there is a 20% likelihood that the case is decided wrongly.

In sum, using a probabilistic analysis as a normative basis for decision-making is not only an important paradigm shift from a theoretical point of view, but it also raises important concrete questions. This new approach could be called legal determinism since it determines future outcomes on probabilistic calculations based on past data. As shown in this chapter, it has a number of implications for judicial decision-making which need to be considered carefully.

IV   CONCLUSION

This chapter explores the use of AI in arbitral or judicial decision-making. While AI modules have shown the ability to predict legal decision-making accurately, their use in real-life international arbitration scenarios is likely to face various hurdles. These include the unavailability of sufficient data and the inability of providing satisfactory legal reasons. Going beyond these hurdles, the use of AI does not fit easily in existing legal theories on judicial decision-making. AI models elevate probabilistic inferences to be the normative basis for legal decision-making. This chapter argues that this not only constitutes a paradigm shift from a theoretical point of view but also raises important questions as to whether and how the outcome of future decisions should be determined on probabilistic calculations.

These conclusions, however, should not detract from the most obvious point: AI will fundamentally affect the legal profession and legal activities, including judicial decision-making. It is therefore important to further study how to best use AI, even with the limitations, barriers and issues highlighted in this chapter.

As early as 1963, Lawlor speculated that computers would one day become able to analyse and predict judicial decisions, but noted that reliable prediction would

---

52. *See*, for instance, the discussion in the US Supreme Court case of *McCleskey v. Kemp*, 481 U.S. 279, 287 et seq. (1987).
53. *See, e.g.*, Emily Sherwin, 'A Comparative View of Standards of Proof', 50(2) Am. J. Comp. L. (2002) p. 243.
54. For instance, in *Miller v. The Minister of Pensions*, the UK Supreme Court (then House of Lords) elaborated the balance of probabilities concept, stating that if 'the evidence is such that the tribunal can say "We think it is more probable than not", the burden is discharged, but if the probabilities are equal, then it is not.' *See* House of Lords, [1947] 2 All ER 372 (opinion delivered by Lord Denning).

depend on a 'scientific' understanding of the ways the law and the facts impact the judges' decisions.[55] This chapter hopes to contribute to a 'scientific' – or one could say enlightened – understanding of the use of AI within arbitral decision-making.

---

55. Reed C. Lawlor, 'What Computers Can Do: Analysis and Prediction of Judicial Decisions', 49 ABA J. (1963) p. 337.

CHAPTER 40

Decentralized Justice Systems: A New Player in the Field of Alternative Dispute Resolution?

Julie Raneda[*]

TABLE OF CONTENTS

I   INTRODUCTION

A new world based on blockchain technology is emerging. The growing adoption of blockchain technology in many sectors of the economy is accompanied by a paradigm shift, from traditional written contracts to smart contracts.[1] The question of the right mechanism for the resolution of disputes arising out of this new form of contract is thus relevant.

The flexibility of proceedings and the enforceability of awards make international arbitration a prime candidate to resolve disputes arising out of blockchain. But a new

---

[*] Partner in the International Arbitration Group of Schellenberg Wittmer in Singapore.
     The author would like to thank Andreas Wehowsky, Associate at Schellenberg Wittmer, for his valuable input in the preparation of this chapter.
1. Peter L. Michaelson and Sandra A. Jeski, "A Guidebook to Arbitrating Disputes Involving Blockchains and Smart Agreements," 39 Alternatives to the High Cost of Litigation (April 2021) 4 p. 60.

form of dispute resolution mechanism based on blockchain technology is developing. The decentralized justice systems (DJS) claim to offer a cost-efficient, rapid and immediately enforceable dispute resolution mechanism and ambition to become a preferred dispute resolution method for blockchain-related disputes.[2]

This chapter discusses whether the DJS are a legitimate player in the field of alternative dispute resolution and may offer a credible alternative to traditional dispute resolution mechanisms such as international arbitration in some cases.

This chapter first addresses the features of blockchain technology, its practical uses in the new economy and the types of disputes that arise in this context (section II). Section III presents the DJS and their main characteristics, including the challenges they pose, in particular in terms of the integrity of the process. Section IV concludes this chapter by considering whether the DJS represent a valid alternative for the resolution of smart contract disputes.

II   THE WORLD OF SMART CONTRACTS, NFTS AND CRYPTOCURRENCIES: A COMPLEX TERRITORY FOR DISPUTE RESOLUTION

1   The World of Blockchain Technology

a   *The Basics of Blockchain Technology*

An overview of blockchain technology and its key features is necessary to understand its importance for the new economy and the underlying problems envisaged in this chapter.

In simple terms, blockchain technology is a distributed (decentralized) ledger technology. The ledger allows the storage of information in an unalterable way and provides a record of all transactions and data pertaining to a digital asset and other data.[3]

Blockchain technology is based on the following key features:[4]

– Decentralization: no central authority validates and stores individual transactions on a blockchain. The transfer of virtual assets or currency requires no oversight by regulatory institutions or intervention by third parties. Each participant in a blockchain holds a full copy of the ledger.

---

2. Some even go further and consider that DJS should become the preferred dispute resolution method even for disputes unrelated to the blockchain economy. Kleros, "White Paper" at https://kleros.io/static/whitepaper_en-8bd3a0480b45c39899787e17049ded26.pdf (last accessed August 15, 2022).
3. Hans Rudolf Trüeb, "Smart Contracts," in Pascal Grolimund, Alfred Koller, Leander D. Loacker and Wolfgang Portmann (eds), Festschrift für Anton K. Schnyder zum 65. Geburtstag (2018), p. 727.
4. Peter L. Michaelson and Sandra A. Jeskie, "Arbitrating Disputes Involving Blockchains, Smart Contracts, and Smart Legal Contracts," 74 Disp. Resol. J. (2020) 4, p. 105.

– Consensus: for a transaction to be valid, a majority of the participants on the blockchain ("miners") must agree on its validity. Without miner consensus, a transaction will not appear on the ledger.[5]
– Anonymity: unless the user chooses to identify him- or herself, transactions are performed anonymously or via pseudonyms, or more accurately through a unique string of characters personalized to a specific user (cryptographic key).[6] This provides the basis for digital identity.[7]
– Provenance: each and every transaction affecting a digital asset is recorded into the blockchain so that all participants know where the asset comes from and how its ownership has changed over time.
– Immutability: no participant can tamper with a transaction after it has been entered into the blockchain. In case of mistake, a new transaction must be entered to reverse the mistake and both transactions are visible on the blockchain.

These features are said to enhance efficiency and trust in the system and explain the success of blockchain technology in practice.

The most common applications of blockchain technology are cryptoassets and smart contracts. Cryptoassets are made up of a (or several) token(s) whose existence and exchange are recorded and secured through a blockchain.[8] Cryptocurrency (such as Bitcoin or Ethereum) is a prime example of such an asset. It is a token used as a currency. Cryptoassets can also represent tangible or intangible assets existing "off-chain."[9]

Smart contracts are automated contracts written in computer code that embed the key contractual terms. This means that as soon as predefined conditions in the smart contract are fulfilled, the smart contract terms will be executed automatically in a self-verifying and self-executing manner ("if this, then that"), without the need for an intermediary (whether human or institutional).[10] Because they benefit from the blockchain's immutability, smart contracts are impossible to unilaterally reverse or alter.[11] Accordingly, unless the parties have incorporated the possibility to amend or

---

5. Michael Buchwald, "Smart Contract Dispute Resolution: The Inescapable Flaws of Blockchain-Based Arbitration," 168 U. Pa. L. Rev. (2020) p. 1376.
6. *Ibid.*, p. 1378.
7. Matthew Townsend, "Five Web3 Predictions for the NFT Age," Global Arbitration Review (May 12, 2022), at https://globalarbitrationreview.com/article/five-web3-predictions-the-nft-age (last accessed August 9, 2022).
8. Armin Varmaz, Nermin Varmaz, Steffen Günther and Thorsten Poddig, "Kryptowährungen und Token," in: Sebastian Omlor and Mathias Link (eds), Deutscher Fachverlag, paras. 35 et seqq.
9. Brenda Horrigan and Guillermo Garcia-Perrote, "Is International Arbitration Ready for Smart Contract and Blockchain Related Disputes?," in: 'International Arbitration in the Age of the Technological Revolution," Volume 1, 2020.
10. P.L. Michaelson and S.A. Jeskie, "Arbitrating Disputes Involving Blockchains, Smart Contracts, and Smart Legal Contracts," p. 93.
11. Rolf Weber, "Leistungsstörungen und Rechtsdurchsetzung bei Smart Contracts, Eine Auslegeordnung möglicher Problemstellungen," Jusletter (December 4, 2017) para. 3.

terminate the contract in the code, there is in principle no way to stop the execution of a smart contract.[12]

That said, the execution of a smart contract may depend on events taking place in the real world ("off-chain"), such as a due date, the delivery of an item, the occurrence of a natural event or an insured risk, etc. The execution based on an "off-chain" event takes place through oracles, which are third-party services (individuals or programs) that provide the smart contract with external information, as a means to interact with the real world.[13]

More complex forms of smart contracts integrated into a broader contract law-based relationship are developing, which comprise both "smart" (computer-executed) and "non-smart" (traditional text-based) clauses, contracts written in code incorporating by reference to the terms of a natural language master agreement, or contracts written in natural language with encoded performance for certain aspects.[14]

b   Use Cases of Blockchain Technology

Blockchain and smart contracts have a growing importance in certain sectors of the economy.[15] Practical applications (so-called use-cases) concern the exchanges of cryptocurrencies and other assets represented digitally, such as non-fungibles tokens (or NFTs) and digital stock certificates, deeds, bills, etc.[16] Blockchain technology is impacting a variety of industries, from trading and finance to the use of smart contracts in sectors like government and voting, healthcare, licensing and royalty collection, real estate, cybersecurity, inventory management, supply chain management, and the "Internet of Things" (IoT).[17]

The common denominator of these and other use cases is that they benefit from the protection against unauthorized use of data on the blockchain and the automated functioning of smart contracts, which gives greater confidence to the parties

---

12. Ibrahim Mohamed Nour Shehata, "Smart Contracts & International Arbitration" at https://papers.ssrn.com/sol3/papers.cfm?abstract_id = 3290026 (last accessed August 12, 2022).
13. Maxime Chevalier, "From Smart Contract Litigation to Blockchain Arbitration, a New Decentralized Approach Leading Toward the Blockchain Arbitral Order," 12 J.I.D.S. (2021), p. 559.
14. Smart Contracts Alliance, "Smart Contracts: Is the Law Ready?," Chamber of Digital Commerce (2018) at https://digitalchamber.s3.amazonaws.com/Smart-Contracts-Whitepaper-WEB.pdf (last accessed August 13, 2022); B. Horrigan and G. Garcia-Perrote, "Is International Arbitrations Ready for Smart Contract?," p. 3680.
15. According to a specialized source, the global blockchain market is projected to grow from USD 7.18 billion in 2022 to USD 163.83 billion by 2029, at a CAGR of 56.3% in forecast period, 2022-2029. See Fortune Business Insights, at https://www.fortunebusinessinsights.com/industry-reports/blockchain-market-100072 (last accessed August 19, 2022).
16. P.L. Michaelson and S.A. Jeskie, "Arbitrating Disputes Involving Blockchains, Smart Contracts, and Smart Legal Contracts," p. 100.
17. Sam Daley, "34 Blockchain Applications and Real-World Use Cases" (updated by Brenna Whithfield), August 10, 2022, at https://builtin.com/blockchain/blockchain-applications (last accessed August 16, 2022); KPMG Ireland, Strategic Blockchain Practical use cases and lost causes in the blockchain gold rush, 2022, pp. 6-9, available at https://assets.kpmg/content/dam/kpmg/ie/pdf/2022/04/ie-blockchain.pdf (last accessed August 16, 2022).

involved.[18] According to some commentators, smart contracts will revolutionize social and commercial relations and are the "beginning of the end of classic contract law."[19]

2   The Inevitable Rise of Blockchain Disputes and Their Challenges

With the development of blockchain technology and use cases, it is likely that smart contracts will become increasingly complex and capable of dealing with more sophisticated transactions. While the technology may reduce the likelihood of disputes thanks to its inherent features, the increase in blockchain-related disputes is inevitable.[20]

In the blockchain environment, disputes may be of a highly technical nature and involve complex questions pertaining to bugs in the smart contract, the underlying technology, the execution of software codes, or security vulnerabilities (the so-called on-chain disputes).[21] But disputes can also be due to humans, who write the codes and are naturally prone to errors. They may involve a link between the blockchain and the real world and may concern, e.g., the information received by the oracles, i.e., the facts underlying the transaction, by allowing human error to penetrate the blockchain ledger (the "off-chain" disputes).[22]

Furthermore, the code may not be able to encompass all contingencies for more complex contracts. Disputes may thus require some degree of human determination because they concern the validity, operation and effect of the smart contracts or the interpretation of legal terms, such as "unforeseeable', or the implementation of legal principles, such as liability, breach of contract, misrepresentation, negligence or good faith.[23]

That said, blockchain-related disputes have common characteristics that are directly linked to the nature of the technology: they are transnational, often anonymous, and relate to autonomous and immutable transactions.[24]

---

18. Johannes Landbrecht and Andreas Wehowsky, "Arbitrating Blockchain and Smart Contract Disputes: Lessons to Be Learnt from Commodities and Shipping Arbitration?," 40 ASA Bulletin (2022) p. 314.
19. Alexander Savelyev, "Contract Law 2.0. "Smart" Contracts as the Beginning of the End of Classic Contract Law," National Research University Higher School of Economics, WP BRP 71/LAW/2016.
20. M. Buchwald, "Smart Contract Dispute Resolution," p. 1371.
21. Leonel Constantino Ferreira, "La résolution des litiges *blockchain* Vers un arbitrage décentralisé?" (January 2021) p. 21, at https://papers.ssrn.com/sol3/papers.cfm?abstract_id = 3920872 (last accessed September 9, 2022).
22. Darcy W.E. Allen, Aaron M. Lane and Marta Poblet, "The Governance of Blockchain Dispute Resolution," 25 HNLR (2019), p. 82; M. Buchwald, "Smart Contract Dispute Resolution," p. 1381.
23. Falco Kreis and Markus Kaulartz, "Smart Contracts and Dispute Resolution: A Chance to Raise Efficiency?," 37 ASA Bulletin (2019) p. 339. *See also* P.L. Michaelson and S.A. Jeskie, "Arbitrating Disputes Involving Blockchains, Smart Contracts, and Smart Legal Contracts," p. 116.
24. L.C. Ferreira, "La résolution des litiges *blockchain*', p. 14.

III THE EMERGENCE OF DJS

1 The New Kids on the Block

International arbitration has positioned itself as a natural candidate to resolve blockchain-related disputes. This is not surprising given the key benefits of international arbitration, such as its cross-border nature, party autonomy, the possibility to choose arbitrators with the right expertise, confidentiality, and the enforceability of arbitral awards, which fit naturally with the nature of blockchain-related disputes.

However, some proponents of blockchain technology claim that smart contracts will render courts and arbitral tribunals obsolete.[25] For the adepts of the new economy, the reliance on a centralized third party, such as a national court or an arbitral institution, to resolve a dispute undermines the fundamentals of blockchain technology.

A number of projects based on a decentralized justice model and using blockchain technology and smart contracts are emerging. While still in their infancy, the DJS, or on-chain adjudication, decentralized applications (DApps), on-chain arbitration, blockchain arbitration—depending on the terminology used[26]—emerge as go-to mechanisms for the resolution of smart contracts and blockchain-related disputes.[27]

The DJS share the same premise: traditional systems of justice, such as litigation or international arbitration, are cumbersome, too onerous, and disconnected from the immediacy and decentralized nature of the blockchain.[28] By contrast, DJS are in line with the demands of blockchain users: they claim to be fast, fully automated, inexpensive, reliable, decentralized and suited for every kind of contract.[29]

While the DJS do not provide uniform procedures, they share some common features. Platforms such as Kleros, Jur, Aragon and CodeLegit have created protocols permitting blockchain disputes to be resolved directly on the blockchain. The protocols are encoded in the smart contract as an oracle. They allow a party to freeze the performance of the smart contract and trigger the application of the dispute resolution mechanism.[30] The systems are decentralized with no intermediaries involved and use escrow mechanisms to guarantee enforcement on the blockchain.[31]

---

25. M. Buchwald, "Smart Contract Dispute Resolution," p. 1371.
26. In this chapter, DJS is used as a generic term for the applications permitting the resolution of disputes on the blockchain. For the reasons developed herein, the author considers that the reference to "blockchain arbitration" may be misleading.
27. Matthew Townsend, "Five Web3 Predictions for the NFT Age" (May 12, 2022) Global Arbitration Review at https://globalarbitrationreview.com/article/five-web3-predictions-the-nft-age (last accessed August 9, 2022).
28. Kleros, "White Paper" at https://kleros.io/static/whitepaper_en-8bd3a0480b45c39899787e170 49ded26.pdf (last accessed August 15, 2022).
29. Ibid.
30. M. Buchwald, "Smart Contract Dispute Resolution," p. 1386.
31. M. Chevalier, "Toward the Blockchain Arbitral Order," p. 559.

Kleros is a pioneer in the field and seems to have been operational since 2019.[32] It reports more than a thousand registered disputes.[33] It describes itself as an "open source online dispute resolution protocol which uses blockchain and crowdsourcing to fairly adjudicate disputes."[34] Kleros' premise is that users who vote consistently with the majority, make money on average and those who dissent, lose money on average. This mechanism is based on the game theory model elaborated by Professor Thomas Schelling in the 1950s.

In essence, the Kleros system is organized as follows: the contract indicates a specialized court and the number of decision-makers (called jurors) for the first-instance decision.[35] As soon as a dispute arises, a notice is sent to the court. Any user of Ethereum, the blockchain on which Kleros is built, can become a juror. A juror does not need to hold any kind of expertise or reveal his or her identity. The aspiring jurors bid within Ethereum to serve on a dispute. The selection of jurors is made at random but the probability of being selected as a juror for a dispute increases with the number of tokens the juror stakes within the platform.[36]

Jurors independently analyze the evidence which is generally not limited in terms of quantity or permissible data but is uploaded in a single round onto the blockchain. They vote anonymously for the party that they think is right, without deliberation or communication among themselves. The party with the majority of votes wins. The jurors in the majority are rewarded with a bonus; those jurors who vote against the prevailing decision lose tokens. There is thus a clear economic incentive for the jurors to converge on one viewpoint.[37] According to this model, "jurors are expected to vote the true answer because they expect the other jurors to vote the true answer."[38]

Aragon follows a similar system of decisions which is not based on merits but on the party that the majority thinks is the likely winner.[39] The potential jurors post a certain amount of cryptocurrency called a "bond." The higher the bond, the higher the chances that a user will be chosen as juror.[40] The decision is made by voting for one of

32. Kleros, "White Paper" at https://kleros.io/static/whitepaper_en-8bd3a0480b45c39899787e170 49ded26.pdf (last accessed August 15, 2022).
33. Kleros, available at https://kleros.io/ (last accessed September 2, 2022).
34. Kleros, "About Kleros" available at https://kleros.io/about/ (last accessed August 15, 2022).
35. Kleros, "Dispute Revolution: The Kleros Handbook of Decentralized Justice," p. 41 at https:// kleros.io/book/ (last accessed August 16, 2022).
36. Ibid., p. 44 at p. 46 at https://kleros.io/book/ (last accessed August 16, 2022).
37. Sophie Nappert and Federico Ast, "Decentralised Justice: Reinventing Arbitration for the Digital Age?," (May 1, 2020) Global Arbitration Review at https://globalarbitrationreview.com/article /decentralised-justice-reinventing-arbitration-the-digital-age (last accessed August 4, 2022).
38. Kleros, "Dispute Revolution: The Kleros Handbook of Decentralized Justice," p. 40 at https:// kleros.io/book/ (last accessed August 16, 2022).
39. According to its website, "Aragon Court guardians are not asked to rule impartially on disputes but instead are asked to rule the way they expect the plurality of guardians to rule. Aragon Court attempts to find what the subjective truth is (i.e., the most correct outcome of a dispute) with a Schelling point." "What Is Aragon Court?," at https://documentation.aragon.org/products/ aragon-court/aragon-court (last accessed August 15, 2022).
40. Aragon White Paper, at https://github.com/aragon/whitepaper (last accessed September 1, 2022).

the predetermined possible remedies.[41] The jurors that vote like the majority will receive a share of the bonds of the jurors that cast a minority vote.[42]

CodeLegit offers a different system of blockchain dispute resolution, more akin to traditional arbitration proceedings. CodeLegit's Blockchain Arbitration Library provides a set of coded provisions to be incorporated into smart legal contracts (the "Blockchain Arbitration Rules" based on the UNCITRAL Rules), which allow the parties to pause, resume, modify and end the contract. CodeLegit also provides a database of specialized arbitrators. The arbitrator does not have to be a jurist and can be a blockchain technician. The award is self-enforced by establishing a new transaction on the blockchain.[43]

JUR promotes itself as "The New Jurisdiction for the Digital Economy,"[44] providing an answer to the problem of access to justice and offering solutions to the challenges posed by traditional dispute resolution mechanisms, in particular the length and costs of proceedings. According to JUR's website, its Open Justice Platform (OJP) is in line with the 1958 New York Convention and the UNCITRAL Model Law. It claims to be the fast and fair go-to system for "small to medium sized disputes with values of up to USD 1 million [which] can be resolved quickly and at a fraction of the cost because of the digital aspect of the platform."[45]

Most DJS provide an opportunity to appeal the decision, although under different formats and costs. They generally imply an increase in fees, with the aim to deter the parties from engaging in frivolous appeals.[46]

2   The Obstacles to a Fair and Legitimate Process

The question arises whether DJS align with the basic tenets of a fair dispute resolution process. The following elements represent the main obstacles to their recognition as legitimate dispute resolution mechanisms:

- Selection of jurors: The principle of jurors selected at random by crowdfunding is difficult to reconcile with the selection of independent and impartial arbitrators. In international arbitration, an arbitrator who has a financial interest in the dispute is immediately disqualified to resolve the dispute.[47]

---

41. *Ibid.*
42. *Ibid.*
43. "CodeLegit Conducts First Blockchain-Based Smart Contract Arbitration Proceeding" at https://datarella.com/codelegit-conducts-first-blockchain-based-smart-contract-arbitration-proceeding/ (last accessed August 25, 2022); "CodeLegit White Paper on Blockchain Arbitration" at https://docs.google.com/document/d/1v_AdWbMuc2Ei70ghlTC1mYX4_5VQsF_28O4PsLckNM4/edit, p. 3 (last accessed August 25, 2022).
44. < Jur - Network State > (last accessed August 25, 2022).
45. JUR, "White Paper 3: The Open Justice Platform and the Justice Problem in the Pandemic" at https://jur.io/blog/white-paper-3-the-open-justice-platform-and-the-justice-problem-in-the-pandemic/ (last accessed August 25, 2022.
46. M. Buchwald, "Smart Contract Dispute Resolution," p. 1391.
47. IBA Guidelines on conflict of interests in international arbitration, Articles 1.3 and 1.4.

- Integrity of the process: a system where jurors have a financial interest in the outcome may seem hard to reconcile with the requirements of impartiality and independence of arbitrators. According to one of Kleros' funders, however, the "game theory" mechanism is what ensures that potential jurors perform their duties in a professional and honest manner.[48] Yet, a majority vote is not necessarily equivalent to a vote for the correct legal result.[49] This increases the risks of inconsistent, incorrect or arbitrary decisions.[50]
- Due process: this is the cornerstone of most dispute resolution systems, including international arbitration.[51] Some DJS report that compliance with due process is a "built-in feature" of the protocol.[52] However, criticisms are raised, in particular in relation to evidence, where the discovery process is often limited to parties unilaterally uploading what they deem fit, including an optional "submission," with no opportunity for rebuttal, further clarifications or orders for document production.[53]

Last but not least, the success of a mechanism for dispute resolution is often judged on its ability to enforce its decisions. While directly enforceable on the blockchain, it is doubtful that the decisions arising out of DJS qualify as international arbitral awards within the meaning of the New York Convention. DJS decisions may be difficult to reconcile with the territorial approach and the idea of circulation of awards among member states of the Convention since they do not emanate from a specific seat (unless one is specified).[54] For the same reasons, DJS proceedings and awards escape from the supervision of national courts.[55]

Other obstacles to enforcement relate to the coded nature of the decision, which may be problematic in light of the requirement to produce a duly authenticated original award under Article IV(1)(a) New York Convention, or to the inability to identify the parties to the proceedings, given that they are usually unknown or use pseudonyms.

Adaptations could be considered to reduce some of the issues identified. Smart contracts could incorporate a choice-of-law provision, which would avoid decisions based only on the perception of other jurors' judgments and provide a legal framework for the decision-making process.[56] Due consideration should also be given to the arbitration agreement included in the smart contracts and the choice of seat by making

48. S. Nappert and F. Ast, "Decentralised Justice," at https://globalarbitrationreview.com/article/decentralised-justice-reinventing-arbitration-the-digital-age (last accessed August 4, 2022).
49. M. Buchwald, "Smart Contract Dispute Resolution', p. 1404.
50. *Ibid.*, p. 1408.
51. Joe Tirado and Gabriela Cosio, "Lex Cryptographia: Guidelines for Ensuring Due Process in Transnational Blockchain-Based Arbitration" (March 4, 2022) at https://www.ibanet.org/lex-cryptographia-due-process-blockchain-based-arbitration (last accessed August 16, 2022).
52. Kleros, "Dispute Revolution: The Kleros Handbook of Decentralized Justice," p. 277 at https://kleros.io/book/ (last accessed August 16, 2022). According to Kleros, "stages such as proper notice of the parties, the composition of the jurors' tribunal, exchange of evidence and comments of the parties are executed automatically by smart contracts. As a result, Kleros rulings are a hard target for judicial review."
53. M. Buchwald, "Smart Contract Dispute Resolution," pp. 1394 et seq.
54. M. Chevalier, "Toward the Blockchain Arbitral Order," p. 569.
55. *Ibid.*, p. 570.
56. M. Buchwald, "Smart Contract Dispute Resolution," p. 1421.

sure that the law of the seat recognizes the validity of smart contracts and the arbitration agreement contained therein.

To the author's knowledge, only one reported case relates to the enforcement of a Kleros decision "off-chain." In this case, which is reported by Kleros itself, a Mexican court enforced for the first time an arbitral award relying on the Kleros protocol.[57] The dispute arose out of a lease agreement for a property in Mexico which was subject to Mexican law and provided for arbitration by a sole arbitrator, who was required to refer the dispute to the Kleros protocol for decision on the merits. Three jurors (whose identity is unknown) rendered a short decision containing summary reasons. The sole arbitrator incorporated the Kleros decision in the award. Subsequently, the landlord sought enforcement of the award before a Mexican state court.[58] According to Kleros, the court enforced the award without providing specific reasons relating to the nature of the decision or whether the decision respected the parties' due process rights.

This unique decision enforcing an award resulting from a hybrid process provides little guidance as to the possibility to enforce DJS decisions in the real world and whether such mechanisms can be used for non-digital assets. Without proper data available, the role that DJS (will) play in the world of blockchain disputes remains difficult to assess.

IV   CONCLUSION: A NECESSARY (R)EVOLUTION?

The use of cryptocurrencies and smart contracts on a wide scale is giving rise to a growing number of disputes, which present new legal and technical challenges for their resolution.

DJS take a radical new approach to the resolution of blockchain-related disputes. They introduce protocols encoded in smart contracts for the resolution of blockchain disputes and offer a dispute resolution process in line with the principles of blockchain technology, i.e., decentralized, fully automated, inexpensive and immediately enforceable on the blockchain. Some DJS provide for the selection of jurors based on the number of tokens they stake, offer a decision-making process driven by financial gain, and limit the evidence-taking process. As a result, the DJS offer a system that has little to do with the basic tenets of a fair and impartial dispute resolution process.

DJS are just emerging, and many are still in the development stage. As a result, no empirical data demonstrating the attractiveness of the DJS are available. They may

---

57. Mauricio Virues Carrera, "Accommodating Kleros as a Decentralised Dispute Resolution Tool for Civil Justice Systems: Theoretical Model and Case of Application," https://ipfs.kleros.io/ipfs/QmfNrgSVE9bb17KzEVFoGf4KKA1Ekaht7ioLjYzheZ6prE/Accommodating%20Kleros%20as%20a%20Decentralized%20Dispute%20Resolution%20Tool%20for%20Civil%20Justice%20Systems%20-%20Theoretical%20Model%20and%20Case%20of%20Application%20-%20Maur icio%20Virues%20-%20Kleros%20Fellowship%20of%20Justice.pdf (last accessed on September 1, 2022).
58. Maxime Chevalier, "Arbitration Tech Toolbox: Is a Mexican Court Decision the First Stone to Bridging the Blockchain Arbitral Order with the National Legal Orders?" (March 4, 2022) Kluwer Arbitration Blog at http://arbitrationblog.kluwerarbitration.com/2022/03/04/arbitration-tech-toolbox-is-a-mexican-court-decision-the-first-stone-to-bridging-the-blockchain-arbitral-order-w ith-national-legal-orders/ (last accessed August 29, 2022).

prove useful in resolving low-value disputes on simple facts or clear contractual obligations on the blockchain in an efficient and cost-effective manner. In the future, they may even capture a number of disputes unrelated to the new economy which would otherwise remain unresolved. For parties involved in small-scale disputes, the risks relating to the integrity of the process or due process considerations may be less critical compared with the advantages of simplicity, immediacy and efficiency of the process.

However, in the current state of their development, DJS are inadequate for more complex smart contract disputes requiring extensive review of evidence and an analysis by decision-makers familiar with the issues in dispute and the underlying law.[59] For these disputes, traditional dispute resolution mechanisms such as international arbitration should remain the norm.

Ultimately, it will be for the parties to choose the method that fits best with their needs in an increasingly on-chain world, bearing in mind the values that blockchain technology carries. The success of smart contracts and the development of technology in the future will dictate whether DJS can transform into a legitimate and reliable mechanism for the resolution of smart contract disputes.

---

59. *Ibid.*, p. 1412.

Artificial Intelligence and the Face of the Arbitrations of Tomorrow

Kathryn Khamsi[*]

TABLE OF CONTENTS

I   INTRODUCTION

I was tasked for ICCA 2022 to speak to 'artificial intelligence in international arbitration' (AI in IA). It is a subject that bears addressing from multiple angles. In one direction, one can consider the use of international arbitration to resolve AI and other technology disputes; for instance, much interest has been said about using arbitration to resolve cryptocurrency or smart contract disputes.[1] From the other direction – considering how artificial intelligence can be deployed in international arbitration – one can consider the use of artificial intelligence in document production,[2] or the use

---

[*] Partner at Three Crowns LLP.

1. The subject was, for instance, the subject of a recent webinar hosted by the Singapore International Arbitration Centre: see 'ArbXTalk – Session 1 and Cryptocurrency, Blockchain And NFTs ("CBNFT") – What Do They Mean For Arbitration Practitioners', YSIAC Conference 2021.
2. It is a subject that I addressed at the most recent ICC Institute Annual Conference, on the panel 'Retiring the Redfern schedule: document production and the need for new models', November 2021, Paris. *See also* K. Khamsi, 'Compliance with Document Production Orders: Traditional Paradigm and New Questions', Proceedings of the ICC Institute, forthcoming 2022.

of artificial intelligence to predict the outcome of arbitrations.[3] Much important thinking remains to be done on all of those subjects, and my co-panellists have the ground well covered. So in this piece, I will consider a topic that has received somewhat less attention: the role that AI-based technology can play in establishing the merits of a claim.

For context, I will first describe the technology (section II) and consider how it might be deployed in establishing or testing the merits of a claim (section III). The majority of this piece will then consider how that may change the 'face' of arbitration (section IV).

II   THE TECHNOLOGY

In April 2010, the following diagram appeared on the front page of the New York Times.[4]

---

3. *See, e.g.*, H. Carlson, 'AI as Facilitator and Disruptor', ICCA 2018; M. Scherer, 'Artificial Intelligence and Legal Decision-Making: The Wide Open? A Study Examining International Arbitration', Kluwer Law International BV 2019; L. Reed, 'AI vs IA: End of the Enlightenment?'; *see* Chapter 5 AI Versus IA: End of the Enlightenment? by Lucy Reed in this volume.
4. E. Bumiller, 'We Have Met the Enemy and He Is PowerPoint', New York Times, 26 April 2010.

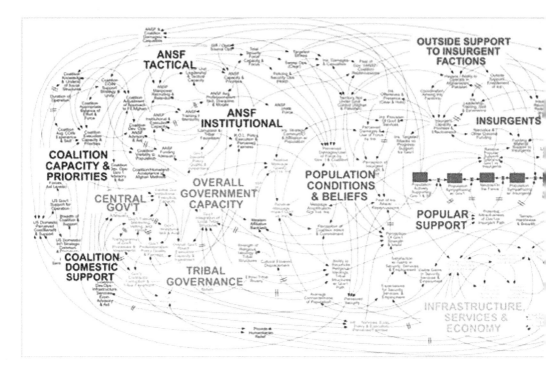

This was in the throes of the US army's 'surge' in Afghanistan. According to the article, the diagram – reproduced on a PowerPoint slide – was shown to General Stanley McChrystal. The reader may remember General McChrystal – he was the leader of American and NATO forces in Afghanistan at the time. And apparently, or so the article reports, McChrystal said: 'When we understand that slide, we'll have won the war.' We now know how that turned out, but that is a subject for another time.

For present purposes, I note the piece because of the underlying technology. The title of the article was: 'We Have Met the Enemy and He Is PowerPoint'. In fact, though, the diagram is not a PowerPoint diagram. It was generated by a methodology called 'system dynamics' – also known as 'dynamic simulation'. And it is interesting for present purposes because system dynamics relies on artificial intelligence, and is a type of modelling that can be deployed (and that I have deployed) to establish the merits of a claim.

To understand how that type of modelling can be deployed, and the new issues it may raise in the arbitrations of tomorrow, the reader will need to understand how it works. I will use the Afghanistan example to that end since the matter in which I deployed system dynamics is confidential; I confess also to finding the Afghanistan example particularly interesting, having spent two years living and working in Kabul.

The above diagram is a visual depiction of a system dynamics model (the diagram can be created automatically using the system dynamics software). In the event, it is a model of the various factors then affecting NATO coalition efforts in Afghanistan. As such, one sees things like: NATO coalition capacity (in black on the left); the tactical and institutional capacity of the Afghan national security force (at the top and to the right); and outside support to the insurgents (on the top right) – at the time, mostly Taliban (ISIS came later).

The model represents in mathematical form how the various factors influence each other, and ultimately how they influence the success of NATO efforts. Each line in the diagram represents a mathematical equation in the model. For instance, a line going from outside support to insurgents – and another line going from narcotics to insurgents – means that both are influencing the success of the insurgents in the model. And as can be seen from the diagram above, some of the relationships are circular; this form of modelling can capture 'feedback' loops, which is why it is referred to as *dynamic* simulation.

For purposes of our discussion, one also needs to understand a bit about how one creates these models. As is typical of AI, a tremendous amount of data is used. However, the data is not an input to the model. Rather, one builds the model by first investigating the parts of the system; and by hypothesizing as to the relationships between those parts. That hypothesis is then tested against the benchmark of the data and is refined in an iterative process until the model can independently reproduce the data.

To illustrate the Afghanistan model and stay with the above relationships, the model builders started with interviews of knowledgeable individuals. They will have heard multiple times that support from Pakistan, compounded by opium money, strengthens the Taliban. The modellers would therefore have created a first version of the model reflecting these basic dynamics. The next question the modellers would have asked is: how much and how do those factors strengthen the Taliban? Basically, the modellers reflect an educated guess in the first instance. That guess is then checked against the data; adjusted if it does not independently reproduce the data; and checked and adjusted again and again in an iterative process until the model does reproduce the data.

Once the model independently reproduces the data (and assuming the right data is used, a subject to which I return below), the idea is that the model is reliably capturing the dynamics of the system. That is interesting – including for arbitration – because once a model is reliably capturing the dynamics of the system, and reliably reproducing what actually happened, one can use it to determine what will happen in alternative scenarios. For the NATO model, the idea was to determine what policies and military strategies would be most effective in combatting the insurgency in Afghanistan. Is it a surge of military troops; or increasing the capacity of the government; or combatting the opium trade; or some combination of the three? Thus, the idea was to determine what would happen in various scenarios *in the future*. But one can also use a dynamic simulation model to determine what would have happened in alternative scenarios *in the past*. And that is perhaps particularly interesting for arbitration because we frequently have to answer 'what if'-type questions in relation to past events.

III WHEN TO DEPLOY: ANSWERS TO 'WHAT IF' QUESTIONS

One would be hard-pressed to identify an arbitration that does not require the tribunal to answer at least one 'what if'-type question.

Perhaps the most common of those questions arise in relation to remedies. That is because most legal systems – including the international one – require a respondent to remedy a breach, and in so doing to place the claimant in the situation it would have been in 'but for' the breach. To illustrate, the International Law Commission's (ILC) Articles on State Responsibility (which are understood to capture the relevant international law principles), provide in Article 31 ('Reparation') that:

> 1. The responsible State is under an obligation to make full *reparation for the injury caused by the internationally wrongful act.*
> 2. Injury includes any damage, whether material or moral, *caused by the internationally wrongful act* of a State.

Article 31 thus poses a causation question. And while answering that question may be simple in some cases, it may be prohibitively difficult in others – for example, in cases involving the impact of disruption on complex first-of-a-kind infrastructure projects. It is in those cases that the causation analysis may be assisted by AI-based tools.

Those same tools can also address 'what if'-type questions relating to the establishment of breach. Like many others, I have spent quite some time considering the various cases arising out of Argentina's 2001 financial crisis, including the near-identical cases in the gas transportation and distribution sector.[5] All of those cases considered the application of Article 25 of the ILC Articles, which sets out the defence of necessity at international law. The principles will be well known to the reader. I recall them here, to underline the 'what if' question that the language poses. Article 25 provides:

> 1. *Necessity may not be invoked* by a State as a ground for precluding the wrongfulness of an act not in conformity with an international obligation of that State *unless the act:*
>   (a) *is the only way for the State to safeguard an essential interest against a grave and imminent peril*; and
>   (b) does not seriously impair an essential interest of the State or States towards which the obligation exists, or of the international community as a whole.
> 2. In any case, necessity may not be invoked by a State as a ground for precluding wrongfulness if:
>   (a) the international obligation in question excludes the possibility of invoking necessity; or
>   (b) the State has contributed to the situation of necessity.[6]

Thus, Article 25 – and specifically its first paragraph – requires consideration of what would have happened if the State had taken measures less restrictive of the claimant's rights. More specifically, Article 25(1) requires consideration of whether such measures would have been sufficient to safeguard the relevant State interest against a grave and imminent peril.

That can be quite a difficult question to answer, as we saw in the Argentine cases. Indeed, what is perhaps most remarkable about those cases is how little attention is given in the awards to answering that fundamental question. What follows is an excerpt from the first of the awards, in the claim brought by CMS:

> A different issue, however, is whether the measures adopted were the 'only way' for the State to safeguard its interests. This is indeed debatable. The views of the parties and distinguished economists are wide apart on this matter, ranging from the support of those measures to the discussion of a variety of alternatives, including dollarization of the economy, granting of direct subsidies to the affected population or industries and many others. Which of these policy alternatives would have been better is a decision beyond the scope of the Tribunal's task, which is to establish whether there was only one way or various ways and thus whether the requirements for the preclusion of wrongfulness have or have not been met.
>
> The International Law Commission's comment to the effect that the plea of necessity is 'excluded if there are other (otherwise lawful) means available, even

5. K. Khamsi, 'Compensation for Non-expropriatory Investment Treaty Breaches in the Argentine Gas Sector Cases: Issues and Implications', in: *The Backlash Against Investment Arbitration: Perceptions and Reality* (Kluwer, 2010); J.E. Alvarez and K. Khamsi, 'The Argentine Crisis and Foreign Investors: A Glimpse into the Heart of the Investment Regime', *Yearbook on International Investment Law & Policy* (Oxford, 2009).
6. International Law Commission, Draft articles on Responsibility of States for Internationally Wrongful Acts, with commentaries, UN Doc. No. A/56/10, Yearbook of the International Law Commission, 2001.

if they may be more costly or less convenient,' is persuasive in assisting this Tribunal in concluding that the measures adopted were not the only steps available.[7]

That is the full extent of the tribunal's analysis of the fundamental question posed by Article 25, which is remarkable. It may be that the tribunal did not feel equipped by the evidence to answer in any greater detail. This would perhaps not be surprising, given that answering the question in any greater detail would have required the tribunal to determine the impact of alternative economic measures on a complex macroeconomic system, in which not only domestic but also international forces were at play.

It is in relation to that type of question that one might envisage looking to AI in international arbitration. And there is no shortage of disputes raising similarly challenging questions as to how impugned action or inaction may have affected the behaviour of complex systems. To name only a few topical examples, one is already seeing – or can readily envisage – disputes relating to climate change; epidemiology (e.g., Ebola, COVID); and forestry management.

The question, then, becomes: what will be the impact of using AI-based evidence on the face of arbitration?

IV   AI IN IA: THE FACE OF THE ARBITRATIONS OF TOMORROW

It would be a vast overstatement to claim that arbitration will be revolutionized by the use of AI-based evidence. But there will inevitably be an evolution in the types of arguments advanced and how they are put. I consider, below, three features of these arbitrations of tomorrow: challenges to the new methodology (1), arguments about model boundaries, data and its processing (2), and logistical issues relating to the presentation of evidence (3).

1   Challenges to the Methodology

History teaches that dispute resolution has a natural tendency to conservatism, sticking to tried and true methods and methodologies. This reflex against change extends to new technologies: they are not readily adopted upon their introduction but rather are typically subject to challenge. One can expect the same as and when AI-based tools are introduced. And those challenges can, of course, be more or less blunt.

At their bluntest, the opponent may try to avoid engaging with the technology altogether. One can expect this in particular where the new technology will measure or reveal facts that traditional techniques will ignore, as is the case for system dynamics. An adversary may therefore deploy a 'traditional' expert using the old techniques that suit its case. The testimony from that expert will be essentially this: since your new methodology does not do what my traditional methodology does, or does not do it in

---

7. *CMS Transmission Co. v. Argentine Republic*, ICSID Case No. ARB/01/8 (US-Argentina BIT), Award, 12 May 2005, ¶¶ 323-324.

the same way, it must be wrong or otherwise unreliable. On one of our matters, we managed to demonstrate the fundamentally false premise of this 'traditional' expert approach using an analogy to the Battle of Britain: the expert conceded that the invention of radar had been a game-changer for locating inbound aircraft, but admitted that he would have been 'the guy' looking out through the fog over the Channel, saying there were no planes if he could not see them with his binoculars.

Whether and to what extent such an argument will get traction is hard to say; it will undoubtedly depend on the tribunal's constitution. In any event, there are less blunt means of methodological attack that I anticipate will be more prevalent, at least as the new technology is introduced. The attack may, for instance, take the form of an allegation that the methodology lacks sufficient 'transparency' or is a 'black box'.

When one uses standard software – Excel, say – one does not have to prove that the software works. And although not everyone may understand *how* the software works – like: who can say how Excel's 'goal seek' works? What is the programming behind it? – one does not typically have opponents claiming that Excel is a 'black box'.

Ironically, though, the more sophisticated the analysis, the more prone it is to such an attack – at least, in my experience. One example: as noted, a system dynamics model will represent relationships in mathematical form. Our opponent made a great fuss about the alleged complexity of the equations in the model that our experts had presented. In particular, they had complained in their pleadings about the use of so-called dimensionless measures, terminology that of course suggests something ephemeral and unknowable. This was pressed again in their examination of our experts. But in cross-examination of their experts, we were able to debunk the idea that there is anything particularly unknowable or unreliable about a 'dimensionless measure': a percentage, for instance, is a 'dimensionless measure'.

Since AI-based tools are fundamentally knowable, I anticipate that most 'black box'-type arguments will have a response, albeit perhaps not so simple a response. But that will leave more profound questions – and potential sources of attack – in relation to the data used in model creation.

2   Data and Other Evidentiary Issues: 'Garbage In, Garbage Out'

The reader will be aware that artificial intelligence relies on large amounts of data. The reader will also be familiar with the maxim 'garbage in, garbage out' and have heard their fair share of 'garbage in, garbage out'-type arguments in arbitration. It is precisely that type of argument that one can expect when deploying AI in arbitration, given its reliance on large amounts of data. And that type of argument can take various forms, relating among other things to the scope of the model, the choice of data and its processing, and whether or not witness evidence is required for model hypotheses that are tested against the data. I consider each, in turn, using the NATO Afghanistan model to illustrate.

There will inevitably be debates about a model's scope – or the model's 'boundaries', in the parlance. To illustrate: the scope of the NATO Afghanistan model can be seen by looking at its elements, each of which is labelled in the diagram above.

For instance, the model captures what is referred to as 'outside support to insurgent factions'. Presumably, that would have covered support from Pakistan and Iran. However, the model does not appear to differentiate between the support coming from Pakistan and Iran, although they have traditionally supported different insurgent factions in Afghanistan. Neither does the model attempt to capture in a dynamic way how internal politics in Pakistan or Iran are affecting support by those countries to the insurgents. The model's boundaries, in essence, correspond to the boundaries of Afghanistan. In an arbitration, an adversary might allege that that makes the model unreliable because the model is too limited in scope to identify what is really driving NATO's prospects of success in Afghanistan. For instance, that adversary would say, the model cannot tell us whether a comprehensive agreement between the US and Iran – or an agreement relating to, say, nuclear weapons – will help NATO in Afghanistan.

That question of scope is strongly related to the question of what data to use, which in turn is also driven by the question of whether that data can be processed for use in modelling. Both are fundamental questions given that the data is used as a benchmark for the model, but both are potentially quite vexing.

As it stands, system dynamics has been deployed principally in complex con-struction arbitrations involving allegations of delay and disruption. In such arbitra-tions, one will typically be measuring progress on tasks, and resources and time spent to achieve progress. There may be data that correlates relatively well with what one wants to measure: regular reporting of progress; recorded labour hours. Even there, though, there may be challenges. For instance, there may be imperfections in the data: people may be slow about recording their labour, or do it in a lump at year-end; or, data may not exist for some periods or places. That data needs to be 'smoothed'; and how that is done can be quite contentious, as well as unfamiliar to a typical tribunal.

Then of course there will be situations where there is no clear data set for model elements, creating an even greater scope for challenge. That will, for instance, have been the case for many of the elements of the NATO Afghanistan model. Under the rubric of modelling 'overall government capacity', one assumes that the modellers will have attempted to model the strength of the judicial system and respect for the rule of law. Yet one was hard-pressed at the time even to find written decisions from the judiciary. And even if the modellers had had a complete body of jurisprudence, one can readily see how reducing that to a data set for modelling purposes might be controver-sial: how does one count respect for the rule of law?

Last point, still on the 'garbage in, garbage out' theme: as noted, a model will be based initially on hypotheses about the system being modelled. Practically speaking, that means that expert modellers are going to have to rely – at least in the first instance – on input from people knowledgeable about the system. For the Afghanistan model, the experts themselves interviewed knowledgeable individuals (from the Aga Khan Foundation, I understand). Initial hypotheses may also come from counsel.

The question, then, is this: does one need to evidence those hypotheses in an arbitration? Our instinct as lawyers may be 'yes': if an expert relies on a position unless it is *de minimis* or self-evident, then it typically needs to be evidenced. But the answer from the AI field is arguably 'no', and for two reasons. First, the positions are overtaken by the modelling process itself: as noted, the hypotheses in the model are adjusted until the models can independently recreate the data. And second, the fact that the model recreates the data is itself arguably the proof of the model hypotheses, as adjusted. Which of course then underscores the importance of arguments as to whether one has used the right data.

3   Logistics

The final point that bears noting about the face of the arbitrations of tomorrow is perhaps a more mundane one, relating to the logistics of presenting evidence in relation to AI-based analyses.

We arbitration practitioners are not the most tech-forward bunch: we have only recently moved away from paper filings (thanks notably to the Green Arbitration Pledge), and we have all more or less mastered Zoom ('thanks' notably to COVID). But the reality is that our evidence still looks much like what it looked like a generation ago (mostly written documents, albeit now provided in electronic format, and with some Excel spreadsheets in the mix), as does our manner of testing that evidence and recording that testimony (mostly in written transcripts with only words; no images, much less video). That little has changed was underscored for me by a recent experience: I had prepared questions for the opposing expert about the assumptions inherent in the 'macros' of his Excel model ('macros' being the math behind the model). The approach was so unexpected that the expert was unable to answer the questions: a junior had designed the model, and the expert had never looked at the macros.

As technology becomes more sophisticated, though, so too must counsel. Inevitably, there will be points that can only be made – or at least can only be made compellingly, or in a manner that effectively 'pins down' the witness or expert – 'live' in the software.

That then gives rise to logistical questions about the performance and recording of hearing testimony. In particular, it really is not that effective to record in words an examination involving live modelling in the software. The approach presumes that tribunal members will, using the words, themselves recreate the live modelling if necessary to recall what was accomplished. It would be much more effective to have a video recording of the modelling or at least a visual snapshot of the results.

Indeed, it may be that these more mundane logistical changes are the most revolutionary changes that we might anticipate to the 'face' of arbitration. Time will tell.

PANEL 12   New Frontiers II: The Subject
Matters of the Disputes of Tomorrow

CHAPTER 42

Harmonious Interpretation of Investment Treaties and International Human Rights Instruments Considering the Climate Change

Değer Boden[*]

TABLE OF CONTENTS

I   INTRODUCTION

Climate change is not a threat to the future anymore,[1] it is a reality and already harming our lives. Climate change has detrimental consequences on a wide range of universally

---

*   Managing Partner of Boden Law. She received her Law degree (LL.B) from Galatasaray Univer-
    sity, School of Law (2000). She holds an LL.M. degree in International Business Law from the
    University of Minnesota, School of Law (2005) and another LL.M. degree in Law of Economics
    from Istanbul Bilgi University, School of Law (2004). She is a member of the Advisory Board of the
    Center for Energy and Sustainable Development (CESD) of Kadir Has University in Istanbul. She
    is Chair of the Energy Commission of Istanbul Arbitration Center (ISTAC). I would like to thank
    ICCA for giving me this opportunity.
1. "The IPCC Special Report on Global Warming of 1.5°C," Sect. Summary for Policy Makers,
    (October 2018) (the IPCC Special Report), p. 15, it states that "it will 'require rapid and
    far-reaching transitions of energy, land, urban and infrastructure (including transport and

recognized fundamental rights, such as the rights to life, food, adequate housing, health, and water.[2] Therefore, climate change itself affects human rights.[3]

Foreign investments protected by bilateral investment treaties (BITs) and other investment treaties entail a considerable risk to the climate. Foreign investment has a positive impact on economic growth in host states. However, it also leads to environmental degradation.[4] While the number of BITs including treaties with investment provisions are exceeding 3,000 and foreign investments are significantly increasing,[5] our world is greatly suffering from climate change. Accordingly, international investment law and climate change inevitably inter-react. International investments not only risk the climate but eventually, each and every human right specified by the Universal Declaration of Human Rights (UDHR). While corporations' investment activities have detrimental impacts on human rights and climate, only states are held accountable for human rights violations under international law. Human rights are increasingly in conflict with the rights of foreign investments and there is a clear need for coordination between human rights and international investment law.[6]

The first-generation BITs have been criticized as being one-sided and asymmetric, protecting only the interests of the investors and bringing obligations only to the states, not to the investors. The criticism was mostly related with regards to the negative effects of foreign investments on the environment and human rights. They have been criticized for not holding investors accountable for the environmental, social and economic consequences of their activities. Conventionally, investment arbitration

buildings) and industrial systems' to avoid the worst effects of climate change," available at https://www.ipcc.ch/site/assets/uploads/sites/2/2019/05/SR15_SPM_version_report_LR.pdf (last accessed April 8, 2022).

2. "Understanding Human Rights and Climate Change," Submission of the Office of the High Commissioner, "News and Events: Climate Change and for Human Rights," to the 21st Conference of the Parties to the United Nations Framework Convention on Climate Change, available at https://www.ohchr.org/sites/default/files/Documents/Issues/ClimateChange/COP21.pdf (last accessed April 10, 2022).

3. UN Environment Programme, "News and Stories: Human rights are at threat from climate change, but can also provide solutions," it states that "according to climate change experts climate change and its impacts threaten a broad range of human rights and as a result states and private actors have extensive human rights obligations and responsibilities," available at https://www.unenvironment.org/news-and-stories/story/human-rights-are-threat-climate-change-can-also-provide-solutions (last accessed April 10, 2022).

4. Anh Hoang To, Dao Thi-Thieu Ha, Ha Minh Nguyen and Duc Hong Vo, "The Impact of Foreign Direct Investment on Environment Degradation. Evidence from Emerging Markets in Asia," May 10, 2019, Int. J. Environ. Res. Public Health, available at https://www.ncbi.nlm.nih.gov/pmc/articles/PMC6539116/ (last accessed August 10, 2022). The study shows the correlation between economic growth and environmental degradation and emission growth. According to the study, they are in positive correlation until the level of industrialization. Only once a country has been industrialized, then investment is directed towards less carbon-intensive industries.

5. UNCTAD, International Investment Agreements Navigator, statistics shows while the number of effective BITs is 2231, that of *treaties with investment provisions* (TIPs) is 335, available at https://investmentpolicy.unctad.org/international-investment-agreements (last accessed August 14, 2022).

6. Christina Binder, "The UNDRIP's Relationship to Existing International Law, Ch. 4, The UNDRIP and Interactions with International Investment Law," from the UN Declaration on the Rights of Indigenous Peoples: A Commentary, edited by Jessie Hohmann and Marc Weller, March 22, 2018, it analyses the same question from the perspective of indigenous peoples' rights.

has always been a tool for investors to hold States liable.[7] It is now undisputed that there is a need to rebalance BITs considering public interests such as environmental rights and human rights.

This chapter aims to analyze whether it is mandatory to have hard law instruments to ensure the coordination between human rights and international investment law considering climate change.

This chapter argues the following basic point: Although lawmaking seems to be the best approach, a harmonious interpretation of investment treaties and international human rights instruments by arbitral tribunals might be a solution to the rebalancing need.

This chapter is organized as follows: section II elaborates on climate change, its consequences and its interaction with human rights, while section III examines in which situations climate change and investment arbitration interact. Section IV discusses which tools are available to rebalance foreign investor rights and human rights.

II   CLIMATE CHANGE

1   Climate Change Facts

There is a scientific consensus that climate change is caused by human activity.[8] As known, greenhouse gas emissions, primarily CO_2 emissions cause global warming.[9] Today, global warming is at $1.1\,°C$. According to the reports of the Intergovernmental Panel on Climate Change, if global warming reaches $2\,°C$, climate change will reach an irreversible level. The reports suggest that stabilizing greenhouse gases in the atmosphere at a level of about 450 ppm in 2,100 would give us a chance of more than 50% in order for the rise in global warming to remain below $2\,°C$.

As also known, parties to the Paris Agreement agreed to try to limit global warming to "well below" $2\,°C$. According to the Paris Agreement, the ideal scenario is to limit it to $1.5\,°C$. In this regard, signatories of the Paris Agreement declare nationally determined contributions (NDCs). However, according to studies, the NDCs of the parties to the Paris Agreement are insufficient for limiting global warming to $1.5\,°C$.[10] In order to limit global warming to $1.5\,°C$, global greenhouse gas emissions need to be

---

7. Saarthak Jain, "Bridging the Gap Between Investment Arbitrations and Environmental Concerns: Can Inclusion of Counterclaims Help?," March 26, 2019, it states that "Investor-state arbitrations have been generally viewed as a "one-way street," available at http://blogs2.law.columbia.edu /aria/bridging-the-gap-between-investment-arbitrations-and-environmental-concerns-can-inclu sion-of-counterclaims-help/ (last accessed April 11, 2022).
8. https://www.theguardian.com/science/2019/jul/24/scientific-consensus-on-humans-causing-global-warming-passes-99 (last accessed July 22, 2022).
9. The Hague District Court, the Judgment of May 26, 2021, case number/cause list number: C/09/571932 / HA ZA 19-379 ("*Milieudefensie et al versus ROYAL DUTCH SHELL PLC*"), available at http://climatecasechart.com/wp-content/uploads/sites/16/non-us-case-documents /2021/20210526_8918_judgment-1.pdf, p. 6 (last accessed August 14, 2022).
10. *Milieudefensie et al. v. ROYAL DUTCH SHELL PLC*, p. 11. Also *see* "Climate Commitments Not on Track to Meet Paris Agreement Goals" as NDC Synthesis Report is Published, February 26,

reduced by 45 % by 2030 in comparison to 2010 and by 100 % by 2050.[11] While climate change is already affecting humans and ecosystems, with the steady increase of global warming, the risks would be even greater such as food insecurity, water scarcity, deterioration of water quality, droughts, floods, loss of biodiversity, loss of species and sea-level rise.[12]

2   Interrelationship Between Climate Change and Human Rights

The UN Human Rights Council (UNHRC) having been raising awareness of the links between human rights and climate change has adopted several resolutions on climate change over the years. In its 2008 resolution, the UNHRC stated that climate change "poses an immediate and far-reaching threat to people and communities around the world" and in its 2009 resolution, the UNHRC noted that "climate change-related impacts have a range of implications, both direct and indirect, for the effective enjoyment of human rights ... ." Climate change is considered to be the most pervasive threat to the environmental and human rights.[13] As it has adverse effects on clean water, natural resources, food and other basic needs,[14] has detrimental consequences on a wide range of universally recognized fundamental rights, such as the rights to life,[15] food, adequate housing, health, and water.[16] Therefore, climate change itself affects human rights.[17] The UNHRC recently adopted a resolution recognizing that a clean, healthy, and sustainable environment is a human right.[18] Although it is not binding, it is likely to have a catalyst effect to hold countries and companies liable.

2021, available at https://unfccc.int/news/climate-commitments-not-on-track-to-meet-paris-agreement-goals-as-ndc-synthesis-report-is-published (last accessed August 10, 2022).

11. *Milieudefensie et al. v. ROYAL DUTCH SHELL PLC,* p. 11. Also *see* "Climate Commitments Not on Track to Meet Paris Agreement Goals" as NDC Synthesis Report is Published, February 26, 2021, available at https://unfccc.int/news/climate-commitments-not-on-track-to-meet-paris-agreement-goals-as-ndc-synthesis-report-is-published (last accessed August 10, 2022).

12. UNEP's Report on Climate Change and Human Rights, p. 7 available at https://wedocs.unep.org/bitstream/handle/20.500.11822/9530/-Climate_Change_and_Human_Rightshuman-rights-climate-change.pdf.pdf?sequence = 2&%3BisAllowed (last accessed August 14, 2022). Also *see* https://www.cfr.org/backgrounder/paris-global-climate-change-agreements (last accessed August 14, 2022).

13. UNEP's Report on Climate Change and Human Rights, p. 1.

14. UNEP's Report on Climate Change and Human Rights, p. 1.

15. Extreme whether events, drought, increased heat are considered as threats to the enjoyment of right to life.

16. "Understanding Human Rights and Climate Change," Submission of the Office of the High Commissioner for Human Rights to the 21st Conference of the Parties to the United Nations Framework Convention on Climate Change, available at https://www.ohchr.org/sites/default/files/Documents/Issues/ClimateChange/COP21.pdf (last accessed April 10, 2022).

17. UN Environment Programme, "News and Stories: Human rights are at threat from climate change, but can also provide solutions," it states that "according to climate change experts climate change and its impacts threaten a broad range of human rights and as a result states and private actors have extensive human rights obligations and responsibilities," available at https://www.unenvironment.org/news-and-stories/story/human-rights-are-threat-climate-change-can-also-provide-solutions (last accessed April 10, 2022).

18. https://news.un.org/en/story/2021/10/1102582 (last accessed August 10, 2022).

III CLIMATE CHANGE AND INVESTMENT ARBITRATION INTERACTION

Climate change and investment arbitration interact not only to hold states liable for breach of their environmental commitments[19] but also for climate change-related regulatory measures implemented by the States. Investors also bring cases against damages to the environment by a State.[20] In addition, States started to bring counterclaims against damages to the environment by the investors. As this chapter aims to show the instances where there is a need for rebalance between private and public benefits, it focuses only on the claims by investors against a state's climate change-related measures and states' counterclaims against damages to the environment by the investors where the rebalance need is more obvious.

1 Claims by the Investors Against States' Climate Change-Related Measures

The first interaction showing the rebalancing need between the environment and investor rights occurs when investors (mostly carbon-intensive investors) challenge the environmental measures of the States. Investment treaties are used by carbon-polluter energy generators against States' environmental measures. For example in

---

19. These are the cases brought by clean technology investors. Cases brought against European countries such as Spain, Italy and Check Republic after their revocation or modification of PV solar incentivization schemes are the most common examples of such cases. Spain implemented a renewable energy reform in 2010 and adopted regulatory measures modifying the feed-in tariff regime for the photovoltaic sector. At the first arbitration award, arbitral tribunal constituted under the Stockholm Chambers of Commerce Rules ruled that the regulatory measures in Spain did not amount to an indirect expropriation and did not violate the investors' legitimate expectations. The Tribunal followed the principle adopted in the case of *Electrabel S.A. v. Republic of Hungary* (ICSID Case No. ARB/07/19), Award, November 25, 2015, according to which "While the investor is promised protection against unfair changes, it is well established that the host State is entitled to maintain a reasonable degree of regulatory flexibility to respond to changing circumstances in the public interest. Consequently, the requirement of fairness must not be understood as the immutability of the legal framework [...]." Another point raised by the tribunal was the need to carry out a due diligence analysis of the legal framework of the host country on the part of the investors, in order to shape expectations. On the other hand, in *Eiser Infrastructure Limited and Energía Solar Luxembourg S.à r.l. v. Kingdom of Spain* (ICSID Case No. ARB/13/36), Award, May 4, 2017, it was ordered Spain to pay EUR 128 million plus interest to Eiser Infrastructure Ltd., Solar Energy Luxembourg, which invested in thee Concentrated Solar Power (CSP) plants in Spain. *Eiser* case was based on the measures taken in 2013-2014, while *Charanne* case was based on 2010 measures. The quarantees provided by the Royal Decree were not eliminated by 2010 measures. Tribunal in *Eiser* compared two cases and stated that the measures in *Charanne* had far less dramatic effects than those at issue here. The Tribunal further mentioned that 2013-2014 measures breached legitimate expectations of the investors that the measures will not destroy the value of the investment.
20. A good example of this type of claim can be found in *Peter A. Allard v. The Government of Barbados* (PCA Case No. 2012-06). Award, June 27, 2016. The case was brought by an investor who made an investment in eco-tourism in Barbados. Investor argued that the State caused degradation of the environment and accordingly damaged its investment. The tribunal analyzed the issue under Fair and Equitable Treatment (FET), Full Protection and Security (FPS) and expropriation claims and dismissed the claims of the Claimant.

Vattenfall AB, Vattenfall Europe AG, Vattenfall Europe Generation AG&Co KG v. Federal Republic of Germany, ICSID Case No. ARB/09/6 (March 30, 2009) a Swedish investor, owner of a coal-fired power plant in Germany, made an arbitration request against Germany before ICSID based on the Energy Charter Treaty and claimed that the environmental restrictions to reduce the plant pollution imposed after the provisional acceptance of the project constitutes a violation of its rights to fair and equitable treatment and such measures render the investment economically not feasible. In *Methanex Corporation v. USA*, the challenged act was a ban on a fuel additive. Similarly, in *S.D. Myers, Inc. v. Canada*, a ban on the importation of waste material, Polychlorinated Biphenyl (PCB) was the challenged act. In *Westmoreland Mining Holdings v. Canada*, new climate change policies that included phasing out coal-generated electricity were challenged.[21] As recent examples of this trend, challenges by five energy and exploration companies can also be shown. The challenges were against the decisions of the governments of the Netherlands, Italy, Poland and Slovenia that are planning to phase out the coal-fired power plants or block projects. RWE and Uniper from Germany, Rockhopper from the United Kingdom and two other firms initiated cases based on the Energy Charter Treaty.[22] According to such examples, it is understood that investment treaties have been used as a tool for carbon-polluting investors to challenge the States' environmental measures. Investment claims thereto are mostly unlawful expropriation arguing that the environmental measures reduce the economic value of an investment project, breaches of fair and equitable treatment standards, non-discrimination, full protection and security clauses.

The more the States implement the necessary legal framework to achieve the Paris Agreement commitments to reduce greenhouse gases, including in relation to tariffs, taxation or greater constraints, the more the capital-intensive investors may bring investment arbitration claims against the states.[23]

2 Environmental or Human Rights Counterclaims

Recently environmental or human rights counterclaims started to take a significant role in investment arbitration. Host States rely on international human rights to pursue a human rights counterclaim. For example, in the *Urbaser v. Argentina* case, the counterclaim by the Argentine Republic was related to the Claimants' investment obligations under the concession contract for water and sewage services in the Province of Greater Buenos Aires. Respondent alleged that by failing to make the agreed investments, Claimants violated the principles of good faith and *pacta sunt servanda* under both Argentine law and international law, but more importantly – basic human rights to water and sanitation, which affected the health and the environment

---

21. *Westmoreland Mining Holdings v. Canada* (ICSID Case No. UNCT/20/3), Notice of Arbitration and Statement of Claim para. 6, available at https://www.italaw.com/cases/7002 (last accessed on August 10, 2022).
22. Available at https://balkangreenenergynews.com/energy-firms-sue-four-eu-countries-for-disrupting-their-fossil-fuel-projects/ (last accessed August 14, 2022).
23. ICC, "Arbitration of Climate Change Related Disputes" (henceforth the Task Force), p. 17.

of people in that area. The Tribunal found itself competent to hear Argentina's counterclaim but rejected it on its merits.

In *Burlington* and *Peronco* cases, Ecuador asserted in its counterclaims that the investor(s) breached Ecuadorian environmental laws. The cases were brought by oil production companies against the State's tax applied on oil production. *Burlington* and *Peronco* cases show that private companies can be held liable for the environmental harm they caused to the Ecuadorian Amazon.

Although counterclaims seem to be a tool to address the criticism about the structural bias of investment arbitration against host states,[24] there are many conceptual difficulties regarding counterclaims. The first issue is whether the arbitral tribunal has jurisdiction over counterclaims. When deciding whether they have jurisdiction over a counterclaim, the tribunals mostly consider whether there is consent of the parties and a close connection between claim and counterclaim.[25] Therefore, the treaty wording is essential in determining whether states' counterclaims are covered. Some treaties allow arbitration only for investors. The jurisdiction provision of the treaty should be sufficiently broad (such as "any disputes between the investor and the host State relating to the investment") and the claim should be related to the investment.[26] Arbitral rules referred to in the treaty would also be taken into consideration. For example, both ICSID and UNCITRAL allow counterclaims of States. Rule 46 of the Arbitration Rules of ICSID provides that a party may present a counterclaim arising directly out of the subject matter of the dispute.

IV   REBALANCING TOOLS

Both globalization of the world economy and privatization show a shift in many fields from public to private. Today, not only states but also non-state actors act in a way to threaten the enjoyment of human rights. Such groups of non-state actors include foreign investors through their investments. The human rights system is based on the responsibility of states. However, the threat to human rights and environment coming from non-state actors should also be tackled.[27]

The most effective tool to hold an investor accountable for a breach of human rights and environmental protection would be through adopting hard law instruments bringing obligations to respect environmental rights and human rights at the

---

24. Saarthak Jain, "Bridging the Gap Between Investment Arbitrations and Environmental Concerns: Can Inclusion of Counterclaims Help?," March 26, 2019, it states that "Investor-state arbitrations have been generally viewed as a *'one-way street'*," available at http://aria.law.columbia.edu/bridging-the-gap-between-investment-arbitrations-and-environmental-concerns-can-inclusion-of-counterclaims-help/?cn-reloaded = 1 (last accessed April 11, 2022).
25. Anne K. Hoffmann, "Counterclaims" Building International Investment Law, the First 50 Years of ICSID, Wolters Kluwer, p. 518.
26. *Urbaser S.A. and Consorcio de Aguas Bilbao Bizkaia, Bilbao Biskaia Ur Partzuergoa v. The Argentine Republic* (ICSID Case No. ARB/07/26), Award (December 8, 2016), paras. 1143-1155.
27. Andrew Clapham, "Human Rights Obligations of Non-State Actors," Oxford University Press, Vol. XV/1, 2006, p. 25.

international law level as well as incorporating explicit references to environmental rights and human rights in investment treaties.[28]

1   International Law and International Investment Law

a   *Climate Change Related International Documents*

The 1972 Stockholm Conference on the Human Environment was the first conference recognizing the interrelation between human rights and environmental protection. The Declaration made at the end of the conference (the Declaration of the United Nations Conference on the Human Environment), in its Principle 1 recognizes that the protection of environment for present and future generations is vital for the enjoyment of many human rights.[29]

In 1992 the UN Framework Convention on Climate Change (UNFCCC) was concluded and ratified by 197 countries. It was the first global treaty addressing climate change. It seeks to protect the climate system for present and future generations. Accordingly, it aims to stabilize greenhouse gas emissions at a level to prevent dangerous anthropogenic interference with the climate system.[30] The UNFCCC established the Conference of the Parties (COP) in its Article 7 which usually convenes annually. These conferences produced the Kyoto Protocol and the Paris Agreement.

The Kyoto Protocol was adopted in 1997 and entered into force in 2005. It was the first legally binding climate treaty. The Kyoto Protocol made a distinction between industrialized (Annex 1) and developing counties (non-Annex 1). While industrialized countries were required to reduce emissions by an average of 5% below 1990 levels, all other (non-Annex I) countries had no such obligations.

The Paris Agreement was adopted in 2015. Instead of rigid differentiation of countries, the Paris Agreement introduces self-determination of countries' responsibilities through their national climate action plans, known as NDCs with the goal of preventing the global average temperature from rising 2°C above preindustrial levels and pursuing efforts to keep it below 1.5°C.

b   *International Human Rights Treaties*

As explained above, climate change and environmental and human rights are interrelated and the right to be protected from the effects of climate change is not only arising from the Paris Convention but also from the international human rights documents. The 1948 UDHR was the first detailed expression of the basic rights and fundamental

---

28. Andreea Nica, "David Aven v. Costa Rica: An Aftershock of Urbaser v. Argentina?," December 12, 2018, available at http://arbitrationblog.kluwerarbitration.com/2018/12/12/david-aven-v-costa-rica-an-aftershock-of-urbaser-v-argentina/ (last accessed April 10, 2022).
29. "Man has the fundamental right to freedom, equality and adequate conditions of life, in an environment of a quality that permits a life of dignity and well-being, and he bears a solemn responsibility to protect and improve the environment for present and future generations."
30. Article 2 of the Convention.

freedoms to which all human beings are entitled. There are also other international human rights instruments such as the International Covenant on Civil and Political Rights (ICCPR) and the International Covenant on Economic, Social and Cultural Rights ("Covenants"). Together, the UDHR and these two Covenants are known as the International Bill of Human Rights. The International Bill of Human Rights covers among others, rights such as the rights to life, food, adequate housing, health, and water.

Whether non-state actors have human rights obligations or not is also a problem of human rights law.[31] There is no multilateral human rights treaty explicitly holding the corporations liable for human rights abuses nor for international environmental violations or climate change. Although there is no hard law document yet, there is a clear trend toward imposing human rights and environmental obligations on investors. UN Guiding Principles (UNGPs) on Business and Human Rights adopts soft law principles regarding corporate responsibility to respect human rights.[32] The Human Rights Council at its 26th session, on June 26, 2014, adopted resolution 26/9 by which it decided "to establish an open-ended intergovernmental working group [(OEIGWG)] on transnational corporations and other business enterprises with respect to human rights … to elaborate an international legally binding instrument to regulate, in international human rights law, the activities of transnational corporations and other business enterprises."[33]

The open-ended intergovernmental working group (OEIGWG) has had five sessions and evolved to the release of a revised draft legally binding instrument on business activities and human rights so far. The revised draft served as the basis for direct substantive intergovernmental negotiations during the fifth session of the OEIGWG (October 14-18, 2019).

As another recent development, on December 12, 2019, the Hague Rules on Business and Human Rights Arbitration was officially launched. This was a project initiated by the Business and Human Rights Arbitration Working Group, a private group of international practicing lawyers and academics. The Hague Rules aims to create an international private judicial dispute resolution mechanism to solve business

---

31. Andrew Clapham, "Human Rights Obligations of Non-State Actors," Oxford University Press, Vol. XV/1, 2006, p. 25.
32. The UNGPs on Business and Human Rights do not directly address climate change. However, we understand that not only states but also business enterprises are under certain duty to mitigate climate change effects. States are under duty to take effective measures to protect against business-related climate change within their territory and/or jurisdiction. Business enterprises may not be able to discharge their responsibility to respect all internationally recognized human rights unless they integrate climate change considerations into their human rights due diligence processes.

    Building on existing climate change standards, its prior work and sessions organized at the UN Forum in 2019 and 2018, the Working Group on Business and Human Rights will develop an Information Note on what all three pillars of the UNGPs entail for States and business enterprises in relation to climate change, available at https://www.ohchr.org/EN/Issues/Business/Pages/Climate-Change-and-the-UNGPs.aspx (last accessed April 11, 2022).
33. UN Human Rights Council, Resolution 26/9, 26th Session, June 26, 2014, available at https://www.ohchr.org/EN/HRBodies/HRC/WGTransCorp/Pages/IGWGOnTNC.aspx (last accessed April 11, 2022).

and human rights issues.[34] Although it is a private initiative and it is not referring to binding hard law instruments imposing human rights obligations for non-state actors, it clearly demonstrates the need for imposing high human rights standards on investors and it may add to the trend towards imposing human rights obligations on investors.[35]

c Climate-Based Litigation

Climate-based litigation[36] also imposes pressure on countries and corporations to align with the standards of the Paris Convention, international human rights instruments and constitutional rights. Accordingly, national courts or institutions, as the case may be, hold states or corporations liable for climate change. *Urgenda climate* case was the first case in which the Dutch Supreme Court ruled in December 2019 that the state owes a duty of care to protect its citizens from the effects of climate change in accordance with its obligations under the European Convention for the Protection of Human Rights and Fundamental Freedoms.[37] Such landmark decision inspired many other cases in countries such as Belgium, Canada, the UK, France, Germany, Colombia, New Zealand, Norway, and Switzerland.

Not only governments but also corporations are held liable for their role in contributing to climate change by institutions or the courts. As an example, in December 2019, the Commission on Human Rights of the Philippines announced that the world's biggest carbon polluters could be held liable for their role in contributing to climate change. The Commission ruled that even if current international human rights law does not explicitly hold major fossil fuel companies liable, they are morally obligated to respect human rights, as stated in the UNGPs on Business and Human Rights. Similarly, in a suit filed by the Dutch foundation Milieudefensie and co-plaintiffs against Royal Dutch Shell, the Hague District Court ordered Royal Dutch Shell to reduce greenhouse gas (GHG) pollution across its entire product chain (including sold products) by 45% by 2030 relative to 2019 levels. By ruling so, the Dutch District Court interpreted the Dutch unwritten standard of duty of care (Dutch Civil Code Book 6, section 162) on the basis of "the relevant facts and circumstances, the best available science on dangerous climate change and how to manage it, and the widespread international consensus that human rights offer protection against the impacts of

---

34. Center for International Legal Cooperation, The Hague Rules on Business and Human Rights Arbitration, available at https://www.cilc.nl/project/the-hague-rules-on-business-and-human-rights-arbitration/ (last accessed April 11, 2022).

35. Ylli Dautaj, "Roll Out the Red Carpet: The Hague Rules on Business and Human Rights Arbitration are Finally Here!," December 26, 2019, available at http://arbitrationblog.kluwerarbitration.com/2019/12/26/roll-out-the-red-carpet-the-hague-rules-on-business-and-human-rights-arbitration-are-finally-here/ (last accessed April 10, 2022).

36. As of July 2022, total number of cases is over 2,000 which includes cases filed before courts in 43 countries and 15 international or regional courts or tribunals, available at https://www.lse.ac.uk/granthaminstitute/publication/global-trends-in-climate-change-litigation-2022/ (last accessed August 10, 2022).

37. Urgenda decision is available at https://www.urgenda.nl/en/themas/climate-case/ (last accessed on August 10, 2022).

dangerous climate change and that companies must respect human rights."[38] The decisions show us that there is a growing trend that not only the states but also the global carbon-polluter companies are also held liable for their contribution to global warming. In such cases, courts benefit from the developments in climate science as it is becoming easier to establish the relationship between historical carbon emissions and climate change events.

d   *Other International Law Sources*

According to Article 31(3)(c) of the Vienna Convention on the Law of Treaties (VCLT) "any relevant rules of international law applicable in the relations between the parties" will be taken into consideration when interpreting a treaty. This principle is considered to be a principle of "systematic interpretation" and "principle of integration" by scholars and is read as requiring "unity" when interpreting a treaty provision in a way that "rules should not be considered as isolation of general international law."[39] Similarly, Article 42 of the Convention on the Settlement of Investment Disputes between States and Nationals of Other States (ICSID Convention) provides that "in the absence of [an agreement of the parties], the Tribunal shall apply the law of the Contracting State party to the dispute (including its rules on the conflict of laws) and such rules of international law as may be applicable."

As peremptory or *jus cogens* norms also constitute a part of international law, they should also be taken into consideration by arbitrators when interpreting a treaty in line with systematic interpretation principle of the VCLT. Although there are no generally accepted criteria to identify norms of *jus cogens*, they are considered to be norms of general international law accepted and recognized by the international community of states as a whole, non-derogable and capable of modification only by a similar norm of the same character.[40] *Jus cogens* are accepted as part of international law but may fall within different forms, i.e., customary law, treaty law, and general principles of law.[41] According to Article 31(3)(c) of the VCLT peremptory or *jus cogens* norms are hierarchically superior norms.[42] It is stated that violations of *jus cogens*

---

38. The Hague District Court the Judgement of 26 May 2021, case number / cause list number: C/09/571932 / HA ZA 19-379 ("*Milieudefensie et al. v. ROYAL DUTCH SHELL PLC*"), available at http://climatecasechart.com/wp-content/uploads/sites/16/non-us-case-documents/2021/2 0210526_8918_judgment-1.pdf, p. 21 (last accessed August 14, 2022).

39. Valentina Vadi, "*Jus Cogens* in International Investment Law and Arbitration," Netherlands Yearbook of International Law, 2015 (pp. 357-388), p. 363, available at https://www.researc hgate.net/profile/Valentina-Vadi-2/publication/306320072_Jus_Cogens_in_International_Inve stment_Law_and_Arbitration/links/5bd318be4585150b2b88b80a/Jus-Cogens-in-International-Investment-Law-and-Arbitration.pdf?origin=publication_detail (last accessed on August 10, 2022).

40. R.W. Muzangaza, "Normative Hierarchy in International Environmental Law: A Constitutional Reading," Chapter 9: Constitutional Conversations in the Anthropocene: In Search of Environmental Jus Cogens Norms, Prof. Louis J. Kotze, mini-dissertation submitted for the partial fulfillment of Master of Law in Environmental Law and Governance at Northwest University, November 2016, p. 68.

41. Valentina Vadi, p. 360.

42. Article 53 of the VCLT states "A treaty is void, if at the time of its conclusion, it conflicts with a peremptory norm of general international law. For the purposes of the present Convention, a

would result not only in accountability of states, but, also non-state actors.[43] To date, no international court or tribunal pronounced any environmental norms of *jus cogens*.[44] However, there is an evolving doctrine stating that four norms in international environmental law might have the potential to become environmental *jus cogens* norms namely: the no-harm principle;[45] the right to a healthy environment, the prohibition of willful serious damage to the environment during armed conflict, the general prohibition of causing or not preventing environmental damage that threatens the international community as a whole.[46] Although what rights fall within the norms of *jus cogens* is a vague issue, international courts or tribunals may contribute to the development of investment law by interpreting, applying and making concrete the peremptory norms.[47]

e   New Generation IIAs

International investment law has been highly criticized for being one-sided and protecting only the interests of foreign investors.[48] However, a growing number of international investment treaties (IIAs) make reference to environmental and human rights concerns.

Some new generation IIAs emphasize sustainable development public policy concerns, such as those related to health, safety, security and environmental protection in their preambles. For instance, the preamble of the Brazil-Mozambique BIT acknowledges the "essential role of investment in the promotion of sustainable development, economic growth, poverty reduction, job creation, expansion of productive capacity and human development." The US-Rwanda BIT, while recognizing the importance of stimulating the flow of mutual capital between the parties, notes that parties desire to achieve this goal "in a manner consistent with the protection of health, safety, and the environment, and the promotion of internationally recognized labor rights."

In some of them, there are certain exceptions where the treaty or certain provisions of the treaty will not apply. With the carve-outs, the regulatory power of the State in the public interest is preserved. These circumstances include measures relating to public order, human, animal, plant life, protection of environment and natural resources. For instance, the Switzerland-Mexico BIT states: "The Parties recognize that

peremptory norm of general international law is a norm accepted and recognized by the international community of States as a whole as a norm from which no derogation is permitted and which can be modified only by a subsequent norm of general international law having the same character."
43. Andrew Clapham, "Human Rights Obligations of Non-State Actors," Oxford University Press, Vol. XV/1, 2006, p. 90.
44. R.W. Muzangaza, p. 67.
45. R.W. Muzangaza, p. 60, No-harm principle is considered as having customary law status, however, not have *jus cogens* status yet.
46. R.W. Muzangaza, p. 68.
47. Valentina Vadi, p. 383.
48. Patrick Abel, "Counterclaims Based on International Human Rights Obligations of Investors in International Investment Arbitration: Fallacies and Potentials of the 2016 ICSID Urbaser v. Argentina Award," Vol. 1, November 28, 2018, available at https://brill.com/view/journals/bol/1/1/article-p61_61.xml (last accessed April 11, 2022).

it is inappropriate to encourage investment by relaxing domestic health, safety or environmental measures."

Some treaties make reference to corporate social responsibility standards, although not obligatory on investors such as OECD Guidelines for Multinational Enterprises and UNGPs on Businesses and Human Rights (Dutch Model BIT, Turkey-Uruguay BIT).

Model 2015 BIT of India was incorporating detailed provisions for environmental protection obligations of investors.[49] The Final BIT took a number of steps back from the March 2015 draft and diluted counterclaim and environmental obligations for the investors. 2017 Intra-Mercosur Agreement provides the best effort obligation to respect human rights including the right to a clean environment. The 2008 ECOWAS Supplementary Act on Investments introduces certain investor responsibilities (e.g., to comply with environmental assessment standards).[50] The Southern African Development Community (SADC) Model requires investors not to operate their investments "in a manner inconsistent with international environmental, labour, and human rights obligations binding on the Host State or the Home State, whichever obligations are higher."[51]

There is an obvious trend to balance investment protection with public policy concerns such as environmental protection and human rights. Even if the IIAs bring obligations to the investors, it will take some time to phase out the old IIAs due to survival provisions.

2   Interpretation by the Investment Arbitration Tribunals

Another means of rebalancing between private and public benefits is the interpretation by the tribunals. Some tribunals seem to follow an approach balancing the tension between evolving environmental and human rights considerations and investment protection.

a   Interpretation in Cases Where States' Environmental Measures Are Challenged

The investors when challenging the States' environmental measures make an unlawful expropriation claim. There are two approaches adopted by the tribunals whilst evaluating expropriation claims: effect-based approach and purpose-based approach. Under the effect-based approach, the tribunals did not take into account whether the State's action was for legitimate purposes, for the public's benefit such as environmental purposes. The tribunals decided that the State's obligation to pay compensation remains regardless of the purpose of the action. The tribunals did not consider the

---

49. BITs do not explicitly allow raising counterclaims. There was an attempt to include raising counterclaim right in the Indian March 2015 Model BIT.
50. Articles 11-16.
51. Article 15. SADC Model Bilateral Investment Treaty Template with Commentary, available at https://www.iisd.org/itn/wp-content/uploads/2012/10/sadc-model-bit-template-final.pdf.

State's purpose. There is ample case law in support of this proposition. For example, in the *Compania del Desarrollo de Santa Elena SA v. Republic of Costa Rica* case, the award includes the following paragraph:

> 72. Expropriatory environmental measures—no matter how laudable and beneficial to society as a whole—are, in this respect, similar to any other expropriatory measures that a state may take in order to implement its policies: where property is expropriated, even for environmental purposes, whether domestic or international, the state's obligation to pay compensation remains.[52]

Similar to the *Santa Elena SA v. Republic of Costa Rica* decision, in the Metalclad decision, the Tribunal did not decide or consider the motivation or intent of the adoption of the Ecological Decree, the Tribunal only considered whether the implementation of the Ecological Decree would constitute an act tantamount to expropriation.[53]

Under the purpose-based approach, bona fide regulations such as nondiscriminatory environmental regulations aimed at general welfare (the so-called police Powers of the state) are considered non-compensable. There is also ample case law in support of this proposition. For example, in Saluka the tribunal adopted the principle that "'a State does not commit an expropriation and is thus not liable to pay compensation to a dispossessed alien investor when it adopts general regulations that are 'commonly accepted as within the police power of States'" and considered this principle as forming part of customary international law." The tribunal in *Methanex Corp. v. USA* stated in its final award, "[i]t is a principle of customary international law that, where economic injury results from a *bona fide* regulation within the police powers of a State, compensation is not required."

Even if an act of the State is considered non-compensable under expropriation evaluation, it would still need to meet the requirements of fair and equitable treatment in order to be in line with investment treaties. Interpretations of the fair and equitable treatment standard vary from case to case, notably with regard to the notion of an investor's legitimate expectations. Are the States required to ensure a stable, predictable framework for the investment? Or may the State's policy change over time?

In cases, such as *MTD v. Chile*, *Tecmed v. Mexico*, *CMS v. Argentina*, *Enron v. Argentina*, and *PSEG v. Turkey*, the Tribunals decided that States are required to ensure a stable environment for the investors.

The recent approach tends to accept the fact that the State's policies may change over time and even if recognized in the preamble of the BITs, stability is not considered to be an obligation in itself. In other words, aside from clear stabilization clauses, BITs are not interpreted as guaranteeing "freezing" of the law such as tribunals of *Unglaube v. Costa Rica*, *Parkering v. Lithuania*, *Continental Casualty v. Argentina*, *EDF v. Romania*, *Glamis Gold v. US*, and *Plama v. Bulgaria*. While states' regulatory powers

---

52. *Compañia del Desarrollo de Santa Elena S.A. v. Republic of Costa Rica* (ICSID Case No. ARB/96/1), Award, February 17, 2000, para. 1317.
53. For similar approach, you can also *see Azurix Corp. v. The Argentine Republic* (ICSID Case No. ARB/01/12), Award, July 14, 2006 and *Tecnicas Medioambientales Tecmed S.A. v. United Mexican States* (ICSID Case No. ARB(AF)/00/2), Award, May 29, 2000.

are generally accepted, whether changes in regulations may be tantamount to a violation of legitimate expectations would depend on the facts of each case. For instance, in *Impreligo v. Argentina* "unreasonable modifications"[54] and in *Toto Costruzioni Generali v. Lebanon* "a drastic or discriminatory change"[55] are considered as reasons from which investors must be protected.

b   Interpretation in Environmental/Human Rights Counterclaims

The *Urbaser v. Argentina* decision is the first ICSID decision admitting the possibility of bringing a human rights counterclaim. Followed by *David Aven v. Costa Rica* decision, there is an obvious trend toward: (i) accepting certain international human rights obligations for the investors, (ii) integrating human rights obligations into investment arbitration.[56]

In the *Urbaser* case, the Tribunal first confirmed the principal wrongness of the categorical understanding of BITS' nature as asymmetric and only protecting investments through rights exclusively granted to investors.[57] It was also confirmed that BITs are not international investment law in isolation, fully independent from other sources of law (both national and international) that might provide for rights the respondent can invoke before an international arbitral tribunal.[58]

The 1948 UDHR, after proclaiming fundamental human rights to be universally protected, states in Article 30 that "Nothing in this Declaration may be interpreted as implying for any State, group or person any right to engage in any activity or to perform any act aimed at the destruction of any of the rights and freedoms set forth herein." The Covenant, ICCPR, European Convention on Human Rights (ECHR) and American Convention on Human Rights (ACHR) provide similar provisions. Whether the Declaration and the abovementioned other soft law instruments may be interpreted as bringing human rights obligations to non-state actors is an interpretation issue. The Urbaser tribunal interpreted these provisions as bringing "an obligation on all parts, public and private parties, not to engage in activity aimed at destroying such rights."[59] Scholars criticize this interpretation with the argument that the preparatory works show that the aim was not to impose human rights obligations on private parties but to foreclose them to use any right with the sole purpose of destroying the human rights of another right holder.[60] The principle of systematic integration of Article 31(3)(c) of the

---

54. *Impreligo v. Argentina* (ICSID Case No. ARB/07/17), Award, June 21, 2011, para. 291.
55. *Toto Costruzioni Generali v. Lebanon* (ICSID Case No. ARB/07/12), Award, June 7, 2012, para. 244.
56. Patrick Abel, "Counterclaims Based on International Human Rights Obligations of Investors in International Investment Arbitration: Fallacies and Potentials of the 2016 ICSID Urbaser v. Argentina Award," Vol. 1, November 28, 2018, available at https://brill.com/view/journals/bol/1/1/article-p61_61.xml (last accessed April 12, 2022).
57. *Urbaser S.A. and Consorcio de Aguas Bilbao Bizkaia, Bilbao Biskaia Ur Partzuergoa v. The Argentine Republic* (ICSID Case No. ARB/07/26), Award, December 8, 2016, para. 1183.
58. *Ibid.*, para. 1186.
59. *Ibid.*, para. 1199.
60. Patrick Abel, "Counterclaims Based on International Human Rights Obligations of Investors in International Investment Arbitration: Fallacies and Potentials of the 2016 ICSID Urbaser v.

VCLT is of relevance in terms of referring to international human rights in investment arbitration cases. According to this provision, when interpreting an investment treaty "any rules of international law applicable in the relations between the parties" shall be taken into account. The Urbaser Tribunal stated that "[t]he BIT has to be construed in harmony with other rules of international law of which it forms part, including those relating to human rights" based on Article 31(3)(c) of the VCLT.[61] Certain scholars argue that this principle is only to interpret a provision of the treaty not to import a missing investor obligation.[62]

The doctrine criticizes the Urbaser decision by stating that it is not convincing to read the BIT provision in a way to include obligations for investors merely because it allegedly exists under a human rights treaty.[63]

The Urbaser Tribunal, although decided that non-state actors are under a negative obligation not to engage in activity aimed at destroying human rights, stated that in terms of obligation to enforce the human right to water, there is no clear obligation of investors to perform.[64]

In the *David Aven v. Costa Rica* case, the tribunal went one step further and found that although "the enforcement of environmental law is primarily to the States, it cannot be admitted that a foreign investor could not be subject to international law obligations in this field."[65]

The *David Aven v. Costa Rica* case was based on the Dominican Republic-Central America Free Trade Agreement (DR-CAFTA) which is a new generation IIA addressing environmental concerns. DR-CAFTA Article 10.9.3(c), Article 10.11 and Chapter Seventeen show the environmental language approach of the treaty. Article 10.11 establishes that "Nothing in this Chapter shall be construed to prevent a Party from adopting, maintaining, or enforcing any measure otherwise consistent with this Chapter that it considers appropriate to ensure that investment activity in its territory is undertaken in a manner sensitive to environmental concerns." The Tribunal interpreted these provisions as representing a basis for the investors' obligation to comply with the environmental domestic laws and regulations and any corresponding measures adopted by the host state. According to the Tribunal; any breach thereof would result in a violation of domestic and international law.[66] The tribunal's

---

Argentina Award," Vol. 1, November 28, 2018, available at https://brill.com/view/journals/bol/1/1/article-p61_61.xml (last accessed April 11, 2022).

61. *Urbaser S.A. and Consorcio de Aguas Bilbao Bizkaia, Bilbao Biskaia Ur Partzuergoa v. The Argentine Republic* (ICSID Case No. ARB/07/26), Award, December 8, 2016, para. 1200.

62. Patrick Abel, "Counterclaims Based on International Human Rights Obligations of Investors in International Investment Arbitration: Fallacies and Potentials of the 2016 ICSID Urbaser v. Argentina Award," Vol. 1, November 28, 2018, available at https://brill.com/view/journals/bol/1/1/article-p61_61.xml (last accessed April 12, 2022).

63. *Ibid.*

64. *Urbaser S.A. and Consorcio de Aguas Bilbao Bizkaia, Bilbao Biskaia Ur Partzuergoa v. The Argentine Republic* (ICSID Case No. ARB/07/26), Award, December 8, 2016, paras. 1199 and 1210.

65. *David R. Aven and Others v. Republic of Costa Rica* (ICSID Case No. UNCT/15/3), Award, September 18, 2018, para. 737.

66. Andreea Nica, "David Aven v. Costa Rica: An Aftershock of Urbaser v. Argentina?," December 12, 2018, available at http://arbitrationblog.kluwerarbitration.com/2018/12/12/david-aven-v-costa-rica-an-aftershock-of-urbaser-v-argentina/ (last accessed April 11, 2022).

conclusion that a foreign investor could be subject to international law obligations in environmental law was primarily based on the environmental language of DR-CAFTA.

In the *Cortec Mining v. Republic of Kenya* case, the Tribunal decided that environmental regulatory obligations on which the Claimants defaulted were of "fundamental importance."[67] The Tribunal, therefore, concludes that the Claimants' failure to comply with the legislature's regulatory regime governing the Mrima Hill forest and nature reserve, and the Claimants' failure to obtain an Environmental Impact Assessment (EIA) license (or approval in any valid form) concerning the environmental issues involved in the proposed removal of 130 million tons of material from Mrima Hill, constituted violations of Kenyan law that, in terms of international law, warrant the proportionate response of a denial of treaty protection under the BIT and the ICSID.[68]

V   CONCLUSION

Climate change is not a threat to the future anymore, it is a reality and already harming our lives. COVID-19 has shown us that we globally need to work together to tackle global challenges. The next global challenge will likely be climate change related. Accordingly, there is an apparent need for a balance between investment protection and environmental protection. In terms of climate change, drastic action is needed and it takes time to address environmental and climate issues in the investment treaties. Although there is a growing trend to address environmental considerations in IIAs, even in cases where there are no explicit legal obligations for corporations in investment treaties, arbitral tribunals can be enthusiastic in the harmonious reading of the human rights system and investment law. As the Urbaser tribunal stated, a categorical understanding of BITs as asymmetric and only protecting investments through rights exclusively granted to investors should be left. There may be no need to wait until new generation IIAs enter into force. IIAs should be interpreted taking into account the needs of today.

In *David Aven v. Costa Rica*, DR-CAFTA was a new generation IIA addressing environmental concerns. The Tribunal did not have to analyze the integration of international human rights into IIAs, nor human rights obligations of non-state actors arising from international law as was the case in *Urbaser*. Even in cases where the IIA is not a new generation treaty, there should be room for interpreting the IIA in line with international human rights. Severe environmental damages by foreign investments may well require considering certain human rights as *jus cogens* such as the right to a healthy environment over time may help tribunals in terms of integration of international human rights into IIAs.

---

67. *Cortec Mining Kenya Limited, Cortec (Pty) Limited and Stirling Capital Limited v. Republic of Kenya* (ICSID Case No. ARB/15/29), Award, October 22, 2018.
68. *Ibid.*, para. 365.

The International Court of Justice (ICJ) often states that existing environmental norms and standards should be taken into consideration when interpreting a treaty.[69] In the *Gabčíkovo-Nagymaros* case, the ICJ stated that "the Treaty is not static and is open to adapt to emerging norms of international law."[70] In the Iron Rhine Arbitration, the Tribunal cited Article 31(3)(c) of the VCLT as the legal basis for a contemporaneous interpretation of the treaties at issue and considered principles of international environmental law in their current forms at the time of its decision.[71] Such case law may be inspirational for investment arbitral tribunals.

In this regard, arbitrators' expertise in human rights is gaining importance as human rights and investment arbitration increasingly interact with one another. We need to find a balance between economic development and public health and welfare. International human rights law is likely to be transformed to cover environmental rights, and investment law will likely interact more with human rights law.

One of the reasons for investment arbitration tribunals' reluctance to refer to international human rights treaties and instruments might be the fact that many investment arbitrators have a private law background.[72] Article 11 of the recently launched Hague Rules requires the proven expertise of the presiding or the sole arbitrator in areas relevant to the dispute such as human rights law. If the tribunal contains an arbitrator with a background in public international law, it might be beneficial in terms of a harmonious reading of the human rights system and investment law.[73]

69. Laurence Boisson de Chazournes, "Environmental Protection and Investment Arbitration: Yin and Yang?" Anuario Colombiano de Derecho Internacional, Vol. 10, pp. 371-399, 2017, available at https://www.redalyc.org/journal/4295/429552542012/html/#fn8 (last accessed August 10, 2022).

70. *Case Concerning the Gabčíkovo-Nagymaros Project (Hungary/Slovakia)*, para. 112, available at https://jusmundi.com/en/document/decision/en-gabcikovo-nagymaros-project-hungary-slovakia-judgment-thursday-25th-september-1997 (last accessed August 10, 2022).

71. Laurence Boisson de Chazournes, "Environmental Protection and Investment Arbitration: Yin and Yang?" Anuario Colombiano de Derecho Internacional, Vol. 10, pp. 371-399, 2017, available at https://www.redalyc.org/journal/4295/429552542012/html/#fn8 (last accessed August 10, 2022). Award in the Arbitration regarding the Iron Rhine ("Ijzeren Rijn") Railway between the Kingdom of Belgium and the Kingdom of the Netherlands, decision of May 24, 2005 Reports of International Arbitral Awards, Volume XXVII pp. 35-125, para. 58, available at https://legal.un.org/riaa/cases/vol_XXVII/35-125.pdf (last accessed on August 10, 2022).

72. Christina Binder, "The UNDRIP's Relationship to Existing International Law, Ch. 4, The UNDRIP and Interactions with International Investment Law," from the UN Declaration on the Rights of Indigenous Peoples: A Commentary, edited by Jessie Hohmann and Marc Weller, March 22, 2018.

73. *Ibid.*

Chapter 43

New Types of Energy Disputes: In the Era of Low Carbon Transition

Peter D. Cameron[*]

I   INTRODUCTION

I have been invited to consider *energy* disputes as part of our New Frontiers panel. As many of you will know, energy disputes make up a disproportionately high number of claims before the International Centre for Settlement of Investment Disputes (ICSID), the International Chamber of Commerce (ICC), and the London Court of International Arbitration (LCIA) and other arbitral bodies that provide us with statistical data on disputes from time to time. A simple breakdown of this data into sub-sectors or country origin of the parties tells us little or nothing about the single most influential factor that is shaping this category of disputes. This is often known as 'the energy transition', the process by which the balance of energy consumption is to be shifted from fossil fuels to a less carbon-intensive mix, to alleviate the impacts of climate change. Even allowing for the current preoccupation with energy security and affordability issues,

---

[*] Director, Centre for Energy, Petroleum and Mineral Law and Policy, and Professor of International Energy Law and Policy, University of Dundee, UK; Barrister (England & Wales)(Middle Temple), Associate, Landmark Chambers, London; FCIArb and Fellow of the Royal Society of Edinburgh: p.d.cameron@dundee.ac.uk.

this trend towards decarbonization is likely to prove a major source of uncertainty and disruption in this sector for the foreseeable future. It is locked into government policies through the legally binding international climate change treaty, known as the Paris Agreement, signed by 193 states in 2015, with commitments that imply large-scale, multiple interventions by states in the commercial operations of the energy sector. These are likely to be as diverse as the energy priorities and endowments of the many signatories to the Paris Agreement. As a result, the term 'energy transition' in the singular is likely to be less accurate in practice than in the plural. Future investments in any form of energy must now take this factor of 'energy transitions' into account. For international commercial arbitration, the question is whether a policy framework compatible with these international obligations is also compatible with the pre-existing obligations arising from treaty and contractual instruments – which are, after all, designed primarily to protect the interests of investors.

In this chapter, I shall examine this tension in relation to (section II) new kinds of energy or energy-related activity that have generated disputes; and (section III) disputes arising from mandatory closures and phasing out of certain energies as a result of public policy changes. I shall then ask some questions – such as whether the notion of 'legitimate expectations' may be affected by the increased state role that the energy transitions are already leading to – that may be relevant to the panel discussion to which this paper is a contribution.

II NEW ENERGIES AND DISPUTES

When the search for new forms of energy takes place, it is likely that familiar legal mechanisms for granting access such as permitting, or licensing will be central to any arbitral disputes that emerge. If there is a dispute between the foreign investor and the host state, the conditions included in the grant of access may have been breached by subsequent state action. An example is the production of *biofuels* in Panama, where an Italian company registered an ICSID claim against the government for an alleged series of measures that made it impossible for the investor to proceed with a plan to manufacture bioethanol through locally sourced material.[1] The government passed a law requiring gasoline to be mixed with a certain percentage of bioethanol, with the result being a cleaner form of gasoline. The law set the price for the sale of bioethanol, taking care that the price covered the production costs so that the local product was not undercut by any cheaper international version of the product. On this basis, the investor committed capital to purchase land and invested more than USD 100 million, concluding several long-term contracts with parties interested in buying its bioethanol. The investor claimed to have received assurances that this law was stable. A new government took office and set a new price formula for locally produced bioethanol. It also revoked the decree that required a proportion of bioethanol to be mixed with gasoline, in effect destroying the nascent industry in the country. The investor claimed

---

1. *Campos de Pese S.A. v. Republic of Panama*, ICSID Case No. ARB/20/19; GAR, 23 July 2020, 'Details of Panama biofuels dispute emerge'.

that the government's assurances over the stability of the legal framework had created a legitimate expectation that was not met. Among the claims made by Campos under the Italy-Panama Bilateral Investment Treaty (BIT) are expropriation and denial of justice, and others based on the MFN clause. Despite the novelty of the energy element, the legal measures taken are familiar to investment treaty lawyers.

A different kind of energy, yet rarely known to be in commercial use, is *geothermal energy*. It figured in an investor-state arbitration arising from an investment in Kenya.[2] A US-Canadian investor secured a thirty-year licence in 2007 to exploit geothermal resources in southwest Kenya. The government revoked the licence after five years, alleging a lack of performance of the licence duties and a lack of capacity to carry out the work. The claim for USD 340 million was dismissed.[3]

Disputes of a different kind arise from so-called critical minerals. An indirect effect of the transition to lower carbon energy consumption is the recognition that many states depend on imports of a limited range of minerals in quantities that are without precedent. Without their application in batteries for electric vehicles and hardware for solar panels and wind turbines, no comprehensive transition will be possible. Many of these minerals are disproportionately located in a few, not necessarily friendly, states, highlighting the kind of vulnerability familiar in the traditional oil and gas markets. To reduce this dependence and identify new sources, some states have sought to encourage investment in their territories. Two early examples of disputes from such efforts may be noted here.

First, there is a dispute involving rights to mine phosphate sand deposits in waters offshore Mexico. With innovative technologies, these may be extracted commercially in the foreseeable future, and their location in waters offshore hints at the notion of a 'blue economy' that may emerge in future years. A US company, Odyssey Marine Exploration, brought a claim under the North American Free Trade Agreement (NAFTA) on behalf of its Mexican subsidiary, ExO, arising out of a refusal by the Mexican authorities to grant an environmental permit.[4] In relation to NAFTA's successor, the United States-Mexico-Canada Agreement (USMCA), this is a 'pending claim' within the terms of Annex 14-C, paragraphs 1 and 4, for which Mexico has promised to maintain its consent after the expiry of NAFTA.[5] The investor had been granted a mining concession for the deposit with a fifty-year duration, covering about 3,000 square kilometres. It sought to extract the mineral using dredging techniques which, in contrast to terrestrial mining, had both cost advantages and a smaller environmental footprint, they alleged. An environmental impact assessment and development plan involved four years of preparation but was rejected by the authorities, although in the same period, Mexican companies and state agencies were alleged to have secured permission to carry out activities in areas that were more ecologically sensitive than this one. The argument was that Mexico was in breach of Article 1105

2. *WalAm Energy LLC v. Republic of Kenya*, ICSID Case No. ARB/15/7.
3. Award, 10 July 2020, paras 336, 579.
4. *Odyssey Marine Exploration Inc v. United Mexican States*, ICSID Case No UNCT/20/1; Claimant's Memorial, 4 September 2020.
5. Claimant's Memorial, para. 207.

NAFTA which requires Fair and Equitable Treatment (FET) and full protection and security; Article 1110(1) which prohibits indirect expropriations and Article 1102 that requires treatment no less favourable than that which the host state accords to its own investors.[6] The claim sought full compensation reflecting the fair market value of the concession and the claimant's investment in Mexico (USD 2.36 billion, plus interest).[7] Once again, the legal issues are familiar, as is the treaty protection sought, even though the way the natural resource was to be extracted relied upon recently developed and innovative technology.

A second example concerns rare earth and uranium mining. This became a source of dispute in *Greenland Minerals v. Greenland & Denmark* when the claimant's plans to start exploitation of a resource it discovered were cast into doubt by a prohibition on uranium mining.[8] The statutory prohibition led to the claimant's application for a licence to exploit being rejected. This is by the way a claim that is third-party funded.

III   DISPUTES ARISING FROM MANDATORY CLOSURES AND PHASE-OUTS

There are a growing number of energy disputes arising from measures that respond to evolving emission reduction policies. In Europe and North America, there are several examples. In the former, these co-exist with the many Energy Charter Treaty (ECT) cases in which feed-in tariffs have been revised in ways that have triggered international arbitrations involving the Czech Republic, Italy, and Spain. Such claims are prima facie concerned with adaptations to policy in the face of costs that are deemed unsustainable by the governments concerned. Policies that require closure, phasing-out or imposing prohibitions fall into a different category and are closely linked to a shift in energy priorities aligned to a state's climate policy.

Examples of states pursuing climate change mitigation policies despite the risk that investors will initiate arbitral proceedings as a result include policy decisions to phase out coal in the generation of electricity.

The Netherlands faced potential ECT claims because of its decision to phase out coal in electricity generation from 2030. Following a decision of the Supreme Court censoring a lack of action by the Government in addressing climate change issues and the adoption of a Prohibition of Coal in Electricity Generation Act in 2019, a phased ban was introduced on the use of coal to generate electricity. The Act prohibits the use of coal as a fuel in those plants that generate electricity and does not affect other uses of the generating plants (e.g., those that use biomass instead of coal to generate electricity). A transition period is offered until the end of 2029. Subject to certain conditions, compensation is available. This idea of a coal phase-out is not new and is

---

6. *Odyssey Marine Exploration*, at paras 217-352.
7. *Ibid.*, at para. 433.
8. *Greenland Minerals A/S v. Greenland, 2022: Greenland Minerals Limited Press Release, 26 July 2022: Draft Exploitation Licence Decision and White Paper Review.* The prohibition applied to ores that exceeded a specific threshold set out in an Act of Parliament of December 2021.

being planned by both Germany and the UK with dates set for closure of certain plants. However, in this case, the compensation payments were deemed inadequate by RWE, a German-based utility that owned two coal-fired power plants in the country. In January 2021 a claim was submitted by RWE AG and RWE Eemshaven Holding II BV against the Netherlands under the ECT.[9] This is the first-ever claim against the Netherlands before ICSID. A second electricity utility, Uniper, also German-owned, had agreed to build a coal-fired power plant in 2007, following discussions with the Dutch Government. The plant opened in 2016 and cost a reputed EUR 1.6 billion with an expected life of forty years.[10] As if to demonstrate that volatility is a characteristic of energy markets and not just government policy, Uniper was obliged to withdraw the claim following a bail-out package agreed upon with the German Government in mid-2022.

In **Germany**, a similar phase-out decision was taken but with respect to the use of nuclear power, in the aftermath of the Fukushima accident in Japan. The German legislature adopted Nuclear Amendment No. 13, a measure which imposed specific decommissioning dates for each nuclear plant. This triggered an ECT claim in 2012 by a Swedish investor, Vattenfall, for a compensation amount of EUR 4.7 billion.[11] The decision to initiate arbitration was not a challenge to the policy choice itself but rather a request for compensation.[12] In parallel domestic proceedings, initiated by Vattenfall, the German Constitutional Court (*Bundesverfassungsgericht*) held that Nuclear Amendment No. 13 was unconstitutional, affecting Vattenfall's right to distribute their residual energy, and affecting its right to property, guaranteed under the Basic Law.[13]

Germany faced other claims in respect of its renewable energy legislation. Germany amended its Renewable Energy Sources Act in 2016 so that the right to receive fixed feed-in tariffs from the State was replaced by a market-based pricing mechanism for renewable energy producers. In addition, a new Offshore Wind Energy Act required investors in offshore wind projects to participate in tariff auctions managed by the Federal Grid Agency, which would award to bidders according to those offering the cheapest rate to the consumer. In response to the changed regulatory

---

9. *RWE AG and RWE Eemshaven Holding II BV v. Kingdom of the Netherlands*, ICSID Case No ARB/21/4.
10. *Uniper SE, Uniper Benelux Holding BV and Uniper Benelux NV v. Kingdom of the Netherlands*, ICSID Case No. ARB/21/22. *See* Claimant's Memorial, 20 May 2022: www.italaw.com.
11. *Vattenfall AB and others v. Federal Republic of Germany*, ICSID Case No. ARB/12/12. The arbitration was discontinued on 9 November 2021, following the entry into force of a Settlement Agreement. Germany agreed to pay compensation of around EUR 1.4 billion. This is not to be confused with an earlier case with the same parties about a power plant construction project, which was concluded with an award embodying the parties' settlement agreement in 2011: *Vattenfall AB, Vattenfall Europe AG, Vattenfall Europe Generation AG v. Federal Republic of Germany*, ICSID Case No. ARB/09/6. The case concerned environmental restrictions imposed on a EUR 2.6 billion coal-fired power plant under construction on the Elbe River. The final construction permit appears to have been granted by the City of Hamburg authority only subject to certain additional restrictions on the plant's impact on the river.
12. Interestingly, claims pursued by nuclear utilities in German state courts succeeded on their merits, survived appellate review, and entered into the damages phase, all in a very few years.
13. Press Release No. 98/2020 of 12 November 2020; Order of 29 September 2020, 1 BvR 1550/19, 'The Sixteenth Amendment of 10 July 2018 to the Atomic Energy Act has not entered into force; the legislator remains obligated to enact new provisions.'

framework, a claim was brought against Germany by Strabag, a large construction firm, and others, under the ECT on the ground that the regulatory changes combined with the exclusion of their projects from the public auction process meant that they had no alternative but to abandon the investments, which had been made in reliance on the legal regime for offshore wind producers.[14]

A different approach to phasing out fossil fuels has been evident in France and Italy. In **France**, a new law prohibited the production of oil and gas after 2040, and the grant of new hydrocarbon exploration licences with immediate effect in France and its overseas territories. It thereby sought to implement the country's commitments under the Paris Agreement on climate change. An example of how an international treaty can be used to seek to influence such a measure is that a Canadian oil and gas company was reported to be preparing an ECT claim to defend its investment.[15]

In **Italy**, similar legislative actions against hydrocarbon exploration and production went from the proposal stage to law in the form of Act No. 11/2019. Article 11-ter of this Act suspends all exploration permits as well as new applications for production concessions for a period of eighteen months.[16] In effect, it is a moratorium during which time the Government is supposed to determine which areas are suitable for hydrocarbon activities, taking environmental factors into account. Administrative fees were also to be increased by twenty-five times because of the Act. In Italy's case, there is a precedent for arbitration with investors over hydrocarbon operations. In the *Rockhopper v. Italy* arbitration, the investor claimed compensation of EUR 275 million from Italy for a breach of its obligations under the ECT, including legitimate expectations.[17] The tribunal found that a law of December 2015 which strengthened an offshore drilling ban, and the subsequent denial of an application for a production licence amounted to a direct expropriation under Article 13 of the ECT. Italy's right to impose and strengthen a drilling ban was not in question, the tribunal found, and the protection from expropriation in Article 13 was not absolute. However, Italy had failed to pay any compensation for the loss of the right to be granted a concession to produce hydrocarbons. The claimants were awarded EUR 184 million in lost profits plus decommissioning costs of more than EUR 6 million and interest.[18]

In North America, there are examples of similar actions leading to arbitrations by foreign investors. In **Canada**, the decision by the Ontario Power Authority (OPA) to delay the award of permits and authorizations to Windstream Energy led to a claim under NAFTA,[19] which Canada ultimately lost. Following Ontario's enactment of the

14. *Strabag SE, Erste Nordsee-Offshore Holding GmbH and Zweite Nordsee-Offshore Holding GmbH v. Germany*, ICSID Case No. ARB/19/29.
15. GAR, 13 September 2018: 'France threatened over oil and gas bill.' The author is not aware of any claim going forward to arbitral proceedings. The Law (Law No. 2017-1839) was adopted on 30 December 2017. It was not retroactive.
16. Danilo Ruggero Di Bella and Josep Galvez, 13 March 2019, 'Oil & Gas: Is Italy Doing It Wrong All over Again?' at http://arbitrationblog.kluwerarbitration.com/2019/03/13/oil-gas-is-italy-doing-it-wrong-all-over-again/.
17. *Rockhopper Italia SpA, Rockhopper Mediterranean Ltd and Rockhopper Exploration Plc v. Italy*, ICSID Case No. ARB/17/14.
18. Final Award, 23 August 2022, para 335.
19. *Windstream Energy LLC v. Government of Canada*, 27 September 2016, PCA Case No. 2018-54.

Green Energy and Green Economy Act of 2009, and subsequent promulgation of implementing rules, a Feed-in Tariff programme was created for the development of renewable energy projects, including onshore and offshore wind projects. After the award of a Feed-in Tariff Contract to the claimant, the Provincial Government was alleged to have delayed approval of the necessary permits and authorizations for the project, a USD 3.9 billion 300-megawatt offshore wind facility on Lake Ontario. A year later, the Ontario government imposed a moratorium arguing that more scientific research was required on the environmental impact of wind energy projects. This frustrated Windstream's attempts to develop its wind project. The tribunal had to consider whether the acts of the OPA, a state enterprise with responsibility for signing long-term electricity purchasing contracts with companies, could be attributed to Canada, a question that had arisen in another wind energy case, *Mesa Power v. Canada*.[20] The tribunal's answer was that it was not necessary to determine this since the conduct underpinning the NAFTA breach was found to be conduct of the Ontario government directly, not the OPA. The tribunal did not contest the reason given for the moratorium but rather the absence of any subsequent action taken 'to address the scientific uncertainty surrounding offshore wind that it relied upon as the main publicly cited reason for the moratorium'.[21] Canada had also failed to 'address the legal and contractual limbo in which Windstream found itself after the imposition of the moratorium'.[22] Hence, the tribunal found that Windstream had been treated unfairly and inequitably within the meaning of Article 1105(1) of NAFTA when the moratorium had been imposed on offshore wind energy projects. Windstream had claimed USD 460 million in damages, but received only USD 21 million in 2016, including legal costs.[23] In calculating damages, the tribunal found that the project progress was insufficient to justify the use of a Discounted Cash Flow (DCF) method and favoured instead a comparables approach, entailing the examination of comparable projects around the world to determine the usual value of a project at the stage of progress that Windstream's had reached.[24] The investor had also not lost the full value of the project, which for the tribunal was a reason for denying the full value in compensation.

A further claim arose out of Ontario's renewable energy programme in late 2019. In *Tennant Energy v. Canada*, the claims were made (among others) that the administration of the FiT programme was non-transparent and opaque, and that the award of access to the electricity grid was unfair and gave preferential treatment to

---

20. *Mesa Power Group LLC v. Government of Canada*, UNCITRAL, Award, 26 March 2016. The claim centred on a FiT scheme aimed at promoting the use of renewable energy in electricity generation in Ontario. Mesa claimed that Canada had imposed arbitrary requirements through the design and implementation of its FiT programme, preventing Mesa from participating and had given preferential treatment to rival companies. Mesa lost its claim in a majority decision. There was a robust 'concurring and dissenting opinion' by Judge Charles N. Brower.
21. Paragraph 378.
22. Paragraph 379.
23. Windstream Energy Press Release, 25 February 2017. The award was the largest made against Canada under NAFTA at the time.
24. Paragraphs 476-486.

another consortium.[25] An interesting aspect of this case, however, is that Canada sought security for costs and disclosure of third-party funding.[26] This request has its origin in delays it experienced in collecting on a final costs award from the earlier *Mesa* case. It is also a useful reminder that governments can have trouble in recovery of the costs of arbitration from certain investors.

Canada found itself involved in another claim arising from the decision by a different Provincial government, this time Alberta, to phase out greenhouse gas (GHG) emissions and air pollutants produced by coal-fired power generation by 2030 and make transition payments to certain companies in relation to this policy.[27] The decision to phase out coal-fired electricity was part of Alberta's Climate Leadership Plan and addressed its circumstances as the second highest GHG emitting sector in Alberta. Six of the existing coal-fired power plants were expected to operate beyond 2030, so the Provincial Government agreed to pay the operators around USD 1 billion in transition payments, a form of compensation, between 2016 and 2030. It did not propose to pay *suppliers* of coal, only the generation units.

In 2019, Westmoreland Mining Holdings (WMH), a US coal mining company, initiated arbitration proceedings under NAFTA Chapter 11. The allegation by WMH was that it suffered discrimination by the policy and the lack of payments made to it (as a supplier of coal). Most of the recipients of payments were in fact customers of WMH. It argued that its investment in 2014 in two Canadian entities, which directly or indirectly owned three coal mines located adjacent to power generators, had been made at a time when a federal regulatory scheme contemplated a fifty-year term for coal-fired power plants. Its losses were to include revenue from early closure on or before 2030 and accelerated costs arising from the rehabilitation of land after closure. In fact, the dispute arose from an investment made by Westmoreland Coal Company (WCC), which in late 2018 filed for bankruptcy and sent a notice of arbitration to Canada soon after. Some of its assets were transferred to WMH, the claimant in the arbitration, which had been incorporated in early 2019. WCC withdrew its NAFTA claim and WMH filed its notice of arbitration on its own behalf and under NAFTA. In its Award of January 2022, the tribunal found that it lacked jurisdiction since the claimant had to have owned or controlled the relevant investment at the time of the alleged treaty breach to bring a NAFTA claim. Since the claimant did not exist when the underlying measures were adopted, it did not qualify as a successor of an entity that owned the investment at the relevant time. No assignment of the right to bring a NAFTA claim could have taken place, so WMH did not qualify as a protected investor. The tribunal also upheld Canada's objection that the challenged measures did not relate to the claimant or its investment in the terms of NAFTA.[28] The claimant had not undertaken any investment risk since the coal phase-out was widely known at the time

25. *Tennant Energy LLC v. Government of Canada*, PCA Case No. 2018-54, Notice of Arbitration, 1 June 2017. All claims were dismissed after the tribunal found that the claimant was not a qualifying investor under NAFTA: Final Award, 25 October 2022.
26. *Ibid.*: Government of Canada Motion for security of costs and disclosure of third-party funding, 16 August 2019.
27. *Westmoreland Mining Holdings LLC v. Government of Canada*, ICSID Case No. UNCT/20/3.
28. Final Award, 31 January 2022.

when the claimant was incorporated and had even been factored into the purchase price the claimant paid for the assets of WCC.

A very different arbitral claim resulted in an arbitral award against the Caribbean state of **Grenada**.[29] In 2016, the Government of Grenada adopted an Electricity Supply Act that ended the monopoly of Grenada Private Power Limited, partly owned by a US-based company, WRB Enterprises, and altered the rate-setting mechanism, as well as limiting some of the tax advantages. WRB had a Share Purchase Agreement with Grenada under which the latter was obliged to repurchase the shares according to a specified formula if one of several 'repurchase events' occurred. In their claim, WRB argued that following the 2016 measure Grenada was under an obligation to repurchase their 50% stake in the utility, GRENELEC. The tribunal agreed and ordered Grenada to purchase the shares at a price above their fair market value.

The relevance of this contract-based dispute to this paper is the renewable energy dimension that was introduced into the case by Grenada. The electricity utility had done remarkably little to draw upon the country's significant potential in geothermal energy, wind, solar energy and municipal waste-to-energy over a period of many years. Instead, it relied upon the import of expensive diesel fuel with damaging effects on the country's foreign exchange. The 2016 legal measure could be seen as an attempt by the Government to act in a way that implemented its Nationally Determined Contributions under the Paris Agreement. The tribunal was not convinced by this argument, however, and concluded on the evidence 'that neither the Claimants nor the Government pursued renewable energy proposals with as much vigour as they now assert'.[30] The root of the problem in the relationship between the Government and the monopoly utility had nothing to do with the Paris Agreement but rather lay in the weak regulatory framework established many years earlier in 1994 and the failure to set performance standards for renewable energy which would have promoted its development.

IV   QUESTIONS

1   Are Legal Measures Taken by States to Promote Energy Transitions Likely to Be Undermined or Halted by Established Investment Treaty Provisions Such as Those in the Energy Charter Treaty?

If we examine the cases referred to in section III above, we find that in the European cases (the Netherlands, Germany, and Italy), the right of the government to introduce a legal measure for a transition policy was not in question in the disputes. Rather, the origin of the investors' claims was the lack of appropriate compensation. The Canadian cases engaged with the need to pay compensation but the outcomes for investors were hardly indicative of treaty bias towards the investor. In *Windstream*, compensation for a breach of due process was less than a twentieth of what was claimed, while in *Westmoreland* the claim was dismissed on jurisdictional grounds. They also involved

---

29. *Grenada Private Power Limited and WRB Enterprises, Inc. v. Grenada*, ICSID Case No. ARB/17/13, Award, 19 March 2020.
30. *Ibid.*, para. 140.

consideration of the scope of the investment at the core of the dispute, underlining the need to show documented expenditures.

The cases remind us that if, indeed, the claimants are able to prove that they had an investment within the terms of the relevant treaty, the tribunal will then proceed to consider how much was invested and when, under what legal circumstances, with what kind of due diligence and using what professional or commercial judgement: all these are hurdles that an investor/claimant may not find easy to negotiate in a dispute arising from a transition measure taken by a state that affects their investment.

If we turn to the sole international treaty instrument that expressly applies to investments in the energy sector, the ECT, the idea that it is fundamentally biased in favour of fossil fuel investors seems odd.[31] It has a limited membership geographically, lacks among its ratifying states all the major hydrocarbon-producing states and includes only four states as members that are the 'home-states' of internationally operating oil and gas companies (France, Italy, the Netherlands and the UK). Most of the claims leading to arbitration under the ECT have in fact concerned renewable forms of energy, not fossil fuels, and have concerned familiar forms of investment protection in international law. Further, as the cases here demonstrate, where claims have been successful, the claimants have received significantly less compensation than they initially sought and in more than a few cases, delay in payment has followed a challenge to the award from the respondent party.

2   In the Context of the Energy Transitions, How Are Tribunals Likely to Understand the Protections Grounded in the Notion of Legitimate Expectations?

The recent awards in arbitrations concerning renewable energy in Spain, Italy and the Czech Republic, have emphasized that differences of view can arise between and within arbitral tribunals around the notion of Fair and Equitable Treatment and particularly its constituent notion, an investor's legitimate expectation. The uncertainty that the energy transitions are giving rise to – about the state's right to regulate and its limits – seem likely to continue this trend towards arbitrator scrutiny of what expectation can be considered legitimate as a defence for investors against an adverse state measure. Questions that are likely to be asked will include several: are the expectations based on contractual commitments or on the host state's legal order? Are they based on representations, circumstances or context? Separately, but linked to this, there will be questions about possible negligence on the part of the claimant. Article 39 of the Draft ILC Articles on State Responsibility notes that the extent to which the

---

31. This is a view that has acquired much media coverage: for example, the Guardian, 21 June 2022, which refers to a letter to the EU and signed by seventy-six climate scientists that links the ECT investor protections to obstacles to plant closures and prospective large compensation payments: https://www.theguardian.com/environment/2022/jun/21/young-people-go-to-europe an-court-to-stop-treaty-that-aids-fossil-fuel-investors.

claimant's own actions or omissions contributed to the injury is a matter for the tribunal's discretion.[32]

3 Will Transition Policies and Measures Have Effects on Commercial Disputes among Parties to Agreements for Traditional Oil and Gas Projects?

Yes. Even if the state is not a partner to the agreement in question, which might be a Joint Operating Agreement (JOA), this context of state-induced transition seems likely to foster potential for disputes among parties in certain situations. Companies may well have quite different assessments of their obligations in relation to climate change mitigation, differing investment strategies in response to it, and different timetables for implementing these on the road towards Net Zero emissions. These can be expected to evolve and as they do, the potential for conflicting strategies and priorities from those of their partners in a particular project may well grow. This may lead to more than differences over familiar exit issues such as the decommissioning of oil and gas installations. It may concern decisions to proceed or not with appraisal and development, following risk assessments, perhaps favouring withdrawal from a particular project or alternatively, seeking to proceed with commitments that go beyond those required by the relevant regulations. In many countries, such differences among project partners will be complicated by the presence of state energy companies. This is new territory for investors in large, long-term, multi-partner energy projects.

4 What Impact Is This Likely to Have on the Arbitration Process Itself, If Any?

One of the notable features of *energy* disputes is the frequent use of experts in arbitral proceedings. Often, this is understood as the use of expert testimony to contribute specialist knowledge to the development of the tribunal's views on quantum or to assist the tribunal in understanding the highly complex calculations that often arise in gas pricing disputes and sometimes the geological and engineering complexities of petroleum reservoir management. However, it is less commonly observed that this reliance on expertise can also extend to matters that concern industry practice, given the widespread use in petroleum agreements of terms such as 'good international petroleum industry practice.' The lack of standardization or limited recognition of commonly used terms means that there is scope for differences of view. The new trends towards climate and energy transition policies and corporate initiatives mean that how 'good international industry practice' is characterized will change, and in ways that are likely to be uneven. Nor is there any reason why this preoccupation with identifying good industry practice should be restricted to one energy sub-sector. The role of experts in arbitral proceedings can be expected to expand as a result, especially in the renewable energy sub-sector.

---

32. The Tribunals in *MTD v. Chile* and *Occidental v. Ecuador* decided that damages should be reduced because of the claimants' failings.

CHAPTER 44

Access to and Use of Freshwater River Resources

Rodman Bundy[*]

TABLE OF CONTENTS

I   INTRODUCTION

The combination of population increase, climate change, environmental concerns and growth in demand for use of fresh water is likely to lead to an increase in watercourse disputes at the State-to-State and investor-State levels in the future.

At the State-to-State level, the past ten years have already seen a number of such disputes relating to transboundary watercourses and shared rivers submitted to

---

[*] Rodman Bundy is a senior partner in the Singapore office of Squire Patton Boggs LLP specializing in public international law, investment and commercial arbitration and the upstream oil and gas industry. He is a member of the New York Bar and a former member of the Paris Bar. Over the past forty years, Mr. Bundy has made numerous appearances as counsel and advocate before the International Court of Justice, the International Tribunal for the Law of the Sea, the Iran-United States Claims Tribunal and institutional and ad hoc State-to-State, investment and commercial arbitral tribunals.

international adjudication or arbitration. However, the principal multilateral convention dealing with international watercourses – the 1997 United Nations Convention on the Law of Non-navigational Uses of International Watercourses (the 'Watercourses Convention') – suffers from a lack of State Parties from Asia and Latin America and does not contain a compulsory and binding dispute resolution mechanism. Moreover, tensions continue to exist between the two main substantive principles set out in the Watercourses Convention – the 'equitable and reasonable utilization' principle frequently relied on by upstream States and the 'no significant harm' principle that downstream States often favour. What is more, the extent to which a State is obliged to notify and consult with a potentially affected State and take steps to mitigate the risk of transboundary harm with respect to projects impacting an international watercourse can be controversial.

At the investor-State level, the balance between a State's right to regulate and use freshwater resources for the benefit of its population, and an investor that invests in projects that use or impact these resources, will also be likely to be a source of disputes.

Section II of this chapter will touch on the recent case law relating to international river disputes. Section III will then address the key principles and jurisdictional limitations for settling disputes by means of binding arbitration or adjudication embodied in the UN Watercourses Convention. Lastly, section IV will turn to the prospect that disputes relating to the protection or use of freshwater resources may increasingly become the subject matter of investment arbitration.

II   RECENT INTER-STATE CASES RELATING TO INTERNATIONAL WATERCOURSES

1   The *Gabčikovo-Nagymaros Project* Case

The modern, albeit modest, tendency for State-to-State disputes relating to international watercourses to be submitted to international adjudication or arbitration may be said to have started with the case concerning the *Gabčikovo-Nagymaros Project*. The case was instituted by means of the notification of a Special Agreement between Hungary and Slovakia to the International Court of Justice on 2 July 1993. It is principally related to the question of whether either party had breached obligations owing to the other under a Treaty on the Construction and Operation of the Gabčikovo-Nagymaros Barrage System on the Danube River entered into between Hungary and Czechoslovakia in 1977.

While environmental issues were raised with respect to the protection of the river, the Court's 1997 Judgment dealt mainly with issues of treaty interpretation rather than water law.[1] However, in the course of its Judgment, the Court did make reference to the 'equitable and reasonable utilization' principle reflected in Article 5 of the UN Watercourses Convention.[2] It also emphasized the 'need to reconcile economic

---

1. *Gabčikovo-Nagymaros Project (Hungary/Slovakia)*, Judgment, I.C.J. Reports 1997, p. 7.
2. I.C.J. Reports 1997, p. 80, paras 147 and 150.

development with protection of the environment' as expressed in the concept of sustainable development.[3]

Interestingly, the Special Agreement provided that, if the parties could not agree on the modalities for the execution of the Court's Judgment, either party could request the Court to render an Additional Judgment. Slovakia made such a request in 1998 – a year after the Court's original Judgment – but the proceedings were subsequently suspended when the parties notified the Court that they were continuing their negotiations. Those negotiations have not yet reached a conclusion with the result that, some twenty-five years after the Court's Judgment, the case is still listed as pending on the Court's docket – the longest such pending case.

2   Pulp Mills on the River Uruguay

In May 2006, Argentina filed an application instituting proceedings against Uruguay concerning alleged violations by Uruguay of a 1975 Treaty dealing with the utilization of the part of the River Uruguay that constitutes their international boundary. The Court's jurisdiction was based on a compromissory clause in the 1975 Treaty.

This was not a case involving an upstream and downstream State or the question of equitable and reasonable utilization of the waters of the river. Rather, the case concerned environmental issues between two riparian States situated on opposite sides of the same river. Argentina's contentions centred on a claim that Uruguay had proceeded with the construction of two pulp mills on the river without complying with the prior notification and consultation procedures provided for in the Treaty and that the activities of the mills would have an adverse effect on the quality of the waters of the river thereby causing damage to Argentina.

The Court ruled that Uruguay had breached certain procedural obligations in the Treaty by not informing the joint commission established by the parties under the Treaty before issuing initial environmental authorizations for the works, and not notifying Argentina about the plans for the project. However, on the substantive level, the Court held that there was no conclusive evidence that Uruguay had failed to act with due diligence, or that discharges from the mills would have an adverse effect or cause harm to the living resources and quality of the water, or the ecological balance of the river.[4]

3   Construction of a Road in Costa Rica along the San Juan River

The Court was faced with another case between two States situated on opposite sides of a boundary river involving environmental issues in the *Construction of a Road in*

---

3. *Ibid.*, p. 78, para. 140.
4. *Pulp Mills on the River Uruguay (Argentina v. Uruguay)*, Judgment, I.C.J. Reports 2010, p. 75, para. 180, p. 77, para. 189 and p. 101, para. 265.

Costa Rica case brought before the Court by Nicaragua in 2011 pursuant to the compromissory clause contained in Article XXXI of the Pact of Bogotá.[5]

In its pleadings, Nicaragua alleged that, in constructing a road along the banks of the San Juan River in Costa Rican territory, Costa Rica had breached procedural obligations to notify and consult with Nicaragua, and to carry out an environmental impact assessment, before commencing the works. Nicaragua also alleged that Costa Rica had breached the substantive obligation not to cause significant harm to Nicaragua. With respect to this issue, Nicaragua's claims centred on allegations that the construction had harmed Nicaragua by increasing sediment loads in the river, damaging the river's morphology and aquatic ecosystem, and prejudicing Nicaragua's navigational rights and dredging activities.

The Court's Judgment, rendered in 2015, contains important observations with respect to procedural obligations under general international law relating to the protection of the environment. These are clearly relevant to international watercourses, but they also apply more widely to other kinds of projects that give rise to the risk of transboundary harm.

The Court expanded on what it had said in the *Pulp Mills* case with respect to the circumstances that must exist for a State to be obligated to conduct an environmental impact assessment and to notify and consult with a neighbouring State, for projects having the potential to cause significant transboundary environmental harm. In so doing, the Court laid down a three-step approach that a State is obliged to adopt when there is a risk that its activities may cause significant harm to another State:

- First, in order to fulfil its obligation to exercise due diligence in preventing significant transboundary environmental harm, 'a State must, before embarking on an activity having the potential adversely to affect the environment of another State, ascertain if there is a risk of significant transboundary harm'.[6]
- Second, if it is ascertained that there is such a risk, this triggers the requirement for the State to carry out an environmental impact assessment before proceeding with the project.[7] As the Court noted: 'the obligation to conduct an environmental impact assessment requires an *ex ante* evaluation of the risk of significant transboundary harm'.[8] And it further observed, citing from its decision in *Pulp Mills*, that 'it may now be considered a requirement under general international law to undertake an environmental impact assessment where there is a risk that the proposed industrial activity may have a significant adverse impact in a transboundary context, in particular, on a shared resource'.[9]

---

5. *Certain Activities Carried Out by Nicaragua in the Border Area (Costa Rica v. Nicaragua) and Construction of a Road in Costa Rica along the San Juan River (Nicaragua v. Costa Rica)*, Judgment, I.C.J. Reports 2015, p. 665.
6. I.C.J. Reports 2015, pp. 706-707, para. 104; and *see* p. 723, para. 161.
7. *Ibid.*, p. 707, para. 104.
8. *Ibid.*, p. 723, para. 161.
9. *Ibid.*, p. 706, para. 104, citing *Pulp Mills on the River Uruguay (Argentina v. Uruguay)*, Judgment. I.C.J. Reports 2010, p. 83, para. 204. The Court also noted that, although its statement in *Pulp*

– Third, 'If the environmental impact assessment confirms that there is a risk of significant transboundary harm, the State planning to undertake the activity is required, in conformity with its due diligence obligation, to notify and consult in good faith with the potentially affected State, where that is necessary to determine appropriate measures to prevent or mitigate that risk.'[10]

In the operative part of its Judgment, the Court ruled that Costa Rica had violated its obligations under general international law by failing to carry out an environmental impact assessment concerning construction of the road. However, it dismissed Nicaragua's substantive claims because they had not been established or proved.[11]

4   Dispute over the Status and Use of the Waters of the Silala

While both the *Pulp Mills* and *Construction of a Road* cases concerned the environmental obligations of a State bordering a shared river, the Court currently has before it a case involving the status and use of a river – the Silala – where the question arises whether the river is an international watercourse and, if so, what the respective rights and obligations of the upstream and downstream States are with respect to the use of its waters.

The case was brought by Chile against Bolivia by means of an application filed on 6 June 2016. As with the *Construction of a Road* case, the Court's jurisdiction is founded on Article XXXI of the Pact of Bogotá. The Court convened oral hearings in the case in April 2022, and the judgment is currently pending.

The origins of the dispute date back to the 1920s when a Chilean concessionaire constructed a series of channels in Bolivian territory, where the springs that feed the Silala originate, in order to assist in the diversion of part of those waters through a pipeline to Chile for railway, industrial and drinking water purposes. The Silala itself is a very small river, but its importance is enhanced by the fact that it is located in one of the driest places in the world.

Questions arose during the case involving (i) whether Bolivia had the right to dismantle the man-made channels in its territory and, if so, under what conditions; (ii) whether Bolivia had breached customary international law by building some modest structures near the river; and (iii) the mutual rights and obligations of the parties under the 'equitable utilization' and 'no significant harm' principles.

Given my involvement as counsel for one of the parties in this case, it would not be appropriate to comment further on the merits of the case. What can be said is that, if the Court finds that the Silala constitutes an international watercourse, it may well have to address for the first time the respective rights and obligations of an upstream

---

Mills referred to industrial activities, 'the underlying principle applies generally to proposed activities which may have a significant adverse impact in a transboundary context'.

10. *Ibid.*, p. 707, para. 104.

11. I.C.J. Reports 2015, p. 741, para. 229; and *see* p. 731, para. 196, p. 733, para. 204, p. 734, para. 205, p. 734, para. 207 and p. 736, para. 213.

and downstream user, and the interplay between the 'equitable and reasonable utilization' and 'no significant harm' principles.

5   The Indus Waters *Kishenganga Arbitration*

The *Kishenganga Arbitration* was brought by Pakistan against India in 2010 pursuant to the dispute resolution clause in the 1960 Indus Waters Treaty.[12] That Treaty was a remarkable instrument painstakingly negotiated under the auspices of the World Bank. The Treaty governed the division and use of the waters of six major tributaries of the Indus River system, which originated in India and flowed downstream into Pakistan. The fact that the *Kishenganga Arbitration* was the first case brought to arbitration under the Treaty in more than fifty years since the Treaty came into force attests to its comprehensiveness and durability.

The principal issue in the case was whether India was entitled to construct a dam on and divert the waters of the Kishenganga/Neelum River, a tributary of the Jhelum River (one of the six main tributaries making up the Indus system), in order to generate hydroelectric power. The water once diverted would flow through a tunnel to a power plant being constructed by India, and thence would be released via another river and a lake back into the Jhelum some 200 kilometres downstream from where the original diversion occurred. Thus, Pakistan would eventually receive the diverted waters, but only far downstream. However, Pakistan also had plans to use the waters of the Kishenganga/Neelum for its own hydroelectric project before the diverted waters flowed back into the river, and it maintained that India's diversion of the waters would damage the economics of its own project and adversely impact the aquatic environment of the river on its side of the Line of Control in Kashmir.

The arbitration had several unusual, if not unique, features. First, the Court of Arbitration comprised seven members. Each party nominated two members with the remaining three, including the Chairman, appointed through a complex process set out in the Treaty. One of the three had to be a highly qualified engineer; a second was required to be well-versed in international law; and the third was stipulated to be a person qualified by status and reputation to be the Chairman. Ultimately, the selection of the engineer member was made by the Rector of the Imperial College of Science and Technology, London; the Lord Chief Justice of England selected the legal member; and the Secretary-General of the United Nations selected the Chairman (Stephen Schwebel, a former President of the ICJ).

Of particular interest was the requirement for one of the members to be an engineer. The case – indeed, the Indus Waters Treaty as a whole – dealt with numerous highly technical matters, and it is thought that the Court of Arbitration benefitted from having an engineer as one of its members.[13]

---

12. 419 U.N.T.S 126.
13. For an excellent study on the use of experts in freshwater disputes, *see*: Dr Makane Moïse Mbengue and Rukmini Das, 'Use of Experts in International Freshwater Disputes: A Critical Assessment' in *Brill Research Perspectives in International Water Law*, Vol. 4.3 (2019) pp. 1-94.

A second feature of the arbitration was that the Court of Arbitration organized not one, but two, site visits to the area. This included visiting both the Indian and Pakistani dam locations along the river, which formed part of their hydroelectric projects. Needless to say, the organization of these visits required substantial logistical arrangements to be put in place.

The case was decided mainly on the basis of the Treaty provisions. However, the Treaty did provide that the Court of Arbitration could apply customary international law whenever necessary for the interpretation or application of the Treaty. In its Partial Award rendered on 18 February 2013, the Court of Arbitration referred to a number of general principles that informed its interpretation of the Treaty. These included:

- Reference to what it termed 'a foundational principle of customary international law' that had already been enunciated in the *Trail Smelter* arbitration to the effect that, 'no State has the right to use or permit the use of its territory in such a manner as to cause injury by fumes in or to the territory of another or the properties or persons therein, when the case is of serious consequence and the injury is established by clear and convincing evidence'.[14]
- Principle 21 of the 1972 Stockholm Declaration, which the Court of Arbitration described as embodying a 'broader restatement of the duty to avoid transboundary harm … pursuant to which States, when exploiting natural resources, must 'ensure that activities within their jurisdiction or control do not cause damage to the environment of other States or of areas beyond the limits of national jurisdiction'.[15]
- The fact that principles of international environmental law must be taken into account even when interpreting treaties concluded *before* the development of that body of law.[16]

The Kishenganga River was characterized by highly variable seasonal flows. In the wet (monsoon) season, there was plenty of water to enable India to divert an amount necessary for its hydroelectric plant while still leaving an adequate flow to sustain the aquatic environment downstream and allow Pakistan to operate its own hydroelectric project. During the dry season, however, flows were much lower. Consequently, the Court of Arbitration concentrated on a minimum flow that India would be required to release during the dry season so as not to cause significant harm to the downstream environment and to enable Pakistan to operate its plant, even if at a reduced capacity. In its Partial Award, the Court of Arbitration expressly requested the parties to provide more information on the effect a range of flows would have on power generation and the environment before making a final decision.

---

14. *Indus Waters Kishenganga Arbitration (Pakistan v. India)*, Partial Award dated 18 February 2013, para. 448; citing *Trail Smelter arbitration*, 16 April 1938 and 11 March 1941, 13 R.I.A.A. 1905, at 1965, which was reaffirmed in the *Legality of the Threat or Use of Nuclear Weapons*, *Advisory Opinion*, I.C.J. Reports 1996, p. 226, p. 242.
15. *Ibid.*, para. 448; referring to Stockholm Declaration of the United Nations Conference on the Human Environment, 16 June 1972, UN Doc. A/CONF. 48/14/Rev 1, 3.
16. *Ibid.*, para. 452.

In its Final Award, the Court of Arbitration did not refer to the principle of 'equitable and reasonable utilization' per se; it gave more detailed treatment to the environmental factors at issue. Nonetheless, it seems likely that the Court of Arbitration had the notion in mind in applying a balanced approach to each Party's interests reflected in the 1960 Treaty when it ruled that India was obligated to ensure that a specified minimum flow would be released below its dam during the driest months so as to take into account Pakistan's interests.[17]

| III | THE UNITED NATIONS CONVENTION ON THE LAW OF THE NON-NAVIGATIONAL USES OF INTERNATIONAL WATERCOURSES AND ITS JURISDICTIONAL LIMITATIONS FOR DISPUTE SETTLEMENT[18] |

1 The States Parties to the Convention

The UN Watercourses Convention was a long time in the making. After some twenty years of study, the International Law Commission adopted Draft Articles on the subject in 1994. This formed the basis for negotiations in the Sixth Committee, which culminated in the adoption of the Convention by the UN General Assembly on 21 May 1997 by a vote of 103 in favour, 3 against and 27 abstentions.[19]

Despite this sizeable majority, the Convention did not come into force until 17 August 2014 when Viet Nam became the thirty-fifth party to ratify or accede to the Convention. As of 2020, there were thirty-seven State Parties to the Convention. Obviously, this falls well short of the number of States that voted in favour of the Convention in the General Assembly in 1997.

The geographic composition of the State Parties to the Convention is revealing. As of 2020, there were only two Asian States that were parties – Viet Nam and Uzbekistan – and no Latin American States, although both Paraguay and Venezuela signed the Convention in the late 1990s but did not thereafter ratify it. Moreover, a cursory review of the list of States Parties suggests that outside of Europe – i.e., particularly in the Middle East and Africa – the vast preponderance of parties appear to be downstream States with respect to one or more international watercourses. This raises the question of whether upstream States are less comfortable with the Convention.

2 Equitable and Reasonable Utilization

For purposes of this chapter, Articles 5 ('Equitable and reasonable utilization and participation'), Article 6 ('Factors relevant to equitable and reasonable utilization'),

---

17. *Indus Waters Kishenganga Arbitration (Pakistan v. India)*, Final Award dated 20 December 2013, paras 114-116.
18. This chapter does not address the 1996 Convention on the Protection and Use of Transboundary Watercourses and International Lakes or the ILC's 2008 Draft Articles on the Law of Trans-boundary Aquifers, the latter of which includes the 'equitable and reasonable utilization' and 'no significant harm' principles found in the UN Watercourses Convention.
19. General Assembly resolution 51/229, annex, *Official Records of the General Assembly*, Fifty-first session, Supplement No. 49 (A/51/49).

Article 7 ('Obligation not to cause significant harm') and Article 33 ('Settlement of disputes') are of particular interest.

Article 5, paragraph 1, which Professor Stephen McCaffrey suggests many regard as the 'cornerstone of the law in this field',[20] provides as follows:

> Watercourse States shall in their respective territories utilize an international watercourse in an equitable and reasonable manner. In particular, an international watercourse shall be used and developed by watercourse States with a view to attaining optimal and sustainable utilization thereof and benefits therefrom, taking into account the interests of the watercourse States concerned, consistent with adequate protection of the watercourse.

Paragraph 2 of Article 5 provides that the Watercourse States shall participate in the use, development and protection of an international watercourse. Participation in this sense relates to Article 8, which contains a general obligation for States to cooperate in good faith to obtain the optimal utilization and adequate protection mentioned in Article 5(1).

A non-exhaustive list of factors relevant to equitable and reasonable utilization is contained in Article 6 of the Convention. Most of these factors appear in Article 5(2) of the 1966 Helsinki Rules adopted by the International Law Association as guidelines, although that document lists some additional factors as well. However, the scope of the 'equitable and reasonable' utilization principle has not been addressed by the International Court of Justice (ICJ) or an inter-State arbitral tribunal to date, and there is limited State practice on the issue. The extent to which these factors reflect customary international law therefore remains open.

3   No Significant Harm

Article 7 of the UN Watercourses Convention is entitled 'Obligation not to cause significant harm'. Paragraph 1 provides that 'Watercourse States shall, in utilizing an international watercourse in their territories, take all appropriate measures to prevent the causing of significant harm to other watercourse States.' Article 7(2) then places an obligation on a State that causes significant harm to another watercourse State to take all appropriate measures in consultation with the affected State to eliminate or mitigate such harm and, where appropriate, to discuss the question of compensation.

Once again, the meaning and scope of this provision have not yet been tested in international litigation or arbitration. For his part, McCaffrey suggests that the no-harm principle 'is not, and has never been, conceived as absolutely prohibiting the causing of significant harm in all circumstances'.[21] Moreover, as can be seen from the case law referred to above, the International Court of Justice has addressed the general obligation to prevent significant transboundary environmental harm in its judgments in the *Pulp Mills* and *Construction of a Road* cases, and the Court of Arbitration dealt

---

20. Stephen C. McCaffrey, *The Law of International Watercourses Non-navigational Uses* (Oxford University Press, 2019), p. 305.
21. S. McCaffrey, *supra* n. 20, p. 347.

with environmental issues in its awards in the *Kishenganga Arbitration*. However, none of those decisions specifically dealt with the UN Watercourses Convention as part of the applicable law. That being said, the issue may well arise in the pending case concerning the *Dispute over the Status and Use of the Waters of the Silala (Chile v. Bolivia)*.

4   Dispute Resolution

Article 33 of the UN Watercourses Convention addresses the settlement of disputes. It provides that, if the parties concerned cannot reach an agreement by negotiation requested by one of them, they may jointly seek the good offices of, or request mediation or conciliation by, a third party, including submitting the dispute to arbitration or the ICJ. This provision does not provide for compulsory third-party settlement. It simply says that the parties *may* jointly request a particular procedure.

In the event the parties have not been able to settle their dispute within six months from the time of the request for negotiations, the dispute may be submitted unilaterally by a party to an impartial fact-finding procedure set out in paragraphs 4-9 of Article 33. The fact-finding Commission established under these procedures is composed of three members unless a party fails to nominate a member, in which case the other party may request the Secretary-General of the United Nations to appoint a person who shall constitute a single-member Commission. After undertaking its fact-finding mission, the Commission shall adopt a report by majority vote and submit it to the parties concerned setting out its findings and such recommendations as it deems appropriate for an equitable solution of the dispute. The parties concerned are obliged to consider the report in good faith, but the report does not create any binding obligations on them.

It follows that, unlike a multilateral convention such as the United Nations Convention on the Law of the Sea, the UN Watercourses Convention does not contain any compulsory dispute resolution procedure that is legally binding.

As discussed earlier, thus far river disputes at the State-to-State level have gone to third-party adjudication or arbitration either by virtue of a multilateral convention such as the Pact of Bogotá that provides for the general jurisdiction of the ICJ (e.g., disputes over 'any question of international law'), or by Special Agreement, or by a specific bilateral treaty dealing with the river in question (the *Kishenganga Arbitration*).

IV   INVESTOR-STATE DISPUTES INVOLVING FRESHWATER

A number of investor-State disputes relating directly or indirectly to freshwater have emerged over the past fifteen years. In the author's view, this trend is likely to continue due to the risk of a future scarcity of freshwater resources.

As Ursula Kriebaum points out in discussing the relevant jurisprudence in her timely article on 'The Right to Water before Investment Tribunals', these disputes have often centred on disagreements between an investor and State authorities over water tariffs and their effect on the affordability of water, including privatization of the water, perceived shortcomings by the investor, and threats of pollution coupled with protection of the quality of water.[22]

One of the issues that have arisen in connection with these kinds of disputes, particularly as they relate to water fees, is the relationship between protecting a foreign investor's rights under an investment treaty and what may be considered a basic human right to affordable water. These issues have been addressed in cases such as *Aguas del Tunari, SA v. Bolivia*,[23] *Azurix v. Argentina*[24] and the *Suez* arbitrations.[25] While tribunals have not laid down hard and fast rules for how these interests should be balanced, the tribunal in *SAUR v. Argentina* noted that a State's prerogatives under human rights law 'are compatible with the rights of investors to receive protection offered by the BIT'. It observed:

> The fundamental right to water and the right of an investor to benefit from the protection offered by the BIT operate on different levels: the concessionary company of a basic public service is in a situation of dependency on the public administration, which has special powers to guarantee its enjoyment by virtue of the fundamental right to water; but the exercise of these powers is not absolute and must be combined with respect for the rights and guarantees granted to the foreign investor under the BIT. If the government decides to expropriate the investment, treat the investor unfairly or inequitably, or deny the promised protection of full security, all this by violating the BIT, the investor will be entitled to be compensated under the terms of the Treaty.[26]

With respect to the protection of the quality of water, a similar balancing of interests is at play. As Kriebaum observes, in cases such as *MethanexCorp v. USA* and *Clayton/Bilcon v. Canada*, 'legitimate expectations played a key role in the decisions of investment tribunals. Both cases demonstrate that *bona fide* regulation to ensure that water resources are protected against pollution will not lead to a violation of investment protection standards, except where specific promises to the contrary have been made'.[27]

A different question arose in *Bayview Irrigation District et al. v. United Mexican States*. The central issue was whether US entities that relied on waters from the Rio Grande, the apportionment of which was governed by a 1944 treaty between the United States and Mexico, could claim that Mexico's failure to let sufficient volumes flow into

---

22. Ursula Kriebaum, 'The Right to Water Before Investment Tribunals', *Brill Open Law* 1 (2018) 16-36. *See also*, Bree Farrugia, 'The Human Right to Water: Defences to Investment Treaty Violations', *Arbitration International*, 2015, 31, pp. 261-282.

23. *Aguas del Tunari, SA v. Bolivia*, ICSID Case No. ARB/02/3, Decision on Respondent's Objections to Jurisdiction, 21 October 2005.

24. *Azurix Corp. v. Argentina*, ICSID Case No. ARB/01/12, Award, 14 July 2006.

25. *Suez, Sociedad General de Aguas de Barcelona, S.A. and InterAgua Servicios Integrales del Agua, S.A. v. Argentina*, ICSID Case No. ARB/03/17, Decision on Liability, 30 July 2010, *AWG Group Ltd. Argentine Republic*, UNCITRAL, Decision on Liability, 30 July 2010, *Suez, Sociedad General de Aguas de Barcelona, S.A. and Vivendi Universal, S.A. v. Argentine Republic*, ICSID Case No. ARB/03/19, Decision on Liability, 30 July 2020.

26. *SAUR v. Argentina*, ICSID Case No. ARB/04/4, Decision on Jurisdiction and Liability, 6 June 2012.

27. U. Kriebaum, *supra* n. 22, p. 33.

the United States due to severe drought conditions in Mexico had damaged their irrigation operations in Texas in violation of NAFTA. The claimants alleged that Mexico's diversion of water amounted to an expropriation of their investments.[28]

The tribunal initially addressed the case in terms of whether it had jurisdiction over the claims. In particular, the question arose whether the claimant was an investor or had made an investment in the territory of the other State party (Mexico) within the scope of NAFTA. Noting that Chapter 11 of NAFTA is concerned with a 'foreign investment' which must be primarily regulated by the law of the State other than that of the investor's nationality, the tribunal concluded that the claimants were investors in Texas where their irrigation projects were located, but not foreign investors in Mexico.[29] Moreover, in response to the argument that the claimants had a right to water in Mexico pursuant to the 1944 Treaty – in other words, they effectively owned water in Mexico – the tribunal concluded that they did not.[30] The tribunal took the position that the question of whether diversion of the waters of the Rio Grande constituted a breach of the 1944 Treaty would be a matter for the two States that are the only parties to that Treaty (the USA and Mexico), but that 'the 1944 Treaty does not create property rights amounting to investments within the meaning of NAFTA'.[31]

V   CONCLUSION

At the State-to-State level, because of the lack of agreements providing for compulsory third-party settlement of freshwater disputes in the event a negotiated solution is not achieved, future recourse to the ICJ or arbitration is likely to be limited even if there is currently a modest trend for such cases to be litigated. However, it can be hoped that, with the increased scarcity of freshwater coupled with more demands for its use, States will come to accept the proposition that new means are needed to resolve such disputes.

The situation may be different with respect to investor-State interests concerning freshwater resources. While other investment cases involving water rights beyond those that have been referred to above could be cited, it seems clear that, despite anti-investment arbitration sentiments emerging from some States, freshwater-related disputes will probably continue to form the subject matter of future investment arbitrations.

---

28. The case is examined in greater detail in Michael Rand, 'Water-Related International Investment Disputes: A Fresh Look at Bayview Irrigation District v. United Mexican States', *Journal of International Arbitration*, 2012, 29(5), pp. 605-622.
29. *Bayview Irrigation District et al. v. United Mexican States*, ICSID ARB(AF)/05/1, Award dispatched to the parties on 19 June 2007, paras 105-109 and para. 113.
30. *Ibid.*, para. 114.
31. *Ibid.*, para. 121.

CHAPTER 45

New Frontiers II: The Subject Matters of the Disputes of Tomorrow – Cloud Disputes

Ginta Ahrel[*]

TABLE OF CONTENTS

I   **INTRODUCTION**

In the last decade or so, cloud computing has become an integral part of our lives. As private individuals, we use it for everyday actions such as web-based e-mail or remote banking. In a business environment, it is increasingly used for communication and collaboration tools, customer relations management, document handling and storage, to name a few. Governmental institutions, too, are increasingly adopting cloud solutions as public services go online. Notably, even large transnational corporations,

---

[*] Partner at Westerberg & Partners, Stockholm, Sweden; Member of the Board of the SCC Arbitration Institute; Member of the Board of the Swedish Arbitration Association; Member of the Board of the Swedish Women in Arbitration Network.

     The author is grateful to Yaroslava Sushinets, legal intern at Westerberg & Partners, for initial research for this chapter.

including telecom operators, data infrastructure equipment suppliers, as well as IT software houses, are now moving their private IT networks and resources to the cloud.

The growth of the cloud computing industry is well-established through empirical data, as made clear from a report published by Fortune Business Insights in April 2022.[1] This research reveals that the global cloud storage market was valued at USD 70.19 billion in 2021 and is projected to grow from USD 83.41 billion in 2022 to USD 376.37 billion by 2029. It is thus a sizeable market.

Cloud services provide numerous advantages, such as setup speed, scalability, improved agility, and often the total cost of ownership savings. But this is not the only explanation for such a skyrocketing increase. The COVID-19 pandemic and, consecutively, the work-from-home format that followed it, have affected the situation tremendously. Companies and public institutions are now relying more heavily on cloud services (especially cloud storage, databases, and software) that enable their employees to access files and share data remotely. During the pandemic, cloud computing turned out to be an indispensable service, which allowed businesses all over the world to keep on operating and supporting the national as well as the global economy.

However, when using a cloud computing service provided by a public cloud provider, data and applications are normally hosted by a third party. This is a fundamental difference between cloud computing and traditional IT, where most data is held within a self-controlled network. It is often said that cloud is just someone else's computer. Through the use of cloud services, highly valuable and potentially sensitive business assets come to depend on third-party servers. Data safety, integrity, privacy and accessibility all depend on that third-party provider. However, a cloud computing provider can experience service disruptions or security breaches as a result of technical circumstances or a malicious attack. In turn, this will affect the users of the cloud service. Data leaks or loss is thus a common concern. In the cloud, data can be compromised in several ways, most commonly through misconfiguration or deletion due to human error or malicious actions by hackers. The latter became of particular concern during the pandemic. In the words of Tanium, one of the leading cybersecurity and systems management companies: 'Hackers went to town when the world stayed at home'.[2]

Following the unprecedented growth in the use of cloud services, in conjunction with these security concerns, disputes related to delivery and use of cloud services ('cloud disputes') are expected to increase. Disagreements over who is ultimately responsible for data loss and consequential damage that might occur are unavoidable. The solution is far from straightforward, owing especially to the complexity of cloud supply chains, where large numbers of cloud service providers are involved on various levels.

---

1. Fortune Business Insights, 'Cloud Storage Market Size, Share & COVID-19 Impact Analysis', Summary, Key Market Insights (April 2022), available at https://www.fortunebusinessinsights.com/cloud-storage-market-102773 (last accessed 4 August 2022) (henceforth Fortune Business Insights Report).
2. Tanium, 'What Happened When the World Stayed Home?', available at https://world-at-home.tanium.com/ (last accessed 4 August 2022).

This chapter will explore cloud computing starting with a brief description of the service model in question, followed by a discussion of the main legal issues and the types of disputes that arise in cloud computing. It will then provide a high-level analysis of the extent to which international arbitration is a suitable recourse to resolve cloud disputes.

II   CLOUD COMPUTING: DEFINITION, USE, SERVICE AND DEPLOYMENT MODELS

So, what is cloud computing? How did it develop? What service and deployment models are used? And why are private organizations and public bodies all over the globe increasing their use of cloud services?

1   Definition, Development and Use

The term *cloud* is a metaphor for the Internet, based on the cloud drawing used in the past to represent the telephone network, and later to depict the Internet in computer network diagrams as an abstraction for the complex infrastructure it conceals.[3]

Cloud computing is often described as the storing, processing and use of data on remotely located computers accessed over the internet.[4] A more elaborated and precise definition was introduced by the National Institute of Standards and Technology (NIST) in 2011: 'cloud computing is a model for enabling ubiquitous, convenient, on-demand network access to a shared pool of configurable computing resources (e.g., networks, servers, storage, applications, and services) that can be rapidly provisioned and released with minimal management effort or service provider interaction'.[5]

Characteristics of cloud services thus include self-provisioning and elasticity, meaning that users can provision services on an on-demand basis and exit them when no longer necessary. Users typically subscribe to cloud services under monthly billing arrangements or the like, rather than paying for software licenses or supporting server and network infrastructure. Cloud-based technology allows organizations to access software, storage, computing and other IT infrastructure elements without bearing the burden of maintaining and upgrading them.[6]

---

3. Jessie Holliday Scanlon & Brad Wieners, 'The Internet Cloud', Industry Standard (9 July 1999), available at https://web.archive.org/web/20100211133442/http://www.thestandard.com/article/0,1902,5466,00.html (last accessed 19 August 2022).
4. European Commission et al., Communication from the Commission to the European Parliament, the Council, the European Economic and Social Committee and the Committee of the Regions Unleashing the Potential of Cloud Computing in Europe (27 September 2012), available at https://eur-lex.europa.eu/legal-content/EN/TXT/?uri = celex:52012DC0529 (last accessed 17 August 2022).
5. Peter Mell, Tim Grance, 'The NIST Definition of Cloud Computing', The National Institute of Standards and Technology (NIST) at the U.S. Department of Commerce (September 2011), available at https://csrc.nist.gov/publications/detail/sp/800-145/final (last accessed 19 August 2022).
6. John Moore, 'Cloud Services', TechTarget (December 2016), available at https://www.techtarget.com/searchitchannel/definition/cloud-services (last accessed 17 August 2022) (henceforth Moore, 'Cloud Services').

Cloud computing had its watershed moment in 1999, as the business application Salesforce[7] debuted. It demonstrated the great business potential of cloud computing. Just a few years later, in 2002, Amazon's web-based retail services were launched on a global scale. In 2006, Amazon introduced Amazon Web Services, allowing users to access online services and rent virtual resources to run their applications. Around the same time, Google launched its Google Docs services.[8]

As security concerns hampered the public cloud's widespread acceptance, the development of private clouds spurred. In 2010, Microsoft, OpenStack, and Amazon Web Services created usable private clouds, and 2011 saw the development of hybrid clouds (private and public clouds used together).[9]

The key market driver in cloud computing is the exponential growth in data volumes. Remote sensing,[10] the Internet of Things[11] and improved video quality such as high-definition cameras have resulted in the collection of large amounts of data. As a result, demand for cloud-based storage and networking technology is increasing. Similarly, the growing use of artificial intelligence is projected to increase storage demand and improve data security.[12]

Data privacy and confidentiality are crucial elements of the cloud storage ecosystem. Because the data resides outside the organization's infrastructure, the organisation necessarily relinquishes the physical control over its data and the ability to directly supervise the barriers against security breaches. Such privacy and security concerns are still recognized as barriers to adopting cloud-based services.[13]

2   Service Models

When Oracle introduced the Oracle Cloud in 2012, this was a game-changing idea in cloud computing: this concept rolled out three service models: Infrastructure as a Service (IaaS), Platform as a Service (PaaS) and Software as a Service (SaaS); all offered as standard packages for Oracle cloud subscriptions.[14] These standard models quickly became the norm, with some public clouds offering all of these services, while others focused on offering only one. Software as a service, in particular, became quite popular.[15]

---

7. Salesforce is a popular customer relationship management (CRM) platform.
8. Simplilearn, 'Ten U.S. Cloud Computing Companies to Consider Working For' (28 March 2022), available at https://www.simplilearn.com/cloud-computing-companies-in-usa-article (last accessed 17 August 2022) (henceforth Simplilearn).
9. *Ibid.*
10. The term remote sensing generally refers to the use of satellite- or aircraft-based sensor technologies to detect and classify objects on Earth.
11. The term Internet of things is used to describe physical objects with sensors, processing ability, and software that connect and exchange data with other devices and systems over the Internet, for example, lighting fixtures, thermostats, home security systems, cameras, and other home appliances.
12. Fortune Business Insights Report.
13. Fortune Business Insights Report.
14. Simplilearn.
15. Keith D. Foote, 'A Brief History of Cloud Computing', Dataversity (17 December 2021), available at https://www.dataversity.net/brief-history-cloud-computing/# (last accessed 19 August 2022).

Each model provides a different level of control, flexibility and management, allowing the user to select the right set of services for their needs. Each model has a similar component stack. The difference lies in which parts of the stack of services are managed by the provider and which are handled by the user, as shown in Figure 45.1.[16]

Figure 45.1   Component Stacks

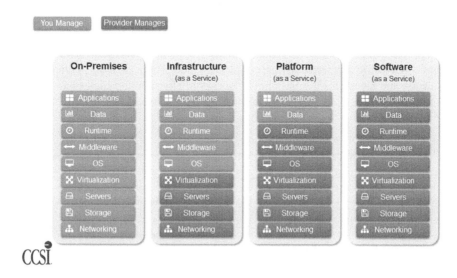

Today, these service models have become an industry standard. They are often referred to as 'layers'. Together, they are the components that enable cloud computing.

It should be underlined that cloud computing is a business model; it is not a new technology. Cloud services should thus also be distinguished from novel digital technology which itself often depends on cloud computing, such as the Internet of Things, Artificial Intelligence, cryptoassets, cryptocurrency, smart contracts, distributed ledger technology, fintech and biotech applications.

a   Infrastructure as a Service (IaaS)

IaaS contains the basic building blocks for cloud IT. It typically provides access to networking features, computers (virtual or on dedicated hardware), and data storage space. This model is most closely similar to the existing IT resources with which IT departments and developers are long since familiar. IaaS products however allow organizations to manage their business resources – such as their network, servers, and data storage – on the cloud. The user does not manage or control the underlying cloud

---

16. Contemporary Computer Services Inc (CCSI), 'Cloud Computing Basics', available at https://www.ccsinet.com/blog/cloud-computing-basics/ (last accessed 19 August 2022).

infrastructure[17] but maintains control over operating systems and deployed applications. Examples of this model include Amazon Web Services, IBM Bluemix and Microsoft Azure.

b   Platform as a Service (PaaS)

PaaS removes the need for the user to manage the underlying infrastructure as well as the operating systems and middleware.[18] PaaS refers to the delivery of operating systems and associated services over the Internet without downloads or installation. The approach enables users to create and deploy applications without having to invest in the underlying infrastructure. Examples include Amazon Web Services' Elastic Beanstalk and Salesforce's App Cloud.[19] PaaS products allow businesses and developers to host, build and deploy consumer-facing applications.

c   Software as a Service (SaaS)

SaaS is by far the most common cloud service. This is a software distribution model in which applications are hosted by a service provider and made available to customers over a network, typically the Internet.[20] Examples include Microsoft Office 365, SharePoint, Dropbox, Salesforce and Workday. With a SaaS offering, the user does not have to think about software maintenance or how the operating systems or underlying infrastructure is managed.

d   Anything as a Service (XaaS)

Outside of the three basic models, further models have developed, generally called 'Anything-as-a-service' (XaaS). XaaS describes a general category of services related to cloud computing and remote access. It recognizes the vast number of products, tools and technologies that are now delivered to users as a service over the Internet. This category includes services as varied as disaster recovery as a service (DRaaS), communications as a service (CaaS), network as a service (NaaS), database as a service

---

17. Cloud infrastructure as explained by NIST: 'The cloud infrastructure can be viewed as containing both a physical layer and an abstraction layer. The physical layer consists of the hardware resources that are necessary to support the cloud services being provided, and typically includes server, storage and network components. The abstraction layer consists of the software deployed across the physical layer, which manifests the essential cloud characteristics.' Available at https://nvlpubs.nist.gov/nistpubs/Legacy/SP/nistspecialpublication800-145.pdf (last accessed 19 August 2022).
18. Middleware is software that lies between an operating system and the applications running on it. *See* more here – https://azure.microsoft.com/en-us/resources/cloud-computing-dictionary/what-is-middleware/ (last accessed 17 August 2022).
19. Moore, 'Cloud Services'.
20. *Ibid.*

(DBaaS), storage as a service (STaaS), desktop as a service (DaaS), and monitoring as a service (MaaS).[21]

3   Deployment Models

Cloud providers may deploy these service models in several different ways: through a public cloud, a private cloud, a community cloud or a hybrid cloud.

a   *Public Cloud*

The SaaS, PaaS and IaaS providers noted above may all be said to be providing public cloud-based services. This form of cloud computing is delivered via the internet, shared across organizations and open for use by the general public. The physical infrastructure is located on the premises of the cloud provider. Public clouds are owned by cloud service providers, who charge users for the use of cloud resources.

According to market research published in April 2022, the public cloud segment is expected to account for a major market share due to growing cloud spending.[22] The major public cloud providers are Amazon Web Services, Microsoft Azure, Google Cloud Platform, Oracle Cloud Infrastructure, IBM Cloud and Alibaba Cloud.

b   *Private Cloud*

A private cloud involves cloud computing provisioned for exclusive use by a single organization comprising multiple consumers (e.g., business units). It may be owned, managed and operated by the organization, a third party, or some combination of them, and it may exist on or off premises. The computing resources are isolated and delivered via a secure private network and are not shared with other customers.

A private cloud can be customized to meet the unique business and security needs of the organization. With greater visibility and control over the infrastructure, organizations can operate compliance-sensitive IT workloads without compromising the security and performance that could previously be achieved only through reliance on dedicated on-premises data centres.

Private clouds are typically used by government agencies, financial institutions, and other mid-to-large-size organizations, which involve business-critical operations that require enhanced control over their IT environment.

c   *Community Cloud*

In a community cloud, the cloud infrastructure is shared by several organizations, but access is limited to a specific community with shared concerns (e.g., a shared mission,

---

21. NetApp, 'What Is XaaS (Anything as a Service)?', available at https://www.netapp.com/cloud-services/what-is-anything-as-a-service-xaas/ (last accessed 17 August 2022).
22. Fortune Business Insights Report.

security requirements, policy, or compliance considerations). It may be managed by the organizations themselves or by a third party and it may exist on-premise or off-premise.[23]

d   Hybrid Cloud

A hybrid cloud is a type of cloud that combines on-premises infrastructure (or a private cloud) with a public cloud. In a hybrid cloud, data and applications can move between the two environments. Many organizations use a hybrid cloud approach because of the need to take full advantage of on-premises technology investment or meet regulatory and data sovereignty requirements. When computing and processing demand fluctuates, the hybrid cloud allows the organization to scale up the on-premises infrastructure to the public cloud to handle any overflow. This flexibility of resources can be obtained without giving third-party data centres access to the organisation's entire data.[24]

4   Complexity of the Cloud Supply Chains

What makes cloud computing services complex as compared to other IT services, is the number of providers in the cloud supply chain. The combination of different layers of service and deployment models allows additional flexibility to the providers. However, it complicates things for the end-user.

For example, most users of SaaS do not know if their provider uses its own infrastructure and do not know the location of the servers and data, who has access to it and what kind of physical security measures are in place to protect their data. For example, a SaaS may be built upon the Microsoft Azure platform (PaaS) but deployed on Amazon Web Services (IaaS). The terms for data processing and storing could depend on several service providers in different jurisdictions. Most such details of the underlying layers of the service remain unknown to ordinary users.[25] A layered service which employs several sub-contractors will invariably pose a higher risk for complex disputes and liability issues to arise than situations where the service is supplied in full by only one party.

Even well-known cloud providers, such as Apple's iCloud, do use third-party servers, like Google Cloud, for storage needs.[26] The question of whether Apple was

---

23. NIST, NIST Cloud Computing Standards Roadmap, *Special Publication 500-291* (July 2011) available at https://tsapps.nist.gov/publication/get_pdf.cfm?pub_id = 909024 (last accessed 17 August 2022), p. 15.
24. Noah Jackson, 'Cloud Migration Simply Explained: What Is It, Why Business Needs It, and More', *CMC Global* (20 August 2021) available at https://cmcglobal.com.vn/cloud-migration/cloud-migration-simply-explained-what-is-it-why-business-needs-it-and-more/ (last accessed 17 August 2022).
25. Dusco Martic, 'Dispute Resolution for Cloud Services: Access to Justice and Fairness in Cloud-Based Low-Value Online Services' (2017), available at http://amsdottorato.unibo.it/826 1/1/MARTIC_DUSKO_tesi.pdf (last accessed 17 August 2022), p. 61.
26. Mary Jo Foley, 'Apple May No Longer Be Using Microsoft's Azure' (26 February 2018) https://www.zdnet.com/article/apple-may-no-longer-be-using-microsofts-azure/ (last accessed 17 August 2022).

contractually entitled to do so was brought before the United States District Court for the Northern District of California in a 2019 class action in *Williams v. Apple Inc.*[27] The plaintiffs brought a claim for breach of contract regarding Apple's iCloud Service, contending that Apple had breached the iCloud Terms and Conditions by storing user data on third-party servers. Apple maintained that it did nothing wrong and denied that it breached the contract. In January 2022, Apple agreed to pay USD 14.8 million to settle the lawsuit.

III   MAIN LEGAL ISSUES ARISING FROM CLOUD COMPUTING

Many legal issues may arise from cloud computing. The most frequent liability situations will likely include issues pertaining to the delivery of service, regulatory issues and intellectual property (IP) issues.

1   Delivery of Service

Problems with delivery of the service, such as service interruptions, are inevitable, regardless of the size of the cloud service provider. When a cloud service goes down, users lose access to their data. If the user itself is offering processing capabilities, it may be unable to provide services to its own customers and may thus be exposed to significant liability for such failure. Worse still, data may be lost or corrupted. The information itself may contain trade secrets or other sensitive data, making the fact of its loss a potential security issue.

Such performance issues raise even more complex questions if the cloud outage is caused by hacking. Is hacking a circumstance out of the service provider's control? Can it qualify as a force majeure event? Or was hacking possible due to gross negligence of the service provider, for example, by failing to install commonly known safeguards?

Besides hacking a disruption of online services can occur also through a software malfunction leading to a telecommunication network (carrier) outage or a data centre's outage with similar consequences for the users as cyber-attacks. Furthermore, with the Internet of Things technology on the rise, an internet failure has the potential of affecting the manufacturing industry on a global scale, as machines are unable to communicate via network as intended. This can carry consequences for the production process and supply chains and give rise to consequential liability issues in the next step.

Cloud service providers typically attempt to avoid or significantly limit their liability in case of loss of data or loss of business due to performance issues. After all, an IaaS or PaaS provider only furnishes a specific service, such as infrastructure or storage. It has no way of knowing whether the data in its custody contains critical trade

---

27. *Williams v. Apple Inc.,* Case No. 19-cv-04700-LB, United States District Court for the Northern District of California, Information website available at https://www.storageclassactionsettle ment.com (last accessed 17 August 2022).

secrets or sensitive personal data. Therefore, the current standard contract terms of the biggest cloud providers (Microsoft, Amazon, Google) contain wide liability exclusion clauses.[28]

Another aspect to be taken into account is the chains of responsibility the cloud service provider in a SaaS model engages sub-contractors. For example, the file-sharing service Dropbox uses Amazon Web Services for its data storage in Europe. Dropbox naturally does not want to take more responsibility for the customer's data than Amazon is willing to offer Dropbox. Disclaimers in supplier agreements regarding the supplier's sub-contractors are thus common.

Private individuals generally lack the bargaining power to change these terms. However, big publicly traded corporations and municipalities have started to negotiate and successfully adapt standard cloud contracts to their needs. For example, the City of Los Angeles was successful in adjusting the standard contract terms of Google's cloud service to include a USD 7.7 million cap on damages caused by the loss or destruction of data.[29]

2   Regulatory Issues

Multiple regulatory issues can arise in cloud computing. These include, on the more complex side, competition and antitrust matters, but overall compliance with data protection laws is arguably the major issue for cloud computing providers as well as users. Cloud services have an inherent cross-border nature and providers often must adhere to multiple rapidly evolving foreign data protection frameworks. Privacy and data protection regulations restrict the transfer of personal information across national borders: both physical transfer of data and remote access to the data.

The cloud-based products and services provided by businesses in industries like healthcare, software, financial services and social media offer unprecedented convenience and mobility but also create unprecedented risks.[30] If a third party obtains unauthorized access to private information about the service provider's clients, this may harm the provider's reputation and lead to liability to compensate customers for violations of their data privacy.

While cloud providers maintain basic compliance standards and provide basic security capabilities and tools, the user retains responsibility for the security on its side of the cloud network, and in particular its hybrid network, and must secure data and applications stored there. Cloud providers and users thus share the responsibility to ensure a safe and secure network environment.

Unauthorized secondary usage of private information is another regulatory issue of some notoriety. It is part of the standard business model of some cloud service

---

28. R.H. Weber & D.N. Staiger, 'Cloud Computing: A Cluster of Complex Liability Issues', (2014) 20(1) Web JCLI, available at https://www.zora.uzh.ch/id/eprint/108609/1/418# (last accessed 17 August 2022).
29. *Ibid.*
30. Morningstar Law Group, 'The Laws of Cloud Computing: Weathering the Storms of Cyberpiracy, Hacking, and IP Infringement' (15 March 2015) available at https://morningstarlawgroup.com/insights/cloud-computing-legal-issues/ (last accessed 17 August 2022).

providers that the service provider may use users' data in certain authorized secondary ways to gain revenue, most commonly the targeting of advertisements. Users should therefore exercise caution before submitting sensitive data into the cloud and must ensure that no such undesirable access right is granted to the cloud provider. In a worst-case scenario, a cloud provider could use confidential financial information stored on a cloud server (i.e., financial statements) to trade on a company's stock, thus potentially making the company liable for breach of securities regulations as well as other laws.

Another regulatory aspect pertains to litigation before national courts in civil and criminal proceedings. A cloud service provider may be forced to hand over data stored in the cloud upon a court order if the data is considered to be of importance as evidence. This, too, should give users pause before placing sensitive information into the cloud.

3   IP Issues

Issues relating to IP rights may for example arise in the areas of copyright, trademark or patent law. A customer using a PaaS or SaaS cloud environment must be aware of a variety of IP rights questions, such as the required cloud software licences or other third-party IP rights.

When a cloud customer uses a cloud software solution which potentially infringes third-party IP rights, the obligations and the conduct of each party must be closely analysed. Pinpointing an exact location of an IP breach is also challenging: the processing may take place in one country, storage and transmission in another. Given the complexity of cloud supply chains, a number of sub-contractors (cloud provider, server centres, software distributor) may be equally involved in a provider's potential infringement, thus in theory requiring liability for the infringement to be apportioned accordingly.

IV   DISTINGUISHING CLOUD DISPUTES FROM TELECOM, MEDIA, TECHNOLOGY DISPUTES

A 2016 survey by the Queen Mary University of London (the 'QMUL 2016 survey') demonstrated that IT and telecom companies were less in favour of arbitration, preferring litigation and expert determination, respectively.[31] Since there is an overlap between the cloud service providers and IT and telecom companies, this is an interesting finding, worth exploring.[32]

---

31. International Dispute Resolution Survey, Pre-empting and Resolving Technology, Media and Telecoms Disputes by Queen Mary University of London (2016), available at https://arbitration .qmul.ac.uk/research/2016/ (last accessed 19 August 2022) (henceforth QMUL 2016 Survey) p. 7.
32. *See also* Patricia Shaughnessy, Paul Cohen & Duarte G Henriques, 'SVAMC Task Force on Tech Disputes, Tech Companies & International Arbitration', White Paper, 25 September 2020

The sceptical approach of telecom operators towards arbitration can be explained by the type of disputes they are engaged in. Telecom operators operate in highly regulated environments, under specific approval regimes and frameworks handed down by government authorities. The telecoms industry is heavily concentrated and highly competitive, due to historically long periods of monopoly, scarcity of frequencies (in mobile networks) and immense investments in the core infrastructure. Furthermore, only a handful of suppliers of telecom equipment and software can provide the core networks necessary to run a nationwide telecom service. Hence, the competition authorities are particularly vigilant when it comes to the telecoms industry. Moreover, telecom operators handle personal and sensitive data of their customers, raising issues of personal data and public safety, all under the watchful eye of data protection authorities.[33] These types of disputes are arguably not well-suited for international arbitration (apart from investment arbitration) due to the limitations of the arbitrators' mandate. Issues pertaining to regulatory, tax and competition law are typically not arbitrable.

According to the QMUL 2016 survey, litigation was the most favoured dispute resolution mechanism in the IT sector, scoring 50 % approval, while arbitration scored 27 %. By contrast, respondents from the Energy, Construction and Manufacturing industries all rated arbitration as the most favoured dispute resolution mechanism. The fact that IT suppliers favour litigation over arbitration, while the opposite is true of some of their potential customers from other sectors, may cause problems: when customers and suppliers draw up commercial contracts, the drafting of the dispute resolution clause could be a contentious point.[34]

The QMUL 2016 survey also showed that when asked about the suitability of international arbitration for Telecom, Media, Technology (TMT) disputes (present and future), a staggering 92 % of all respondents indicated that international arbitration is well suited for such disputes and 82 % believed there will be an increase in the use of international arbitration. As discussed below, arbitration offers the potential for time and cost savings as well as confidentiality, specialised expertise, international enforcement, and delocalisation.

V INTERNATIONAL ARBITRATION AND CLOUD DISPUTES

1 Time to Resolution

According to a survey conducted in 2017 by the Global Technology Dispute Resolution Council and the Silicon Valley Arbitration & Mediation Center (the GTDRC/SVAMC

---

available at https://secureservercdn.net/198.71.233.183/3d0.328.myftpupload.com/wp-con tent/uploads/White-Paper-SVAMC-Task-Force-on-Tech-Disputes-Tech-Companies-and-Interna tional-Arbitration-1.pdf (last accessed 19 August 2022) (henceforth SVAMC White Paper).

33. Nasser Ali Khasawneh, Maria Mazzawi and Ricardo Christie, 'The Guide to Telecoms Arbitrations, Arbitration and the Advent of New Technologies', *Global Arbitration Review*, Eversheds Sutherland (29 July 2022) available at https://globalarbitrationreview.com/guide/the-guide-telecoms-arbitrations/first-edition (last accessed 17 August 2022) p. 10.

34. QMUL 2016 Survey, p. 19.

study), time to resolution is viewed as a major issue with litigation involving technology companies: 57% of survey respondents listed this as one of the top three problems with litigation.[35] This comes as no surprise because quick dispute resolution allows the parties to remove uncertainty and revert to their core business more rapidly.

Another issue is that the speed of judicial decision-making often does not keep pace with advances in technology, resulting in technology becoming obsolete before the dispute is resolved in court. While it is recognized that arbitration offers a much speedier dispute resolution mechanism than that of national courts, criticism nonetheless centres on it not being quick enough. Arbitral institutions have sought to address these concerns by the introduction of expedited and emergency procedures.

2   Flexibility

A major advantage of arbitration that appears to be universally recognized is its flexibility. The parties can select procedural rules, institutions and arbitrators with their specific efficiency interests in mind. The parties can also define the length of proceedings and the extent of expenditure that is appropriate for the case. During the arbitral proceedings, the parties continue to have substantial opportunities to adapt the procedures and formulate the contested issues to suit their needs.[36]

Many arbitral institutions now use electronic case management systems providing secure access to the case file and communications with the arbitral tribunal. In this respect, one may note that arbitral institutions, too, offer their services by means of cloud computing.

3   Expertise

Litigation can be unpredictable when decided by judges with limited cloud computing industry and technology law expertise. In arbitration, the parties are free to appoint arbitrators with specialized expertise required for the dispute.

According to the GTDRC/SVAMC study, 76% of the survey respondents identified specialized expert decision-making as the greatest benefit of arbitration involving technology companies. Correspondingly, inexperienced and unqualified judges were viewed as a recurring problem in litigations involving technology companies, with 46% of the respondents listing it as one of the top three problems.

4   Confidentiality

International cloud computing disputes will often involve many sensitive issues, whether in relation to the data in question, the software and its IP or trade secrets, to

---

35. Gary Benton et al., 'Cost Is the Top Tech Litigation Problem, Survey Shows', Silicon Valley Arbitration and Mediation Center and Global Technology Dispute Resolution Council Survey Report (2017) available at https://svamc.org/wp-content/uploads/SVAMC-2017-Survey-Report .pdf (last accessed 19 August 2022) p. 1.
36. SVAMC White Paper, p. 4.

name a few. Arbitration offers a private decision-making process that is particularly well-suited for disputes where confidential business information or trade secrets are at issue. Arbitral proceedings under the rules of the vast majority (if not all) arbitration institutes are administered under confidentiality unless parties have agreed otherwise.

Confidentiality is often presented as one of the key decisive factors in opting for arbitration instead of resorting to state courts. The use of cloud computing services is a strategic business issue for the user, as service suppliers gain detailed knowledge of the user's business strategy and procedures. Users will want to ensure that this information remains confidential and is not disclosed in the course of public hearings.

Yet, it is not only the users that may be keen on the dispute being resolved confidentially. Cloud service providers may also be interested in keeping disputes private. The reputation of a cloud service provider will undoubtedly impact cloud users' choice of cloud services. Consequently, like for example financial institutions, cloud providers seek to build and maintain a strong and solid reputation. If a company's reputation is sullied by, for example, a cloud security breach, it may experience a significant loss of customers as a result, which could of course be harmful to the company's financial standing.

A telling example is the infamous cloud security scandal involving Cambridge Analytica in 2018. It was revealed that the company had harvested millions of Facebook profiles of US voters, in one of the tech giant's biggest data breaches and used them to build a powerful software program to predict and influence voters' choices during the presidential elections. When Facebook announced to investors that user growth had slowed in the wake of the Cambridge Analytica scandal and that 3 million European users had abandoned the social network following the revelation of the breach, this brought on a 19% downturn in the value of Facebook's shares and a diminution of the company's market value of more than USD 119 billion.[37]

5   Internationally Enforceable

Cloud computing contracts and supply chains are inherently international and commonly lead to multi-jurisdictional disputes. The need for legal instruments that facilitate enforcement in multiple foreign jurisdictions is therefore critical.

An arbitral award is enforceable in 170 countries under The Convention on the Recognition and Enforcement of Foreign Arbitral Awards of 1958 (the New York Convention).[38] By contrast, the enforcement of national court decisions typically requires that specific bilateral treaties are in force between the involved countries. For example, the United States of America has no treaties providing for enforcement of its court judgments abroad. In nearly all jurisdictions, it is necessary to initiate a new

---

37. Rupert Neate, 'Over USD 119bn Wiped Off Facebook's Market Cap after Growth Shock', *The Guardian* (26 July 2018) available at https://www.theguardian.com/technology/2018/jul/26/facebook-market-cap-falls-109bn-dollars-after-growth-shock (last accessed 19 August 2022).
38. Convention on the Recognition and Enforcement of Foreign Arbitral Awards (New York, 1958), *Status*, UNCITRAL available at https://uncitral.un.org/en/texts/arbitration/conventions/foreign_arbitral_awards/status2 (last accessed 19 August 2022).

litigation to enforce a foreign judgment.[39] This naturally speaks in favour of international arbitration.

6   Neutrality of Forum

Neutrality of forum – as in a non-national, delocalised forum – is one of the key advantages of international arbitration. International parties will often be hesitant to agree to a foreign court's jurisdiction for a number of reasons, one being a perceived potential bias in favour of the party that is of the same nationality as the local court. Arbitration offers a neutral and non-state-based forum of dispute resolution and is therefore more likely to instil confidence in international parties dealing with disputes involving cloud-based cross-border personal and sensitive data than litigation before local courts.

VI   CONCLUSIONS

Many traditional industries including construction, energy, healthcare, finance, automotive and industrial manufacturing, have moved their core activities and offerings to cloud-based solutions and services. Companies seated in one country can provide services and support users worldwide using global cloud infrastructure, third-party storage and multiple cloud service sub-providers. Such business model is bound to lead to technically complicated cross-border disputes. The exposure to potential cloud disputes affects not only businesses in the traditional technology sector but also companies in nearly every major business sector.

In an industry where the main asset is constantly evolving and moving instantly around the world, as the case is for data, there is a significant need for international protection and enforcement of rights associated with this asset. While some types of controversies are best resolved in local courts (regulatory, data protection and competition issues), many types of disputes in this area would benefit from international arbitration. This is particularly true for disputes arising under various cloud computing contracts involving service delivery issues and sub-contractors in several jurisdictions. National courts are ill-equipped for such disputes, for one, because their jurisdiction is limited to the country of their location and, two, their judgments are seldom enforceable in other jurisdictions. By comparison, arbitration is delocalized, and flexible and awards are enforceable in 170 countries. Two other key advantages of arbitration are the opportunity to select arbitrators with specialised expertise in technology-related disputes and the ability to preserve the confidentiality of the proceedings.

---

39. Gary L. Benton, Steven K. Andersen, 'Technology Arbitration Revisited', Dispute Resolution Journal July Vol. 74 No. 4, American Arbitration Association (2020) p. 10, available at https://go.adr.org/rs/294-SFS-516/images/Benton%20and%20Andersen%20-%20Technolog y%20Arbitration%20Revisited.pdf (last accessed 19 August 2022).

PANEL 13   Renaissance Arbitrator

CHAPTER 46

Aristotle's Virtue Ethics in Arbitration

Melanie van Leeuwen [*]

TABLE OF CONTENTS

I   INTRODUCTION

During the fifteenth and sixteenth centuries, scientists, writers, philosophers, states-men, artists, and architects in Western Europe went back to classical antiquity and sought to revive and build upon classical ideas, notions and achievements. Seeking to break with the stagnation that was characteristic of the Middle Ages, the 'Renaissance man' aimed to progress through the rediscovery of classical philosophy, literature and art. The rebirth ('*renaissance*') and the revival of classical learning and wisdom led to a period in history of significant development, during which the sciences, the arts and commerce thrived and enabled European nations to pursue their global exploration.[1]

The Organising Committee of the ICCA Congress of 2022 likely proposed the topic of the Renaissance Arbitrator with that objective in mind. We live and practise in an era where legal excellence no longer suffices. In addition to legal issues, arbitrators increasingly have to deal with complex technical issues that require a sound under-standing of financial and economic models, engineering techniques, sanctions, tech-nology, cyber-security and data protection. In the exercise of their duties, arbitrators

---

[*] Partner, Derains & Gharavi AARPI, Paris, France; Chair of the ICC Commission on Arbitration and
     ADR.
1. *See*, for example, Will Durant, *The Renaissance: The Story of Civilization, Volume V, Book II*
    (Simon & Schuster 2011).

are expected to display impeccable case management skills and conduct proceedings in a fair, impartial and efficient manner, while staying well clear of the pitfalls of corruption, money laundering and other vices that are afflicting today's globalized economy.

In the face of this myriad of challenges, it is useful to reflect on how classical notions, ideas and achievements can provide an impetus for innovation in present-day international dispute resolution. Can classical wisdom help the much younger, 150-year-old, arbitration discipline[2] ensure that it meets the twenty-first-century needs and expectations of users around the globe?

II   ARISTOTLE'S VIRTUE ETHICS

Together with the Roman concept of *humanitas*, classical Greek philosophy provided the intellectual basis of the Renaissance. The protagonist of ancient Greek thought leadership is Aristotle. With a strong focus on logic and cogent reasoning, Aristotle made foundational contributions to a wide range of sciences (physics, biology, mathematics, psychology, metaphysics, rhetoric, ethics, politics, analytics).[3] As a result, Aristotle is considered to have been one of the first *homines universales* – the archetype of the Renaissance man.[4]

Ethics is the study of how one can live life well and virtue ethics is the theory that focuses on the role that character and virtue play in moral philosophy. These theories address questions such as 'How should one live?', 'What is the good life?' and 'What are proper social values?'

Aristotle's teachings and writings, notably the *Nicomachean Ethics*, are among the oldest available sources of virtue ethics.[5] According to Aristotle, virtue is the key to a life well-lived and the ultimate goal in life is '*eudaimonia.*'[6] The Aristotelian notion of *eudaimonia* is a state of being, in which one's rational, social and emotional skills are applied to the achievement of happiness through virtuous conduct. *Eudaimonia*

---

2. Modern day international arbitration practice dates back at least to 1871 when an international arbitral tribunal was constituted in Geneva to hear the Alabama claims of the United States of America against Great Britain, *see* United Nations Reports on International Arbitral Awards Volume XXIX, pp. 124-134, Award rendered on 14 September 1872 by the tribunal of arbitration established by Article I of the Treaty of Washington of 8 May 1871, available at https://legal.un .org/rIaa/cases/vol_XXIX/125-134.pdf (last accessed 20 October 2015); *see also* Chapter 2 A Search for International Enlightenment Through Arbitration: Andrew Carnegie, the *Alabama* Claims Arbitration, and the 'Temple of Peace' by J. Christopher Thomas KC in this volume.
3. Justin Humphreys, 'Aristotle (384–322 B.C.E.)', *Internet Encyclopedia of Philosophy*, available at https://iep.utm.edu/aristotle/ (last accessed on 20 October 2022).
4. New World Encyclopedia contributors, 'Polymath', *New World Encyclopedia*, available at https: //www.newworldencyclopedia.org/p/index.php?title = Polymath&oldid = 988043 (last accessed on 20 October 2022).
5. Aristotle, *Nicomachean Ethics*, in H. Rackham (transl.), *Aristotle in 23 Volumes,* Vol. XIX (Harvard University Press 1934) available at http://www.perseus.tufts.edu/hopper/text?doc = Perseus%3atext%3a1999.01.0054 (last accessed on 20 October 2022). *See generally* Alex John London, 'Moral Knowledge and the Acquisition of Virtue in Aristotle's "Nicomachean" and "Eudemian Ethics"', 54 The Review of Metaphysics (2001) p. 553.
6. Mark Dimmock and Andrew Fisher, *Ethics for A-Level* (Open Book Publishers 2017) p. 51.

encompasses happiness, contentment and fulfilment; it is the best kind of life – an end in and of itself, as well as the path to living and faring well.[7]

What sets man apart from other beings is reason. A life worth living is a life in which one reasons well. So, the Aristotelian ideal of *eudaimonia* revolves around a life of virtuous conduct in accordance with reason.[8]

Aristotle considered a virtuous person to have ideal character traits. While to a degree character traits derive from a person's natural disposition, in Aristotle's view internal tendencies need to be developed, controlled, and nurtured through upbringing, education, and practice, all grounded in reason. In his theory, a virtue, once acquired, will become part of a person's habits and that person will henceforth act consistently, predictably and appropriately in all situations.[9]

Aristotle identified twelve virtues that are the quintessential ingredients for a full and meaningful life (*eudaimonia*): courage, moderation, generosity, magnificence, magnanimity, ambition, patience, truthfulness, humour, kindness, modesty and justice. Each of those virtues lies in the mean – commonly referred to as the golden mean[10] – between the extremes of deficiency and excess. The right behaviour follows a bright – though perhaps fine – line between too much and too little.

III   THE VIRTUES OF A GOOD ARBITRATOR

The virtues Aristotle identified are fundamental civic values which at the time (384-322 BC) provided guidance and structure for citizens of the Greek city-states. Although the world has changed since Aristotle's days, the basic civic values that were essential in classical Greece retain their foundational validity: the same values need to be observed and aspired to in order for society and the economy to flourish.

Since it is the responsibility of the arbitration community to resolve the disputes that the current globalized economy generates, those who aspire to be Renaissance arbitrators may benefit from a brief review of Aristotelian virtues, to understand how these virtues may be the lodestars for international arbitrators in administering justice.

1   Courage (ανδρεία, andreia)

Aristotle considered courage to be a prime marker of moral excellence. In *Nicomachean Ethics*, courage is broadly defined as the median between fear and confidence.[11] According to Aristotle, someone who exaggerates their confidence is not courageous but audacious or reckless; whereas someone who yields to fear and lacks confidence is

---

7. *Ibid.*
8. *Ibid.*
9. Nafsika Athanassoulis, 'Virtue Ethics', *Internet Encyclopedia of Philosophy,* available at https://iep.utm.edu/virtue/ (last accessed on 20 October 2022).
10. Aristotle, *Nicomachean Ethics, supra* n. 5, p. 1107a.
11. Aristotle, *Nicomachean Ethics, supra* n. 5, p. 1107a. *See also* Denise Vigani, 'Artistotle's Account of Courage', 34 History of Philosophy Quarterly (2017) p. 313 at p. 320.

a coward. Courage enables a person to take appropriate action in challenging situations. Both overwhelming fear and overwhelming confidence may blur one's judgment, driving their subsequent action or inaction.

Arbitration is all about exercising good judgment, at the right time, taking into consideration all circumstances and interests at stake in the case. Arbitrators work in an inherently tense field, where most parties vigorously pursue their opposed interests. The need for the right degree of courage is indispensable for arbitrators in two types of situations.

First, as the importance of the interests at stake increases, so does the frequency of tactical procedural applications that put pressure on arbitrators. Especially when faced with applications principally directed to create a foundation for challenges to arbitrators, annulment applications and bids to resist the enforcement of arbitral awards at a later stage, arbitrators have to strike the right balance between the short-term satisfaction of the applicant or the defendant and the long game, in which arbitrators bear the ultimate responsibility for rendering an enforceable award.[12]

Although arbitrators have the duty to manage the arbitral process efficiently and do justice throughout the proceedings (not just in the final award),[13] there are cases in which tribunals need to go through procedural hoops – with the attendant frustration of additional costs and delay – to ensure the enforceability of the award at the end of the road.[14] While arbitrators must take complaints about due-process paranoia

---

12. Günther J. Horvath, 'The Duty of the Tribunal to Render an Enforceable Award', 18 Journal of International Arbitration (2001) p. 135.
13. UNCITRAL Model Law on International Commercial Arbitration (2006), Article 18: 'The parties shall be treated with equality and each party shall be given a full opportunity of presenting his case.' UNCITRAL Arbitration Rules (2021), Article 17(1): 'Subject to these Rules, the arbitral tribunal may conduct the arbitration in such manner as it considers appropriate, provided that the parties are treated with equality and that at an appropriate stage of the proceedings each party is given a reasonable opportunity of presenting its case. The arbitral tribunal, in exercising its discretion, shall conduct the proceedings so as to avoid unnecessary delay and expense and to provide a fair and efficient process for resolving the parties' dispute.'; ICC Rules of Arbitration (2021), Article 22(1): 'The arbitral tribunal and the parties shall make every effort to conduct the arbitration in an expeditious and cost-effective manner, having regard to the complexity and value of the dispute.'; SCC Arbitration Rules (2017), Article 23(2) 'In all cases, the Arbitral Tribunal shall conduct the arbitration in an impartial, efficient and expeditious manner, giving each party an equal and reasonable opportunity to present its case.'; LCIA Arbitration Rules (2020), Article 14(1): 'Under the Arbitration Agreement, the Arbitral Tribunal's general duties at all times during the arbitration shall include: [...] (ii) a duty to adopt procedures suitable to the circumstances of the arbitration, avoiding unnecessary delay and expense, so as to provide a fair, efficient and expeditious means for the final resolution of the parties' dispute'; SIAC Rules (2016), Rule 19(1): 'The Tribunal shall conduct the arbitration in such manner as it considers appropriate, after consulting with the parties, to ensure the fair, expeditious, economical and final resolution of the dispute.'; HKIAC Administered Arbitration Rules (2018), Article 13(1): 'Subject to these Rules, the arbitral tribunal shall adopt suitable procedures for the conduct of the arbitration in order to avoid unnecessary delay or expense, having regard to the complexity of the issues, the amount in dispute and the effective use of technology, and provided that such procedures ensure equal treatment of the parties and afford the parties a reasonable opportunity to present their case.'
14. Claudia Salomon, 'Maslow's Hammer: An Over-Reliance on Familiar Tools', Tel-Aviv Arbitration Week Keynote (2020) available at https://iccwbo.org/content/uploads/sites/3/2022/03/tel-aviv-arbitration-week-keynote-claudia-salomon-140322-1.pdf (last accessed on 20 October 2020).

seriously,[15] there are cases where the mean of courage may lie in not granting instant relief but in timing decisions so that the arbitral process does not get unnecessarily disrupted and delayed.

Second, arbitrators must have the courage of their own conviction. After consideration of all submissions and evidence in the record, arbitrators must express their own reasoned views in the deliberations, as well as in their decisions. After all, the function of an arbitrator is *intuitu personae*.[16] Apart from hard work, it takes courage if one's convictions go against the views of one's fellow arbitrators and consensus cannot immediately be found. It takes even more courage if one's convictions go against the tide of jurisprudential trends.

A recent example is provided by the tribunal that rendered the award in the *Green Power v. Spain* arbitration.[17] That was the first tribunal ever to uphold an intra-EU jurisdictional objection, holding that the ECT does not include a valid offer to arbitrate intra-EU investment disputes. The findings of the *Green Power* tribunal are based on Swedish law, as the arbitration was seated in Stockholm, leading to the applicability of Swedish law (incorporating EU law) as the law governing subject-matter arbitrability.[18] The tribunal's analysis of the ECT's acknowledgement and incorporation of EU law is in stark contrast with prior decisions of other tribunals that dismissed EU Member States' jurisdictional objections (e.g., the tribunals in *Slovakia v. Achmea*, *Moldova v Komstroy and Poland v. PL Holdings* cases)[19] and exercised jurisdiction. Whether the decision is right is the topic of fierce debate;[20] but what is clear is that the arbitrators in that case had the courage of their own conviction.

2 Moderation (σωφροσύνη, sophrosyne)

The second Aristotelian virtue encompasses the notions of moderation and temperance – the mean state between insensitivity and indulgence. In Aristotelian times the focus

---

15. Lucy F. Reed and Shaparak Saleh, 'Bon Courage, TRIBUNALS!', 2 BCDR International Arbitration Review (2015) p. 1.
16. Marcel Huys and Guy Keutgen, *L'arbitrage en droit belge et international* (Bruylant 1981) p. 199.
17. *Green Power K/S and SCE Solar Don Benito APS v. Kingdom of Spain* (SCC Case No. V2016/135), Award (16 June 2022).
18. *Green Power K/S and SCE Solar Don Benito APS v. Kingdom of Spain* (SCC Case No. V2016/135), Award (16 June 2022) para. 172.
19. *Achmea B.V. v. The Slovak Republic (II)* (PCA Case No. 2013-12), Award on Jurisdiction and Admissibility (20 May 2014) paras 162-188; *Republic of Moldova v. Komstroy* (Case C-741/19 – ECLI:EU:C:2021:655), Judgment of the Court (Grand Chamber) (2 September 2021), paras. 46, 49-50; *PL Holdings S.a.r.l. v. Poland* (SCC Case No. V 2014/163), Partial Award (28 June 2017) paras 306-317.
20. Federica I. Paddeu and Christian J. Tams, 'Interpreting Away Treaty Conflicts? Green Power, ISDS and the Primacy of EU Law' (23 August 2022) available at http://arbitrationblog. kluwerarbitration.com/2022/08/23/interpreting-away-treaty-conflicts-green-power-isds-and-the-primacy-of-eu-law/ (last accessed on 12 December 2022); Daniel Müller, 'EU Law and Arbitration under International Investment Instruments: The Surprising Award in Green Power v. Spain' (28 June 2022) available at https://blog.jusmundi.com/eu-law-and-arbitration-under-international-investment-instruments-the-surprising-award-in-green-power-v-spain/ (last accessed on 12 December 2022).

of moderation was on striking a balance between suffering, pleasure and avoiding excessive indulgence.[21]

In the context of present-day arbitration, the virtue of moderation reminds arbitrators to fulfil their duties dispassionately. They must not act on first impression, belief or instinct. They should not let their personal preferences, views or feelings carry them away. Moderation requires arbitrators to exercise self-restraint and to fulfil their tasks in a composed manner. It requires arbitrators to test the submissions against the evidence and to test their own perceptions against the views of others (the parties, the witnesses, the experts and the other arbitrators). Moderation is an essential attribute in order for arbitrators to take the right measures, that are proportionate to the issues and interests at stake.

The powers and duties vested in arbitrators should be exercised in two particular respects with the virtue of moderation in mind.

First, arbitrators owe a duty of independence and impartiality.[22] The subjective standard of impartiality goes to the state of mind of the arbitrator and requires them to hear and decide the case in a neutral, unbiased, fair-minded manner without prejudice with respect to any of the issues in dispute and without a predisposition towards any of the parties involved in the arbitration.[23] The requirement of independence is an objective one and is aimed at ensuring the absence of unacceptable relations or links between an arbitrator and parties or counsel involved in the arbitration.[24]

The combination of these twin requirements seeks to ensure that arbitrators approach and discharge their duties with an open mind and without bias, thereby giving the parties the confidence that they are open to being convinced by sound arguments, irrespective of which party is putting those arguments forward.[25] Only if arbitrators are completely truthful about their predispositions and their past and

---

21. Aristotle, *Nicomachean Ethics*, *supra* n. 5, pp. 1107a-1108b.
22. UNCITRAL Model Law on International Commercial Arbitration (2006), Article 12(2): 'An arbitrator may be challenged only if circumstances exist that give rise to justifiable doubts as to his impartiality or independence [...]'; UNCITRAL Rules (2021), Article 12(1): 'Any arbitrator may be challenged if circumstances exist that give rise to justifiable doubts as to the arbitrator's impartiality or independence'; ICC Rules of Arbitration (2021), Article 11(1): 'Every arbitrator must be and remain impartial and independent of the parties involved in the arbitration.'; SCC Arbitration Rules (2017), Article 18.1: 'Every arbitrator must be impartial and independent'; LCIA Arbitration Rules (2020), Article 5(3): 'All arbitrators shall be and remain at all times impartial and independent of the parties; and none shall act in the arbitration as advocate for or authorised representative of any party. No arbitrator shall give advice to any party on the parties' dispute or the conduct or outcome of the arbitration'; SIAC Rules (2016), Rule 13.1: 'Any arbitrator appointed in an arbitration under these Rules, whether or not nominated by the parties, shall be and remain at all times independent and impartial.'; HKIAC Administered Arbitration Rules (2018), Article 11(1): 'An arbitral tribunal confirmed under these Rules shall be and remain at all times impartial and independent of the parties.'
23. Mélanie van Leeuwen, 'Pride and Prejudice in the Debate on Arbitrator Independence', in Christoph Muller and Antonio Rigozzi, eds, *New Developments in International Commercial Arbitration 2013* (Schulthess 2013), p. 1 at pp. 12-13.
24. Loretta Malintoppi, 'Independence, Impartiality, and Duty of Disclosure of Arbitrators', in Peter Muchlinski, Federico Ortino and Christoph Schreuer, eds, *The Oxford Handbook of International Investment Law* (Oxford University Press 2008) p. 789 at p. 807.
25. Gary B. Born, 'Rights and Duties of International Arbitrators' in *International Commercial Arbitration*, 3rd edn (Kluwer Law International 2022), p. 2132.

present relations to the other actors in the arbitral process, will arbitrators be capable of discharging their duties and deciding the dispute in a moderate manner – that is to say, on the basis of the relevant facts and the applicable law alone.[26]

Second, save for limited exceptions, arbitrators' decisions must be reasoned.[27] For the legitimacy of the arbitral process and its outcome, it must be readily understandable from the tribunal's reasoning why, and on which factual and legal bases, the tribunal decided the contentious issues in the manner it did.[28] It is crucial for litigants and their counsel to see that arbitrators have considered the parties' respective positions and analysed the relevant evidence on record in relation to a particular disputed issue.[29] Good reasoning bears out that all contentious matters that must be decided to resolve a dispute, have been analysed objectively and decided dispassionately.[30] A moderate yet courageous approach to reasoning will demonstrate that the

---

26. See, e.g., Gary B. Born, 'Selection, Challenge and Replacement of Arbitrators in International Arbitration' in *International Commercial Arbitration*, 3rd edn (Kluwer Law International 2022), pp. 1908-1910.

27. The obligation to provide reasons for example does not apply to consent awards, see Gary Born, 'Form and Contents of International Arbitral Awards', in *International Commercial Arbitration*, 3rd edn (Kluwer Law International 2022), p. 3271. UNCITRAL Model Law on International Commercial Arbitration (2006), Article 31(2); UNCITRAL Arbitration Rules (2021), Article 36(1): 'If, before the award is made, the parties agree on a settlement of the dispute, the arbitral tribunal shall either issue an order for the termination of the arbitral proceedings or, if requested by the parties and accepted by the arbitral tribunal, record the settlement in the form of an arbitral award on agreed terms. The arbitral tribunal is not obliged to give reasons for such an award.'; SCC Arbitration Rules (2017), Article 42(1): 'The Arbitral Tribunal shall make its award in writing, and, unless otherwise agreed by the parties, shall state the reasons upon which the award is based.'; LCIA Arbitration Rules (2020), Article 26(9): 'In the event of any final settlement of the parties' dispute, the Arbitral Tribunal may decide to make an award recording the settlement if the parties jointly so request in writing (a "Consent Award") [...]. A Consent Award need not contain reasons or a determination in relation to the Arbitration Costs or Legal Costs.'; HKIAC Administered Arbitration Rules (2018), Article 37(2)(a): 'If, after the arbitral tribunal is constituted and before the final award is made: (a) the parties settle the dispute, the arbitral tribunal shall either issue an order for the termination of the arbitration or, if requested by the parties and accepted by the arbitral tribunal, record the settlement in the form of an arbitral award on agreed terms. The arbitral tribunal is not obliged to give reasons for such an award. [...].' Parties can also waive the reasoning requirement, see for example UNCITRAL Model Law Article 31(2): 'The award shall state the reasons upon which it is based, unless the parties have agreed that no reasons are to be given [...].'; UNCITRAL Arbitration Rules (2021), Article 34(3): 'The arbitral tribunal shall state the reasons upon which the award is based, unless the parties have agreed that no reasons are to be given.'; LCIA Arbitration Rules (2020), Article 26(2): 'The Arbitral Tribunal shall make any award in writing and, unless all parties agree in writing otherwise, shall state the reasons upon which such award is based.'; SIAC Rules (2016), Rule 32(4): 'The Award shall be in writing and shall state the reasons upon which it is based unless the parties have agreed that no reasons are to be given.'; HKIAC Administered Arbitration Rules (2018), Article 35(4): 'An award shall state the reasons upon which it is based unless the parties have agreed that no reasons are to be given.'

28. Giuditta Cordero-Moss, 'Reasoning in Arbitration: What Do Users Want or Need?' in Antonio Crivellaro and Mélida Hodgson, eds, *Explaining Why You Lost: Reasoning in Arbitration*, 18 Dossiers of the ICC Institute of World Business Law (Kluwer Law International 2020) p. 93 at pp. 97-100.

29. Gary B. Born, 'Procedures in International Arbitration' in *International Commercial Arbitration*, 3rd edn (Kluwer Law International 2022) p. 2283.

30. Giuditta Cordero-Moss, 'Reasoning in Arbitration: What Do Users Want or Need?' in Antonio Crivellaro and Mélida Hodgson, eds, *Explaining Why You Lost: Reasoning in Arbitration*, 18 Dossiers of the ICC Institute of World Business Law (Kluwer Law International 2020) p. 93.

right measures have been taken in the circumstances of the case, thereby enhancing the legitimacy of the arbitral award.

3   Generosity (γενναιοδωρία, gennaiod<u>o</u>ría)

Aristotle defined the virtue of generosity – also rendered as liberality – by reference to wealth,[31] as the mean between the deficiency of parsimony and the excess of prodigality or extravagance.[32] Where the extravagant exceeds in giving and is deficient in getting, a stingy, parsimonious person exceeds in getting and is deficient in giving.

Aristotle was of the view that citizens should not focus on the protection of their own interests alone but learn to be liberal by contributing generously to worthwhile causes.[33] The virtue of generosity is found in the proper management of economic resources and the distribution of wealth.

Generosity on the part of arbitrators is not about awarding relief to the underdog. Arbitrators' generosity is in the first place linked to the need for efficiency in arbitration. Unfortunately, from time to time one sees arbitrators in action, who comport themselves like divas, who will only travel and dine first class, who expect to be served like royalty and who order complex submissions on demanding issues to be prepared overnight. The moral hazard of wasting parties' time and money on facilities and tasks that are not necessary to resolve the dispute is unacceptable. It must be eradicated from the international arbitration practice.[34] To that end, arbitral institutions have rightly increased the level of scrutiny of arbitrators' time and expenses.[35] Arbitrators should not have to be reminded of the fact that they are service providers and that appropriate professional conduct does not involve excess at the expense of others.

In the second place, there is a need for generosity in reasoning. Still too frequently one receives awards where the reproduction of the parties' positions runs over hundreds of pages, while the arbitrators' reasoning is set out over a couple. Or, equally bad, reasoning in which arbitrators forget to engage with the legal arguments actually advanced by the parties because they are too busy dealing with issues of particular interest to them, citing their own awards and publications. It is incumbent on arbitrators to be generous when explaining how the tribunal arrived at the decision it did, by clearly articulating its analysis of the facts and the law. For the legitimacy of the

---

31. Salvatore Giammusso, 'Friendship with Oneself and the Virtues of Giving in Aristotle's Ethics', 58 Archiv für Begriffsgeschichte (2016) p. 7 at p. 7.
32. Aristotle, *Nicomachean Ethics*, *supra* n. 5, p. 1107b.
33. Judith Swanson, 'Aristotle on Liberality: Its Relation to Justice and Its Public and Private Practice', 27 Polity (1994) p. 3 at pp. 14-15.
34. *See generally* Klaus Sachs, 'Time and Money: Cost Control and Effective Case Management' in Loukas A. Mistelis and Julian D.M. Lew, eds, *Pervasive Problems in International Arbitration*, 15 International Arbitration Law Library (Kluwer Law International 2006) pp. 103-115 (discussing the issue of excessive costs in arbitral proceedings and potential remedies to address that issue).
35. Jean Kalicki, 'Controlling Time and Costs in Arbitration: A Progress Report (Part 2 of 2)' (22 November 2011) available at http://arbitrationblog.kluwerarbitration.com/2011/11/22/contr olling-time-and-costs-in-arbitration-a-progress-report-part-2-of-2/ (last accessed on 20 October 2022).

award it is essential that both parties – especially the losing party – understand why the tribunal decided as it decided.[36] For the enforceability of the award, it is essential that the annulment instance or enforcement court can readily understand the factual and legal foundation for the tribunal's decision(s).

Lastly, there is a need for generosity in spirit. Having established themselves professionally, generosity in spirit requires arbitrators to invest in their younger colleagues, in colleagues from other regions, and in colleagues with different professional backgrounds.[37] Training the next generation of arbitrators, fostering professional opportunities for others, and working with colleagues beyond the small circle of trusted colleagues requires an open mind and a generous spirit. That generosity is necessary to ensure that tomorrow's disputes – from small- and medium-sized enterprises to large multinationals and states – will be efficiently resolved by a diverse pool of well-equipped and experienced arbitrators.

4   Magnificence (μεγαλοπρέπεια, megaloprépeia)

According to Aristotle, the virtue of magnificence is the mean found between the excess of vulgarity and the defect of paltriness.[38] Magnificence is about making oneself useful to society with graciousness, style and charisma. The soul of the magnificent person is reflected in their solemn conduct.

Arbitrators are servants of justice. They carry responsibility for access to justice and for the administration of justice in the international context. Arbitration is a people's business *par excellence*.

It is the author's submission that arbitrators ought to conduct themselves and the proceedings graciously. All involved in the arbitral process deserve to be treated with respect. It is important to be benevolent and accommodating when arbitrators see a first-time advocate struggle during an examination, when they hear the testimony of a nervous witness who has difficulty finding the right words when the manner in which foreign counsel express themselves is not as eloquent as that of a native speaker when a participant in the process is hampered by a disability. Magnificent arbitrators exercise their function with humaneness, and humaneness is the core of Aristotle's benevolence. They treat all involved in the arbitral process with goodwill, make the effort to facilitate their participation in the process and ensure that all participants are heard and understood.

---

36. Mélida Hodgson, 'Conclusion' in Antonio Crivellaro and Mélida Hodgson, eds, *Explaining Why You Lost: Reasoning in Arbitration*, 18 Dossiers of the ICC Institute of World Business Law (Kluwer Law International 2020) p. 123 at pp. 123-124.
37. Eduardo Silva Romero, 'Challenging the Premises of Diversity: Opening Speech PAW 2021', ICC Dispute Resolution Bulletin 2021 Issue 3; Mélanie van Leeuwen, 'Diversity in Action: Opening Speech PAW 2021', ICC Dispute Resolution Bulletin 2022 Issue 2.
38. Aristotle, *Nicomachean Ethics, supra* n. 5, pp. 1107b and 1122a.

5   Magnanimity (μεγαλοψυχία, megalopsychia)

In the sphere of honour and dishonour, Aristotle places the mean of magnanimity between the excess of vanity and the defect of spinelessness.[39] Magnanimity is the virtue of being confident about one's position, without displaying vanity or falling short on the responsibilities that come with the position.[40] As Aristotle explained in the *Nicomachean Ethics*, honour is the prize of virtue and it is an honour that the magnanimous strive for in particular – and indeed deserve.[41] In that pursuit, the magnanimous therefore live a life of great virtue.

Accordingly, good arbitrators confidently perform their duties and exercise the powers that come with their function. In the process, they comport themselves in a calm, dignified and respectful manner, which will instil in the parties a sense of confidence in the conduct of the arbitral process, and a sense of trust among the members of a tribunal that is conducive to fruitful deliberation and collegial decision-making.

6   Ambition (φιλοδοξία, filodoxía)

Aristotle defined those who achieve their goals as ambitious persons who may take pride in their achievements. The virtue of ambition – found somewhere in the middle between laziness and single-mindedness – is about being industrious towards a higher goal. In Aristotelian theory, the only achievements that lead to glory are the achievements brought about by one's own virtuous activity and sheer hard work. There is no pride to be taken or glory to be had in respect of other person's achievements.[42]

Transposed into today's arbitration world, the virtue of proper ambition reinforces the '*intuitu personae*' character of arbitral appointments. Arbitrators are selected by parties and their counsel – often after extensive due diligence, discussion and consideration – for their expertise, their experience and their skills. None of their substantive and decision-making tasks may be delegated to tribunal secretaries. As Constantine Partasides KC put it eloquently twenty years ago, the parties did not agree to appoint a fourth arbitrator.[43] In line with Aristotle's ethics, ambitious arbitrators must perform their own analysis and must write their own decisions. No glory is due to arbitrators who pass the secretary's reasoning for their own.

In addition, it is worth recalling that arbitrators who sit in a plural formation, typically of three, all carry individual responsibility for the soundness of the reasoning and the quality of the decision. While the presiding arbitrator leads the process, co-arbitrators must equally be industrious and weigh in during the deliberations, and

39. *Ibid.*, p. 1107b; *see generally* Salvatore Giammusso, 'Friendship with Oneself and the Virtues of Giving in Aristotle's Ethics', 58 Archiv für Begriffsgeschichte (2016) p. 7.
40. Aristotle, *Nicomachean Ethics*, supra n. 5, p. 1123b.
41. *Ibid.*, pp. 1123b, 1124a and 1125a.
42. Aristotle, *Nicomachean Ethics*, supra n. 5, p. 1123b.
43. Constantine Partasides, 'The Fourth Arbitrator', 18 Arbitration International (2002) p. 147.

indeed also the drafting of the award, to ensure that it contains fair, comprehensive and logical reasoning on all issues in disputes.[44]

7   Patience (πραότητα, praótita)

Patience – or good temper – is identified by Aristotle as a key characteristic that is necessary for a person to make a meaningful contribution to society. Patience is the key driver of moderation. It holds the middle between the defect that can be described as a lack of spirit and the excess of hot temper.[45] In Aristotle's view, a good citizen is capable of hearing people out and will only protest if the need arises, at the right moment, on the right grounds, against the right person, in the right manner and for the right length of time.[46]

In the framework of arbitration, there is an infinite number of situations in which arbitrators have to employ the virtue of patience. Naturally, the fundamental principles of due process require arbitrators to ensure that all parties are afforded a reasonable opportunity to present their cases, to adduce their evidence and to respond to the other parties' pleaded case and evidence.[47] In that process, arbitrators must treat the parties professionally, with respect and in good faith, without irritation or dismissal.[48]

Only after arbitrators have heard all parties and considered all aspects of the issues in dispute, should they proceed to make a decision and reflect their considerations comprehensively in the reasoning thereof.

8   Truthfulness (αλήθεια, alítheia)

Unsurprisingly, truthfulness is one of the key virtues identified by Aristotle. He defined it as the need to have regard for the truth as objectively as possible, as opposed to acting on instinct or impression. In the middle between being boastful and self-deprecating, a truthful citizen would not succumb to the temptation of distorting the objective truth.[49]

Truthfulness goes to the heart of arbitral duty, now as always. Arbitrators have to search for and establish the truth as objectively as possible. To that end, arbitrators need to consider and analyse the entirety of the evidence before them and inquire with

---

44. *See generally* Charles Jarrosson, 'Reasoning in Arbitration' in Antonio Crivellaro and Mélida Hodgson, eds, *Explaining Why You Lost: Reasoning in Arbitration*, 18 Dossiers of the ICC Institute of World Business Law (Kluwer Law International 2020) p. 16 (discussing the essential qualities of an arbitral award and its reasoning).
45. Aristotle, *Nicomachean Ethics, supra* n. 5, p. 1108a.
46. Aristotle, *Nicomachean Ethics, supra* n. 5, pp. 1105b and 1125b-1126a; Nicolas Bommarito, 'Patience and Perspective', 64 Philosophy East and West (2014) p. 269 at p. 272.
47. Bernardo M. Cremades, 'The Use and Abuse of "Due Process in International Arbitration"', 9 Arbitraje: Revista de Arbitraje Comercial y de Inversiones (2016) p. 661.
48. Irene Welser and Samuel Mimnagh, 'The Arbitrator and the Arbitration Procedure: An Arbitrator's Imperative – How to Avoid Disappointing the Parties, Preventing Surprises and Enabling Efficient and Progressive Arbitral Proceedings' in Christian Klausegger and Peter Klein, eds, *Austrian Yearbook on International Arbitration 2021* (Manz'sche Verlags- und Unversitatsbuch-handlung 2021), p. 127 at p. 151.
49. Aristotle, *Nicomachean Ethics, supra* n. 5, p. 1108a.

the parties if they perceive gaps, inconsistencies or limitations in their respective cases, to satisfy themselves that they have fully understood the position.

That may be easier said than done. In cases that involve highly complex technical, economic or financial expertise, arbitrators may struggle because of limitations to their own knowledge, experience and understanding.[50] One must not sweep one's own failure to understand under the rug. One must confront it and address it. In such cases, truthfulness demands arbitrators not to retreat into familiar habits and practices or succumb to biases that will necessarily narrow their perception. Instead, arbitrators must acknowledge their limitations and seek additional explanation or even education in the relevant field. They should make an effort to acknowledge their biases and consider how debiasing techniques can be used.[51]

Furthermore, the duty of truthfulness in relation to the parties requires arbitrators to draw consequences in case of non-compliance with document production orders or in cases where parties hold back information to advance a selective explanation only.

Finally, the duty of truthfulness in relation to the other members of the tribunal requires arbitrators to be open, honest, reasonable and forthcoming in the deliberations about the reasons for the direction they wish to take, in a manner that is well-founded in fact and in law.

9   Humor (εὐτραπελία, eutrapelia)

As the right measure of enjoyment in social interaction is essential to achieving *eudaimonia*, Aristotle also identified good humour – or wit – as one of the twelve virtues.[52] Where the deficient person is boorish and the excessive person a buffoon, the golden mean is found in a person who is capable of taking a step back from serious matters to lighten up the spirit of those engaging in the interaction.[53]

Laughter relieves stress and boredom, boosts engagement and well-being, and spurs not only creativity and collaboration but also analytical precision and productivity.[54] Most people welcome a smile – not to say a good laugh – during a hearing.

In the professional setting where arbitrators interact with parties, lawyers, witnesses, experts, interpreters and court reporters, the work experience will be more enjoyable for all involved if arbitrators are engaging, keep a healthy perspective and lead the proceedings with a light touch of wit. If applied in the right measure at the right time, good humour can be extremely effective in defusing tension between litigants, as well as tension within a tribunal.

---

50. Kathleen Paisley, presentation at the ICCA Edinburgh 2022 Congress.
51. *See* Chapter 48 Some "Wh"s of Training of Arbitrators on Bounded Rationality and Debiasing Techniques: Taking the Future of Arbitral Decision-Making Seriously, by Bruno Guandalini in this volume; Bruno Guandalini, 'Freeing the Arbitrator from Limited Rationality: Some Proposed Solutions' in *Economic Analysis of the Arbitrator's Function*, 55 International Arbitration Law Library (Kluwer Law International 2020) p. 367.
52. John Lombardini, 'Civic Laughter: Aristotle and the Political Virtue of Humor', 41 Political Theory (2013) p. 203 at p. 209.
53. Aristotle, *Nicomachean Ethics*, *supra* n. 5, p. 1108a.
54. Alison Beard, 'Leading with Humor', Harvard Business Review (May 2014) available at https://hbr.org/2014/05/leading-with-humor (last accessed on 20 October 2022).

However, a word of caution is in order. One should be careful not to overdo it and be aware of the fact that an attempt at humour may get lost in translation in an arbitration that involves persons from different cultural backgrounds. Unlike laughter, humour is unfortunately not a universal language.[55] In order to stay within the bounds of good humour and avoid unnecessary challenges, good arbitrators require social intelligence and skills.[56]

Good humour is closely connected to the next Aristotelian value, which is kindness.

10 Kindness (φιλία, philia)

Much like good humour is required to make social interactions pleasant, in Aristotelian virtue theory kindness among interlocutors will foster the state of happiness and contentment that we strive for in a full, meaningful, *'eudaimonian'* life. In Aristotle's writings, the importance of kindness and amity is significant.[57] It is considered a complex and multifaceted aspect of human life.[58]

A kind person occupies the middle ground between the deficient, who are cantankerous, and the overly friendly, who are servile.[59]

How the virtue of kindness will enhance arbitrators' performance of their tasks, coincides with the reflections above on good humour, generosity, magnificence and magnanimity.

11 Modesty (αιδώς, aidós)

About the eleventh virtue, modesty, Aristotle said that it is a feeling rather than a disposition.[60] It is the fear of falling into disrepute.[61] Modesty is about preventing embarrassment to oneself and to others.

In the arbitration context, the classical notion of modesty will remind arbitrators to ensure that all arbitral participants are treated with respect and are able to leave the proceedings with their dignity intact. This is naturally important for the legitimacy of the arbitral process.

---

55. Kluwer Arbitration Blog, 'Young ICCA Interview: Amanda Lee' (September 2019) available at http://arbitrationblog.kluwerarbitration.com/2019/09/10/young-icca-interview-amanda-lee/ (last accessed on 20 October 2022).
56. *Meyer v. Kalanick*, Memorandum and Order, United States District Court, Southern District Court of New York, Case 1:15-cv-09796-JSR at p. 8, available at https://www.sdnyblog.com/files/2020/08/15-Civ.-09796-2020.08.03-Order-Upholding-Uber-Arbitration-Win.pdf (last accessed on 20 October 2022).
57. Elena Irrera, 'Between Advantage and Virtue: Aristotle's Theory of Political Friendship', 26 History of Political Thought (2005) p. 565.
58. *Ibid.*, pp. 565, 573 and 576.
59. Aristotle, *Nicomachean Ethics*, *supra* n. 5, p. 1108a.
60. *Ibid.*, p. 1128b.
61. *Ibid.*

Modesty in the modern sense of the word will remind arbitrators of the fact that they are service providers. That the purpose of the process is not their own gratification, but the administration of justice through fair and efficient dispute resolution. Being apprehensive of the risk of shame or, worse, disrepute is often an important driver for colleagues starting out as arbitrators, who have the ambition of building their reputation and who want to get things right. However, in order to achieve the moral progress that Aristotle thinks every virtuous person should be striving for throughout their lifetime, some of the more senior members of the arbitration bar may wish to work on the rebirth – or rediscovery – of their modesty skills.

12 Justice (δικαιοσύνη, dikaiosúní)

The ultimate, all-encompassing Aristotelian virtue for present purposes is justice.[62] Justice is the ability to distinguish right from wrong; and the readiness to protest against injustice. A just character is found in the middle ground between envy and malice, which are sentiments experienced in relation to other people's fortunes.[63] The envious person is afflicted by the good fortune of others, while the malicious person will actually experience joy over the misfortune of others.[64]

Those who master the virtue of justice are troubled by undeserved good fortune. The purpose of justice is to preserve or re-establish equality. As inequality breeds a sense of injustice, Aristotle was firmly of the view that society cannot move forward unless there is demonstrable equality, and that can only be achieved through the application of the law.

The law needs to steer citizens towards virtue and away from vice by forbidding certain actions and imposing others. Laws need to be enforced in order to ensure that inequality will not undermine the coherence of society.[65] To that end, Aristotle was the first to advocate that like cases should be treated alike, while unlike cases should be distinguished and treated differently, in accordance with and in proportion to their different conditions. In philosophical terms, this is referred to as distributive justice.[66]

As the law applies equally to all, Aristotelian virtue theory places great importance on equality in distribution. That does not mean that everyone should have an identical share to everyone else. Rather, equality is defined in terms of the proportional mean between the participants' respective worth and their respective needs. Thus, in distributive justice, equality consists of each participant receiving a share that is proportional to his relative worth.[67]

---

62. *Ibid.*, p. 1129b.
63. *Ibid.*, p. 1108b.
64. *Ibid.*
65. Xianzhong Huang, 'Justice as a Virtue: An Analysis of Aristotle's Virtue of Justice', 2 Frontiers of Philosophy in China (2007) p. 266.
66. David Johnston, 'Aristotle's Theory of Justice' in *A Brief History of Justice* 1st edn (John Wiley & Sons 2011) p. 64.
67. Delba Winthrop, 'Aristotle and Theories of Justice', 72 The American Political Science Review (1978) p. 1201.

That is a challenge that arbitrators will increasingly face in disputes generated by a globalized economy where inequalities are growing due to climate change, access to natural resources, energy, health care, et cetera.

The generation of Renaissance arbitrators that is reborn in Edinburgh during the ICCA Congress of 2022 will hopefully be courageous, moderate, generous, magnificent, magnanimous, ambitious, patient, truthful, witty, kind, modest and just enough to resolve the complex and challenging disputes that the twenty-first century will generate.

CHAPTER 47

The Renaissance Arbitrator: Lessons from the Construction Industry and Statutory Adjudication

Janey L. Milligan LLM FRICS FCIArb[*]

TABLE OF CONTENTS

I   INTRODUCTION

Translated directly from French to English, "renaissance" means "rebirth"; however, the term is also typically understood as referring to a revival or renewed interest in

---

[*] Since 1997, having qualified with a Masters' in Construction Law from the University of Strathclyde, Janey has been Managing Director of Construction Dispute Resolution. Janey also currently serves as a Director of the Scottish Arbitration Centre.

Initially qualifying as a Chartered Quantity Surveyor and after fifteen years in private practice, Janey later lectured at Glasgow Caledonian University (GCU) on professional practice, construction contracts and dispute resolution. Janey has wide experience in construction contracts specializing in providing contract advice to contractors and consultants in the construction industry, and in dispute resolution in the roles of Adjudicator and Arbitrator.

With her extensive and varied experience, Janey has been appointed to provide Expert Opinion in the areas of quantum in relation to construction contract claims for extension of time and loss and expense; contract administration; and professional negligence.

Always actively involved with the Royal Institution of Chartered Surveyors (RICS), Janey is a Past Chairman of RICS Scotland (2007-2008) and currently sits on the RICS Conflict Avoidance Process Working Group.

something. In addition, the term is often understood to be a reference specifically to the Renaissance period, which saw a revival of European art and literature under the influence of classical models;[1] many contributions to the sciences and architecture; and new religious and political ideas.[2]

During the Renaissance period, knowledge was viewed as central to value creation, and particularly knowledge sharing, where the Italian "bottega" of the fifteenth century was a community hub renowned for exchanges of ideas, creativity, and innovation.[3] The Renaissance Arbitrator can therefore be understood in the context of knowledge sharing to foster value creation.

This chapter draws upon the author's own experience as both an arbitrator and adjudicator in the UK construction industry to explore lessons arbitrators can learn from statutory adjudication; introduced to the UK construction industry under the Housing Grants, Construction and Regeneration Act 1996; to improve their practice for the benefit of the end-users—the parties to the dispute.

II   THE CONSTRUCTION INDUSTRY IN THE UK

1   Economic Significance

The most recently published statistics indicate that the construction industry contributes more than GBP 110 billion per annum to the UK economy equating to around 7% of the gross domestic product (GDP).[4] However, when the annual contribution is combined with further inputs to the construction process, using 2018 figures by example, such as manufacturing, mining and energy (GBP 60 billion contribution), professional services (GBP 25 billion contribution), finance and real estate (GBP 8 million contribution), and distribution (GBP 5 billion contribution), it becomes apparent that the construction industry has an even greater influence on the UK economy as a whole.[5]

This influence can, of course, have a negative impact, and from the 1970s onward, it has been recognized that the UK construction industry has a problem with insolvency.[6] The UK construction sector remains the most significant contributor to the

---

1. LEXICO, "Renaissance," available at https://www.lexico.com/en/definition/renaissance (last accessed June 18, 2022).
2. The Editors of Encyclopaedia Britannica, "Renaissance—European History" (February 7, 2020), available at https://www.britannica.com/event/Renaissance (last accessed June 18, 2022).
3. Piero Formica, "The Innovative Coworking Spaces of 15th-Century Italy" (April 27, 2016), available at https://hbr.org/2016/04/the-innovative-coworking-spaces-of-15th-century-italy (last accessed June 18, 2022).
4. Office of National Statistics for Construction, available at https://www.google.com/search?q = 0 office + of + national + statistics + for + construction + gdp + figures&oq = &aqs = chrome.0.69i59i 45ol8.249649276j0j15&sourceid = chrome&ie = UTF-8 (last accessed June 22, 2022).
5. Brian Green, "The Real Face of Construction 2020: Socio-Economic Analysis of the True Value of the Built Environment" (2020), available at https://policy.ciob.org/wp-content/uploads/2020/0 2/The-Real-Face-of-Construction-2020.pdf (last accessed June 18, 2022).
6. John G. Lowe & Elias Moroke, "Insolvency in the UK Construction Sector" In: Egbu, C., ed. *Procs 26th Annual ARCOM Conference* (Association of Researchers in Construction Management, 2010) pp. 93-100.

insolvency numbers representing 16% of all insolvencies in December 2021, with 407 construction companies becoming insolvent. Year to date, construction accounts for 16% of all company insolvencies in 2021.[7] The most common cause of insolvency is a lack of cash, and even profitable companies can fail due to a lack of funds.[8] The construction industry has been consistently plagued with uncertainty and ambiguity regarding cash flow,[9] and so contracting parties have typically been unable to adequately manage cash flow, exacerbating problems with insolvency.[10,11,12]

As early as 1971 the Courts recognized the importance of cash flow in the construction industry, and the difficulties faced in the event of poor cash flow. In the judgment in *Dawnays v. Minter*,[13] Lord Denning famously stated: "cash flow was the very lifeblood of the enterprise."[14] This statement is as true today as it was then.

Notwithstanding this, there was also a recognized lack of sanction for non-payment of sums applied for and properly due. Indeed, the judgment in *Gilbert-Ash (Northern) Ltd v. Modern Engineering (Bristol) Ltd*[15] held that to avoid making payment to a contractor, all that was required by the employer/client was the advance of a counterclaim, in any amount. If the contractor wished to contest this non-payment, the only available option was court or arbitration.[16] In this respect, one famous quote from more recent years provides:

> One of the greatest threats to cash flow is the incidence of disputes. Resolving them by litigation is frequently lengthy and expensive. Arbitration in the construction context is often as bad or worse.[17]

The issue came to a head in the wake of the UK recession of 1989-1990, when the rapid growth experienced in the UK construction industry throughout the course of the 1980s came to an abrupt end, with devastating consequences for the UK economy.[18] Recognizing the key role played by the construction industry in the success of the

7. CREDITSAFE Business Insolvency Statistics, Company insolvency figures for December 2021, available at https://www.creditsafe.com/gb/en/blog/reports/insolvencies.html (last accessed June 22, 2022).
8. Henry A. Odeyinka, John Lowe & Ammar Kaka, "An Evaluation of Risk Factors Impacting Construction Cash Flow Forecast" (2008) *Journal of Financial Management of Property and Construction*, 13(1), pp. 5-17.
9. Henry A. Odeyinka, John Lowe & Ammar Kaka, "A Construction Cost Flow Risk Assessment Model" In: Greenwood, D., ed. *18th Annual ARCOM Conference* (University of Northumbria, 2002), Vol. 1, pp. 3-12.
10. Richard E. Calvert, *Introduction to Building Management*, 5th ed. (1987).
11. Abdel H. Boussabaine & Ammar P. Kaka, "A Neural Networks Approach for Cash Flow Forecasting" (1998), *Construction Management and Economics*, 17, pp. 745-55.
12. Frank Harris, Ronald McCaffer & Francis Edum-Fotwe, *Modern Construction Management*, 6th ed. (Oxford 2006)
13. [1971] 1 WLR 1205.
14. Peter Coulson LJ, *Coulson on Construction Adjudication*, 4th ed. (Oxford 2018) pp. 3.
15. [1974] A.C. 689.
16. James Pickavance, *A Practical Guide to Construction Adjudication* (West Sussex 2016).
17. Denise Bowes, "Practitioners' Perception of Adjudication in UK Construction" In: Boyd, D., ed. *Procs 23rd Annual ARCOM Conference* (Association of Researchers in Construction Management, 2007) pp. 117-125, p. 117.
18. Mike Murray & David Langford, *Construction Reports 1944-98* (Wiley-Blackwell 2008).

economy as a whole, the UK government commissioned the Latham Report,[19] seeking recommendations on how best to make improvements to the industry, with the ultimate aim of managing risks to the UK economy as a whole.[20]

2   Dispute Resolution in the Construction Industry in the UK

a   *Introduction of the Housing Grants, Construction and Regeneration Act 1996*

A number of Latham's recommendations were carried forward into the drafting of the Housing Grants, Construction and Regeneration Act 1996 ("the 1996 Act")—setting down key legislative measures to achieve specific aims: in particular, to improve cash flow across the construction industry, and provide access to a *quick and cost-effective* means of resolving construction disputes.[21,22]

The 1996 Act is said to be the "most significant piece of legislation to affect the construction industries" in recent years.[23] However, commentators across the industry highlighted loopholes in the 1996 Act and shortcomings which negatively impacted the ability of the Act to reach its full potential.[24,25] Accordingly, amendments to the Act were introduced under the Local Democracy, Economic Development and Construction Act 2009 ("the 2009 Act") to address these issues.

i   *Adjudication under the Housing Grants, Construction and Regeneration Act 1996*

The 1996 Act provides for statutory adjudication at section 108, expressly providing that a dispute under a construction contract can be referred to adjudication "at any time," and that the decision of the adjudicator is binding until final determination by litigation, arbitration, or agreement by the parties. Parties cannot contract out of adjudication,[26] as confirmed in the judgment of HHJ Kirkham in *CommSuite Projects*

---

19. Michael Latham, *Constructing the Team: Final Report of the Government / Industry Review of Procurement and Contractual Arrangements in the UK Construction Industry* (HMSO 1994).
20. Mike Murray & David Langford., *Construction Reports 1944-98* (Wiley-Blackwell 2008).
21. Colin M. Darch, "The Construction Act Overview: Take Control of Subcontractor Payments" (March 9, 2017), available at https://openecx.co.uk/uk-construction-act-overview-take-control -of-subcontractor-payments/ (last accessed June 18, 2022).
22. Steven Evans, "Payment under the New 'Construction' Act: A Practical Guide" (April 2013) http://www.stevencevans.com/payment-under-the-new-construction-act-a-practical-guide/ (last accessed June 18, 2022).
23. John Redmond, *Adjudication in Construction Contracts* (Wiley 2001), p. 1.
24. Gary F. Sinden, James R. Mason, David G. Proverbs & Colin A. Booth, "The New Construction Act: Views and Perceptions of Construction Industry Stakeholders" (2012) *Structural Survey*, 30(4), pp. 333-343.
25. Janey Milligan, Amy Jackson & Lisa Cattanach, "UK Construction Payment Legislation—Clarity or Chaos?" In: RICS, ed. *RICS COBRA 2016 Conference*. Royal Institution of Chartered Surveyors, 2016).
26. Richard Anderson, *A Practical Guide to Adjudication in Construction Matters* (W.Green 2000).

Ltd v. Andritz AG.[27] The industry generally agrees with this requirement, with the strongly held belief that such an ability would be to the detriment of sub-contractors in particular, having less sway in negotiations.[28]

Where a construction contract does not provide for adjudication, Regulation 2 of the Scheme for Construction Contracts (England and Wales) Regulations 1998,[29] and Regulation 3 of the Scheme for Construction Contracts (Scotland) Regulations 1998,[30] provide that Part 1 of the applicable Scheme (dependent on the relevant UK jurisdiction), and the rules set out therein, shall apply to any adjudication entered into by the parties to the contract. This provides statutory certainty for parties entering into more informal arrangements, or where contracts are simply not up-to-date with the legislative requirements.

The 2009 Act amended the 1996 Act to expressly include wholly or partly oral contracts in the definition of a construction contract. Generally, this is thought of as a "move in the right direction,"[31] allowing sub-contractors and less contractually aware small main contractors access to the provisions of the 1996 Act which they could not previously benefit from. In late 2017 a consultation was carried out by the UK Government's Department for Business, Energy, and Industrial Strategy to support a Post-Implementation Review of the 2009 Amendments to the 1996 Act ("the 2017 Consultation"). The results of the consultation were published in February 2020 and indicated that respondents to the consultation considered the inclusion of oral contracts to be a positive, eliminating what was once one of the principal grounds for challenging an adjudicator's jurisdiction.[32]

b Reception of Statutory Adjudication

The 1996 Act was an extreme measure as it contradicted the overriding common law principle of the parties' freedom to contract.[33] In this respect, the 1996 Act was unique, being the first legislation to intervene in a sector of the economy which was generally thought to be performing well and contributing effectively.[34]

---

27. [2003] EWHC 958 (TCC).
28. D. Bowes, "Practitioners' Perception of Adjudication in UK Construction" supra n. 17.
29. Scheme for Construction Contracts (England and Wales) Regulations 1998, No. 649.
30. Scheme for Construction Contracts (Scotland) Regulations 1998, No. 687 (S.34).
31. G. Sinden, J. Mason, D. Proverbs & C. Booth, "The New Construction Act," supra n. 24.
32. Department for Business, Energy & Industrial Strategy, "2011 Changes to Part 2 of the Housing Grants, Construction and Regeneration Act 1996—A consultation to support a Post-Implementation Review—Summary of responses" (February 26, 2020), available at https://assets. publishing.service.gov.uk/government/uploads/system/uploads/attachment_data/file/868629/2011-changes-to-part-2-of-the-housing-grants-construction-and-regeneration-act-1996-summary-responses.pdf (last accessed June 18, 2022).
33. Douglas Wood, Paul Chynoweth, Julie Adshead & Jim Mason, *Law and the Built Environment*, 2nd ed. (Wiley-Blackwell2011).
34. G. Sinden, J. Mason, D. Proverbs & C. Booth, "The New Construction Act", supra n. 24.

Notwithstanding this, the importance of the 1996 Act was recognized by the industry from its inception,[35] regarded as the "most significant piece of legislation to affect the construction industries" in recent years.[36]

Particularly, the introduction of adjudication caused a "revolution" in construction disputes and the manner in which they are resolved.[37] Only one year following the introduction of the 1996 Act, adjudication was the top form of dispute resolution for construction disputes.[38] Since its introduction in 1998, there have been 33,529 referrals to Adjudicator Nominating Bodies (ANBs) up to April 2020.[39] This equates to an average of around 1,500 adjudications per year. It is anticipated that there will be many more appointments by the direct agreement of the parties.

The 2017 Consultation, as discussed above, provided that, in the five years prior to the consultation, 40% of respondents had used adjudication on more than one-fifth of disputes; a further 30% had used adjudication on between 1% and 20% of disputes; and 30% had not used adjudication on any disputes.[40]

The popularity of statutory adjudication in the UK construction industry following its introduction even led to such a pronounced decline in the use of arbitration in the industry that, in 2005, arbitration was removed as the default method of dispute resolution in the Scottish Building Contract Committee (SBCC)'s standard form construction contracts,[41] with litigation replacing arbitration as the tribunal of final determination. However, arbitration was reinstated in these contracts in 2016, marking a key distinction between the SBCC and its English counterpart, the Joint Contracts Tribunal where litigation remains the default.[42]

c   *The Changing Face of Statutory Adjudication*

As above, parties can refer "any dispute" arising under a construction contract to adjudication, and in recent years, there has been a marked shift from disputes referred to adjudication concerning only simple payment disputes to disputes concerning more complex, technical matters.[43]

---

35. Tony Bingham, *"10 Years of the Construction Act"* (April 25, 2008), available at http://www.building.co.uk/10-years-of-theconstruction-act/3111844.article (last accessed June 18, 2022).

36. J. Redmond, *Adjudication in Construction Contracts, supra* n. 23, p. 1.

37. J. Pickavance, *A Practical Guide to Construction Adjudication, supra* n. 16.

38. J. Pickavance, *A Practical Guide to Construction Adjudication, supra* n. 16.

39. Janey Milligan & Amy Jackson, "Report No. 19—Research Analysis of the Development of Adjudication November 2020), available at Adjudication-Report-19-November-1-Dec-2020.pdf (cdr.uk.com) (last accessed June 18, 2022).

40. Department for Business, Energy & Industrial Strategy, "2011 Changes to Part 2 of the Housing Grants, Construction and Regeneration Act 1996," *supra* n. 32.

41. Iain Drummond, "The Arbitration (Scotland) Act 2010" (November 4, 2011), available at https://shepwedd.com/knowledge/arbitration-scotland-act-2010-0. Last accessed June 18, 2022.

42. Kirstin Beattie, "SBCC D&B 2016 Is Here! 4 Key Changes" (June 29, 2017), available at https://www.burnesspaull.com/insights-and-events/news/sbcc-d-and-b-2016-is-here!-4-key-changes (last accessed June 18, 2022).

43. Peter Kennedy, Janey Milligan, Lisa Cattanach & Edward McCluskey, "The Development of Statutory Adjudication in the UK and Its Relationship with Construction Workload" In: RICS, ed. *RICS COBRA 2010 Conference* (Royal Institution of Chartered Surveyors, 2010).

There has also been an increase in high-value disputes being referred to adjudication, speaking to the increasing confidence in adjudication as an effective means of resolving a range of construction disputes.[44] Further, in recent years, a trend has emerged toward an increasing number of lawyer adjudicators, whereas in the past quantity surveyors were the most common discipline of adjudicators.[45] This has been attributed to and said to be characteristic of, an increasingly legalistic approach to adjudication, possibly indicating a shift away from the technical focus of adjudication initially intended.

This has all resulted in a corresponding increase in costs,[46] characterized by an increase in adjudicator's hourly fees,[47] as well as an increase in parties' own costs, which are non-recoverable regardless of success.

The 2017 Consultation found, in this regard, that the costs of adjudication were one of the principal grounds cited by parties for avoiding adjudication; with 38% of respondents believing costs had prevented them from opting for adjudication in between 1% and 20% of their disputes, and a further 23% believing this to be the case for more than one-fifth of their disputes.[48] The 2017 Consultation also found that the average cost of an adjudication in 2017 was GBP 28,000,[49] equivalent to around GBP 30,220 in 2021 when adjusted for inflation at an average of 1.9% per year.[50] Continuing at 1.9% per annum relates to approximately GBP 30,800 in 2022.

3   Arbitration in Scotland

Arbitration has a long history in Scotland, spanning some seven hundred years, and yet in the Arbitration (Scotland) Act 2010 ("the Scottish Act") Scotland has one of the most modern systems of arbitration in the world.[51] The Scottish Act provides parties with the utmost confidence in the confidentiality of proceedings, with limited grounds for appeal, as well as the ability to enforce arbitral awards made in the region across the globe. The founding principles enshrined in the Act reflect the key aims of the legislation and provide:

(a) that the object of arbitration is to resolve disputes fairly, impartially and without unnecessary delay or expense;

---

44. J. Milligan & A. Jackson, "Report No. 19," *supra* n. 39.
45. J. Milligan & A. Jackson, "Report No. 19," *supra* n. 39.
46. D. Bowes, "Practitioners' Perception of Adjudication in UK Construction," supra n. 17.
47. J. Milligan & A. Jackson, "Report No. 19," *supra* n. 39.
48. Department for Business, Energy & Industrial Strategy, "2011 Changes to Part 2 of the Housing Grants, Construction and Regeneration Act 1996," *supra* n. 32.
49. Department for Business, Energy & Industrial Strategy, "2011 Changes to Part 2 of the Housing Grants, Construction and Regeneration Act 1996," *supra* n. 32.
50. Bank of England, "Inflation Calculator," available at https://www.bankofengland.co.uk/monetary-policy/inflation/inflation-calculator (last accessed June 18, 2022).
51. Scottish Arbitration Centre, "About Arbitration and Arbitration in Scotland," available at About Arbitration and Arbitration in Scotland—Scottish Arbitration Centre (last accessed June 22, 2022).

(b) that parties should be free to agree on how to resolve disputes subject only to such safeguards as are necessary for the public interest; and

(c) that the court should not intervene in an arbitration except as provided by the Act.

a   *Similarities Between Arbitration and Adjudication*

In many ways, both being processes of alternative dispute resolution (ADR), arbitration bears many of the hallmarks of adjudication which, as above, has proven hugely popular in the UK construction industry. In particular, fast-track or short-form arbitration is virtually indistinguishable from adjudication.[52]

In the first instance; and like adjudicators; whilst the arbitrator acts as a 'judge' in the arbitration, they differ from a court judge in that they are an expert in their own right[53] considering and deciding disputes from the perspective of their technical background, and bringing this expertise to the parties' dispute.

Arbitration also offers strict confidentiality, like adjudication, this being supported by express statutory provision in the Arbitration (Scotland) Act 2010.[54] However, the notion of arbitral confidentiality under the Scottish system is further strengthened in that any challenges made to the courts on the basis of an arbitral award will also be subject to principles of confidentiality, with parties afforded anonymity in any proceedings related to the arbitration.[55] This is not the case in adjudication, where judgments in enforcement proceedings publish parties' names as well as details of the contract and the dispute.

Finally, both adjudication under the 1996 Act and arbitration under the 2010 Act afford parties limited grounds for appeal. Under the 2010 Act, the courts will not enforce the arbitrator's award: (i) if the award is under appeal or is subject to a process of correction under Rule 58 of the Scottish Arbitration Rules; or (ii) if the court is satisfied that the arbitrator did not have jurisdiction.[56] In the context of adjudication, the court will enforce the adjudicator's decision unless: (i) the adjudicator had no jurisdiction to make the decision; or (ii) there was a serious breach of the rules of natural justice.[57] This reinforces the view that the courts will support both adjudication and arbitration as effective, enforceable means of dispute resolution.

---

52. Rupert Choat, "Arbitration and Adjudication: A Tale of Two Acts" (October 9, 2015), available at https://www.building.co.uk/communities/arbitration-and-adjudication-a-tale-of-two-acts/5 078023.article (last accessed June 18, 2022).
53. CIARB, "Arbitration," available at https://www.ciarb.org/disputes/dispute-appointment-serv ice/arbitration/ (last accessed June 18, 2022).
54. Schedule 1 to the Act—Scottish Arbitration Rules, Rule 26: *Confidentiality.*
55. Scottish Arbitration Centre, "Advantages of Scottish Arbitration," *supra* n. 51.
56. Arbitration (Scotland) Act 2010, section 12.
57. Thomas Reuters, "Adjudication: A Quick Guide to Challenging the Enforcement of an Adjudicator's Decision," available at https://uk.practicallaw.thomsonreuters.com/7-386-8631?transi tionType = Default&contextData = (sc.Default)&firstPage = true&bhcp = 1# (last accessed June 18, 2022).

III   LESSONS TO BE LEARNED

1   Adjudication Principles of Benefit to Arbitration

As in the Renaissance, knowledge sharing remains a valuable tool to drive innovation across industries, and arbitrators can learn valuable lessons by looking to other forms of ADR and considering features which would translate well to arbitration to best meet users' needs. The arbitration community must be agile and willing to review its processes and adapt to the changing landscape of the disputes market. In this respect, the needs of users of international arbitration can be summarized as:

- (i)   fair resolution of their dispute;
- (ii) a private and flexible process;
- (iii) an internationally enforceable result; and
- (iv) a result provided at a reasonable cost.[58]

Anecdotally, the popularity of adjudication in the UK construction industry is credited to the technical focus of proceedings and industry expertise of adjudicators, as well as the expedited process and consequent reduction in fees when compared to other forms of ADR, primarily arbitration and litigation. Arbitration already has a number of similarities with adjudication which can be highlighted and drawn upon to consider where improvements in the process can be made, to the benefit of the end-users—the parties in dispute.

a   *The Decision Maker*

As is the case in arbitration, construction adjudicators come from a range of different professional backgrounds and the adjudicator nominated to a particular dispute will normally have technical expertise aligned to the matter in dispute. For instance, disputes could concern highly technical engineering, architectural, or quantum issues which require a very specific set of skills and knowledge to effectively decide the dispute.

Although research has indicated a shift toward more lawyer adjudicators;[59] and of course, there is most definitely a place for lawyers in all forms of ADR, which by their very nature are rooted in the law; to distinguish ADR from litigation, and to continue providing optimum value to parties in dispute, arbitration must maintain a strong focus on arbitrators with technical expertise. In the construction context, this means continuing and increasing efforts to recruit more engineers, architects, surveyors, and other construction professionals as arbitrators. A decision maker's background and experience will influence the key factors that stand out to them when reviewing a

---

58. Colin Hutton, Rob Wilson & Laura West, "Innovation and Technology in International Arbitration: What Lies Ahead?" (November 26, 2019), available at https://cms.law/en/gbr/publication/innovation-and-technology-in-international-arbitration-what-lies-ahead (last accessed June 18, 2022).
59. J. Milligan & A. Jackson, "Report No. 19," *supra* n. 39.

dispute. Knowledge in the particular area of the dispute informs the process and allows the decision maker to identify and examine the issues with the ability to ask piercing questions. Often the very nub of the matter in dispute, being a technical point, becomes engulfed in periphery issues and unnecessary legal arguments which are distracting and costly to the process.

An essential component of any dispute resolution process is that it is provided at a reasonable cost. Appointing arbitrators with a wealth of experience in the parties' industry—the inherent understanding of the relevant processes, contract forms, and technical matters which the arbitrator brings to the dispute allows for its more efficient, and ultimately more cost-effective, resolution.

Whilst appointing arbitrators with a wealth of experience is important, the need to consider how to bring a more diverse mix of arbitrators into the process and be more inclusive remains a significant issue. At the 2020 Roebuck Lecture, Cherie Blair commented:

> Our arbitration community must better reflect our clients and society if we are to avoid group-think, benefit from a diversity of talents and perspectives, and foster greater trust in the system ... To be genuinely inclusive we must also set our sights on pulling down other barriers—those concerning race, socio-economic background and age.[60]

Society is evolving and perception of who an arbitrator should be is properly advancing. We must move with that change to make it a reality and continue the transformation of arbitration. Some progress has been made in terms of gender diversity on arbitral tribunals over the past three years. But despite the increased focus on diversity issues and initiatives, respondents clearly feel that this has not as yet translated into actual or sufficient positive change.[61]

Dispute resolvers need to possess many skills and abilities; these include experience in the area of the dispute, understanding of the parties' legal rights and the capability to approach the dispute in an open and unbiased manner. A diverse spectrum of talents involving people from a range of different social and ethnic backgrounds, gender identities and other diverse groups is essential to this aim.

b   Timetable, Procedure, and Costs

Adjudication is a fast-track process that is much quicker than arbitration, with the adjudicator required to reach a decision within twenty-eight days of the dispute being referred. Whilst there is provision for the decision date to be extended; initially by the referring party to forty-two days, and with subsequent extensions possible with the agreement of both parties; typically an adjudicator will issue their decision in a much

---

60. Cherie Blair "CIArb 2020 Roebuck Lecture page 9-10," available at https://www.ciarb.org/media/10078/20200611-ciarb-2020-roebuck-lecture-by-cherie-blair-cbe-qc-mciarb.pdf (last accessed June 22, 2022).
61. White & Case "Diversity on Arbitral Tribunals: What's the Prognosis? (2021)," available at https://www.whitecase.com/publications/insight/2021-international-arbitration-survey/diversity-arbitral-tribunals (last accessed June 2022).

shorter timescale than an arbitral award. The published research in this regard indicates that over half of the decisions are issued within the initial twenty-eight-day period; a further one-third are issued within forty-two days; and only 14% are issued in a longer period. This research indicated that this final category covered a range of periods, from 7 to 20 weeks in total (or an extension to the statutory period of 3 to 16 weeks).[62] Anecdotally, very few adjudicators' decisions are extended by a significant period of several months.

Encouragingly, findings from a survey of Scottish arbitrations indicate that the vast majority of arbitration awards were issued either within 6 months (42%) or in 6-12 months (28%),[63] however, this is still a marked increase in the periods for adjudicator's decisions.

Notwithstanding this, we cannot lose sight of the requirement to balance the need for a resolution of the dispute efficiently and cost-effectively with the need for the award to be (internationally) enforceable. With regard to adjudication, the very tight timescales imposed by the 1996 Act have the potential to place the parties to a dispute under extreme pressure in the production of submissions within a matter of days, in turn placing a real strain on the business and its other projects as resources (both financial and in the form of key personnel) are diverted to the adjudication. This has led to criticisms of adjudication as providing "rough justice."[64] Whilst such a perception is not necessarily fatal to adjudication as providing a temporarily binding resolution to parties' disputes, arbitration; providing a final binding resolution of the dispute; must avoid such perceptions. Arbitration cannot be fast-tracked at the expense of its reputation. It is however of note that most adjudications are the final say on the matter of the material dispute with parties accepting the decision or using it to negotiate a final settlement.

To meet the key needs of users of international arbitration, the arbitration community must provide a flexible process. Perhaps one way to expedite the arbitration procedure and reduce costs while maintaining the authority afforded to arbitration is to promote the use of short-form processes published by recognized and respected bodies, particularly those which promote reaching an award on a "documents-only" basis, foregoing a hearing where this is neither necessary nor appropriate. By way of example, the CIArb published the Scottish Short Form Arbitration Rules in 2012, which include the following provisions:

4.1 The arbitrator and the parties shall conduct the arbitration without unnecessary delay and without incurring unnecessary expense...

4.4 The arbitration shall be conducted on a 'documents-only' basis where the arbitrator and the parties so decide. Notwithstanding the foregoing, the

---

62. J. Milligan & A. Jackson, "Report No. 19," *supra* n. 39.
63. Derek P. Auchie, Richard Farndale, Chris MacKay & Coral Riddell, "The Scottish Arbitration Survey: Report No. 1" (June 2015), available at https://www.abdn.ac.uk/law/documents/Scottish_Arbitration_Survey_June_2015.pdf (last accessed June 18, 2022).
64. Jonathan Cope, "Has the 'Rough Justice' Principle of Adjudication Been Extended Too Far?" (February 6, 2018), available at http://constructionblog.practicallaw.com/has-the-rough-justice-principle-of-adjudication-been-extended-too-far/ (last accessed June 18, 2022).

arbitrator may order a hearing of whatever kind at his discretion if he considers it is necessary for the purpose of reaching a decision...

5.1 The arbitrator shall publish his award within fourteen (14) days, of the later of:
   (i) the date upon which he received the last documents or submissions; or
   (ii) the close of any hearing; or
   (iii) any site visit or inspection.

5.2 The time period stipulated in article 5.1 shall, subject to intimation by the arbitrator to the parties prior to its expiry, be capable of being extended by the arbitrator by seven (7) days. The arbitrator may request a further extension of the time and with the agreement of the parties the time specified may be extended.[65]

In the construction sector, many arbitrators also act as adjudicators and are therefore used to operating to the tight timescales of adjudication and can therefore utilize this skill in arbitrations. Importantly, the same can be said for party representatives who have adapted their methods and practice to meet the tight timescales of adjudication yet still fulfill their clients' needs and expectations. Representatives must be encouraged to transfer their expertise to fully blend with fast-track and cost-effective arbitration processes driven by all participants and a proactive arbitrator.

Although accepting there has to be a balance between the fact that arbitration is final and binding and the time afforded for submissions; the process and publication of the arbitration award must move with the times if it is to continue with its rebirth. More emphasis should be put on adopting fixed timescales for the vast majority of arbitrations with all parties and the arbitrator agreeing on them from the outset. A compromise may be to agree on a fixed duration for the award to be published following the completion of all submissions.

Mandatory timescales, at least by agreement, could make the arbitration process more appealing to parties for construction disputes in the United Kingdom. By reducing the duration of the arbitration, the parties' representatives and arbitrator's fees are also likely to be reduced.

It is not controversial that the examination of witnesses, both of factual and expert evidence, is extremely time-consuming and costly to the arbitration process. It is interesting to note that hearings are not frequent in adjudications which is partly down to the restricted timescales. However, they do on occasion occur. In my experience and anecdotally, in the majority of cases, the adjudicator will not permit cross-examination of the witnesses, preferring to question the witnesses themselves based on the key points that they have identified need to be examined to determine the dispute. This diversion from the norm can save an immense amount of time and it is suggested should be encouraged in more arbitration proceedings.

As above, it is said that adjudications are more often conducted on a documents-only basis even for fairly complex disputes. This has not diminished the success of adjudication and often submissions are in electronic copy only, reducing the administrative burden and printing costs associated with hard copy submissions. This is an evolution that has moved forward quickly in adjudication due to the impact of

---

65. CIARB, "Scottish Short Form Arbitration Rules" (2012), available at https://www.ciarb.org/media/5829/scottish-short-form-arbitration-rules-2012.pdf (last accessed June 18, 2022).

COVID-19 and arbitration must be agile to the benefits of this not only in costs but also in green credentials.

A word of caution—it is arguable that a danger of electronic copies can be to encourage the parties to make lengthy submissions with voluminous supporting (and irrelevant) documentation. This consequence must be controlled as any benefits are lost to the greater number of hours being spent by the arbitrator examining potentially unnecessary material. It is key, therefore, that the parties are encouraged to keep submissions refined and focused on the salient points in dispute which echoes an earlier point encouraging party representatives to refine their methods and practice.

In the past, the arbitration community has been reluctant to instigate change and move from its tried and tested procedures. COVID-19 has been credited with changing that aspect of dispute resolvers' behavior at astonishing speed. As the world shut down on an unprecedented scale people's ability to meet, travel to different countries and even commute to the office was curtailed and, in some instances, prevented. However, Zoom and Teams meetings became the new normal. From there, progress was made to electronic submissions and virtual hearings for many forms of ADR. This enabled the arbitration community to continue with business despite the restrictions imposed. Although meeting in person is often preferable, the continued adoption of virtual meetings and hearings, particularly procedural ones, could assist in the rebirth of arbitration and certainly in the reduction of costs.

What can the arbitration community learn from adjudication about costs? In adjudication, parties must bear their own costs of going to adjudication, win or lose, and are only required under the legislation, except in very limited circumstances,[66] to pay for adjudicator's time. This has made adjudication very accessible for the disgruntled party that previously had to consider not only its own costs but a proportion of its opponent's costs if it raised an arbitration and was subsequently unsuccessful. The wealthier opponent often had the threat of financial advantage even if its case was weak.

Perhaps there is an opening in arbitration for similar rules with regard to costs to be adopted at least in particular circumstances, types or parts of disputes.

It is not disputed that adjudication in the UK is considerably removed from international arbitration but that is not to say lessons cannot be learned. Complex and high-value disputes are efficiently resolved using adjudication with experts in the field adopting new techniques and technologies in doing so. Generations of the future across the globe, where many jurisdictions have introduced domestic adjudication, are learning these practices. Sharing the successes of these and applying them to an international dispute, or even just parts or individual issues that lend themselves to alternative methods, could offer significant rewards, particularly financially. New entrants to dispute resolution are particularly enthusiastic and energetic to move forward with developing trends which is inspiring and contagious. This is a renaissance which must be allowed to flourish rather than keeping with tradition for tradition's sake.

---

66. Housing Grants, Construction and Regeneration Act 1996, section 108A Adjudication costs; effectiveness of provision.

IV   CONCLUSIONS

The construction industry in the United Kingdom is a massive contributor to the GDP and has many facets to it. Cash flow has always been the "lifeblood of the industry" but frequently disputes arise as a result of negative cashflow exacerbated for many different reasons.

This position resulted in the UK government passing the Housing Grants, Construction and Regeneration Act in 1996 to improve cash flow and resolve construction disputes in a quick and cost-effective way with statutory adjudication.

The introduction of adjudication caused a "revolution" in resolving construction disputes within one year of the Act coming into force.

The popularity of adjudication is, in part, credited to the technical focus of proceedings and industry expertise of adjudicators. There is real value in employing experts in specific disciplines to get quickly to the heart of the matter for resolving technical disputes efficiently. Decision makers with a wealth of experience in the parties' industry have an inherent understanding of the relevant processes, contract forms, and technical matters which they bring to the dispute promoting a more efficient, and ultimately more cost-effective, resolution.

Society is evolving and perception of who an arbitrator should be is properly advancing. The arbitration community must move with that change to make it a reality and continue the transformation of arbitration.

Adjudication has shown that the arbitration community could provide a more flexible and quicker process by adopting fixed durations for the process, or end dates tied to final submissions with more emphasis on documents-only proceedings. Where it is incumbent on the decision maker to hear from witnesses, cross-examination can be effectively replaced by the decision maker directly asking the questions that need to be answered.

As a result of the COVID-19 experience adjudicators and arbitrators adapted swiftly to the use of virtual hearings. This in turn increased the use of electronic documents only with both techniques offering reductions in costs. However, it is imperative that the temptation to include more information electronically is tempered by keeping submissions succinct and eliminating irrelevant material.

Appointing arbitrators with a wealth of experience in the discipline of the dispute and streamlining the processes will help to reduce costs. It may be that only a part of the whole dispute or an individual issue can benefit from a streamlined approach adopting the techniques discussed in reaching an overall conclusion.

Costs are always a prominent feature in deciding how to approach the resolution of a dispute. Adjudication legislation requires the parties to normally bear their own costs. It is thought that some arbitrations may welcome this as an option; again this is a feature that could be implemented in the circumstances where one part of the dispute is separated out for streamlining and more cost-effective resolution.

Whilst Scotland has a very modern arbitration system enshrined in the Arbitration (Scotland) Act 2010, recognizing the success of adjudication and being alert to the fact that shared knowledge creates value, lessons can be learned from that success and transferred to the arbitration community.

In all, the arbitration community must be agile and willing to review its processes and adapt to the changing landscape of the disputes market. Knowledge sharing remains a valuable tool to drive innovation across industries and it is imperative that traditional arbitration processes are not maintained only for tradition's sake.

CHAPTER 48

Some "Wh"s of Training of Arbitrators on Bounded Rationality and Debiasing Techniques: Taking the Future of Arbitral Decision-Making Seriously

Bruno Guandalini[*]

TABLE OF CONTENTS

I   INTRODUCTION

Arbitral decision-making is subject to errors that stem from the very essence of human nature. Bounded rationality or cognitive bias is a particular source of these errors. Thus, preventing and correcting bounded rationality or cognitive bias is essential to improve arbitral decision-making. This text assumes this premise.

The theory of bounded rationality and cognitive bias is grounded in behavioral science, psychology, and behavioral economics. It is said to have begun when

---

[*] Partner at Guandalini, Isfer e Oliveira Franco Advogados, Brazil. PhD Université Côte d'Azur. LL.M. Georgetown University Law Center. Master II Université de Paris II (Panthéon-Assas). Former President of the ARBITAC—Mediation and Arbitration Chamber of the Paraná State Commerce Association.

psychologists started questioning the rational choice theory. Simon explained the problems with decisions that are adopted intuitively,[1] but the cornerstone is an article by Amos Taversky and Daniel Kanheman[2] explaining that decision-makers may be affected by heuristics and bias.

Since then, a whole line of thinking has been developed around the bounded rationality of economic actors more commonly known as behavioral economics.[3] Rational choice theory was therefore thrown into doubt. With this recent development, psychology has encountered and engaged with microeconomics, and the limitation of rationality has gained a special place in every economic analysis. If traditional law and economics used the premises of microeconomics to read law, behavioral law and economics—or law and economics mitigated by psychology and behavioral sciences—would explain bounded rationality in several decision-making situations.

Alice Stocker recently noted that "WIKIPEDIA alone lists nearly 200 unconscious biases that tamper with a supposedly rational way of thinking."[4] Although many different manifestations have been described by scientists, in fact, bounded rationality or unconscious bias is extremely difficult to demonstrate in the context of an arbitrator's function. Bias is a naturally unobservable phenomenon.[5] This is perhaps the reason why few studies have attempted to conduct empirical research on arbitral decision-making. Others, naturally, conducted deductive analysis and explained different possibilities on how bounded rationality may affect an arbitrator's decision-making process.[6]

1. Hebert A. Simon, "A Behavioral Model of Rational Choice," 69(1) The Quarterly Journal of Economics (February 1955), 99-118.
2. Daniel Kahneman and Amos Tversky, "Judgment under Uncertainty: Heuristics and Biases," in *Judgment Under Uncertainty: Heuristics and Biases* (Daniel Kahneman, Paul Slovic and Amos Tversky, eds), Cambridge University Press, 1982.
3. *See* Cass R. Sunstein, *Behavioral Law and Economics*, Cambridge University Press, 2000; *see also* Eyal Zamir and Doron Teichman, *The Oxford Handbook of Behavioral Economics and the Law*, Oxford University Press, 2014.
4. Alice Stocker, "De-biasing Counsel: A Call for Agile Minds in Arbitration," 39(1) Journal of International Arbitration 117-128, p. 119 (2022).
5. Stavros Brekoulakis, "Systemic Bias and the Institution of International Arbitration: A New Approach to Arbitral Decision-Making," 4(3) Journal of International Dispute Settlement 553-585 (2013).
6. Some commentators have already discussed limitations on rationality of arbitrators: *See* Shari Diamond, "Psychological Aspects of Dispute Resolution: Issues for International Arbitration," *International Commercial Arbitration: Important Contemporary Questions* 327-342 (2003); *see also* Tereza Giovannini, "The Psychological Aspects of Dispute Resolution: Commentary," *International Commercial Arbitration: Important Contemporary Questions*, The Hague, Kluwer Law International, 2003, p. 348; Christian R. Drahozal, "A Behavioral Analysis of Private Judging: Law and Contemporary Problems," 2004, available at: https://ssrn.com/abstract=380021; Daphna Kapeliuk, "The Repeat Appointment Factor: Exploring Decision Patterns of Elite Investment Arbitrators," 96 Cornell L. Rev. 47 (2010); Gus Van Harten, "Arbitrator Behavior in Asymmetrical Adjudication: An Empirical Study of Investment Treaty Arbitration," 50 Osgoode Hall Law Journal (2012); Ricardo Dalmaso Marques, Carmine Pascuzzo and Ana Weber, "Challenging the Splitting the Baby Myth in International Arbitration," (719) J. Int'l Arb. (2014); Lucy Reed, "The 2013 Hong Kong International Arbitration Centre Kaplan Lecture: 'Arbitral Decision-Making: Art, Science or Sport?," 85 J. Int'l Arb. (2013); *see also* Edna Sussman, "Arbitrator Decision-Making: Unconscious Psychological Influences and What You Can Do about Them," 24 American Review of International Arbitration 487, 514 (2013); Naomi Gershoni, "Singles vs. Panels: Do More Arbitrators Induce Less Bias?" [preliminary and incomplete],

Of the research conducted so far, some studies are worth highlighting. Flader et al. conducted interviews in 2008 and 2011 and published results in 2012,[7] which were then reassessed in 2017.[8] Also in 2017, Franck et al. focused on international arbitrators, in research during an ICCA Congress.[9] Research conducted by Sussman in 2018 provided some empirical evidence.[10] More recently, in 2019, Franck published remarkable research, particularly on international treaty arbitration.[11] On this same path, we have recently consolidated a few kinds of limitations on the arbitrator's rationality.[12]

Despite the lack of consistent empirical research on the decision-making of arbitrators, according to general theory, we may sustain that arbitrators suffer from bounded rationality making them—and the parties—victims of consequent errors. Arbitrators are, after all, human beings.[13]

We bring some clarification. First, cognitive illusions are decision-making models that can lead to distorted perceptions. That is, an inaccurate judgment or an illogical interpretation of reality, which also comprises intuition. It also includes heuristics, which are mental shortcuts that allow human beings to solve problems, make

---

November 18, 2015. Available at: http://naomigershoni.weebly.com/uploads/5/3/2/0/5320512 5/singlesvspanels_nov15.pdf; *see also* Sergio Puig and Anton Strehnev, "Affiliation Bias in Arbitration: An Experimental Approach," *Arizona Legal Studies*, Discussion Paper No. 16-31, 2016. Available at https://papers.ssrn.com/sol3/papers.cfm?abstract_id = 2830241. *See also* Rebecca Helm, Jeffrey Rachlinski and Andrew Wistrich, "Are Arbitrators Human?," 13(4) Journal of Empirical Legal Studies 666-693 (2016). *See also* Ank van Aaken and Tomer Broude, "Arbitration from a Law & Economics Perspective," *The Oxford Handbook of International Arbitration*, Working Paper No. 2016-07, 2016. Available at https://papers.ssrn.com/sol3/papers .cfm?abstract_id = 2860584. *See also* David Collins, "Loss Aversion Bias or Fear of Missing Out: A Behavioral Economics Analysis of Compensation in Investor-State Dispute Settlement," 9 Journal of International Dispute Settlement 460-482 (2017). *See also* Edna Sussman, "The Arbitrator Survey: Practices, Preferences and Changes on the Horizon," 26 The American Review of international Arbitration 517-538 (2018). *See also* Susan Franck, Ank van Aaken, James Freda, Chris Guthrie, and Jeffrey Rachlinski, "Inside the Arbitrator's Mind," 66 Emory Law Journal (2017). *See also* Tony Cole, Pietro Ortolani and Sean Wright, "Arbitration in Its Psychological Context: A Contextual Behavioral Account of Arbitral Decision-Making," *University of Leicester School of Law Research Paper*, 30 April 2018. Available at SSRN: https://ssrn.com/abstract = 31 51107. Susan Franck, *Arbitration Costs, Myths and Realities in Investment Treaty Arbitration* (Oxford University Press 2019).
7. *See* Dieter Flader, Sophie Nappert and Jansen Calamita, 'The Psychological/Communicative Preconditions for the International Arbitral Process: Initial Findings of a Research Project and its Methodology," *ISPSW Strategy Series: Focus on Defense and International Security*, August 2012, Issue No. 200. Available at https://www.files.ethz.ch/isn/152191/200_Flader_Nappert_Jansen. pdf.
8. *Ibid.*
9. *See* Susan Franck et al., "Inside the Arbitrator's Mind," 66 Emory Law Journal (2017).
10. *See* Edna Sussman, "Arbitrator Decision-Making: Unconscious Psychological Influences and What You Can Do about Them," 24 American Review of International Arbitration 487, 514 (2013).
11. *See* Susan Franck, *Arbitration Costs, Myths and Realities in Investment Treaty Arbitration* (Oxford University Press 2019).
12. Bruno Guandalini, *Economic Analysis of the Arbitrator's Function* (Wolters Kluwer 2020).
13. *See* Rebecca Helm, Jeffrey Rachlinski and Andrew Wistrich, "Are Arbitrators Human?," 13(4) Journal of Empirical Legal Studies 666-693 (2016).

decisions, and react to situations quickly and efficiently[14] without thinking about each decision based on its cost-benefit or its consequences. Some examples that affect an arbitrator's behavior are extremeness aversion, anchoring, loss aversion, availability heuristic, optimistic bias, tendency to the status quo, and hindsight bias.[15]

In addition, external factors such as emotions, prosocial incentives and cultural influences irrationally affect an arbitrator's decision-making. Emotions, although an internal psychological issue, are classified as an external influence. The reason relies on the fact that emotions are activated by external influences. The crucial element here is not the constraints that emotions will internally generate in the arbitrator as a rational actor, but that external influences might modify the arbitrator's rational behavior by creating feelings that will automatically and unconsciously impact their decision-making processes.

Limitations could also occur with altruistic behavior and social and cultural influences. The situations that are envisaged are those in which individuals tend to help strangers or help people in general, even if they are not known to the decision-maker. Brekoulakis explains that the altruistic behavior of a decision-maker is rather a behavior that prefers society first, rather than individual rights or commercial activities.[16] On this same path, culture is a response and consequence of the repeated behavior of actors in society. It is also modified by the conduct of the members within the community and might not be rational. Bias may also be cultural, in the sense that actors—or arbitrators—may have their own cultural understanding of trading practices[17] or legal principles.[18] Likewise, limitation of rationality is also driven by the instinct of reciprocity, which is an irrational behavior and a consequence of social interaction. This instinct occurs particularly when people feel the necessity to reciprocate other members of society and their network.

Thus, all these limitations on an arbitrator's rationality can affect arbitral decision-making, the quality of the award, parties' expectations, and, at the end of the day, the efficiency of the arbitrator's contract. But what could be done to improve arbitral decision-making and reduce such transaction costs?

Just a few commentators have already offered solutions. First, in 2013, Sussman proposed a checklist of techniques that arbitrators could adopt during the proceedings.[19] In 2017, ELM analyzed debiasing strategies for arbitrators, specifically looking

---

14. Edna Sussman, "Arbitrator Decision-Making: Unconscious Psychological Influences and What You Can Do about Them," 24 American Review of International Arbitration 487, 514 (2013) at 495.
15. *See* Bruno Guandalini, *Economic Analysis of the Arbitrator's Function*, Wolters Kluwer, 2020, Chapter 7.
16. Stavros Brekoulakis, "Systemic Bias and the Institution of International Arbitration: A New Approach to Arbitral Decision-Making," *supra*.
17. Ilias Bentekas, "The Psychological Anthropology of International Arbitration," in *The Roles of Psychology in International Arbitration* (Tony Cole ed.), Wolters Kluwer, 2017, p. 379.
18. *See* Joshua Karton, *The Culture of International Arbitration and the Evolution of Contract Law*, Oxford University Press, 2014, p. 21. *See also* Won L. Kindane, *The Culture of International Arbitration*, Oxford University Press, 2017.
19. Edna Sussman, "Arbitrator Decision-Making: Unconscious Psychological Influences and What You Can Do about Them," *supra*, p. 507.

at how to design behaviorally improved arbitration clauses.[20] In 2019, Franck discussed debiasing of arbitrators under the investment arbitration environment according to Fischoff's three techniques to correct faulty decision-makers: replace incorrigible individuals, give notice of the degree of illusions, and, finally, prepare for inevitable errors.

Among those techniques, for the arbitrator's decision-making, we argue that training and education should be given more attention. Few commentators emphasize—or even understand—the importance of training and education. Franck notes that arbitrators could train themselves to minimize errors.[21] Others expressly recognized that training and education are crucial steps for arbitrators[22] and decision-makers.[23] Recently, we described training as a first and important step.[24]

However, no literature regarding an arbitrator's decision-making has deeply considered training and education of arbitrators in behavioral economics and cognitive psychology. We argue that training and education are of the utmost importance and a necessary step if the arbitration community wants to take the improvement of arbitrators' decision-making seriously. This chapter further discusses Why (section II), What (section III), Who, Where, When and How (section IV) arbitrators should be trained and educated. We will also consider some inherent difficulties to be overcome (section V) and offer a conclusion (section VI).

II   WHY?

We address at least four reasons *why* arbitrators should be trained and educated.

The *first reason* is that arbitrators are in general not aware of their bounded rationality; arbitrators are all human beings. Actors are usually unaware of their cognitive limitations. It is also called "unconscious bias." Only with enough knowledge of how the human mind works would arbitrators be able to identify and avoid limitations on rational decision-making. Arbitrators should be aware that limitations exist.

Taking confirmation bias as an example, arbitrators should be able to understand that their intuitive thinking might lead them to form an initial belief in relation to the case and then seek evidence to confirm the position. Thus, arbitrators should be able

---

20. Jan-Philip Elm, "Behavioral Insights into International Arbitration: An Analysis of How to De-Bias Arbitrators," 27 *The American Review of International Arbitration* 49 and the followings (24 May 2017).
21. Susan Franck, *Arbitration Costs, Myths and Realities in Investment Treaty, supra*, p. 61.
22. *See also* Tony Cole, Pietro Ortolani and Sean Wright, "Arbitration in Its Psychological Context: A Contextual Behavioral Account of Arbitral Decision-Making," *supra*, p. 35. *See also* Rebecca Helm, Jeffrey Rachlinski and Andrew Wistrich, "Are Arbitrators Human?," *supra*, p. 691.
23. Specially in the EU Judicial context: Christoph K. Winter, "The Value of Behavioral Economics for EU Judicial Decision-Making," 21 German Law Journal 240-264, at 263 (2020).
24. *See* Richard P. Larrick, "Debiasing," in *Blackwell Handbook of Judgment and Decision Making* (Derek J. Koehler and Nigel Harvey, eds), Blackwell Publishing, 2011, pp. 316-338. *See also* Scott Lilienfield, Rachel Ammirati and Kristin Landfield, "Giving Debiasing Away: Can Psychological Research on Correcting Cognitive Errors Promote Human Welfare?," *Association for Sociological Science*, 2009, pp. 390-398.

to understand that if they use intuitive reasoning, they could be wrongly looking for additional evidence of their initial beliefs.[25]

There are other examples. Arbitrators should be aware that they might have extremeness aversion in order to avoid a possible unconscious tendency to split the baby; that they suffer from anchoring in order to avoid adjusting their reasoning towards irrational references or anchors; that they suffer from availability heuristic in order to avoid miscalculating disproportionate odds of events just because they have already had some previous experiences; that they suffer from hindsight bias and avoid considering that an *ex ante* inevitable event wrongly appears evitable *ex post* just because it has just occurred;[26] to mention but a few. Finally, when social influences and networks are considered, arbitrators should be aware that affiliation bias exists so that they might have an unconscious tendency to favor the party that has appointed them.

A *second reason* is that arbitrators are normally smart and experienced people who hardly ever consider that they could make a mistake or that their decision-making process is not good enough or, in other words, that they could not be 100% rational.

Just to shed some light on the problem, empirical research we developed in 2017[27] asked twenty experienced arbitrators whether that had bounded rationality or unconscious bias. Only nine answered that they do have cognitive limitations (as does every human being). Eleven of the interviewees—more than half (!)—answered that they did not have any cognitive bias or limitation on rationality (or did not understand the question or gave completely unrelated answers), demonstrating that they do not understand the topic and would be perfect candidates for the discussed training.

There is an easy explanation for this result. Cognitive psychology and behavioral economics are taught in schools of psychology, and to a degree in economics and management, but there is little emphasis on limitations of rationality and how to overcome these limitations,[28] especially in law schools. Arbitrators, the majority of whom are trained in law—and several years ago—are usually not trained on the topic.

Besides the lack of training, their level of experience might induce them to make decisions intuitively. The problem is that experience leads to overconfidence, which could reduce an arbitrator's attention to limitations of rationality rendering them even more exposed. The adoption of System 1[29] or intuitive reasoning allows limitations to act and affect rational reasoning. As experience is a form of knowledge accessibility

---

25. Mark Lepper, Charles Lord and Lee Ross, "Assimilation and Attitude Polarization: The Effects of Prior Theories on Subsequently Considered Evidence," 37 Journal of Personality & Social Psychology 2098 (1979).
26. Lucy Reed, "The 2013 Hong Kong International Arbitration Centre Kaplan Lecture: 'Arbitral Decision-Making: Art, Science or Sport?'," *supra*, at 91.
27. *See* Bruno Guandalini, *Economic Analysis of the Arbitrator's Function*, Wolters Kluwer, 2020, p. 341.
28. Richard P. Larrick, "Debiasing," 316-338 (Derek J. Koehler and Nigel Harvey, eds., Blackwell Publishing 2011), p. 326.
29. System 1 and System 2 are different forms that the human brain uses to process decisions. System 1 is said to operate automatically and quickly, without effort and without a sense of voluntary control. System 2 emphasizes all mental attention, which includes complex computations and is frequently associated with choice and concentration. *See* is explained in Daniel Kahneman, *Thinking, Fast and Slow*, Farrar, Straus, and Giroux, 2015, pp. 20-21.

and arbitrators are usually very experienced individuals, it is natural that they frequently use intuition. Posner recognizes that "experiences nourish intuitions."[30] Thus, it is natural to conclude that highly demanded arbitrators will use intuition because they are either very busy and need to make quick decisions—by definition—not adapted to System 2, or familiar with legal problems of a case having already dealt with many similar facts on similar cases.

The *third reason* can be summarized in a single sentence: specialized training may help mitigate the influence of cognitive bias.[31] Only the knowledge about cognitive science and behavioral economics—including all different limitations of rationality and debiasing techniques—would allow arbitrators to act and employ debiasing techniques themselves, which will improve certainty in arbitral decision-making and efficiency in the arbitrator's contract.

An important technique of bias correction and prevention is the use of one's own biases or limitations of rationality to obtain efficiency instead of eliminating them.[32] It is not about moving arbitrators from System 1 to System 2 but rather using System 1 as a better *choice architect*.[33] To illustrate, the extremeness aversion may be used or considered by an arbitrator to correct anchoring should the arbitrator consider that parties are trying to impose anchors. However, to be aware that parties are trying to impose anchors and to consider that extreme aversion could prevent anchoring, arbitrators should understand the concepts and how they work.

Likewise, arbitrators should be able to understand the limitations and importance of adopting for themselves other debiasing techniques to certify better legal reasoning. We bring two examples. First, Sussman recommends the creation of columns for each party during the procedure and award drafting and listing facts and arguments of each subsequent claim as they are found according to the perspective of each party might help reduce intuitive thinking.[34] The second is the acceptance by arbitrators of the utility of using technology to confirm the arbitrator's decision as a double-check mechanism.[35] We are not advocating for a "machine arbitrator," as if the machine would decide; rather, artificial intelligence could be used not only to facilitate the arbitrator's life but as a tool through which a human tribunal would be able to consult with a computer program as a supplement to validate decisions.[36]

---

30. Richard A. Posner, *How Judges Think*, Harvard University Press, 2008, at 107.
31. D. Kim Rossmo and Joycelyn M. Pollock, "Confirmation Bias and Other Systemic Causes of Wrongful Convictions: A Sentinel Events Perspective," 11(2) Northeastern University Law Review 832 (2019), *apud* Carey K. Morewedge et al., "Debiasing Decisions: Improved Decision Making with a Single Training Intervention," 2 Pol'y Insights from Behav. and Brain Sci. 129, 129, 131, 134, 136-137 (2015).
32. Eyal Zamir and Doron Teichman, *The Oxford Handbook of Behavioral Economics and the Law*, *supra*, 158.
33. M.L. Milkman, D. Chugh and M.H. Bazerman, "How Can Decision Making Be Improved?," *supra*, p. 8.
34. *Ibid.*
35. Christine Sim, "Will Artificial Intelligence Take over Arbitration?," 14(1) Asian International Arbitration Journal 1-14, 4/5, 3 (2018).
36. Paul Cohen and Sophie Nappert, "The March of the Robots," *GAR*, 5 February 2017. Available at: https://globalarbitrationreview.com/article/1080951/the-march-of-the-robots.

Lastly, the *fourth reason* is that training might be necessary and important to maintain appointments. Bounded rationality has gained the arbitral community's attention in the last decade. Commentators are starting to denounce the possibility of errors in decision-making that might affect the quality of the award[37] and as a source of inefficiency in the arbitrator's contract.[38] Thus, participating in training and education may be a signaling tool to the arbitration market that the educated arbitrator presents lower risks of errors due to bounded rationality.

Thus, since there are several good reasons why arbitrators should be trained, it is worth discussing other "Wh"s.

III   WHAT?

The content of training and education should be in economics, cognitive psychology, behavioral economics, specifically topics of cognitive bias, bounded rationality, and the effect of debiasing techniques on legal decision-making.

To begin with, it should especially comprise training in cognitive psychology. Arbitrators should all understand how the human mind works and "the study of individual-level mental processes such as information processing, attention, language use, memory, perception, problem-solving, decision-making, and thinking"[39] should be largely mastered.

It should comprise concepts of microeconomics and an understanding of an arbitrator's own utility function. Understanding what motivates them would help arbitrators to focus more on the costs and benefits of the utility function forcing them to concentrate on incentives, and increasing incentives is also a strong debiasing technique because it helps the actors to focus on System 2 of reasoning. However, arbitrators should first be aware of their utility function.

Behavioral law and economics are also important because it studies and demonstrates the impact of intuitive decisions, heuristics, cognitive bias, and cultural and social influences on legal decision-making.

In addition to the limitations of rationality on decision-making, arbitrators should be taught different methods for prevention and correction of bounded rationality and its effects on decision-making considering motivational, cognitive, and technical debiasing strategies. This topic includes the knowledge of debiasing techniques themselves. The increase in incentives and in an arbitrator's liability, the reduction in information asymmetries, the strategy to consider the opposite, the use of other biases, the increase in obligation to reason the award, the facilitation of the arbitrator's life, the use of group decisions, the appointment of arbitrators who are not natives in the language of the arbitration, the addition by the arbitral tribunal of techniques to better certify legal reasoning, controlling the party's representative and counsel, taking care

37. Susan Franck, *Arbitration Costs, Myths and Realities in Investment Treat*, *supra*, p. 33.
38. Bruno Guandalini, *Economic Analysis of the Arbitrator's Function*, *supra*.
39. Richard J. Gerrig and Philip G. Zimbardo, *Psychology and Life*, 16th ed., Pearson Scott Foresman, 2002.

of the arbitrator's comfort and biological needs, and blind decisions as a form of correction.[40]

IV   WHO, WHERE, WHEN AND HOW?

The training and education of arbitrators could be done in numerous places and forms, by trained and experienced instructors and professors, by arbitrators themselves and even by lawyers during the procedures. Here we consider and offer some solutions.

To begin with, arbitrators should educate themselves through readings on the appropriate topics (*see* section III). Irrespective of how deep they go into the topic, all knowledge counts towards their awareness of their limitation on rationality and should already have a debiasing effect. Publications on the general topic are extensive.[41]

Arbitrators should though first be aware of their ignorance. An introduction to and awareness of the importance of the topic would be best done at conferences and congresses in international arbitration and arbitration in general. Among those events, it would be a terrific opportunity to call participants' attention to the topic and convince them about the Why (*see* section II) and the importance of the knowledge of the topic and employment of debiasing techniques.

Once aware, arbitrators should be better trained. Specific courses and workshops on debiasing are perhaps the most valuable tools. Arbitral institutions worldwide and independent organizations such as the International Council for Commercial Arbitration – (ICCA),[42] the Chartered Institute of Arbitrators (CIArb),[43] the Institute for Transnational Arbitration (ITA),[44] and national committees[45] are good institutions to sponsor such initiatives. These institutions have been providing training and reports on other topics[46] and are the best placed, especially because they can "create an opportunity for addressing the training of arbitrators on cognitive biases in a way that is responsive to the social context in which arbitrators operate."[47] Those institutions have an interest in improving arbitral decision-making but more importantly, they have the credibility to spread the word and tell experienced arbitrators they should be aware of their limitations on rationality. A commentator explains that the institution's "central role as a norm-representer within its arbitral community would ensure that taking such a training course would be seen as adhering to the community's norms of

---

40. Bruno Guandalini, *Economic Analysis of the Arbitrator's Function, supra*, Chapter 8.
41. *See supra* n. 6.
42. Available at https://www.arbitration-icca.org/. Last accessed on June 1, 2022.
43. Available at https://www.ciarb.org/. Last accessed on June 1, 2022.
44. Available at https://www.cailaw.org/Institute-for-Transnational-Arbitration/About-Us/index. html. Last accessed on June 1, 2022.
45. Such as Comité Français de l'Arbitrage (available at http://www.cfa-arbitrage.com/) and Brazilian Arbitration Committee (http://cbar.org.br/site/). Last accessed on June 1, 2022.
46. Available at https://iccwbo.org/training/online-training-and-certificates/. Last accessed on June 1, 2022.
47. Tony Cole, Pietro Ortolani and Sean Wright, "Arbitration in Its Psychological Context: A Contextual Behavioral Account of Arbitral Decision-Making," *supra*, p. 35.

good arbitral practice, rather than as acknowledging a personal deficiency that deviated from those norms.[48]

In addition to training courses and workshops, institutions might disseminate knowledge by preparing specific studies and initiatives, which could be credible literature. The ICCA, for instance, maintains different important task forces[49] and a task force on the subject would be an excellent step. A "Debiasing Arbitrators Task-Force" could reach important conclusions and perhaps provide must-adopt recommendations with a profound impact on arbitral decision-making. Experienced and busy arbitrators might be easier to reach with this path.

The good news is that courses with several sessions might not be really necessary. A study found through controlled experiments that a "single debiasing intervention could effectively produce immediate and persistent improvements in decision-making."[50] Thus, one single training session could arguably be of some value to arbitrators. And since short training courses should work, it is feasible that arbitrators be trained in short workshops during virtual or in-person congresses, conferences, or seminars.

Professional and specialized instructors and professors would be the most adequate professionals to conduct specific debiasing workshops. However, one should not ignore the need for experienced arbitrators who could call their colleagues' attention to debiasing.

Finally, there is the possibility that the parties and attorneys themselves educate arbitrators during the arbitration procedure. Put differently, parties themselves could draw the arbitrator's attention to their possible cognitive bias.[51] It does not mean that parties should bring a scientific text without any correspondence to the case. The argument is that parties and attorneys could alert arbitrators on the written and oral statements of the counterparties' use of anchoring or extremeness aversion against arbitrators; i.e., counsels may indicate that that specific anchoring is being used and arbitrators might now avoid that anchoring.

Likewise, counsels should be trained too. Although training counsels could give them weapons for exploring arbitrator's bounded rationality and the problem could in theory be worsened, it is still worthwhile for two reasons: one, debiasing and education during the procedure requires trained attorneys; two, counsels usually wear the arbitrator's hat and therefore more people in the market for arbitrators would be trained in debiasing.

V   DIFFICULTIES AND CHALLENGES

There is considerable difficulty and costs in adopting and implementing arbitrator's training and education on debiasing.

---

48. *Ibid.*
49. Available at https://www.arbitration-icca.org/projects.html.
50. Carey K. Morewedge et al., "Debiasing Decisions: Improved Decision Making with a Single Training Intervention," 2 Pol'y Insights from Behav. and Brain Sci. 4 (2015).
51. M.L. Milkman, D. Chugh and M.H. Bazerman, "How Can Decision Making Be Improved?," Working Paper, 2008, https://www.hbs.edu/faculty/Publication%20Files/08-102_1670bc7e-dc 3c-49c8-bc5f-1eba2e78e335.pdf, p. 3.

First, there may be considerable resistance from arbitrators to accept such training and education. As said, arbitrators are usually experienced, busy, and professionally mature people who will probably not be willing to hear a younger scientist saying that their rationality is limited and that they might have problems with their decision-making.

In addition, if experienced people attend courses, they may consider incurring the risk of signaling the market that they need to improve their decision-making process and perhaps threaten the legitimacy of their current procedures and the most recently rendered awards.

Regarding those difficulties, the very first, important step is the challenge of convincing arbitrators to deflate their egos. An author discussed solutions to correct the implicit bias of judges and noted that the very first move perhaps should be to "deflate our egos" since "we must recognize that we are not as objective, as fair, as virtuous as we view ourselves to be."[52] The same author also describes embarrassing evidence (because mathematically impossible) that "87% of (non-senior) federal district judges and 92% of senior federal district judges view themselves as in the top 25% of their colleagues in their ability to make decisions free from racial bias."[53] It is not difficult to imagine that among arbitrators similar research would arrive at similar results.

Also, to deplete the ego and train yourself on debiasing should not signal any personal weakness or mediocre quality; quite the contrary. The content of the training is getting knowledge about the limitations of rationality that all human beings are said to have. Learning correction and prevention techniques and how to not be trapped by such bounded rationality could never be understood as a recognition of bad decision-makers. On the contrary, not seeking such training might signal that a decision-maker is a person that is able to be trapped by implicit bias, implying a decision-maker who makes reliable errors.[54]

That said, we do not ignore the great difficulty that is overcoming the direct and indirect costs that training might have for arbitrators, parties, and institutions. However, the forces of the market for arbitrators will confirm whether it is worth bearing them. Technology and artificial intelligence in the decision-making context are booming and will certainly play a role in this training; at least the competition threats of the non-human robot arbitrator will be a great incentive to human training for better decision-making.

Other issues and concerns may arise shortly. Could empirical research or the machine demonstrate evidence of arbitrator's bounded rationality that would give grounds for annulment of awards? Perhaps one day the culture of arbitration might impose on arbitrators a best effort obligation to demonstrate that they have taken

---

52. Study cited by Jerry Kang, "What Judges Can Do about Implicit Bias," 57 Court Review (2021), *apud*, Mark W. Bennett, "The Implicit Racial Bias in Sentencing: The Next Frontier," Yale L.J. Forum (January 31, 2017).
53. Study cited by Jerry Kang, What Judges Can Do about Implicit Bias, 57 Court Review (2021), *apud* Mark W. Bennett, *The Implicit Racial Bias in Sentencing: The Next Frontier*, Yale L.J. Forum (January 31, 2017).
54. Susan D. Franck, *Arbitration Costs, Myths and Realities in Investment Treaty*, *supra*, p. 59.

measures to prevent and correct bounded rationality as a mandatory compliance obligation of the arbitrator's function.

VI   CONCLUSION

Any user of any jurisdictional procedure envisages better and more precise decision-making. In times when we start discussing greater competition in the market for arbitrators, and possible competition from machine arbitrators, improvement of arbitral decision-making should be taken seriously now more than ever.

Jurists, economists, and cognitive psychologists have demonstrated that humans do suffer from limitations on rationality and that legal decision-makers like judges and arbitrators also do.

As commentators have demonstrated, training and educating arbitrators on bounded rationality and debiasing techniques may improve arbitral decision-making, reduce error costs, and render arbitration more efficient.

We sustained that the best kick-off towards more training has already been made by several commentators with the publications. The next step should now be taken, as arguably said, by institutions during congresses and conferences. The offer of such workshops on this training could incentivize the first players to adhere and then the parties and market forces would dictate the real importance; it is all a matter of costs.

Thus, it is time for the arbitral community to take arbitral decision-making more seriously by supporting further studies and by training arbitrators on prevention and correction of limitations of rationality.

PANEL 14   Different Perspectives

CHAPTER 49

Enlightened, but under Siege?: A User's Perspective on the International Commercial Arbitration Market

Patrick Baeten[*]

I   INTRODUCTION

This chapter is a user's response to the ICCA 2021 Congress' Programme Committee invitation to "take stock of achievements and explore ideas to adapt to a fast-changing environment, and shape the future of international arbitration."[1] International commercial arbitration being a market, the classical concepts of competition law (customer, seller, product, and neighboring markets) offer a useful analytical framework to better understand its dynamics in general and the users' positioning in particular

---

[*] Patrick Baeten graduated in law from the University of Ghent and holds a *magna cum laude* LLM in international law from the University of Louvain-la-Neuve. He joined ENGIE as in-house counsel in 1996, where he held legal management positions in Europe and Brazil and served i.a. as chief counsel for global disputes. He is now general secretary of Besix Group.. Patrick lectured European energy law at the University of Leuven. He is a member of the Scientific Committee of the CEPINA and of the Advisory Board of the *Climate Change Arbitration Monitor,* and a Belgian delegate to the ICC Commission on arbitration and ADR.
1. Prof. Dr. Gabrielle Kaufmann-Kohler, "Invitation from the ICCA President" at < https://icca2020.scot/ > (last accessed on October 22, 2022).

(section II). The customers' expectations in terms of product characteristics (cost, duration, flexibility, and diversity) have been described in quite some detail by the successive Queen Mary University of London International Arbitration Surveys,[2] which provide insights into the users' somewhat ambiguous attitude vis-à-vis international commercial arbitration—although most of those insights are probably second-hand, given the regrettable underrepresentation of private sector in-house counsel among the respondents: 7% only in the 2021 edition[3] (section III). To conclude, the chapter reflects on whether international commercial arbitration's competitive edge has eroded, to the benefit of other, competing dispute resolution mechanisms; and whether, should that be the case, this is problematic from the customer's perspective (section IV).

II   A COMPLEX MARKET

Commercial arbitration is a means to resolve business disputes among market operators. Provided all parties involved have given their consent, a private neutral (or college of neutrals) is called upon by the parties to take a final and binding decision on the issues at stake. The neutral(s) organize(s) and preside(s) over the proceedings, examine(s) the case and the evidence, hear(s) the parties, their counsel, witnesses and experts and renders an award whereby the dispute is settled. The neutral(s) is/are remunerated for this. As such, commercial arbitration is basically a service, proposed by arbitrators to disputing parties. Price setting is mostly free. Most states do provide for a legal framework, on top of institutional rules and some level of self-regulation by soft law, but this does not fundamentally alter the analysis: commercial arbitration is a free market.

Whereas a scientific economic approach to the international commercial arbitration market is clearly beyond the ambit of this chapter,[4] basic yet classical notions of competition law[5] can help analyze the interactions between the market actors and shed some light on the role the users play or could play.

1   The Customer

The notion of "customer" is, in its sight, probably the simplest to define: any party to a commercial arbitration is, quite obviously, a customer, as it is that

2. All Queen Mary University of London International Arbitration Surveys (hereinafter "QMUL Survey [year]") are available at http://www.arbitration.qmul.ac.uk/research/ (last accessed on October 22, 2022).
3. QMUL Survey 2021, p. 35.
4. For a recent in-depth analysis of the market from the arbitrators' perspective, *see* Bruno Guandalini, *Economic Analysis of the Arbitrator's Function*, International Arbitration Law Library, Volume 55 (Kluwer Law International, 2020).
5. *See*, among others, the European Commission Notice on the definition of relevant market for the purposes of Community competition law (97/C 372/03), *OJ* C372, 9.12.97, p. 5, available at https://eur-lex.europa.eu/legal-content/EN/TXT/PDF/?uri = CELEX:31997Y1209(01)&from = EN (last accessed on October 22, 2022) (hereinafter "European Commission Notice").

party—corporation, individual, or, in some cases, public authority or even sovereign state—which buys the product.[6]

This, however, must be qualified in at least two respects.

First, choosing arbitration as a dispute resolution service is almost always a consensual choice, made by *two* users. This highly unusual feature in a competitive market trickles down in various aspects of the arbitral procedure, starting with the choice of the arbitrator. It is not because one party is a customer that it chooses autonomously who will be the seller/arbitrator. The most common case is the one where a party nominates or appoints one party arbitrator, its counterparty nominates the other party arbitrator, and both party arbitrators (or the appointing parties) then agree on which third arbitrator will chair the tribunal. But a wealth of other possibilities exist, depending on what has been provided in the arbitration clause or agreement, whether it is institutional or ad hoc arbitration and what the arbitral rules provide, whether the dispute is entrusted to a sole arbitrator or a college of arbitrators, etc. Nonetheless, from a customer perspective, the reality is that one (almost) never chooses on its own who will be the actual provider of the service one is looking for.[7] If there is a third-party funder, this funder will also look for trust and predictability and, hence, will more likely than not intervene in if not downright steer the party's "decision" on the constitution of the tribunal—even if the third-party funder and the funded party generally share the same interest and should thus, logically, look for the same "ideal" potential arbitrator. The counterparty of course also intervenes, and often so does the arbitral institution.[8] To overestimate the value of one of the main features of commercial arbitration, the so-called ability to choose the adjudicator[9] can hence prove hazardous. This comes with consequences. No sophisticated user of commercial arbitration doubts the importance of the choice of the arbitrator(s), but an individual party has only a limited impact on who will actually adjudicate the dispute. This increases the uncertainty the user is confronted with regarding availability and quality of the sellers/arbitrators, effective conduct of the proceedings, dynamics of the deliberation, and, ultimately, the outcome of the dispute. More fundamentally, it also somehow weakens the "bargaining" position or market power the individual user/customer has, probably to the benefit of the sellers/arbitrators, and maybe to the benefit of actors in other, neighboring markets.[10]

Second, there is no such thing as "the" user or, for that matter, customer. The needs, market behavior, market power and so forth vary highly from one user to the

---

6. On that notion, *see* further below, II.1.c.
7. What Sophie Nappert calls "a significant degree of control over the selection of the decision-makers" is exactly that: significant (at least compared to the quasi absence of control on the appointment of the adjudicator in judicial proceedings), but far from total; Sophie Nappert and Avani Agarwal, "Twenty-First Century Arbitration: Who Do You Trust?", Kluwer Arbitration Blog, March 2, 2020, available at http://arbitrationblog.kluwerarbitration.com/2020/03/02/twenty-first-century-arbitration-who-do-you-trust/ (last accessed on October 22, 2022).
8. The "lack of insight into how institutions select and appoint arbitrators" has been ranked as the seventh worst characteristic of international arbitration by the respondents to the QMUL Survey 2018, p. 8.
9. *See,* for instance, QMUL Survey 2006, p. 6.
10. *See* further below, II.d.

other, depending on a wide variety of factors: size of the corporation; degree of sophistication of its organization, management, and teams; sector of activity; positioning on its own markets, strategy, objectives, culture, and values; frequency of its use of arbitration and other dispute settlement mechanisms; ... The list is probably endless. Out of those factors, the internal decision-making process on key questions[11]—start arbitration proceedings or not, in stand-alone or in combination with settlement discussions (whether mediated or not), when, supported by which attorney, nominating which party arbitrator—is critical when analyzing the functioning of the commercial arbitration market(s) and its adequacy from a user's perspective. Depending on who, within a company, is deciding on what, the company's perspective on commercial arbitration may differ—as may actions that other players, arbitrators, counsel, and institutions, can take to respond to this decision maker's expectations.[12]

2   The Seller

The seller side of the market[13] looks, again on its face, simple enough as well. There appears to be a vast offer of potential arbitrators, with a growing diversification in terms of profile: age, gender, and geographical origin.[14] This should—at least in theory—necessarily benefit the customer, as it widens the offer, hence increases competition between sellers, which, in turn, should exert a downward pressure on the price and an upward pressure on the quality of the product offered.

In my experience, however, some structural barriers to entry, maybe embedded in or deriving from the very essence of international commercial arbitration as we know it today, tend to annihilate this positive effect.

First, access to information about potential sellers/arbitrators is unsatisfactory.[15] Despite recent initiatives, commercial or not, prospects for an in-house counsel to gain direct access, in any foreseeable future, to structured, objective and reliable information about candidate arbitrators seem slim. This is especially true for relatively less sophisticated users, or less frequent users of commercial arbitration. It is true as well for nonspecialized counsel, or counsel who do not belong to a global firm with a vast arbitration practice. This is potentially even more detrimental to an optimal functioning of the market, as in-house counsel and corporations in general rely heavily on advice from external counsel to choose the party arbitrator.[16] A certain level playing field in terms of available information is indispensable and would, among other benefits, greatly contribute to avoiding the repeat appointments "snowball effect."

---

11. QMUL Survey 2013, pp. 16-18. *See also* QMUL 2016, p. 23.
12. Whether despite this, one may nevertheless distinguish common features and general trends will be further discussed under section III below.
13. "The lucrative arbitrators' market," as Daphna Kapeliuk calls it: "The Repeat Appointment Factor: Exploring Decision Patterns of Elite Investment Arbitrators," 96 Cornell L. Rev. 47 (2010), p. 79 (available at https://scholarship.law.cornell.edu/cgi/viewcontent.cgi?article=31 85&context=clr; last accessed on October 22, 2022).
14. On the question of diversity, *see* below, III.4.
15. *See* below, III.4.
16. QMUL Survey 2010, p. 27.

Second, there is a certain degree of vertical integration between the market for legal services in the field of litigation, a de facto if not legal monopoly of the bar, and arbitration. The proportion of international arbitrators exercising in parallel activity as external counsel is and stays relatively high. For multinational companies with a global reach, this vertical integration can give rise to delicate situations—as it does for the law firms concerned. In that respect, the high sensitivity parties, arbitrators, and institutions nowadays show in relation to conflicts of interest is welcome, even if it can contribute to due process paranoia. Yet, a certain level of autoregulation[17] (some might even advocate what competition law calls full unbundling) in respect of the arbitrator/counsel combination may be beneficial for the users and, more widely, the commercial arbitration market *in globo*, even if it were only in terms of image and legitimacy.

3   The Product

As indicated above, the product offered by arbitrators is a final and binding decision on the issues at stake between the parties, crystalized in a motivated[18] and readily enforceable award.

But is this product sufficiently non-substitutable to create a stand-alone "relevant market," as defined by European competition law, comprising "all those products and/or services which are regarded as interchangeable or substitutable by the consumer, by reason of the products' characteristics, their prices and their intended use"?[19]

In terms of product's characteristics, one may refer to the list used by the Queen Mary University of London in its 2018 International Arbitration Survey: enforceability, avoidance of specific legal systems or national courts, flexibility, ability to select the arbitrators, confidentiality and privacy, neutrality, finality, speed, cost, possibility of effective sanctions during the arbitral process, power in relation to third parties, efficiency, possibility of national court intervention, etc.[20] The list could be extended and refined, but the essentials are there and provide a useful frame of reference to compare international commercial arbitration with other means of dispute settlement.

The price element—usually euphemistically referred to as "cost"—comes with a certain degree of complexity. Obviously, there are the arbitrators' fees, which, depending on the rules and agreements applicable, and often depending on the amounts at stake in the dispute at hand, can differ both in absolute terms and in the way they are calculated. More will be said about price/cost under III.1 below, but as far as

---

17. *See* for instance, for investment arbitration, Article 4 of the third draft Code of Conduct for Adjudicators in Investment Disputes, offering three options: "Full Prohibition," "Modified Prohibition" and "Full Disclosure (with Option to Challenge)": https://icsid.worldbank.org/sites/default/files/documents/Code_of_Conduct_V3.pdf (last accessed on October 22, 2022).

18. Although in some relatively rare instances, parties can agree or arbitration rules can provide that the award does not need to be motivated, or not *in extenso*; this is the case, for instance, in Portugal.

19. European Commission Notice, no. 7.

20. QMUL Survey 2018, pp. 7-8.

competitive pressure is concerned, one must bear in mind that the arbitrators' fees are but a (small?) part of the overall price a user/customer will, in the end, pay to obtain an award. There are internal costs—time spent, management distraction, provisions for risks, and so forth—[21] as well as the costs for the services the user needs to acquire on neighboring markets: legal advice and representation, experts, and institutions.[22] Limiting the price of commercial arbitration to the sole arbitrators' fees would be reductive and bias any analysis of product substitutability.

The third criterion for a proper product definition is the intended use, the purpose for which users/customers buy the product. This criterion is particularly critical when analyzing international commercial arbitration because, depending on whether one retains a narrow description ("obtain a final and enforceable award") or a broader description ("put an end to the dispute"), one will obtain diametrically opposed conclusions. In a narrow description, there would probably be no real substitute for international commercial arbitration; if on the contrary one considers that commercial arbitration is but one of the means to terminate a dispute, a wide variety of other dispute resolution mechanisms would come into play (party negotiations, mediation, dispute boards, litigation, etc.), with all the consequences this would entail for commercial arbitration providers—arbitrators, institutions and, to some extent, external counsel and experts—who would be confronted with "competitors."[23]

4   Neighboring Markets

As already alluded to above, the user/arbitrator relationship does not suffice for a functional commercial arbitration market. In modern international commercial arbitration, other players have indispensable roles as well, and it is the combination of those relationships/markets which allows disputing parties to turn to commercial arbitration to have their dispute settled. Those relationships and interactions need to be fully considered to analyze commercial arbitration and assess whether it is effective and efficient from a potential customer's perspective.

---

21. Compare Philippe Cavalieros, "In-House Counsel Costs and Other Internal Party Costs in International Commercial Arbitration," Arbitration International, Vol. 30, No. 1, p. 145, available at https://www.winston.com/images/content/7/6/v2/76523/ARBI-30-1-Philippe-Cavalieros-Offprint-In-House-Counsel-costs-in.pdf (last accessed on October 22, 2022).
22. *See* below, II.1.d.
23. For the sake of completeness, geography-related elements can come into play as well: "The relevant geographic market comprises the area in which the undertakings concerned are involved in the supply and demand of products or services, in which the conditions of competition are sufficiently homogeneous and which can be distinguished from neighbouring areas because the conditions of competition are appreciably different in those area" (European Commission Notice, no. 8). One can think of the (absence of?) competition between global and local arbitral institutions, of the impact of language and training of arbitrators, of ethnic and racial diversity, etc.

a   The Market for External Advice

External counsel play obviously a critical role in commercial arbitration, as they do in dispute resolution in general.[24] They provide advice on strategy and tactics, on legal questions, on the choice of arbitrators; they draft, file and plead; they often intervene in the document gathering and analysis phase; they interact with the institution, if any; they liaise with counterparty counsel; they represent their client before national jurisdictions in enforcement and other proceedings; etc. It is fair to say that external counsel is, in virtually all cases, almost as indispensable as the arbitrators themselves.

In technically or legally complex cases, expert advice may prove indispensable as well. This is the case for most construction arbitrations, gas price reviews, and so forth.

A recent study has shown that the so-called party costs, which comprise legal costs and other expenses incurred by a party for the arbitration, including the fees and expenses of outside counsel, party-appointed experts, witnesses, translators, etc. amount to 83% of the global cost of international arbitration.[25] The bulk of those party costs consists of external counsel fees.

b   The Market for the Administration of Commercial Arbitration Proceedings

Arbitration institutions play a major role as well. By offering administration services—on top of drafting and promoting arbitration rules—and for some of them additional services (scrutiny of awards, rosters of arbitrators, …), most of the institutions have become full-blown and sometimes powerful actors on the commercial arbitration market(s), not in the least because corporations have a tendency to favor[26] institutional arbitration over ad hoc arbitration.[27] In my experience, ad hoc arbitration is a relatively weak competitor of institutional arbitration, or at least not one which exerts meaningful competitive pressure on the major institutions, for several reasons. First and foremost, large corporations, especially those who are frequent and sometimes quite sophisticated users of commercial arbitration, tend to avoid uncertainty and risks—hence are reluctant to jump into the often unknown and to a certain extent uncharted territory of ad hoc arbitration, but will rather turn to renowned and tested institutions and their rules. Second, the value proposition of the institutions—pay a

---

24. Although this may be nuanced for some alternative dispute resolution mechanisms, especially mediation and dispute boards; also, external counsel role may be far less important in party negotiations than in arbitration.
25. ICC Commission Report "Decisions on Costs in International Arbitration," ICC Dispute Resolution Bulletin 2015, Issue 2, para. 2, available at https://www.iccwbo.be/wp-content/uploads/2012/03/20151201-Decisions-on-Costs-in-International-Arbitration.pdf (last accessed on October 22, 2022).
26. *See* further below, III.3.
27. On this dichotomy and borderline cases, see Ulrich G. Schroeter, "Ad Hoc or Institutional Arbitration—A Clear Cut Distinction? A Closer Look at Borderline Cases," (2021) 10 Contemporary Asia Arbitration Journal 141.

relatively small price[28] for the professional administration of sensitive proceedings—is appealing to users. Third, the choice to be made between ad hoc and institutional arbitration needs to be agreed on by both parties; logically, the mainstream choice will likely be more acceptable to both actual or future opponents than any out-of-the-box solution proposed by one of them, as innovative, flexible, and efficient that solution may be.[29]

The wide variety of institutions—global, regional, or national; generalist or sector-specific—does not materially alter this finding. Rather, they tend to adequately "cover" the demand, by collectively (albeit naturally) proposing specific responses to specific demands. In a sense, there may be different markets or submarkets for arbitration case management. The emergence of more regional institutions like the Singapore International Arbitration Centre and the Hong Kong International Arbitration Centre, for example, next to the traditional global players like the ICC International Court of Arbitration and the London Court of International Arbitration, shows that there is room for multiple and different players.[30] This is, by definition, beneficial for the users.

Another noteworthy trend is the convergence of institutional arbitration rules.[31] Whether that is a curse or a blessing for users, and whether that will weaken the innovative edge of arbitration institutions by decreasing the competitive pressure among them or, to the contrary, create a virtuous circle of user-friendly innovations intended to compete for users' favor, is yet unclear.

c   *The Market for Third-Party Funding*

The significance of third-party funding[32] is growing. Recent years have seen an upsurge in the number of third-party funders, the number of funded cases, the number of law firms working with third-party funders, and the number of reported cases involving issues relating to funding.[33] It has been argued that four main forces drive the sharp increase in the demand for dispute financing: the public policy ideal of increasing access to justice, the slew of companies seeking a means to pursue a meritorious claim

---

28. In the case of the ICC, 2% of the total arbitration cost, according to the ICC Commission Report referred to under *supra* n. 25.
29. There may, as such, be a self-reinforcing factor here: the more an institution manages cases, the more it will probably attract new cases. *See* below, III.3.
30. QMUL Survey 2018, pp. 13-15.
31. *See* further below, III.3.
32. "The term 'third-party funding' refers to an agreement by an entity that is not a party to the dispute to provide a party, an affiliate of that party or a law firm representing that party, a) funds or other material support in order to finance part or all of the cost of the proceedings, either individually or as part of a specific range of cases, and b) such support or financing is either provided in exchange for remuneration or reimbursement that is wholly or partially dependent on the outcome of the dispute, or provided through a grant or in return for a premium payment." *Report of the ICCA-Queen Mary Task Force on Third-Party Funding in International Arbitration*, p. 50, available at https://cdn.arbitration-icca.org/s3fs-public/document/media_document/Third-Party-Funding-Report%20.pdf, last accessed on 22 October 2022.
33. *Ibid.*, p. 1.

while also maintaining enough cash flow, the "worldwide market turmoil and uncertainty following the 2008 global financial crisis" and what would be "the newly-developed (...) demand for third-party funding as corporate finance."[34]

Third-party funding is not only demanded in cases where a party does not have sufficient financial means to pay for the costs of an arbitration but is increasingly used as a risk allocation mechanism (the party allocating the cost of the proceedings to a funder in exchange for a portion of the amount awarded), or even as an insurance or an intercompany loan. Some have stated that "[i]nstitutions specialized in the financing of arbitration costs are now part of the market and definitely play a speculative role. (...) Speculation by TPFs has a known consequence in the market for arbitrators: it increases the number and cost of procedures."[35]

Third-party funding in any event has a bearing on several features of the arbitration market and among others via the potential encouragement of less-meritorious claims, the potential discouragement of settlement in favor of fighting for a larger recovery, the risk that the funder may put its own interests ahead of the user's interests, the potential conflicts of interests that may arise if the funder meddles in the attorney-client relationship,[36] etc.[37]

5 First Provisional Finding: The Individual User Is a Customer Highly Dependent on Other Actors

The commercial arbitration market—simple on its face—thus shows some quite unique and complex features.

The buy decision-making process by the user cannot be apprehended correctly if one loses sight of the fact that the individual user's ability as a "customer" to choose arbitration as a "product" and a particular arbitrator as the "seller" is weakened by the fact that the counterparty, as another "customer", systematically has its say on the product first, on its provider second. In institutional arbitration, the institution itself, as "seller" on another market, may also play a critical role. This relatively weak position of the individual user/customer is exacerbated by some opacity on the sellers' side, as free access to objective information on potential arbitrators remains, to a certain extent and for the time being, an objective rather than an achievement. The fact that the pool of sellers/arbitrators significantly overlaps with the offerors of external legal advice can, in that respect, raise questions as well.

The question of substitutability is even more complex. Whether the determining factor for the product market definition is linked to the characteristics of international commercial arbitration (and if so, which characteristics) or its price (which includes a variety of other cost elements than the mere arbitrators' fees), or its intended use, or a

---

34. Lisa Bench Nieuwveld and Victoria Shannon Sahani, *Third-Party Funding in International Arbitration*, Kluwer Law International, 2017, p. 11, available at https://www.kluwerarbitration .com/document/KLI-KA-Nieuwveld-2017-Ch01, last accessed on October 22, 2022.
35. Bruno Guandalini, *supra* n. 4, pp. 110-111.
36. *See*, for instance, https://globalarbitrationreview.com/king-spalding-sued-client-in-funded-bit-case, last accessed on October 22, 2022.
37. Lisa Bench Nieuwveld and Victoria Shannon Sahani, *supra* n. 34, p. 16.

combination thereof, is probably highly depending on the specificities of the dispute at hand. Geographical elements may also come into play.

Finally, neighboring markets play a critical role as well, as without those, international commercial arbitration as we know it today would probably not exist. In particular, the impact of external counsel and especially the global firms on the one hand, the global arbitration institutions on the other hand, should not be underestimated—even less so since their number is quite limited.

This leads us to the following provisional finding: international commercial arbitration is a quite specific assemblage of neighboring and interacting markets, on which market power is extremely diluted among the various, interdependent actors. In this complex (combination of) market(s), the individual customer has virtually no influence, let alone a determining one. In this respect, one may wonder whether opting for international arbitration is indeed, and without nuance, the "ultimate form of forum shopping."[38]

Yet, other actors may want to consider the users' aspirations, to avoid seeing customers, deprived of any real say and potentially dissatisfied with some product features (as will now be illustrated), investigate other options and leave the market altogether.

III   THE USER: A REASONABLY SATISFIED BUT CRITICAL CUSTOMER

The Queen Mary University of London International Arbitration Survey 2018[39] has revisited earlier empirical studies to ascertain changes in user preferences and perceptions.[40] The findings do not diverge in any substantial way from the results of the 2015 survey: international arbitration is still, and by far, the preferred method for resolving cross-border disputes.[41]

Its most valuable product characteristics, according to respondents, are the enforceability of awards, the possibility to avoid specific legal systems and/or national courts, the flexibility, the ability of parties to select arbitrators, and confidentiality and privacy (which scores particularly high among the in-house counsel subgroup). Cost, the lack of effective sanctions during the arbitral process, the lack of power in relation to third parties, the lack of speed and the lack of insight into arbitrators' efficiency are perceived as being the worst characteristics of international arbitration.[42]

From a user perspective, most of the concerns expressed relate to efficiency: commercial arbitration is often perceived as "too expensive, too slow," procedural rules as flexible indeed but too complex, and arbitrators as too "pale, male and

---

38. Catherine A. Rogers, "A Window into the Soul of International Arbitration: Arbitrator Selection, Transparency and Stakeholder Interests," Victoria U. Wellington L. Rev. Vol. 46 (2015), p. 1179.
39. The survey covers both "commercial" and "investment treaty" or investor-State arbitration—although we do not think this distorts in any way the findings as far as commercial arbitration is concerned.
40. Paul Friedland, introducing the QMUL Survey 2018, p. 1.
41. "With a twist," says the report; QMUL Survey 2018, p. 5.
42. Ibid., pp. 7-8.

stale"[43]—although the latter, as we will see, is essentially due to users and external counsel and may, on top, not be a real, hardcore concern for individual users.

1 Cost

As from the very first QMUL Survey, in 2006, the feedback from users[44] was clear:

> Corporations are not entirely satisfied with the process of international arbitration. We asked participants in the online study to list their three most significant concerns associated with the use of international arbitration. The expense of the international arbitration process (including the costs of arbitration lawyers, arbitrators, and the arbitration institution that may be involved)[45] was the most widely recognized disadvantage. 70 out of 80 respondents cited it as one of their top three concerns, with 50% of respondents ranking it as their primary concern. This challenges one of the common myths surrounding international arbitration, that it is less expensive than transnational litigation.[46]

Later surveys have confirmed this finding.[47]

As indicated above,[48] the notion of cost covers multiple components. Several categorizations are possible: the QMUL Survey 2006, for instance, distinguishes between arbitration costs and counsel's fees;[49] the ICC report published in 2015 makes a distinction between (a) party's costs (which include lawyers' fees and expenses, expenses related to witness and expert evidence, and other costs incurred by the parties for the arbitration), (b) arbitrators' fees and (c) case administration;[50] one could as well

---

43. On the specific issue of diversity, *see*, among others, Susan D. Franck et al., "The Diversity Challenge: Exploring the 'Invisible College' of International Arbitration", Colum. J. Transnational L. Vol. 53 (2015), 429, available at https://pdfs.semanticscholar.org/e40d/8ae91ceec4c526ee4f36c7cb73bb65cb135c.pdf (last accessed on October 22, 2022); Susan D. Franck et al., "International Arbitration: Demographics, Precision and Justice", in *Legitimacy: Myths, Realities, Challenges*, ICCA Congress Series no. 18 (2015), p. 33.
44. Who made up a full 100% of the respondents; QMUL Survey 2006, p. 24.
45. At the risk of over-interpreting, this list is interesting as it seems to suggest that in-house counsel do not regard internal costs as being determining—or at least that those costs do not fundamentally differ for arbitration and judicial proceedings.
46. *Ibid.*, pp. 6-7 and 19.
47. QMUL Survey 2008, p. 5: "[Participants'] concerns stemmed from their experience of the increased costs of arbitration (...).", *see also* pp. 8-9 on the link with post-arbitral settlements. QMUL Survey 2010, p. 21: regarding the choice of arbitration institution: "Cost remains an extremely important issue (...)." QMUL Survey 2013, p. 21: "Many respondents and interviewees expressed concern over related issues of costs and delays experienced in international arbitration proceedings." QMUL Survey 2015, p. 24: "Cost [is] ranked by respondents as amongst the worst characteristics of international arbitration." QMUL Survey 2016, p. 28: "We asked respondents what changes might make international arbitration a more appealing option. Unsurprisingly, lower costs took the lead (...)," being suggested by 58% of the participants. QMUL Survey 2018, p. 7: "The current survey continues to confirm this trend as 'cost' is yet again the most selected option [for the worst characteristic of arbitration], and by a significant margin" (64%!). QMUL Survey 2019, p. 3: "(...) the perception is undoubtedly that it (...) costs more than it should to pursue an arbitration to a final award (and sometimes to enforce that award)."
48. Above, II.1.c.
49. QMUL Survey 2006, p. 19.
50. *Supra* n. 22.

distinguish between internal costs and external costs, and in the latter, advice costs and procedural costs, for instance. But whatever the relevance of those distinctions, the overall perception remains and should be addressed: in the eyes of the users, commercial arbitration is expensive, too expensive.

However, this apparent truism should be nuanced.

First, cost is a necessary criterium to determine whether, for users, it makes sense to turn to arbitration, both in general terms ("Should I opt for arbitration in my dispute resolution clause, or not?") and in concrete terms ("Should I file a request for arbitration or should I try to resolve this dispute in another way?"). But it is not a sufficient one. What really matters is the "value," the potential "return on investment," which is a relative notion. The "value" is highly dependent on several factors. As highlighted by the QMUL Survey 2019 on construction arbitration, the amount at stake in the dispute is one of the determining elements: the lower the amount at stake, the less appealing may be arbitration.[51] In other words, users ask themselves the question of whether it is "commercially sensible to pursue through commercial arbitration."[52] It may well be that the current trend to introduce expedited proceedings and to make them the default choice below a certain amount at stake,[53] is partly inspired by the willingness of arbitral institutions to capture that part of the dispute resolution market. The sector in which the dispute arises has an impact as well: for instance, for 81% of the participants in the QMUL Survey 2016 "if international arbitration is not well suited for TMT [technology, media and telecom] disputes, it is because [it is] more costly than alternatives";[54] in international construction disputes, to the contrary, arbitration is still perceived as the best available process for resolving disputes in international projects,[55] despite its relatively high cost.

The way in which costs are ultimately allocated is not neutral either. Assuming there is a relatively high likelihood that costs will be allocated to the defeated party,[56] one may expect that the relative weight of the cost factor in choosing commercial arbitration will be low, or at least lower. But whereas this might be true in theory, it neglects at least two key elements: one, in most cases, the contractual choice of arbitration as a dispute resolution mechanism is made well before the dispute arises, at a time, parties cannot in any way predict if a conflict will arise, and even less so whether they will have the relatively stronger case, or not. Second, even if a party feels comfortable with its case, there is always a degree of uncertainty regarding (a) the ultimate outcome on the merits, (b) the costs the arbitrators will consider and the way in which they will allocate those, and (c) the likelihood of effectively recouping those allocated costs from the counterparty, via voluntary compliance with the award and

---

51. QMUL Survey 2019, p. 15.
52. *Ibid.*
53. Which corresponds to a demand expressed by users: QMUL Survey 2015, p. 26.
54. QMUL Survey 2016, p. 26.
55. QMUL Survey 2019, p. 5. Most respondents considered that the amount above which it makes commercial sense to opt for arbitration lies between USD 1 million and USD 10 million; in-house counsel considered the minimum amount to be higher, between USD 11 million and USD 25 million.
56. QMUL Survey 2012, p. 40.

cost decision or via enforcement. The importance of cost allocation thus should not be overestimated when it comes to evaluating the impact of cost on the attractiveness of commercial arbitration.

Finally, this impact is probably limited in and of itself, as other elements may interfere. For instance, reputational issues or issues of confidentiality may lead to the choice of arbitration rather than court litigation, even if the cost is higher. Technical complexity is another element that may justify not choosing the cheaper option, as may the need for perfect (real and perceived) neutrality, etc. Basically, all characteristics of commercial arbitration may well, in this or the other case, gain more weight than the pure cost element.[57] As the QMUL Survey 2013 put it, cost is a "frequent concern but with limited impact (...) respondents did not rank costs among the most important factors when deciding whether to initiate arbitration proceedings. Costs are a concern but on their own are not usually a deterrent to initiating arbitration proceedings."[58] Important, but probably not critical per se.

However, this concern about costs may well grow in importance as other, cheaper ways of resolving disputes gradually emerge.[59] In competition law terms, the product substitutability—allowing a switch from commercial arbitration to the judiciary or a form of ADR—is likely to increase, and a negative cost perception by the customers may well reinforce, if not trigger this evolution.

2 Duration

Costs are, to a non-negligible extent, linked to the length of the proceedings or, expressed negatively, the "delay."

The QMUL Survey 2018 notes in this respect that "lack of speed" is the fourth worst characteristic of international arbitration. The "various dilatory tactics employed by counsel that go unsanctioned either because the arbitrators are reluctant to order appropriate sanctions or because they do not possess the right instruments to do so"[60] is obviously linked to delay as well.

The point was raised in 2006[61] and consistently mentioned since.[62]

But as for costs, delay is a recurring although non-systematic and multiform concern and its deterrent effect is quite limited.

---

57. The same is true for delay, as confirmed, for construction disputes, by the QMUL Survey 2019, p. 23; *see* further below, under III.2.
58. QMUL Survey 2013, p. 21.
59. Third-party funding as well has been labeled as "one potential solution to th[e] problem" of high costs of commercial arbitration (*Report of the ICCA-Queen Mary Task Force on Third-Party Funding in International Arbitration, supra* n. 32, p. 6). This is doubtful: indeed, as in most cases the funded party will accept to transfer part of the proceeds (if any) to the funder, and this part necessarily includes a risk premium, my view is that third-party funding, ultimately, increases the cost for the prevailing funded party.
60. QMUL Survey 2018, pp. 6 and 27.
61. "A related concern is the time the arbitration process takes from filing the award, which was the second most commonly expressed concern," in QMUL Survey 2006, p. 7.
62. QMUL Survey 2008, p. 5; QMUL Survey 2013, p. 21; QMUL Survey 2015, p. 24.

The respondents to the QMUL Survey 2010 were asked to rank the top three stages of the arbitration that contribute to delay. According to the participants, disclosure of documents is the longest stage (24%), followed by written submissions (18%) and the constitution of the tribunal (18%). Other stages that may potentially lengthen considerably the proceedings are the hearings, the rendering of the award and, to a lesser extent, enforcement actions.[63] The QMUL Surveys 2015 and 2019 went a step further in analyzing those elements. The 2015 edition looked at it from the angle of potential improvements and found the following innovations to be most effective according to the respondents: a requirement that tribunals commit to and notify parties of a schedule for deliberations and delivery of award; a stronger pre-appointment scrutiny of arbitrators' availability; introduction and use of sanctions for dilatory conduct by parties or their counsel; a requirement for an early procedural conference; and a pre-hearing preparatory meeting of the arbitral tribunal. Other means also relate to the procedure itself (with the notable exceptions of "sanctions for dilatory conduct by arbitrators" and "deadline for rendering the award," which relate to the conduct of arbitrators rather than to procedural features).[64] The 2019 survey focused on the problem itself, rather than on potential solutions, by asking respondents the following question: "In your experience in the last five years, what makes or can make international construction arbitration inefficient?", giving participants twenty-three different responses to choose from. Interestingly, at least six of those relate almost exclusively to or derive from party conduct, including the first one: "party tactics." Other party conduct and duration-related responses include large amounts of evidence, challenges to arbitrators, experts, etc., and requirements to pursue non-arbitral procedures. Arbitrator-related factors play a role as well: poor case management, inexperience in construction arbitration and limited availability of specialized arbitrators, etc., next to general procedural issues.[65]

If users thus contribute to a considerable extent to the duration problem commercial arbitration is facing[66] and should thus urgently start to act, the issue will not be solved without the proper intervention of counsel,[67] arbitrators and arbitration institutions, which are perceived as best placed to reduce delay.[68] As it is unlikely that two (or more) opposing parties will have the natural tendency to agree on sensitive points that may speed up the arbitral process once started, the way in which the procedural rules are crafted and implemented is of utmost importance. Institutions have made considerable efforts in the last years,[69] the effectiveness of which still needs

---

63. QMUL Survey 2010, p. 32.
64. QMUL Survey 2015, p. 25.
65. QMUL Survey 2019, p. 25.
66. QMUL Survey 2018, p. 35.
67. "Respondents believe that arbitration counsel could be better at working together with opposing counsel to narrow down issues and limit document production, encouraging settlement (including the use of mediation) during an arbitration, and not 'overlawyering'," in QMUL Survey 2015, pp. 24 and 30-31. *See also* QMUL Survey 2019, p. 32.
68. Comp. QMUL Survey 2010, p. 32.
69. *See* for instance the 2018 ICC Commission Report on *Controlling Time and Costs in Arbitration*, available at https://iccwbo.org/publication/icc-arbitration-commission-report-on-techniques-for-controlling-time-and-costs-in-arbitration/ (last accessed on 22 October 2022).

to be quantified. Perhaps the most striking example (next to the various relatively new rules on expedited proceedings) is the Arbitration Institute of the Stockholm Chamber of Commerce initiative dubbed "SCC Express," which in May 2021 published Rules for Express Dispute Assessment, that "may be useful, for instance, where the parties are willing to reduce the scale of their process and forgo certain procedural steps in favour of time and cost efficiency."[70]

3 Flexibility

For Yves Derains, "arbitration proceedings are standardized proceedings. Whatever the place of arbitration, whoever the parties, we have, in general, the same type of proceedings."[71]

Yet, flexibility—the ability of parties to tailor the arbitral procedure to their own, specific needs—consistently ranks in the top three attractive features of commercial arbitration, irrespective of the subgroup being interviewed:[72] "International business people agree to arbitration with the objective of obtaining fair, neutral and *flexible* procedures that are capable of efficiently solving their disputes."[73] One would thus expect that users tend to turn to ad hoc arbitration, or at least that they carefully select the institutional rules which are best suited to the particularities of their dispute, that they take advantage of the wealth of possibilities most of the institutional rules offer, that they make an educated and thought through choice of the institution (if any) that will administer their case, and so forth.

Data, however, seem to indicate that, quite to the contrary, most of the time the force of habit (or the fear of the unknown?) prevails and that users turn to the mainstream options. Since the first QMUL Survey, in 2006, a clear majority (76%) of respondents indicated that their favorite choice was institutional arbitration rather than ad hoc proceedings, for various reasons: a strong reputation for managing the proceedings, familiarity with proceedings and an understanding of costs and fees.[74] And not only do users favor institutional arbitration over ad hoc arbitration, but users also tend to be conservative in their choice of the institution and the applicable rules—and rarely resort to "exotic" choices. The main reasons for choosing a particular institution do not come as a surprise: high level of administration, neutrality and internationalism, global presence and ability to administrate arbitrations worldwide.[75]

---

70. Article 2(1) of said rules, available at https://sccinstitute.com/media/1800129/scc-rules-for-express-dispute-assessment_20210524.pdf (last accessed on October 22, 2022).
71. Quoted by Claudia Salomon in "Maslow's Hammer: An Over-reliance on Familiar Tools", March 14, 2022, available at https://iccwbo.org/publication/maslows-hammer-an-over-reliance-on-familiar-tools/#: ~ :text = Drawing%20parallels%20with%20Maslow%27s%20Hammer,other %20tools%20may%20be%20required (last accessed on October 22, 2022).
72. QMUL Survey 2015, p. 6; QMUL Survey 2018, p. 7.
73. QMUL Survey 2012, introduction (no page number); emphasis added.
74. QMUL Survey 2006, p. 12. Noteworthily, the other 24% were primarily from corporations with a gross annual turnover of more than USD 5 billion, so probably more sophisticated or at least with more means, including in-house.
75. QMUL Survey 2015, p. 18.

We see at least four reasons why users, paradoxically, plebiscite flexibility and choice while having the tendency, in real life, to systematically turn to the same, straightforward, tested and risk-averse options. For one, there is the so-called midnight clause syndrome.[76] Having spent long days (and nights) in arduous discussions about a complex agreement, negotiators often lack the energy and grit to open yet another front of negotiations by proposing original solutions for dispute resolution. Standard and tested choices are the most likely to be accepted without much discussion by the counterparty. This is even more true, and that is the second element, for a clause which intrinsically envisages the worst possible situation: that the agreement which has been the object of so arduous discussions ends up in nasty legal proceedings is an eventuality that no negotiator is happy to envisage; here again, a standard choice will allow to proceeding swiftly to more pleasant subjects. Third, it is of course impossible, at the time of negotiating the dispute resolution clause, to predict eventual future advantages of specific procedural options. Last but not least, corporate templates for contracts (including dispute resolution clauses) or corporate dispute resolution policies play a role as well, by "imposing" some sort of one-fits-all choice in terms of arbitration rules and institutions.

An additional element may also be that arbitration rules, at least those of the major institutions, have become increasingly uniform: already back in 2002, because the requirements of businesses—and thus potential litigants—are the same the world over, it was "perhaps unsurprising that, with each successive modification, the arbitration rules of each of these institutions have become increasingly harmonized."[77] The trend is there for global institutions, but for regional institutions as well.[78] This logically decreases, if not the importance of making an informed choice,[79] at least the natural tendency of the average negotiator (not necessarily familiar with the subtleties of the various rules) to pay a lot of attention to the subject. The fact that "specific institutional features seem to preoccupy respondents [of the QMUL Survey 2018] to a significantly lesser extent" confirms this.[80]

---

76. An allusion to this can be found in the QMUL Survey 2016, p. 23: "(...) at the procurement stage when the terms and conditions are being negotiated, the parties may give little or no time to the D[ispute] R[esolution] provisions, partly because of time constraints and partly because neither anticipates a major dispute arising."

77. Jonathan L. Greenblatt, Peter Griffin, "Towards the Harmonization of International Arbitration Rules: Comparative Analysis of the Rules of the ICC, AAA, LCIA and CIETAC," *Arbitration International*, Vol. 17(1), March 1, 2001, p. 101.

78. *See* for instance the IBA report on *The Current State and Future of International Arbitration: Regional Perspectives*, August 2015, p. 7: "First, there is a growing standardisation of international arbitration practice. The biggest indicators of this are the convergence of arbitral institutional rules (...)"; the report is available at https://www.ibanet.org/LPD/Dispute_Resolution_Section/Arbitration/Publications.aspx (last accessed on October 22, 2022).

79. "Although the rules of the above institutions are now broadly similar, important differences remain. Parties must still consider whether, in light of their particular needs, one institution offers more suitable services than another.": Jonathan L. Greenblatt, Peter Griffin, *supra* n. 77.

80. QMUL Survey 2018, p. 15.

The call of some interviewees for the QMUL Survey 2010 for "more streamlined and disciplined arbitration proceedings to provide an entirely effective form of dispute resolution"[81] is in stark contradiction with a finding from 2013:

> A recurrent theme in interviews with respondents from various sectors was the risk of "judicialisation" of arbitration. Interviewees expressed concern about their perception that the process of arbitration has become more sophisticated and more "regulated," with "control" over the process moving towards law firms—and away from the actual users of this process. Several interviewees linked concerns over increases in the costs of arbitration with this encroaching judicialisation.[82,83]

This debate has been addressed directly by the 2015 survey, where "a clear majority (70%) expressed that international arbitration currently enjoys an adequate amount of regulation, thereby indicating a preference for the status quo." 17% though felt that there is too much regulation. This regulation would restrict the flexibility of the arbitral process and stifle independent thought. Moreover, tribunals may have the tendency to apply guidelines and soft law rigidly.[84] The 2018 edition then considered whether the two opposing demands by users—prescription on one hand and flexibility on the other—can be reconciled. Again, a large majority of respondents believed that the existing sets of arbitration rules contained the right level of prescription (77%) while 18% indicated that they were not prescriptive enough. Only 5% considered them as being too prescriptive. An analysis of the subgroups interviewed revealed no change in these standings.[85]

This paradox—users want flexibility but do not actively use it—may well find its explanation in the fact that, for good or bad reasons, the average user of arbitration is of the opinion that it is up to others to tailor and steer the proceedings according to the specific needs of the case before them. There seems indeed to be a "notable dissatisfaction with respect to the 'lack of creativity' shown by both arbitrators and counsel" in that respect.[86] For instance, as regards early case management conferences, arbitrators and counsel should "get creative" rather than using a standardized template for the initial and subsequent procedural orders.[87] The pot calls the kettle black.

4 Diversity

As already alluded to above,[88] the clear lack of direct, preferably free, detailed, readily available, and reliable information about arbitrators is a major concern for users. In

---

81. QMUL Survey 2010, p. 32.
82. QMUL Survey 2013, p. 22, confirmed by QMUL Survey 2021, p. 14: "A recurring theme in interviews was the sense that arbitration is becoming increasingly over-formalistic, *at the expense of efficiency.*" (emphasis added).
83. For a detailed—and empirical—analysis of the judicialization phenomenon, *see* Rémy Gerbay, "Is the End Nigh Again? An Empirical Assessment of the 'Judicialization' of International Arbitration," The American Review of International Arbitration, Vol. 25, No. 2 (2014), p. 223.
84. QMUL Survey 2015, p. 34.
85. QMUL Survey 2018, p. 33.
86. QMUL Survey 2018, p. 38.
87. *Ibid.*, p. 26.
88. *Supra*, II.1.b.

2010, 68% of the in-house counsel interviewed indicated not to routinely gather information about arbitrators whom they may appoint to arbitrate potential disputes. The cost such gathering entails is one of the elements explaining this. Reflective of this, a same 68% said they did not feel they had a satisfactory level of information to make an informed choice about arbitrators independently of external counsel help—while 67% felt they did with the input of counsel. In the words of the authors of the study:

> [t]his raises a potential issue for the 'arbitration system' as a whole. It may be questioned whether the influence of external counsel over arbitrator selection gives those firms disproportionate influence over the participants in the process, making them virtual 'gatekeepers'. This may reduce the diversity of the arbitration community and mean that undue importance is placed on arbitrator relationships with law firms.[89]

Later surveys confirmed this information deficit: the QMUL Survey 2018 indicates that, indeed, the access to sufficient information about arbitrators' profiles is "problematic for some," "some" referring manifestly to in-house counsel as a mere 57% of them responded that they had sufficient information (without the help of external counsel), whereas 70% among the total pool of respondents declared themselves satisfied with the information they have access to and 80% of the arbitrators' subgroup reported their satisfaction about the information they have access to regarding their peers.[90] Rather than a straightforward information deficit, there is thus a clear *information unbalance*—to the detriment of users and, no doubt, especially to the detriment of less sophisticated or less frequent users.

Users' notorious (and perfectly normal) risk aversion, as expressed by their preferred selection criteria, contributes as well to a narrowed pool of repeat arbitrators. For the last fifteen years, users consistently indicated that the importance of reputation when selecting an arbitrator cannot be overestimated.[91] The way in which users make their choice is not neutral either: the impact of rankings, recommendations,[92] word of mouth and exchanges with colleagues[93]—on top of external counsel advice, most of the time based on the same information channels—further contributes to the pre-existing difficulty to expand the pool of potential arbitrators from which to choose, certainly in the short term.[94]

The combination of these two factors, lack of information on the one hand, and willingness to stick to no-brainer choices on the other hand (the "safe bet syndrome"), leads to what may well be a particularly vicious[95] circle: even as the demand for

---

89. QMUL Survey 2010, p. 27.
90. QMUL Survey 2018, pp. 20-21.
91. QMUL Survey 2006, p. 16, QMUL Survey 2010, pp. 25-26; QMUL Survey 2016, p. 33; reputation is also essential in assessing most of the criteria listed in the QMUL Survey 2019, p. 13: experience, expertise, confidence in decision-making, ...
92. QMUL Survey 2016, p. 33.
93. QMUL Survey 2018, p. 21.
94. QMUL Survey 2006, p. 17.
95. Even if there may be positive effects there as well. *See* for instance Christophe Seraglini, "Who Are the Arbitrators? Myths, Reality and Challenges", in *Legitimacy: Myths, Realities, Challenges*, ICCA Congress Series no. 18 (2015), p. 593: "There should be a 'virtuous' circle there", referring to the positive effects of experience on the "quality of justice" delivered.

arbitrators grows,[96] users tend to limit themselves to the very reputable "happy few," which creates a snowball effect of repeat appointments, with a long list of unwanted collateral effects: an increased risk of conflicts of interest, whether real or perceived; a lower availability of those repeat arbitrators; hence, more delay, potentially less qualitative decisions and awards; the need for overloaded arbitrators to outsource and resort to tribunal secretaries with a sometimes unclear or even disputed[97] role; etc.

It should thus not come as a surprise that, while it may be argued that the arbitration community, including users, does not desire further macro-regulation, corrective micro-regulation is to be welcomed in some specific areas,[98] starting with the conduct of the arbitrators themselves. The QMUL Survey 2015 learns that, if there is a small majority of participants who feels that the conduct of arbitrators should be regulated more (55%), the results differ to quite an extent depending on the subgroups—with an unsurprising 33% minority of arbitrators who think their conduct should be regulated more. When asked what exactly should be regulated, conflicts are not seen as requiring specific regulation in commercial arbitration,[99] but repeat appointments are considered problematic by a decisive majority, regardless of whether the appointments are made by parties or—de facto—by their counsel.[100] This, how-ever, forms no basis for further regulation, as interviewees generally felt the existing instruments, and notably the IBA Guidelines on Conflicts of Interest,[101] offer sufficient guidance to deal with the issue. Interestingly, one suggested topic for regulation as far as arbitrators are concerned, was the setting up of databases that would provide parties with information about an arbitrator's performance in past cases. While this is clearly linked with the information unbalance discussed above, some interviewees noted that such databases would be welcome, but not necessarily the most effective way to regulate arbitrators. Rather, databases were better used in conjunction with other methods.[102] The 2018 survey asked respondents whether they would welcome the

---

96. *Ibid.*: "As the popularity of international arbitration increases, so will the demand for the scarce specialists at the top of the arbitration community."
97. For a high-profile example in investment arbitration: Dmytro Galagan, "The Challenge of the Yukos Award: An Award Written by Someone Else—A Violation of the Tribunal's Mandate?", Kluwer Arbitration Blog, February 27, 2015, available at http://arbitrationblog.kluwera rbitration.com/2015/02/27/the-challenge-of-the-yukos-award-an-award-written-by-someone-else-a-violation-of-the-tribunals-mandate/ (last accessed on October 22, 2022). *See also* the recent judgment of the Brussels Court of First Instance of June 17, 2021, available at https:// jusmundi.com/fr/document/decision/fr-european-commission-v-emek-insaat-sti-and-wte-was sertechnik-jugement-du-tribunal-de-premiere-instance-francophone-de-bruxelles-thursday-17 th-june-2021 (last accessed on October 22, 2022), commented by Benoît Allemeersch, Hannelore Buelens, "Delegations of Tasks to Arbitral Secretaries: Striking the Right Balance?", *Kluwer Arbitration Blog*, August 22, 2021, available at http://arbitrationblog.kluwerarbitration.com/2 021/08/22/delegation-of-tasks-to-arbitral-secretaries-striking-the-right-balance/ (last accessed on October 22, 2022); the case is now pending before the Belgian *Cour de Cassation.*
98. QMUL Survey 2015, p. 49.
99. But they do in investment treaty arbitration.
100. Which is consistent with the finding discussed above that most of the appointments are "inspired" by external counsel.
101. Available at https://www.ibanet.org/ENews_Archive/IBA_July_2008_ENews_ArbitrationMu ltipleLang.aspx (last accessed on October 22, 2022).
102. QMUL Survey 2015, pp. 37-40.

opportunity to evaluate arbitrators at the end of the proceedings. An overwhelming part of the respondents indicated that they would (80%), with nine out of ten in-house counsel eager to be given that possibility.[103] The 2018 edition also offered a wealth of other issues for consideration, as far as arbitrator regulation is concerned: standards of independence and impartiality; consequences for delay by arbitrators; deadlines for issuing awards; and use of tribunal secretaries.[104,105]

This appointment snowball effect may as well explain, at least in part,[106] the recent calls for more diversity in the arbitration "community." It however remains unclear whether that is a genuine concern of users, or rather a (welcome) side-effect from the more general calls for (especially gender) diversity in society at large. The 2010 survey noticed that, as to what drives decisions about arbitrators' appointment, "[t]he least important factors were gender, religion/faith and nationality."[107] One author notes, in the same vein, that "the 'rights' of women, minorities, and young people to be nominated are not the dominant concern of counsel in nominating arbitrators."[108] The survey of 2018 did a deep dive into what it labels the "diversity dilemma" and the main findings were as follows: (i) respondents were unsure whether there is any causal link between the diversity across a panel of arbitrators and the quality of its decision-making, or whether this is even a relevant enquiry to make; (ii) progress has been made on gender diversity, but probably not in terms of geography, age, cultural and ethnic diversity;[109] (iii) to encourage diversity, all stakeholders should expand and diversify the pools from which they select arbitrators.[110] On that last point, it is striking—but logical, once more[111]—that "a vast majority of interviewees across all

---

103. QMUL Survey 2018, p. 22; those results are broadly in line with the findings of the QMUL Survey 2010, p. 28.
104. QMUL Survey 2018, p. 34.
105. The role and need for potential regulation of tribunal secretaries has been analyzed in more detail in the QMUL Survey 2012, pp. 11-12 and in the QMUL Survey 2015, pp. 42-45.
106. Concerns of the arbitration community regarding legitimacy play a role as well. It is telling that the 2020 Report of the Cross-Institutional Task Force on Gender Diversity in Arbitral Appointments and Proceedings mentions legitimacy as one of the four reasons "why [gender diversity] matters" (p. 12; available at https://www.kluwerarbitration.com/book-toc?title = ICCA + Reports + No. + 8%3a + Report + of + the + Cross-Institutional + Task + Force + on + Gender + Diversity + in + Arbitral + Appointments + and + Proceedings, last accessed on October 22, 2022). *See also Legitimacy: Myths, Realities, Challenges,* ICCA Congress Series no. 18 (2015) and the late V.V. Veeder quote on p. 660: "Discrimination is wrong; and, if allowed to continue, it will bring arbitration into disrepute."
107. QMUL Survey 2010, p. 25.
108. Elizabeth Oger-Gross, as quoted in the 2020 Report of the Cross-Institutional Task Force on Gender Diversity in Arbitral Appointments and Proceedings, footnote 127.
109. It might be worthwhile investigating as well if there is any diversity in terms of training or if, to the contrary, most appointees share, to some extent, the same education in the top league law schools first, and in the tier one global law firms next. *See,* among others, Luke Nottage, Nobumichi Teramura and James Tanna, "Lawyers and Non-Lawyers in International Arbitration: Discovering Diminishing Diversity," September 20, 2021, available at https://papers.ssrn.com/sol3/papers.cfm?abstract_id = 3926914 (last accessed on October 22, 2022).
110. QMUL Survey 2018, pp. 16-20.
111. Comp. QMUL Survey 2019, p. 12: "When choosing an arbitrator, as many [sic] as 17% of respondents also took account of the diversity of the resulting tribunal." *See also* Payel Chatterjee and Vyapak Desai, "Is Increasing Gender and Ethnic Diversity in Arbitral Tribunals a Valid Concern?", *Kluwer Arbitration Blog,* March 1, 2020, available at http://arbitrationblog

subgroups based on primary role provided a clear indication of the fact that diversity meets its fiercest resistance from parties and, by extension, their in-house or external counsel (...)."[112] The follow-up questioning in the 2021 edition of the survey offered the following additional insights: (i) progress has been made, at least as far as gender diversity is concerned;[113] (ii) it is unclear if there is any connection between diversity on a tribunal and perceived independence and impartiality; and (iii) commitment by counsel to suggest a diverse list of arbitrators to their client would be a welcome addition to efforts made by the institutions—and would bring in-house counsel to do their part when exercising their "ultimate power to choose between potential arbitrator candidates."[114] As noted by Professor Seraglini:

> There should also be a balance between diversity and the parties' wishes and autonomy. Diversity cannot really be imposed on the parties by their counsel. It is rather a question of recommendation to the parties, of educating them to the merits of new practices. More generally, there is a need to be realistic with respect to the solutions proposed.[115]

5 Second Provisional Finding: The User Is a Reasonably Satisfied, but Potentially Disengaged Customer

Maybe paradoxically, the users remain deeply satisfied with the status of international commercial arbitration. As noted above, international commercial arbitration is still, and by far, our preferred method for resolving cross-border disputes. Users, however, struggle seriously with several issues on which, in my opinion, some progress only has been made in recent years, despite clear empirical evidence that there was (and still is) a call for change by "the customer."

Our lack of real market power, as illustrated under II above, may be part of an explanation. This would be consistent with one of the conclusions of the QMUL Survey 2018: arbitral institutions are perceived as being best placed (80%) to make an impact

---

.kluwerarbitration.com/2020/03/01/is-increasing-gender-and-ethnic-diversity-in-arbitral-trib unals-a-valid-concern/ (last accessed on October 22, 2022): "While selecting arbitrators, the last thing on anyone's mind is promoting gender and ethnic diversity rather [sic] appointing the best person for the job whom they deem fit (...)." Likewise, Bruno Guandalini, *supra* n. 4, p. 125: "(...) parties' unilateral appointments of women will happen when and to the extent the market considers it more efficient to the case, irrespective, once again, of gender characteristics—male, female, or non-binary people."

112. *Ibid.*, p. 19. For an analysis of the recent statistics of the major institutions in this respect, please refer to Kathryn Sanger and Marco de Sousa, "Trendspotting: What Do Recent Arbitration Statistics Tell Us about What's to Come in International Arbitration in 2020 and Beyond?", in *Inside Arbitration—Perspectives on Cross-Border Disputes*, issue 9, February 28, 2020, p. 19, available at https://www.herbertsmithfreehills.com/latest-thinking/inside-arbitration (last accessed on October 22, 2022), finding that "[p]arties continue to lag behind the institutions in the gender diversity of their appointments."

113. For a critical analysis of the most recent statistics: Archismita Raha, Shreya Jain and Juhi Gupta, "Growing Gender Diversity in International Arbitration: a Half Truth?", *Kluwer Arbitration Blog*, September 28, 2021, http://arbitrationblog.kluwerarbitration.com/2021/09/28/ growing-gender-diversity-in-international-arbitration-a-half-truth/ (last accessed on October 22, 2022).

114. QMUL Survey 2021, pp. 15-19.

115. Christophe Seraglini, *supra* n. 95, p. 606.

on the future evolution of international arbitration, followed by arbitration interest groups/bodies like CIArb, ICCA, etc. (56%), arbitrators (42%) and external counsel (40%). Parties (nonlegal personnel) and in-house counsel ranked sixth and seventh only, with respectively 21% and 20%, the in-house counsel subgroup giving comparable answers. The reading by the researchers is that "[p]erhaps this may suggest that it is the stakeholders whose existence is essentially symbiotic with the system of international arbitration who are seen to have the ultimate stewardship of it."[116] In more straightforward—and less positive—terms, "the parties themselves can feel sidelined to their own dispute." = [117]

Another reading may be that the users group suffers from a too high level of entropy and lacks the necessary energy (or time, or sense of priority) to overcome inertia.

The worst of cases for international commercial arbitration would be that users are gradually losing interest and turning, when possible, to other, less costly, swifter, genuinely flexible ways to have their disputes resolved by a more diverse pool of neutrals.

IV   THE USER: A CUSTOMER LOOKING FOR AN ALTERNATIVE PRODUCT?

Is that so? Is commercial arbitration under siege? Are other ways of resolving disputes—and especially non-adjudicative methods—gradually eroding the market share of commercial arbitration?

The data gathered by the successive QMUL surveys indicate without any ambiguity that, while international arbitration is still the preferred ultimate dispute resolution mechanism, most of the users prefer a combination of international arbitration and so-called alternative dispute resolution methods[118] in a multi-tiered, or escalating, dispute resolution process: 44% in 2006, when only in-house counsel participated in the survey,[119] 34% in 2015, for a wider and more diverse respondent group,[120] up again to 49% in 2018—when the in-house counsel subgroup reflected a clear preference for international arbitration together with ADR (60%) over international arbitration as stand-alone (32%)—and 59% in 2021.[121] For the authors of the study, this significant increase in the overall popularity of arbitration combined with alternative dispute resolution methods[122] "suggests that, even though arbitration

---

116. QMUL Survey 2018, pp. 36-37.
117. Claudia Salomon, "Maslow's Hammer: An Over-reliance on Familiar Tools", *supra* n. 71.
118. Other empirical studies come to the same conclusion. *See*, for example, the SIDRA International Dispute Resolution Survey 2020 Final Report (available at https://sidra.smu.edu.sg/sites/sidra.smu.edu.sg/files/survey/index.html, last accessed on October 22, 2022).
119. QMUL Survey 2006, p. 5.
120. QMUL Survey 2015, p. 5.
121. "This year's findings *once again* reveal a *noticeable* increase over recent years in the overall popularity of arbitration used in conjunction with ADR," QMUL Survey 2021, p. 5, emphasis added.
122. For an analysis of this in the construction sector, traditionally eager to safeguard commercial relations, see QMUL Survey 2019, pp. 18-21.

continues to be the go-to dispute resolution mechanism, parties are increasingly resorting to various forms of ADR *in the hope that a swifter and more cost-efficient resolution can be found* to disputes before having them resolved by arbitration."[123,124] Interestingly, there's a notable gap here between the private practitioners and full-time arbitrators subgroups which still show a slight preference for arbitration stand-alone (respectively 51% and 54%).

This tendency is confirmed when one analyses the corporate dispute resolution policies, which frequently include clauses promoting multi-tiered or escalating dispute resolution procedures promoting the active search for a settlement.[125] In the TMT sector, for instance, mediation is the most encouraged mechanism (50%), with arbitration coming next (47%).[126]

The frequency of settlements before or after the award,[127] and the reasons why parties pursue such settlements, point to the same phenomenon. The four main reasons that motivate corporations to settle before the award are, in decreasing order of importance: to preserve business relationships, to avoid high costs, a weak case and to avoid excessive delay. The same reasons, although in a slightly different order, are invoked to explain post-award settlements: avoid costs, save time, and preserve a sound working relationship.[128,129] An improved cooperation by arbitration counsel in encouraging settlement, including the use of mediation during an arbitration, was the third most selected improvement by the respondents to the 2018 survey, and the number one option selected by the in-house counsel subgroup when asked what counsel could do better.[130]

---

123. QMUL Survey 2018, p. 5; emphasis added. Some interviewees however indicated that multi-tier escalation clauses may well lead to the arbitration/ADR-mix ending up being more costly and time-consuming than simply resolving disputes through arbitration only (*ibid.*, p. 6); although this is probably true in some cases, in general this is not our experience. One can also refer to the survey of 2013 which found that "[w]hen asked whether the 2008 financial crisis had changed their choice of dispute resolution mechanisms, the most frequently mentioned change was an increase in the use of mediation post crisis. Interviewees indicated that this was due to the increased pressure in litigation budget"; QMUL Survey 2013, p. 10.

124. The growing tension between transparency and confidentiality/privacy, an essential feature of arbitration for the user, may push for more ADR as well.

125. QMUL Survey 2006, p. 9.

126. QMUL Survey 2016, p. 19.

127. A high-profile and striking example is the settlement entered into between Areva, Siemens and TVO putting an end to their protracted dispute related to the construction of the Olkiluoto nuclear power plant in Finland; http://www.sa.areva.com/news/liblocal/docs/CP_groupe/2 018/PR_Global%20Settlement%20Agreement%20between%20TVO%20and%20AREVA%20 Siemens.pdf (last accessed on October 22, 2022). See also the settlement announced by EDF and Areva on June 30, 2021: https://www.edf.fr/en/the-edf-group/dedicated-sections/jou rnalists/all-press-releases/edf-and-areva-reach-a-settlement-agreement (last accessed on October 22, 2022). These are of course not isolated examples.

128. QMUL 2008, pp. 7-9.

129. In practice, the party that prevails thus is prepared to abandon part of the damages awarded in exchange for a swifter and secured payment—hence accepts to *pay* for the certainty and swiftness of a (partial) voluntary execution.

130. QMUL Survey 2018, p. 31.

Mediation especially gains traction among users. Even if the actual impact of the Singapore Convention[131] is yet unclear,[132] one fails to see how it could possibly not reinforce, even marginally, this pro-settlement trend. Also, the arbitration community, true to its reputation of creativity, regularly comes up with new initiatives and tools in ADR, as lately for instance the Arbitration Institute of the Stockholm Chamber of Commerce with its "SCC Express."[133]

The results of other empirical studies, starting with the large-scale Global Pound Conference Series of 2016 and 2017, are telling. The four key global themes identified were: "Efficiency is the key priority of parties in choice of dispute resolution processes," "Parties expect greater collaboration from advisors in dispute resolution," "Global interest in the use of pre-dispute protocols and mixed-mode dispute resolution (combining adjudicative and non-adjudicative processes)" and "In-house counsel are the agents to facilitate organisational change. External lawyers are the primary obstacles to change."[134]

The last point may come as a surprise when referring to the relative demobilization of in-house counsel which we concluded under III above. We see, however, no inconsistency. Users of arbitration in general and in-house counsel in particular may feel they do not have the means to be agents of change in *arbitration* (as the arbitration process appears to be predominantly dependent on if not "monopolized" by the other actors), that does not necessarily mean they cannot and are not eager to cause major evolutions of *dispute resolution in general*. 42% of the respondents to the Global Pound Conferences—parties, advisors, adjudicative providers, non-adjudicative providers, and influencers—indicated that in their view, in-house lawyers have the potential to be the most influential in bringing about change in commercial dispute resolution practice.[135] Such re-appropriation of dispute resolution by in-house counsel is to be welcomed. As stated by one of the driving forces behind the Global Pound Conferences:

> [d]isputes are generally not an academic exercise but are about protecting corporate value. In-house counsel has the right to demand change as custodian of this value and they also have the ability to drive change as they hold the purse strings. They represent a key link between the legal world and the commercial one, balancing the need for effective dispute resolution with the hard-earned experience of how best to get results.[136]

This call for a paradigm shift should not be perceived by the arbitral community as a threat. Rather, it offers an opportunity for this community—including the

131. United Nations Convention on International Settlement Agreements Resulting from Mediation of December 20, 2018, available at https://uncitral.un.org/sites/uncitral.un.org/files/media-documents/EN/Texts/UNCITRAL/Arbitration/mediation_convention_v1900316_eng.pdf (last accessed on October 22, 2022).
132. *See* for instance QMUL Survey 2018, p. 31.
133. *Rules for Express Dispute Assessment*, May 2021, available at scc-express-guidelines_2021.pdf (sccinstitute.com) > (last accessed on October 22, 2022).
134. Global Pound Conference Series—Global Data Trends and Regional Differences, pp. 9-18, available at https://www.imimediation.org/research/gpc/series-data-and-reports/ (last accessed on October 22, 2022).
135. *Ibid.*, p. 17.
136. *Ibid.*, p. 18.

users!—to make sure arbitration, "as a species of dispute resolution mechanisms" is not systematically "supplanted by other species." If there is to be no "tale of extinction," commercial arbitration will have to evolve and adapt; not only making sure it "migrat[es] into new areas (...) where a more hospitable habitat (i.e., complex/high value claims) offers it a brighter outlook for survival"[137] but also accepting to share its existing habitat (or market) with other species (or competitors), to learn from them and to adapt to the ongoing "climate change" in the dispute resolution cosmos.

As for us, in-house counsel, we must do our part, and positively respond to calls for engagement. Back in 2014 already, the ICC made a strong case for in-house counsel engagement in its *Guide for In-House Counsel on Effective Management of Arbitration*,[138] and this invitation to partake has been reiterated since by many. Let us help the arbitration community, *our* arbitration community, to overcome "the bias of stakeholder engagement."[139]

---

137. All quotes from Rémy Gerbay, "Is the End Nigh Again?", *supra* n. 83, p. 247.
138. At p. 5, available at https://iccwbo.org/publication/effective-management-of-arbitration-a-guide-for-in-house-counsel-and-other-party-representatives/ (last accessed on October 22, 2022).
139. Claudia Salomon, "Maslow's Hammer: An Over-reliance on Familiar Tools," *supra* n. 71.

CHAPTER 50

State Perspective on International Commercial Arbitration: State as a Policymaker and State as a User of the System

*Mariam Gotsiridze**

I   INTRODUCTION

Despite increased criticism and heated debate in reference to international arbitration, the demand for this private method of dispute resolution is constantly growing among businesses. The use of Arbitration has also increased with respect to transactions and projects involving states and state entities. It seems that arbitration is not only popular among commercial users but also has greatly benefited from the support of states and public institutions.

---

* Principal Research Fellow, Singapore International Dispute Resolution Academy (SIDRA), Singapore Management University. Email: mgotsiridze@smu.edu.sg. Former Head of the Department of State Representation in Arbitration and Foreign Courts, Ministry of Justice of Georgia.
     The views expressed in this chapter and the statements made therein are the author's own, and not necessarily those of the SIDRA or the Ministry of Justice of Georgia.

There is a general trend among states around the world to support the development of international commercial arbitration. Many states have revised their legislation and have put in place framework and infrastructure to facilitate the development or continued successful use of arbitration. Some states went even further by promoting the creation of regional arbitration centres and attempting to position themselves as a favourable arbitration venue. For these purposes, states would enter into cooperation agreements with international arbitral institutions, the academic world and other governments to support development, research and capacity building in this field; in the same manner, some governments would strongly advocate for their own arbitration structures to help them grow and to boost the reputation of their respective jurisdictions.

Arbitral institutions have not been standing still either; they put a lot of effort into remaining attractive and to compete with courts or other domestic means of dispute resolution. We recently saw many institutions revising their rules, and adopting some soft law instruments or procedural mechanisms to respond to recent trends or contemporary challenges of international arbitration. Institutions have also been focusing on arbitrations involving states. Some institutions have revised their rules or have put in place separate instruments to respond specifically to the needs of arbitration matters involving sovereigns and their instrumentalities.

While there is an evident tendency of governments supporting the development of international commercial arbitration on a policy level, certain criticism has also been voiced by the latter as users of the system. The set of concerns that are, in fact, shared by many governments around the world, relate both to arbitration procedure as well as material aspects of handling arbitration matters involving state parties. These concerns include time and cost, parallel proceedings and frivolous claims as well as the capacity and qualification of arbitrators and arbitral institutions to deal with matters involving state parties and public interest.

The aim of this article is to discuss recent trends, problems and possible solutions with respect to international commercial arbitration. We will do so from the perspective of the state and therefore, focus more on some of the issues that arise in commercial arbitration both on the state policy level as well as in the context of matters involving state entities, without any attempt at being exhaustive, however. Where possible, we will also share some specific experiences of Georgia and other jurisdictions. We shall first look at trends and developments in international commercial arbitration in recent years and the state's role and perspective thereto. Then we shall focus our attention on arbitration of state contracts[1] and discuss whether and to what extent is arbitration suitable and capable of adjudicating matters involving state entities.[2] Finally, we shall briefly look at the role of states themselves in addressing

---

1. We shall use terms 'state contract' and 'public-private contract' interchangeably to refer to the commercial or investment contracts involving the state or state entities and the public interest.
2. For the purposes of this chapter, under state entity we contemplate a state or any state body or instrumentality that is either established under the statute or is exercising public functions delegated to it by state authorities or by virtue of a statute.

some of the concerns in order to make international arbitration a more reliable, effective and efficient process.

II CURRENT TRENDS AND POLICIES IN INTERNATIONAL ARBITRATION

In recent years, awareness, support and demand for international commercial arbitration have been steadily augmenting. Commercial arbitration remains more favourable than national courts[3] or other domestic administrative procedures. International arbitral institutions have been publishing impressive statistics regarding the number and value of disputes referred to arbitration in past years.[4]

The results of yet another Queen Mary University Survey entitled 'Adapting Arbitration to a Changing World', are indeed a good demonstration of this evolutionary success of commercial arbitration. As the Survey has revealed, 90% of interviewed users of the system consider arbitration as their preferred means of dispute settlement.[5] It is noteworthy that the strong preference for arbitration has not been affected by COVID-19[6] as the reasons for such trust[7] have not changed over time, including during the pandemic.[8]

It is noteworthy that governments from around the world have been expressing unparalleled support for arbitration. Promotion and development of international

---

3. *See*, Tom Jones, 'Bermann on Commercial Arbitration and Its Critics', 4 December 2019, Global Arbitration Review, *found at* https://globalarbitrationreview.com/article/1210713/bermann-on -commercial-arbitration-and-its-critics (last visited 15.02.2020). As Professor George A. Berman suggested at GAR Live Atlanta in 2019, the reasons for this favoritism would include the ability to appoint decision-makers, confidentiality, finality, neutrality, ease of negotiation and enforcement.
4. The ICC International Court of Arbitration has been announcing a record numbers of referrals in recent years. In 2019, the ICC has registered 869 applications in total, at the same time marking registration of the 25,000th case in ICC arbitration history. Found at ICC celebrates case milestone, announces record figures for 2019 – ICC – International Chamber of Commerce (iccwbo.org) (last visited 12 February 2020). That number has increased to 946 new cases in 2020 reaching the second-highest number of cases ever registered with ICC. Found at ICC Dispute Resolution Statistics: 2020 - ICC - International Chamber of Commerce (iccwbo.org) (last visited 21 June 2022).
    Similarly, the London Court of International Arbitration announced receipt of a record number of cases in 2020 totaling 444 referrals for all services with the slight decline in 2021 with 387 referrals in total. Found at https://www.lcia.org/lcia/reports.aspx (last visited 21 June 2022).
5. '2021 International Arbitration Survey: Adapting Arbitration to a Changing World', Queen Mary University of London & White & Case LLP, p. 5. Found at https://arbitration.qmul.ac.uk/media /arbitration/docs/LON0320037-QMUL-International-Arbitration-Survey-2021_19_WEB.pdf (last visited 20 June 2022).
6. In 2018, 97% of interviewed respondents considered arbitration as a preferred means of dispute resolution. '2018 International Arbitration Survey: the Evolution of International Arbitration', Queen Mary University of London & White & Case LLP, p. 2. Found at http://www.arbitration. qmul.ac.uk/media/arbitration/docs/2018-International-Arbitration-Survey---The-Evolution-of-International-Arbitration-(2).PDF (last visited 15 February 2020).
7. According to the results of 2018 Queen Mary University Survey, arbitration was favoured primarily because of 'enforceability of awards' and the possibility to avoid 'specific legal systems/national courts' as well as flexibility and ability to select decision-makers. *See*, '2018 International Arbitration Survey', p. 7.
8. '2021 International Arbitration Survey', p. 5.

arbitration have been raised at a state policy level. Some countries simply aim at attracting cross-border trade and investment while others go much further by promoting their arbitration structures and jurisdictions.

1   Arbitration as a Tool to Attract Cross-Border Trade and Investment

In order to attract cross-border trade and investment and to establish themselves on the global economic map as a business- and investment-friendly jurisdiction, states are prepared to offer relevant guarantees and protection. Dispute settlement provisions among those guarantees are almost non-negotiable in state contracts involving foreign commercial or investment parties. Arbitration seems to become some kind of trade-off that states need to provide in order to negotiate the deal. In Georgia's reality, the vast majority of state contracts with foreign counterparts in commercial and investment transactions contain arbitration as a method of dispute resolution.

According to the Secretary-General of the Commonwealth, Honourable Patricia Scotland:

> A robust framework for resolving cross-border commercial disputes can unlock valuable trade and investment opportunities for Commonwealth countries. … agreeing frameworks for international commercial arbitration sends strong message to foreign investors that the business environment of countries is stable, efficient and fair.[9]

Asia Development Bank (ADB) has funded a regional development technical assistance program to help South Pacific countries 'create better investment climate'; the latter believe that promotion of international commercial arbitration in the region could facilitate more cross-border trade and investment.[10]

Arbitration is considered to be the most appropriate and therefore, preferred method of dispute resolution especially in cross-border transitions or foreign investment projects. It is claimed that such forms of commercial and investment relationships might involve parties of different nationalities, different applicable laws and different jurisdictions; courts of a particular state could not be prepared or qualified to deal with such matters; judges might lack qualifications in different applicable laws that might be in conflict with one another, as well as particular technical or industry expertise required for the matters to be examined in dispute. Arbitration, on the other hand, gives parties the possibility to select arbitrators who are qualified in particular jurisdictions and/or possess special expertise in relevant areas. It is also claimed that the possibility of obtaining a final enforceable award before the tribunal within one set

---

9. The Rt Hon Patricia SCOTLAND QC, Secretary-general of the Commonwealth, 'How a Robust International Legal Framework Can Boost Global Trade and Economic Growth', 11 November 2019. Found at https://thecommonwealth.org/blog/blog-how-robust-international-arbitration-framework-can-boost-global-trade-and-economic-growth (last visited 17 February 2020).
10. Tamlyn Mills and Mrithula Shanker, 'Promoting Investment Trough Arbitration: Recent Reform in the South Pacific' in 'International Arbitration Report', Issue 17, Norton Rose, December 2021, p. 8.

of proceedings is indeed a luxury for businessmen for whom uncertainty in business relations for a prolonged period of time could be detrimental.

From Georgia's policy perspective, in recent years, specifically with an idea to improve further its business environment, the government has attempted to reform the existing system in three directions: judiciary, arbitration and mediation.[11] This way, the Georgian government intends to provide businesses operating in Georgia or in the region with a suite of options – three possible means for the resolution of their disputes. Eventually, it would be the choice of the parties which method of dispute resolution they consider more appropriate and trustworthy for their business affairs.

2 States Promoting Regional Centres and Their Jurisdictions as Arbitration Venues

In view of this increased demand for arbitration, states have been extending notable support to the development of international commercial arbitration. Although international and autonomous in nature, international arbitration is still significantly attached to domestic jurisdictions and its success can be determined by the realities on a national level. Thus, support or, conversely, disapprobation of arbitration on a legislative or policy level in respective jurisdictions can trigger major developments in the field of arbitration. We can certainly observe more positive trends in terms of the government's commitment and support towards arbitration in the past years. This support has been demonstrated in various forms, be it the adoption of arbitration-friendly legislation and the development of relevant institutions or the promotion of their arbitration structures and their respective jurisdictions as a venue for international arbitration. What is interesting is that the competition among states in this field is so high that these new trends involve not only countries with little practice in international arbitration and underdeveloped institutional and legal structures but also those with developed arbitration centres and a high reputation in this field.

Countries have been modernising their legislation to create a robust legal framework for arbitration all-round the globe. After a long period of consideration, Switzerland has revised Chapter 12 of its Private International Law Act (PILA), the aim of which is to modernise Swiss arbitration law to ensure the continued attractiveness and competitiveness of Switzerland as a long-recognised international arbitration venue.[12] Likewise, other states in Europe have made important attempts to re-establish themselves as attractive arbitration jurisdictions; this would include Sweden which

11. Georgia has undertaken serious reform of its judicial system in past years. Georgia had revised its arbitration legislation to align it with international standards and practices; Georgia has been promoting its jurisdiction as a venue for arbitration in the region and has been cooperating with local and international institutions to bring in more expertise and experience in the country in this area. In September 2019 Georgian parliament passed the Mediation Act of Georgia; in August 2019 Georgia signed the UN Convention on International Settlement Agreements Resulting from Mediation.
12. Chapter 12 of Swiss Private International Law Act (PILA) came into force on 1 January 2021. *See*, Vanessa Alarcon DUVANEL, King & Spalding, 'Update PILA: Switzerland Revamps Arbitration Law', 20 January 2021, found at http://arbitrationblog.practicallaw.com/updated-pila-switzerland-revamps-arbitration-law/ (last visited 20 June 2022).

had revised its Arbitration Act in 2019 – twenty years after its enactment, to adapt it to recent developments and to fill in some legal gaps.[13]

Georgia, being a corridor between Europe and Asia for centuries and part of the historic Silk Road, heavily depended on and benefited from international trade, cross-border economic ties and foreign direct investment. Therefore, Georgia always understood the importance of putting in place a legal regime and dispute settlement infrastructure for local and foreign businesses. Georgia became a party to all major international investment and trade agreements in the early nineties, immediately after its independence from the Soviet Union.[14] In the same period, Georgia started to conclude Bilateral Investment Agreements with its major trading and investment partners. It enacted its first arbitration act as early on as in 1997, when it was rebuilding its entire legal framework from scratch in post-Soviet Union times. In order to bring its legal framework closer to modern international arbitration practices, in 2009, Georgia adopted a new Arbitration Act based on the Model Law of the United Nations Conference on International Trade Law (UNCITRAL). In 2015, Georgia further amended its Arbitration Act to align it with modern international developments and best practices.[15]

In 2016, Korea likewise revised its Arbitration Act to make it more compliant with the UNCITRAL Model Law, and in 2017, it issued the Arbitration Industry Promotion Act creating a legal basis for the government to support arbitration through expanding its facilities, cultivating experts and professionals and supporting research and development.[16] Singapore and Hong Kong have passed so-called third-party funding legislation in 2017 and 2018, receptively, abolishing common law torts of maintenance and champerty with an idea to promote more liberal use of third-party funding and thus, ensure increased access to arbitration.[17] Thailand went as far as introducing a Smart Visa program to streamline the application process, among others, with the aim to attract more foreign arbitrations to their jurisdiction.[18] In 2021, Uzbekistan adopted a

---

13. 'The Revised Swedish Arbitration Act: Noteworthy Development of *Lex Arbitri* of a Leading Jurisdiction for International Arbitration', Cleary Gottlieb Steen & Hamilton LLP, 12 March 2019, Found at https://www.clearygottlieb.com/-/media/files/alert-memos-2019/the-revised-swedish-arbitration-act.pdf (last visited 18 February 2020).
14. Georgia signed and ratified the ICSID Convention on 7 August 1992; it acceded to the 1958 New York Convention on the Recognition and Enforcement of Foreign Arbitral Awards on 2 June 1994 and on 17 December 1994 signed and later, on 22 February 1995, ratified 1994 Energy Charter Treaty.
15. 2015 amendments have introduced the following changes to arbitration legislation in Georgia: some form requirements for the arbitration agreement have been removed; the duty of the courts to decline their jurisdiction in favor of arbitration has been enhanced; the power of the courts to assist the arbitration process, including with respect to the appointment of arbitrators as well as the adoption and enforcement of provisional measures, has been further strengthened; lodging fees for the recognition and enforcement of arbitral awards have been significantly reduced, etc.
16. Sue Hyun Lim, 'Innovating the Future: Recent Changes and Developments in Global and Regional Arbitration Institutes', KCAB International, Global Arbitration Review, 11 June 2019, Found at https://globalarbitrationreview.com/insight/the-asia-pacific-arbitration-review-2020/1193887/innovating-the-future-recent-changes-and-developments-in-global-and-regional-arbitral-institutions (last visited 15 February 2020).
17. *Ibid.*
18. *Ibid.*

new law on international commercial arbitration based on the UNCITRAL Model Law as part of the broader goal to promote arbitration and develop this central Asian state into a regional disputes hub.[19]

Similar developments can be observed on the African continent. In 2017, South Africa adopted the UNCITRAL Model Law on International Commercial Arbitration.[20] Here again, the aim of the reform was to align the practice of arbitration in South Africa with international standards and thus contribute to the promotion of the country as an arbitration hub in Africa. There are many more examples of states implementing similar reforms in the field of arbitration that we could not exhaustively cover here.

Governments seem to have also realised that they can further strengthen their image as a favourable business environment by putting in place dispute settlement structures that are more favourable to business than local courts are. States must have also realised that there are some additional benefits that come with the practice of international arbitration in their jurisdictions; that would include the economic benefits of providing various services, as well as a reputational benefit – developed international arbitration practice sends a broader message about the rule of law and the stability of the legal and political environment of the country. It is probably with this motivation that many states have been positioning themselves as favourable venues for international arbitration through various attempts at strengthening the image of their dispute settlement structures and their respective jurisdictions.

In 2017, Spain's three largest arbitration institutions signed a memorandum of understanding preparing for their future merger with the aim to boost Spain's profile as a centre for international arbitration.[21] In 2018, new Arbitration Rules of the German Arbitration Institute (DIS) came into force, introducing high flexibility for the parties of the proceedings, which further increased the popularity of Germany in arbitration.[22] Georgia, as a country located at the crossroad between Asia, Europe and the Middle East, is a natural venue for various business encounters, including as a neutral place to resolve disputes between the commercial and investment actors in the region. This is why the Georgian Government has been promoting the country as a venue for international arbitration and alternative dispute resolution (ADR) in the region. While

---

19. Alison Ross, 'Uzbekistan's Offering on Show at First Arbitration Week', Global Arbitration Review, 12 October 2021, found at https://globalarbitrationreview.com/article/uzbekistans-offering-show-first-arbitration-week (last visited 5 June 2022).
20. Michael Ostrov, Ben Sanderson and Andrea Lapunzina Veroneli, 'Developments in African Arbitration', DLA Piper, 10 May 2018, Global Arbitration Review, found at https://globalarbitrationreview.com/insight/the-middle-eastern-and-african-arbitration-review-2018/1169293/developments-in-african-arbitration (last visited 18 February 2020).
21. The idea behind the initiative is to unify three centers in order to create a single arbitration center in Madrid that could administer international arbitration. The authors of the idea claim that Madrid as 'an important financial Centre' has a potential to administer cases from Europe and Latin America. *See*, Cosmo Sanderson, 'Spain's Big Three Arbitration Centers Work towards Unification', Global Arbitration Review, 19 December 2017, found at https://globalarbitrationreview.com/article/1151897/spain%E2%80%99s-big-three-arbitration-centres-work-towards-unification (last visited 15 February 2020).
22. Daniel Froesch, 'Recent Developments in the Framework of Arbitration in Germany', Heuking Kuöhn Luöer Wojtek, Global Arbitration Review, 17 November 2021, found at https://globalarbitrationreview.com/review/the-european-arbitration-review/2022/article/recent-developments-in-the-framework-of-arbitration-in-germany (last visited 5 June 2022).

the primary aspiration of the Georgian government is to create a favourable legal and business environment for cross-border trade and investment, it is also convinced that the development of dispute settlement services in Georgia would greatly contribute to the development of the legal culture and the market for legal services.

A series of reforms have been undertaken for the recognition of Malaysia as the hub of international arbitration that finalised with the rebranding of its main arbitral institute the Asian International Arbitration Centre (AIAC).[23] In 2019, the Shenzhen Court of International Arbitration (SCIA) introduced an optional appellate procedure for arbitration matters, possibly to be the first to respond to a line of criticism of arbitration for the lack of possibility of further review of arbitral awards.[24] SCIA has even won a GAR Award for best innovation in 2019 for this initiative. Japan's desire to promote itself as seat of arbitration has been demonstrated by establishing the Japan International Dispute Resolution Center (JIDRC) in 2018 as well as opening a new JIDRC hearing facility in Tokyo in October 2020.[25]

As part of its ambitious project to develop itself as a regional disputes hub, in 2018 Uzbekistan created the Tashkent International Arbitration Centre (TIAC).[26] In order to increase the Centre's marketing chances the Government issued a decree whereby parties do not have to pay value added tax (VAT) on TIAC's services, and foreign arbitrators hearing cases in Uzbekistan are released from income tax on their fees; TIAC is also exceptional by not charging parties for administering arbitration proceedings.[27]

Likewise in Africa, several jurisdictions from all parts of the continent have been making serious efforts to promote their jurisdictions. Thus, the Casablanca International Mediation and Arbitration Centre has been expressing its ambition to become a centre for dispute settlement not only for the region but also for all of Africa, appealing to its strategic location as a gateway between Africa, Europe and North America.[28] The Kigali International Arbitration Centre in Rwanda[29] and the Nairobi Centre for International Arbitration in Kenia have also been keen to get a share of the African arbitration market.[30]

Exaggeration and overdoing things are not beneficial for any industry or any system. As Professor Bermann has very sensibly pointed out, 'something as apparently pro-arbitration ... may actually move us in the opposite direction, to the point of being

---

23. Andre Yeap SC, Avinash Pradhan, 'The Asia-Pacific Arbitration Review 2020', 24 May 2019, found at https://globalarbitrationreview.com/insight/the-asia-pacific-arbitration-review-2020/1193380/malaysia (last visited 5 March 2020).
24. S.H. Lim, 'Innovating the Future'.
25. Sangyub (Sean) Lee, Ji Yoon (June) Park, 'Innovating the Future: Recent Changes and Developments in Global and Regional Arbitration Institutions', Global Arbitration Review, 7 July 2021, found at https://globalarbitrationreview.com/review/the-asia-pacific-arbitration-review/2022/article/innovating-the-future-recent-changes-and-developments-in-global-and-regional-arbitral-institutions (last visited 5 June 2022).
26. A. Ross, 'Uzbekistan's Offering on Show at First Arbitration Week'.
27. *Ibid.*
28. M. Ostrov, B. Sanderson and A.L. Veroneli, 'Developments in African Arbitration'.
29. *Ibid.*
30. *Ibid.*

arbitration-unfriendly.'[31] Is there paranoia about being arbitration-friendly and how is this affecting the commercial arbitration system? It is because of the proliferation of arbitral institutions and other dispute settlement forums and the increased competition in this market, that the possibility of cooperation or joining forces is intensely discussed in the arbitration world.[32]

3 Tension Between Promoting International Arbitration and Developing Domestic Court Litigation

While all the justifications for favouring arbitration discussed in part I.1. are self-explanatory, we were wondering whether the current trend of overwhelming favouritism for arbitration and the perceived inadequacy of national courts to resolve cross-border trade or investment disputes has been too extreme and somewhat unfair to national dispute settlement systems.

It is true that in the modern era of globalisation, the borders between countries for international trade and investment activities have faded, which resulted in an increase in the complexity of disputes; but this is the everyday reality not only with respect to major business or investment activities but even for ordinary individuals on a day-to-day basis; for instance, consumers that can purchase goods and services from any part of the world. In order to be competitive or to be able to survive in this globalised environment all actors in the field need to, and they in fact do, change their behaviours – they learn, practice and adapt. Why then should national courts be left out of this global process of adaptation – why couldn't judges educate themselves, learn languages, qualify in more than one jurisdiction, etc. – especially when technology makes it so easy to access information and opportunities around the globe?

There is indeed serious tension between states wanting to reform and improve the judiciary, the quality of processes and the decisions in their local courts, and, on the other hand, in order to attract cross-border trade and investment, feeling obliged to opt for international arbitration. In parallel with the development of a legal and institutional framework for arbitration, many states have undertaken serious reforms to their judiciary specifically to address the needs of international commercial and investment matters. One of the strong reflections of this tension, however, is the current trend of setting up specialised commercial courts within a domestic legal system.[33] What is interesting in this development is the fact that most of these courts are established with

---

31. Professor Bermann developed this view with respect to arbitrability of disputes, arguing that taking as many disputes as possible within the system of arbitration might seem as a pro-arbitration stance, but in fact, the system would be much better off if some categories of disputes did not come to arbitration, such as, for instance consumer disputes. *See*, T. Jones, 'Bermann on Commercial Arbitration'.

32. *See* Tom Jones, Alison ROSS, 'Mourre Calls for Institutionalization to Join Forces', 9 March 2018, GAR, found at https://globalarbitrationreview.com/article/1166513/mourre-calls-for-instituti ons-to-join-forces (last visited 5.3.2020).

33. In recent years, several states have created specialised commercial courts within their domestic system of judiciary. In 2015, Singapore officially launched its International Commercial Courts. In 2018, China established two commercial courts in Xian and in Shenzhen respectively, to deal with certain types of disputes within China's Belt and Road Initiative. In 2018, Kazakhstan

the idea to deal with international commercial and investment disputes and thus, to obtain a share of the dispute settlement market that is currently occupied by international arbitration. Many of these courts have been designed with due consideration of the merits and demerits of international arbitration, with an idea to mimic all the favourable features of the current system of arbitration, but at the same time, avoid the problems identified therein.[34] For instance, many newly set up commercial courts would bring in the pull of international judges, provide the possibility of representation by a foreign lawyer of a party's choice, allow the conduct of proceedings in foreign language/s, subject jurisdiction of the court to the consent of the parties,[35] design procedure in a way to speed up the litigation process and reduce costs, allow for the confidentiality of the process, enhance the authority of judges to decide matters under foreign law, provide appeal but limit it to only one appearance subject to party choice, etc. In addition, governments are trying to promote their judicial structures by elevating the well-established civil procedural law mechanisms that concern areas where arbitration has attracted some criticism. This would include, for instance, the joinder of third parties, transparency and rule of precedent or, for civil law countries, the possibility of interpreting law by court decisions to increase predictability and consistency, etc. All this is the demonstration of strong competition between arbitration and domestic court litigation.

The idea of bringing national courts back into the business of cross-border trade and investment dispute resolution might become more relevant in the context of current criticism of international arbitration. It is a matter of serious consideration whether certain perceived benefits of arbitration in comparison with national courts have diminished or disappeared over time.[36] The Queen Mary Survey has identified cost as the major downside of arbitration, followed by 'lack of efficiency in sanctions during the arbitration process', lack of powers with respect to third parties and 'lack of speed'.[37]

Professor George Bermann has organised criticism of international commercial arbitration in three categories: (1) the speed, cost and increasing formality of the process, (2) the decision-makers – arbitration is concentrated in few hands, arbitrators

---

opened the Astana International Financial Centre's Court the primary aim of which is to offer protection to foreign investments. There are specialised courts in United Arab Emirates.

    Several European states have also consider setting up similar commercial courts within their domestic legal systems. For example, on 1 January 2019, Netherlands Commercial Court was created to 'swiftly and effectively resolve international business disputes'. *See* the website of the Netherlands Commercial Court (NCC), found at https://www.rechtspraak.nl/English/NCC/Pages/default.aspx (last visited 3 March 2020).

34. The Singapore International Commercial Court has been designed in a way to avoid problems identified in the international arbitration system. *See* Akira Saito, 'International Commercial Arbitration and International Commercial Courts: Towards a Competitive and Cooperative Relationship', p. 45, found at https://www.victoria.ac.nz/__data/assets/pdf_file/0004/118697 8/Saito.pdf (last visited 3 March 2020).

35. *Ibid.*, p. 46.

36. We have seen increased debate and criticism towards the system of investor-state dispute settlement (ISDS). Although, the criticism of ISDS could not directly translate to commercial arbitration in all aspects, there are, however, certain commonalities between the two processes and therefore some concerns identified in one system could be equally applicable to the other.

37. '2018 International Arbitration Survey', p. 5.

are insufficiently diverse and accountable, and (3) the suitability of the commercial arbitration for certain types of disputes.[38]

The reality is that despite this criticism, arbitration is still the most preferred dispute resolution mechanism and for national courts taking a significant share of business disputes seems to be yet a remote perspective. Notwithstanding the above-mentioned tension between supporting their own court systems and promoting alternative methods of dispute resolution, states continue to demonstrate strong support for international commercial arbitration. We will discuss below whether arbitration is in fact the most appropriate method of dispute resolution for matters involving state parties.

Despite the strong desire and impressive efforts, these various jurisdictions, arbitration centres and commercial courts have different challenges to overcome, and whether they will eventually succeed is the subject of a different discussion. The important thing for our analyses is to have identified certain trends in international commercial arbitration and to have asked the right questions from the perspective of the state as policymaker.

III   THE STATE AS USER OF ARBITRATION: ARBITRATION UNDER
         STATE CONTRACTS

It has been several decades already that we are witnessing an increased interaction between the public and private sectors. Governments and state entities have been increasingly relying on private actors to administer a wide variety of public functions. Thus, in the modern-day world, it is quite common to outsource the performance of public services and privatise certain industries that were in the hands of state entities or government-controlled monopolies in the past. These types of industries can involve, for instance, utilities, public infrastructure, transportation, education, health-care, natural resources etc. Hence, these contracts could entail the provision of essential public services or the implementation of important state policies in social, economic, industrial or other sectors. These developments naturally have led to the increase of state contracts with private entities.

Privatisation or outsourcing does not, however, release the government of its ultimate functions and responsibilities. State entities continue to play an important role as active participants in this private-public collaboration. Public bodies remain responsible and accountable to the public for the fulfilment of public functions or policies for the purposes for which they entered into contractual relationships. Thus, they are the ones who carry the primary duty to procure relevant services and infrastructure for the population and to ensure their proper functioning. Some state contracts require continued government administration and supervision as well; for instance, in the utilities business responsible state entities would continuously engage to ensure safety and quality standards as well as the administration of its tariff-fixing and pricing policies.[39]

---

38. *See* T. Jones, 'Bermann on Commercial Arbitration'.
39. *See* Nigel Blackaby, 'Utilities, Government Regulations and Energy Investment Arbitrations', J. William Rowley QC, Doak Bishop and Gordon Kaiser, eds, 'The Guide to Energy Arbitrations',

The development of public-private partnerships, the delegation of government functions and the privatisation of industries, on the one hand, and the fact that arbitration is the most preferred method of dispute settlement for foreign businesses and investors, on the other hand, have led to the increased use of arbitration in public-private contractual relationships. The use of arbitration is also prevalent in state contracts. Many standard contract forms already contain arbitration as a dispute settlement method. For instance, the FIDIC suite of contracts provides for a multi-tiered dispute settlement clause that ends in ICC arbitration.

We have analysed the recent trends of state support for international arbitration. In some countries, the use of arbitration in state contracts has been established as a policy requirement. With the aim to attract private investment in infrastructure development projects, Brazil has officially authorised the use of international arbitration in public contracts in the port, road, rail, waterway and airport sectors. On 20 September 2019, the President of Brazil issued Decree No. 10.025 authorising the settlement of disputes by means of arbitration between the state or federal public entities and concessionaires and other private contractors in the above-mentioned sectors.[40] In 2017, a new Egyptian Investment Law provided for a whole new institutional setup to deal with investment-related disputes. The Egyptian Mediation and Arbitration Centre that is yet to be established is supposed to examine disputes between investors or investors and state or state's public or private entities.[41] Thus, disputes under state contracts related to investment will be resolved within the Centre through mediation or arbitration procedure.

The increased use of arbitration in state contracts has led to an increase in commercial arbitration disputes involving states and state entities. It is our observation that in practice the matters arising out of such contracts are usually considered as any other commercial arbitration case between two private entities. The specificities of arbitration involving state entities have not been given much attention and the distinction between this type of case and the ones involving two private actors has not been considered important in practice. In this part of the chapter, we will try to identify a few distinctive features of commercial arbitration matters involving states and analyse the challenges associated with the examination of this type of case in commercial arbitration proceedings.

1   Nature of State Contracts

We would like to argue that the nature of state contracts is different from ordinary business-to-business transactions. We have identified several important features of

3rd ed., January 2019, found at https://globalarbitrationreview.com/chapter/1178839/utilities-government-regulations-and-energy-investment-arbitrations (last visited 13 February 2020).

40. Orlando Kabrera, 'Brazil Allows Arbitration in Public Contracts in the Port, Road, Rail, Waterway and Airport Sectors', Kluwer Arbitration Blog, 12 October 2019, found at http://arbitrationblog.kluwerarbitration.com/2019/10/12/brazil-allows-arbitration-in-public-contracts-in-the-port-road-rail-waterway-and-airport-sectors/ (last visited 12 February 2020).

41. M. Ostrov, B. Sanderson and A.L. Veroneli, 'Developments in African Arbitration'.

state contracts that in our view differentiate them from ordinary commercial agreements and therefore, might warrant different considerations and legal analyses in arbitration. This includes the subject matter of the contract, the legal capacity and status of state parties and the implications of the breach of contract.

a Subject Matter of State Contracts: Public Interest Element

The subject matter of a state contract is different from that of an ordinary commercial agreement. The public interest element of the transaction or a project makes it distinct both from commercial and legal point of view.

State interests differ from the interests of an ordinary commercial party; besides purely commercial and monetary considerations, there can be many other important interests and stakes attached to the underlying public-private transition, which from the state's perspective can even supersede commercial aspects of the deal. In many cases, these transactions are never confined to one particular contract or one particular commercial relation; normally, such state contracts are part of a wider governmental policy or project. For example, a contract for the construction of a section of a highway could be yet another commercial deal for the contractor, under which it expects to generate certain profit, while for the state entity, this could be one section of a highway that itself is part of a bigger infrastructure project, the completion and operation of which could be directly connected to the realisation of other projects in different sectors and the long-term economic goals of the country. The delay or failure to deliver performance under one such contract could be a reason for the delay of many other projects that depend on it and the loss of opportunities for the state attached thereto.

From the commercial perspective, the goals and expectations of the parties to a public-private contract can be dramatically different. If the private contractor, free from any accountability towards the public, is essentially concerned with maximising its profit at a minimum cost, the state entity's goal is to ensure the existence and public access to vital social services and infrastructure and to ensure reasonable spending and long-term preservation of public resources. For instance, state contracts could provide access to such essential social utilities as heating, electricity, water and sewage, etc. as well as social infrastructure and other important services. A State party shall also ensure that in the process of performance of contractual obligations under state contracts other important public policies such as protection of public health and safety, human rights, the environment, sustainable development, etc., are also fulfilled. This does not mean that the state is not interested in the commercial or monetary side of the project, but what we argue is that the state may also have many other interests that are completely non-commercial, and sometimes such interests might be more crucial than the financial side of the deal. For example, in cases where the concessionaire under a concession agreement related to the mining of natural resources violates environmental regulations, the protection of human life and health and environment could become for the state an interest of much higher importance than the royalties, taxes and duties collected or the wealth and investment generated from the project. Other such non-commercial interests might be important drivers behind the decisions of state entities and are therefore important to consider when determining the will of the parties under the contract or when investigating the facts of the case in the arbitration.

Now let us look at the legal side of state contracts. Although governed by private law norms, contracts concluded with state entities cannot be considered in isolation from public administrative law. These are the set of public law norms that regulate the status and functions of the state entity and the industry covered by the contract. Under Georgian law, this type of state contract would be categorised as a 'contract under public law'[42] because of its public-law nature. Such contracts, although governed by the Civil Code of Georgia, shall in addition to the principles of civil law be interpreted in accordance with the fundamental principles of public law. These fundamental principles include the rule of law and the protection of the public interest, legality, equality before law, and proportionality between public and private interests.[43] Since state contracts operate in the realm of public law and the authority derived therefrom, they cannot run counter to fundamental principles of public law and public order. Therefore, when dealing with such contracts, competing private and public interests should be analysed not only under private law norms governing the contract but also against applicable public law norms; Such analyses shall ensure that the right balance is found between the interest of the public in receiving services or performance covered by the contract and the interest of the private party in making a profit.

In view of the above, although, arbitration disputes between public and private entities arise out of contractual relationships in the same way as commercial arbitration between private parties does, what differentiates the former from the latter is the public interest element and related implications. It is this important distinction that makes it crucial to differentiate commercial arbitration disputes involving states from purely private commercial arbitration matters.

b   *State and State Entities as Parties*

The state or state entity is not an ordinary private litigant – the State is not a commercial entity. It is 'a sovereign authority with a special character and responsibilities'.[44] The State has multiple overlapping or parallel roles and interests that can affect the decisions it makes.[45] Although in contractual relationships the state acts under private law in its private capacity, it also retains its status and public responsibilities under the governing public law. It is important for the adjudicator in disputes involving such entities to have a good understanding of the peculiar nature of state parties and their legal status and capacity.

---

42. Article 2(1)(g) of the General Administrative Code of Georgia (GACG) defines a contract under public law as 'a civil law contract concluded by an administrative body with a natural or legal person or another administrative body for the purposes of exercising public authority'. General Administrative Code of Georgia, Article 2(1)(g), No 21821-IIs, 25 June 1996.
43. These principles are laid out in General Administrative Code of Georgia. *See* General Administrative Code of Georgia, Articles 1, 4, 5, 7.
44. Jeremy K. Sharpe, 'The Agent's Indispensable Role in International Investment Arbitration', (ICSID Review 2018), Oxford University Press, p. 2.
45. *Ibid.*

The state can enter into contractual relationships in its own name or through its entities and instrumentalities. State entities may have distinct legal personality, which means that they may independently enter into contractual relationships and may sue or be sued in their own name.[46] Who shall be a party to a particular state contract is an issue of careful consideration for the state when entering into a contractual relationship – sometimes it is the state itself or its organs or entities with distinct legal personality. The issue of authority of the relevant state entity is equally important – is the entity vested with the power to bind the state to the contractual terms or does it act in its own capacity? Have the relevant requirements and procedures to obtain the authority been complied with? Does the entity at issue have legal and administrative capacity to comply with the contractual obligations? Etc.

It happens quite often in practice that a private party would initiate arbitration proceedings against a wrong state party or a long list of state instrumentalities whether they are named parties to the contract or not, for the tactical reasons of publicity or in order to put some pressure or procedural burden on the state. For example, in Georgia's experience, there have been cases where a contract was entered into by a state agency with a distinct legal personality, but the claimant decided to sue the state and its organs even though their involvement in the contract was either none or was limited to endorsing the conclusion of the contract upon the request of the private party in the first place. Such publicity could be a huge reputational problem for the state that cares about the image of its business and legal environment; representing several entities in arbitration, even until the issue of the proper party is resolved, could be related to a significant waste of time and human and financial resources for the state that could be directed to a more meaningful public activity.

Public law norms i.e. the personal law of the state entity will play an important role in determining its authority to enter into contractual relationships on terms provided therein and thus, the legality of the contract. It might be that the state agency or official signing the contract was not authorised to make certain commitments – for instance, to agree to a certain type of stabilisation clause or waive certain rights on behalf of the state. The public law norms governing this entity and its activities as well as the norms regulating public function or interest underlying the contract will be decisive in determining the legality of and enforceability of contractual norms. The above analysis would also be important in determining the proper party to the contract, the possibility of extending arbitration clause to non-signatory state parties[47] and thus, the jurisdiction of the arbitral tribunal *ratione personae*.

In view of the above, it is absolutely indispensable that arbitrators have a good understanding of the nature of the state party and its instrumentalities and that they conduct proper legal analyses under the personal law of these entities regarding their

---

46. Veijo Heiskanen, 'State as a Private: the Participation of States in International Commercial Arbitrating' (Transnational Dispute management 2010), p. 3.
47. The issues of the proper state party to the contract and the extension of the arbitration clause to state parties have been raised in courts at the enforcement stage with regard to several arbitration awards and some of which resulted in the refusal to enforce. *See* V. Heiskanen, 'State as a Private', pp. 6-8.

legal status, capacity and the authority with respect to a given contractual relationships.

c   *Implication of the Breach and the Issue of Damages*

Important considerations would arise also in the context of the consequences of the breach of state contract and the related issue of damages. In arbitrations involving state entities, the damages incurred by the state in case of non-performance by a private party might be much greater or different in nature than damages normally incurred by a private party to the contract. Apart from purely monetary damages or lost profit, the failure to perform under a state contract can have serious public interest implications and jeopardise long-term state policies and objectives. The state's claims or counterclaims could provide a basis for different types of damages in arbitration. As an example, in the case of a failed infrastructure project it is not only an unearned advance payment, delay damages or damages for the correction of defect that a state could suffer, but this could lead to other types of damages such as loss of use of infrastructure and loss of opportunities to accomplish state policies or other important public projects that were directly dependent upon or attached to the completion of this very project. In addition, some projects might also involve far-reaching implications related to the series of social, political and reputational problems caused by the failure of the responsible state entity to deliver the relevant infrastructure or public service. In the author's experience arbitrators are not willing to recognise the broader picture and seriously consider such other possible damages suffered by state parties.

d   *Procedural Issues in Arbitrations Arising from State Contracts*

The participation of state entities in arbitration proceedings raises some procedural issues as well that we need to mention here to make our discussion complete. These issues include some very practical as well as material procedural matters. It is not surprising that a state or state entity operating under a big bureaucratic mechanism might require more time to coordinate internally for the purposes of ongoing arbitration matters. This could include the collection of relevant documents and information, the identification of witnesses, retaining outside counsel, allocating state funds for representation in arbitration, obtaining mandate and/or instructions with respect to the strategy of the representation on a particular case, etc.[48] This is especially true for expedited procedures such as emergency arbitration, where tight time limits and concise procedures could make it very strenuous for states to ensure proper representation on their matters. Material procedural issues might involve such matters as the protection of privileged information, transparency and publicity issues, provisional measures in terms of possible interference in the conduct of sovereign state activities (such as collection of taxes or state policy and regulation, issuance of licences and permits or retendering of project), etc.

---

48. *Ibid.*, pp. 9-10.

This does not mean that the state should be granted special treatment or procedural privileges in the course of arbitration, however, arbitrators should be cognisant of these nuances of the operation of state machinery in order to adequately and fairly deal with the procedural issue on the matter and ensure basic due process and fair trial requirements for both parties.

2 Challenges of Arbitrating Matters Involving State Entities

In our view proper analyses are required as to what distinguishes arbitrations with state entities from private disputes, how the public interest element affects the factual and legal analysis of the case and whether such disputes require a different approach. We have tried to identify certain aspects of the current system of international commercial arbitration that could be indicative of inadequacy of the system in dealing with matters involving state entities.

a Lack of Distinction Between Private-to-Private Arbitrations and Those Involving State Entities

In the majority of commercial arbitration cases, arbitral institutions and arbitrators seem to fail to differentiate commercial arbitration disputes involving public entities and tend to treat them as any other commercial arbitration matter between private parties. In an interesting study, professors at Queen Mary University have explained this attitude with respect to arbitrations under English law by the fact that due to 'the historical development of arbitration as an exclusive private mode of dispute resolution, the current legal framework of arbitration in England has developed around the private law paradigm of a commercial dispute involving private actors'.[49] A thorough analysis would be required to determine the reasons why arbitration involving state entities developed the way it did. This could be the private nature of international commercial arbitration or some historical developments, an issue of qualification of arbitrators or the ignorance of arbitrators and arbitral institutions or all of the above.

Arbitrations involving state entities are mostly not distinguished from ordinary commercial arbitration between private parties neither under domestic laws nor by arbitration rules or arbitral institutions. Some institutions have recently started to think about the special nature of such arbitrations and have even attempted to revise their arbitration rules and procedures according to the specificities of such arbitrations. However, such reforms mostly cover some purely procedural and technical matters to streamline the process rather than substantively deal with the matter, especially by giving due consideration to the public interest element involved. For example, the 2012 ICC revised Arbitration Rules, which have specifically claimed to take account of the needs of matters involving state entities, do not seem to substantively address the core

---

49. *See* S. Brekoulakis and M. Devaney, 'Public-Private Arbitration', p. 3.

difference of such matters.[50] The amendments to the Rules do not go beyond some procedural matters. For instance, the Rules do not deal with such important issues as qualification of arbitrators, confidentiality and protection of privileged information, applicable law, etc. The 2017 revisions to the ICC Rules do not address any matter relevant to arbitrations involving states or state entities whatsoever,[51] while the 2021 revisions introduce special provisions with regard to arbitrations arising from treaties only with respect to the nationality of arbitrators and the exclusion of emergency arbitration for such matters.[52]

The Singapore International Arbitration Centre (SIAC) has introduced a whole set of rules for investment arbitration matters that can be applied in all arbitrations including those arising out of investment contracts. While the Rules, inspired by the UNCITRAL and ICSID Arbitration Rules, seem to have considered many nuances of arbitration involving state entities such as the issue of state immunities, third-party funding, early dismissal procedures, third-party submissions, etc., they also seem to have neglected some public interest implications. For instance, the Rules are silent with respect to the qualifications of the arbitrator; although the Rules oblige the Court to seek the parties' views on the qualifications of the arbitrators when making default appointments,[53] the Rules themselves do not provide any qualification requirements, let alone prescribe credentials required for matters involving state entities specifically.[54]

Neither of the two sets of Rules discussed above accounts for the particular needs of states in allowing some flexibility in procedure and time limits given their bureaucratic nature of governance, the strict division of functions and responsibilities, the formalities related to procuring relevant services and the allocation of funds for representation in arbitration, etc. As an example, from the Author's experience, the well-known international arbitral institutions would refuse to give more than a standard extension of time to state parties to file an answer to the request for arbitration and would not consider the state procurement procedure for retaining external counsel and the formalities to allocate funds from state budget for state representation as good enough reasons for a longer extension; this is especially difficult when any such

---

50. See 'States, State Entities and ICC Arbitration', ICC Commission Report (ICC 2010), found at https://iccwbo.org/content/uploads/sites/3/2016/10/ICC-Arbitration-Commission-Report-on-Arbitration-Involving-States and State-Entities pdf (last visited 20 February 2020).

51. The 2017 revisions to the ICC Arbitration Rules address the following issues: communication of reasons with respect to the decisions regarding the formation of the arbitral tribunal, time limit for finalising Terms of Reference, jurisdictional objections, schedule of fees. See, Steven P. Finizio, Wen-Chuan Dai, Daria Sakhno and Michael Lee, '2017 Revisions to the ICC Rules of Arbitration and Comparison of Expedited Procedures under Other Institutional Rules', International Arbitration Alert, WilmerHale, 28 February 2017, found at 2017 Revisions to the ICC Rules of Arbitration and Comparison of Expedited Procedures Under Other Institutional Rules | WilmerHale (last visited 15 June 2022).

52. See ICC Arbitration Rules 2017 & 2021 – Compared Version, ICC International Court of Arbitration, found at https://iccwbo.org/content/uploads/sites/3/2020/12/icc-2021-2017-arbit ration-rules-compared-version.pdf (last visited 15 June 2022).

53. Investment Arbitration Rules of the Singapore International Arbitration Centre, Article 8(a), 1st ed. (1 January 2017).

54. Ibid., Article 10.

extension would be conditional upon state's nomination of its party-appointed arbitrator – a decision that could determine the fate of the entire arbitration process and the outcome thereof, which in this case the state would have to make without having the possibility to consult its counsel.

b   Qualification and Capacity of Decision-Makers

Although arbitration allows parties to appoint decision-makers who may possess special expertise in the matters governed by the contract, these private decision-makers may not always understand the peculiarities of state contracts and public governance. We tried to demonstrate that state contracts are not ordinary business-to-business agreements for various reasons discussed above.

During the discussion on the issue of decision-makers in UNCITRAL Working Group III on the reform of Investor-State Dispute Settlement (ISDS), the delegates ascribed special importance to the qualifications of arbitrators required to deal specifically with investor-state disputes. The delegates have agreed that arbitrators 'should have an understanding of the different policies underlying investment, of issues of sustainable development, of how to handle ISDS cases and of how governments operated'.[55] Likewise, the Guide on Investment Mediation adopted by the Energy Charter Conference requires that mediators have 'government experience or experience in dealing with governments'.[56] We argue that the same approach is required in commercial arbitration cases involving state entities.

The realities in which the state or state entities operate are totally different from the ones in which commercial parties function. Understanding legal systems, regional specificities, cultural characteristics and methods of doing business, as well as social, political, economic or other policies of the country, would be of great significance for the adjudication of the matter since these are the realities that underlie the contractual relationships at hand and determine parties' behaviour. It is highly questionable whether arbitrators always understand these peculiarities of dealing with cases involving state entities or consider it important to conduct relevant analysis on a particular case, with respect to a particular state. Arbitrators dealing with disputes involving state entities should be qualified in public administrative law matters or at least have experience in dealing with matters involving states and state entities and have a good understanding of public governance; familiarity with the realities of a particular country or region could definitely be an asset.

c   Limited Scope and Mandate of Decision-Makers

The jurisdiction of an arbitral tribunal is limited to the scope of an arbitration agreement in a contract as well as arbitrability under applicable statutory norms.

---

55. 'Report of Working Group III (Investor-State Dispute Settlement Reform) on the Work of its Resumed Thirty-eighth Session' (Vienna, 20-24 January 2020) UNCITRAL, 38th Sess., UN Doc. A/CN.9/1004/Add. 1 (28 January 2020), p. 16, ¶97.
56. Guide on Investment Mediation, ECT, CCDEC 2016 12 INV, 19 July 2016, Brussels, p. 13.

Commercial or investment contracts would very rarely cover legitimate measures that a state would take for the purposes of public interest in times of political, economic, security or other changes; likewise, contracts would rarely extend to measures that a state takes against the regulatory violations by the contractor, related, for instance, to environmental protection, labour, human rights, safety or other standards. These measures that allegedly interfere with the contractual relationships could constitute a legitimate basis for the defence or counterclaim of a state entity in arbitration. Although arbitrators in commercial arbitration might be able to consider these matters by relying on general principles of law, they may be constrained by the limits of the scope of the arbitration clause or the arbitrability that determines its jurisdiction on the matter.[57]

Even the broadest arbitration clauses might not go beyond the disputes related to or arising out of the contract at hand. The restricted subject-matter jurisdiction might not allow the tribunal to go beyond the contractual framework and examine other related public policy interests of the state that were the reason for the conclusion of the contract and later dictated the performance of the state. Even if the contract allowed going beyond contractual terms by extending the jurisdiction of the arbitral tribunal to matters of violation of law or through applying general principles of law, arbitrators might be reluctant to do so out of fear of not exceeding their mandate. In addition in some jurisdictions matters pertaining to public governance or concerning public policy in general might not be arbitrable.[58]

IV   THE STATE'S ROLE IN REDUCING THE RISKS AND IN BETTER MANAGING DISPUTES

It would not be entirely fair to put all the burden on the system and the adjudicators; States and state entities involved in arbitration cases could do so much to limit or mitigate all the downsides of the process they complain about by preventing or better managing the process of arbitration.

The measures that states could take to reduce the number of disputes can vary at different stages of their involvement with private contractors. They include:

- introducing proper procedure for the selection of a contractor/investor for a particular project, whether through tender or direct negotiations, to guarantee that a contractor has the relevant experience and resources to implement the project;
- making sure that their contracts, including dispute settlement provisions, are properly drafted, including with respect to risk allocation and necessary guarantees;
- designating the responsible state agency that will ensure effective communication and coordination of processes internally after the dispute arises; the

---

57. *See* N. Blackaby, 'Energy Investment Arbitrations'.
58. For instance, in France, parties may not enter in an arbitration agreement regarding 'disputes relating to public bodies and institutions, and, more generally, in all matters in which public policy is concerned'. Article 2060, Civil Code of France, as amended in 2016.

agent's role is also crucial in accumulating experience on all such matters for the prevention of disputes in the future and for policy consideration of the government.[59]
- engaging external assistance (counsel, expert, etc.) from early on in the process;
- considering the possibility of amicable settlement of the dispute with the aim of: (1) maintaining business and investment relationships and corresponding economic benefits and opportunities in the country, and/or (2) reducing significant costs of the proceedings and avoiding a worse outcome of the case.
- learning important lessons from its own experience, as well as from that of other states involved in arbitration matters, to educate its organs and agencies accordingly, in order to prevent disputes in the future.

In our times many states hand over their disputes entirely to external counsel and maintain very limited or no involvement or control in the process themselves. It is true that for many states arbitrating disputes under state contracts might still be a novelty, and the arbitration procedure is highly specialised and requires relevant expertise and resources to represent party in dispute; it is also true that such disputes might often involve high financial, social or political stakes. Obviously, it is not suggested that states should completely forgo using external assistance and expertise to ensure proper representation on arbitration matters. However, the support and cooperation of the relevant state officials or state agency can play a crucial role in better managing the process and in achieving a better outcome for the case. Thus, the designated state agency could provide tremendous support in coordinating internally with relevant government authorities, working with witnesses, providing domestic law advice, and explaining to counsel the realities, the culture, and the mode of operation in the country that can be so significant for both the procedural and substantive aspects of the matter. External counsel may not be able to easily grasp how state bureaucracy works or understand the culture, customs, human characters and other specificities of the country. Such support is important not only for strategic management of the matter but also for the smooth organisation of the works that can be such a huge cost and time saver in the process of arbitration.

Settlement of disputes could be another very wise way for a state to save itself huge expenses and reputational costs, and to retain business and economic opportunities within the country. Sometimes disputes between state agency and its commercial or investment partners may paradoxically arise in situations when both parties are serious and determined to execute their contractual commitments. Sometimes the reasons for the parties' failure under the contract can be some major misunderstandings, thoughtless or uncoordinated conduct, lack of experience in the specific industry, mismanagement of investment, failure to properly assess risks or do due diligence, etc. Therefore, the possibility of meeting and discussing things could be a good opportunity

---

59. On the state agent's indispensable role for the purposes of arbitrations involving states, please see J. Sharpe, 'The Agent's Indispensable Role'.

for the parties to clarify some misunderstandings, better understand underlying goals and policies on both sides, better allocate risks and responsibilities, etc.

It is not necessary that settlement only contemplates a monetary payment in exchange for the withdrawal of the matter, but this could be a good opportunity to find some creative solutions that can help parties to preserve their contractual relationships, i.e., to find ways to modify and eventually execute their contractual commitments. Even if the contractual relationships are to end, parties could still manage to find some creative and mutually satisfactory way of exit.

Georgia has been open to the possibility of settling cases. In its experience, there have been matters that could only result in a monetary settlement, but there were other cases where some creative solutions could be found, such as restructuring of the deal, renegotiation of the contract, relocation of the project or substitution of the investor or the contractor, return of privatised state property that was later retendered for something that turned out to be a successful project, etc.

V   CONCLUSIONS

As demonstrated above, commercial arbitration has gained much traction in recent years, with the overwhelming policy support of governments all around the world. Motivation behind such a strong interest of states towards international arbitration could, in fact, be very positive and sincere. Some countries are trying to attract foreign business and investment opportunities, to remain competitive payers in regional and international trade markets. Many others are competing for a share of the international dispute settlement market, being mesmerised by the potential reputational fame as well as financial benefits attached thereto. However, the level and intensity of activities around the world are so frenetic and unnaturally high that it creates some legitimate questions as to the true nature and possible implications of this tendency.

Looking at all these developments, including the mushrooming of new dispute settlement centres and institutions, a series of interesting questions arise: What is the ultimate idea behind these changes and where is this all heading? Is there a true demand for so many arbitration centres, institutions and courts? And what does this mean for the future of international arbitration? This aggressive process will need to chill down at some point and these questions would need to be addressed sooner or later. This increased interest and paranoia of arbitration-friendliness on the one hand, and increased criticism and call for reforms, on the other hand, might suggest that the system of international arbitration is on the verge of a serious restructuring process which, we could only hope, will result in a positive outcome for the future of commercial arbitration.

One positive side of these developments, however, is the fact that the awareness and expertise with respect to international commercial arbitration, including on the governmental policy level, is increasing around the world. This intense competition between arbitral institutions, jurisdictions and national courts could be an important driver to contribute to further sophistication of the system and more consistency in the procedure and practice of international arbitration and commercial litigation.

On the user side, involvement of states and state entities in international arbitration as parties raises a variety of specific issues, both procedural and conceptual. The public interest element and nature of state parties make state contracts a unique type of agreement that requires a special approach and different legal and factual analyses. Unfortunately, this distinction is not properly recognised or accounted for in commercial arbitration practice. The lack of specialised approach, qualification or competence of arbitral institutions and arbitrators in dealing with matters involving state entities may lead to incomplete examination of matters and imbalance in addressing competing public and private interests. This could in turn seriously jeopardise public interests underlying the public-private contractual relationships at hand. However, we believe that the concerted efforts of all the actors in the system can effectively deal with the challenges identified above. The role of arbitral institutions as well as the states and state entities would be decisive. Arbitral institutions could put in place procedures or soft law instruments to ensure that the arbitration procedures adequately address the peculiarities of the matters involving public interest and state entities and that decision-makers possess relevant qualifications and are prepared to conduct necessary legal and factual analyses. States and state entities could significantly contribute to the successful examination of disputes involving public interest by properly drafting their arbitration clauses as well as selecting arbitrators with relevant qualifications. They could further assist their counsel in understanding public interest and public policy matters as well as in determining important factual circumstances so that counsel adequately present their case to the arbitrators.

Our primary goal was to identify major trends and development in international commercial arbitration from the perspective of the state as a policymaker and as a user of the system. We also tried to identify some problems and pose the right questions. It is not our ambition to answer all the questions or find all the solutions, it simply would not be possible; however, we hope that this chapter could be useful food for thought and a modest contribution to future discussions.

CHAPTER 51

Protecting Party Consent: The Role of the UK Courts in International Arbitration

Lord Hodge[*]

TABLE OF CONTENTS

I   INTRODUCTION

Sitting in the House of Lords in 1856, Lord Campbell observed that English judges had traditionally 'had great jealousy of arbitrations'.[1] In his 2019 Roebuck Lecture, Professor Stavros Brekoulakis preferred to characterise the historical relationship as one of 'cautious trust'.[2] Whatever the truth of the matter, in more recent history before the enactment of the Arbitration Act 1996, the English courts have certainly drawn international criticism for intervening 'more than they should in the arbitral process'.[3]

---

[*] Lord Hodge is the Deputy President of The Supreme Court of the United Kingdom. He acknowledges with thanks the assistance which he received from his former Judicial Assistants, Francesca Ruddy and Thomas Watret, in the preparation of this chapter.
1. *Scott v. Avery and others* [1843-60] All ER Rep 1 at p. 7.
2. Stavros Brekoulakis, 'The 2019 Roebuck Lecture: 14 June 2019: The Unwavering Policy Favouring Arbitration under English Law', Arbitration, Vol. 86(1) (2020) p. 97 at p. 101.
3. Departmental Advisory Committee on Arbitration Law, '1996 Report on the Arbitration Bill', Arbitration International, Vol. 13(3) (1997) p. 275 at p. 280.

To the casual observer, it might seem that such intrusion upon the realm of arbitrators is continuing, with the UK Supreme Court having decided five substantial arbitration-related appeals, and the Judicial Committee of the Privy Council another three, the beginning of the 2019 legal year and each has another judgment in the pipeline. However, in my view, this belies the true attitude of the UK courts towards their relationship with arbitration.

Much has changed in the world of arbitration since the periods described by Lord Campbell and Professor Brekoulakis. Most obviously, the number and range of cases now arbitrated far exceeds what was ever contemplated in the past. Arbitration is no longer administered by 'a small and select group' upholding 'a code of unwritten rules shaped by common values'.[4] Rather, the modern arbitration community is global, with arbitrators, institutions and arbitration users from a wide range of legal cultures resolving disputes according to a complex mixture of contractual terms, institutional rules, national laws and non-binding guidance.

The growth of arbitration has increased the number of arbitration-related questions coming before national courts. Matters arising from arbitration make up a significant proportion of the claims issued in the Commercial Court: around 25% in 2020-2021.[5] Yet, the proportion of UK-seated arbitrations involving any recourse to the courts remains low.[6] How, then, does the modern arbitration user conceive of the role of the UK courts in international arbitration? And do the UK courts share this view?

In this chapter, I examine the contention that the UK courts have come to support rather than supervise the arbitral process. Through an analysis of the legislative framework in England[7] and Scotland and recent trends in the case law of these jurisdictions, I consider the readiness of UK courts to take up the invitation to intervene in arbitral proceedings. Drawing out the principles which emerge from the case law, I offer some reflections for the future.

II THE STATUTORY FOUNDATIONS OF THE MODERN RELATIONSHIP BETWEEN UK COURTS AND INTERNATIONAL ARBITRATION

1 England, Wales and Northern Ireland

In 1985, the United Nations Commission on International Trade Law (UNCITRAL) published its Model Law on International Commercial Arbitration ('Model Law'),[8]

---

4. Sundaresh Menon, 'Adjudicator, Advocate or Something in Between? Coming to Terms with the Role of the Party-Appointed Arbitrator', Arbitration, Vol. 83(2) (2017) p. 185 at p. 189.
5. Commercial Court Annual Report (2020-2021) (February 2022), para. 3.1, available at https://www.judiciary.uk/wp-content/uploads/2022/02/14.50_Commercial_Court_Annual_Report_20 20_21_WEB.pdf (last accessed 13/06/2022).
6. Kieron O'Callaghan and Jerome Finnis, 'Chapter 20: Support and Supervision by the Courts' in Julian D.M. Lew et al. (eds), *Arbitration in England, with chapters on Scotland and Ireland* (Kluwer Law International 2013), paras. 20-21.
7. References to England are to England, Wales and Northern Ireland unless otherwise stated.
8. 'UNCITRAL Model Law on International Commercial Arbitration' (1985) Official Records of the General Assembly, Fortieth Session, Supplement No. 17 (UN Doc. A/40/17), annex I.

which has now been adopted in various forms in at least eighty States.[9] As is apparent from the *travaux préparatoires*,[10] the Model Law was intended to reflect international consensus on key aspects of international arbitration practice and to assist States in modernising their laws on arbitral procedure. A key aim of the Model Law was to limit the scope for court intervention in the arbitral process, with Article 5 providing that: '[i]n matters governed by this law, no Court *shall* intervene except where so provided in this law' (emphasis added).

At the UNCITRAL drafting meetings in 1985, the UK delegation expressed some concern that the Model Law would not represent a complete code and that, as such, it was not clear which matters it would 'govern' for the purposes of Article 5.[11] Although many of the other delegates agreed with the UK's position, it was not clear that these concerns could be allayed by any drafting changes. Thus, despite the debate, Article 5 was adopted unamended.

In 1989, the UK Departmental Advisory Committee on Arbitration Law (DAC) considered whether to recommend the implementation of the Model Law in the UK. The Chairman of the DAC, Lord Mustill, had been part of the UK delegation to UNCITRAL during the Model Law drafting sessions and remained troubled by the lack of clarity as to the matters governed by the Model Law and, therefore, the extent of the exclusion of the court's powers under Article 5.[12] He also expressed concern that the homogenous legal regime for arbitration in England and Wales would be disrupted by the introduction of an incomplete code and that the operation of a dual system of arbitration rules would generate uncertainty, not least because of the ambiguity of Article 5.[13] Thus, his report on behalf of the DAC recommended against implementing the Model Law.[14]

In 1995, the DAC considered the position again. Whilst expressing support for the underlying principle that the English courts should 'only intervene in order to support rather than displace the arbitral process',[15] the DAC remained of the view that Article 5 was too broad and uncertain. Thus, in domesticating the principles of the Model Law in the Arbitration Act 1996 (the '1996 Act'), the mandatory language of Article 5 (i.e., no Court 'shall' intervene) was softened. Section 1(c) of the 1996 Act now provides that 'in matters governed by this Part the court *should not* intervene except as provided by this Part' (emphasis added).

---

9. *See*: https://uncitral.un.org/en/texts/arbitration/modellaw/commercial_arbitration/status (last accessed 14/06/2022).
10. *See*: https://uncitral.un.org/en/texts/arbitration/modellaw/commercial_arbitration/travaux (last accessed 14/06/2022).
11. https://uncitral.un.org/sites/uncitral.un.org/files/media-documents/uncitral/en/309meeting-e.pdf (last accessed 14/06/2020). Significantly, the UK delegation did not include any Scots lawyers (*see*: Professor Fraser Davidson, *Arbitration*, 2nd edn (Thomson Reuters 2012) at para. 1.06).
12. Lord Justice Mustill, 'A New Arbitration Act for the United Kingdom? The Response of the Departmental Advisory Committee to the UNCITRAL Model Law', Arbitration International Vol. 6(1) (1990) p. 3 at para. 13.
13. Lord Justice Mustill, 'A New Arbitration Act for the United Kingdom?', *supra* n. 12, p. 22.
14. Lord Justice Mustill, 'A New Arbitration Act for the United Kingdom?', *supra* n. 12, p. 29.
15. DAC, '1996 Report on the Arbitration Bill', *supra* n. 3, para. 22.

This difference in language was considered by the Commercial Court in *Vale Do Rio Doce Navegacao v. Shanghai Bao Steel Ocean Shipping Co.*[16] Noting the views expressed in the 1996 DAC report, Thomas J accepted that the replacement of 'shall' with 'should' indicated that Parliament had not intended 'an absolute prohibition' on intervention by the court in circumstances other than those specified in Part 1 of the 1996 Act. However, he added that it was 'clear that the general intention was that the Courts should usually not intervene outside [those] general circumstances'. The same general intention is evident from sections 1(a) and (b) of the 1996 Act, which note the importance of avoiding 'unnecessary delay or expense'[17] and of respecting the parties' freedom to agree how their disputes are resolved, 'subject only to such safeguards as are necessary in the public interest'.[18]

In furtherance of these general principles, the 1996 Act provides for a number of situations in which the court's powers may not be exercised unless all arbitral remedies have been exhausted. For instance, the court may not intervene to extend the time for commencement of an arbitration,[19] to require a party to comply with a peremptory order of the arbitral tribunal,[20] or to hear any challenge to an arbitral award[21] unless the applicant has exhausted any available arbitral processes. The 1996 Act also imposes time limits on parties for recourse to certain court powers[22] and requires the agreement of the parties, or else the permission of the tribunal, before others can be accessed.[23] In addition, parties are able to opt out of a number of default provisions which would otherwise give power to the courts. For instance, the parties may exclude the court's statutory power to enforce the tribunal's peremptory orders,[24] to support the taking or preservation of evidence, or to grant interim relief.[25] It is possible to exclude by agreement any right to appeal an arbitral award on a point of law.[26]

Certain powers are reserved to the court by section 81 of the 1996 Act (i.e., to determine matters which are not arbitrable, to determine the effect of oral arbitration agreements, and to refuse to recognise or enforce arbitral awards on public policy grounds). Beyond these limited powers, the court retains an inherent jurisdiction to stay proceedings brought in breach of an arbitration agreement and to grant injunctive and declaratory relief. Whilst the extent of these retained powers is a source of concern for some within the international arbitration community, the general trend of the 1996 Act is to maximise party autonomy and minimise the role of the English courts. As Lord Steyn acknowledged in *Lesotho Highlands v. Impregilo SpA*, the ethos of the 1996 Act

---

16. [2000] 2 All E.R. (Comm) 70.
17. 1996 Act, section 1(a).
18. 1996 Act, section 1(b).
19. 1996 Act, section 12(2).
20. 1996 Act, section 42(3).
21. 1996 Act, section 70(2).
22. For example, section 70(3), which imposes a twenty-eight-day limit on applications and appeals under sections 67-69.
23. For example, the determination of a preliminary point of jurisdiction under section 32 and non-urgent applications for supportive court orders under section 44.
24. 1996 Act, section 42(1).
25. 1996 Act, section 44(1).
26. 1996 Act, section 69(1).

was to effect a radical rebalancing of the relationship between arbitrators and the courts by conferring 'only those essential powers which ... the Court should have, that is rendering assistance when the arbitrators cannot act in the way of enforcement or procedural steps, or, alternatively, in the direction of correcting very fundamental errors'.[27]

2   Scotland

Many of the criticisms made of the English courts prior to the 1996 Act did not apply equally in Scotland, where arbitration was (and remains) governed by an entirely separate legal regime. Prior to the publication of the Model Law, there was remarkably little statutory control of arbitration in Scotland,[28] whereas arbitration in England had been the subject of successive enactments since 1698.[29] Some commentators have indicated that this distinctive approach derives from 'the civil law origins of Scots law',[30] although it is notable that most developed civilian systems deal with arbitration in their civil codes.[31] Whatever the reason, the practice and procedure of arbitration in Scotland were governed almost exclusively by case law and academic writing.[32]

    Whilst the absence of statutory controls might suggest a significant role for the Scottish judiciary in the management of arbitrations, in fact, the powers of the courts were strictly circumscribed by their own case law.[33] To the extent that the subject matter was arbitrable, Scottish judges were very ready to exercise their coercive powers in support of arbitration.[34] Nor was there great scope to challenge arbitral awards before the Scottish courts.[35] Until 1972, it was not possible to refer a point of law to the courts for determination. Even when such a power was introduced, it was capable of being excluded by agreement of the parties and, in any case, only subsisted during the arbitration and not after the award was rendered.[36] Thus the question of judicial overreach did not arise in the same way as it had in England. The principal difficulty with the Scottish approach – and it was a substantial difficulty – was that, depending as it did on case law from the nineteenth century and earlier, it was

---

27. [2005] UKHL 43 at para. 18, quoting Lord Wilberforce during the parliamentary debates on the Arbitration Bill (Hansard (HL Debates), 18 January 1996, col. 778).
28. Only three statutes directly regulated arbitration in Scotland: Article 25 of the Articles of Regulation 1695, section 3 of the Administration of Justice (Scotland) Act 1972 and the Arbitration (Scotland) Act 1894.
29. Stavros Brekoulakis, 'The 2019 Roebuck Lecture', *supra* n. 2, pp. 100-101.
30. Lord Justice Mustill, 'A New Arbitration Act for the United Kingdom?', *supra* n. 12, p. 8.
31. Professor Davidson, *Arbitration, supra* n. 11, para. 1.12.
32. Professor Davidson, *Arbitration, supra* n. 11, para. 1.05.
33. Lord Justice Mustill, 'A New Arbitration Act for the United Kingdom?', *supra* n. 12, para. 30.
34. *Sanderson & Son v. Armour & Co* 1922 SC (HL) 117, 126, per Lord Dunedin 'If the parties have contracted to arbitrate, to arbitration they must go'.
35. *See, e.g.,* the dicta of Lord Watson in *Caledonian Railway Co v. Turcan* (1898) 25 R (HL) 7, at p. 17.
36. Section 3 of the Administration of Justice (Scotland) Act 1972, described as a 'drafting mishap' by Hew Dundas and David Bartos, *Dundas & Bartos on the Arbitration (Scotland) Act 2010,* 2nd edn (Thomson Reuters 2010) p. 1.

relatively inaccessible (particularly to foreign users) and failed to address modern commercial realities.[37]

In Scotland, as in the rest of the UK, the publication of the Model Law provided a spur to modernise the relationship between the courts and arbitration. In 1990, Scotland adopted the Model Law, on the recommendation of the Scottish Advisory Committee on arbitration law, in relation to international commercial arbitration.[38] This was, in many ways, a step forward. However, it was not a comprehensive code; nor did it address serious lacunae in the Scots law of arbitration in domestic and non-commercial cases. There remained significant gaps and uncertainties in the legal landscape, with a lack of clarity about arbitrators' powers producing avoidable and expensive litigation.[39] It would also appear that Scotland's adoption of the Model Law had, at best, a neutral impact on its reputation as a seat for international commercial arbitration, with anecdotal evidence suggesting that only a 'tiny handful' of arbitrations took place under the Model Law in the twenty years during which it was in force.[40]

Following an unsuccessful attempt by the Scottish Council for International Arbitration and the Scottish Branch of the Chartered Institute of Arbitrators to modernise the law in 2002,[41] Scottish legislators eventually enacted the Arbitration (Scotland) Act 2010 (the '2010 Act'). The 2010 Act created a modern, comprehensive and accessible arbitration code for Scotland. It was largely modelled on the 1996 Act in England and is underpinned by the same principles of non-intervention and respect for party autonomy. For instance, the 2010 Act adopts the English approach of enabling parties to exclude the default statutory powers of the court to vary time limits,[42] to provide interim relief[43] and to hear appeals on points of law.[44] The 2010 Act also provides that certain court powers may only be exercised as a last resort, after the exhaustion of any arbitral remedies,[45] and imposes time limits for invoking the court's jurisdiction.[46] However, as in England, the court retains an inherent jurisdiction over the matters addressed in the 2010 Act, with section 1(c) providing that 'the court *should* not intervene in an arbitration except as provided by this Act' (emphasis added).

In fact, the 2010 Act goes further than its English equivalent in restricting the role of the courts in arbitration, providing only limited scope for appellate courts to consider

---

37. Hew R. Dundas, 'Chapter 27: Arbitration in Scotland' in Julian D.M. Lew et al., *Arbitration in England, supra* n. 6, para. 27-1.

38. Lord Dervaird, 'Scotland and the UNCITRAL Model Law: The Report to the Lord Advocate of the Scottish Advisory Committee on Arbitration Law', Arbitration International, Vol. 6(1) (1990), pp. 63-74. Law Reform (Miscellaneous Provisions) (Scotland) Act 1990, section 66.

39. For example, *McCrindle Group Ltd v. Maclay, Murray & Spens* [2013] CSOH 72.

40. Hew Dundas and David Bartos, *Dundas & Bartos on the Arbitration (Scotland) Act 2010, supra* n. 36, p. 3.

41. Lord Dervaird, John Campbell, Steven Walker and Hew Dundas, 'Arbitration in Scotland: A New Era Dawns', Arbitration, Vol. 70(2) (2004) p. 115.

42. Rule 43 of the Scottish Arbitration Rules contained in Schedule 1 to the 2010 Act.

43. Rule 46, Scottish Arbitration Rules.

44. Rule 69, Scottish Arbitration Rules.

45. For example, Rule 71(2), Scottish Arbitration Rules.

46. For example, Rule 71(4), Scottish Arbitration Rules.

arbitration-related questions. Decisions of the Outer House of the Court of Session on applications to challenge arbitral awards may only be appealed with the leave of the Outer House.[47] Where leave is refused, that is 'the end of it'.[48] Where leave is granted, the 2010 Act expressly precludes any subsequent appeal to the UK Supreme Court.[49] For all other matters referable to the Outer House, the 2010 Act provides that there is no right of appeal whatsoever.[50]

Scotland's restrictive approach to arbitration-related appeals has been hailed as an improvement upon the English regime, where appeals can often be lengthy and costly.[51] However, the same measures necessarily reduce the ability of appellate courts to scrutinise and clarify the law relating to arbitration in Scotland. Whilst the 2010 Act codified English jurisprudence on certain aspects of the 1996 Act which had generated uncertainty,[52] important questions as to the application of the 2010 Act are still liable to arise. The effect of restricting access to appeals is compounded by the relative paucity of first-instance cases which are likely to be brought in Scotland, given the relatively small size of the jurisdiction and its commercial centres. As such, it is welcome that the 2010 Act adopts the principles, approaches and terminology of the 1996 Act since this enables Scots lawyers to draw on English jurisprudence as persuasive authority.[53] Given the perennial popularity of London as a seat for international arbitration,[54] this is a considerable resource.

III   SUPPORTING THE MODERN ARBITRATION USER IN PRACTICE

Notwithstanding the statutory provisions in the 1996 Act and 2010 Act which limit the role of the UK courts in arbitration, it is important to recognise that 'at least in some

---

47. Rule 71(13). Under Rule 71(15), leave will only be granted where the Outer House considers that an appeal would raise an important point of principle or practice or that there is another compelling reason to hear the appeal. In England, there are similar restrictions on granting leave to appeal from the decision of a first-instance court on a point of law challenge, but not in respect of jurisdiction or serious irregularity challenges (*see* section 69(3) of the 1996 Act).
48. *Arbitration Application No.3 of 2011* [2011] CSOH 164, per Lord Glennie at para. 16. However, some commentators have suggested that the Inner House nonetheless retains a residual discretion to grant relief in cases of unfairness, reasoning by analogy with English authority to that effect (e.g., Professor Davidson, *Arbitration, supra* n. 11, para. 19.37).
49. Rules 67(7), 68(8), 70(12), 71(17), Scottish Arbitration Rules.
50. For example, Rule 42(4), discussed in Hew R. Dundas, 'Chapter 27: Arbitration in Scotland' in Julian D.M. Lew et al., *Arbitration in England, supra* n. 7, at paras 27-11, 27-12. This can be contrasted with the English position, which allows for appeals with the leave of the High Court (*see* section 45(6) of the 1996 Act).
51. Hew Dundas and David Bartos, *Dundas & Bartos on the Arbitration (Scotland) Act 2010, supra* n. 36, p. 5.
52. For example, Rule 46(4)D. *See*: Professor Davidson, *Arbitration, supra* n. 11, paras 27-92.
53. 'There is no point in re-inventing the (arbitration) wheel' *Arbitration Application No.3 of 2011, supra* n. 48, per Lord Glennie at para. 8. Accordingly, in the following analysis, English case law is treated as representing the likely position in Scots law unless otherwise stated.
54. In the 2021 International Arbitration Survey produced by White & Case LLP and the Queen Mary University of London School of International Arbitration (available at https://arbitration.qmul.ac.uk/media/arbitration/docs/LON0320037-QMUL-International-Arbitration-Survey-2021_19_WEB.pdf, last accessed 14/06/2022) London was identified by respondents as the 'most preferred' seat for arbitration (jointly with Singapore).

instances the intervention of the Court may not only be permissible but highly beneficial'.[55] Indeed, there are cases in which the intervention of national courts is not only desirable but necessary to give effect to the parties' agreement to arbitrate.

With the growth of international arbitration has come a proliferation of arbitral institutions and rules, more or less prescriptive of tribunal powers and procedures. The participation of arbitrators and arbitration users from an ever-widening range of legal cultures has also increased the scope for clashing expectations where the arbitration agreement or arbitral rules are silent.[56] Increasingly, national courts are being called upon to hold the ring between warring arbitration parties. This is borne out by the results of the 2021 International Arbitration Survey, in which respondents listed 'Greater support for arbitration by local courts and judiciary' (56%), 'Increased neutrality and impartiality of the local legal system' (54%), 'Better track record in enforcing agreements to arbitrate and arbitral awards' (47%), and 'Ability to enforce decisions of emergency arbitrators or interim measures ordered by arbitral tribunals' (39%) as the four adaptations which would make arbitral seats more attractive to users.[57] It appears that many in the arbitration world do not support a further retreat of the courts from the field of arbitration.

There are three phases of the arbitral process during which arbitration users seek the support and intervention of the courts; namely, at the outset, in the course of the arbitral proceedings and after the tribunal has delivered its award. In the following sections, I address these phases in turn, considering the nature of the interventions sought in recent cases and how the UK courts have responded to attempts to expand their role.

1   Policing the Threshold of Arbitration

At the 2016 ICCA Conference in Mauritius, George Bermann described how the role played by national courts at the threshold of arbitration is 'anything but standard across jurisdictions'.[58] Whereas there is some international convergence as to the proper role of the court at the recognition and enforcement stages, he opined that national courts are 'much less well-aligned' as to their role prior to the commencement of arbitration.[59]

In the UK, legislators have sought to balance respect for the legitimacy of the arbitral tribunal with the need for supportive court powers to ensure the effectiveness of arbitration. Thus, arbitral tribunals are generally granted the first opportunity to determine the enforceability of an arbitration agreement, with the parties having an

---

55. S.A. Coppée-Lavalin N.V. v. Ken-Ren Chemicals and Fertilisers Ltd (in liquidation) [1995] 1 AC 38 (HL), per Lord Mustill at pp. 60-61.
56. Sundaresh Menon, 'Adjudicator, Advocate or Something in Between?', supra n. 4, p. 190.
57. 2021 International Arbitration Survey, supra n. 54.
58. George Bermann, 'The Role of National Courts at the Threshold of Arbitration', in International Arbitration and the Rule of Law: Contribution and Conformity, ICCA Congress Series no. 19 (henceforth ICCA Congress Series no. 19) p. 456.
59. George Bermann, 'The Role of National Courts at the Threshold of Arbitration', supra n. 58, p. 443.

immediate but strictly time-limited right to invite the court to review the tribunal's assessment.[60] Whilst the standard of review to be adopted by the court has proved contentious[61] (with the English courts undertaking a *de novo* rather than a prima facie review of the tribunal's decision and the Scottish courts expected to take the same approach[62]), this model gives positive effect to the *Kompetenz-Kompetenz* principle and, at least in theory, reduces the scope for lengthy and expensive arbitral proceedings to be undermined by post-award jurisdiction challenges.

The enforceability of an arbitration agreement will turn on its particular terms. However, the UK courts have developed a strong reputation for being pro-arbitration when it comes to addressing this question. In part, this reputation derives from the principles which the courts have developed over time, such as the doctrine of separability[63] and the generous interpretation of the scope of arbitration agreements,[64] in order to refer the parties to arbitration wherever possible. The UK Supreme Court has delivered two important judgments in the last few years addressing those issues.

In *Enka Insaat Ve Sanayi AS v. OOO Insurance Co Chubb*,[65] the Supreme Court addressed the law governing the validity and scope of an arbitration agreement prior to the commencement of the arbitration. The parties had not chosen a governing law, and the law applicable to the contract containing the arbitration agreement, which in this case was Russian law, differed from the law of the seat of the arbitration, which was English law. The question of which law should govern the arbitration agreement in those circumstances had long been divisive, primarily because of the separability principle. As Mr Justice Baker had put it at first instance, '[t]he separability of an arbitration agreement makes it a natural candidate for at least the possibility that it might be governed by a system of law different to that which governs the contract generally'.[66]

A majority of the Supreme Court held that in the absence of choice, the arbitration agreement was governed by the law with which it was most closely connected. Where the parties had chosen a seat of arbitration, that would generally be the law of the seat, even if that differed from the law applicable to the contract containing the arbitration agreement. Notably, the majority also stated the purposive principle to 'validate if possible' has a role to play when looking for the parties' choice of law at the first stage of the analysis. A court should hesitate to apply a law potentially identified by the terms if it would impair the arbitration agreement. If a potentially applicable law would give narrow scope to the arbitration agreement, that might be a reason for applying another law instead.

---

60. Sections 32 and 73 (1996 Act) and Rule 21 (Scottish Arbitration Rules).
61. Gary Born, *International Commercial Arbitration*, 3rd edn (Kluwer Law International 2020) pp. 1174-1179.
62. Professor Davidson, *Arbitration*, *supra* n. 11, para. 8.19.
63. First recognised in *Heyman v. Darwins Ltd* [1942] A.C. 356.
64. *See, e.g.*, the approach adopted by the House of Lords in *Fiona Trust & Holding Corpn v. Privalov* [2007] UKHL 40.
65. [2020] UKSC 38.
66. [2019] EWHC 3568 (Comm), at [48].

In *Kabab-Ji v. Kout Food Group*,[67] the Supreme Court applied the principles in *Enka* at the enforcement stage of the arbitral process. One party was resisting enforcement of an award in England on the basis that it was not a party to the arbitration agreements. The Supreme Court held that the principles identified in *Enka* applied with equal force at the enforcement stage. The parties' choice of English law as the governing law of the agreement extended to the law governing the validity of the arbitration agreement. As a matter of English law, the defendant was not a party to the arbitration agreement and thus the arbitral award was not valid. The Supreme Court therefore refused recognition and enforcement of the award under section 103(2)(b) of the 1996 Act. The Supreme Court also confirmed that in appropriate cases the English courts could determine an application for recognition and enforcement by way of summary judgment.

In these judgments, the Supreme Court sought to bring clarity to the critical but long-contentious issue of the law governing arbitration agreements, both prior to commencement of arbitration proceedings and after the award is rendered. This clarity appears to have been welcomed by practitioners. In reaching our decisions, the Supreme Court had regard to the expectations of reasonable commercial parties and adopted approaches that would where possible uphold arbitration agreements. Both judgments recognise the principle identified by the House of Lords in *Fiona Trust & Holding Corpn v. Privalov*[68] that reasonable commercial parties are likely to have intended any dispute arising out of their relationship to be decided by the same tribunal and that commercial parties are generally unlikely to have intended a choice of governing law for the contract to apply to an arbitration agreement if there is at least a serious risk that a choice of that law would significantly undermine that agreement: the 'one-stop-shop' principle.

The same principle was applied in a different context in two recent decisions of the Commercial Court. In both *NWA v. FSY*[69] and *Sierra Leone v. SL Mining Ltd*,[70] the Commercial Court held that the failure of a party to comply with a term of an arbitration agreement, requiring the parties to attempt to mediate or to settle their dispute for a specified period before referring it to arbitration, went only to the admissibility of the claim and not the tribunal's jurisdiction. In both cases, the Commercial Court referred to the principle in *Fiona Trust* as relevant to interpreting the arbitration agreement. The commercial construction, consistent with the parties' intentions, was that all disputes arising from the relevant contracts were to be referred to arbitration. It was for the arbitration tribunal to determine the consequences of the alleged breach of the procedural pre-condition that the parties should first attempt to mediate or settle their dispute.

In addition to adopting a pro-arbitration approach to the interpretation of arbitration agreements, the English courts have demonstrated a willingness to use their

---

67. [2021] UKSC 48.
68. *See supra* n. 64.
69. [2021] EWHC 2666 (Comm).
70. [2021] EWHC 286 (Comm).

coercive powers to suspend and injunct litigation in order to keep parties to their commitments to refer disputes to arbitration. It is to those powers that I now turn.

a   Suspending Proceedings

Under section 9 of the 1996 Act and section 10 of the 2010 Act, on the application of any party to an enforceable arbitration agreement, the court must suspend any domestic proceedings brought in breach of that agreement, regardless of the seat specified for the arbitration.[71]

There has been a flurry of recent Scottish cases considering the application of section 10 of the 2010 Act. In *Heart of Midlothian Football Club PLC v. Scottish Professional Football League Ltd*,[72] the Outer House considered section 10(1)(d), which stipulates that the party applying for the sist (i.e., a stay) must not have waived its right to insist on arbitration by answering a substantive claim in the court proceedings. Referring to various English authorities on the equivalent provision in the 1996 Act,[73] Lord Clark held that if a party's responses to substantive claims in court proceedings are subject to the clear qualification that a sist for arbitration is requested, then that party has not taken a step which bars the request for arbitration. In *Peter Morton and others v. British Polar Engines Limited*,[74] the Outer House applied the approach set out by Lord Clark in *Heart of Midlothian*, refusing to sist the court proceedings on the basis that the defender had taken a substantive step in the court proceedings and therefore did not meet the requirements of section 10(1). And in *Fraserburgh Harbour Commissioners v. McLaughlin & Harvey Ltd*,[75] the Inner House took the opportunity to reiterate the established position that an arbitration agreement does not wholly oust the court's jurisdiction. The court may not entertain the merits of the dispute, but it may support the arbitration, for example by enforcing the parties' arbitration agreement. It also may be necessary for a party to commence court proceedings to prevent the operation of prescription, or to obtain interim measures to secure its claim such as diligence on the dependence. Should the arbitration fail for any reason, the court's jurisdiction revives. The Inner House also held that when court proceedings had been commenced in breach of an arbitration agreement, the court is required by section 10 to sist, rather than dismiss, the court proceedings.[76]

Whilst the application of the statutory rule requiring the suspension of domestic court proceedings is relatively straightforward, there will be scenarios falling outside

---

71. Section 9 of the 1996 Act and section 10 of the 2010 Act. In England, this suspension is referred to as a 'stay' of proceedings, whereas in Scotland the relevant term is 'sist'.
72. [2020] CSOH 68.
73. Namely *Patel v. Patel* [2000] QB 551, *Capital Trust Investments Ltd v. Radio Design TJ AB* [2002] 2 All ER 159 and *Bilta (UK) Ltd (in liquidation) v. Nazir and others* [2010] Bus L R 1634. That approach was again adopted by the English High Court in the case of *The Deposit Guarantee Fund for Individuals v. Bank Frick & Co AG and others* [2021] EWHC 3226 (Ch).
74. [2021] CSOH 118.
75. [2021] CSIH 58.
76. And *see also* the case of *Greater Glasgow Health Board v Multiplex Construction Europe Limited and others* [2021] CSOH 115, where the Outer House adopted the same approach with regards to an adjudication clause.

its scope where it may nonetheless be desirable to suspend those proceedings, such as where the existence or scope of an arbitration agreement is disputed and the tribunal has yet to make its own determination.

In England, it has long been recognised that the court has an inherent power to stay proceedings where justice requires, even if the requirements of section 9 of the 1996 Act are not met.[77] However, the English courts have stressed that this inherent jurisdiction should be exercised only in 'rare and compelling circumstances',[78] or in cases which are 'not contemplated by the statutory provisions'.[79] In practice, the English courts have held that this jurisdiction may be exercised to halt wasteful, duplicative proceedings which are contingent on the outcome of a related arbitration,[80] but that a mere overlap between court and arbitration proceedings will not, without more, be sufficient.[81] In borderline cases, it is likely to be significant whether an arbitration has yet been commenced.[82]

In addition, the English courts have wide case management powers under Rule 3.1(2) of the Civil Procedure Rules 1998 (CPR), including the right to stay domestic proceedings. Perhaps as a result of the English courts' reluctance to invoke their inherent jurisdiction to stay proceedings outside of the statutory scheme, arbitration parties have begun to invite the courts to use these broad case-management powers instead. For instance, in a recent case arising out of the 1MDB scandal in Malaysia,[83] the defendants sought a stay of the claimants' challenges to an arbitral award on three alternative bases; namely, section 9 of the 1996 Act, the court's inherent jurisdiction, and the court's case management power under CPR 3.1(2)(f). At first instance, despite holding that there could be no stay under section 9 of the 1996 Act, the Commercial Court was persuaded to grant a stay under its case management powers, finding that the claimants' challenges to the award raised questions which a separate arbitral tribunal should have the first opportunity to consider.

The defendants' victory in *1MDB* was short-lived. The Court of Appeal over-turned the decision to grant a stay, holding that the CPR 3.1(2)(f) power to stay proceedings should not be used by the court to delay its consideration of the sections 67 and 68 challenges under the 1996 Act, where related arbitrations raised similar jurisdictional issues.[84] The Court of Appeal stressed that challenges to awards are not merely an extension of the consensual arbitration process but, rather, involve the determination of a statutory right in an adversarial context by a court which operates

---

77. This power is recognised in section 49(3) of the Senior Courts Act 1981 and has been cited in cases such as *Channel Tunnel Group Ltd v. Balfour Beatty Construction Ltd* [1993] AC 334.

78. *Reichhold Norway ASA v. Goldman Sachs International* [2000] 1 W.L.R 173 per Lord Bingham of Cornhill CJ at 186C.

79. *Etri Fans Ltd v. NMB (UK) Ltd* [1987] 2 All ER 763.

80. *Stemcor UK Ltd v. Global Steel Holdings Ltd and another* [2015] EWHC 363 (Comm).

81. *PPF Capital Source v. Singh and another* [2016] EWHC 3097 (Ch).

82. *In the matter of Fenox (UK) Limited sub nom J & W Sanderson Limited v. (1) Fenox (UK) Limited (2) Fenox Automotive Limited (3) Vitali Arbuzov. (4) Ihar Putitski (5) Uladzimir Khrystsich* [2014] EWHC 4322 (Ch).

83. *Minister of Finance (Incorporated) and another v. International Petroleum Investment Company* [2019] EWHC 1151 (Comm) (henceforth *1MDB*).

84. *Minister of Finance (Incorporated) and another v. International Petroleum Investment Company* [2019] EWCA Civ. 2080 (henceforth *AMC*).

as a branch of the state. Accordingly, the Court of Appeal held that it would not be appropriate to delay the determination of a challenge to an arbitral award in order to favour the progress of other, ongoing arbitrations. Similarly, in *AMC III Purple BV. v. Amethyst Radiotherapy Ltd*,[85] the Commercial Court refused to grant a case management stay of proceedings pending the outcome of a related arbitration in Cyprus, finding that the claimant was not a party to the arbitration and should not be denied the benefit of exclusive jurisdiction agreements in its favour simply because the defendant was engaged in an ongoing arbitration involving related issues.

Thus, whilst arbitration users have sought to find innovative ways to circumvent the court's narrow statutory powers to suspend proceedings, the courts have been cautious to examine the wider impact of the sought suspensions. As *1MDB* and *AMC* make plain, the courts are prepared to assess the substance of the arbitration said to be hampered by the ongoing litigation before determining whether to grant a case management stay. Taken alone, the results in these cases may suggest to some that the courts are failing to step in to defend arbitrations. However, the approach of the courts has been more nuanced, favouring arbitration only to the extent that there is valid and continuing party consent to do so.

b   *Anti-suit Injunctions*

There is at first sight a contrast between the apparent reluctance in recent case law to stay domestic proceedings and the traditional willingness of the English courts to exercise their inherent jurisdiction[86] to restrain foreign proceedings brought in breach of arbitration agreements.[87] To explain this apparent contradiction, it is important to consider the statutory context. Whereas section 9 of the 1996 Act sets clear limitations on the availability of a stay, which the courts ought not to circumvent by the use of general powers, there is no such express restriction on the availability of injunctive relief for breaches of an arbitration agreement.[88] Indeed, there is a compelling legal basis for such injunctions where foreign proceedings amount to a breach of the contract to arbitrate. As Lord Millet famously expressed in *The Angelic Grace*, '[t]here is no good reason for diffidence in granting an injunction to restrain foreign proceedings on the clear and simple ground that the defendant has promised not to bring them'.[89]

---

85. [2019] EWHC 1503 (Comm).
86. Under section 37 of the Senior Courts Act 1981.
87. The Scottish courts have never been invited to grant an interdict to restrain foreign proceedings (Professor Davidson, *Arbitration, supra* n. 11, para. 15.02). It is likely that the Scottish courts would exercise their discretionary power to grant interdicts (under the Civil Jurisdiction and Judgments Act 1982 Schedule 8 Rule 2(j)) in line with English jurisprudence in this area.
88. Section 44, which is a non-mandatory provision of the 1996 Act, confers on the court a power to grant interim injunctions on the same basis as in other legal proceedings but does not specify any circumstances in which the court would be required to exercise this power. In any case, this provision has no application where there is no arbitration on foot (*Ust-Kamenogorsk Hydropower Plant JSC v. AES Ust-Kamenogorsk Hydropower Plant LLP* [2013] UKSC 35 at para. 40).
89. [1995] 1 Lloyd's Rep 87 at p. 96.

Yet it is important to recognise that anti-suit injunctions can offend principles of comity (when issued to restrain foreign court proceedings) and *Kompetenz-Kompetenz* (when issued to restrain arbitral proceedings). Indeed, as is well-known, such was the perceived damage caused by the anti-suit injunction to the mutual trust between EU legal systems that, in 2009, the Grand Chamber of the European Court of Justice in *Allianz SpA v. West Tankers* prohibited Member States from issuing such injunctions in respect of proceedings before the national courts of other Member States or signatories to the Lugano Convention.[90] Of course, with the departure of the UK from the EU and the instruments governing jurisdiction and enforcement of judgments between EU Member States, UK courts are no longer constrained by *West Tankers* from granting anti-suit injunctions in cases involving parallel proceedings before the courts of EU Member States.[91] And in any event, even prior to Brexit, UK courts retained the power to injunct proceedings brought outside the EU/Lugano area in breach of a domestic arbitration clause, as the UK Supreme Court made clear in the later case of *Ust-Kamenogorsk Hydropower Plant JSC v. AES Ust-Kamenogorsk Hydropower Plant LLP.*[92] Echoing the sentiments of Lord Millet in *The Angelic Grace*, my colleagues held that: '[a]n agreement to arbitrate disputes has positive and negative aspects. A party seeking relief within the scope of the arbitration agreement undertakes to do so in arbitration in whatever forum is prescribed. The (often silent) concomitant is that neither party will seek such relief in any other forum'.[93]

More recently, perhaps buoyed by robust decisions such as *Ust-Kamenogorsk*, arbitration users in England have sought to push the boundaries of the anti-suit injunction. In 2019, the Commercial Court was invited to continue an anti-suit injunction against a non-party to an arbitration agreement, in support of London Court of International Arbitration (LCIA) arbitration proceedings.[94] Dismissing that application, the Commercial Court stressed that it would not hesitate to exercise its inherent jurisdiction to prevent a party to an arbitration agreement from breaching that agreement by commencing proceedings in a forum that was not specified in the arbitration agreement. However, despite a strong indication of collusion between the respondent and the counterparty to the ongoing arbitrations, the Commercial Court held that the respondent was not a party to the arbitration agreement and that the Russian courts were the proper and natural forum for its claims. Whilst the Commercial Court has previously issued injunctions against non-parties which were in common control with arbitration parties and had initiated foreign proceedings in order to frustrate those arbitrations,[95] in the present case it was the arbitrations which appeared to be 'questionable'. That the issues in the court proceedings were the same as or

---

90. Case EUECJ C-185/07 [2009] *Allianz SpA v. West Tankers SAb* (10 February 2009).
91. *See, e.g.*, the recent decisions in *Pescatore v. Valentino* [2021] EWHC 1953 (Ch) and *Dream International Cooperatief UA v. Ragnar Investment Ltd* [2022] 2 WLUK 189, which proceeded on that basis.
92. *Supra* n. 88.
93. Per Lord Mance at para. 1.
94. *Evison Holdings Ltd v. International Co Finvision Holdings, Orient Express Bank Public Joint Stock Company* [2019] EWHC 3057 (Comm).
95. *BNP Paribas v. Open Joint Stock Company Russian Machines* [2011] EWHC 308 (Comm) and *Mace (Russia) Ltd v. Retansel Enterprises Ltd* [2016] EWHC 1209 (Comm).

related to those raised in the ongoing arbitration did not render it just and convenient to take the 'remarkable' step of restraining the foreign proceedings when the respondent was the proper claimant and was pursuing its own legitimate claims.[96]

However, the Commercial Court will move with alacrity to grant anti-suit injunctions to restrain court proceedings brought in breach of an arbitration clause in appropriate cases, with numerous and varied examples from the last few years. These examples also illustrate the geographical diversity of parties from around the world which choose to arbitrate in the UK. For example, in *Africa Finance Corporation and others v. Aiteo Eastern E & P Company Ltd*,[97] the Commercial Court granted a final anti-suit injunction notwithstanding a substantial delay in making the application of thirteen months, in part because of a recognition of the desirability of upholding rights under an arbitration agreement. In *ZHD v. SQO*,[98] the Commercial Court granted a mandatory injunction requiring a party to an arbitration agreement which had issued proceedings in Vietnam to use its best endeavours to procure a stay of the Vietnamese proceedings. In *VTB Bank (PJSC) v. Mejlumyan*,[99] the English Commercial Court granted a final mandatory injunction that the defendant discontinue Armenian court proceedings where an earlier injunction prohibiting the defendant from taking steps in those proceedings had proved ineffective, in part because the defendant had issued an invitation to the Armenian court to continue the proceedings in his absence. And in *Riverrock Securities Ltd v. International Bank of St Petersburg (Joint Stock Company)*,[100] the Commercial Court issued an anti-suit injunction to restrain Russian proceedings brought by the liquidator of an insolvent company in breach of a London-seated arbitration agreement governed by English law.

The English courts, therefore, remain ready to issue anti-suit injunctions in appropriate cases. However, they have so far held firm against expanding the circumstances in which such an injunction will be available against someone who is not a party to an arbitration agreement. As with case management stays, the courts have demonstrated a willingness to look behind the mere existence of an arbitration and to consider the substance of the parties' rights and interests in the litigation.

2   Topping up the Tribunal's Powers During the Arbitral Proceedings

At the time of concluding an agreement to arbitrate, the parties will rarely have applied their minds to detailed questions of arbitral procedure, such as the nature and extent of evidence gathering and the penalties for non-compliance with orders of the tribunal. Nor will the parties typically have considered how evidence or property in the hands of third parties should be protected for the purposes of the arbitration. The institutional rules (if any) and default provisions in the law of the seat may provide some general

---

96. *Supra* n. 94, per Mr Justice Phillips at para. 29.
97. [2022] EWHC 768 (Comm).
98. [2021] EWHC 1262 (Comm).
99. [2021] EWHC 3053 (Comm).
100. [2020] EWHC 2483 (Comm).

guidance in relation to the former.[101] However, the consensual nature of arbitration prevents the tribunal from having any competence in respect of third parties. Indeed, in the 2018 International Arbitration Survey, participants identified the 'lack of effective sanctions during the arbitral process' and the 'lack of power in relation to third parties' as two of the three 'worst characteristics' of international arbitration.[102] Since the powers of the UK courts are not generally so limited, arbitration users are increasingly calling upon them to 'fill the gaps'[103] in tribunal powers and support the efficacy of the arbitral process.

a   Evidence Gathering

In England, section 34(1) of the 1996 Act provides that '[i]t shall be for the tribunal to decide all procedural and evidential matters, subject to the right of the parties to agree any matter'. In Scotland, equivalent powers are conferred by section 28 of the 2010 Act. Whilst these broad powers reflect the reluctance of many jurisdictions to constrain the parties' freedom to agree the parameters of any evidence taking within the arbitration,[104] the provisions by themselves lack the granularity necessary to address many of the detailed questions which will arise in practice, such as the nature, extent and timing of disclosure, the search terms and methodology to be employed by the parties, the individual custodians whose documents should be searched, and the issues in relation to which documentary evidence should be provided. The same problems arise in respect of institutional rules, which are invariably drafted with a similar degree of generality.[105] Even the International Bar Association rules,[106] which seek to balance the typically broad view of disclosure in common law jurisdictions with the narrower view taken in civil law countries,[107] are substantially lighter in detail than the extensive CPR provisions governing disclosure in English civil litigation.

More fundamentally, assuming that the parties can agree upon a set of framework procedural rules for evidence gathering and taking, arbitral tribunals lack the coercive powers of the courts to hold the parties to such a bargain and to enforce their procedural decisions against relevant third parties. The importance of this point cannot be overstated. The success or failure of an arbitration in achieving a just result will often depend on parties disclosing material, including prejudicial evidence, to the

---

101. Discussed further in Carine Dupeyron, 'Shall National Courts Assist Arbitral Tribunals in Gathering Evidence?', *ICCA Congress Series no. 19*, pp. 458-480.
102. 2018 International Arbitration Survey produced by White & Case LLP and the Queen Mary University of London School of International Arbitration (available at https://arbitration.qmul.ac.uk/media/arbitration/docs/2018-International-Arbitration-Survey---The-Evolution-of-International-Arbitration-(2).PDF last accessed 19/03/2020), p. 8. This question did not appear in the 2021 International Arbitration Survey.
103. Emilia Onyema, 'The Jurisdictional Tensions Between Domestic Courts and Arbitral Tribunals', *ICCA Congress Series no. 19*, p. 488.
104. Gary Born, *International Commercial Arbitration*, supra n. 61, p. 2498.
105. Carine Dupeyron, 'Shall National Courts Assist Arbitral Tribunals', *supra* n. 101, p. 461.
106. https://www.ibanet.org/MediaHandler?id=def0807b-9fec-43ef-b624-f2cb2af7cf7b (last accessed 14/06/2020).
107. Carine Dupeyron, 'Shall National Courts Assist Arbitral Tribunals', *supra* n. 101, p. 462.

tribunal. Yet, beyond the usual remedy of drawing an 'adverse inference' where known evidence is not provided,[108] the tribunal has no means of penalising or disincentivising the destruction or withholding of important documents. Nor can the tribunal direct the parties to preserve relevant evidence before it has been constituted.

The statutory regimes in Scotland and England enable parties to an arbitration to avail themselves of the same court procedures as are available in relation to civil litigation for the purposes of securing documentary or witness evidence.[109] The Court of Appeal in *A and B v. C, D and E*[110] recently addressed a 'long-standing controversy' by concluding, contrary to a line of first-instance authority,[111] that the courts have the same powers under section 44(2)(a) of the 1996 Act to order the taking of evidence from a non-party witness to an arbitration as it has in relation to civil proceedings before the court. While the Court of Appeal expressly declined to overrule earlier cases restricting the other powers in section 44(2) to parties to the arbitration agreement,[112] some commentators,[113] as well as Mr Justice Foxton at first instance,[114] have suggested that those other powers should also be available against non-parties. It remains to be seen whether the law on those provisions will develop further.

b   *Interim Relief*

Similar issues arise in relation to the court's powers to grant interim relief under section 44 of the 1996 Act. In that regard, I note that it is unusual for the English courts to be asked to provide injunctive relief in respect of non-parties. Most commonly, such relief under section 44 is sought against the counterparty to the arbitration, with the most contentious question being whether the application must be made on notice and with the permission of the tribunal, or whether the urgency exception in section 44(3) is satisfied.

As to urgency, it will not be sufficient that section 44(3) was satisfied at the time of an initial application for interim relief. Where the applicant seeks a continuation of interim measures, or to secure compliance with those measures, recent decisions of the High Court indicate that the applicant must demonstrate that the situation remains

---

108. Gary Born, *International Commercial Arbitration, supra* n. 61, pp. 2563-2564.
109. Sections 43 (mandatory) and 44 (non-mandatory) of the 1996 Act, Rules 45 (mandatory) and 46 (non-mandatory) of the Scottish Arbitration Rules.
110. [2020] EWCA Civ 409.
111. *Commerce and Industry Insurance v. Certain Underwriters at Lloyd's* [2002] 1 W.L.R. 1323; *Cruz City I Mauritius Holdings v. Unitech Limited* [2014] EWHC 3704 (Comm); *DTEK Trading SA v. Mr Sergey Morozov and another* [2017] EWHC 94 (Comm); *Trans-Oil International SA v. Savoy Trading KP* [2020] EWHC 57 (Comm).
112. At [35], [49].
113. *See, e.g.,* Jack Alexander and Daniel Brinkman, 'Non-party Orders in Support of Arbitral Proceedings', LQR Vol. 136 (2020), p. 539; Masoon Ahmed, 'Taking Evidence from Non-parties in International Commercial Arbitration', Int. ALR, Vol. 24(1) (2021), p. 57; George Burn and Kevin Cheung, 'Section 44 of the English Arbitration Act 1996 and third parties to arbitration', Arbitration International, Vol. 37(1) (2021) p. 287. For a different view, *see* Sara Cockerill, 'Orders in Support of Arbitration: Section 37 Senior Courts Act, Section 44 of the Arbitration Act 1996', JBL Vol. 3 (2021) p. 246.
114. [2020] EWHC 258 (Comm) at [14].

urgent. In the recent case of *VTB Commodities Trading DAC v. JSC Antipinsky Refinery*,[115] the English Commercial Court made an order continuing a worldwide freezing order but dismissed an application to continue an injunction restraining the defendant from disposing of cargo. It held that where a party had obtained an urgent without notice injunction under section 44(3) to preserve evidence or assets in relation to arbitral proceedings, and it then applied to continue the injunction once the urgency had ceased, it was required under section 44(4) to obtain the tribunal's permission or the consent of all parties before making the application. In another case, *Schillings International LLP v. Scott*,[116] the High Court refused an application to secure compliance with an injunction which had been ordered one year earlier. Whereas, at the time of the original application, arbitral proceedings had yet to commence and there was an imminent risk of the respondent breaching the terms of a partnership agreement in order to obtain an unfair 'springboard advantage',[117] those factors were no longer present at the time of the subsequent application. As such, the High Court concluded that there was a 'fatal' absence of urgency.[118]

3   Handling Complaints after an Award Has Been Rendered

Bingham J observed in *Zermalt Holdings SA v. Nu-Life Upholstery Repairs Ltd* that 'the courts strive to uphold arbitration awards. They do not approach them with a meticulous legal eye endeavouring to pick holes, inconsistencies and faults in awards with the object of upsetting or frustrating the process of arbitration. Far from it. The approach is to read an arbitration award in a reasonable and commercial way, expecting, as is usually the case, that there will be no substantial fault that can be found with it'.[119]

The same cannot typically be said for the disappointed party in an arbitration. Notwithstanding the absence of a litigation-style appeal mechanism for arbitral awards in the UK, and the high hurdles placed in the way of challenges to awards under both the Scottish and English regimes, the UK courts face frequent, meritless applications from disgruntled arbitration users seeking to overturn unfavourable awards. The Commercial Court's hearing statistics are especially revealing in this regard.[120] Of the 79 challenges brought under section 68 of the 1996 Act (for serious irregularity) in the 2019-2021 legal years, three were successful and two were partially successful.[121] Of the 126 applications brought under section 69 of that Act (appeals on a point of law) during the same period, only six were successful.[122]

---

115. [2020] EWHC 72 (Comm).
116. [2019] EWHC 1335 (Ch).
117. Paragraph 38.
118. Paragraph 40.
119. [1985] 2 EGLR 14.
120. Commercial Court Annual Report (2020-2021), pp. 11-14, *supra* n. 5.
121. These statistics do not take into account fourteen applications which had not been determined by the time of publication of the Annual Report.
122. These statistics do not take into account five cases which were granted permission to appeal but which had not been determined by the time of publication of the Annual Report.

Faced with challenges to the award, its enforceability, or the tribunal itself, the court's jurisdiction is plainly supervisory. At first glance, this would appear to sit uncomfortably alongside the restrained, supportive role which the courts typically adopt during the life of the arbitration. However, as the Court of Appeal noted in *1MDB*, when the court's jurisdiction to hear challenges is invoked, its function is to administer justice as a branch of the state, not to seek to promote the arbitration agreement. That a challenge has been made to the court indicates that the parties' consensual relationship has broken down.

a   *Challenges to Arbitrators*

As Sundaresh Menon SC noted in a thoughtful article in 2017, the roles and responsibilities attached to arbitrators and the significance of party appointments are matters on which reasonable minds may differ, both within and between legal cultures.[123] Some have described the phenomenon of the party-appointed arbitrator as a 'moral hazard', setting the public good of the proper administration of justice against the personal incentive to secure repeat business from satisfied customers.[124] Others have noted with alarm the frequency of dissents penned by arbitrators appointed by the unsuccessful party.[125] There are also those who consider that parties should have a 'right' to appoint their own arbitrator, and that the existence of such an appointee represents a safeguard for the interests of that party.[126] The debate between these factions has produced considerable uncertainty as to the proper role of party-appointed arbitrators and whether they are to be held to the same ethical standards as arbitrators not so appointed. Such is the confusion that 80% of respondents to the 2018 International Arbitration Survey expressed the view that arbitration rules (whether institutional or ad hoc) should include provisions dealing with 'standards of independence and impartiality for arbitrators'.[127] In fact, this was the most popular of all the provisions suggested in the survey.

It was against this backdrop that the UK Supreme Court decided *Halliburton Company v. Chubb Bermuda Insurance Ltd*,[128] which involved an application under section 24 of the 1996 Act to remove an arbitrator on the ground that circumstances existed that gave rise to justifiable doubts as to his impartiality.

In essence, the case concerned the failure of the chairman of an arbitral tribunal to disclose that, six months after his appointment, he had been appointed by the

---

123. Sundaresh Menon, 'Adjudicator, Advocate or Something in Between?', *supra* n. 4, pp. 194-195.
124. Jan Paulsson 'Moral Hazard in International Dispute Resolution', ICSID Rev., Vol. 25(2) (2010), p. 339.
125. Albert Jan van den Berg, 'Dissenting Opinions by Party-Appointed Arbitrators in Investment Arbitration' in Mahnoush Arsanjani et al. (eds), *Looking to the Future: Essays on International Law in Honor of W. Michael Reisman* (Koninklijke Brill NV 2010) pp. 821-843.
126. Charles Brower and Charles Rosenberg, 'The Death of the Two-Headed Nightingale: Why the Paulsson van den Berg Presumption that Party-Appointed Arbitrators Are Untrustworthy Is Wrongheaded', Arbitration International Vol. 29(1) (2013), p. 7.
127. *Supra* n. 102, p. 34. This question did not appear in the 2021 International Arbitration Survey.
128. [2020] UKSC 48.

respondent as an arbitrator in separate proceedings arising out of the same environmental disaster and involving the same type of insurance contract. The key question was whether this non-disclosure amounted to apparent bias such that the tribunal's award (which had favoured the respondent) should be set aside. There were also significant ancillary questions to address, such as the appropriate test for apparent bias, including what the 'fair-minded and informed' observer should be treated as knowing, and whether multiple overlapping appointments are in themselves suggestive of bias. By the time the appeal reached us, much ink had been spilled by commentators and interested parties on the Court of Appeal's approach to these questions.

We held that the courts below were correct to hold that the fair-minded and informed observer would not have concluded that there was a real possibility of bias or circumstances that gave rise to justifiable doubts about the chairman's impartiality. We emphasised that impartiality was a 'cardinal duty' of both judges and arbitrators, but that it was important to bear in mind not only the special characteristics of arbitration and the differences in nature and circumstances between judicial determination of disputes and arbitral determination of disputes but also the characteristics of a particular type of arbitration. It was a notable aspect of this appeal that the Supreme Court received interventions from several interested parties, including the International Chamber of Commerce (ICC) and LCIA, as well as detailed written submissions from the London Maritime Arbitrators Association (LMAA), Chartered Institute of Arbitrators (CIArb) and the Grain and Free Trade Association (GAFTA), which assisted us in reaching a decision that was sensitive to the context of the particular arbitration and recognised that parties' expectations and arrangements may differ in different forms of arbitration.

b   Challenges to Awards

The 1996 Act provides three mechanisms by which parties may challenge a tribunal's award and the 2010 Act makes equivalent provision for Scotland. A party may require the court to determine whether the tribunal had the substantive jurisdiction to make its award,[129] whether there has been a 'serious irregularity' in the proceedings such that the award should be set aside,[130] and (unless the parties have agreed otherwise) whether the tribunal has made an error of law.[131]

None of these avenues is designed to make it easy for applicants to overturn arbitral awards. However, it is especially difficult to succeed in a challenge based on

---

129. Section 67 (1996 Act), Rule 67 (Scottish Arbitration Rules).
130. Section 68 (1996 Act), Rule 68 (Scottish Arbitration Rules).
131. Section 69 (1996 Act), Rule 69 (Scottish Arbitration Rules). *See* the case of *Arbitration Appeal No 4 of 2020* [2021] CSOH 14 for a recent example of the Outer House of the Court of Session considering whether an arbitration agreement providing for an award to be 'final and binding' was sufficient to exclude a right of appeal under Rule 69. The restrictive approach to appeals on a point of law can be seen in the requirement of obtaining the leave of the court and the conditions which must be met for the court to grant such leave.

'serious irregularity' under section 68, which has been recognised as imposing a 'high threshold' or 'high hurdle'.

In *RAV Bahamas Ltd & Bimini Bay Resort Management Limited v. Therapy Beach Club Incorporated*,[132] the Judicial Committee of the Privy Council upheld a successful challenge to an arbitral award on the grounds of serious irregularity under section 90 of the Bahamas Arbitration Act 2009 (which is materially identical to section 68 of the Arbitration Act 1996). The Board held that to establish serious irregularity, the applicant needs to show both that there has been an irregularity of one or more of the kinds listed in section 90 and that that has caused or will cause substantial injustice to the applicant. However, while it is good practice and should be encouraged, it is not a requirement that a party challenging an award makes a separate and express allegation of and that the court separately and expressly considers and finds, substantial injustice. It is sufficient that, as a matter of substance, substantial injustice be established. Some irregularities may be so serious that substantial injustice is inherently likely and indeed self-evident. In this case, the applicant succeeded on two grounds: that the arbitrator did not deal with two of the applicant's arguments, leading her to award damages for a six-year period rather than a three-year period, and that the arbitrator had improperly quantified the claimant's losses.

Where the alleged irregularity is an excess of the tribunal's powers, it is not sufficient that the tribunal has wrongly exercised its powers. The applicant must establish that the tribunal has purported to exercise a power it does not have.[133] This may be difficult when the English courts are inclined to read arbitration agreements liberally in light of the 'one-stop-shop' principle. Thus, in the case of *Filatona Trading Ltd and another v. Navigator Equities Ltd and others*,[134] although it was common ground that the tribunal did not have the power to make a buy-out award under section 48(5) of the 1996 Act, the court read the parties' shareholders agreement as providing the tribunal with the necessary power.

Even if a 'serious irregularity' can be established, the requirement that the irregularity caused the applicant 'substantial injustice' is a considerable hurdle. For instance, in *Chantiers de l'Atlantique SA v. Gaztransport & Technigaz SAS*,[135] the applicants established that there had been fraud in the arbitration, but still could not convince the Commercial Court that it would suffer substantial injustice.

There were eleven reported challenges under section 68 in 2021, only one of which was successful: *PBO v. DONPRO and others*.[136] The applicant succeeded on the grounds that the tribunal wrongly refused to allow the applicant to amend its statement of case, which prevented it from advancing potentially determinative arguments in circumstances in which there would be no (or minimal) prejudice to the other party, and that the tribunal departed from the way in which the case was presented without

---

132. [2021] UKPC 8.
133. *Abuja International Hotels Ltd v. Meridien SAS* [2012] EWHC 87 (Comm).
134. [2019] EWHC 173 (Comm), upheld in [2020] EWCA Civ 109.
135. [2011] EWHC 3383 (Comm).
136. [2021] EWHC 1951 (Comm).

warning and without giving the parties the opportunity to address the tribunal on those issues.

It is unusual for challenges to succeed under section 68 and the example of *PBO* demonstrates quite how serious a procedural flaw must be before the court will consider granting relief. That the bar is set so high reflects the court's continued deference to the legitimacy of the arbitral tribunal, even when exercising a supervisory jurisdiction. However, the success of the applicant in *PBO* should provide some comfort to arbitration users that their rights under section 68 are not illusory.

c   Challenges to Enforcement

Since 1975, the UK has been a signatory to the New York Arbitration Convention on the Recognition and Enforcement of Foreign Arbitral Awards. Whilst the principal aim of the Convention is to enable seamless recognition and enforcement of awards in contracting States, Article II(3) recognises that some awards may be unenforceable and that national courts have a necessary role in determining such cases.

The question of enforceability of foreign arbitral awards was the subject of detailed consideration by the UK Supreme Court in the 2010 case of *Dallah Real Estate and Tourism Holding Co v. The Ministry of Religious Affairs of Pakistan.*[137] In that case, the Supreme Court refused to enforce an award made by an ICC arbitral tribunal sitting in Paris, although the same award was later enforced by the French courts. The Supreme Court found that the State of Pakistan, against whom the arbitral award had been made, was not party to any contract or arbitration agreement. The Supreme Court also refused to stay the claimant's appeal in circumstances where it had subsequently brought parallel enforcement proceedings in France. This judgment has been described as 'a pathological international arbitration',[138] with the Supreme Court accused of undermining the fundamental objectives of the Convention by disagreeing with the courts of the arbitral seat over the application of its own law. Yet its result was merely to protect the autonomy of the respondent against submission to the outcome of arbitral proceedings to which it had not consented. As *Dallah* demonstrated powerfully, the enforcement of arbitral awards is far from a 'rubber-stamping' exercise.[139] Where there are grounds for refusing enforcement, UK courts must consider whether it is in the interests of justice to exercise their discretion to enforce the award.

More recently, the Judicial Committee of the Privy Council in *Betamax Ltd v. State Trading Corporation (Mauritius)*[140] considered the extent to which a court can set aside or refuse to enforce an international arbitration award on the basis that it conflicts with public policy – in this case, the public policy of Mauritius. The appeal concerned the relevant provision of the Mauritian International Arbitration Act, which enacts

137. [2010] UKSC 46.
138. Gary Born, 'Dallah and the New York Convention', Kluwer Arbitration Blog, 7 April 2011 (available at http://kluwerarbitrationblog.com/2011/04/07/dallah-and-the-new-york-convention/, last accessed 14/06/2022).
139. The relevant powers are found in section 66 (1996 Act) and section 12 (2010 Act).
140. [2021] UKPC 14.

Article 34 of the Model Law and which is also reflected in sections 68(2)(g) and 103(3) of the 1996 Act and in Article V(2)(b) of the New York Convention, and is therefore of wider significance. In *Betamax*, the Supreme Court of Mauritius had set aside an award in Betamax's favour on the basis that the underlying contract was in conflict with the public policy of Mauritius. That issue was within the jurisdiction of the tribunal and had been determined in favour of Betamax in the award. The Board held that the Supreme Court was not entitled to review the tribunal's decision on the validity of the contract. Such an approach would be inconsistent with the purpose of the Mauritian International Arbitration Act and the Model Law, which are premised on the finality of the tribunal's decision. The proper question for the court was whether, on the findings of law and fact made in the award, there was any conflict between the award and public policy. The Board reiterated that the policy of modern international arbitration law is to uphold the finality of the tribunal's decision on the contract made within the tribunal's jurisdiction, whether right or wrong in fact or in law, absent the specified vitiating factors enumerated in the relevant Act.

Whereas it will generally be straightforward to determine the enforceability of a money award, the position with respect to mandatory injunctions is more complex. In the case of *Sterling v. Rand and Another*,[141] the High Court held that specific performance would not be granted if it interfered with the rights of third parties, or if a party had not come to court with clean hands. In that case, new evidence had been presented to the High Court which undermined the award made by the London Beth Din. In the circumstances, notwithstanding that the award was unchallenged, the High Court concluded that it would be inequitable to enforce it.

Considering only the outcomes of those cases, some observers may be inclined to agree with Gary Born's critique that the UK courts interfere pathologically in the enforcement of arbitral awards. However, as with the court's interventions at earlier stages of the arbitral process, I would suggest that the position is much more nuanced. Whilst it may be an affront to the tribunal and, indeed, to other national courts, the readiness of UK courts to refuse enforcement in appropriate cases is an important check on the abuse of arbitration by unscrupulous parties.

IV   CONCLUSION

Thomas LCJ has spoken of the need for the UK courts to balance 'maximum support' with 'minimum intervention' if they are to exist harmoniously alongside arbitration.[142] From my assessment of the recent case law, it would appear that the UK courts are broadly succeeding in this endeavour at all stages of the arbitral process.

Looking to the future, I expect that there will continue to be calls from within the arbitration community for 'delocalisation', perhaps better described by Kerr LJ as 'arbitral procedures floating in the transnational firmament, unconnected with any

---

141. [2019] EWHC 2560 (Ch).
142. https://www.judiciary.uk/wp-content/uploads/2017/04/lcj-speech-national-judges-college-beijing-april2017.pdf at p. 6 (last accessed 14/06/2022).

municipal system of law'.[143] On the other side, I am confident that litigators and some judges will still lament the steady diversion of claims from the courts to arbitration and the attendant risk of ossification of the common law.[144] In my view, what is needed is a careful equilibrium. The 'great paradox' of arbitration is said to be its reliance on the cooperation of national courts.[145] The effectiveness and attraction of arbitration depend upon the possibility of court intervention at potentially critical points. Yet the obverse is much overlooked. A thriving arbitration market in the UK jurisdictions increases the attraction of our laws and ultimately of our courts. Issues arising from arbitrations, when they do reach the courts, can raise novel points, assisting in the development of English commercial law.

It is possible for the UK courts to have a symbiotic relationship[146] with arbitration. However, to do so, we must stay abreast of the latest developments in each other's realm. Whilst conferences and lectures undoubtedly have a role to play, it will also be helpful for the courts to receive targeted contributions from arbitration bodies in appropriate cases. Indeed, a notable aspect of the recent *Halliburton* appeal in the UK Supreme Court was the informative and useful interventions from interested arbitral institutions.[147] I note that similar interventions were made in the seminal case of *Jivraj v. Hashwani* in 2011.[148] It has been said that the role of the UK Supreme Court is principally one of thought leadership, with the small number of arbitration-related cases which we hear having a ripple effect on other practitioners.[149] No doubt our arbitration-related judgments will continue to spark debate and, in some quarters, disagreement. However, I am hopeful that we will continue the dialogue with the international arbitration community so that we might forge a deeper relationship of trust and collaboration between our respective jurisdictions.[150]

---

143. *Bank Mellat v. Helliniki Techniki SA* [1984] QB 291.
144. *See supra* n. 142, p. 10.
145. Paulsson, 'Arbitration in Three Dimensions' (2010) http://eprints.lse.ac.uk/32907/1/WPS20 10-02_Paulsson.pdf at p. 2 (last accessed 14/06/2022).
146. Dame Elizabeth Gloster, 'Symbiosis or Sadomasochism? The Relationship Between the Courts and Arbitration', Arbitration International, Vol. 34(3) (2018) pp. 321-339.
147. As stated above, we received helpful oral submissions from the LCIA and the ICC, as well as detailed written submissions from the LMAA, ClArb and GAFTA.
148. [2011] UKSC 40.
149. Jan Kleinheisterkamp and Shaurya Upadhyay, 'The UK Supreme Court and International Commercial Arbitration', Belgian Review of Arbitration, Vol. 2019(2) (2019), pp. 501–520.
150. I hope that by the time this chapter is published, the Supreme Court and the Judicial Committee of the Privy Council will each have handed down a judgment on the circumstances in which legal proceedings may be stayed for arbitration under section 9 of the Arbitration Act 1996 and the equivalent provision in the Cayman Islands: *Republic of Mozambique v. Privinvest Shipbuilding SAL* and *Ting Chuan (Cayman Islands) Holding Corp. v. FamilyMart China Holding Co Ltd.*

PANEL 15   The Great Debate: 'A World Without Investment Arbitration?'

THE ICCA DEBATE:

'The institution of ISDS is under attack. As the world of arbitration reacts, it is not yet clear what reforms will ultimately look like – or whether we'll see the extinction of the system as we know it today. In this great debate, speakers will offer different answers to the fundamental question of whether the world would be better with or without investment arbitration.'

CHAPTER 52

A World Without Investment Arbitration? An Introduction to Debate

Jan Kleinheisterkamp[*]

The Great Debate was an important moment of introspection for the arbitration community in 2022: can – and should – we imagine, and prepare for, a world without investment arbitration? Already in his 2011 Freshfields Lecture, Toby Landau pointed at the need to see the community's own responsibility for much of the challenges that investment arbitration is facing and in a Cassandrian way urged it to think about 'Saving Investment Arbitration From Itself'.

The issues haunting investment arbitration have been fermenting underground since at least 1907,[1] shaping the Latin American Calvo doctrine throughout the twentieth century.[2] They have emerged as *#firstworldproblems* since the political repercussions of the Methanex case in 2001 in the US, leading to the limitations of the 2002 Trade Act[3] that foreshadowed similar reservations of the European Union in 2013.[4] Things have critically accelerated since: fuelled by reports like 'Profiting from

---

[*] Arbitrator & Mediator, Visiting Professor in Practice at the London School of Economics School of Law.

1. For one of the very early stumbling stones see the 1907 Drago-Porter Convention, the first treaty to codify the prohibition of use of armed force, in particular for the recovery of debt owed to foreign nationals, but (upon the insistence of US delegate General Horace Porter) making this prohibition of use of force conditional on the host state accepting arbitration – a condition that Philip Jessup described as 'a loophole through which a fleet of warships could sail', Ph. Jessup, *A Modern Law of Nations: An Introduction* (New York, NY: MacMillan, 1948) 113.

2. For a classic analysis *see* D. Shea, *The Calvo Clause: A Problem of Inter-American and International Law and Diplomacy* (Minneapolis, MN: University of Minnesota Press, 1955).

3. Section 2102(b)(3) of the Trade Act 2002, 19 USC 3802, Public Law 107-210, making fast-track authority for negotiating investment agreements contingent on 'ensuring that foreign investors in the United States are not accorded greater substantive rights with respect to investment protections than United States investors in the United States'.

4. Regulation (EU) No. 912/2014 of the European Parliament and of the Council of 23 July 2014 establishing a framework for managing financial responsibility linked to investor-to-state dispute

Injustice',[5] protests against ISDS in the (aborted) EU-US Transatlantic Trade and Investment Partnership (TTIP) and the EU-Canadian Comprehensive Economic Trade Agreement (CETA) (still not fully ratified) shook much of Europe in 2016; the *Achmea* and *Komstroy* judgments of the European Court of Justice in 2018 and 2021 have not yet been digested by everyone,[6] let alone the subsequent axing of intra-EU bilateral investment treaties (BITs) and, most recently since ICCA 2022, the ever more probable obliteration of the Energy Charter Treaty.[7]

Indeed, the word 'legitimacy crisis' has pervaded not only the last ten years of literature on investment arbitration[8] but also the panels of ICCA 2022, ranking on top together with the more topical catch-words 'war', 'inflation', 'bias' or 'climate catastrophe'.[9] And yet, this crisis was announced as early as 1995. In his seminal article 'Arbitration Without Privity', Jan Paulson famously warned: 'A single incident of an adventurous arbitrator going beyond the proper scope of his jurisdiction in a sensitive case may be sufficient to generate a backlash.' So here we are, and it is what it is.

---

settlement tribunals established by international agreements to which the European Union is party, OJ L 257, 28 October 2014, pp. 121-134, at Recital 4: 'Union agreements should afford foreign investors the same high level of protection as Union law and the general principles common to the laws of the Member States grant to investors from within the Union, but not a higher level of protection.'

5. P. Eberhardt & C. Olivet, *Profiting from Injustice: How Law Firms, Arbitrators and Financiers Are Fuelling an Investment Arbitration Boom* (Brussels/Amsterdam: CEO/TNI November: 2016), https://corporateeurope.org/sites/default/files/publications/profiting-from-injustice.pdf.

6. CJEU judgment of 6 March 2018, *Slowakische Republik v. Achmea BV*, ECLI:EU:C:2018:158; and Judgment of the Court (Grand Chamber) of 2 September 2021, *République de Moldavie v, Komstroy LLC*, ECLI:EU:C:2021:655.

7. *See, e.g.*, European Parliament Resolution of 24 November 2022 on the outcome of the modernisation of the Energy Charter Treaty (2022/2934(RSP), https://www.europarl.europa.eu/doceo/document/RC-9-2022-0498_EN.html: 'having regard to the announcements by the Spanish Government of 12 October 2022, by the Dutch Government of 19 October 2022, by the French Government of 21 October 2022, by the Slovenian Government of 10 November 2022, by the German Government of 11 November 2022, and by the Luxembourgish Government of 18 November 2022 of their intention to withdraw from the ECT ... 11. Recalls its position that the EU and its Member States should not sign or ratify investment protection treaties that include the ISDS mechanism; regrets the fact that the modernised ECT maintained this outdated dispute settlement mechanism and stresses the considerable evidence of investment arbitrators disregarding state's intent to protect their public policy objectives').

8. The Kluwer Arbitration databases produce 236 results for the search for 'legitimacy crisis' and 1,646 results for the search 'legitimacy AND investment arbitration'. For the early voices, *see* S. Frank, 'The Legitimacy Crisis in Investment Treaty Arbitration: Privatizing Public International Law Through Inconsistent Decisions' (2005) 73 Fordham L. Rev. 1521, 1584-1587; M. Sornarajah, 'A Coming Crisis: Expansionary Trends in Investment Treaty Arbitration', in: K.P. Sauvant (ed.), *Appeals Mechanism in International Investment Disputes* (Oxford: OUP 2008) 39, 41; S.W. Schill, *International Investment Law and Comparative Public Law* (Oxford: OUP 2010) 4-7; M. Waibel et al., (eds), *Backlash Against Investment Arbitration: Perceptions and Reality* (Oxford: OUP 2010).

9. For discussions of legitimacy of investment arbitration at previous ICCA congresses, *see, e.g.*, S. Schill, 'Developing a Framework for the Legitimacy of International Arbitration', in: A.J. van den Berg (ed.), *ICCA Congress Series No. 18 (Miami 2014): Legitimacy: Myths, Realities, Challenges* (The Hague: Kluwer International 2015) 789-827; T. Schultz, 'Legitimacy Pragmatism in International Arbitration: A Framework for Analysis', in: J. Kalicki & A. Raouf (eds), *ICCA Congress Series No. 20 (Sydney 2018): Evolution and Adaptation: The Future of International Arbitration* (The Hague: Kluwer International 2019) 25-51.

That means that we cannot avoid facing the uncomfortable question of whether a world without investment arbitration would be a better place. Just how critical things are can be gleaned from an arguable link between two intriguing speeches on the first day of the ICCA Conference: Louise Arbour's keynote address about the eroding effects of international arbitration for justice in the Global South,[10] on the one hand, and Jan Paulsson's analysis of the International Court of Justice's (ICJ) *Barcelona Traction* case,[11] with his reference to the 'wretched of the world' as the title of Franz Fanon's revolutionary book of 1961 (a cornerstone of anti-colonialist literature),[12] on the other hand. (Indeed, the mere fact that Jan Paulsson feels the need to go as far as to conjure the first line of *The International*, the socialist anthem, to plead for the protection of foreign shareholders under international law, probably already says quite something about the state of affairs ... .)

Louise Arbour pointed us to the effects of taking profitable disputes out of desperately underfunded national courts and taking them to arbitration. She invited us to think about a form of tax on international arbitration to finance the dilapidated court systems in at least the poorest countries, akin to the Tobin tax on international currency transactions. Jan Paulsson's proposition of guaranteeing access to arbitration to those deprived of their rights when engaging in international transactions,[13] in contrast, could be taken just a nudge further (some may say *ad absurdum*): why do we not extend the right to go to arbitration to all the wretched of the Earth? Not only to shareholders investing abroad but also to those who did not voluntarily expose themselves to the risks of globalization – and arguably do not really stand to win much, if anything, from the foreign investments that affect their lives and destroy their livelihood. So, should not the wretched of the Earth, whose human rights have been trampled on by foreign investors with the complicity of their governments, also get equal access to that first-class justice system of international arbitration, in the name of global rule of law? Those, to whose home courts foreign investors do not want to submit, requesting investment arbitration – but to whose home courts the same foreign investors, when sued, wish to confine wretched of the Earth?[14]

---

10. *See* Chapter 1, Arbitration's Age of Enlightenment: A Celebration or a Challenge?, by Louise Arbour in this volume.
11. *See* Chapter 9, Why Investment Treaties Should Not Be Subverted by *Barcelona Traction*, by Jan Paulsson in this volume.
12. F. Fanon, *Les damnés de la terre – avec un preface de Jean-Paul Sarte* (Paris: Maspero 1961).
13. *See*, in a similar vein, J. Basedow, 'The Law of Open Societies: Private Ordering and Public Regulation of International Relations' (2012) 360 RdC 9, 202 (para. 253): 'the efforts of individual contracting partners to create legal certainty by means of a choice-of-law selection ... represents, as it were, *a human right in a globalized world* that is typically directed against not only one, but several affected States, specifically those States whose courts share the judicial competence to resolve a dispute arising from a contractual relationship' (emphasis added). For a critical discussion in the light of investment treaty law, *see* J. Kleinheisterkamp, 'Mehr Freiheit wagen mit Menschenrechten: Ein Versuch zur Rechtssicherheit durch Investitionsschutz', in: A. Dutta & C. Heinze (eds), *Mehr Freiheit wagen – Beiträge zur Emiritierung von Jürgen Basedow* (Tübingen: Mohr Siebeck 2018) 173-193.
14. *See*, for example, the attempts of a British mining company to invoke *forum non conveniens* and abuse of Article 4 of the Brussels I Regulation to avoid the jurisdiction of English courts in a 'case seek[ing] compensation for a large number of extremely poor Zambian residents for negligence or breach of Zambian statutory duty in connection with the escape within Zambia of noxious

It is not difficult to polarize on this subject. Polarization is, indeed, what debate is about. And having a public debate is not for the sake of entertainment but for making people think. It is by polarizing that we sometimes can see issues more clearly by not hearing 'truths' but position, artefacts of the mind – and each of us must form her or his own ideas on the subject. It is in this spirit that Toby Landau and Carolyn Lamm have agreed to entertain the ICCA 2022 audience: for the sake of thought. The positions they have defended – and, indeed, have been attributed to them by us – are obviously not necessarily their own conviction or views. The written elaborations of their motions are a testimony of the rich research upon which they have based their arguments, and they are an invitation to everyone in the arbitral community to engage more deeply with the problems that investment arbitration both creates and faces.

Irrespective of whether one is convinced by Toby Landau's ever-so-enticing arguments, a serious engagement is profoundly and urgently needed, at the very least to avoid an even larger backlash against arbitration. It would, indeed, be daunting to have to announce at a future ICCA Conference a Great Debate on 'a world without commercial arbitration?'. Certain is only that the future will bring significant changes to investment arbitration. What those changes will be is not only up to governments that are negotiating collectively in the UNCITRAL Working Group III or bilaterally negotiating new generations of investment treaties. It will also be up to the arbitration community to take responsibility for how investment arbitration is practised and thus perceived, and that will depend a lot on what deeper intentions are reflected by the shaping of its practice: is it really about contributing to a balanced development of the rule of law, or is it just about growing business opportunities? This Great Debate of ICCA 2022 has certainly contributed for everyone to see a bit clearer what is at stake for arbitration altogether.

substances arising in connection with the operation of a Zambian mine', *Vedanta Resources PLC & Anor v. Lungowe & Ors* [2019] UKSC 20 at [87], where Coulson J. at first instance, 'doing [his] best to assess that evidence, [was] bound to conclude [...] that the claimants would almost certainly not get access to justice if these claims were pursued in Zambia', *Lungowe & Ors v. Vedanta Resources Plc & Anor* [2016] EWHC 975 (TCC) at [198].

CHAPTER 53

For the Proposition: A World Without Investment Arbitration?[*]

Toby Landau KC, Chester Brown & Michael Waibel[**]

TABLE OF CONTENTS

I   INTRODUCTION: THE CURRENT PRACTICAL REALITY

Ever since the emergence of investment arbitration, there have been criticisms as to its fairness, justification and legitimacy. Such criticisms began as rumblings which were easily dismissed as ill-informed and ill-focused. They were said to be no more than the rants of anti-globalists, anti-capitalists, and other interest groups, or wayward academics with specific agendas but no actual experience in this form of dispute resolution.

---

[*]   This is a pedagogical piece, drafted for the purposes of a debate, and does not necessarily reflect the opinions of its authors.

[**] Toby Landau KC, Governing Board Member of ICCA, is a barrister, advocate and arbitrator, practising at Duxton Hill Chambers (Singapore Group Practice) in Singapore and in sole practice at the English Bar. Chester Brown is Professor of International Law and International Arbitration, University of Sydney Law School; Barrister, 7 Wentworth Selborne Chambers, Sydney; and Overseas Member, Essex Court Chambers, London. Michael Waibel is Professor of International Law, University of Vienna.

     The authors thank Sam Wordsworth KC for detailed comments on an earlier draft, and Andrijana Mišović and Rebecca McMenamin for research assistance. All errors are those of the authors alone.

They were said to be demonstrably wrong as a matter of fact. Hence, notwithstanding their growing volume and momentum, the criticisms were given little or no credence as the world of investment arbitration continued to develop.

But the situation has now changed. We have firmly and irretrievably arrived at a *Reality Checkpoint*.[1] Whereas practitioners in investment arbitration will continue to discount the criticisms as simply incorrect, the debate outside of this specialist pool has already – in large measure – been lost. The view of informed, experienced insiders no longer matters, because the outside world has now lost confidence in the arbitration process in its current form. Whether we like it or not, the rumblings have matured into a full backlash. There is widespread disquiet and a fundamental concern about legitimacy. Most states have now confirmed (e.g., at UNCITRAL) that the current system is simply no longer sustainable. So it is that, according to the UNCTAD Investment Policy Hub, there have been 512 terminations of investment treaties to date.[2] And the pace of terminations per year is accelerating. In 2019, there were 37; in 2020, there were 43; in 2021, there were 87. From 2015 to 2022 alone, there were 310 terminations. In 2017, the number of effective terminations of bilateral investment treaties (BITs) exceeded the number of new treaties for the first time. And that has been the position in the years since.[3]

The exodus has comprised a wide range of countries, and political and economic profiles. By way of example only, at least four G20 Member States have terminated investment treaties (Australia, India, Indonesia, and South Africa). Indeed, if the termination of intra-EU BITs by France, Germany and Italy is included, the total number of G20 member countries to terminate investment treaties is seven. Another G20 country – Brazil – has not ratified any BIT with investment arbitration provisions, preferring instead investment facilitation and state-to-state dispute settlement. Indonesia began to terminate its BITs in early 2014 (with the Netherlands-Indonesia BIT (1992)). Since then, it has terminated twenty-three agreements. India gave notice in 2016 that it would terminate fifty-eight BITs, and to date has terminated seventy-four of them. Bolivia has terminated sixteen BITs since 2009. South Africa has terminated twelve BITs since 2013. Ecuador established an investment treaties audit commission, CAITISA,[4] to audit all its BITs and its foreign investment policy. In 2017, CAITISA recommended that Ecuador terminate its remaining sixteen BITs and negotiate new instruments. Since 2017,

---

1. The large cast-iron lamppost in the middle of Parker's Piece, Cambridge, England, at the intersection of the park's diagonal paths.
2. https://investmentpolicy.unctad.org/international-investment-agreements.
3. UNCTAD IIA Issues Note, August 2021 (Issue 3). Both in 2019 and 2020, the number of effective treaty terminations exceeded the number of new IIAs. In 2020 alone, 42 terminations came into effect (of which 10 were unilateral terminations, of which seven were replacements (through the entry into force of a newer treaty), 24 IIAs were terminated by mutual consent, and 1 expired. Of the 42 terminations, 20 were the consequence of the entry into force of the agreement to terminate all intra-EU BITs on 29 August 2020. Moreover, as in 2019, India was particularly active in terminating treaties, with six BITs terminated, followed by Australia with three, and Italy and Poland with two each.
4. Comisión para la Auditoría Integral Ciudadana de los Tratados de Protección Recíproca de Inversiones y del Sistema de Arbitraje Internacional en Materia de Inversiones (Commission for the Comprehensive Citizen Audit of the Reciprocal Investment Protection Treaties and the International Investment Arbitration System).

Ecuador has terminated fourteen BITs. In 2009 and 2010, the Czech Republic terminated its BITs with Denmark, Italy, Malta and Slovenia by mutual agreement. In 2020, EU Member States agreed to terminate intra-EU BITs via a termination agreement. On 5 May 2020, twenty-three of twenty-seven EU Member States (excluding Austria, Finland, Ireland, and Sweden) signed a treaty to terminate all intra-EU BITs between them.[5] Member States that are parties to this plurilateral treaty have agreed to terminate all intra-EU BITs (124) between them listed in Annex A to the agreement. The termination agreement implements the March 2018 European Court of Justice decision in *Slovak Republic v Achmea* that investment arbitration clauses within intra-EU BITs are incompatible with the Treaty on the Functioning of the European Union.[6] The signatories of the termination agreement are Belgium, Bulgaria, Croatia, the Republic of Cyprus, the Czech Republic, Denmark, Estonia, France, Germany, Greece, Hungary, Italy, Latvia, Lithuania, Luxembourg, Malta, Netherlands, Poland, Portugal, Romania, Slovakia, Slovenia and Spain. Italy withdrew from the Energy Charter Treaty (ECT) in January 2016. Diplomatic minutes leaked from a 12 July 2022 Council of the EU meeting reveal that some governments have been contemplating a joint withdrawal from the ECT, regardless of the revised ECT deal set to be negotiated at the Energy Charter Conference on 22 November 2022.[7] At the Council meeting, Spain said it regarded leaving the ECT as the best option available, echoing the words of the country's deputy Prime Minister, Teresa Ribera, who said prior to the 24 June summit that she favoured a withdrawal. This was based on doubt that European ambitions have been achieved with regard to the Paris Agreement and sustainable development. In Poland, a draft law on the 'termination of the Energy Charter Treaty' and its protocols was agreed by the Polish Government on 10 August 2022 and sent to the country's lower chamber, the Sejm, by Prime Minister Mateusz Morawiecki on 25 August 2022. It states that the ECT's investor-State dispute settlement (ISDS) clause constitutes 'a threat to the autonomy of EU law and the principle of mutual trust between Member States' and should be terminated 'to ensure legal certainty in the EU legal order'. On 6 October 2022, the Polish Sejm voted in favour of the draft law.[8] In mid-October 2022, Spain initiated a procedure to withdraw from the ECT.[9] The Netherlands promptly followed.[10] France followed on 21 October

---

5. Agreement for the Termination of Bilateral Investment Treaties between the Member States of the European Union, signed 5 May 2020, *Official Journal of the European Union*, L 169/1 (29 May 2020).
6. *Slovak Republic v. Achmea BV* (Case C-284/16, Judgment of the Court of 6 March 2018).
7. On the prospects for modernising the ECT, *see* Johannes Tropper and Maximilian Wagner, 'Don't Pull the Plug on the Energy Charter Treaty: Why EU Member States Should Modernise Rather than Abandon It' (*Völkerrechtsblog: International Law and International Legal Thought*, 16 May 2022) https://voelkerrechtsblog.org/ accessed 8 November 2022.
8. Lisa Bohmer, 'Poland's Lower House Votes in Favour of Withdrawing from Energy Charter Treaty', *IA Reporter* (9 October 2022), available at www.iareporter.com (last accessed 20 November 2022).
9. Lisa Bohmer, 'Spain Is Set to Withdraw from the Energy Charter Treaty, Following in Poland's Footsteps', *IA Reporter* (13 October 2022), available at www.iareporter.com (last accessed 20 November 2022).
10. Lisa Bohmer, 'Dutch Government Announces Intention to Withdraw from Energy Charter Treaty', *IA Reporter* (18 October 2022), available at www.iareporter.com (last accessed 20 November 2022).

2022, having put EU withdrawal from the ECT on the table in February 2021.[11] Germany has also confirmed that it intends to withdraw,[12] as have Slovenia,[13] and Luxembourg.[14] In light of these national withdrawals, the EU has confirmed that the Commission is not planning a coordinated withdrawal and that the EU itself will remain a party to the ECT.[15]

This exodus from investment agreements does not take account of current and threatened treaty renegotiations.[16] Nor does it take account of the full force of the current backlash, with all its popular support, which has not yet manifested in actual terminations (for a variety of reasons, including the difficulty of negotiating terminations and the lack of bargaining power of many states – an important constraint that is not to be confused with acceptance of the current system).[17] Nor does it take account of the fact that some of the most economically significant investment agreements – such as the Transatlantic Trade and Investment Partnership (TTIP) – have failed to secure agreement.

This dramatic picture does not mean that all the criticisms have been proven correct. Instead, it means that over the past twenty or so years, there has been a monumental failure of advocacy on our part – the collective of investment arbitration specialists – to explain and justify our current system. Negative perceptions have now firmly taken hold, and it is *perceptions* that, ultimately, have and will continue to dictate whether the process remains viable.

Persuading investment arbitration specialists of the demerits of the current system of arbitration has all the flavour of persuading turkeys of the merits of Christmas or Thanksgiving. But in truth, we are all now faced with no choice. We cannot bury our heads in the arbitral sands. If we continue to cling to the existing system, refuse to think afresh, and wheel out the same counter-arguments already long

---

11. Damien Charlotin, 'France Will Also Withdraw from Energy Charter Treaty, French President Announces', *IA Reporter* (21 October 2022), available at www.iareporter.com (last accessed 20 November 2022).
12. Lisa Bohmer, 'Germany's Governing Coalition Reaches Agreement on Trade Issues – Including Withdrawal from the ECT, Ratification of CETA, and Initiating Negotiations with the USA for a Free Trade Agreement', *IA Reporter* (11 November 2022), available at www.iareporter.com (last accessed 20 November 2022).
13. Lisa Bohmer, 'Another EU State Announces its Withdrawal from the ECT, as EU Commission Stands Its Ground', *IA Reporter* (10 November 2022), available at www.iareporter.com (last accessed 20 November 2022).
14. Damien Charlotin, 'The Latest EU State to Leave the Energy Charter Treaty: Luxembourg', *IA Reporter* (18 November 2022), available at www.iareporter.com (last accessed 20 November 2022).
15. European Commission, 'Proposal for a Council Decision on the Position to Be Taken on Behalf of the European Union in the 33rd Meeting of the European Energy Conference', Brussels (5 October 2022), Doc No COM(2022) 521 final, 2022/0324 (NLE).
16. *See* Figure 8.1 and Table 8.1 in Wolfgang Alschner, *Investment Arbitration and State-Driven Reform: New Treaties, Old Outcomes* (Oxford University Press 2022) 248-249, based on mid-2021 data. *See also* Clint Peinhardt and Rachel L. Wellhausen, 'Withdrawing from Investment Treaties but Protecting Investment' (2016) 7 Global Policy 571-576.
17. *See* the explanation for constraints on reform offered by Tuuli-Anna Huikuri, 'Constraints and Incentives in the Investment Regime: How Bargaining Power Shapes BIT Reform' (2022) The Review of International Organizations 361.

deployed to rebut the criticisms, we will be faced in any event with a 'world without investment arbitration'.

Critically, however, the question for debate is 'a world without investment arbitration'. It is not 'a world without ISDS'. The argument that follows from the current crisis is certainly not that all forms of investor-State dispute resolution should be abandoned, with a reversion to the exhaustion of local remedies or the diplomatic protection models. Rather, it is that the current system of investment arbitration must be replaced with something else. And it is suggested that a large and diverse body of dispute resolution specialists such as is now in place, in the exercise of its collective imagination, must be able to come up with other possible models that meet and quell the widespread disquiet.

This argument will proceed in three stages:

(i) That the current economic and political rationales for investment arbitration provide no basis to justify the continuation of the current model.
(ii) That the current system of investment arbitration suffers from a range of perceived weaknesses that require a fundamental re-think.
(iii) That given viable alternatives, a 'world without investment arbitration' in its current form is neither unattractive nor unrealistic.

II   CURRENT ECONOMIC AND POLITICAL RATIONALES

There are two rationales most commonly deployed to justify investment arbitration. First, the 'Credible Commitment' rationale: that investment arbitration is a crucial ingredient for host states to make credible commitments to foreign investors, and so attract investment flows. Second, the 'De-Politicisation' rationale: that investment arbitration provides a mechanism for the de-politicisation of investment disputes.

Each rationale is flawed, and neither provides a justification for the continuation of our current arbitration model as the only available system. Each is addressed in turn.

1   The 'Credible Commitment' Rationale

The first frequently invoked rationale is that the host state's consent to international arbitration in investment treaties creates credible commitments vis-à-vis foreign investors and thus helps host states to attract foreign capital. The costs that can be imposed by arbitral tribunals in case of treaty breach assure investors either that such breaches will not occur or, if they occur, that arbitral tribunals will promptly remedy them. Based on a host state's commitment to international arbitration in advance, the investor commits capital. Investment arbitration is therefore an important means to an end. It helps countries that need foreign capital attract such capital at reasonable cost.

Despite its theoretical appeal, this economic rationale does not withstand scrutiny. It fails for at least two reasons:

a   *Lack of Historical Support*

It is a virtually universal assumption that modern international investment law is about investment arbitration. This is simply wrong. For at least the first thirty years of investment law, international arbitration was not an active feature of investment treaties. Capital-exporting countries did not consider international arbitration to be an essential element of the investment treaties that they concluded (in large numbers). Indeed, they were perfectly content to conclude investment treaties without any recourse to arbitration. It is only since the 1980s that we have seen the proliferation of investment arbitration clauses in treaties and since the beginning of this century that the field has been shaped by arbitral decisions. In fact, modern investment law has existed *without* arbitration for a considerably longer time than with it.

Lauge Poulsen has demonstrated that the European and United States architects of Friendship, Commerce and Navigation (FCN) agreements and BITs did not conceive of these treaties as credible commitments, that is, obligations enforceable through international arbitration. Rather, they regarded the substantive treaty standards primarily as salient focal points for largely informal dispute settlement that could support the crystallisation of customary international law to promote the rule of law[18] and produce a body of case law that would further develop international law.[19]

According to Poulsen, the drafters of first-generation FCNs and BITs only occasionally included international arbitration provisions because they considered them unimportant, focusing instead on the coordinating role of the agreements.[20] This is also supported by Vandevelde, who emphasises that the US did not see the substantive protections as concessions granted by other countries but as reflections of 'right principles' that both countries had already embraced.[21]

It is well known that Germany and Pakistan signed the first bilateral investment treaty on 25 November 1959.[22] Less well-known is that the first investment treaty that provided the host state's advance consent to investment arbitration was the Chad-Italy BIT of 1969.[23] In the 1960s and 1970s, states included investment arbitration provisions only occasionally in their investment treaties. Moreover, even when they did include this method of dispute resolution, investment treaty arbitration remained a 'sleeping beauty' until the 1990s.[24]

---

18. Lauge N. Skovgaard Poulsen, 'Beyond Credible Commitments: (Investment) Treaties as Focal Points' (2020) International Studies Quarterly.
19. Kenneth J. Vandevelde, *The First Bilateral Investment Treaties: US Postwar Friendship, Commerce, and Navigation Treaties* (Oxford University Press 2017) 385-388.
20. Lauge N. Skovgaard Poulsen, 'Beyond Credible Commitments: (Investment) Treaties as Focal Points' (2020) International Studies Quarterly.
21. Kenneth J. Vandevelde, *The First Bilateral Investment Treaties: US Postwar Friendship, Commerce, and Navigation Treaties* (Oxford University Press 2017) Ch. 6.
22. For example, Rudolf Dolzer and Yun-I Kim, 'Germany', in Chester Brown (ed.), *Commentaries on Selected Model Investment Treaties* (Oxford University Press, 2013), 289, 289.
23. Federico Ortino, 'Italy', in Chester Brown (ed.), *Commentaries on Selected Model Investment Treaties* (Oxford University Press, 2013), 321, 341.
24. Arguably, the sleeping beauty was awoken by Jan Paulsson, in his 1995 seminal article: 'Arbitration Without Privity' (Fall 1995) 10(2) *ICSID Review – Foreign Investment Law Journal* pp. 232-257.

The very first investment treaty award was handed down on 27 June 1990 in *Asian Agricultural Products Ltd v. Sri Lanka* (*AAPL*) under the Sri Lanka-UK BIT – thirty-one years after the first BIT was signed. Nevertheless, it took another decade for investment treaty arbitration to become common.

The first NAFTA tribunals in the late 1990s established modern assumptions about how investment law is intended to work. Only at this point did international arbitration come to be seen by some as a necessary feature of investment treaties and the contemporary narrative took hold among many in the international investment community.[25]

But even then, crucially, the existing empirical evidence demonstrates that foreign investors cared little, and were often unaware, of investment arbitration before the year 2000.[26]

The critical question then is: why did arbitration provisions begin to proliferate in treaties in the late 1980s? This is obviously a central enquiry if one is to contemplate a 'world without' such provisions. Critically, it is far from evident that the proliferation of arbitration provisions had anything to do with the narrative of credible commitment that is common today.

Archival research does not show that capital-exporting countries were concerned about the ineffectiveness of investment treaties without investment arbitration, and nor does it show that investors ever called for such protection.[27]

Rather, three completely different factors, all unrelated to the common narrative, likely contributed to the emergence and success of investment arbitration.

First, the role of the World Bank. Starting in the 1970s, the World Bank put considerable effort into promoting ICSID arbitration, among other forms of arbitration, by encouraging states to adopt arbitration clauses in their investment treaties.[28] International civil servants at the World Bank believed in the utility of this method of dispute resolution and encouraged states to adopt it.

Second, the Iran-US Claims Tribunal, which was set up in 1981, also helped to promote the idea of international arbitration as 'de-politicised' dispute resolution (see below on de-politicisation).

Third, there was a key competitive dynamic. Capital-exporting countries did not want their own investors to enjoy lesser protection than investors of other states that already benefited from arbitration under investment treaties.[29] This competitive dynamic helped diffuse arbitration provisions in investment treaties.

---

25. Jarrod Hepburn et al., 'Investment Law before Arbitration', (2020) 23 Journal of International Economic Law 929. .

26. Lauge Poulsen, Jonathan Bonnitcha and Jason Yackee, *Transatlantic Investment Treaty Protection* (Centre for European Policy Studies 2015) 4; for an overview *see* Jonathan Bonnitcha, Lauge Poulsen and Michael Waibel, *The Political Economy of the Investment Treaty Regime* (Oxford University Press 2017) 164-165.

27. Lauge N. Skovgaard Poulsen, 'Beyond Credible Commitments: (Investment) Treaties as Focal Points' (2020) International Studies Quarterly; Jarrod Hepburn et al., 'Investment Law Before Arbitration' (2020) 23 Journal of International Economic Law 929.

28. Taylor St. John, *The Rise of Investor-State Arbitration: Politics, Law, and Unintended Consequences* (Oxford University Press 2018).

29. Poulsen 12.

It follows from the true genesis and history of this field that a 'world without investment arbitration' cannot be viewed as a betrayal or frustration of states' or investors' essential interests in the investment treaty regime.

b   Lack of Empirical Support

Under the 'Credible Commitment' rationale, investment arbitration plays a crucial role in giving investment treaties more bite, resulting in more investor confidence – and therefore more investment. If this were true, one would expect a positive and statistically significant impact of investment arbitration on investment inflows. This is to be measured by comparing the effect of investment treaties with international arbitration provisions on investment inflows with investment treaties that lack host state consent to arbitration. This is a narrower question than the wider issue as to whether investment treaties more generally are causal for increased investment inflows.

As to the wider issue, more than forty studies have been done to date, with ambiguous results.[30] As to the narrower issue, the studies to date are unambiguous. Crucially, *none* of the existing studies shows that the inclusion of international arbitration provisions in investment treaties leads to increased investment inflows.[31] The results of these studies simply do not support the view that international arbitration in investment treaties helps countries attract foreign capital, even if (as has yet to be convincingly shown) the presence of an investment treaty may do so.

c   Conclusion

It follows that the 'Credible Commitment' rationale is simply not a viable justification for a world with the investment arbitration model as we currently know it.

2   The 'De-politicisation' Rationale

A second, common narrative suggests that investment arbitration has de-politicised investment disputes and thereby contributed to peaceful international relations. The theory is that investment arbitration helps states avoid or minimise political conflict in their relations because investors can turn to international arbitral tribunals directly, rather than having to rely on the political and military protection of their home state: in short, a viable alternative to 'gunboat diplomacy'. An attendant benefit is that it

---

30. Lauge Poulsen, Jonathan Bonnitcha and Jason Yackee, *Transatlantic Investment Treaty Protection* (Centre for European Policy Studies 2015) 4; for an overview *see* Bonnitcha, Poulsen and Waibel, Ch. 6, and Table A.6.1.
31. Axel Berger et al., 'More Stringent BITs, Less Ambiguous Effects on FDI? Not a Bit!' (2011) 112 Economics Letters 270; Axel Berger et al., 'Do Trade and Investment Agreements Lead to More FDI? Accounting for Key Provisions Inside the Black Box' (2013) 10 International Economics & Economic Policy 247; Clint Peinhardt and Todd Allee, *Devil in the Details? The Investment Effects of Dispute Settlement Variation in BITs* (2010).

insulates home states from pleas by investors to intervene or resort to diplomatic protection.

There are two dimensions to this rationale. The first dimension is whether the drafters of investment treaties attached importance to de-politicisation or saw international arbitration as a means to avoid gunboat diplomacy. The second is whether international arbitration has in fact de-politicised investment disputes. The rationale lacks strong empirical support in both respects.[32]

First, even though de-politicisation was an important goal for the framers of the ICSID Convention,[33] there is little evidence that de-politicisation prompted governments to include arbitration provisions in investment treaties since ICSID was created (setting to one side the World Bank's aforementioned lobbying efforts on behalf of arbitration). On the contrary, the available evidence suggests that the protection of investments has been a much more important objective of governments. For instance, archival records in Germany and the United Kingdom show that the drafters of first-generation investment treaties did not attach any importance to de-politicisation. Rather, with remarkable prescience, they were concerned that international arbitration could 'turn every case of expropriation into an international litigation with political relevance',[34] that is, that international arbitration would *increase* the politicisation of investment disputes.

Second, the evidence as to whether international arbitration has, in fact, de-politicised investment disputes is at best mixed. For example, the availability of investment arbitration to US investors has had no significant effect on whether, or the extent to which, the US Government raises the issue of the treatment of US investors at the inter-governmental level. The US Government has routinely intervened in investment disputes to promote broader foreign policy agendas.[35] The US is unlikely to be an outlier among capital-exporting states. Future research will likely show that home states more generally do not refrain from diplomatic intervention where important political interests are involved.

More anecdotally, as the nature of investment disputes becomes ever more sensitive (including topics such as nuclear power, renewable energy, climate change, economic policy, sanctions, the effects of war, etc.), it is increasingly difficult to argue that the current system of investment arbitration avoids 'politicisation'. On the contrary, the very limitations of the current arbitral system have projected the entire field into an increasingly politically treacherous situation.[36]

It follows that the 'De-Politicisation' rationale is also not a viable justification for a world with the investment arbitration model as we currently know it. And if

---

32. Bonnitcha, Poulsen and Waibel, 193-198.
33. Convention on the Settlement of Investment Disputes Between States and Nationals of Other States (International Centre for Settlement of Investment Disputes (ICSID).
34. Lauge Poulsen, *Bounded Rationality and Economic Diplomacy: The Politics of Investment Treaties in Developing Countries* (Cambridge University Press 2015).
35. Gertz, Jandhyala and Poulsen 2016; *see also* Bonnitcha, Poulsen and Waibel 197.
36. *See, e.g.,* the widespread political fallout from such cases as *Vattenfall v. Germany (I) & (II)*; *Phillip Morris v. Uruguay*; *Phillip Morris v. Australia*; *White Industries v. India*; *Tethyan Copper v. Pakistan.*

'De-Politicisation' is a goal, there is nothing to suggest that the current Anglo-US adversarial model of arbitration is the only way to achieve this.

III   PERCEIVED PROBLEMS WITH THE CURRENT SYSTEM OF INVESTMENT ARBITRATION

The now widespread attack on the current system of investment arbitration comprises two categories of criticism.

First, a now familiar list of defects in the way in which investment arbitration is currently operated, as elaborated (in particular) by UNCITRAL Working Group III. Some of these criticisms may be more accurate than others. But as already noted, the view of specialists and insiders on the accuracy of these points is now less important than the widespread perception, and consensus amongst many states, that the current system is broken and no longer delivering what is expected of it.

Second, a more fundamental, but less commonly articulated, question as to the suitability of the current arbitration model itself.

Each category is addressed in turn.

1   Six Standard Criticisms

UNCITRAL decided at its 50th session, which was held from 3 to 21 July 2017, to entrust UNCITRAL's Working Group III with a broad mandate to work on the possible reform of investor-State dispute settlement.[37] In carrying out that mandate, Working Group III was to ensure that its deliberations, 'while benefiting from the widest possible breadth of available expertise from all stakeholders, would be Government-led, with high-level input from all Governments, consensus-based and fully transparent'.[38] The approach of Working Group III was to proceed in three stages: (i) it would 'identify and consider concerns regarding ISDS'; (ii) it would 'consider whether reform was desirable in light of any identified concerns'; and (iii) if the Working Group concluded that reform was desirable, it would 'develop any relevant solutions to be recommended to the Commission'.[39]

Working Group III's conclusions, after the first two phases of this programme of work, are well known and cannot be ignored: namely that there are several concerns with the present system that are in need of reform.[40] But these conclusions sit alongside

---

37. Report of the United Nations Commission on International Trade Law, 50th Session (3-21 July 2017), UN Doc No A/72/17, UNGAOR, 72nd Session, Supplement No 17, paras 240-265.
38. Report of the United Nations Commission on International Trade Law, 50th Session (3-21 July 2017), UN Doc No A/72/17, UNGAOR, 72nd Session, Supplement No 17, para. 264; *see also* Report of UNCITRAL Working Group III on the Work of its Thirty-Sixth Session (Vienna, 29 October-2 November 2018), UN Doc No A/CN.9/930/Rev.1 (19 December 2017), para. 6.
39. Report of UNCITRAL Working Group III on the Work of its Thirty-Sixth Session (Vienna, 29 October-2 November 2018), UN Doc No A/CN.9/930/Rev.1 (19 December 2017), para. 6.
40. Report of UNCITRAL Working Group III on the Work of its Thirty-Sixth Session (Vienna, 29 October-2 November 2018), UN Doc No A/CN.9/964 (6 November 2018), paras 25-133.

a wider body of scholarship and commentary that raise other issues that must also be considered. The following list distils some of the key points from all sources.

a   *Investment Arbitration Produces Inconsistent Decisions That Result in a Lack of Predictability for Investors and Host States*

The concern that investment arbitration produces inconsistent decisions that result in a lack of predictability arises from three issues particular to investment arbitration. First, investment tribunals, because of their *ad hoc* character and because of the absence of a doctrine of precedent, produce inconsistencies in their decision-making with respect to interpretations of commonly recurring substantive standards of protection, issues of jurisdiction and admissibility, as well as procedural issues.[41] Second, there is no framework in investor-state cases to address multiple proceedings.[42] Third, there is no mechanism to address inconsistencies between, and the incorrectness of, arbitral decisions.[43]

All three issues lead to a lack of predictability for investors and host states alike.[44] Given its fundamentally different nature as compared to commercial arbitration, the defence that private dispute resolution does not require consistent decisions is simply no longer sustainable in this field.

This concern goes well beyond the infamous *Lauder* and *CME* awards of the early 2000s. Problems of inconsistency and incoherence in international investment law now arise in just about every case, given that just about every case will involve one or more commonly recurring issues. This includes every case involving the interpretation of the fair and equitable treatment (FET) obligation, including the nature and confines of legitimate expectations; the scope of the most favoured nation (MFN) clause; and the effect of the umbrella clause, to name but a few. There are of course cases in which inconsistent outcomes can be understood by reference to different formulations of the various standards from one BIT to another.[45] But Working Group III has focused on instances of 'unjustified inconsistency', that is, 'where the same investment treaty standard or same rule of customary international law was interpreted differently in the absence of justifiable ground for the distinction'.[46]

---

41. Report of UNCITRAL Working Group III on the Work of its Thirty-Sixth Session (Vienna, 29 October-2 November 2018), UN Doc No A/CN.9/964 (6 November 2018), paras 27-40.
42. Report of UNCITRAL Working Group III on the Work of its Thirty-Sixth Session (Vienna, 29 October-2 November 2018), UN Doc No A/CN.9/964 (6 November 2018), paras 41-53.
43. Report of UNCITRAL Working Group III on the Work of its Thirty-Sixth Session (Vienna, 29 October-2 November 2018), UN Doc No A/CN.9/964 (6 November 2018), paras 54-63.
44. Report of UNCITRAL Working Group III on the Work of its Thirty-Sixth Session (Vienna, 29 October-2 November 2018), UN Doc No A/CN.9/964 (6 November 2018), paras 25-63.
45. Julian Arato, Chester Brown and Federico Ortino, 'Parsing and Managing Inconsistency in Investor-State Dispute Settlement' (2020) 21 *Journal of World Investment and Trade* 336; *see also* Julian Arato, Chester Brown and Federico Ortino, 'Lack of Consistency and Coherence in the Interpretation of Legal Issues', Blogpost published on *EJIL: Talk!* (5 April 2019), available at https://www.ejiltalk.org/lack-of-consistency-and-coherence-in-the-interpretation-of-legal-issues/.
46. *Report of UNCITRAL Working Group III on the Work of its Thirty-Sixth Session*, UN Doc No A/CN.9/964 (6 November 2018), para. 29, referring to Note by the Secretariat, 'Possible reform

If the investment treaty regime aspires to be governed by the rule of law and not by the rule of arbitrators, consistency in decisions is important. Without consistency states are unable, despite their best efforts, to comply with their treaty obligations in advance;[47] foreign investors do not know in advance what protections under investment treaties they enjoy; and arbitral decisions can have limited impact in raising standards or establishing norms going forward. To this end, the uncertainty is not only inefficient because neither investors nor host states can plan, it also undermines one of the key purposes of the international investor-state system.

It is important to note that these concerns affect all users of the investment arbitration regime, not just states. It is often assumed that only certain states and members of civil society consider the current system needs reform. This is incorrect. The business community also recognises that there are serious costs inherent in, for instance, a system in which the interpretation of legal issues can differ widely, and in which diametrically opposed conclusions can be reached by different tribunals on the same issues. This results in a system that is inconsistent, unpredictable, and extremely inefficient. The lack of predictability and legal certainty creates an incentive (and for many counsel, a professional obligation) to run every possible argument for their client, even if the argument has been rejected by most tribunals which have considered the issue. The obvious result is that parties generally submit lengthy pleadings, covering all issues and arguing every possible point, on the off chance that the tribunal that has been constituted for the case might be persuaded where previous tribunals were not.

Given the pressing importance of these points, it ought to be an uncontroversial requirement that the current system of investment arbitration be replaced by a system that produces consistent decisions that can guide the conduct of states and foreign investors in advance.

b   *Problems with the Decision-Makers*

Working Group III has identified four problems with the decision-makers in investment arbitration. First, an apparent lack of independence and impartiality of certain arbitrators in investor-State cases.[48] Second, inadequate or ineffective methods of challenging arbitrators in investor-State cases.[49] Third, a lack of appropriate diversity among arbitrators.[50] Fourth, a lack of uniform qualifications for arbitrators, which raises concerns over the methods of constituting arbitral tribunals.[51]

---

of investor-State dispute settlement (ISDS): Consistency and related matters', UN Doc No A/CN.9/ WG.III/WP.150 (28 August 2018), para. 9.

47. Bonnitcha, Poulsen and Waibel 250.

48. Report of UNCITRAL Working Group III on the Work of its Thirty-Sixth Session (Vienna, 29 October-2 November 2018), UN Doc No A/CN.9/964 (6 November 2018), paras 66-83.

49. Report of UNCITRAL Working Group III on the Work of its Thirty-Sixth Session (Vienna, 29 October-2 November 2018), UN Doc No A/CN.9/964 (6 November 2018), paras 84-90.

50. Report of UNCITRAL Working Group III on the Work of its Thirty-Sixth Session (Vienna, 29 October-2 November 2018), UN Doc No A/CN.9/964 (6 November 2018), paras 91-98.

51. Report of UNCITRAL Working Group III on the Work of its Thirty-Sixth Session (Vienna, 29 October-2 November 2018), UN Doc No A/CN.9/964 (6 November 2018), paras 99-108.

Again, we amalgamate the concerns of Working Group III with other concerns and commentary from others in the community, in elaborating on these four specific issues.

i   The Problem of Party-Appointed Arbitrators

According to supporters of the existing model of party-appointed arbitrators, alternative arrangements 'may undermine the very foundations of arbitration (and of justice): the equality of arms between the parties'.[52] This normative argument has uncomfortable implications. If one accepts that 'justice' and 'the equality of arms' require that states have no greater influence than plaintiffs over the choice of tenured judges, it seems to follow that most courts, whether they be the German Constitutional Court, the UK Supreme Court or the United States Supreme Court, are illegitimate fora to resolve claims against states.[53]

The issue here concerns arbitrator moral hazard: the idea that party appointments encourage disputing parties to identify and appoint individuals who are (or are at least perceived to be) sympathetic to their position.[54] Their appointment for a single investment dispute undercuts the independence of arbitrators and increases their dependence on the disputing parties. This is all the more so when arbitrators are full-time, with (arguably) an eye on future appointments. Accordingly, the interests of party-appointed arbitrators may be closely aligned with their appointing party, and perhaps too closely aligned when arbitrators have often assumed the mantle of advocates for their appointing parties.[55]

ii   The Perception of Career/Financial Incentives

There is a perception that when interpreting and applying investment treaty provisions, arbitrators (who earn fees for each arbitration) may have an incentive to expand the scope of the regime to facilitate more arbitrations and thus potential appointments for themselves.[56] A particular concern may arise when arbitrators wear 'multiple hats' in investment arbitration by also representing investors. An analogous situation in domestic legal systems would be if a judge could also represent claimants against the state (or the state against claimants), in which case the neutrality of the judge could be

---

52. Thomas W Wälde, 'Procedural Challenges in Investment Arbitration under the Shadow of the Dual Role of the State: Asymmetries and Tribunals' Duty to Ensure, Pro-actively, the Equality of Arms' (2010) 26 Arbitration International 3; On equality of arms, *see* further IDI resolution.
53. This paragraph draws on Bonnitcha, Poulsen and Waibel 254.
54. Paulsson 2010; *see also* Malcolm Langford, Daniel Behn and Maria Chiara Malaguti, 'The Quadrilemma: Appointing Adjudicators in Future Investor-State Dispute Settlement', Academic Forum on ISDS Concept Paper 2019/12, 32.
55. Karen J Alter, 'Agents or Trustees' International Courts in Their Political Context' (2008) 14 European Journal of International Relations 33; Yuval Shany, 'Squaring the Circle-Independence and Impartiality of Party-Appointed Adjudicators in International Legal Proceedings' (2008) 30 Loyola LA International and Comparative Law Review 473.
56. Christopher R Drahozal, 'A Behavioural Analysis of Private Judging' (2004) 67 Law and Contemporary Problems 105.

placed in doubt.[57] Another concern, even where arbitrators do not also represent states before other arbitral tribunals, is that arbitrators may potentially affiliate themselves to a particular perspective. Building a reputation as a pro-investor or pro-state arbitrator could be more valuable for future appointments in the competitive market for arbitrators (especially for party appointments).

iii   *Lack of Diversity*

There is an issue with the homogenous backgrounds and lack of diversity among arbitrators.[58] Homogeneity relates to diverse aspects including professional and educational background. For example, commercial lawyers and those educated at leading universities in the UK and the US are arguably over-represented among arbitrators.

The gender gap, in particular, is wide: as of 2014, 93% of all arbitral appointments were men, and just two women accounted for three-quarters of all female appointments.[59] More recent data shows that this is improving, at least in the arbitrators appointed by the ICC, where there has been an increase in the appointment of female arbitrators from 10.4% of appointments in 2015 to 24.3% of appointments in 2021.[60] However, the gender imbalance remains stark: a 2022 ICCA report records that nearly half of all three-member tribunals appointed were single-gender, of which 97.5% were all-men tribunals and 2.5% were all-women tribunals.[61]

Arbitrators of Asian or African nationality are markedly under-represented, despite significant investment flows to and from Asia in particular and associated investment treaty disputes. The 2022 ICCA report – the first time the Task Force has reported on the nationality of female arbitrators – shows that the significant majority of appointees were from Western Europe and the United Kingdom (45.4%); a smaller proportion of women were Asian nationals (18.1%); and women from Africa (2.5%) and the Middle East (1.9%) were the least represented.[62] This homogeneity of investment arbitrators is all the more striking when compared with WTO panellists and other international courts and tribunals.[63] Further, even if this does not have a

---

57. Bonnitcha, Poulsen and Waibel 255.
58. *See, e.g.*, Malcolm Langford, Daniel Behn and Maria Chiara Malaguti, 'The Quadrilemma: Appointing Adjudicators in Future Investor-State Dispute Settlement', Academic Forum on ISDS Concept Paper 2019/12, 27.
59. Sergio Puig, 'Social Capital in the Arbitration Market' (2014) 25 European Journal of International Law 387, 405; *see generally* Nienke Grossman, 'Achieving Sex-Representative International Court Benches' (2016) 110 American Journal of International Law 82.
60. Report of the Cross-Institutional Task Force on Gender Diversity in Arbitral Appointments and Proceedings: 2022 update (2nd ed., International Council for Commercial Arbitration, 2022), 22.
61. Report of the Cross-Institutional Task Force on Gender Diversity in Arbitral Appointments and Proceedings: 2022 update, 59.
62. Report of the Cross-Institutional Task Force on Gender Diversity in Arbitral Appointments and Proceedings: 2022 update, 66.
63. Jóse Augusto Fontura, 'Comparing WTO Panellists and ICSID Arbitrators: The Creation of International Legal Fields' (2011) 1 Oñati Socio-Legal Series 1; Joost Pauwelyn, 'The Rule of Law Without the Rule of Lawyers? Why Investment Arbitrators Are from Mars, Trade Adjudicators from Venus' (2015) 109 American Journal of International Law 761.

significant effect on outcomes, it is undoubtedly a legitimacy problem given that 80% of investment arbitration cases are against non-Western respondent states.[64]

From the outside looking in, these characteristics of the body of arbitrators have a palpable impact on perceptions, in particular when arbitrators are seen to look for answers to difficult and novel questions, and when interpreting and applying open-ended standards of treatment such as indirect expropriation or FET.[65] A background, for instance, in commercial law might render some arbitrators less sympathetic to interests outside their traditional domains, such as human rights law, or less willing to consider the impact of their awards on other legal systems. More broadly, the current homogeneity among arbitrators has fuelled a widespread perception of pro-investor bias which – even if the perception is out of step with reality – undermines confidence in the current system[66] and constitutes an incentive for states to withdraw from treaties and/or exclude investment arbitration clauses in any new treaty.

iv   Lack of Accountability

Arbitral awards (indeed any decision of an arbitral tribunal) cannot be appealed in the current investment arbitration system. In the absence of an appeal or review mechanism, there is an accountability gap. This may be mitigated to an extent either through transparent decision-making (again, not an intrinsic feature of the current investment arbitration system, although many decisions are published) or a sustained reputation on the part of arbitrators as even-handed. But although even-handedness of arbitrators may restore some sense of accountability in the arbitral system, a reputation for even-handedness may also be the basis on which an arbitrator builds a career and secures further appointments. So even this potential answer to accountability may be impugned.

These four elements inevitably lead to the conclusion that the current system needs to be replaced by a process helmed by independent and diverse adjudicators that represent the contemporary world economy, driven not by financial and career incentives, but aspiring collectively towards the rule of law.

c   **Cost and Duration**

According to UNCITRAL, the average duration of an investment arbitration claim is 3 to 4 years.[67] This, on any view, is surprising for a system of dispute settlement

---

64. Malcolm Langford, Daniel Behn and Maxim Usynin, 'The West and the Rest: Geographic Diversity and the Role of Arbitrator Nationality in Investment Arbitration' in Daniel Behn, Ole Kristian Fauchald and Malcolm Langford (eds), *The Legitimacy of Investment Arbitration* (Cambridge University Press 2022) 283.
65. *See also* Olof Larsson et al., 'Selection and Appointment in International Adjudication: Insights from Political Science', Academic Forum on ISDS Concept Paper 2019/10, 15.
66. Susan D. Franck et al., 'The Diversity Challenge: Exploring the Invisible College of International Arbitration' (2015) 53 Columbia Journal of Transnational Law 429.
67. Note by the Secretariat, 'Possible reform of investor-State dispute settlement (ISDS) – cost and duration', UN Doc No A/CN.9/WG.III/WP.153 (31 August 2018), paras 54-59.

supposed to be faster than traditional litigation and which does not have the right of appeal.

Further, the current system of investment arbitration is expensive – a feature exacerbated by the lack of consistency in decision-making and lack of predictability, which naturally causes counsel to run every available argument. The average tribunal costs are around USD 1 million; the average cost for the claimant is around USD 6 million and the average cost for the respondent state is around USD 4.8 million.[68] There are concerns that the resource-intensive nature of investment arbitration proceedings is untenably costly for developing states with scarce financial and human resources. Likewise, small to medium enterprises with limited financial resources have, in effect, reduced access to investment arbitration.[69]

According to Working Group III, problematic features include:[70] (i) the lack of a mechanism to address frivolous or unmeritorious cases;[71] (ii) the inadequacy of rules on the allocation of costs;[72] and (iii) concerns relating to the availability of security for costs.[73] Working Group III has been exploring the possibility of a new legal test to address frivolous or unmeritorious claims as part of its procedural reforms. The proposal is for inclusion of a rule on early dismissal, empowering the arbitral tribunal to make a prima facie assessment of whether the case is 'manifestly without merit'.[74] Likewise, Working Group III discussions have developed into a proposal for including a default rule that the unsuccessful party would bear the costs of the proceedings, with the arbitral tribunal having the discretion to decide otherwise.[75] Reform on security for costs is still underway, with recognition of the need to balance protection for states against a claimant's inability or unwillingness to pay and for certain investors, particularly small- and medium-sized enterprises, to remain able to access justice.[76] These, however, are incomplete and disparate patches on what is a far-reaching underlying problem with the current system.

---

68. Note by the Secretariat, 'Possible reform of investor-State dispute settlement (ISDS) – Cost and Duration', UN Doc No A/CN.9/WG.III/WP.153 (31 August 2018), paras 38-53.
69. Report of UNCITRAL Working Group III on the Work of its Thirty-Sixth Session (Vienna, 29 October-2 November 2018), UN Doc No A/CN.9/964 (6 November 2018), para. 112.
70. Report of UNCITRAL Working Group III on the Work of its Thirty-Sixth Session (Vienna, 29 October-2 November 2018), UN Doc No A/CN.9/964 (6 November 2018), paras 109-133.
71. Report of UNCITRAL Working Group III on the Work of its Thirty-Sixth Session (Vienna, 29 October-2 November 2018), UN Doc No A/CN.9/964 (6 November 2018), paras 110-123.
72. Report of UNCITRAL Working Group III on the Work of its Thirty-Sixth Session (Vienna, 29 October-2 November 2018), UN Doc No A/CN.9/964 (6 November 2018), paras 124-127.
73. Report of UNCITRAL Working Group III on the Work of its Thirty-Sixth Session (Vienna, 29 October-2 November 2018), UN Doc No A/CN.9/964 (6 November 2018), paras 128-133.
74. Report of UNCITRAL Working Group III on the Work of its Forty-Third Session (Vienna, 5-16 September 2022), paras 107-119; and UNCITRAL Working Group III, 'Possible reform of investor-State dispute settlement (ISDS): Draft provisions on procedural reform' UN Doc A/CN.9/WG.III/WP.219 (2022).
75. Report of UNCITRAL Working Group III on the Work of its Forty-Third Session (Vienna, 5-16 September 2022), paras 120-124; UNCITRAL Working Group III, 'Possible reform of investor-State dispute settlement (ISDS): Draft provisions on procedural reform' UN Doc A/CN.9/WG.III/WP.219 (11 July 2022).
76. Report of Working Group III on the Work of its Thirty-Ninth Session (Vienna, 5-9 October 2020), UN Doc A/CN.0/1044 (10 November 2020), paras 74-77.

d　　*The Ease of Commencing Arbitration and the Impact on States' Resources*

The number of investment arbitrations is inefficiently high under the *status quo*. Investors are quick to initiate investment arbitrations as third-party funders often cover their downside risk. Such investors have only upside risk.[77] The result is a plethora of arbitrations, some with doubtful prospects, that stretch the resources of respondent states.

e　　*A Preferential Forum for Foreign Investors Distorts the Market for Foreign Investment*

To the extent a host state has a well-developed and independent judicial system, investment arbitration may unnecessarily introduce a new source of inefficiency. Domestic investors are limited to domestic courts, whereas foreign investors receive preferential treatment. In such cases, providing a new forum exclusively for foreign investors appears unjustified.[78] By establishing a new forum exclusively for foreign investors and thus providing greater rights to foreign investors, the market for investments is distorted.

By contrast, such a forum may be justified on economic grounds if the host country lacks a well-functioning legal system because the second distortion may correct the first distortion.

Thus, if the host state has a robust domestic legal system, there is no need for a separate, preferential system for resolving investment disputes for foreign investors. Even if domestic courts lack independence and a forum outside the host state is desirable, it does not follow that foreign investors themselves should be able to influence the composition of investment treaty tribunals.

f　　*Investment Arbitration Chills Regulation in the Public Interest That Is Compatible with Investment Treaties*

Certain characteristics of the current investment arbitration system have the effect of deterring states from adopting measures in the public interest that are compatible with their obligations under investment treaties, in particular: (a) the lack of predictability in the system (as above); and (b) the threat of expensive, cumbersome proceedings (even if there is a prospect of a successful outcome). Not all states have the resources to defend measures over years of arbitration.

---

77. Report of UNCITRAL Working Group III on the Work of its Thirty-Sixth Session (Vienna, 29 October-2 November 2018), UN Doc A/CN.9/964 (6 November 2018), para. 134; and Report of UNCITRAL Working Group III on the Work of its Thirty-Seventh Session (New York, 1-5 April 2019), UN Doc No A/CN.9/970 (9 April 2019), paras 17-25.

78. *See* the 2005 Australia-US Free Trade Agreement; *see also* Jan Kleinheisterkamp and Lauge Poulsen, 'Investment Protection in TTIP: Three Feasible Proposals' (2014) Global Economic Governance Programme and Blavatnik School of Government (https://www.geg.ox.ac.uk/publication/policy-brief-investment-protection-ttip-three-feasible-proposals).

The example of plain-packaging tobacco legislation is instructive. While Australia had the resources to defend its measure against Philip Morris,[79] New Zealand delayed the implementation of an equivalent measure until the arbitration with Australia was concluded.[80] Uruguay's ability to defend its tobacco control measures regarding packaging depended on millions of dollars of legal and technical support provided by Michael Bloomberg and the Gates Foundation.[81]

In other instances, countries do not refrain from adopting general measures in pursuit of the public interest but abandon them due to investment arbitration. Examples include the cases of *SD Myers v. Canada* and *Ethyl v. Canada*, both under NAFTA. The first case concerned a Canadian ban on hazardous waste exports to the US. After a US investor initiated arbitration, the Canadian Government revoked the measure.[82] In the second case, the claim of the US investor regarding an environmental measure played at least some role in the abandonment of the measure.[83]

Regulatory chill as in the examples above is a significant concern. Governments refrain from or abandon measures in the public interest due to the shadow and uncertainties of investment arbitration, even for measures that arguably, or actually, do not breach the applicable investment treaty. The inevitable, and it is suggested entirely reasonable, conclusion is that the current system should be replaced by a system that does not curb regulation in the public interest.

2   Fundamental Issues with the Current Model

But there are much more fundamental issues with respect to the very design of the current arbitral model.

Traditionally, arbitration has been conceived as a form of private dispute settlement that remains within the control of the immediate disputing parties.[84] In the field of ISDS, the system of arbitration invariably deployed embodies what is a traditional Anglo-US adversarial procedural model that was developed to resolve commercial disputes. According to this, the arbitral tribunal sits as an essentially passive umpire, waiting to be educated by the disputing parties and mandated to

---

79. *Philip Morris Asia Ltd v. Australia* (UNCITRAL, Award on Jurisdiction and Admissibility of 17 December 2015).
80. Cabinet Social Policy Committee (NZ), 'Tobacco Plain Packaging: Approval for Drafting (13 August 2013); *see also* Jane Kelsey, 'Regulatory Chill: Learnings from New Zealand's Plain Packaging Tobacco Law' (2017) 17 QUT Law Review 21.
81. Council of Foreign Relations 2012; *see Philip Morris Brands SARL v. Uruguay* (Award) ICSID Case No. ARB/10/7 (8 July 2016).
82. *SD Myers, Inc v. Canada* (Final Award of 30 December 2002).
83. *Ethyl Corporation v. Canada* (Award on Jurisdiction of 24 June 1998). *See also* Kyla Tienhaara, *The Expropriation of Environmental Governance: Protecting Foreign Investors at the Expense of Public Policy* (Cambridge University Press 2009); and Poulsen, Bonnitcha and Yackee 28.
84. Stephen Ware, 'Default Rules from Mandatory Rules: Privatizing Law Through Arbitration' (1999) 88 Minn. L. Rev. 703; Claire A. Cutler, *Private Power and Global Authority: Transnational Merchant Law in the Global Political Economy* (Cambridge University Press 2003); Doreen Lustig and Eyal Benvenisti, 'The Multinational Corporation as "the Good Despot": The Democratic Cost of Privatization in Global Settings' (2014) 15 Theoretical Inquiries in Law 125; and *ibid.*, 246.

resolve the dispute within the confines of the submissions and materials which the immediate parties choose to present to it.

There are three problems with this model when transplanted into the world of investor-State treaty disputes.

a   The Impact on Wider Interests

The mandate of investment arbitration tribunals is to adjudicate upon the exercise of sovereign discretion. The nature of such disputes is not 'horizontal' in nature, as is commercial arbitration, in the sense of parties that have contracted with each other on the same level. Rather, it is 'vertical', or more akin to administrative adjudication, whereby an individual investor questions the policy or conduct of a state which may affect not only the investor, but a wide range of interests, a whole community, or even an entire population.

As the nature of investment disputes becomes ever more sensitive, this difference becomes ever more marked. Cases questioning a state's policy on nuclear power, cigarette packaging, economic or fiscal policy, climate change, sanctions, war, water and other topics will inevitably bear upon substantial interests that will not be represented in an investment arbitration. The scope for an arbitral tribunal to widen its mission to take account of such interest is extremely limited, and the prevailing arbitral mindset is notably opposed to this in any event. There is a fundamental mismatch between the procedural model that is now in use and the interests that may be affected.

b   The Development of International Investment Law

Investment treaty tribunals do not only find facts and settle commercial disputes, although this is the purpose for which the current procedural model was designed. Investment treaty arbitrators also develop international investment law by articulating and clarifying vague legal principles and standards found in investment treaties. These in turn affect the behaviour of the disputing parties and third parties prospectively.[85]

Considering (a) how frequently tribunals rely on awards of other tribunals and (b) how arbitrators' conceptions of the appropriate exercise of public power inform the way they develop and apply international investment law,[86] investment tribunals also

---

85. Heinrich Kronstein, 'Business Arbitration: Instrument of Private Government' (1994) 54 Yale L.J. 36; Samantha Besson, 'Legal Philosophical Issues of International Adjudication: Getting over the Amour Impossible Between International Law and Adjudication' in Cesare P.R. Romano, Karen J. Alter and Yuval Shany (eds) *The Oxford Handbook of International Adjudication* (Oxford University Press 2014); Armin von Bogdandy and Ingo Venzke, *In Whose Name? A Public Law Theory of International Adjudication* (OUP 2014); Stephan W Schill, 'Conceptions of legitimacy' in David D Caron and others (eds), *Practising Virtue: Inside International Arbitration* (Oxford University Press, 2015); and *ibid.*

86. That investment arbitral tribunals have such a judicial function has also been the subject of controversy and is the subject of debate in Working Group III: *see*, e.g., Report of Working Group III on the Work of its Thirty-sixth Session (Vienna, 29 October-2 November 2018), UN Doc A/CN.9/964; and Yanwen Zhang, 'The Judicial Function of Investment Tribunals: Taking Foundational Assumptions Seriously' (2022) 25(1) JIEL 129.

engage, in effect, in governance.[87] In this way, the findings of investment tribunals have consequences reaching far beyond a single investment dispute, and the current arbitral system has produced conflicts and negative spill-overs for other legal systems. And yet the current system encourages arbitrators to proceed as if they were operating in splendid isolation, despite the reality that they are creating law and exercising governance functions.[88]

c Limitations of the Adversarial Model

As noted above, the prevailing form of arbitration utilised in ISDS is a commercial model, which has been transplanted without modification to resolve disputes governed by public international law. This form of dispute resolution has a tendency to escalate disputes and sever business relations permanently.[89] But more than this, the adversarial model all too often leads to a polarisation of the competing parties' positions – often exacerbated by the use of party-appointed experts. The result can be an environment singularly ill-suited for a tribunal to grapple with highly sensitive and nuanced issues of policy, which have increasingly become the subject of arbitral claims.

3 Conclusion

Standing back, the criticisms of the current system are far-reaching, profound, and voiced with increasing urgency. The call for change is now simply too loud to ignore. And this is a change in the fundamental structure and nature of the process. Light tweaks to the existing system patently will not suffice to meet the breadth and depth of the current disquiet and stem the current exodus.

And the attempt to sustain the current system is all the more unjustified given the existence of viable alternatives – to which we now turn.

IV VIABLE ALTERNATIVES TO THE CURRENT SYSTEM

1 Local Remedies

The first alternative is for investors to make use of what is really the default option that exists in the absence of investment arbitration, namely the possibility of seeking

---

87. Von Bogdandy and Venzke; José E. Alvarez, 'What Are International Judges For? The Main Functions of International Adjudication' in Cesare P.R. Romano, Karen J. Alter and Yuval Shany (eds), *The Oxford Handbook of International Adjudication* (Oxford University Press 2014); *ibid.*
88. *Waste Management v. Mexico (II)* (Award) Case no ARB(AF)/00/3 (30 April 2004); and *see* Michael Reisman, 'International Arbitration and Sovereignty' (2002) 18(3) Arbitration International 231. On indirect and passive investments, *see* Michael Waibel, 'Subject Matter Jurisdiction: The Notion of Investment' in Jorge Viñuales and Michael Waibel (eds), *ICSID Reports*, vol. 19 (Cambridge University Press 2021) [58]. *See* further J. Ho, 'Passive Investments', (2020) 34(3) ICSID Rev - FILJ 1. On structured, indirect investments, *see* Jorun Baumgartner, *Treaty Shopping in International Investment Law* (Oxford University Press 2016) Ch. 5.
89. Ilija Mitrev Penusliski, 'A Dispute Systems Design Diagnosis of ICSID', in Michael Waibel et al. (eds), *The Backlash Against Investment Arbitration* (Kluwer, 2010).

dispute settlement before the host state's local courts. This argument has been made in the context of Working Group III, with South Africa in particular questioning whether there is any need for ISDS at all. South Africa has argued that states 'must not rush into assuming that ISDS policies must be a part of their investment agreements and must be mindful of the origins of the ISDS', which was 'never seen as a substitute for domestic legal dispute settlement, but as a stopgap in cases of extreme maladministration carried out by governments'.[90]

It is noteworthy that this is precisely what happens in the case of certain investor-state disputes already, such as those arising under Chapter 14 of the Japan–Australia Economic Partnership Agreement;[91] disputes under Chapter 11 of the Australia–United States Free Trade Agreement;[92] disputes arising under the Protocol on Investment to the Australia–New Zealand Closer Economic Relations Trade Agreement;[93] and (prospective) disputes arising under Chapter 13 of the Australia–United Kingdom Free Trade Agreement.[94] As between states that have key economic and strategic partnerships with each other, this seems a perfectly viable and reasonable approach, obviating the need for a special mechanism. Indeed, even beyond such key partnerships, some authors suggest there is an emerging trend towards no investment arbitration provisions or limited investment arbitration provisions in new agreements.[95] An example is Chapter 14 of the United States-Mexico-Canada Agreement, which entered into force in 2020 and requires a foreign investor to litigate in domestic courts for at least a period of thirty months before it can submit an arbitral claim.[96]

2   Diplomatic Protection

The second concrete alternative is the possibility of traditional diplomatic protection. This involves investors relying on their state of nationality to espouse their claim and to present it on the international plane against the host state. A recent example without investment arbitration is the Regional Comprehensive Economic Partnership Agreement (RCEP), a free trade agreement (FTA) among Australia, Brunei, Cambodia, China, Indonesia, Japan, South Korea, Laos, Malaysia, Myanmar, New Zealand, the Philippines, Singapore, Thailand and Vietnam, which entered into force on 1 January 2022.

---

90. *Submission from the Government of South Africa*, UN Doc No A/CN.9/WG.III/WP.176 (17 July 2019), para. 37.
91. Japan – Australia Economic Partnership Agreement, signed 8 July 2014, [2015] ATS 2 (entered into force 15 January 2015), Ch. 14.
92. Australia – United States Free Trade Agreement, signed 18 May 2004, [2005] ATS 1 (entered into force 1 January 2005), Ch. 11.
93. Protocol on Investment to the Australia – New Zealand Closer Economic Relations Trade Agreement, signed 16 February 2011, [2013] ATS 10 (entered into force 1 March 2013).
94. Australia – United Kingdom Free Trade Agreement, signed 17 December 2021, available at https://www.dfat.gov.au/trade/agreements/not-yet-in-force/aukfta (not yet in force).
95. *See, e.g.*, Prabhash Ranjan, 'Emerging Trends in Investor-State Dispute Settlement in New Free Trade Agreements' (2022) 17 Global Trade and Customs Journal 332.
96. United States-Mexico-Canada Agreement (USMCA) (entered into force 1 July 2020), Article 14.D.5(1)(b). This provision applies only as between United States and Mexico as Canada is not a party to the USMCA's chapter on ISDS.

But the state of nationality might not wish to espouse the diplomatic protection claim and cannot be forced to do so.[97] Further, under customary international law, a diplomatic protection claim is only possible if two conditions are met, namely: first, that the investor, whether a natural or legal person, actually has the nationality of the state in question (although the International Law Commission has suggested that a state may also exercise diplomatic protection in respect of a person who is stateless or a refugee who is lawfully resident in the state);[98] and second, that the investor in question has exhausted local remedies unless a relevant exception to that rule applies.[99]

In the specific context of investment treaty claims, there is usually the possibility of state-to-state dispute settlement proceedings, a possibility to which most BITs already cater. There have been at least three such state-to-state disputes under investment treaties, namely *Italy v. Cuba*;[100] *Chile v. Peru* (although this state-to-state dispute, which was commenced in the context of the *Lucchetti v. Peru* claim, does not appear to have progressed very far);[101] and *Ecuador v. United States*.[102]

So most investment treaties, including those which do not have investment arbitration clauses, already make provision for the resolution of disputes. And such BITs confirm that the absence of an investment arbitration provision does not need to be regarded as an absence of efficacy as regards investor protection. State-to-state arbitration provisions provide a natural home for claims that the host state has misapplied the BIT regarding a given investor. And all this underscores the point made earlier that investment treaties without investment arbitration provisions are not toothless. Such treaties still have the important function of establishing substantive standards as salient focal points for the crystallisation of customary international law.[103]

3   **Dispute Prevention, and Submission to a Joint Committee, with Inter-State Arbitration as a Last Resort**

The third possibility is for an alternative model that embraces dispute prevention as a critical element of the procedure, and which culminates in the facilitation of dispute

---

97. *See, e.g., Van Zyl v. South Africa* [2007] ZASCA 109, [2007] SCA 109 (RSA). This dispute related to the cancellation of five mining leases in the basin of the Khatse Dam by Lesotho in 1991. Van Zyl and others requested South Africa to provide them with diplomatic protection against Lesotho. The South African Government refused to do so on the understanding there was no obligation to do so. The Supreme Court of South African upheld the Government's decision, holding that there was neither a domestic nor international law obligation to diplomatic protection in the particular circumstances of the case. *See also Abbasi v. Secretary of State for Foreign and Commonwealth Affairs* [2002] EWCA Civ 1598.
98. International Law Commission Articles on Diplomatic Protection (2006), Article 8.
99. International Law Commission Articles on Diplomatic Protection (2006), Articles 14-15.
100. *Italian Republic v. Republic of Cuba* (Final Award of 1 January 2008).
101. *See, e.g., Empresas Lucchetti SA and Lucchetti Peru SA v. Peru* (Award) ICSID case no ARB/03/4 (7 February 2005) [7].
102. *Ecuador v. United States* (Award) PCA case no 2012/05 (29 September 2012).
103. *Supra* nn. 19 & 20.

settlement. In the context of Working Group III, Brazil has promoted this approach,[104] which reflects its policy of negotiating investment treaties known as 'Cooperation and Facilitation Investment Agreements' or 'CFIAs'.[105] These treaties emerged in the context of increasing dissatisfaction with the traditional approach to ISDS. As Brazil has explained it:

> The lack of evidence that BITs promote FDI, the controversial nature of investment agreements that unduly protect investors at the expense of the right of host countries to regulate in the public interest and the growing demand for a more balanced approach between investors and States reinforced Brazil's decision to develop a model that would overcome the shortcomings of traditional BITs.[106]

Brazil's approach is based on a preference for dispute prevention, rather than adversarial litigation. The dispute settlement procedure involves the use of two institutions, namely the 'Joint Committee' (which is a committee consisting of representatives of the two states parties to the treaty) and the 'National Focal Point' (which is an Ombudsman-type role, with one person appointed by each state). This can be seen in the provisions of Brazil's most recent CFIA, the Investment Cooperation and Facilitation Treaty between Brazil and India signed on 25 January 2020 (not yet in force).[107]

Beginning with the 'Joint Committee':

(i) Under Article 13 of the Brazil–India CFIA, the parties agree to establish a 'Joint Committee' for the administration of the treaty, which is comprised of government representatives of both parties appointed by their respective governments.[108]

(ii) The Joint Committee has the functions of: (i) supervising the implementation and execution of the treaty; (ii) discussing and making known opportunities for the expansion of mutual investment; (iii) coordinating the implementation of mutually agreed cooperation and facilitation agendas; (iv) consulting with investors and relevant stakeholders, when applicable, on their views on specific issues related to the work of the Joint Committee; (v) discussing issues and seeking to resolve disputes concerning investments of investors of a Party in an amicable manner; and (vi) supplementing the rules for arbitral dispute settlement between the Parties.[109]

---

104. *Submission from the Government of Brazil*, UN Doc A/CN.9/WG.III/WP.171 (11 June 2019).
105. *See* especially Henrique Choer Moraes and Pedro Mendonca Cavalcante, 'The Brazil – India Investment Cooperation and Facilitation Treaty: Giving Concrete Meaning to the "Right to Regulate" in Investment Treaty Making' (2021) 36 *ICSID Review – Foreign Investment Law Journal* 304.
106. *Submission from the Government of Brazil*, UN Doc No A/CN.9/WG.III/WP.171 (11 June 2019).
107. Investment Cooperation and Facilitation Treaty between Brazil and India, signed 25 January 2020 (not yet in force) ('Brazil – India CFIA'); see Choer Moraes and Mendonca Cavalcante (cited above).
108. Brazil – India CFIA, Articles 13(1)-(2).
109. Brazil – India CFIA, Article 13(4).

As for the 'National Focal Point' or 'Ombudsman':[110]

(i) Under Article 14 of the treaty, each Party is to designate 'a single National Focal Point … whose main responsibility shall be to support investors from the other Party in its territory'.[111]

(ii) The function of the National Focal Point includes: (i) following 'the recommendations of the Joint Committee and interact[ing] with the National Focal Point … of the other Party'; (ii) following up 'on requests and enquiries of the other Party or of investors of the other Party with the competent authorities, including in the state and local levels, and inform[ing] them on the results of its action'; (iii) assessing suggestions 'to improve the investment environment and complaints received from the other Party or investors of the other Party'; (iv) addressing 'differences in investment matters, in collaboration with government authorities and relevant investors, with a view to helping in the prevention of disputes'; (v) providing information 'on regulatory issues on general investment or on specific projects, to the extent possible'; and (vi) reporting to the Joint Committee.[112]

Turning then to the dispute settlement procedure under Brazil's CFIAs (called a 'Dispute Prevention Procedure'):[113]

(i) First, if a party (being one of the state parties, i.e., Brazil or India) considers that a specific measure adopted by the other party constitutes a breach of the treaty, it may initiate a dispute prevention procedure within the Joint Committee.[114]

(ii) The Joint Committee is to meet within 90 days to consider the request and to prepare a report within 120 days of the date of its first meeting.[115]

(iii) The Joint Committee's Report is to (i) identify the complaining party; (ii) describe the measure in question and the alleged breach of the treaty; and (iii) state its findings.[116]

(iv) If the measure in question relates to a specific investor, then representatives of the affected investor may be invited to appear before the Joint Committee.[117]

(v) In all cases, the Joint Committee may invite other interested stakeholders to appear before the Joint Committee and to present their views on the measure in question, if it considers this would be relevant to the measure in question.[118]

---

110. In some of Brazil's other CFIAs, the gender-neutral term 'Ombudsperson' is used: see, e.g., Brazil – UAE CFIA, signed 15 March 2019, Article 19 (not yet in force).
111. Brazil – India CFIA, Article 14(1).
112. Brazil – India CFIA, Article 14(4).
113. Brazil – India CFIA, Article 18.
114. Brazil – India CFIA, Article 18(1).
115. Brazil – India CFIA, Article 18(2).
116. Brazil – India CFIA, Article 18(2).
117. Brazil – India CFIA, Article 18(3).
118. Brazil – India CFIA, Article 18(4).

(vi) The meetings of the Joint Committee, and all materials submitted to the Joint Committee, are confidential, although this confidentiality does not apply to the Joint Committee's Report.[119]

If the Joint Committee's Report does not resolve the dispute, then the next step is an ad hoc inter-state arbitration, in accordance with Article 19(1):

(i) The purpose of the ad hoc arbitration is 'to decide on interpretation of [the] Treaty or the observance by a Party of the terms of [the] Treaty'.[120]

(ii) The ad hoc tribunal has jurisdiction to consider whether the Parties have complied with their substantive obligations under the treaty (with two minor exceptions, namely the obligation on states to ensure that their laws are publicly available, and the obligation on states to adopt measures to combat corruption, money laundering and terrorism financing).[121] The treaty makes it clear that the tribunal may not award compensation.[122]

(iii) The tribunal is to be constituted by each party appointing one arbitrator, and the two party-appointed arbitrators selecting a national of a third state who, on approval by the two parties, is appointed Chairman of the tribunal.[123] The arbitrators must meet certain qualification requirements, including that they have to be independent and impartial, and that they have relevant expertise or experience in public international law, international investment law and trade, or in the resolution of investment disputes.[124]

This is a real and effective alternative to the traditional model of investment arbitration. And, notably, it has done Brazil no harm in its ability to attract foreign investment. If one looks at UNCTAD's World Investment Report for 2022, Brazil is the world's sixth-highest recipient of foreign direct investment (FDI), having attracted USD 50 billion in 2021.[125] In the COVID-19-affected year of 2020, it attracted USD 25 billion in FDI (and was in 11th place), and in 2019, Brazil was the sixth highest recipient of FDI, having attracted USD 65 billion.[126] The figures for the previous years show a consistent story: in 2018, it attracted USD 61 billion of FDI; in 2017, it attracted USD 68 billion of FDI;[127] in 2016, it attracted USD 59 billion of FDI (and was again in seventh place); and in 2015, it attracted USD 64 billion of FDI (and was in eighth place).[128]

The focus on dispute prevention and management has been picked up more broadly in Working Group III's most recent work. At its 38th session in October 2019, there was general support in the Working Group for further consideration of the

---

119. Brazil – India CFIA, Article 18(5).
120. Brazil – India CFIA, Article 19(1).
121. Brazil – India CFIA, Article 19(3) (*see* Articles 8 and 10(1)).
122. Brazil – India CFIA, Article 19(2).
123. Brazil – India CFIA, Article 19(4).
124. Brazil – India CFIA, Article 19(6).
125. UNCTAD, World Investment Report 2022 (2022) 9.
126. UNCTAD, World Investment Report 2021 (2021) 5.
127. UNCTAD, *World Investment Report 2019* (2019) 4 (Figure I.3).
128. UNCTAD, *World Investment Report 2017* (2017) 12 (Figure I.11).

establishment of an Advisory Centre on International Investment Law usefully complementing other reform options.[129] In the September 2022 session, it was suggested that express reference be made to the Centre providing dispute-prevention-related services.[130] Financing was discussed in the 38th session but remains undecided and on Working Group III's agenda. Possible options are: (i) through contributions from Member States, which could take into account the level of economic development of members, and through voluntary contributions, and/or (ii) user-pays, with fees charged to states adjusted based on their level of economic development.[131] Financing options should be sustainable in the long term, maintain the independence of such a centre to preserve its legitimacy, balance tensions between various stakeholders, and provide equal opportunity to all states to defend their interests in ISDS.[132] Again, this is a viable, and radically different, approach to dispute resolution in this field.

4   Multilateral Investment Court and Appellate Tribunal

Another option, and the one which deserves the most serious consideration, is the establishment of a permanent adjudicatory body, in the form either of a multilateral investment court (MIC) with or without an appellate tier, to replace the current system of ad hoc tribunals or a self-standing appellate mechanism for the existing system of ad hoc tribunals. Both of these variants are under active review by Working Group III, driven by states who believe that the systemic problems identified earlier cannot be resolved with mere incremental reforms, or tweaking of the current arbitral model. These states include the European Union and its Member States;[133] Canada; and China, which has recently announced its support for research into an appellate structure.[134]

The most radical of the variants – the proposal for a MIC – is much broader than the conclusion of individual investment agreements that provide for the creation of a permanent tribunal for a single treaty. Rather, the proposal is to replace the current system of investment arbitration with a truly permanent MIC, which would have two levels, a first-instance tribunal, and an appellate tribunal. The first instance tribunal would hear disputes; conduct fact-finding much as arbitral tribunals do under the present system; and apply the applicable law to the facts. The first instance tribunal would also dispose of cases remanded back to it by the appellate tribunal.[135] The appellate tribunal would hear appeals from the first-instance tribunal. As currently

129. Report of Working Group III on the Work of its Thirty-Eighth Session (Vienna, 14-18 October 2019), UN Doc A/CN.9/1004, paras 26-49.
130. Report of UNCITRAL Working Group III on the Work of its Forty-Third Session (Vienna, 5-16 September 2022), paras 52 and 198.
131. Report of Working Group III on the Work of its Thirty-Eighth Session (Vienna, 14-18 October 2019), UN Doc A/CN.9/1004, para 38.
132. Report of Working Group III on the Work of its Thirty-Eighth Session (Vienna, 14-18 October 2019), UN Doc A/CN.9/1004, paras 37-39.
133. *Submission by the EU and its Member States*, UN Doc No A/CN.9/WG.III/WP.159/Add.1 (24 January 2019).
134. *Submission from the Government of China*, UN Doc No A/CN.9/WG.III/WP.177 (19 July 2019).
135. *Submission by the EU and its Member States*, UN Doc No A/CN.9/WG.III/WP.159/Add.1 (24 January 2019), para. 13.

conceived, the grounds of appeal would include error of law (including serious procedural shortcomings); manifest errors in the appreciation of the facts; as well as typical grounds for setting aside (under domestic legislation on international arbitration) or annulment (under the ICSID Convention). The appellate tribunal would therefore have the power to uphold, modify, or reverse the decision of the first instance tribunal. The appellate tribunal could also remand cases to the first instance tribunal where the factual record before it did not permit it to dispose of the case (although this may be conferred as a discretionary power). Importantly, the appellate tribunal would not undertake a *de novo* review of the facts.[136] Parties would not have the right to appeal a decision or award of the first instance tribunal (which may otherwise result in the appellate tribunal being overwhelmed); instead, a party would have to apply for leave to appeal, and the appellate tribunal would exercise discretion in granting such leave.

The opposition to this proposal, to date, has centred upon three key issues: (i) the problem of who the adjudicators would be, and how they would be elected or appointed; (ii) the problem of the interaction between the proposed MIC and the New York Convention[137] and the ICSID Convention; and (iii) the problem of financing. None of these concerns is sufficient to undermine the viability of this proposal.

a   *Who Would Be the Adjudicators?*

Beginning with the composition of both the MIC and its appellate tribunal, and a self-standing appellate body, much work has been done on possible solutions. The key principles (as so far suggested by the EU) may be summarised as follows.[138]

Adjudicators would be full-time; not have any outside activities;[139] and would be paid salaries comparable to the salaries of judges on other international courts and tribunals.[140] They would have to comply with a strict code of ethics[141] and their independence from governments would be assured by having a 'long-term, non-renewable term of office [e.g., nine years] … combined with a robust and transparent appointment process'.[142]

---

136. *Submission by the EU and its Member States*, UN Doc No A/CN.9/WG.III/WP.159/Add.1 (24 January 2019), para. 14.
137. Convention on the Recognition and Enforcement of Foreign Arbitral Awards (adopted 10 June 1958, entered into force 7 June 1959) 300 UNTS 38 ('New York Convention').
138. Note by the Secretariat, Possible Reform of Investor-State Dispute Settlement: Standing Multilateral Mechanism – Selection and Appointment of ISDS Tribunal Members and Related Matters, UN Doc No A/CN.9/WG.III/WP.123 (8 December 2021); *see also* Note by the Secretariat, Possible Reform of Investor-State Dispute Settlement: Selection and Appointment of ISDS Tribunal Members, UN Doc No A/CN.9/WG.III/WP.203 (16 November 2020).
139. *Submission by the EU and its Member States*, UN Doc No A/CN.9/WG.III/WP.159/Add.1 (24 January 2019), para. 16.
140. *Submission by the EU and its Member States*, UN Doc No A/CN.9/WG.III/WP.159/Add.1 (24 January 2019), para. 17.
141. *Submission by the EU and its Member States*, UN Doc No A/CN.9/WG.III/WP.159/Add.1 (24 January 2019), para. 18.
142. *Submission by the EU and its Member States*, UN Doc No A/CN.9/WG.III/WP.159/Add.1 (24 January 2019), para. 19.

Adjudicators would have to possess certain qualifications, as is the case with judges of other international courts and tribunals. For instance, adjudicators would typically have to demonstrate 'the qualifications required in their respective countries for appointment to the highest judicial offices' or be 'juriconsults of recognised competence in international law', as is the case of judges of the International Court of Justice.[143]

The appointment process for adjudicators would be robust and transparent in order to ensure independence and impartiality and to avoid the polarisation of tribunals that is so often generated by the current system of party appointments in arbitration. In this regard, protests at the MIC/appellate body proposal are commonly encountered from those who typically act for claimants, and who argue that if states appoint all members of the MIC, claimants will be prejudiced or discriminated against. But this position ignores the reality that if states indeed make all appointments to the MIC and/or an appellate body (which they may not), they would have to take a longer-term perspective, not simply driven by a one-off case, in order to protect the interests of their own investors when in the position of claimant. In other words, states 'would be expected to appoint objective adjudicators, rather than ones that are perceived to lean too heavily in favour of investors or states, because they are expected to internalize not only their defensive interests, as potential respondents in investment disputes, but also their offensive interests, i.e., the necessity to ensure an adequate level of protection to their investors'.[144] Furthermore, the position ignores the reality that ISDS in any form requires a minimum level of state support (and the decay of this support forms the background to the current discussions).

In any event, finding a neutral and objective way for the members of the MIC and/or an appellate body to be appointed is of paramount importance for all stake-holders to have confidence in the new institution. And there are certainly ways to achieve this, by removing the appointment process from the direct control of the state parties. For example:

(a) Appointments could be made by an independent commission, which would be one step removed from the state parties in question. This sort of independent commission is used for the appointment of judges to the Caribbean Court of Justice, whose selection process 'is not dominated by member states or their representatives ... judges are appointed by an independent commission, the Regional Judicial and Legal Services Commission', and the President of the Caribbean Court of Justice is appointed by 'a qualified majority of member

---

143. *Submission by the EU and its Member States*, UN Doc No A/CN.9/WG.III/WP.159/Add.1 (24 January 2019), para. 20.
144. *Submission by the EU and its Member States*, UN Doc No A/CN.9/WG.III/WP.159/Add.1 (24 January 2019), para. 23; *see* especially Anthea Roberts, 'Would a Multilateral Investment Court Be Biased? Shifting to a Treaty Party Framework of Analysis', *EJIL: Talk!* (27 April 2017), available at https://www.ejiltalk.org/would-amultilateral-investment-court-be-biased-shifting-to-a-treaty-party-framework-of-analysis/.

states upon the advice of the same commission'.[145] The independent commission includes representatives from bar associations, civil society, and academics.

(b) Alternatively, it could involve the use of screening mechanisms (consisting of independent members, including perhaps ex officio members, such as recently retired senior judges of other international courts and tribunals, or judges of domestic supreme courts) to ensure that the adjudicators appointed meet the agreed criteria. Such a screening mechanism is used for judicial appointments to the International Criminal Court[146] as well as for appointments to the Court of Justice of the European Union.[147] This type of process would be one way to increase judicial independence, whilst at the same time arguably accommodating the principle of party autonomy.[148]

A mechanism would be established to ensure both geographical and gender diversity among the adjudicators. This could be modelled on the approach of the Rome Statute of the International Criminal Court, which requires, at the nomination stage, that there be 'a minimum of six male and six female candidates, a minimum of three candidates from each region as defined by the UN system, as well as a minimum of nine candidates with a criminal law background and a minimum of five candidates with an international law background'.[149]

The number of adjudicators would depend on the projected workload of the MIC or appellate body,[150] and there would be more adjudicators than the number that would hear each case (in much the same way that the Iran–US Claims Tribunal consists of nine judges, who used to sit in Chambers of three for the mixed claims brought by individuals against one of the two states).[151] For each case, the adjudicators would be appointed to divisions of the MIC or appellate body 'on a randomised basis' to ensure

---

145. Olof Larsson et al., 'Selection and Appointment in International Adjudication: Insights from Political Science', *Academic Forum on ISDS Concept Paper 2019/10*, p. 13.

146. The International Criminal Court's screening mechanism is the 'Advisory Committee on nominations of judges of the International Criminal Court': *see* especially James Devaney, 'Selecting Investment Arbitrators: Reconciling Party Autonomy and the International Rule of Law', *KFG Working Paper Series No 33* (May 2019), pp. 15-16; and Olof Larsson et al., 'Selection and Appointment in International Adjudication: Insights from Political Science', *Academic Forum on ISDS Concept Paper 2019/10*, pp. 22-24; *see also Submission by the EU and its Member States*, UN Doc No A/CN.9/WG.III/WP.159/Add.1 (24 January 2019), para. 22.

147. This is the 'Article 255 Panel': Olof Larsson et al., 'Selection and Appointment in International Adjudication: Insights from Political Science', *Academic Forum on ISDS Concept Paper 2019/10*, pp. 22-23.

148. James Devaney, 'Selecting Investment Arbitrators: Reconciling Party Autonomy and the International Rule of Law', *KFG Working Paper Series No 33* (May 2019).

149. Olof Larsson et al., 'Selection and Appointment in International Adjudication: Insights from Political Science', *Academic Forum on ISDS Concept Paper 2019/10*, p. 16; *see also Submission by the EU and its Member States*, UN Doc No A/CN.9/WG.III/WP.159/Add.1 (24 January 2019), para. 21. On the Rome Statute's election procedure, *see* Rome Statute, Article 36.

150. *Submission by the EU and its Member States*, UN Doc No A/CN.9/WG.III/WP.159/Add.1 (24 January 2019), para. 16.

151. *Submission by the EU and its Member States*, UN Doc No A/CN.9/WG.III/WP.159/Add.1 (24 January 2019), para. 24.

that the disputing parties would not be in a position to know in advance who would hear their case.[152]

b   *What Would Be the Relationship Between the MIC or Appellate Body and the New York Convention/ICSID Convention?*

Another frequent protest at the proposed MIC and appellate body concerns their relationship with the New York Convention of 1958, and the ICSID Convention of 1965. In particular, it is said that the proposal would lead to a system that lacks all the benefits of these very successful treaties. This, once again, is a misplaced protest.

At the outset, it is to be noted that there is a view that an appellate body cannot be established in respect of ICSID arbitrations because to do so would be inconsistent with the ICSID Convention.[153] It is right that the ICSID Convention provides in Article 53 that '[t]he award shall be binding on the parties and shall not be subject to any appeal or to any other remedy except those provided for in this Convention'. But it is also right that the ICSID Convention is capable of amendment. This may be done with the consent of all Contracting Parties.[154] But – perhaps more realistically – it may also be done by those Contracting Parties who wish to amend Article 53 of the ICSID Convention *inter se*, in accordance with Article 41 of the Vienna Convention on the Law of Treaties. This provides that:

(1) Two or more of the parties to a multilateral treaty may conclude an agreement to modify the treaty as between themselves alone if
   (a) the possibility of such a modification is provided for by the treaty; or
   (b) the modification in question is not prohibited by the treaty and:
      (i) does not affect the enjoyment by the other parties of their rights under the treaty or the performance of their obligations;
      (ii) does not relate to a provision, derogation from which is incompatible with the effective execution of the object and purpose of the treaty as a whole.

There is nothing in the ICSID Convention which provides for such an *inter se* amendment within the meaning of Article 41(1)(a). Thus the question is whether the conditions of Article 41(1)(b) are met. The ICSID Convention does not 'prohibit' the proposed amendment of Article 53 within the meaning of Article 41(1)(b). Nor would such an amendment affect 'the enjoyment by the other parties of their rights under the treaty or the performance of their obligations' within the meaning of Article 41(1)(b)(i), because the amendment would only apply among the states which had agreed to it. The remaining issue is whether the proposed amendment to Article 53 'relates to a provision, derogation from which is incompatible with the effective execution of the object and purpose of the treaty as a whole' within the meaning of

---

152. *Submission by the EU and its Member States*, UN Doc No A/CN.9/WG.III/WP.159/Add.1 (24 January 2019), para. 24.
153. *See, e.g.,* N Jansen Calamita, 'The (In)Compatibility of Appellate Mechanisms with Existing Instruments of the Investment Treaty Regime' (2018) *Journal of World Investment and Trade*, p. 19.
154. ICSID Convention, Article 66(1).

Article 41(1)(b)(ii). Calamita has argued that the establishment of an appellate body would amount to such a derogation from Article 53.[155] But other views are certainly tenable, as noted for example by Gabrielle Kaufmann-Kohler and Michele Potestà.[156] Indeed, the object and purpose of the ICSID Convention are evident (a) from its preamble and (b) from its Article 1(2). As to (a), it is readily apparent from the preamble that the Convention reflected the desire of Contracting States to establish an effective and impartial dispute resolution mechanism – with no preference whatsoever as to whether this would include an appellate mechanism. As to (b), Article 1(2) provides that '[t]he purpose of the Centre shall be to provide facilities for conciliation and arbitration of investment disputes between Contracting states and nationals of other Contracting states in accordance with the provisions of this Convention'. As August Reinisch has noted, the proviso in Article 1(2) that the conciliation or arbitration be carried out 'in accordance with' the terms of the ICSID Convention cannot be understood as requiring that such conciliation or arbitration take place 'exactly' as provided for in the Convention, for otherwise it would 'make any inquiry into the compatibility of modifications of the Convention superfluous'.[157] The better view is, therefore, that Article 53 does not pose an obstacle.

Returning to the relationship between the MIC/appellate body, current systems for challenges to awards, and the enforcement of awards, the starting point is that there will be no need for a review of awards at the domestic level or through *ad hoc* international mechanisms such as ICSID annulment tribunals because this function can be exercised by the broader review provided by the MIC appellate tribunal or separate appellate body.[158] Thus, in case of challenges to the award (as set forth, for instance, in Article 52 of the ICSID Convention, or Article 34 of the UNCITRAL Model Law), the appellate mechanism will be able to decide on such applications as a part of its appellate jurisdiction. This is indeed the case in the investment chapter of CETA, which provides that the Appellate Tribunal has the power to 'uphold, reverse, or modify the Tribunal's award' based on '(a) errors in the application or interpretation of applicable law'; '(b) manifest errors in the appreciation of the facts, including the appreciation of relevant domestic law'; and '(c) the grounds set out in Article 52(1)(a)-(e) of the ICSID

---

155. N. Jansen Calamita, 'The (In)Compatibility of Appellate Mechanisms with Existing Instruments of the Investment Treaty Regime' (2018) *Journal of World Investment and Trade*, pp. 21-28.
156. ICSID Convention, Article 1(2); Gabrielle Kaufmann-Kohler and Michele Potestà, 'Can the Mauritius Convention Serve as a Model for the Reform of Investor-State Arbitration in Connection with the Introduction of a Permanent Investment Tribunal or an Appeal Mechanism? Analysis and Roadmap' (Centre for International Dispute Settlement, 2016), pp. 84-85, paras 243-245.
157. August Reinisch, 'Will the EU's Proposal Concerning an Investment Court System for CETA and TTIP Lead to Enforceable Awards? – The Limits of Modifying the ICSID Convention and the Nature of Investment Arbitration' (2016) 19 *Journal of International Economic Law* 761, 776; noted in N. Jansen Calamita, 'The (In)Compatibility of Appellate Mechanisms with Existing Instruments of the Investment Treaty Regime' (2018) *Journal of World Investment and Trade*, p. 28.
158. *Submission by the EU and its Member States*, UN Doc No A/CN.9/WG.III/WP.159/Add.1 (24 January 2019), para. 30.

937

Convention, insofar as they are not covered by paragraphs (a) and (b)'.[159] Although there is no express reference in the CETA to the Model Law grounds for challenging an award, there is no reason why this could not be made clear. The appellate mechanism would therefore supplant the role of the courts of the seat of the arbitration in the case of challenges to awards (whether of the MIC or ad hoc tribunals) – leading to greater consistency in the application of procedural and substantive standards.

As for enforcement, awards issued by the MIC and an appellate body would be capable of enforcement in accordance with provisions of the treaty establishing both. Such awards would also be capable of enforcement under the New York Convention, which also applies to awards issued by 'permanent arbitral bodies'.[160] Both the MIC and an appellate body could be established in terms that would ensure that awards issued by each would satisfy this definition.

As for awards issued by arbitral tribunals under treaties other than the treaty which establishes the MIC or appellate body, or in respect of states which have not 'opted in' with respect to either, such awards would remain enforceable under the provisions of the New York Convention or the ICSID Convention, as appropriate.

Once again, the protests under this head are without force.

c   *How Would the MIC Be Financed?*

A final protest concerns the financing model for the MIC and appellate body. Should their financing be: (i) a user-pays model (which would reflect the current norm in investment arbitration), or (ii) funded by the states which are parties to the founding treaty, and if so, how should each state's contributions be assessed?[161] The EU has suggested the latter model, i.e., that the contracting states should pay contributions 'weighted in accordance with their respective level of development so that developing or least developed countries would bear a lesser burden than developed countries'.[162] The EU is open to the idea that users of the MIC and appellate body pay certain fees, 'although care should be taken not to tie these fees directly to the remuneration of the adjudicators and should not be so high as to become a hurdle for small and medium sized enterprises to bring a case'.[163]

In short, this is an issue perfectly capable of a sensible solution.

As a final point, it is possible that a MIC or appellate body will be upon us one way or another in any event – notwithstanding the protests. This is because the EU has already successfully proposed the inclusion of an investment court system during the negotiation of the Comprehensive Economic Trade Agreement (CETA) with Canada in

---

159. EU – Canada CETA, Article 8.28(2).
160. New York Convention, Article 1(2).
161. On this issue, *see also* 'Cost and Financing of a Permanent Multilateral Body' (unofficial draft only), available at https://uncitral.un.org/en/working_groups/3/investor-state (last accessed 20 November 2022).
162. *Submission by the EU and its Member States*, UN Doc No A/CN.9/WG.III/WP.159/Add.1 (24 January 2019), para. 33.
163. *Submission by the EU and its Member States*, UN Doc No A/CN.9/WG.III/WP.159/Add.1 (24 January 2019), para. 33.

2014,[164] and put forward the proposal during the negotiation of the Transatlantic Trade and Investment Partnership (TTIP) with the United States in 2015.[165] Further, it has already negotiated the inclusion of a permanent tribunal, with an appellate mechanism, in its investment agreements with Canada, Mexico,[166] Singapore,[167] and Vietnam,[168] and it is also currently negotiating with Australia (the July 2022 in-principle agreement includes no investment arbitration), China, Indonesia, Japan, and Mercosur, which negotiations may also include such a permanent tribunal. It is entirely conceivable that, in time, the EU will have negotiated the creation of permanent tribunals and appellate bodies with many important trade and investment partners. At some point, a critical mass will be reached, and the EU and its various treaty partners may well agree to amalgamate the existing entities into one body, resulting in the creation of a two-tiered MIC.

5   Incremental Reforms to Investment Arbitration

A final possibility is that, rather than embarking on structural reform of ISDS, states could tinker with and make incremental improvements to the current arbitral regime. The states that favour this approach (including Chile, Japan, Russia, Israel, Peru, the United States and Mexico in particular) view criticisms of the investment arbitration regime as overblown and consider that the current system of *ad hoc* tribunals to resolve investment disputes is the best option available (subject to targeted reforms). This is an approach fuelled by the view that states need not adopt a 'one size fits all' approach and instead should retain flexibility to tailor solutions to each state's policy needs and preferences, in the context of varying (and varied) pre-existing agreements and bilateral relationships.[169] There is also a pragmatic view that Working Group III should focus on areas where there is already the least divergence of views among the Member States.[170]

---

164. The negotiation of the CETA was completed in August 2014, although the text was not finalised until 2016, and it provisionally entered into force on 21 September 2017: EU, 'EU-Canada Comprehensive Economic and Trade Agreement', available at https://ec.europa.eu/trade/policy/in-focus/ceta/.

165. EU Proposal for Investment Protection and Resolution of Investment Disputes, Transatlantic Trade and Investment Partnership, Trade in Services, Investment, and E-Commerce (12 November 2015), available at http://trade.ec.europa.eu/doclib/docs/2015/november/tradoc_153955.pdf.

166. EU – Mexico Agreement (Agreement in Principle announced on 21 April 2018), Chapter 19 (Resolution of Investment Disputes).

167. EU – Singapore Investment Protection Agreement, signed 19 October 2018, Article 3.9.

168. EU – Vietnam Investment Protection Agreement, signed 30 June 2019, Article 3.38. As at the current date, according to the EU's trade and investment policy website (https://policy.trade.ec.europa.eu/eu-trade-relationships-country-and-region/negotiations-and-agreements_en), it appears that there are no further trade and investment agreements which contain the Investment Court System proposal, although such agreements are in negotiation with Australia, China, Indonesia, Japan, Mercosur, New Zealand, and the UK. Some of these will probably ultimately include the ICS proposal, but this is not yet clear.

169. *See, e.g., Submission by the Governments of Chile, Israel, Japan, Mexico and Peru*, UN Doc No A/CN.9/WG.III/WP.182 (2 October 2019), 5.

170. Submission from the Government of the Russian Federation, UN Doc No A/CN.9/WG.III/WP.188, 2; and Submission by the Governments of Chile, Israel and Japan UN Doc No A/CN.9/WG.III/WP.163 (15 March 2019), 4.

The types of 'incremental' reforms proposed by these states include such issues as the dismissal of frivolous claims; the admissibility of non-disputing party submissions on treaty interpretation, the introduction of a Code of Conduct for arbitrators, limitations on standing for reflective loss; limitations on treaty shopping; and provisions requiring claimants to waive their right to continue or initiate claims in other forums.[171]

Although these proposals have merit, would no doubt improve the current system, and have gained traction in Working Group III, they simply do not provide any solution to the breadth and depth of the current concerns, as now squarely recognised in Working Group III, and summarised above. And nor will they safeguard ISDS from more fundamental change.

V CONCLUSION

Those who are participating in the Working Group III debates now recognise that there has been a marked change of mood in the room and an acknowledgement that something must be done. And behind this is a stark truth: the users of the current ISDS system are not the owners of that system. The current regime is not theirs to protect. It is a system that was built by states from the 1960s through the 1990s, and if states decide that they want to reform the system that they created, that is surely up to them. The object of the exercise must be to enhance the rule of law, not the ability of private corporations to sue states.

We can continue to try to uphold and justify our current system. But the arguments deployed to this end have already been deployed for years. And they have failed. A new approach is now urgently required. And if we miss this moment, we will then surely be heading for a world without investment arbitration.

---

171. *See* especially *Submission by the Governments of Chile, Israel, Japan, Mexico and Peru*, UN Doc No A/CN.9/WG.III/WP.182 (2 October 2019).

CHAPTER 54

The World Is Better with Investment Arbitration

Carolyn B. Lamm, Rocío Digón & Caitlin Walczyk[*]

TABLE OF CONTENTS

I   INTRODUCTION

Investment arbitration is the past, present and future of global investment and international business. Indeed, international arbitration is the tool that has enabled capital-importing States to actively compete for investors from capital exporting States, to offer international legal protection and an agreed method to resolve investment disputes.

---

[*] Carolyn Lamm, Partner, White & Case LLP, Chair International Arbitration of the Americas. Lead Counsel in international arbitrations in ICSID, ICC and other fora and related litigation in U.S. Courts for foreign states, foreign state-owned companies, and foreign corporate entities. Arbitrator on the ICSID List, first nominated by the United States and by the Government of Uzbekistan. Served as arbitrator in ICSID proceedings, ICC proceedings, SAIC proceedings, ICDR proceedings,

At present, we find ourselves in the midst of a period of reform to the investment treaty system, including the scope of international protections offered and the fora for dispute resolution. This call for change requires an evolution of the system—not a revolution—and is not dissimilar from the reforms witnessed at various points in previous decades. Investment arbitration has depoliticized the resolution of investment disputes by displacing gunboat diplomacy and espousal of claims through diplomatic protection. It also has displaced the need to rely on national courts, which may be perceived as (or in some cases actually are) biased. History has demonstrated that the system is not static; and it is precisely its ability to adapt to the changing socioeconomic realities and demands of investors, States, and their counsel that ensures its relevance and livelihood.

For example, the longstanding legal and economic gap between capital-importing and capital-exporting States was bridged by the Convention on the Settlement of Investment Disputes between States and Nationals of Other States of 1965, establishing the International Centre for Settlement of Investment Disputes ("ICSID Convention") and subsequent decades of Bilateral Investment Treaties (BITs) and multilateral conventions guaranteeing treatment at an international level and international dispute resolution. In recent years, the ICSID Arbitration Rules have been amended again, the

---

AAA proceedings, etc. Distinguished Faculty Co-Chair, White & Case LLM International Arbitration at the University of Miami School of Law. Immediate Past President, American Bar Endowment. Member, Advisory Council and previously Governing Board of ICCA; Council of the American Law Institute (elected 1999): Counselor for the Restatement 4th of Foreign Relations; Advisory Committee for the Restatement of International Commercial and Investment Arbitration. Past President: DC Bar; American Bar Association. Frequent lecturer and author in the field of international arbitration. Chairman of the Board of the American-Uzbekistan U.S. Chamber of Commerce. Member Board of Trustees, University of Miami (2020-2023); honorary Professor Tashkent State University, School of Law. Rocío Digón is a legal consultant at White & Case. Based in Rome, Rocío has experience as counsel in commercial and investment treaty arbitration under the rules of leading arbitral institutions, including ICSID, ICC and ICDR/AAA and has acted as sole arbitrator under the rules of the CAM. Prior to joining White & Case, she was an Associate Research Scholar at Yale Law School and previously spent three years as the first Managing Director and Counsel of the ICC International Court of Arbitration, SICANA, Inc., where she was responsible for administering cases for the North America region and directing SICANA's promotional activities. Rocío writes and speaks frequently on topics in international and commercial arbitration. Additionally, Rocío co-founded the Rising Arbitrators Initiative and is Co-Chair of the Arbitral Appointments committee of Racial Equality for Arbitration Lawyers (REAL). Rocío holds a J.D. from Yale Law School, an LL.M. from Leiden University in Public International Law, and a B.A. from Amherst College (*summa cum laude*). She speaks English, French, Spanish and Italian and is admitted to practice in Massachusetts and New York. Caitlin Walczyk is an associate in the White & Case's International Arbitration and Litigation Groups, and is resident in the Washington, DC office. She represents and advises private companies and foreign sovereigns in the resolution of international disputes, including before arbitral tribunals constituted under the International Centre for the Settlement of Investment Disputes (ICSID) and the International Chamber of Commerce (ICC). Her experience also includes litigation related to the Foreign Sovereign Immunities Act. During law school, Caitlin was a member of the Harvard International Law Journal and Harvard National Security Law Journal.

   The opinions expressed here and in the Great Debate are those assigned by ICCA and do not necessarily reflect, in all respects, the views of the authors, White & Case LLP, or its clients. This chapter is for general information purposes and is not intended to be and should not be taken as legal advice.

United States-Mexico-Canada Agreement (USMCA) has evolved from the North Atlantic Free Trade Agreement (NAFTA), and treaties such as the Dominican Republic-Central American Free Trade Agreement (CAFTA-DR), the Comprehensive and Progressive Agreement for Trans-Pacific Partnership (CP-TPP) and the United Nations Convention on International Settlement Agreements Resulting from Mediation ("Singapore Convention") have been adopted. In each "generation" of investment treaty reform, the main tenets of investment arbitration have been preserved—providing a neutral forum for investors and States to resolve their disputes, providing substantive protections to investors and their investments while preserving the host State's right to regulate, upholding due process rights, ensuring the finality of awards with limited grounds for refusal of enforcement and set aside, and having independent and impartial arbitrators.

Section II of this chapter assesses the contributions of States and investors to the proliferation of BITs and other treaties with investment chapters and to the expansion of investment protections over time. Sections III and IV demonstrate that investment arbitration is a necessity for States and investors, respectively, and section V debunks the myths surrounding the alleged pitfalls of investment treaty arbitration. Finally, section VI offers our conclusions.

II   BOTH STATES AND INVESTORS HAVE CONTRIBUTED TO THE PROLIFERATION OF BITs AND OTHER TREATIES WITH INVESTMENT CHAPTERS AND TO THE EXPANSION OF INVESTMENT PROTECTIONS OVER TIME

While BITs are the predominant mechanism for regulating international investment, this has not always been the case. Rather, BITs as they exist today did not develop until the last few decades, and their provisions and protections developed from both investors' and States' needs that were not met by the modern BITs' predecessors. This section discusses the early use of military power to resolve investment disputes; the end of gunboat diplomacy and the introduction of friendship, commerce, and negotiation (FCN) treaties; the development of early BITs and the transition into modern BITs; the development of multilateral treaties; and the development of investment protections in modern BITs.

1   Gunboat Diplomacy and Military Force as Means to Resolve Investment Disputes

Prior to the promulgation of BITs, investors did not have the individual right under international law to bring claims against host States for breaches of international protections with respect to their investments and the related harm; rather, investors had to depend on their home State's willingness to exercise diplomatic protection vis-à-vis the host State, and the host State's willingness to comply with the limited provisions aimed at promoting foreign direct investment in its own domestic laws. This left investors vulnerable, especially to politically motivated measures of the host State, and they often suffered harm as a result.[1]

In certain situations, the investors' home States would become involved and the dispute would turn from an investor-State dispute to a State-State dispute.[2] Prior to the end of World War II, however, there was limited diplomatic recourse between States for disputes relating to foreign investment, trade, or commerce and the primary practice of capital-exporting nations was the use of military force, otherwise known as "gunboat diplomacy."[3] For example, in 1900, the U.S. Secretary of State dispatched a vessel to Venezuela to prevent the destruction of the property of an American investor following the collapse of foreign companies in Latin America and serious economic loss by foreign investors caused by the Latin American bonds default.[4] Similarly, France invaded Mexico from 1861 to 1862 when a French investor was unable to obtain compensation in Mexican courts after the Mexican government defaulted on a loan.[5]

Military conflict reached its peak during the first half of the 20th century with the breakout of World War I and World War II, which indirectly laid the groundwork for the end of gunboat diplomacy. Many foreign policy leaders concluded that the wars were a result of the lack of an open world economy and thus sought to establish a more open international economic framework which would promote cooperation and peace.[6]

2   The End of Gunboat Diplomacy and Introduction of Treaties of Friendship, Commerce and Navigation

In an attempt to establish a more cooperative economic framework, the United States began entering into FCN treaties. FCN treaties focused on developing political and

1. *See* Stephan W. Schill, *Private Enforcement of International Investment Law: Why We Need Investor Standing in BIT Dispute Settlement, in* THE BACKLASH AGAINST INVESTMENT ARBITRATION (Waibel, Kaushal, Chung, et al., eds., January 2010), *available at* https://www.kluwerarbitration .com/document/KLI-KA-201011004-n.
2. *See* Stephan W. Schill, *Private Enforcement of International Investment Law: Why We Need Investor Standing in BIT Dispute Settlement, in* THE BACKLASH AGAINST INVESTMENT ARBITRATION (Waibel, Kaushal, Chung, et al., eds., January 2010), *available at* https://www.kluwerarbitration .com/document/KLI-KA-201011004-n.
3. Borzu Sabahi et al., *History and Limitations of the Traditional System for Resolving Investment Disputes, in* INVESTOR-STATE ARBITRATION (2d ed., September 2019), ¶¶ 2.31-2.33, *available at* https://www.kluwerarbitration.com/document/KLI-KA-Sabahi-2020-Ch02.
4. S Borzu Sabahi et al., *History and Limitations of the Traditional System for Resolving Investment Disputes, in* INVESTOR-STATE ARBITRATION (2d ed., September 2019), ¶ 2.32, *available at* https:// www.kluwerarbitration.com/document/KLI-KA-Sabahi-2020-Ch02.
5. Borzu Sabahi et al., *History and Limitations of the Traditional System for Resolving Investment Disputes, in* INVESTOR-STATE ARBITRATION (2d ed., September 2019), ¶ 2.33, *available at* https:// www.kluwerarbitration.com/document/KLI-KA-Sabahi-2020-Ch02.
6. Robert E. Baldwin, *The Changing Nature of U.S. Trade Policy Since World War II, in* THE STRUCTURE AND EVOLUTION OF RECENT U.S. TRADE POLICY (Baldwin, Krueger eds., 1984), p. 7, *available at* https://www.nber.org/system/files/chapters/c5828/c5828.pdf.

economic ties between countries and often were entered into between major developed countries, such as France, Italy, and the U.S.[7]

The earliest FCN treaty dates back to the U.S. Civil War, during which the U.S. and France signed an alliance treaty.[8] Thereafter, the U.S. entered into similar agreements with other European and South American countries. These early FCNs, which focused primarily on commercial and trade matters, established the most-favored-nation (MFN) status, which requires a host State to provide a foreign investor the most favorable treatment offered to other foreign nationals.[9] After World War I, the scope of these treaties began to expand and offer protections to company rights abroad, including through the protection of private property.[10]

The scope of these treaties expanded even further after the end of World War II. The General Agreement on Tariffs and Trade (GATT) was established in 1947, which subjected international trade to multilateral rules.[11] Gradually, GATT contracting parties and other multilateral institutions put a heavier emphasis on promotion of foreign investment.[12] In this way, the focus of FCN treaties began to shift to foreign investment, which became primarily comprised of investment-related provisions.[13] From 1946 to 1966, the U.S. alone entered into twenty-one FCN treaties heavily focused on investment.[14]

While current BITs hold many similarities to FCN treaties, FCN treaties tended to cover a much broader array of complex subject matters, including human rights, immigration policy, or religious practice. As Professor Bergmann noted in his seminal

---

7. Wolfgang Alschner, *Americanization of the BIT Universe: The Influence of Friendship, Commerce and Navigation (FCN) Treaties on Modern Investment Treaty Law*, 5(2) GOETTINGEN JOURNAL OF INTERNATIONAL LAW 455, 464-466 (2013), *available at* https://www.gojil.eu/issues/52/52_article_walschner.pdf.

8. Wolfgang Alschner, *Americanization of the BIT Universe: The Influence of Friendship, Commerce and Navigation (FCN) Treaties on Modern Investment Treaty Law*, 5(2) GOETTINGEN JOURNAL OF INTERNATIONAL LAW 455, 461 (2013), *available at* https://www.gojil.eu/issues/52/52_article_walschner.pdf.

9. Wolfgang Alschner, *Americanization of the BIT Universe: The Influence of Friendship, Commerce and Navigation (FCN) Treaties on Modern Investment Treaty Law*, 5(2) GOETTINGEN JOURNAL OF INTERNATIONAL LAW 455, 461 (2013), *available at* https://www.gojil.eu/issues/52/52_article_walschner.pdf.

10. Jeswald W. Salacuse, *BIT by BIT: The Growth of Bilateral Investment Treaties and Their Impact on Foreign Investment in Developing Countries*, 24(3) THE INTERNATIONAL LAWYER 655, 656 (1990), *available at* https://scholar.smu.edu/cgi/viewcontent.cgi?article = 2743&context = til.

11. Wolfgang Alschner, *Americanization of the BIT Universe: The Influence of Friendship, Commerce and Navigation (FCN) Treaties on Modern Investment Treaty Law*, 5(2) GOETTINGEN JOURNAL OF INTERNATIONAL LAW 455, 462 (2013), *available at* https://www.gojil.eu/issues/52/52_article_walschner.pdf.

12. *Agreement on Trade Related Investment Measures*, WORLD TRADE ORGANIZATION, *available at* https://www.wto.org/english/tratop_e/invest_e/invest_info_e.htm#top (last accessed November 6, 2022).

13. Wolfgang Alschner, *Americanization of the BIT Universe: The Influence of Friendship, Commerce and Navigation (FCN) Treaties on Modern Investment Treaty Law*, 5(2) GOETTINGEN JOURNAL OF INTERNATIONAL LAW 455, 462 (2013), *available at* https://www.gojil.eu/issues/52/52_article_walschner.pdf.

14. Wolfgang Alschner, *Americanization of the BIT Universe: The Influence of Friendship, Commerce and Navigation (FCN) Treaties on Modern Investment Treaty Law*, 5(2) GOETTINGEN JOURNAL OF INTERNATIONAL LAW 455, 462 (2013), *available at* https://www.gojil.eu/issues/52/52_article_walschner.pdf.

article on the evolution of treaty protections, "the attempt to address very complex issues in the context of such a broad spectrum of relations detracted from the utility of the FCN [treaty] as an investment protection device."[15] The negotiations surrounding these treaties were also often highly politicized and prone to fail.[16] In addition, FCN treaties' protections were typically directly enforceable in domestic courts—the potential for this to intrude on national sovereignty restricted States' willingness to bind themselves to certain provisions, particularly with respect to investment protection.[17] The prospect of having national courts decide cases arising out of a state's alleged breach of an international standard was not acceptable. By 1966, developing countries were hesitant to agree to FCN treaties due to their broad nature and strict enforcement provisions.[18]

At the same time, many investors also were hesitant to make significant investments and enter into investment agreements with dispute resolution limited to the national courts of developing countries with unstable legal regimes. FCN treaties did not have any provisions for host States to maintain their investment protections after entering into agreements with foreign investors, thus host countries were able to change their local laws after an investment was made that would harm the investor and its investment.[19] There were virtually no consequences for such changes to the laws and/or adverse behaviors. Another risk investors faced was that host States had the potential to impose onerous conditions on foreign-owned businesses in an arbitrary and discriminatory manner.[20] This risk was a reality for many investors throughout the 1960s and 1970s. In 1977, the U.S. Department of State estimated that there were 102 existing investment disputes between U.S. investors and foreign governments, and the United Nations identified 875 distinct government takings of foreign property across 62 countries from 1960 to 1974.[21]

---

15. M.S. Bergmann, *Bilateral Investment Protection Treaties: An Examination of the Evolution and Significance of the U.S. Prototype Treaty*, 16 New York University Journal of International Law 1, 1, 7 (1983).

16. Wolfgang Alschner, *Americanization of the BIT Universe: The Influence of Friendship, Commerce and Navigation (FCN) Treaties on Modern Investment Treaty Law*, 5(2) Goettingen Journal of International Law 455, 463 (2013), *available at* https://www.gojil.eu/issues/52/52_article_walschner.pdf.

17. Wolfgang Alschner, *Americanization of the BIT Universe: The Influence of Friendship, Commerce and Navigation (FCN) Treaties on Modern Investment Treaty Law*, 5(2) Goettingen Journal of International Law 455, 465 (2013), *available at* https://www.gojil.eu/issues/52/52_article_walschner.pdf.

18. Jeswald W. Salacuse, *BIT by BIT: The Growth of Bilateral Investment Treaties and Their Impact on Foreign Investment in Developing Countries*, 24(3) The International Lawyer 655, 656-657 (1990), *available at* https://scholar.smu.edu/cgi/viewcontent.cgi?article = 2743&context = til.

19. Jeswald W. Salacuse, *BIT by BIT: The Growth of Bilateral Investment Treaties and Their Impact on Foreign Investment in Developing Countries*, 24(3) The International Lawyer 655, 659 (1990), *available at* https://scholar.smu.edu/cgi/viewcontent.cgi?article = 2743&context = til.

20. Jeswald W. Salacuse, *BIT by BIT: The Growth of Bilateral Investment Treaties and Their Impact on Foreign Investment in Developing Countries*, 24(3) The International Lawyer 655, 659 (1990), *available at* https://scholar.smu.edu/cgi/viewcontent.cgi?article = 2743&context = til.

21. Jeswald W. Salacuse, *BIT by BIT: The Growth of Bilateral Investment Treaties and Their Impact on Foreign Investment in Developing Countries*, 24(3) The International Lawyer 655, 659, n. 32 (1990), *available at* https://scholar.smu.edu/cgi/viewcontent.cgi?article = 2743&context = til.

In addition, at this time, there was no international legal regime with binding mechanisms for dispute resolution. As a consequence, there was no remedy available to investors, who never received compensation for these government takings and/or other misconduct that violated minimum international standards. This inevitably chilled investment, leading to a lose-lose situation for both host States and investors.[22] While developed, capital-exporting countries attempted to put into place an international regime that recognized protections for foreign investors, developing, capital-importing countries rejected this attempt and emphasized their sovereign right to handle investments as they chose.[23] This prevented any multilateral solution from arising to resolve the issue.

3   Introduction to the Early BITs

To combat the issues faced by investors in the FCN treaty regime, European countries began looking to bilateral solutions with individual developing States which offered investment protections and a method of international dispute resolution. In the late 1950s, Europe began negotiating a new type of treaty that dealt exclusively with foreign investment, now known as the BIT. Germany led these negotiations, and the first BIT was adopted in 1959 between Germany and Pakistan.[24] That treaty and others negotiated in the 1960s provided for dispute resolution only between States and did not provide for investor-State dispute resolution.[25] This discord—and need for collective change—inspired the efforts of Dr. Aron Broches (former General Counsel of the World Bank) to reconcile the interests of capital exporting and importing states with a mutually acceptable set of standards to resolve international investment disputes.[26] By

---

22. Jeswald W. Salacuse, *BIT by BIT: The Growth of Bilateral Investment Treaties and Their Impact on Foreign Investment in Developing Countries*, 24(3) THE INTERNATIONAL LAWYER 655, 659 (1990), *available at* https://scholar.smu.edu/cgi/viewcontent.cgi?article=2743&context=til.
23. In the 1970s, capital-exporting countries claimed that customary international law imposed an obligation on host states to provide for a minimum standard of protection toward foreign investors, but developing countries rejected this view. Jeswald W. Salacuse, *BIT by BIT: The Growth of Bilateral Investment Treaties and Their Impact on Foreign Investment in Developing Countries*, 24(3) THE INTERNATIONAL LAWYER 655, 660 (1990), *available at* https://scholar.smu.edu/cgi/viewcontent.cgi?article=2743&context=til.
24. Jeswald W. Salacuse, *BIT by BIT: The Growth of Bilateral Investment Treaties and Their Impact on Foreign Investment in Developing Countries*, 24(3) THE INTERNATIONAL LAWYER 655, 657 (1990), *available at* https://scholar.smu.edu/cgi/viewcontent.cgi?article=2743&context=til; Judge Stephen M. Schwebel, *Keynote Address: In Defense of Bilateral Investment Treaties*, p. 4 (2014).
25. *See* Germany-Pakistan BIT, done at Bonn November 25, 1959, Article 11 (providing for State-State dispute resolution before the International Court of Justice, "if both parties so agree" and, failing such agreement, before an arbitral tribunal).
26. *See* Antonio R. Parra, THE HISTORY OF THE ICSID CONVENTION 22 (2d ed. 2017) ("The experience of the [World] Bank helped to convince its management to pursue the dispute settlement approach to the encouragement of foreign investment. Leading the way under the President of the Bank was its [then] General Counsel, Aron Broches. He raised the topic with the Executive Directors of the bank in a note he sent to them at the end of August 1961. Further elaboration was provided in additional notes to the Executive Directors, one sent by the Bank's President Blank in December 1961, and another by Broches in January 1962. The notes together sketched out the rationale for main features of an international agreement that the Bank might help draw upon the settlement of investment disputes."); *see also ibid.*, pp. 34-35 ("A convention, [Broches]

providing a procedural and institutional framework for investor-State arbitration that was agreed upon among both developed and developing countries, the conclusion of the ICSID Convention in 1968 led to the negotiation of BITs that also contained the host State's offer of consent to investor-State arbitration.[27] By the end of 1970, over 170 BITs had been concluded between European countries and developing countries. The U.S. eventually adopted Europe's approach; in 1981, the U.S. began negotiating BITs with developing countries and entered into sixteen BITs by 1990.[28] By the end of 1999, 1,857 BITs had been concluded across the world.[29]

Rather than focusing on the relationship between already developed countries, the early BITs shifted focus to developing a relationship between a developed, capital-exporting country and a developing, capital-importing country.[30] This allowed for a greater flow of capital worldwide and promoted development within developing countries. From 1980 to 1995, foreign direct investment (FDI) grew from USD 40 billion to USD 315 billion.[31] At nearly the same time, the number of BITs "quintupled" from "385 at the end of the 1980s to a total of 1,857 BITs ... at the end of the 1990s."[32] A vast majority of this growth occurred in developing countries which were parties to BITs, and which experienced increases in FDI inflow as much as 42% to 104% compared to the total FDI inflow in developing countries.[33] Indeed, BITs "concluded between developing countries; between developing countries and countries in Central and Eastern Europe; and between Central and Eastern European countries grew sharply,

explained, would be needed to establish that the agreements to resort to conciliation or arbitration would be valid international obligations. Governments, he added, might be reluctant to accept international procedures for the settlement of investment disputes if they would still be subject to diplomatic representations or claims by the home State of the foreign investor. A convention would eliminate that problem by, in effect, excluding such representations or claims when an arbitration agreement was in effect and being carried out by the host State. A convention would also provide rules to assure that a conciliation or arbitration agreement could not frustrated by a party and that, in the case of arbitration, the award would be complied with.").

27. *See, e.g.*, Italy-Chad BIT, done at Rome June 11, 1969, Article 7 (providing for ICSID arbitration); Judge Stephen M. Schwebel, *Keynote Address: In Defense of Bilateral Investment Treaties*, p. 3 (2014).

28. Jeswald W. Salacuse, *BIT by BIT: The Growth of Bilateral Investment Treaties and Their Impact on Foreign Investment in Developing Countries*, 24(3) THE INTERNATIONAL LAWYER 655, 657-659 (1990), *available at* https://scholar.smu.edu/cgi/viewcontent.cgi?article=2743&context=til.

29. Bilateral Investment Treaties 1959-1999, UNCTAD/ITE/IIA/2, UNITED NATIONS, p. 1 (2000), *available at* https://unctad.org/system/files/official-document/poiteiiad2.en.pdf.

30. Bilateral Investment Treaties 1959-1999, UNCTAD/ITE/IIA/2, UNITED NATIONS, p. 1 (2000), *available at* https://unctad.org/system/files/official-document/poiteiiad2.en.pdf.

31. Susan D. Franck, *Foreign Direct Investment, Investment Treaty Arbitration, and the Rule of Law*, 19 PAC. MCGEORGE GLOBAL BUS. & DEV. L.J. 337, 338 n. 4 (2006), *available at* https://scholarl ycommons.pacific.edu/globe/vol19/iss2/3/?utm_source=scholarlycommons.pacific.edu%2F globe%2Fvol19%2Fiss2%2F3&utm_medium=PDF&utm_campaign=PDFCoverPages.

32. *Bilateral Investment Treaties Quintupled During The 1990s*, UNCTAD Press Release TAD/INF/PF/077 dated December 15, 2020, *available at* https://unctad.org/press-material/ bilateral-investment-treaties-quintupled-during-1990s.

33. Eric Neumayer and Laura Spess, *Do Bilateral Investment Treaties Increase Foreign Direct Investment to Developing Countries?* LONDON: LSE RESEARCH ONLINE, 28 (2005), *available at* http://eprints.lse.ac.uk/627/1/World_Dev_%28BITs%29.pdf (originally published in 33(1) WORLD DEVELOPMENT 1565).

from 63 at the end of the 1980s to 833 at the end of the 1990s."[34] The more BITs that the developing country was a party to, the higher the FDI inflow was likely to be.[35]

In contrast to their FCN treaty predecessors, BITs were much more concise and focused primarily on investment policy and protection, rather than on trade and foreign policy. This allowed the treaties to put a heavier focus on providing clear and enforceable investment protections, such as those preventing expropriation and discriminatory treatment. For example, the Germany-Malaysia BIT, which entered into force in 1963, provides:

> The investments of nationals or companies of either Contracting Party in the territory of the other Contracting Party shall not be expropriated except for a public purpose, nor shall they be expropriated without prompt, adequate and effective compensation which shall be freely transferable between the territories of the two Contracting Parties. The legality of any such expropriation and the quantum of compensation shall be subject to review by due process of law in the territory of the Contracting Party in which the investment has been expropriated.[36]

This benefited both foreign investors and host States, because host States could promote investment within their territories, and investors could ensure that these investments would remain protected.[37]

This narrow focus solely on foreign investment seen in early BITs, however, had its drawbacks. For example, early BITs did not directly address human rights, environmental, or cultural issues.[38] Moreover, in BITs drafted prior to 1990, fair and equitable treatment (FET) clauses were drafted in an open-ended way, such that it would become necessary to interpret the meaning and scope of the protections offered.[39] This open-ended drafting is evident, for example, in the Germany-Mauritius BIT, which entered into force in 1973 and requires Contracting Parties to "accord such investments fair and equitable treatment," without defining what is considered fair and equitable.[40] Some of the definitions of investment protections in early BITs sought to limit treatment of investments (not investors) to that accorded with foreign investments in "like circumstances" or "similar situations." For example, in *Içkale v.*

34. *Bilateral Investment Treaties Quintupled During The 1990s*, UNCTAD Press Release TAD/INF/PF/077 dated December 15, 2020, *available at* https://unctad.org/press-material/bilateral-investment-treaties-quintupled-during-1990s.
35. Eric Neumayer and Laura Spess, *Do Bilateral Investment Treaties Increase Foreign Direct Investment to Developing Countries?* London: LSE Research Online, 28 (2005), *available at* http://eprints.lse.ac.uk/627/1/World_Dev_%28BITs%29.pdf.
36. Germany-Malaysia BIT, done at Kuala Lumpur December 22, 1960, *entered into force* July 6, 1963, Article 4(1).
37. Jeswald W. Salacuse, *BIT by BIT: The Growth of Bilateral Investment Treaties and Their Impact on Foreign Investment in Developing Countries*, 24(3) The International Lawyer 655, 660 (1990), *available at* https://scholar.smu.edu/cgi/viewcontent.cgi?article=2743&context=til.
38. Wolfgang Alschner, *Americanization of the BIT Universe: The Influence of Friendship, Commerce and Navigation (FCN) Treaties on Modern Investment Treaty Law*, 5(2) Goettingen Journal of International Law 455, 467 (2013), *available at* https://www.gojil.eu/issues/52/52_article_walschner.pdf.
39. *Recent Policy Developments and Key Issues, in* World Investment Report 2022: International Tax Reforms and Sustainable Investment 89 (2022), *available at* https://unctad.org/system/files/official-document/wir2022_ch02_en.pdf.
40. Germany-Mauritius BIT, done at May 25, 1971 *entered into force* August 27, 1973, Article 1.

Turkmenistan, which arose under the 1992 Turkey-Turkmenistan BIT, the claimant sought to import FET treatment through the treaty's MFN clause, which stated:

> Each Party shall accord to these investments, once established, treatment no less favorable than that accorded in similar situations to investments of its investors or to investments of investors of any third country, whichever is most favorable.[41]

The claimant alleged that, although the Turkey-Turkmenistan BIT did not have an FET clause, it was entitled to rely on the FET provisions set out in other BITs concluded by Turkmenistan, including with Egypt, Bahrain, and the UK.[42] The tribunal, however, rejected this argument and reasoned that claimant's investment could not be considered in a "similar situation" to that of investments created under BITs with an FET clause:

> The terms "treatment accorded in similar situations" therefore suggest that the MFN treatment obligation requires a comparison of the factual situation of the investments of the investors of the home State and that of the investments of the investors of third States, for the purpose of determining whether the treatment accorded to investors of the home State can be said to be less favourable than that accorded to investments of the investors of any third State. It follows that, given the limitation of the scope of application of the MFN clause to "similar situations," it cannot be read, in good faith, to refer to standards of investment protection included in other investment treaties between a State party and a third State."[43]

Since the late 1960s and early 1970s, one of the most salient features of these early BITs has been that they afforded (and continue to afford in their modern version) investors a direct right to seek dispute resolution against capital-importing States. BITs provide foreign investors with the assurances necessary to induce investment into what may then have been considered "risky" countries while at the same time, they allow States to promote and protect foreign investment by providing a neutral judicial forum for the resolution of investment disputes based on the rule of law or any alleged denial of the minimum standard of international protections—to the extent offered by the state.[44] This is an alternative to the host State's courts, which might be perceived as biased or otherwise unlikely to resolve disputes based on the rule of law and the international standards of protection. This new, neutral, alternative dispute resolution (ADR) mechanism induces investment, which, in turn, benefits the States.[45]

As investors took advantage of this new, neutral dispute resolution mechanism, the undefined nature of substantive investment protections in BITs became more

---

41. Turkey-Turkmenistan BIT, done at May 2, 1992, *entered into force* March 13, 1997, Article II(2).
42. *Içkale İnşaat Limited Şirketi v. Turkmenistan*, ICSID Case No. ARB/10/24, Award dated March 8, 2016 ¶ 314.
43. *Içkale İnşaat Limited Şirketi v. Turkmenistan*, ICSID Case No. ARB/10/24, Award dated March 8, 2016 ¶ 329.
44. *See* Jeswald W. Salacuse, *BIT by BIT: The Growth of Bilateral Investment Treaties and Their Impact on Foreign Investment in Developing Countries,* 24(3) THE INTERNATIONAL LAWYER 655, 673 (1990), *available at* https://scholar.smu.edu/cgi/viewcontent.cgi?article = 2743&context = til.
45. *See* Jeswald W. Salacuse, *BIT by BIT: The Growth of Bilateral Investment Treaties and Their Impact on Foreign Investment in Developing Countries,* 24(3) THE INTERNATIONAL LAWYER 655, 674 (1990), *available at* https://scholar.smu.edu/cgi/viewcontent.cgi?article = 2743&context = til.

evident and problematic, and States began to consider how they could revise BITs to address these new challenges. In the 1980s and 1990s, there were only a few disputes annually arising out of BITs, Foreign Investment Laws[46] and Individual Investment Agreements;[47] since the mid-1990s, however, this number has increased markedly, and in 2021, ICSID alone saw sixty-six cases registered under the ICSID Convention.[48] These difficulties led States to reconsider the streamlined nature of these early BITs, and they began to negotiate more complex, comprehensive agreements that take into consideration social welfare and provide more comprehensive definitions of investor and State rights but also maintained the neutral dispute resolution and substantive protections seen in early BITs.[49] These latter agreements became the basis of what we now know as the modern BIT.

4 The Development of the Modern BIT

Over the course of the last several decades, BITs have transitioned from single-issue agreements with open-ended terms to agreements with defined protections encompassing a wider range of issues that reflect the emerging socioeconomic realities of today's world.

There have been several developments leading to the modern-day BIT. First, as more countries see the benefits that BITs bring with respect to foreign investment, more BITs are entering into force. The current numbers speak for themselves. Currently, there are over 3,300 investment treaties, over 2,800 of which are BITs.[50] A careful analysis of the current landscape demonstrates that States continue to conclude new treaties and renegotiate old treaties, while the number of terminated investment treaties remains low. In 2021, thirteen new investment treaties, including six new BITs,

---

46. For example, in *Southern Pacific Properties (Middle East) Limited v. Arab Republic of Egypt*, the ICSID tribunal rendered a decision for a claim brought on August 24, 1984 under Egypt's foreign investment Law No. 43 "Concerning the Investment of Arab and Foreign Funds and Free Zones." *See* ICSID Case No. ARB/84/3, Award dated May 20, 1992 ¶¶ 1, 43, 78.

47. For example, in *Amco Asia Corporation and others v. Republic of Indonesia*, the ICSID tribunal rendered a decision for a claim brought on January 15, 1981 arising from the Indonesian government's approval of Amco's Investment Application. *See* ICSID Case No. ARB/81/1, Award dated November 20, 1984 ¶¶ 1, 20-32, 48.

48. ICSID, 2021-2 THE ICSID CASELOAD-STATISTICS 22 (2021), *available at* https://icsid.worldbank.org/sites/default/files/Caseload%20Statistics%20Charts/The%20ICSID%20Caseload%20Statistics%202021-2%20Edition%20ENG.pdf.

49. Wolfgang Alschner, *Americanization of the BIT Universe: The Influence of Friendship, Commerce and Navigation (FCN) Treaties on Modern Investment Treaty Law*, 5(2) GOETTINGEN JOURNAL OF INTERNATIONAL LAW 455, 480 (2013), *available at* https://www.gojil.eu/issues/52/52_article_walschner.pdf.

50. *Recent Policy Developments and Key Issues, in* WORLD INVESTMENT REPORT 2022: INTERNATIONAL TAX REFORMS AND SUSTAINABLE INVESTMENT 65 (2022), *available at* https://unctad.org/system/files/official-document/wir2022_ch02_en.pdf. This number encompasses all BITs. There are currently 2,207 bilateral investment treaties in force. *See International Investment Agreements Navigator*, UNCTAD INVESTMENT POLICY HUB, *available at* https://investmentpolicy.unctad.org/international-investment-agreements/advanced-search (last accessed November 15, 2022).

were concluded, and four were renegotiated and replaced with a new treaty.[51] In addition, the nature of international trade and the global economy as they exist today means that there is less distinction between capital-importing and capital-exporting States. Rather, foreign investment has become increasingly bi-directional, and developing, formerly capital-importing countries are now exporting capital to developed countries.[52] This means that all countries feel the regulatory burden, providing developing countries with a more equal and reciprocal opportunity when negotiating BITs. In addition, BITs no longer exist primarily between one developed and one developing country. Since 1999, the UNCTAD Secretariat has been promoting cooperation between developing countries in negotiating BITs with each other.[53] By the end of the 1980s, 10% of BITs were between two developing countries;[54] now, 23% of BITs are between developing countries, representing 519 agreements currently in force.[55] Modern treaties are also more innovative, as they introduce new provisions seeking to safeguard, for example, social welfare, the environment, or human rights. They also offer the host State more flexibility to implement measures that may negatively impact foreign investment but are done for public policy purposes.[56] Of the twenty-nine new treaties concluded in 2018, nineteen contain general exceptions for the protection of human, animal, or plant life or health, or the conservation of exhaustible natural resources; in twenty-five of the treaties, the preamble refers to the protection of health and safety, labor rights, the environment, water resources and development; and corporate social responsibility provisions appear in thirteen of the twenty-nine treaties.[57] In 2021, all four publicly available, newly concluded treaties clarify the FET standard; all four include clauses to prevent host States from lowering labor and environmental standards; three provide for exceptions for the protection of human,

---

51. *Recent Policy Developments and Key Issues, in* WORLD INVESTMENT REPORT 2022: INTERNATIONAL TAX REFORMS AND SUSTAINABLE INVESTMENT 65 (2022), *available at* https://unctad.org/system/files/official-document/wir2022_ch02_en.pdf.

52. Wolfgang Alschner, *Americanization of the BIT Universe: The Influence of Friendship, Commerce and Navigation (FCN) Treaties on Modern Investment Treaty Law,* 5(2) GOETTINGEN JOURNAL OF INTERNATIONAL LAW 455, 477 (2013), *available at* https://www.gojil.eu/issues/52/52_article_walschner.pdf.

53. Bilateral Investment Treaties 1959-1999, UNCTAD/ITE/IIA/2, UNITED NATIONS (2000), p. 2, *available at* https://unctad.org/system/files/official-document/poiteiiad2.en.pdf.

54. Bilateral Investment Treaties 1959-1999, UNCTAD/ITE/IIA/2, UNITED NATIONS (2000), p. 4, *available at* https://unctad.org/system/files/official-document/poiteiiad2.en.pdf.

55. International Investment Agreements Navigator, UNCTAD INVESTMENT POLICY HUB (last accessed November 7, 2022), *available at* https://investmentpolicy.unctad.org/international-investment-agreements/advanced-search. This statistic was created by using the UNCTAD Navigator Tool, viewing BITs in force "intra" developing economies including least developing countries ("LDCs").

56. *Recent Policy Developments and Key Issues, in* WORLD INVESTMENT REPORT 2022: INTERNATIONAL TAX REFORMS AND SUSTAINABLE INVESTMENT 90 (2022), *available at* https://unctad.org/system/files/official-document/wir2022_ch02_en.pdf.

57. *Recent Policy Developments and Key Issues, in* UNCTAD WORLD INVESTMENT REPORT 2019: SPECIAL ECONOMIC ZONES 105 (2022), *available at* https://unctad.org/en/PublicationChapters/WIR2019_CH3.pdf.

animal, or plant life or health; two incorporate provisions on corporate social responsibility standards; and one, the Australia-United Kingdom Foreign Trade Agreement, promotes gender equality and women's economic empowerment.[58]

Tribunals themselves have recognized the particular socioeconomic realities of contracting parties. As the tribunals in *El Paso Energy International v. Argentina* and *Plama v. Republic of Bulgaria* have recognized, a balanced approach to treaty interpretation is needed, "taking into account both State sovereignty and the State's responsibility to create an adapted and evolutionary framework for the development of economic activities, and the necessity to protect foreign investment and its continuing flow."[59]

In addition, arbitral tribunals have played a critical role in developing consistent jurisprudence protecting the rule of law and defining investor rights. Although tribunals are not bound under the doctrine of *stare decisis*, and there may be significant variation in treaty language, over the years they have interpreted substantive treaty standards, supported by elaborate definitions of treaty terms, in a consistent manner across their jurisprudence. To the extent that tribunals diverge from prevailing interpretations, they feel compelled to explain this divergence. As the tribunal in *Saipem v. Bangladesh* explained:

> The Tribunal considers that it is not bound by previous decisions. At the same time, it is of the opinion that it must pay due consideration to earlier decisions of international tribunals. It believes that, subject to compelling contrary grounds, *it has a duty to adopt solutions established in a series of consistent cases*. It also believes that, subject to the specifics of a given treaty and of the circumstances of the actual case, *it has a duty to seek to contribute to the harmonious development of investment law and thereby to meet the legitimate expectations of the community of States and investors towards certainty of the rule of law*.[60]

---

58. *Recent Policy Developments and Key Issues, in* WORLD INVESTMENT REPORT 2022: INTERNATIONAL TAX REFORMS AND SUSTAINABLE INVESTMENT 66 (2022), *available at* https://unctad.org/system/files/official-document/wir2022_ch02_en.pdf.

59. *El Paso Energy International Co. v. The Argentine Republic*, ICSID Case No. ARB/03/15, Decision on Jurisdiction dated April 27, 2006 ¶ 70; *El Paso Energy International Co. v. The Argentine Republic*, ICSID Case No. ARB/03/15, Award dated October 31, 2011 ¶ 650; *Plama Consortium Ltd. v. Republic of Bulgaria*, ICSID Case No. ARB/03/24, Award dated August 27, 2008 ¶ 167.

60. *Saipem S.p.A v. The People's Republic of Bangladesh*, ICSID Case No. ARB/05/07, Decision on Jurisdiction and Recommendation on Provisional Measures dated March 21, 2007 ¶ 67 (emphasis added); *see also Infrastructure Services Luxembourg S.à.r.l. and Energia Termosolar B.V. (formerly Antin Infrastructure Services Luxembourg S.à.r.l. and Antin Energia Termosolar B.V.) v. Kingdom of Spain*, ICSID Case No. ARB/13/31, Decision on Annulment, July 30, 2021 ¶ 156 ("First, while the Committee is not bound by previous decisions, it should nonetheless 'pay due consideration to earlier decisions of international tribunals' so as to 'contribute to the harmonious development of investment law and thereby to meet the legitimate expectations of the community of States and investors towards certainty of the rule of law'.") (emphasis removed); *Saba Fakes v. Republic of Turkey*, ICSID Case No. ARB/07/20, Award, July 14, 2010 ¶ 96 ("The Tribunal is not bound by the decisions adopted by previous ICSID tribunals. At the same time, it believes that it should pay due regard to earlier decisions of such tribunals. The present Tribunal shares the opinion of the Tribunal in the *Bayindir v. Pakistan* case that, unless there are compelling reasons to the contrary, it ought to follow solutions established in a series of consistent cases that are comparable to the case at hand, subject to the specificity of the treaty under consideration and the circumstances of the case. By doing so, it will fulfill its duty to seek

Finally, to address the issues arising from the vague, broad language seen in early BITs, many modern BITs provide for clearer, qualified definitions of the protections afforded in them.[61] This has allowed investors and host States a clearer understanding of their rights and obligations, and it increases the transparency of the dispute resolution process. While a laudatory goal, however, it is important to remember that, while States are free to agree to amend their treaties to formulate any new international protections they wish to offer, only they—and not tribunals—may extend these protections. Tribunals must balance their approach to defining treaty rights by developing a consistent jurisprudence with the established admonition that tribunals cannot rewrite treaty provisions, but must accept those the States have agreed to.[62]

5 Development of Multilateral Investment Treaties

Another way that the international community has adapted to challenges in the investment sphere is by introducing multilateral treaties that offer international dispute resolution. NAFTA entered into force in 1994, and, similar to modern BITs, it takes a more comprehensive approach to commercial matters by regulating matters of investment in the context of other issues surrounding social welfare, the environment, and human rights.[63] Also similar to modern BITs, disputes arising under NAFTA were

---

to contribute to the harmonious development of investment law and thereby meet the legitimate expectations of the community of States and investors towards certainty of the rule of law.").

61. Wolfgang Alschner, *Americanization of the BIT Universe: The Influence of Friendship, Commerce and Navigation (FCN) Treaties on Modern Investment Treaty Law,* 5(2) GOETTINGEN JOURNAL OF INTERNATIONAL LAW 455, 481 (2013), *available at* https://www.gojil.eu/issues/52/52_article_walschner.pdf.

62. *See Içkale İnşaat Limited Şirketi v. Turkmenistan,* ICSID Case No. ARB/10/24, Partially Dissenting Opinion of Carolyn B. Lamm ¶ 7 ("A fundamental rule of treaty interpretation is that meaning must be afforded to provide meaning to the entire clause. [...] The investor's option [to select among the international arbitral fora] provided in the chapeau cannot be deprived of any meaning by interpreting a subsidiary clause as effectively depriving the investor of any choice."); *Territorial Dispute Case (Libya v. Chad)* (1994) ICJ 6 ¶ 41 ("[I]nterpretation must be based above all upon the text of the treaty."); *Wintershall Aktiengesellschaft v. Argentine Republic,* ICSID Case No. ARB/04/14, Award December 8, 2008 ¶ 78 ("[T]he text must be presumed to be the authentic expression of the intention of the parties. The starting point of all treaty-interpretation is the elucidation of the meaning of the text, not an independent investigation into the intention of the parties from other sources."); *Nasib Hasanov v. Georgia,* ICSID Case No. ARB/20/44, Decision on Respondent Inter-State Negotiation Objection, April 19, 2022 ¶ 88(i) ("The intention of the Contracting Parties as expressed in the text of the BIT is the best guide to their common intentions. This does not preclude the possibility that the textual approach may itself lead to a choice of possible meanings, and that in exercising its choice a tribunal will need to pay particular attention to the treaty's objects and purposes (of which there may also be a range of policies in play). However, it should not be presumed, as a starting point, that a certain type of instrument—here, an investment protection treaty—entails a certain formulation, and if the text does not reflect that formulation, it should further be presumed that the Contracting Parties have made a drafting error. In short, neither intentions nor mistakes should be presumed; the text should be examined.").

63. Wolfgang Alschner, *Americanization of the BIT Universe: The Influence of Friendship, Commerce and Navigation (FCN) Treaties on Modern Investment Treaty Law,* 5(2) GOETTINGEN JOURNAL OF INTERNATIONAL LAW 455, 480 (2013), *available at* https://www.gojil.eu/issues/52/52_article_walschner.pdf.

subject to international arbitration.[64] This influenced the negotiation of more multilateral, preferential trade and investment agreements (PTIAs) between countries like Australia, Canada, Chile, Japan, Mexico, Singapore, and Taiwan, among others.[65] As a further example, the CAFTA-DR entered into force for seven countries in 2009. It removes tariff barriers and promotes stability throughout Central America, and disputes arising thereunder are subject to international arbitration.[66]

These PTIAs are still being negotiated and concluded. Between 2018 and 2021, the CP-TPP, for example, entered into force between six countries.[67] The CP-TPP covers a wide range of issues in addition to investment, including technical barriers to trade, sanitary and phytosanitary measures, customs administration, transparency and State-owned enterprises, protection of environment and labor rights, regulatory coherence, and economic development.[68] Like the other PTIAs, the CP-TPP refers investment disputes to investor-State arbitration.[69]

6   Protections Offered by BITs

In addition to facilitating cross-border investment, BITs play an active role in shaping global governance.[70] BITs originally were "designed to cover an asymmetrical relationship between developed, capital exporting countries and developing, capital importing countries,"[71] meaning that, on the one hand, BITs encourage investment in developing countries while on the other hand also protecting the interests of investors from

---

64. North American Free Trade Agreement, *entered into force* January 1, 1994, Article 1116. NAFTA was replaced by the USMCA agreement on July 1, 2020. *See* United States-Mexico-Canada Agreement, *entered into force* July 1, 2020, Preamble ¶ 1. The USMCA limits the ability to bring investor-State arbitration to disputes between parties in the United States and Mexico, and it imposes limits to arbitration not typically seen in PTIAs or BITs. *See generally* Daniel Garcia-Barragan et al., *The New NAFTA: Scaled-Back Arbitration in the USMCA*, 36 JOURNAL OF INTERNATIONAL ARBITRATION 739 (2016).

65. Wolfgang Alschner, *Americanization of the BIT Universe: The Influence of Friendship, Commerce and Navigation (FCN) Treaties on Modern Investment Treaty Law*, 5(2) GOETTINGEN JOURNAL OF INTERNATIONAL LAW 455, 481 (2013), *available at* https://www.gojil.eu/issues/52/52_article_walschner.pdf.

66. Dominican Republic-Central America Free Trade Agreement, *entered into force* January 1, 2009, Article 20.22.

67. Comprehensive and Progressive Agreement for the Trans-Pacific Partnership, NEW ZEALAND FOREIGN AFFAIRS & TRADE, *available at* https://www.mfat.govt.nz/en/about-us/who-we-are/treaties/comprehensive-and-progressive-agreement-for-tpp/ (last accessed November 7, 2022).

68. CP-TPP Explained, GOVERNMENT OF CANADA, *available at* https://www.international.gc.ca/trade-commerce/trade-agreements-accords-commerciaux/agr-acc/cptpp-ptpgp/cptpp_explained-pt pgp_apercu.aspx?lang = eng (last accessed November 7, 2022).

69. Comprehensive and Progressive Agreement for Trans-Pacific Partnership, *entered into force* December 30, 2018, Article 9.19.

70. Stephan W. Schill, *Private Enforcement of International Investment Law: Why We Need Investor Standing in BIT Dispute Settlement, in* THE BACKLASH AGAINST INVESTMENT ARBITRATION (Waibel, Kaushal, Chung, et al., eds., January 2010), *available at* https://www.kluwerarbitration.com/document/KLI-KA-201011004-n.

71. Wolfgang Alschner, *Americanization of the BIT Universe: The Influence of Friendship, Commerce and Navigation (FCN) Treaties on Modern Investment Treaty Law*, 5(2) GOETTINGEN JOURNAL OF INTERNATIONAL LAW 455, 465 (2013), *available at* https://www.gojil.eu/issues/52/52_article_walschner.pdf.

developed countries. This has resulted in BITs being heavily focused on specific and enforceable investment protections. The asymmetry present at the time of the drafting of early BITs, along with their lack of specificity in defining investment treaty protections has been replaced over time with a more symmetrical relationship between BIT parties and a focus on establishing specific and enforceable investment protections. There are several protections that have become commonplace in modern BITs.

a   *Fair and Equitable Treatment*

The obligation to provide Fair and Equitable Treatment (FET) has become one of the fundamental protections offered in BITs.[72] Out of the 2,584 investment treaties made publicly available by UNCTAD, 2,453 (94%) contain FET clauses.[73]

While this term is broad and has been subject to interpretation by many tribunals over the decades, it generally means that an investor has a claim against a host State if the host State violates the investor's right to procedural fairness, due process, transparency, legitimate expectations, or otherwise coerces, harasses, or denies the investor justice.[74] A key element of FET is the right of the investor against discrimination; the host State is prevented from treating a foreign investor or investment from being treated differently from other investors without any justified purpose, i.e., the host State cannot treat the foreign investor or investment in an arbitrary, grossly unfair, or unjust manner in a way that targets the foreign investor or investment or is otherwise based on "other manifestly wrongful grounds such as gender, race or religious belief."[75]

BITs concluded prior to 1990 often defined FET in an open-ended way, but more recent BITs address issues of regulatory stability and compliance with investors' legitimate expectations, transparency and participation in State decision-making on behalf of the investor, and proportionality requirements for any measures taken against the investor or investment.[76] In addition, recent Model BITs have sought to clarify further the definition of the FET standard by including an explicit reference to the

---

72. See Jeswald W. Salacuse, *BIT by BIT: The Growth of Bilateral Investment Treaties and Their Impact on Foreign Investment in Developing Countries*, 24(3) THE INTERNATIONAL LAWYER 655, 667 (1990), *available at* https://scholar.smu.edu/cgi/viewcontent.cgi?article=2743&context=til.

73. *International Investment Agreements Navigator*, UNCTAD INVESTMENT POLICY HUB, *available at* https://investmentpolicy.unctad.org/international-investment-agreements/iia-mapping (last accessed November 7, 2022). This number encompasses all Investment treaties publicly available by UNCTAD. There are currently 1,848 investment treaties in force that are publicly available by UNCTAD, 1,767 (95%) of which contain MFN clauses. *Ibid.* These statistics were created using the UNCTAD Navigator Tool, viewing all treaties containing the FET standard of treatment.

74. Dr. Markus Burgstaller, *Fair and equitable treatment in international investment law*, THOMPSON REUTERS, *available at* https://uk.practicallaw.thomsonreuters.com/5-385-7129?transitionType=Default&contextData=(sc.Default)&firstPage=true (last accessed November 6, 2022).

75. *Fair and Equitable Treatment*, UNCTAD SERIES ON ISSUES IN INTERNATIONAL INVESTMENT AGREEMENTS II, p. 82 (2012), *available at* https://unctad.org/system/files/official-document/unctaddiaeia2011d5_en.pdf.

76. *Recent Policy Developments and Key Issues, in* WORLD INVESTMENT REPORT 2022: INTERNATIONAL TAX REFORMS AND SUSTAINABLE INVESTMENT 89 (2022), *available at* https://unctad.org/system/files/official-document/wir2022_ch02_en.pdf.

customary international law standard or enumerating measures that would constitute a breach of the standard.[77] Many of these new BITs refer to the international minimum standard of treatment (IMST), a rule of customary international law which provides for "a minimum set of principles which States, regardless of their domestic legislation and practices, must respect when dealing with foreign nationals and their property."[78] Moreover, as the tribunal in *ADF v. United States* recognized, "both customary international law and the minimum standard of treatment of aliens it incorporates[] are constantly in a process of development."[79]

As an example of the evolution of the FET standard, the Benin-Canada BIT, which entered into force in 2014, obligates the host State to accord investors IMST and FET, as defined below:

> (1) Each Contracting Party shall accord to a covered investment treatment in accordance with the customary international law minimum standard of treatment of aliens, including fair and equitable treatment and full protection and security.
>
> (2) The concepts of "fair and equitable treatment" and "full protection and security" in paragraph 1 do not require treatment in addition to or beyond that which is required by the customary international law minimum standard of treatment of aliens.[80]

In contrast, the Canada-Slovakia BIT, which entered into force in 1992, stated only:

> Investments or returns of investors of either Contracting Party shall at all times be accorded fair and equitable treatment in accordance with principles of international law and shall enjoy full protection and security in the territory of the other Contracting Party.[81]

Since then, Canada and Slovakia have negotiated a new BIT, which entered into force in 2012 and contains an FET provision that is substantially identical to that in the Benin-Canada BIT.[82]

---

77. *See, e.g.*, U.S. Model Bilateral Investment Treaty (2012), Art. 5 ("For greater certainty, paragraph 1 prescribes the customary international law minimum standard of treatment of aliens as the minimum standard of treatment to be afforded to covered investments. The concepts of 'fair and equitable treatment' and 'full protection and security' do not require treatment in addition to or beyond that which is required by that standard, and do not create additional substantive rights. …"); Netherlands Draft Model BIT (2019), Article 9(2).

78. OECD, *Fair and Equitable Treatment Standard in International Investment Law*, OECD WORKING PAPERS ON INTERNATIONAL INVESTMENT 2004/03 (2004), p. 8 n. 32, *available at* https://www.oecd.org/daf/inv/investment-policy/WP-2004_3.pdf.

79. *ADF Group Inc. v. United States of America*, ICSID Case No. ARB (AF)/00/1, Award dated January 9, 2003 ¶ 179.

80. Benin-Canada BIT, done January 9, 2013, *entered into force* May 12, 2014, Article 7(1)-(2).

81. Canada-Slovakia BIT, done November 15, 1990, *entered into force* March 9, 1992, Article 3.

82. Canada-Slovakia BIT, done July 20, 2010, *entered into force* March 14, 2012, Article III(1)(a)-(b).

b   *National Treatment and Most-Favored-Nation Treatment*

National treatment clauses require the host State to treat foreign investors or investments not less favorably than it treats its local investors and investments.[83] These clauses typically prohibit any discriminatory treatment, whether it is by law (de jure) or in fact (de facto).[84] Out of the 2,584 investment treaties made publicly available by UNCTAD, 2,196 (84%) contain national treatment clauses.[85]

MFN clauses complement national treatment clauses by affording foreign investors and their investments the best protections offered by the host State to investors and/or investments from other States.[86] These clauses are designed to create an even playing field between foreign investors within a host State.[87] Out of the 2,584 investment treaties publicly available by UNCTAD, 2,540 (98%) contain MFN clauses.[88]

Moreover, parties often seek to expand the jurisdictional and substantive protections offered in the basic treaty through operation of its MFN clause in reliance on the protections offered in a third treaty. While the application of MFN provisions to dispute settlement is "highly controversial, it is widely accepted that investors may rely on MFN clauses to claim a better substantive treatment."[89] As in the case of the FET standard described above, States have recently sought to exclude the application of MFN to procedural provisions "by stating the exception in an appropriate way in the text or the negotiating history of newer agreements."[90]

---

83. Jeswald W. Salacuse, *BIT by BIT: The Growth of Bilateral Investment Treaties and Their Impact on Foreign Investment in Developing Countries,* 24(3) THE INTERNATIONAL LAWYER 655, 668 (1990), *available at* https://scholar.smu.edu/cgi/viewcontent.cgi?article = 2743&context = til.
84. RUDOLF DOLZER AND CHRISTOPH SCHREUER, PRINCIPLES OF INTERNATIONAL INVESTMENT LAW 201 (2d ed. 2012).
85. *International Investment Agreements Navigator,* UNCTAD INVESTMENT POLICY HUB, *available at* https://investmentpolicy.unctad.org/international-investment-agreements/iia-mapping (last accessed November 7, 2022). This number encompasses all Investment treaties made publicly available by UNCTAD. There are currently 1,848 Investment treaties in force that are made publicly available by UNCTAD, 1,588 (85%) of which contain national treatment clauses. *Ibid.* These statistics were created using the UNCTAD Navigation Tool, viewing all investment treaties with national treatment clauses.
86. Jeswald W. Salacuse, *BIT by BIT: The Growth of Bilateral Investment Treaties and Their Impact on Foreign Investment in Developing Countries,* 24(3) THE INTERNATIONAL LAWYER 655, 668 (1990), *available at* https://scholar.smu.edu/cgi/viewcontent.cgi?article = 2743&context = til.
87. Rudolf Dolzer and Christoph Schreuer, PRINCIPLES OF INTERNATIONAL INVESTMENT LAW 206 (2d ed. 2012).
88. *International Investment Agreements Navigator,* UNCTAD INVESTMENT POLICY HUB, *available at* https://investmentpolicy.unctad.org/international-investment-agreements/iia-mapping (last accessed November 7, 2022). This number encompasses all Investment treaties publicly available by UNCTAD. There are currently 1,848 Investment treaties in force that are publicly available by UNCTAD, 1,820 (98%) of which contain MFN clauses. *Ibid.* These statistics were created using the UNCTAD Navigation Tool, viewing all investment treaties with MFN standards of treatment.
89. RUDOLF DOLZER, URSULA KREIBAUM, AND CHRISTOPH SCHREUER, PRINCIPLES OF INTERNATIONAL INVESTMENT LAW (3d ed. 2022), p. 269.
90. Andreas R. Ziegler, *Most Favoured-Nation (MFN) Treatment,* in Standards of Investment Protection (Ed. August Reinisch), 2008, p. 86.

c   *Full Protection and Security*

Full protection and security (FPS) is another protection commonly granted in BITs. FPS generally requires the host State to protect investors and investments against harmful State action, especially actions that threaten the life and physical integrity of persons.[91] Similar to FET clauses, FPS clauses were previously drafted in a very broad manner, subject to multiple interpretations, including extending them to cover legal protection of enterprises.[92] However, there has been a shift toward drafting more qualified FPS clauses in recently negotiated BITs.[93] Out of the 2,584 investment treaties publicly available by UNCTAD, 2,174 (99%) contain FPS clauses.[94]

d   *Provisions Against Expropriation*

Direct expropriation is the physical seizure or transfer of title of property.[95] Indirect expropriation occurs when the investor experiences a substantial deprivation of the investment but without any physical seizure of the investment.[96] Nearly all BITs contain provisions reflecting the customary international law standard for expropriation, i.e., that the host State may not expropriate property of a foreign investor absent a public purpose, without due process, in an arbitrary or discriminatory manner, or without providing just compensation.[97] Out of the 2,584 investment treaties publicly available by UNCTAD, 2,575 (84%) contain clauses regulating expropriation.[98]

---

91. Rudolf Dolzer and Christoph Schreuer, Principles of International Investment Law 161 (2d ed. 2012).
92. *Recent Policy Developments and Key Issues, in* World Investment Report 2022: International Tax Reforms and Sustainable Investment 89 (2022), available at https://unctad.org/system/files/official-document/wir2022_ch02_en.pdf.
93. Marcela Klein Bronfman, *Fair and Equitable Treatment: An Evolving Standard,* University of Heidelberg, *in* Max Planck Institute for Comparative Public Law and International Law and the University of Chile 610, 635 (March 2005), *available at* https://www.mpil.de/files/pdf3/15_marcela_iii1.pdf.
94. *International Investment Agreements Navigator,* UNCTAD Investment Policy Hub, *available at* https://investmentpolicy.unctad.org/international-investment-agreements/iia-mapping (last accessed November 7, 2022). This number encompasses all Investment treaties publicly available by UNCTAD. There are currently 1,848 investment treaties in force that are publicly available by UNCTAD, 1,609 (87%) of which contain FPS clauses. *Ibid.* These statistics were created using the UNTAD Navigation Tool, viewing all investment treaties with FPS standards of treatment.
95. Expropriation: A Sequel, UNCTAD Series on Issues in Investment Agreements II 6 (2012), *available at* https://unctad.org/system/files/official-document/unctaddiaeia2011d7_en.pdf.
96. Expropriation: A Sequel, UNCTAD Series on Issues in Investment Agreements II 7 (2012), *available at* https://unctad.org/system/files/official-document/unctaddiaeia2011d7_en.pdf.
97. Campbell McLachlan et al., *Expropriation, in* International Investment Arbitration: Substantive Principles ¶ 8.03 (2d. ed., 2017), *available at* https://www.kluwerarbitration.com/document/KLI-KA-McLachlan-2020-Ch08; Expropriation: A Sequel, UNCTAD Series on Issues in Investment Agreements II 5 (2012), *available at* https://unctad.org/system/files/official-document/unctaddiaeia2011d7_en.pdf.
98. *International Investment Agreements Navigator,* UNCTAD Investment Policy Hub, *available at* https://investmentpolicy.unctad.org/international-investment-agreements/iia-mapping (last accessed November 7, 2022). This number encompasses all Investment treaties publicly available by UNCTAD. There are currently 1,848 investment treaties in force that are publicly

e   *Neutral Dispute Resolution Mechanisms*

Perhaps one of the most beneficial provisions in BITs is their establishment of neutral, independent and impartial dispute resolution by international arbitration, which does not require the investor to seek recourse through the host State's legal system. Instead, the investor may submit a dispute to international arbitration and seek a binding award against the host State.[99]

As of January 1, 2022, the total number of publicly known investor-State dispute settlement (ISDS) cases pursuant to treaties reached 1,190,[100] 130 countries and one economic grouping have been respondents, five of which were respondents for the first time.[101] By the end of 2021, at least 807 ISDS proceedings had been concluded;[102] approximately 38% of the cases concluded in favor of the State, 28% concluded in favor of the investor, 19% of the cases settled, 12% were discontinued, and 3% found a breach but did not provide compensation.[103] In 2021, at least forty-two new treaty-based investor-State disputes were filed.[104]

In addition, while, traditionally, the provisions for dispute resolution envisioned investors as the claimants, recent arbitral decisions suggest that certain modern investment treaties also give States a cause of action against investors for breaches of the treaties' environmental or other regulations. In *David Aven v. Costa Rica*, for example, Costa Rica brought a counterclaim against the claimants under the CP-TPP, alleging that the claimants unlawfully caused environmental damage to the wetland on the project site.[105] The tribunal held that it had jurisdiction to hear Costa Rica's counterclaim:

> Article 10.1 makes it clear that Article 10.11 covers all investments in the territory of the Party. A logical effect of Article 10.11 could be that the "measures" adopted by the host State for the protection of the environment should be deemed to be

available by UNCTAD, 1,841 (99%) of which contain clauses regulating expropriation. *Ibid.* These statistics were created using the UNCTAD Navigation Tool, viewing all investment treaties with protections for expropriation.

99. Jeswald W. Salacuse, *BIT by BIT: The Growth of Bilateral Investment Treaties and Their Impact on Foreign Investment in Developing Countries*, 24(3) THE INTERNATIONAL LAWYER 655, 672 (1990), *available at* https://scholar.smu.edu/cgi/viewcontent.cgi?article=2743&context=til.

100. *Recent Policy Developments and Key Issues, in* WORLD INVESTMENT REPORT 2022: INTERNATIONAL TAX REFORMS AND SUSTAINABLE INVESTMENT 73 (2022), *available at* https://unctad.org/system/files/official-document/wir2022_ch02_en.pdf.

101. *Recent Policy Developments and Key Issues, in* WORLD INVESTMENT REPORT 2022: INTERNATIONAL TAX REFORMS AND SUSTAINABLE INVESTMENT 73 (2022), *available at* https://unctad.org/system/files/official-document/wir2022_ch02_en.pdf.

102. *Recent Policy Developments and Key Issues, in* WORLD INVESTMENT REPORT 2022: INTERNATIONAL TAX REFORMS AND SUSTAINABLE INVESTMENT 75 (2022), *available at* https://unctad.org/system/files/official-document/wir2022_ch02_en.pdf.

103. *Recent Policy Developments and Key Issues, in* WORLD INVESTMENT REPORT 2022: INTERNATIONAL TAX REFORMS AND SUSTAINABLE INVESTMENT 75 (2022), *available at* https://unctad.org/system/files/official-document/wir2022_ch02_en.pdf.

104. *Investor-State Dispute Settlement Cases: Facts and Figures 2020*, UNCTAD IIA ISSUES NOTE (September 2021), *available at* https://unctad.org/system/files/official-document/diaepcbinf2021d7_en.pdf.

105. *David R. Aven and others v. Republic of Costa Rica*, ICSID Case No. UNCT/15/3, Award ¶¶ 698, 721 dated September 18, 2018.

compulsory for everybody under the jurisdiction of the State, particularly the foreign investors. Therefore, following said interpretation the investors have the obligation, not only under domestic law but also under section A of Chapter 10 of DR-CAFTA to abide and comply the environmental domestic laws and regulations, including the measures adopted by the host State to protect human, animal, or plant life or health. *No investor can ignore or breach such measures and its breach is a violation of both domestic and international law, so that the perpetrator cannot be exempt of liability for the damages caused.*[106]

The tribunal's decision suggests that investment treaties and investment arbitration will continue to evolve and adapt to the changing socioeconomic realities and demands of both investors *and* States.

III   INVESTMENT ARBITRATION IS A NECESSITY FOR STATES

Investment arbitration is important to States on the domestic and international planes, as it is critical to the establishment of a stable investment climate for foreign investment and facilitates economic growth. The overwhelming majority of treaties include provisions for international dispute settlement: of 2584 treaties mapped by UNCTAD, 2449 contain ISDS clauses.[107] A meaningful number of treaties—627—also include provisions for voluntary ADR methods, such as conciliation or mediation.[108] Nevertheless, certain States have also included provisions for exhaustion of local remedies in their recent model BITs, in part in response to the backlash against investment arbitration. For example, the Indian Model BIT and the South African Development Community Model BIT both require exhaustion of local remedies or a demonstration of their futility prior to submitting the dispute to arbitration.[109] While some may argue the inclusion of these provisions on exhaustion of local remedies reflects States' backlash against investment arbitration, in reality, it demonstrates an evolution of the ISDS system and a balance of State interests by providing States the opportunity to resolve a dispute domestically, while also guaranteeing investors the protections of investment arbitration.

---

106. *David R. Aven and others v. Republic of Costa Rica,* ICSID Case No. UNCT/15/3, Award ¶¶ 734, 742 dated September 18, 2018 (emphasis added).
107. *International Investment Agreements Navigator,* UNCTAD INVESTMENT POLICY HUB, *available at* https://investmentpolicy.unctad.org/international-investment-agreements/iia-mapping (last accessed November 15, 2022). These statistics were created using the UNCTAD Navigation Tool, viewing all investment treaties including provisions for ISDS.
108. *International Investment Agreements Navigator,* UNCTAD INVESTMENT POLICY HUB, *available at* https://investmentpolicy.unctad.org/international-investment-agreements/iia-mapping (last accessed November 15, 2022). These statistics were created using the UNCTAD Navigation Tool, viewing all investment treaties with provisions for either voluntary or compulsory conciliation or mediation.
109. Indian Model BIT (2015), Article 14.3, *available at* https://www.mygov.in/sites/default/files/master_image/Model%20Text%20for%20the%20Indian%20Bilateral%20Investment%20Treaty.pdf (last accessed November 30, 2022); South African Community Development Model BIT (2012), Article 28.4, (last accessed November 30, 2022), *available at* https://www.iisd.org/itn/wp-content/uploads/2012/10/sadc-model-bit-template-final.pdf.

It is well established that the proliferation of investment treaties during the 1990s was accompanied by a global increase in FDI flows.[110] Moreover, a recent World Bank report found that 25% of all investors in developing States discontinue FDI projects due to unresolved grievances.[111] Thus, a viable and robust international system of treaty protections and dispute resolution is essential to attracting and retaining FDI. Indeed, access to impartial third-party dispute settlement has been identified as one of the main factors for Ease of Doing Business Indices by multilateral organizations.[112] The benefits of increased and retained FDI that result, in part, from the availability of effective international dispute settlement provisions are multi-fold. Domestically, job growth usually follows from an increase in foreign direct investment. For example, in Latin America, nearly 1.4 million jobs were created between 2013 and 2018 as a result of FDI in new projects. Specifically, jobs created by FDI represented "45% of new jobs in Mexico and 14% of new jobs in Brazil."[113] Such job growth is not limited to Latin America: "[i]n 2018, more than 170,000 jobs were created across the African continent as a result of 710 FDI projects, comprising $75.5 billion in capital";[114] in 2016 FDI contributed to the creation of 6.1 million jobs in the United States;[115] and a 2006 study concluded that there was a direct relationship between FDI flows and employment based on data from twenty Caribbean countries.[116]

Further, a 2020 World Bank study analyzed FDI and employment outcomes in developing countries and likewise found positive results. In 2018, greenfield FDI projects were responsible for the creation of 2.3 million jobs in developing countries and it was held that "about 68% more jobs" were generated "for MNC affiliates in targeted sectors as compared to non-targeted sectors."[117] More broadly, the study

110. Susan D. Franck, *Foreign Direct Investment, Investment Treaty Arbitration, and the Rule of Law*, 19 Pac. McGeorge Global Bus. & Dev. L.J. 337, 338 n. 4 (2006), *available at* https://scholarlycommons.pacific.edu/globe/vol19/iss2/3/?utm_source=scholarlycommons.pacific.edu%2Fglobe%2Fvol19%2Fiss2%2F3&utm_medium=PDF&utm_campaign=PDFCoverPages.

111. World Bank Group & European Commission, Retention and Expansion of Foreign Direct Investment, Political Risk and Policy Responses, Summary of Research Findings and Policy Implications 1 (2019).

112. Investor-State Dispute Settlement (ISDS) Reform, submitted by the Corporate Counsel International Arbitration Group (CCIAG) to UNCITRAL Working Group III 2 (December 18, 2019), *available at* https://uncitral.un.org/sites/uncitral.un.org/files/cciag_isds_reform.pdf.

113. Investor-State Dispute Settlement (ISDS) Reform, submitted by the Corporate Counsel International Arbitration Group (CCIAG) to UNCITRAL Working Group III 1-2 (December 18, 2019), *available at* https://uncitral.un.org/sites/uncitral.un.org/files/cciag_isds_reform.pdf.

114. Investor-State Dispute Settlement (ISDS) Reform, submitted by the Corporate Counsel International Arbitration Group (CCIAG) to UNCITRAL Working Group III 1-2 (December 18, 2019), *available at* https://uncitral.un.org/sites/uncitral.un.org/files/cciag_isds_reform.pdf.

115. Investor-State Dispute Settlement (ISDS) Reform, submitted by the Corporate Counsel International Arbitration Group (CCIAG) to UNCITRAL Working Group III 1-2 (December 18, 2019), *available at* https://uncitral.un.org/sites/uncitral.un.org/files/cciag_isds_reform.pdf.

116. World Bank Report, Foreign Direct Investment and Employment Outcomes in Developing Countries 4 (2020).

117. World Bank Report, Foreign Direct Investment and Employment Outcomes in Developing Countries 4 (2020).

reported that the "targeted investment promotion in developing countries has been found to reduce asymmetries and lower bureaucratic burden to attract FDI inflows."[118]

Indeed, evidence demonstrates that States typically also benefit from an increase in living standards, foreign expertise in local business, development of human capital, transfer of technology, and host country tax revenues.[119] For example, with regard to technology, FDI is seen as a channel to enable technological transfer, directly impacting technological development in the host State (technological spillover), and promoting domestic productivity.[120] FDI increases likewise benefit human capital, leading to higher productivity and profitability.[121]

On the international plane, States equally benefit at different levels. Economically, there are more opportunities for States to engage in bilateral or multilateral transactions when they have entered into BITs. According to a recent study, the probability and dollar volume of cross-border mergers between two countries significantly increases after signing a BIT, going from 1.6% before the signature of the treaty to 4.5% after the treaty is signed.[122] The study concludes that BITs contribute, in overall terms, to a reduction in political risk.[123]

At the same time, when signing BITs, States are more likely to seek to join multilateral treaties in areas such as human rights, labor, health or environment,[124] as well as enter into other bilateral agreements such as double taxation treaties.[125] Furthermore, BITs can also contribute to the international rule of law by prompting

---

118. World Bank Report, Foreign Direct Investment and Employment Outcomes in Developing Countries 4 (2020).
119. Investor-State Dispute Settlement (ISDS) Reform, submitted by the Corporate Counsel International Arbitration Group (CCIAG) to UNCITRAL Working Group III 1-2 (December 18, 2019), *available at* https://uncitral.un.org/sites/uncitral.un.org/files/cciag_isds_reform.pdf.
120. Bernard M. Hockman et al., *Transfer of Technology to Developing Countries: Unilateral and Multilateral Policy Options*, World Bank Research Working Papers 3332, p. 9 (2004); Lise Johnson, Lisa Sachs and Nathan Lobel, *Aligning Investment Agreements with the Sustainable Development Goals*, Columbia Journal of Transnational Law 61 (February 5, 2020), *available rociat* https://www.jtl.columbia.edu/journal-articles/aligning-international-investment-agre ements-with-the-sustainable-development-goals ("FDI can be an efficient and effective way to transfer capital and technologies across borders and [...] to spur [...] economic growth and development through employment, infrastructure development, technology transfer, tax revenues, and other economic linkages."); Jacob Jordaan et al., Foreign Direct Investments, Backwards Linkages and Productivity Spillovers, World Bank 9 (2020).
121. Jonathan Michi, *The Impact of FDI on human Capital Enhancement in Developing Countries*, Report for the OECD 4 (2001).
122. Vineet Bhagwat, Jonathan Brogaard and Brandon Julio, *A BIT Goes a Long Way: Bilateral Investment Treaties and Cross-Border Mergers*, Journal of Financial Economics 140, 515 (2021).
123. Vineet Bhagwat, Jonathan Brogaard and Brandon Julio, *A BIT Goes a Long Way: Bilateral Investment Treaties and Cross-Border Mergers*, Journal of Financial Economics 140, 526, 529, 532 (2021).
124. OECD, The Future of Investment Treaties, Background Note on Potential Avenues for Future Policies ¶¶ 18-21 (2021), *available at* https://www.oecd.org/daf/inv/investment-policy/Note -on-possible-directions-for-the-future-of-investment-treaties.pdf.
125. Tax treaties are bilateral agreements made between two States to "facilitate cross-border trade and investment by eliminating the tax impediments too these cross-border flows," which is most commonly done by eliminating double taxation. Brian J. Arnold, *An Introduction to Tax Treaties*, United Nations Department of Economic and Social Affairs (June 2020) ¶ 44, *available at* https://www.un.org/development/desa/financing/sites/www.un.org.developm ent.desa.financing/files/2020-06/TT_Introduction_Eng.pdf.

host States to abide by international law. As BITs are international treaties, international law governs principles of treaty interpretation. This means that substantive treaty rights, such as FET, are interpreted using principles of international law.[126] Moreover, international law often becomes a crucial source of applicable law, whether directly (as specified in the language of the BIT) or indirectly (as incorporated into the selected State law).[127] In cases where parties have not agreed on the applicable law, ICSID Convention Article 42(1) provides for the application of the law of the host State and international law as may be applicable.[128] In this context, tribunals will apply the host State's law and, to the extent that the host State's law is undeveloped or where there is a *lacuna*,[129] international law will be applied.[130] International law thus plays a critical role in the development of investment protections, even when it is not expressly chosen as an applicable law under the BIT.

The presence of effective dispute resolution mechanisms in treaties is particularly important to smaller and mid-size corporations seeking to invest in a foreign country, who do not have the same negotiating power as larger corporations to secure by alternative means the protections guaranteed in investment treaties. Larger companies may be able to negotiate investment protections in their investment agreements and thus may still invest, but they will require a higher rate of return, a quicker horizon for the investment, or "other incentives to mitigate the added risk of uncertainty with

---

126. *Ceskoslovenska Obchodni Banka, A.S. v. The Slovak Republic*, ICSID Case No. ARB/97/4, Award dated December 19, 2004 ¶ 63 ("[T]he BIT ... has to be interpreted in the context of the legal system under which it has been drafted. Consequently the incorporation of the BIT includes the rues of international law that are relevant for its interpretation.").

127. *See* Emmanuel Gaillard and Yas Banifatemi, *The Meaning of "and" in Article 42(1), Second Sentence, of the Washington Convention: The Role of International Law in the ICSID Choice of Law Process*, 18 ICSID REVIEW—FOREIGN INVESTMENT LAW JOURNAL 375, 376 (2003).

128. ICSID Convention, Article 42(1) ("The Tribunal shall decide a dispute in accordance with such rules of law as may be agreed by the parties. In the absence of such agreement, the Tribunal shall apply the law of the Contracting State party to the dispute (including its rules on the conflict of laws) and such rules of international law as may be applicable."); *see also* Emmanuel Gaillard and Yas Banifatemi, *The Meaning of "and" in Article 42(1), Second Sentence, of the Washington Convention: The Role of International Law in the ICSID Choice of Law Process*, 18 ICSID REVIEW— FOREIGN INVESTMENT LAW JOURNAL 375, 379-380 (2003) (noting that, when there is no party agreement on the applicable law under an ICSID arbitration, "[i]nternational law is thus part of the equation from the outset").

129. A *lacuna* arises when there is a gap in the host State's law on a given issue. ICSID tribunals will apply international law when this occurs. *See*, W. Michael Reisman, *The Regime for Lacunae in the ICSID Choice of law Provision and the Question of its Threshold*, 15 ICSID REVIEW—FOREIGN INVESTMENT LAW JOURNAL 362, 375 (2000).

130. *Klöckner Industrie-Anlagen GmbH and others v. United Republic of Cameroon and Société Camerounaise des Engrais*, ICSID Case No. ARB/81/2, Excerpts of Ad hoc Committee Decision on Annulment dated May 3, 1985 ¶ 69; *Amco Asia Corp. et al. v. Republic of Indonesia*, ICSID Case No. ARB/81/1, Annulment Decision dated May 16, 1986, reprinted in 1 ICSID REPORTS 509, 542 (1993), p. 515; Aron Broches, Observations on the Finality of ICSID Awards, 6 ICSID REV. FILJ 321, p. 342. *Ceskoslovenska Obchodni Banka, A.S. v. The Slovak Republic, ICSID Case No. ARB/97/4*, Award dated December 19, 2004 ¶ 63; *PSEG Global, Inc., The North American Coal Corporation, and Konya Ingin Electrik Üretim ve Ticaret Limited Sirketi v. Republic of Turkey*, ICSID Case No. ARB/02/5, Decision on Jurisdiction dated June 4, 2004 ¶¶ 167-174.

negative consequences for civil society."[131] Without an investment treaty in place, mid-size and small companies may be deterred entirely from investing.

Moreover, investment treaties provide States with guidance for sovereign conduct at an internationally acceptable level. States can offer the level of international investment protection they are comfortable with to other States. Recent investment treaties are characterized by the inclusion of provisions that raise the level of protection in relation to human rights, environment or labor rights.[132] Additionally, this new generation of investment treaties contains clauses aimed at combatting corruption, either directly, or indirectly through the inclusion of corporate social responsibility clauses.[133] In this sense, new investment treaties can act as an incentive for host States to adhere to and implement internationally accepted standards, and to adopt and enforce domestic policies aimed at providing a more stable business framework for investors.[134]

IV   INVESTMENT ARBITRATION IS A NECESSITY FOR INVESTORS

For investors, investment arbitration is crucial to obtain the reassurance of making investment decisions among the various capital-importing States. Investors rely on foreign investment to access markets, customers, and innovation, among other resources.[135] However, investors, and their investments, are placed at risk when there is no neutral dispute resolution mechanism for investors to enforce their international rights under the treaties. Investment arbitration affords investors a neutral arbitral

---

131. Investor-State Dispute Settlement (ISDS) Reform, submitted by the Corporate Counsel International Arbitration Group (CCIAG) to UNCITRAL Working Group III 2 (December 18, 2019), *available at* https://uncitral.un.org/sites/uncitral.un.org/files/cciag_isds_reform.pdf.

132. *See, e.g.*, Chile-Brazil BIT (2015), Article 15 ("Investors [...] shall develop their best efforts to abide by the OECD Guidelines for Multinational enterprises [...] [including] to respect internationally recognized human rights of people involved in the corporations activities") (unofficial translation); India-Kyrgyzstan BIT (2019), Article 12 ("Investors and their enterprises operating within its territory of each Party shall endeavour to voluntarily incorporate internationally recognized standards of corporate social responsibility [...] These principles may address issues such as labour, the environment, human rights, community relations, and anti-corruption."); 2021 Canada Foreign Investment Promotion and Protection Agreement (FIPA) Model, Article 16 ("The Parties reaffirm that investors and their investments shall comply with domestic laws and regulations of the host State, including laws and regulations on human rights, the rights of Indigenous peoples, gender equality, environmental protection and labour.").

133. *See, e.g.*, Morocco-Nigeria BIT (2016), Art. 17 ("Each Contracting Party shall ensure that measures and efforts are undertaken to prevent and combat corruption regarding matters covered by this Agreement in accordance with its laws and regulations."); India-Kyrgyzstan BIT (2019), Article 12 ("Investors and their enterprises operating within its territory of each Party shall endeavour to voluntarily incorporate internationally recognized standards of corporate social responsibility [...] These principles may address issues such as labour, the environment, human rights, community relations, and anti-corruption.").

134. OECD, The Future of Investment Treaties, Background Note on Potential Avenues for Future Policies ¶¶ 18-21 (2021), *available at* https://www.oecd.org/daf/inv/investment-policy/Note-on-possible-directions-for-the-future-of-investment-treaties.pdf.

135. Investor-State Dispute Settlement (ISDS) Reform, submitted by the Corporate Counsel International Arbitration Group (CCIAG) to UNCITRAL Working Group III 2 (December 18, 2019), *available at* https://uncitral.un.org/sites/uncitral.un.org/files/cciag_isds_reform.pdf.

forum for the resolution of investment disputes based on the rule of law, likely more balanced than the host State's courts, which might be perceived as biased or otherwise unlikely to resolve disputes based on the rule of law.[136] The reality is that there would be far less FDI without investment arbitration, particularly in developing countries, as investors tend to be reluctant to direct resources into countries with an unstable investment climate, and as explained above, smaller and mid-size corporations would be further deterred from entering these markets.

When deciding whether to invest in developing countries, the existence of legal protections is a fundamental decision element for investors. According to a "Global Investment Competitiveness" survey commissioned by the World Bank, over 90% of investors consider investment protection guarantees as "critical for retaining and expanding investments in the long term across all types of FDI."[137] Indeed, an uncertain political climate and inadequate investment policies can negatively affect investment decisions by foreign investors.[138]

Numerous studies confirm that ISDS provisions stimulate FDI, providing investors with a neutral forum for dispute resolution, as well as an effective enforcement mechanism. When ISDS is an available mechanism, investors feel more confident in making investment decisions, particularly those involving large amounts of capital with long-term implications.[139] Further, several studies point to the positive effect of ISDS provisions on increased investment flows.[140] For example, according to one study, FDI inflows in South-, East-, and South-East Asia can increase by 2.3% as a result of investment treaties.[141] Moreover, investment treaties contribute to increasing

---

136. *See* Jeswald W. Salacuse, *BIT by BIT: The Growth of Bilateral Investment Treaties and Their Impact on Foreign Investment in Developing Countries,* 24(3) THE INTERNATIONAL LAWYER 655, 673 (1990), *available at* https://scholar.smu.edu/cgi/viewcontent.cgi?article=2743&context=til.

137. Peter Kusek and Andrea Silva, *What Matters to Investors in Developing Countries: Findings from the Global Investment Competitiveness Survey, in* GLOBAL INVESTMENT COMPETITIVENESS REPORT 19, 20 (2018).

138. Peter Kusek, Abhishek Saurav and Ryan Kuo, *Outlook and Priorities for Foreign Investors in Developing Countries: Findings from the 2019 Global Investment Competitiveness Survey in 10 Middle Income-Countries,* WORLD BANK 24; *see also* The Role of International Investment Agreements in Attracting Foreign Direct Investment to Developing Countries, UNCTAD Series, p. XIV (2009), *available at* https://unctad.org/system/files/official-document/diaeia20095_en .pdf.

139. APEC Policy Support Unit, *Policy Support Brief No. 28, ISDS as an Instrument for Investment Promotion and Facilitation* 3 (October 2019) *available at* https://www.apec.org/docs/default -source/publications/2019/11/isds-as-an-instrument-for-investment-promotion-and-facilitati on/psu-policy-brief_isds_final-rev2.pdf?sfvrsn=47526d77_1.

140. Rose-Ackerman, Susan, and Jennifer Tobin, *When BITs Have Some Bite: The Political-Economic Environment for Bilateral Investment Treaties,* THE REVIEW OF INTERNATIONAL ORGANIZATIONS 6, No. 1: 1-32, p. 4 (2011); The Role of International Investment Agreements in Attracting Foreign Direct Investment to Developing Countries, UNCTAD Series 15, 53, 55 (2009), *available at* https://unctad.org/system/files/official-document/diaeia20095_en.pdf.

141. Kim Sokchea, Bilateral Investment Treaties, Political Risk and Foreign Direct Investment, 11 Asia Pacific Journal of Economics & Business No. 1, 22 (June 2007) *available at* https://papers .ssrn.com/sol3/papers.cfm?abstract_id=909760.

the number of multinational firms and the number of plants per firm.[142] Access to international arbitration increases investor confidence because host States typically make a "strong commitment to honour their obligations."[143]

In addition, scholars have analyzed the effect of ISDS provisions on FDI through the lens of investment arbitration and its role in promoting the rule of law. One scholar notes that ISDS can create a "race to the top" prompting national courts of the host State to adjudicate disputes in a more impartial and just way, supporting the development of rule of law in developing countries.[144]

In terms of the number of investment treaties containing ISDS provisions, other scholars point to a sharp increase, from six BITs in 1978 to about one-third of BITs sampled, in 1990.[145] More recently, between 2000 and 2022, out of 682 BITs signed and currently in force, 597 included ISDS provisions. Only two agreements (signed by Brazil in 2015) did not contain or otherwise excluded ISDS mechanisms.[146]

These studies unequivocally demonstrate that the impact of ISDS is mutually beneficial to both investors and States. Investors have increased confidence as a result of ISDS provisions in BITs, which in turn stimulates FDI, and States seek to honor the obligations set forth in BITs, which stimulates domestic growth.

V   THE CRITICISMS OF ISDS MISREPRESENT THE ACTUAL REALITY

As discussed above in section II, ISDS has changed and evolved over time in light of changing expectations and thereby has avoided becoming an anachronism. ISDS is now again at one of those turning points.

A vast majority of international disputes have arisen under the early investment treaties developed prior to 2000. As of 2022, out of 1190 disputes, 969 (or 81%) of disputes arose from these old treaties.[147] However, as explained, a careful analysis of

---

142. APEC Policy Support Unit, *Policy Support Brief No. 28, ISDS as an Instrument for Investment Promotion and Facilitation* 3 (Oct. 2019) *available at* https://www.apec.org/docs/default-source/publications/2019/11/isds-as-an-instrument-for-investment-promotion-and-facilitation/psu-policy-brief_isds_final-rev2.pdf?sfvrsn=47526d77_1.

143. The Role of International Investment Agreements in Attracting Foreign Direct Investment to Developing Countries, UNCTAD Series 15 (2009), *available at* https://unctad.org/system/files/official-document/diaeia20095_en.pdf.

144. Susan D. Franck, "Foreign Direct Investment, Investment Treaty Arbitration, and the Rule of Law," 19 Pac. McGeorge Global Bus. & Dev. L.J. 337, 367 (2006), *available at* https://scholarlycommons.pacific.edu/globe/vol19/iss2/3

145. Axel Berger et al., "More Stringent BITs, Less Ambiguous Effects on FDI? Not a Bit!", World Trade Organization Economic Research and Statistics Division 3-4 (May 2010) *available at* https://www.wto.org/english/res_e/reser_e/ersd201010_e.pdf.

146. International Investment Agreements Navigator, UNCTAD Investment Policy Hub, *available at* https://investmentpolicy.unctad.org/international-investment-agreements/iia-mapping (last accessed November 9, 2022). This statistic was calculated using the UNTAD Navigator Tool, viewing all BITs signed between 2000 and 2022, which are currently in force and contain ISDS provisions.

147. International Investment Dispute Settlement Navigator, UNCTAD Investment Policy Hub, *available at* https://investmentpolicy.unctad.org/investment-dispute-settlement (last accessed November 10, 2022). This statistic was created by using the UNCTAD Navigator Tool, viewing all disputes initiated under investment treaties signed before 2000.

the current landscape demonstrates that States continue to conclude new treaties and renegotiate old treaties.[148] In doing so, ISDS is alleviating and tackling concerns over the quality and review of awards, arbitrator conflicts and incentives, transparency, and costs, including in relation to State parties. In fact, many of the revisions to modern investment treaties provide greater protections to States and even provide them with the opportunity to bring claims against investors who violate the social welfare, environmental, or human rights provisions of the IIA.[149]

Proponents of abandoning ISDS have not provided a single, widely supported alternative to ISDS. Rather, the proposed alternatives, such as establishing a permanent court or an appellate mechanism, are destabilizing and unnecessary. Indeed, the selection of a permanent court or appellate mechanism with all of the jurists selected by states would not provide any reassurance to investors, nor would they define the international standards each state would provide. The proposals fail to remedy the criticisms and would take years of negotiating and legislation to implement. Implementing such mechanisms runs the risk of toppling the entire international legal system governing foreign investment. There is simply no clear substitute for the system of investment treaty arbitration.

A room full of intelligent people redesigning the system, as some may support, ignores the political reality of eschewing the existing system rather than reforming it and ignores the time and effort it would take to design any new system, including obtaining the agreement of 156 countries, running it through national approval processes to obtain ratification and subsequently implementing it. At best, such a process would take twenty to thirty years, if it were even possible to realize, without even mentioning what would happen to investment protections and international dispute resolution in the interim. The far better solution is to revise the current system, which has provided many benefits over the decades. Even defining the real frailties in a mutually agreed way and the acceptable remedies will take years.

This section addresses some of the common misconceptions used in support of abandoning the ISDS system and shows that these arguments are wrong, based on unfounded concerns regarding ISDS, or would be better addressed by improving the current system in place, not stripping it in its entirety.

1   **The Outside World Has Not Lost Confidence in the ISDS System**

The myth that there has been a "mass exodus" from the ISDS system due to concerns about fairness and consistency is far from correct. There is no evidence of any mass exodus. Rather, the statistics demonstrate that more investment treaties and PTIAs are entered into each year. As explained above, there are currently over 2,500 investment

---

148. *Recent Policy Developments and Key Issues, in* WORLD INVESTMENT REPORT 2022: INTERNATIONAL TAX REFORMS AND SUSTAINABLE INVESTMENT 65 (2022), *available at* https://unctad.org/system/files/official-document/wir2022_ch02_en.pdf.

149. *Recent Policy Developments and Key Issues, in* WORLD INVESTMENT REPORT 2022: INTERNATIONAL TAX REFORMS AND SUSTAINABLE INVESTMENT 90 (2022), *available at* https://unctad.org/system/files/official-document/wir2022_ch02_en.pdf.

treaties in force over 2,200 of which are BITs.[150] In 2021 alone, thirteen new investment treaties, including six new BITs, were concluded, and four were renegotiated and replaced with a new treaty.[151] In contrast, the number of terminated treaties remains relatively low over time.[152]

While it is true that there have been a few pushbacks to certain investment treaties, most notably the U.S.'s pushback on NAFTA during the Trump Administration, this does not signify a loss of confidence in the ISDS system. Rather, this sharp change in the approach to NAFTA demonstrates the Trump Administration's shift in trade policy toward that of economic protectionism.[153] Moreover, the new USMCA contains an ISDS provision. In the same vein, in 2020, the U.S. Trade Representative issued a report accusing the WTO Appellate Body of "judicial overreach"[154] and proceeded to block the appointment of new Appellate Body judges, rendering WTO members unable to make new appeals.[155] The solutions presented by critics of the current ISDS system (*i.e.*, implementing an appellate mechanism) would do nothing to resolve these concerns coming from States with economic protectionist policies.

2 The Current ISDS System Is Not Inconsistent

Contrary to critics' assertions, the ISDS system has evolved into one that is internally consistent, promotes certainty of the rule of law, assures due process and ensures that investors can rely on States' legitimate expectations. For the most part, considering the different facts, circumstances, and treaty provisions in each dispute that must be considered, arbitral awards are consistent, and there is a system of annulment or set-aside proceedings that addresses any problems that may arise. This ensures investor confidence and is one contributing factor to foreign investment.

As explained in section II, arbitral jurisprudence has developed substantive treaty standards that are consistent. For example, it is undisputed that there is consistency

---

150. International Investment Agreements Navigator, UNCTAD INVESTMENT POLICY HUB (last accessed November 7, 2022), *available at* https://investmentpolicy.unctad.org/international-investment-agreements/advanced-search.
151. *Recent Policy Developments and Key Issues, in* WORLD INVESTMENT REPORT 2022: INTERNATIONAL TAX REFORMS AND SUSTAINABLE INVESTMENT 65 (2022), *available at* https://unctad.org/system/files/official-document/wir2022_ch02_en.pdf.
152. Of the 3,204 investment treaties mapped by UNCTAD, only 524 have been terminated. 164 of these treaties were replaced by new treaties. International Investment Agreements Navigator, UNCTAD INVESTMENT POLICY HUB, *available at* https://investmentpolicy.unctad.org/international-investment-agreements/advanced-search (last accessed November 14, 2022). These statistics were calculated using the UNCTAD Navigation Tool, viewing all investment treaties terminated and all investment treaties replaced by new treaties.
153. Dominic Rushe, *More Than 1,000 Economists Warn Trump His Trade Views Echo 1930s Errors,* THE GUARDIAN (May 3, 2018) *available at* https://www.theguardian.com/us-news/2018/may/03/donald-trump-trade-economists-warning-great-depression.
154. United States Trade Representative, Report on the Appellate Body of the World Trade Organization 51 (February 2020) *available at* https://ustr.gov/sites/default/files/Report_on_the_Appellate_Body_of_the_World_Trade_Organization.pdf.
155. United States Continues to Block New Appellate Body Members for the World Trade Organization, Risking the Collapse of the Appellate Process, 113 AMERICAN JOURNAL OF INTERNATIONAL LAW 822, 822-823 (2019).

when it comes to the distinction between treaty and contract claims, and when it comes to fair and equitable treatment.[156] Arbitrators have a responsibility to uphold the rule of law, and they attempt to remain consistent when it is possible to do so. Divergences in outcomes, when they do arise, are often the result of differences in the treaty language or the facts of the case at hand, rather than a different legal standard applied by a new tribunal. In *Metal-Tech v. Uzbekistan*, the tribunal described its duty to promote the rule of law and explain any divergences:

> [The Tribunal] is of the opinion that it should pay due regard to earlier decisions of international tribunals. The Tribunal is further of the view that, *unless there are compelling reasons to the contrary, it has a duty to follow solutions established in a series of consistent cases comparable to the case at hand,* but subject, of course, to the specifics of a given treaty and of the circumstances of the actual case. By doing so, it will meet its duty to contribute to the *harmonious development of investment law and thereby to meet the legitimate expectations of the community of States and investors towards certainty of the rule of law.*[157]

In addition, ISDS has even further protections in place, through treaty jurisprudence, post-award remedies and set-aside proceedings, to promote the rule of law and legitimate expectations and to condemn investment born or implemented with fraud and corruption.[158] In ICSID Convention arbitration, for example, after an award is rendered, a party may (i) request a supplementary decision if it believes the tribunal did not decide a question in the award or request a rectification of an error; (ii) request interpretation of an award if the party believes that there is a dispute as to the award's scope or meaning; (iii) request revision of an award if there is a new fact that could affect the award; or (iv) request annulment of an award if the tribunal violated fundamental due process principles.[159] Parties also have the ability to set aside non-ICSID Convention awards in the national courts of the seat of arbitration and to

---

156. Gabrielle Kaufmann-Kohler, *Is Consistency a Myth?, available at* https://www.arbitration-icca.org/media/4/92392722703895/media0123191413607200095062.pdf.
157. *Metal-Tech Ltd. v. Republic of Uzbekistan,* ICSID Case No. ARB/10/3, Award dated October 4, 2013, ¶ 116 (emphasis added); *see also, e.g., Burlington Resources Inc. v. Republic of Ecuador,* ICSID Case No. ARB/08/5, Decision on Reconsideration and Award dated February 7, 2017 ¶ 46 (finding that, "subject always to the specifics of a given treaty and to the circumstances of the actual case, it has a duty to adopt solutions established in a series of consistent similar cases, if such exist, absent compelling contrary grounds"); *Churchill Mining Plc v. Republic of Indonesia,* ICSID Case No. ARB/12/14 and 12/40, Award dated December 6, 2016 ¶ 253 ("[I]n its judgment [the Tribunal] must pay due consideration to earlier decisions of international tribunals. Specifically, it believes that, subject to compelling grounds to the contrary, it has a duty to adopt principles established in a series of consistent cases. It further believes that, subject always to the text of the BITs and the circumstances of each particular case, it has a duty to contribute to the harmonious development of international investment law, with a view to meeting the legitimate expectations of the community of States and investors towards legal certainty and the rule of law.").
158. In *Metal-Tech v. Uzbekistan,* for example, the tribunal found that it did not have jurisdiction over the dispute because, since the investment was obtained through corruption, "the investment has not been 'implemented in accordance with the laws and regulations of the Contracting Party in whose territory the investment is made' as required by Article 1(1) of the Israel-Uzbekistan BIT." ICSID Case No. ARB/10/3, Award dated October 4, 2013 ¶ 372.
159. *Post-Award Remedies,* ICSID (last accessed November 8, 2022), *available at* https://icsid.worldbank.org/node/12236.

challenge awards in the enforcing jurisdiction on the bases set forth in Article V of the New York Convention: procedural flaws, public policy and excess of power.[160]

States also can preemptively resolve any issues of inconsistency in tribunal interpretations by providing their own binding interpretations of standards—and they have exercised this right.[161] Treaties since the original NAFTA provide for binding interpretation of standards by the treaty parties. In 2018, Colombia and India signed a joint interpretive declaration on their 2009 BIT, and in 2017 Bangladesh and India and Colombia and France, respectively, signed binding declarations.[162] Other parties have entered into agreements to include mandates to issue binding interpretations of standards, including the Australia–Peru FTA (2018), the Belarus–India BIT (2018), the Central America–Republic of Korea FTA (2018), the CP-TPP (2018), the EU–Singapore IPA (2018), the proposed EU–Viet Nam IPA, the 2018 amendments to the Republic of Korea–United States FTA (2007), the USMCA (2018), and the Netherlands model BIT (2018).[163] These binding interpretations of standards ensure the participating States and investors that they understand the rights afforded under the treaty prior to the investment.

Arbitration rules can also address any issues of inconsistent results, for example, those that may result from parallel proceedings. For example, Rule 46 of the ICSID Arbitration Rules, as amended in 2022, provides that "[p]arties to two or more pending arbitrations administered by the Centre may agree to consolidate or coordinate these arbitrations."[164] Additionally, the US Model BIT, the Canada Model BIT and the Australian-Chile FTA all make reference to consolidation.[165] The reality is that contract and treaty claims may arise from the same dispute or multiple parties may commence separate arbitrations concerning the same State action, and there are existing mechanisms such as these to prevent the likelihood of inconsistent results.

Implementing a rule of *stare decisis*, as suggested by opponents of the current ISDS system, would be inconsistent with the system of international adjudication and the rules governing other international courts and tribunals. Each arbitration has different facts and evidence, and different applicable host state laws, and arbitrators decide on this basis. Moreover, many States following the civil law tradition would not accept the implementation of *stare decisis*. Finally, implementing a rule of *stare decisis* is unnecessary because, as explained above, tribunals have established a consistent body of jurisprudence, substantive treaty standards, and elaborate definitions of treaty

---

160. Borzu Sabahi et al., *Annulment, Set Aside, and Refusal to Enforce*, INVESTOR-STATE ARBITRATION (2d ed. 2019) ¶ 22.72, *available at* https://www.kluwerarbitration.com/document/kli-ka-sabahi-2020-ch22.
161. For further discussion of binding interpretive notes and other tools to clarify treaties, please see the IBA's Investment Treaty Arbitration Report 2018, "Consistency, Efficiency and Transparency in Investment Treaty Arbitration."
162. UNCTAD, World Investment Report 109-110 (2019) *available at* https://unctad.org/en/PublicationChapters/WIR2019_CH3.pdf.
163. UNCTAD, World Investment Report 110 (2019) *available at* https://unctad.org/en/PublicationChapters/WIR2019_CH3.pdf.
164. ICSID Convention, Regulations and Rules 113 (July 2022) *available at* https://icsid.worldbank.org/sites/default/files/documents/ICSID_Convention.pdf.
165. Giovanni Zarra, *Parallel Proceedings in Investment Arbitration*, 80 n. 93 (2016).

terms, and tribunals in actual practice follow the standards set forth by earlier decisions to the extent possible.

3   There Are Procedures in Place to Address Arbitrator Bias and Conflicts

Proponents of dismantling the ISDS system often point to the selection of and purported perverse incentives for arbitrators to prolong proceedings, in spite of the emphasis on efficiency, time, and costs, or to decide that the tribunal has jurisdiction when there is none. This is contrary to simple facts and reality. Cases are dismissed on jurisdictional grounds, arbitrators are more frequently agreeing to address issues of jurisdiction and admissibility preliminarily, and arbitrators are aware that delays have a significant effect on their reputation.[166] In reality, arbitrators have the responsibility to promote and uphold the rule of law, which they do. If arbitrators fail to adhere to the standards, they can be challenged during the proceeding, or a party may use this as a basis to set aside the award under the Federal Arbitration Act (FAA) Article 10 and/or the New York Convention Article V.[167]

Steps are continuously being taken to make proceedings more efficient. Certain institutions such as the ICC are penalizing arbitrators for delays in rendering awards, and institutional rules are entering into effect on expedited proceedings. ICSID's newly amended rules were approved on January 20, 2022, by ICSID member States and went into effect on July 1, 2022.[168] The approved amendments include broader access to ICSID's services such as allowing regional economic integration organizations to be

---

166. Queen Mary University and White & Case, Presentation: *2010 International Arbitration Survey: Choices in International Arbitration*, p. 26 (2010), *available at* https://arbitration.qmul.ac.uk /media/arbitration/docs/2010_InternationalArbitrationSurveyReport.pdf.

167. 9 U.S.C. § 10(a) ("In any of the following cases the United States court in and for the district wherein the [arbitration] award was made may make an order vacating the award upon the application of any party to the arbitration—[...] (2) where there was evident partiality or corruption in the arbitrators, or either of them; where the arbitrators were guilty of misconduct in refusing to postpone the hearing, upon sufficient cause shown, or in refusing to hear evidence pertinent and material to the controversy; or of any other misbehavior by which the rights of any party have been prejudiced; or (4) where the arbitrators exceeded their powers, or so imperfectly executed them that a mutual, final, and definite award upon the subject matter submitted was not made."); New York Convention (1958) Article V(1) ("Recognition and enforcement of the award may be refused, at the request of the party against whom it is invoked, only if that party furnishes to the competent authority where the recognition and enforcement is sought, proof that: [...] (b) he party against whom the award is invoked was not given proper notice of the appointment of the arbitrator or of the arbitration proceedings or was otherwise unable to present his case; or (c) The award deals with a difference not contemplated by or not falling within the terms of the submission to arbitration, or it contains decisions on matters beyond the scope of the submission to arbitration, provided that, if the decisions on matters submitted to arbitration can be separated from those not so submitted, that part of the award which contains decisions on matters submitted to arbitration may be recognized and enforced; or (d) The composition of the arbitral authority or the arbitral procedure was not in accordance with the agreement of the parties, or, failing such agreement, was not in accordance with the law of the country where the arbitration took place.").

168. ICSID Convention, Regulations and Rules (July 2022), *available at* https://icsid.worldbank. org/resources/rules-amendments.

parties to proceedings, increased transparency, and disclosure of third-party funding. UNCITRAL and ICSID are currently still working on a code of conduct for arbitrators, that will not be ready in 2022.[169] The ICSID amendments and the ICC award delay penalties are steps in the right direction, and more institutions should insist on rules that awards should be prompt and balanced. The willingness of ICSID Member States to approve the amendment of the ICSID rules in early 2022 signals the current vitality of the investment arbitration regime and a willingness to amend further as needed to address issues that may arise.

In addition, while critics allege that conflicts of interest are created by "double hatting" and an arbitrator's interest in repeat appointments, in reality, this does not result in any more conflicts than for those who will "single hat" as arbitrators, but also only ever rule in favor of either respondents or claimants. Regardless, efforts are underway to clarify the standards governing arbitrators' conflicts of interest, and ICSID and other arbitral institutions have already instituted more rigorous disclosure requirements. These are steps towards resolving any issues, to the extent that they exist. In any event, given party autonomy, it is for the parties to consider whether to nominate an arbitrator who will "double hat." There is no reason to abolish ISDS.

Finally, statistics demonstrate that the criticism regarding arbitrator bias is far overblown. Parties have the opportunity to challenge an arbitrator who they believe is biased or conflicted out of participating in the proceeding. Only 1% to 5% of arbitrators have been successfully challenged.[170]

4 ISDS Does Not Chill Public Interest or Regulatory Control

Critics' allegations that ISDS chills public interest in regulatory control or public interest ring hollow. First, these allegations rest on the assumption that ISDS impacts legislative process; however, only 9% of ICSID cases relate to legislative acts.[171] Moreover, most studies have not found any concrete evidence of a correlation between ISDS and regulatory chill.[172] Rather, these studies have found that there is no way to

---

169. UNCITRAL, Report of Working Group III (Investor-State Dispute Settlement Reform) A/CN.9/1092, 13-20 (March 23, 2022) *available at* https://uncitral.un.org/sites/uncitral.un.org/files/media-documents/uncitral/en/final_report_acn.9.1092_with_annex_45.pdf.

170. *Mohammed Bedjaoui from the Victor Pey Casado v. Chile* case in 2006 (*Victor Pey Casado and President Allende Foundation v. Republic of Chile*, ICSID Case No ARB/98/2); Christian Albanesi, *Some reflections on unmeritorious challenges to arbitrators* (August 22, 2017) *available at* https://www.linklaters.com/en-us/insights/blogs/arbitrationlinks/2017/august/some-reflections-on-unmeritorious-challenges-to-arbitrators; 2021 ICSID Annual Report, World Bank Group, *available at* https://icsid.worldbank.org/sites/default/files/publications/ICSID_AR21_CRA_bl1_web.pdf. In PCA cases, only seven of twenty-eight challenges have been upheld. Sarah Grimmer, *The Determination of Arbitrator Challenges by the Secretary-General of the Permanent Court of Arbitration, in* Challenges and Recusals of Judges and Arbitrators in International Courts and Tribunals 82-83 (2015).

171. *A response to the criticism against ISDS*, European Federation for Investment Law and Arbitration (EFILA) dated May 17, 2015 ¶ 7.2, available at https://efila.org/wp-content/uploads/2015/05/EFILA_in_response_to_the-criticism_of_ISDS_final_draft.pdf.

172. Christine Côté, *A Chilling Effect? The Impact of International Investment Agreements on National Regulatory Autonomy in the Areas of Health, Safety and the Environment* 187 (2014) *available at* http://etheses.lse.ac.uk/897/8/Cote_A_Chilling_%20Effect.pdf (last accessed November 14, 2022).

actually examine the extent to which draft legislation is halted on the basis of risks related to ISDS.[173] Some studies have even found that, in some States, having more ISDS cases actually increases the frequency of regulatory acts.[174] There are numerous reasons why a State may choose to enact (or not enact) certain legislation, including political debate or the local judiciary.[175]

In reality, the States that negotiate and enter into the IIA define all aspects of the applicable substantive law, the protections they wish to offer, and the dispute system they wish to offer. In addition, as explained above in section II, rather than scrap investment treaties altogether, States are concluding new treaties and renegotiating old treaties with more defined investor protections and increased protections relating to social welfare, the environment, and human rights.[176] States can, at the same time, revise their BITs to provide additional provisions to deal with the challenges noted above.

| 5 | Multilateral Investment Courts Will Not Make International Dispute Resolution More Consistent but Will Cause Unnecessary Delays and Burdensome Costs |

Opponents of the current ISDS system argue for the establishment of standing investment courts, appellate courts, or a multilateral investment court (MIC).[177] Contrary to their contentions, this proposal—which was first raised at the European Union[178]—will not provide greater consistency in international dispute resolution. Rather, it will only weaken the system. There is no evidence that an appellate body appointed by States would instill greater confidence than the present system or would actually solve the alleged inconsistency of awards.[179] As Professor Schreuer explained, "[e]ven a central body that operates in chambers or divisions will not necessarily develop the desired degree of consistency. Experience from domestic supreme courts,

---

173. Gloria Maria Alvarez et al., *A Response to the Criticism against ISDS by EFILA*, 33 JOURNAL OF INTERNATIONAL ARBITRATION 1, 24-25 (2016).
174. Tarald Berge and Axel Berger, *Do Investor-State Dispute Settlement Cases Influence Domestic Environmental Regulation? The Role of Respondent State Bureaucratic Capacity*, 12 JOURNAL OF INTERNATIONAL DISPUTE SETTLEMENT 1, 25 (2021).
175. Gloria Maria Alvarez et al., *A Response to the Criticism Against ISDS by EFILA*, 33 JOURNAL OF INTERNATIONAL ARBITRATION 1, 24-25 (2016).
176. *Recent Policy Developments and Key Issues, in* WORLD INVESTMENT REPORT 2022: INTERNATIONAL TAX REFORMS AND SUSTAINABLE INVESTMENT 65 (2022), *available at* https://unctad.org/system/files/official-document/wir2022_ch02_en.pdf.
177. The MIC, proposed by the European Commission, would be a series of courts consisting of a first instance tribunal, appeal tribunal, and a permanent body of judges. *See Multilateral Investment Court project*, EUROPEAN COMMISSION, *available at* https://policy.trade.ec.europa.eu/enforcement-and-protection/multilateral-investment-court-project_en (last accessed November 30, 2022).
178. *See Multilateral Investment Court project*, EUROPEAN COMMISSION, *available at* https://policy.trade.ec.europa.eu/enforcement-and-protection/multilateral-investment-court-project_en (last accessed November 30, 2022) ("Since 2015, the European Commission has been working to establish a Multilateral Investment Court.").
179. Albert Jan van den Berg, *Appeal Mechanism for ISDS Awards: Interaction with the New York and ICSID Conventions*, 34 ICSID REVIEW 156, 188-189 (2019).

and from the European Court of Human Rights, shows that even unitary judicial bodies that adjudicate in varying composition are not always consistent."[180]

In addition, implementing the MIC proposal would only lead to fragmentation; it would not resolve it. The MIC proposal, which only contemplates a review of disputes arising under BITs, would require the establishment of a global multilateral treaty or the amendment of all existing bilateral and plurilateral treaties, neither of which is realistic. As explained above, designing a new system, which would require the consent of 156 countries, would be nearly impossible and span over several decades. There is also no consideration of how these grounds for appeal and the appellate mechanism would interact with the New York Convention or ICSID annulment procedures. Professor Schreuer notes that Article 53 of the ICSID Convention envisions the:

> theoretical possibilities of an amendment to the Convention and of an *inter se* modification of the ICSID Convention among the States establishing the appeals mechanism. Amendment would require the positive assent of all existing Parties, which is unlikely to occur.[181]

Professor Schreuer further notes that it would not be possible to apply Article 54 of the ICSID Convention, which deals with recognition and enforcement, to awards subject to appeal because "[t]he States establishing the new appeals mechanism can provide for enforcement in the same manner as under the ICSID Convention but that would only bind these States and not all Parties to the ICSID Convention."[182] In sum, establishing an appellate mechanism like the one proposed would require stripping the entire ISDS system as it currently exists. This simply is not feasible.

Finally, introducing an appellate mechanism will only cause unnecessary delays and increase already burdensome costs. The WTO's appellate body is an example of this. As of December 31, 2021, a panel had been established in respect of 365 disputes, leading to panel reports in 277 of these disputes. Of those 277 panel reports, 189 disputes were appealed—in other words, 68% of all cases in which there was a panel report.[183] When parties are afforded an additional mechanism to reargue their case, and statistics suggest that two-thirds of parties will choose to do so, that only delays the final outcome of the proceeding and unreasonably increases costs. This is entirely unnecessary, particularly when there are existing control mechanisms in annulment proceedings under the ICSID Convention or in set-aside proceedings under the domestic law of the arbitral seat, as referenced in the New York Convention. Parties do not need further opportunities to reargue their cases. While the ICSID annulment

---

180. C.H. Schreuer and A. de la Brena, "Does ISDS Need an Appeals Mechanism?" 2 TDM 6 (2020) *available at* www.transnational-dispute-management.com.
181. C.H. Schreuer and A. de la Brena, "Does ISDS Need an Appeals Mechanism?" 2 TDM 4 (2020) *available at* www.transnational-dispute-management.com.
182. C.H. Schreuer and A. de la Brena, "Does ISDS Need an Appeals Mechanism?" 2 TDM 5 (2020) *available at* www.transnational-dispute-management.com.
183. World Trade Organization, *Dispute Settlement Activity: Some Figures* (December 31, 2021) *available at* https://www.wto.org/english/tratop_e/dispu_e/dispustats_e.htm#orpanel_abp, *see also* Chart 4.

system has seen a few "generations," as described by Professor Schreuer,[184] we are now in a moment of appropriate deference to the finality of awards. An April 2016 ICSID report observes that the percentage of total awards annulled declined from 8% (2001-2010) to 3% (2011-2016).[185]

6 UNCITRAL's Working Group III Demonstrates That There Is No Agreement on Dissolving the System of ISDS

Another way to address the concerns arising in ISDS is through the UNCITRAL Working Group III established in 2017, which identifies issues in ISDS and evaluates whether and what reform would be beneficial.[186] Working Group III is comprised of States, observer States, observer international governmental organizations, and non-governmental international bodies, whose aim is to find the solutions that are the most beneficial for investors, States, and the ISDS system as a whole.[187] Unfortunately, the reality is that the Working Group III process has been protracted and marked by virtually no consensus on the issues the Working Group was intended to tackle.

Currently, Working Group III has identified three core areas to target for reform: (a) concerns with the consistency and coherence of arbitral decisions; (b) concerns regarding the independence and impartiality of arbitrators; (c) and concerns related to the cost and duration of the arbitration proceedings.[188]

To address issues of consistency and coherency, the Working Group is working on strengthening ADR mechanisms through the use of mediation in ISDS and reshaping existing mechanisms to avoid frivolous claims, for instance, through providing a more predictable framework for security for costs, allocating the arbitration costs to the party that brought frivolous proceedings, or by ensuring early dismissal mechanisms.[189] In respect of allegedly inconsistent or incoherent awards, Professor van den Berg explained that "the contradictory decisions of arbitral tribunals are limited to a few instances."[190]

---

184. Christoph Schreuer, *Three Generations of ICSID Annulment Proceedings*, in Annulment of ICSID Awards 17 (Emmanuel Gaillard and Yas Banifatemi, eds., 2004).
185. ICSID 'Updated Background Paper on Annulment for the Administrative Council of ICSID' 11 (May 5, 2016) 11 *available at* https://icsid.worldbank.org/sites/default/files/Background%2 0Paper%20on%20Annulment%20April%202016%20ENG.pdf.
186. Report of the UNCITRAL, July 3-21, 2017, General Assembly, A/72/17, ¶ 264. https:// documents-dds-ny.un.org/doc/UNDOC/GEN/V17/058/89/PDF/V1705889.pdf?OpenElement.
187. United Nations Commission on International Trade Law, Working Group III, Fortieth session, A/CN.9/WG.III/WP.200, *available at* https://uncitral.un.org/sites/uncitral.un.org/files/med ia-documents/uncitral/en/acn9_wg.iii_wp.200.pdf.
188. United Nations Commission on International Trade Law, Working Group III, Possible Reform of Investor-State Dispute Settlement (ISDS), Note by the Secretariat, Thirty-fourth session, A/CN.9/WG.III/WP.142, p. 6, *available at* https://documents-dds-ny.un.org/doc/UNDOC/ LTD/V17/067/48/PDF/V1706748.pdf?OpenElement.
189. UNCITRAL Working Group III: Investor-State Dispute Settlement Reform (April 21, 2021), *available at* https://www.ohchr.org/sites/default/files/Documents/Issues/Business/WG/Su bmissions/Others/UNCITRAL.pdf.
190. Albert Jan van den Berg, *Appeal Mechanism for ISDS Awards: Interaction with the New York and ICSID Conventions*, 34 ICSID Review 156, 157 (2019).

To address concerns over arbitrator independence and impartiality, the Working Group has drafted a Code of Conduct for Adjudicators for International Investment Disputes. This Code of Conduct addresses several topics identified as potential issues related to arbitrator independence and impartiality, including, *inter alia*, "double hatting,"[191] "issue conflicts,"[192] and limited repeat appointments for arbitrators.[193] After publishing four versions of the Code beginning in 2020, in November 2022, the drafters had to split the Code into two separate codes—one for arbitrators and one for judges—given the ongoing disagreements over a Standing Multilateral Mechanism and its judges.[194] The Code of Conduct for Arbitrators in International Investment Arbitration ("Code of Conduct for Arbitrators") was adopted at UNCITRAL's 56th session.[195] The Code of Conduct For Arbitrators includes a prohibition on double-hatting in cases involving the same measures, the same or related parties, or the same provisions in the same instrument of consent during a one to three-year "cooling-off" period.[196] At the same session, the Code of Conduct for Judges was adopted "in principle," pending a decision by the Working Group on a Standing Multilateral Mechanism.[197] Despite their passage, the need to split the original Code into two separate ones confirms the controversial nature of the proposed reforms, and in any event, there is no enforcement mechanism for either code. Moreover, it is unclear how the Code for Arbitrators (drafted in collaboration between ICSID and UNCITRAL) will apply to other arbitral institutions or intersect with existing rules.[198]

---

191. Draft Code of Conduct for Adjudicators in International Investment Disputes, Version Four, Article 4, Limit on Multiple Roles; Code of Conduct, Background Papers, Double Hatting, ICSID, *available at* https://icsid.worldbank.org/sites/default/files/Background_Papers_Dou ble-Hatting_(final)_2021.02.25.pdf.

192. Draft Code of Conduct for Adjudicators in International Investment Disputes, Version Four, Article 10, Disclosure Obligations; Code of Conduct, Background Papers, Issue Conflict ICSID, *available at* https://icsid.worldbank.org/sites/default/files/Background_Papers_Issue_Conf lict_Final_2.26.2021.pdf.

193. Draft Code of Conduct for Adjudicators in International Investment Disputes, Version Four, Articles 3, 10, Article 6; Code of Conduct, Background Papers, Repeat Appointments, ICSID, *available at* https://icsid.worldbank.org/sites/default/files/Background_Papers_Repeat_App ointments_final_25.2.2021.pdf.

194. Brodlija, Fahira. The Draft Code of Conduct for Adjudicators in International Investment Disputes: Low-Hanging Fruit or Just An Appetizer?, Kluwer Arbitration Blog, 7 June 2023, *available at:* https://arbitrationblog.kluwerarbitration.com/2023/06/07/the-draft-code-of-con duct-for-adjudicators-in-international-investment-disputes-low-hanging-fruit-or-just-an-appet izer/.

195. UN Commission on International Trade Law finalizes four legal texts during the first week of its 56th Session in Vienna, UNIS/L/344, 13 July 2023.

196. Giorgetti, Chiara. Habemus Codicem! UNCITRAL WGIII Agrees on Final Versions of Codes of Conduct for Arbitrators and Judges in ISDS, Kluwer Arbitration Blog, 28 May 2023, *available at* https://arbitrationblog.kluwerarbitration.com/2023/05/28/habemus-codicem-uncitral-wgiii-agrees-on-final-versions-of-codes-of-conduct-for-arbitrators-and-judges-in-isds/.

197. UN Commission on International Trade Law finalizes four legal texts during the first week of its 56th Session in Vienna, UNIS/L/344, 13 July 2023.

198. Investor-State Dispute Settlement (ISDS) Reform, Draft Code of Conduct: Means of Implementation and Enforcement, Note by the Secretariat, September 2, 2021 (A/CN.0/WG.III/WP.208), proposing different ways of incorporating the provisions of the future Code of Conduct for Adjudicators to arbitral institutions.

The Working Group has also considered proposals for creating a Standing Multilateral Mechanism, a multilateral standing tribunal that would have a first instance and an appellate level.[199] It has been difficult to reach a consensus on this Mechanism, as reflected in the stalled discussions during Working Group meetings. In the 43rd formal session, the Working Group discussed the possible structure and scope of application of a multilateral instrument, but no consensus was reached.[200] In the 44th formal session, the Working Group considered issues relating to the development of the appellate mechanism, including with respect to interactions with existing review mechanisms and models for implementation, and determined that the advantages and disadvantages "would need to be further examined."[201] The Working Group is expected to hold an intersessional meeting in September 2023 to discuss further the standing multilateral mechanism and appellate mechanism.[202] Moreover, while this is just one option being considered by the Working Group, it is important to keep in mind that, as explained above in section V.5, introducing an appellate mechanism will only cause unnecessary delays and increase already burdensome costs.

Finally, at its September 2022 meeting, the Working Group discussed the possibility of creating a multilateral instrument that would include core provisions and additional protocols/annexes, that States would be able to opt into and thereby devise a customized ISDS regime. There was no agreement among the Working Group members as to whether this new multilateral instrument and its protocol would have the effect of modifying existing investment treaties.[203]

The starts and stops of Working Group III, together with its difficulty in making progress over the past several years since it received its mandate, confirm that the better solution is to reform the system currently in place, rather than creating all new

---

199. Lino Torgal and Cláudia Saavedra Pinto, *The Multilateral Investment Court Project: The "Judicialization" of Arbitration?* (July 24, 2019) *available at* https://www.lexology.com/library/detail.aspx?g=318efe3f-e1db-473e-b21b-de423d8109d8; UNCITRAL, Report of Working Group III (Investor-State Dispute Settlement Reform) A/CN.9/1092, 7 (March 23, 2022), *available at* https://uncitral.un.org/sites/uncitral.un.org/files/media-documents/uncitral/en/final_report_acn.9.1092_with_annex_45.pdf.

200. UNCITRAL, Report of Working Group III (Investor-State Dispute Settlement Reform), A/CN.9/1124 § III (October 7, 2022), *available at* https://documents-dds-ny.un.org/doc/UNDOC/GEN/222/285/3E/PDF/2222853E.pdf?OpenElement.

201. UNCITRAL, Report of Working Group III (Investor- State Dispute Settlement Reform), A/CN.9/1130 § IV (February 7, 2023), *available at* https://documents-dds-ny.un.org/doc/UNDOC/GEN/V23/007/33/PDF/V2300733.pdf?OpenElement. Additionally, the European Economic and Social Committee recently published an opinion expressing "regret[]" that the Working Group III negotiations "are focusing more on procedural issues rather than substantive ones" and "urge[d] the European Commission . . . to continue pursuing the reform of substantive law issues" including, *inter alia*, with respect to limiting the scope of FET provisions. *See* Opinion of the European Economic and Social Committee on Multilateral investor-State arbitration court: assessment of the UNCITRAL process and its achievements in light of civil society recommendations, 2023/C 75/18, Official Journal of the European Union ¶¶ 1.2-1.4 (February 28, 2023), *available at* https://eur-lex.europa.eu/legal-content/EN/TXT/HTML/?uri=CELEX:52022IE1963&from=EN.

202. UNCITRAL, Report of Working Group III (Investor-State Dispute Settlement Reform) A/CN.9/1131 ¶ 88 (April 14, 2023), *available at* https://documents-dds-ny.un.org/doc/UNDOC/GEN/V23/024/83/PDF/V2302483.pdf?OpenElement.

203. BIICL Blog, https://www.biicl.org/blog/44/uncitral-investor-State-dispute-settlement-reform-group-makes-progress-despite-disagreements.

mechanisms such as a standing court that would be anachronistic almost from the start.

7   Concerns over Damages Calculations in Arbitral Awards Can Be Resolved Within the Current ISDS System

Following the tribunal awards in *Yukos v. Russia* and *Tethyan v. Pakistan* in the amount of over USD 50 billion[204] and USD 4 billion,[205] respectively, the critics of ISDS voiced their concerns over the calculation of damages in investment arbitration. These concerns, to the extent they are valid, may be addressed within the current system. For example, changes can be made such that the standard for quantum calculation is more concrete and accessible, similar to the evolution that has occurred in the development of substantive standards. Moreover, in the event of an anomalous award, the system has corrective mechanisms already in place: possible annulment by an ICSID committee or challenge before a national court.

The criticism surrounding the calculation of a few damages awards is insufficient as a basis to strip an entire system that has been developed over several decades. There is no evidence that a new multilateral court would be better placed than tribunals currently are to calculate damages because no such evidence exists. The current ISDS system should be improved, including with respect to the standards for the calculation of damages, but not replaced.

8   The Overarching Realities Demonstrate That ISDS Is Necessary and Beneficial

Investment arbitration is the past, present, and future of global investment and international business. It has long displaced gunboat diplomacy, espousal of claims via diplomatic protection, or the use of national courts to resolve international investment disputes.

Capital-importing States incentivize foreign investors by offering investment arbitration as a neutral dispute resolution mechanism under the rule of law. In turn, investors rely on the protections offered in investment treaties when making their investment decisions, knowing that, in the event of a dispute, they can bring a claim to a neutral adjudicator and avoid the potential bias of national courts.

We currently find ourselves in the midst of a period of reform of limited aspects of a very viable investment treaty system. Such renewal of the system is a symbol of its strength, and its ability to adapt to the changing socioeconomic realities and to the demands of investors and States.

At each "generational" step of investment treaty reform, the main tenets of investment arbitration have been preserved—providing a neutral, balanced forum for

---

204. *Yukos Universal Ltd. (Isle of Man) v. The Russian Federation*, UNCITRAL, PCA Case No. 2005-04/AA227, Final Award dated July 18, 2014 ¶ 1827.
205. *Tethyan Copper Company Pty Ltd. v. Islamic Republic of Pakistan*, ICSID Case No. ARB/12/1, Award dated July 12, 2019 ¶ 1858.

investors and States to resolve their disputes, providing substantive protections to parties—that the States wish to offer, upholding due process rights, ensuring the finality of awards with limited grounds for annulment and set aside, and having independent and impartial arbitrators. Investment arbitration is a necessity for both States and investors.

VI   CONCLUSION

The ISDS system is robust and dynamic, representing our future. There is not any legitimacy crisis facing ISDS that would displace the current system of international dispute resolution. In ISDS, the investor and the State are on the same plane, and now, developed and developing countries are increasingly on equal grounds when it comes to treaty negotiations. In reality, the current system is working for all parties involved by promoting FDI, offering investment protections, and promising a neutral dispute mechanism.

While some reforms are needed to continue improving the efficiency and neutrality of the current ISDS system, there is not any alternative better than the system in place. It is easy to assert that the ISDS system is broken, yet no attempt to devise a new system has succeeded—because it cannot. Returning to gunboat diplomacy is not an option, nor are national courts or other local remedies replete with issues of sovereign immunity and perceptions of bias or home court advantage. The UNCITRAL WG III proposals have stalled before even getting off the ground and any other attempts to devise a new system are infeasible.

ISDS has shown through the decades that it is capable of improving itself to fit new needs that arise in international investment, as demonstrated through the renegotiation or replacement of investment treaties to further define treaty protections; incorporation of social welfare, environmental, and human rights concerns into treaties; and changes to arbitration rules to incorporate disclosure requirements and delay penalties for arbitrators. Put simply, the ISDS system and investment arbitration are necessary to preserve global investment and economies.

CHAPTER 55

The Great Debate: A Commentator's Perspective

Chin Heng Ong[*]

TABLE OF CONTENTS

I   SETTING THE CONTEXT

After witnessing this delightfully brilliant and epic gladiatorial clash of the Titans, I'm sorry that it falls to me to serve as your 'musical interlude'. I am to undertake the decidedly more boring and bland janitorial duty of picking up the pieces and stitching together the severed limbs – scattered around our arena – in the course of this Great Debate.

I propose to make *two* broad sets of comments in reaction to the many scintillating arguments advanced by Toby Landau KC[1] and Carolyn Lamm.[2] I will pick up on certain points raised by each speaker that I felt resonated with me. And I do so, from the perspective of a State which relies upon *both* the import *and* export of capital for its economic survival, that is to say – a country with both offensive and defensive

---

[*] Senior State Counsel and Senior Director (International Economic Law) in the International Affairs Division of the Attorney-General's Chambers of Singapore.
1. *See* Chapter 53, For the Proposition: A World Without Investment Arbitration?, by Toby Landau KC, Chester Brown and Michael Waibel, in this volume.
2. *See* Chapter 54, The World Is Better with Investment Arbitration, by Carolyn B. Lamm, Rocío Digón and Caitlin Walczyk, in this volume.

interests in roughly equal measure. And thus I hope to convey some observations to make for a balanced and pragmatic commentary.

II   THE LATEST STATE OF PLAY IN THE ACTUAL REAL-TIME ISDS DEBATE

My *first* observation seeks to bridge the currently polarised positions (and necessarily so by design) which have been advanced by our two protagonists, by addressing first the Motion of this House as it has been presented, that is to say 'Would the World be a Better Place *Without* Investment Arbitration?'

The world would *indeed* be a better place without investment arbitration. That is however premised upon us living in an ideal and enlightened world. But because we find ourselves in an imperfect world, we must reluctantly acknowledge the existence of investment arbitration as a necessary 'evil'.

The challenge before us, though, is to ask ourselves – are there newer or better alternatives to that? Carolyn has argued that investment arbitration is a necessity for States, as well as a necessity for investors. She spoke about the equality of arms between investors and States, recalling that access to investment arbitration puts the former on the same plane as the latter.

To a large extent, it is the *perception* – rightly or wrongly – that this equality of arms has increasingly shifted out of balance, too far against States, which has led to the current global debate on the reform of investor-State dispute settlement (ISDS).

And thus – as was covered in much greater detail in yesterday morning's panel featuring Secretary of the United Nations Commission on International Trade Law (UNCITRAL) Anna Joubin-Bret[3] and Secretary-General of the International Centre for Settlement of Investment Disputes (ISCID) Meg Kinnear[4] – over the past 4 years at UNCITRAL's Working Group III, States have identified several issues in investment arbitration needing to be addressed:

- costs & duration of proceedings;
- issues relating to correctness and consistency of arbitral decisions; and
- issues relating to the independence, impartiality and diversity of arbitrators.

Having identified these, the Working Group has embarked on an iterative process of developing reform options on various fronts in parallel. Just in the preceding two weeks at UNCITRAL in Vienna, the Working Group discussed:

- various selection and election methods for adjudicators in a possible permanent multilateral tribunal;
- the possible features of an advisory centre for investment law;

---

3. *See* Chapter 23, 'State of the World': New Developments and Reform in International Investment Arbitration – The UNCITRAL ISDS Reform, by Anna Joubin-Bret and David Nikolaus Probst, in this volume.
4. *See* Chapter 22, A User's Guide to What's New in the ICSID Rules 2022, by Meg Kinnear, in this volume.

- draft clauses on matters like cost allocation, early dismissal and third-party funding;
- draft clauses on investor-State mediation;
- a draft Code of Conduct for adjudicators in ISDS; and
- to tie all these bits and pieces together, the possibility of a delivery platform such as a multilateral treaty to implement these various reform options.

As you can see, these reform options run the gamut from procedural enhancements, all the way through to exploring deeper structural reform involving even the possible creation of new institutions.

My delegation has adopted a constructive, supportive and open-minded position on all these possibilities. Now taking a step back to look at the overall picture, in my own view, a dispute settlement option is only as good as it is ultimately *enforceable*. So to me, enforceability is a key consideration to bear in mind when exploring our reform options.

So in that regard, I recognise that the existing legal framework – comprising both the *ICSID Convention* and *New York Convention* – does help to anchor the current investment arbitration regime, precisely because of the underlying assurance of enforceability of arbitral awards. So for all of Toby's critiques earlier about the 'Anglo-US' adversarial model being potentially ill-suited or an unnatural fit, minimally the enforcement regime seems to have been one element that has maintained the use-case of investment arbitration.

In time to come, with the advent of the *Singapore Convention on Mediation*, we can hopefully also start saying the same about mediated settlements, as regards *their* enforceability. By extension, any other reform option, including any structural reform option such as a multilateral investment tribunal, will also need to bear in mind this key question of enforcement and how it is to be achieved: e.g., whether it is amenable to being plugged into the existing framework of the aforementioned Conventions; or whether a self-contained enforcement regime is to be developed alongside the reform option in-question.

III A THIRD DIMENSION: THE OVERLOOKED VALUE OF DISPUTE AVOIDANCE

My *second* observation involves actually challenging the very premise of this Motion itself. I believe I am allowed to do that since I serve as Commentator, rather than a Debater. As currently structured, the arguments lend themselves to an obvious dichotomy – that is to say, should we have investment arbitration or not?

But I would like to submit that this is a false, or at least a *forced*, dichotomy. It is a dichotomy that is seen through the lens of, exclusively, dispute *settlement*. I would like to introduce a 'third dimension', and in an august gathering of the arbitration community like the present one, I fear it is a dimension that is sometimes overlooked, underrated, or possibly even unpopular. And that is to view things through the lens of dispute *avoidance* and upstream risk management. On this note, I recall that Toby did also allude to this element, when he talked about dispute prevention, with investment arbitration only as a last resort. Likewise, Carolyn mentioned it in passing in her arguments. So I would like to take this a step further and expand upon this element based on my own experience.

What I have in mind is dispute avoidance through proper adherence to international commitments. Dispute avoidance through capacity building. Dispute avoidance through good governance and disciplined policy-making. Dispute avoidance through enhancing the international reputation and credibility of the host State. Dispute avoidance through pre-action/pre-arbitration resolution options.

In the work that we do, our office is like a one-stop shop – my colleagues and I run the gamut from treaty *negotiations*; to international investment law *advisory* services; all the way through to *representation* in defence against claims, if that should ever become necessary.

We spend the overwhelming majority of time investing in the first two tasks, which are more upstream in nature. This is in a concerted and deliberate effort to *avoid* the third task ever having to arise. Or even if a dispute *does* arise, at least we want to be in a position, not just substantively, but also evidentially and procedurally, to fall on the correct side of a tribunal's scrutiny.

So my office supports the policymakers in negotiating investment treaty texts, crafting substantive and procedural provisions that are informed by the latest developments in international investment law and reflecting best drafting practices.

Having negotiated by now over sixty investment treaties and free trade agreements over the course of our history, we also spend a very significant amount of time guiding, advising and hand-holding our client ministries and agencies. When they craft and implement measures in the exercise of regulatory power, we partner closely with our clients in order to make sure that these measures are developed in a manner that is sensitive to the disciplines set out in our treaties, as shaped by current international jurisprudence on, e.g., notions such as fair & equitable treatment, indirect expropriation, etc. We also work to make sure that all the documentation and records are in order if ever needed to be produced as evidence.

UNCITRAL Working Group III is, amongst other things, discussing the establishment of an Advisory Centre on Investment Law. One of the key functions which I personally hope such a Centre will give adequate weight to is that of capacity building – and by that, I mean *not just* capacity building in terms of defending against claims, but capacity building to help States, including line ministries and municipal authorities, to fully understand and properly implement their treaty obligations in the first place.

With greater awareness, understanding and discipline, hopefully, the number and the complexity of disputes actually arising will then be far smaller and less intense.

IV   CIRCLING BACK

And in this sense, even if we are unable to create that ideal world without any investment arbitration whatsoever, we can nonetheless transition into a world where there is less need for, or less reliance upon, investment arbitration, and at least one without this crisis of legitimacy faced by the system.

PART VII   Closing Session

CHAPTER 56

Closing Keynote Address

Colin Sutherland, The Right Hon Lord Carloway*

TABLE OF CONTENTS

Good afternoon to everyone, and thank you for this opportunity to talk to you at the close of the Congress.

It has been a hectic few weeks in Edinburgh. The end of the summer was, as usual, marked by the annual cultural festivals, bringing with them large numbers of visitors from across the globe. The entertainments were almost literally mired in rubbish as a result of industrial action. It was not a pretty site. The autumn opened sadly with the death of Her Majesty the Queen, with all the tears and reminiscences that such a momentous event inevitably brings. It has been a busy time for those of us involved in the constitutional arrangements which followed. It is only now that we can settle down in expectation of things to come.

What then are we awaiting? Global tensions continue to dominate the international scene with today's speech by President Putin but one example. War and sanctions are disturbing the world's equilibrium and its trade routes. The economic

---

* Lord President of the Court of Session and Lord Justice General of Scotland. I am grateful to my law clerk, Ysabeau Middleton, and to the Lord Justice Clerk's law clerk, Alannah McGinley, for preparing the first drafts of this talk.

effects of that, the pandemic which is still a major feature, especially in the Far East, and Brexit in Europe are all factors which are playing daily on the world stage. It is a time at which the importance of arbitration on an international scale can hardly be overemphasised.

Your focus has quite rightly been on arbitration on the international stage. As the President of the Court of Session, our supreme civil court in Scotland, this is not an area in which I can claim an extensive knowledge; far less any experience or expertise. I can but apologise for that. Before looking at the material for the congress, I doubt whether I would have passed an examination based on my knowledge of the Abu Dhabi Oil award in the 1950s, the Barcelona Traction case in the 1970s or the Mitsubishi case in the 1980s.

I accept without reservation that a little learning is a dangerous thing[1] upon which to address you at such a significant, international congress. That said, I have read, with interest, several of the papers prepared by the panellists. I have been impressed with the quantity of papers which the conference has produced. I have been even more impressed by their quality and encouraged by their forward-looking themes. I have only been able to dip into some of those, but they have given me a far greater insight, than I have ever had before, into the advantages which international commercial arbitration has, especially in relation to confidentiality, and the problems which face international arbitration practitioners across the borders not only of nations but in particular subject areas. I would like to try to draw together some of the subjects discussed in the papers and to provide some local Scottish context which may be of value when it comes to deciding which way to go in relation to future procedures and practice in the international arbitration process.

I INTERNATIONAL ARBITRATION IN SCOTLAND

Before 1990, it is not unreasonable to comment that Scotland was unique in the developed world in that it lacked a single comprehensive statutory basis or code for arbitration. This was so even though its introduction was coeval with the foundation of Scots law. As sometimes happened in Scottish jurisprudence, the law was caught between the two stools of the civil or European *ius commune* and the English or Norman common law. Without a set of clear procedural rules, arbitration in Scotland was conducted under inappropriate court-like procedures. It acquired a reputation, even when compared with Court of Session litigation, for expense and delay. It became little used.[2] The conditions were just right, then, for Scotland to adopt the Model Law in 1990.[3]

---

1. Alexander Pope: *An Essay in Criticism.*
2. In the foreword to the Scottish Arbitration Survey, Report No 1 Covering the Period 1 July 2013 to 30 June 2014, available at: https://www.abdn.ac.uk/law/documents/Scottish_Arbitration_Survey_June_2015.pdf.
3. Section 66 of and Schedule 7 to the Law Reform (Miscellaneous Provisions) (Scotland) Act 1990.

A more comprehensive set of rules was introduced by the Arbitration (Scotland) Act 2010. That Act now applies to all arbitrations that are seated in Scotland.[4] However, the Model Law remains relevant, as most of the provisions of the 2010 Act are default rules, which can be varied or replaced by parties with the Model Law if they so choose to do that. In addition, the Model Law is broadly reflected in the Act's fundamental principles[5,6] that:

(1) the object of arbitration is to resolve disputes fairly,[7] impartially[8] and without unnecessary delay or expense;
(2) parties should be free to agree how to resolve disputes subject only to such safeguards as are necessary in the public interest; and
(3) the court should not intervene in an arbitration except as provided by the Act.[9]

It is a curiosity that Scotland is the first, and maybe only, country to discard the Model Law after having adopted it. The reasoning behind that decision is straightforward. It is logical to have a single statutory regime applicable to both domestic and international arbitration. International parties, who are designating Scotland as the seat of a potential arbitration, need look no further than the Scottish Arbitration Rules set out in the Act.

II   ARBITRATION VERSUS LITIGATION

Sir David Edward's paper on constitutionalism and populism in the Americas and Europe cautions against the replacement of Investor/State Dispute Settlement arbitration with a judicial system. This is in response to the European Commission's proposal for a Multilateral Investment Court. I express no view on the Commission's proposal, but Sir David's paper did prompt me to reflect on the overall place of arbitration within a developed legal system. Why does such a system require a supplement?

When I spoke on the topic of arbitration in 2016,[10] I mentioned the anti-litigation rhetoric which was then alive and well amongst politicians, practitioners and some providers of ADR services. I identified one of the reasons for this as being that the civil court process was lacking in terms of its information technology. The procedure did not, at that stage, meet public expectations; much less those of well-informed and commercially minded clients. The position has changed dramatically; mostly because of the progress which was achieved out of the necessity in light of the pandemic, but

---

4. Whether Scotland is to be so designated is a matter to be agreed between parties, or determined by a third party authorised to do so, failing which, the arbiter or the court may designate Scotland as the seat of the arbitration, section 3, 2010 Act.
5. *See* Chapter 26 The Americas and Europe Between Constitutionalism and Populism: European Challenges to ISDS by Sir David Edward in this volume
6. Section 1.
7. *See* Article 18, Model Law (as enacted 1985).
8. *See* Article 12, Model Law (1985).
9. *See* Article 5, Model Law (1985).
10. 'TO AN ARBITRATOR: Reflections on ADR, arbitration, and the role of the court', 13 October 2016.

also because of the groundwork that the Scottish Courts and Tribunals Service had been putting in place since 2016 through its Digital Strategy.

Our civil courts are now well-equipped to host fully remote or hybrid hearings. That said, the pandemic placed the court system, at least in its early months, under enormous strain. On the criminal side, we are still catching up on the backlog. It all serves as a reminder that alternative forms of dispute resolution can be useful during periods of extraordinary pressure upon the courts. An arbiter is unlikely to have the same restrictions on his or her time as the courts. This enables them to case manage closely and to set short timescales throughout the process.

The potential to appoint an arbiter with specialist knowledge is a strong reason why arbitration must be given its place within any developed legal system. As any judge, who has required to grapple with evidence concerning the precise cause of the collapse of the main tunnel of a hydroelectric dam,[11] or whether fish damaged by sea lice are 'diseased' or merely 'physically disabled' for the purposes of an insurance claim,[12] may very well appreciate, having pre-existing knowledge of a technical subject may make it far easier to apply the law to the case. In her paper which explores what lessons arbitrators can take from the adjudication regime, Janey Milligan suggests that specialist decision-makers may more readily ask piercing questions, which get to the heart of the dispute, and can help to prevent the nub of the matter from becoming engulfed by peripheral issues.[13] It is all part of that most dangerous of concepts, common sense. A fact-finder has first to know what it is that they don't know, in order to unravel the case.

In Scotland, it has recently, if obviously, been recognised that the right of access to the courts is one of the most basic of legal principles. A provision in a contract will not be interpreted as excluding the court's jurisdiction unless by clear words or necessary implication.[14] The court will remain a party's ultimate recourse, but, where an arbitration has taken place, that recourse is available only in limited circumstances. The Rules make it clear that an arbiter's decisions may only be challenged in the Court of Session on limited grounds. The first is that the tribunal did not have jurisdiction.[15] The second is that there has been a serious irregularity[16] and the third is where there has been a legal error.[17] Jurisdictional and serious irregularity appeals can generally be made to the Court of Session as of right, but the court will only consider a legal error appeal either with the agreement of the parties or where the leave of the court has been granted. Leave will only be granted where: the point will substantially affect a party's rights; the tribunal had been asked to decide that point; and, based on the findings of fact made by the tribunal, its decision was obviously wrong or, when the point is of general importance, is open to serious doubt. Where parties have agreed to enter into

---

11. *SSE Generation v. Hochtief Solutions* 2017 G.W.D. 3-39.
12. *Green Island Organics v. QBE Insurance (Europe)* 2011 SCLR 266.
13. *See* Chapter 47, The Renaissance Arbitrator: Lessons from the Construction Industry and Statutory Adjudication by Janey L. Milligan in this volume
14. *Fraserburgh Harbour Commissioners v. McLaughlin & Harvey* 2022 SC 84.
15. 2010 Act, Schedule 1, Part 8, Rule 67.
16. *Ibid.*, Rule 68.
17. *Ibid.*, Rule 69.

arbitration, it is important that that process takes precedence.[18] In restricting the power of the court to interfere in an arbiter's decision, the system affords significant deference to the parties' selection of forum.

Lord Hodge, in his paper on the role of the United Kingdom courts in international arbitration, describes the relationship of the court to arbitration as being one of support rather than supervision.[19] The Scottish Arbitration Rules seek to strike that balance. As Sir Michael Kerr once put it: '… when parties agree to arbitration they buy the right to get the wrong answer'.[20] The first-instance courts here[21] have essentially adopted the English courts' approach to what is meant by 'obviously wrong'. The decision 'must involve something in the nature of a major intellectual aberration, or making a false leap in logic or reaching a result for which there was no reasonable explanation'.[22] On serious irregularity, they have explained, first, that this is a long stop which is available only in extreme cases where justice calls out for the matter to be corrected. Secondly, as is often said in the context of appeals, the court will not intervene just because it might have done things differently. Thirdly, a challenge can only succeed if there has been substantial injustice; that is that the arbitral decision would have been different. A dissatisfied party has a high test to meet.[23] An award need only deal with the essential issues, not with every point raised. Reasons, which are 'very brief', may still be adequate.[24]

Prior to the 2010 Act, arbitration was a relatively unpopular and misunderstood method of alternative dispute resolution in Scotland. The courts were seen to be in competition, or even conflict, with arbitration.[25] The Act changed that and alleviated previous tension between the respective aims and purposes of litigation and arbitration. The court's role is very clearly set out as a supervisory one. There is a mutual respect for the different roles. Cases are decided on the basis of the founding principle of minimal intervention. The role of the court enhances confidence in the private arbitration process. Lord Glennie put it well when he summarised the relationship as follows:

> The court friendship with arbitration is not a blind one, but rather that of a wise and trusted friend, willing where appropriate to speak his mind and give advice to the arbitrator, who is asked to rethink and make amends for any significant failings on his part.[26]

---

18. See *Heart of Midlothian Football Club* v *Scottish Professional Football League* 2020 SLT 736 at paras 9-16.
19. See Chapter 51 Protecting Party Consent: The Role of the UK Courts in International Arbitration by Lord Hodge in this volume.
20. As cited by Joshua Rozenberg in 'Family awards can be overruled', available at: https://www.lawgazette.co.uk/commentary-and-opinion/family-awards-can-be-overruled/5106205.article.
21. *Arbitration Application No.2 of 2011* [2011] CSOH 186.
22. *Arbitration Application 1 of 2013* [2014] CSOH 83 at para. 32.
23. *Ibid.*, at para. 18.
24. *Ibid.*, at paras [23]-[24].
25. See, e.g., *ERDC Construction Ltd v. HM Love & Co (No 2)* 1997 SLT 175 and the various McCrindle arbitration cases (*McCrindle Group v. Maclay Murray & Spens* 2013 CSOH 72 and *Macroberts LLP v. McCrindle Group Limited* 2014 CSOH 99).
26. Scottish Arbitration Survey, Report No 1 (*supra*) at para. 6.2.3.

III   THE ROLE OF ETHICS

Carole Malinvaud's proposal of a principle of 'Loyauté', with which I broadly agree, raises some powerful questions in relation to the duty of practitioners to act in a fair manner and in good faith; in the sense of not seeking to use procedural or other devices to delay or to cause greater expense than is necessary for the resolution of a dispute.[27]

The experience of the courts here and elsewhere has been to introduce a variety of mechanisms to ensure fair play; even if these may not always work, especially when dealing with an imbalance of financial capacity between the parties. In countries where there is a split profession, between advocates (the Scottish equivalent of barristers) and solicitors (or law agents, as they have been traditionally known here) there is at least an expectation that the members of the Bar, at least, will act independently with a view to the expeditious progress of the cause. The primary duty of the Scottish advocate is to the court and not to the party whose case they are instructed to advance. That may sometimes sound pompous and, to some clients, come as an unpleasant surprise, but it is an important ethical rule which ultimately enhances confidence in the decision-making process. The interest of the client must not be put before providing the tribunal with the correct information on the applicable law and the known facts. There can be a tendency to be over-confident in the way that this principle is perceived to operate in practice, but it remains a good one.

It is, in the world of court litigation and no doubt arbitration, by no means unheard of to hear one party's counsel or agent being accused of sharp practice, or worse, by the opposing advocate. Sometimes these accusations amount to little more than a terrible misunderstanding, and sometimes they reflect back on the accusing party as an attempt to obfuscate the merits of the dispute by focusing on how the procedure has operated. The tribunal has to be vigilant to ascertain whether there is a substantive reason behind the complaint, but that is usually better considered after the substantive decision on the merits has been reached.

There are ethical rules, set by the Faculty of Advocates and the Law Society of Scotland, which attempt to define, albeit in general terms, what is or is not acceptable. The problem is that the tribunal is generally well advised to avoid being side-tracked into the ethical protest and away from the merits of the case. Such arguments are better ventilated at the stage of expenses (or costs). In the courts here, there is a relatively sophisticated expenses regime which is designed to secure the progress of a case in an efficient and cost-effective manner. In the event of failure on the merits, there is likely to be an adverse award of expenses, but the amounts awarded are kept within relatively strict bounds if all that has happened is that one party has lost. Some solicitors complain about the parsimonious levels of recoverable fees, but they are kept at a modest level for good reason. If there has been unreasonable or improper behaviour in the conduct of the case, the scale of costs may change to a much heavier one designed to express the court's disapproval of the way in which the litigation has been conducted.

---

27. *See* Chapter 4, "Loyauté": A Tool for Enlightenment? by Carole Malinvaud in this volume.

Despite these protections, the potential for the more affluent party to be able to take advantage of procedure devices, without any fear of a sanction which truly bites in economic terms, remains a real one. Equally, when considering ethical issues, the divergence of standards between jurisdictions is significant. This is especially so in commercial disputes in which the litigation lawyers may have a different view of what is acceptable not only to their colleagues at the commercial bar but also to the clients who may want a 'no holds barred' approach to securing victory.

In this context, one feature which some of the papers, including Lucy Reed's on Artificial Intelligence,[28] cover is the use of aggression in the context of what is intended to be a civilised way of resolving disputes. I agree that this is something which all systems ought to guard against. If it is being taught or encouraged in some circles, and it may well be judging from some of the correspondence which we see passing between firms of what are supposed to be civilised legal practitioners, that ought to be identified and addressed. Bullying and harassment ought to play no part in the dispute resolution process. If we could invent a system of free kicks, or even penalties, beyond the application of the costs' regimes, for aggressive conduct, I would be most interested in it. Sending counsel off the field of play would be a curious, a few might say attractive, alternative, but that is some distance away from reality.

IV   YOUNG PRACTITIONERS AND THE FUTURE OF ARBITRATION

I noticed from the programme that one of the panels was discussing young practitioners and the future of arbitration. I have not seen any of the papers from that session, but I read the summary with interest.[29] In Scotland, we are fortunate that our pool of legal talent continues to grow. In 2020/2021, the 774 legal traineeships which were commenced represented a 71% increase on the previous practice year.[30] Twenty-eight lawyers passed advocate (joined the bar) this year, twelve in 2021, and twenty-six in 2020. These are large year groups. Young and new lawyers have an important role to play in the future of arbitration and the courts.

The legal profession, like a number of others, is often resistant to change. Yet the profession is often the first branch of society to become aware of when the law is no longer fit for purpose or the system is no longer working as it should. It can be detrimental to the system as a whole when the profession does not reflect on why things are the way that they are.

That is where the young, or at least, the new, come in. The profession needs young or new practitioners to look at the way things are done with fresh eyes. Ji En Lee's paper on 'How to Win Instructions in the Post-Pandemic World' discusses the value which younger lawyers have tended to place on mobility in their world.[31] They

---

28. See Chapter 5 AI Versus IA: End of the Enlightenment? by Lucy Reed in this volume.
29. See Chapter 37 Report of the Moderator for the Young Practitioners and Our Future Panel by Yuet Min Foo in this volume.
30. Trainee Statistics, Practice Year 2020-2021, Law Society of Scotland, Trainee statistics | Law Society of Scotland (lawscot.org.uk)
31. Chapter 38 How to Win Instructions in the Post-pandemic World by Lee Ji En in this volume.

found virtual hearings and paperless systems more attractive during the pandemic. Whilst every jurisdiction will have made different decisions about the extent to which to retain those innovations, I do not think that it is controversial to say that these were essential innovations, which brought with them the added advantage of environmental benefits. In the sphere of arbitration, organisations such as the Chartered Institute of Arbitrators' Young Members Group, as well as events like today's can be important spaces in which ideas can be exchanged and temperatures gauged.

It is always of great benefit to see how the young lawyer operates, especially in researching the law. Old judges like me are still often thirled to their books. They find it easier to pick up a textbook or a hard copy law report rather than search for the same things online. I have no doubt that the young are baffled by the way that I do things, but it does have its advantages.

V   CASE MANAGEMENT: PREVENTING DELAY AND EXPENSE

Arbitration is intended to be quicker and cheaper than litigation through the courts. Whether it is will depend on speed and cost in the particular jurisdiction. James Hope's paper on Exploring the Way Forward outlines the difficulties which he has identified in international arbitration.[32] These include counsel requesting, and in the arbitration context setting, lengthy timetables and producing written submissions of gargantuan proportions. Mr Hope correctly points out that there are a myriad of case management solutions available to the tribunal which can deal with this if it chooses to use them. He points to Winston Churchill's memorandum of 1940, which called for shorter briefing papers on the basis that a lot of time was being wasted in reading ones containing irrelevant or unnecessary material. He was, and is, right.

It has to be recognised by the profession that, in all contexts, whether courtroom or arbitration, although the advocates will attempt to use their reasonable endeavours to win the case, the fundamental purpose of any form of submission, whether written or oral, is to assist the tribunal in reaching its decision. The duty on practitioners is to present their cases in as clear, cogent and concise a form as is reasonably practicable. It is not about obfuscating the issues, especially if that is thought to be the only tactic remaining available on the facts. It is not about demonstrating the genius or learning of the advocate or impressing the client. How is this problem to be addressed? Mr Hope has some very useful ideas. I offer some from the Scottish experience.

Restrictions on the length of both written and oral argument have been introduced in the appellate Divisions of the Court of Session, with much success. Cases which used to last several days, now take a few hours. Thus, although parties can ask to vary the impact of the rules in a particular case of complexity, as a generality, they are asked to provide a Note of Argument, which is a beastie that has more flesh than a skeleton but is less extensive than a written submission. It ought to be in the region of twenty pages. Yes, we have to specify the font and line spacing and prohibit footnotes in order to block attempts to circumvent the purpose of the practice. One

---

32. *See* Chapter 7, Some Thoughts on Progress by James Hope in this volume.

thing that good lawyers are exceedingly good at is abiding by the rules, whilst still attempting to deliver value to the client in the strength of the submission. Give them a page restriction and they will not only abide by it, they will excel in it.

A similar approach has been taken to oral submissions. In the Scottish, and I suspect other, courts, we are going through an era of transition away from full oral discussion at a hearing, which is an exceedingly expensive way of doing things, onto one which is a hybrid of written and oral presentation. The need to keep the oral argument within reasonable bounds is relatively easily achievable by limiting it not only to the points which have been raised in the written Note but also by strict control of the allocated time by the tribunal. Once again, provided that the parties have advanced notice of the timetable and each is given a fair kick at the ball, the lawyers will be extremely effective in putting over the relevant points in a clear, concise and understandable manner. This type of system is not difficult to devise. It is not difficult to enforce, but there must be a consensus amongst those engaged in the process, notably the members of the tribunal. It does require a determined consistency in approach.

To return to an earlier point, one aggressive method of conducting litigation, and it is not so much aggressive to the other party but to the tribunal, is the excessive citation of cases which a party has trawled up from the depths of a search engine's ocean of cases from all over the world. I am sure the Scottish contingent amongst you will be singing the praises of the Scottish legal system which, at least in theory, is based upon principle rather than precedent. It is deductive rather than inductive. What Mr Justice X said in a first instance decision in 1826 about horse-drawn carriages is unlikely to be of much relevance to the sinking of an oil rig in 2020.

The Scottish system, or at least most of us within it, seek first to derive the general principle from which more specific applicable rules might be drawn. The principle is likely to have come from the European *ius commune* as later interpreted under the light of the strong influence of Anglo-American common law. In commercial matters, Scots and English law have common themes, largely developed as global trade developed in the nineteenth century. The principles are set out with remarkable clarity and brevity in the textbooks of that time, if not earlier.

It may well be that, if a case is to reach not just a first instance arbitration or court litigation but the highest court in a particular jurisdiction, an in depth exploration of domestic and international decisions may be of some value, if the point is truly a novel one. These are very rare indeed. Generally, the decisions at first instance will turn upon the facts or on well-known principles of law. I was interested in the papers to see a discussion, especially in Professor Hi-Taek Shin's presentation, about how Artificial Intelligence can be useful at least in connection with proofreading, research and translation.[33] I would also be interested to see how it might be used as a tool to gauge the credibility and reliability of witnesses. One judge in the House of Lords in the early part of the last century[34] was of the view that decisions on these aspects might depend

---

33. Chapter 3, How Does International Arbitration Fare in a World Creeping Towards Unilateralism, Protectionism and Nationalism? by Hi-Taek Shin in this volume.
34. *Clarke v. Edinburgh and District Tramways Co* 1919 SC (HL) 35, Lord Shaw of Dunfermline at 37.

on 'the turns of the eyelid'. I am not sure whether many practising in the international or domestic field now would subscribe to that theory, given the multicultural aspects of global trade and industry. Yet it is still regularly quoted in support of an argument not to interfere with the first instance tribunal's determinations of fact. In the modern world, we can record evidence in sound and vision. The trial judge has no great advantage over an appellant tribunal in observing the witnesses as they give evidence. Would we benefit from a machine's assessment of the witnesses' demeanour and its value? Maybe.

The excessive citation of precedent in the appellate Divisions in Scotland is something which we have been actively fighting against for some years. There is good reason for this. First, it waters the pitch; it slows down the debate by forcing the tribunal, not to mention the other parties, to read an excessive, sometimes ridiculous, amount of material. By excessive, I mean that it is material which the tribunal does not need in order to reach a fair decision. Secondly, experience has shown that much of the material is of peripheral, if any, value. Very often, the cited cases are just examples of the application of a well-known principle. In the appellate courts, we have adopted some simple expedients.[35] Restrict the number of cases that can be cited.[36] Make it a rule that cases are not cited for propositions of law which are not in dispute. Do not permit the citation of more than one authority per proposition.

Some of these ideas, which have no doubt been adopted or created elsewhere, take a while to bed in, but they work. Arbiters, too, should guard against such tactics by making appropriate case management orders.

VI   CONFIDENTIALITY VERSUS TRANSPARENCY

I read Paula Hodges' contribution on confidentiality (In defence of Party Choice) with great interest.[37] Once more, I found myself in broad agreement with that panellist and with the not-dissimilar paper of Anke Sessler (How Confidential Is Confidential?).[38] Arbitration is regarded largely as a private matter in Scotland and rightly so. In recognition of this, section 15 of the 2010 Act provides that, where court proceedings have challenged the arbitral award, the court can prohibit the disclosure of the identity of the parties to the arbitration in any report of the court case. The court must grant an application for anonymity unless disclosure would be: in the public interest; necessary in the interests of justice; required to protect a party's lawful interests; or to enable the proper performance of public functions. That being said, in one case,[39] the court refused one such application where relevant information was already in the public

---

35. Court of Session Practice Note No 3 of 2011: *Causes in the Inner House,* para 86 (accessible at: Practice Note No 3 of 2011 (scotcourts.gov.uk)).
36. *Ibid,* para 91.
37. *See* Chapter 14 In Defence of Party Choice: The Continuing Importance of Confidentiality in Commercial Arbitration by Paula Hodges KC in this volume.
38. *See* Chapter 16 How Confidential Is Confidential?: Safeguards, Obstacles, and Boundaries of Confidentiality in International Commercial Arbitration by Anke Sessler in this volume.
39. *North Lanarkshire Council* v *Stewart and Shields* 2017 SLT 741.

domain. It is implicit in the court's power to grant anonymity that it is something which still requires to be protected.

The issue of confidentiality, albeit in a different context, arose in a case in which a party moved the court to disclose documents relating to private arbitral proceedings.[40] In granting the motion, the court acknowledged that arbitral proceedings were private and therefore confidential, but that the court should seek to strike a balance between confidentiality and the public interest in the fair administration of justice. The recovery of the documents was reasonably necessary to allow the party seeking recovery to prepare for trial.

Nevertheless, as a generality, there is little reason for most arbitrations to be made public when the parties do not want that to happen. There may be an exception to this where there is a positive need for transparency in order to provide the public, as distinct from some commentators, with confidence in a series of arbitrations on the same subject matter being carried on by the same institution. For the courts to retain legitimacy, as they must do in the eyes of the public, they must be transparent. This principle does not apply to individual arbitrations but it could do so in circumstances in which legitimacy is important in connection with a number of linked cases. I noted with interest the comments on the investment trading arbitrations in that regard.

I take on board Lord Thomas's observations on the potential damage which confidential arbitrations might cause to the development of the common law.[41] For the reasons which I have given in relation to the development of Scots law, this is not a problem which we should be too worried about. There are many court litigations in which public pronouncements on the law and the facts will be given; perhaps more than ever. The law will continue to be developed as and when that needs to happen.

I have mentioned the obligation on parties to focus their submissions and to assist the tribunal. It is equally the tribunal's duty to keep the expression of its decisions within proper bounds. The object of a decision is what it says on the tin. It is to express a decision; albeit to give reasons for that decision. It is about adjudicating between the parties. With the possible exception of decisions of the supreme courts of a particular jurisdiction, there is no need to explore why or how the law may have developed in a particular way. That does not matter to the parties. The tribunal should find the facts, state simply what it considers the law to be and apply it. Its function does not extend to demonstrating how clever the tribunal may be. At an appellate level in this jurisdiction, we are dedicated to producing short, easily read and understandable decisions. That may be swimming against the tide in other tribunals, but swim we will.

VII   CONCLUDING REMARKS: THE FUTURE FOR ARBITRATION IN SCOTLAND?

As I mentioned earlier, our civil courts are now well-equipped to host fully remote or hybrid hearings. This capability allows applications or appeals in arbitrations with a

---

40. *Gray Construction* v *Harley Haddow* 2012 SLT 1035.
41. The Rt. Hon. The Lord Thomas of Cwmgiedd, 'Developing Commercial Law Thorugh the Courts: Rebalancing the Relationship Between the Courts and Arbitration', The Bailii Lecture, 9 March 2019 (Lord Chief Justice speech: The Bailii Lecture 2016 (judiciary.uk)).

global element to be dealt with expeditiously and in a cost-efficient manner. Reliance on electronic processes produces a similar result. These improvements, and there are more to come, ensure that the Scottish courts are well placed to play a role in assisting in the resolution of any disputes arising either during or post-arbitration. At the Accession Council in London a week or so ago, I required to witness the King's Oath to protect the Church of Scotland. On seeing this happening, one member of the legal profession, who had a good handle on my approach to the use of technology, tweeted 'Could have been on WebEx'. Fair comment indeed.

There is considerable scope for the subject matter of arbitrations in Scotland to be widened. Historically, most arbitration has taken place in the sphere of construction contracts, development agreements and commercial leases. Arbitration is becoming particularly popular in renewable energy contracts. No doubt a number of these cases will come before the courts.

The fact that we are all here today and that Edinburgh is hosting the 25th Congress of the International Council for Commercial Arbitration speaks to the appetite of our jurisdiction to embrace the potential which arbitration has to offer. In conjunction with the role played by the courts, Scotland remains a contender as a centre for the resolution of international commercial disputes. This is demonstrated by the significant increase in the number of lawyers training to become arbitrators and a general increase in interest from other professions. It is an exciting time for our jurisdiction. I am sure that this event and many more to come will continue to drive the momentum forwards.

I hope that those of you unfamiliar with Edinburgh and Scotland will have some time to enjoy all that the city and the country have to offer. The conference will have prompted new ideas and promoted personal and professional friendships. I wish you all the best for the future.

Thank you for listening.

ICCA Edinburgh Congress List of Participants[*]

Albania

Mucaj, Xhuljana
University of Sheffield
Tirana

Andorra

Raoul-Duval, Pierre
Tribunal d'Arbitratge del Principat
d'Andorra (TAPA)
Andorra la Vella

Angola

Nogueira, Itweva
Dentons Lead
Luanda

Argentina

Bordaçahar, Julian
Permanent Court of Arbitration
The Hague

Ostrower, Ricardo
Marval, O'Farrell, Mairal
Buenos Aires

Rivera Jr., Julio Cesar
Marval, O'Farrell, Mairal
Buenos Aires

Sivak, Federico
Delos Dispute Resolution
Buenos Aires

Australia

Brown, Chester
Essex Court Chambers and
7 Wentworth Selborne Chambers
Sydney

Davidson, Ben
Corrs Chambers Westgarth
Melbourne

Einfeld, Alexandra
Corrs Chambers Westgarth
Sydney

Freeman, Christopher
Culwulla Chambers Sydney
Sydney

---

[*] The List of Participants is based on information provided by the participant upon registering for the Congress.

Horrigan, Brenda
Independent Arbitrator (Singapore)
Sydney

Kelly, KC, Anthony
Victorian Bar
Melbourne

Khan, Faraz
Law In Order
Melbourne

Levine, Judith
Levine Arbitration
Paddington NSW

Lincoln, Mark
SJA
Melbourne

Lincoln, Bronwyn
Thomson Geer
Melbourne

Morrison, James
Peter & Kim
Mullengudgery

Moxham, Tom
Peter & Kim
Sydney

Newbold, Beverley
Minter Ellison
Sydney

Paffey, Joshua
Corrs Chambers Westgarth
Brisbane

Quan-Sing, Jeremy
Allens
Perth

Quick, Georgia
Ashurst Australia / ACICA
5 Martin Place

Redwood, Jonathon
Twenty Essex
Rose Bay

Ross, Donna
Donna Ross Dispute Resolution
Melbourne

Rudge, Nick
Allens
Melbourne

Stephenson, Andrew
Corrs Chambers Westgarth
Melbourne

Suhadolnik, Nastasja
Corrs Chambers Westgarth
Melbourne

Thiagarajan, Premala
Victorian Bar
Hawthorn

Tomkinson, Deborah
Australian Centre for International Commercial Arbitration
Sydney

Xie, Dan
University of New South Wales
Shanghai

Austria

Bielesz, Holger
CERHA HEMPEL Rechtsanwälte GmbH
Vienna

Burgstaller, Markus
Hogan Lovells International LLP
London

Feher, Lili Hanna
Schoenherr Rechtsanwälte GmbH
Vienna

Karollus-Bruner, Daniela
CMS Reich-Rohrwig Hainz Rechtsanwälte GmbH
Vienna

Klausegger, Christian
Binder Grösswang Rechtsanwälte GmbH
Vienna

Konrad, Christian W.
Konrad & Partner Rechtsanwälte GmbH
Vienna

Kopecky, Leon
Schönherr Rechtsanwälte GmbH
Vienna

Krepil, Paul
CERHA HEMPEL Rechtsanwälte GmbH
Vienna

Kutschera, Michael
Binder Grösswang Rechtsanwälte GmbH
Vienna

Leinwather, Niamh
VIAC
Vienna

Liebscher, Christoph
Liebscher Dispute Management
Vienna

Lindinger, Christoph
Schönherr Rechtsanwälte GmbH
Vienna

Lukic, Sebastian
Schönherr Rechtsanwälte GmbH
Vienna

Pernt, Victoria
Schönherr Rechtsanwälte GmbH
Vienna

Pitkowitz, Nikolaus
Pitkowitz & Partners
Vienna

Riegler, Stefan
Wolf Theiss Rechtsanwälte GmbH & Co
KG
Vienna

Riznik, Peter
Konrad Partners
Vienna

Schwendinger, Jasmin
Schönherr Rechtsanwälte GmbH
Vienna

Stanisavljevic, Marina
Schönherr Rechtsanwälte GmbH
Vienna

Tsaturyan, Sona
Schoenherr Rechtsanwälte GmbH
Vienna

Welser, Irene
CERHA HEMPEL Rechtsanwälte GmbH
Vienna

Bahamas

Nottage, Theominique
Government of The Bahamas
Nassau

Bahrain

Al Zayed Al Jalahma, Fatema
Bahrain Chamber for Dispute Resolution
Manama

Husain, Ahmed
Bahrain Chamber for Dispute Resolution
Manama

Mutaywea, Aysha
Mena Chambers
Manama

Paulsson, Jan
Honorary President and
Advisory Member of ICCA
Three Crowns
Manama

Zimmo, Aseel
Supreme Judicial Council- Bahrain
Manama

Belgium

Baeten, Patrick
ENGIE SA
Paris La Défense

Bassiri, Niuscha
Hanotiau & van den Berg
Brussels

van den Berg, Albert Jan
Honorary President and
Advisory Member of ICCA
Hanotiau & van den Berg
Brussels

Eyskens, Werner
Crowell & Moring LLP
Brussels

Hanotiau, Bernard
Advisory Member of ICCA
Hanotiau & van den Berg
Brussels

Hay, Emily
Hanotiau & van den Berg
Brussels

Iancu, Iuliana
Hanotiau & van den Berg
Brussels

Kleinheisterkamp, Jan
JK-ADR / London School of Economics
Brussels

Kohl, Benoit
University of Liège
Embourg

Kovacs, Zsuzsanna
CMS
Brussels

Lefevre, Francoise
Francoise Lefevre SRL
Brussels

Paisley, Kathleen
Paisley Bvba
Boechout

van Houtte, Hans
Van Houtte Partners
Leuven

van Houtte, Vera
Advisory Member of ICCA
Van Houtte Partners
Leuven

Van Tornout, Beatrice
Liedekerke
Brussels

Vijra, Tarunima
Hanotiau & van den Berg
Brussels

Bermuda

Elkinson, Jeffrey
Conyers Dill & Pearman
Hamilton

Bolivia

Wayar, Bernardo
Wayar & von Borries Abogados S.C.
La Paz

Botswana

Luke, Edward
Luke & Associates
Gaborone

Brazil

Beneti, Ana Carolina
Beneti Advocacia
São Paulo

Casoretti, Simone
Tribunal de Justiça de São Paulo
São Paulo

Coelho, Eleonora
CAM-CCBC
São Paulo

Damião Gonçalves, Eduardo
ICCA Governing Board Member
Mattos Filho
São Paulo

Furtado, Ana Flavia
CAM-CCBC
São Paulo

Godoy, Luciano
Luc Advogados
São Paulo

Gomes, Marcus
Felsberg Advogados
São Paulo

Gonzalez Cronemberger Parente,
Arthur
Mattos Filho, Veiga Filho,
Marrey Jr E Quiroga Advogados
São Paulo

Kobayashi, Patricia
CAM-CCBC
São Paulo

Kömel, Luiza
CAM-CCBC
São Paulo

Mastrobuono, Cristina
FCIArb Brasil Branch
São Paulo

Peixinho Gomes Correa, Fabio
Tauil & Chequer Advogados
São Paulo

Pestilla Fabbri, Maurício
Cescon, Barrieu, Flesch & Barreto Sociedade De Advogados
São Paulo

Ribas, Leonardo
Felsberg Advogados
São Paulo

Santini FCIArb, Christine
Christine Santini Sociedade Individual De Advocacia
São Paulo

Tepedino, Ricardo
Tepedino, Berezowski e Poppa Advogados
São Paulo

Bulgaria

Hristova, Velislava
American Bar Association
Sofia

Canada

Alvarez, Henri
Vancouver Arbitration Chambers
Mission

Arbour, Louise
Borden Ladner Gervais
Montreal

Badri, Kishan
Investor-State LawGuide
Vancouver

Barrington, Louise
Arbitration Place
Toronto

Bédard, Julie
ICCA Governing Board Member
Skadden, Arps, Slate, Meagher &
Flom LLP
New York

Bienvenu, Pierre
IMK LLP
Montreal

Birks, Cristina
Borden Ladner Gervais LLP
Montreal

Casey, J. Brian
Bay Street Chambers
Toronto

Cherkezov, Stanislav
Huvepharma
Sofia

Chiasson, Craig
Borden Ladner Gervais LLP
Vancouver

Darche, Jacques S.
Borden Ladner Gervais LLP
Montreal

Deane, Robert
Borden Ladner Gervais LLP
Vancouver

Drymer, Stephen L.
Woods LLP
Montreal

Ferris, Craig
Lawson Lundell LLP
Vancouver

Gélinas, Fabien
McGill University
Montreal

Haigh, David R.
Burnet, Duckworth & Palmer LLP
Calgary

Harrison, Douglas
Harrison ADR Professional Corporation
Toronto

Judge, John
Arbitra International
Toronto

Leblanc, Christian
Fasken
Montreal

Louyeh, Soheila Ebrahimi
Investor-State LawGuide
Vancouver

McArthur, Joe
Blake, Cassels & Graydon LLP
Vancouver

McLaren, Richard
Western University
London

Moon, Paul
Investor-State LawGuide
Vancouver

Nirala, Chintan
McGill University
Montreal

Oghigian, Haig
Fasken
Montreal

Reynolds, Bruce
Singleton Urquhart Reynolds Vogel LLP
Toronto

Riley, Dawn
c/o Burnet, Duckworth & Palmer LLP
Calgary

Rosen, Howard
Secretariat Advisors (Canada) Limited
Toronto

Thomas, Christopher
J C Thomas Law Corporation
Vancouver

Vogel, Sharon
Singleton Urquhart Reynolds Vogel LLP
Toronto

Von Kumberg, Wolf
Arbitra
London

Walker CM, Janet
Toronto Arbitration Chambers
Toronto

Weiler, Todd
Independent
London

Chile

Mereminskaya, Elina
Wagemann Lawyers & Engineers
Santiago

China PR

Sun, Wei
Zhong Lun Law Firm
Beijing

Yang, Ling
Hong Kong International Arbitration Centre
Shanghai

Zhang, Yuejiao
Tsinghua University School of Law
Beijing

Colombia

Benavides, Claudia
Baker McKenzie
La Calera

Zuleta, Eduardo
Advisory Member of ICCA

Zuleta Abogados
Bogotá

Costa Rica

Filloy, Marcela
LatinAlliance Costa Rica
San José

Jiménez, Dyalá
ICCA Governing Board Member
DJ Arbitraje
San José

Cyprus

Dimitriou, Charis
Charis D. Demetriou & Co LLC
Limassol

Hadjisoteriou, Marina
Michael Kyprianou & Co LLC
Limassol

Michaelides, Andreas
Scordis, Papapetrou & Co LLC
Limassol

Czech Republic

Belohlavek, Alexander
Law Offices Belohlavek
Prague

Mareš, Alexandr
MAREŠ PARTNERS
Prague

Qureshi, Sirshar
PwC Czech Republic
Prague

Wilkinson, John
EY
Prague

Denmark

Christensen, Peter Clemmen
Lundgrens Law Firm P/S
Hellerup

Dalgaard-Knudsen, Frants
Plesner Lawfirm
Copenhagen

Nedergaard Thomsen, Henrik
Poul Schmith / Kammeradvokaten
Copenhagen

Pihlblad, Steffen
The Danish Institute of Arbitration
Copenhagen

Terkildsen, Dan
Lundgrens Law Firm P/S
Hellerup

Egypt

Abdel Wahab, Mohamed
ICCA Governing Board Member
Zulficar & Partners
Cairo

El-Nashar, Salma
Khodeir & Partners
Cairo

Hussein, Dalia
Cairo Regional Centre for
International Commercial Arbitration and
Faculty of Law- Zakazik University
Cairo

Nassar, Nagla
NassarLaw
Cairo

Finland

Forss, Anders
Castrén & Snellman Attorneys Ltd
Helsinki

Hentunen, Marko
Castrén & Snellman Attorneys Ltd
Helsinki

Lehtinen, Jussi
Dittmar & Indrenius
Helsinki

Lehto, Helen
Dittmar & Indrenius
Helsinki

Pohjanpalo, Maria
Ministry for Foreign Affairs of Finland
Helsinki

Saarikivi, Aapo
Roschier, Attorneys Ltd
Helsinki

Toivonen, Oskar
Baker Hughes
Lohja

Turunen, Santtu
Leale Conflict Management
Espoo

Wallgren-Lindholm, Carita
Lindholm Wallgren, Attorneys Ltd
Helsinki

France

Achtouk-Spivak, Laurie
Cleary Gottlieb Steen & Hamilton
Paris

El-Ahdab, Jalal
Bird & Bird AARPI
Paris

Berger Baton-Vermeersch,
Marie-Caroline
Allianz Technology
Paris

Blumrosen, Alexander
Polaris Law
Paris

Borde, Fabienne
Kroll Advisory Ltd
Paris

Cabrol, Emmanuelle
Ashurst LLP
Paris

Carducci, Guido
Carducci Arbitration
Paris

CASTELLANE, Béatrice
CCA
Paris

Cavalieros, Philippe
Simmons & Simmons LLP
London

Charlotin, Damien
IAReporter
Paris

Charlton, Anthony
HKA
Paris

Chessa, Valentine
MGC Arbitration
Paris

Crevon, Anna
Dentons
Paris

de Pouzilhac, Cédric
Aramis
Paris

Degos, Louis
K&L Gates LLP
Paris

Diawara, Diamana
ICC International Court of Arbitration
Paris

El Kara, Myriam
Verkor
Grenoble

ELKESLASSY, Frédéric
EY Services France
Paris La Défense

Elliot, Simon
Three Crowns LLP
Paris

Fathallah, Raed
Bredin Prat
Paris

Flower, Andrew
Alvarez & Marsal
Paris

Fortoul, Celine
Grant Thornton Conseil
Neuilly-sur-Seine

Fouchard Papaefstratiou, Athina
AFP Arbitration
Paris

Fox, Emily
Herbert Smith Freehills LLP
Paris

Franc-Menget, Laurence
Herbert Smith Freehills LLP
Paris

Garaud, Jean-Yves
Cleary Gottlieb Steen & Hamilton LLP
Paris

Gouiffès, Laurent
Hogan Lovells
Paris

Grisel, Florian
University of Oxford
Montreuil

Gurdova, Shirin
Young ICCA
Levallois-Perret

Hascher, Dominique
Advisory Member of ICCA
Supreme Judicial Court (France)
Paris

Honlet, Jean-Christophe
Honlet Legum Arbitration
Paris

Joubin-Bret, Anna
UNCITRAL
Vienna

Khamsi, Kathryn
Three Crowns LLP
Paris

Khosla, Sumit
Accuracy
Paris

Kleiman, Elie
Jones Day
Paris

Koba, Dmytro
Jus Mundi
Paris

Kouassi, Yannick
University of Strasbourg
Illkirch-Graffenstaden

Laborde, Gustavo
Laborde Law
Paris

Le Bars, Benoit
Lazareff Le Bars SARL
Paris

Lecuyer-Thieffry, Christine
Independent arbitrator
Paris

Legum, Barton
Honlet Legum Arbitration
Paris

Maffei, Antoine
De Pardieu Brocas Maffei
Paris

Malinvaud, Carole
ICCA Governing Board Member
Gide Loyrette Nouel AARPI
Paris

Mantilla-Serrano, Fernando
ICCA Governing Board Member
Latham & Watkins
Paris

McDougall, Andrew
White & Case
Paris

McKenny, Iain
Profile Investment
Paris

McNutt, J Michael
Lazareff Le Bars SARL
Paris

Mourre, Alexis
ICC International Court of Arbitration
Paris

Nunez-Lagos, Carmen
Nunez-Lagos Arbitration
Paris

Obamuroh, Tolu
White & Case
Paris

Oger-Gross, Elizabeth
White & Case
Paris

Ordonez, Melissa
Hogan Lovells
Paris

Pérez, José María
Bredin Prat
Paris

Peterson, Patricia
Peterson//ADR
Paris

Plump, Andrew
Linklaters LLP
Paris

Portwood, Timothy
Bredin Prat
Paris

Prevot, Clemence
Jus Mundi
Paris

Rosher, Peter
Reed Smith LLP
Paris

Shelbaya, Mohamed
Gaillard Banifatemi Shelbaya Disputes
Paris

Shirinyans, Alveen
My Arbitration
Saint Germain En Laye

Spinelli, Julie
Le 16 Law
Paris

Stern, Brigitte
University of Paris 1 Pantheon-Sorbonne
Paris

Stoyanov, Marie
Allen & Overy LLP
Paris

Thieffry, Patrick
Independent arbitrator and consultant
Paris

Thorp, Peter
Thorp Arbitration
Paris

Tomasi, Thierry
Herbert Smith Freehills
Paris

Turner, KC, Peter J.
Freshfields Bruckhaus Deringer LLP
Paris

Vagenheim, Alexandre
Jus Mundi
Paris

Van Hooft, Annet
Van Hooft
Paris

Virjee, Hafez
Delos Dispute Resolution
Paris

Von Dewall, Sophia
Derains & Gharavi
Paris

Weiss, Marina
Bredin Prat
Paris

Wetmore, Todd
Three Crowns LLP
Paris

Younan, Jennifer
Shearman & Sterling LLP
Paris

Zalmanova, Maria
Jus Mundi
Paris

Ziadé, Marie-Aude
CBR & Associés
Paris

Ziadé, Roland
Linklaters LLP
Paris

Zukova, Galina
ZUKOVA.Legal
Paris

Georgia

Edilashvili, David
Georgian International Arbitration Centre
Tbilisi

Injia, Beka
Georgian International Arbitration Centre
Tbilisi

Germany

Ahrens, Jan-Michael
Siemens Aktiengesellschaft
Erlangen

Brödermann, Eckart
Brödermann Jahn RA GmbH
Hamburg

Bryant, Jennifer
Noerr Partnerschaftsgesellschaft mbB
Düsseldorf

Bülau, Maximilian
Hengeler Mueller Partnerschaft von Rechtsanwaelten mbB
Frankfurt am Main

Gantenberg, Ulrike
Gantenberg Dispute Experts
Düsseldorf

Grothaus, Julia
Linklaters LLP
Frankfurt am Main

Hadding, Matthias
Dentons Europe LLP
Düsseldorf

Herzberg, Axel Benjamin
Bodenheimer
Berlin

Hirth, René-Alexander
Buse Heberer Fromm RA Stb PartG mbB
Stuttgart

Hoesch, Antonia
Hengeler Mueller
Frankfurt

Hunter, Robert
Osborne Clarke
Cologne

Keller, Moritz
Clifford Chance Partnerschaft mbB
Frankfurt

Knott, Hermann
Kunz Law
Cologne

Koch, Olena
Rothorn Legal Rechtsanwälte Trittmann & Partner mbB
Frankfurt

Krotten, Nicolas
Armesto & Asociados
Tholey

Lissner, Benjamin
CMS Hasche Sigle
Cologne

Loercher, Torsten
CMS Hasche Sigle
Cologne

Mogendorf, Mathaeus
Hengeler Mueller
Berlin

Norton, Henry
ABB
Mannheim

Novikova, Irina
PwC Germany
Eschborn

Perkams, Markus
Addleshaw Goddard LLP
Frankfurt

Pickrahn, Guenter
Baker McKenzie
Frankfurt

Pika, Maximilian
Morgan Lewis
Frankfurt

Reeg, Axel
Reeg Rechtsanwälte mbB
Mannheim

Sachs, Klaus
ICCA Governing Board Member
CMS Hasche Sigle
Munich

Schäfer, Erik
Cohausz & Florack, Patent- und Rechtsan-
wälte, Partnerschaftsgesellschaft mbB
Düsseldorf

Schmitt, Moritz
Rothorn Legal
Frankfurt

Sessler, Anke
Advisory Member of ICCA
Skadden, Arps, Slate, Meagher & Flom
LLP
Frankfurt

Simma, Bruno
Iran-United States Claims Tribunal
The Hague

Thejraj Mallar, Dhanya
Clyde & Co., Hamburg
Kannur

Trippel, Pierre
Morgan Lewis & Bockius LLP
Frankfurt

Wachtel, Svenja
Willkie Farr & Gallagher LLP
Frankfurt

Whitener, Robert
Greenberg Traurig Germany, LLP
Berlin

Ghana

Amartey, Maxwell Bruce
Reindorf Chambers
Accra

Ayanru, Anne-Marie
Office of the Attorney-General
Accra

Fleischer, Alexa
Reindorf Chambers
Accra

Hayfron-Benjamin Boaten, Sally
Reindorf Chambers
Accra

Kumi, Samuel Kwame
Ghana School of Law
Makola, Accra

Owusu-Ankomah, Nania
Bentsi-Enchill, Letsa & Ankomah
Accra

Greece

Skoufari, Eleni
Zepos & Yannopoulos
Halandri

Vassardanis, Ioannis
I. Vassardanis & Partners Law Firm
Athens

Honduras

Villeda Corona, Fabián José
Lexincorp Central American Law Firm
La Ceiba

Hong Kong SAR

Boltenko, Olga
Fangda Partners
Hong Kong SAR

Branson, David
BW ArbIntl
Hong Kong SAR

Caldwell, Peter Scott
Caldwell Ltd
Hong Kong SAR

Chan, Elizabeth
Allen & Overy LLP
London

Charlesworth, Margaret
Caldwell Ltd
Sha Tin

Cheung, Venus
Department of Justice
Hong Kong SAR

Cohen, Julian
Resolution Chambers International
Hong Kong SAR

D'Agostino, Justin
Herbert Smith Freehills LLP
Hong Kong SAR

Denton, Gavin
Arbitration Chambers
Hong Kong SAR

Dimsey, Mariel
Hong Kong International Arbitration
Centre
Hong Kong SAR

Gearing, Matthew
Allen & Overy
Hong Kong SAR

Johnson, Mark Douglas
Debevoise & Plimpton LLP
Hong Kong SAR

Ladharam, Kirti
Hong Kong International Arbitration Centre
Hong Kong SAR

Lau, Joanne
Allen & Overy
Hong Kong SAR

Losari, Junianto James
City University of Hong Kong/
UMBRA
Hong Kong SAR

McDonald, Damien
Outer Temple Chambers and
Prince's Chambers
Hong Kong SAR

Moser, Michael
ICCA Governing Board Member
Michael Moser
Hong Kong SAR

Munro, Susan
K&L Gates
Hong Kong SAR

Poon, Emily
Hong Kong International Arbitration
Centre
Hong Kong SAR

Rigden-Green, Andrew
Stephenson Harwood LLP
Hong Kong SAR

Rhoda, Robert
Dentons Hong Kong LLP
Hong Kong SAR

Rooney, Kim
Gilt Chambers, Hong Kong
Hong Kong SAR

So, Wing
Rede Chambers
Hong Kong SAR

Ta, Pui-Ki Emmanuelle
eBRAM International Online Dispute Resolution
Centre Limited
Hong Kong SAR

Thomson, Mary
Pacific Chambers, 36 Stone Chambers
Hong Kong SAR

Tung, Sherlin
Withers
Hong Kong SAR

Uyar, Gokce
Hong Kong International Arbitration Centre
Hong Kong SAR

Uyar, Gökçe
Hong Kong International Arbitration Centre
Hong Kong SAR

Walsh, Thomas
Clifford Chance
Hong Kong SAR

Wiegand, Nicolas
CMS
Hong Kong SAR

Willems, Jane
BWArb Intl Ltd
Hong Kong SAR

Yang, Ing Loong
Akin Gump Strauss Hauer & Feld
Hong Kong SAR

Yeoh, Friven
Sidley Austin
Hong Kong SAR

Yeung, Man Sing
Li & Partners
Hong Kong SAR

Hungary

Damjanovic, Gabor
Forgó, Damjanovic & Partners
Budapest

Kun, Diana
SMARTLEGAL Schmidt & Partners
Budapest

Okanyi, Zsolt
CMS Cameron McKenna Nabarro Olswang LLP
Budapest

Schmidt, Richard
SMARTLEGAL Schmidt & Partners
Budapest

India

Aggarwal, Vishal
Independent Arbitration Practitioner
Delhi

Asapu, Ramalingeswara Rao
Judiciary
Hyderabad

Bagaria, Prateek
Singularity Legal LLP
Mumbai

Bakhru, Vibhu
High Court of Delhi
New Delhi

Banerjee, Kingshuk
Khaitan & Co.
Mumbai

Banerji, Gourab
Chambers of Gourab Banerji
New Delhi

Basur, Aanchal
AB Law
New Delhi

Baya, Madhur
LexArbitri
Mumbai

Bhan, Ashish
Trilegal
New Delhi

Chhatrapati, Bijal
J. Sagar Associates
Ahmedabad

Damodaran, Pooja
Glimstedt Partners/ Vilnius University
Chennai

Datta, Sachin
High Court of Delhi
New Delhi

Datta, Siddhartha
Shardul Amarchand Mangaldas & Co
Kolkata

Dave, Ami
New Delhi

Dave, Dushyant
Advisory Member of ICCA
Senior Advocate
New Delhi

Garg, Shashank
Chambers of Shashank Garg
New Delhi

Jain, Sameer
PSL Advocates & Solicitors
New Delhi

Karia, Tejas
Shardul Amarchand Mangaldas & Co
New Delhi

Khambata, Darius
One Essex Court
Mumbai

Lahoti, Divyakant
Lahoti Advocates
Noida

Lavu, Nageswara Rao
Retired Justice, Supreme Court Of India
Uttar Pradesh

Mathur, Dinesh
Advocate
New Delhi

Mukerjee, Vishrov
Trilegal
New Delhi

Nair, Dheeraj
J. Sagar Associates
New Delhi

Narula, Sanjeev
Delhi High Court
Delhi

Parikh, Shaneen
Cyril Amarchand Mangaldas
Mumbai

Prabha, Vinod Kumar
J. Sagar Associates
Chennai

Puri, Gaganpreet Singh
Alvarez and Marsal India Private Limited
New Delhi

Sengupta, Shankh
Trilegal
New Delhi

Shiralkar, Yash
Shardul Amarchand Mangaldas & Co
Mumbai

Sorabjee, Farhad
JSA, Advocates & Solicitors
Mumbai

Thacker, Siddharth
Mulla & Mulla & Craigie Blunt & Caroe
Mumbai

Ireland

Adam, Stephen
Transperfect
Dublin

Ahern, Susan
The Bar of Ireland
Dublin

Conlon, Éamonn
Éamonn Conlon
Dublin

Fisher, Rose
Arbitration Ireland & Ireland for Law
Dublin

Leonard SC, Patrick
The Bar of Ireland
Dublin

McGoldrick BL, Cian
The Bar of Ireland/Ireland for Law
Dublin

Nagle BL, Katie
The Bar of Ireland/ Ireland for Law
Dublin

Purcell, Kevin
A & L Goodbody
Dublin

Tissa, Remi
Mainstream Renewable Power
Dublin

Israel

Apfelbaum, Chavah
Asserson Law Offices
Tel Aviv

Sharvit, Shai
Gornitzky & Co.
Tel Aviv

Italy

Azzali, Stefano
Milan Chamber of Arbitration
Milan

Benedettelli, Massimo
Arblit - Radicati Di Brozolo Sabatini
Benedettelli Torsello
Milan

Cicogna, Michelangelo
De Berti Jacchia
Milan

Concolino, Barbara
BonelliErede
Milan

Crivellaro, Antonio
BonelliErede
Milan

Deli, Maria Beatrice
Associazione Italiana Per L'arbitrato
Rome

Digón, Rocio
White & Case LLP
Rome

Garcia Bel, Marta
Freshfields Bruckhaus Deringer LLP
Milan

Harris, Dan
Brattle Group
Rome

Lampo, Giuliana
University Of Naples Federico II
Procida

Landi, Niccolo
Beecheyarbitration
Milan

Malintoppi, Loretta
Vice President of ICCA

39 Essex Chambers
Singapore

Mauro, Benedetta
D|R Arbitration & Litigation
Rome

Radicati Di Brozolo, Luca
ARBLIT - Radicati di Brozolo Sabatini
Benedettelli Torsello
Milan

Rojas Elgueta, Giacomo
D|R Arbitration & Litigation
Rome

Santoro, Carlo
Cleary Gottlieb Steen & Hamilton LLP
Rome

Japan

Kodama, Masafumi
Kitahama Partners
Osaka

Markert, Lars
Nishimura & Asahi
Tokyo

Nakahara, Chié
Nishimura & Asahi
Tokyo

Ohara, Yoshimi
ICCA Governing Board Member
Nagashima Ohno & Tsunematsu
Tokyo

Takatori, Yoshihiro
Kasumigaseki International Law Office,
International Arbitration Chambers
Tokyo

Tezuka, Hiroyuki
Nishimura & Asahi
Tokyo

Kenya

Ahmed, Leyla
TripleOKLaw LLP
Nairobi

Aluoch, Joyce
Nairobi

Cetina, Luisa
Anjarwalla & Khanna LLP
Nairobi

Kamau, Ndanga
Ndanga Kamau Law
The Hague

Ohaga, John
ICCA Governing Board Member
TripleOKLaw LLP
Nairobi

Korea, Republic of

Baek, Yun Jae
Yulchon LLC
Seoul

Christensen, Matthew
Kim & Chang
Seongnam-shi

Eernisse, Arie
Shin & Kim
Seoul

Jung, Woo Suk
Yulchon
Seoul

Kim, David
Lee & Ko
Seoul

Kim, Kap-You (Kevin)
Advisory Member of ICCA
Peter & Kim
Seoul

Kim, Joongi
Yonsei Law School
Seoul

Kim, Junu
Bae, Kim & Lee LLC
Seoul

Lee, Chul-won
Kim & Chang
Seoul

Lee, Hangil
Bae, Kim & Lee LLC
Seoul

Lee, Hyun Jung
Bae, Kim & Lee LLC
Seoul

Lee, Young Seok
Rosetta Legal
Seoul

Lim, Sungwoo
Lee & Ko
Seoul

Park, Eun Young
Park Arbitration Chambers
Seoul

Shin, Hi-Taek
ICCA Governing Board Member
Seoul National University/Twenty Essex
Seoul

Shin (Kim), Young-Hyun
KCAB
Seoul

Yoon, Byung Chol
Kim & Chang
Seoul

Lebanon

Obeid, Ziad
Obeid & Partners
Beirut

Lithuania

Audzevičius, Ramūnas
PLP Motieka & Audzevicius
Vilnius

Vaitkute Pavan, Vilija
Ellex Law Firm
Vilinius

Vilcinskaite, Solveiga
Law Firm GLIMSTEDT Bernotas &
partners
Vilnius

Luxembourg

Forrester KC, Ian
General Court of the European Union
2015-2020
Luxembourg

Malaysia

Lee, Ji En
Chambers Lab
Kuala Lumpur

Mauritius

Adamjee, Ali
Chambers of Sir Hamid Moollan KC
Port Louis

Assou, Clemence
Mauritius International Arbitration Centre (MIAC)
Port Louis

Luximon, Smita
Mauritius International Arbitration Centre
Port Louis

Namdarkhan, Mushtaq
BLC Robert & Associates
Ebene

Mexico

Brown De Vejar, Kate
Dla Piper México, S.C.
Mexico City

Flores Rueda, Cecilia
FloresRueda Abogados
Mexico City

Gonzalez De Cossio, Francisco
Gonzalez De Cossio Abogados
Mexico City

Llano, Rafael
White & Case
Mexico City

Magallanes, Adrian
Von Wobeser Y Sierra S.C.
Mexico City

Velázquez, Jorge A.
University of Cambridge
Mexico City

Monaco

Forgione, Luca
Forgione Law
Monaco

Montenegro

Bozovic, Vesko
VMB law firm
Podgorica

Netherlands

Abeln, Rufus
Ysquare
Amsterdam

Acquaisie-Maison, Araba
ICCA
The Hague

Ambast, Ashwita
Permanent Court of Arbitration
The Hague

Ameli, Koorosh
Ameli Arbitration
The Hague

Ameli, Shiva
Ameli Arbitration
The Hague

van Baren, Willem
Independent Arbitrator
Amsterdam

Bartolone, David
Wolters Kluwer
Netherlands

Beckmann, Martin
Adviesbureau Beckmann B.V.
Kerkrade

van den Berg, Roelien
SSHJ Advocaten
Amsterdam

Bingham, Lisa
ICCA
The Hague

Borelli, Silvia
ICCA
The Hague

Bosman, Lise
Executive Director of ICCA
ICCA
The Hague

Burns, Lucy
ICCA
The Hague

Czepelak, Marcin
Permanent Court of Arbitration
The Hague

Daly, Brooks
Permanent Court of Arbitration
The Hague

de Haas, Emilie
ICCA
The Hague

De Ly, Filip
EUR
Utrecht

de Vries, Gwen
Wolters Kluwer
Alphen aan den Rijn

de Wit, Camilla Perera
Nederlands Arbitrage Instituut
Rotterdam

Di Giacomo Toledo, Tulio
Permanent Court of Arbitration
The Hague

Doe Rodriguez, Martin
Permanent Court of Arbitration
The Hague

Faienza, Valentina
ICCA
The Hague

Goriatcheva, Evgeniya
Permanent Court of Arbitration
The Hague

Gritsenko, Maria
Veon
Amsterdam

van de Hel, Mirjam
NautaDutilh NV
Amsterdam

Van Hooijdonk, Marieke
Allen & Overy LLP
Amsterdam

Knottenbelt, Dirk
Houthoff
Rotterdam

Krzeminski, Kasper
NautaDutilh NV
Rotterdam

van Leeuwen, Melanie
Derains & Gharavi
Paris

Leijten, Marnix
De Brauw Blackstone Westbroek
Amsterdam

van Leyenhorst, Max
Legaltree
Leiden

Macpherson, Camilla
P.R.I.M.E. Finance
The Hague

Naudin ten Cate, Robin
The Hague Hearing Centre
The Hague

van den Nieuwendijk, Isabelle
Houthoff
Rotterdam

Oorthuys, Sander
Legaltree
Leiden

Paoletta, Sofia
Netherlands Arbitration Institute
Rotterdam

Peters, Niek
Simmons & Simmons LLP
Amsterdam

Robbins, Tim
Robbins Arbitration
The Hague

Sabanogullari, Levent
Permanent Court of Arbitration
The Hague

Schellaars, Rogier
Van Doorne N.V.
Amsterdam

Schill, Stephan
ICCA General Editor
University of Amsterdam
Amsterdam

Schluep, Alexandra
SSHJ Advocaten
Amsterdam

Schofield, Garth
Permanent Court of Arbitration
The Hague

Seok, Jinyoung
Permanent Court of Arbitration
The Hague

Smith, Fedelma
Permanent Court of Arbitration
The Hague

Stouten, Thomas
Houthoff
Rotterdam

Verhoeven, Martje
De Brauw Blackstone Westbroek
Amsterdam

Verkerk, Remme
Houthoff
Rotterdam

Wilinski, Piotr
Erasmus University
Rotterdam

Williams, Bryce
Permanent Court of Arbitration
The Hague

van Zelst, Bastiaan
Van Doorne N.V.
Amsterdam

Nigeria

Adekoya, Olufunke
ICCA Governing Board Member
Aelex
Lagos

Akeredolu, Abimbola
Banwo and Ighodalo
Lagos

Fagbohunlu, Olurotimi Babatunde
Aluko & Oyebode
Lagos

Kadiri SAN, Yusuf Asamah
Jackson, Etti & Edu
Lagos

Mohammed, Safiya
Ukiri Lijadu
Maitama Abuja

Nweke-Eze, Stanley U
The University of Hong Kong | Templars
Victoria Island, Lagos State

Okala, Ajuma Patience
Nigerian Investment Promotion Commission
Abuja

Omoaka, Godwin
Templars
Lagos

Philip-Idiok, Oluwaseun
Aelex
Lagos

Rhodes-Vivour, Adedoyin
Doyin Rhodes-Vivour & Co
Lagos

Tunde-Olowu, Adedapo
Aelex
Lagos

Ufot, SAN, Dorothy
Dorothy Ufot & Co.
Victoria Island

Ukaejiofor, Harry
Ukiri & Lijadu
Victoria Island Lagos

Norway

Langford, Malcolm
University of Oslo
Oslo

Oman

Al Azri, Moosa
Oman Commercial Arbitration Centre
Al Mawalih South

Pakistan

Naqvi, Feisal
BNR
Lahore

Peru

Oriundo Melgar, Silvana Esperanza
Lima

Philippines

De Los Angeles, Dino Ricardo
Romulo Mabanta Buenaventura Sayoc &
De Los Angeles
Makati City

de Vera, Christianne Noelle
Follosco Morallos & Herce
Quezon

Flores, Sienna
Romulo Mabanta Buenaventura Sayoc &
De Los Angeles
Makati City

King Kay, Catherine Beatrice
Romulo Mabanta Buenaventura Sayoc De
Los Angeles
Mandaluyong City

Ongkiko, Ricardo
Sycip Salazar Hernandez & Gatmaitan
Makati City

Poland

Cudna-Wagner, Anna
CMS Cameron McKenna Nabarro
Olswang Pośniak i Bejm Sp.k.
Warsaw

Frontczak, Maja
Gessel, Koziorowski Kancelaria Radców
Prawnych i Adwokatów Sp.p.
Warsaw

Gessel, Beata
Gessel, Koziorowski Sp.k.
Warsaw

Goledzinowski, Piotr
Wardynski & Partners
Warsaw

Kieszczynski, Jan
Ligit
Warsaw

Korzeniewski, Arkadiusz
CMS Cameron McKenna Nabarro
Olswang Pośniak i Bejm Sp.k.
Warsaw

Kruzewski, Bartosz
Clifford Chance
Warsaw

Kucharczyk, Katarzyna
CMS Cameron Mckenna Nabarro
Olswang Pośniak i Bejm Sp.k.
Warsaw

Morek, Rafal
DWF LLP
Warsaw

Nowaczyk, Piotr
Independent Arbitrator
Warsaw

Plesinski, Wojciech
BSJP Brockhuis Jurczak Prusak Sroka
Nilsson
Poznan

Tujakowska, Anna
Sołtysiński Kawecki & Szlęzak – Kancelaria Radców Prawnych i Adwokatów
Sp.k
Warsaw

Portugal

Gouveia, Mariana
PLMJ
Lisbon

Henriques, Duarte
Victoria Associates
Lisbon

Martins, Sofia
Miranda & Associados
Lisbon

Qatar

Al Eidan, Saad
Ashghal
Doha

Al-Hamad, Alya Jumah
Ashghal
Doha

Al-Marri, Abdulla
Ashghal
Doha

Al-Qadi, Sara Masoud
Ashghal
Doha

Jones, Andrew
Dentons & Co
Doha

Romania

Vasile, Cosmin
Zamfirescu Racoti Vasile & Partners Attorneys at Law
Bucharest

Russian Federation

Dyakin, Dmitry
Rybalkin, Gortsunyan and Partners
Moscow

Khvalei, Vladimir
ICCA Governing Board Member
Mansors
Moscow

Mullina, Yulia
Russian Arbitration Center at the
Russian Institute of Modern Arbitration
Moscow

Zagonek, Julia
White & Case LLC
Moscow

Rwanda

Manzi, Christian
Rwanda Convention Bureau
Kigali

Mugabe, Victor
Kigali International Arbitration Centre
Kigali

Murangwa, Frank
Rwanda Convention Bureau
Kigali

Saudi Arabia

Alberti, Christian P.
SCCA
Riyadh

Alduhaim, Abdulaziz
Ministry of Commerce
Riyadh

Al-Kherb, Mosaad
SCCA
Riyadh

Alrasheed, Majed

Majed Alrasheed Law Firm
Riyadh

Alshehri, Sara
NCC
Riyadh

Colvin, Timothy
Saudi Aramco
Dhahran

Dutson, Jason
Saudi Aramco
Dhahran

Hamad Aljaid, Mohannd
SCCA
Riyadh

Ismail, Ahmed
NCC
Riyadh

MacPherson, James
SCCA
Riyadh

Mahfooz, Yasmina
NCC
Riyadh

Merah, Hamed
SCCA
Riyadh

Singapore

Apostolova, Kate
Kate Apostolova
Singapore

Artero, Christine
The Arbitration Chambers
Singapore

Bailey, Christopher
Stephenson Harwood LLP
Singapore

Ban, Jiun Ean
Maxwell Chambers
Singapore

Bao, Chiann
Arbitration Chambers
Singapore

Bell, Gary F.
National University of Singapore
Singapore

Bhushan, Abhinav
39 Essex Chambers
Singapore

Bundy, Rodman
Squire Patton Boggs (Singapore) LLP
Singapore

Chan, Hock Keng
WongPartnership LLP
Singapore

Chew, Daryl
Three Crowns LLP
Singapore

Chou, Sean Yu
WongPartnership LLP
Singapore

Chung, Katie
Norton Rose Fulbright
Singapore

Cooke, Timothy
Reed Smith LLP
Singapore

Foo, Yuet Min
Drew & Napier LLC
Singapore

Gill, Judith
ICCA Governing Board Member
Twenty Essex
Singapore

Grief, David
David Grief International Consultancy Pte
Ltd

Grimmer, Sarah
Twenty Essex
Singapore

Jeremiah, Herman
Dentons Rodyk & Davidson LLP
Singapore

Koh, Swee Yen
WongPartnership LLP
Singapore

Kronenburg, Edmund
Braddell Brothers LLP
Singapore

Landau KC, Toby
ICCA Governing Board Member
Duxton Hill Chambers, Singapore
Singapore

Lee, Michael
Twenty Essex
Singapore

Lees, Amanda
King & Wood Mallesons
Singapore

Lim, Jonathan
Wilmer Cutler Pickering Hale and Dorr
LLP
London

Lingard, Nicholas
Freshfields Bruckhaus Deringer LLP
Singapore

Loh, Derek
TSMP Law Corporation
Singapore

Margetson, Gavin
Mishcon de Reya LLP
London

Ong, Chin
Attorney-General's Chambers, Singapore
Singapore

Pradhan, Avinash
Rajah & Tann Singapore LLP
Singapore

Pullen, Andrew
Fountain Court Chambers
Singapore

Rai, Mahesh
Drew & Napier LLC
Singapore

Raneda, Julie
Schellenberg Wittmer
Singapore

Singh, Kirindeep
Dentons Rodyk And Davidson LLP
Singapore

Tan, Karen
Supreme Court of Singapore
Singapore

Teh, Lawrence
Dentons Rodyk & Davidson LLP
Singapore

Thio, SC, Shen Yi
TSMP Law Corporation
Singapore

Xavier, Francis
Rajah & Tann Singapore LLP
Singapore

Slovakia

Raimanová, Lucia
Allen & Overy Bratislava, s.r.o.
Bratislava

Slovenia

Menard, Maja
Fatur Menard Law Firm
Ljubljana

South Africa

Alp, Nick
Webber Wentzel
Johannesburg

Daya, Priyesh
Webber Wentzel
Johannesburg

Mkiva, Clement
Bowmans
Johannesburg

Movshovich, Vlad
Webber Wentzel
Johannesburg

Ripley-Evans, Jonathan
Herbert Smith Freehills SA LLP
Johannesburg

Versfeld, Trevor
Webber Wentzel
Johannesburg

Vivian, Stephen
Pretoria Society of Advocates
Pretoria

Spain

Baptista, Krystle
KB | International Law & Arbitration
Madrid

Bonnin, Victor
VBArbitration
Madrid

Bottini, Gabriel
Uría Menéndez Abogados
Madrid

Cremades Sanz Pastor, Bernardo M.
Advisory Member of ICCA
B. Cremades Y Asociados S.L.
Madrid

Fortún Costea, Alberto
Cuatrecasas
Madrid

Gual Grau, Cristian
Uría Menéndez Abogados, SLP
Barcelona

Jankowski, Adam
Armesto & Asociados Arbitraje S.L.
Madrid

Navarro, Seguimundo
Club Español del Arbitraje
Madrid

Vicien Milburn, Maria
Independent Arbitrator
Madrid

Sweden

Ahrel, Ginta
Westerberg & Partners Advokatbyrå AB
Stockholm

Bogegård, Erik
Norburg & Scherp Advokat
Stockholm

Ewerlöf, Pontus
Hannes Snellman Attorneys Ltd
Stockholm

Falconer, Caroline
Arbitration Institute of the
Stockholm Chamber of Commerce
Stockholm

Foerster, Alexander
Advokatfoerster AB
Stockholm

Goldman, Björn
MAQS Advokatbyrå
Göteborg

Hope, James
Vinge
Stockholm

Johard, Andreas
Hammarsköld & Co
Stockholm

Linton-Wahlgren, Mikael
Lindmark Welinder
Lund

Nilsson, Bo G.H.
Westerberg & Partners Advokatbyrå AB
Stockholm

Norburg, Fredrik
Norburg & Scherp Advokatbyrå AB
Stockholm

Permyakova, Polina
Advokatfirman Delphi
Stockholm

Petrik, Natalia
SCC
Stockholm

Rifall, Martin
Hannes Snellman Attorneys Ltd
Stockholm

Shaughnessy, Patricia
Stockholm University
Lidingö

Sidklev, Johan
Roschier, Attorneys Ltd
Stockholm

Söderlund, Christer
Adv Christer Söderlund AB
Stockholm

Wikström-Hermansen, Rikard
Roschier, Attorneys Ltd
Stockholm

Switzerland

Akikol, Diana
Walder Wyss Ltd
Geneva

Amigues-MacRae, Rona
Lalive
Geneva

Athanasiou, Maria
Bureau Pierre Tercier
Fribourg

Bernet, Martin
Bernet Arbitration / Dispute Management
Zurich

Boog, Christopher
Schellenberg Wittmer
Zurich

Brown-Berset, Dominique
Brown & Page SA
Geneva

Chalkias, Panagiotis
White & Case
Geneva

Dasser, Felix
Homburger AG
Zurich

Devitre, Dilber
Homburger AG
Zurich

Dickenmann, Philipp
CMS Cameron McKenna Nabarro
Olswang LLP
Zurich

Donde, Rahul
Lévy Kaufmann-Kohler
Geneva

Favre Bulle, Xavier
Lenz & Staehelin
Geneva

Frey, Harold
Lenz & Staehelin
Zurich

George, Anya
Schellenberg Wittmer
Zurich

Gunter, Pierre-Yves
Bär & Karrer
Geneva

Habegger, Philipp
Habegger Arbitration
Zurich

Hochstrasser, Daniel
Bär & Karrer
Zurich

Johnson, Alexandra C.
Pestalozzi Attorneys at Law
Geneva

Kaufmann-Kohler, Gabrielle
Honorary President and

Advisory Member of ICCA
Lévy Kaufmann-Kohler
Geneva

Killias, Laurent
Pestalozzi Attorneys at Law
Zurich

Kolwas, Patrycja
Cofco International
Rolle

Kozmenko, Anna
Schellenberg Wittmer
Zürich

Landon, Tanya
Sidley Austin LLP
Geneva

Lenggenhager, Fadri
Lenz & Staehelin
Zurich

Marugg, Daniel
Marugg Dispute Resolution
Zurich

Maurer, Anton
Anton Maurer International Legal
Services GmbH
St. Moritz

Mazuranic, Alexandre
White & Case SA
Geneva

McQuillen, Monika
Lustenberger + Partners
Zurich

Mohs, Florian
Pestalozzi Attorneys at Law
Zurich

Nater-Bass, Gabrielle
Homburger AG
Zurich

Potestà, Michele
Lévy Kaufmann-Kohler
Geneva

Radjai, Noradèle
Lalive
Geneva

Roney, David
Sidley Austin LLP
Geneva

Schneider, Michael E.
Lalive
Geneva

Schramm, Dorothee
Swiss Arbitrator
Geneva

Shylova, Daria
Rothorn Legal AG
Zurich

Sievi, Nino
Lex Futura
Zurich

Tercier, Pierre
Advisory Member of ICCA
Bureau Pierre Tercier
Fribourg

Tran Thang, Nhu-Hoang
Peter & Kim
Geneva

Triebold, Claudius
Lustenberger + Partners
Zurich

Voser, Nathalie
Rothorn Legal
Zurich

Weber-Stecher, Urs
Weber-Stecher, Arbitration / Mediation
Zurich

Wehland, Hanno
Lenz & Staehelin
Geneva

Yasseen, Rabab
Mentha Avocats
Geneva

Zaugg, Niklaus
CMS von Erlach Partners AG
Zurich

Zuberbühler, Tobias
Lustenberger + Partners
Zurich

Tanzania

Bhojani, Fayaz
FB Attorneys
Dar Es Salaam

Tunisia

Kemicha, Fathi
Advisory Member of ICCA
Kemicha Legal Consulting K.L.C.
Tunis

Turkey

Akuzum, Huseyin Ural
Kabine Law Office
Istanbul

Blythe, Jonathan
Senguler Law and
Eurasia Consultants
Istanbul

Boden, Değer
Boden Law
Istanbul

Çetinkaya, Ceyda Sila
Baker McKenzie
Istanbul

Çoşar, Utku
Cosar Avukatlik Burosu
Istanbul

Durlu Gürzumar, Derya
University of Neuchatel
Ankara

Karlı, Mehmet
Kabine Law Office
Istanbul

Yalım, Tuvan
Kabine Law Office
Istanbul

Yıldız Üstün, Esra
Atatürk University
Erzurum

Ukraine

Droug, Olexander
Sayenko Kharenko
Kyiv

Slipachuk, Tatyana
Sayenko Kharenko
Kyiv

United Arab Emirates

Al Tamimi, Essam
Al Tamimi and Company
Dubai

Al Zaabi, Ahmed
ADGM Courts
Abu Dhabi

Alsawalehi, Shamlan
DIFC Courts
Dubai

Cole, Adrian
Independent Arbitrator
Abu Dhabi

Dennehy, Hannah
ADGM Arbitration Centre
Abu Dhabi

Emmerson, Alec
ADR Management Consultancies
Dubai

Ghaffari, Amir
Vinson & Elkins LLP
Dubai

Heitzmann, Pierre
Jones Day
Dubai

Hoffmann, Anne K.
Independent Arbitrator
Dubai

Hope, The Right Honourable Lord David
Abu Dhabi Global Market
Abu Dhabi

Kazim, Jehad
DIAC
Dubai

Lovett, Graham
Akin Gump
DIFC

O'Connell, Kirsten
Allen & Overy LLP
Dubai

Oogorah, Reshma
Niyom Legal
Dubai

Saey, Ayman
DIFC Courts
Dubai

Saoud, Ritta
Dubai International Arbitration Centre
Dubai

Sharratt, Nicholas
Stephenson Harwood LLP
Dubai

Sibbald, Greg
CMS Cameron McKenna Nabarro
Olswang LLP
Dubai

Snider, Thomas
Al Tamimi and Company
Dubai

Tannous, Sami
Freshfields Bruckhaus Deringer LLP
Dubai

Whelan, Ryan
Akin Gump Strauss Hauer & Feld LLP
Dubai

United Kingdom

England

Adesokan, Jide
Stephenson Harwood LLP
London

Adeyemi, Tope
33 Bedford Row
London

Aggarwal, Manish
Three Crowns LLP
London

Aglionby, Andrew
Aglionby ADR
London

Ahmad, Jawad
Mayer Brown International LLP
London

Alabi, IfeOluwa
University of Sussex
Brighton

Albert, Francesca
Enyo Law LLP
London

Allan, Brian
Bristol

Ambrose, Hannah
Herbert Smith Freehills LLP
London

Ambrose, Clare
Twenty Essex
Sevenoaks

Antoon, Wilson
King & Wood Mallesons
London

Anurov, Kirill
Alvarez & Marsal
London

Armes, Murray
Sense Studio
London

Ashford, Peter
Fox Williams
London

Aswani, Ravi
36 Stone
London

Auchecorne, Taryn
Opus 2
London

Awosika, Afolarin
Stephenson Harwood LLP
London

Azpiroz, Maddi
Claimtrading
London

Bagshaw, Duncan
Howard Kennedy LLP
London

Baltag, Crina
Stockholm University
Hitchin

Barnes, David
Atkin Chambers
London

Barnes, Jessica
Kroll
London

Barsalou, Nicolas
Accuracy
London

Bastin, Lucas
Essex Court Chambers
London

Beechey, John
ICCA Governing Board Member
Arbitration Chambers
London

Bellamy, Jonathan
39 Essex Chambers
London

Bevan, Alex
Shearman & Sterling LLP
London

Bharucha, Arish
Howard Kennedy LLP
London

Bhatty, Saadia
Gide Loyrette Nouel
London

Bhuckory, Sandip
Allen & Overy LLP
London

Bigelow-Nutall, Clea
Pinsent Masons
London

Bilbow, Angela
Grant Thornton UK LLP
London

Blackaby, Nigel
Freshfields Bruckhaus Deringer LLP
Washington, DC

Blair, Sir William
3 Verulam Buildings
London

Blake, Conway
Debevoise & Plimpton LLP
London

Blower, Susan
BDO LLP
London

Boden, Daniel
CMS Cameron McKenna Nabarro
Olswang LLP
London

Boon, Daniel
Stephenson Harwood LLP
London

Braby, Alexandra
Chartered Institute of Arbitrators
London

Bradfield, Michelle
Jones Day
London

Bradshaw, Robert
Lalive
London

Brady, James
Cleary Gottlieb
London

Brekoulakis, Stavros
ICCA Governing Board Member
Queen Mary University of London and
3 Verulam Buildings
London

Bridgeman, James
4-5 Gray's Inn Square
London

Briercliffe, Naomi
Allen & Overy LLP
London

Bruton, Leilah
Three Crowns LLP
London, UK

Burder, Matt
FTI Consulting
London

Burgess, Tony
Brick Court Chambers
London

Burstyn, Jack
Mishcon de Reya LLP
London

Byrne, Ruth
King & Spalding
London

Caher, Charlie
WilmerHale
London

Caldwell, Richard
The Brattle Group
London

Campbell, Maya
Everlaw
London

Campbell, Mark
University of Bristol Law School
Bristol

Cannon, Andrew
Herbert Smith Freehills LLP
London

Carroll, Ben
Linklaters LLP
London

Carter, Bianca
Epiq
London

Carter, Sam
Outer Temple
London

Cartwright, Charlotte
Linklaters LLP
London

Carvalho, Carlos
Opus2
London

Cawdron, Steven
Ernst & Young LLP
London

Chandrasekera, Rovine
Stephenson Harwood LLP
London

Chaplin, Jacqueline
Linklaters LLP
London

Charles, Philippa
Stewarts
London

Chataud, Line
Mayer Brown International LLP
London

Chauhan, Hemant
Global Arbitration Review
London

Cheema, Jas
Accuracy
London

Chesney, Gavin
Debevoise & Plimpton LLP
London

Child, Nick
Secretariat International
London

Clanchy, James
James Clanchy, Arbitrator
London

Clark, Joanna
CMS Cameron McKenna Nabarro
Olswang LLP
London

Cliff, Paul
Grant Thornton UK LLP
London

Cohen, Paul
4-5 Gray's Inn Square Chambers
London

Coles, Nikki
Alvarez & Marsal Disputes and
Investigations, LLP
London

Cooke, Uliana
PCB Byrne LLP
London

Cooper KC, Nigel
Quadrant Chambers
London

Cordara KC SC, Roderick
Essex Court Chambers
London

Cox, Johanne
Shoosmiths
London

Craig, Nicholas KC
3VB
London

Cumming, Samantha
Sidley Austin LLP
London

Daele, Karel
Taylor Wessing LLP
London

Davies, Katharine
Pinsent Masons LLP
London

Davies, Gwendoline
Walker Morris LLP
Leeds

De Boisséson, Matthieu
Arbitration Chambers
London

De Germiny, Lorraine
Lalive (London) LLP
London

Dearman, David
Ankura
London

Dechamps, Jean Paul
Dechamps International Law
London

Deniger, Christiane
Burford Capital
London

Dennison, Paul
Brick Court Chambers
London

Devenish, Philip
Jones Day
London

Dhillon, Inderpal
BDO LLP
London

Diver, Andrew
Farrer & Co LLP
London

Dixon, Catherine
Chartered Institute of Arbitrators
London

Doeh, Doran
36 Stone
London

Van Duijvenoorde, Erik
Accuracy
London

Dutson, Stuart
Simmons & Simmons LLP
London

Dymond, Tony
Debevoise & Plimpton LLP
London

Edworthy, Chloe
Macfarlanes LLP
London

El Housan, Asel
AEH UK Limited
Glasgow

Escobar, Alejandro
Baker Botts (UK) LLP
London

Everson, Colin
Kroll
London

Farren, Ania
Omnia
London

Fawke, Alexander
Linklaters LLP
London

Fenn, Michael
Pinsent Masons LLP
London

Finizio, Steven
Wilmer Cutler Pickering Hale and Dorr
London

Fisher, Toby
Global Arbitration Review
London

Flannery KC, Louis
Mishcon de Reya LLP
London

Fletcher, Nicholas
4 New Square
London

Fleuren, Bart
Linklaters LLP
London

Fox, Andrew
Sidley Austin LLP
London

Foxton, Tom
One Essex Court
London

Freeman, James
Allen & Overy LLP
London

Fritzsche, Matthew
Ernst & Young LLP
London

Ganz, Sarah
Wilmer Cutler Pickering Hale and Dorr
LLP
London

Garcia, Augusto
WilmerHale
London

Gardiner, Daniel
Pinsent Masons
London

Gearing KC, Matthew
Fountain Court
Bath

Gendler, Howard
HKA
London

Ghaly, Karim
39 Essex Chambers
London

Giaretta, Ben
Fox Williams LLP
London

Gibbons-Jones, Charlotte
CMS Cameron McKenna Nabarro
Olswang LLP
London

Gibbs, Stewart
4 Pump Court
London

Gilfedder, Catherine
Dentons UK and Middle East LLP
London

Gimblett, Jonathan
Covington & Burling LLP
London

Goch, Rylan
TransPerfect Legal Solutions
Harpenden

Goddard KC, Andrew
Atkin Chambers
London

Godman, Camilla
Omni Bridgeway
London

Goh, Nelson
Pallas Partners LLP
London

Goldberg, David
White & Case LLP
London

Goldsmith, Peter
Debevoise & Plimpton LLP
London

Gonin, Emilie
Brick Court Chambers
London

González Garcíá, Luis
Matrix Chambers
London

Grebenkova, Valeriya
Resolut
London

Greenwood, Lucy
GreenwoodArbitration
Alresford

Greer, Shan
Arbitra International
London

Griffith, Gavan
Essex Court Chambers
London

Grunwald, Dora
Osborne Partners
London

Gunn, Jane
Chartered Institute of Arbitrators
London

Haeri, Hussein
Withers LLP
London

Van Haersolte van Hof, Jacomijn
LCIA
London

Hambury, Jason
Pinsent Masons
London

Harrison, Jamie
LCIA
London

Harrison, Luke Tucker
Keidan Harrison LLP
London

Hawes, Julian
International Arbitration Centre
London

Hayman KC, George
Maitland Chambers
London

Heilbron, Hilary
Brick Court Chambers
London

Hesmondhalgh, Serena
The Brattle Group
London

Hickinbottom, Gary
39 Essex Chambers
London

Hickman, Damian
International Dispute Resolution Centre
London

Hodge, Patrick
UK Supreme Court
London

Hodges KC, Paula
Herbert Smith Freehills LLP
London

Holland, Ben
K&L Gates LLP
London

Holmes, Pamela
Cleary Gottlieb Steen & Hamilton LLP
London

Honey, Damian
HFW
London

Hollander de Groot, Yael
Wolters Kluwer
London

Hooker, Will
Pallas Partners
London

Hoose, Robert
Debevoise & Plimpton LLP
London

Horn, Schellion
Grant Thornton UK LLP
London

Hornan, Ben
Hogan Lovells International LLP
London

Horne, Lois
Macfarlanes LLP
London

Howick, Adrian
Alvarez & Marsal
London

Hunt, David
Boies Schiller Flexner LLP
London

Iyer, Shobana
Swan Chambers
London

Jain, Srishti
Keidan Harrison LLP
London

Jain, Maanas
Three Crowns LLP
London

James, Rebecca
Linklaters LLP
London

Johnston, Lewis
Chartered Institute of Arbitrators
London

Jones, Robert
Ankura
London

Joseph, David
Essex Court Chambers
London

Kadioglu Kumtepe, Cemre
University of Leicester
Leicester

Kalisz, Aleksander
King's College London
London

Kalnina, Eva
Arbitration Chambers
London

Kapoor, Vivek
39 Essex Chambers
London

Kapoor, Priyanka
Fieldfisher
London

Karl, Kai-Uwe
GE Renewable Energy
London

Kavanagh KC, David
Skadden Arps Slate Meagher &
Flom (UK) LLP
London

Kazmi, Samar Abbas
Atkin Chambers
London

Key, Paul
Essex Court Chambers
London

Kleist, Paul
Cleary Gottlieb Steen & Hamilton LLP
London

Koepp, Johannes
Baker Botts (UK) LLP
London

Kotick, Brian
M.B. Kemp LLP
London

Kotrly, Michael
One Essex Court
London

Kurdi, Suzi
RPC
London

Laboucarie-Polak, Teresa
Linklaters LLP
London

Lafferty, Jonathan
Sidley Austin LLP
London

Lake, Chris
Ankura
London

Lancaster, Sarah
Arbitration Chambers
London

Langley, James
Dentons
London

Laufer, Helin
Van Bael & Bellis (London) LLP
London

Laurendeau, Tsegaye
Signature Litigation
London

Lawn, Nicholas
Van Bael & Bellis (London) LLP
London

Lawrence, Owen
Arbitra International
London

Le Gal, Jean-francois
Pinsent Masons LLP
London

Leaver, Peter
One Essex Court
London

Lee, Amanda
myArbitration
London

Lew, Julian
Twenty Essex Street
London

Lightfoot, Charlie
Jenner & Block
London

Limond, Katrina
Allen & Overy LLP
London

Lloyd-Williams, Mark
Arbitration Chambers
London

Lodebo, Yemi
Ethiopian Ministry of Revenues
London

Lord KC, Richard
Brick Court Chambers
London

Macdoombe, Jason
BDO LLP
London

MacPhee, Michelle
ICCA Governing Board Member
BP
London

Macpherson, Scott
Hogan Lovells International LLP
London

Madden, Penny
Gibson Dunn & Crutcher LLP
London

Maidment, Simone
TLT Solicitors
Bristol

Malas, Salah
Curtis, Mallet-Prevost, Colt & Mosle
London

Marquand, Charles
4 Stone Buildings
London

Martignoni, Andrea
Independent
London

Martinez, Lucy
Martinez Arbitration
London

Matthews, Noel
FTI Consulting
London

Mawkin, Sunil
Allen & Overy
Reading

Mayal, Montek
Osborne Partners Limited
London

McAllister, Gordon
Crowell & Moring
London

McBrayer, Mercy
Chartered Institute of Arbitrators
London

McDevitt, Matthew
BDO LLP
London

McEntegart, Tom
TLT LLP
Bristol

McKenzie, James
King & Wood Mallesons
London

McKeown, Emily
Stephenson Harwood LLP
London

McQueen, Peter
ArbDB Chambers
London

McQueen, Nick
Walker Morris LLP
Leeds

McQuitty, Jonathan
Innsworth Advisors Limited
London

Meijer, Gerard
Linklaters LLP
London

Menaker, Andrea
White & Case LLP
London

Meredith, Ian
K&L Gates LLP
London

Minaeva, Tatiana
RPC
London

Mistelis, Loukas
Clyde & Co LLP and QMUL
Virginia Water

Mitchell, David
BDO LLP
London

Mitchell, James
Maitland Chambers
London

Mizner, Andrew
CDR News
London

Moger, Christopher
4 Pump Court Chambers
London

Molloy, Matthew
MCMS
London

Montpetit, Elizabeth
Taylor Wessing LLP
London

Moollan, Salim
Brick Court Chambers
London

Moore, Christopher
Cleary Gottlieb Steen & Hamilton LLP
London

Morel, Claire
Bryan Cave Leighton Paisner
London

Morgan, Sir Paul
Wilberforce Chambers
London

Morris, Rosie
Howard Kennedy LLP
London

Mukherjee, Elora
Fieldfisher LLP
London

Murphy, Cameron
Profile Investment
London

Murphy, David
Smith & Williamson LLP
London

Nagapetyan, Lilit
CANDEY / Queen Mary University of
London
London

Nardell KC, Gordon
Twenty Essex
London

Nazzini, Renato
King's College London
London

Nesbitt KC, Simon
Maitland Chambers
London

Newing, Neil
Signature Litigation LLP
London

Nicholson KC, FCIArb, Jeremy
4 Pump Court
London

Noury, Sylvia
ICCA Governing Board Member
Freshfields Bruckhaus Deringer LLP
London

Nsofor, Amaechi
Grant Thornton UK LLP
London

Nwosu, Ugochi
Reading University
Reading

O'Callaghan, Kieron
Hogan Lovells International LLP
London

O'Donoghue, Monique
Covington
London

O'Grady, Rachael
Mayer Brown International LLP
London

Onyema, Emilia
SOAS University of London
London

O'Reilly, Ronan
Jenner & Block London LLP
London

Osman, Nesreen
Pinsent Masons LLP
Dubai

Outram, Rob
Ankura
London

Pacht, Roni
Asertis
London

Parker KC, Chris
Herbert Smith Freehills LLP
London

Parrott, Simon
EY
Bisley

Partasides KC, Constantine
ICCA Governing Board Member
Three Crowns LLP
London

Patel, Millie
Chartered Institute of Arbitrators
London

Paterson, Christopher
HKA
London

Patterson KC, Lindy
39 Essex Chambers
London

Pe, Robert
Arbitration Chambers
London

Peacock, Nick
Bird & Bird LLP
London

Peacock, Nicholas
Herbert Smith Freehills LLP
London

Pellew, Dominic
Dentons UK and Middle East LLP
London

Perry, Ben
Essex Court Chambers
London

Perry, Sebastian
Global Arbitration Review
London

Petit, Sherina
Norton Rose Fulbright LLP
London

Pillai, Rajesh
3 Verulam Buildings
London

Poirier, Genevieve
Lalive
London

Poloni, Flore
Signature Litigation
London

Pullum, Stuart
3 Verulam Buildings
London

Qureshi KC, Khawar
Mcnair International
London

Rad, Jonyar
Global Arbitration Review
London

Rahman, Ashique
Fietta LLP
London

Ramadoss, Arunn
Opus 2
London

Rawding KC, Nigel
Twenty Essex
London

Rees KC, Peter
39 Essex Chambers
London

Reeves, Catherine
Twenty Essex
London

Richards, Edmond
Accuracy
London

Rigby, Benjamin
Global Legal Post and
Arbitra International
Brentwood

Rogers, James
Norton Rose Fulbright LLP
London

Roos, Hanna
Aavagard LLP
London

Ros, Ciara
Vinson & Elkins LLP
London

Rowe, Samantha
Debevoise & Plimpton LLP
London

Rowley, William
20 Essex Chambers
London

Rubinina, Evgeniya
Enyo Law LLP
London

Ryan, Daniel
Berkeley Research Group UK Ltd
Guildford

Sabharwal KC, Dipen
White & Case LLP
London

Sachdeva, Vikram
39 Essex Chambers
London

Sanderson, Cosmo
Global Arbitration Review
London

Sanghi, Shivani
Fieldfisher LLP
London

Saunders, Matthew
Ashurst LLP
London

Scherer, Maxi
ICCA Governing Board Member
WilmerHale
London

Schuetz, Christina
Clifford Chance LLP
London

Schwarz, Franz
WilmerHale
London

Scott, Lindsay
39 Essex Chambers
London

Searle, Nathan
Hogan Lovells International LLP
London

Segal, Zachary
Mishcon de Reya LLP
London

Selvaratnam KC, Vasanti
36 Stone
London

Shah, Chiraag
Morrison & Foerster UK LLP
London

Shah, Kamal
Stephenson Harwood LLP
London

Sheppard, Audley
Vice President of ICCA
Clifford Chance LLP
London

Short, Adam
Travers Smith LLP
London

Simpson, Henry
Stephenson Harwood LLP
London

Sinclair, Anthony
Quinn Emanuel Urquhart & Sullivan, LLP
Plaxtol

Slade, Alexander
Mishcon de Reya LLP
London

Slattery, Simon
Quadrant Chambers
London

Smith, Vincent
ESCP
London

Soady, Robert
Grant Thornton UK LLP
London

Spears, Suzanne
Paxus LLP
London

Stanic, Ana
E&A Law Limited
London

Stewart, Alex
Clyde & Co LLP
London

Stokes, Paul
Mishcon De Reya LLP
London

Tarawali, Naomi
Cleary Gottlieb Steen & Hamilton LLP
London

Taylor, Patrick Samuel
Debevoise & Plimpton LLP
London

Taylor, Travis
Secretariat
Dedham

Tevendale, Craig
Herbert Smith Freehills LLP
London

Theau Laurent, Anthony
Accuracy
London

Thomas, David Brynmor
39 Essex Chambers
London

Thomas KC, Will
Freshfields Bruckhaus Deringer LLP
London

Tjegulla, Euridisa
International Arbitration Centre
London

Tonova, Sylvia
Jones Day
London

Torrealba, Jose Gregorio
Lega
London

Triantafilou, Nontas
Quinn Emanuel
London

Tse, Nicholas
Brown Rudnick LLP
London

Tune, Chris
Grant Thornton UK LLLP
London

Turner, Daniel
Grant Thornton UK LLP
Manchester

Tweedale, Jon
Addleshaw Goddard LLP
London

Uff, Alexander
Quadrant Chambers
London

Vail, Tomas
Vail Dispute Resolution
London

Vasani, Sarah
CMS Cameron McKenna Nabarro
Olswang LLP
London

Veeder, Marie
Essex Court Chambers
London

Veit, Marc
Lalive
London

Verhoosel, Gaetan
Three Crowns LLP
London

Walker, David
Deminor
London

Walmsley, Tom
Addleshaw Goddard LLP
London

Walsh, Heidrun
Mishcon De Reya LLP
London

Wasiak, Bart
Arnold & Porter
London

Wasunna, Mark
SOAS University of London
London

Webster, Peter
Essex Court Chambers
London

Weiniger, Matthew
Linklaters LLP
London

West, Chris
Grant Thornton UK LLP
London

Wheal, Robert
White & Case LLP
London

Williams, Justin
Akin Gump LLP
London

Wilmot, Daniel
Stewarts
London

Wilson, Jeremy
Covington & Burling LLP
London

Winter, Henry
Mishcon De Reya LLP (Singapore)
London

Wood, Myfanwy
Ashurst
London

Woods, Louise
Vinson & Elkins LLP
London

Yildiz, Heidi
36 Stone
London

Young, Briana
London

Yusuf, Guled
Allen & Overy LLP
London

Zaman, Rebecca
3 Verulam Buildings
London

Scotland

Andrew, Roy
FTI Consulting
Stirling

Beattie, Andy
Scottish Government
Edinburgh

Boyack, Graham
Scottish Mediation
Edinburgh

Brannigan, Gerry
HKA
Glasgow

Calvert, Julia
University of Edinburgh
Edinburgh

Cameron, Peter
University of Dundee
Edinburgh

Carmichael Lemaire, Gillian
Carmichael Lemaire Ltd
Twickenham

Clark, Alistair
College of Justice
Edinburgh

Clark, Iain
Gilson Gray LLP
Glasgow

Connal KC, Craig
RCCQC
Glasgow

Crockett, Jody
Burness Paull
Glasgow

D'Aleo, Davide
Scottish Arbitration Centre
Inverness

Daza Vargas, Ana Maria
University of Edinbugh
Newport on Tay

Devlin, Mark
RICS Scotland
Lanark

Dodds, Juliet
Scottish Arbitration Centre
Edinburgh

Douglas, Eilidh
CMS Cameron McKenna Nabarro
Olswang LLP
Edinburgh

Drennan, Andrew
HKA
Glasgow

Edward, KCMG KC, Sir David
Scottish Arbitration Centre
Edinburgh

Entwistle, Liam
Wright, Johnston & Mackenzie LLP
Glasgow

Glennie, Angus
Scottish Courts
Edinburgh

Goldie, Stephen
Brodies LLP
Edinburgh

Grahame KC FCIArb, Angela
Faculty of Advocates
Edinburgh

Hutton, Colin
CMS Cameron McKenna Nabarro
Edinburgh

Jago, Ysella
RICS
Edinburgh

Kalaitsoglou, Konstantina
University of Aberdeen
Aberdeen

Kotelnikov, Andrey
Robert Gordon University
Aberdeen

Little, Andrew
Burness Paull
Glasgow

Lockwood, Sophie
Faculty of Advocates
Edinburgh

Macdonald, Ken
Brodies LLP
Aberdeen

Macdonald KC, Alison
Essex Court Chambers
London

Mackay, Chris
Burness Paull
Edinburgh

Mackenzie, Andrew
Scottish Arbitration Centre

Mackinnon, Donny
Mackinnon Consult
Glasgow

Macneill, Calum
Faculty of Advocates
Edinburgh

Malone, Brandon
Scottish Arbitration Centre

Marks, Adam
Law Society of Scotland
Edinburgh

McCartney, Alison
CMS Cameron McKenna Nabarro
Olswang LLP
Edinburgh

Mcgiffen, Diane
Law Society of Scotland
Edinburgh

Mcmillan, Alan
Burness Paull
Edinburgh

Menzies, Fiona
Law Society of Scotland
Edinburgh

Michelakakis-Howe, Emmanuel
Scottish Arbitration Centre
Edinburgh

Milligan, Janey
Scottish Arbitration Centre
Edinburgh

Murray, Torquil
Chartered Institute of Arbitrators
Bridge of Weir

Nicolson, John
Nicolson & Co Consulting Ltd
Mauchline

Nolan, Brandon
Scottish Arbitation Centre
Edinburgh

O'Carroll, Maurice
33 Bedford Row Chambers
Edinburgh

Oyston, Jared
Brodies LLP
Edinburgh

Parratt KC, David
Faculty of Advocates / 3PB Barristers
Edinburgh

Reeves, Brian
Brian Reeves & Co
Edinburgh

Robertson, Allan
Allan Robertson Consulting Limited
Linlithgow

Rutherford, Iain
Brodies LLP
Edinburgh

Saeed, Rahaf
Scottish Arbitration Centre
Edinburgh

Struckmeier, Anne
Addleshaw Goddard LLP
Edinburgh

Sutherland, Colin
Senator of the College of Justice
Edinburgh

Sutherland, Robert
Robert Sutherland
Edinburgh

Tams, Christian J.
University of Glasgow and
Matrix Chambers
Glasgow

Tanner KC, Susanne
Ampersand Advocates
Edinburgh

Taylor, Patricia
DWF LLP and
Scottish Young Lawyers' Association
Glasgow

Thomson, James
Gilt Chambers
Edinburgh

Tyre, Colin
Scottish Supreme Courts
Edinburgh

Waughman, Kirsty
MBM Commercial LLP
Edinburgh

Webster, Sheila
Davidson Chalmers Stewart LLP
Edinburgh

Williamson, Brian
LMAA
Edinburgh

Zivkovic, Patricia
University of Aberdeen, School of Law
Aberdeen

United States

Aitelaj, Kamel
Milbank
Washington, DC

Alexandrov, Stanimir
President of ICCA
Stanimir A Alexandrov PLLC
Washington, DC

Alford, Roger
Notre Dame Law School
Notre Dame

Amirfar, Catherine
ICCA Governing Board Member
Debevoise & Plimpton LLP
New York

Aragaki, Hiro
UC Hastings College of Law & JAMS
San Francisco

Baker, Mark
Norton Rose Fulbright US LLP
Houston, Texas

Bastos Oliveira, Matheus
Freshfields Bruckhaus Deringer LLP
Washington, DC

Bejarano, Santiago
Latham & Watkins LLP
New York

Bermann, George
Columbia Law School
New York

Bishop, R. Doak
Advisory Member of ICCA
King & Spalding
Houston

Bloomenthal, Jeremy
Jeremy M. Bloomenthal, Esq.
Waltham

Bogart, Christopher
Burford Capital
New York

Borofsky, Niki
JAMS
New York

Borrasso, Ava
Ava J Borrasso PA
Miami

Bouchenaki, Amal
Herbert Smith Freehills Ny LLP
New York

Boykin, James
Hughes Hubbard & Reed LLP
Washington, DC

Brower, Charles N
International Court of Justice and
Iran-United States Claims Tribunal
Chevy Chase, Maryland

Cardani, Andrea
BRG
New York

Carter, James
Carter Arbitration
New York

Cheng, Tai-Heng
Sidley Austin LLP
New York

Chepiga, Geoffrey
Paul, Weiss, Rifkind, Wharton &
Garrison LLP
New York, NY

Chung, Kyongwha
Covington & Burling LLP
Baltimore

Cicchetti, Tina
Vancouver Arbitration Chambers
Frisco

Collins, Michael
Hanscom & Collins PA
Rockland

Commission, Jeffery
Burford Capital
Washington, DC

Compres, Tiffany
Fisherbroyles LLP
Miami

Conlon, John
Mayer Brown LLP
New York

Davidson, Robert
JAMS
New York

Day, Pete
Mercer Island Arbitration Chambers
Int'l LLC
Mercer Island

de Gramont, Alexandre
Dechert LLP
Washington, DC

Dekker, Stuart
Secretariat International

Washington, DC

Donovan, Donald
Honorary President,
Honorary Vice President and
Advisory Member of ICCA
Arbitration Chambers
New York

Draper, Matthew
Draper & Draper LLC
New York

Elul, Hagit Muriel
Hughes Hubbard & Reed LLP
New York

Enix-Ross, Deborah
Debevoise & Plimpton LLP
New York

Farhang, Suzz
American University
Washington, DC

Franck, Susan
American University
Washington College of Law
Washington, DC

Friedman, Mark W.
Debevoise & Plimpton LLP
New York

Fucci, Fred
Fucci Law & ADR, PLLC
New York

Gans, Kiera
DLA Piper LLP
New York

Gardiner, John
Skadden, Arps, Slate, Meagher & Flom
LLP
New York

Gastrell, Lindsay
Arbitration Chambers
New York

George, Glenn
Bates White Economic Consulting
Washington, DC

Gilley, Ellen
Ropes & Gray
Boston

Gilman, Luke
Jackson Walker
Houston

Glover, Aasiya
Debevoise & Plimpton LLP
New York

Gohary, Michelle
Auwcl
Oxon Hill

Goldstein, Marc
MJG Arbitration
New York

Gonzalez, Katie
Cleary Gottlieb Steen & Hamilton LLP
New York

Gusy, Martin
Bracewell LLP
New York

Hamilton, Jonathan C.
White & Case LLP
Washington, DC

Harvey, Donald T.
Secretariat
Atlanta

Haworth McCandless, Jennifer
Sidley Austin LLP
Washington, DC

Hellmann, Betsy
Skadden Arps Slate Meagher & Flom LLP
New York

Hendrix, Glenn
Arnall Golden Gregory LLP
Atlanta

Herrmann, Gerold
Honorary President and
Advisory Member of ICCA
UNCITRAL
Hillsboro Beach

Hodge, Rachael
IMS Consulting & Expert Services
Pensacola

Hodgson, Melida
Arnold & Porter Kaye Scholer LLP
New York

Hosking, James
ICCA Governing Board Member
Chaffetz Lindsey LLP
New York

Hossain, Nilufar
Omni Bridgeway
San Francisco

Howes, B. Ted
Mayer Brown LLP
New York

Hunnefeld, Angelika
Greenberg Traurig, P.A.
Miami

Isernia Dahlgren, Anna
Colorado Judicial Branch
Fort Collins

Ivers, Jennifer
White & Case LLP
Washington, DC

Johnson, Nicholas
Washington College of Law
Washington, DC

Kahn, Sherman
Mauriel Kapouytian Woods LLP
New York

Kalicki, Jean
ICCA Governing Board Member
Arbitration Chambers
New York

Kern, Jackson
ALG LLP
Washington, DC

Kerstein, Dave
Validity Finance
New York

Kinnear, Meg
Advisory Member of ICCA
ICSID
Washington, DC

Klaas, Paul
Maitland Chambers
Minneapolis, Minnesota

Klaas, Barbara
North Coast Arbitration Chambers
Minneapolis, Minnesota

Ksenofontova, Sveta
Senogles & Co
New York

Kuck, Lea Haber
Skadden, Arps, Slate, Meagher & Flom
LLP
New York

Kunsman, Isabel
Alixpartners
Washington, DC

Lahlou, Yasmine
Chaffetz Lindsey LLP
New York

Laird, Ian A.
Crowell & Moring LLP
Washington, DC

Lee, Mimi
Chevron
San Ramon

Litt, Gregory
Skadden, Arps, Slate, Meagher &
Flom LLP
New York

Llamzon, Aloysius
King & Spalding
Washington, DC

MacKinnon, Ari D.
Cleary Gottlieb
New York

Maniatis, Alexis
The Brattle Group
Washington, DC

Martinez, Luis
International Centre for Dispute Resolution
New York

Mastin, Deborah
Law Office of Deborah Mastin
Miami

Meddin, Elisabeth
Pryor Cashman
New York

Meyendorff, Anna
Bates White Economic Consulting
Washington, DC

Miles, Craig
King & Spalding
Houston

Morantz, Matthew
Paul Hastings LLP
New York

Morril, Mark
Morriladr
New York

Mouawad, Caline
Chaffetz Lindsey
New York

Nelson, Timothy
Skadden, Arps, Slate, Meagher &
Flom LLP
New York

Nolan, Michael
Arbitration Chambers
New York

Norton, Patrick M.
Arbitration Chambers
Darien

Nyer, Damien
White & Case LLP
New York

Orta, David
Quinn Emanuel Urquhart & Sullivan, LLP
Washington, DC

Oxford, Neil
Hughes Hubbard & Reed LLP
Philadelphia

Pearsall, Patrick
Allen & Overy LLP
Washington, DC

Peart, Nicola
Three Crowns LLP
Washington, DC

Permesly, Jennifer
Skadden, Arps, Slate, Meagher & Flom LLP
New York

Pierce, John V.H.
Latham & Watkins LLP
New York

Polasek, Martina
ICSID
Washington, DC

Polasek, Petr
White & Case LLP
Washington, DC

Popova, Ina
Debevoise & Plimpton LLP
New York

Prager, Dietmar
Debevoise & Plimpton LLP
New York

Ramos-Klee, Camille
Independent Tribunal Secretary
New York

Rassi, Justin
Debevoise & Plimpton LLP
New York

Reed, Lucy
Honorary President and
Governing Board Member of ICCA
Arbitration Chambers
New York

Rivkin, David W.
Debevoise & Plimpton LLP
New York

Robertson, Ann Ryan
Locke Lord LLP
Houston

Roe, Bailey
Arnold & Porter
Washington, DC

Rush, Garrett
Secretariat International
Washington, DC

Saeger, Steve
Analysis Group
Washington, DC

Schaner, Lawrence
Schaner Dispute Resolution LLC
Chicago

Schiefelbein, Lester
Schiefelbein Global Dispute Resolution
Los Gatos

Schierholz, LL.M, Miroslava
International Centre For Dispute Resolution
New York

Schill, James
Galloway Arbitration
Cle Elum

Schwartz, Eric
Schwartz Arbitration
New York

Sequeira, Kiran
Secretariat International
Washington, DC

Sicard-Mirabal, Josefa
Sicard-Mirabal ADR/
Fordham Law School
New York

Sikora, Tomasz J.
Institute For Transnational Arbitration
Humble

Silberman, Mallory
Arnold & Porter Kaye Scholer LLP
Washington, DC

Silver, Nicole
Validity Finance
New York

Simmons, Josh
Wiley Rein LLP
Washington, DC

Simson, Caroline
Law360
Manorville

Skulnik, Steven
Practical Law-Thomson Reuters
New York

Smith, Stephen
Steve Smith ADR LLC
Denver

Smutny, Abby Cohen
ICCA Treasurer
White & Case LLP
Washington, DC

Strick, Stephen
StrickADR
New York

Sussman, Edna
Sussmanadr LLC
Scarsdale

Tahbaz, Christopher
Debevoise & Plimpton LLP
New York, NY

Taylor, Greig
AlixPartners
Little Silver

Teitelbaum, Ruth
Ruth Teitelbaum PLLC
Bayside

Townsend, John
Hughes Hubbard & Reed LLP
Washington

Tuchmann, Eric
American Arbitration Association –
International Centre for Dispute
Resolution
New York

Utterback, Mary
King and Wood Mallesons
New York

Wang, Clemency
White & Case
New York

Ward, Daniel
Ropes & Gray
Boston

Weil, Kristen
Dentons
New York

Weiner, Conna
Arbitrator and Mediator
Boston

West, Briana
Cobham Advanced Electronic
Solutions Inc.
San Jose

Wilson, David
Sherman & Howard L.L.C.
Denver

Wöss, Herfried
Wöss & Partners
Washington, DC

Yeum, June
Pillsbury Winthrop / UPenn Law School
New York

Uruguay

Diaz, Soledad
FERRERE
Montevideo

Virgin Islands

Doumal, Hana
BVI International Arbitration Centre
Tortola

Leon, Barry
Arbitration Place and
33 Bedford Row
Road Town

Stephenson, Jodi-Ann
Agon Litigation
Saint Catherine

Estrada, Fransua
Superior Court of the Virgin Islands
St. Thomas

Zambia

Rattray, Suzanne
Rankin Engineering Consultants
Lusaka

1053

INTERNATIONAL COUNCIL FOR
COMMERCIAL ARBITRATION (ICCA)

Correspondence address:
ICCA Bureau
Peace Palace, Carnegieplein 2
Phone: + 31 70 302 2834
E-mail: bureau@arbitration-icca.org

LIST OF ICCA OFFICERS AND GOVERNING BOARD MEMBERS

SEPTEMBER 2023

OFFICERS

President

DR. STANIMIR A. ALEXANDROV (Washington, DC, USA)
Dr. Stanimir Alexandrov serves as an arbitrator in numerous cases administered by the International Centre for Settlement of Investment Disputes (ICSID), the International Chamber of Commerce (ICC), the London Court of International Arbitration (LCIA), and the Permanent Court of Arbitration (PCA), as well as ad hoc arbitrations under the UNCITRAL Rules. He has been appointed to the ICSID Panel of Arbitrators and is also a member of the panel of arbitrators of the Hong Kong International Arbitration Center (HKIAC), the Dubai International Arbitration Center (DIAC), the Chinese International Economic and Trade Arbitration Commission (CIETAC), and the Arbitration Center at the Institute of Modern Arbitration (Moscow).

Vice Presidents

MS. LORETTA MALINTOPPI (Singapore)
Ms. Loretta Malintoppi is dually qualified (Paris and Rome Bars) and has been registered to practise as a Foreign Lawyer in Singapore since 2012. She practised in the Paris office of Eversheds from 1991 until 2012 and thereafter in the Singapore office until 2016. Loretta joined 39 Essex Chambers in January 2017. She acts as counsel, advocate and arbitrator in international commercial and investment arbitration and has represented private companies, States and State entities in proceedings under a variety of arbitration rules, including ICSID, ICC, UNCITRAL SIAC, LCIA and DIAC.

MR. AUDLEY WILLIAM SHEPPARD KC (London, United Kingdom)
Mr. Audley Sheppard KC is a Partner of Clifford Chance LLP. He is an advocate and an arbitrator in infrastructure and investment disputes. He is also a Member of the Governing Board of ICCA, and Chair of the Advisory Council at the School of International Arbitration, Queen Mary University of London. He has been Chair of the LCIA Board and a Vice President of the LCIA Court, a Member of the ICC Court, Co-Chair of the IBA Arbitration Committee, and Rapporteur of the ILA Arbitration Committee.

Treasurer

MS. ABBY COHEN SMUTNY (Washington, DC, USA)
Ms. Abby Cohen Smutny is the Global Head of White & Case's International Arbitration Practice. She is widely recognized as one of the leading international arbitration practitioners globally. Abby's leadership positions have included: Chair of the Institute of Transnational Arbitration (ITA); Vice President of the American Society of International Law; President of LCIA North American Users Council; AAA Advisory Board Member; Vice Chair of IBA Arbitration Committee and Chair of IBA Investment Treaty Sub-Committee; ALI Adviser on US Restatement on International Arbitration; co-Chair of the ICCA Task Force on Standards of Practice in International Arbitration; and Chair International Law Section of Washington DC Bar. Abby is a member of the Court of Arbitration of the Singapore International Arbitration Centre and is a member of the Board of the Saudi Center for Commercial Arbitration.

ICCA General Editor (Ex Officio)

PROF. DR. STEPHAN W. SCHILL (Amsterdam, The Netherlands)
Prof. Dr. Stephan W. Schill is the General Editor of ICCA Publications, the Yearbook Commercial Arbitration, and the ICCA Awards Series. He is a Professor

of International and Economic Law and Governance at the University of Amsterdam, specializing in international investment law and investor-State dispute settlement and its connections to general public international law, specialized international legal regimes, such as human rights or international environmental law, regional economic integration, as well as domestic administrative and constitutional law and international commercial arbitration. He is admitted as a Rechtsanwalt to the bar in Germany and as an Attorney-at-Law in the State of New York, is a Member of the ICSID Panel of Arbitrators, and regularly sits as arbitrator in investor-State proceedings under all major institutional and ad hoc rules. He is the General Editor of *Schreuer's Commentary on the ICSID Convention* (3d ed., CUP 2022), has served as Editor-in-Chief of The Journal of World Investment and Trade (2014-2023), and has published widely on international investment law and investment arbitration.

Executive Director

MS. LISE BOSMAN (The Hague, The Netherlands)

Ms. Lise Bosman is Senior Legal Counsel at the Permanent Court of Arbitration and the Executive Director and Executive Editor at ICCA. She is also an Adjunct Professor at the University of Cape Town, a Fellow at the Association of Arbitrators (Southern Africa), serves on the Editorial Board of Tijdschrift voor Arbitrage and is a Series Editor of the PCA Award Series. She is the General Editor and contributing author to *Arbitration in Africa: A Practitioners' Guide* (2d ed., Kluwer Law International, September 2021).

GOVERNING BOARD MEMBERS

PROF. DR. MOHAMED SALAH ELDIN ABDEL WAHAB (Cairo, Egypt)

Prof. Dr. Mohamed Abdel Wahab served as Arbitrator, Legal Expert and Counsel in more than 245 cases, involving parties from Africa, Asia, Canada, Europe, the Middle East and the United States. He received the LAW Magazine 2017 Best Legal Practitioner Award, the 2018 ASA International Arbitration Advocacy Prize, the 2019 AYA Hall-of-Fame African Arbitrator Award, and the 2020 and 2021 Client Choice International Awards. He is listed in Who's Who Global Elite Thought Leaders: International Arbitration (2021 and 2022); selected among the Legal 500 Africa Powerlist (2021) and the AYA's Africa's Top 30 Powerlist (2021). He is the coeditor (with Prof Maxi Scherer and Ms Niuscha Bassiri) of *International Arbitration and the COVID-19 Revolution* (2020); co-editor (with Prof Ethan Katsh and Mr Daniel Rainey) of *Online Dispute Resolution: Theory and Practice* (2021).

MS. FUNKE ADEKOYA (Lagos, Nigeria)

Olufunke Adekoya is an independent arbitrator, having retired as Head of the Disputes Practice Group at AELEX, a Lagos, Nigeria-based law firm. She is regularly appointed as an arbitrator in commercial and investment-related disputes in the energy and construction sectors. She is a Fellow and Chartered Arbitrator of the Chartered Institute of Arbitrators and sits on the Court of the Singapore International Arbitration Centre. She is listed on the panel of arbitrators of the Kigali International Arbitration Centre, SIAC, ICSID and CIETAC amongst others. She is also a member of the African Users Council of the London Court of International Arbitration and ArbitralWomen.

MS. CATHERINE M. AMIRFAR (New York, USA)

Catherine Amirfar is Co-Chair of the International Disputes Resolution and Public International Law Groups at Debevoise & Plimpton LLP and sits as a member of the Firm's Management Committee. She is the immediate Past President of the American Society of International Law, the pre-eminent learned society in the United States dedicated to international law. With over twenty years of experience, Ms Amirfar is recognized as a top practitioner in international disputes globally. Her practice focuses on international commercial and treaty arbitration, international litigation and public international law. She regularly appears in U.S. courts and before international courts and arbitration tribunals, including the International Court of Justice (ICJ). Ms Amirfar serves as a Member of the US Department of State's Advisory Committee on International Law, the Council on Foreign Relations, the Advisory Committees of the American Law Institute for the Restatement (Fourth) of Foreign Relations Law of the United States and for the Restatement of the US Law of International Commercial Arbitration. She also serves as Co-Chair of the ICCA-ASIL Task Force on Damages in International Arbitration. She is a member of the Court of Arbitration of the Singapore International Arbitration Centre and the International Centre for Dispute Resolution of the American Arbitration Association. From 2014 to 2016, Ms Amirfar served as a Counsellor on International Law to the Legal Adviser at the US Department of State in the Obama Administration, for which she received the State Department's Superior Honour Award in recognition of her contributions to the Department.

MS. DOMITILLE BAIZEAU (Geneva, Switzerland)

Domitille Baizeau is a partner at LALIVE, based in Geneva. She has been acting as counsel and arbitrator in proceedings governed by civil law and common law and international law for over twenty years. Her areas of specialization include joint venture, M&A, shareholders, sales, distribution and investment disputes in the energy (oil & gas, solar), mining, finance and pharmaceutical sectors, as well as infrastructure projects. Domitille is a member of the International Court of Arbitration of the ICC, Vice President of the Board of Directors of the Swiss

Arbitration Centre (and past Vice President of its Arbitration Court). She also chairs the Management Board of LALIVE.

MS. JULIE BÉDARD (New York, USA)

Julie Bédard is head of Skadden's International Litigation and Arbitration Group for the Americas. Fluent in French, Spanish and Portuguese, Ms Bédard practises in four languages in complex disputes and investigations. Trained in both civil and common law, she has a doctorate in conflict of laws and represents clients in connection with litigation and arbitration proceedings throughout the world, raising disputes on governing law, jurisdiction, the enforcement of arbitration agreements, extraterritoriality and international judgment enforcement. Ms Bédard has repeatedly been recognized as a leading lawyer in a variety of legal publications, including Chambers Global, Chambers USA, Chambers Latin America, Euromoney and Latinvex.

MR. JOHN BEECHEY (London, United Kingdom)

Mr. John Beechey CBE, a past President of the ICC International Court of Arbitration, has served as chairman, party-appointed arbitrator, or sole arbitrator on international arbitral tribunals in both 'ad hoc' (including UNCITRAL) and institutional arbitrations under the Rules of all major arbitral institutions including, inter alia, the European Development Fund (EDF), ICC, ICDR/AAA, ICSID, LCIA, PCA, SIAC and Stockholm Chamber. He is the current Chairman of the Board of the British Virgin Islands International Arbitration Centre. In June 2016, he was appointed CBE (Commander of the Order of the British Empire) for services to international arbitration.

PROF. STAVROS BREKOULAKIS (London, United Kingdom)

Stavros is a Professor in International Arbitration at the Queen Mary University of London and an arbitrator practising at 3 Verulam Buildings (Gray's Inn). He has been involved in international arbitration for more than twenty years and is widely recognised as a leading authority in the field. He is regularly listed in Who's Who Legal: Arbitration, Who's Who Legal: Construction and Who's Who Legal: Thought Leader, being included in the Legal 500 Arbitration Power List and ranked as a WWL Arbitration: Global Elite Thought Leader and one of the twenty-five most highly regarded arbitrators in the EMEA region. He has been shortlisted twice for the Global Arbitration Review Best Prepared and Most Responsive Arbitrator Award and received the 2020 GAR Award for Best Public Speech.

MR. CAVINDER BULL SC (Singapore)

Mr. Cavinder Bull SC is the Chief Executive Officer of Drew & Napier LLC. He is also Vice-President of the SIAC Court of Arbitration. He is called to the bars of Singapore, New York and England and Wales. He handles both investor-state cases and commercial cases as arbitrator or counsel. He has published work in the areas of international arbitration and contract law. Beyond arbitration, he has held a number of appointments including being a member of the Securities Industries Council of Singapore and the Advisory Council to the Faculty of Law of the National University of Singapore.

PROF. DR. NAYLA COMAIR-OBEID (Dubai, United Arab Emirates)

Prof. Dr. Nayla Comair-Obeid is the Founding Partner of Obeid & Partners where she heads the firm's dispute resolution practice. She is also an associate member of 3VB Chambers in London and a Professor of International Arbitration. She has been actively involved in over 170 domestic and international commercial and investment arbitrations conducted in Arabic, French and English language whether ad hoc and or institutional (ICSID, ICC, LCIA, DIAC, CRCICA, BCDR, DIFC-LCIA, UNCITRAL, etc). Throughout her career, Professor Comair-Obeid has held and continues to hold pre-eminent positions. She has been elected the Vice Chair of the ICC Global (as of June 2022) and appointed the Chair of the Jury of the ICC Institute Prize (2023 edition). She sits, among others, as a member of the ICC Executive Board, former member of the LCIA Court, member of the CRCICA Board of Trustees, Companion of the CIArb, and member of the international commercial expert committee of China's Supreme People's Court. She has authored numerous publications, including the book 'The Law of Business Contracts in the Middle East', among others.

MR. EDUARDO DAMIÃO GONÇALVES (São Paulo, Brazil)

Mr. Eduardo Damião Gonçalves holds a Law Degree from the University of São Paulo (1994); DEA in International Private Law and International Trade from the University of Paris II - Pantheon-Assas (1997); PhD. in Private International Law from the University of São Paulo (2008) with final thesis on 'Objective Arbitra-bility'; he was a Founding Partner of BKBG Advogados (from 2004 thru 2010); and is a Partner of Mattos Filho Advogados (since 2010)

MR. NING FEI (Beijing, People's Republic of China)

Mr. Ning Fei has been practising as counsel and arbitrator in the international commercial disputes arena for over thirty years. He is a co-founder and the managing partner of Hui Zhong Law Firm, the first and leading international dispute resolution boutique based in China. He served as a member (from 2013 to 2019) of the HKIAC Council, a title vested for the first time in history to individuals from Mainland China. He is a vice chair of the International Chamber of Commerce's Belt and Road Commission. He led the endeavour to amend SCIA's arbitration rules, the first of its kind that fully integrates with international standards. During the revision of China's Arbitration Law, he directed and coordinated the submission of a thorough opinion of over 30,000 words to the Chinese legislature. He has taught a series of lectures on international arbitration at Peking University. He also frequently conducts training for young practitioners and arbitrators in the Greater China region.

DR. JUAN FERNANDEZ-ARMESTO (Madrid, Spain)

Dr. Juan Fernandez-Armesto is a professional arbitrator and specializes in commercial, investment and construction arbitration. He has extensive experience in both Spanish domestic arbitrations as well as international arbitrations administered by bodies such as the ICC, LCIA, VIAC, DIAC and ad hoc arbitrations under the UNCITRAL Rules. He has been President of the Spanish Securities and Exchange Commission (CNMV) (1996-2000), partner of Uría Menéndez (1983-1996) and Chaired Professor of Commercial Law (1988-2009).

MS. JUDITH GILL KC (Singapore)

Ms. Judith Gill is recognised as one of the leading practitioners in international arbitration. She was a partner in the global law firm Allen & Overy for more than twenty-five years and was Head of the International Arbitration Group for eleven years. She moved to Singapore in September 2015 and joined Twenty Essex Chambers in Singapore in May 2018. Since May 2022, she has practised exclusively as an independent arbitrator and has extensive experience in matters involving construction, energy contracts, manufacturing, distributorship agreements and other commercial agreements. She is the immediate past President of the LCIA Court. She was the second female solicitor-advocate to be appointed KC in England.

MS. SAMAA A. HARIDI (New York, USA)

Samaa A. Haridi is a common and civil law-trained, trilingual partner at King & Spalding. Ms Haridi has significant experience representing clients in multi-jurisdictional international commercial and investment arbitration proceedings under the arbitration rules of all the major arbitral institutions. Ms Haridi also frequently sits as an arbitrator in international commercial and investment disputes. Ms Haridi is a member of the bars of New York, California, and England and Wales. She is fluent in French and Arabic and is also conversant in Spanish.

MR. KARL HENNESSEE (Blagnac, France)

Karl Hennessee, FRAeS, is Senior Vice President, Litigation, Investigations & Regulatory Affairs at Airbus, where he leads the Group's global activities in these areas. Separately, he occasionally sits as arbitrator and serves on the board of directors of companies and nonprofits. Until July 2019, he also served as Chairman of the Governing Body of the ICC Court of International Arbitration and is now a member of the HKIAC Council as well as its Proceedings Committee. He also serves on the Advisory Council for the School of International Arbitration at the Queen Mary University of London.

MR. JAMES HOSKING (New York, USA)

James Hosking has been practising in the international disputes arena for over twenty-five years. As co-founder of the international dispute resolution boutique Chaffetz Lindsey, he leads the firm's international arbitration team. James's practice has seen him appear in over one hundred arbitrations as counsel, while he also sits as arbitrator in commercial and investor-state cases. He is an adjunct professor at NYU School of Law, co-author of the leading Commentary on the ICDR International Rules, and a Fellow of the Arbitrators and Mediators Institute of New Zealand. James was previously a partner in a leading international firm and also practised in New Zealand.

MR. ANDRÉS JANA (Santiago, Chile)

Mr. Andrés Jana is a litigation and arbitration partner at the Chilean law firm of Bofill Mir & Alvarez Jana and a Professor at Universidad de Chile. He has wide experience in international disputes, as a lawyer, arbitrator, and expert. These disputes involved international arbitration as well as international public law issues and have been carried out, among others, before the ICJ, ICSID, ICC, LCIA, AAA, and SCC. He is the Chilean delegate before UNCITRAL and has been elected to Chair the WGII work on Expedited Proceedings in International Arbitration. He is on the Chilean List of Arbitrators for ICSID, is a former member of the LCIA, former Vice Chair of the IBA Arbitration Committee, and former Chair of the ITA Americas Initiative.

MS. DYALÁ JIMÉNEZ (San José, Costa Rica)

Dyalá Jiménez is a Costa Rican national who specializes in international arbitration. She is frequently appointed as arbitrator in institutional and ad hoc arbitrations, both in commercial and investor-State disputes. She is a member of the ICSID panel of conciliators and arbitrators for Costa Rica and of the ICC International Court of Arbitration. She is a Fulbright Scholar and alumnus of Georgetown University Law Center, is the author of numerous publications (visit www.djarbitraje.com) and has taught at several universities. Dyalá served as Minister of Foreign Trade of Costa Rica (2018-2020).

MS. JEAN ENGELMAYER KALICKI (New York, USA)

Jean Kalicki is an independent arbitrator associated with Arbitration Chambers, specializing in investment disputes and complex international cases; until 2016, she was a Partner at Arnold & Porter LLP. She is a member of the ICC Commission and formerly was a Vice President of the LCIA and member of the AAA Board and Council. She is regularly ranked in Chambers' Band 1 ('Most In-Demand' Arbitrators) for both Global Arbitration and Public International Law and was its only 'Star Arbitrator' (above Band 1) in the USA for 2019-2020. Best Lawyers in America has named her 'Lawyer of the Year' five times in her jurisdiction and practice; Who's Who Legal annually lists her as a 'Thought Leaders: Global Elite'; and Global Arbitration Review named her the 'Best Prepared/Most Responsive Arbitrator' worldwide in 2017.

MR. VLADIMIR KHVALEI (Moscow, Russian Federation)

Mr. Vladimir Khvalei is a senior partner at Mansors Law Firm. Mr Khvalei has significant experience participating in litigation both in Russia and abroad and representing Russian and foreign companies operating in various industries, including oil and gas, construction, banking and others in complex international disputes. Mr Khvalei has also acted as counsel and arbitrator in international cases under a wide range of arbitration rules including those of UNCITRAL, ICC, LCIA, SCC, MKAS, HKIAC, ICAC, CRCICA, ICSID and other arbitration institutions. Mr Khvalei is included in the lists of various arbitral institutions in Russia, Austria, Azerbaijan, the Republic of Belarus, Kazakhstan, Kyrgyzstan, UAE, China, Hong Kong, South Korea, Malaysia, Singapore, Vietnam, the US and Israel.

MR. TOBY LANDAU KC (Singapore)

Mr. Toby Landau KC is a barrister, advocate and arbitrator practising as a sole practitioner in London and as a member of Duxton Hill Chambers (Singapore Group Practice) in Singapore. He specialises in international arbitration and has argued hundreds of major international commercial, investor-State and inter-state arbitrations, as well as ground-breaking cases in the courts of numerous jurisdictions. As Arbitrator, he has extensive experience under most of the world's leading ad hoc and institutional rules and is a member of various panels including ICSID. He is on the Panel of Advisers to the Attorney-General of Singapore; Visiting Professor at Kings College London; Vice President of the SIAC Court of Arbitration; and a draftsman of arbitration legislation in a number of jurisdictions.

MS. MICHELLE AMANDA MACPHEE (London, United Kingdom)

Ms. Michelle MacPhee has over twenty-five years of experience in international commercial arbitration and dispute resolution. She is currently the Managing

Counsel of BP Legal's London-based Dispute Resolution Team and also heads BP Legal's International Arbitration Centre of Expertise. Prior to joining BP in 2010, she was of Counsel in Freshfields Bruckhaus Deringer's London International Arbitration Group. Her current responsibilities at BP include identifying, evaluating and managing legal, financial, business operation and reputational risks relating to all manner of major commercial disputes and potential disputes arising from BP's global businesses and Group level activities.

MS. CAROLE MALINVAUD (Paris, France)

Ms. Carole Malinvaud is a partner at Gide in Paris, where she co-heads the international arbitration section of the firm and chairs the Gide Pro Bono Foundation. She is a member of the Paris and New York Bars and has acted as counsel or arbitrator in over eighty international arbitration proceedings either ad hoc or institutional, as well as before domestic French courts in relation to international litigations and arbitrations. She is the current Vice Chair of the ICC Court (2021-2024); she was Chair of the ICC France (2013-2020), a member of the LCIA Court, a member of the International Council of Arbitration for Sport (ICAS), and Chair of the Ordinary Chamber of the Court for Arbitration for Sport (CAS).

MR. FERNANDO MANTILLA-SERRANO (Paris, France)

Mr. Fernando Mantilla-Serrano is a partner and co-chair of the International Arbitration Practice at Latham & Watkins. He has served as both lead counsel and arbitrator under the ICC, ICSID, LCIA, SCC, ICDR, IACAC, UNCITRAL and EDF arbitration rules. Mr Mantilla-Serrano is fellow of the Chartered Institute of Arbitrators (FCIArb), member of the International Law Association (ILA) and of the Court of Arbitration of the Singapore International Arbitration Centre (SIAC). Mr Mantilla-Serrano is admitted to the bars of Colombia, New York (USA), Paris (France) and Madrid (Spain).

MS. ZIA JAYDEV MODY (Mumbai, India)

Ms. Zia Mody is the Founder and Senior Partner of AZB & Partners. She was the former Deputy Chairman and a Non-Executive Director, HSBC Asia Pacific Board, a former Member of the World Bank Administrative Tribunal, and former Vice President and member of the LCIA. She was also a member of the Committee on Corporate Governance formed by the Securities and Exchange Board of India (SEBI), the Godrej Committee on Corporate Governance and the Reserve Bank of India Committee on Comprehensive Financial Services for Small Businesses and Low-Income Households.

DR. MICHAEL JOSEPH MOSER (Hong Kong SAR)

Dr. Michael Moser practises as an international arbitrator with 20 Essex Street Chambers and is a Chartered Arbitrator and Fellow of the Chartered Institute of Arbitrators. He is a current board member of the Singapore International Arbitration Centre (SIAC), the Vienna International Arbitral Centre (VIAC) and a Commission Member of CIETAC. He is an Honorary Past Chairman of the Hong Kong International Arbitration Centre and a past member of the LCIA Court and of the Stockholm SCC Arbitration Institute Board. He is the author of many books and articles, co-editor of *The Asia Arbitration Handbook* (Oxford Univ. Press, 2011) and former General Editor of the Journal of International Arbitration.

MS. SYLVIA NOURY KC (London, United Kingdom)

Ms. Sylvia Noury is a partner at Freshfields Bruckhaus Deringer where she heads the International Arbitration Group in London. Her practice focuses on high-stakes international commercial and treaty arbitration in high-risk jurisdictions. She is a Member of the Board of the Arbitration Institute of the Stockholm Chamber of Commerce (SCC); the Advisory Council of Africa Arbitration; the ITA Advisory Board and a former Member of the Arbitration Committee and Nominations Sub-Committee of the ICC UK. She is the Founder and Co-Chair of the Equal Representation in Arbitration Pledge.

MR. JOHN MORRIS OHAGA (Nairobi, Kenya)

John Ohaga is the Managing Partner in the law firm of TripleOKLaw LLP. He holds an LLM in International Dispute Resolution from the Queen Mary University of London. He is a Senior Counsel and a Chartered Arbitrator.

MS. YOSHIMI OHARA (Tokyo, Japan)

Ms. Yoshimi Ohara is a partner at Nagashima Ohno & Tsunematsu in Tokyo, Japan. She served as counsel in international arbitration under the rules of the ICC, ICSID, AAA/ICDR, SIAC and JCAA. She also served as co-arbitrator, sole arbitrator, and presiding arbitrator under rules of the ICC, SIAC, JCAA, KCAB, ICDR and UNCITRAL. She is a member of the Board of the Swiss Arbitration Association (ASA) and a member of the Executive Director of the Japan Association of Arbitrators (JAA). She is a former Vice President of the London Court of International Arbitration (LCIA) and the ICC International Court of Arbitration. She is admitted to the Japanese Bar and the New York Bar and has an LLM from Harvard Law School.

MR. CONSTANTINE PARTASIDES KC (London, United Kingdom)

Mr. Constantine Partasides KC has appeared as counsel on some of the largest commercial arbitrations of the last decade, many of which relate to the energy sector. He has been named as one of the 'top 20' individuals in the world of arbitration each year since 2011 in 'Who's Who' of Commercial Arbitration. He is a co-author of the fourth, fifth and sixth editions of the leading textbook on international arbitration, *Redfern and Hunter on International Arbitration*. He is a solicitor-advocate (Higher Courts Civil) and was appointed Queen's Counsel in 2014.

MS. LUCY REED (New York, USA)

Ms. Lucy Reed, the Immediate Past President of ICCA, currently is an independent arbitrator with Arbitration Chambers in New York. From 2016-2019, Lucy was the Director of the Centre for International Law and Professor of Practice at the National University of Singapore and, before her retirement in 2016, led the global international arbitration group of Freshfields Bruckhaus Deringer. Now the President of the SIAC Court, Lucy has served as a Vice President of the ICC Court, Chair of the Institute for Transnational Arbitration, and President of the American Society of International Law.

PROF. DR. KLAUS SACHS (Munich, Germany)

Prof. Dr. Klaus Sachs is a senior partner at CMS Hasche Sigle and an honorary professor of international arbitration law at the Ludwig-Maximilian-University of Munich. He has more than twenty-five years of experience as chairman, sole arbitrator, co-arbitrator and counsel in more than 200 national and international arbitrations concerning commercial and investment disputes. He is a member of the board of the German Arbitration Institute (DIS). He is a former Vice President of the ICC International Court of Arbitration and a former Vice President of the London Court of International Arbitration. He is also on the Panel of Arbitrators maintained by ICSID and is a co-editor of the German Arbitration Journal.

PROF. DR. MAXI SCHERER (London, United Kingdom)

Professor Maxi Scherer is a Special Counsel at Wilmer Cutler Pickering Hale and Dorr LLP in London and a Professor of Law at the Queen Mary University of London, where she holds the Chair for International Arbitration, Dispute Resolution and Energy Law. She has practised international arbitration for more than twenty years and represented clients, serving as arbitrator or legal expert in more than 120 commercial and investor-State arbitrations. She is Vice President of the London Court of International Arbitration (LCIA), a member of the Governing Board of International Council for Commercial Arbitration (ICCA), a co-chair of the IBA Investment Arbitration Subcommittee and holds many other public appointments and commissions of trust, including being a member of the panel of arbitrators (ICSID). Maxi has been regularly ranked by Who's Who Legal, Chambers, The Legal 500, BestLawyer etc. as leading arbitration practitioner and is identified amongst the top 'Global Elite Thought Leaders' in the field.

PROF. HI-TAEK SHIN (Seoul, Republic of Korea)

Prof. Hi-Taek Shin is a professor (emeritus) at Seoul National University School of Law. He is an arbitrator at Twenty Essex Chambers (practice based in Seoul). He has taught the resolution of commercial and investment disputes arising from cross-border transactions. Prior to moving to academia, he was a partner at Kim & Chang, the leading Korean law firm. He regularly sits as an arbitrator both in international investment treaty arbitrations and international commercial arbitrations.

MR. EDUARDO SIQUEIROS (Mexico City, Mexico)

Mr. Eduardo Siqueiros is an independent arbitrator and a part-time Professor and lecturer in Mexican law schools. He has authored articles on the subject of arbitration, corporate law, trade and investment. He has been included in Band 1 in Chambers and Partners Global and Latin America (2010-2015), and Legal 500 Latin America (2013-2015). He is also a member of the Mexican Arbitration Institute (IMA), the Mexican Arbitration Committee (ICC) and is on the Panel of Arbitrators, ICSID.

DR. CLAUS WERNER VON WOBESER (Mexico City, Mexico)

Claus von Wobeser is the Founding Partner of Von Wobeser y Sierra. He has acted in over 200 international arbitration proceedings and has served as Vice President of the International Court of Arbitration of the ICC, Co-Chair of the IBA Arbitration Committee, President of the Arbitration Commission of ICC Mexico, Member of the Panel of Arbitrators of ICSID, Member of the London Court of International Arbitration, Member of the Board of Directors of the AAA, and as a Member of the ICC Court. In 1994 he founded and since teaches in the diploma course on arbitration co-organized by the Escuela Libre de Derecho and ICC México. Currently, he serves as President of ALARB and ICC Mexico. He studied law at Escuela Libre de Derecho in Mexico City and for a PhD at Université de Paris 2, Sorbonne.

Honorary Presidents

PROF. ALBERT JAN VAN DEN BERG (Brussels, Belgium)

Professor Albert Jan van den Berg is a partner at Hanotiau & van den Berg (Brussels, Belgium). He served as President of ICCA from 2014-2016. He is a Visiting Professor at Georgetown University Law Center, Tsinghua University School of Law and University of Miami School of Law; Emeritus Professor (Arbitration Chair) at Erasmus University, Rotterdam; and member of the faculty of the University of Geneva Master in International Dispute Settlement Program. He is Honorary President of the Netherlands Arbitration Institute and former Vice President of the London Court of International Arbitration. Professor van den

Berg has published extensively on international arbitration (see www.hvdb.com), in particular, the New York Convention of 1958 (see www.newyorkconvention.org).

MR. DONALD FRANCIS DONOVAN (New York, USA)

Mr. Donovan is Co-Head of the International Disputes Group at Debevoise & Plimpton LLP and teaches International Arbitration and International Investment Law and Arbitration at the New York University School of Law. He is also a visiting professor at the School of International Arbitration at the Queen Mary University of London. He serves as a member of the U.S. Secretary of State's Advisory Committee on International Law, a member of the Advisory Committees of the American Law Institute for the Restatement of US Foreign Relations Law and for the Restatement of the US Law of International Commercial Arbitration (ITA), and he has also served as an Alternate Member of the ICC International Court of Arbitration.

DR. GEROLD HERRMANN (Vienna, Austria)

Dr. Gerold Herrmann was President of ICCA from 2002 until 2010. Until his retirement in 2001, he worked for twenty-six years for UNCITRAL (United Nations Commission on International Trade Law), the last ten years thereof as its Director. His major achievement was the elaboration and promulgation of the UNCITRAL Model Law and the concomitant assistance in establishing or internationalising arbitration centres all over the world. Dr Herrmann is Honorary Professor of Vienna University, Honorary Vice President of the LCIA Court and former President of the LCIA Court. In 2001, INSOL International presented to him the Scroll of Honour and the International Insolvency Institute honoured him in 2006 with the Outstanding Contributions Award.

PROF. DR. GABRIELLE KAUFMANN-KOHLER (Geneva, Switzerland)

Prof. Dr. Gabrielle Kaufmann-Kohler is a Founding Partner of Lévy Kaufmann-Kohler and has extensive experience as an international arbitrator. She is also Professor Emerita at Geneva University, and Visiting Professor at various universities, including NUS, Sciences Po Paris and MIDS. She is Honorary President of ICCA, the Swiss Arbitration Association (ASA), as well as the founder and former director of the Geneva LLM in International Dispute Settlement (MIDS).

MR. FALI S. NARIMAN (New Delhi, India)

Mr. Fali Nariman is a Senior Advocate of the Supreme Court of India and President Emeritus of the Bar Association of India. He is an Honorary Member of the International Commission of Jurists; a past President of the Law Association for Asia and the Pacific (LAWASIA); a Member of the Court of the LCIA; a past

Vice Chairman International Court of Arbitration of the International Chamber of Commerce (ICC); and a past Co-Chair of the Human Rights Institute of the IBA.

PROF. JAN PAULSSON (Manama, Bahrain)
Judge, Bahrain Court of Cassation (authorised to act in personal capacity in international arbitrations). Past positions: Partner successively in Coudert Frères, Freshfields Bruckhaus Deringer. and Three Crowns; President, ICCA, LCIA & World Bank Administrative Tribunal; Vice-President, ICC Court of International Arbitration; Member, SIAC Court of Arbitration; tenured professor at the University of Miami; Centennial Professor, London School of Economics. Law degrees: Yale, Paris.

MS. LUCY REED (New York, USA)
[Governing Board Member; see details at p. 1066.]

Honorary Vice Presidents

MR. DONALD FRANCIS DONOVAN (New York, USA)
[Honorary President, Honorary Vice President and Advisory Board Member; see details at p. 1068.]

DR. MICHAEL HWANG SC (Singapore)
Dr. Michael Hwang SC currently practises as a Barrister, primarily servicing lawyers as International Arbitrator and (selectively) as Leading Counsel. He has served as Chief Justice of the Dubai International Financial Centre (DIFC) Courts, as a Judicial Commissioner (Contract Judge for a fixed period) of the High Court of Singapore, as President of the Law Society of Singapore, and as Singapore's Non-Resident Ambassador to Switzerland and Argentina.

MRS. TINUADE OYEKUNLE (Lagos, Nigeria)
Mrs. Tinuade Oyekunle is the managing partner and founder of Tinuade Oyekunle & Co, (Now known as Sonotina Chambers). She is a seasoned Chartered Arbitrator, handling complex national and international commercial arbitration disputes. She has been appointed in disputes under the auspices of the ICC, ICSID, and other arbitration institutions. She is a member of the Governing Council of the Lagos International Centre for Commercial Arbitration. Tinuade is an ardent participant in discussions dealing with issues relating to development of ADR and enforcement of Awards. Mrs Tinuade Oyekunle, with her colleague Chief Bayo Ojo SAN, co-authored the 'Handbook on Arbitration and ADR Practice in Nigeria', published by LexisNexis in January 2019.

Honorary Secretary General

MR. ANTONIO RICARDO PARRA (Easton, USA)
> Mr. Antonio R. Parra was Secretary General of ICCA from 2004 to 2010. He is currently an Ethics Adviser under the Code of Conduct for Board Officials of the World Bank Group. His earlier positions include Deputy Secretary-General, ICSID, Legal Adviser, ICSID, Senior Counsel, World Bank, and Counsel, World Bank.

Advisory Members

DR. MOHAMED ABDEL RAOUF (Sheikh Zayed, Egypt)
> Partner, Abdel Raouf Law Firm (Egypt); Associate Professor, Université Paris 1 Panthéon-Sorbonne; Vice Chairman of the Board of Trustees and Member of the Advisory Committee of the CRCICA; Alternate Member ICC Court; Chairman of the Egypt Branch of the Chartered Institute of Arbitrators (CIArb); Member of the Arbitration Committee of the Lagos Court of Arbitration (LCA); Member of the Board of Directors of the Saudi Center for Commercial Arbitration (SCCA); Arbitrator, Court of Arbitration for Sport (CAS); Conciliator, ICSID Panel of Conciliators; CEDR Accredited Mediator; Director of the CRCICA (2012-2016); Member of the Board of the Arbitration Institute of the Stockholm Chamber of Commerce, SCC (2012-2017); Vice President, the International Federation of Commercial Arbitration Institutions, IFCAI (2011-2015).

MR. CECIL WILBERT MOHANARAJ ABRAHAM (Kuala Lumpur, Malaysia)
> Cecil Abraham, Senior Partner of Cecil Abraham & Partners, is a Barrister and a Bencher of the Middle Temple. He is a Fellow of Queen Mary & Westfield College, the Chartered Institute of Arbitrators U.K., Malaysian Institute of Arbitrators, Singapore Institute of Arbitrators, and the Australian Centre for International Commercial Arbitration. He is a Chartered Arbitrator and is a member of various arbitral tribunals. Cecil has an extensive arbitration practice and appears as counsel in domestic and international arbitrations. Cecil is a Member of the ICSID panel.

MR. MAKHDOOM ALI KHAN (Karachi, Pakistan)
> Mr. Makhdoom Ali Khan is a Senior Advocate of the Supreme Court of Pakistan and a former Attorney General for Pakistan. He has appeared in many important commercial cases before the High Courts and the Supreme Court. He also sits as an arbitrator in ad hoc and institutional domestic, international commercial, and investment arbitrations. He was a member of the Court of the London Court of International Arbitration and is a member of the Board of AAA. He is a former

Member of the Board of DIAC. He is on the panel of arbitrators of SIAC and KLRCA and has been designated as an arbitrator on the ICSID panel.

PROF. ALBERT JAN VAN DEN BERG (Brussels, Belgium)
[Honorary President of ICCA; see details at p. 1067.]

MR. DOAK BISHOP (Houston, USA)

Mr. Doak Bishop is a partner in King & Spalding's Houston office and co-chairs the Firm's International Arbitration Practice Group. He has served as both an arbitrator and counsel under the auspices of ICSID, the ICC, LCIA, UNCITRAL, ICDR, AAA, IACAC, and CPR, as well as in ad hoc arbitrations. He has served as Chairman of the Institute of Transnational Arbitration, Advisor to the American Law Institute's Restatement of Law (3rd) of International Commercial Arbitration, a member of the Board of Directors of AAA, as a member of the Courts of the LCIA and of the Singapore International Arbitration Centre, as a member of the Executive Committee of ASIL, and others.

PROF. DR. KARL-HEINZ BÖCKSTIEGEL (Frankenforst, Germany)

Prof. Dr. Karl-Heinz Bockstiegel is an arbitrator, sole practitioner and member of the Law Faculty of the University of Cologne as Professor Emeritus. He has practised as parties' counsel, as mediator, and as arbitrator and president of arbitration tribunal in many national and international arbitrations of the ICC, ICSID, NAFTA, AAA, SCC, UNCITRAL, and others. He is a Past Patron of the Chartered Institute of Arbitrators; Honorary Chairman (Chairman 1996-2012), German Arbitration Institute (DIS); President, International Law Association (ILA) 2004-2006; and President, German Association for International Law 1993-2006. In view of his age, in 2018 he stopped accepting new arbitrator appointments, and by the end of 2019, he resigned from the remaining cases still pending at that time. In 2021, the https://khboeckstiegel-foundation was created.

MS. ADRIANA BRAGHETTA (São Paulo, Brazil)

Ms. Adriana Braghetta is the founding partner at Adriana Braghetta Advogados. She was formerly the Co-Head of the arbitration group at LOBaptista-SVMFA. She also formerly served as President of CBAr - 'Comitê Brasileiro de Arbitragem' (2009-2013), having previously served as Vice-President (2005-2009) and co-founding member. She is a member of the ILA International Arbitration Committee, ICC Arbitration Commission, ICC Latin-American Arbitration Commission, and ICDR/AAA Board for Latin America. She is also a member of different commissions in other institutions such as CCBC, CIESP, and AMCHAM-SP. She is a Professor at FGV/SP and CEU-IICS and a member of the editorial council of CBAr journal.

PROF. DR. NAEL GEORGES BUNNI (Dublin, Ireland)

Prof. Dr. Nael G. Bunni is a Chartered Engineer, Chartered Arbitrator, Conciliator/Mediator, and Visiting Professor in Construction Law and Contract Administration at Trinity College Dublin. He is currently a member of the Commission on International Arbitration of the ICC and is involved in many of its Standing Committees; since September 2009, a special advisor of FIDIC's Contracts Committee.

MS. TERESA CHENG (Hong Kong SAR)

Ms. Teresa Cheng is Senior Counsel of Hong Kong SAR and served as the founding Chairman of the Asian Academy of International Law. She was the Vice President of ICCA, Deputy President in 2007 and President in 2008 of the Chartered Institute of Arbitrators, and Vice-President, the ICC Court of International Arbitration. She established the International Arbitration and Dispute Settlement Program at the Law School of Tsinghua University and served as Course Director and adjunct Professor. She also sat as a Recorder in the Court of First Instance of the High Court and served as the Secretary for the Justice of Hong Kong.

PROF. BERNARDO CREMADES (Madrid, Spain)

Prof. Bernardo Cremades is a lawyer, arbitrator and senior partner of B. Cremades y Asociados. He is a Professor of International Business Law at Universidad de Madrid and is a member of the Institute of World Business Law of the ICC. He is the leading Spanish international arbitration practitioner ('number one practitioner in Spain for commercial arbitration legal expertise' and 'one of the top names in the industry', Who's Who Legal, July 2005). His international recognition includes Germany's distinguished Verdienstkreuz award and the French distinction of Chevalier de l'Ordre National du Mérite.

MR. DUSHYANT DAVE (New Delhi, India)

Mr. Dushyant Dave is a Senior Lawyer practising in the Supreme Court of India and the High Courts across the country. He joined the Bar in 1978 and practised in the Gujarat High Court till 1986 and then moved to Delhi. His practice over a span of more than four decades involves various branches of law including Civil Laws, Criminal Laws and Corporate Laws. He has appeared in a large number of matters involving Constitutional and Public Law issues as well as issues including Fundamental Rights and Civil Liberties of citizens. He has defended many citizens and their causes pro bono. He actively participates in the field of International Commercial Arbitration and has been on the board of the American Arbitration Association (AAA') and the London Court of International Arbitration (LCIA).

MR. YVES DERAINS (Paris, France)

Mr. Yves Derains is Partner of Derains & Gharavi, Paris. Honorary Chairman of the ICC Institute of World Business Law, former Chairman of the Comité Français de l'Arbitrage and Co-Chairman of the ICC Working Group on the reduction of costs and time in international Arbitration. Past Secretary General, International Court of Arbitration of the International Chamber of Commerce (ICC) and Member of the Paris Bar. He has acted as counsel or arbitrator in more than 200 international proceedings throughout the world. He is the author of many publications on international arbitration.

MR. DONALD FRANCIS DONOVAN (New York, USA)

[Honorary President, Honorary Vice President and Advisory Board Member; see details at p. 1067.]

HON. L. YVES FORTIER, PC, CC, OQ, KC (Montréal, Canada)

Hon. L. Yves Fortier is currently the judge ad hoc of the International Court of Justice in The Hague. He was Chairman Emeritus and Senior Partner of Norton, Rose, Fulbright until 2012. In 2013, he became the Founding Partner of the Cabinet Yves Fortier in Montreal. Since 1992, he has acted as arbitrator and mediator in many major international arbitrations under the auspices of the ICC, LCIA, AAA, ICSID, CAS and others. From 1988 to 1992, he was Canada's Ambassador and Permanent representative to the United Nations in New York. In 1989, he was President of the Security Council. From 1998 to 2001, he was President of the LCIA. From 2013 to 2017, he was Chairman of the Sanctions Board of the World Bank and he presently serves as Chairman of the Enforcement Committee of the European Bank for Reconstruction and Development. Mr Fortier is a Companion of the Order of Canada (C.C.) and an officer of the Ordre du Québec (O.Q.).

PROF. DR. BERNARD HANOTIAU (Brussels, Belgium)

Prof. Dr. Bernard Hanotiau is a member of the Brussels and Paris Bars. He is a founding partner of Hanotiau & van den Berg. Since 1978, he has been actively involved in more than 600 international arbitration cases as party-appointed arbitrator, chairman, sole arbitrator, counsel and expert in all parts of the world. He is professor emeritus of the law school of Louvain University (Belgium). He is a member of the Council of the ICC Institute. He is also a former Vice-President of the Institute of Transnational Arbitration (Dallas) and a former Vice President of the LCIA Court. He is a member of the Court of Arbitration of SIAC, of the Consultative Board of HKIAC and a former Vice President of the Governing Board of DIAC (Dubai).

HON. DOMINIQUE T. HASCHER (Paris, France)

Judge Dominique Hascher is a Judge on the Supreme Judicial Court of France. Previously, he served as General Counsel and Deputy-Secretary General at the International Court of Arbitration of the International Chamber of Commerce, Hon. Bencher of Gray's Inn in London.

DR. GEROLD HERRMANN (Vienna, Austria)

[Honorary President of ICCA; see details at p. 1068.]

DR. MICHAEL HWANG SC (Singapore)

[Honorary Vice President of ICCA; see details at p. 1069.]

MR. NEIL KAPLAN CBE, KC, SBS (Melbourne, Australia)

Mr. Neil Kaplan is an arbitrator with Arbitration Chambers in both England and Hong Kong. Mr Kaplan was the Chairman of Hong Kong's WTO Review Body on Bid Challenges from 2000 to 2004 and was formerly Chairman of Hong Kong's Telecommunications (Competition Provision) Appeal Board. He is a Fellow of the Chartered Institute of Arbitrators and is a Chartered Arbitrator. He is also a Fellow of the Hong Kong Institute of Arbitrators as well as a panellist of CIETAC. In June 2001, he was awarded a CBE for services to international arbitration. In 2007, he was awarded the Silver Bauhinia Star by the Chief Executive of the Hong Kong SAR.

PROF. GABRIELLE KAUFMANN-KOHLER (Geneva, Switzerland)

[Honorary President of ICCA; see details at p. 1068.]

DR. FATHI KEMICHA (Les Berges du Lac, Tunis, Tunisia)

Dr. Fathi Kemicha is the founder of Kemicha Legal Consulting K.L.C. He has acted as arbitrator and counsel in numerous institutional and ad hoc commercial arbitrations. He is a former member of the United Nations International Law Commission (ILC) and the World Bank Group Sanctions Board. He served as Vice-Chairman of the Commission on Arbitration at the International Chamber of Commerce (ICC) and was also a member of the Dubai International Arbitration Centre (DIAC) Board of Trustees. He was made Knight of the French Legion of Honor by President Jacques Chirac, President of the French Republic, and awarded by His Majesty King Hamad Bin Isa Al Khalifa, the King of the Kingdom of Bahrain, 'The Order of Bahrain' (First Class).

MR. KAP-YOU (Kevin) Kim (Seoul, Republic of Korea)

Kap-You (Kevin) is a senior founding partner at Peter & Kim in Seoul, a dispute resolution practice with offices in Korea, Switzerland, Australia and Singapore. Over the past thirty years, he has acted as counsel, presiding arbitrator, co-arbitrator and sole arbitrator in more than 300 cases of international arbitration under various arbitration rules.

MS. MEG KINNEAR (Washington, DC, USA)

Ms. Meg Kinnear is currently the Secretary-General of the International Centre for Settlement of Investment Disputes (ICSID) at the World Bank. She was formerly the Senior General Counsel and Director General of the Trade Law Bureau of Canada, where she was responsible for the conduct of all international invest-ment and trade litigation involving Canada. Prior to this, she was Executive Assistant to the Deputy Minister of Justice of Canada and Counsel at the Civil Litigation Section of the Canadian Department of Justice.

PROF. ALEXANDER SERGEEVICH KOMAROV (Moscow, Russian Federation)

Prof. Alexander Komarov is currently Professor of International Private Law Chair at the Russian Academy of Foreign Trade and a Member of the Consultative Council at the Supreme Court of the Russian Federation. He is a CIArb Fellow and Chartered Arbitrator. He is also a member of the Presidium of the International Commercial Arbitration Court at the Chamber of Commerce and Industry of the Russian Federation. He was a Vice-President of the International Federation of Commercial Arbitration Institutions, an LCIA Member, and a Member of the Board of the Arbitration Institute of the Stockholm Chamber of Commerce.

MS. CAROLYN BETH LAMM (Washington, DC, USA)

Ms. Carolyn Lamm is a Partner at White & Case LLP and Distinguished Faculty Chair of the LLM Program in International Arbitration and Visiting Professor at the University of Miami. She is also the Chair of International Arbitration Americas and of the American-Uzbekistan Chamber of Commerce. She is a Member of the Board of the American-Turkish Council and American Indonesian Chamber of Commerce. She is a Member of the ICSID Panel of Arbitrators, a member of the ICDR International List, the American Law Institute's Council and its Advisory Committee on Restatement on International Arbitration and the US member of the NAFTA 2022 Committee.

CHIEF JUSTICE SUNDARESH MENON (Singapore)

Chief Justice of the Supreme Court of Singapore, Sundaresh Menon previously held office as Judge of Appeal and as Attorney-General of Singapore. He is a former Judicial Commissioner of the Supreme Court of Singapore. He previously served as Dy Chairman of the Singapore International Arbitration Centre and worked as Managing Partner at Rajah & Tann LLP, Partner at Jones Day and Head of International Litigation and Arbitration for Asia.

MR. FALI S. NARIMAN (New Delhi, India)
[Honorary President of ICCA; see details at p. 1068.]

MR. CARLOS NEHRING NETTO (São Paulo, Brazil)
Mr. Carolos Nehring Netto is the Founder of Nehring & Associados – Advocacia and teaches arbitration at FGV University. He has been nominated a Chevalier de l'Ordre du Merite in recognition of legal services rendered to French enterprises. He was the Brazilian member of the International Court of Arbitration of the ICC for three mandates (from 1987 through 1996). He has served twice as Chairman of the Arbitration Center of the American Chamber of Commerce in S. Paulo.

MS. ELLEN GRACIE NORTHFLEET (Rio de Janeiro, Brazil)
Justice Ellen Gracie Northfleet is an attorney in private practice, an arbitrator in Rio de Janeiro and Former Chief Justice at the Brazilian Federal Supreme Court. She currently acts as Vice-President of the Arbitration Chamber of the Federation of Industries of São Paulo - FIESP. She serves on the Board of the Brazilian Committee of Arbitration (CBAr) and on the Board of Directors of the World Justice Project. Gracie has acted as a member of the World Bank's Sanctions Board from 22 April 2013 until the end of her second term on 21 April 2019. She is also a member of the International Council of Arbitration for Sport and of the Inter-American Dialogue.

MS. TINUADE OYEKUNLE (Lagos, Nigeria)
[Honorary Vice President of ICCA; see details at p. 1069.]

PROF. WILLIAM W. PARK (Cohasset, USA)
Prof. William W. (Rusty) Park is Professor of Law at Boston University, where he lectures on tax, banking and international business transactions. He is the former General Editor of Arbitration International. He has served on the Appeals Tribunal for the International Commission on Holocaust Era Insurance Claims and as Arbitrator on the Claims Resolution Tribunal for Dormant Accounts in Switzerland. Prof. Park is also the past President of the London Court of International Arbitration and past Chair of the ABA Committee on International Commercial Dispute Resolution.

MR. ANTONIO RICARDO PARRA (Easton, USA)
[Honorary Secretary General of ICCA; see details at p. 1070.]

PROF. JAN PAULSSON (Manama, Bahrain)
Honorary President of ICCA; see details at p. 1069.]

PROF. DR. MICHAEL PRYLES (Toorak, Australia)
Prof. Dr. Michael Pryles was the Founder President of the SIAC Court of Arbitration and Chairman of the Board of SIAC. Prior to that, he was President of the Australian Centre for International Commercial Arbitration and the founding President of the Asia Pacific Regional Arbitration Group Centre for International Commercial Arbitration. He also served as a member of the Board of Trustees of the Dubai International Arbitration Centre, a Commissioner of the United Nations Compensation Commission and a Court member of the London International Court of Arbitration. For his services to international arbitration, he was appointed an Officer in the Order of Australia. For several years he was also a member of the Australian Government delegation to the Hague Conference on Private International Law.

HON. ANDREW JOHN ROGERS KC (Sydney, Australia)
The Hon. Andrew Rogers currently acts as an international legal consultant, specialising in the area of arbitration, meditation and dispute resolution, with his expertise spanning relevant legislation in the UK, US, Asia and Europe as well as Australian Law. He has acted as Chairman, Sole Arbitrator and member of Arbitral Tribunals and has been a Judge of the Supreme Court of New South Wales in charge of the Commercial List, as well as the foundation Chief Judge of that court's Commercial Division.

DR. ANKE SESSLER (Frankfurt am Main, Germany)
Dr. Sessler is a Partner in the Frankfurt office of Skadden, Arps, Slate, Meagher & Flom LLP. She is widely recognized as one of Germany's leading dispute lawyers, with extensive experience in international and domestic arbitration and complex litigation proceedings. She represents industrial corporations and financial service providers in disputes relating to inter alia M&A and supply contracts, joint ventures and other commercial agreements, as well as in shareholder litigation and disputes to corporate boards. She also represents states and investors in treaty arbitration proceedings. Dr Sessler holds positions in various arbitration institutions, including the ICC Court of Arbitration, the ICC Commission on Arbitration and the AAA board.

PROF. YASUHEI TANIGUCHI (Tokyo, Japan)

Prof. Yasuhei Taniguchi is Professor Emeritus at Kyoto University in Japan. He is a Judge of the Singapore International Commercial Court and Counsel at Matsuo & Kosugi. He is a former member of the Appellate Body of the World Trade Organization Dispute Settlement Body; Special Advisor of the Japan Commercial Arbitration Association and Former President, Japan Association of Arbitrators, and Civil Procedure Association. He is internationally recognized for his expertise in comparative and transnational legal studies. He is a leading scholar in several areas of law including Civil Procedure, Alternative Dispute Resolution, Insolvency Law, and International Trade Law.

PROF. DR. GUIDO SANTIAGO TAWIL (Punta del Este, Uruguay)

Prof. Dr. Guido Tawil is an Independent Arbitrator, former Chair Professor of Administrative Law at the University of Buenos Aires School of Law and Senior Partner at M. & M. Bomchil in Buenos Aires, where he headed the International Arbitration, Administrative Law and Regulatory Matters Practices for over twenty-five years. He is Honorary President, Founding Member and Past Chair of the Latin American Arbitration Association (ALARB), Past Co-Chair of the IBA´s Arbitration Committee and Latin American Fora; Past Council Member of the IBA´s Legal Practice Division, Past Court Member of the LCIA, of the Institute for Transnational Arbitration (ITA) Academic Council, of the ICC Latin American Arbitration Group, and of the ICC Institute of World Business Law, current member of SIAC's Court of Arbitration, among other positions.

PROF. DR. PIERRE TERCIER (Fribourg, Switzerland)

Prof. Dr. Pierre Tercier is Professor Emeritus at the University of Fribourg, Switzerland and was Chairman of the International Court of Arbitration of the International Chamber of Commerce. He has extensive international arbitration and dispute resolution experience, having served on numerous occasions in ICC, ICSID and other cases. He is highly respected in the international legal and business community as an arbitrator, lecturer and author. Prof. Tercier is a visiting professor of law at numerous universities, including Geneva and Paris. He has recently joined the law firm Peter & Kim, in Geneva, as Senior Counsel.

MS. VERA VAN HOUTTE (Leuven, Belgium)

Ms. Vera Van Houtte is a Belgian lawyer (Dr Juris of the University of Leuven and LL.M. of Harvard Law School). Till the end of 2012, she was a partner at the Benelux firm Stibbe in Brussels, heading the construction and energy law department. She has been active in international arbitration for more than thirty-five years, first as counsel, and later as arbitrator, sitting in both commercial and investment arbitrations. Since 2013, she has acted exclusively as an arbitrator. She is a listed ICSID Panel arbitrator and has handled cases under a variety of arbitration rules (ICC, ICSID, LCIA, DIAC, UNCITRAL, Arbitration Institute of the Finnish and of the Hungarian Chambers of Commerce, CEPANI...) and ad hoc.

HON. S. AMOS WAKO FCIArb, SC (Nairobi, Kenya)

The Hon. S. Amos Wako is a Fellow of the Chartered Institute of Arbitrators and was elected a member of the International Law Commission at the 61st Session of the United Nations General Assembly. He is a chairman of the Association of Professional Societies in East Africa and (founding) chairman of the Public Law Institute. His appointments have included: representative to the Board of Trustees of the United Nations Voluntary Fund for Victims of Torture, special Rapporteur of the U.N. Commission on Human Rights on the Question of Summary or Arbitrary Executions and special Envoy of the Secretary General to East Timor to investigate the 12th November 1991 incident in DILI.

DR. SHENGCHANG WANG (Beijing, People's Republic of China)

Dr. Shengchang Wang is the Former Vice Chairman and Former Secretary General, China International Economic and Trade Arbitration Commission (CIETAC); Former Vice Chairman, China Maritime Arbitration Commission (CMAC); Former Member, London Court of International Arbitration (LCIA) and the Arbitration Institute of the Stockholm Chamber of Commerce (SCC). He is currently the senior consultant at Beijing Hui Zhong Law Firm and the Director of Proarb LLC. As an arbitrator, he has handled more than 200 international arbitration cases in various arbitration centres. As a counsel, he advises clients on commercial and maritime arbitration, investment treaty arbitration and sports arbitration.

SIR DAVID WILLIAMS KNZM, KC (Auckland, New Zealand)

Prof. David Williams currently practises as a Barrister with Bankside Chambers in Auckland, New Zealand. For some years he taught international arbitration at the University of Auckland Law School. He was a member of the IBA Working Group which produced the IBA Guidelines on Conflicts of Interest in International Arbitration 2004; a member International Law Association, Committee on International Arbitration and an Honorary Professor of Law, University of Auckland 2010.

MS. ARIEL YE (Nanshan District, Shenzhen, People's Republic of China)

Ms. Ariel Ye is a seasoned arbitration practitioner and arbitrator. She is a senior partner of King & Wood Malleson's Cross-border Dispute Resolution Practice and a recognized expert on PRC-related dispute resolution in the Asia Pacific region. She frequently handles arbitration cases before CIETAC, HKIAC, ICC, and other international arbitration institutions. Ms Ye is a panel arbitrator of CIETAC, HKIAC, SIAC and the Shenzhen Court of International Arbitration. She is also an SIAC Board Member.

DR. JIANLONG YU (Beijing, People's Republic of China)

Dr. Jianlong Yu is the Vice Chairman of the China Council for the Promotion of International Trade (CCPIT) and Executive Vice Chairman of the China Chamber of International Commerce (CCOIC); Vice Chairman of the World Chambers Federation. He is the former Vice-Chairman of the China International Economic and Trade Arbitration Commission (CIETAC); Vice-Chairman of the China Maritime Arbitration Commission (CMAC). He is also a Former President of the Asia Pacific Arbitration Group (APRAG) and Former Vice-Chairman of the China Academy of Arbitration Law (CAAL).

JUDGE ABDULQAWI AHMED YUSUF (The Hague, The Netherlands)

Judge Abdulqawi Ahmed Yusuf serves as the Vice-President of the International Court of Justice. He is a Member of the ICSID panel of arbitrators, a Member of the Institute of International Law (Institut de droit international), as well as a Founder and General Editor of the African Yearbook of International Law (Annuaire africain de droit international), and a Founding Member and Chairman of the Executive Committee of the African Foundation for International Law. He has previously served as Chief Legal Counsel to various international organizations including UNESCO and UNIDO.

PROF. EDUARDO ZULETA (Bogotá, Colombia)

Prof. Eduardo Zuleta is an independent arbitrator. He has acted as chair and co-arbitrator in a vast number of commercial and investment cases under, *inter alia*, ICC, ICDR, ICSID, UNCITRAL, LCIA, OIC and IACAC as well as in ICSID annulment committees. Disputes in which Prof Zuleta has acted include infrastructure, M&A, energy, financial products and distribution and involve parties, including state parties from Latam, Europe, Asia and the Middle East. Prof. Zuleta is a member of the Sanctions Board of the World Bank and Adjunct Professor at Georgetown Law.

ICCA Membership
now open

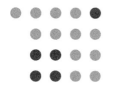

**Membership of ICCA
is now open to all law
graduates specializing
in dispute resolution.**

Membership benefits include:

- Listing in a fully searchable electronic membership directory on
  the ICCA website
- Listing in a hard-copy membership directory, to be distributed
  to members once per year
- 10% discount on the purchase price of ICCA Publications
  (including the Yearbook Commercial Arbitration, the
  International Handbook on Commercial Arbitration and the
  Congress Series)
- 10% discount to attend biennial ICCA Congresses and
  Conferences
- Regular electronic and hard copy newsletters
- Advance notice of ICCA-sponsored events and activities
- ICCA members are also entitled to take part in the activities of
  ICCA interest groups and projects, and are eligible for
  appointment to the ICCA Governing Board.

How to apply:

- On-line via www.arbitration-icca.org
- Via email to membership@arbitration-icca.org

www.arbitration-icca.org